Industry Spending Projections 2005-2009

Veronis Suhler Stevenson

MEDIA • COMMUNICATIONS • INFORMATION

Communications Industry Forecast

Nineteenth Edition

Historical and Projected Expenditures for 12 Industry Segments

The 2005 Veronis Suhler Stevenson Communications Industry Forecast was prepared by:

For *Veronis Suhler Stevenson:* James P. Rutherfurd, Executive Vice President, Managing Director
Chris Baffa, Director of Research
Brooke T. Suhler, Associate Director of Marketing
Tanya Dessereau, Marketing Coordinator

For *PQ Media:* Patrick Quinn, President & Publisher
Leo Kivijarv, Ph.D., Vice President & Research Director

Composition by: *NK Graphics*
West Chesterfield, New Hampshire

Printed by: *Applause Printing & Graphics Ltd.*
New York, New York

Veronis Suhler Stevenson Communications Industry Forecast
First edition published in 1987
Nineteenth edition published in 2005
ISBN 0-9711310-5-8

Veronis Suhler Stevenson
350 Park Avenue
New York, NY 10022
212-935-4990
212-381-8168 (Fax)
www.vss.com
researchpubs@vss.com

Summary of Contents

* Graphs appear in italics.

Recent Fund III Portfolio Exit

FUND III INVESTMENTS: YBR Group Transactions

VS&A Communications Partners III, L.P.
an affiliate of Veronis Suhler Stevenson LLC
has co-invested with
3i Plc
and the company's management
to acquire
Fonecta Group Ltd.
(formerly Sonera Info Communications, Ltd.)
a leading provider of directory services
in Finland and France
for
€111,500,000
Veronis Suhler Stevenson International Ltd., the London-based
affiliate of Veronis Suhler Stevenson LLC, acted
as financial advisor to and exclusive representative of
VS&A Communications Partners III, L.P.
March 2002

VS&A Communications Partners III, L.P.
an affiliate of Veronis Suhler Stevenson LLC
has co-invested with
3i Group Plc and management
to acquire
Telefoongids Media B.V.
(formerly Telemedia Nederland B.V.)
a division of Royal KPN N.V.
a leading provider of directory services in the Netherlands

for
€500,000,000
Veronis Suhler Stevenson International Ltd., an affiliate of
Veronis Suhler Stevenson LLC, acted as financial advisor to
and exclusive representative of
VS&A Communications Partners III, L.P.
February 2003

VS&A Communications Partners III, L.P.
an affiliate of Veronis Suhler Stevenson Partners LLC
has acquired the European directory operations of

Verizon Information Services

HEROLD Get the Information. MEDIATEL  Polskie Książki Telefoniczne GTE Yellow Pages

with
3i Group plc and management
$260,000,000
Veronis Suhler Stevenson International Ltd., an affiliate of
Veronis Suhler Stevenson, acted as financial advisor to and
representative of VS&A Communications Partners III, L.P.
July 2003

a portfolio company of
VS&A Communications Partners III, L.P.
has completed a recapitalization
in the amount of
€110,000,000
Veronis Suhler Stevenson International Ltd.,
an affiliate of Veronis Suhler Stevenson,
acted as financial advisor to and assisted in the negotiations
as the representative of Fonecta Oy.
January 2004

VS&A Communications Partners III, L.P.
the private equity affiliate of Veronis Suhler Stevenson
is pleased to announce the merger and refinancing of

FONECTA • De Telefoongids MEDIATEL

Recapitalisation
€1,040,000,000
April 2004

Private Equity Capital / Mezzanine Capital / Industry Research and Forecasts

Veronis Suhler Stevenson
MEDIA • COMMUNICATIONS • INFORMATION

350 Park Avenue, New York, NY 10022
212-935-4990 212-381-8168 fax
www.vss.com

Activities requiring securities industry registration will be performed by Veronis Suhler Stevenson Partners LLC wholly-owned broker-dealer affiliate, Veronis Suhler Stevenson LLC. Veronis Suhler Stevenson LLC is a member of NASD and SIPC.

De Telefoongids

Business Overview

YBR Group was formed by Veronis Suhler Stevenson and 3i Group, leading private equity investors with extensive interests in media and publishing, in March 2004. It consists of four principal operations: De Telefoongids, headquartered in Amsterdam; Fonecta, based in Helsinki, Finland; Herold, headquartered in Vienna; and Mediatel, based in Prague. In April 2004, VSS's Fund III, along with 3i, completed the merger and debt recapitalization of three European directory businesses and arranged for €765.0 million of senior secured credit facilities and a €275.0 million mezzanine term loan facility.

Background

Fonecta Oy ("Fonecta") is the leading Finnish directory publisher and provider of associated directory services with call center operations in France. Formerly a subsidiary of Sonera, Finland's largest fixed line and mobile telco, the division was renamed Fonecta after the acquisition by Fund III and 3i. Fonecta was acquired in March 2002.

De Telefoongids BV ("Telefoongids") is one of the two leading directory publishers in the Netherlands. It currently publishes 50 printed directories in 50 regional editions, each of which encompass both white pages (residential listings) and pink pages (the yellow page equivalent or business classifieds). Telefoongids also utilizes CD-ROM technology for business-to-consumer solutions and provides an online directory service through its own portal. Telefoongids was acquired in February 2003.

Mediatel GmbH ("Mediatel") operates regional/local directories businesses primarily in Austria and the Czech Republic and certain other adjacent markets. The group publishes a total of 233 directories with a total circulation of 19.1 million copies. Mediatel which is headquartered in Vienna, Austria was acquired in July 2003.

Strategy & Rationale

The creation of a pan European directories group resulted in:

- scale (combined 2003 revenue of €369.5 million and EBITDA of €146.5 million and combined 2004 revenue of €383.7 million and EBITDA of €155.3 million), on an EBITDA basis it is the 7th largest publisher in Europe;
- balance (low cyclicality, strong cash flow, and good teleco relationships);
- management (the combination brings together some of the most talented directory professionals in Europe);
- synergies (both through complimentary product portfolios, best practices and printing and production savings);
- diversity (geographic footprint, product mix and technical platforms).

Exit

In July 2005, VSS and 3i closed on their sale of YBR to a consortium led by Macquarie Capital Alliance Group and including Macquarie Bank Limited, Caisse de dépôt et placement du Québec and Nikko Principal Investments Limited for €1,825 billion. This resulted in a 4.3x return of capital and a 119% IRR.

About
Veronis Suhler Stevenson

A Private Equity Investor Serving the Global Media, Communications and Information Industries

- Advertising, Specialty Media & Marketing Services
- Broadcast Television
- Cable & Satellite TV
- Broadcast & Satellite Radio
- Entertainment Media
- Consumer Internet
- Newspapers
- Consumer Books
- Consumer Magazines
- Business-to-Business Media
- Educational & Training Media
- Professional & Business Information Services

Veronis Suhler Stevenson (VSS) is a private equity and mezzanine capital investment firm dedicated to serving the media, communications and information industries (collectively, "Media") in North America and Europe. Veronis Suhler Stevenson was founded in 1981 by John J. Veronis and John S. Suhler with the premise that the investment process is better informed with the combination of seasoned industry professionals with hands-on operating and transactional experience together with Media-focused investment banking and investment professionals. Jeffrey T. Stevenson, who joined the Firm in 1982 and subsequently managed the Firm's first private equity fund, became a name partner of the Firm in December 2001. In March 2003, S. Gerard Benford, Marco Sodi and Scott J. Troeller were named Partners. VSS has grown to more than 60 professionals and support staff with offices in New York and London.

Since 1987, VSS has managed four private equity funds and a mezzanine fund exclusively dedicated to investments in the media, communications, and information industries. Over the past 18 years, VSS has managed funds with commitments exceeding $2 billion and has invested in 38 platform companies, which have completed over 190 add-on acquisitions.

Financial Expertise, Industry Experience

VSS prides itself on the depth of its media industry, financial, and transaction experience. This experience provides a platform for our Firm to work with media company owners and management on a peer level.

The Firm continues to attract top media industry and Wall Street media-focused financial professionals. VSS's managing directors are drawn from the ranks of such distinguished companies as Time Warner, Viacom, NBC, Merrill Lynch, JP Morgan Chase, PRIMEDIA, CBS, Westinghouse Broadcasting, McGraw-Hill, Scholastic, CS First Boston, Ziff Davis, UBS Warburg, Penton Media, Miller Freeman and PricewaterhouseCoopers.

Cross-Border Services: Veronis Suhler Stevenson International Limited

In an industry that has become increasingly global, we are especially proud of the multi-transactional relationships the Firm enjoys with many of the world's premier media companies, including those based in Europe, Canada and Australia.

Since inception, approximately 30 percent of VSS's transactions have involved international participants. In 2000, the Firm established a London-based affiliate, Veronis Suhler Stevenson International Limited (VSSIL), to conduct European-based transactions and private equity investments.

Private Equity And Mezzanine Funds

PRIVATE EQUITY INVESTING

Since 1987, VSS has managed four private equity buyout funds with 38 portfolio companies including over 190 add-on acquisitions in the media, communications and information industries. Typical transaction structures which VSS private equity funds have used historically include: (i) management buyouts and buy-ins; (ii) expansion or acquisition financings; (iii) leveraged recapitalizations; (iv) leveraged buildups; (v) "going private" transactions and (vi) strategic and corporate partnerships. The equity funds' strategy is to make control investments across a diverse group of media industry segments in North America and Europe. Typical transaction size involves companies which have an enterprise value of $50 million to $250 million at the time of the VSS Fund initial investment. We target companies for which there are significant add-on acquisition opportunities and a likelihood of sale upon exit to a strategic buyer.

MEZZANINE INVESTING

VSS began investing its first Mezzanine Fund in April 2005. The VSS Mezzanine Fund targets investments in mezzanine securities in middle market media companies. Types of transactions include (i) expansion or acquisition financing; (ii) leveraged recapitalizations; (iii) management buyouts or buy-ins; or (iv) other growth initiatives requiring mezzanine capital. Types of investment structures for the VSS Mezzanine Fund generally include debt and non-control equity participation. The Mezzanine Fund works closely with its portfolio companies to source add-on acquisition opportunities and to otherwise assist the company with growth initiatives.

Few private equity firms specialize in media, communications and information. Fewer still cover as many industry segments as does VSS, including radio, television, cable,

Seated, from left to right: John J. Veronis, John S. Suhler, Jeffrey T. Stevenson.
Standing: Marco Sodi, S. Gerard Benford, Scott J. Troeller.

wireless communications towers, business-to-business and consumer publishing, trade shows, database information, professional information and services, education and training, yellow pages directories, newspapers, advertising and marketing, and entertainment. This broad industry segment and served market coverage reduces investment risks through diversification.

The Limited Partners who provide capital for the VSS Funds represent a diverse group of institutional investors from the U.S., Canada, Europe, the Middle East and Asia including local and state government-sponsored pension funds, corporate pension funds, financial institutions, endowments, foundations and family offices. In addition, there are several media companies and media families in North America and Europe who are investors in VSS Funds.

THE VSS DIFFERENTIATION

Four important factors differentiate VSS from other private equity managers:

1) The combination of a proven investment team composed of former communications industry executives and corporate finance professionals; 2) the successful investment strategies and philosophies that have been developed and refined through Funds I, II, III and IV spanning more than 18 years; 3) the Firm's exclusive focus on opportunities within the attractive media, communications and information industries; and 4) its consistent focus on investing in both North America and Europe.

The affiliation with VSS allows its portfolio companies to benefit from the industry relationships, operating expertise, and resulting flow of transaction opportunities of the Firm. Structuring investments around platform companies has allowed VSS to maximize the managerial and entrepreneurial insight of the cadre of its managing directors and portfolio company management.

VSS has an active involvement in influencing the major decisions and key factors that drive the portfolio businesses. As such, the Fund seeks to maintain a significant equity and/or control position in its portfolio companies. Senior managers/partners of the Fund's portfolio companies are also provided with meaningful equity incentives.

INVESTMENT STRATEGY: PLATFORM BUILDUPS

The Funds have employed similar strategies that have proved successful: Invest in growth-oriented platform companies with positive cash flow that exhibit strong "buildup" potential; strong management partners; flexible transaction structures; and the potential for operational improvements and strategic add-on acquisitions, which provide merger benefit opportunities and, in turn, generate attractive exit options.

This disciplined investment philosophy has given the Funds a competitive advantage in locating, purchasing, financing and growing investments to the benefit of its limited partners. By investing in companies with capable management and the ability to grow both organically and through follow-on acquisitions, the Funds create expandable platform companies that can enhance returns through the efficiencies inherent in attaining critical mass and leveraging scale economies. These platform businesses build the critical mass necessary to achieve incremental operating efficiencies by leveraging the core infrastructure of their base business, especially management's core competency. Critical mass also enhances the financing and exit alternatives for the platform business.

PARTNERING WITH MANAGEMENT

VSS assists its portfolio companies by working with management to determine objectives, to develop strategic plans, to identify acquisitions, and to structure and finance transactions. Given its operating and financial expertise, the Fund shares with management a common perspective on how value is created through improving operating performance and targeting strategic acquisition opportunities.

VSS Communications Partners IV, L.P. Portfolio Companies

Company	Description
DOAR Communications, Inc.	A premium provider of comprehensive litigation support solutions to major law firms and Fortune 1000 companies involved in complex commercial litigation in which there are typically multiple parties involved. The company is a single-source provider of a full range of solutions including scanning and coding, electronic discovery, online repository, jury research, trial graphics and at-trial support.
Facts On File, Inc.	Facts On File is one of the leading independent publishers of print and online reference materials for the school and library markets. FOF produces high-quality encyclopedias, dictionaries, directories, atlases, chronologies, almanacs, and biographies under three imprints: Facts On File (core reference), Ferguson Publishing (career-oriented), and Checkmark Books (adult trade).
**Riviera Broadcast Group, LLC	Headquartered in Scottsdale, Arizona, Riviera Broadcast Group is a newly formed entity that will operate and acquire stations within the top 100 radio markets, with a focus on the top 50 markets. The initial station acquisition of the Company was KEDJ-FM in Phoenix, Arizona. Riviera was founded by Chris Maguire, former CFO of GoldenState Towers, and by Tim Pohlman, a senior radio industry executive who most recently served as Market Manager for Infinity Broadcasting's LA cluster.
Southern Theatres, LLC	Southern Theatres was formed in 2003 as a developer and operator of multiplex stadium-seating movie theatres. Headquartered in New Orleans, Louisiana, Southern Theatres currently operates multiplex stadium-seating movie theatres with 52 screens in Louisiana and Mississippi. The company has additional locations under construction that are scheduled to open in June 2005, at which point Southern Theatres will own five stadium-seating multiplex movie theatres across Louisiana, Mississippi and Texas with a total of 72 screens. CEO George Solomon was previously CEO of Gulf States Theatres, a family-owned business, which was sold to AMC Entertainment and Entertainment Properties Trust for over $100 million in 2002.

**Fund investment pending regulatory approval.

VS&A Communications Partners III, L.P. Portfolio Companies

Access Intelligence, LLC	Formerly PBI Media, LLC, Access Intelligence is a leading business media company serving the aviation, broadband, chemicals, defense, media and satellite industries. AI was formed in 2004 by the merger of PBI Media, LLC and Chemical Week Associates.
Ascend Media, LLC	Primarily a provider of education, publishing and marketing services to the medical and healthcare industries. Ascend publishes professional magazines and journals, and operates conferences and trade shows, and Internet properties and databases serving the medical, healthcare, tradeshow services, gaming, food and transportation industries.
Birch Telecom, Inc.	A competitive local exchange carrier serving the southern and central United States, deploying a next-generation network to provide broadband communication services to small and medium-sized businesses with over 450,000 access lines.
*Data Transmission Network Corp.	A business information services company which provided real-time information delivery systems and proprietary content to subscribers in four separate divisions: agriculture (DTN Ag Services), weather (Meteorlogix), energy (DTN Energy Services) and financial (DTN Market Access).
*GoldenState Towers, LLC	A wireless communications tower owner/operator of more than 200 towers in Idaho, Washington, Oregon, Missouri, Arizona, California and Iowa.
*Hanley Wood, LLC	The leading business-to-business media company serving the housing and construction industries with products that included 23 trade magazines, 12 trade shows (four of which are among the 200 largest in the U.S.), nine conferences and multiple Web sites.
Hemscott, plc (formerly CoreData, LLC)	A leading financial data publisher serving the financial information needs of financial institutions, major corporations, universities and sophisticated individual investors through proprietary data assets covering the United States, United Kingdom and Canada.
ITE Group plc	A leading organizer of trade shows and exhibitions in emerging markets such as Russia and the CIS, Eastern Europe and Turkey, the Middle East, South Africa, the United Kingdom, Germany, Holland and France, as well as within numerous industries such as automotive products, travel and tourism, oil and gas, and construction.
Pepcom GmbH	Consolidator of small cable TV operators in Germany, Europe's largest cable market. Pepcom is one of Germany's fastest-growing cable TV companies, having aggregated nearly 400,000 subscribers since November 2001.
Solucient, LLC	A leading provider of comprehensive, intelligent market data to assist in the management of hospitals, managed care facilities, and pharmaceutical companies in the U.S.
User-Friendly Phone Book, LLC	A U.S.-based directory publishing company operating in Louisiana, Texas, Kentucky, Oklahoma, Ohio, California and Indiana publishing 27 directories with an annual circulation of approximately 3.6 million.
Xtreme Information Ltd.	Based in the U.K., Xtreme Information is a global business information services company providing global advertising monitoring and press monitoring services across most media formats.

*Portfolio company or Fund investment interest that has been sold or liquidated.

*Yellow Brick Road Group	The combination of the three European directories businesses owned jointly by Fund III and 3i Group PLC ("3i") to form Yellow Brick Road Group ("YBR").
*De Telefoongids BV	One of two leading directory companies in The Netherlands. The Company's core product portfolio includes combined white pages and yellow pages-type directories in 48 regional printed editions with a circulation of over 8.3 million, and electronic directory services such as CD-ROM technology and online products. Telefoongids' online search site is one of the five most visited sites in the country.
*Fonecta Oy	An international smart directory solutions provider for mobile and fixed line operators, content providers, mobile portals and other service providers. The company also provides state-of-the-art directory assistance services to meet the needs of a variety of customer segments in Finland and France. Fonecta currently publishes 30 directories with an annual circulation of approximately 3 million.
*Mediatel GmbH	A group of directory publishing businesses that includes the dominant providers of white and yellow pages directories in Austria and the Czech Republic. Mediatel currently publishes 207 directories with an annual circulation of approximately 14.7 million.

VS&A Communications Partners II, L.P. Portfolio Companies

Access Intelligence, LLC	Formerly PBI Media, LLC, Access Intelligence ("AI") is a business media company serving the aviation, broadband, chemicals, defense, media and satellite industries. AI was formed in 2004 by the merger of PBI Media, LLC and Chemical Week Associates.
*Broadcasting Partners Holdings, L.P.	The twenty-fifth-largest radio group in the U.S. Owned and operated 37 radio stations in 12 markets including Buffalo, NY, Syracuse, NY and Atlantic City, NJ.
*Canon Communications LLC	Leading business media magazine publisher and trade show producer company serving the medical equipment and high-tech manufacturing industries. Canon published 14 trade magazines and was the organizer and manager of 14 trade shows.
*Centaur Communications Ltd.	U.K.-based business-to-business communications company that produced 17 magazines, over 100 conferences and nine exhibitions. Served markets included marketing and design, finance, law, and engineering and construction.
*The Official Information Company	A diversified communications, information services, publishing, and marketing firm that served the convention and tradeshow and investigative services industries.
*Rifkin Acquisition Partners, L.L.L.P.	The twenty-fifth-largest U.S. cable television multiple system operator ("MSO"), with 200,000 subscribers primarily located in suburban Atlanta and Nashville.
*SNL Securities LC	Leading supplier of proprietary financial and regulatory database information relating to 1,800 publicly traded entities in the financial services industry.
*Spectrum Resources Towers, L.P.	Owned freestanding towers serving the wireless telecommunications industry.
*Triax Midwest Associates. L.P.	The twenty-third-largest U.S. cable television MSO with 350,000 subscribers in the rural markets of Illinois, Indiana, Iowa, Minnesota and Wisconsin.
*Yellow Book USA, L.P.	Largest independent publisher of yellow pages directories in the U.S. Published over 250 directories with a combined circulation of 13 million in New York, New Jersey, Pennsylvania, Florida, Delaware, Maryland, Virginia, and Washington, DC.

*Portfolio company or Fund investment interest that has been sold or liquidated.

VS&A Communications Partners, L.P. Portfolio Companies

*B&B Merger Corporation	Published program guide magazines and specialty publications, including *Stagebill*, serving major performing arts centers nationwide.
*Broadcasting Partners, Inc.	Group owner of radio stations in New York, Chicago, Detroit, Charlotte and Dallas.
*Cable Management Ireland	Owned cable systems in the Republic of Ireland.
*Hughes Broadcasting Partners	Owned television stations KUTV-TV, the NBC affiliate serving Salt Lake City, UT, and WOKR-TV, the ABC affiliate serving Rochester, NY.
*International Media Partners	Published specialty newspapers and organizer of conferences related to international trade, business and finance.
*Kansas Broadcasting System, L.P.	Owned television station KWCH-TV, the CBS affiliate serving Wichita and the state of Kansas through a statewide network of satellite stations.
*PJS Publications Inc.	Published special-interest consumer magazines and newsletters.
*Triax Southeast Associates, L.P. TRIAX TELECOMMUNICATIONS COMPANY, L.L.C.	Owned cable systems in Kentucky, West Virginia, Pennsylvania, Maryland, Virginia and South Carolina serving 54,000 subscribers.

THE VSS MEZZANINE FUND

VSS closed on its first Mezzanine Fund, VSS Mezzanine Partners, L.P. (the "Mezzanine Fund") on January 31, 2005. The Mezzanine Fund's primary objective is to invest in the mezzanine securities of middle market media, communications and information companies. As detailed in the following company profile, the Mezzanine Fund made its first investment in April 2005 in Schofield Media, a business-to-business publisher operating in the U.K. and the U.S.

VSS Mezzanine Partners, L.P.—Portfolio Investment

Schofield Media Group Schofield Media Ltd.	Established in 2000, Schofield Media Group is a publisher of 15 business-to-business controlled circulation magazines in the U.S., and U.K. Schofield's magazines cover industry areas such as manufacturing and services, general business, food service, construction, design and healthcare. The funds from the Mezzanine Fund investment were used for Schofield's acquisition of four business-to-business magazines from VNU Business Media Inc.: *Restaurant Business*; *Food Service Network*; *Retail Merchandiser*; and *Beverage World*.

*Portfolio company or Fund investment interest that has been sold or liquidated.

Communications Industry Research/ Databases

"The yearly [*Communications Industry Forecast*] is viewed as a must-have research and planning tool by media executives."

—*USA Today*, August, 2003

"Veronis Suhler Stevenson's annual report on the communications industry is always chockfull of revealing statistics about the media business."

—*MediaPost*, August, 2003

"The report has become as durable a resource for number crunchers in New York and Hollywood as *The Almanac of American Politics* is in Washington. And there are several controversial findings, if you read between the numbers."

—*USA Today*, August 5, 2002

"The 369-page forecast from New York-based media merchant bank Veronis Suhler is a kind of state-of-the-art report on all communications media, including the consumer Internet."

—*Newsbytes*, August 7, 2001

"When media executives want detailed sales and profit projections for sectors in their industry, they turn to the latest forecast of Veronis, Suhler & Associates."

—*Broadcasting & Cable*, September 18, 2000

- **Communications Industry Forecast**—Reflecting our commitment to the industries we serve, Veronis Suhler Stevenson has become a prominent source of authoritative media and communications industry data. Each year, the Firm relates five-year historical and five-year forward forecasting by segment of advertiser, consumer, and business end-user spending patterns with the key market forces driving industry growth in its highly acclaimed *Communications Industry Forecast* (*CIF*). This comprehensive research report provides critical demographic, economic, technological, institutional, behavioral, and competitive served-market data that have immediate implications for strategic planning, corporate development, budgeting and forecasting.
- **Investment Considerations for the Communications Industry, A Thirty-Year Review: 1977-2007**—The *ICCI* is a comprehensive review of key data, trends and drivers impacting the media industry for the past 25 years. Results from the 2004 *ICCI* indicate that the communications industry has enjoyed steady and impressive growth for the past 25 years, consistently surpassing broader economic growth and outperforming most other U.S. industries. The report examines historical and forecast spending data, and compares the strong financial performance of leading publicly reporting media companies against the S&P 500. In addition, the *ICCI* includes relevant analytics that evaluate the communication industry's performance during economic slowdowns and recoveries.
- **The VSS Media 100™** is an index of 100 major U.S. public media and communications companies that represent all 12 major segments of the industry. It is the latest addition to the media financial tools provided by VSS, which has long focused on five-year industry historical and forecast trends in its annually produced *VSS Communications Industry Forecast*. Provided to the purchasers of the *CIF* on the subscription-only portion of its Web site (www.vss.com), the VSS Media 100 prominently displays a performance chart, updated throughout each week, showing how the media-weighted composite index compares with the Dow Jones Industrial Average, as well as the S&P 500 and NASDAQ indices. Also updated throughout each week is a list of the top 10 media and communications stock gainers and losers. The highlight of the index is weekly stock quotes of 100 leading media companies that can be sorted by industry segment, market cap, highest or lowest share price, or alphabetically, among other search criteria. In addition, the year-to-date historical graphs show industry trends. Rather than using conventional means to track companies by sheer size or market cap, the VSS

Media 100 represents a weighted representation of prominent companies from all 12 major media and communications segments.

- **Transactions Database**—Since 1984, Veronis Suhler Stevenson has maintained a comprehensive database of completed transactions in the media and communications industries. This proprietary compilation, the Veronis Suhler Stevenson Transactions Database, can be accessed by industry segment and can yield an analysis of transaction activity and valuation multiple trends over a specified period of time.
- **The Veronis Suhler Stevenson Domestic 1000 and International 500**—The Veronis Suhler Stevenson Domestic 1000 is a database, updated continuously, that tracks the leading public and private media companies in the United States. The Veronis Suhler Stevenson International 500 tracks the top international media companies. Information in these two key tracking databases includes ownership, contact history, and detailed segment revenue data.
- **Consumer Magazine Database**—In addition to general industry research, Veronis Suhler Stevenson maintains a comprehensive, proprietary database focusing on all major consumer magazines. Our Consumer Magazine Database, drawn from the Audit Bureau of Circulation, BPA International, Publishers Information Bureau, and syndicated readership research, enables analysis of share-of-market and served-market/editorial category trends by title, category, parent company and revenue stream by year and five-year trends.
- **Ongoing Industry Data Mining**—As a complement to its published reports, the Research Department maintains the Veronis Suhler Stevenson Database, which contains extensive records on all communications industry companies, their holdings, management, past transactions, ownership, finances, and contact history.

BROADCASTING AND ENTERTAINMENT

- Alternative Radio
- Cable Television Systems and Networks
- Direct Broadcast Satellite
- Electronic Games and Interactive Software
- Filmed Entertainment
- Interactive Television/Video-on-Demand
- Mobile Content
- Music Publishing
- Radio Stations and Networks
- Recorded Music
- Satellite Radio
- Television Production
- Television Stations and Networks

BUSINESS-TO-BUSINESS MEDIA

- Business-to-Business E-media
- Business Custom Publishers
- Business Newsletters
- Business Trade Shows and Exhibitions
- Business-to-Business Magazines
- Seminar/Conference Organizers

CONSUMER INTERNET

- Internet Content Providers
- Internet Search Engines
- Internet Service and Infrastructure Providers

CONSUMER PUBLISHING

- Calendars and Greeting Cards
- Comic Books and Trading Cards
- Consumer Book Publishing
- Consumer Custom Publishers
- Consumer Magazines
- Consumer Newsletters
- Yellow Page Directories

EDUCATIONAL PUBLISHING AND CORPORATE TRAINING

- College Textbooks
- Corporate Training
- K-12 Textbooks
- Library Reference Publishing
- Supplemental Publishing

NEWSPAPER PUBLISHING

- Alternative Newspapers
- Daily and Weekly Newspapers
- Financial Newspapers
- Local Business Journals
- Local Legal Newspapers
- Shoppers
- Traders

PROFESSIONAL AND BUSINESS INFORMATION SERVICES

- Credit and Risk Management Data and Services
- Financial and Economic Data and Services
- General Business and Industry Data and Services
- Journal Publishing
- Marketing Data and Services
- Payroll and Human Resources Data and Services
- Professional and Business Health and Life Science Data and Services
- Professional and Business Legal and Regulatory Data and Services
- Professional and Business Science and Technical Data and Services

SPECIALTY MEDIA AND MARKETING SERVICES

- Affinity Membership Organizations
- Alternative Advertising
- Billboards
- Branded Entertainment
- Catalogs
- Coupons
- Direct Mail
- In-Store and Promotion Services
- Interactive Advertising
- Marketing Communications
- Marketing Services
- Public Relations
- Telesales

The Partners

JOHN J. VERONIS

John J. Veronis, Co-Founder and Managing Partner, is also Chairman and Co-Chief Executive Officer of Veronis Suhler Stevenson and a Senior Managing Member of the General Partner of the Fund. Mr. Veronis' involvement in Media spans over four decades and reflects a rare combination of corporate and entrepreneurial success. He has founded, owned, operated, served on the Board of Directors and/or served as an executive across a broad spectrum of Media, including magazine and book publishing, radio and television broadcasting, cable television, college textbook publishing, book clubs, educational films and newsletters. Prior to co-founding VSS in 1981, Mr. Veronis co-founded *Psychology Today*, one of the most successful magazine launches of its time, which expanded its operations into textbooks, book clubs and educational films. He subsequently started *Book Digest* magazine, which grew to a circulation of one million under his direction. Earlier in his career, he was President of Curtis Magazines, publisher of *Ladies' Home Journal* and served as a general corporate executive at Interpublic Group of Companies.

Mr. Veronis previously served on the Boards of Hanley Wood, Centaur Communications, The Official Information Company, Rifkin Acquisition Partners, Triax Midwest Associates, Broadcasting Partners Holdings, Cable Management Ireland, B&B Merger Corporation, Triax Southeast Associates, and International Media Partners.

Mr. Veronis is a Director of the Metropolitan Opera and a Trustee of Carnegie Hall. He is a past Director of the United States Chamber of Commerce, the Magazine Publishers of America, Curtis Circulation Company and WRGB-TV, the CBS affiliate in Schenectady, New York. Mr. Veronis received his BA from Lafayette College and attended the New York University Graduate School of Business.

JOHN S. SUHLER

John S. Suhler, Co-Founder and Managing Partner, is also President and Co-Chief Executive of Veronis Suhler Stevenson and a Senior Managing Member of the General Partner of the Fund. He has been actively involved in raising the capital of Veronis Suhler Stevenson's private equity funds. Mr. Suhler, for the majority of his operational career, was a Senior Manager/Publisher/President in consumer, educational (el-hi, college, supplemental materials), and professional publishing; weekly newspapers, consumer magazines and books, professional (medical and healthcare) journals, monographs, and newsletters. Mr. Suhler was trained early on as a direct marketing and periodical subscription marketing analyst and was instrumental later as a circulation manager and publisher in the application of mathematical modeling to the business of circulation and print order planning and optimization of customer acquisition. Mr. Suhler participates in the management presentations and due diligence reviews of nearly all portfolio companies and significant add-ons, and he has served on the Board of Directors of most of the Fund's portfolio companies. Prior to co-founding VSS in 1981, Mr. Suhler was President of CBS Publishing Group, a $550 million (1980) revenue multinational operation and one of the four operating groups of CBS, Inc., and previously was publisher of the *Psychology Today* group at Ziff Davis Publishing and CRM, Inc.

Mr. Suhler has been a member of the Board of Directors of the Association of American Publishers and the Magazine Publishers of America, and an affiliate member of the American Newspaper Publishers Association and WRGB-TV, the CBS affiliate in Schenectady, New York. Mr. Suhler currently sits on the Board of Access Intelligence. Previously, he has served on the Boards of PJS Publications, International Media Partners, Hughes Broadcasting Partners, Kansas Broadcasting System, Broadcasting Partners Holdings, Yellow Book USA, Spectrum Resources Towers, Solucient, The Official Information Company, Triax Southeast Cable,

Canon Communications and Hanley Wood. Mr. Suhler created the *Veronis Suhler Stevenson Communications Industry Report* and the *Veronis Suhler Stevenson Communications Industry Forecast*, published since 1984 and 1987, respectively.

Mr. Suhler received his BS from the University of Kansas, where he attended the William Allen White School of Journalism and was Chairman of The University Daily Kansan Board. He is currently a Trustee of the William Allen White Foundation and the recipient of the University of Kansas Journalism School Legacy Achievement Award.

JEFFREY T. STEVENSON

Jeffrey T. Stevenson, a Managing Partner, is also Co-Chief Executive Officer of Veronis Suhler Stevenson and a Senior Managing Member of the General Partner of the Fund. He joined the Firm in 1982 shortly after its formation and has been the head of its private equity business since its first investment in 1989. Mr. Stevenson serves as the President of each of the Equity Funds, approves all capital commitments, and directs the investment activities of the Equity Funds. Previously, Mr. Stevenson was Executive Vice President in charge of corporate finance at VSS, a department he founded.

Mr. Stevenson currently serves as a Director of Xtreme Information, Access Intelligence, Facts On File and Southern Theatres. Previously, he served as a Director of The Official Information Company, Centaur Communications, Birch Telecom, ITE Group, Pepcom, Yellow Book USA, Rifkin Acquisition Partners, Triax Midwest Associates, Broadcasting Partners Holdings, Spectrum Resources Towers, PJS Publications, Kansas Broadcasting Systems, B&B Merger Corporation, Cable Management Ireland, International Media Partners, Hughes Broadcasting Partners, Triax Southeast Associates, Canon Communications, Hanley Wood, De Telefoongids, Mediatel and Broadcasting Partners. Mr. Stevenson holds a BA from Rutgers College.

S. GERARD BENFORD

S. Gerard Benford is a Partner of Veronis Suhler Stevenson and a Managing Member of the General Partner of the Fund. He was actively involved in all aspects of each of the Equity Funds' investments from 1990 until September 2000 with particular emphasis on Hanley Wood, Birch Telecom, Solucient, Hughes Broadcasting Partners, Broadcasting Partners Holdings, Spectrum Resources, Canon Communications, Chemical Week Associates, Rifkin Acquisition Partners, The Official Information Company, Triax Midwest Associates, and Yellow Book USA. From September 2000 until July 2002 he provided part-time consulting services to the Equity Funds, and in August 2002 he rejoined the Equity Funds on a full-time basis. He currently serves as a Director of Pepcom, Solucient, and User-Friendly. Prior to joining VSS, Mr. Benford served for several years as a Director and Chief Financial Officer of HiShear Industries, a New York Stock Exchange listed company. Before working for HiShear, Mr. Benford was the Corporate Vice President of Warner Communications, where he specialized in mergers, acquisitions, divestitures, and other corporate development activities. During his 17-year career at Warner, Mr. Benford was involved in the acquisitions of Warner Brothers, Franklin Mint Corporation, The Garden State National Bank, numerous cable television businesses, the formation of the Warner-Amex cable joint-venture and many other Media-related businesses as well as the startup phase of many new business enterprises. He was also responsible for overseeing and monitoring Warner's venture capital investment portfolio. In addition, Mr. Benford was involved in the divestiture of all of Warner's non-entertainment businesses, including Warner's interests in National Kinney Corporation, the Eastern Mountain Sports retail business, and Uris Buildings Corporation, a New York City commercial real estate business, which was sold to Olympia & New York Ltd. Before joining Warner, he was a Principal at Arthur Young & Company. Mr. Benford holds a BBA from

St. Francis College and is a Certified Public Accountant. Since 1964, he has been a member of the American Institute of Certified Public Accountants.

MARCO SODI

Marco Sodi heads VSS's London-based affiliate, Veronis Suhler Stevenson International, is a Partner of Veronis Suhler Stevenson, and a Managing Member of the General Partner of the Fund. Mr. Sodi developed VSS's international activities throughout the 1990s and established the Firm's London office in 2000. Mr. Sodi has been active with each of the Equity Funds. In 2004 he led the merger and recapitalization of three directory companies into The Yellow Brick Road Group and the sale of Centaur Communications through an accelerated IPO. Mr. Sodi led the investments in De Telefoongids, Pepcom, Centaur Communications and Fonecta. Additionally, Mr. Sodi played an important role in the Equity Funds' investments in Hanley Wood, ITE, Hughes Broadcasting Partners, Triax Southeast Associates, and the acquisition of Yellow Book USA, as well as its subsequent sale to British Telecommunications in 1999. Mr. Sodi currently serves as a Director of ITE Group plc, Hemscott plc, and Pepcom. Previously he has served on the Boards of YBR Group, De Telefoongids, Fonecta and Mediatel. Prior to joining Veronis Suhler Stevenson in 1988, Mr. Sodi was a Partner at Salem Solutions, a consulting firm, and worked at Exxon Enterprises, the venture capital arm of ExxonMobil. Born and raised in Florence, Italy, Mr. Sodi received a BS from Cornell University.

SCOTT J. TROELLER

Scott J. Troeller is a Partner of Veronis Suhler Stevenson and a Managing Member of the General Partner of the Fund. He is actively involved in all aspects of VSS's fund-related activities, including originating and developing investment opportunities, transaction structuring, arranging debt financing and portfolio company monitoring. Mr. Troeller has investment and transactional experience in numerous media sectors, such as business information services, business media, radio and television broadcasting, consumer magazine publishing and wireless communications towers. Mr. Troeller has played an active role in several of the Equity Funds' investments, including GoldenState Towers, The Official Information Company and its separate subsidiaries Total Information Services (TISI), CoreSearch, Atwood Publishing, ExpoExchange, and GEM Communications. Mr. Troeller is currently a Director of Ascend Media and Hemscott and previously served as a Director of GoldenState Towers and The Official Information Company. Prior to joining VSS in 1996, Mr. Troeller was an investment banker with JP Morgan & Co., where his primary focus was on merger and acquisition advisory work in the Media industry. During his time at JP Morgan, he also served as a sell-side equity analyst and was a member of an *Institutional Investor*-ranked "All-American" analyst team. Mr. Troeller is a graduate of Rutgers College.

MANAGING DIRECTORS

Managing Directors include professionals dedicated primarily to the activities of the Equity and Mezzanine Funds, as well as professionals dedicated primarily to mezzanine investing or industry specialists who assist the Fund's Partners and Managing Directors in sourcing, analyzing and monitoring portfolio companies. Each Managing Director is highly incentivized to actively participate in the success of the Fund by having an opportunity to share in the General Partner's carried interest.

DAVID F. BAINBRIDGE

David F. Bainbridge Mr. Bainbridge specializes in professional and educational publishing and business information services for mezzanine debt investments and private equity investment opportunities. He is active with Fund IV's investments in Facts On File and DOAR. Mr. Bainbridge joined VSS in October 2003, having spent the previous 10 years as an investment banking professional, most recently with Berkery Noyes where he was a Managing Director, specializing in various institutional publishing and information segments. In the mid-1990s he worked with Scott-Macon, a New York-based M&A boutique, as a Vice President in the Media, Communications and Publishing Group. In 2000 he returned to school to get his MBA at New York University. Some of the transactions that he has participated in during the past few years include the sale of Novartis Medical Education Group to MediMedia, the acquisition of both Parthenon Publishing and Transcender Corp. by Information Holdings, Inc., the acquisition of Educational Design by Haights Cross Communications, and the purchase of Wave Technologies by Thomson Corporation. Mr. Bainbridge is a graduate of Cornell and an honors graduate of the Stern School of Business at New York University.

ROBERT J. BROADWATER

Robert J. Broadwater Mr. Broadwater leads VSS's activities in newspapers, books and educational publishing. Among his notable transactions are the 2004 sale of Saxon Publishers to Harcourt Achieve, the sale of Transcender LLC to Kaplan, Inc., the sale of seven regional newspapers owned by The New York Times Company, the sale of Fox Valley Press, a group of daily and weekly newspapers owned by The Copley Press, Inc., the sale of Sterling Publishing Company to Barnes & Noble, the sale of Running Press Book Publishers, the sale of Hemmings Motor News, the sale of Stern Publishing, Inc. (publisher of *The Village Voice*), the acquisition of the Thomson Corporation's Arizona newspaper group by Freedom Communications, Inc., the acquisition by Community Newspaper Holdings of 45 newspapers from Hollinger Inc. and the sale of The Orion Publishing Group, a leading British consumer book publisher, to Hachette Livre. Mr. Broadwater joined VSS in 1988 after a 10-year career on Wall Street. He previously served in the corporate finance department of EF Hutton and as an equity options trader at First Boston. He holds a BA from Yale University and an MBA from Columbia University.

ANDREW J. BUCHHOLTZ

Mr. Buchholtz focuses on magazine publishing, printing, direct marketing, yellow pages directory publishing and other consumer media and service transactions. Mr. Buchholtz joined VSS in 1995 and was promoted to Managing Director in 2000. During his tenure, Mr. Buchholtz has worked on the successful sale of White Directory Publishers, Inc. to The Hearst Corporation, the sale of Clipper Magazine, Inc. to Gannett Co., Inc., the sale of Zuckerman Group's *Fast Company* magazine to Gruner + Jahr USA, the sale of National Directory Company to the Yell Group Limited, the sale of the Devon Publishing Group to Lynx Private Equity, the sale of Time Warner's Little, Brown Professional Publishing Group, Inc. to Wolters Kluwer US Corporation, the formation of a 50-50 joint-venture between Liberis Publications of Greece and Edipresse, S.A. of Switzerland, as well as numerous other transactions. Mr. Buchholtz previously served as Vice President of Business Development at PRIMEDIA Special Interest Publications. Mr. Buchholtz graduated from Boston University magna cum laude with a BA in economics and an MBA in management.

J. MORGAN CALLAGY

Mr. Callagy joined VSS in 1996 in New York and is currently based in the Firm's London office, which oversees all of VSS's international activities. Mr. Callagy is responsible for the sourcing, negotiation and oversight of private equity transactions across media segments. Mr. Callagy was actively involved in Fund II's acquisitions and subsequent sales of both Yellow Book USA and Centaur Communications. Mr. Callagy was involved in helping the Firm establish its presence in London, and since joining the Firm's London office, has played a key role in each international transaction, including: ITE Group, Xtreme Information, Pepcom, Fonecta, De Telefoongids, the acquisition of Verizon Information Services' European directories business (Mediatel) and the formation of Yellow Brick Road, which encompassed the combination and refinancing of Fonecta, Mediatel and De Telefoongids. Mr. Callagy is a member of the Board of Directors of Yellow Brick Road and was previously a member of the Board of Directors of YBR Group. Mr. Callagy is a graduate of Georgetown University.

GEORGE L. COLE

Mr. Cole is Co-Manager of VSS Mezzanine Partners, L.P. He is responsible for the origination, underwriting, structuring and management of all portfolio investments. Mr. Cole currently serves on the Board of directors of Schofield Media. Prior to the formation of VSS Mezzanine Partners while serving as a Principal of Fund III, Mr. Cole was active in the acquisitions of Pepcom and CoreData LLC, and served on the latter's Board of Directors. Prior to joining VSS in 2000, Mr. Cole served as Co-Head and Managing Director of First Union Securities' Media & Entertainment Investment Banking Group. Mr. Cole's group was responsible for the origination of investment banking and leveraged finance activity for all of the media and entertainment industry relationships of First Union. While at First Union, Mr. Cole's team led the origination, structuring, underwriting and syndication of senior loans, subordinated debt and bridge financings for seven VSS Portfolio Companies totaling over $1.3 billion, including Rifkin Acquisition Partners, Canon Communications, Centaur Communications, The Official Information Company and Hanley Wood. Mr. Cole joined First Union Securities in 1987, beginning his career at First Union in Leveraged Finance at the firm's New York office. Mr. Cole earned a BBA from the University of Texas and an MBA from the University of Houston.

JONATHAN D. DRUCKER

Mr. Drucker is the General Counsel and a Managing Director of Veronis Suhler Stevenson. Prior to joining VSS in 1999, Mr. Drucker spent 11 years with the New York law firm Rubin, Baum, Levin, Constant & Friedman, where he was a Partner. He was also an Associate for three years with the New York law firm Cadwalader, Wickersham & Taft. Mr. Drucker supports VSS's private investment activities by participating in investment negotiations involving mergers, recapitalizations, acquisitions, financings and joint ventures. He also plays a principal role in the formation and structuring of VSS's various investment funds. He received his JD from Stanford University Law School and his BA, magna cum laude, from the University of Pennsylvania.

HAL R. GREENBERG

Mr. Greenberg is Co-Manager of VSS Mezzanine Partners, L.P.. He is responsible for the origination, underwriting, structuring and management of portfolio investments for the Mezzanine Fund and for the private equity funds. As a member of the Board, Mr. Greenberg has been particularly active with Canon Communications, Access Intelligence and Ascend Media and is a Board Observer of Xtreme Information, a U.K.-based company. Mr. Greenberg joined Veronis Suhler Stevenson in 1988 from his position as Director of Planning and Acquisitions at McGraw-Hill Book Company. He has also held various positions at CBS, successively as Manager of Strategic Planning for the CBS Broadcast Group, Director of Market Analysis for the CBS Television Network and Director of Acquisitions for CBS, Inc. Mr. Greenberg earned a BA in economics from Lake Forest College and holds a JD from the New England School of Law and an MBA from New York University.

THOMAS L. KEMP

Mr. Kemp specializes in business media. He is active with Fund III's Access Intelligence investment and with the Mezzanine Fund's Schofield Media investment. Mr. Kemp joined the Firm in 2004 from Penton Media, Inc., where he served as Chairman and Chief Executive Officer since 1996. He began his career at Miller Freeman in San Francisco, where he worked for over 20 years and served as President and Chief Operating Officer. Mr. Kemp served as Chairman of the Board of Directors of Penton Media, Inc., and as a Board member of

Miller Freeman, Inc., American Business Media, BPA International and Association of Medical Publishers. He was named to *B-to-B* magazine's "Who's Who in the B-to-B Industry" in 2003, as well as to *Tradeshow Week* magazine's "Power Pack 100: The 100 Most Influential People in the Tradeshow Industry" for the past four years. In 1997, *MIN* magazine named Mr. Kemp "Business Magazine Person of the Year." Mr. Kemp graduated cum laude from Amherst College and studied in the Executive Management Programs at the Johnson School of Management at Cornell University and the London School of Business.

MICHAEL B. KESSLER

Mr. Kessler specializes in the business information services sector, which in recent years has become a key focus for VSS in its investment banking transactions as well as its private equity investments. He participated in the acquisition of CoreData, serving on its Board of Directors, and has assisted in the development of Hemscott PLC. Mr. Kessler has over 18 years of experience in investment banking. He joined the Firm in 2003 from CIBC World Markets, where he served as a senior member of the Enterprise Software and eBusiness Services group, primarily focused on business services and software-related transactions. He has executed numerous financing transactions, raising an aggregate of over $2.8 billion, and closed over 30 mergers and acquisitions transactions aggregating over $2.0 billion in value. Prior to CIBC, Mr. Kessler was a Managing Director at Oppenheimer & Co. (acquired by CIBC in 1997), where he served as a senior member of the media and business services investment banking group. Prior to joining Oppenheimer in 1993, he was a Director at Barclays Capital responsible for originating, structuring and distributing private placements of debt, equity and mezzanine securities. Mr. Kessler has an MBA in finance from The Wharton School of the University of Pennsylvania and a BA in economics from the University of Pennsylvania.

CHRISTOPHER J. RUSSELL

Mr. Russell is responsible for originating, structuring and monitoring U.S. and international investment opportunities. Since joining VSS in 1994, Mr. Russell has been active in private equity investments, merger and acquisition advisory, and corporate finance across all targeted Media sectors. He played a key role in the firm's investments in Hanley Wood, ITE Group Plc, Xtreme Information, and Facts On File and currently serves on the Board of Directors of each, and was also involved with the firm's investments in YBR Group and Centaur Communications. Mr. Russell established the Firm's London office in 2000 in order to accelerate European investment activity, and is now based in New York. Prior to becoming Managing Director, Mr. Russell was a Director in both the Firm's Equity Funds and the Investment Bank, and was also the Firm's Director of Research. Previously, he worked in various corporate positions at NBC Television. Mr. Russell earned a BA from Georgetown University and an MBA from Columbia Business School.

JAMES P. RUTHERFURD

Mr. Rutherfurd is Executive Vice President of Veronis Suhler Stevenson and Managing Director responsible for Limited Partner communications, investor relations, fundraising and the Fund co-investment program. Mr. Rutherfurd joined VSS in January 1999 from JP Morgan & Co., where he served as a Managing Director in the Mergers & Acquisitions Group and Co-Head of JP Morgan's Media Group. He was previously a Director in The First Boston Corporation's Media Group. Prior to First Boston, he was a corporate and securities lawyer at Rogers & Wells in New York. Mr. Rutherfurd has worked with companies across many segments of the Media industry, including newspapers, television, cable, magazines, radio, information services, Internet services and entertainment. Mr. Rutherfurd holds a JD from the University of Virginia School of Law and a BA from Princeton University.

MARVIN L. SHAPIRO

Mr. Shapiro concentrates his activities on television and radio broadcasting and cable television. His many advisory transactions include the sale of KSTU-TV (Salt Lake City, UT) to FOX Television Stations, the sale of WICS-TV (Springfield, IL) to Guy Gannett Co., the sale of New Jersey Broadcasting Partners to Greater Media, Odyssey Partners' acquisition of WPCQ-TV (Charlotte, NC) and the formation of Queen City Broadcasting (WKBW-TV, Buffalo, NY) and Telemundo Group. Additionally, Mr. Shapiro played a key role in the formation of Cable Management Ireland, Broadcasting Partners Holdings, and Spectrum Resources Towers, and served each as a Director. Mr. Shapiro joined VSS in 1983 after 22 years at Westinghouse Broadcasting Company (Group W), where he was a Director, member of the Executive Committee, and as Executive Vice President, Chief Operating Officer, was President-Station Group. He served as both Chairman and a Director of the Television Bureau of Advertising and as a Director of the Radio Bureau of Advertising. Mr. Shapiro graduated from Syracuse University with a BS degree and completed executive courses at Williams College and Columbia Business School.

JOHN R. SINATRA

John R. Sinatra is the Chief Financial Officer and a Managing Director of Veronis Suhler Stevenson. He supports VSS's private investment activities by participating in accounting, tax planning, structural issues and technical due diligence. He serves on the Board of Directors of Access Intelligence and Solucient. He was previously a Director of Yellow Book USA and Hanley Wood. Mr. Sinatra oversees all VSS financial functions including accounting and controls, budgeting, risk management and tax planning. Previously, Mr. Sinatra served as Controller at James D. Wolfensohn Inc., a broker-dealer specializing in investment banking services and was a Senior Manager at Spicer & Oppenheim, an international accounting firm. Mr. Sinatra graduated cum laude from Baruch College with a BBA in accounting. He is a Certified Public Accountant.

JOHANNES VON BISMARCK, PH.D.

Dr. von Bismarck is responsible for sourcing, executing and monitoring private equity investments in Europe across all media segments, with particular focus on the German, Austrian and Swiss markets. He led the add-on acquisition of Kabelfernsehen München (KMS) for Fund III's investment in German cable TV operator Pepcom, and sits on the Board of Directors of KMS. Prior to joining VSS's London office in 2004, Dr. von Bismarck was a Director at the U.S. and European media-focused investment bank Communications Equity Associates (CEA, now Goetzpartners), within the European media and entertainment industry group, where he specialized in television broadcasting, cable television, film production, film distribution, sports rights and publishing. Prior to CEA, he was part of the investment banking team at the German private merchant bank Joh. Berenberg, Gossler & Co. (Berenberg Bank) in Hamburg, working on mergers and acquisitions, structured finance and leveraged buyout transactions. Dr. von Bismarck gained his first M&A experience as an attorney at the German Trustee Agency (Treuhandanstalt), advising on the privatization of former East German companies. He started his banking career with a two-year training program at Deutsche Bank. Dr. von Bismarck is a trained attorney-at-law with degrees from the University of Munich and Berlin Department of Justice. He holds a diploma in banking and earned a Ph.D. in international comparative law from Humboldt University of Berlin.

KEVIN S. WALDMAN

Since joining Veronis Suhler Stevenson in 1996, Mr. Waldman has worked on a broad range of transactions in numerous sectors within the media and communications industries including directory publishing, radio and television broadcasting, cable television, business information, wireless communication towers and telecommunication services. Mr. Waldman has been active across a range of VSS portfolio companies, including DOAR Communications Inc., Riviera Broadcast Group, GoldenState Towers, User-Friendly Phone Book, Birch Telecom, Broadcasting Partners Holdings, Spectrum Resources Towers and Triax Midwest Associates. Mr. Waldman currently serves as a member of the Board of User-Friendly, DOAR Communications Inc. and Riviera Broadcast Group. He previously served as a member of the Boards of GoldenState Towers and ionex Telecommunications. Prior to joining VSS, Mr. Waldman spent four years at JP Morgan & Co., culminating as an associate in the Media, Telecommunications and Technology Group. He holds a BS degree from Syracuse University.

DIRECTORS

Supporting the Firm's Partners and Managing Directors is a team of Directors, Associates and Analysts as well as research staff. Directors include professionals dedicated to the activities of the Equity and Mezzanine Funds as well as professionals specializing in one or more industries who assist the Fund in sourcing, analyzing and monitoring portfolio companies. All professionals are highly incentivized to lend execution support and source transactions.

R. TRENT HICKMAN

Mr. Hickman's responsibilities include developing investment opportunities, conducting due diligence, arranging debt financing for portfolio investments, structuring investments and monitoring portfolio companies. He was actively involved in Fund III's acquisitions of Hanley Wood, Access Intelligence, Pepcom, Mediatel and Ascend Media. Mr. Hickman is a member of the Board of Managers of Access Intelligence. Prior to attending business school, Mr. Hickman was an Analyst and Associate in the Media & Entertainment Investment Banking Group of First Union Securities where he was involved in underwriting senior and subordinated debt financing for a number of Fund II portfolio companies, including Rifkin Acquisition Partners, Canon Communications, Centaur Communications and The Official Information Company. Mr. Hickman earned an AB in history and French literature from Duke University and an MBA in finance from The Wharton School of the University of Pennsylvania.

DAVID R. HOLLAND

Mr. Holland joined Veronis Suhler Stevenson in December 2000 as part of VSS's International team and is based in the Firm's London office. He worked on the merger and €1 billion refinancing of Fund III's European directory portfolio into YBR Group, having previously been involved in Fund III's acquisitions of each of the directory platforms, Fonecta (Finland), De Telefoongids (The Netherlands) and Mediatel (Austria, Czech Republic). Mr. Holland also worked on the sale of YBR Group, and has also worked with companies in the radio, newspaper and magazine sectors. Prior to joining VSS, Mr. Holland worked in the Sydney and London offices of PricewaterhouseCoopers as part of the firm's Transaction Services team. He has a Bachelor of Business (accounting and finance) degree from the University of Technology, Sydney, and is a member of the Institute of Chartered Accountants in Australia.

SETH E. ROSENFIELD

Mr. Rosenfield has been involved in both buy-side and sell-side transactions across many Media segments, with particular emphasis on business, consumer and professional media. During his tenure at Veronis Suhler Stevenson, Mr. Rosenfield has completed nearly 30 transactions, including Readers Digest's $760 million acquisition of Reiman Publications, and the sales of White Directory Publishers to Hearst, Saxon Publishers to Harcourt, and Carnegie Communications to Alloy. Prior to joining VSS in 1998, Mr. Rosenfield held senior financial positions at Scholastic and Simon & Schuster, a division of Viacom, Inc.

Mr. Rosenfield earned an MBA in marketing and operations and a BS in finance from New York University.

ERIC VAN ERT

Mr. Van Ert's responsibilities include sourcing new investment opportunities, structuring investments, valuation and financial analysis, due diligence and monitoring of portfolio companies. He was a member of the Board of Directors of Hanley Wood and GoldenState Towers. Prior to joining Veronis Suhler Stevenson in 2001, Mr. Van Ert was Director of Corporate Development at Hanley Wood. Previously, he was a Financial Analyst for Lockheed Martin. A CFA Charterholder, Mr. Van Ert earned an MBA from American University and a BS with honors from Saint Michael's College.

NICK VERONIS

Mr. Veronis's responsibilities include sourcing new investment opportunities, structuring investments, conducting financial analysis and due diligence, and monitoring portfolio companies. He focuses primarily on business information services and participated in the acquisition of Hemscott, a Fund III investment, and DOAR, a Fund IV investment. He has been involved in numerous buy-side and sell-side transactions at VSS, including the sales of Clipper Magazine, The Official Information Company, and Roper Starch Worldwide. Prior to joining the Firm in 1999, Mr. Veronis first gained Media experience as a reporter for *The Boston Business Journal* and then as a general assignment reporter for *The Star-Ledger* in New Jersey. He also was Associate Director of Newhouse Newspapers New Media Department. Mr. Veronis holds a BA degree in economics from Trinity College.

MARGARET V. YOUNG

Mrs. Young specializes in the newspaper, book and educational publishing industries. She joined VSS in 1996 as an Associate and spent the ensuing eight years working with VSS's Private Equity funds. She has been responsible for several platform investments in Fund II, including Canon Communications and Chemical Week Associates, monitoring operational and financial results and supervising bank relationships. Prior to joining VSS, Mrs. Young worked at S.G. Warburg with responsibility for strategic planning. From 1981 to 1991, she worked for Manufacturers Hanover Trust Company, where she was Vice President-Group Executive in the bank's Media Group. Mrs. Young earned a BA in music from Smith College and an MBA from Columbia University.

Board of Advisors

The Veronis Suhler Stevenson Board of Advisors comprises leaders from the Media industry and international politics. They play a key role for the Firm in new business development, provide strategic guidance to portfolio companies and lend their industry expertise for the benefit of the Fund.

DAVID ARCULUS

David Arculus is a member of the Board of Advisors of Veronis Suhler Stevenson and is currently non-executive Chairman of Earls Court & Olympia, The Better Regulation Task Force, and Severn Trent. He was Chairman of IPC Group from 1998 until its acquisition in 2001 by Time Warner, and served as COO of United News & Media. Prior to that, he was Group Managing Director of EMAP. In 1997 he became a non-executive Director of Barclays, and in 2002 a Delegate for the Finance Committee at Oxford University Press, as well as a member of the CBI Council and an associate of the Prime Minister Delivery Unit.

REGINALD K. BRACK

Reginald K. Brack is a member of the Board of Advisors of Veronis Suhler Stevenson and is the former Chairman and CEO of Time, Inc. He also served as publisher of *Time* magazine and Chairman and CEO of Time-Life Books. A former Chairman of the Magazine Publishers of America and the Advertising Council, Mr. Brack is a Director of the Interpublic Group of Companies and Bristol Hotels and Resorts.

LAWRENCE M. CRUTCHER

Lawrence M. Crutcher is a member of the Board of Advisors of Veronis Suhler Stevenson. From 1990 through 2004 he was a Managing Director at VSS specializing in direct marketing-related businesses and the consumer magazine and book industries, both in the U.S. and abroad. He completed the joint venture agreement between American Express Publishing Co. and Time Inc., wherein Time manages the American Express properties. Mr. Crutcher has long-term relationships in the catalog, list management and juvenile publishing industries, as well as in the magazine and trade publishing categories. His work now also includes newsletters and medical education companies. Mr. Crutcher joined VSS after a 22-year career at Time Inc., where he served as President and Chief Executive Officer of Book-of-the-Month Club. He holds a BA from Yale College and an MBA from Harvard Business School.

JAN O. FROESHAUG

Jan O. Froeshaug is a member of the Board of Advisors of Veronis Suhler Stevenson and previously served as the Chief Executive of the Egmont Foundation and its business enterprise, the Egmont Group, a position he held for 14 years. The Egmont Group, a Danish publishing and media corporation, comprising 100 companies in 29 countries. Mr. Froeshaug was also the Managing Director of Norsk Hydro, one of the leading Danish oil companies. He was the Chief Operating Officer of Great Nordic, a telecommunications and electronics group with activities and companies in Europe, Asia and the USA. He is currently a non-executive Director of AG Holding, Small-Cap Denmark and Torsana Oncology Systems. Additionally, Mr. Froeshaug is a non-executive Director of Ringier, a VSS limited Partner, and non-executive Chairman of Mediatel, a portfolio company of Fund III.

HERBERT A. GRANATH

Herbert A. Granath is a member of the Board of Advisors of Veronis Suhler Stevenson and is Chairman Emeritus of ESPN. He has held numerous senior management positions in the television industry, including Chairman of Walt Disney International Television, Board Chairman of ESPN, A&E, The History Channel, and Lifetime television networks, as well as Founding Partner of Eurosport. While at ABC, Mr. Granath served as Corporate Senior Vice President of the International Academy of Television Arts and Sciences. He is the recipient of two Emmy and two Tony awards.

GENE F. JANKOWSKI

Gene F. Jankowski is a member of the Board of Advisors of Veronis Suhler Stevenson. From 1995 through 2004 he was an Advisor Managing Director of VSS. Mr. Jankowski focuses his activities on television broadcasting, filmed entertainment, radio broadcasting, and subscription video services. In 1994, Mr. Jankowski joined VSS after a 28-year career at CBS. In 1970 he was appointed General Sales Manager of WCBS-TV, the CBS flagship station in New York. He then became Vice President of Sales for the nationwide CBS Television stations division and was later named Vice President and Controller for CBS Inc. In 1977, Mr. Jankowski became President and Chairman of the CBS Broadcasting Group, a position he held for 12 years until 1989, when he left CBS to form his own company. Mr. Jankowski graduated from Canisius College and Michigan State University with a master's degree in radio, television and film. He holds honorary doctorate degrees from Canisius College and Michigan State. Mr. Jankowski is Chairman of the Board at the Trans-Lux Corporation. He is the co-author of *Reflections on Television: It Won't Be What You Think.*

THE RIGHT HONORABLE BRIAN MULRONEY

The Right Honourable Brian Mulroney is a member of the Board of Advisors of Veronis Suhler Stevenson. Mr. Mulroney was Prime Minister of Canada from 1984 to 1993. Now a Senior Partner with the law firm of Ogilvy Renault, Mr. Mulroney also serves as a Director of a variety of companies, including Archer Daniels Midland Company, Quebecor Printing, Independent Newspapers, Barrick

Gold, and Cendant. He is a member of numerous international advisory Boards, including those of the Power Corporation of Canada (a VSS limited partner), JP Morgan Chase (a VSS limited partner), the China International Trust, and the Hicks Muse Tate and Furst Latin American Strategy Board.

JOHN R. PURCELL

John R. Purcell is a member of the Board of Advisors of Veronis Suhler Stevenson and is Chairman and CEO of Grenadier Associates, a venture banking firm. He served as Chairman of Donnelley Marketing, and of Mindscape. Formerly, Mr. Purcell was Chairman and President of SFN Companies, Executive Vice President of CBS, and Senior Vice President, finance of Gannett Co. He is a Director of several companies, including Bausch & Lomb, Omnicom Group, Technology Solutions Co. and Journal Register Company.

FRANÇOIS R. ROY

François R. Roy is a member of the Board of Advisors of Veronis Suhler Stevenson. Mr. Roy is a Senior Executive with extensive experience working with Canadian media companies, as well as technology companies, industrial companies and financial firms in both Canada and the United States. He has served as Chief Financial Officer for Quebecor Inc., Telemedia Corporation and Avenor, Inc. For over two decades, Mr. Roy has developed additional investment experience in Canada and the United States with firms such as the Bank of Nova Scotia and Société générale de financement du Québec, and most recently serving as Advisor to François de Gaspé Beaubien, a prominent shareholder of Telemedia. Mr. Roy serves on the Board of Directors of MDC Partners Inc., Advanced Fiber Technologies Inc. and Macquarie Power Income Fund, and is a member of the Advisory Board of Dessau-Soprin. He has served on the Board of Trustees of several not-for-profit organizations such as the Montreal Museum of Fine Arts, Canadian Centre for Architecture, International Festival of Art Films, and continues to serve on the Board of Trustees of the Opéra de Montréal.

INQUIRIES

Veronis Suhler Stevenson welcomes inquiries regarding its private equity and mezzanine activities in the United States and abroad. Interested parties may contact James P. Rutherfurd, Executive Vice President, or Jeffrey T. Stevenson, Managing Partner and Co-Chief Executive Officer, in New York, or Marco Sodi, Partner, at the Firm's London address noted below or via email:

VERONIS SUHLER STEVENSON PARTNERS LLC
350 Park Avenue
New York, NY 10022
www.vss.com
Tel: 212-935-4990
Fax: 212-381-8168
E-mail: *rutherfurdj@vss.com*
stevensonj@vss.com

VERONIS SUHLER STEVENSON INTERNATIONAL LIMITED
8th Floor, Buchanan House
3 St. James's Square, London SW1Y 4JU
Tel: +44 (0) 20 7484 1400
Fax: +44 (0) 20 7484 1410
E-mail: *sodim@vss.com*

Fund III Investments: Xtreme Add-ons and Transactions

VS&A Communications Partners III, L.P.
an affiliate of Veronis Suhler Stevenson LLC

has acquired
along with the company's management

Xtreme Information Services Ltd.
a leading global advertising and press monitoring service

Veronis Suhler Stevenson International Ltd.,
the London-based affiliate of Veronis Suhler Stevenson LLC,
initiated the transaction, acted as financial advisor to,
and is the exclusive representative of
VS&A Communications Partners III, L.P.

August 2001

Xtreme Information Services Ltd.
a leading global advertising and press monitoring services firm
and a portfolio company of
VS&A Communications Partners III, L.P.

has acquired

TVR Australia

Veronis Suhler Stevenson International Ltd.,
an affiliate of Veronis Suhler Stevenson, acted as
financial advisor to Xtreme Information Services Ltd.

August 2002

Xtreme Information Services Ltd.
a leading global advertising and press monitoring services firm
and a portfolio company of
VS&A Communications Partners III, L.P.

has acquired

Veronis Suhler Stevenson International Ltd.,
an affiliate of Veronis Suhler Stevenson LLC, acted as
financial advisor to Xtreme Information Services Ltd.

May 2002

Xtreme Information Services Ltd.
a leading global advertising and press monitoring services firm
and a portfolio company of
VS&A Communications Partners III, L.P.

has acquired

a U.K. AIM-listed company providing press monitoring services

for approximately

£7,600,000

Veronis Suhler Stevenson International Ltd.,
an affiliate of Veronis Suhler Stevenson LLC, acted as
financial advisor to Xtreme Information Services Ltd.

January 2002

Xtreme Information Services Ltd.
a leading global competitive monitoring company
and a portfolio company of
VS&A Communications Partners III, L.P.

has acquired

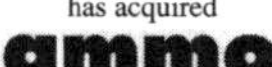

Advanced Media &Marketing Opportunities
a U.K. marketing information company

Veronis Suhler Stevenson International Ltd.,
an affiliate of Veronis Suhler Stevenson, acted as
financial advisor to Xtreme Information Services Ltd.

November 2004

Xtreme Information Services Ltd.
a leading global advertising and press monitoring services firm
and a portfolio company of
VS&A Communications Partners III, L.P.

has sold

Xtreme News

to

Durrants Press Cuttings Limited

Veronis Suhler Stevenson International Ltd.,
an affiliate of Veronis Suhler Stevenson, acted as
financial advisor to Xtreme Information Services Ltd.

May 2004

Private Equity Capital / Mezzanine Capital / Industry Research and Forecasts

Veronis Suhler Stevenson
MEDIA • COMMUNICATIONS • INFORMATION

350 Park Avenue, New York, NY 10022
212-935-4990 212-381-8168 fax
www.vss.com

Activities requiring securities industry registration will be performed by Veronis Suhler Stevenson Partners LLC wholly-owned broker-dealer affiliate, Veronis Suhler Stevenson LLC. Veronis Suhler Stevenson LLC is a member of NASD and SIPC.

Forecast Summary

Communications Industry Spending And Nominal GDP Growth, 2000-2009

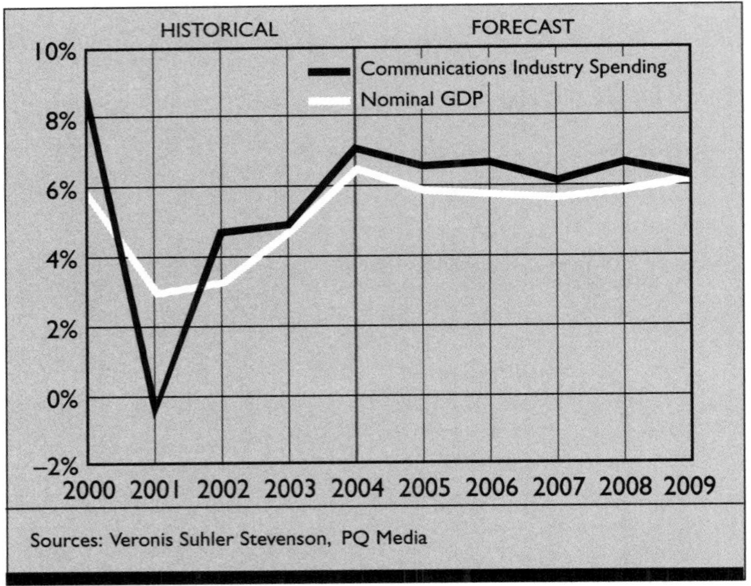

Sources: Veronis Suhler Stevenson, PQ Media

MAJOR TRENDS IMPACTING THE COMMUNICATIONS INDUSTRY IN 2004 AND 2005

While the cyclical segments of the communications industry transitioned from recovery to expansion mode in 2004, following a devastating economic recession in 2001 and two years of sluggish recovery in the advertising sector, the industry is undergoing a fundamental change. This transformation, the likes of which have not been seen in decades, is being driven by several important developments, and was predicted by Internet pundits a decade ago. Although these predictions may have been self-serving or at least premature—as the dot-com bubble burst in 2000, hastening the recession that ravaged the advertising business—those dot-com soothsayers are looking quite deft. Five years later, the economic recession appears to have been a blip in a new order that has emerged from the ashes of the worst advertising contraction since the Great Depression.

This New Media Order began to take shape in 2001 and 2002, when companies large and small were forced to cut budgets, reduce staff and curtail expenses in an effort to shore up profit margins exposed to one of the worst economic downturns in decades. As part of their fiscal restraint, corporations, including major advertisers, decided to significantly scale back plans for new ventures and new media expansion in favor of refocusing on core businesses and conventional mar-

Growth of U.S. Communications Industry Spending

	Advertising Spending	*Specialty Media And Marketing Services Spending*	*Consumer End-User Spending*	*Institutional End-User Spending*	*Total*
2004 Expenditures ($ Millions)	$188,187	$257,145	$186,301	$171,082	$802,715
1999-2004 Compound Annual Growth (%)	3.0%	4.9%	7.6%	5.6%	5.2%
2004-2009 Projected Compound Annual Growth (%)	6.8%	6.7%	6.3%	7.0%	6.7%
2009 Projected Expenditures ($ Millions)	$260,897	$355,154	$252,801	$239,820	$1,108,672

Sources: Veronis Suhler Stevenson, PQ Media

keting methods while they evaluated their business development and media expenditures. But instead of simply hunkering down and spending their limited media budgets on traditional advertising vehicles until the storm passed, marketers took a hard look at their media spending patterns, and decided that they needed stronger measurements of their return on investment (ROI) in advertising and marketing campaigns. This growing belief was only accentuated by the tough economic times that had befallen corporate America.

Meanwhile, a revolution was taking place in the consumer end-user sector, which was flourishing in 2001 and 2002 in the wake of the economic recession, the advertising market contraction and the September 11 terrorist attacks. Consumers, and families in particular, went into a sort of cocoon mode, in which they began spending more time at home, or doing things together, and more of that time was being spent on non-advertising-based media, such as home videos, videogames and movies, as well as the Internet. At the same time, technology innovations fueled the consistent rollout of new consumer-based media, which drove accelerated audience fragmentation and increased consumer multitasking. In addition, the advent of the digital video recorder (DVR) ushered in the era of consumer empowerment over media, in which consumers not only have a multitude of media choices, but they can now completely skip ads delivered through one of the most powerful advertising tools on the planet: television.

While consumers were becoming accustomed to their newfound power over media, advertisers were becoming increasingly frustrated by the lack of effective ROI measurements and the pushback that media were receiving from consumers complaining about increased ad clutter, due to marketers using all available opportunities to reach ever more elusive audiences. The result of this torrent of activity in the communications industry over the past five years has been a gradual shift of time spent away from advertising-based to consumer-supported media, and a steady transfer of spending away from traditional to new media advertising. Marketers in recent years have considerably increased their use of non-conventional media, such as videogames, cell phones and movies in their ardor to reach desirable markets like the 18- to 34-year-old demographic, which is not accepting traditional media in the recovery-to-expansion period the way past generations did. For example, newspaper readership and broadcast television viewership by young adults were down substantially in 2004 compared with two decades ago, while videogame usage and Internet consumption are up significantly.

From a statistical perspective, advertising-based media, including broadcast television, broadcast and satellite radio, daily newspapers and consumer magazines, accounted for 63.6 percent of all consumer time spent with media in 1999, compared with 36.4 percent for consumer-supported media, such as cable and satellite television, box office, home video, interactive television (ITV), recorded music, videogames, consumer Internet and consumer books. By the end of 2004, however, ad-based media's share of consumer time spent declined more than 7 percentage points to 56.4 percent, versus 43.6 percent for consumer-supported media. At the conclusion of 2009, we expect the gap to close further—although at a progressively decelerating pace in the forecast period—as ad-based media will comprise 54.1 percent of consumer time spent, while consumer-supported media will command a 45.9 percent share.

On the advertising spending front, expenditures on new media advertising, such as cable and satellite television, satellite radio, business-to-business e-media, consumer Internet, movie screens and videogames, grew at a double-digit rate in 2004, while spending on traditional media, including broadcast television, newspapers, broadcast radio, yellow pages, consumer magazines, business-to-business magazines and out-of-home, expanded only at a single-digit rate, much slower than new media. Traditional media advertising accounted for 89.7 percent of all ad expenditures in 1999, while new media comprised the other 10.3 percent of total ad spending that year. But at year-end 2004, traditional media advertising's share of total ad expenditures

Highlights

The cyclical segments of the communications industry transitioned from recovery to expansion mode in 2004, as the industry posted accelerated growth for the third consecutive year and outpaced nominal GDP expansion for the third straight year. Total communications spending climbed 7.3 percent to $802.72 billion, driven by accelerated growth in three of the four broad sectors of the industry—advertising, specialty media and marketing services, and institutional end user. While the fourth sector, consumer end user, posted decelerated growth for the second consecutive year in 2004, this sector still recorded relatively solid expansion at 6.2 percent. Total communications spending grew at a compound annual rate of 5.2 percent from 1999 to 2004, exceeding nominal GDP and making communications the seventh-fastest-growing industry of the U.S. economy in the period.

■

Specialty media and marketing services was the largest sector of the communications industry in 2004, growing 6.9 percent to $257.15 billion and accounting for 32.0 percent of all communications spending for the year. The advertising sector expanded 7.6 percent to $188.19 billion and comprised 23.4 percent of all media expenditures in 2004, while the consumer end-user sector grew 6.2 percent to $186.30 billion and accounted for 23.2 percent of all spending. Although the consumer end-user sector grew more slowly than the other three in 2004, this sector posted the fastest compound annual growth in the 1999-2004 period at 7.6 percent. Meanwhile, institutional end-user spending rose the fastest of all four sectors in 2004, climbing 8.8 percent to $171.08 billion, but was the smallest of all sectors with a 21.3 percent share for the year.

■

The communications industry is in the midst of a fundamental change, driven by technology innovation, the emergence of new media delivery and channel options, quickening audience fragmentation, more multitasking, increased demand for customization and tighter focus on return on investment (ROI). This new order, which began to take shape during the recession, will usher in major changes in all four communications sectors, particularly advertising. Part of this transformation will be the gradual shift of time spent away from advertising-based to consumer-supported media, as well as a steady transfer of spending away from traditional to new media advertising.

had dropped more than 6 percentage points to 83.3 percent, while new media's share grew to 16.7 percent for the year. We expect this trend to continue in the forecast period, as marketers shift ad dollars to new media that reach younger audiences more effectively and provide better ROI measurement. Consequently, spending on traditional advertising is projected to lose almost 10 share points to new media by the end of 2009.

Traditional advertising media are facing competition from new advertising options that generally cost less and are doing a better job meeting marketers' demands for proof of ROI. The product sampling and in-store media markets, for instance, are anticipated to surpass overall growth in spending on advertising and specialty media over the next five years, due in part to a tighter focus on delivering ROI. In early 2005, one provider of in-store sampling and retail entertainment events introduced a system that tracks the

Meanwhile, in the consumer end-user sector, technology innovations will continue to fuel the rollout of new consumer media, driving increased audience fragmentation and multitasking. In the specialty media and marketing services, and institutional end-user sectors, new technology, ROI requirements, end-user empowerment and growing demand for customization will speed the growth of alternative marketing and stimulate the development of creative multimedia workflow solutions.

■

Total communications spending in the first half of 2005 was pacing behind the industry's growth in the similar period of 2004, mainly due to the absence of political and Olympics advertising and decelerated growth in the professional and business information services segment, which was hard pressed to match the strong growth of the previous year. As a result, communications spending growth is expected to decelerate somewhat to 6.8 percent for full-year 2005, with expenditures reaching $857.59 billion.

■

We expect overall communications spending to grow at an accelerated compound annual rate of 6.7 percent from 2004 to 2009, surpassing the trillion-dollar mark in 2008, and reaching $1.109 trillion in 2009. The industry's expansion will outperform nominal GDP growth of 6.0 percent in the forecast period, driven by mid- to high-single-digit growth in all four industry sectors. Institutional end-user spending will outpace the other three sectors with compound annual growth of 7.0 percent from 2004 to 2009. Specialty media and marketing services will remain the largest sector of the communications industry in 2009 with expenditures of $355.15 billion. Communications will become the fourth-largest sector of the U.S. economy by 2009, as well as improve to the fourth-fastest-growing sector of the economy during the five-year period.

■

Overall, consumers increased time spent with media by only 0.3 percent in 2004 to 3,480 hours per person for the year, slightly less than 10 hours a day per person. Since 1999, overall use has increased 200 hours per person annually, up a half-hour per day. Overall usage increased at a compound annual rate of 1.2 percent from 1999 to 2004. The increase in time spent with media has been the subject of numerous debates over the past two years, leading to the launch of a cavalcade of studies regarding the occurrence and impact of media multitasking. From 2004 to 2009, overall time spent with media will expand to 3,555 hours per person per year, posting compound annual growth of 0.4 percent.

sales performance of individual demonstrators at sampling events. Another retail marketing services company launched an in-store broadcast radio service that demonstrates the measurability of in-store promotion. And market research firms have created systems for measuring ROI in product placements. Alternative marketing vehicles, as well as non-traditional advertising media, are also more adept at reaching the coveted 18- to 34-year-old market, an elusive group because they divide their time among a variety of media. As a result, non-traditional ad media that attract younger audiences, such as consumer Internet, videogames and movie screens, are benefiting greatly from this development. Alternative marketing vehicles that reach young audiences are also generating strong growth, such as sponsorships at concerts and sporting events, and product placements in television shows with youth appeal.

Time Spent with Media

Category	Hours per Person per Year						Percent Change	
	1999	Percent Share	2004	Percent Share	2009	Percent Share	1999-2004	2004-2009
Media with Significant Advertising Support*	2,075	63.3%	1,976	56.8%	1,951	54.9%	−4.8%	−1.2%
Media Supported Predominantly By Consumers†	1,204	36.7	1,504	43.2	1,604	45.1	24.9	6.6

Sources: Veronis Suhler Stevenson, PQ Media

*Broadcast television, broadcast & satellite radio, daily newspapers, consumer magazines.

†Cable & satellite television, box office, home video, interactive television, recorded music, videogames, consumer Internet, consumer books.

The primary result of these critical trends is that media buying has become more complicated. Buyers have been pressed to develop complex purchasing plans that use a variety of advertising and marketing strategies integrating the use of conventional and nontraditional media to reach more cagey audiences. For example, marketers are demanding that their buyers develop approaches that ensure their brand messages cut through increased ad clutter, which has led to the surging growth of alternative marketing tactics like product placement. At the same time, advertisers want better ROI measurement, which has fueled the strong expansion of ad categories such as Internet keyword search. In addition, during the 2004 political elections, both presidential candidates used tightly targeted direct mail and e-mail campaigns to reach niche demographic and psychographic groups based on zip code characteristics.

As a result of technology innovations, the surfacing of new media choices, and the subsequent changes in consumer and advertiser behavior, the New Media Order has emerged and will change the advertising business fundamentally. As the forecast period progresses, advertising will take one of two forms: It will be integrated directly into media content that is relevant to the consumer, and that the consumer chooses to read, view or listen to; or it will be a message that the consumer actively seeks as part of a product or service.

The new order, however, has not only affected the advertising and consumer sectors of the industry, but has also had a notable impact on the specialty media and marketing services, and institutional end-user sectors. In the specialty media and marketing services sector, the important change catalysts of technology innovation, the tighter focus on ROI, end-user empowerment and growing demand for customization have led marketers to embrace alternative marketing strategies, ranging from product placement and custom publishing to event sponsorship and interactive direct marketing. These key drivers will continue to stimulate solid growth in this sector throughout the forecast period as marketers use alternative marketing tactics to break through the clutter of competing advertising messages. This will result in strong growth in the key segments of direct marketing, custom publishing, branded entertainment and public relations over the next five years.

In the institutional sector, the same key trends are spurring some of the most remarkable innovation, growth and change in a sector once known for its stodginess. A common theme in all four of the institutional end-user

Advertising in Traditional and New Media

	Advertising Spending ($ Millions)						Compound Annual Growth	
Category	*1999*	*Percent Share*	*2004*	*Percent Share*	*2009*	*Percent Share*	*1999-2004*	*2004-2009*
Traditional Media Advertising*	$145,698	89.7%	$156,822	83.3%	$192,281	73.7%	1.5%	4.2%
New Media Advertising†	16,753	10.3	31,365	16.7	68,616	26.3	13.4	16.9

Sources: Veronis Suhler Stevenson, PQ Media

*Includes broadcast television, newspapers, broadcast radio, yellow pages, consumer magazines, business-to-business magazines, and out-of-home.

†Includes cable and satellite television, satellite radio, business-to-business e-media, consumer Internet, movie screen advertising, and videogame advertising.

segments is that the escalating demand for ROI measurement is being met through the creative use of technology. Nowhere in the media industry is this more apparent than in the professional and business information services (PBIS) segment, where publishers were a decade ahead of the rest of the industry in developing and delivering ingenious technology solutions to end users through integrated multimedia workflow tools. And each year, the PBIS segment has improved on its arsenal of workflow gear by creating more advanced value-added products and services that combine enhanced functionality with flexible delivery, progressive analytics and innovative ROI measurement instruments. In the meantime, educational and training media providers have used technology advances to create original online courseware and learning environments designed to improve education and training opportunities on campuses, at work and at home, as well as to connect learners and educators communicating at a distance. And in the business-to-business media segment, leading companies are transforming themselves from simply magazine publishers to multimedia business information providers delivering mission-critical content via print, live events and e-media formats that end users need to do their jobs better.

THE COMMUNICATIONS INDUSTRY BY THE NUMBERS: 1999 TO 2009

Transitioning from recovery to expansion mode, the communications industry grew at its fastest rate in four years in 2004, expanding 7.3 percent to $802.72 billion, driven by accelerated growth in three of the four broad sectors of the industry. Communications spending growth accelerated for the third consecutive year in 2004 and outpaced nominal GDP expansion for the third straight year. While the advertising, specialty media and marketing services, and institutional end-user sectors each posted faster year-over-year growth in 2004, the consumer end-user sector—which outperformed the other sectors for three consecutive years from 2001 to 2003—recorded decelerating growth for the year, although still solid in the mid-single digits.

Total communications spending grew at a compound annual rate of 5.2 percent from 1999 to 2004, making communications the seventh-fastest-growing industry out of the 15 that comprised the U.S. economy in the five-year period. The communications industry's growth exceeded nominal GDP expansion of 4.8 percent in the period.

In order for Veronis Suhler Stevenson to provide the most accurate, up-to-date and valuable data and information available to

Top 15 Economic Sectors Ranked by Five-Year Growth

	1999-2004		2004-2009	
Economic Sector	*CAGR**	*Rank*	*CAGR**	*Rank*
Mining	11.5%	1	5.2%	12
Finance, Insurance and Real Estate	6.1	2	6.7	3
Construction	5.9	3	6.4	7
Services	5.5	4	6.4	8
Electric, Gas and Sanitary Services	5.4	5	6.9	2
Federal Government	5.2	6	7.1	1
Communications	**5.2**	**7**	**6.7**	**4**
State and Local Government	5.0	8	6.4	9
Retail Trade	4.6	9	6.6	5
Agriculture, Forestry and Fishing	4.4	10	6.6	6
Wholesale Trade	3.6	11	5.3	11
Transportation	3.3	12	4.7	13
Nondurable Goods	3.0	13	5.3	10
Telephone and Telegraph	2.8	14	3.7	14
Durable Goods	1.0	15	1.5	15
Nominal GDP	4.8	6.0		

Sources: Veronis Suhler Stevenson, PQ Media, Bureau of Economic Analysis
*Compound annual growth rate.

our subscribers, we made a number of substantive changes to the 2005 edition of the *Forecast* which changed the size and structure of the communications industry compared with the 2004 edition. In particular, there were several changes made that had significant impacts on the size, growth and shares of each of the four broad sectors of the communications industry in 2004. Among these were the additions of several new spending categories to the direct marketing segment of the specialty media and marketing services sector, which made this sector the largest of the four in 2004. There were also important additions and revisions of data made to several segments of the advertising, consumer end-user and institutional end-user sectors, which changed their respective shares of the overall communications industry. For all of the details regarding these changes and their impact on this edition of the *Forecast*, please consult the Appendix that is located at the end of this report.

As a result, specialty media and marketing services grew 6.9 percent to $257.15 billion and accounted for 32.0 percent of all communications spending for the year. The specialty media and marketing services sector includes spending on direct marketing, business-to-business promotion, consumer promotion, custom publishing, public relations and branded entertainment, which includes event sponsorship, promotional licensing and product placement. Spending on alternative marketing methods, such as product placement, custom publishing and interac-

Top 15 Economic Sectors Ranked by Dollar Sales*

	2004		2009	
Economic Sector	*$ Billions*	*Rank*	*$ Billions*	*Rank*
Services	$ 2,798	1	$ 3,815	1
Finance, Insurance and Real Estate	2,341	2	3,235	2
State and Local Government	959	3	1,306	3
Durable Goods	832	4	895	6
Communications	**803**	**5**	**1,109**	**4**
Retail Trade	770	6	1,060	5
Wholesale Trade	665	7	860	7
Nondurable Goods	564	8	730	8
Construction	522	9	711	9
Federal Government	448	10	632	10
Transportation	327	11	411	11
Electric, Gas and Sanitary Services	233	12	325	12
Telephone and Telegraph	219	13	263	13
Mining	142	14	183	14
Agriculture, Forestry and Fishing	112	15	154	15
Nominal GDP	11,735		15,689	

Sources: Veronis Suhler Stevenson, PQ Media, Bureau of Economic Analysis
*Dollar amounts reflect final sales of goods and services to consumers and businesses in each of the sectors. Communications spending data are taken from this *Forecast*, not from the annual BEA data, which is for the 1988-2003 period. The data for 2004 were calculated from historical data using the post-1998 linear trend. To avoid double counting the sectors, the following communications segments were not included in the following BEA categories: printing and publishing not included in nondurable goods; motion pictures not included in services.

tive direct marketing, fueled growth in this sector from 1999 to 2004, as the combined market grew at a compound annual rate of 4.9 percent in the period. Many of the trends that stimulated the advertising sector in 2004 to its highest growth rate since 2000 drove the specialty media and marketing services sector, as well. Marketers have been embracing non-conventional marketing strategies, including the aforementioned tactics, at an increasing rate in recent years, and we expect this trend to continue to drive solid growth in this sector in 2005 and during the forecast period as marketers utilize more alternative means of breaking through the growing advertising clutter. Accordingly, spending growth in the specialty media and marketing services sector in 2005 is projected to increase slightly over 2004, rising 7.0 percent to $275.11 billion for the year. Double-digit growth is expected in custom publishing, product placement, public relations, and ITV promotions and advertising, while mid- to high-single-digit gains are anticipated in event sponsorship, direct marketing, business-to-business promotion, and trade show fees, sponsorship and promotion. Marketers will continue to seek out alternative marketing vehicles, placing those most affected by the federal Do Not Call Registry, partly spurring compound annual growth of 6.7 percent in the 2004-2009 period to $355.15 billion in 2009.

For the first time in at least a decade, institutional end-user spending grew the fastest of the four media sectors in 2004,

Advertising, Specialty Media and Marketing Services, and End-User Spending

($ MILLIONS)

Year	Advertising Spending	Specialty Media And Marketing Services Spending	Total Advertising, Specialty Media And Marketing Services Spending	Consumer End-User Spending	Institutional End-User Spending	Total End-User Spending	Total
1999	$162,451	$202,389	$364,840	$129,153	$130,436	$259,589	$ 624,429
2000	181,248	220,805	402,053	135,902	141,383	277,285	679,338
2001	167,168	218,866	386,034	147,671	143,332	291,003	677,037
2002	170,060	228,627	398,687	163,132	149,356	312,488	711,175
2003	174,871	240,598	415,469	175,479	157,306	332,785	748,254
2004	188,187	257,145	445,332	186,301	171,082	357,383	802,715
2005	199,670	275,110	474,780	199,336	183,473	382,809	857,589
2006	214,586	293,615	508,201	212,697	196,259	408,956	917,157
2007	227,916	311,788	539,704	226,676	209,706	436,382	976,086
2008	245,509	332,971	578,480	240,204	224,656	464,860	1,043,340
2009	260,897	355,154	616,051	252,801	239,820	492,621	1,108,672
Five-Year Change							
1999-2004	25,736	54,756	80,492	57,148	40,646	97,794	178,286
2004-2009	72,710	98,009	170,719	66,500	68,738	135,238	305,957

Sources: Veronis Suhler Stevenson, PQ Media

climbing 8.8 percent to $171.08 billion, but was the smallest communications sector with a 21.3 percent share of all spending. The institutional end-user sector includes spending on PBIS; television programming; educational and training media; and business-to-business magazine circulation and trade show exhibition space. Institutional spending grew at a compound annual rate of 5.6 percent from 1999 to 2004, as strong growth during the past two years was moderated by weaker performances in 2001 and 2002. The institutional sector is expected to be the fastest-growing area of the communications business again in 2005, climbing at a strong, albeit slightly decelerated, rate of 7.2 percent to expenditures of $183.47 billion for the year. Institutional spending growth will be fueled mainly by solid gains in the PBIS segment, which accounted for nearly 60 percent of all institutional expenditures in 2004. PBIS spending is predicted to increase 8.1 percent in 2005, followed by 7.2 percent growth in educational and training media and 6.0 percent upside in television programming. Going forward, institutional spending on communications will grow at a compound annual rate of 7.0 percent from 2004 to 2009, reaching $239.82 billion, sparked by continued technology innovation, a tighter focus on ROI, end-user empowerment and growing demand for customization.

The consumer end-user sector, in the meantime, posted its slowest growth rate in four years in 2004, rising 6.2 percent to $186.30 billion, due to slowing growth in the videogames segment, which has been hurt by the lack of a new console release since 2002, and a home video segment that was severely impacted by the rapid decline of the VHS market. Nevertheless, the consumer sector logged respectable mid-single-digit growth for the year and accounted for 23.2 percent of all communications spending. The consumer end-user sector includes expendi-

Growth of Advertising, Specialty Media and Marketing Services, and End-User Spending

Year	*Advertising Spending*	*Specialty Media And Marketing Services Spending*	*Total Advertising, Specialty Media And Marketing Services Spending*	*Consumer End-User Spending*	*Institutional End-User Spending*	*Total End-User Spending*	*Total*
2000	11.6%	9.1%	10.2%	5.2%	8.4%	6.8%	8.8%
2001	–7.8	–0.9	–4.0	8.7	1.4	4.9	–0.3
2002	1.7	4.5	3.3	10.5	4.2	7.4	5.0
2003	2.8	5.2	4.2	7.6	5.3	6.5	5.2
2004	7.6	6.9	7.2	6.2	8.8	7.4	7.3
2005	6.1	7.0	6.6	7.0	7.2	7.1	6.8
2006	7.5	6.7	7.0	6.7	7.0	6.8	6.9
2007	6.2	6.2	6.2	6.6	6.9	6.7	6.4
2008	7.7	6.8	7.2	6.0	7.1	6.5	6.9
2009	6.3	6.7	6.5	5.2	6.7	6.0	6.3
Compound Annual Growth							
1999-2004	3.0	4.9	4.1	7.6	5.6	6.6	5.2
2004-2009	6.8	6.7	6.7	6.3	7.0	6.6	6.7

Sources: Veronis Suhler Stevenson, PQ Media

tures on cable and satellite television subscriptions, home video, Internet access and content, consumer books, recorded music, newspaper circulation, consumer magazine circulation, box office admissions, videogames, ITV and wireless content, and satellite radio subscriptions. Although the consumer sector grew more slowly than the other three in 2004, this market posted the fastest compound annual growth in the 1999-2004 period at 7.6 percent, and the market's growth is expected to accelerate in 2005, climbing 7.0 percent to $199.34 billion. Growth will be driven by expansion in new media, fueled by expected double-digit gains in satellite radio subscriptions, ITV and wireless content, consumer Internet and home video, as well as solid single-digit upside in cable and satellite television. Many of the other consumer end-user segments—consumer books, consumer magazines, box office and videogames—will experience low-single-digit growth, while expenditures on recorded music and newspaper circulation are expected to decline in 2005. Consumer media spending will slow slightly during the forecast period as a number of newer media, such as the Internet, begin to reach market saturation. Accordingly, consumer end-user spending will grow at a compound annual rate of 6.3 percent from 2004 to 2009, reaching $252.80 billion.

Due to solid gains during the recession, the consumer end-user sector surpassed advertising in 2003 as the second-largest communications sector, but was unable to sustain this momentum in 2004. The advertising sector expanded 7.6 percent to $188.19 billion in 2004, and regained its position as the second-largest sector of the communications industry by capturing 23.4 percent of all media expenditures for the year. Growth was fueled by political and Olympics advertising, as well as double-digit gains in new media advertising such as the Internet, business-to-business e-media, videogames, movie screens,

Shares of Advertising, Specialty Media and Marketing Services, and End-User Spending

Year	*Advertising Spending*	*Specialty Media And Marketing Services Spending*	*Total Advertising, Specialty Media And Marketing Services Spending*	*Consumer End-User Spending*	*Institutional End-User Spending*	*Total End-User Spending*
1999	26.0%	32.4%	58.4%	20.7%	20.9%	41.6%
2000	26.7	32.5	59.2	20.0	20.8	40.8
2001	24.7	32.3	57.0	21.8	21.2	43.0
2002	23.9	32.1	56.1	22.9	21.0	43.9
2003	23.4	32.2	55.5	23.5	21.0	44.5
2004	23.4	32.0	55.5	23.2	21.3	44.5
2005	23.3	32.1	55.4	23.2	21.4	44.6
2006	23.4	32.0	55.4	23.2	21.4	44.6
2007	23.3	31.9	55.3	23.2	21.5	44.7
2008	23.5	31.9	55.4	23.0	21.5	44.6
2009	23.5	32.0	55.6	22.8	21.6	44.4

Sources: Veronis Suhler Stevenson, PQ Media

and alternative out-of-home media. Advertising spending rose at a compound annual rate of only 3.0 percent in the 1999-2004 period, primarily due to the 7.8 percent contraction in 2001 and slow recovery in the ensuing two years. The advertising sector includes spending on broadcast television, cable and satellite television, broadcast and satellite radio, daily and weekly newspapers, consumer and business-to-business magazines and e-media, the Internet, yellow pages, out-of-home, and advertising on new media previously reserved for consumers, such as videogames, movie screens and wireless content. Advertising in new media will continue to be a key growth driver in this market in 2005 and beyond as marketers look to alternative marketing methods, especially those that supply strong ROI metrics, to accentuate growth in a more competitive marketplace. Advertising expenditures are expected to increase 6.1 percent to $199.67 billion in 2005, a slightly decelerated growth rate owing to the absence of political and Olympics advertising.

We project spending on advertising to grow at a compound annual rate of 6.8 percent from 2004 to 2009, reaching $260.90 billion, driven mainly by the migration of ad dollars from traditional to new media. Although the advertising industry will continue to post gains during the forecast period, growth will not surpass that of GDP by as wide a margin as in the past, due to competition with alternative marketing vehicles and the several other aforementioned trends. After the advertising market emerged from the recession of the early 1990s, annual spending growth exceeded GDP by 2.0 to 6.0 percentage points from 1994 through 2000. But from 2004 to 2009, annual spending growth is anticipated to exceed GDP by only 0.1 of a point to 1.7 points.

The Outlook for The Communications Industry

While total spending on communications in the first half of 2005 was pacing slightly behind the prior year, as a result of the absence of political and Olympics advertising and somewhat decelerated growth in several recently strong specialty and institutional media segments, industry expenditures are expected to post comparatively robust growth at 6.8 percent for the full year. The communications industry will settle into a similar growth pattern throughout the forecast period, rising at a compound annual rate of 6.7 percent from 2004 to 2009. Communications spending is projected to surpass the trillion-dollar mark in 2008 and reach $1.109 trillion in 2009. Compound annual growth in the five-year period will accelerate over the 5.2 percent upside posted in the 1999-2004 timeframe. The industry's expansion will also outperform nominal GDP growth of 6.0 percent in the forecast period, driven by solid mid-single-digit growth in all four industry sectors over the next five years. Institutional end-user spending will outpace the other three sectors with compound annual growth of 7.0 percent from 2004 to 2009, while specialty media and marketing services will remain the largest sector of the industry in 2009 with expenditures of $355.15 billion. Communications will become the fourth-largest industry of the U.S. economy in 2009, as well as improve to the fourth-fastest-growing sector of the economy during the period.

We remain optimistic about the communications industry's prospects over the next five years because historical trends support our assumptions regarding the health of the economy. U.S. Government data indicate that economic expansions since World War II have had an average length of about five years. The two most recent expansions, however, extended nearly 10 years each. The current expansion is in its fourth year in 2005.

The fastest-growing communications segments over the next five years will be consumer Internet, which will post compound annual growth of 14.5 percent from 2004 to 2009; custom publishing, which will record compound annual expansion of 12.1 percent in the forecast period; public relations, which will log upside of 8.9 percent; and branded entertainment, which will surge 8.2 percent. On the downside, consumer books will be the slowest-growing segment in the period with compound annual growth of only 2.1 percent, while newspapers will grow a mere 2.8 percent and broadcast television will expand 4.3 percent.

Average Length of Business Cycles Since 1854, in Months

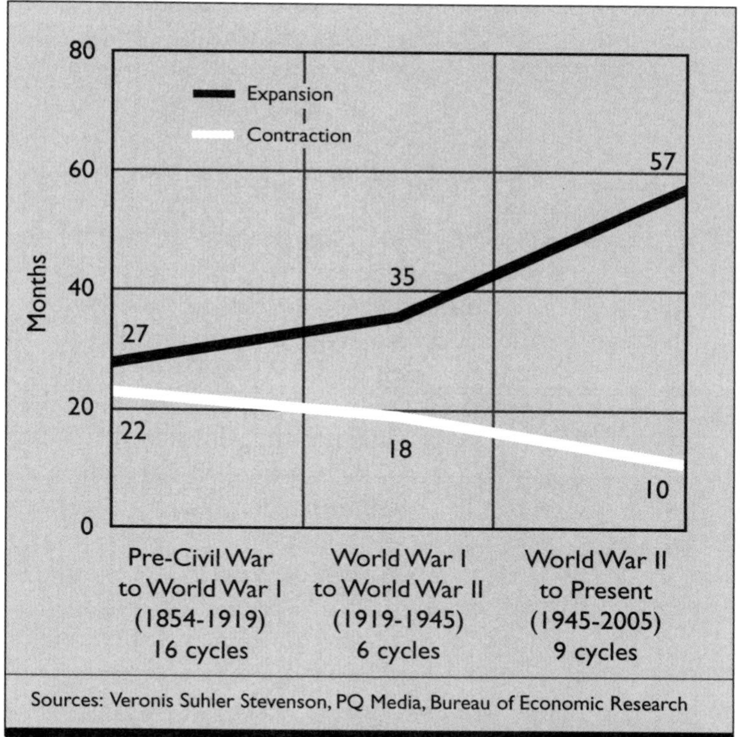

Sources: Veronis Suhler Stevenson, PQ Media, Bureau of Economic Research

MEDIA USAGE BY CONSUMERS

In recent decades, consumers have increased their time spent with media significantly, mainly as a result of the presence of new digital media, like satellite radio, home video, DVRs, videogames and the Internet. The growth in time spent has been decelerating, however, due to penetration rates of new media reaching saturation. For example, many consumers have transitioned to DVD from VHS, slowly expanding their video libraries in the new format. For other digital media, there has been a struggle to gain a foothold in American households. A possible cause for this slower adoption rate is format confusion. That is, media that are offered in more than one format, such as the ill-fated laser disks of the early 1980s, are less likely to achieve rapid acceptance by consumers. Historical data show that media lacking a format war, such as DVDs, have traditionally reached adoption rates of over 30 percent in seven years while multiple-format media, like satellite radio, have struggled to attain a 10 percent penetration rate during the same period.

Consumers are becoming more empowered through the advent of various new media choices and on-demand technology, such as VOD and DVRs, as technology has played a significant role in the strong growth of consumer spending on media in recent years. Our data show that households increase their discretionary spending on media when there is the perception of added value in the new technology, such as the addition of behind-the-scenes material in home videos or the inclusion of technology supporting quicker speeds. In order to be competitive with new media, traditional media like newspapers and radio must extend brands to the Internet and wireless applications. New formats, delivery modes and distribution channels often supplant older ones—as was the case when DVDs replaced VHS—but consumer expenditures usually shift to the new technology rather than disappear altogether. As a result, consumption and expenditures of consumer media continue to grow.

Television remains the most popular medium, accounting for slightly more than 40 percent of all time spent with media. A recent Labor Department study found that television trailed only work and sleep as the activity most often performed by consumers. Broadcast television experienced a resurgence in 2004, driven by the launch of popular new shows such as *Desperate Housewives* and *Lost*, while cable television also increased its time spent as a result of new programs like *The Daily Show* and *Chappelle's Show*. Total television usage increased at a compound annual rate of 1.6 percent from 1999 to 2004, reaching 1,546 hours annually per consumer in 2004. The growth of TV use by consumers, however, is decelerating, up only 0.2 percent in 2004, after increases of 1.5 percent or more annually since 2000, due primarily to a decline in the launch of new cable and satellite networks, as well as the slower rollout of original cable programming, which had been pushing up usage figures in recent years.

Radio is the second choice of consumers at 986 hours in 2004; however, consumers spent less time with radio in 2004 than in the prior year, as listenership declined 1.7 percent, the first downturn in a number of years. Listeners have become increasingly frustrated with advertising clutter and generic formats, leading top radio group Clear Channel to introduce a plan in 2004 to reduce the amount of commercial time aired per hour on its stations. Despite the 2004 decline, radio listenership rose at a compound annual rate of 1.0 percent from 1999 to 2004, mainly fueled by satellite radio gains, longer commutes and the growing Hispanic population and the number of stations catering to this demographic. Together, radio and television accounted for 72.8 percent of all consumer time spent with media in 2004. As younger audiences continue to migrate to newer media such as videogames and the Internet, broadcast media's share of time spent is expected to decline to 71.6 percent at the conclusion of 2009.

The largest increases in consumer time spent with media in 2004 were attained by new media like the Internet, home video, ITV and wireless content. While consumer use of ITV and wireless content skyrocketed 59.7 percent in 2004, the 11 hours devoted to this medium accounted for 0.3 percent of all time spent with media. Conversely, the growth of wireless content and Internet usage is somewhat misleading. A significant portion of time spent with these two media is on activities that don't compete with traditional media usage. For example, e-mail and instant messaging are really substitutes for letter writing and phone calls, rather than newspaper reading or radio listening. Regardless of the type of Internet activity, online usage is growing, up 7.5 percent to 176 hours in 2004, mainly as a result of the transition from dial-up to broadband. The growth of another digital medium, home video, was up 12.0 percent to 67 hours in 2004, driven by the migration to the DVD format by households that tend to purchase disks rather than rent them.

Two media that have endured declining usage patterns in recent years experienced unexpected gains in 2004. Recorded music inched up 0.8 percent to 185 hours and consumer magazine readership grew 1.9 percent to 124 hours (this does not include listening to Internet downloaded music on iPods and via computers). Music's increase was fueled by a number of hot new titles, while consumer magazine growth was fueled by the renewed marketing of and subsequent interest in single copy purchases at newsstands. Other print media were not so lucky in stemming years of declining consumption, as time spent with newspapers fell 2.1 percent to 188 hours and consumer books dropped 1.0 percent to 108 hours in 2004.

Other media experiencing usage declines in 2004 were box office, down 4.3 percent to 12 hours, the second straight year of falling admissions. High theater ticket prices and low DVD prices have led many consumers to wait to see movies on DVD. Meanwhile, the videogame industry, awaiting the release of new console platforms, experienced a minor 2.4 percent increase in usage to 77 hours, although consumption of handheld games climbed after Nintendo's GameBoy Advance and Sony's PlayStation Portable became available.

Overall, consumers increased time spent with media by only 0.3 percent in 2004 to 3,480 hours per person for the year, slightly less than 10 hours a day per person. Since 1999, overall use has increased 200 hours per person annually, up a half-hour per day. Overall usage increased at a compound annual rate of 1.2 percent from 1999 to 2004. The increase in time spent with media has been the subject of numerous debates over the past two years, leading to the launch of a cavalcade of studies regarding the occurrence and impact of media multitasking. Most media analysts accept that high levels of multitasking occur during the use of television and the Internet, as well as with the simultaneous consumption of recorded music and reading material. However, there is inconclusive evidence related to how often multitasking occurs within a particular medium and the level of consumer engagement with the primary or secondary medium, despite the expenditure of millions of dollars by various media trade organizations trying to prove their particular medium is the most often used, the more engaging and/or the one that provides the strongest ROI. Another trend being monitored closely is the U.S. demographic shift. Marketers often target the 18- to 34-year-old market, despite the fact that the share of older audiences is rising. Additionally, the Hispanic market in recent years has surpassed the African-American market as the second-largest demographic group in the U.S. behind European Americans, a major shift that has caught the attention of many in the media industry.

Media supported by consumers continued to gain market share on media supported by advertisers in 2004 and throughout the 1999-2004 period, although the latter still commands a larger share of total time spent with media. Advertising-based media, including broadcast television, broadcast and satellite radio, daily newspapers and consumer magazines, accounted for 63.6 percent of all consumer time spent with media in 1999, compared with 36.4 percent for consumer-supported media, such as cable and satellite television, box office, home video, ITV, recorded music, videogames, consumer Internet and consumer books. By the end of 2004, however, ad-based media's share of consumer time spent declined more than 7 percentage points to 56.4 percent, versus 43.6 percent for consumer-supported media. By the end of 2009, we expect the gap to close further, although at a decelerating rate in the forecast period, as ad-based media will

Hours per Person per Year Using Consumer Media

Year	Network-Affiliated Stations	Independent & Public Stations	Total Broadcast Television	Basic Cable & Satellite Networks	Premium Cable & Satellite Services	Total Cable & Satellite TV#	Total TV**	Broadcast & Satellite Radio‡
1999*	604	193	797	540	90	630	1,427	939
2000†	700	93	793	555	119	674	1,467	942
2001	651	93	744	611	133	744	1,488	952
2002	624	95	719	664	136	800	1,519	991
2003	601	95	696	697	150	847	1,543	1,003
2004	583	95	678	719	149	868	1,546	986
2005	584	95	679	733	136	869	1,548	978
2006	590	94	684	737	134	871	1,555	975
2007	585	93	678	731	146	877	1,555	974
2008	580	95	675	742	149	891	1,566	984
2009	587	94	681	747	134	881	1,562	984
Five-Year Change								
1999-2004	–21	–98	–119	178	59	237	118	47
2004-2009	4	–1	3	29	–16	13	16	–2

Sources: Veronis Suhler Stevenson, PQ Media, Adams Media Research, Alexander & Associates, Arbitron, Audit Bureau of Circulations, Book Industry Study Group, Daily Variety, Datamonitor, *Editor & Publisher*, Entertainment Media Association, *The Financial Post*, The Gallup Organization, Insight Research, Kagan Research, Kinetic Strategies, Magazine Publishers of America, Motion Picture Association of America, National Cable & Telecommunications Association, Newspaper Association of America, Nielsen Media Research, NPDFunworld, Online Publishers Association, Recording Industry Association of America, Scarborough Research, Time Warner, U.S. Census Bureau, Video Software Dealers Association, Yankee Group

Note: Estimates for time spent were derived using rating data for television, cable & satellite television, radio survey research and consumer purchase data (units, admissions, access) for books, home video, Internet, interactive television, magazines, movies in theaters, newspapers, recorded music and video games. Adults 18 and older were the basis for estimates for newspapers, consumer books, consumer magazines, and home video. Persons 12 and older were the bases for estimates for broadcast television, cable & satellite television, radio, recorded music, movies in theaters, video games, consumer Internet and ITV & wireless content.

*In 1999, independent and public stations included UPN, WB, PAX, Telemundo and Univision affiliates, as well as cable superstations except TBS. Basic cable & satellite networks included TBS, pay-per-view, interactive channels, home shopping and audio-only feeds.

†In 2000, UPN, WB, and PAX moved to network affiliated stations. Telemundo and Univision affiliates remain independent. Cable superstations, including TBS and WGN, included in basic cable & satellite networks. Pay-per-view, interactive channels, home shopping and audio-only feeds included with premium cable & satellite services.

Forecast Summary

Newspapers[‡**]	*Recorded Music*[‡#]	*Consumer Internet*	*Consumer Magazines*[‡]	*Consumer Books*[‡]	*Videogames*[‡]	*Home Video*[§‡]	*Box Office*	*Interactive TV & Wireless Content*[‖]	*Total*[***]
205	281	65	134	117	58	41	13	—	3,280
201	258	104	135	107	64	43	12	—	3,333
197	229	131	127	106	66	47	13	—	3,356
194	200	147	125	109	70	57	14	4	3,430
192	184	164	121	109	75	60	13	7	3,471
188	185	176	124	108	77	67	12	11	3,480
183	179	183	124	106	78	76	12	15	3,483
179	175	190	122	106	82	84	12	19	3,499
175	175	195	122	106	86	91	12	26	3,518
170	169	200	122	106	93	95	12	32	3,549
165	165	203	121	106	96	99	12	42	3,555
–17	–96	111	–10	–9	19	26	0	—	200
–23	–20	27	–2	–2	19	32	0	31	75

§Playback of prerecorded VHS cassettes and DVDs only.

‖Wireless content only. Digital video recorders (DVRs) included in total TV. Pay-per-view and video-on-demand included in premium cable & satellite services.

‡Does not include Internet-related use of traditional media. Examples of traditional media being used on the Internet include: listening to downloaded music directly on the computer or from a burned disk on an MP3 player, reading a downloaded e-book, listening to a radio station transmitted by a Windows media player, reading a Web-based newspaper article, taking a Web-based magazine survey, gathering product information also found in the printed version, or playing an Internet single- or multiplayer videogame. All the examples listed are included in the time spent data under consumer Internet, although the media content was originally provided on a traditional medium.

#Some subsegments appear in two or more chapters. To avoid double counting, VOD is included in cable & satellite TV, not in ITV & wireless content; online music and online games are included in consumer Internet, not in recorded music or video games, respectively.

**Methodology to determine time spent with this medium revised. Television expanded to include teenagers as well as adults; and newspapers expanded to include weekly papers as well as dailies.

***Can include media multitasking, such as using the Internet and television simultaneously.

Forecast Summary

Growth of Hours per Person per Year Using Consumer Media

Year	*Network-Affiliated Stations*	*Independent & Public Stations*	*Total Broadcast Television*	*Basic Cable & Satellite Networks*	*Premium Cable & Satellite Services*	*Total Cable & Satellite TV*[#]	*Total TV***	*Broadcast & Satellite Radio*[‡]
2000*†	15.9%	–52.0%	–0.6%	2.7%	32.2%	6.9%	2.7%	0.4%
2001	–7.0	0.5	–6.1	10.2	11.7	10.4	1.5	1.0
2002	–4.2	2.0	–3.4	8.7	2.0	7.5	2.0	4.2
2003	–3.7	0.6	–3.1	4.8	10.8	5.8	1.6	1.1
2004	–3.0	–0.5	–2.7	3.1	–0.7	2.5	0.2	–1.7
2005	0.1	0.1	0.1	2.0	–8.9	0.1	0.1	–0.8
2006	1.1	–1.3	0.7	0.6	–1.3	0.3	0.5	–0.3
2007	–0.9	–0.9	–0.9	–0.9	9.1	0.7	0.0	–0.1
2008	–0.8	1.6	–0.4	1.5	1.6	1.6	0.7	1.0
2009	1.2	–1.1	0.9	0.7	–10.1	–1.1	–0.3	0.0
Compound Annual Growth								
1999-2004	–0.7	–13.2	–3.2	5.9	10.6	6.6	1.6	1.0
2004-2009	0.1	–0.3	0.1	0.8	–2.2	0.3	0.2	0.0

Sources: Veronis Suhler Stevenson, PQ Media, Adams Media Research, Alexander & Associates, Arbitron, Audit Bureau of Circulations, Book Industry Study Group, Daily Variety, Datamonitor, *Editor & Publisher*, Entertainment Media Association, *The Financial Post*, The Gallup Organization, Insight Research, Kagan Research, Kinetic Strategies, Magazine Publishers of America, Motion Picture Association of America, National Cable & Telecommunications Association, Newspaper Association of America, Nielsen Media Research, NPDFunworld, Online Publishers Association, Recording Industry Association of America, Scarborough Research, Time Warner, U.S. Census Bureau, Video Software Dealers Association, Yankee Group

Note: Estimates for time spent were derived using rating data for television, cable & satellite television, radio survey research and consumer purchase data (units, admissions, access) for books, home video, Internet, interactive television, magazines, movies in theaters, newspapers, recorded music and video games. Adults 18 and older were the basis for estimates for newspapers, consumer books, consumer magazines, and home video. Persons 12 and older were the bases for estimates for broadcast television, cable & satellite television, radio, recorded music, movies in theaters, videogames, consumer Internet and ITV & wireless content.

*In 1999, independent and public stations included UPN, WB, PAX, Telemundo and Univision affiliates, as well as cable superstations except TBS. Basic cable & satellite networks included TBS, pay-per-view, interactive channels, home shopping and audio-only feeds.

Newspapers‡**	*Recorded Music*‡#	*Consumer Internet*	*Consumer Magazines*‡	*Consumer Books*‡	*Videogames*‡	*Home Video*§‡	*Box Office*	*Interactive TV & Wireless Content*‖	*Total****
–2.1%	–8.2%	59.1%	0.7%	–8.2%	11.4%	4.5%	–5.0%	—	1.6%
–1.8	–11.2	26.1	–5.8	–1.4	2.0	11.2	3.4	—	0.7
–1.5	–12.4	12.1	–1.9	3.0	6.7	20.8	8.1	—	2.2
–1.2	–8.2	11.5	–2.7	–0.2	7.4	4.9	–4.3	90.3%	1.2
–2.1	0.8	7.5	1.9	–1.0	2.4	12.0	–4.3	59.7	0.3
–2.3	–3.3	4.1	0.4	–1.3	0.5	13.4	–1.5	41.4	0.1
–2.3	–2.5	3.6	–1.8	–0.3	5.7	10.2	–0.2	26.9	0.5
–2.6	0.1	2.8	–0.1	0.2	5.5	8.2	–0.6	35.3	0.5
–2.8	–3.4	2.3	0.1	0.1	7.9	4.9	–1.1	20.6	0.9
–3.0	–2.3	1.9	–0.4	–0.2	2.5	3.8	0.5	33.4	0.2
–1.7	–8.0	21.9	–1.6	–1.6	5.9	10.5	–0.6	—	1.2
–2.6	–2.3	2.9	–0.4	–0.3	4.4	8.0	–0.6	31.3	0.4

†In 2000, UPN, WB, and PAX moved to network affiliated stations. Telemundo and Univision affiliates remain independent. Cable superstations, including TBS and WGN, included in basic cable & satellite networks. Pay-per-view, interactive channels, home shopping and audio-only feeds included with premium cable & satellite services.

§Playback of prerecorded VHS cassettes and DVDs only.

‖Wireless content only. Digital video recorders (DVRs) included in total TV. Pay-per-view and video-on-demand included in premium cable & satellite services.

‡Does not include Internet-related use of traditional media. Examples of traditional media being used on the Internet include: listening to downloaded music directly on the computer or from a burned disk on an MP3 player, reading a downloaded e-book, listening to a radio station transmitted by a Windows media player, reading a Web-based newspaper article, taking a Web-based magazine survey, gathering product information also found in the printed version, or playing an Internet single- or multiplayer videogame. All the examples listed are included in the time spent data under consumer Internet, although the media content was originally provided on a traditional medium.

#Some subsegments appear in two or more chapters. To avoid double counting, VOD is included in cable & satellite TV, not in ITV & wireless content; online music and online games are included in consumer Internet, not in recorded music or video games, respectively.

**Methodology to determine time spent with this medium revised. Television expanded to include teenagers as well as adults; and newspapers expanded to include weekly papers as well as dailies.

***Can include media multitasking, such as using the Internet and television simultaneously.

Forecast Summary

Hours per Person per Year Using Consumer Media, by Media Type

Year	*Total Broadcasting and Cable Media**	*Total Print Media†*	*Total Entertainment Media‡*	*Total Consumer Internet Medium*
1999	2,366	456	392	65
2000	2,409	443	377	104
2001	2,440	430	354	131
2002	2,510	428	345	147
2003	2,546	422	339	164
2004	2,532	419	353	176
2005	2,525	414	360	183
2006	2,530	407	372	190
2007	2,529	402	391	195
2008	2,550	398	401	200
2009	2,546	392	414	204
Five-Year Change				
1999-2004	165	–37	–39	111
2004-2009	14	–27	61	27

Sources: Veronis Suhler Stevenson, PQ Media

*Broadcast television, cable & satellite television, broadcast & satellite radio.

†Newspapers, consumer books, consumer magazines.

‡Box office, home video, interactive TV & wireless content, recorded music, videogames.

Growth of Hours per Person per Year Using Consumer Media, by Media Type

Year	*Total Broadcasting and Cable Media**	*Total Print Media†*	*Total Entertainment Media‡*	*Total Consumer Internet Medium*
2000	1.8%	–2.8%	–3.9%	59.1%
2001	1.3	–2.9	–6.0	26.1
2002	2.9	–0.5	–2.7	12.1
2003	1.4	–1.4	–1.7	11.5
2004	–0.6	–0.7	4.1	7.5
2005	–0.2	–1.3	2.1	4.1
2006	0.2	–1.7	3.3	3.6
2007	0.0	–1.1	4.9	2.8
2008	0.8	–1.2	2.7	2.3
2009	–0.2	–1.4	3.2	1.9
Compound Annual Growth				
1999-2004	1.4	–1.7	–2.1	21.9
2004-2009	0.1	–1.3	3.2	2.9

Sources: Veronis Suhler Stevenson, PQ Media

*Broadcast television, cable & satellite television, broadcast & satellite radio.

†Daily newspapers, consumer books, consumer magazines.

‡Box office, home video, interactive TV & wireless content, recorded music, videogames.

Shares of Hours per Person per Year Using Consumer Media, by Media Type

Year	Total Broadcasting and Cable Media*	Total Print Media†	Total Entertainment Media‡	Total Consumer Internet Medium
1999	72.1%	13.9%	12.0%	2.0%
2000	72.3	13.3	11.3	3.1
2001	72.7	12.8	10.6	3.9
2002	73.2	12.5	10.1	4.3
2003	73.4	12.2	9.8	4.7
2004	72.8	12.0	10.1	5.1
2005	72.5	11.9	10.3	5.3
2006	72.3	11.6	10.6	5.4
2007	71.9	11.4	11.1	5.5
2008	71.9	11.2	11.3	5.6
2009	71.6	11.0	11.6	5.7

Sources: Veronis Suhler Stevenson, PQ Media
*Broadcast television, cable & satellite television, broadcast & satellite radio.
†Daily newspapers, consumer books, consumer magazines.
‡Box office, home video, interactive TV & wireless content, recorded music, videogames.

comprise 54.1 percent of consumer time spent that year, while consumer-supported media will command a 45.9 percent share.

The segments expected to achieve the highest growth in time spent over the next five years are ITV and wireless content, with compound annual growth of 31.3 percent; home video, which will increase 8.0 percent on a compound annual basis; and videogames, which will rise 4.4 percent. Consumer usage of television and the Internet will expand in the low single digits, while radio listenership will be flat, and recorded music, box office, newspapers, consumer magazines and consumer books all will continue to decline at low-single-digit rates. From 2004 to 2009, overall time spent with media will expand to 3,555 hours per person per year, posting compound annual growth of 0.4 percent. The average person is projected to use media almost 10 hours a day in 2009.

The average consumer spent $794.78 per year on media content and access in 2004, an increase of 4.9 percent. Compound annual growth from 1999 to 2004 was 6.3 percent. Media that exhibited triple- and double-digit growth in 2004 were satellite radio, ITV and wireless content, and consumer Internet. Annual consumer spending per person on media will break the $1,000 barrier for the first time in 2009. Spending per person per year on media will rise at a compound annual rate of 5.2 percent during the forecast period to $1,023.69 in 2009. Growth will be driven by increased spending on the emerging wireless content and satellite radio segments, in addition to other digital-based media, such as home video, videogames and consumer Internet.

Consumer Spending per Person per Year

Year	*Broadcast TV*	*Cable & Satellite TV*	*Total TV*	*Home Video*	*Consumer Internet*	*Consumer Books*
1999	$0.00	$179.75	$179.75	$ 80.21	$ 34.08	$87.34
2000	0.00	189.45	189.45	81.49	49.47	85.84
2001	0.00	204.74	204.74	92.50	68.81	84.35
2002	0.00	224.30	224.30	108.22	85.84	87.64
2003	0.00	240.53	240.53	122.19	100.63	89.69
2004	0.00	255.36	255.36	125.31	113.48	89.67
2005	0.00	269.85	269.85	138.60	125.43	91.39
2006	0.00	282.92	282.92	151.09	138.83	91.27
2007	0.00	296.02	296.02	161.14	151.91	93.26
2008	0.00	308.40	308.40	171.63	165.60	93.23
2009	0.00	320.81	320.81	180.27	177.42	93.90

Sources: Veronis Suhler Stevenson, PQ Media, Adams Media Research, Alexander & Associates, Arbitron, Audit Bureau of Circulations, Book Industry Study Group, Business 2.0, comScore Networks, Datamonitor, Digital Entertainment Group, DirecTV, DSL Forum, EchoStar, *Editor & Publisher*, Entertainment Software Association, Federal Communications Commission, *The Financial Post*, The Gallup Organization, In Demand, Insight Research, In-Stat/MDR, Jupiter Media Metrix, Kagan Research, Kinetic Strategies, Leichtman Research Group, Lexis/Nexis, LodgeNet, Magazine Publishers of America, Motion Picture Association of America, National Cable & Telecommunications Association, Newspaper Association of America, Nielsen Media Research, NPDFunworld, Online Publishers Association, Recording Industry Association of America, Replay TV, Scarborough Research, Sirius Satellite Radio, Smith Travel Research, SRDS, Time Warner, Telecommunications Industry Association, TiVo, U.S. Census Bureau, *Video Business*, Video Software Dealers Association, XM Satellite Radio, Yankee Group

Newspapers	*Recorded Music*	*Consumer Magazines*	*Box Office*	*Videogames*	*Interactive TV & Wireless Content*	*Broadcast & Satellite Radio*	*Total*
$52.26	$62.95	$47.98	$32.15	$28.21	$ 0.03	—	$ 585.71
51.93	61.04	47.54	32.64	27.89	0.10	—	608.31
52.40	57.85	46.90	35.41	29.17	0.22	$ 0.001	652.89
53.00	52.47	46.86	39.59	32.34	3.35	0.07	712.64
52.68	48.73	46.08	39.01	32.65	7.40	0.37	757.49
51.62	49.39	46.88	38.76	32.94	13.31	1.15	794.78
50.17	47.65	47.82	38.82	33.49	20.10	2.65	841.48
48.97	45.77	47.59	39.11	36.13	26.95	4.68	888.06
47.95	45.35	48.50	39.70	38.87	32.96	6.91	936.75
47.13	43.49	49.19	40.17	42.63	37.94	9.13	982.56
46.47	42.39	49.57	41.04	44.30	42.41	11.16	1,023.69

Forecast Summary

Growth of Consumer Spending per Person per Year

Year	*Broadcast TV*	*Cable & Satellite TV*	*Total TV*	*Home Video*	*Consumer Internet*	*Consumer Books*
2000	—	5.4%	5.4%	1.6%	45.2%	–1.7%
2001	—	8.1	8.1	13.5	39.1	–1.7
2002	—	9.6	9.6	17.0	24.8	3.9
2003	—	7.2	7.2	12.9	17.2	2.3
2004	—	6.2	6.2	2.5	12.8	0.0
2005	—	5.7	5.7	10.6	10.5	1.9
2006	—	4.8	4.8	9.0	10.7	–0.1
2007	—	4.6	4.6	6.7	9.4	2.2
2008	—	4.2	4.2	6.5	9.0	0.0
2009	—	4.0	4.0	5.0	7.1	0.7
Compound Annual Growth						
1999-2004	—	7.3	7.3	9.3	27.2	0.5
2004-2009	—	4.7	4.7	7.5	9.4	0.9

Sources: Veronis Suhler Stevenson, PQ Media, Adams Media Research, Alexander & Associates, Arbitron, Audit Bureau of Circulations, Book Industry Study Group, Business 2.0, comScore Networks, Datamonitor, Digital Entertainment Group, DirecTV, DSL Forum, EchoStar, *Editor & Publisher*, Entertainment Software Association, Federal Communications Commission, *The Financial Post*, The Gallup Organization, In Demand, Insight Research, In-Stat/MDR, Jupiter Media Metrix, Kagan Research, Kinetic Strategies, Leichtman Research Group, Lexis/Nexis, LodgeNet, Magazine Publishers of America, Motion Picture Association of America, National Cable & Telecommunications Association, Newspaper Association of America, Nielsen Media Research, NPDFunworld, Online Publishers Association, Recording Industry Association of America, Replay TV, Scarborough Research, Sirius Satellite Radio, Smith Travel Research, SRDS, Time Warner, Telecommunications Industry Association, TiVo, U.S. Census Bureau, *Video Business*, Video Software Dealers Association, XM Satellite Radio, Yankee Group

Newspapers	Recorded Music	Consumer Magazines	Box Office	Videogames	Interactive TV & Wireless Content	Broadcast & Satellite Radio	Total
–0.6%	–3.0%	–0.9%	1.5%	–1.2%	182.0%	—	3.9%
0.9%	–5.2	–1.3	8.5	4.6	132.1	—	7.3
1.1	–9.3	–0.1	11.8	10.8	1,413.5	8,299.3%	9.2
–0.6	–7.1	–1.7	–1.5	1.0	121.0	429.1	6.3
–2.0	1.3	1.7	–0.6	0.9	79.9	208.5	4.9
–2.8	–3.5	2.0	0.2	1.7	51.0	130.0	5.9
–2.4	–3.9	–0.5	0.7	7.9	34.1	76.3	5.5
–2.1	–0.9	1.9	1.5	7.6	22.3	47.7	5.5
–1.7	–4.1	1.4	1.2	9.7	15.1	32.0	4.9
–1.4	–2.5	0.8	2.2	3.9	11.8	22.3	4.2
0.2	–4.7	–0.5	3.8	3.1	230.4	—	6.3
–2.1	–3.0	1.1	1.1	6.1	26.1	57.4	5.2

Forecast Summary

Communications Industry Spending

Year	Broadcast Television*	Cable & Satellite Television*†‡	Broadcast & Satellite Radio*	Entertainment Media*†‡	Consumer Internet*‡	Newspaper Publishing*	Consumer Book Publishing	Consumer Magazine Publishing	Business-to-Business Media†
1999	$37,751	$ 58,290	$17,681	$ 66,848	$12,517	$61,511	$18,087	$21,369	$21,063
2000	42,420	64,288	19,848	69,661	19,700	64,267	18,012	22,345	22,790
2001	36,642	70,329	18,369	72,192	23,482	60,228	17,924	21,061	20,810
2002	39,993	77,708	19,428	78,631	26,650	60,478	18,849	21,074	19,599
2003	39,559	85,136	19,698	83,169	31,746	61,596	19,529	21,468	19,886
2004	43,176	93,376	20,306	88,564	37,552	63,527	19,761	22,452	20,911
2005	43,982	101,539	21,231	94,862	43,816	65,266	20,359	23,442	22,143
2006	47,241	109,346	22,434	102,693	50,936	67,300	20,570	24,281	23,411
2007	48,244	117,204	23,874	109,712	58,541	69,054	21,256	25,462	24,728
2008	52,185	125,314	25,756	117,783	66,464	71,071	21,495	26,687	26,176
2009	53,251	134,220	27,449	124,349	74,038	72,926	21,903	27,936	27,684
Five-Year Change									
1999-2004	5,425	35,086	2,625	21,716	25,035	2,016	1,674	1,083	–152
2004-2009	10,075	40,844	7,143	35,785	36,486	9,399	2,142	5,484	6,773

Sources: Veronis Suhler Stevenson, PQ Media

*A number of similar tables were found in two chapters to reflect changes in the media industry. To avoid double counting, below are the segments in which the spending was or was not included: a) Barter syndication spending was included in Entertainment Media, not in Broadcast Television b) Video-on-demand (VOD) spending was included in Cable & Satellite Television, not in Entertainment Media c) Digital video recorders spending was included in Entertainment Media, not in Cable & Satellite TV d) Online music and online game spending were included in Consumer Internet, not in Entertainment Media e) Local online newspaper advertising was included in Consumer Internet, not in Newspaper Publishing f) Internet yellow page advertising was included in Yellow Pages, not in Consumer Internet g) Cable modem spending was included in Consumer Internet, not in Cable & Satellite Television.

†Data were revised or added for the 2005 edition to reflect changes in the media landscape. They include: a) Data were available for the first time for custom publishing, product placement in branded entertainment, wireless content and console videogame rentals in Entertainment Media, and e-media in Business-to-Business Media b) Due to the availability of data from new sources, the methodology used to determine historical spending data were revised for home video in Entertainment Media, b-to-b magazine advertising in Business-to-Business Media, outsourced training in Educational & Training

THE COMMUNICATIONS INDUSTRY SEGMENTS BY THE NUMBERS: 1999 TO 2009

It is important to note here that in order to reflect the multitude of changes in the communications industry, we have developed several new exclusive methodologies and subsegments for this edition of the *Forecast,* as well as numerous new data tables, in addition to partnering with research firms, such as PQ Media, to license exclusive original content on emerging media segments that is not available from other sources. Additionally, some data were placed in two segments due to cross-branding trends that have become common in the communications industry. To avoid double counting, however, the data were included in the overall spending figures of only one segment. We believe that these accessories have added significant value to this year's *Forecast,* providing our subscribers with a most engaging and insightful communications industry analysis. For a comprehensive description of all of the changes, see the Appendix at the end of this report.

Educational & Training Media[†]	*Professional & Business Information Services*[†]	*Yellow Pages**	*Out-of-Home Advertising*	*Direct Marketing*[†]	*Business-to-Business Promotions*	*Consumer Promotion*[†]	*Custom Publishing*	*Branded Enter-tainment*[†]	*Public Relations*	*Total*
$15,838	$ 75,190	$13,196	$4,832	$106,854	$36,676	$27,971	$11,650	$14,760	$2,345	$ 624,429
17,106	80,846	14,267	5,235	115,279	40,129	30,689	12,981	16,357	3,118	679,338
17,601	81,326	15,035	5,233	115,555	38,161	28,815	14,288	17,086	2,900	677,037
17,553	84,156	15,231	5,232	120,705	38,535	29,617	16,982	17,827	2,927	711,175
17,939	89,175	15,366	5,504	127,703	40,165	30,293	18,284	18,993	3,045	748,254
18,694	97,822	15,928	5,834	135,367	41,658	31,639	22,009	20,729	3,410	802,715
20,048	105,757	16,522	6,144	144,166	44,001	33,198	24,629	22,730	3,754	857,589
20,914	113,662	17,274	6,481	152,816	46,435	34,778	27,904	24,574	4,107	917,157
21,910	122,766	18,067	6,849	161,374	49,032	36,405	30,806	26,374	4,428	976,086
22,955	132,049	18,975	7,234	170,733	51,941	38,239	34,996	28,497	4,790	1,043,340
24,037	142,325	19,973	7,623	180,978	54,957	40,206	38,881	30,724	5,212	1,108,672
2,856	22,632	2,732	1,002	28,513	4,982	3,668	10,359	5,969	1,065	178,286
5,343	44,503	4,045	1,789	45,611	13,299	8,567	16,872	9,995	1,802	305,957

Media, and all categories of Professional & Business Information Services c) VOD spending data were included in Cable & Satellite TV rather than Entertainment Media d) Direct mail was expanded to include direct marketing spending in all media, such as telesales and infomercials e) Two chapters were reorganized. Professional information data, previously in Professional, Educational & Training Media, were combined with Business Information Services, forming two new chapters: Educational & Training Media and Professional & Business Information Services f) Subsegments were rearranged and a new segment was formed. Branded entertainment spending has been added by incorporating event sponsorships, promotional licensing (formerly in consumer promotion) and a new subsegment, product placement.

‡As in past editions, spending tables are included in some chapters, but the data are not included in overall Communications Industry spending because these subsegments are not content. a) Cable telephony in Cable & Satellite TV, t-commerce in Entertainment Media, and consumer e-commerce and business-to-business e-commerce in consumer Internet.

BROADCAST TELEVISION

Record presidential election spending and Olympics-related advertising boosted spending on broadcast television 9.1 percent to $43.18 billion in 2004. But heading into 2005, the industry faced a number of challenges that threatened to chip away at broadcast TV advertising expenditures in the near term. Among them were the emergence of ad-skipping technology and less reliance on the 30-second spot, increased competition with cable television and the Internet for consumer attention, and heightened interest among advertisers in non-traditional marketing vehicles. Spending increased at a compound annual rate of 2.7 percent from 1999 to 2004.

The news on the programming front was positive in the 2004-05 season. Television networks won back audiences thanks to breakout hits *Desperate Housewives* and *Lost* on ABC, and the enduring success of *CSI* and reality favorites *Survivor*, *American Idol* and *The Apprentice*. Prime-time network ratings increased 2.3 points to 31.2 through January 2005. However, the increase is not

Growth of Communications Industry Spending

Year	Broadcast Television	Cable & Satellite Television	Broad-cast & Satellite Radio	Enter-tainment Media	Consumer Internet	Newspaper Publishing	Consumer Book Publishing	Consumer Magazine Publishing	Business-to-Business Media
2000	12.4%	10.3%	12.3%	4.2%	57.4%	4.5%	–0.4%	4.6%	8.2%
2001	–13.6	9.4	–7.4	3.6	19.2	–6.3	–0.5	–5.7	–8.7
2002	9.1	10.5	5.8	8.9	13.5	0.4	5.2	0.1	–5.8
2003	–1.1	9.6	1.4	5.8	19.1	1.8	3.6	1.9	1.5
2004	9.1	9.7	3.1	6.5	18.3	3.1	1.2	4.6	5.2
2005	1.9	8.7	4.6	7.1	16.7	2.7	3.0	4.4	5.9
2006	7.4	7.7	5.7	8.3	16.2	3.1	1.0	3.6	5.7
2007	2.1	7.2	6.4	6.8	14.9	2.6	3.3	4.9	5.6
2008	8.2	6.9	7.9	7.4	13.5	2.9	1.1	4.8	5.9
2009	2.0	7.1	6.6	5.6	11.4	2.6	1.9	4.7	5.8
Compound Annual Growth									
1999-2004	2.7	9.9	2.8	5.8	24.6	0.6	1.8	1.0	–0.1
2004-2009	4.3	7.5	6.2	7.0	14.5	2.8	2.1	4.5	5.8

Sources: Veronis Suhler Stevenson, PQ Media

Shares of Communications Industry Spending

Year	Broadcast Television*	Cable & Satellite Television	Broad-cast & Satellite Radio	Enter-tainment Media	Consumer Internet	Newspaper Publishing	Consumer Book Publishing	Consumer Magazine Publishing	Business-to-Business Media
1999	6.0%	9.3%	2.8%	10.7%	2.0%	9.9%	2.9%	3.4%	3.4%
2000	6.2	9.5	2.9	10.3	2.9	9.5	2.7	3.3	3.4
2001	5.4	10.4	2.7	10.7	3.5	8.9	2.6	3.1	3.1
2002	5.6	10.9	2.7	11.1	3.7	8.5	2.7	3.0	2.8
2003	5.3	11.4	2.6	11.1	4.2	8.2	2.6	2.9	2.7
2004	5.4	11.6	2.5	11.0	4.7	7.9	2.5	2.8	2.6
2005	5.1	11.8	2.5	11.1	5.1	7.6	2.4	2.7	2.6
2006	5.2	11.9	2.4	11.2	5.6	7.3	2.2	2.6	2.6
2007	4.9	12.0	2.4	11.2	6.0	7.1	2.2	2.6	2.5
2008	5.0	12.0	2.5	11.3	6.4	6.8	2.1	2.6	2.5
2009	4.8	12.1	2.5	11.2	6.7	6.6	2.0	2.5	2.5

Sources: Veronis Suhler Stevenson, PQ Media

*Not including barter syndication

Educational & Training Media	*Professional & Business Information Services*	*Yellow Pages*	*Out-of-Home Advertising*	*Direct Marketing*	*Business-to-Business Promotions*	*Consumer Promotion*	*Custom Publishing*	*Branded Enter-tainment*	*Public Relations*	*Total*
8.0%	7.5%	8.1%	8.3%	7.9%	9.4%	9.7%	11.4%	10.8%	33.0%	8.8%
2.9	0.6	5.4	0.0	0.2	–4.9	–6.1	10.1	4.5	–7.0	–0.3
–0.3	3.5	1.3	0.0	4.5	1.0	2.8	18.9	4.3	0.9	5.0
2.2	6.0	0.9	5.2	5.8	4.2	2.3	7.7	6.5	4.0	5.2
4.2	9.7	3.7	6.0	6.0	3.7	4.4	20.4	9.1	12.0	7.3
7.2	8.1	3.7	5.3	6.5	5.6	4.9	11.9	9.7	10.1	6.8
4.3	7.5	4.6	5.5	6.0	5.5	4.8	13.3	8.1	9.4	6.9
4.8	8.0	4.6	5.7	5.6	5.6	4.7	10.4	7.3	7.8	6.4
4.8	7.6	5.0	5.6	5.8	5.9	5.0	13.6	8.0	8.2	6.9
4.7	7.8	5.3	5.4	6.0	5.8	5.1	11.1	7.8	8.8	6.3
3.4	5.4	3.8	3.8	4.8	2.6	2.5	13.6	7.0	7.8	5.2
5.2	7.8	4.6	5.5	6.0	5.7	4.9	12.1	8.2	8.9	6.7

Educational & Training Media	*Professional & Business Information Services*	*Yellow Pages*	*Out-of-Home Advertising*	*Direct Marketing*	*Business-to-Business Promotions*	*Consumer Promotion*	*Custom Publishing*	*Branded Enter-tainment*	*Public Relations*
2.5%	12.0%	2.1%	0.8%	17.1%	5.9%	4.5%	1.9%	2.4%	0.4%
2.5	11.9	2.1	0.8	17.0	5.9	4.5	1.9	2.4	0.5
2.6	12.0	2.2	0.8	17.1	5.6	4.3	2.1	2.5	0.4
2.5	11.8	2.1	0.7	17.0	5.4	4.2	2.4	2.5	0.4
2.4	11.9	2.1	0.7	17.1	5.4	4.0	2.4	2.5	0.4
2.3	12.2	2.0	0.7	16.9	5.2	3.9	2.7	2.6	0.4
2.3	12.3	1.9	0.7	16.8	5.1	3.9	2.9	2.7	0.4
2.3	12.4	1.9	0.7	16.7	5.1	3.8	3.0	2.7	0.4
2.2	12.6	1.9	0.7	16.5	5.0	3.7	3.2	2.7	0.5
2.2	12.7	1.8	0.7	16.4	5.0	3.7	3.4	2.7	0.5
2.2	12.8	1.8	0.7	16.3	5.0	3.6	3.5	2.8	0.5

expected to be as pronounced when the full-year results are tabulated because the networks always enjoy an initial boost at the start of the TV season and during the winter when people tend to stay indoors.

Broadcast television advertising is expected to grow only 1.9 percent to $43.98 billion in 2005, due mainly to the absence of political and Olympics advertising, as well as the erosion of drug advertising and pricing pressures. Broadcast television advertising typically surpasses nominal GDP growth in even years due to political and Olympics advertising, and lags GDP growth in odd years due to the lack of such spending. The gap between GDP and broadcast television growth is starting to shrink, and this trend is expected to continue in the forecast period as advertisers reevaluate their TV ad budgets and seek non-traditional media options. Television's share of political advertising is diminishing as candidates employ alternative marketing vehicles, such as the Internet and public relations, pursuing a strategy similar to that of other TV advertisers. Despite these problems, broadcast television continues to be considered the optimal medium for advertisers to reach large audiences at one time. For example, Super Bowl ad rates climbed at high-single-digit rates for the third consecutive year in 2005, up to $2.4 million per 30-second spot. Spending will increase at a compound annual rate of 4.3 percent from 2004 to 2009, reaching $53.25 billion in 2009.

CABLE & SATELLITE TELEVISION

Driven by growth in cable advertising and direct broadcast satellite (DBS) subscribers, as well as subscription rate hikes for cable and DBS, and increased spending on license fees, total expenditures on cable and satellite television climbed 9.7 percent to $93.38 billion in 2004. Following two years of sluggish ad spending growth in 2001 and 2002, the market rebounded in 2003 and continued to expand in 2004, posting compound annual growth of 9.9 percent for the 1999-2004 period. Growth in 2004 and in the five-year period easily outpaced that of GDP, a trend we expect to continue in the forecast period.

The DBS subsegment has experienced dramatic subscriber growth over the past five years, due primarily to the ability of satellite providers to deliver local channels. However, DBS's subscriber growth is expected to decelerate during the forecast period because most major television markets are now fully served by DBS. In addition, cable operators have stepped up their game to fend off the DBS threat and stem the migration of subscribers. Cable companies are also increasing their investment in original and syndicated programming to maintain subscriber loyalty, grow ratings and attract more advertisers. Additionally, cable providers are investing in new technology to offer advanced services in bundled packages, such as telephony, Internet access and video on demand (VOD). Not to be outdone, DBS providers are pursuing partnerships with telephone companies in an effort to offer similar services.

Overall spending on cable and satellite television subscriptions, advertising and license fees will increase 8.7 percent to $101.54 billion in 2005, fueled by growth in license fees and advertising rates. Growth in the forecast period will be driven by increased ratings and audience share, continued investment in technology and programming, economic expansion and lower CPMs compared with broadcast television.

Total spending on wired cable will grow at a compound annual rate of 6.4 percent in the forecast period to $60.22 billion in 2009, due mainly to increased expenditures on local advertising and growing use of VOD services. Meanwhile, spending on satellite television will increase at a compound annual rate of 7.7 percent over the next five years to $23.38 billion in 2009 as satellite providers seek to increase their subscription base, add more DBS advertising inventory and upgrade technology in order to offer more bundled services.

Overall cable and satellite subscription spending will be driven by the bundling of multiple interactive services by cable providers, extended channel capacity due to the availability of digital cable, and new investments in the DBS market. Subscriber spending on basic, premium and pay-per-view (PPV) services will grow at a compound annual rate of 5.9 percent from 2004 to

2009, reaching $74.83 billion in 2009. Cable subscriber spending on basic, premium, PPV and VOD services will grow at a compound annual rate of 5.1 percent in the 2004-2009 period to $50.50 billion, while satellite subscriptions for these services will grow at a slightly higher rate of 7.4 percent to $22.94 billion.

Total cable and satellite television advertising expenditures are expected to expand at a compound annual rate of 12.0 percent from 2004 to 2009, reaching $33.36 billion in 2009. Investments in programming will drive increased ratings and audience share, while continued outlays for new technology and favorable CPMs will bolster ad spending in the forecast period. In the local advertising arena, new demographic targeting services and the expansion of regional sports networks will spur growth going forward. As digital cable develops a larger installed base, its proven ability to deliver vastly increased channel offerings and programming will come into play, and the continued success of original programming on both analog and digital channels will attract new ad spending in the cable network sector. Total spending on cable and satellite television will grow at a compound annual rate of 7.5 percent from 2004 to 2009, reaching $134.22 billion, driven chiefly by strong increases in advertising spending and more moderate growth in license fees.

BROADCAST & SATELLITE RADIO

Overall spending on broadcast and satellite radio increased 3.1 percent in 2004 to $20.31 billion, mainly on the strength of consumer spending on satellite radio subscriptions. As a result of the weak advertising market during the recession, and decelerating growth in recent years, spending on broadcast and satellite radio grew at a compound annual rate of 2.8 percent from 1999 to 2004.

Broadcast radio advertising expenditures increased 2.1 percent to $20.01 billion in 2004, accelerating only slightly over the growth pace in 2003 despite faster GDP growth, record spending on political and Olympics advertising, and additional advertising related to a plethora of new car launches. Local advertising, which accounted for 77.3 percent of all broadcast radio spending, grew 2.5 percent to $15.48 billion in 2004, while national spot expenditures declined 0.5 percent to $3.45 billion and network spending increased 4.6 percent to $1.08 billion. Broadcast radio growth lagged GDP growth for the second consecutive year.

We believe the broadcast radio sector is transitioning from a growth business to a mature one, as a result of near-term pricing issues due to overcapacity, the lack of a sophisticated local sales management system and increased competition from local cable and satellite radio. Additionally, we don't foresee a significant event similar to the Internet advertising boom of the late 1990s. Therefore, we expect the growth of broadcast radio advertising to be more in line with, if not trailing, that of GDP over the next five years. As a result, broadcast radio will perform only slightly better in 2005 versus 2004, with advertising increasing 2.7 percent to $20.55 billion. We project spending on terrestrial radio advertising to grow at a compound annual rate of 4.0 percent from 2004 to 2009, reaching $24.34 billion in 2009, driven by 4.0 percent compound annual growth in local ad spending, 3.8 percent growth in national spot and 4.8 percent growth in network.

Meanwhile, satellite radio spending, including subscriptions and advertising, rose 208.6 percent in 2004 to $293.0 million, as subscription expenditures grew 212.5 percent to $284.0 million and advertising spending increased 124.8 percent to $9.0 million for the year. Subscriptions, which accounted for 96.8 percent of all spending, are the primary driver of the satellite radio business, and OEM, content and licensing deals are driving more subscribers to the medium. With a cadre of OEM, licensing and retail deals already completed or in negotiation, and a subscriber churn rate in the low single digits, we anticipate the number of subscribers to satellite radio will continue to grow at strong rates in 2005 and throughout the forecast period. Driven by this trend, subscription and advertising expenditures will again climb at triple-digit rates in 2005. While growth will decelerate over the next five years, the expansion will outpace all other media segments. Satellite radio subscription spending will grow at a compound annual rate of 59.0 percent from 2004 to 2009, reaching $2.88 billion, while advertising expenditures will increase at a compound annual rate of 88.2 percent in the period to $222.0 million in 2009. Total satellite radio spending will grow 60.3 percent on a compound annual basis from 2004 to 2009, reaching $3.11 billion.

We project overall broadcast and satellite radio spending will grow at a compound annual rate of 6.2 percent from 2004 to 2009, reaching $27.45 billion, as the unprecedented expansion of satellite radio accentuates the relatively tempered growth of broadcast radio advertising.

ENTERTAINMENT MEDIA

Total spending on entertainment media grew 6.5 percent to $88.56 billion in 2004, fueled by strong growth in the filmed entertainment segment as a result of increased investment in broadcast and cable TV programming, and strong consumer spending on DVD rentals and sales. The burgeoning market for ITV and wireless content also contributed to filmed entertainment's growth. While expenditures on in-home filmed entertainment posted solid growth in 2004, box office spending was comparatively sluggish. Meanwhile, spending on recorded music rebounded in 2004, driven by successful album releases, attractive CD pricing and growing demand for legal online music downloads. However, spending on interactive entertainment, or videogames, was hampered by the lack of a new console system launch during the year.

The largest subsegment of the entertainment segment, filmed entertainment, grew 7.7 percent to $68.18 billion in 2004, due primarily to increased household penetration of DVD players, falling DVD software prices and growth in the television programming sector. The number of DVD households grew 40.0 percent to 65.4 million in 2004. The growing popularity of DVDs somewhat suppressed box office spending in 2004, as consumers waited for films to come out on DVD rather than view them in theaters. Box office expenditures, including movie screen advertising, grew only 1.3 percent to $9.98 billion in 2004, due to a decline in attendance. Rising ticket prices helped offset the drop in attendance and pushed 21 movies past the $100 million revenue mark, while five exceeded $200 million, and three were among the 10 highest-grossing movies of all time. Box office spending is expected to show modest growth in 2005, due to the success of *Star Wars: Episode III: Revenge of the Sith* and new versions of *The Pink Panther* and *The Dukes of Hazzard*, and *Charlie and the Chocolate Factory*, a remake of the 1971 classic *Willy Wonka & the Chocolate Factory*.

The television programming subsegment of filmed entertainment expanded 9.3 percent to $27.36 billion in 2004, as networks invested more money in expensive scripted dramas and relied less on low-budget reality shows. This trend will continue in 2005, when we expect television and cable broadcasters to boost spending 4.3 percent to $28.52 billion. Although broadcast TV's share of programming is declining slightly as cable networks invest in more original shows, the broadcast networks represent approximately 45 percent of the market. This investment in Hollywood production keeps the pipeline filled and the system sustained. Meanwhile, the growing adoption of ITV and wireless content services fueled a 78.0 percent gain in spending on these services to $3.23 billion in 2004, not including VOD. The pace of growth in this subsegment is projected to remain in the double digits throughout the forecast period as household penetration of ITV technology expands and more consumers download wireless content.

Meanwhile, recorded music spending rebounded in 2004 to post a gain of 2.5 percent to $12.15 billion, the market's first gain in five years. The music business continues to be driven by hit titles, as the top 10 albums of 2004 outsold the 10 bestselling albums of the previous year, spurring growth in the market. CD sales rose partly as a result of a 0.9 percent decrease in the average price of a music album to $14.93. CD sales represented more than 94 percent of all music revenues in

2004. Despite the music industry's 2004 recovery, we expect recorded music expenditures to decline during the forecast period, owing to the heavy reliance on blockbusters to drive growth and continued losses to digital piracy.

The videogame subsegment continues to draw consumer attention and dollars away from other entertainment media, such as box office and music. The typical gamer plays for nearly seven hours a week and no longer fits the stereotype of being a teenage boy; in contrast, 40.0 percent of gamers are women, and the average age of a gamer is now 26. Interactive entertainment spending, which includes expenditures on console videogames, computer game and entertainment software, and videogame advertising, increased 2.5 percent to $8.23 billion in 2004. Growth was tempered by the lack of a new major videogame console release, which typically fuels new hardware and software sales. New videogame consoles from Sony and Microsoft will not be released until the second half of 2005, but will help drive a 3.4 percent increase in spending to $8.51 billion in 2005.

Although the entertainment market's growth in 2004 accelerated from the 5.8 percent performance the previous year, it trailed nominal GDP slightly—a minor disappointment considering the market's growth exceeded that of GDP in three of the previous four years. Nevertheless, strong growth in filmed entertainment in the first half of 2005 foreshadowed accelerated growth in the overall entertainment media market for the full year, as the market is expected to outpace GDP upside once again. Deeper ITV penetration, growing demand for wireless content and increased spending on new scripted programs by television networks were driving the gains in filmed entertainment in the first half of 2005. The growth of videogame spending is also expected to quicken in 2005 when new console systems are released later in the year, and new titles are developed for the PlayStation Portable. However, recorded music's rebound will be short-lived, as spending will decline again in 2005. Overall expenditures on entertainment media are projected to increase 7.1 percent to $94.86 billion in 2005, and grow at a compound annual rate of 7.0 percent in the 2004-2009 period, reaching $124.35 billion in 2009.

CONSUMER INTERNET

Consumer Internet expenditures, including spending on Web access, advertising and content, rose at a double-digit rate for the fifth consecutive year in 2004, as total spending in this market surged 18.3 percent to $37.56 billion for the year. Driven by several key trends in the three major subsegments, consumer Internet spending growth significantly outpaced that of nominal GDP in 2004 and in the 1999-2004 period, when expenditures grew at a compound annual rate of 24.6 percent.

Consumer Web access spending continued to account for the largest share of the overall market in 2004, with expenditures of $25.58 billion, a 13.0 percent increase compared with the previous year. The double-digit gain was due to the increasing penetration of broadband access, which includes both cable modem and digital subscriber line (DSL) installations. Household spending on cable modem access increased 35.1 percent to $9.30 billion in 2004, while DSL household spending climbed 35.8 percent to $6.56 billion for the year. Meanwhile, household spending on dial-up dropped 15.4 percent to $8.22 billion in 2004. Total spending on consumer Internet access grew at a compound annual rate of 26.5 percent from 1999 to 2004.

Consumer Internet advertising, the second-largest subsegment, grew the fastest in 2004 as spending surged at an accelerated rate of 32.5 percent to $9.63 billion for the year. The strong gain was driven by increased demand for keyword search advertising, which pushed prices up, as well as an expanded amount of searchable content that generated more advertising opportunities. Among the major drivers pushing continued double-digit growth in Internet advertising, and keyword search in particular, is demand from advertisers that media increasingly provide detailed and timely ROI data. Greater broadband penetration drove up growth in rich media advertising, since it allowed more users to view these larger files more rapidly. Total spending on consumer Internet advertising grew at a compound annual rate of 15.8 percent from 1999 to 2004.

Content spending, the smallest of the three consumer Internet subsegments, expanded 27.9 percent to $2.35 billion in 2004. Of the three content categories—general content, online games and digital music—general content accounted for the largest share with $1.36 billion in 2004 expenditures. However, general content spending—which includes news, personals, greeting cards and research—declined 3.6 percent for the year. Digital music posted the strongest gain in the content segment, with spending up 312.5 percent to $330.0 million in 2004.

Total consumer Internet spending is projected to increase 16.7 percent to $43.82 billion in 2005, driven by double-digit growth in advertising and content spending, while Internet access expenditures will post high-single-digit growth for the year. The expansion of the overall consumer Internet market, which will again outpace that of the broader economy in 2005, will be spurred by several critical drivers, including the shift of advertising dollars to media that provide marketers with detailed ROI data in a timely fashion. Overall consumer Internet expenditures are expected to maintain a double-digit growth rate throughout the 2004-2009 period, consistently beating nominal GDP, as advertisers move to more effectively reach target audiences and track the benefits of media buys, and consumers ratchet up their use of online games and digital music downloads. Total consumer Internet spending will grow at a compound annual rate of 14.5 percent from 2004 to 2009, reaching $74.04 billion in 2009.

While the growth in overall Internet households is expected to slow down over the next three years, cable modem and DSL installations will continue to increase in the low-double-digit range. Total spending on Internet access will increase 9.3 percent in 2005 to $27.97 billion, as a result of broadband's higher pricing compared with dial-up. Spending on broadband access will continue to drain spending from the dial-up market, causing steady declines in dial-up expenditures. Internet advertising is expected to grow 31.2 percent in 2005, and post compound annual growth of 24.0 percent from 2004 to 2009, with spending reaching $28.20 billion. Keyword search advertising and rich media will continue to fuel Internet advertising growth, while the use of banner ads will drop, as advertisers increasingly look for ways of engaging consumers in an interactive experience that drives loyalty. Internet content spending will increase in the double digits throughout the forecast period, generating compound annual growth of 27.1 percent. Spending will reach $7.76 billion in 2009. Growth will be driven by digital music downloads and online gaming.

NEWSPAPERS

Total newspaper spending, including daily and weekly advertising and circulation, posted accelerated growth for the third consecutive year in 2004, increasing 3.1 percent to $63.53 billion, driven by the fastest advertising growth in four years. Although still trailing nominal GDP growth, newspaper advertising expenditures advanced 4.0 percent to $52.15 billion in 2004, fueled by the strengthening economy, expanding job market and gains in each of the three major ad categories. Retail advertising grew on the strength of several subcategories, including home supplies and furniture, financial, and the automotive aftermarket, while classified advertising was driven by double-digit gains in the employment category. Meanwhile, strong growth in the publishing and media, and political and government categories fueled upside in national advertising. The weekly newspaper subsegment also contributed to the overall newspaper segment's growth in 2004, as weeklies continue to deliver the attractive young and affluent demographic.

Overall newspaper spending grew a slim 0.6 percent on a compound annual basis in the 1999-2004 period, suppressed by the 6.3 percent decline in the 2001 recession year, but also because of a slower-than-expected recovery in the ensuing years, a trend that affected most ad-based media. Going forward, we expect newspapers and other traditional media will be challenged like never before to prove their ROI to major advertisers, who are increasingly skeptical of the value of their conventional advertising buys, a development that will hamper ad growth in the forecast period.

On the circulation front, total spending decreased 0.8 percent to $11.38 billion in 2004, due to declining unit circulation at major daily and weekly newspapers, and a downturn in prices of weekday and Sunday papers. Aggregate unit circulation of U.S. newspapers dropped 1.1 percent to 55.97 million in 2004, as readership of daily newspapers continued its decades-long decline among adults across different age groups, especially younger adults who prefer online news sources.

Overall daily newspaper spending, including advertising and circulation, grew 3.0 percent to $57.69 billion in 2004, driven by an increase in all three major advertising categories, but tempered by a decrease in circulation spending. While each of the three key ad categories posted growth in 2004, upside was slower than in prior years during recovery intervals, another reason for the scanty overall expansion. Daily ad spending, which accounted for 81.2 percent of all newspaper expenditures in 2004, increased 3.9 percent to $46.70 billion. Circulation spending declined 0.9 percent to $10.99 billion, as both unit circulation and prices fell. Daily newspaper unit circulation has declined every year since 1994.

Weekly newspaper spending, including advertising and circulation at weekly and shopper publications, grew 4.9 percent to $5.84 billion in 2004, driven by the fourth straight year of accelerating gains in advertising expenditures. Ad spending increased 5.1 percent to $5.45 billion, outpacing daily growth, with most of the expansion coming from the entertainment and specialty merchandise categories, accentuated by the trend of weeklies delivering a coveted younger and affluent demographic. Paid unit circulation declined 1.4 percent to 20.9 million in 2004, but an increase in prices led to growth in circulation spending. Total weekly newspaper spending grew at a compound annual rate of 4.2 percent from 1999 to 2004.

Total spending on daily and weekly newspapers is expected to grow just 2.7 percent to $65.27 billion in 2005. The increase will be driven by the anticipated economic expansion and more robust job market during the year, tempered by a deceleration in the growth of retail and national advertising. Both unit circulation and circulation spending are expected to decline over the forecast period, as consumers increasingly turn to electronic media, such as the Internet and cable television, for their news. The decline in circulation is expected to hinder advertising spending, as marketers perceive diminishing returns from shrinking audiences. As a result, even as the general advertising market expands, total newspaper spending will grow at a tepid compound annual rate of 2.8 percent in the 2004-2009 period, reaching $72.93 billion in 2009.

CONSUMER BOOKS

Strong consumer book sales at the start of 2004 and a respectable holiday season offset a weak summer and fall, resulting in a 1.2 percent increase in book spending to $19.76 billion for the year. Spending growth was driven primarily by a 3.4 percent hike in prices, which offset a 2.1 percent decline in unit sales for the year.

The fastest-growing consumer book segment in 2004 was religion, which posted a 10.7 percent increase in spending. *The Purpose-Driven Life* continued to be a phenomenon in 2004, selling more than 7 million copies after selling over 11 million in 2003. Growth in religious book spending was fueled by an aging American public that continues to shift toward spirituality and conservatism, a trend that became more pronounced after the terrorist attacks of September 2001. To capitalize on the public's heightened interest in religious books, more mainstream bookstores have expanded their inventories of religious books, and religious books are also among the top sellers at superstores such as Wal-Mart. The only other consumer book segment to achieve a meaningful increase in spending in 2004 was the adult trade category, which posted an increase of 4.3 percent for the full year. Spending in the university press segment rose 1.3 percent, but expenditures fell in the juvenile, mass-market paperback, book club and mail order categories.

Consumer book spending was sluggish in the first quarter of 2005, due to the post-election decline in spending on political books, coupled with the lack of a new fiction blockbuster. The U.S. Census Bureau reported that bookstore sales were down 4.6 percent in the first two months of 2005. Monthly estimates from the Association of American Publishers showed sales down in all consumer book categories in the first two months of 2005, with the exception of juvenile hardcover. A modest rebound is expected to occur toward mid-year, although spending growth is expected to increase only 3.0 percent for full-year 2005, driven by growth in the juvenile hardcover and religious book segments, which will be offset somewhat by a decline in the mass-market paperback and book club categories. Spending in the adult hardcover segment, the industry's largest category, will increase 2.3 percent for the year, while total units will be flat at 1.66 billion.

We project total spending on consumer books will grow at a 2.1 percent compound annual rate from 2004 to 2009, a slight acceleration from the 1999-2004 period. Expenditures are expected to reach $21.90 billion in 2009, compared with $19.76 billion in 2004. The higher growth rate in the forecast period will be driven primarily by a minor increase in units and moderate price hikes. Unit sales are projected to rise at a 0.5 percent compound annual rate over the next five years, compared to a 1.1 percent decline in the 1999-2004 timeframe. Price increases are projected to rise at a compound annual rate of 1.4 percent from 2004 to 2009, slower than the 2.9 percent increase in the previous five-year interval.

The strongest spending growth in the forecast period is expected to come from the religious segment, with expenditures projected to increase 3.8 percent on a compound annual basis from 2004 to 2009. Spending in the juvenile trade category is also forecast to beat the 2.1 percent industry average, growing at a compound annual rate of 3.1 percent from 2004 to 2009. The weakest performing segments will be book clubs and mail order.

CONSUMER MAGAZINES

The consumer magazine market continued its recovery in 2004 as total spending increased at an accelerated 4.6 percent rate to $22.45 billion for the year, driven by gains in both advertising and circulation. Overall consumer magazine spending grew at a compound annual rate of 1.0 percent from 1999 to 2004, lagging nominal GDP by almost 4 percentage points, primarily as a result of the significant downturn in 2001 and the relatively flat performance in 2002.

Advertising expenditures, which accounted for 54.0 percent of total segment spending, rose 6.0 percent to $12.12 billion in 2004, fueled by the improving economy and strong gains in the retail, financial and travel categories. Comparatively strong advertising growth in 2004 offset the declines in 2001 and 2002, resulting in compound annual growth of 1.2 percent for the 1999-2004 period. The accelerated upswing in ad spending was the fastest growth posted by consumer magazines in four years and followed a 4.0 percent rise in 2003. Improving retail sales and higher personal incomes drove double-digit spending gains in the three aforementioned categories, combined with increases, albeit smaller ones, in six other major ad categories. General business and regional magazines also notched strong growth, as consumers once again started paying attention to financial markets, and many local economies revitalized.

Circulation spending, which comprised 46.0 percent of total segment expenditures, was up 3.0 percent to $10.33 billion in 2004, the largest increase in seven years. Circulation spending increased despite the lack of price growth, as an upswing in unit circulation spurred the overall gain. Circulation expenditures experienced an up-and-down period from 1999 to 2004 that resulted in compound annual growth of only 0.8 percent for the five-year timeframe. The average single-copy price increased 3.1 percent to $3.36 in 2004, as publishers found newsstand buyers more receptive to higher prices. The average annual subscription price decreased 0.7 percent to $23.06, while the average per-unit price was flat at $1.56 for the year.

As GDP growth slows a bit in 2005, consumer magazine advertising growth also is expected to decelerate somewhat to 5.5 percent, with expenditures reaching $12.79 billion for the year. Growth will be driven primarily by the continued expansion of the economy and the overall ad market, as well as by the magazine industry's extensive marketing and research campaigns designed to tout consumer magazines as an engaging alternative to other media. Nevertheless, we expect magazine advertising growth to outpace nominal GDP growth in 2006 for the first time in six years, although it will do so by only a slim margin. Overall, we expect spending on consumer magazine advertising to grow at an accelerated pace during the forecast period, compared with the 1999-2004 timeframe, but level with the broader economic expansion. Magazine ad expenditures will grow at a compound annual rate of 6.2 percent from 2004 to 2009, exceeding the 1.2 percent compound annual growth in the previous five-year period, but close to the 6.1 percent expansion in nominal GDP.

As non-traditional media grab larger shares of advertising budgets and consumer leisure time, magazines will attempt to fight back on several fronts. The industry, through its primary trade organization, began aggressively marketing itself to advertisers in 2004 in an effort to raise awareness and market share of consumer magazines. The industry is spending millions of dollars to promote itself as the "engagement" medium, meaning that although magazine time spent has been steadily declining for a decade, this has to do with new formats of magazines that are shorter and include more graphics. In addition, the industry claims these data don't take into account that consumers often read magazines exclusive of other media, meaning that consumers can be more engaged with magazines than with other forms of media that are involved in heavy multitasking by consumers. Publishers are also honing their subscription and newsstand strategies, searching for unconventional means of reaching potential subscribers. Finally, to improve consumer targeting, magazine executives are seeking to serve new demographic and editorial niches, creating magazines that resonate with these readers, such as the Hispanic audience.

Along with these drivers, the strength of the economy will play a role in the industry's performance over the next five years. With the economy cooling somewhat in 2005, total spending on consumer magazines is expected to increase 4.4 percent to $23.44 billion, while ad spending will grow 5.5 percent to $12.79 billion, fueled by a resurgence in the food, finance, media, direct response and automotive categories. Circulation expenditures will grow at a slower rate in 2005, increasing 3.1 percent to $10.65 billion. Over the forecast period, we expect magazine advertising spending to come under further pressure from newer media. As a result, compound annual growth will be 6.2 percent from 2004 to 2009, barely higher than the 6.1 percent rate for nominal GDP. Advertising expenditures will reach $16.37 billion in 2009. Circulation spending over the forecast period will be slowed by a contraction in 2006. As a result, the compound annual growth rate will be 2.3 percent. Total consumer magazine expenditures are projected to increase at a compound annual rate of 4.5 percent from 2004 to 2009, reaching $27.94 billon in 2009.

BUSINESS-TO-BUSINESS MEDIA

Total business-to-business media spending, including expenditures on magazines, electronic media and trade shows, grew at an accelerated rate for the third consecutive year in 2004, as spending in all three market subsegments increased. Overall b-to-b media expenditures climbed 5.2 percent to $20.91 billion in 2004, driven by surging e-media spending—the smallest subsegment—which grew 25.9 percent to $1.47 billion, and trade show expenditures, which escalated 5.8 percent to $9.15 billion for the year. Solid growth in these two subsegments, however, was tempered by only 2.2 percent expansion in the largest subsegment—b-to-b magazine spending, including expenditures on advertising and circulation—which combined to produce spending of $10.29 billion in 2004.

Total business-to-business media spending was essentially flat on a compound annual basis from 1999 to 2004, as this segment took a severe blow from the economic recession in 2001, declined for the second consecutive year in 2002 and posted relatively meager growth in 2003, mostly due to two straight years of double-digit declines in magazine advertising in 2001 and 2002. B-to-b market growth trailed that of both GDP and the overall advertising sector in the 1999-2004 period. Similar to past recessions, marketers cut magazine advertising budgets as profits began to fall and waited more than a year to ensure profits returned before spending on b-to-b magazine advertising.

Spending on b-to-b magazine advertising, which was the hardest hit media sector during the 2001 recession, continued to rebound in 2004, posting growth of 3.4 percent to $8.37 billion, the sector's first positive growth in four years and its fastest expansion since 2000. Circulation spending, however, declined 2.9 percent for the year to $1.92 billion, although this represented a deceleration in the rate of decline compared with the 2003 downturn. Meanwhile, e-media expenditures raced up 25.9 percent in 2004 to $1.47 billion, and grew at a compound annual rate of 40.0 percent from 1999 to 2004. Growth was spurred by a surfeit of new online advertising and content initiatives launched by b-to-b publishers over the past five years, as they scrambled to provide end users with comprehensive electronic alternatives to help them do their jobs more efficiently. On the trade show front, spending growth outpaced that of b-to-b magazines in 2004 and in the 1999-2004 period by several percentage points, fueled by the expansion in corporate travel budgets and the availability of low-cost airlines that don't charge additional fees for last-minute bookings. As travel budgets and overall business information budgets increased over the past two years, trade show organizers have been able to amplify vendor-related costs without much backlash. Spending on trade shows increased at a compound annual rate of 1.4 percent from 1999 to 2004.

We expect the growth of the overall business-to-business media segment to accelerate in 2005, fueled by solid gains in the trade show subsegment and a double-digit increase in e-media spending. Growth in business-to-business magazine expenditures will be modest, as falling circulation spending offsets gains in advertising spending. Total b-to-b media spending growth is expected to match GDP expansion in 2005 for the first time since 2000. In the b-to-b magazine market, increased advertising in healthcare, banking, automotive and construction publications is expected to drive an overall spending gain of 2.7 percent in 2005 to $10.57 billion. We expect magazine advertising to rise 3.8 percent to $8.70 billion in 2005, driven partially by increased ad expenditures in automotive titles, as manufacturers promote overstocks to the fleet and trucking industries. Overall b-to-b magazine spending will reach $12.12 billion in 2009, growing 3.3 percent on a compound annual basis from 2004 to 2009.

In the trade show segment, an increase in business-related travel in the first half of 2005 led to record gains in attendance and exhibitors at several shows, and we expect this trend to continue through the rest of the year. Trade show spending growth will continue to surpass magazine expenditure growth in 2005, with an accelerated increase of 6.1 percent to $9.71 billion, as corporate profits continue upward and show organizers attract more attendees and exhibitors through exclusive, invitation-only events. With rising exhibit space costs, organizers are offering packages that include supplementary brand marketing opportunities, such as prominent placement in marketing brochures, to meet ROI demands of exhibitors. Spending on trade shows and exhibitions will increase 5.8 percent on a compound annual basis from 2004 to 2009, reaching $12.10 billion in 2009. E-media, in the meantime, will continue to be the fastest-growing subsegment of the b-to-b media market in 2005, with a projected increase in spending of 26.5 percent to $1.86 billion for the year. The gain will result from the efforts of traditional publishers to build their e-media operations in order to meet the growing demand for faster delivery and more targeted information.

Total b-to-b media spending, including expenditures on magazines, trade shows and e-media, is expected to increase 5.9 percent to $22.14 billion in 2005, the market's best gain in five years. Although the increasing use of e-media will continue to pilfer dollars from traditional print-based advertising and circulation, b-to-b publishers will benefit as they become more accustomed to their new roles as providers of mission-critical multimedia information. Growth in the overall business-to-business media market over the next five years will surpass the gain in the 1999-2004 interval, as traditional publishers continue to create new revenue streams through the Internet. Online offerings, such as e-newsletters, weekly e-mail blasts and Webcasts, will increasingly become part of the basic subscription model, as publishers address reader demand for instant access to information. The ability to more accurately measure ROI with the help of online tools will also fuel the market's growth in the forecast period. The overall b-to-b media market is projected to grow at a compound annual rate of 5.8 percent from 2004 to 2009, reaching $27.68 billion.

EDUCATIONAL & TRAINING MEDIA

Total spending on educational and training media rose 4.2 percent in 2004 to $18.69 billion, the market's largest increase since 2000. The gain was driven by the outsourced corporate training subsegment, which benefited from the robust economy and improved job market, as companies invested more capital in training new employees and developing existing ones. The rebound in spending on outsourced corporate training, however, was offset somewhat by a more sluggish gain in the educational segment, resulting in combined spending growth that trailed that of nominal GDP for the fourth consecutive year.

The K-12 instructional materials market, including spending on basal, supplemental and electronic learning materials, turned in the worst performance of the three subsegments included in this segment—K-12, college and outsourced corporate training—with spending flat at $4.06 billion in 2004. A decline of about 29 percent in spending by textbook adoption states in 2004 to approximately $530 million was offset by higher spending in open territories, strong funding from the federal government and higher expenditures on supplementary materials. The K-12 market's growth in 2004 lagged GDP expansion for the third consecutive year.

Spending on college instructional materials, which includes textbooks, coursepacks, software and online services, grew 1.5 percent to $4.71 billion in 2004, due to students' reluctance to pay for expensive new textbooks. High tuition costs and negative publicity about college textbook prices spurred students to find alternatives to buying new texts.

After a three-year slump, spending on outsourced corporate training increased 7.4 percent to $9.92 billion in 2004, driven by growth in the information technology (IT) subsegment, the largest sector of the corporate training market. The gain in the IT sector offset spending declines in the other three training subsegments.

Total spending on educational and training media grew at a compound annual rate of 3.4 percent from 1999 to 2004, trailing nominal GDP growth by more than one percentage point in the period. Following the recession of 2001, corporations trimmed their corporate training budgets, while state budget cuts and a lack of textbook adoptions limited spending gains in the K-12 instructional materials sector. Rising enrollments and moderate price increases drove spending gains in the college instructional materials market early in the 1999-2004 period, but high prices curbed spending and hindered growth in 2003 and 2004.

We project the growth of spending on educational and training media will accelerate in 2005, rising 7.2 percent to $20.05 billion. The strong economy and robust job market will drive another gain in the outsourced corporate training subsegment in 2005, while healthier state budgets and more adoption opportunities will spur double-digit upside in the K-12 market for the year. Meanwhile, high prices and a slow transition from the use of print materials to electronic learning materials will limit growth in the college market in 2005. Mid-single-digit gains are projected for the remainder of the forecast period for the overall educational and training media segment, resulting in a compound annual growth rate of 5.2 percent from 2004 to 2009. Total segment spending will reach $24.04 billion in 2009.

PROFESSIONAL & BUSINESS INFORMATION SERVICES

Driven by strong demand for workflow solutions, creative online delivery options and a growing national economy, spending on PBIS surged 9.7 percent to $97.82 billion in 2004, as expenditures in both subsegments expanded at healthy rates during the year. Spending in the largest subsegment, business information services (BIS), grew at a faster rate than expenditures in the other subsegment, professional information, as solutions complete with real-time, analytical functionality were purchased at a faster rate, due in part to increased corporate budgets. This trend drove up spending on BIS 10.2 percent to $78.09 billion in 2004. Meanwhile, the continued launch of online products and the introduction of services that complement new technology, such as wireless devices, spurred a gain of 7.9 percent in professional information to $19.73 billion in 2004 as all three categories—legal and regulatory; scientific and technical; and health and life science—recorded relatively strong growth.

The overall PBIS market outgrew nominal GDP by 3.1 percentage points in 2004, and the market grew at a compound annual rate of 5.4 percent from 1999 to 2004, also surpassing the broader economy's growth. The PBIS market's growth rate in 2004 also exceeded its peak 2000 expansion pace of 7.5 percent, which was followed by a deceleration in growth of 0.6 percent in the 2001 recession year. The market grew at an accelerated rate in each of the next three years.

Total spending on professional information increased 7.9 percent in 2004 to $19.73 billion, and grew at a compound annual rate of 6.4 percent from 1999 to 2004. Key growth drivers were the expanded use of digital content delivery and the development of solutions compatible with the latest technological advances. Spending on legal and regulatory information increased 7.2 percent to $8.71 billion in 2004, driven by the rollout of new online delivery options, acquisitions that created larger customer bases and the integration of popular PDA-supported products into providers' slate of offerings. Content delivery via PDAs is beginning to supplant CD-ROM delivery in this market, and we expect spending on legal and regulatory information to grow another 6.2 percent to $9.25 billion in 2005. One of the chief growth drivers will be the launch of more online tools that promote increased functionality supporting an array of Internet-based products and services.

Growth in the BIS subsegment in 2004 was driven primarily by the marketing information services category, which expanded faster than all other categories for the year, growing 14.7 percent to $23.55 billion. Key growth drivers in this category included escalating demand for real-time, analytical information and research services. At the same time, content providers have had to address the changing nature by which users find and analyze their information. Research suggests that professionals are relying less on Internet searches and more on colleagues and peers, as well as various other information alerting services.

The forecast period for PBIS is projected to be one of strong, sustained growth, with many opportunities emerging. Perhaps most important will be the surfacing of new customers with more money to spend and higher demands, which will drive the research and development of creative multimedia workflow solutions that transform this market at a brisker rate than during the past five years. The demand for mission-critical content from end-user companies has been steady, and will only strengthen as the economy expands and corporations increase their budgets for BIS. Growth in the labor market will continue to correlate with growth in PBIS spending. Anecdotal evidence, based on 2002 data, suggests that PBIS spending fell during the recession, along with related labor segments, and the market's recovery corresponded with an increase in hiring the following year. As mentioned previously, this new climate will offer BIS vendors an expanded market in which to launch new products and services that provide end-to-end solutions for their customers.

We expect the PBIS segment to post an 8.1 percent spending increase in 2005, reaching $105.76 billion, outpacing GDP growth of 6.0 percent. This trend is expected to continue over the next five years, as GDP is projected to rise at a compound annual rate of 6.0 percent in the period compared with 7.8 percent upside for PBIS from 2004 to 2009, with expenditures reaching $142.33 billion in 2009.

YELLOW PAGES

The yellow pages market consists of spending in local telephone company directories, competitive directories from independent publishers and Internet yellow pages (IYP) services. Yellow pages advertising spending increased 3.7 percent to $15.93 billion in 2004, due to strong growth for independent yellow pages publishers and IYP services. Competitive print directories and online directories also drove the 3.8 percent compound annual spending growth in the 1999 to 2004 period. Because of the long lead time between sales and recognition of yellow pages directory revenues, the economic recession of 2001 did not impact the market until 2002 and 2003, when revenues were relatively flat.

Spending in local telephone company directories fell 0.1 percent to $12.39 billion. Although the segment's performance represented an improvement over the 3.2 percent decline experienced in 2003, telephone company directories continue to lose market share to competitive directories from independents. The independent directory market grew 16.7 percent in 2004 to $2.76 billion and expanded its market share to 18.2 percent from 16.0 percent the prior year. New directory launches and expanding penetration in existing markets are fueling growth in the independent yellow pages market.

Local advertising continues to represent the bulk of print yellow pages spending, accounting for 84.2 percent, or $12.76 billion in 2004. The national advertising channel, representing only 15.8 percent of print spending, or $2.39 billion, has strong potential for growth. Because national media were more dramatically impacted by the weak economy than were local media, national yellow pages advertising declined 1.4 percent in 2003 compared with a 0.7 percent decline for local. National advertising rebounded in 2004 to post a 2.9 percent gain, compared with 2.5 percent growth for local. National advertising is expected to outpace local for the remainder of the forecast period.

IYP also represents a growth opportunity for yellow pages publishers. Print publishers' online revenues are included in their print revenues. Other online directory spending increased 29.9 percent to $775.0 million in 2005. Although yellow pages publishers face competition from search engines and pure-plays in the online yellow pages arena, a study released in 2005 by the Yellow Pages Association and comScore Networks showed yellow pages publishers may have an advantage over competitors. IYP spending is expected to increase 24.6 percent to $966.0 million in 2005, and grow at a compound annual rate of 17.1 percent in the forecast period.

Print yellow pages spending will increase 2.7 percent to $15.56 billion in 2005, and grow at a compound annual rate of 3.8 percent from 2004 to 2009. IYP and independent directories will continue to drive growth in the forecast period. Independent directory expenditures are expected to increase 13.7 percent to $3.14 billion in 2005, while spending on telephone company directories will grow 0.2 percent to $12.42 billion for the year. Overall, yellow pages spending will increase 3.7 percent to $16.52 billion in 2005, and grow at a compound annual rate of 4.6 percent from 2004 to 2009, reaching $19.97 billion.

OUT-OF-HOME ADVERTISING

Out-of-home advertising includes traditional roadside billboards, as well as non-traditional forms of out-of-home media, such as bus stations, subways, urban furniture and shelters. It does not include point-of-purchase advertising, which is included in consumer promotion, or movie screen advertising, which is a separate subsegment of the entertainment media segment. Out-of-home advertising spending grew 6.0 percent to $5.83 billion in 2004, driven by an influx of new advertisers and growth in alternative out-of-home advertising. Double-digit growth in the media and advertising, insurance and real estate, and financial categories fueled the gains, as did strong political advertising during the 2004 elections. Spending in the 1999-2004 period grew at a compound annual rate of 3.8 percent.

Spending on traditional billboard advertising increased 6.0 percent to $3.62 billion in 2004, fueled by price hikes rather than volume increases because zoning regulations prohibit the building of new billboards. Alternative out-of-home advertising climbed 32.5 percent to $292.0 million in 2004, as advertisers shifted spending from transit and street furniture—also forms of non-traditional out-of-home advertising—to experiment with newer options. Transit advertising growth was on par with the overall industry at 6.0 percent, while street furniture declined 1.1 percent. Non-traditional out-of-home advertising now accounts for nearly 40 percent of out-of-home advertising spending. Local out-of-home advertising increased 5.5 percent to $3.51 billion in 2004, due to strong growth in small boards. National advertising grew 6.8 percent to $2.33 billion, fueled by double-digit gains in media and advertising, financial, and insurance and real estate.

Out-of-home advertising spending is expected to increase 5.3 percent to $6.14 billion in 2005, due to continued strong growth in alternative media. Compound annual growth will be 5.5 percent in the forecast period, with spending reaching $7.62 billion in 2009.

DIRECT MARKETING

The direct marketing segment includes direct mail, telesales, catalogs and interactive advertising, as well as direct-response advertising in traditional media, such as television, radio, newspapers and magazines. Direct marketing spending increased 6.0 percent to $135.38 billion in 2004, due in part to the growing use of niche database marketing, which is making it easier for marketers to target specific zip codes and neighborhoods. According to one survey of marketing executives, direct mail was ranked as the most effective of the major media in reaching target demographics and providing measurable ROI. Another example of direct mail's growing importance in marketing campaigns was its increased use in many 2004 political campaigns that used targeted databases. Mainly due to increased spending on direct mail by both presidential candidates, especially in the battleground states, spending on direct mail surged 93.7 percent to $648.0 million in 2004 compared with 2002 expenditures, according to exclusive research from PQ Media.

Despite the implementation of the federal Do Not Call Registry—which fines companies that make telephone sales calls to consumers who have voluntarily placed their names on the list—spending on telesales to consumers increased 4.7 percent to $29.47 billion in 2004. Comparatively, spending on consumer direct mail rose 4.6 percent to $30.50 billion. One reason for the increase in telesales spending is the rise in costs—including telesales and new automated systems—which are being passed on to clients. But companies continue to invest in telesales because it delivers results. A Direct Marketing Association survey released in late 2004 found that telesales generated the highest response rate compared to other direct marketing tactics, and the strongest ROI.

The trend toward multichannel marketing will drive growth in direct mail and overall direct marketing spending in the forecast period, as marketers often use direct mail to support campaigns combining traditional print advertising with alternative advertising and marketing tools. Spending will increase 6.5 percent to $144.17 billion in 2005, and grow at a compound annual rate of 6.0 percent from 2004 to 2009, reaching $180.98 billion in 2009.

BUSINESS-TO-BUSINESS PROMOTION

Business-to-business promotion, which includes incentives and promotional products, increased 3.7 percent to $41.66 billion in 2004, reflecting the rise in corporate profits, which allowed companies to reward employees and clients.

Growth in spending on employee incentives increased 2.2 percent to $24.35 billion in 2004. The gain is attributable to a tight job market, which prompted employers to reward loyal employees across their organizations. Research on the results of employee recognition programs provides proof that incentive programs improve employee productivity, boost customer satisfaction and increase profits. Customer satisfaction has been found to directly impact employee morale, even for employees who have no direct contact with customers. As in the market for consumer incentives, gift certificates and electronic products were among the most popular items used to reward employees in 2004. Spending on employee incentives is expected to accelerate in 2005 and remain in the 4.0 percent to 5.0 percent range during the 2004-2009 period. Compound annual growth will be 4.7 percent in the period, surpassing the 2.3 percent gain posted in the 1999-2004 timeframe. Spending will reach $30.63 billion in 2009.

Growth in promotional products spending accelerated in 2004, growing 5.9 percent to $17.31 billion in 2004, compared to 4.6 percent growth in 2003. Growth was driven, in part, by gains among luxury brands, such as Coach, which manufactures accessories such as handbags and watches. Corporations are thanking clients with such high-end merchandise to convey the client's value. Spending on promotional products will continue to expand during the forecast period, rising 6.5 percent to $18.44 billion in 2005, and growing at a compound annual rate of 7.0 percent from 2004 to 2009. Spending will reach $24.32 billion in 2009.

Spending on business-to-business promotion is expected to increase 5.6 percent to $44.0 billion in 2005, driven by gains in both employee incentives and promotional products. Spending is expected to grow at a compound annual rate of 5.7 percent from 2004 to 2009, reaching $54.96 billion in 2009.

CONSUMER PROMOTION

Consumer promotion includes point-of-purchase (P-O-P) displays, premiums, product sampling, in-store media and coupons. Spending on consumer promotion increased 4.4 percent to $31.64 billion in 2004, as marketers sought less expensive alternatives to advertising, pursued marketing tactics that directly impact sales, and focused on improving ROI. Growth was driven by strong gains in product sampling and in-store media. Compound annual growth was 2.5 percent from 1999 to 2004.

Spending on P-O-P advertising, including traditional cardboard displays and new interactive kiosks, increased 6.0 percent to $16.64 billion in 2004, driven by the general trend toward bringing marketing inside the retail store. P-O-P advertising allows marketers to reach consumers while they are making purchases, when they tend to be more receptive to promotional messages. Spending is expected to grow at a steady pace in 2005 and during the remainder of the forecast period. According to one survey, about 40 percent of brand marketers expect to increase their P-O-P budgets in 2005. The trend toward more sophisticated displays will fuel 5.8 percent growth to $17.60 billion in 2005, and spur 5.7 percent compound annual growth in the forecast period.

Growth in coupon spending slowed in 2004, as marketers de-emphasized the tactic's role in the marketing mix, most likely because coupon use tends to decline when the economy is strong. Only 16.7 percent of brand marketers reported that coupons and free-standing inserts (FSI) ranked in their top three spending categories in 2004, down from 18.4 percent in 2003. Spending increased only 2.2 percent to $6.90 billion in 2004, but distribution climbed 7.7 percent. The top 20 manufacturers represented about 60 percent of all coupons distributed. Consumer packaged goods manufacturers accounted for 71.4 percent of FSI pages in 2004. But franchise coupons and direct response posted the largest gains in FSI pages, up 14.4 percent and 10.3 percent, respectively. Spending on coupons is expected to increase only 3.1 percent to $7.11 billion in 2005, and grow at a compound annual rate of 2.7 percent from 2004 to 2009, hitting $7.90 billion.

Spending on consumer premiums was flat in 2004 at $5.48 billion, as marketers were more concerned about measuring ROI and directly impacting consumer purchases than with thanking consumers for a previous purchase. Gift certificates and electronic items, such as cameras and home entertainment devices, were among the most popular items used in consumer incentive programs in 2004. Spending on premiums is expected to increase in 2005 due to the emergence of online loyalty programs, which reward consumers with gifts and prizes. Spending is

Communications Industry Segments Ranked by Five-Year Growth

Segment	1999-2004 CAGR*	1999-2004 Rank	2004-2009 CAGR*	2004-2009 Rank
Consumer Internet	24.6%	1	14.5%	1
Custom Publishing	13.6	2	12.1	2
Cable & Satellite Television	9.9	3	7.5	6
Public Relations	7.8	4	8.9	3
Branded Entertainment	7.0	5	8.2	4
Entertainment Media	5.8	6	7.0	7
Professional & Business Information Services	5.4	7	7.8	5
Direct Marketing	4.8	8	6.0	9
Out-of-Home Advertising	3.8	9	5.5	12
Yellow Pages	3.8	10	4.6	15
Educational & Training Media	3.4	11	5.2	13
Broadcast & Satellite Radio	2.8	12	6.2	8
Broadcast Television	2.7	13	4.3	17
Business-to-Business Promotion	2.6	14	5.7	11
Consumer Promotion	2.5	15	4.9	14
Consumer Books	1.8	16	2.1	19
Consumer Magazines	1.0	17	4.5	16
Newspapers	0.6	18	2.8	18
Business-to-Business Media	–0.1	19	5.8	10

Sources: Veronis Suhler Stevenson, PQ Media
*Compound annual growth rate.

forecast to increase 2.6 percent to $5.62 billion in 2005, and grow at a compound annual rate of 3.0 percent from 2004 to 2009, reaching $6.34 billion in 2009.

Spending on product sampling increased 12.5 percent to $1.66 billion in 2004, the highest growth rate among the consumer promotion segments. Marketers are implementing the tactic to target the 18- to 25-year-old demographic, which often has not developed loyalty to particular products or brands. Spring Break has become a prime opportunity for sampling because students will bring products and information back to their campuses, perpetuating the marketing effort at no additional cost. Spending growth is expected to outpace the other consumer promotion segments in the forecast period because marketers view product sampling as an opportunity to drive sales directly. As a result, expenditures are projected to increase 9.8 percent to $1.82 billion in 2005, and grow at a compound annual rate of 9.3 percent in the forecast period to $2.59 billion in 2009.

Spending on in-store media grew 8.0 percent to $962.0 million in 2004, driven by growth in the burgeoning market for in-store television network advertising. In-store media also includes in-store radio networks, on-

Communications Industry Segments Ranked by Size

	2004		2009	
Segment	*$ Millions*	*Rank*	*$ Millions*	*Rank*
Direct Marketing	$135,367	1	$180,978	1
Professional & Business Information Services	97,822	2	142,325	2
Cable & Satellite Television	93,376	3	134,220	3
Entertainment Media	88,564	4	124,349	4
Newspapers	63,527	5	72,926	6
Broadcast Television	43,176	6	53,251	8
Business-to-Business Promotion	41,658	7	54,957	7
Consumer Internet	37,552	8	74,038	5
Consumer Promotion	31,639	9	40,206	9
Consumer Magazines	22,452	10	27,936	12
Custom Publishing	22,009	11	38,881	10
Business-to-Business Media	20,911	12	27,684	13
Branded Entertainment	20,729	13	30,724	11
Broadcast & Satellite Radio	20,306	14	27,449	14
Consumer Books	19,761	15	21,903	16
Educational & Training Media	18,694	16	24,037	15
Yellow Pages	15,928	17	19,973	17
Out-of-Home Advertising	5,834	18	7,623	18
Public Relations	3,410	19	5,212	19

Sources: Veronis Suhler Stevenson, PQ Media

shelf promotional messages, on-shelf coupon dispensers and floor graphics.

In-store media spending is expected to grow 7.8 percent in 2005 to surpass the $1 billion mark. Spending will grow at a compound annual rate of 7.8 percent from 2004 to 2009, reaching $1.40 billion in 2009.

Total spending on consumer promotion is expected to increase 4.9 percent in 2005 to $33.20 billion, bolstered by spending on product sampling and in-store media. Compound annual growth will be 4.9 percent from 2004 to 2009, surpassing the 2.5 percent gain achieved in the previous five-year period. Spending will reach $40.21 billion in 2009.

CUSTOM PUBLISHING

Spending on custom publishing increased 20.4 percent to $22.01 billion in 2004, driven by strong gains in spending on custom magazines for internal use and electronic publications. These figures reflect only production and distribution costs, excluding salaries for personnel. Marketers are shifting funding from traditional advertising vehicles to custom publishing because of the medium's highly targeted approach and its ability to establish ongoing relationships with target audiences and customer groups.

Custom publishing spending is expected to continue to grow at double-digit rates annually during the forecast period, due to interest in establishing solid relationships with clients, the transition from short newsletters to more in-depth four-color magazines, demand for more titles and increased page volume per issue. Among the new custom publications produced in 2005 was the U.S. Postal Service's (USPS) new magazine, *Deliver*, designed to promote the use of direct mail to marketers. The publication is a 32-page bimonthly magazine mailed to a targeted audience of 350,000 CEOs, corporate marketing executives and marketing agencies. Custom publishing spending is expected to increase 11.9 percent to $24.63 billion in 2005, and grow at a compound annual rate of 12.1 percent from 2004 to 2009, hitting $38.88 billion in 2009.

BRANDED ENTERTAINMENT

Branded entertainment includes event sponsorship, promotional licensing and product placement. Due to increased audience fragmentation, the migration to consumer-controlled media through ad-skipping technologies and complaints about advertising clutter, marketers are seeking alternative methods to reach their target audiences in unique ways. Branded entertainment is currently one of the major solutions to meet these criteria, particularly its use in media that engage the 18- to 34-year-old market. As a result, spending on branded entertainment increased 9.1 percent in 2004 to $20.73 billion, and grew at a compound annual rate of 7.0 percent from 1999 to 2004.

Event sponsorship is the largest of the three subsegments of branded entertainment with expenditures of $11.12 billion in 2004, and includes efforts to heighten brand awareness through strategic placements, mainly at sporting and entertainment events such as NASCAR races and music concerts. Promotional licensing is the second-largest subsegment of branded entertainment, generating $6.15 billion in 2004. Promotional licensing includes brand logo placement on purchased products, like T-shirts, or promotional giveaways, such as children's toys at fast food restaurants. Product placement is the smallest, but fastest-growing sector of branded entertainment, up 30.5 percent in 2004 to $3.46 billion, according to exclusive research from PQ Media. It entails the seamless integration of products into television programs, films and other media, such as newspapers, magazines, videogames and the Internet.

Spending on branded entertainment is expected to increase 9.7 percent to $22.73 billion in 2005, driven by double-digit growth in product placement spending, as well as strong gains in sponsorship expenditures. Compound annual growth will be 8.2 percent from 2004 to 2009, fueled by the product placement and sponsorship subsegments. Spending will reach $30.72 billion in 2009.

PUBLIC RELATIONS

The public relations segment has also been positively impacted by the trend toward alternative marketing methods, which fueled a 12.0 percent increase in spending to $3.41 billion in 2004. The growth rate represented a substantial improvement over the market's performance during the previous three years. Spending increased a modest 4.0 percent in 2003, after a disappointing 0.9 percent gain in 2002 and a 7.0 percent slide in 2001. The public relations segment has begun to see the benefits of consolidation that led to full-service advertising and marketing agencies that offer a multitude of strategic services along with media buying, including public relations.

Spending on public relations by the consumer and retail industry, as well as the healthcare industry, fueled growth in 2004. The consumer and retail category posted the strongest growth rate, up 20.7 percent, followed by healthcare, up 19.6 percent. The technology category, which experienced an increase in spending for the first time since 2000, continued to account for the largest share of spending at 27.4 percent.

Spending is expected to increase 10.1 percent to $3.75 billion in 2005, as corporations continue to invest in alternative marketing tactics. Public relations is expected to play a larger role in corporate marketing efforts based on a survey of senior marketers who stated that public relations was most effective in raising awareness, and that it is most valuable in supporting product marketing and product launches. Public relations firms are becoming more proactive in selling to organizations multiple services from brand loyalty campaigns to crisis management. Spending is expected to grow at a compound annual rate of 8.9 percent from 2004 to 2009, surpassing the 7.8 percent growth rate achieved in the prior five-year interval. Spending will reach $5.21 billion in 2009.

2004 Communications Industry Forecast Compared with Actual Growth

Industry Segment	*2004 Forecasted Growth**	*Actual 2004 Growth†*
Broadcast Television	8.5%	9.1%
Cable & Satellite Television	8.8	9.7
Broadcast & Satellite Radio	7.8	3.1
Entertainment Media	7.9	6.5
Consumer Internet	13.1	18.3
Newspaper Publishing	4.7	3.1
Consumer Book Publishing	1.8	1.2
Consumer Magazine Publishing	2.5	4.6
Business-to-Business Media	1.7	5.2
Educational & Training Media	NA	4.2
Professional & Business Information Services	NA	9.7
Yellow Pages	4.7	3.7
Out-of-Home Advertising	4.6	6.0
Direct Marketing	NA	6.0
Business-to-Business Promotion	5.9	3.7
Consumer Promotion	3.4	4.4
Custom Publishing	NA	20.4
Branded Entertainment	NA	9.1
Public Relations	6.8	12.0
Total Advertising	7.2	7.6
Total Marketing Services & Specialty Media	5.1	6.9
Total Consumer End User	7.3	6.2
Total Institutional End User	5.7	8.8
Total Communications Industry	6.4	7.3

*Veronis Suhler Stevenson 2004 Communications Industry Forecast & Report
†Veronis Suhler Stevenson, PQ Media

Veronis Suhler Stevenson Communications Industry Forecast

Industry Segment	1999 Gross Expenditures ($ Millions)	Annual Growth Rate (%) 2000	2001	2002	2003	2004	1999-2004 Compound Annual Growth (%)
Broadcast Television	$37,751	12.4%	–13.6%	9.1%	–1.1%	9.1%	2.7%
Television Networks	14,571	14.0	–8.7	5.2	0.8	9.1	3.8
Television Stations	23,180	11.3	–16.8	11.9	–2.4	9.1	2.0
Cable & Satellite Television	58,290	10.3	9.4	10.5	9.6	9.7	9.9
Subscription Fees	37,225	6.8	9.4	10.9	8.6	7.5	8.6
Advertising	11,624	18.6	3.1	3.7	10.6	16.1	10.2
License Fees	9,441	13.8	17.3	16.8	11.7	10.4	14.0
Broadcast & Satellite Radio	17,681	12.3	–7.4	5.8	1.4	3.1	2.89
Radio Networks	878	17.2	–10.7	8.8	3.3	4.6	4.2
Radio Stations	16,803	12.0	–7.3	5.5	0.9	1.9	2.4
Satellite Radio	—	—	—	4,212.6	388.8	208.6	—
Entertainment Media	66,848	4.2	3.6	8.9	5.8	6.5	5.8
Filmed Entertainment	45,723	6.7	5.6	13.0	8.8	7.7	8.3
Box Office	7,577	3.7	10.2	13.4	0.3	1.3	5.7
Home Video	16,610	3.0	14.9	18.4	14.3	3.8	10.7
Interactive Television & Wireless Content	7	571.4	157.4	615.4	109.7	78.0	241.1
Television Programming	21,529	10.4	–3.0	5.1	3.2	9.3	4.9
Recorded Music	14,585	–1.8	–4.1	–8.2	–6.0	2.5	–3.6
Interactive Entertainment	6,540	0.2	6.1	12.5	2.6	2.5	4.7
Videogames	4,647	–0.3	11.9	18.0	6.5	6.0	8.2
PC Games	1,890	1.2	–8.6	–5.2	–13.9	–15.9	–8.7
Videogame Advertising	3	200.0	144.4	100.0	79.5	51.9	109.1
Consumer Internet	12,517	57.4	19.2	13.5	19.1	18.3	24.6
Online Access	7,896	47.1	33.7	23.2	18.4	13.0	26.5
Internet Content	—	—	—	85.0	21.0	27.9	—
Advertising	4,621	75.0	–11.8	–15.8	20.9	32.5	15.8
Newspaper Publishing	61,511	4.5	–6.3	0.4	1.8	3.1	0.6
Daily Newspapers	56,759	4.3	–7.0	0.1	1.6	3.0	0.3
Advertising	46,287	5.2	–9.0	–0.5	1.9	3.9	0.2
Circulation	10,472	0.7	2.3	2.3	0.6	–0.9	1.0
Weekly Newspapers	4,752	6.4	1.7	4.1	4.1	4.9	4.2
Advertising	4,402	6.8	1.9	3.9	4.2	5.1	4.4
Circulation	350	1.4	–0.8	6.0	1.9	1.8	2.0
Consumer Book Publishing	18,087	–0.4	–0.5	5.2	3.6	1.2	1.8
Consumer Magazine Publishing	21,369	4.6	–5.7	0.1	1.9	4.6	1.0
Advertising	11,433	8.2	–10.3	–0.9	4.0	6.0	1.2
Circulation	9,936	0.4	–0.1	1.1	–0.5	3.0	0.8
Business-to-Business Media	21,063	8.2	–8.7	–5.8	1.5	5.2	–0.1
Business-to-Business Magazines	12,251	8.9	–14.0	–11.3	–0.9	2.2	–3.4
Advertising	10,218	8.8	–15.8	–13.3	–0.2	3.4	–3.9
Circulation	2,033	9.3	–5.4	–2.6	–3.7	–2.9	–1.2
E-media	274	98.5	33.1	26.1	28.0	25.9	40.0
Trade Shows & Exhibitions	8,538	4.3	–3.2	–1.2	1.5	5.8	1.4
Educational & Training Media	15,838	8.0	2.9	–0.3	2.2	4.2	3.4
K-12 Instructional Materials	3,314	13.3	7.8	–5.0	3.5	0.0	4.2
College Instructional Materials	3,645	3.5	6.7	9.5	3.6	1.5	5.2
Outsourced Corporate Training	8,880	7.9	–0.7	–3.7	0.9	7.4	2.2
Professional & Business Information Services	75,190	7.5	0.6	3.5	6.0	9.7	5.4
Professional Information	14,496	8.6	2.8	7.0	5.6	7.9	6.4
Legal & Regulatory Information	6,307	11.2	3.7	6.1	5.3	7.2	6.7
Scientific & Technical Information	4,943	6.8	1.9	8.1	6.4	8.5	6.3
Health & Life Science Information	3,246	6.3	2.4	7.0	5.0	8.5	5.8
Business Information Services	60,694	7.3	0.1	2.6	6.1	10.2	5.2
Marketing Information Services	17,179	6.8	1.9	3.3	6.4	14.7	6.5
Payroll & Human Resource Services	16,347	7.8	–1.1	3.4	6.1	6.0	4.4
Financial & Economic Information	13,032	7.5	–1.5	–0.9	6.8	10.0	4.3
Credit & Risk Information	10,422	7.0	1.7	4.2	5.1	10.0	5.6
General Business Industry News	3,714	7.2	–2.5	3.7	4.5	8.0	4.1

2004 Gross Expenditures ($ Millions)	*Annual Growth Rate (%)* 2005	2006	2007	2008	2009	*2004-2009 Compound Annual Growth (%)*	*2009 Gross Expenditures ($ Millions)*
$ 43,176	1.9%	7.4%	2.1%	8.2%	2.0%	4.3%	$ 53,251
17,563	2.3	7.3	2.0	8.9	1.8	4.4	21,799
25,613	1.6	7.5	2.2	7.7	2.2	4.2	31,452
93,376	8.7	7.7	7.2	6.9	7.1	7.5	134,220
56,276	6.8	6.1	5.8	5.4	5.2	5.9	74,829
18,925	14.6	11.9	10.8	10.6	12.2	12.0	33,361
18,175	8.6	8.0	7.2	7.1	6.4	7.4	26,030
20,306	4.6	5.7	6.4	7.9	6.6	6.2	27,44
1,081	3.3	4.0	4.5	6.5	5.5	4.8	1,363
18,932	2.7	3.2	3.8	5.6	4.6	4.0	22,980
293	131.8	80.4	51.0	34.6	24.6	60.3	3,106
88564	7.1	8.3	6.8	7.4	5.6	7.0	124,349
68,183	9.3	9.8	7.5	8.2	6.3	8.2	101,150
9,977	2.0	2.6	3.2	2.8	3.6	2.8	11,467
27,615	11.8	10.3	7.8	7.7	6.3	8.8	42,048
3,231	52.6	37.0	24.3	17.6	14.0	28.4	11,255
27,360	4.3	7.3	4.8	8.0	5.1	5.9	36,380
12,154	–2.5	–2.9	0.0	–3.2	–1.6	–2.1	10,953
8,227	3.4	9.9	9.8	12.1	6.4	8.3	12,246
6,906	5.3	11.9	10.6	12.6	5.9	9.2	10,737
1,201	–12.1	–10.8	–8.9	–9.7	–8.5	–10.0	709
120	48.3	50.0	50.6	47.8	34.7	46.1	800
37,552	16.7	16.2	14.9	13.5	11.4	14.5	74,038
25,581	9.3	9.1	7.9	7.9	7.2	8.3	38,076
2,345	37.3	35.5	28.5	22.6	13.0	27.1	7,764
9,626	31.2	27.1	24.6	20.3	17.2	24.0	28,198
63,527	2.7	3.1	2.6	2.9	2.6	2.8	72,926
57,687	2.5	2.8	2.5	2.5	2.4	2.5	65,357
46,699	3.5	3.7	3.2	3.2	2.9	3.3	54,941
10,988	–1.9	–1.4	–1.1	–0.7	–0.3	–1.1	10,416
5,840	5.5	6.2	3.8	6.7	4.4	5.3	7,569
5,453	5.8	6.5	4.0	7.0	4.5	5.6	7,145
387	1.5	2.0	1.2	2.5	1.9	1.8	424
19,761	3.0	1.0	3.3	1.1	1.9	2.1	21,903
22,452	4.4	3.6	4.9	4.8	4.7	4.5	27,936
12,121	5.5	6.0	6.3	6.5	6.7	6.2	16,374
10,331	3.1	0.7	3.0	2.6	1.9	2.3	11,562
20,911	5.9	5.7	5.6	5.9	5.8	5.8	27,684
10,290	2.7	3.1	3.4	3.6	3.8	3.3	12,117
8,373	3.8	4.1	4.3	4.5	4.7	4.3	10,336
1,917	–2.2	–1.8	–1.1	–1.3	–0.9	–1.5	1,781
1,472	26.5	22.1	17.3	15.8	12.2	18.7	3,466
9,149	6.1	5.5	5.4	5.8	6.0	5.8	12,101
18,694	7.2	4.3	4.8	4.8	4.7	5.2	24,037
4,063	11.5	3.1	5.0	4.5	3.0	5.4	5,279
4,708	2.0	2.2	2.8	3.0	3.5	2.7	5,378
9,923	8.0	5.8	5.5	5.6	5.9	6.2	13,380
97,822	8.1	7.5	8.0	7.6	7.8	7.8	142,325
19,729	8.3	8.4	8.0	7.8	8.1	8.1	29,166
8,711	6.2	6.8	7.3	7.1	7.9	7.1	12,252
6,713	10.4	9.2	8.5	8.8	8.3	9.0	10,346
4,305	9.4	10.3	8.5	7.7	8.2	8.8	6,568
78,093	8.1	7.2	8.0	7.5	7.7	7.7	113,159
23,554	7.1	6.4	7.7	7.2	6.8	7.0	33,096
20,264	5.1	7.2	6.9	6.7	7.4	6.7	27,968
16,068	12.6	8.5	9.1	8.8	9.2	9.6	25,446
13,666	9.4	7.2	9.1	7.7	7.6	8.2	20,263
4,541	6.1	7.2	7.1	6.8	8.1	7.1	6,386

(Continued)

Veronis Suhler Stevenson Communications Industry Forecast (continued)

Industry Segment	*1999 Gross Expenditures ($ Millions)*	*Annual Growth Rate (%)* 2000	2001	2002	2003	2004	*1999-2004 Compound Annual Growth (%)*
Yellow Pages	$ 13,196	8.1%	5.4%	1.3%	0.9%	3.7%	3.8%
Local Advertising	11,038	6.9	5.3	0.8	–0.7	2.5	2.9
National Advertising	2,056	7.7	6.1	0.4	–1.4	2.9	3.1
Internet Yellow Pages	102	152.0	2.1	32.3	71.9	29.9	50.0
Out-of-Home Advertising	4,832	8.3	0.0	0.0	5.2	6.0	3.8
Local	2,890	8.7	0.6	–0.3	5.5	5.5	3.9
National	1,942	7.8	–1.1	0.5	4.7	6.8	3.7
Direct Marketing	106,854	7.9	0.2	4.5	5.8	6.0	4.8
Telesales	46,311	7.5	–1.5	4.4	5.4	5.5	4.2
Direct Mail	42,091	5.9	0.3	3.0	5.7	5.6	4.1
Catalog	11,470	12.8	3.4	6.1	4.7	4.9	6.3
Television	3,960	7.8	0.0	3.8	6.1	6.0	4.7
Interactive	938	54.4	43.3	33.1	20.6	24.9	34.7
Magazines	1,610	8.1	–6.7	0.4	6.2	6.0	2.7
Newspapers	278	6.1	–8.1	2.6	5.4	5.1	2.1
Radio	196	13.3	–11.7	4.6	7.3	6.8	3.7
Business-to-Business Promotion	36,676	9.4	–4.9	1.0	4.2	3.7	2.6
Incentives	21,736	2.5	–3.0	6.0	4.0	2.2	2.3
Promotional Products	14,940	19.5	–7.3	–5.6	4.6	5.9	3.0
Consumer Promotion	27,971	9.7	–6.1	2.8	2.3	4.4	2.5
Point-of-Purchase	14,399	18.1	–8.8	0.0	1.2	6.0	2.9
Coupons	6,708	–0.9	–6.1	4.5	3.5	2.2	0.6
Premiums	4,874	1.2	1.0	7.9	2.0	0.0	2.4
Product Sampling	1,120	7.1	2.5	9.0	10.0	12.5	8.2
In-Store Media	870	3.9	–5.6	2.0	2.4	8.0	2.0
Custom Publishing	11,650	11.4	10.1	18.9	7.7	20.4	13.6
Branded Entertainment	14,760	10.8	4.5	4.3	6.5	9.1	7.0
Event Sponsorship	7,631	14.0	6.9	3.8	6.2	8.4	7.8
Promotional Licensing	5,502	5.0	0.4	3.0	2.0	1.0	2.3
Product Placement	1,627	15.6	5.6	11.0	20.2	30.5	16.3
Public Relations	2,345	33.0	–7.0	0.9	4.0	12.0	7.8
Total Spending	624,429	8.8	–0.3	5.0	5.2	7.3	5.2
Total Advertising	162,451	11.6	–7.8	1.7	2.8	7.6	3.0
Local Advertising	89,469	7.3	–5.0	2.1	2.0	6.1	2.4
National Advertising	72,982	16.8	–10.9	1.3	3.8	9.4	3.7
Total Specialty Media & Marketing Services	202,389	9.1	–0.9	4.5	5.2	6.9	4.9
Total Consumer End-User	129,153	5.2	8.7	10.5	7.6	6.2	7.6
Total Institutional End-User	130,436	8.4	1.4	4.2	5.3	8.8	5.6
GDP	9,268,400	5.9	3.2	3.5	4.9	6.6	4.8
Communications as a % of GDP	6.7	6.9	6.7	6.8	6.8	6.8	—

2004 Gross Expenditures ($ Millions)	*Annual Growth Rate (%)* 2005	2006	2007	2008	2009	*2004-2009 Compound Annual Growth (%)*	*2009 Gross Expenditures ($ Millions)*
$ 15,928	3.7%	4.6%	4.6%	5.0%	5.3%	4.6%	$ 19,973
12,759	2.5	3.4	3.5	4.1	4.4	3.6	15,199
2,394	3.3	4.9	5.6	5.8	5.9	5.1	3,069
775	24.6	19.2	15.7	13.5	12.8	17.1	1,705
5,834	5.3	5.5	5.7	5.6	5.4	5.5	7,623
3,506	5.8	5.2	6.0	5.3	5.7	5.6	4,604
2,328	4.6	5.9	5.2	6.1	4.9	5.3	3,019
135,367	6.5	6.0	5.6	5.8	6.0	6.0	180,978
56,901	5.9	5.5	5.0	5.5	5.6	5.5	74,412
51,359	6.1	5.9	5.2	5.7	5.8	5.8	67,948
15,584	5.5	4.8	5.4	4.8	5.6	5.2	20,101
4,986	6.3	4.2	5.7	4.3	5.6	5.2	6,436
4,159	24.1	18.1	16.0	13.3	12.2	16.7	8,991
1,835	5.8	5.1	5.4	5.5	5.9	5.5	2,403
308	5.2	4.7	4.9	4.7	4.9	4.9	391
235	5.4	4.5	5.0	4.4	4.5	4.8	297
41,658	5.6	5.5	5.6	5.9	5.8	5.7	54,957
24,348	5.0	4.4	4.7	4.9	4.5	4.7	30,634
17,310	6.5	7.1	6.8	7.3	7.5	7.0	24,323
31,639	4.9	4.8	4.7	5.0	5.1	4.9	40,206
16,637	5.8	5.5	5.3	5.9	6.1	5.7	21,971
6,900	3.1	2.8	3.0	2.5	2.3	2.7	7,899
5,481	2.6	3.1	2.4	3.3	3.4	3.0	6,341
1,659	9.8	8.7	10.1	9.2	8.9	9.3	2,592
962	7.7	7.7	7.6	7.9	8.2	7.8	1,403
22,009	11.9	13.3	10.4	13.6	11.1	12.1	38,881
20,729	9.7	8.1	7.3	8.0	7.8	8.2	30,724
11,117	8.8	7.9	7.5	8.4	8.7	8.3	16,534
6,154	3.8	2.7	2.1	3.9	4.2	3.3	7,251
3,458	22.8	16.9	13.8	12.1	9.7	14.9	6,939
3,410	10.1	9.4	7.8	8.2	8.8	8.9	5,212
802,715	6.8	6.9	6.4	6.9	6.3	6.7	1,108,672
188,187	6.1	7.5	6.2	7.7	6.3	6.8	260,867
100,827	5.2	6.1	5.5	6.5	5.5	5.8	133,464
87,360	7.1	9.0	7.0	9.0	7.0	7.8	127,433
257,145	7.0	6.7	6.2	6.8	6.7	6.7	355,154
186,301	7.0	6.7	6.6	6.0	5.2	6.3	252,801
171,082	7.2	7.0	6.9	7.1	6.7	7.0	239,820
11,735,000	6.0	5.9	5.8	6.0	6.2	6.0	15,689,206
6.8	6.9	7.0	7.0	7.1	7.1	—	7.1

Veronis Suhler Stevenson Communications Industry Forecast

I

Communications in the U.S. Economy

The communications industry transitioned from recovery to expansion in 2004, as the industry posted accelerated growth for the third consecutive year and outpaced nominal GDP growth for the third straight year, as well. Total communications spending in 2004 increased at its fastest rate in four years, rising 7.3 percent to $802.68 billion, exceeding GDP expansion of 6.6 percent, driven by accelerated growth in three of the four broad sectors of the industry, including advertising, specialty media and marketing services, and institutional end user. While the fourth sector—consumer end user—posted decelerated growth for the second consecutive year, the consumer sector still recorded relatively solid expansion at 6.2 percent for 2004.

In order for Veronis Suhler Stevenson to provide the most accurate, up-to-date and valuable data and information available to our subscribers, we made a number of substantive changes to this year's edition of the *Forecast* which changed the size and structure of the communications industry compared with last year's edition. In particular, there were several changes made that had a significant impact on the size, growth and shares of each of the four broad sectors of the communications industry in 2004. Among these were the additions of several new spending categories to the direct marketing segment of the specialty media and marketing services sector, which made this sector the largest of the four in 2004. There were also important additions and revisions of data made to several segments of the advertising, consumer end-user and institutional end-user sectors, which changed their respective shares of the overall communications industry in 2004 and going forward. For all of the details regarding these changes and their impact on this edition of the *Forecast*, please see the Appendix located at the end of the book.

As a result, specialty media and marketing services became the largest sector of the communications industry in 2004, growing 6.9 percent to $257.15 billion and accounting for 32.0 percent of all communications spending for the year. The advertising sector expanded 7.6 percent to $188.15 billion and comprised 23.4 percent of all media expenditures in 2004, while the consumer end-user sector grew 6.2 percent to $186.30 billion and accounted

Top 15 Economic Sectors Ranked By Five-Year Growth

	1999-2004		*2004-2009*	
Economic Sector	*CAGR**	*Rank*	*CAGR**	*Rank*
Mining	11.5%	1	5.2%	12
Finance, Insurance, and Real Estate	6.1	2	6.7	3
Construction	5.9	3	6.4	8
Services	5.5	4	6.4	7
Electric, Gas and Sanitary Services	5.4	5	6.9	2
Federal Government	5.2	6	7.1	1
Communications	**5.2**	**7**	**6.7**	**4**
State and Local Government	5.0	8	6.4	9
Retail Trade	4.6	9	6.6	5
Agriculture, Forestry and Fishing	4.4	10	6.6	6
Wholesale Trade	3.6	11	5.3	11
Transportation	3.3	12	4.7	13
Nondurable Goods	3.0	13	5.3	10
Telephone and Telegraph	2.8	14	3.7	14
Durable Goods	1.0	15	1.5	15
Nominal GDP	4.8		6.0	

Source: Veronis Suhler Stevenson, PQ Media, Bureau of Economic Analysis
*Compound annual growth rate.

Top 15 Economic Sectors Ranked by Dollar Sales*

	2004		2009	
Economic Sector	*$ Billions*	*Rank*	*$ Billions*	*Rank*
Services	$ 2,798	1	$ 3,815	1
Finance, Insurance and Real Estate	2,341	2	3,235	2
State and Local Government	959	3	1,306	3
Durable Goods	832	4	895	6
Communications	**803**	**5**	**1,109**	**4**
Retail Trade	770	6	1,060	5
Wholesale Trade	665	7	860	7
Nondurable Goods	564	8	730	8
Construction	522	9	711	9
Federal Government	448	10	632	10
Transportation	327	11	411	11
Electric, Gas and Sanitary Services	233	12	325	12
Telephone and Telegraph	219	13	263	13
Mining	142	14	183	14
Agriculture, Forestry and Fishing	112	15	154	15
Nominal GDP	11,735		15,689	

Source: Veronis Suhler Stevenson, PQ Media, Bureau of Economic Analysis

*Dollar amounts reflect final sales of goods and services to consumers and businesses in each of the sectors. Communications spending data are taken from this *Forecast*, not from the annual BEA data, which are for the 1988-2003 period. The data for 2004 were calculated from historical data using the post-1998 linear trend. To avoid double counting the sectors, the following communications segments were not included in the following BEA categories: printing and publishing not included in nondurable goods; motion pictures not included in services.

for 23.2 percent of all spending. Although the consumer sector grew more slowly than the other three in 2004, this sector posted the fastest compound annual growth in the 1999-2004 period at 7.6 percent. Meanwhile, institutional end-user spending rose the fastest of all four sectors in 2004, climbing 8.8 percent to $171.08 billion, but was the smallest of all sectors with a 21.3 percent share for the year.

Total communications spending grew at a compound annual rate of 5.2 percent from 1999 to 2004, making communications the seventh-fastest-growing industry out of the 15 that comprised the U.S. economy in the five-year period. The communications industry's growth exceeded nominal GDP expansion of 4.8 percent in the period.

We expect overall expenditures on communications to grow at an accelerated compound annual rate of 6.7 percent from 2004 to 2009, surpassing the trillion-dollar mark in 2008, and reaching $1.109 trillion in 2009. The industry's expansion will outperform nominal GDP growth of 6.0 percent in the forecast period, driven by solid mid-single-digit growth in all four industry sectors over the next five years. Institutional end-user spending will outpace the other three sectors with compound annual growth of 7.0 percent from 2004 to 2009. Communications will become the fourth-largest sector of the U.S. economy in 2009, as well as improve to be the fourth-fastest-growing sector of the economy during the period.

HIGHLIGHTS

The communications industry entered an expansion phase in 2004, as the industry posted accelerated growth for the third consecutive year. Total communications spending increased at its fastest rate in four years, climbing 7.3 percent to $802.68 billion, outpacing GDP expansion for the third year in a row. The key driver was accelerated growth in three of the four broad sectors of the industry, including advertising, specialty media and marketing services, and institutional end user.

■

Total communications spending grew at a compound annual rate of 5.2 percent from 1999 to 2004, making communications the seventh-fastest-growing industry out of the 15 that comprised the U.S. economy in the five-year period, and propelling communications to the fifth-largest of the 15 sectors that comprised the U.S. economy in 2004.

■

In 2004, nominal gross domestic product (GDP) grew 6.6 percent, which compares favorably with nominal GDP compounded growth of 4.8 percent achieved from 1999 to 2004. Real GDP rose 4.4 percent, higher than the real GDP compounded rate of 2.7 percent recorded during the 1999-2004 period. A confluence of unexpected developments supported real and nominal GDP growth in 2004. In the second half of the year, medium-term and long-term interest rates remained stable despite the rise in short-term interest rates, and was a source of unexpected support for the auto and housing industries.

Gross Domestic Product

(BILLIONS OF CURRENT DOLLARS)

Year	*Gross Domestic Product*	*Personal Consumption Expenditures*	*Gross Private Domestic Investment*	*Net Exports of Goods and Services*	*Government Expenditures*	*Percent Change*
Annual Levels						
1994	$ 7,072.2	$4,743.3	$1,097.1	$ –93.6	$1,325.5	6.2%
1995	7,397.7	4,975.8	1,144.0	–91.4	1,369.2	4.6
1996	7,816.9	5,256.8	1,240.3	–96.2	1,416.0	5.7
1997	8,304.3	5,547.4	1,389.8	–101.6	1,468.7	6.2
1998	8,747.0	5,879.5	1,509.1	–159.9	1,518.3	5.3
1999	9,268.4	6,282.5	1,625.7	–260.5	1,620.8	6.0
2000	9,817.0	6,739.4	1,735.5	–379.5	1,721.6	5.9
2001	10,128.0	7,055.0	1,614.3	–367.0	1,825.6	3.2
2002	10,487.0	7,376.1	1,579.2	–424.9	1,956.6	3.5
2003	11,004.0	7,760.9	1,665.8	–498.1	2,075.5	4.9
2004	11,735.0	8,229.9	1,927.3	–606.2	2,183.9	6.6
Quarterly Levels: Seasonally Adjusted						
2004:1Q	11,472.6	8,060.2	1,819.7	–546.8	2,139.5	7.4
2004:2Q	11,657.5	8,153.8	1,920.7	–591.3	2,174.3	6.6
2004:3Q	11,814.9	8,282.5	1,947.0	–611.8	2,197.2	5.5
2004:4Q	11,994.8	8,423.3	2,021.9	–674.8	2,224.5	6.2
Compound Annual Growth Rates						
1994-1999	5.6%	5.8%	8.2%	22.7%	4.1%	
1999-2004	4.8	5.5	3.5	18.4	6.2	

Sources: Veronis Suhler Stevenson, PQ Media, Bureau of Economic Analysis

Nominal GDP and real GDP are forecast to expand by 6.0 percent and 3.7 percent, respectively, in 2005. From 2004 to 2009, nominal GDP is expected to grow at a compound annual rate of 6.0 percent, which corresponds to real GDP growth of 3.6 percent, with some acceleration in the latter half of the forecast period. This compares to real GDP compound annual growth of 3.9 percent recorded from 1994 to 1999, prior to the economic shocks that created a volatile 1999-2004 period for comparison.

■

Despite high oil and commodity prices, inflation will remain moderate in 2005, with the headline and core consumer price indices projected at 2.4 percent and 2.3 percent, respectively. Inflation, as measured by the GDP deflator, will increase at a compound rate of 2.3 percent from 2004 to 2009, compared to a rate of 2.1 percent during the 1999-2004 period.

■

We expect overall expenditures on communications to grow at an accelerated compound annual rate of 6.7 percent from 2004 to 2009, surpassing the trillion-dollar mark in 2008, and reaching $1.109 trillion in 2009. The industry's expansion will outperform nominal GDP growth in the forecast period, driven by solid mid-single-digit growth in all four industry sectors over the next five years.

■

Communications will become the fourth-largest sector of the U.S. economy in 2009, as well as improve to be the fourth-fastest-growing sector of the economy during the period.

Real Gross Domestic Product

(BILLIONS OF 2000 CHAINED DOLLARS)

Year	*Gross Domestic Product*	*Personal Consumption Expenditures*	*Gross Private Domestic Investment*	*Net Exports of Goods and Services*	*Government Expenditures*	*Percent Change*
Annual Levels						
1994	$ 7,835.5	$5,290.7	$1,099.6	$ –79.4	$1,541.3	4.0%
1995	8,031.7	5,433.5	1,134.0	–71.0	1,549.7	2.5
1996	8,328.9	5,619.4	1,234.3	–79.6	1,564.9	3.7
1997	8,703.5	5,831.8	1,387.7	–104.6	1,594.0	4.5
1998	9,066.9	6,125.8	1,524.1	–203.7	1,624.4	4.2
1999	9,470.3	6,438.6	1,642.6	–296.2	1,686.9	4.5
2000	9,817.0	6,739.4	1,735.5	–379.5	1,721.6	3.7
2001	9,890.7	6,910.4	1,598.4	–399.1	1,780.3	0.8
2002	10,074.8	7,123.4	1,560.7	–472.1	1,857.9	1.9
2003	10,381.3	7,355.6	1,628.8	–518.5	1,909.4	3.0
2004	10,841.9	7,632.5	1,843.5	–583.7	1,946.5	4.4
Quarterly Levels: Seasonally Adjusted						
2004:1Q	10,697.5	7,543.0	1,764.5	–550.1	1,935.8	4.5
2004:2Q	10,784.7	7,572.4	1,842.9	–580.3	1,946.5	3.3
2004:3Q	10,891.0	7,667.8	1,853.9	–583.2	1,949.9	4.0
2004:4Q	10,994.3	7,747.0	1,912.6	–621.1	1,954.0	3.8
Compound Annual Growth Rates						
1994-1999	3.9%	4.0%	8.4%	30.1%	1.8%	
1999-2004	2.7	3.5	2.3	14.6	2.9	

Sources: Veronis Suhler Stevenson, PQ Media, Bureau of Economic Analysis

THE ECONOMY IN 2004 AND 2005

Following the 2001 recession, the economy embarked on a recovery marked by progressive acceleration of economic growth. Throughout 2004, economic activity remained buoyant except for a minor soft patch late in the spring, despite record highs in energy prices, uncertainty occasioned by the presidential elections and geopolitical tensions in the Middle East.

A testament to the strength of the economy last year is that the annual growth rate was higher than the compound annual growth rate from 1999 to 2004. However, recent economic indicators and trends suggest that the economy is slowing to a more sustainable growth pace. The slowdown in economic activity is mainly due to weakening productivity growth from the high rate recorded in the last three years, as well as further removal of the highly accommodative monetary and fiscal policy that began in 2001.

There will be some moderation in both household and business spending, although the slowdown in consumer spending will be more pronounced. Rising interest rates imply that the cost of servicing near-record levels of debt will increase for households and that mortgage refinancing—a considerable source of non-income cash in recent years—will become less attractive. Moreover, households will no longer receive a boost from tax rebates. Thus, consumer spending is likely to ease from the pace registered in 2004, despite a stronger job market and wage increases.

The weakening in productivity growth and high commodity prices imply that business profit growth will subside. This trend, in addition to two other developments, will negatively affect investment. First, businesses will no longer benefit from favorable depreciation legislation that expired at the end of last year. Second, the need to invest in equipment and software is expected to diminish this year as businesses complete their upgrading cycle. As a result, business spending will weaken from last year's fast pace, but will remain reasonably strong.

Exports will not compensate for the moderation in growth of domestic demand since major trading partners, such as the European Union and Japan, are expected to register disappointing growth this year. The balance of these factors suggests that GDP growth will slow, but still post a solid nominal and real rate of 6.0 percent and 3.7 percent, respectively, in 2005, compared with 6.6 percent and 4.4 percent in 2004.

Business Investment Remains Strong

After taking off in the second half of 2003, business investment growth was rapid throughout 2004 and is expected to remain the primary driver of the economy in 2005. A key aspect of the current upturn in business spending is that internal cash flow has been adequate to finance all capital spending, in contrast to the business expansion in the second half of the 1990s, which led to massive corporate debts. During the third quarter of 2004, the corporate financing gap stood at an annualized negative $38.6 billion, posting an unprecedented fifth negative reading in six quarters. A negative reading on the financing gap, of course, means that the corporate sector is able to meet all of its investment spending needs, including inventory investment, with internally generated cash flow. This abundance of cash, in addition to high returns on capital, rising business confidence and favorable financial conditions, should ensure that business investment remains robust, on the whole, in 2005.

Capital equipment spending will be strong in the quarters ahead, but will gradually lose some momentum. The modest slowdown expected is due to some fading in the hardware and software replacement cycle, and the expiration of bonus depreciation benefits at the end of last year. Some of the weakening in equipment spending will be partially offset by a pickup in structure investment, which, after being flat since mid-2003, is expected to accelerate in 2005.

Residential investment, which largely exceeded expectations in 2004, will progressively weaken this year, mostly due to higher mortgage rates. In particular, the single-family housing market—which set another string of records last year—has nowhere to go but down. Home sales zoomed, hitting about 8 million annualized units. Construction of new

Annual Growth in Real GDP Components

Year	Gross Domestic Product	Personal Consumption Expenditures	Gross Private Domestic Investment	Exports of Goods and Services	Imports of Goods and Services	Government Expenditures
Annual Rates						
1995	2.5%	2.7%	3.1%	10.1%	8.0%	0.5%
1996	3.7	3.4	8.9	8.4	8.7	1.0
1997	4.5	3.8	12.4	11.9	13.6	1.9
1998	4.2	5.0	9.8	2.4	11.6	1.9
1999	4.5	5.1	7.8	4.3	11.5	3.9
2000	3.7	4.7	5.7	8.7	13.1	2.1
2001	0.8	2.5	–7.9	–5.4	–2.7	3.4
2002	1.9	3.1	–2.4	–2.3	3.4	4.4
2003	3.0	3.3	4.4	1.9	4.4	2.8
2004	4.4	3.8	13.2	8.6	9.9	1.9
Quarterly Rates: Seasonally Adjusted						
2004:1Q	4.5	4.1	12.3	7.3	10.6	2.5
2004:2Q	3.3	1.6	19.0	7.3	12.6	2.2
2004:3Q	4.0	5.1	2.4	6.0	4.6	0.7
2004:4Q	3.8	4.2	13.3	3.2	11.4	0.9

Sources: Veronis Suhler Stevenson, PQ Media, Bureau of Economic Analysis

homes also proceeded at an exceptional pace, reaching about 1.6 million units. Strong demand sent home prices soaring, with the median existing home price gaining 8.0 percent, topping a four-year run of house price appreciation that well exceeds the pace of inflation. Thanks to the strong housing market, home ownership hit an all-time high of 69.5 percent in 2004. Clearly, the housing market cannot continue this stellar performance. Higher mortgage rates will lead to some moderation in residential investment in 2005, with a more pronounced weakening in 2006.

Consumer Spending Wanes

The transition from a consumer-led recovery to a business-driven expansion began in 2004. Indeed, for the first time since 1997, consumer spending expanded at a pace that was slower than overall economic activity, as real GDP grew 4.4 percent but real consumer spending expanded 3.8 percent. It is expected that overall demand will grow at a faster clip than consumer demand in 2005, as well.

In 2005, consumer spending will be negatively affected by a confluence of factors. The chief positive development for consumer demand will be the continued improvement in the labor market. Strong hiring activity will lift consumer confidence, and boost wage and income growth. There are several adverse factors, however, that will more than offset the positive impact of job creation on consumer spending. Transfer payment receipts will slow as the labor market firms and fewer people depend on the government for assistance. Moreover, the volatile proprietor's income will grow at a slower rate, and growth in asset income will moderate as economic growth slows down. Thus, while growth in wages and salaries—which constitute 55 percent of personal income—will accelerate, this will be partly offset by weakness in non-wage income, which will rise at a slower rate. The end-effect is that consumers will rein in discretionary

Annual Growth in Real Gross Private Domestic Investment Components

Year	*Gross Private Domestic Investment*	*Fixed Investment*	*Nonresidential Investment*	*Nonresidential Structures*	*Nonresidential Equipment and Software*	*Residential*
Annual Rates						
1995	3.1%	6.5%	10.5%	6.4%	12.0%	–3.2%
1996	8.9	9.0	9.3	5.6	10.6	8.0
1997	12.4	9.2	12.1	7.3	13.8	1.9
1998	9.8	10.2	11.1	5.1	13.3	7.6
1999	7.8	8.3	9.2	–0.4	12.7	6.0
2000	5.7	6.5	8.7	6.8	9.4	0.8
2001	–7.9	–3.0	–4.2	–2.3	–4.9	0.4
2002	–2.4	–4.9	–8.9	–17.8	–5.5	4.8
2003	4.4	5.1	3.3	–5.6	6.4	8.8
2004	13.2	10.3	10.6	1.4	13.6	9.7
Quarterly Rates: Seasonally Adjusted						
2004:1Q	12.3	4.5	4.2	–7.6	8.0	5.0
2004:2Q	19.0	13.9	12.5	6.9	14.2	16.5
2004:3Q	2.4	8.8	13.0	–1.1	17.5	1.6
2004:4Q	13.3	10.5	14.5	2.1	18.4	3.4

Sources: Veronis Suhler Stevenson, PQ Media, Bureau of Economic Analysis

spending, leading to a weakening in consumer spending growth.

Restrictive economic policies will also have an impact on households. Rising interest rates will undermine consumer spending growth through several channels. First, it will increase the cost of financing durable goods purchased, such as automobiles, and make it more costly for retailers to offer financing incentives such as zero percent financing. Second, rising interest rates will slow asset appreciation, reducing the growth of household wealth. Third, the refinancing window will be completely closed. And finally, rising interest rates will gradually increase the cost of carrying consumer debt. Fiscal policy will also move from being stimulative to being restrictive; while consumers received some direct benefit from fiscal stimulus last year, primarily limited to larger-than-normal tax refunds, there will be none this year.

Interestingly, for many big-ticket items such as vehicles and houses, consumers have bought ahead of their normal cycle to take advantage of low interest rates and other apparently unique deals. This, too, will contribute to a noticeable decline in household spending in 2005.

The Job Market Turns the Corner

For the expansion to sustain itself, the economy needs to generate annual job gains of approximately 1.8 million, since the pace of job growth will generate just enough wage and salary income to keep consumers spending and the economy moving forward. After a disappointing job market recovery, the employment level at long last surpassed the March 2001 pre-recession peak of 132.5 million in January 2005. In 2004, 2.2 million jobs were created—the most since the 2.8 million hirings of 2000—and employment gains were broad-based across industries.

Annual Growth in Real Personal Consumption Components

Year	*Personal Consumption Expenditures*	*Durable Goods*	*Nondurable Goods*	*Services*
Annual Rates				
1995	2.7%	4.4%	2.2%	2.6%
1996	3.4	7.8	2.6	2.9
1997	3.8	8.6	2.7	3.3
1998	5.0	11.3	4.0	4.2
1999	5.1	11.7	4.6	4.0
2000	4.7	7.3	3.8	4.5
2001	2.5	4.3	2.0	2.4
2002	3.1	6.5	2.6	2.6
2003	3.3	7.4	3.7	2.2
2004	3.8	6.7	4.6	2.8
Quarterly Rates: Seasonally Adjusted				
2004:1Q	4.1	2.2	6.7	3.3
2004:2Q	1.6	–0.3	0.1	2.7
2004:3Q	5.1	17.2	4.7	3.0
2004:4Q	4.2	3.9	5.9	3.4

Sources: Veronis Suhler Stevenson, PQ Media, Bureau of Economic Analysis

As is typically the case at this point in the business cycle, productivity growth will continue to fade in the coming quarters. Moreover, the cost of capital will continue to rise due to the expiration in the accelerated depreciation of tax benefits at the end of 2004 and the removal of monetary policy accommodation. Therefore, about 2.2 million jobs are expected to be created in 2005 despite a slowdown in growth.

With the prospect of finding jobs increasing, workers who had previously given up looking for employment will resume their job search. Due to these returning workers, the unemployment rate will remain fairly steady despite robust hiring activity. Job gains should be just large enough to absorb new entrants and some of those who have been out of a job. But overall, the labor market will retain enough slack for wages and salaries to grow only moderately in 2005.

Dollar Decline Will Not Mitigate the Trade Deficit

After depreciating significantly against major currencies in 2003, the dollar weakened only slightly in 2004. This, together with the fastest growth in the global economy in two decades, led to real exports growing 8.6 percent for the year. At the same time, however, real imports rose 9.9 percent due to strong domestic demand. The net effect is that the trade deficit worsened to a record $583.7 billion, which corresponds to 5.4 percent of the real GDP, from $518.5 billion, or 5.0 percent, of real GDP in 2003.

The expansion of the trade deficit has seemingly defied economic theory, which postulates that a depreciating dollar makes exports cheaper and imports more expensive, and that, in time, this should lead to a correction in the trade deficit. Despite the dollar depreciation since early 2002, the American trade deficit has continued to increase and is expected to reach a new record high this year. The balance of U.S. trade has not conformed to textbook economic theory largely because American firms are increasingly producing overseas to take advantage of cheaper labor and favorable tax laws. Thus, imports, which are 1.5-fold exports, continue to rise in spite of the weakening dollar. Based on this trend, it is debatable whether U.S. imports will decrease this year, especially if oil prices remain elevated. At the same time, the growth of major importers of U.S. products, such as Canada and the European Union, will be modest in 2005, making it unlikely that American exports will match 2004's performance.

Given the outlook for U.S. exports and imports, our forecast is for a further expansion of the trade deficit in 2005. While the dollar will benefit from rising short-term interest rates over the next two years, the end-product will be a continued weakening of the dollar in 2005.

Energy Prices Remain a Key Risk

A key feature of the trade deficit and the economic landscape, in general, over the last few years has been the high price of oil. After averaging $19 a barrel from 1994 to 1999, crude oil averaged $31 a barrel from 2000 to 2004. Last year, the average price of a barrel of crude oil surged to $41 from $31 in 2003, and through the first quarter of 2005, the price of a barrel of crude oil was 40 percent higher than the price in the first quarter of 2004. This sharp upturn in energy prices can be attributed mainly to low inventory levels and uncertainty over supplies from the Middle East, Nigeria, Russia and Venezuela.

Still, supply growth kept up with demand growth in terms of barrels of crude oil in 2004; nevertheless, crude prices soared as markets were concerned about the lack of spare capacity in the event of supply disruptions. Such concerns should be somewhat alleviated in 2005 by rising inventory levels, an expansion in global extraction and refining capacities, and completion of the U.S. Strategic Petroleum Reserve filling.

Although the price of crude oil will likely remain elevated by historical standards in 2005, the price is expected to modestly decline as the year unfolds. Indeed, while the price of oil was elevated in the first few months of the year, the price is expected to start declining as demand for heating oil diminishes. In the second half of the year, weakening U.S. and global oil demand, due to more moderate economic growth, will also cause downward pressure on oil prices. All in all, high oil prices may dampen growth this year, but it is likely they will not threaten the expansion. Elevated crude prices, nonetheless, remain one of the most significant threats to the economic outlook, with each $5 increase in price shaving about one-third of a percentage point off of GDP growth.

Removal of Monetary and Fiscal Accommodation Continues

Despite the rise in the price of crude oil and the increase in the price of imports through a weakening of the dollar, inflation remained contained in 2004. This is because limited pricing-power from businesses restricted price pass-through to consumers. The implicit price deflator, a measure of inflation, grew 2.2 percent, only slightly faster than the 1.8 percent pace of 2003.

Subdued inflation notwithstanding, the Federal Open Market Committee (FOMC) started raising the Federal Funds rate from a 46-year low of 1.00 percent in June 2004 in a bid to stave off any eventual pickup in inflation and to prevent excessive risk-taking in financial markets. The FOMC has eight meetings scheduled for 2005 and is expected to take the Federal Funds rate to at least 3.75 percent by year's end. The rise in interest rates will make borrowing increasingly less attractive and, therefore, weaken household and business spending.

The resulting slowdown in growth of aggregate demand will keep inflation in check in 2005. While headline inflation inched higher in the first months of 2005, most notably due to a surge in commodity prices, there was no acceleration in wages and earnings, which remains the prerequisite for a broad-based and sustained pickup in inflation. Given the outlook for job creation, a more persistent pickup in inflation seems likely by mid-2006 when the nation's still

Annual Growth of GDP and GDP Deflator

Year	Gross Domestic Product (Current Dollars)	Gross Domestic Product (Chained 2000 Dollars)	GDP Implicit Price Deflator	Percent Increase Implicit Price Deflator
Annual Levels				
1994	$ 7,072.2	$ 7,835.5	90.3	2.1%
1995	7,397.7	8,031.7	92.1	2.0
1996	7,816.9	8,328.9	93.9	1.9
1997	8,304.3	8,703.5	95.4	1.7
1998	8,747.0	9,066.9	96.5	1.1
1999	9,268.4	9,470.3	97.9	1.4
2000	9,817.0	9,817.0	100.0	2.2
2001	10,128.0	9,890.7	102.4	2.4
2002	10,487.0	10,074.8	104.1	1.7
2003	11,004.0	10,381.3	106.0	1.8
2004	11,735.0	10,841.9	108.2	2.2
Quarterly Levels: Seasonally Adjusted				
2004:1Q	11,472.6	10,697.5	107.2	2.9
2004:2Q	11,657.5	10,784.7	108.1	3.3
2004:3Q	11,814.9	10,891.0	108.5	1.5
2004:4Q	11,994.8	10,994.3	109.1	2.4
Compound Annual Growth Rates				
1994-1999	5.6%	3.9%	1.6%	
1999-2004	4.8	2.7	2.1	

Sources: Veronis Suhler Stevenson, PQ Media, Bureau of Economic Analysis

weak job market will eventually tighten. This said, core inflation appears set to eventually peak near 3 percent, which, in the larger historical scheme of things, is a rather benign outcome.

The federal government is also moving from being a source of stimulus for the economy to a weight on growth. The tax cutting that has characterized fiscal policy over the past few years appears to have come to an end. There might be small changes in 2005, such as a temporary fix for the Alternative Minimum Tax, but no large tax cuts like those seen over the past few years are in the offing. On the spending side, growth will remain positive in real terms, but will slow from the very rapid pace seen over the past few years. In particular, defense spending growth will decelerate as the U.S. maintains its current troop levels in Iraq and Afghanistan. Thus, fiscal policy will be a source of economic restraint this year.

The major federal policy initiative on the agenda in 2005 is the proposal of the inclusion of private accounts as part of Social Security, a centerpiece of President Bush's vision of an "ownership society." Currently, only broad lines of the reform have been laid out and no political consensus has been reached. Social Security reform will therefore have only modest, if any, material impact on the economy this year.

Compound Annual Growth of GDP and Inflation

Year	*Nominal GDP Growth*	*Real GDP Growth*	*Percent Change in GDP Chain Weighted Price Index*
1999	6.0%	4.4%	1.4%
2000	5.9	3.7	2.2
2001	3.2	0.8	2.4
2002	3.5	1.9	1.7
2003	4.9	3.0	1.8
2004	6.6	4.4	2.2
2005	6.0	3.7	2.3
2006	5.9	3.5	2.4
2007	5.8	3.5	2.3
2008	6.0	3.7	2.3
2009	6.2	3.8	2.4
Compound Annual Growth			
1999-2004	4.8	2.7	2.1
2004-2009	6.0	3.6	2.3

Sources: Veronis Suhler Stevenson, PQ Media, Bureau of Economic Analysis

Annual Growth of Consumer Price Index Inflation

Year	*Headline CPI*	*Core CPI*
1994	2.6%	2.8%
1995	2.8	3.0
1996	2.9	2.7
1997	2.3	2.4
1998	1.6	2.3
1999	2.2	2.1
2000	3.4	2.4
2001	2.8	2.7
2002	1.6	2.3
2003	2.3	1.5
2004	2.7	1.8
2005	2.4	2.3
2006	2.2	3.0
2007	2.5	2.6
2008	2.2	2.4
2009	2.1	2.3

Sources: Veronis Suhler Stevenson, PQ Media, Bureau of Labor Statistics

The Outlook For The Economy

In 2004 and early 2005, there was some evidence of a modest slowdown in the economy, from the rapid pace that typically marks a recovery phase to a more sustainable growth pace that is characteristic of a mature expansion. For instance, consumer spending was not particularly strong during the holiday season, and spending on vehicle purchases in the first few months of 2005 were disappointing. Against this background of a slowing economy, the three main risks over the coming year are the possibility of a sharp increase in the already-high price of oil, a geopolitical crisis that would necessitate U.S. engagement and a sharper-than-expected fall in the dollar. Materialization of any of these risks would affect economic fundamentals, such as GDP growth, but also undermine consumer and business confidence.

In 2005, consumer spending growth will weaken to a rate that is in line with income growth, due to the erosion of non-income sources of cash like mortgage refinancing and tax rebates. On the other hand, business investment will continue to lift the economy, and exports will be an additional source of strength. However, these two factors will not fully offset the decelerating growth of consumer spending. Overall, the pace of real GDP growth is forecast to weaken to 3.7 percent in 2005 from 4.4 percent in 2004. Taking into account an inflation rate of about 2.3 percent, this means that the pace of nominal GDP growth will slow to 6.0 percent in 2005 compared with 6.6 percent in 2004.

Economic growth during the forecast period is expected to moderate as the cyclical rebound fades and economic growth settles into its long-term potential. Real GDP is expected to increase at a compound annual rate of 3.6 percent in the 2004-2009 period, while inflation as measured by the GDP deflator will rise at a compound annual rate of 2.3 percent in the period. As a result, nominal GDP will accelerate to a compounded rate of 6.0 percent during the forecast period.

FORECAST ASSUMPTIONS

- Business investment emerged as the main growth driver of the economy in 2004, largely due to spending on information technology, and it will continue to be a key source of growth in 2005. Strong corporate profit growth should continue to support business spending.
- Consumer spending will continue to support the economy in 2005, although to a lesser extent than in recent years. Consumers remain saddled with debt, and with rising interest rates, borrowing is becoming increasingly less attractive. As a result, households are expected to bring their spending back in line with income growth this year.
- Because of higher energy demands associated with heating needs, energy prices remained elevated during the first few months of the year. However, energy prices will gradually decrease in the second half of the year due to the moderation in economic activity, an increase in extraction and refining capacity, and replenishment of reserves.
- We expect that geopolitical tensions will not escalate. Deterioration in Afghanistan and/or Iraq, or an increase in the diplomatic tension with Iran or Korea, could lead to uncertainty over oil supplies and, hence, a sharp rise in the price of oil. Prolonged military engagement in Afghanistan and Iraq, or interventions elsewhere around the globe, would further strain the federal budget, which could lead to a higher-than-expected rise in interest rates.
- The dollar depreciation is projected to be gradual, as has been the case since 2002. Although there is no sign indicating that this may occur in the near or distant future, a sudden fall in foreign appetite for U.S. assets would lead to a steep fall in the dollar. This would, in turn, require the Federal Reserve to sharply raise interest rates to support foreign demand for American assets and limit the fall of the dollar. High interest rates have a negative impact on the housing industry and indebted American households.

2004 Communications Industry Forecast Compared with Actual Growth

Category	*2004 Forecasted Growth**	*Actual 2004 Growth†*
Nominal GDP	5.7%	6.6%
Real GDP	4.2	4.4
Consumer Price Index	1.5	2.2

*Veronis Suhler Stevenson 2004 Communications Industry Forecast & Report
†Veronis Suhler Stevenson, PQ Media

2

Advertising, Specialty Media & Marketing Services

Growth of U.S. Spending on Advertising, Specialty Media and Marketing Services

	Advertising	*Specialty Media And Marketing Services*	*Total*
2004 Expenditures ($ Millions)	$188,187	$257,145	$445,332
1999-2004 Compound Annual Growth (%)	3.0%	4.9%	4.1%
2004-2009 Projected Compound Annual Growth (%)	6.8%	6.7%	6.7%
2009 Projected Expenditures ($ Millions)	$260,897	$355,154	$616,051

Sources: Veronis Suhler Stevenson, PQ Media

Summary

Following a decade of hype about the sea change the Internet and other emerging technologies would usher in, hastening the demise of print media and traditional advertising, the dot-com crash of 2000 and the subsequent economic recession in 2001 forced many companies to rethink their grand plans for new media expansion and refocus on core businesses and marketing methods. But as the economy recovered, corporate profits returned and the job market strengthened, several key trends have begun to take shape that may just prove the pre-Internet crash prognosticators correct. Among these critical developments is the acceleration in the rate of audience fragmentation driven by the surfacing of various technology innovations, new media and consumer multitasking. Second is the increased advertising clutter fueled by marketers trying every available avenue to reach more elusive audiences. Third is the gradual shift of advertising dollars away from traditional media to newer media and alternative marketing techniques as a result of marketers becoming more skeptical of their return on investment (ROI) in conventional advertising and increasingly wary of ad-skipping technology. Fourth is a more empowered consumer who has myriad media choices, can skip ads with the touch of a button and is steadily increasing the use of non-traditional media. And finally, marketers are demanding stronger ROI for each advertising dollar they spend and more precise measurements to prove effectiveness.

The upshot of these crucial trends is that media buying has become much more complicated, and media buyers have been forced to develop extremely sophisticated purchasing plans that utilize a variety of advertising and marketing strategies that incorporate the use of both conventional and alternative media outlets in order to reach more cagey audiences. For example, marketers are demanding that their buyers develop approaches that ensure their brand messages cut through the increased clutter, which has led to the surging growth of alternative marketing tactics like product placement. At the same time, advertisers want better ROI measurement, which has fueled the strong expansion of ad categories such as Internet keyword search. In addition, during the 2004 political campaign, both presidential candidates used direct mail that was extraordinarily targeted to the point of reaching niche audiences via demographic and psychographic mailings based on zip code characteristics.

Meanwhile, marketers have also ratcheted up their use of non-conventional media, including videogames, cell phones and movie theatres, in their fervor to reach coveted markets such as the 18- to 34-year-old demographic, which is not embracing traditional media in the post-recession period the way past generations had done. For example, newspaper readership and broadcast television viewership by young adults are down significantly since 1975, while videogame usage and Internet consumption are up substantially. Finally, in this era of ad-skipping technology, increased audience fragmentation and consumer empowerment, our media usage data covered in detail in the End-User Spending chapter of this *Forecast* clearly indicates a consistent shift from advertising-supported media to consumer-supported media over the past two decades. As a result, so-called traditional media, including broadcast television and radio, newspapers, yellow pages, magazines and out-of-home, have seen their share of communications spending deteriorate at alarming levels in recent years, something that has not occurred during past economic recovery-and-expansion periods when the size of the advertising and marketing pie rose and all media benefited.

Accordingly, spending on new media, such as cable and satellite television, satellite radio, business-to-business e-media, consumer Internet, movie screen advertising and videogame advertising, grew 21.7 percent to $31.37 billion in 2004, while conventional media rose only 5.2 percent to $156.82 billion. Going forward, we expect marketers will continue to shift dollars to new media advertising options as they continue to reach younger audiences more effectively and strengthen their ROI measurement tools. New media advertising will grow 20.7 percent in 2005 compared

Advertising, Specialty Media And Marketing Services Spending And Nominal GDP Growth, 2000-2009

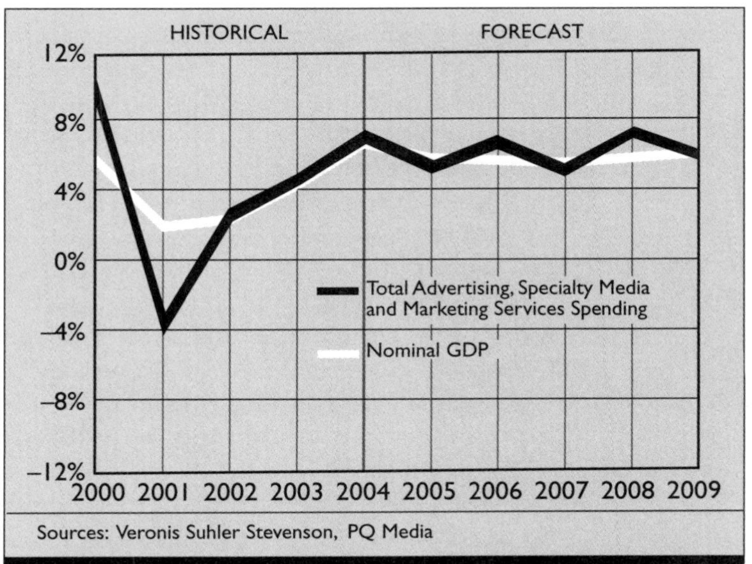

Sources: Veronis Suhler Stevenson, PQ Media

2004 Communications Industry Forecast Compared With Actual Growth

Category	*2004 Forecasted Growth**	*Actual 2004 Growth†*
Advertising	7.2%	7.6%
Yellow Pages Advertising	4.7	3.7
Out-of-Home	4.6	6.0
Specialty Media & Marketing Services	5.1	6.9
Direct Marketing	NA	6.0
Business-to-Business Promotions	5.9	3.7
Consumer Promotions	3.4	4.4
Custom Publishing	NA	20.4
Branded Entertainment	NA	9.1
Public Relations	6.8	12.0
Total	6.3	7.2

*Veronis Suhler Stevenson 2004 Communications Industry Forecast & Report
†Veronis Suhler Stevenson, PQ Media

with only 3.2 percent for traditional media, as broadcast radio, newspapers and magazine advertising continue to struggle or post relatively slow growth, exacerbated by an odd year for broadcast television in the absence of political and Olympics advertising. Spending on new media advertising will grow at a compound annual rate of 16.9 percent from 2004 to 2009, reaching $68.62 billion, while traditional media advertising will rise only 4.2 percent on a compound annual basis in the forecast period to $192.28 billion in 2009. Consequently, the new media sector will grow its share of the total advertising pie from 16.7 percent in 2004 to 26.3 percent in 2009, while the traditional media segment's share will decline in the same period from 83.3 percent to 73.7 percent.

Meanwhile, total advertising spending is expected to increase 6.1 percent to $199.67 billion in 2005, compared to an increase of 7.6 percent to $188.19 billion in 2004. Spending growth in 2004 was fueled by broadcast television advertising—which benefited from political and Olympics spending—as well as double-digit gains from new media options, including cable and satellite television, the Internet, and movie screen and videogame advertising. Election campaigns spent a record $1.85 billion on advertising media in 2004, a 58.9 percent increase from the 2002 election cycle and a 112.1 percent increase from the 2000 cycle, according to exclusive research from PQ Media. Of the total $1.85 billion, $1.45 billion was spent on broadcast and cable television.

In the absence of political and Olympics advertising in 2005, new media will be largely responsible for driving growth. Political advertising will continue to drive growth during even years in the forecast period, but the advertising market's share of political spending is shrinking, as election campaigns pursue alternative marketing strategies. Advertising media received 67.5 percent of political advertising spending in 2004, down from 71.6 percent in 2002 and 72.0 percent in 2000, according to PQ Media. Direct mail, public relations and promotion boosted their share of political spending from a combined 28.0 percent in 2000 to 32.5 percent in 2004. Thus, new media will be a key growth driver in the advertising market from 2005 to 2009. And although the advertising industry will continue to post gains during the forecast period, growth will not surpass GDP by as wide a margin as in the past, as a result of competition with alternative marketing vehicles and the several other aforementioned trends. After the advertising market emerged from the recession of the early 1990s, annual spending growth exceeded GDP by 2.0 to 6.0 percentage points from 1994 through 2000. But from 2004 to 2009, annual spending growth will exceed GDP by only 0.1 of a point to 1.7 points.

It is important to note here that in order to reflect the multitude of changes in the advertising sector and the media industry in general in recent years, we have developed several new exclusive methodologies and subsegments for this edition of the *Forecast*, as well as numerous new data tables, in addition to partnering with research firms, such as PQ Media, to license exclusive original content on emerging media segments that is not available from any other source. We believe that these accessories have added significant value to this year's *Forecast*, providing our subscribers with what we hope will be the most engaging and insightful communications industry analysis ever. For example, in the advertising sector, we have developed what we believe is the first business-to-business e-media data and analysis ever published. In addition, we have added videogame advertising to the Entertainment Media chapter for the first time, and we have included a new table in this chapter comparing the growth of new media versus traditional media to illustrate this major market shift. Among other new features is the addition of the first comprehensive analysis of political advertising and marketing spending in all media, and the first history, analysis and forecast ever compiled on the growing market for product placement spending in all media, both of which are provided through an exclusive licensing agreement with PQ Media. For all changes, consult the Appendix at the end of this *Forecast*.

On the specialty media and marketing services front, spending in this sector is expected to increase 7.0 percent to $275.11

Political Media Buying, 2004, 2002 and 2000*

($ MILLIONS)

		Advertising								*Marketing*		
	Total	*Broadcast TV*	*Cable & Satellite TV*	*Radio*	*News-Papers*	*Out-of-Home*	*Internet*	*Magazines & ITV*	*Total*	*Direct Mail*	*PR & Promotions*	*Total*
Spending ($ Millions)												
2004	$2,744	$1,450	$103	$175	$61	$34	$29	$2	$1,853	$648	$243	$891
2002†	1,629	912	35	155	34	25	5	1	1,166	334	128	463
2000	1,213	676	19	128	26	21	3	1	874	242	97	339
Growth												
04 vs. 02†	68.5%	59.0%	192.4%	13.5%	81.5%	36.3%	506.3%	12.6%	58.9%	93.7%	89.3%	92.5%
04 vs. 00	126.1	114.5	432.5	36.8	132.4	62.8	998.1	82.0	112.1	167.5	149.7	162.4
Share												
2004	—	52.8	3.7	6.4	2.2	1.2	1.1	0.1	67.5	23.6	8.8	32.5
2002†	—	56.0	2.2	9.5	2.1	1.5	0.3	0.1	71.6	20.5	7.9	28.4
2000	—	55.7	1.6	10.6	2.2	1.7	0.2	0.1	72.0	20.0	8.0	28.0

Source: PQ Media

*These data were licensed exclusively to Veronis Suhler Stevenson from PQ Media's *Political Media in 2004*.

†There was no presidential election in 2002, and there were 34 gubernatorial races in 2002 vs. 11 races in 2000 and 2004.

billion in 2005, surpassing the advertising industry's growth rate. Spending will grow at a compound annual rate of 6.7 percent from 2004 to 2009, reaching $355.15 billion. Similar to the advertising section, there have been a number of changes instituted in the specialty media and marketing section of this *Forecast*. Two new segments have been added—custom publishing and the above-mentioned product placement. Due to the inclusion of product placement, the previously existing segments and subsegments of event sponsorship and promotional licensing have been combined into a new section called branded entertainment. Also, we have expanded the direct mail segment to include all direct marketing spending. Additionally, specialty media and marketing services includes business-to-business promotion, consumer promotion and public relations.

According to one survey released in late 2004, the percentage of marketers who expected to boost advertising spending in major media in 2005 was smaller than the percentage in 2004, indicating advertising spending growth will be limited as marketers pursue less expensive alternatives to traditional advertising. Although more than half of all marketers expected to increase online advertising, the percentage declined by 3.0 points compared to 2004. Respondents ranked the Internet as the most effective medium for acquiring and retaining customers. Another survey reported that nearly 85 percent of advertisers expect to increase their online advertising budgets in 2005, with the average increase at 25 percent. As a result, more than 40 percent of these advertisers plan to reduce spending on traditional media, such as magazines, newspapers and direct mail.

Traditional advertising media are at a disadvantage when it comes to advertisers'

Advertising, Specialty Media and Marketing Services Spending

($ MILLIONS)

	Advertising			*Specialty Media & Marketing Services*			*Total*		
Year	*Consumer*	*Business-to-Business*	*Total*	*Consumer*	*Business-to-Business*	*Total*	*Consumer*	*Business-to-Business*	*Total*
1999	$151,695	$10,756	$162,451	$113,584	$ 88,805	$202,389	$265,279	$ 99,561	$364,840
2000	169,305	11,943	181,248	123,815	96,990	220,805	293,120	108,933	402,053
2001	156,783	10,385	167,168	122,992	95,874	218,866	279,775	106,259	386,034
2002	160,729	9,331	170,060	128,810	99,817	228,627	289,539	109,148	398,687
2003	165,300	9,571	174,871	134,616	105,982	240,598	299,916	115,553	415,469
2004	178,023	10,164	188,187	143,672	113,473	257,145	321,695	123,637	445,332
2005	188,782	10,888	199,670	153,254	121,856	275,110	342,036	132,744	474,780
2006	202,910	11,676	214,586	162,949	130,666	293,615	365,859	142,342	508,201
2007	215,441	12,475	227,916	172,272	139,516	311,788	387,713	151,991	539,704
2008	232,167	13,342	245,509	183,198	149,773	332,971	415,365	163,115	578,480
2009	246,695	14,202	260,897	194,638	160,516	355,154	441,333	174,718	616,051

Sources: Veronis Suhler Stevenson, PQ Media, AdScope, *Advertising Age*, Agricom, American Business Media, Association of Directory Publishers, Borrell Associates, BPA International, Cabletelevision Advertising Bureau, Cinema Advertising Council, Council of Public Relations Firms, *Custom Publishing Council*, Direct Marketing Association, Forrester, Global Insight, *IEG Sponsorship Report*, IMS/The Auditor, In Demand, Incentive Marketing Association, Insight Research, In-Store Marketing Institute, Interactive Advertising Bureau, Kagan Research, Magazine Publishers of America, McMurry, Media Networks Inc., Myers Mediaenomics, Newspaper Association of America, NCH NuWorld Marketing Limited, *O'Dwyer's Directory of Public Relations Firms*, Oetting & Company, Outdoor Advertising Association of America, PERQ, Point-of-Purchase and Advertising Institute, *Promo Magazine*, Promotional Products Association International, *Response Magazine*, Screenvision, Simba Information, Sirius Satellite Radio, TNS Media Intelligence/CMR, *Tradeshow Week*, UBS Warburg, Universal McCann, XM Satellite Radio, Yankee Group

Growth of Advertising, Specialty Media and Marketing Services Spending

	Advertising			*Specialty Media & Marketing Services*			*Total*		
Year	*Consumer*	*Business-to-Business*	*Total*	*Consumer*	*Business-to-Business*	*Total*	*Consumer*	*Business-to-Business*	*Total*
2000	11.6%	11.0%	11.6%	9.0%	9.2%	9.1%	10.5%	9.4%	10.2%
2001	–7.4	–13.0	–7.8	–0.7	–1.2	–0.9	–4.6	–2.5	–4.0
2002	2.5	–10.1	1.7	4.7	4.1	4.5	3.5	2.7	3.3
2003	2.8	2.6	2.8	4.5	6.2	5.2	3.6	5.9	4.2
2004	7.7	6.2	7.6	6.7	7.1	6.9	7.3	7.0	7.2
2005	6.0	7.1	6.1	6.7	7.4	7.0	6.3	7.4	6.6
2006	7.5	7.2	7.5	6.3	7.2	6.7	7.0	7.2	7.0
2007	6.2	6.8	6.2	5.7	6.8	6.2	6.0	6.8	6.2
2008	7.8	6.9	7.7	6.3	7.4	6.8	7.1	7.3	7.2
2009	6.3	6.5	6.3	6.2	7.2	6.7	6.3	7.1	6.5
Compound Annual Growth									
1999-2004	3.2	–1.1	3.0	4.8	5.0	4.9	3.9	4.4	4.1
2004-2009	6.7	6.9	6.8	6.3	7.2	6.7	6.5	7.2	6.7

Sources: Veronis Suhler Stevenson, PQ Media, AdScope, *Advertising Age*, Agricom, American Business Media, Association of Directory Publishers, Borrell Associates, BPA International, Cabletelevision Advertising Bureau, Cinema Advertising Council, Council of Public Relations Firms, *Custom Publishing Council*, Direct Marketing Association, Forrester, Global Insight, *IEG Sponsorship Report*, IMS/The Auditor, In Demand, Incentive Marketing Association, Insight Research, In-Store Marketing Institute, Interactive Advertising Bureau, Kagan Research, Magazine Publishers of America, McMurry, Media Networks Inc., Myers Mediaenomics, Newspaper Association of America, NCH NuWorld Marketing Limited, *O'Dwyer's Directory of Public Relations Firms*, Oetting & Company, Outdoor Advertising Association of America, PERQ, Point-of-Purchase and Advertising Institute, *Promo Magazine*, Promotional Products Association International, *Response Magazine*, Screenvision, Simba Information, Sirius Satellite Radio, TNS Media Intelligence/CMR, *Tradeshow Week*, UBS Warburg, Universal McCann, XM Satellite Radio, Yankee Group

Shares of Advertising, Specialty Media and Marketing Services Spending

	Advertising			*Specialty Media & Marketing Services*			*Total*	
Year	*Consumer*	*Business-to-Business*	*Total*	*Consumer*	*Business-to-Business*	*Total*	*Consumer*	*Business-to-Business*
1999	41.6%	2.9%	44.5%	31.1%	24.3%	55.5%	72.7%	27.3%
2000	42.1	3.0	45.1	30.8	24.1	54.9	72.9	27.1
2001	40.6	2.7	43.3	31.9	24.8	56.7	72.5	27.5
2002	40.3	2.3	42.7	32.3	25.0	57.3	72.6	27.4
2003	39.8	2.3	42.1	32.4	25.5	57.9	72.2	27.8
2004	40.0	2.3	42.3	32.3	25.5	57.7	72.2	27.8
2005	39.8	2.3	42.1	32.3	25.7	57.9	72.0	28.0
2006	39.9	2.3	42.2	32.1	25.7	57.8	72.0	28.0
2007	39.9	2.3	42.2	31.9	25.9	57.8	71.8	28.2
2008	40.1	2.3	42.4	31.7	25.9	57.6	71.8	28.2
2009	40.0	2.3	42.3	31.6	26.1	57.7	71.6	28.4

Sources: Veronis Suhler Stevenson, PQ Media, AdScope, *Advertising Age*, Agricom, American Business Media, Association of Directory Publishers, Borrell Associates, BPA International, Cabletelevision Advertising Bureau, Cinema Advertising Council, Council of Public Relations Firms, *Custom Publishing Council*, Direct Marketing Association, Forrester, Global Insight, *IEG Sponsorship Report*, IMS/The Auditor, In Demand, Incentive Marketing Association, Insight Research, In-Store Marketing Institute, Interactive Advertising Bureau, Kagan Research, Magazine Publishers of America, McMurry, Media Networks Inc., Myers Mediaenomics, Newspaper Association of America, NCH NuWorld Marketing Limited, *O'Dwyer's Directory of Public Relations Firms*, Oetting & Company, Outdoor Advertising Association of America, PERQ, Point-of-Purchase and Advertising Institute, *Promo Magazine*, Promotional Products Association International, *Response Magazine*, Screenvision, Simba Information, Sirius Satellite Radio, TNS Media Intelligence/CMR, *Tradeshow Week*, UBS Warburg, Universal McCann, XM Satellite Radio, Yankee Group

growing demands for ROI. Alternative marketing vehicles generally cost less and are doing a better job of proving ROI to marketers. The product sampling and in-store media markets, for example, are expected to surpass overall growth in spending on advertising and specialty media in the forecast period, due in part to a tighter focus on delivering ROI. PromoWorks, a provider of in-store sampling and retail entertainment events, introduced in early 2005 a system that tracks the sales performance of individual demonstrators at sampling events. Mass Connections, a retail marketing services company, launched in 2005 an in-store broadcast radio service that demonstrates the measurability of in-store promotion. And information technology company iTVX has created a system for measuring ROI in product placements.

Alternative marketing vehicles, as well as non-traditional advertising media, are also more adept at reaching the coveted 18- to 34-year-old demographic, which is an elusive group because they divide their time among a variety of media options. Therefore, non-traditional advertising media that tend to attract younger audiences are benefiting from this trend, including Internet, videogame and movie screen advertising. Alternative marketing vehicles that reach young audiences are also generating strong growth, such as sponsorships at concerts and sporting events, and product placements in television shows with youth appeal. It should be noted, however, that some of these newer forms of advertising and marketing, such as movie screen advertising and product placement, have faced a relatively small degree of backlash from consumer groups, who view them as deceptive and intrusive. For example, critics of product placement have claimed the tactic is tantamount to illusory advertising. At the behest of watchdog groups, such as Commercial Alert, The Federal Trade Commission and Federal Communications Commission have addressed the subject, but declined to take any action at press time of this *Forecast*.

Traditional, advertiser-supported media are also facing the growing trend of consumer migration toward media that are primarily user-supported. Consumers have been spending less time with ad-supported media for years, while boosting the amount of time and money they spend on media they pay for, such as cable and satellite television, the Internet and, more recently, satellite radio. New media options that are primarily user-supported continue to emerge, creating more competition for advertising dollars. The latest trend in advertising is to target consumers wherever they are through cell phones or handheld games. For example, Sony and Heavy.com, a Web host of short films and animation, are giving advertisers the opportunity to reach consumers through Sony's PlayStation Portable handheld game system. Heavy.com is providing free clips for the gaming device, hoping advertisers will pay to run commercial messages before and after downloads or use product placements. Unilever was the first advertiser to sign on, running a series of branded shorts promoting Axe body spray. Unilever says it took advantage of the opportunity because traditional advertising vehicles, such as 30-second TV spots and magazine ads, are no longer enough to reach its target audience—men ages 18 to 24, who spend time with a variety of media and often multitask.

Top 100 National Advertisers' Share Of Overall Advertising Spending

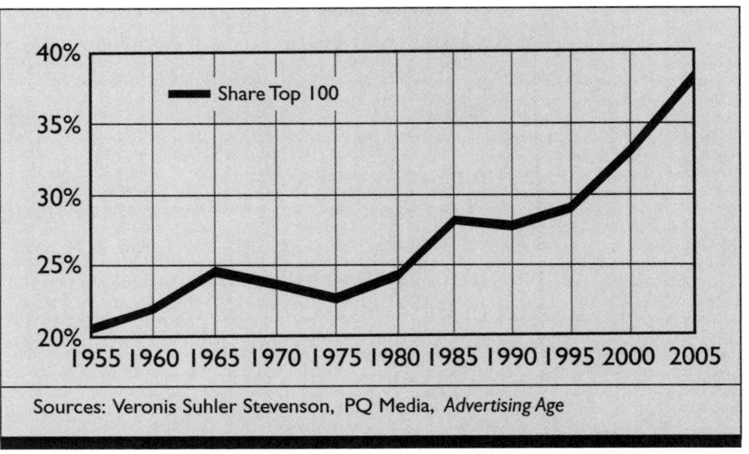

Sources: Veronis Suhler Stevenson, PQ Media, *Advertising Age*

Advertising, Specialty Media & Marketing Services

To combat the negative impact of these trends, media companies are reinventing themselves as information companies to reach users via multiple platforms and offer advertisers a variety of options. For example, business-to-business media companies have expanded into e-media, and radio broadcasters are offering Internet podcasting.

Consolidation among major advertisers is also adversely affecting traditional advertising media because these companies are able to pool their advertising budgets and reduce overall spending. The effect of retail consolidation, including the merger of Kmart and Sears, Roebuck & Co., and that of Federated Department Stores and May Department Stores, is particularly evident in the newspaper industry. But the overall advertising sector is also being impacted by mega-mergers in a variety of other categories, such as Procter & Gamble and Gillette in household products, and Cingular and AT&T Wireless in telecommunications.

Due to this consolidation, the leading national advertisers' share of total advertising spending is climbing. The top 100 national advertisers are expected to account for 38.1 percent of advertising spending in 2005, compared to 33.1 percent in 2000. The advertising market's reliance on major advertisers is a liability, since financial difficulties and budget cuts at a handful of individual companies can make a serious dent in overall ad spending. This situation makes the advertising industry particularly vulnerable during a recession. For example, the largest advertiser in 1991, Procter & Gamble, and the largest advertiser in 2001, General Motors, reduced their ad budgets by more than the overall advertising market's decline in those years, indicating that these cuts affected overall spending patterns.

Overall, spending on advertising, specialty media and marketing services (ASMMS) increased 7.2 percent to $445.33 billion in 2004, driven by solid growth in both segments. Total business-to-business advertising, which includes business-to-business magazines and yellow pages, increased 6.2 percent to $10.16 billion in 2004, due in part to strong growth in the emerging business-to-business e-media market. Advertising targeted at consumers increased 7.7 percent to $178.02 billion for the year. Growth in business-to-business marketing spending increased 7.1 percent to $113.47 billion, while marketing spending aimed at consumers grew 6.7 percent to $143.67 billion in 2004. Business-to-business marketing includes promotional products, incentives and trade show fees, sponsorships and advertising, as well as a portion of public relations and a share of direct marketing.

Total ASMMS sector spending is expected to increase 6.6 percent to $474.78 billion in 2005, fueled by gains in both segments, although marketing spending will grow more rapidly. Many companies are pursuing a multichannel marketing strategy, incorporating traditional advertising media for building brand name awareness, while utilizing alternative marketing vehicles to directly impact sales. As a result, both segments will experience solid growth during the forecast period, although advertising growth will be slower than in the past because traditional media will have to share budgets with alternative marketing. Advertising media will continue to benefit in even years from political and Olympics advertising during the forecast period, outpacing marketing spending in those years. Total ASMMS growth will surpass GDP growth by 0.2 to 0.9 of a percentage point over the next five years. Overall compound annual growth in ASMMS spending will be 6.7 percent from 2004 to 2009, reaching $616.05 billion in 2009.

The Advertising Market in 2004 and 2005

Spending on advertising increased 7.6 percent to $188.19 billion in 2004, driven by new media categories, such as consumer Internet advertising and cable and satellite television. The new advertising categories of videogame advertising, wireless advertising and business-to-business e-media have been added to the advertising segment this year, as mentioned previously. These emerging advertising vehicles helped fuel growth in the advertising industry in 2004, although they represent a small share of the overall market. Traditional media vehicles generally posted low- to mid-single-digit growth, except for broadcast television advertising, which climbed 9.1 percent due to Olympics and political advertising. Compound annual growth for the 1999 to 2004 period was 3.0 percent, driven down by the ad recession in 2001 and sluggish recovery in 2002 and 2003.

It should be noted that many media are beginning to branch out from their traditional roots. Newspaper and yellow pages publishers, as well as television and radio stations, have become active in the local Internet ad market. To avoid double counting, these advertising dollars are captured in the Internet chapter, except for yellow pages.

Growth of national advertising outpaced that of local advertising in 2004, with national up 9.4 percent compared with 6.1 percent for local. Double-digit gains in new national

HIGHLIGHTS

Advertising

Advertising spending increased 7.6 percent to $188.19 billion in 2004, driven primarily by gains in broadcast television, cable and satellite television, and consumer Internet advertising. The emerging markets for movie screen and videogame advertising also contributed to growth. The overall advertising market grew at a compound annual rate of 3.0 percent from 1999 to 2004.

■

Spending on broadcast and cable television, the largest advertising segment, increased 11.2 percent to $62.10 billion in 2004. The gain can be attributed to record political advertising on broadcast television and double-digit growth in cable advertising, due to the growing availability of interconnects, increased ratings and audience share, and continued investment in technology.

■

Videogame advertising, the smallest ad category, posted the strongest growth rate, up 51.9 percent to $120.0 million. The nascent category is beginning to appeal to major advertisers because of its ability to reach the elusive 18- to 34-year-old demographic.

■

Spending on new advertising media—including cable and satellite television, satellite radio, business-to-business e-media, consumer Internet, movie screen advertising and videogame advertising—grew 21.7 percent to $31.37 billion in 2004. Meanwhile, traditional ad media—such as broadcast television, newspapers, magazines, yellow pages and out-of-home—rose only 5.2 percent to $156.82 billion.

■

Advertising spending is expected to rise to 6.1 percent to $199.67 billion in 2005, driven by non-traditional advertising vehicles, such as the Internet and cable television. Broadcast TV ad growth will decelerate in 2005 due to the absence of political and Olympics advertising.

■

Advertising in new media will fuel compound annual growth of 6.8 percent in the 2004 to 2009 period, with spending reaching $260.90 billion in 2009.

Advertising Spending

Year	Broadcast Television*	Cable & Satellite Television	Total Television†	Newspapers†	Broadcast & Satellite Radio†	Yellow Pages‡
1999	$37,751	$11,624	$49,375	$50,689	$17,681	$13,196
2000	42,420	13,788	56,208	53,371	19,848	14,267
2001	36,642	14,214	50,856	49,093	18,369	15,035
2002	39,993	14,736	54,729	49,079	19,411	15,231
2003	39,559	16,304	55,863	50,126	19,607	15,366
2004	43,176	18,925	62,101	52,152	20,022	15,928
2005	43,982	21,686	65,668	54,090	20,571	16,522
2006	47,241	24,258	71,499	56,262	21,258	17,274
2007	48,244	26,888	75,132	58,126	22,120	18,067
2008	52,185	29,746	81,931	60,204	23,419	18,975
2009	53,251	33,361	86,612	62,086	24,565	19,973

Sources: Veronis Suhler Stevenson, PQ Media, AdScope, Agricom, American Business Media, Association of Directory Publishers, Borrell Associates, BPA International, Cabletelevision Advertising Bureau, Cinema Advertising Council, Corzen, IMS/The Auditor Interactive Advertising Bureau, Kagan Research, Magazine Publishers of America, Media Networks Inc., Newspaper Association of America, Outdoor Advertising Association of America, PERQ, Radio Advertising Bureau, Screenvision, Simba Information, Sirius Satellite Radio, Television Bureau of Advertising, TNS Media Intelligence/CMR, Universal McCann, XM Satellite Radio, Yankee Group

*Excludes barter syndication.

†To avoid double counting, advertising on television, newspapers and radio Web sites is included in the Consumer Internet chapter.

‡Includes Internet yellow pages.

§Includes business-to-business e-media.

media, such as videogames and movie screens, as well as the high-double-digit growth of Internet advertising, fueled growth. The double-digit growth of local Internet advertising was unable to compensate for weak growth in the newspaper retail category, radio and yellow pages, three of the four largest local ad media. National advertising accounted for 46.4 percent of total advertising spending in 2004, compared to 44.9 percent in 1999. National advertising spending growth is expected to continue to outpace local advertising spending growth in the forecast period, expanding at a compound annual rate of 7.8 percent compared with 5.8 percent for local. By 2009, national advertising will account for a 48.8 percent share of the advertising market.

BROADCAST TELEVISION

Record presidential election spending and Olympics-related advertising boosted spending on broadcast television 9.1 percent to $43.18 billion in 2004. But heading into 2005, the industry faces a number of challenges that threaten to chip away at broadcast television advertising expenditures in the near term. Among them are the emergence of ad-skipping technology and less reliance on the 30-second spot, increased competition with cable television and the Internet for consumer

Consumer Magazines	Business-to-Business Magazines[§]	Consumer Internet[†]	Out-of-Home	Movie Screen Advertising	Videogame Advertising	Total
$11,433	$10,492	$ 4,621	$4,832	$129	$ 3	$162,451
12,370	11,659	8,087	5,235	194	9	181,248
11,095	10,085	7,134	5,233	246	22	167,168
10,995	9,028	6,010	5,232	301	44	170,060
11,435	9,263	7,267	5,504	361	79	174,871
12,121	9,845	9,626	5,834	438	120	188,187
12,788	10,558	12,629	6,144	522	178	199,670
13,555	11,330	16,052	6,481	608	267	214,586
14,409	12,115	20,002	6,849	694	402	227,916
15,346	12,962	24,062	7,234	782	594	245,509
16,374	13,803	28,198	7,623	863	800	260,897

attention, and heightened interest among advertisers in non-traditional marketing vehicles. Spending increased at a compound annual rate of 2.7 percent from 1999 to 2004.

The news on the programming front was positive in the 2004-05 season. Television networks won back audiences, thanks to breakout hits *Desperate Housewives* and *Lost* on ABC, and the enduring success of *CSI* and reality favorites *Survivor*, *American Idol* and *The Apprentice*. Prime-time network ratings increased 2.3 points to 31.2 through January 2005. However, the increase is not expected to be as pronounced when the full-year results are tabulated because the networks always enjoy an initial boost at the start of the TV season and during the winter when people tend to stay indoors.

Broadcast television advertising is expected to grow only 1.9 percent to $43.98 billion in 2005, due mainly to the absence of political and Olympics advertising, as well as the erosion of drug advertising and pricing pressures. Broadcast television advertising typically surpasses nominal GDP growth in even years due to political and Olympics advertising, and lags GDP growth in odd years due to the lack of such spending. The gap between GDP and broadcast television growth is starting to shrink, and this trend is expected to continue in

Growth of Advertising Spending

Year	*Broadcast Television**	*Cable & Satellite Television*	*Total Television†*	*Newspapers†*	*Broadcast & Satellite Radio†*	*Yellow Pages‡*
2000	12.4%	18.6%	13.8%	5.3%	12.3%	8.1%
2001	–13.6	3.1	–9.5	–8.0	–7.5	5.4
2002	9.1	3.7	7.6	0.0	5.7	1.3
2003	–1.1	10.6	2.1	2.1	1.0	0.9
2004	9.1	16.1	11.2	4.0	2.1	3.7
2005	1.9	14.6	5.7	3.7	2.7	3.7
2006	7.4	11.9	8.9	4.0	3.3	4.6
2007	2.1	10.8	5.1	3.3	4.1	4.6
2008	8.2	10.6	9.0	3.6	5.9	5.0
2009	2.0	12.2	5.7	3.1	4.9	5.3
Compound Annual Growth						
1999-2004	2.7	10.2	4.7	0.6	2.5	3.8
2004-2009	4.3	12.0	6.9	3.5	4.2	4.6

Sources: Veronis Suhler Stevenson, PQ Media, AdScope, Agricom, American Business Media, Association of Directory Publishers, Borrell Associates, BPA International, Cabletelevision Advertising Bureau, Cinema Advertising Council, Corzen, IMS/The Auditor Interactive Advertising Bureau, Kagan Research, Magazine Publishers of America, Media Networks Inc., Newspaper Association of America, Outdoor Advertising Association of America, PERQ, Radio Advertising Bureau, Screenvision, Simba Information, Sirius Satellite Radio, Television Bureau of Advertising, TNS Media Intelligence/CMR, Universal McCann, XM Satellite Radio, Yankee Group

* Excludes barter syndication.

†To avoid double counting, advertising on television, newspapers and radio Web sites is included in the Consumer Internet chapter.

‡Includes Internet yellow pages.

§Includes business-to-business e-media.

Consumer Magazines	*Business-to-Business Magazines*[§]	*Consumer Internet*[†]	*Out-of-Home*	*Movie Screen Advertising*	*Videogame Advertising*	*Total*
8.2%	11.1%	75.0%	8.3%	50.4%	200.0%	11.6%
–10.3	–13.5	–11.8	0.0	26.8	144.4	–7.8
–0.9	–10.5	–15.8	0.0	22.4	100.0	1.7
4.0	2.6	20.9	5.2	19.9	79.5	2.8
6.0	6.3	32.5	6.0	21.3	51.9	7.6
5.5	7.2	31.2	5.3	19.3	48.3	6.1
6.0	7.3	27.1	5.5	16.4	50.0	7.5
6.3	6.9	24.6	5.7	14.2	50.6	6.2
6.5	7.0	20.3	5.6	12.6	47.8	7.7
6.7	6.5	17.2	5.4	10.4	34.7	6.3
1.2	–1.3	15.8	3.8	27.7	109.1	3.0
6.2	7.0	24.0	5.5	14.5	46.1	6.8

Shares of Advertising Spending

Year	*Broadcast Television**	*Cable & Satellite Television*	*Total Television*†	*Newspapers*†	*Broadcast & Satellite Radio*†	*Yellow Pages*‡
1999	23.2%	7.2%	30.4%	31.2%	10.9%	8.1%
2000	23.4	7.6	31.0	29.4	11.0	7.9
2001	21.9	8.5	30.4	29.4	11.0	9.0
2002	23.5	8.7	32.2	28.9	11.4	9.0
2003	22.6	9.3	31.9	28.7	11.2	8.8
2004	22.9	10.1	33.0	27.7	10.6	8.5
2005	22.0	10.9	32.9	27.1	10.3	8.3
2006	22.0	11.3	33.3	26.2	9.9	8.0
2007	21.2	11.8	33.0	25.5	9.7	7.9
2008	21.3	12.1	33.4	24.5	9.5	7.7
2009	20.4	12.8	33.2	23.8	9.4	7.7

Sources: Veronis Suhler Stevenson, PQ Media, AdScope, Agricom, American Business Media, Association of Directory Publishers, Borrell Associates, BPA International, Cabletelevision Advertising Bureau, Cinema Advertising Council, Corzen, IMS/The Auditor Interactive Advertising Bureau, Kagan Research, Magazine Publishers of America, Media Networks Inc., Newspaper Association of America, Outdoor Advertising Association of America, PERQ, Radio Advertising Bureau, Screenvision, Simba Information, Sirius Satellite Radio, Television Bureau of Advertising, TNS Media Intelligence/CMR, Universal McCann, XM Satellite Radio, Yankee Group

*Excludes barter syndication

†To avoid double counting, advertising on television, newspapers and radio Web sites is included in the Consumer Internet chapter.

‡Includes Internet yellow pages.

§Includes business-to-business e-media.

the forecast period as advertisers reevaluate their TV ad budgets and seek non-traditional media options. Television's share of political advertising is shrinking as candidates employ alternative marketing vehicles, such as the Internet and public relations, pursuing a strategy similar to that of other TV advertisers. Despite these problems, broadcast television continues to be considered the optimal medium for advertisers to reach large audiences at one time. For example, Super Bowl ad rates climbed at high-single-digit rates for the third consecutive year in 2005, up to $2.4 million per 30-second spot. Spending will increase at a compound annual rate of 4.3 percent from 2004 to 2009, reaching $53.25 billion in 2009.

Consumer Magazines	Business-to-Business Magazines[§]	Consumer Internet[†]	Out-of-Home	Movie Screen Advertising	Videogame Advertising
7.0%	6.5%	2.8%	3.0%	0.1%	0.0%
6.8	6.4	4.5	2.9	0.1	0.0
6.6	6.0	4.3	3.1	0.1	0.0
6.5	5.3	3.5	3.1	0.2	0.0
6.5	5.3	4.2	3.1	0.2	0.0
6.4	5.2	5.1	3.1	0.2	0.1
6.4	5.3	6.3	3.1	0.3	0.1
6.3	5.3	7.5	3.0	0.3	0.1
6.3	5.3	8.8	3.0	0.3	0.2
6.3	5.3	9.8	2.9	0.3	0.2
6.3	5.3	10.8	2.9	0.3	0.3

CABLE & SATELLITE TELEVISION

Spending on cable and satellite television advertising increased 16.1 percent to $18.93 billion in 2004, spurred by the growing availability of interconnects, increased ratings and audience share, continued investment in technology and programming, and favorable CPMs when compared with broadcast television. An expanding array of channels, meanwhile, allows advertisers to target consumers by demographic segment or special interest. Spending increased 10.2 percent on a compound annual basis from 1999 to 2004. Additionally, local cable has become more attractive to advertisers due to the reorganization of local interconnects, a sales service that combines multiple systems in one market, allowing advertisers to make one media buy instead of several.

Prime-time ratings for ad supported (basic) cable programs rose 1.5 points to 30.9 in the 2003-04 season, primarily as a result of the industry's continuing investment in original programming. For the same period, prime-time ratings for pay cable programs dropped 0.2 of a point to 3.4, due to the absence of HBO hits *Sex and the City* and *The Sopranos*. Combined, cable ratings rose 1.3 points to 34.3 in the 2003-04 season. Cable's prime-time audience share grew 3.0 percentage points to 63.0 in the 2003-04 season, with basic cable accounting for 52.0 percent, premium making up 6.0 percent, and other cable representing 5.0 percent.

We expect the market for cable and satellite TV advertising will grow 14.6 percent to $21.69 billion in 2005. Annual ad spending throughout the remainder of the forecast period will be robust, with compound annual growth of 12.0 percent to $33.36 billion in 2009. Comcast, Time Warner, Cox and Charter are touting technology that will eventually enable them to target advertising as precisely as direct mail, segregating ads that send different messages to different neighborhoods within their viewing areas. Time Warner and Charter Communications are currently testing services that target ads to homes based on subscriber spending patterns.

NEWSPAPERS

Newspaper advertising spending, including dailies and weeklies, increased 4.0 percent to $52.15 billion, driven by classified and retail advertising. The growing economy sparked the job market in 2004 for the first time in three years, and the pace of job creation continued into 2005, fueling growth in employment classifieds. In the 1999 to 2004 period, spending increased at a compound annual rate of 0.6 percent. In addition, circulation scandals at several publishers in 2004 and 2005, as well as the continued decline in overall subscriptions, has led to advertiser concerns about the viability of newspaper advertising.

Daily newspaper advertising spending increased 3.9 percent to $46.70 billion in 2004, fueled by gains in the national, retail and classified categories. Nevertheless, the growth rate was among the weakest in the advertising-based media sector, as total ad market expenditures increased 7.6 percent for the year. National newspaper advertising, which surged in 2003 due to an increase in telecommunications spending, slowed down in 2004 as the telecommunications category contracted, while media and political and government advertising increased. Classified advertising grew, thanks to strong employment and real estate spending, turning positive for the first time since 2000, when the category expanded 5.1 percent. Retail advertising benefited from increases in the automotive aftermarket, home supplies and furniture, and apparel categories. The improvement in classified advertising spending continued into the first quarter of 2005. Several newspapers reported double-digit gains in employment advertising, along with continued strength in real estate listings. The strength in the real estate market, however, is not expected to last as the forecast period progresses, according to several studies released at press time of this *Forecast*.

Spending on newspaper advertising is expected to increase only 3.7 percent to $54.09 billion in 2005. Retail, classified and national advertising growth will decelerate in 2005. Retail and national advertising will be adversely impacted by retail consolidation and the trend toward increasing brand awareness, which will prompt advertisers to divert spending to mass market vehicles such as television and the Internet. Newspapers have been extremely aggressive in increasing their presence in the local Internet advertising market, accounting for approximately one-third of this space. However, pure-play Internet sites like Craigslist and Realestate.com are starting to siphon off ad revenues. As a result of the Internet threat, as well as the backlash from declining circulation, spending will only increase at a compound annual rate of 3.5 percent from 2004 to 2009, reaching $62.09 billion in 2009.

BROADCAST & SATELLITE RADIO

Broadcast and satellite radio advertising increased 2.1 percent to $20.02 billion in

2004, following a 1.0 percent gain in 2003. Spending grew at a compound annual rate of 2.5 percent from 1999 to 2004. Despite the sector's relatively lackluster performances in 2003 and 2004, broadcast radio has maintained its share of total advertising industry spending over the past five years, and the segment is still considered a leading indicator of the traditional advertising industry's health. While satellite radio accounted for less than 0.1 percent share of overall broadcast and satellite radio ad spending in 2004, the medium is growing rapidly. In 2004, satellite radio advertising spending increased 124.8 percent to $9.0 million for the year, compared to a 2.1 percent gain for broadcast to $20.01 billion.

Spending growth is expected to remain in the low single digits in 2005, growing 2.7 percent to $20.57 billion. Spending is expected to increase at a compound annual rate of 4.2 percent during the forecast period, reaching $24.57 billion in 2009. With near-term pricing issues due to overcapacity, the lack of sophisticated local sales management systems, and increasing competition from local cable and satellite radio, the terrestrial radio sector is transitioning from a growth business to a mature one. Nevertheless, several factors indicate the potential for broadcast radio to experience accelerated growth in the forecast period, such as Clear Channel's inventory tightening initiative called "Less Is More," the rollout of digital radio technologies, and the launch of Internet podcasts, which will allow listeners to download exclusive radio programs and live concert performances. While satellite radio advertising will increase at a compound annual rate of 88.1 percent from 2004 to 2009 to $222.0 million, it will account for slightly less than 1.0 percent of overall radio ad spending.

YELLOW PAGES

The yellow pages market consists of spending in local telephone company directories, competitive directories from independent publishers—which are not affiliated with telephone companies—and Internet yellow pages (IYP) services. Yellow pages advertising spending increased 3.7 percent to $15.93 billion in 2004, due to strong growth for independent yellow pages publishers and Internet yellow pages. Competitive print directories and online directories also drove the 3.8 percent compound annual spending growth in the 1999 to 2004 period. Because of the long lead time between sales and recognition of yellow pages directory revenues, the economic recession of 2001 did not impact the market until 2002 and 2003, when revenues were relatively flat.

Spending in local telephone company directories fell 0.1 percent to $12.39 billion. Although the segment's performance represented an improvement over the 3.2 percent decline experienced in 2003, telephone company directories continue to lose market share to competitive directories from independents. Independent publishers grew revenues 16.7 percent to $2.76 billion and expanded their market share to 18.2 percent from 16.0 percent in 2003. New directory launches and expanding penetration in existing markets are fueling growth in the independent yellow pages market.

Independent publishers have benefited from merger and acquisition activity, as well as investments from media companies and private equity firms. The consolidation that has taken place in the independent yellow pages market for the past several years culminated in May 2005 with a deal between Yellow Book, the nation's largest independent, and TransWestern, the second-largest. U.K. publisher Yell, Yellow Book's parent company, announced that Yellow Book agreed to acquire TransWestern for $1.58 billion, or 15.9 times EBITDA. The acquisition would expand Yellow Book's reach from 43 states to 45 and solidify its foothold in many of its existing markets. It would also cement Yellow Book's position as the fifth-largest yellow pages publisher in the U.S., behind the four RBOCs. Yellow Book has been expanding aggressively for years through start-ups and acquisitions. Earlier in 2005, the company announced the acquisition of books in Wisconsin and Arizona, along with plans to launch start-ups in several states.

Yellow Book's acquisition of TransWestern would be the second deal involving a major independent within the past year. In late 2004, media conglomerate The Hearst

Local and National Yellow Pages Advertising

($ MILLIONS)

Year	Print Directories* Local	Print Directories* National	Total Print Yellow Pages	Internet Yellow Pages‡	Total Yellow Pages
1999	$11,038	$2,056	$13,094	$ 102	$13,196
2000	11,796	2,214	14,010	257	14,267
2001	12,424	2,349	14,773	262	15,035
2002	12,525	2,359	14,884	347	15,231
2003†	12,443	2,326	14,769	597	15,366
2004	12,759	2,394	15,153	775	15,928
2005	13,083	2,473	15,556	966	16,522
2006	13,527	2,596	16,123	1,151	17,274
2007	13,994	2,741	16,735	1,332	18,067
2008	14,565	2,899	17,464	1,511	18,975
2009	15,199	3,069	18,268	1,705	19,973

Sources: Veronis Suhler Stevenson, PQ Media, Association of Directory Publishers, Borrell Associates, Simba Information
*Includes print publishers' Internet yellow pages operations.
†Local carrier publishers changed accounting methodology in 2003 to amortize revenues over the life of a directory, rather than recognizing revenues on the publication. The publishers did not restate 2002 data. Local carrier spending declined in 2003, but the accounting anomaly increased the rate of decline.
‡To avoid double counting, Internet yellow pages spending is included here rather than in the Consumer Internet chapter.

Growth of Local and National Yellow Pages Advertising

Year	Print Directories* Local	Print Directories* National	Total Print Yellow Pages	Internet Yellow Pages‡	Total Yellow Pages
2000	6.9%	7.7%	7.0%	152.0%	8.1%
2001	5.3	6.1	5.4	2.1	5.4
2002	0.8	0.4	0.8	32.3	1.3
2003†	–0.7	–1.4	–0.8	71.9	0.9
2004	2.5	2.9	2.6	29.9	3.7
2005	2.5	3.3	2.7	24.6	3.7
2006	3.4	4.9	3.6	19.2	4.6
2007	3.5	5.6	3.8	15.7	4.6
2008	4.1	5.8	4.4	13.5	5.0
2009	4.4	5.9	4.6	12.8	5.3
Compound Annual Growth					
1999-2004	2.9	3.1	3.0	50.0	3.8
2004-2009	3.6	5.1	3.8	17.1	4.6

Sources: Veronis Suhler Stevenson, PQ Media, Association of Directory Publishers, Borrell Associates, Simba Information
*Includes print publishers' Internet yellow pages operations.
†Local carrier publishers changed accounting methodology in 2003 to amortize revenues over the life of a directory, rather than recognizing revenues on the publication. The publishers did not restate 2002 data. Local carrier spending declined in 2003, but the accounting anomaly increased the rate of decline.
‡To avoid double counting, Internet yellow pages spending is included here rather than in the Consumer Internet chapter.

Corporation acquired White Directory Publishers, the largest privately held, family-owned independent in the U.S. Hearst made its first foray into the yellow pages industry in 1994 with its acquisition of Associated Publishing, which will be combined with the White Directory operation. With access to Hearst's vast resources, White stepped up its expansion plans, announcing start-up directories in Virginia, New Hampshire, New York and Georgia, as well as the acquisition of directories in Florida.

Another major media company, Gannett Company, also renewed its interest in the yellow pages market, announcing its acquisition of HomeTown Directories as part of its purchase of HomeTown Communications Network, a regional newspaper publisher. Gannett first entered the yellow pages industry in the late 1980s, but cancelled five Florida books in 1993 and sold 40 directories in New Jersey and New York in 1996.

Meanwhile, RBOC publisher Verizon Information Services' efforts to publish independent directories in competition with the other RBOCs faced setbacks in 2004 and 2005 when the company said it would sell three competitive directories and cancel seven in Georgia, Ohio and Kentucky. Including two directories in Wisconsin and Missouri that Verizon previously cancelled, the company discontinued or sold 12 of the 44 directories it announced over the past three years. The company later confirmed it decided to discontinue 16 directories in Alabama, Missouri and Kentucky, which serve markets where Verizon sold access lines in 2002 and 2003. The company had initially decided to retain the directories and continue to publish them as an independent. Despite the withdrawals, the company said it remains committed to its expansion effort and even announced in December 2004 that it would expand in Florida with new competitive directories in Ocala and Gainesville. User-Friendly Phone Book, a Texas-based independent yellow pages publisher owned by Veronis Suhler Stevenson, purchased Verizon's three Ohio books, marking its entrance into the Ohio yellow pages market.

Telephone companies also continued to divest directories serving their telephone operating areas. SBC Communications agreed to sell its DonTech yellow pages operations in Illinois and northwest Indiana for $1.42 billion to R.H. Donnelley, the sales agent for the books. SBC said it would retain the rest of its yellow pages operation. Donnelley acquired Sprint's yellow pages unit in 2003 for $2.23 billion, marking its return to yellow pages publishing, six years after it began selling off its independent directories. Also in 2003, Qwest sold its yellow pages unit to private equity firms.

Yellow pages publishers banded together in 2004 to initiate syndicated usage research, which would enable the yellow pages to compete more effectively with other measured media for national advertising dollars. The industry's Syndicated Research Committee retained Knowledge Network/SRI in October 2004 to conduct the research, which is scheduled to begin in 2005, with reports due in 2006. Local advertising continues to represent the bulk of print yellow pages spending, accounting for 84.2 percent, or $12.76 billion in 2004. The national advertising channel, representing only 15.8 percent of print spending, or $2.39 billion, has strong potential for growth. Because national media were more dramatically impacted by the weak economy than local media, national yellow pages advertising declined 1.4 percent in 2003 compared with a 0.7 percent decline for local. National advertising rebounded in 2004 to post a 2.9 percent gain, compared with 2.5 percent for local. National advertising is expected to outpace local for the remainder of the forecast period.

Internet yellow pages also represents a growth opportunity for yellow pages publishers. Print publishers' online revenues are included in their print revenues. Other online directories increased 29.9 percent to $775.0 million in 2005. Although yellow pages publishers face competition from search engines and pure-plays in the online yellow pages arena, a study released in 2005 by the Yellow Pages Association and comScore Networks showed yellow pages publishers may have an advantage over competitors. Although about 66 percent of consumers use Web search engines when looking for local information, compared to about 34 percent

Yellow Pages Advertising, By Print Publisher

($ MILLIONS)

Year	*Local Carrier Publishers**	*Independent Competitive Publishers*	*Total*
1999	$11,750	$1,344	$13,094
2000	12,327	1,683	14,010
2001	12,888	1,885	14,773
2002	12,811	2,073	14,884
2003*	12,404	2,365	14,769
2004	12,392	2,761	15,153
2005	12,417	3,139	15,556
2006	12,541	3,582	16,123
2007	12,691	4,044	16,735
2008	12,882	4,582	17,464
2009	13,114	5,154	18,268

Sources: Veronis Suhler Stevenson, PQ Media, Simba Information, Association of Directory Publishers

*Local carrier publishers changed accounting methodology in 2003 to amortize revenues over the life of a directory, rather than recognizing revenues on the publication. The publishers did not restate 2002 data. Local carrier spending declined in 2003, but the accounting anomaly increased the rate of decline.

Growth of Yellow Pages Advertising, By Print Publisher

Year	*Local Carrier Publishers**	*Independent Competitive Publishers*	*Total*
2000	4.9%	25.2%	7.0%
2001	4.6	12.0	5.4
2002	–0.6	10.0	0.8
2003*	–3.2	14.1	–0.8
2004	–0.1	16.7	2.6
2005	0.2	13.7	2.7
2006	1.0	14.1	3.6
2007	1.2	12.9	3.8
2008	1.5	13.3	4.4
2009	1.8	12.5	4.6
Compound Annual Growth			
1999-2004	1.1	15.5	3.0
2004-2009	1.1	13.3	3.8

Sources: Veronis Suhler Stevenson, PQ Media, Simba Information, Association of Directory Publishers

*Local carrier publishers changed accounting methodology in 2003 to amortize revenues over the life of a directory, rather than recognizing revenues on the publication. The publishers did not restate 2002 data. Local carrier spending declined in 2003, but the accounting anomaly increased the rate of decline.

for Internet yellow pages sites, those using Internet yellow pages sites are more likely to buy and to spend more money, the study showed. Thus, consumers using Internet yellow pages sites are ready to make a purchase. The report also found that Internet yellow pages sites are more efficient than local searches on search engines because it takes only 4.6 clicks to find the desired result on IYP sites, compared to 7.6 clicks on search engines.

Yellow pages publishers have attempted to gain a competitive edge in the online yellow pages market by joining forces and rolling out new advertising options. SBC Smart Yellow Pages and BellSouth Advertising and Publishing Corporation formed a joint venture in 2004 to combine their Internet units and to acquire national Internet yellow pages site YellowPages.com. Meanwhile, Verizon Information Services and Dex Media are offering pay-per-click advertising to be competitive with search engines, which represent formidable competitors in the Internet yellow pages arena because they have built-in traffic and have introduced local search offerings.

Internet yellow pages spending is expected to increase 24.6 percent to $966.0 million in 2005, and grow at a compound annual rate of 17.1 percent in the forecast period. Print yellow pages spending will increase 2.7 percent to $15.56 billion in 2005, and grow at a compound annual rate of 3.8 percent from 2004 to 2009. Internet and independent directories will continue to drive growth in the forecast period. Independent directories are expected to increase 13.7 percent to $3.14 billion in 2005, while telephone company directories will grow 0.2 percent to $12.42 billion. Overall, yellow page spending will increase 3.7 percent to $16.52 billion in 2005, and grow at a compound annual rate of 4.6 percent. Spending will reach $19.97 billion in 2009.

CONSUMER MAGAZINES

Consumer magazine advertising increased 6.0 percent to $12.12 billion in 2004, fueled by the improving economy and strong gains in the retail, financial and travel categories. Spending increased at a compound annual rate of 1.2 percent in the 1999 to 2004 period. The magazine industry continues to promote the value of magazines in the media mix through advertising campaigns and research studies. In early 2005, the MPA kicked off a three-year, $40.0 million marketing campaign targeting advertisers and advertising agencies. The campaign represents the industry's effort to improve the attitudes of advertisers and media buyers toward magazines, with the expectation that an attitudinal shift will ultimately result in higher advertising spending for magazines.

The industry hopes that such marketing efforts will mitigate the increasing skepticism of many marketers about their ROI in traditional media advertising. While it remains to be seen how effective the industry's marketing campaign will be, we anticipate that advertisers will progressively shift more ad dollars out of print media, such as consumer magazines, and into electronic media and alternative marketing methods. This shift will moderate spending growth in consumer magazine advertising, which will grow more in line with that of nominal GDP over the next five years, instead of exceeding economic growth by 2 to 3 percentage points as in previous expansion periods.

Nevertheless, we expect magazine advertising growth to outpace nominal GDP growth in 2006 for the first time in six years, although it will do so by only a slim margin. Overall, we expect spending on consumer magazine advertising to grow at an accelerated pace during the forecast period, compared with the 1999-2004 timeframe, but level with the broader economic expansion. Spending will increase 5.5 percent to $12.79 billion in 2005, and grow at a compound annual rate of 6.2 percent in the forecast period. Spending will reach $16.37 billion in 2009.

BUSINESS-TO-BUSINESS MAGAZINES

Spending on business-to-business magazine advertising increased 6.3 percent to $9.85 billion in 2004, fueled primarily by the industry's transition to e-media, which rose at a double-digit pace, as well as solid expansion in five of Veronis Suhler Stevenson's 15 leading print ad categories. Among these key categories was the second-largest, business and financial, which grew 5.9 percent in 2004, in addition to an 8.0 percent increase in the health and life science category, a 7.5 percent rise in retail advertising, an 8.7 percent climb in architecture and construction, and a 19.8 percent surge in automotive advertising for the year. Of the 15 top categories, only four reported spending declines in 2004. Despite the increase in 2004, b-to-b ad spending declined at a compound annual rate of 1.3 percent from 1999 to 2004, driven down by the double-digit contractions in 2001 and 2002.

Spending on e-media climbed 25.9 percent to $1.47 billion in 2004 compared with a 3.4 percent gain in print advertising to $8.37 billion. It should be noted that the majority of e-media spending comes from advertising, but the figures include some non-advertising dollars. E-media accounted for 15.0 percent of business-to-business advertising in 2004, up from 2.6 percent in 1999. Growth was spurred by new online advertising and content initiatives launched by b-to-b publishers, such as Reed Elsevier and Hanley-Wood, over the past five years, as they scrambled to provide end users with comprehensive electronic alternatives to help them do their jobs more efficiently. Also contributing to this growth were technological developments at pure-play e-media companies like CNET Networks, which have helped shape the evolution of the online advertising market. While the majority of spending during the early stages of the migration to e-media involved advertising, additional tools have been added in more recent years as leading b-to-b media companies steadily transform their businesses from simply magazine publishers to multimedia business information providers.

Continued strong growth in e-media spending, as well as increased print advertising in healthcare, banking, construction and automotive publications, are expected to drive a 7.2 percent increase to $10.56 billion in 2005. In the business-to-business magazine market, increased advertising in healthcare, banking, automotive and construction publications is expected to contribute to growth. Advertising expenditures in automotive titles will increase as manufacturers promote overstocks to the fleet and trucking industries. Through the first quarter of 2005, concern that higher interest rates would drive down spending in the housing market was unproven, and the strength of this market will actually drive spending gains in the architecture, engineering and construction segments, as well as in the home design and furnishing category. Healthcare will continue to post strong gains in 2005, due to advertising to promote new medical technology and new trade shows launched by healthcare-related associations. Declines in the largest category, information technology (IT) and telecommunications, will slow in 2005, posting the slowest decline since 2000. Overall, spending will grow at a compound annual rate of 7.0 percent from 2004 to 2009 to reach $13.80 billion in 2009. E-media will continue to siphon ad dollars away from print and account for a 25.1 percent share of business-to-business advertising in 2009.

CONSUMER INTERNET

Spending on consumer Internet advertising surged 32.5 percent to $9.63 billion in 2004, due to increased demand for keyword search advertising, which has driven prices up, and the increase in searchable content, which has produced more advertising opportunities. The major driver pushing the gains in keyword search has been advertiser demand for detailed and timely ROI data. Spending grew at a compound annual rate of 15.8 percent from 1999 to 2004.

The Internet's popularity with 18- to 34-year-olds, along with its ability to measure usage and ROI, has prompted many advertisers to either shift dollars away from traditional media or funnel budget increases to online advertising instead. Keyword search is the largest category of online advertising, and it continued to post strong growth in 2004. Keyword search ad spending increased 51.0 percent to $3.85 billion for the year, accounting for 40.0 percent of all online advertising expenditures. Keyword search ads, which generate revenues based on the number of click-throughs they receive, are directly measurable and their value in the market has increased in recent years as advertisers seek ways in which to prove ROI in their media buys. While keyword search advertising generated the most spending in 2004, referrals posted the strongest growth, up 140.8 percent to $193.0 million. This trend is being fueled by the growth of the Federal Trade Commission's Do Not Call Registry—which has more than 92 million phone numbers—the need to have consumers opt-in to receive e-mail, and the ability of consumers to skip over commercials, all of which limit advertisers' acquisition options. Customer response and retention rates are generally higher for referral programs than other forms of advertising because they are sent by a trusted associate.

Consumer Internet spending growth is expected to continue to be in the double digits in the forecast period, with spending up 31.2 percent to $12.63 billion in 2005. The market is expected to expand at a compound annual rate of 24.0 percent in the forecast period, with spending reaching $28.20 billion in 2009.

OUT-OF-HOME ADVERTISING

Out-of-home advertising includes traditional roadside billboards, as well as non-traditional forms of out-of-home media, such as bus stations and street furniture. It does not include point-of-purchase advertising, which is included in consumer promotion, or movie screen advertising, which is a separate category. Out-of-home advertising spending grew 6.0 percent to $5.83 billion in 2004, driven

Local and National Out-of-Home Advertising Spending ($ MILLIONS)

Year	Local	National	Total
1999	$2,890	$1,942	$4,832
2000	3,141	2,094	5,235
2001	3,161	2,072	5,233
2002	3,150	2,082	5,232
2003	3,324	2,180	5,504
2004	3,506	2,328	5,834
2005	3,709	2,435	6,144
2006	3,902	2,579	6,481
2007	4,136	2,713	6,849
2008	4,356	2,878	7,234
2009	4,604	3,019	7,623

Sources: Veronis Suhler Stevenson, PQ Media, Outdoor Advertising Association of America

Growth of Local and National Out-of-Home Advertising Spending

Year	Local	National	Total
2000	8.7%	7.8%	8.3%
2001	0.6	–1.1	0.0
2002	–0.3	0.5	0.0
2003	5.5	4.7	5.2
2004	5.5	6.8	6.0
2005	5.8	4.6	5.3
2006	5.2	5.9	5.5
2007	6.0	5.2	5.7
2008	5.3	6.1	5.6
2009	5.7	4.9	5.4
Compound Annual Growth			
1999-2004	3.9	3.7	3.8
2004-2009	5.6	5.3	5.5

Sources: Veronis Suhler Stevenson, PQ Media, Outdoor Advertising Association of America

Advertising, Specialty Media & Marketing Services

Top 10 Out-of-Home Advertising Categories

Category	2003 Spending ($ Millions)	2004 Spending ($ Millions)	Percent Change
Local Services & Amusements	$ 776.1	$ 816.8	5.2%
Media & Advertising	473.4	624.3	31.9
Public Transportation, Hotels & Resorts	528.4	530.9	0.5
Retail	528.4	513.4	–2.8
Insurance & Real Estate	390.8	449.3	15.0
Financial	407.3	560.1	37.5
Automotive Dealers & Services	407.3	379.2	–6.9
Restaurants	423.8	373.4	–11.9
Automotive Accessories & Equipment	308.2	332.6	7.9
Telecommunications	220.2	239.2	8.6
Top 10 Total	4,463.9	4,819.2	8.0
Total	5,504.0	5,834.0	6.0
Top 10 as a Percentage of Total	81.1%	82.6%	

Sources: Veronis Suhler Stevenson, PQ Media, Outdoor Advertising Association of America

Spending and Growth of Out-of-Home Advertising, by Type

	Traditional Billboard		*Street Furniture*		*Non-Traditional Transit*		*Alternative*		*Total*	
Year	*Spending ($ Millions)*	*Growth*	*Spending ($ Millions)*	*Growth*	*Spending ($ Millions)*	*Growth*	*Spending ($ Millions)*	*Growth*	*Spending ($ Millions)*	*Growth*
2003	$3,413	—	$825	—	$1,046	—	$220	—	$5,504	—
2004	3,617	6.0%	816	−1.1%	1,109	6.0%	292	32.5%	5,834	6.0%

Sources: Veronis Suhler Stevenson, PQ Media, Outdoor Advertising Association of America

by an influx of new advertisers and growth in alternative out-of-home advertising. Double-digit growth in the media and advertising, insurance and real estate, and financial categories fueled gains, as did strong political advertising during the 2004 elections. Spending in the 1999 to 2004 period grew at a compound annual rate of 3.8 percent.

Spending on traditional billboard advertising increased 6.0 percent to $3.62 billion in 2004, fueled by price hikes rather than volume increases because zoning regulations prohibit the building of new billboards. Alternative out-of-home advertising climbed 32.5 percent to $292.0 million in 2004, as advertisers shifted spending from transit and street furniture—also forms of non-traditional out-of-home advertising—to experiment with newer options. Transit advertising growth was on par with the overall industry at 6.0 percent, while street furniture declined 1.1 percent. Non-traditional out-of-home advertising now accounts for nearly 40 percent of out-of-home advertising spending.

Alternative out-of-home advertising includes a wide range of vehicles, such as transit, street furniture, coffee cup sleeves, bars and restaurants. New opportunities for out-of-home advertising continue to emerge, such as restrooms and gas station pumps, as advertisers take advantage of every opportunity to reach consumers. For example, Captivate Networks, a division of Gannett, has placed more than 5,400 digital screens in office elevators to deliver news, entertainment and advertising to riders.

Local out-of-home advertising increased 5.5 percent to $3.51 billion in 2004, due to strong growth in small boards. National advertising grew 6.8 percent to $2.33 billion, fueled by double-digit gains in media and advertising, financial, and insurance/real estate.

All but three of the top 10 out-of-home advertising categories increased spending in 2004. Local services and amusements generated the most spending, with $816.8 million, up 5.2 percent. Media and advertising rose to second from fourth, due to 31.9 percent growth, the highest among the top 10. Public transportation, hotels and resorts dropped to third with spending about flat at $530.9 million.

Out-of-home advertising spending is expected to increase 5.3 percent to $6.14 billion in 2005, due to continued strong growth in alternative media. Compound annual growth will be 5.5 percent in the forecast period, with spending reaching $7.62 billion in 2009.

MOVIE SCREEN ADVERTISING

Lackluster growth in consumer spending at the box office was offset by strong growth in advertising, as marketers continue to explore this emerging medium, which offers them a captive audience. Advertising spending on movie screens increased 21.3 percent to $438.0 million in 2004, and grew at a compound annual rate of 27.7 percent from 1999 to 2004. Total box office expenditures grew a modest 1.3 percent to $9.98 billion in 2004, as escalating prices suppressed admissions. Growth in movie screen advertising spending is expected to accelerate in 2005, posting a gain of 19.3 percent to $522.0 million. Growth in movie ad spending will help fuel a 2.0 percent increase in total box office spending. In the 2004 to 2009 period, spending is expected to increase 14.5 percent on a compound annual basis, reaching $863.0 million in 2009.

VIDEOGAME ADVERTISING

Videogame advertising spending escalated 51.9 percent to $120.0 million in 2004, posting the strongest growth rate in the advertising industry. Spending grew at a compound annual rate of 109.1 percent from 1999 to 2004. Still in its infancy, the videogame advertising market is emerging as a strong competitor to traditional advertising vehicles because of its strength in the youth market. Major advertisers have begun to recognize the potential of the medium as an advertising vehicle, as some games sell as many as 5 million units. Companies such as McDonald's, Coca-Cola and Nokia are partnering with videogame makers to incorporate more advertising messages into their software. In-game advertising typically ranges from a few cents to more than 50 cents per unit sold, depending on the product placement and overall sales of the game. Spending is expected to jump 48.3 percent in 2005, the fastest growth of any advertising media, to $178.0 million in 2005, and grow at a compound annual rate of 46.1 percent from 2004 to 2009.

OTHER ADVERTISING TRENDS

LOCAL VERSUS NATIONAL ADVERTISING

As a result of double-digit gains in several electronic advertising media, such as the Internet, network cable television, business-to-business e-media, satellite radio and videogames, the growth of national advertising outpaced that of local advertising in 2004. National ad spending rose 9.4 percent to $87.36 billion, while local advertising rose 6.1 percent to $100.83 billion. Due to the recent growth spurt that compensated for a dramatic decline in 2001, national advertising grew at a compound annual rate of 3.7 percent from 1999 to 2004. Local advertising expenditures rose 2.4 percent during the same period.

The growth in national advertising is the result of a number of factors, led by the ROI measurements available through the Web's keyword search technology. Other factors include marketers seeking to effectively target niche audiences through targeted cable net-

National and Local Advertising Spending ($ MILLIONS)

Year	*Local Advertising*	*National Advertising*	*Total Advertising*
1999	$ 89,469	$ 72,982	$162,451
2000	96,019	85,229	181,248
2001	91,249	75,919	167,168
2002	93,141	76,919	170,060
2003	95,002	79,869	174,871
2004	100,827	87,360	188,187
2005	106,071	93,599	199,670
2006	112,531	102,055	214,586
2007	118,726	109,190	227,916
2008	126,465	119,044	245,509
2009	133,464	127,433	260,897

Sources: Veronis Suhler Stevenson, PQ Media

Growth of National and Local Advertising Spending

Year	Local Advertising	National Advertising	Total Advertising
2000	7.3%	16.8%	11.6%
2001	–5.0	–10.9	–7.8
2002	2.1	1.3	1.7
2003	2.0	3.8	2.8
2004	6.1	9.4	7.6
2005	5.2	7.1	6.1
2006	6.1	9.0	7.5
2007	5.5	7.0	6.2
2008	6.5	9.0	7.7
2009	5.5	7.0	6.3
Compound Annual Growth			
1999-2004	2.4	3.7	3.0
2004-2009	5.8	7.8	6.8

Sources: Veronis Suhler Stevenson, PQ Media

Shares of National and Local Advertising Spending

Year	Local Advertising	National Advertising
1999	55.1%	44.9%
2000	53.0	47.0
2001	54.6	45.4
2002	54.8	45.2
2003	54.3	45.7
2004	53.6	46.4
2005	53.1	46.9
2006	52.4	47.6
2007	52.1	47.9
2008	51.5	48.5
2009	51.2	48.8

Sources: Veronis Suhler Stevenson, PQ Media

works, as well as business magazine publishers expanding brands through e-media initiatives. Lastly, advertisers are beginning to look at alternative media, favored by young adults, that weren't thought of as advertising vehicles until recently, such as videogames and box office advertising.

Meanwhile, strong growth in local Web advertising, as well as in local cable and magazines, was unable to compensate for weaker growth in local radio and the retail sector of newspapers. Cable interconnects, in particular, have been credited with siphoning dollars away from radio. Meanwhile, newspapers have been able to weather the drop in retail advertising by proactively becoming a dominant force in the local Internet market, leading many publishers to develop separate online sales divisions from their print sales units.

The trend of marketers shifting budgets to emerging national media will continue in 2005 and during the forecast period. National advertising will grow 7.1 percent to $93.60 billion in 2005, while local advertising is expected to increase 5.2 percent to $106.07 billion. Furthermore, national advertising will climb at a compound annual rate of 7.8 percent during the 2004-2009 period, reaching $127.43 billion, while local advertising expands 5.8 percent to $133.46 billion in 2009.

TRADITIONAL VERSUS NEW MEDIA ADVERTISING

Traditional media, including broadcast television, newspapers and magazines, are seemingly under attack. Marketers are questioning the ROI measurements offered by traditional media in this era of multitasking and increased advertising clutter. Concurrently, younger audiences that are attractive to advertisers are not embracing traditional media as past generations had done. For example, newspaper readership by young adults is down significantly since 1975. Additionally, some non-advertising traditional media like videogames and movies, have expanded revenue streams to include advertising. Finally, a number of concerns have been raised about the transition from advertising-controlled media to consumer-controlled media. Media usage data found elsewhere in this *Forecast* clearly demonstrates the shift of time spent from advertising-supported media to consumer-supported media. Also raising concerns are technological advances that favor consumers, such as digital video recorders that have made ad-skipping more prevalent than in the past. As a result, so-called traditional media, including broadcast television and radio, magazines, newspapers and print yellow pages, and more traditional out-of-home, have seen their share of communications spending deteriorate at alarming levels in recent years, something that has not occurred during past economic recovery-and-expansion periods when the size of the advertising and marketing pie rose and all media benefited.

Accordingly, spending on new advertising media, which includes media that have offered advertising since 1980, such as cable and satellite television, satellite radio, business-to-business e-media, consumer Internet, movie screens and videogames, rose 21.7 percent to $31.37 billion in 2004. Meanwhile, conventional media increased only 5.2 percent to $156.82 billion for the year. Going forward, we expect marketers will continue to shift dollars to new media advertising options as they continue to reach younger audiences more effectively and strengthen their ROI measurement tools. New media advertising will grow 20.7 percent in 2005 compared with only 3.2 percent for traditional media, as broadcast radio, newspapers and magazine advertising continue to struggle or post relatively slow growth, exacerbated by an odd year for broadcast television in the absence of political and Olympics advertising. Spending on new media advertising will grow at a compound annual rate of 16.9 percent from 2004 to 2009, reaching $68.62 billion, while traditional media advertising will rise only 4.2 percent on a compound annual basis in the forecast period to $192.28 billion in 2009. Consequently, the new media sector will grow its share of the total advertising pie from 16.7 percent in 2004 to 26.3 percent in 2009, while the traditional media segment's share will decline in the same period from 83.3 percent to 73.7 percent.

Traditional Media and New Media Advertising Spending

($ MILLIONS)

Year	*Traditional**	*New*†	*Total*
1999	$145,698	$16,753	$162,451
2000	158,369	22,879	181,248
2001	144,566	22,602	167,168
2002	147,707	22,353	170,060
2003	149,090	25,781	174,871
2004	156,822	31,365	188,187
2005	161,807	37,863	199,670
2006	169,925	44,661	214,586
2007	175,833	52,083	227,916
2008	185,569	59,940	245,509
2009	192,281	68,616	260,897

Sources: Veronis Suhler Stevenson, PQ Media

*Includes broadcast television, newspapers, broadcast radio, print yellow pages, consumer magazines, business-to-business magazines, and out-of-home.

†Includes cable and satellite television, satellite radio, business-to-business e-media, consumer Internet, Internet yellow pages, movie screen advertising, and videogame advertising.

Growth of Traditional Media and New Media Advertising Spending

Year	*Traditional**	*New*†	*Total*
2000	8.7%	36.6%	11.6%
2001	–8.7	–1.2	–7.8
2002	2.2	–1.1	1.7
2003	0.9	15.3	2.8
2004	5.2	21.7	7.6
2005	3.2	20.7	6.1
2006	5.0	18.0	7.5
2007	3.5	16.6	6.2
2008	5.5	15.1	7.7
2009	3.6	14.5	6.3
Compound Annual Growth			
1999-2004	1.5	13.4	3.0
2004-2009	4.2	16.9	6.8

Sources: Veronis Suhler Stevenson, PQ Media

*Includes broadcast television, newspapers, broadcast radio, print yellow pages, consumer magazines, business-to-business magazines, and out-of-home.

†Includes cable and satellite television, satellite radio, business-to-business e-media, consumer Internet, Internet yellow pages, movie screen advertising, and videogame advertising.

Shares of Traditional Media and New Media Advertising Spending

Year	*Traditional**	*New*†
1999	89.7%	10.3%
2000	87.4	12.6
2001	86.5	13.5
2002	86.9	13.1
2003	85.3	14.7
2004	83.3	16.7
2005	81.0	19.0
2006	79.2	20.8
2007	77.1	22.9
2008	75.6	24.4
2009	73.7	26.3

Sources: Veronis Suhler Stevenson, PQ Media

*Includes broadcast television, newspapers, broadcast radio, print yellow pages, consumer magazines, business-to-business magazines, and out-of-home.

†Includes cable and satellite television, satellite radio, business-to-business e-media, consumer Internet, Internet yellow pages, movie screen advertising, and videogame advertising.

The Outlook For Advertising

The advertising segment is experiencing myriad changes due to a number of reasons, ranging from consumer empowerment through new technology such as digital video recorders to marketers seeking stronger ROI measurements for their marketing dollars. Some of the first signs of these changes are becoming more evident as advertisers are turning to the Internet with its strong keyword search ROI measurements and alternative media like videogames and movie screen advertising in order to reach younger audiences. As a result, advertising spending is expected to increase 6.1 percent to $199.67 billion in 2005, although growth in broadcast TV and newspapers, the two largest categories, will decelerate. Spending on broadcast television will be adversely affected by the absence of political and Olympics advertising in 2005, which fueled strong growth the prior year. Newspapers will experience slower growth in retail, national and classified spending. Double-digit gains in cable and satellite television, consumer Internet, movie screen ads and videogame ads will offset the slowdown in the broadcast television and newspaper markets.

Spending is expected to increase at a compound annual rate of 6.8 percent from 2004 to 2009, reaching $260.90 billion in 2009 and surpassing the 3.0 percent growth rate achieved in the previous five-year period. The market will benefit from the emergence of new advertising vehicles, including movie screens, videogames and satellite radio, which will fuel overall growth. Cable and satellite television and consumer Internet spending will also post double-digit gains during the forecast period, as these markets have not yet reached maturity. Traditional media vehicles will benefit from the strength of the U.S. economy in the forecast period, but will post low- to mid-single-digit growth due to competition from new media and alternative marketing vehicles.

FORECAST ASSUMPTIONS

- A solid economy will bolster advertising spending gains in the forecast period, but the market will struggle to achieve growth rates that exceed GDP expansion. Traditional advertising media, which represent the lion's share of advertising spending, are facing heightened competition from new media advertising options and alternative marketing practices. Marketers are shifting spending to non-traditional advertising and marketing tactics to directly impact sales and drive return on investment (ROI).
- Marketers are also pursuing multichannel marketing strategies to accomplish a number of goals, from fostering brand name awareness to motivating purchases. This trend is forcing traditional media to share advertising budgets with a variety of new media options, which will lead to slower growth during the forecast period compared with historic growth rates.
- Political campaign spending and Olympics-related advertising will fuel broadcast television spending growth in even-numbered years during the forecast period, followed by slowdowns in growth in odd-numbered years. However, television's share of political advertising is diminishing, and Olympics viewership in the U.S. may be dampened by time differences with the foreign countries hosting the games.
- The broadcast radio sector is transitioning from a growth business to a mature one due to near-term pricing issues stemming from overcapacity, the lack of a sophisticated local sales management system and increasing competition from local cable and satellite radio.
- Consolidation among retailers will result in a reduction of retail newspaper advertising in the 2004-2009 period, as merged companies combine and trim their marketing budgets. They will also shift spending to broadcast television to better reach their larger customer bases across a wider geographic area.
- Consumer magazines, like other traditional print media, are expected to lose advertising dollars to electronic media and alternative marketing methods, which will temper spending growth in the forecast period. The consumer magazine industry, led by its major trade organization, will combat this challenge by aggressively promoting the effectiveness of the medium to advertisers through marketing campaigns and research projects.
- In the business-to-business magazine market, the automotive and recreational vehicles category will experience double-digit growth in 2005, as an inventory glut forces advertisers to target fleet buyers and trucking companies more aggressively. The health and life sciences category will experience healthy single-digit growth, driven by consistent efforts to promote new medical devices and diagnostics to healthcare professionals. The information technology and telecommunications category will recover from the recession and begin to post slow growth in the forecast period, spurred by an increase in equipment purchases that were postponed when the economy slowed.
- The Internet advertising market will benefit from the migration of advertising dollars to media that provide detailed and timely ROI data. In addition, the availability of more searchable content will create more keyword search advertising opportunities. Local advertising growth will outpace national advertising growth as local businesses begin to embrace Web advertising.
- Internet yellow pages and independent directories will fuel spending growth in the yellow pages market during the forecast period.
- Alternative non-traditional out-of-home advertising vehicles, such as transit, street furniture, bars and restaurants, will drive growth in out-of-home advertising spending. Growth in billboard spending will be slow due to limited inventory.
- Emerging advertising instruments—such as movie screens, interactive television and satellite radio—will post strong growth during the forecast period.

HIGHLIGHTS

Specialty Media and Marketing Services

Spending on specialty media and marketing services increased 6.9 percent in 2004 to $257.15 billion, driven by custom publishing, branded entertainment and public relations.

■

Direct marketing, the largest category, grew 6.0 percent to $135.37 billion, due in part to the growing use of niche database marketing, which is making it easier for marketers to target specific zip codes and neighborhoods. The trend toward measuring the effectiveness of advertising and improving ROI also drove gains.

■

Business-to-business promotion spending increased 3.7 percent to $41.66 billion in 2004, reflecting the rise in corporate profits, which allowed companies to reward employees and clients.

■

Consumer promotion spending increased 4.4 percent to $31.64 billion in 2004, as marketers sought less expensive alternatives to advertising, pursued marketing tactics that directly impact sales, and focused on improving ROI. Strong gains in product sampling and in-store media drove overall growth.

■

Spending on custom publishing increased 20.4 percent to $22.01 billion in 2004, driven by strong gains in spending on magazines and the growing use of electronic publications.

■

Branded entertainment spending increased 9.1 percent to $20.73 billion, fueled by the trend toward alternative marketing tactics that engage and entertain the consumer, particularly the 18- to 34-year-old demographic. Product placement spending posted the strongest gain in the segment, outpacing sponsorship and licensing spending.

■

The public relations segment has also been positively impacted by the trend toward alternative marketing, which fueled a 12.0 percent increase in spending to $3.41 billion in 2004. The growth rate represented a substantial improvement over the market's performance during the past three years.

■

Strong growth in custom publishing, branded entertainment and public relations spending will fuel a 7.0 percent gain in marketing spending to $275.11 billion in 2005. Spending will grow at a compound annual rate of 6.7 percent in the 2004 to 2009 period, reaching $355.15 billion in 2009.

The Specialty Media & Marketing Services Market in 2004 and 2005

Specialty media and marketing services spending expanded in 2004, as marketers pursued alternatives to advertising that targeted specific audiences, provided a measurable impact on sales, and delivered a stronger ROI. Specialty media spending increased 6.9 percent to $257.15 billion in 2004, and grew at a compound annual rate of 4.9 percent from 1999 to 2004.

As stated earlier, we have added custom publishing to the specialty media and marketing services segment this year, and expanded the direct mail segment to include all of direct marketing, such as telesales and catalogs, among others. We also added a new branded entertainment segment, which incorporates the new product placement category, as well as the existing categories of sponsorships and promotional licensing. Strong gains in custom publishing, public relations and branded entertainment fueled growth in the period, reflecting the trend toward marketing vehicles that engage and entertain the consumer. Heavy political spending on direct mail, public relations and promotion helped drive growth in 2004, according to exclusive PQ Media research. In the consumer promotion category, strong growth in product sampling and in-store media was spurred by the trend toward measuring a marketing campaign's effect on sales.

DIRECT MARKETING

Direct marketing includes direct mail, telemarketing, catalogs and interactive advertising, as well as direct-response advertising in traditional media, such as television, radio, newspapers and magazines. Direct marketing spending increased 6.0 percent to $135.37 billion in 2004, due in part to the growing use of niche database marketing, which is making it easier for marketers to target specific zip codes and neighborhoods. According to one survey of marketing executives, direct mail was ranked as the most effective of the

Advertising, Specialty Media & Marketing Services

Specialty Media and Marketing Services Spending ($ MILLIONS)

Year	*Direct Marketing*	*Business-to-Business Promotion*	*Consumer Promotion*	*Custom Publishing*	*Branded Entertainment*	*Public Relations*	*Promotional Spending In Other Media**	*Total*
1999	$106,854	$36,676	$27,971	$11,650	$14,760	$2,345	$2,133	$202,389
2000	115,279	40,129	30,689	12,981	16,357	3,118	2,252	220,805
2001	115,555	38,161	28,815	14,288	17,086	2,900	2,061	218,866
2002	120,705	38,535	29,617	16,982	17,827	2,927	2,034	228,627
2003	127,703	40,165	30,293	18,284	18,993	3,045	2,115	240,598
2004	135,367	41,658	31,639	22,009	20,729	3,410	2,333	257,145
2005	144,166	44,001	33,198	24,629	22,730	3,754	2,632	275,110
2006	152,816	46,435	34,778	27,904	24,574	4,107	3,001	293,615
2007	161,374	49,032	36,405	30,806	26,374	4,428	3,369	311,788
2008	170,733	51,941	38,239	34,996	28,497	4,790	3,775	332,971
2009	180,978	54,957	40,206	38,881	30,724	5,212	4,196	355,154

Sources: Veronis Suhler Stevenson, PQ Media, *Advertising Age*, Council of Public Relations Firms, Custom Publishing Association, Direct Marketing Association, Forrest, Global Insight, *IEG Sponsorship Report*, Incentive Marketing Association, In Demand, Insight Research, In-Store Marketing Institute, McMurry, Myers Mediaenomics, NCH NuWorld Marketing Limited, *O'Dwyer's Directory of Public Relations Firms*, Oetting & Company, Point-of-Purchase and Advertising Institute, *Promo Magazine*, Promotional Products Association International, *Response Magazine*, *Tradeshow Week*, UBS Warburg, Universal McCann, Yankee Group

*Includes interactive television advertising and promotions; mobile advertising and promotions; and trade show fees, sponsorships and advertising.

Growth of Specialty Media and Marketing Services Spending

Year	*Direct Marketing*	*Business-to-Business Promotion*	*Consumer Promotion*	*Custom Publishing*	*Branded Enter-tainment*	*Public Relations*	*Promotional Spending In Other Media**	*Total*
2000	7.9%	9.4%	9.7%	11.4%	10.8%	33.0%	5.6%	9.0%
2001	0.2	–4.9	–6.1	10.1	4.5	–7.0	–8.5	–0.9
2002	4.5	1.0	2.8	18.9	4.3	0.9	–1.3	4.5
2003	5.8	4.2	2.3	7.7	6.5	4.0	4.0	5.2
2004	6.0	3.7	4.4	20.4	9.1	12.0	10.3	6.9
2005	6.5	5.6	4.9	11.9	9.7	10.1	12.8	7.0
2006	6.0	5.5	4.8	13.3	8.1	9.4	14.0	6.7
2007	5.6	5.6	4.7	10.4	7.3	7.8	12.2	6.2
2008	5.8	5.9	5.0	13.6	8.0	8.2	12.1	6.8
2009	6.0	5.8	5.1	11.1	7.8	8.8	11.2	6.7
Compound Annual Growth								
1999-2004	4.8	2.6	2.5	13.6	7.0	7.8	1.8	4.9
2004-2009	6.0	5.7	4.9	12.1	8.2	8.9	12.5	6.5

Sources: Veronis Suhler Stevenson, PQ Media, *Advertising Age*, Council of Public Relations Firms, Custom Publishing Association, Direct Marketing Association, Forrester, Global Insight, *IEG Sponsorship Report*, Incentive Marketing Association, In Demand, Insight Research, In-Store Marketing Institute, McMurry, Myers Mediaenomics, NCH NuWorld Marketing Limited, *O'Dwyer's Directory of Public Relations Firms*, Oetting & Company, Point-of-Purchase and Advertising Institute, *Promo Magazine*, Promotional Products Association International, *Response Magazine*, *Tradeshow Week*, UBS Warburg, Universal McCann, Yankee Group

*Includes interactive television advertising and promotions; mobile advertising and promotions; and trade show fees, sponsorships and advertising.

major media for reaching a target audience and providing measurable ROI. Another example of direct mail's growing importance in marketing campaigns was its increased use in many 2004 political campaigns using targeted databases. Mainly due to increased spending on direct mail by both presidential candidates, especially in the battleground states, spending on direct mail surged 93.7 percent to $648.0 million compared with 2002 expenditures, according to PQ Media.

Despite the implementation of the federal Do Not Call Registry—which fines companies that make telephone sales calls to consumers who have voluntarily placed their names on the list—spending on telemarketing to consumers increased 4.7 percent to $29.47 billion in 2004. Comparatively, spending on consumer direct mail rose 4.6 percent to $30.50 billion. One reason for the increase in telemarketing spending is the rise in costs—including telephone charges and

Shares of Specialty Media and Marketing Services Spending

Year	Direct Marketing	Business-to-Business Promotion	Consumer Promotion	Custom Publishing	Branded Enter-tainment	Public Relations	Promotional Spending In Other Media*
1999	52.8%	18.1%	13.8%	5.8%	7.3%	1.2%	1.1%
2000	52.2	18.2	13.9	5.9	7.4	1.4	1.0
2001	52.8	17.4	13.2	6.5	7.8	1.3	0.9
2002	52.8	16.9	13.0	7.4	7.8	1.3	0.9
2003	53.1	16.7	12.6	7.6	7.9	1.3	0.9
2004	52.6	16.2	12.3	8.6	8.1	1.3	0.9
2005	52.4	16.0	12.1	9.0	8.3	1.4	1.0
2006	52.0	15.8	11.8	9.5	8.4	1.4	1.0
2007	51.8	15.7	11.7	9.9	8.5	1.4	1.1
2008	51.3	15.6	11.5	10.5	8.6	1.4	1.1
2009	51.0	15.5	11.3	10.9	8.7	1.5	1.2

Sources: Veronis Suhler Stevenson, PQ Media, *Advertising Age*, Council of Public Relations Firms, Custom Publishing Association, Direct Marketing Association, Forrester, Global Insight, *IEG Sponsorship Report*, Incentive Marketing Association, In Demand, Insight Research, In-Store Marketing Institute, McMurry, Myers Mediaenomics, NCH NuWorld Marketing Limited, *O'Dwyer's Directory of Public Relations Firms*, Oetting & Company, Point-of-Purchase and Advertising Institute, *Promo Magazine*, Promotional Products Association International, *Response Magazine*, *Tradeshow Week*, UBS Warburg, Universal McCann, Yankee Group

*Includes interactive television advertising and promotions; mobile advertising and promotions; and trade show fees, sponsorships and advertising.

Advertising, Specialty Media & Marketing Services

new automated systems—which are being passed on to clients. But companies continue to invest in telemarketing because it delivers results. A Direct Market Association survey released in late 2004 found that telemarketing generated the highest response rate compared to other direct marketing tactics, and the strongest ROI.

E-mail marketing, covered in more detail in the Consumer Internet chapter of this *Forecast*, has not significantly impacted spending on traditional direct mail because of the backlash against spam. The CAN-SPAM Act of 2003 succeeded in curtailing unsolicited, promotional e-mail messages. The average consumer received 78 spam e-mails per week in February 2005, down from 137 a year earlier. The percentage of e-mails considered spam dropped from 60.4 percent in February 2004 to 53.1 percent in February 2005.

However, a postage rate hike slated for 2006 is expected to hamper the growth of

Direct Marketing Spending, by Medium and Market

	Telesales			*Direct Mail*			*Catalog*			*Television*		
Year	*Consumer*	*B-to-B*	*Total*	*Consumer*	*B-to-B*	*Total*	*Consumer*	*B-to-B*	*Total*	*Consumer*	*B-to-B*	*Total*
1999	$24,737	$21,574	$46,311	$25,997	$16,094	$42,091	$ 7,540	$3,930	$11,470	$3,667	$293	$3,960
2000	26,365	23,436	49,801	27,433	17,128	44,561	8,611	4,331	12,942	3,950	319	4,269
2001	25,982	23,062	49,044	27,181	17,518	44,699	8,912	4,465	13,377	3,950	319	4,269
2002	27,081	24,103	51,184	27,998	18,026	46,024	9,286	4,904	14,190	4,103	330	4,433
2003	28,144	25,784	53,928	29,166	19,477	48,643	9,700	5,155	14,855	4,345	357	4,702
2004	29,466	27,435	56,901	30,501	20,858	51,359	10,154	5,430	15,584	4,604	382	4,986
2005	30,939	29,301	60,240	32,087	22,422	54,509	10,702	5,740	16,442	4,895	406	5,301
2006	32,424	31,147	63,571	33,692	24,059	57,751	11,162	6,072	17,234	5,095	430	5,525
2007	33,786	32,984	66,770	35,107	25,647	60,754	11,709	6,449	18,158	5,385	458	5,843
2008	35,341	35,095	70,436	36,722	27,519	64,241	12,213	6,816	19,029	5,611	481	6,092
2009	36,931	37,481	74,412	38,447	29,501	67,948	12,848	7,253	20,101	5,925	511	6,436

Sources: Veronis Suhler Stevenson, PQ Media, Direct Marketing Association, Forrester, Oetting & Company, *Response Magazine*, Universal McCann

Growth in Direct Marketing Spending, by Medium and Market

	Telesales			*Direct Mail*			*Catalog*			*Television*		
Year	*Consumer*	*B-to-B*	*Total*	*Consumer*	*B-to-B*	*Total*	*Consumer*	*B-to-B*	*Total*	*Consumer*	*B-to-B*	*Total*
000	6.6%	8.6%	7.5%	5.5%	6.4%	5.9%	14.2%	10.2%	12.8%	7.7%	8.9%	7.8%
2001	–1.5	–1.6	–1.5	–0.9	2.3	0.3	3.5	3.1	3.4	0.0	0.0	0.0
2002	4.2	4.5	4.4	3.0	2.9	3.0	4.2	9.8	6.1	3.9	3.4	3.8
2003	3.9	7.0	5.4	4.2	8.0	5.7	4.5	5.1	4.7	5.9	8.2	6.1
2004	4.7	6.4	5.5	4.6	7.1	5.6	4.7	5.3	4.9	6.0	7.0	6.0
2005	5.0	6.8	5.9	5.2	7.5	6.1	5.4	5.7	5.5	6.3	6.4	6.3
2006	4.8	6.3	5.5	5.0	7.3	5.9	4.3	5.8	4.8	4.1	5.8	4.2
2007	4.2	5.9	5.0	4.2	6.6	5.2	4.9	6.2	5.4	5.7	6.4	5.7
2008	4.6	6.4	5.5	4.6	7.3	5.7	4.3	5.7	4.8	4.2	5.1	4.3
2009	4.5	6.8	5.6	4.7	7.2	5.8	5.2	6.4	5.6	5.6	6.2	5.6
Compound Annual Growth												
1999-2004	3.6	4.9	4.2	3.2	5.3	4.1	6.1	6.7	6.3	4.7	5.4	4.7
2004-2009	4.6	6.4	5.5	4.7	7.2	5.8	4.8	6.0	5.2	5.2	6.0	5.2

Sources: Veronis Suhler Stevenson, PQ Media, Direct Marketing Association, Forrester, Oetting & Company, *Response Magazine*, Universal McCann

Interactive			*Magazines*			*Newspapers*			*Radio*			*Total*		
Consumer	*B-to-B*	*Total*	*Consumer*	*B-to-B*	*Total*	*Consumer*	*B-to-B*	*Total*	*Consumer*	*B-to-B*	*Total*	*Consumer*	*B-to-B*	*Total*
$ 315	$ 623	$ 938	$632	$ 978	$1,610	$210	$ 68	$278	$160	$36	$196	$63,258	$43,596	$106,854
474	974	1,448	677	1,064	1,741	222	73	295	181	41	222	67,913	47,366	115,279
668	1,407	2,075	642	982	1,624	203	68	271	160	36	196	67,698	47,857	115,555
1,039	1,722	2,761	652	978	1,630	208	70	278	167	38	205	70,534	50,171	120,705
1,264	2,067	3,331	685	1,046	1,731	217	76	293	179	41	220	73,700	54,003	127,703
1,579	2,580	4,159	722	1,113	1,835	227	81	308	191	44	235	77,444	57,923	135,367
1,921	3,240	5,161	760	1,182	1,942	238	86	324	201	47	248	81,742	62,424	144,166
2,263	3,833	6,096	789	1,252	2,041	248	91	339	209	50	259	85,883	66,933	152,816
2,596	4,476	7,072	824	1,327	2,151	260	96	356	220	52	272	89,886	71,488	161,374
3,002	5,008	8,010	856	1,413	2,269	271	101	372	229	55	284	94,244	76,489	170,733
3,426	5,564	8,990	895	1,508	2,403	284	107	391	239	58	297	98,996	81,982	180,978

Interactive			*Magazines*			*Newspapers*			*Radio*			*Total*		
Consumer	*B-to-B*	*Total*	*Consumer*	*B-to-B*	*Total*	*Consumer*	*B-to-B*	*Total*	*Consumer*	*B-to-B*	*Total*	*Consumer*	*B-to-B*	*Total*
50.5%	56.3%	54.4%	7.1%	8.8%	8.1%	5.7%	7.4%	6.1%	13.1%	13.9%	13.3%	7.4%	8.6%	7.9%
40.9	44.5	43.3	–5.2	–7.7	–6.7	–8.6	–6.8	–8.1	–11.6	–12.2	–11.7	–0.3	1.0	0.2
55.5	22.4	33.1	1.6	-0.4	0.4	2.5	2.9	2.6	4.4	5.6	4.6	4.2	4.8	4.5
21.7	20.0	20.6	5.1	7.0	6.2	4.3	8.6	5.4	7.2	7.9	7.3	4.5	7.6	5.8
24.9	24.8	24.9	5.4	6.4	6.0	4.6	6.6	5.1	6.7	7.3	6.8	5.1	7.3	6.0
21.6	25.6	24.1	5.2	6.2	5.8	4.9	5.9	5.2	5.2	6.4	5.4	5.6	7.8	6.5
17.8	18.3	18.1	3.9	5.9	5.1	4.3	5.7	4.7	4.1	6.1	4.5	5.1	7.2	6.0
14.7	16.8	16.0	4.4	6.0	5.4	4.7	5.3	4.9	4.9	5.5	5.0	4.7	6.8	5.6
15.6	11.9	13.3	3.9	6.5	5.5	4.4	5.6	4.7	4.3	4.8	4.4	4.8	7.0	5.8
14.1	11.1	12.2	4.6	6.7	5.9	4.5	5.8	4.9	4.4	5.1	4.5	5.0	7.2	6.0
38.0	32.9	34.7	2.7	2.6	2.7	1.6	3.6	2.1	3.6	4.1	3.7	4.1	5.8	4.8
16.8	16.6	16.7	4.4	6.3	5.5	4.6	5.7	4.9	4.6	5.6	4.8	5.0	7.2	6.0

Business-to-Business Promotion Spending ($ MILLIONS)

Year	Incentives	Promotional Products	Total
1999	$21,736	$14,940	$36,676
2000	22,279	17,850	40,129
2001	21,611	16,550	38,161
2002	22,908	15,627	38,535
2003	23,824	16,341	40,165
2004	24,348	17,310	41,658
2005	25,566	18,435	44,001
2006	26,691	19,744	46,435
2007	27,945	21,087	49,032
2008	29,315	22,626	51,941
2009	30,634	24,323	54,957

Sources: Veronis Suhler Stevenson, PQ Media, Incentive Marketing Association, *Promo Magazine*, Promotional Products Association International

Growth of Business-to-Business Promotion Spending

Year	Incentives	Promotional Products	Total
2000	2.5%	19.5%	9.4%
2001	–3.0	–7.3	–4.9
2002	6.0	–5.6	1.0
2003	4.0	4.6	4.2
2004	2.2	5.9	3.7
2005	5.0	6.5	5.6
2006	4.4	7.1	5.5
2007	4.7	6.8	5.6
2008	4.9	7.3	5.9
2009	4.5	7.5	5.8
Compound Annual Growth			
1999-2004	2.3	3.0	2.6
2004-2009	4.7	7.0	5.7

Sources: Veronis Suhler Stevenson, PQ Media, Incentive Marketing Association, *Promo Magazine*, Promotional Products Association International

direct mail spending in 2006 and 2007. In April 2005, the U.S. Postal Service (USPS) filed for a 5.4 percent rate hike for almost all classes of mail. The impact is not expected to be significant since the rate hike requested is lower than the double-digit figures previously considered, and the USPS has not implemented a rate hike since 2002. Interestingly, the USPS launched a custom publication in March 2005, aimed at marketing executives, that promotes the use of direct mail in multichannel marketing campaigns because of its ability to deliver measurable ROI.

The trend toward multichannel marketing will drive growth in direct mail and overall direct marketing spending in the forecast period, as marketers often use direct mail to support campaigns combining traditional print advertising with alternative advertising and marketing tools. Spending will increase 6.5 percent to $144.17 billion in 2005, and grow at a compound annual rate of 6.0 percent from 2004 to 2009, reaching $180.98 billion in 2009.

BUSINESS-TO-BUSINESS PROMOTION

Business-to-business promotion, which includes incentives and promotional products, increased 3.7 percent to $41.66 billion in 2004, reflecting the rise in corporate profits, which allowed companies to reward employees and clients.

Incentives

Growth in spending on employee incentives increased 2.2 percent to $24.35 billion in 2004. The gain is attributable to a tight job market, which prompted employers to reward loyal employees across their organizations. Research on the results of employee recognition programs provide proof that incentive programs improve employee productivity, boost customer satisfaction and increase profits. One study found customer satisfaction was directly related to employee morale, even for employees who have no direct contact with customers. As in the market for consumer incentives, gift certificates and electronic items were among the most popular items used to reward employees in 2004.

Spending on employee incentives is expected to accelerate in 2005 and remain in the 4.0 percent to 5.0 percent range during the 2004-2009 period. Compound annual growth will be 4.7 percent in the period, surpassing the 2.3 percent gain posted in the 1999-2004 timeframe. Spending will reach $30.63 billion in 2009.

Promotional Products

Growth in promotional products spending accelerated in 2004, growing 5.9 percent to $17.31 billion in 2004, compared to 4.6 percent growth in 2003. Growth was driven, in part, by gains among luxury brands, such as Coach, which manufactures accessories such as handbags and watches. Corporations are thanking clients with such high-end merchandise to convey the client's value.

The number of small companies distributing promotional products increased from 20,150 to 20,249. Meanwhile, the number of distributors with sales of $2.5 million or more rose from 815 in 2003 to 919 in 2004. Apparel and accessories, or wearables, accounted for the largest share of sales in 2004 at nearly 30 percent, followed by writing instruments at 10.6 percent and calendars at 7.5 percent. (Because three new categories were introduced in 2004, the figures are not comparable to 2003.) Wearables include, among other items, T-shirts, golf shirts, aprons, uniforms, blazers, caps, hats, headbands and jackets.

Spending on promotional products will continue to expand during the forecast period, rising 6.5 percent to $18.44 billion in 2005, and growing at a compound annual rate of 7.0 percent from 2004 to 2009. Spending will reach $24.32 billion in 2009.

The Outlook for Business-to-Business Promotion

Spending on business-to-business promotion is expected to increase 5.6 percent to $44.0 billion in 2005, driven by gains in both employee incentives and promotional products. Spending is expected to grow at a compound annual rate of 5.7 percent from 2004 to 2009, reaching $54.96 billion in 2009.

CONSUMER PROMOTION

Consumer promotion includes point-of-purchase displays, premiums, product sampling, in-store media and coupons. Spending on consumer promotion increased 4.4 percent to $31.64 billion in 2004, as marketers sought less expensive alternatives to advertising, pursued marketing tactics that directly impact sales, and focused on improving ROI. Growth was driven by strong gains in product sampling and in-store media. Compound annual growth was 2.5 percent from 1999 to 2004.

Point-of-Purchase

Spending on point-of-purchase (P-O-P) advertising, including traditional cardboard displays and new interactive kiosks, increased 6.0 percent to $16.64 billion in 2004, driven by the general trend toward bringing marketing inside the retail store. P-O-P advertising allows marketers to reach consumers while they are making purchases, when they tend to be more receptive to promotional messages.

Spending is expected to grow at a steady pace in 2005 and during the remainder of the forecast period. According to one survey, about 40 percent of brand marketers expect to increase their P-O-P budgets in 2005. Many respondents are pitching ideas for new, innovative displays to retailers and are embracing new technology, such as touch screens, digital signs, and interactive displays, which will fuel spending growth in the forecast period. In the face of increasing competition from superstores and warehouse clubs, supermarket chains are attempting to improve the ambience in their stores and create a more upscale image, making them more receptive to new P-O-P concepts and interactive displays. The trend toward more sophisticated displays will fuel 5.8 percent growth to $17.60 billion in 2005, and spur 5.7 percent compound annual growth in the forecast period.

Coupons

Growth in coupon spending slowed in 2004, as marketers de-emphasized the tactic's role in the marketing mix, most likely because coupon use tends to decline when the economy is strong. Only 16.7 percent

Advertising, Specialty Media & Marketing Services

Consumer Promotion Spending

($ MILLIONS)

Year	*Point-of-Purchase*	*Coupons*	*Premiums*	*Product Sampling*	*In-Store Media*	*Total*
1999	$14,399	$6,708	$4,874	$1,120	$ 870	$27,971
2000	17,005	6,648	4,932	1,200	904	30,689
2001	15,509	6,242	4,981	1,230	853	28,815
2002	15,509	6,523	5,374	1,341	870	29,617
2003	15,695	6,751	5,481	1,475	891	30,293
2004	16,637	6,900	5,481	1,659	962	31,639
2005	17,602	7,114	5,623	1,822	1,037	33,198
2006	18,570	7,313	5,798	1,980	1,117	34,778
2007	19,554	7,532	5,937	2,180	1,202	36,405
2008	20,708	7,721	6,133	2,380	1,297	38,239
2009	21,971	7,899	6,341	2,592	1,403	40,206

Sources: Veronis Suhler Stevenson, PQ Media, Incentive Marketing Association, In-Store Marketing Institute, NCH NuWorld Marketing Limited, Point-of-Purchase and Advertising Institute, *Promo Magazine*

of brand marketers reported that coupons and FSIs (free-standing inserts) ranked in their top three spending categories in 2004, down from 18.4 percent in 2003, according to one survey. Spending increased only 2.2 percent to $6.90 billion, but distribution climbed 7.7 percent. The top 20 manufacturers represented about 60 percent of all coupons distributed. Consumer packaged goods manufacturers accounted for 71.4 percent of FSI pages in 2004. But franchise coupons and direct response posted the largest gains in FSI pages, up 14.4 percent and 10.3 percent, respectively.

Procter & Gamble and General Mills, the largest distributors of coupons, helped drive gains in overall distribution by increasing volume 15.8 percent and 10.7 percent, respectively. Johnson & Johnson and Campbell Soup also boosted volume in the double digits. Coupons for personal care products represented the highest distribution volume, followed by pet foods and household cleaning products.

Marketers attempted to drive coupon use by increasing face value and reducing expiration timeframes. The average face value of coupons distributed through FSIs in newspapers increased 8.1 percent to $1.03 in 2004, representing the first time average face value has exceeded $1. Meanwhile, the length of time between distribution and expiration was reduced 0.2 percent to 10.1 weeks. The increasing marketing power of retailers led to an increase in co-marketing programs in 2004.

Spending on coupons is expected to increase only 3.1 percent to $7.11 billion in 2005, and grow at a compound annual rate of 2.7 percent from 2004 to 2009. Spending is expected to reach $7.90 billion in 2009.

Premiums

Spending on consumer premiums was flat in 2004 at $5.48 billion, as marketers were more concerned about measuring ROI and directly impacting consumer purchases than with thanking consumers for a previous purchase. Gift certificates and electronic items, such as cameras and home entertainment devices, were among the most popular items used in consumer incentive programs in 2004.

Spending on premiums is expected to increase in 2005 due to the emergence of online loyalty programs, which reward con-

Growth of Consumer Promotion Spending

Year	Point-of-Purchase	Coupons	Premiums	Product Sampling	In-Store Media	Total
2000	18.1%	–0.9%	1.2%	7.1%	3.9%	9.7%
2001	–8.8	–6.1	1.0	2.5	–5.6	–6.1
2002	0.0	4.5	7.9	9.0	2.0	2.8
2003	1.2	3.5	2.0	10.0	2.4	2.3
2004	6.0	2.2	0.0	12.5	8.0	4.4
2005	5.8	3.1	2.6	9.8	7.8	4.9
2006	5.5	2.8	3.1	8.7	7.7	4.8
2007	5.3	3.0	2.4	10.1	7.6	4.7
2008	5.9	2.5	3.3	9.2	7.9	5.0
2009	6.1	2.3	3.4	8.9	8.2	5.1
Compound Annual Growth						
1999-2004	2.9	0.6	2.4	8.2	2.0	2.5
2004-2009	5.7	2.7	3.0	9.3	7.8	4.9

Sources: Veronis Suhler Stevenson, PQ Media, Incentive Marketing Association, In-Store Marketing Institute, NCH NuWorld Marketing Limited, Point-of-Purchase and Advertising Institute, *Promo Magazine*

sumers with gifts and prizes. Spending is forecast to increase 2.6 percent to $5.62 billion in 2005, and grow at a compound annual rate of 3.0 percent from 2004 to 2009. Spending will reach $6.34 billion in 2009.

Product Sampling

Spending on product sampling increased 12.5 percent to $1.66 billion in 2004, the highest growth rate among the consumer promotion segments. Marketers are implementing the tactic to target the 18- to 25-year-old demographic, which often has not developed loyalty to particular products or brands. Spring Break has become a prime opportunity for sampling because students will bring products and information back to their campuses, perpetuating the marketing effort at no additional cost. Brand marketers are also distributing samples at high schools, colleges, and places where young people congregate, such as malls, concerts and movie theaters. They are using spokesmodels to distribute samples to increase their appeal. For example, during the NBA's All-Star Weekend, McDonald's hired basketball stars to hand out samples of its Chicken Selects chicken strips at its establishments in Denver, where the game was held.

Marketers are not interested in merely generating excitement for their products at sampling events; they are looking for proof that distributing samples leads to sales. To this end, PromoWorks, a provider of in-store sampling and retail entertainment events, introduced in early 2005 a system that tracks the sales performance of individual demonstrators at sampling events. The company used the technology to measure the performance of demonstrators at in-store events for Wal-Mart in late 2004, distributing more than 50,000 PromoPIN cards to demonstrators. Marketers are also distributing coupons with samples to encourage purchases and track results.

Because marketers view product sampling as an opportunity to directly drive sales, spending growth is expected to outpace the other consumer promotion segments throughout the forecast period. Spending is projected to increase 9.8 percent to $1.82 billion in 2005, and grow at a compound annual rate of 9.3 percent from 2004 to 2009. Spending will reach $2.59 billion in 2009.

Custom Publishing Spending, Growth and Share

	Magazines			Newsletters		
Year	*Spending ($ Millions)*	*Growth*	*Share*	*Spending ($ Millions)*	*Growth*	*Share*
1999	$ 3,437	—	29.5%	$7,165	—	61.5%
2000	4,544	32.2%	35.0	6,491	–9.4%	50.0
2001	4,858	6.9	34.0	7,430	14.5	52.0
2002	6,029	24.1	35.5	7,897	6.3	46.5
2003	7,807	29.5	42.7	7,405	–6.2	40.5
2004	10,014	28.3	45.5	8,209	10.9	37.3
Compound Annual Growth						
1999-2004		23.8			2.8	

Sources: Veronis Suhler Stevenson, PQ Media, Custom Publishing Council, McMurry

In-Store Media

Spending on in-store media grew 8.0 percent to $962.0 million in 2004, driven by growth in the burgeoning market for in-store television network advertising. In-store media also includes in-store radio networks, on-shelf promotional messages, on-shelf coupon dispensers and floor graphics.

In-store TV network advertising is being touted as the brand marketer's solution to dwindling audiences for traditional broadcast network advertising. In-store television networks target consumers while they are in the purchasing mode and receptive to advertising messages. Furthermore, customers cannot fast-forward through commercials on in-store TV networks the way they can at home. Premier Retail Networks (PRN), a leading in-store network, delivers programming to more than 5,000 stores nationwide, including Wal-Mart, Best Buy, Costco, Sears, Sam's Club and Circuit City. PRN continues to expand its network to more stores, fueling growth in the in-store media industry.

Growth for in-store television advertising is expected to continue to spur high-single-digit growth for in-store media in 2005. Albertson's announced in April 2005 that PRN will install 15-inch flat-panel LCD screens at checkout lanes in its stores and will provide programming and sell advertising related to health, home and family. Albertson's also retained SignStorey to install 42-inch plasma screens along the perimeter of its stores to provide programming and advertising. Wal-Mart, which has an in-store TV network in 2,620 stores reaching 84.1 million shoppers per week, is installing new plasma and LCD models in 2005, some at eye level.

In-store radio network advertising is also expected to drive growth in 2005. Mass Connections, a retail marketing services company, partnered with In-Store Broadcasting Network in early 2005 to launch a program called Audio Connection, which broadcasts consumer product information during in-store events. Mass Connections expects to hold more than 1 million events in 2005. The program demonstrates the measurability of in-store promotion. Mass Connections reported that sales increase as much as 200 percent in one week when Audio Connection is used. More than 13,000 retail stores began using Audio Connection in April 2005, including Kroger, Albertson's and Safeway.

Spending on in-store media is expected to grow 7.8 percent in 2005 to surpass the $1 billion mark. Spending will grow at a compound annual rate of 7.8 percent from 2004 to 2009, reaching $1.40 billion in 2009.

The Outlook for Consumer Promotion

Spending on consumer promotion is expected to increase 4.9 percent in 2005 to $33.20 billion, bolstered by spending on product sampling and in-store media. Compound annual growth will be 4.9 percent from 2004 to 2009, surpassing the 2.5 percent gain achieved

E-pubs			Tabloids			Total	
Spending ($ Millions)	*Growth*	*Share*	*Spending ($ Millions)*	*Growth*	*Share*	*Spending ($ Millions)*	*Growth*
$ 58	—	0.5%	$ 990	—	8.5%	$11,650	—
909	1,460.0%	7.0	1,039	4.9%	8.0	12,981	11.4%
1,429	57.2	10.0	572	−45.0	4.0	14,288	10.1
1,953	36.7	11.5	1,104	93.1	6.5	16,982	18.9
2,158	10.5	11.8	914	−17.2	5.0	18,284	7.7
2,685	24.5	12.2	1,100	20.4	5.0	22,009	20.4
	115.1			2.1			13.6

in the previous five-year period. Spending will reach $40.21 billion in 2009.

CUSTOM PUBLISHING

Spending on custom publishing increased 20.4 percent to $22.01 billion in 2004, driven by strong gains in spending on magazines for custom publishing projects produced for use within a single organization and the growing use of electronic publications. The figures reflect production and distribution costs, but exclude salaries for personnel. Marketers are shifting funding from traditional advertising vehicles into custom publishing because of the medium's highly targeted approach and its ability to establish ongoing relationships with target audiences.

Titles targeting external audiences accounted for 59.0 percent of publications produced in 2004, compared to 41.0 percent for titles aimed at internal audiences. External publications accounted for only 20.0 percent of titles produced in 1999. The figures indicate that companies have recognized the effectiveness of custom publications as marketing tools, as well as employee communication vehicles.

Among the leaders in the custom publishing field are McMurry, Penton Custom Publishing and Meredith Integrated Marketing. McMurry was selected in 2005 by financial services company USAA to publish *USAA Magazine*, with a circulation of 3.9 million. McMurry is implementing a redesign of the 56-page publication, which is published three times per year. Among Penton Custom Media's clients is Altair Engineering, which distributes a 30,000-circulation publication to upper-level managers and engineering executives.

On the consumer side, Meredith Integrated Marketing publishes several custom magazines for DaimlerChrysler aimed at owners of the car manufacturer's vehicles, including *Chrysler Magazine*, which has a circulation of 1.5 million and is published twice per year; *Jeep* with a circulation of 1.5 million, published twice per year; and *Dodge: The Magazine* with a circulation of 3 million, published twice per year. Meredith also publishes *Currents* for Carnival Cruise Lines (3 million circulation, three times per year), in addition to a number of other publications.

Custom publishing spending is expected to continue to grow at double-digit rates annually during the forecast period, due to an increase in the number of titles produced, page volume per issue and the transition from short newsletters to more in-depth and four-color layout magazines. Among the new custom publications produced in 2005 was the U.S. Postal Service's (USPS) new magazine, *Deliver*, designed to promote the use of direct mail to marketers. The publication is a 32-page bimonthly magazine mailed to a targeted audience of 350,000 CEOs, corporate marketing executives and marketing agencies. The magazine is published for the USPS by Campbell-Ewald Publishing.

Advertising, Specialty Media & Marketing Services

Branded Entertainment Spending

($ MILLIONS)

Year	Event Sponsorship	Promotional Licensing	Product Placement*	Total
1999	$ 7,631	$5,502	$1,627	$14,760
2000	8,700	5,777	1,880	16,357
2001	9,301	5,800	1,985	17,086
2002	9,650	5,974	2,203	17,827
2003	10,251	6,093	2,649	18,993
2004	11,117	6,154	3,458	20,729
2005	12,097	6,388	4,245	22,730
2006	13,053	6,560	4,961	24,574
2007	14,032	6,698	5,644	26,374
2008	15,211	6,959	6,327	28,497
2009	16,534	7,251	6,939	30,724

Sources: Veronis Suhler Stevenson, PQ Media, *Promo Magazine*, *IEG Sponsorship Report*
*These data were licensed exclusively to Veronis Suhler Stevenson from PQ Media's *Product Placement Spending in Media 2005*.

Growth of Branded Entertainment Spending

Year	Event Sponsorship	Promotional Licensing	Product Placement*	Total
2000	14.0%	5.0%	15.6%	10.8%
2001	6.9	0.4	5.6	4.5
2002	3.8	3.0	11.0	4.3
2003	6.2	2.0	20.2	6.5
2004	8.4	1.0	30.5	9.1
2005	8.8	3.8	22.8	9.7
2006	7.9	2.7	16.9	8.1
2007	7.5	2.1	13.8	7.3
2008	8.4	3.9	12.1	8.0
2009	8.7	4.2	9.7	7.8
Compound Annual Growth				
1999-2004	7.8	2.3	16.3	7.0
2004-2009	8.3	3.3	14.9	8.2

Sources: Veronis Suhler Stevenson, PQ Media, *Promo Magazine*, *IEG Sponsorship Report*
*These data were licensed exclusively to Veronis Suhler Stevenson from PQ Media's *Product Placement Spending in Media 2005*.

Custom publishing spending is expected to increase 11.9 percent to $24.63 billion in 2005, and grow at a compound annual rate of 12.1 percent from 2004 to 2009, hitting $38.88 billion in 2009.

Branded Entertainment

Branded entertainment includes event sponsorship, promotional licensing and product placement. Due to increased audience fragmentation, the migration to consumer-controlled media through ad-skipping technologies, and complaints about advertising clutter, marketers are seeking alternative methods to reach their target audiences in unique ways. Branded entertainment is currently one of the major trends in meeting these criteria, particularly using media that engage and entertain the 18- to 34-year-old market. As a result, spending on branded entertainment increased 9.1 percent in 2004 to $20.73 billion, and grew at a compound annual rate of 7.0 percent from 1999 to 2004.

Event sponsorship is the largest of the three subsegments of branded entertainment with expenditures of $11.12 billion in 2004, and includes expanding brand awareness through strategic placements mainly at sporting and entertainment venues, such as NASCAR races and concerts. Promotional licensing is the second-largest subsegment of branded entertainment, generating $6.15 billion in 2004. Promotional licensing includes brand logo placement on purchased products like T-shirts or promotional giveaways, such as children's toys at fast food restaurants. Product placement is the smallest, but fastest-growing sector of branded entertainment, up 30.5 percent in 2004 to $3.46 billion, according to exclusive research from PQ Media. It entails the seamless integration of products into television programs, films and other media, such as newspapers, magazines, videogames and the Internet.

EVENT SPONSORSHIP

Spending on event sponsorship increased 8.4 percent to $11.12 billion in 2004, bolstered by sporting events including the Olympics. Sports is expected to remain the largest category in 2005, with projected spending of $8.39 billion, up 9.4 percent, driven by

Top 5 Sponsors*

Company	*2003 Spending ($ Millions)*	*2004 Spending ($ Millions)*	*Percent Change*
PepsiCo	$ 253	$ 268	5.7%
Anheuser-Busch	243	263	8.0
General Motors	188	208	10.4
Coca-Cola	183	203	10.7
Nike	163	188	15.0
Top 5 Total	1,030	1,128	9.5

Sources: Veronis Suhler Stevenson, PQ Media, *IEG Sponsorship Report*

*Figures estimated based on spending ranges provided by IEG.

Event Sponsorship Spending, by Category

Category	*2004 Spending ($ Millions)*	*2005 Spending ($ Millions)*	*Percent Change*
Sports	$ 7,670	$ 8,391	9.4%
Entertainment, Tours & Attractions	1,060	1,153	8.8
Causes	988	1,077	9.0
Arts	610	630	3.3
Festivals, Fairs, Events	482	507	5.2
Associations	307	339	10.4
Total	11,117	12,097	8.8

Sources: Veronis Suhler Stevenson, PQ Media, *IEG Sponsorship Report*

sponsorship tied to NASCAR, the NFL and the NBA. The associations segment was broken out from the festivals, fairs and events category in 2004 because sponsors are now signing year-round deals with trade groups and professional organizations instead of just sponsoring annual conventions. The associations category is expected to post the strongest growth in 2005, at 10.4 percent to $339.0 million. Sponsorship spending on music tours, concert series and venues is expected to increase 8.5 percent in 2005, following a 21.0 percent increase in 2004, due in part to multicultural marketing efforts, which have prompted sponsors to support Latino acts.

PepsiCo remained the biggest spender on sponsorship in 2004, boosting spending 5.7 percent to about $268 million. Anheuser-Busch ranked second with about $263 million in spending, up 8.0 percent, and General Motors ranked third with about $208 million, up 10.4 percent.

Spending on sponsorship is expected to continue to increase in 2005, as established and emerging categories generate more spending, and existing and new sponsors expand their budgets. According to one survey in 2005, about 65 percent of corporate marketers reported their ROI for sponsorship deals has increased over the past few years, compared to about 47 percent in the 2004 survey.

Videogame system manufacturers, which are already active in the sponsorship arena, are expected to expand their spending in 2005 to support new product launches. Nintendo of America, which introduced the Nintendo DS handheld system in late 2004, signed on with the Taste of Chaos international tour, a multiband concert event. Meanwhile, Sony Computer Entertainment America agreed to sponsor the Dew Action Sports Tour in June 2005 to promote its PlayStation Portable to action sports enthusiasts. While videogame manufacturers are reaching their youth audience through sponsorship, mainstream corporations are also attempting to target young people using this method. For example, State Farm Insurance signed a two-year deal in 2004 with the U.S. Ski & Snowboard Association, and AFLAC signed a deal with Paramount Pictures' *Lemony Snicket's A Series of Unfortunate Events*.

Overall, spending on sponsorship is expected to increase 8.8 percent to $12.10 billion in 2005, and grow at an accelerated compound annual rate of 8.3 percent from 2004 to 2009, compared with the previous five-year period's expansion pace.

Promotional Licensing

Tight retail space, due in part to consolidation, dampened spending on licensing in 2004. Expenditures on licensing increased 1.0 percent to $6.15 billion in 2004. Retailers are also growing more selective about the merchandise they choose to stock, confining themselves to safe and familiar products they know will sell. For example, merchandise based on *The Lord of the Rings* film series generated more than $1 billion in sales worldwide by the middle of 2004.

The weak retail environment precipitated a 1.3 percent decline in sales of licensed products to $70.5 billion. Sales in the two largest categories, sports and trademarks/brands, were off by about 1 percent each. Sales of sports merchandise were hampered by the declining popularity of retro jerseys and the NHL player lockout. However, sales in the sports category were positively impacted by football and baseball merchandise, particularly after the Red Sox won the World Series in 2004. Sales in the licensed corporate trademark and brand segment were dampened by limited available space on retail shelves and retailers' efforts to move their private labels. The third-largest category, entertainment/character, was also off by about 1.0 percent, despite strong sales for Nickelodeon's *Dora The Explorer* and *SpongeBob SquarePants*. Retail sales of licensed products received a boost from musical entertainers in 2004, as a number of stars announced apparel and fragrance deals, driving a 25 percent gain in retail sales of music-related licensed products, the highest growth rate among the top 10 categories of licensed properties. The movie *Spider-Man 2* generated the most film-related sales.

The rate of spending growth on promotional licensing is expected to improve in 2005, due to the expanded opportunities in movie licensing. *Star Wars: Episode III: Revenge of the Sith,* and *Batman Begins* are expected to help rejuvenate spending. Prior to *Revenge of the Sith*'s release, Hasbro introduced a new line of Star Wars toys based on the film at a week-long series of events at selected retailers. The campaign kicked off with "Midnight Madness" events held on April 2 at 12:01 a.m. One participating retailer, Wal-Mart, presented interactive toy and game demonstrations and gave away *Star Wars*-related prizes. Products in Hasbro's *Revenge of the Sith* line included the Darth Vader Voice Changer, lightsabers, action figures, a Trivial Pursuit DVD game, and a trading card game.

Spending on licensing is expected to increase 3.8 percent to $6.39 billion in 2005, and grow at a compound annual rate of 3.3 percent in the forecast period to $7.25 billion in 2009.

Product Placement

While the use of product placement is not new, its role in the marketing mix has increased significantly in recent years, prompting its inclusion in this year's *Forecast.* The emergence of ad-skipping technology, audience fragmentation and increased use of alternative marketing strategies has fueled growth in product placement spending. Spending on product placement in all nine media used for this purpose increased 30.5 percent to $3.46 billion in 2004, and grew at a compound annual rate of 16.3 percent from 1999 to 2004, according to data licensed exclusively to Veronis Suhler Stevenson from PQ Media's *Product Placement Spending in Media 2005.*

While product placement spending is growing in both film and television, spending on television is climbing more rapidly and surpassed film for the first time in 2004. Until recently, film has been the primary recipient of product placement spending, a practice dating back more than 100 years to when movies were first produced. However, the emergence of reality programming has spurred growth in product placement spending on television to levels not seen since advertisers produced programs in the 1950s, a practice that was halted by the quiz show scandals late in that decade. Product placement spending on television has been rising

Shares of Product Placement Spending, By Arrangement, 2004

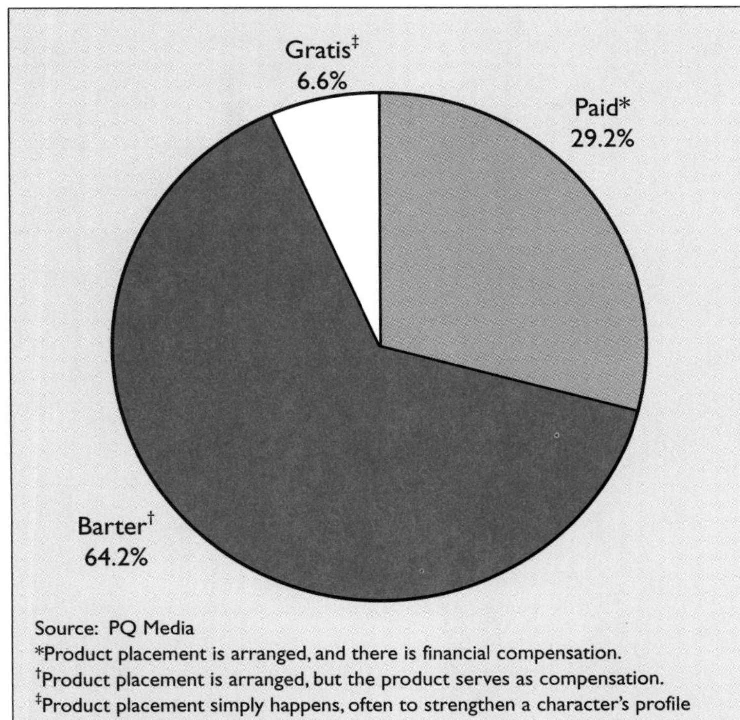

Source: PQ Media
*Product placement is arranged, and there is financial compensation.
†Product placement is arranged, but the product serves as compensation.
‡Product placement simply happens, often to strengthen a character's profile or add richness to the plot.

Product Placement Spending, by Medium*

($ MILLIONS)

Year	Television†	Film‡	Other Media§	Total
1999	$ 709	$ 730	$187	$1,627
2000	833	843	204	1,880
2001	883	886	216	1,985
2002	1,002	964	237	2,203
2003	1,283	1,094	272	2,649
2004	1,878	1,254	326	3,458
2005	2,442	1,418	385	4,245
2006	2,942	1,576	443	4,961
2007	3,402	1,742	500	5,644
2008	3,856	1,919	552	6,327
2009	4,244	2,096	599	6,939

Source: PQ Media

*These data were licensed to Veronis Suhler Stevenson from PQ Media's *Product Placement Spending in Media 2005.*

†Includes network, local, syndication and cable.

‡Includes theatrical releases and home video.

§Includes newspapers, magazines, videogames, consumer Internet, recorded music, consumer books and radio.

steadily since the 1990s, as marketers increasingly seek creative ways to reach the elusive 18- to 34-year-old market, which is spending more time with new media like the Internet and videogames. Coinciding with these trends, ad-skipping technology such as digital video recorders was launched and cable TV continued to grab share from broadcast TV. Spending on product placement in television, including cable, grew at a compound annual rate of 21.5 percent from 1999 to 2004, according to PQ Media. Product placement spending surged in 2004, increasing 46.4 percent to $1.88 billion. Broadcast television, prime-time and local, accounts for the overwhelming majority of product placement spending because network-affiliated programs receive higher ratings than most individual cable shows. Broadcast TV has lost share of product placement spending to cable television in recent years due to the proliferation of cable networks, many of which require producers to have product placement arrangements in place before a program is added to their schedules.

Paid product placement is becoming more prevalent than in the past. While paid arrangements accounted for only 21.5 percent of product placement spending in 1999, such arrangements represented 29.2 percent of total spending in 2004. The increase in paid placements has been the result of more products being integrated into television and film plot lines. For example, advertisers are paying premium prices to feature their brands on *The Apprentice* as contestants develop marketing strategies for the products.

Scripted shows, including comedies and dramas, accounted for the highest product placement spending on television in 2004. Scripted dramas have been the most aggressive in pursuing product placement deals because they can offset their costs through barter arrangements with products used on the show. Spending on reality and game shows is growing the fastest. PQ Media fore-

Growth of Product Placement Spending, by Medium*

Year	*Television*†	*Film*‡	*Other Media*§	*Total*
2000	17.5%	15.4%	8.9%	15.6%
2001	6.0	5.1	5.7	5.6
2002	13.5	8.7	10.2	11.0
2003	28.0	13.6	14.4	20.2
2004	46.4	14.6	19.9	30.5
2005	30.0	13.1	18.1	22.8
2006	20.5	11.1	15.2	16.9
2007	15.7	10.6	12.7	13.8
2008	13.3	10.1	10.5	12.1
2009	10.1	9.3	8.4	9.7
Compound Annual Growth				
1999-2004	21.5	11.4	11.7	16.3
2004-2009	17.7	10.8	12.9	14.9

Source: PQ Media

*These data were licensed to Veronis Suhler Stevenson from PQ Media's *Product Placement Spending in Media 2005*.

†Includes network, local, syndication and cable.

‡Includes theatrical releases and home video.

§Includes newspapers, magazines, videogames, consumer Internet, recorded music, consumer books and radio.

casts that broadcast television product placement spending will grow at a compound annual rate of 17.7 percent from 2004 to 2009, due to rising costs for scripted dramas and continued growth of spending on reality shows. Spending is expected to reach $4.24 billion in 2009.

Although film's share of overall product placement spending has declined over the past five years, it remains strong because it allows marketers to reach the youth market, which makes up half of movie audiences, in a captive space. Spending increased 14.6 percent to $1.25 billion in 2004. Product placement spending in other media, such as videogames and the Internet, is rising faster than in films because of the appeal of the former to younger audiences. Spending increased 19.9 percent to $326.0 million in 2004.

Spending on product placement is expected to increase 22.8 percent in 2005 and continue to expand in the double digits through most of the forecast period. Compound annual growth will be 14.9 percent, with spending reaching $6.94 billion in 2009, according to PQ Media.

The Outlook for Branded Entertainment

Spending on branded entertainment is expected to increase 9.7 percent to $22.73 billion in 2005, driven by double-digit growth in product placement spending, as well as strong gains in sponsorship expenditures. Compound annual growth will be 8.2 percent from 2004 to 2009, fueled by the product placement and sponsorship segments. Spending will reach $30.72 billion in 2009.

PUBLIC RELATIONS

The public relations segment has also been positively impacted by the trend toward alternative marketing methods, which fueled a 12.0 percent increase in spending to $3.41 billion in 2004. The growth rate represented a substantial improvement over the market's

Advertising, Specialty Media & Marketing Services

Public Relations Spending, by Industry Sector, Share and Growth

	1999	*2000*		*2001*		*2002*		*2003*		*2004*	
Industry Sector	*Share*	*Growth*	*Share*	*Growth*	*Share*	*Growth*	*Share*	*Growth*	*Share*	*Growth*	*Share*
Technology	37.2%	46.0%	40.5%	–20.1%	34.1%	–10.1%	30.4%	–1.2%	29.1%	5.8%	27.4%
Consumer & Retail	21.5	21.7	19.5	–8.4	20.9	10.5	23.0	6.6	23.7	20.7	25.5
Healthcare	15.7	29.6	15.1	8.2	18.8	8.4	20.3	8.8	21.3	19.6	22.7
Industrial	7.9	35.6	8.0	1.2	9.0	–4.2	8.5	0.5	8.3	3.7	7.7
Government & Nonprofit	7.2	35.7	7.2	1.0	7.3	8.3	7.9	3.6	7.9	7.4	7.6
Financial Products & Services	6.3	36.7	6.4	–16.8	6.2	6.2	6.5	–0.8	6.2	4.1	5.8
Professional Services	4.2	5.0	3.3	1.8	3.7	–8.0	3.4	4.8	3.4	11.2	3.4

Sources: Veronis Suhler Stevenson, PQ Media, Council of Public Relations Firms

Public Relations Spending and Growth

Year	*Revenues ($ Millions)*	*Growth*
1999	$2,345	—
2000	3,118	33.0%
2001	2,900	–7.0
2002	2,927	0.9
2003	3,045	4.0
2004	3,410	12.0
2005	3,754	10.1
2006	4,107	9.4
2007	4,428	7.8
2008	4,790	8.2
2009	5,212	8.8
Compound Annual Growth		
1999-2004		7.8
2004-2009		8.9

Sources: Veronis Suhler Stevenson, PQ Media, Council of Public Relations Firms, *Advertising Age*, *O'Dwyer's Directory of Public Relations Firms*

performance during the previous three years. Spending increased a modest 4.0 percent in 2003, after a disappointing 0.9 percent gain in 2002 and a 7.0 percent slide in 2001. The public relations segment has begun to see the benefits of consolidation that led to full-service advertising and marketing agencies that offer a multitude of strategic services along with media buying, including public relations.

Spending on public relations by the consumer and retail industry, as well as the healthcare industry, fueled growth in 2004. The consumer and retail category posted the strongest growth rate, up 20.7 percent, followed by healthcare, up 19.6 percent. The technology category, which experienced an increase in spending for the first time since 2000, continued to account for the largest share of spending at 27.4 percent.

Spending is expected to increase 10.1 percent to $3.75 billion in 2005, as corporations continue to invest in alternative marketing tactics. Public relations is expected to play a larger role in corporate marketing efforts based on a survey of senior marketers who stated that public relations was most effective in raising awareness, and that it is most valuable in supporting product marketing and product launches. Public relations firms are becoming more proactive in selling to organizations multiple services from brand loyalty campaigns to crisis management. Spending is expected to grow at a compound annual rate of 8.9 percent from 2004 to 2009, surpassing the 7.8 percent growth rate achieved in the prior five-year interval. Spending will reach $5.21 billion in 2009.

PROMOTIONAL SPENDING IN OTHER MEDIA

Promotional spending in other media includes ITV promotion and advertising; wireless content promotion and advertising; and trade show fees, advertising and sponsorship. Spending grew a combined 10.3 percent to $2.33 billion in 2004, driven by the newer segments of ITV and wireless content advertising and promotion. Expanding use of ITV and wireless devices as advertising vehicles will continue to fuel growth in the forecast period. Spending is expected to increase 12.8 percent to $2.63 billion in 2005, and grow at a compound annual rate of 12.5 percent from 2004 to 2009.

Spending on ITV advertising and promotion increased 19.9 percent to $193.0 million in 2004, driven by renewed interest by advertisers to find interactive methods of generating sales, as well as advances in the enabling technology that brought down price points to use this medium. Spending is expected to grow 31.3 percent to $253.0 million in 2005 and advance at a compound annual rate of 30.6 percent in the forecast period to $759.0 million in 2009.

Surging consumption of new wireless computing and communication technologies is prompting marketers to evaluate the advertising opportunities these new devices offer. Advertisers are eager to approach the market for wireless devices because the technology allows them to reach consumers beyond the confines of the television or movie screen, especially the 18- to 34-year-old market that has embraced this technology. The variety of applications that these devices can hold has opened a window for marketers to send direct and concise messages to consumers. Wireless advertising and promotion spending grew 143.0 percent to $105.0 million in 2004 and is expected to reach $201.0 million in 2005.

Meanwhile, spending on trade show fees, sponsorship and advertising increased 6.5 percent to $2.04 billion in 2004, driven by growth in professional attendance and the ROI measurements that are being developed to help justify costs of exhibiting and attending trade shows. The healthcare category was largely responsible for the 2.7 percent increase in attendance to 40.86 million in 2004. The demand for new technologies, equipment and pharmaceuticals, along with increased specialization, has led several healthcare-related associations to develop new trade shows that focus more on education than on selling. Spending on fees, sponsorship and advertising is expected to increase 7.0 percent to $2.18 billion in 2005.

The Outlook For Specialty Media And Marketing Services

Strong growth in custom publishing, branded entertainment and public relations spending will fuel overall gains in specialty media and marketing services spending in 2005 as it did in 2004. Total market spending is expected to accelerate in 2005, growing 7.0 percent to $275.11 billion. Spending is expected to grow at a faster clip in all segments, except for custom publishing and public relations, which experienced the strongest growth in 2004. However, these segments will continue to grow at double-digit rates. Promotional spending in other media is expected to post the strongest growth rate in 2005, driven by the burgeoning ITV and wireless advertising markets.

Direct marketing spending will rise 6.5 percent to $144.17 billion in 2005 as a result of continued double-digit growth in interactive campaigns, as well as strong growth in catalog and direct mail spending. As marketers continue to seek alternative methods to reach their target audiences, spending on direct marketing is forecast to grow at a compound annual rate of 6.0 percent from 2004 to 2009, reaching $180.98 billion.

Driven by gains in employee incentives and promotional products, spending on business-to-business promotion is expected to grow 5.6 percent to $44.0 billion in 2005. As businesses continue to promote client and employee loyalty, spending is expected to rise at a compound annual rate of 5.7 percent from 2004 to 2009, hitting $54.96 billion in 2009. Meanwhile, spending on consumer promotion is expected to increase 4.9 percent in 2005 to $33.20 billion, bolstered by spending on product sampling and in-store media. Compound annual growth will be 4.9 percent from 2004 to 2009, surpassing the 2.5 percent gain achieved in the previous five-year period. Spending will reach $40.21 billion in 2009.

Marketers will continue to turn to custom publishing in 2005 and during the forecast period as an efficient alternative method to reach niche audiences. Custom publishing spending is expected to increase 11.9 percent to $24.63 billion in 2005, and grow at a compound annual rate of 12.1 percent from 2004 to 2009, hitting $38.88 billion in 2009.

Fueled by double-digit gains in product placement, spending on branded entertainment will climb a healthy 9.7 percent to $22.73 billion in 2005. In addition to product placement, marketers will continue using event sponsorship as an effective means to reach their target audiences, leading to a compound annual growth of branded entertainment of 8.2 percent from 2004 to 2009, reaching $30.72 billion in 2009.

Double-digit advances in advertising and promotion spending on wireless content and ITV will push growth in promotional spending in other media in 2005, up 12.8 percent to $2.63 billion. Promotion in other media will generate a compound annual growth rate of 12.5 percent during the 2004-2009 period, climbing to $4.20 billion as advertisers seek out alternative marketing platforms aimed at the 18- to 34-year-old market during the forecast period, as well as companies using trade show fees, sponsorship and advertising to reach institutional end users.

Total spending on specialty media and marketing services will grow at a compound annual rate of 6.7 percent in the 2004 to 2009 period, 1.8 percentage points faster than compound annual growth in the 1999 to 2004 period. Specialty media and marketing services spending will climb to $355.15 billion by 2009. Promotional spending in other media will post the strongest compound annual growth, followed by custom publishing, public relations and branded entertainment.

FORECAST ASSUMPTIONS

- The growing use of niche database marketing, which allows marketers to target specific geographic and demographic segments, will fuel direct marketing spending in the forecast period. Telemarketing and direct marketing are benefiting from the trend toward measuring the effectiveness of marketing campaigns.
- The growing prominence of luxury brands in the product placement arena is fueling spending growth. Due to the tight job market, spending on employee incentives, including travel and merchandise, will increase at a steady pace during the forecast period.
- In the market for consumer promotion, use of the retail environment as a marketing medium will gain momentum in the forecast period and fuel strong growth in the in-store media segment, particularly for in-store radio and television networks. Spending on product sampling events, both in and out of the retail store, will climb because of the tactic's proven ability to influence sales.
- Marketers are boosting spending on custom publishing because of the medium's highly targeted approach and its ability to establish an ongoing relationship with the audience. The number of publications produced and the pages per issue will continue to increase, as will production quality, including greater use of four-color printing. Small companies will help drive growth since they produce more custom publications and carry more pages per issue than do large companies.
- The growing popularity of ad-skipping technology will drive growth in product placement spending, particularly in television shows that appeal to young audiences. Growth in spending on other branded entertainment vehicles, including event sponsorships and promotional licensing, will also stem from marketing efforts aimed at the 18- to 34-year-old demographic.
- The public relations segment will benefit from the general trend toward alternative marketing, as well as the trend toward full-service advertising and marketing programs. Public relations firms are becoming more proactive in selling to organizations multiple services from brand loyalty campaigns to crisis management.

FUND III INVESTMENTS: User-Friendly Add-ons and Transactions

VS&A Communications Partners III, L.P.
an affiliate of Veronis Suhler Stevenson Partners LLC

has acquired a majority interest in

The User-Friendly Phone Book

an independent yellow pages company
with operations in Louisiana, Texas, Kentucky and Indiana

We acted as financial advisor to and as the exclusive representative of VS&A Communications Partners III, L.P.

October 2003

The User-Friendly Phone Book

a portfolio company of
VS&A Communications Partners III, L.P.

has acquired

the English-language version of the
Blue Book Telephone Directory

from

Cobalt Publishing, LLC

We initiated the transaction and acted as exclusive financial advisor to User-Friendly Phone Book, LLC.

May 2004

The User-Friendly Phone Book

a portfolio company of
VS&A Communications Partners III, L.P.

has acquired the assets of

Rio Grande Valley Publishing, Inc.
publisher of the "Fiesta Pages" directories

We initiated the transaction and acted as exclusive financial advisor to User-Friendly Phone Book, LLC.

June 2004

The User-Friendly Phone Book

a portfolio company of
VS&A Communications Partners III, L.P.

has acquired the assets of

Three directories covering Canton, Youngstown and areas in Northeast Ohio

from

We initiated the transaction and acted as exclusive financial advisor to User-Friendly Phone Book, LLC.

December 2004

The User-Friendly Phone Book

a portfolio company of
VS&A Communications Partners III, L.P.

has acquired the assets of

Champion Directories

We initiated the transaction and acted as exclusive financial advisor to User-Friendly Phone Book, LLC.

June 2005

The User-Friendly Phone Book

a portfolio company of
VS&A Communications Partners III, L.P.

has acquired the assets of

Shaw Publications

and

Diamond Directories

We initiated the transaction and acted as exclusive financial advisor to User-Friendly Phone Book, LLC.

June 2005

Private Equity Capital / Mezzanine Capital / Industry Research and Forecasts

Veronis Suhler Stevenson
MEDIA • COMMUNICATIONS • INFORMATION

350 Park Avenue, New York, NY 10022
212-935-4990 212-381-8168 fax
www.vss.com

Activities requiring securities industry registration will be performed by Veronis Suhler Stevenson Partners LLC wholly-owned broker-dealer affiliate, Veronis Suhler Stevenson LLC. Veronis Suhler Stevenson LLC is a member of NASD and SIPC.

The User-Friendly Phone Book

Business Overview

User-Friendly Phone Book, LLC ("User-Friendly") is a leading independent yellow pages company with directories in Louisiana, California, Ohio, Texas, Kentucky, Oklahoma and Indiana. User-Friendly was started in 1999 by Cameron Communications, a family-owned rural local exchange carrier ("RLEC") based in Sulphur, Louisiana. User-Friendly initially published an independent/competitive yellow page directory in two Louisiana markets and one market in southeast Texas. The current management team was installed in late 1999 to improve operations and expand the yellow page footprint. The management team had successfully grown revenue from $690,000 in 1999 to $10.8 million in 2003, at the time of VSS's acquisition, through the growth of existing publications as well as the successful launch of five new directories. Today we publish 29 directories and will make over $30 million in revenue in 2005.

User-Friendly is headquartered in Houston, Texas and has approximately 50 employees.

Background

In November 2003, VSS's Fund III acquired User-Friendly for approximately $18.4 million including fees and expenses. The transaction was structured as a stock and asset purchase. Fund III funded approximately $10.9 million. Management rolled over approximately $5.6 million in equity and $1.8 million of a seller note. Subsequent transactions have required an additional Fund III capital commitment of $7.9 million increasing Fund III's ownership to 74.4%.

Strategy & Rationale

- Proven track record taking directory usage from incumbent.
- Existing growth opportunities for current products, as well as new product launches and acquisitions.
- Opportunity to leverage company to provide debt financed add-on acquisitions.
- Create contiguous directories geographically clustered around core markets.

Add-on Acquisition Activities

- May 2004—User-Friendly acquired the English-language version of the **Blue Book Telephone Directory** for approximately $2.0 million. The Blue Book Telephone Directory is based outside of Louisville in Shelby County, Kentucky. Approximately 126,000 copies of the yellow pages directory are distributed annually.
- June 2004—User-Friendly acquired the assets of **Rio Grande Valley Publishing LLP**, a yellow page publisher in Texas, for approximately $6.2 million. Rio Grande publishes two directories serving Hidalgo and Cameron counties with approximately 275,000 in circulation.
- May 2005—Acquired 11 directories in Northeast Ohio through three separate transactions.
- July 2005—Acquired two directories in Kentucky with approximately 145,000 in circulation.
- Launched 4 directories in 2005 and planned an additional 3 for 2006.

Private Equity Capital / Mezzanine Capital / Industry Research and Forecasts

Veronis Suhler Stevenson
MEDIA • COMMUNICATIONS • INFORMATION

350 Park Avenue, New York, NY 10022
212-935-4990 212-381-8168 fax
www.vss.com

End-User Spending On Communications

3

End-User Spending On Communications

End-User Spending and Nominal GDP Growth, 2000-2009

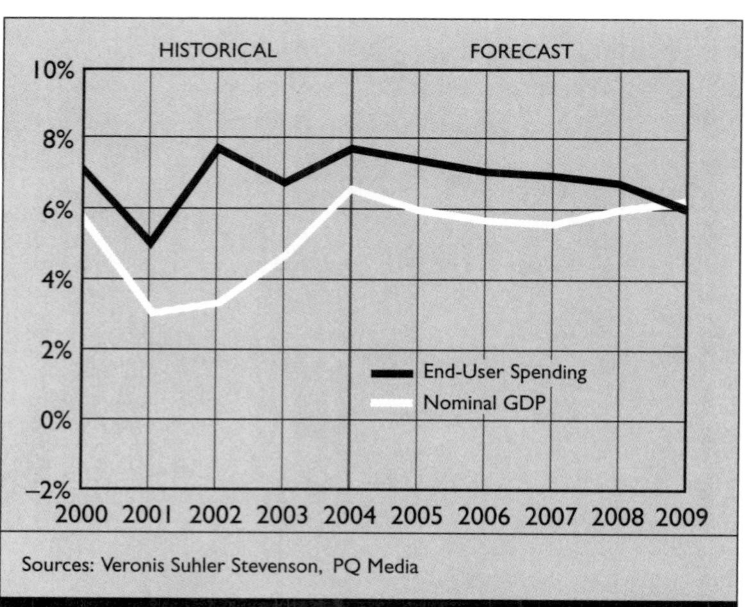

Sources: Veronis Suhler Stevenson, PQ Media

Summary

The end-user media sector is being impacted by many of the same trends transforming the advertising, specialty media and marketing services sector, spurred by technology innovation, the development of multimedia solutions, increased demand for customization and a tighter focus on return on investment (ROI). Consumer and institutional end users continue their migration to on-demand technology ranging from video-on-demand (VOD) and digital video recorders (DVRs) in the consumer market to integrated software suites and e-media in the institutional market. And with the proliferation of new media technologies, consumers and institutional end users are seeking improved metrics to justify their expenditures.

End-user spending continued climbing during the first half of 2005, although at a decelerating rate, after posting another strong year in 2004, fueled by both institutions and consumers increasing expenditures on major end-user media such as professional and business information services and consumer Internet. Total end-user spending on communications is expected to increase 7.1 percent to $382.81 billion for full-year 2005, slightly lower than the 7.4 percent growth in 2004, driven by strong year-over-year growth in both the consumer and institutional sectors. End-user spending on communications grew at a compound annual rate of 6.6 percent from 1999 to 2004, outperforming nominal GDP in every year of the period.

For the first time since the recession, institutional end-user spending on communications outperformed consumer end-user spending in 2004, growing 8.8 percent in 2004 compared with an increase of 6.2 percent for consumer end-user spending. The growth in institutional end-user spending was fueled by solid gains in professional and business information services, television programming, and outsourced training in the educational and training media segment, in addition to trade show exhibit space in the business-to-business media segment. Continued healthy spending on institutional information and services is expected in 2005,

Total End-User Spending On Communications

($ MILLIONS)

Year	Consumer End-User Spending	Institutional End-User Spending	Total End-User Spending
1999	$129,153	$130,436	$259,589
2000	135,902	141,383	277,285
2001	147,671	143,332	291,003
2002	163,132	149,356	312,488
2003	175,479	157,306	332,785
2004	186,301	171,082	357,383
2005	199,336	183,473	382,809
2006	212,697	196,259	408,956
2007	226,676	209,706	436,382
2008	240,204	224,656	464,860
2009	252,801	239,820	492,621

Sources: Veronis Suhler Stevenson, PQ Media, Adams Media Research, Alexander & Associates, Audit Bureau of Circulations, Book Industry Study Group, Business 2.0, comScore Networks, Digital Entertainment Group, DirecTV, DSL Forum, EchoStar, *Editor & Publisher*, Entertainment Software Association, Federal Communications Commission, In Demand, Insight Research, In-Stat/MDR, Jupiter Media Metrix, Kagan Research, Leichtman Research Group, Lexis/Nexis, LodgeNet, Magazine Publishers of America, Motion Picture Association of America, National Cable & Telecommunications Association, Newspaper Association of America, NPDFunworld, Online Publishers Association, Recording Industry Association of America, Rentrak, ReplayTV, Sirius Satellite Radio, SRDS, Smith Travel Research, Telecommunications Industry Association, TiVo, U.S. Census Bureau, *Video Business*, Video Software Dealers Association, XM Satellite Radio, Yankee Group

Growth of Total End-User Spending on Communications

Year	Consumer End-User Spending	Institutional End-User Spending	Total End-User Spending
2000	5.2%	8.4%	6.8%
2001	8.7	1.4	4.9
2002	10.5	4.2	7.4
2003	7.6	5.3	6.5
2004	6.2	8.8	7.4
2005	7.0	7.2	7.1
2006	6.7	7.0	6.8
2007	6.6	6.9	6.7
2008	6.0	7.1	6.5
2009	5.2	6.7	6.0
Compound Annual Growth			
1999-2004	7.6	5.6	6.6
2004-2009	6.3	7.0	6.6

Sources: Veronis Suhler Stevenson, PQ Media, Adams Media Research, Alexander & Associates, Audit Bureau of Circulations, Book Industry Study Group, Business 2.0, comScore Networks, Digital Entertainment Group, DIRECTV, DSL Forum, EchoStar, *Editor & Publisher*, Entertainment Software Association, Federal Communications Commission, In Demand, Insight Research, In-Stat/MDR, Jupiter Media Metrix, Kagan Research, Leichtman Research Group, Lexis/Nexis, LodgeNet, Magazine Publishers of America, Motion Picture Association of America, National Cable & Telecommunications Association, Newspaper Association of America, NPDFunworld, Online Publishers Association, Recording Industry Association of America, Rentrak, ReplayTV, Sirius Satellite Radio, SRDS, Smith Travel Research, Telecommunications Industry Association, TiVo, U.S. Census Bureau, *Video Business*, Video Software Dealers Association, XM Satellite Radio, Yankee Group

Growth of U.S. Consumer And Institutional End-User Spending

	Consumer End-User Spending	Institutional End-User Spending	Total End-User Spending
2004 Expenditures ($ Millions)	$186,301	$171,082	$357,383
1999-2004 Compound Annual Growth %	7.6%	5.6%	6.6%
2004-2009 Projected Compound Annual Growth %	6.3%	7.0%	6.6%
2009 Projected Expenditures ($ Millions)	$252,801	$239,820	$492,621

Sources: Veronis Suhler Stevenson, PQ Media

End-User Spending On Communications

Shares of Total End-User Spending on Communications

Year	*Consumer End-User Spending*	*Institutional End-User Spending*
1999	49.8%	50.2%
2000	49.0	51.0
2001	50.7	49.3
2002	52.2	47.8
2003	52.7	47.3
2004	52.1	47.9
2005	52.1	47.9
2006	52.0	48.0
2007	51.9	48.1
2008	51.7	48.3
2009	51.3	48.7

Sources: Veronis Suhler Stevenson, PQ Media, Adams Media Research, Alexander & Associates, Audit Bureau of Circulations, Book Industry Study Group, Business 2.0, comScore Networks, Digital Entertainment Group, DIRECTV, DSL Forum, EchoStar, *Editor & Publisher*, Entertainment Software Association, Federal Communications Commission, In Demand, nsight Research, In-Stat/MDR, Jupiter Media Metrix, Kagan Research, Leichtman Research Group, Lexis/Nexis, LodgeNet, Magazine Publishers of America, Motion Picture Association of America, National Cable & Telecommunications Association, Newspaper Association of America, NPDFunworld, Online Publishers Association, Recording Industry Association of America, Rentrak, ReplayTV, Sirius Satellite Radio, SRDS, Smith Travel Research, Telecommunications Industry Association, TiVo, U.S. Census Bureau, *Video Business*, Video Software Dealers Association, XM Satellite Radio, Yankee Group

2004 Communications Industry Forecast Compared With Actual Growth

Category	*2004 Forecasted Growth**	*Actual 2004 Growth†*
Consumer	7.3%	6.2%
Institutional	5.7	8.8
Total	6.5	7.4

*Veronis Suhler Stevenson 2004 Communications Industry Forecast & Report
†Veronis Suhler Stevenson, PQ Media

though at a slightly decelerated rate of 7.2 percent to $183.47 billion. The professional and business information services market will record the highest growth at 8.1 percent, followed by 7.2 percent growth in educational and training media and 6.0 percent growth in television programming. The deceleration in growth of overall spending is primarily attributable to a slowdown in business information services spending, although it will still be solid in the mid-single digits.

Also in the institutional sector, a common theme in all four segments is that the escalating demand for ROI measurement is being met through the creative use of technology. Nowhere in the media industry is this more apparent than in the professional and business information services (PBIS) segment, where publishers were a decade ahead of the rest of the communications industry in developing new technology solutions for end users in the form of melded multimedia workflow tools. And each year, the PBIS segment has improved on its slate of workflow solutions by creating more advanced value-added products and services that combine enhanced functionality with flexible delivery, progressive analytics and actionable ROI measurement instruments. In the meantime, educational and training media providers have used technology advances to create original online courseware and learning environments designed to improve education and training opportunities on campuses and at work, as well as to connect learners and educators communicating at a distance. In the business-to-business media segment, leading companies are transforming themselves into multimedia business information providers delivering mission-critical content via print and e-media formats.

In the consumer end-user sector, which weathered the 2001 recession well and has been strong since, consumers continue to spend more time on non-advertising-based media, such as home videos, videogames, movies, and the Internet. At the same time, technology innovations have fueled the consistent rollout of new consumer-based media, which has driven accelerated audience fragmentation and increased consumer multitasking. In addition, the advent of the digital video recorder has given rise to an era of consumer empowerment over media, in which consumers not only have a multitude of media choices, but they can bypass ads completely through one of the most powerful advertising tools on the globe: television.

New media continued to propel spending in the consumer end-user market in the first half of 2005, led by expected double-digit gains in satellite radio subscriptions, interactive television (ITV) and wireless content, consumer Internet, and home video, as well as a solid single-digit increase in cable and satellite television. As a result, consumer spending on media is expected to rise 7.0 percent in 2005 to $199.34 billion. Many of the other consumer end-user segments—consumer books, consumer magazines, box office and videogames—will experience low-single-digit growth, while recorded music and newspaper circulation spending are expected to decline.

It is important to note that to reflect the multitude of changes in the consumer and institutional end-user sectors and the media industry in general in recent years, we have developed several new exclusive methodologies and subsegments for this edition of the *Forecast*, as well as numerous new data tables. We believe that these accessories have added significant value to this year's *Forecast*, providing our subscribers with what we hope will be the most engaging and insightful communications industry analysis ever. For example, in the consumer end-user sector, we have added data and trend analysis in wireless content, such as instant messaging, ringtones and wireless games. In the institutional end-user sector, professional information was combined with business information services and a new proprietary methodology was developed to size the market. We also revised the outsourced training sector based on a new data source that better reflects subsectors in this market. Additionally, a number of similar tables had been found in multiple chapters, such as online music and games in the Consumer Internet and Entertainment Media chapters, but were subtracted out of one of those chapters to avoid double counting.

The consumer end-user sector includes spending on cable and satellite television subscriptions, home video, Internet access and content, consumer books, recorded music, newspaper circulation, consumer magazine circulation, box office admissions, videogames, ITV and wireless content, and satellite radio subscriptions. Consumer end-user expenditures grew at a compound annual rate of 7.6 percent from 1999 to 2004, exceeding growth of the other three communications sectors, due to strong expansion in the cable and satellite television, home video and consumer Internet segments, as well as gains in the emerging segments of ITV and wireless content, and satellite radio.

The institutional end-user sector includes spending on professional and business information services; television programming; educational and training media; and business-to-business magazine circulation and trade show exhibition space. Institutional spending grew at a compound annual rate of 5.6 percent from 1999 to 2004, as strong growth during the past two years was offset by weak performances in 2001 and 2002 resulting from economic recession, lower corporate earnings and institutional budget reductions.

Total end-user spending on communications is projected to grow at a compound annual rate of 6.6 percent in the 2004-2009 period, reaching $492.62 billion. Key growth drivers will be stronger overall economic and budgetary conditions, heightened demand for integrated suites and on-demand media, and more effective ROI metrics that help justify expenditures. Other factors driving growth will include increased demand for customization and a tighter focus on ROI.

The Consumer End-User Spending Market In 2004 and 2005

Spending in the consumer end-user sector began to rebound in the first half of 2005 after two consecutive years of decelerating growth, as spending on new media, such as ITV and wireless content, and the Internet were compensating for declines in recorded music and newspaper circulation. Total consumer spending on media is expected to increase 7.0 percent to $199.34 billion in 2005, fueled by solid growth in the largest segment—cable and satellite television—and even stronger growth in home video, consumer Internet and the smaller ITV and wireless content and satellite radio segments.

However, due to declines in spending in home video and videogames in 2004, the consumer end-user sector was unable to exceed advertising spending as it had in 2003, and grew more slowly than did the other three sectors for the first time since the 2001 recession. As a result, consumer spending on communications underperformed nominal GDP growth for the first time in four years. Total consumer spending on media rose 6.2 percent to $186.30 billion in 2004.

The consumer end-user sector includes spending on cable and satellite television, home video, Internet access and content, consumer books, recorded music, newspaper circulation, consumer magazine circulation, box office admissions, videogames, ITV and wireless content, and satellite radio subscriptions. Consumer spending on communications increased for the thirtieth consecutive year in 2004, despite several economic recessions, the impact of major global events and increased competition during this period. Consumer end-user expenditures grew at a compound annual rate of 7.6 percent from 1999 to 2004, surpassing the growth of the other three communications sectors. Growth in the period was fueled by consistent high-single-digit and double-digit growth in the cable and satellite television, consumer Internet, and ITV and wireless content segments, as consumers dealt with the difficult economic and social climates by enjoying various types of consumer media, particularly entertainment media.

Consumer spending on cable and satellite television services remained the largest segment of the consumer sector in 2004, expanding 7.5 percent to $56.28 billion. While growth decelerated for the second consecutive year, it still outperformed most other communications markets. Consumer spending on the Internet and ITV and wireless content expanded at double-digit rates in 2004 and satellite radio spending increased by triple digits for the year. Videogames struggled for the second straight year as no new video console platforms were introduced, while home video spending decelerated dramatically due to VHS spending falling almost 50 percent. Surprisingly, spending on recorded music and consumer magazines rebounded in 2004 after posting declines in 2003. Meanwhile spending on consumer books and box office remained relatively flat and newspaper subscription spending declined for the first time in this decade.

The consumer media sector posted strong growth throughout the recent economic slowdown, despite the downturn in many other economic sectors, including advertising. Consumers have shown a tendency in tough economic and social climates to escape through entertainment, but several other factors also played roles in this sector's continued strong growth. Among these factors were technological advances that spawned new and improved media, and the emergence of media multitasking.

As a result of the strong growth of consumer spending, there has been a steady increase in the share of disposable income that is spent on media over the past few decades. Despite three recessions since 1980, the share of disposable income spent on communications almost doubled to 2.16 percent in 2004. By 2009, the share of disposable income spent on media content and access is projected to rise slightly to 2.22 percent. Concurrently, consumer spending on communications has grown approximately 2.4 percentage points faster than disposable income on a compound annual basis during the past 30 years.

Average consumer spending on media per person per year grew at a decelerated rate in 2004, advancing 4.9 percent to $794.78,

HIGHLIGHTS

Consumer End-User Spending

Due to declines in home video and videogames spending in 2004, the consumer end-user sector grew more slowly than the other three sectors for the first time since the 2001 recession. As a result, consumer end-user spending on communications underperformed nominal GDP growth for the first time since 2000. Total consumer spending on media rose 6.2 percent to $186.30 billion in 2004.

■

Consumer media expenditures grew more quickly than the other three communications industry sectors from 1999 to 2004, increasing at a compound annual rate of 7.6 percent in the period. Growth in the period was fueled by consistent high-single-digit and double-digit growth in the cable and satellite television, consumer Internet, and interactive television (ITV) and wireless content segments, as consumers dealt with the difficult economic and social climates by enjoying various types of consumer media, particularly entertainment media.

■

Cable and satellite television services remained the largest segment of the consumer sector in 2004, expanding 7.5 percent to $56.28 billion. Growth decelerated for the second consecutive year, but still outperformed most other communications markets. Three of the 11 segments—consumer Internet, ITV and wireless content, and satellite radio—expanded at high rates in 2004.

■

Consumers increased overall media use only 0.3 percent to 3,480 hours per person per year in 2004, slightly less than 10 hours per day per person. Since 1999, overall use has increased 200 hours per person per year, a half-hour more per day compared with five years ago. Overall usage rose at a compound annual rate of 1.2 percent from 1999 to 2004.

■

Average consumer spending on media expanded 4.9 percent in 2004 to $794.78 per person per year. Compound annual growth from 1999 to 2004 was 6.3 percent. Underlying the strong growth of consumer spending over the past three decades has been a steady increase in the share of disposable income spent on media. The share of disposable income spent on communications was 2.2 percent in 2004, double the 1.1 percent share in 1975.

■

Consumer end-user spending on communications began to rebound in the first half of 2005 after two straight years of decelerating growth, as spending on new media like ITV and wireless content, satellite radio, and the Internet compensated for declines in traditional media such as recorded music and newspapers. Total consumer spending on media is expected to increase 7.0 percent to $199.34 billion in 2005.

■

Total consumer end-user spending on communications is forecast to grow at a compound annual rate of 6.3 percent from 2004 to 2009, reaching $252.80 billion. The sector's growth will outperform that of nominal GDP during the early stages of the forecast period, but fall below nominal GDP by 2009 as new media penetration rates near saturation and double-digit growth rates will no longer be the norm.

■

Led by increases in time spent with videogames, the Internet, home videos, and ITV and wireless content, the average consumer will increase time spent with all media per year at a compound annual rate of 0.4 percent to 3,555 hours in 2009. Meanwhile, consumer spending per person per year on media will break $1,000 for the first time in 2009, rising at a compound annual rate of 5.2 percent during the 2004-2009 period to $1,023.69.

End-User Spending On Communications

Consumer Spending on Communications

Year	*Cable & Satellite TV*	*Consumer Internet*	*Home Video*	*Consumer Books*	*Recorded Music*	*Newspapers*
1999	$37,225	$ 7,896	$16,610	$18,087	$14,585	$10,822
2000	39,752	11,613	17,100	18,012	14,327	10,896
2001	43,506	16,348	19,656	17,924	13,745	11,135
2002	48,242	20,640	23,276	18,849	12,615	11,399
2003	52,373	24,479	26,606	19,529	11,855	11,470
2004	56,276	27,926	27,615	19,761	12,154	11,375
2005	60,116	31,187	30,877	20,359	11,849	11,176
2006	63,767	34,884	34,054	20,570	11,502	11,038
2007	67,467	38,539	36,727	21,256	11,505	10,928
2008	71,106	42,402	39,572	21,495	11,135	10,867
2009	74,829	45,840	42,048	21,903	10,953	10,840

Sources: Veronis Suhler Stevenson, PQ Media, Adams Media Research, Alexander & Associates, Audit Bureau of Circulations, Book Industry Study Group, Business 2.0, comScore Networks, Digital Entertainment Group, DIRECTV, DSL Forum, EchoStar, *Editor & Publisher*, Entertainment Software Association, Federal Communications Commission, In Demand, Insight Research, In-Stat/MDR, Jupiter Media Metrix, Kagan Research, Leichtman Research Group, Lexis/Nexis, LodgeNet, Magazine Publishers of America, Motion Picture Association of America, National Cable & Telecommunications Association, Newspaper Association of America, NPDFunworld, Online Publishers Association, Recording Industry Association of America, Rentrak, Replay TV, Sirius Satellite Radio, SRDS, Smith Travel Research, Telecommunications Industry Association, TiVo, U.S. Census Bureau, *Video Business*, Video Software Dealers Association, XM Satellite Radio, Yankee Group

Growth of Consumer Spending on Communications

Year	*Cable & Satellite TV*	*Consumer Internet*	*Home Video*	*Consumer Books*	*Recorded Music*	*Newspapers*
2000	6.8%	47.1%	3.0%	–0.4%	–1.8%	0.7%
2001	9.4	40.8	14.9	–0.5	–4.1	2.2
2002	10.9	26.3	18.4	5.2	–8.2	2.4
2003	8.6	18.6	14.3	3.6	–6.0	0.6
2004	7.5	14.1	3.8	1.2	2.5	–0.8
2005	6.8	11.7	11.8	3.0	–2.5	–1.7
2006	6.1	11.9	10.3	1.0	–2.9	–1.2
2007	5.8	10.5	7.8	3.3	0.0	–1.0
2008	5.4	10.0	7.7	1.1	–3.2	–0.6
2009	5.2	8.1	6.3	1.9	–1.6	–0.2
Compound Annual Growth						
1999-2004	8.6	28.7	10.7	1.8	–3.6	1.0
2004-2009	5.9	10.4	8.8	2.1	–2.1	–1.0

Sources: Veronis Suhler Stevenson, PQ Media, Adams Media Research, Alexander & Associates, Audit Bureau of Circulations, Book Industry Study Group, Business 2.0, comScore Networks, Digital Entertainment Group, DIRECTV, DSL Forum, EchoStar, *Editor & Publisher*, Entertainment Software Association, Federal Communications Commission, In Demand, Insight Research, In-Stat/MDR, Jupiter Media Metrix, Kagan Research, Leichtman Research Group, Lexis/Nexis, LodgeNet, Magazine Publishers of America, Motion Picture Association of America, National Cable & Telecommunications Association, Newspaper Association of America, NPDFunworld, Online Publishers Association, Recording Industry Association of America, ReplayTV, Sirius Satellite Radio, SRDS, Smith Travel Research, Telecommunications Industry Association, TiVo, U.S. Census Bureau, *Video Business*, Video Software Dealers Association, XM Satellite Radio, Yankee Group

($ MILLIONS)

Consumer Magazines	Box Office	Videogames	Interactive TV & Wireless Content	Satellite Radio	Total
$ 9,936	$ 7,448	$ 6,537	$ 7	—	$129,153
9,975	7,661	6,546	20	—	135,902
9,966	8,413	6,931	47	$ 0.2	147,671
10,079	9,520	7,775	720	17	163,132
10,033	9,489	7,943	1,611	91	175,479
10,331	9,539	8,107	2,933	284	186,301
10,654	9,653	8,327	4,478	660	199,336
10,726	9,827	9,079	6,074	1,176	212,697
11,053	10,074	9,862	7,511	1,754	226,676
11,341	10,285	10,916	8,748	2,337	240,204
11,562	10,604	11,446	9,892	2,884	252,801

Consumer Magazines	Box Office	Videogames	Interactive TV & Wireless Content	Satellite Radio	Total
0.4%	2.9%	0.1%	185.7%	—	5.2%
–0.1	9.8	5.9	135.0	—	8.7
1.1	13.2	12.2	1,431.9	8,400.0%	10.5
–0.5	–0.3	2.2	123.8	435.3	7.6
3.0	0.5	2.1	82.1	212.1	6.2
3.1	1.2	2.7	52.7	132.4	7.0
0.7	1.8	9.0	35.6	78.2	6.7
3.0	2.5	8.6	23.7	49.1	6.6
2.6	2.1	10.7	16.5	33.2	6.0
1.9	3.1	4.9	13.1	23.4	5.2
0.8	5.1	4.4	234.5	—	7.6
2.3	2.1	7.1	27.5	59.0	6.3

Shares of Consumer Spending on Communications

Year	*Cable & Satellite TV*	*Consumer Internet*	*Home Video*	*Consumer Books*	*Recorded Music*	*Newspapers*
1999	28.8%	6.1%	12.9%	14.0%	11.3%	8.4%
2000	29.3	8.5	12.6	13.3	10.5	8.0
2001	29.5	11.1	13.3	12.1	9.3	7.5
2002	29.6	12.7	14.3	11.6	7.7	7.0
2003	29.8	13.9	15.2	11.1	6.8	6.5
2004	30.2	15.0	14.8	10.6	6.5	6.1
2005	30.2	15.6	15.5	10.2	5.9	5.6
2006	30.0	16.4	16.0	9.7	5.4	5.2
2007	29.8	17.0	16.2	9.4	5.1	4.8
2008	29.6	17.7	16.5	8.9	4.6	4.5
2009	29.6	18.1	16.6	8.7	4.3	4.3

Sources: Veronis Suhler Stevenson, PQ Media, Adams Media Research, Alexander & Associates, Audit Bureau of Circulations, Book Industry Study Group, Business 2.0, comScore Networks, Digital Entertainment Group, DIRECTV, DSL Forum, EchoStar, *Editor & Publisher*, Entertainment Software Association, Federal Communications Commission, In Demand, Insight Research, In-Stat/MDR, Jupiter Media Metrix, Kagan Research, Leichtman Research Group, Lexis/Nexis, LodgeNet, Magazine Publishers of America, Motion Picture Association of America, National Cable & Telecommunications Association, Newspaper Association of America, NPDFunworld, Online Publishers Association, Recording Industry Association of America, ReplayTV, Sirius Satellite Radio, SRDS, Smith Travel Research, Telecommunications Industry Association, TiVo, U.S. Census Bureau, *Video Business*, Video Software Dealers Association, XM Satellite Radio, Yankee Group

Consumer End-User Spending On Communications as a Percentage Of Disposable Income

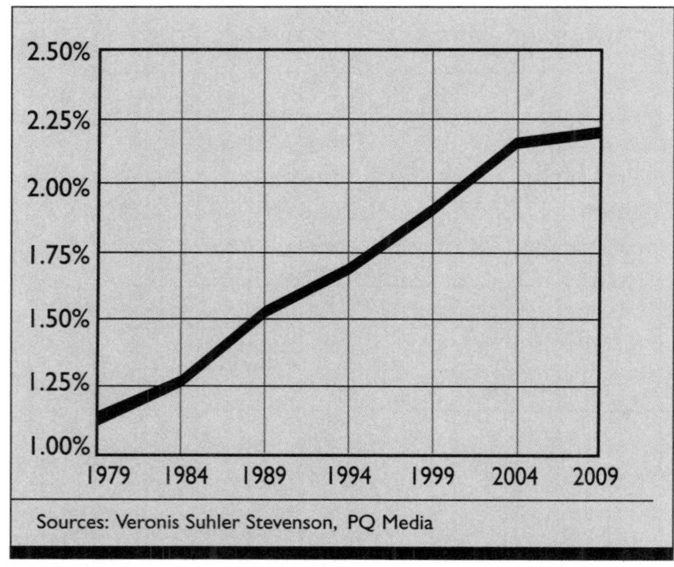

Sources: Veronis Suhler Stevenson, PQ Media

bolstered by increased spending in eight of the 11 segments. Average consumer expenditures on communications rose at a compound annual rate of 6.3 percent from 1999 to 2004. Total consumer spending on media was $186.30 billion in 2004, and is projected to grow to $252.80 billion by 2009, a compound annual growth rate of 6.3 percent. As a result, the average consumer spending on media per person per year is expected to climb over $1,000 for the first time in 2009, reaching $1,023.69.

CONSUMERS BECOME MORE EMPOWERED

The engine of technology innovation has afforded consumers greater flexibility in their media choices and more power over the mar-

Consumer Magazines	Box Office	Videogames	[illegible]	[illegible]
7.7%	5.8%	5.1%	0.0%	[illegible]
7.3	5.6	4.8	0.0	[illegible]
6.7	5.7	4.7	0.0	[illegible]
6.2	5.8	4.8	0.4	0.0%
5.7	5.4	4.5	0.9	0.1
5.5	5.1	4.4	1.6	0.2
5.3	4.8	4.2	2.2	0.3
5.0	4.6	4.3	2.9	0.6
4.9	4.4	4.4	3.3	0.8
4.7	4.3	4.5	3.6	1.0
4.6	4.2	4.5	3.9	1.1

ket due to the rollout of new consumer media, the emergence of ad-skipping technology and additional multitasking, which has fragmented consumer time spent with and expenditures on consumer-supported media as well as advertising-based media. The result has been a shift in consumers' time and money spent from ad-based communications to consumer-supported media for the past two decades. We believe this shift will continue in the forecast period, although the rate of transition will slow over the next five years. The reason for this slowdown will be a deceleration in the VHS market and slower growth of Internet access spending, as well as weaker growth in movie ticket sales because of market maturation and higher prices. This outlook could change with an unforeseen sleeper movie hit in the 2004-2009 period.

While the consumer adoption of on-demand media, such as DVRs and VOD, has been slow, these media have been proactive in responding to the broader media transformation. The broadcast, entertainment and print segments are adding interactive elements such as t-commerce and cross-platform packages to meet consumer demands. As such, consumers have increased their time spent with all media substantially due to the presence of newer electronic and digital media choices, such as cable and satellite television, home video, videogames, the Internet and satellite radio. Concurrently, consumers have become more sophisticated in their media usage, often media multitasking (using two

...the

...dicates ...en indi- ...sic or tele- ...amount of ...nt material is ...rch shows that ...on and the Inter- ...popular means of ...ecause both can be ...ount of concentration, ... reality program and vot- ing ... s online.

Nevertheless, some of this data indicating the demise of traditional media can be exaggerated if not viewed in a broader context. A number of traditional media, such as broadcast television, are hit-driven, and when consumers believe the content is superior, such as a hit sitcom or drama, they will increase their use of the medium. In 2005, broadcast television viewing increased during the winter due to high interest in hot new scripted programs like *Desperate Housewives*, *Lost*, *House*, and the *CSI* and *Law & Order* franchises. General consumer book use was down in 2004 due to the lack of a blockbuster title, but higher growth is expected in 2005 with the release of the latest Harry Potter title in July. The most recent *Star Wars* film generated the highest four-day box office spending in history. Additionally, gains in time spent with newer media can be slightly deceptive. Although Internet usage grew more rapidly than did most other media from 1999 to 2004, time spent with digital versions of traditional media was included in that increase. In other words, consumers will often use the Internet to research information and find it ...tal or Web versions of traditional ... Therefore, while the time consumers ...d with newspapers is declining, total ...ne spent reading newspaper articles is likely increasing because of the proliferation of newspaper Web sites.

Conversely, a high share of the time spent with the Internet and wireless content is due to individual activities, such as e-mail and instant messaging, rather than a mass medium message. These activities have augmented telephone calls and letter writing, instead of broadcast or print media use.

The trends driving increases in consumer time spent, and particularly spending, on media are primarily attributable to new technology. Consumers are migrating their time to the DVD format, broadband Internet access and satellite television. Traditional media, such as magazines, are extending print products online and wired cable providers have reduced churn as a result of their ability to offer bundled services. But contrary to popular belief, while new usage devices, distribution channels and delivery formats often supplant older ones in a cycle, consumer spending on the overall medium doesn't usually end; instead, time spent simply shifts to the new delivery mode.

The strength and influence of the new media such as DVRs and VOD, can also be exaggerated. Penetration rates of both these media have yet to exceed 10 percent. These media are often used by younger demographics, which are already tending away from traditional media, more often used by the older, affluent markets. Currently, the paid VOD market seems to be supplementing the viewing of regularly scheduled programs on broadcast and cable networks, instead of replacing them. But as the market grows, the use of newer media by the younger demographics will increasingly impact overall media use and expenditures, and likely not in a positive fashion. Increases in time spent with VOD are being driven by free programs, mainly aimed at children, like *SpongeBob* on-demand.

Impact of Competing Hardware on Consumer Adoption Cycle of Media

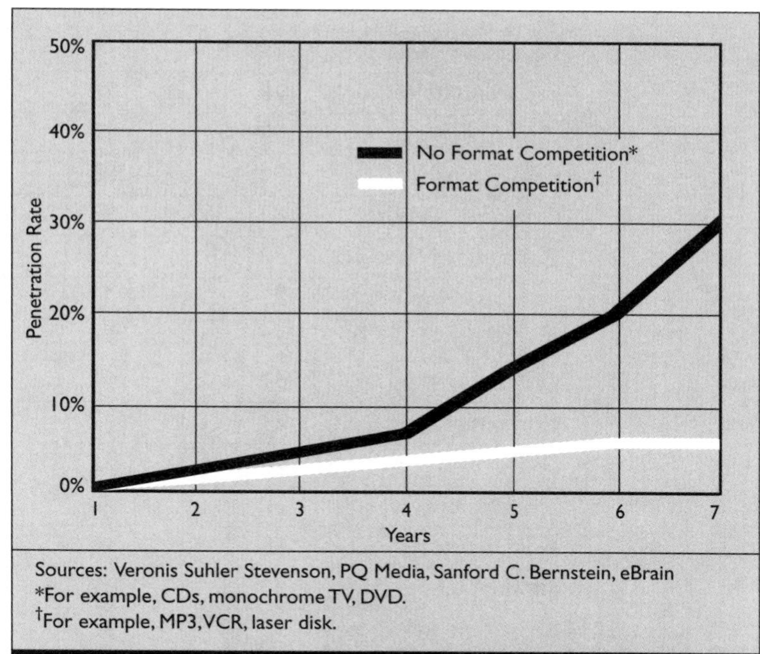

Sources: Veronis Suhler Stevenson, PQ Media, Sanford C. Bernstein, eBrain
*For example, CDs, monochrome TV, DVD.
†For example, MP3, VCR, laser disk.

KEY CONSUMER TRENDS AND TIME SPENT WITH MEDIA

Consumers have increased their time spent with media significantly during the past few decades, owing to the presence of new digital media choices, such as satellite television and radio, home video, DVRs, videogames, the Internet, and portable iPods, cell phones and PDAs. Many families consider some of these media almost mandatory utilities in this day and age.

However, the growth in time spent has been decelerating as penetration rates of new media begin to level off due to several key segments reaching saturation points. For example, most consumers willing to subscribe to the Internet have done so, though the method by which they access the Web is changing from dial-up to broadband. Conversely, there are a number of new media that have struggled to gain a foothold in American households. One possible reason for this lack of adoption is consumer confusion over format. That is, media that are offered in more than one format, such as the early days of home video with Beta and VHS, are less likely to exhibit rapid consumer acceptance. Historical data suggest that the lack of a format war quickens adoption cycles, for example, DVD, reaching a near 30 percent penetration rate within seven years, while media that have multiple formats have difficulty reaching a 10 percent penetration rate during the same period. This trend will most likely serve as an example impacting adoption of the next generation of DVD players that are upgrading memory capacity, but in two different formats.

With all the new media choices, consumers are becoming more empowered through on-demand technologies, such as VOD and DVRs. Additionally, technology has played a significant role in the steady climb of consumer spending on media. Households will increase discretionary spending on media when they perceive an inherent value in the new technology, such as the extra material on DVDs that has led to a decline in VHS use, or broadband Internet replacing dial-up in order to access streaming video and other rich media formats.

To stay competitive, more traditional media, such as newspapers, broadcast TV and radio, have seen the extension of brands into new media like the Internet and wireless content. Cable providers have been somewhat successful in their battle with satellite television due to their ability to offer bundled services not available from direct broadcast satellite (DBS) providers, such as modems and VOD. However, as mentioned previously, when new formats, modes and distribution channels supplant older ones—as was the case when DVDs replaced VHS—consumer expenditures usually shift to the new technology. In general, technology expands content distribution and increases options for consumers. As a result, consumption and expenditures of consumer media continue to grow.

Penetration Rates of Consumer Media*

	2009	*2004*	*2000*	*1990*	*1980*	*1970*
Broadcast Radio	**99%**	**99%**	**99%**	**99%**	**99%**	**99%**
Broadcast Television	**98**	**98**	**98**	**98**	**98**	96
VHS	90	**97**	86	70	3	—
CDs	94	**95**	**95**	48	0.1	—
Consumer Books	82	83	84	81	**88**	83
Consumer Magazines	78	80	80	**81**	**81**	79
Wireless Phones	**83**	78	47	3	0.1	—
Box Office	72	74	**76**	73	66	69
Cable Television	**67**	**67**	66	55	23	7
Computers	**71**	67	51	15	2	—
DVDs	**96**	63	11	—	—	—
Newspapers	50	53	55	62	67	78
Videogames	**55**	49	40	20	3	—
Phonographs	35	42	45	88	**95**	93
Broadband Internet	**56**	32	5	—	—	—
Dial-up Internet	13	31	**37**	1	0.1	—
Satellite Television	**30**	25	19	2	—	—
MP3/iPod	**37**	18	1	—	—	—
HDTV	**29**	4	0.5	—	—	—
DVRs	**12**	4	0.1	—	—	—
Satellite Radio	**10**	2	—	—	—	—

Sources: Veronis Suhler Stevenson, PQ Media LLC, Audits & Survey, Consumer Electronics Association, Gallup, icwhen.com, Motion Picture Association of America, Mediamark Research, National Association of Broadcasters, Newspaper Association of America, *TV Dimensions*, U.S. Bureau of the Census, *Wall Street Journal*

*Based on the number of households with the electronic device (e.g., television set, DVD player, etc.), survey results on the share of the population. that indicated using a medium in a given year (e.g., read newspaper, went to a movie), or estimates based on circulation or unit data.

Note: Penetration rates in bold represent the highest consumer adoption rate for the medium.

1960	1950	1940	1930	1920	1910	1900
96%	95%	81%	46%	0.5%	—	—
87	9	0.1	—	—	—	—
—	—	—	—	—	—	—
—	—	—	—	—	—	—
74	67	61	57	52	41%	35%
75	71	63	58	37	28	15
—	—	—	—	—	—	—
76	87	92	63	24	9	1
0.1	—	—	—	—	—	—
—	—	—	—	—	—	—
—	—	—	—	—	—	—
81	79	72	66	55	46	38
—	—	—	—	—	—	—
84	51	38	20	12	3	0.1
—	—	—	—	—	—	—
—	—	—	—	—	—	—
—	—	—	—	—	—	—
—	—	—	—	—	—	—
—	—	—	—	—	—	—
—	—	—	—	—	—	—
—	—	—	—	—	—	—

Hours per Person per Year Using Consumer Media

Year	*Network-Affiliated Stations*	*Independent & Public Stations*	*Total Broadcast Television*	*Basic Cable & Satellite Networks*	*Premium Cable & Satellite Services*	*Total Cable & Satellite TV*	*Total TV***	*Broadcast & Satellite Radio‡*
1999*	604	193	797	540	90	630	1,427	939
2000†	700	93	793	555	119	674	1,467	942
2001	651	93	744	611	133	744	1,488	952
2002	624	95	719	664	136	800	1,519	991
2003	601	95	696	697	150	847	1,543	1,003
2004	583	95	678	719	149	868	1,546	986
2005	584	95	679	733	136	869	1,548	978
2006	590	94	684	737	134	871	1,555	975
2007	585	93	678	731	146	877	1,555	974
2008	580	95	675	742	149	891	1,566	984
2009	587	94	681	747	134	881	1,562	984

Sources: Veronis Suhler Stevenson, PQ Media, Adams Media Research, Alexander & Associates, Arbitron, Audit Bureau of Circulations, Book Industry Study Group, *Daily Variety*, Datamonitor, *Editor & Publisher*, Entertainment Media Association, *The Financial Post*, The Gallup Organization, Insight Research, Kagan Research, Kinetic Strategies, Magazine Publishers of America, Motion Picture Association of America, National Cable & Telecommunications Association, Newspaper Association of America, Nielsen Media Research, NPDFunworld, Online Publishers Association, Recording Industry Association of America, Scarborough Research, Time Warner, U.S. Census Bureau, Video Software Dealers Association, Yankee Group

Note: Estimates for time spent were derived using rating data for television, cable & satellite television, radio survey research and consumer purchase data (units, admissions, access) for books, home video, Internet, interactive television, magazines, movies in theaters, newspapers, recorded music and videogames. Adults 18 and older were the basis for estimates for newspapers, consumer books, consumer magazines, and home video. Persons 12 and older were the bases for estimates for broadcast television, cable & satellite television, radio, recorded music, movies in theaters, videogames, consumer Internet and ITV & wireless content.

*In 1999, independent and public stations included UPN, WB, PAX, Telemundo and Univision affiliates, as well as cable superstations except TBS. Basic cable & satellite networks included TBS, pay-per-view, interactive channels, home shopping and audio-only feeds.

†In 2000, UPN, WB, and PAX moved to network affiliated stations. Telemundo and Univision affiliates remain independent. Cable superstations, including TBS and WGN, included in basic cable & satellite networks. Pay-per-view, interactive channels, home shopping and audio-only feeds included with premium cable & satellite services.

Despite the emergence of digital technology, certain aspects of the media markets remain unchanged. Television continued to be the most popular medium, accounting for slightly less than half of all time spent with media. A recent Labor Department study found that television trailed only work and sleep as the activity consumers engage in most often. A number of new programs on television has increased the medium's popularity in recent years, highlighting the point made earlier about hits, such as *Desperate Housewives* and *The Apprentice* on broadcast and *The Daily Show* and *Chappelle's Show* on cable television. Total television usage increased at a compound annual rate of 1.6 percent from 1999 to 2004, reaching 1,546 hours annually per consumer. However, the

Newspapers‡**	*Recorded Music*‡#	*Consumer Internet*	*Consumer Magazines*‡	*Consumer Books*‡	*Videogames*‡#	*Home Video*§‡	*Box Office*	*Interactive TV & Wireless Content*‖	*Total****
205	281	65	134	117	58	41	13	—	3,280
201	258	104	135	107	64	43	12	—	3,333
197	229	131	127	106	66	47	13	—	3,356
194	200	147	125	109	70	57	14	4	3,430
192	184	164	121	109	75	60	13	7	3,471
188	185	176	124	108	77	67	12	11	3,480
183	179	183	124	106	78	76	12	15	3,483
179	175	190	122	106	82	84	12	19	3,499
175	175	195	122	106	86	91	12	26	3,518
170	169	200	122	106	93	95	12	32	3,549
165	165	203	121	106	96	99	12	42	3,555

§Playback of prerecorded VHS cassettes and DVDs only.

‖Wireless content only. Digital video recorders (DVRs) included in total TV. Pay-per-view and video-on-demand included in premium cable & satellite services.

‡Does not include Internet-related use of traditional media. Examples of traditional media being used on the Internet include: listening to downloaded music directly on the computer or from a burned disk on an MP3 player, reading a downloaded e-book, listening to a radio station transmitted by a Windows media player, reading a Web-based newspaper article, taking a Web-based magazine survey, gathering product information also found in the printed version, or playing an Internet single- or multiplayer videogame. All the examples listed are included in the time spent data under consumer Internet, although the media content was originally provided on a traditional medium.

#Some subsegments appear in two or more chapters. To avoid double counting, VOD is included in cable & satellite TV, not in ITV & wireless content; online music and online games are included in Consumer Internet, not in recorded music or videogames, respectively.

**Methodology to determine time spent with this medium revised. Television expanded to include teenagers as well as adults; and newspapers expanded to include weekly papers as well as dailies.

***Can include media multitasking, such as using the Internet and television simultaneously.

growth of television usage is decelerating, up only 0.2 percent in 2004, after increases of 1.5 percent or more since 2000. This trend is mainly due to a decline in new cable and satellite networks that had been pushing consumer usage growth in recent years, as well as younger audiences migrating to other media like videogames, wireless content and the Internet.

Research also shows that the heaviest users of television are an older, less educated demographic including fewer children in the household. Meanwhile, studies on affluent audiences conclude that as household income rises, there is less dependency on broadcast media, but increased use of print media and the Internet. Additionally, almost two-thirds of the time spent with television

Growth of Hours per Person per Year Using Consumer Media

Year	Network-Affiliated Stations	Independent & Public Stations	Total Broadcast Television	Basic Cable & Satellite Networks	Premium Cable & Satellite Services	Total Cable & Satellite TV	Total TV**	Broadcast & Satellite Radio‡
2000*†	15.9%	–52.0%	–0.6%	2.7%	32.2%	6.9%	2.7%	0.4%
2001	–7.0	0.5	–6.1	10.2	11.7	10.4	1.5	1.0
2002	–4.2	2.0	–3.4	8.7	2.0	7.5	2.0	4.2
2003	–3.7	0.6	–3.1	4.8	10.8	5.8	1.6	1.1
2004	–3.0	–0.5	–2.7	3.1	–0.7	2.5	0.2	–1.7
2005	0.1	0.1	0.1	2.0	–8.9	0.1	0.1	–0.8
2006	1.1	–1.3	0.7	0.6	–1.3	0.3	0.5	–0.3
2007	–0.9	–0.9	–0.9	–0.9	9.1	0.7	0.0	–0.1
2008	–0.8	1.6	–0.4	1.5	1.6	1.6	0.7	1.0
2009	1.2	–1.1	0.9	0.7	–10.1	–1.1	–0.3	0.0
Compound Annual Growth								
1999-2004	–0.7	–13.2	–3.2	5.9	10.6	6.6	1.6	1.0
2004-2009	0.1	–0.3	0.1	0.8	–2.2	0.3	0.2	0.0

Sources: Veronis Suhler Stevenson, PQ Media, Adams Media Research, Alexander & Associates, Arbitron, Audit Bureau of Circulations, Book Industry Study Group, *Daily Variety*, Datamonitor, *Editor & Publisher*, Entertainment Media Association, *The Financial Post*, The Gallup Organization, Insight Research, Kagan Research, Kinetic Strategies, Magazine Publishers of America, Motion Picture Association of America, National Cable & Telecommunications Association, Newspaper Association of America, Nielsen Media Research, NPDFunworld, Online Publishers Association, Recording Industry Association of America, Scarborough Research, Time Warner, U.S. Census Bureau, Video Software Dealers Association, Yankee Group

Note: Estimates for time spent were derived using rating data for television, cable & satellite television, radio survey research and consumer purchase data (units, admissions, access) for books, home video, Internet, interactive television, magazines, movies in theaters, newspapers, recorded music and videogames. Adults 18 and older were the basis for estimates for newspapers, consumer books, consumer magazines, and home video. Persons 12 and older were the bases for estimates for broadcast television, cable & satellite television, radio, recorded music, movies in theaters, videogames, consumer Internet and ITV & wireless content.

*In 1999, independent and public stations included UPN, WB, PAX, Telemundo and Univision affiliates, as well as cable superstations except TBS. Basic cable & satellite networks included TBS, pay-per-view, interactive channels, home shopping and audio-only feeds.

†In 2000, UPN, WB, and PAX moved to network affiliated stations. Telemundo and Univision affiliates remain independent. Cable superstations, including TBS and WGN, included in basic cable & satellite networks. Pay-per-view, interactive channels, home shopping and audio-only feeds included with premium cable & satellite services.

occurs between 5 p.m. and 11 p.m., when television accounts for almost 75 percent of all media usage. During early morning hours, also known as the graveyard shift, radio is the dominant media. However, by mid-morning, consumers are often switching among various media, mainly television, radio and the Internet. Interestingly, magazine and newspaper readership is also at its highest level at this time of day.

Radio is the second most often used medium at 986 hours in 2004, which represents a 28.3 percent share of time spent with media. However, the figures represent a 1.7 percent decline in radio usage, the first drop since the late 1990s. Consumers have become frustrated with advertising clutter and generic formats that are not targeted to local audiences. Radio groups, such as Clear Channel, reduced their hourly advertising

Newspapers[‡]**	Recorded Music[‡#]	Consumer Internet	Consumer Magazines[‡]	Consumer Books[‡]	Videogames[‡#]	Home Video[§‡]	Box Office	Interactive TV & Wireless Content[‖]	Total***
−2.1%	−8.2%	59.1%	0.7%	−8.2%	11.4%	4.5%	−5.0%	—	1.6%
−1.8	−11.2	26.1	−5.8	−1.4	2.0	11.2	3.4	—	0.7
−1.5	−12.4	12.1	−1.9	3.0	6.7	20.8	8.1	—	2.2
−1.2	−8.2	11.5	−2.7	−0.2	7.4	4.9	−4.3	90.3%	1.2
−2.1	0.8	7.5	1.9	−1.0	2.4	12.0	−4.3	59.7	0.3
−2.3	−3.3	4.1	0.4	−1.3	0.5	13.4	−1.5	41.4	0.1
−2.3	−2.5	3.6	−1.8	−0.3	5.7	10.2	−0.2	26.9	0.5
−2.6	0.1	2.8	−0.1	0.2	5.5	8.2	−0.6	35.3	0.5
−2.8	−3.4	2.3	0.1	0.1	7.9	4.9	−1.1	20.6	0.9
−3.0	−2.3	1.9	−0.4	−0.2	2.5	3.8	0.5	33.4	0.2
−1.7	−8.0	21.9	−1.6	−1.6	5.9	10.5	−0.6	—	1.2
−2.6	−2.3	2.9	−0.4	−0.3	4.4	8.0	−0.6	31.3	0.4

§Playback of prerecorded VHS cassettes and DVDs only.

‖Wireless content only. Digital video recorders (DVRs) included in total TV. Pay-per-view and video-on-demand included in premium cable & satellite services.

‡Does not include Internet-related use of traditional media. Examples of traditional media being used on the Internet include: listening to downloaded music directly on the computer or from a burned disk on an MP3 player, reading a downloaded e-book, listening to a radio station transmitted by a Windows media player, reading a Web-based newspaper article, taking a Web-based magazine survey, gathering product information also found in the printed version, or playing an Internet single- or multiplayer videogame. All the examples listed are included in the time spent data under consumer Internet, although the media content was originally provided on a traditional medium.

#Some subsegments appear in two or more chapters. To avoid double counting, VOD is included in cable & satellite TV, not in ITV & wireless content; online music and online games are included in Consumer Internet, not in recorded music or videogames, respectively.

**Methodology to determine time spent with this medium revised. Television expanded to include teenagers as well as adults; and newspapers expanded to include weekly papers as well as dailies.

***Can include media multitasking, such as using the Internet and television simultaneously.

time in 2004 and 2005 in order to stem the migration of listeners to other media. Despite the decline in 2004, radio listenership rose at a compound annual rate of 1.0 percent from 1999 to 2004, mainly fueled by satellite radio gains, longer commutes and a growing Hispanic demographic embracing various formats aimed at them.

The largest increases in time spent came in new media like the Internet, home video, and ITV and wireless content. Consumer use of ITV and wireless content climbed 59.7 percent in 2004 to 11 hours, which is 0.3 percent of all time spent. Internet use rose 7.5 percent to 176 hours in 2004, due to the transition from dial-up to broadband, which has prompted longer use of the Web and rich media content. It should be noted that a large share of the time spent with ITV and wireless content and the Internet are on activities that

Shares of Hours per Person per Year Using Consumer Media

Year	*Network-Affiliated Stations*	*Independent & Public Stations*	*Total Broadcast Television*	*Basic Cable & Satellite Networks*	*Premium Cable & Satellite Services*	*Total Cable & Satellite TV*	*Total TV***	*Broadcast & Satellite Radio*[‡]
1999*	18.4%	5.9%	24.3%	16.5%	2.7%	19.2%	43.5%	28.6%
2000[†]	21.0	2.8	23.8	16.6	3.6	20.2	44.0	28.3
2001	19.4	2.8	22.2	18.2	4.0	22.2	44.4	28.4
2002	18.2	2.8	21.0	19.4	4.0	23.3	44.3	28.9
2003	17.3	2.8	20.1	20.1	4.3	24.4	44.5	28.9
2004	16.8	2.7	19.5	20.6	4.3	24.9	44.4	28.3
2005	16.8	2.7	19.5	21.0	3.9	24.9	44.4	28.1
2006	16.9	2.7	19.5	21.1	3.8	24.9	44.4	27.9
2007	16.6	2.6	19.3	20.8	4.2	24.9	44.2	27.7
2008	16.4	2.7	19.0	20.9	4.2	25.1	44.1	27.7
2009	16.5	2.6	19.1	21.0	3.8	24.8	43.9	27.7

Sources: Veronis Suhler Stevenson, PQ Media, Adams Media Research, Alexander & Associates, Arbitron, Audit Bureau of Circulations, Book Industry Study Group, *Daily Variety*, Datamonitor, *Editor & Publisher*, Entertainment Media Association, *The Financial Post*, The Gallup Organization, Insight Research, Kagan Research, Kinetic Strategies, Magazine Publishers of America, Motion Picture Association of America, National Cable & Telecommunications Association, Newspaper Association of America, Nielsen Media Research, NPDFunworld, Online Publishers Association, Recording Industry Association of America, Scarborough Research, Time Warner, U.S. Census Bureau, Video Software Dealers Association, Yankee Group

Note: Estimates for time spent were derived using rating data for television, cable & satellite television, radio survey research and consumer purchase data (units, admissions, access) for books, home video, Internet, interactive television, magazines, movies in theaters, newspapers, recorded music and videogames. Adults 18 and older were the basis for estimates for newspapers, consumer books, consumer magazines, and home video. Persons 12 and older were the bases for estimates for broadcast television, cable & satellite television, radio, recorded music, movies in theaters, videogames, consumer Internet and ITV & wireless content

*In 1999, independent and public stations included UPN, WB, PAX, Telemundo and Univision affiliates, as well as cable superstations except TBS. Basic cable & satellite networks included TBS, pay-per-view, interactive channels, home shopping and audio-only feeds.

[†]In 2000, UPN, WB, and PAX moved to network affiliated stations. Telemundo and Univision affiliates remain independent. Cable superstations, including TBS and WGN, included in basic cable & satellite networks. Pay-per-view, interactive channels, home shopping and audio-only feeds included with premium cable & satellite services.

don't compete with traditional media, such as instant messaging, which are really substitutes for letter writing and phone calls, rather than television viewing or reading magazines. Data released by the Online Publishers Association (OPA) show that almost 60 percent of time spent on the Internet in 2004 was on e-mail or e-commerce, and accounted for about 100 hours per person per year. Data are unavailable for previous years, so we are unable to determine whether that share has been falling, but monthly data from the OPA suggest that the shift to content and search is increasing slightly. Growth in home video usage, up 12.0 percent to 67 hours in 2004, is being driven by the migration from the VHS format to DVD. DVD households tend to purchase units more often than do VHS households, which favor renting, allowing DVD consumers to watch titles more often for longer periods of time due to the extra footage.

Surprisingly, two media saw gains in usage in 2004 after a number of years of decline. Recorded music was up 0.8 percent to 185 hours and consumer magazine readership was up 1.9 percent to 124 hours. Music's increase was fueled by a number of popular releases, such as Usher's *Confession* and Norah Jones's *Feels Like Home*. Consumer magazine growth stemmed from renewed consumer interest in single-copy issues, which rose by 1.0 percent to 51.3 million copies after four consecutive years of decline. While magazine readership increased, other print media, such as newspapers and

Newspapers[‡]**	*Recorded Music*[‡#]	*Consumer Internet*	*Consumer Magazines*[‡]	*Consumer Books*[‡]	*Videogames*[‡#]	*Home Video*[§‡]	*Box Office*	*Interactive TV & Wireless Content*[‖]
6.2%	8.6%	2.0%	4.1%	3.6%	1.8%	1.2%	0.4%	—
6.0	7.7	3.1	4.1	3.2	1.9	1.3	0.4	—
5.9	6.8	3.9	3.8	3.1	2.0	1.4	0.4	—
5.7	5.8	4.3	3.6	3.2	2.0	1.7	0.4	0.1%
5.5	5.3	4.7	3.5	3.1	2.2	1.7	0.4	0.2
5.4	5.3	5.1	3.6	3.1	2.2	1.9	0.4	0.3
5.3	5.1	5.3	3.6	3.0	2.2	2.2	0.4	0.4
5.1	5.0	5.4	3.5	3.0	2.3	2.4	0.4	0.6
5.0	5.0	5.5	3.5	3.0	2.5	2.6	0.3	0.7
4.8	4.8	5.6	3.4	3.0	2.6	2.7	0.3	0.9
4.6	4.6	5.7	3.4	3.0	2.7	2.8	0.3	1.2

§Playback of prerecorded VHS cassettes and DVDs only.

‖Wireless content only. Digital video recorders (DVRs) included in total TV. Pay-per-view and video-on-demand included in premium cable & satellite services.

‡Does not include Internet-related use of traditional media. Examples of traditional media being used on the Internet include: listening to downloaded music directly on the computer or from a burned disk on an MP3 player, reading a downloaded e-book, listening to a radio station transmitted by a Windows media player, reading a Web-based newspaper article, taking a Web-based magazine survey, gathering product information also found in the printed version, or playing an Internet single- or multiplayer videogame. All the examples listed are included in the time spent data under consumer Internet, although the media content was originally provided on a traditional medium.

#Some subsegments appear in two or more chapters. To avoid double counting, VOD is included in cable & satellite TV, not in ITV & wireless content; online music and online games are included in Consumer Internet, not in recorded music or videogames, respectively.

**Methodology to determine time spent with this medium revised. Television expanded to include teenagers as well as adults; and newspapers expanded to include weekly papers as well as dailies.

End-User Spending On Communications

Time Spent with Media

	Hours per Person per Year						*Percent Change*	
Category	*1999*	*Percent Share*	*2004*	*Percent Share*	*2009*	*Percent Share*	*1999-2004*	*2004-2009*
Media with Significant Advertising Support*	2,075	63.3%	1,976	56.8%	1,951	54.9%	–4.8%	–1.2%
Media Supported Predominantly By Consumers[†]	1,204	36.7	1,504	43.2	1,604	45.1	24.9	6.6

Sources: Veronis Suhler Stevenson, PQ Media

*Broadcast television, broadcast & satellite radio, newspapers, consumer magazines.

†Cable & satellite television, box office, home video, interactive television & wireless content, recorded music, videogames, consumer Internet, consumer books.

Average Hours per Day in Media Activities, by Selected Demographics

Demographic Characteristic	*Watching TV*		*Reading*		*Playing Games/ Computer*		*Total*	
	Men	*Women*	*Men*	*Women*	*Men*	*Women*	*Men*	*Women*
Age								
Total 15+	2.75	2.41	0.33	0.40	0.36	0.23	3.44	3.04
15 to 24	2.29	2.17	0.14	0.14	0.80	0.43	3.23	2.74
25 to 34	2.33	2.01	0.14	0.18	0.36	0.19	2.83	2.38
35 to 44	2.54	1.87	0.20	0.26	0.21	0.16	2.95	2.29
45 to 54	2.65	2.26	0.30	0.34	0.24	0.18	3.19	2.78
55 to 64	3.06	2.53	0.43	0.55	0.25	0.21	3.74	3.29
65+	4.05	3.70	0.94	1.01	0.26	0.24	5.25	4.95
Ethnicity								
White	2.69	2.39	0.35	0.44	0.34	0.23	3.38	3.06
African-American	3.35	2.72	0.19	0.18	0.45	0.28	3.99	3.18
Hispanic	2.78	2.53	0.15	0.13	0.27	0.12	3.20	2.78
Employment								
Full-Time	2.21	1.76	0.21	0.26	0.26	0.19	2.68	2.21
Part-Time	2.55	2.00	0.34	0.32	0.50	0.24	3.39	2.56
Not Employed	3.98	3.19	0.57	0.57	0.52	0.30	5.07	4.06
Presence of Children in Household*								
None	3.07	2.69	0.40	0.54	0.37	0.25	3.84	3.48
Children under 18	2.21	2.02	0.20	0.21	0.35	0.21	2.76	2.44
13 to 17 Years Only	2.26	2.18	0.28	0.29	0.55	0.22	3.09	2.69
6 to 12 Years Only	2.27	2.02	0.19	0.23	0.33	0.21	2.79	2.46
Youngest under 6	2.14	1.92	0.15	0.14	0.25	0.20	2.54	2.26
Education								
Less Than High School	3.94	3.47	0.29	0.35	0.19	0.12	4.42	3.94
High School Diploma	3.19	2.81	0.25	0.45	0.23	0.21	3.67	3.47
Some College	2.70	2.28	0.37	0.44	0.33	0.23	3.40	2.95
College Graduate†	2.11	1.66	0.52	0.54	0.27	0.17	2.90	2.37

Sources: Veronis Suhler Stevenson, PQ Media, United States Department of Labor
*Children under 18 years of age.
†Bachelor's degree or higher.

consumer books, experienced declines in time spent. Newspaper usage fell 2.1 percent to 188 hours and consumer books dropped 1.0 percent to 108 hours in 2004. Evening papers continue to close and readers are not migrating to the morning papers that replace them. Meanwhile, consumer book readership was suppressed by the lack of a blockbuster title such as *The Da Vinci Code* and *The South Beach Diet*, which drove gains in prior years.

Time spent at the movies fell 4.3 percent to 12 hours, the second straight year of falling admissions. The high cost of seeing a film, including ticket and concession costs, have led many consumers to wait for the DVD release that can be viewed on home theatre systems. The videogame industry experienced its slowest gain since 2001, up only 2.4 percent to 77 hours. Though handheld use increased slightly with the release of Nintendo's advanced GameBoy system and Sony's first foray into this format with PlayStation Portable (PSP), there weren't

Media Habits of Affluent Households

Year 2004	*$75,000-$99,999*	*$100,000-$199,999*	*$200,000 +*
Number of Magazines Read*	6.5	9.1	16.4
Hours per Week, TV†	23.9	21.1	18.4
Hours per Week, Radio	8.3	7.9	7.5
Hours per Week, Internet	5.0	6.6	8.1

Sources: Veronis Suhler Stevenson, PQ Media, Mendelsohn Media
*Consumer and business-to-business magazines over a measured period of time.
†Broadcast and cable television.

End-User Spending On Communications

Shares of Time Spent with Media, by Hour

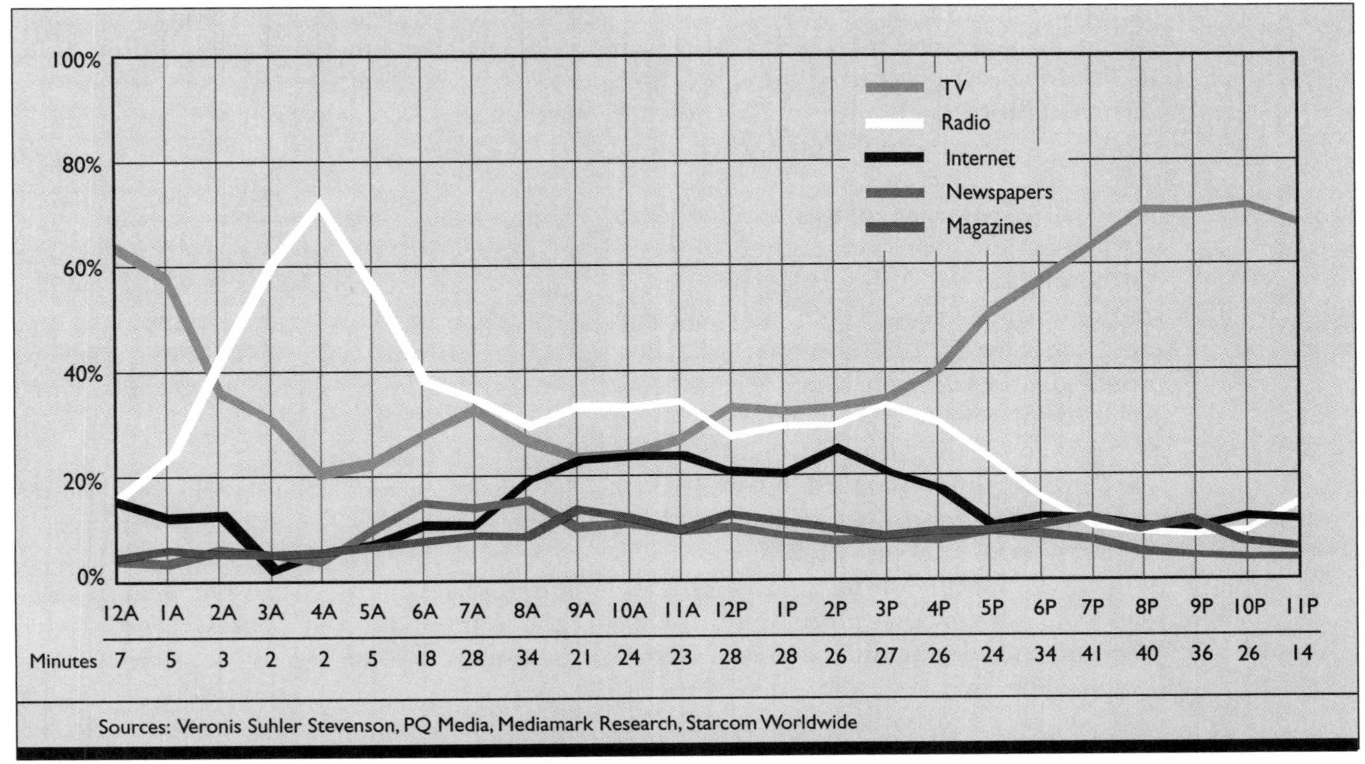

Sources: Veronis Suhler Stevenson, PQ Media, Mediamark Research, Starcom Worldwide

Share of Consumer Time Spent Online in 2004

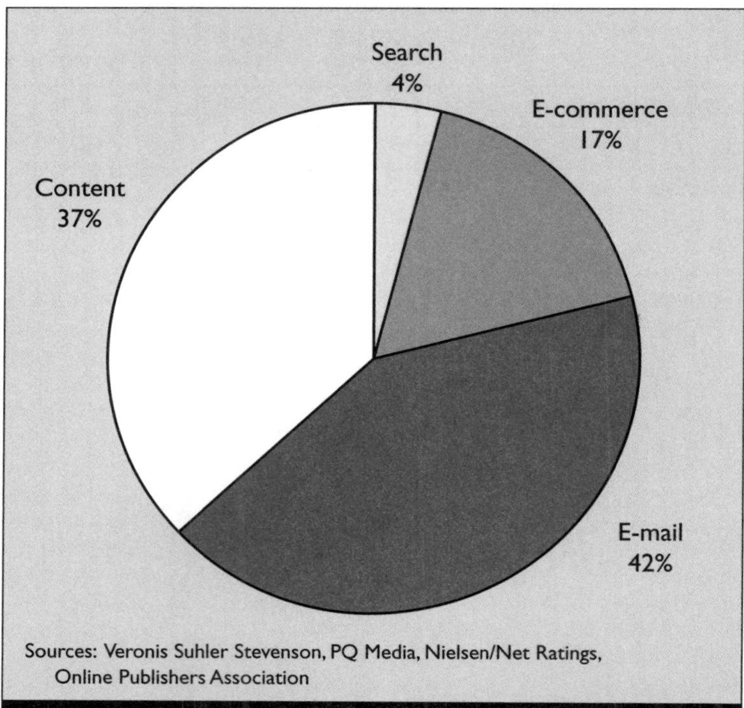

Sources: Veronis Suhler Stevenson, PQ Media, Nielsen/Net Ratings, Online Publishers Association

enough new titles for this format to push growth much higher. Concurrently, the industry is awaiting the release of new console game platforms from Sony, Microsoft and Nintendo, not expected until late 2005 and 2006, but a significant increase in time spent won't occur until 2007 when more titles become available.

Finally, data indicating deceleration or declines in time spent with traditional media can be misleading. Although Internet usage continues to increase more quickly than many other media, time spent with the digital versions of traditional media brands are included in that increase. Consumers spend 37.4 percent of their time on the Web seeking content, often supplied by traditional media companies on their online brands of print products or electronic programs. It is difficult to break out usage according to shares of exact time that consumers spend on Web sites related to traditional media such as downloading music, reading news articles, listening to radio stations, or looking at online magazines. Therefore, while the time consumers spend with analog recorded music has slowed, total time spent with music is likely increasing because of digital music downloads on devices like the iPod.

Consumers increased overall media use only 0.3 percent to 3,480 hours per person per year in 2004, slightly less than 10 hours per day per person. Since 1999, overall use has increased 200 hours per person per year, more than one half-hour a day than five years ago. Overall usage has increased at a compound annual rate of 1.2 percent from 1999 to 2004, and some researchers point to the events of 9/11 as a turning point in increased media usage as consumers stayed home more often.

The increase in time spent with media has also led to skepticism about the overall number of hours individuals spend with media. One explanation for the high numbers is media multitasking, which has been observed in numerous studies, often with conflicting results. The media industry generally accepts that consumers often use TV and the Internet simultaneously, and that they listen to music while using other media, and that print media requires more concentration than electronic media. There is inconclusive evidence of the amount of time consumers spend multitasking while using specific media, and of the level of consumer engagement with the primary medium being used during multitasking. For example, one study suggests high levels of multitasking in DVR households, which contradicts data on the low levels of multitasking in affluent households, the major purchasers of DVRs. Current data on media engagement is also questionable because the sources of much of the data are often trade organizations that tout research that is favorable to their medium. Research from trade groups are often contradicted by similar reports released from trade groups in other media segments.

Another trend being closely monitored by media companies is the shifting demographics in the United States. While marketers covet the 18- to 34-year-old demographic, the share of older audiences is rising. Most research on younger audiences suggests that they are migrating away from traditional print and broadcast media to new media like the Internet, wireless content and video-

Media Multitasking, by Primary Media*

	Other Medium Used to Multitask[†]					
Primary Medium	*Internet*	*Magazines*	*Newspapers*	*Radio*	*Television*[‡]	*Average*
Television[‡]	35.2%	59.8%	64.2%	28.9%	—	47.0%
Radio	57.3	46.5	46.9	—	17.7%	42.1
Newspapers	22.6	—	—	49.6	52.4	41.5
Magazines[§]	23.3	—	—	42.8	51.4	39.2
Internet	—	21.4	20.2	52.1	61.8	38.9
Average	34.6	42.6	43.8	43.4	45.8	42.0

Sources: Veronis Suhler Stevenson, PQ Media, BIGResearch
*Regularly or occasionally.
[†]Second medium chosen in the multitasking process, with maximum concentration on primary medium.
[‡]Broadcast television and cable & satellite television.
[§]No media multitasking data available on books. Anecdotal evidence suggests multitasking parallel to magazine use.

End-User Spending On Communications

games. There are other data suggesting that migration is not as rapid as once thought; for example, television viewership among teenagers has not declined significantly during the past five years, and has even increased in some years due to the popularity of particular programs. Meanwhile, older audiences perform less media multitasking and are among the heaviest users of television and print materials, yet marketers tend to dismiss this audience due to its brand loyalty. Marketers, however, do have heightened interest in one particular subset of this older demographic—those individuals who are defined to be "influentials," consumers who influence the buying habits of others. Influentials are said to be heavy users of print media and the Internet, as indicated by political blog visitors during the recent presidential election.

The other demographic of interest is the burgeoning Hispanic market, which recently became the largest minority, surpassing African-Americans. Attractive to marketers is the trend pushing that growth, young immigrants with children. Meanwhile, recent data

Shares of Consumers Who Media Multitask, by Medium

Medium	*Multitasking*
Print	*48.5%*
Magazines	53.9
Books	47.4
Newspapers	44.4
Music	*45.3*
Cassettes	52.4
CDs	45.0
MP3	31.1
Radio*	21.7
Internet	*43.5*
Web Surfing	43.8
E-mail	38.1
Video	*9.2*
Videogames	26.0
Television[‡]	20.4
VHS	11.4
DVDs	5.7
All Media[†]	*18.1*

Sources: Veronis Suhler Stevenson, PQ Media, International Digital Media & Arts Association
*Includes non-music stations, such as all talk or sports radio.
[†]Includes cell phone and postage mail use.
[‡]Includes broadcast and cable television.

Consumer Spending per Person per Year

Year	Broadcast TV	Cable & Satellite TV	Total TV	Home Video	Consumer Internet	Consumer Books	Newspapers
1999	$0.00	$179.75	$179.75	$ 80.21	$ 34.08	$87.34	$52.26
2000	0.00	189.45	189.45	81.49	49.47	85.84	51.93
2001	0.00	204.74	204.74	92.50	68.81	84.35	52.40
2002	0.00	224.30	224.30	108.22	85.84	87.64	53.00
2003	0.00	240.53	240.53	122.19	100.63	89.69	52.68
2004	0.00	255.36	255.36	125.31	113.48	89.67	51.62
2005	0.00	269.85	269.85	138.60	125.43	91.39	50.17
2006	0.00	282.92	282.92	151.09	138.83	91.27	48.97
2007	0.00	296.02	296.02	161.14	151.91	93.26	47.95
2008	0.00	308.40	308.40	171.63	165.60	93.23	47.13
2009	0.00	320.81	320.81	180.27	177.42	93.90	46.47

Sources: Veronis Suhler Stevenson, PQ Media, Adams Media Research, Alexander & Associates, Arbitron, Audit Bureau of Circulations, Book Industry Study Group, Business 2.0, comScore Networks, Datamonitor, Digital Entertainment Group, DIRECTV, DSL Forum, EchoStar, *Editor & Publisher*, Entertainment Software Association, Federal Communications Commission, *The Financial Post*, The Gallup Organization, In Demand, Insight Research, In-Stat/MDR, Jupiter Media Metrix, Kagan Research, Kinetic Strategies, Leichtman Research Group, Lexis/Nexis, LodgeNet, Magazine Publishers of America, Motion Picture Association of America, National Cable & Telecommunications Association, Newspaper Association of America, Nielsen Media Research, NPDFunworld, Online Publishers Association, Recording Industry Association of America, Rentrak, Replay TV, Scarborough Research, Sirius Satellite Radio, Smith Travel Research, SRDS, Time Warner, Telecommunications Industry Association, TiVo, U.S. Census Bureau, *Video Business*, Video Software Dealers Association, XM Satellite Radio, Yankee Group

Recorded Music	Consumer Magazines	Box Office	Videogames	Interactive TV & Wireless Content	Broadcast & Satellite Radio	Total
$62.95	$47.98	$32.15	$28.21	$ 0.03	—	$ 585.71
61.04	47.54	32.64	27.89	0.10	—	608.31
57.85	46.90	35.41	29.17	0.22	$ 0.001	652.89
52.47	46.86	39.59	32.34	3.35	0.07	712.64
48.73	46.08	39.01	32.65	7.40	0.37	757.49
49.39	46.88	38.76	32.94	13.31	1.15	794.78
47.65	47.82	38.82	33.49	20.10	2.65	841.48
45.77	47.59	39.11	36.13	26.95	4.68	888.06
45.35	48.50	39.71	38.87	32.96	6.91	936.75
43.49	49.19	40.17	42.63	37.94	9.13	982.56
42.39	49.57	41.04	44.30	42.41	11.16	1,023.69

End-User Spending On Communications

Shifting Demographics in the United States (% Share)

	Adults		Race				
Year	18 to 49	50+	White	Hispanic	African-American	Asian & Pacific Islander	American Indian
1999	63.5%	36.5%	71.9%	11.5%	12.1%	3.8%	0.7%
2004	61.5	38.5	69.7	13.0	12.3	4.2	0.8
2009	58.8	41.2	67.7	14.3	12.5	4.7	0.8

Sources: Veronis Suhler Stevenson, PQ Media, U.S. Census Bureau

Growth of Consumer Spending per Person per Year

Year	Broadcast TV	Cable & Satellite TV	Total TV	Home Video	Consumer Internet	Consumer Books	Newspapers
2000	—	5.4%	5.4%	1.6%	45.2%	–1.7%	–0.6%
2001	—	8.1	8.1	13.5	39.1	–1.7	0.9
2002	—	9.6	9.6	17.0	24.8	3.9	1.1
2003	—	7.2	7.2	12.9	17.2	2.3	–0.6
2004	—	6.2	6.2	2.5	12.8	0.0	–2.0
2005	—	5.7	5.7	10.6	10.5	1.9	–2.8
2006	—	4.8	4.8	9.0	10.7	–0.1	–2.4
2007	—	4.6	4.6	6.7	9.4	2.2	–2.1
2008	—	4.2	4.2	6.5	9.0	0.0	–1.7
2009	—	4.0	4.0	5.0	7.1	0.7	–1.4
Compound Annual Growth							
1999-2004	—	7.3	7.3	9.3	27.2	0.5	–0.2
2004-2009	—	4.7	4.7	7.5	9.4	0.9	–2.1

Sources: Veronis Suhler Stevenson, PQ Media, Adams Media Research, Alexander & Associates, Arbitron, Audit Bureau of Circulations, Book Industry Study Group, Business 2.0, comScore Networks, Datamonitor, Digital Entertainment Group, DIRECTV, DSL Forum, EchoStar, *Editor & Publisher*, Entertainment Software Association, Federal Communications Commission, *The Financial Post*, The Gallup Organization, In Demand, Insight Research, In-Stat/MDR, Jupiter Media Metrix, Kagan Research, Kinetic Strategies, Leichtman Research Group, Lexis/Nexis, LodgeNet, Magazine Publishers of America, Motion Picture Association of America, National Cable & Telecommunications Association, Newspaper Association of America, Nielsen Media Research, NPDFunworld, Online Publishers Association, Recording Industry Association of America, Rentrak, Replay TV, Scarborough Research, Sirius Satellite Radio, Smith Travel Research, SRDS, Time Warner, Telecommunications Industry Association, TiVo, U.S. Census Bureau, *Video Business*, Video Software Dealers Association, XM Satellite Radio, Yankee Group

from the Census Bureau show that there are a greater percentage of whites than Hispanics over the age of 65, the opposite of what holds true in those under 18. The problem facing marketers is that data on Hispanic media usage often show differences in Hispanic markets based on country of heritage, such as Mexican, Cuban and Puerto Rican. Advertisers are faced with the challenges of determining which medium will most effectively reach these various audiences, in addition to how to effectively dimension the English-Spanish language preferences in immigrants from these countries.

What is clear from all the factors discussed above is that consumers are becoming more empowered to control content. Media supported by consumers continued to gain market share on media supported by advertisers in 2004, although the latter still commands a larger share of total time spent with media. Time spent with advertising-supported media accounted for 56.8 percent, or 1,975 hours, of the total, while consumer-supported media accounted for the remaining 43.2 percent, or 1,504 hours. Consumer-supported media gained 6.5 share points on advertising-supported media between 1999 and 2004. Over the next five years, the share of media supported by consumers will grow to 45.1 percent, or 1,604 hours per person per year, versus 54.9 percent, or 1,951 hours, for advertising-supported media.

Over the next five years, the media

Recorded Music	Consumer Magazines	Box Office	Videogames	Interactive TV & Wireless Content	Broadcast & Satellite Radio	Total
–3.0%	–0.9%	1.5%	–1.2%	182.0%	—	3.9%
–5.2	–1.3	8.5	4.6	132.1	—	7.3
–9.3	–0.1	11.8	10.8	1,413.5	8,299.3%	9.2
–7.1	–1.7	–1.5	1.0	121.0	429.1	6.3
1.3	1.7	–0.6	0.9	79.9	208.5	4.9
–3.5	2.0	0.2	1.7	51.0	130.0	5.9
–3.9	–0.5	0.7	7.9	34.1	76.3	5.5
–0.9	1.9	1.5	7.6	22.3	47.7	5.5
–4.1	1.4	1.2	9.7	15.1	32.0	4.9
–2.5	0.8	2.2	3.9	11.8	22.3	4.2
–4.7	–0.5	3.8	3.1	230.4	—	6.3
–3.0	1.1	1.2	6.1	26.1	57.4	5.2

expected to show the highest growth in usage are interactive television and wireless content, with compound annual growth of 31.3 percent; home video, which will increase 8.0 percent; and videogames, which will rise 4.4 percent. Usage of total television and consumer Internet will expand in the low single digits, radio listenership will be flat, while recorded music, box office, newspapers, consumer magazines and consumer books will continue to fall in the low single digits. From 2004 to 2009, overall time spent with media will expand to 3,555 hours per person per year, posting compound annual growth of 0.4 percent. The average person is projected to use media almost 10 hours per day by 2009.

Currently, the average consumer is spending $794.78 per year on media content and access, an increase of 4.9 percent over 2003. Compound annual growth from 1999 to 2004 was 6.3 percent. Double-digit growth in the average consumer's spending occurred in 2004 with satellite radio, interactive television and wireless content, and consumer Internet. Going forward, consumer spending per person on media will break $1,000 for the first time in 2009. Spending per person per year on media will rise at a compound annual rate of 5.2 percent during the forecast period to $1,023.69 in 2009. Growth will be driven by increased spending on the emerging wireless content and satellite radio segments, in addition to other digital-based media, such as home video, videogames and consumer Internet.

End-User Spending On Communications

Shares of Consumer Spending per Person per Year

Year	Broadcast TV	Cable & Satellite TV	Total TV	Home Video	Consumer Internet	Consumer Books	Newspapers
1999	0.0%	30.7%	30.7%	13.7%	5.8%	14.9%	8.9%
2000	0.0	31.1	31.1	13.4	8.1	14.1	8.5
2001	0.0	31.4	31.4	14.2	10.5	12.9	8.0
2002	0.0	31.5	31.5	15.2	12.0	12.3	7.4
2003	0.0	31.8	31.8	16.1	13.3	11.8	7.0
2004	0.0	32.1	32.1	15.8	14.3	11.3	6.5
2005	0.0	32.1	32.1	16.5	14.9	10.9	6.0
2006	0.0	31.9	31.9	17.0	15.6	10.3	5.5
2007	0.0	31.6	31.6	17.2	16.2	10.0	5.1
2008	0.0	31.4	31.4	17.5	16.9	9.5	4.8
2009	0.0	31.3	31.3	17.6	17.3	9.2	4.5

Sources: Veronis Suhler Stevenson, PQ Media, Adams Media Research, Alexander & Associates, Arbitron, Audit Bureau of Circulations, Book Industry Study Group, Business 2.0, comScore Networks, Datamonitor, Digital Entertainment Group, DIRECTV, DSL Forum, EchoStar, *Editor & Publisher*, Entertainment Software Association, Federal Communications Commission, *The Financial Post*, The Gallup Organization, In Demand, Insight Research, In-Stat/MDR, Jupiter Media Metrix, Kagan Research, Kinetic Strategies, Leichtman Research Group, Lexis/Nexis, LodgeNet, Magazine Publishers of America, Motion Picture Association of America, National Cable & Telecommunications Association, Newspaper Association of America, Nielsen Media Research, NPDFunworld, Online Publishers Association, Recording Industry Association of America, Rentrak, Replay TV, Scarborough Research, Sirius Satellite Radio, Smith Travel Research, SRDS, Time Warner, Telecommunications Industry Association, TiVo, U.S. Census Bureau, *Video Business*, Video Software Dealers Association, XM Satellite Radio, Yankee Group

Consumer Spending per Person per Hour

Year	Broadcast TV	Cable & Satellite TV	Total TV	Box Office	Home Video	Interactive TV & Wireless Content	Consumer Books
1999	$0.00	$0.29	$0.13	$2.50	$1.96	—	$0.75
2000	0.00	0.28	0.13	2.67	1.91	—	0.80
2001	0.00	0.28	0.14	2.81	1.95	—	0.80
2002	0.00	0.28	0.15	2.90	1.89	$0.95	0.81
2003	0.00	0.28	0.16	2.99	2.03	1.10	0.83
2004	0.00	0.29	0.17	3.11	1.86	1.24	0.83
2005	0.00	0.31	0.17	3.16	1.82	1.32	0.86
2006	0.00	0.32	0.18	3.19	1.80	1.40	0.86
2007	0.00	0.34	0.19	3.25	1.77	1.26	0.88
2008	0.00	0.35	0.20	3.33	1.80	1.20	0.88
2009	0.00	0.36	0.21	3.38	1.82	1.01	0.89

Sources: Veronis Suhler Stevenson, PQ Media, Adams Media Research, Alexander & Associates, Arbitron, Audit Bureau of Circulations, Book Industry Study Group, Business 2.0, comScore Networks, Datamonitor, Digital Entertainment Group, DIRECTV, DSL Forum, EchoStar, *Editor & Publisher*, Entertainment Software Association, Federal Communications Commission, *The Financial Post*, The Gallup Organization, In Demand, Insight Research, In-Stat/MDR, Jupiter Media Metrix, Kagan Research, Kinetic Strategies, Leichtman Research Group, Lexis/Nexis, LodgeNet, Magazine Publishers of America, Motion Picture Association of America, National Cable & Telecommunications Association, Newspaper Association of America, Nielsen Media Research, NPDFunworld, Online Publishers Association, Recording Industry Association of America, Rentrak, Replay TV, Scarborough Research, Sirius Satellite Radio, Smith Travel Research, SRDS, Time Warner, Telecommunications Industry Association, TiVo, U.S. Census Bureau, *Video Business*, Video Software Dealers Association, XM Satellite Radio, Yankee Group

Recorded Music	*Consumer Magazines*	*Box Office*	*Videogames*	*Interactive TV & Wireless Content*	*Broadcast & Satellite Radio*
10.7%	8.2%	5.5%	4.8%	0.01%	—
10.0	7.8	5.4	4.6	0.02	—
8.9	7.2	5.4	4.5	0.03	0.0001%
7.4	6.6	5.6	4.5	0.5	0.01
6.4	6.1	5.1	4.3	1.0	0.05
6.2	5.9	4.9	4.1	1.7	0.1
5.7	5.7	4.6	4.0	2.4	0.3
5.2	5.4	4.4	4.1	3.0	0.5
4.8	5.2	4.2	4.1	3.5	0.7
4.4	5.0	4.1	4.3	3.9	0.9
4.1	4.8	4.0	4.3	4.1	1.1

Consumer Internet	*Videogames*	*Consumer Magazines*	*Newspapers*	*Recorded Music*	*Broadcast & Satellite Radio*	*Total*
$0.52	$0.49	$0.36	$0.25	$0.22	—	$0.18
0.48	0.43	0.35	0.26	0.24	—	0.18
0.52	0.44	0.37	0.27	0.25	—	0.19
0.58	0.46	0.38	0.27	0.26	$0.00007	0.20
0.61	0.43	0.38	0.27	0.27	0.0004	0.22
0.64	0.43	0.38	0.27	0.27	0.0012	0.23
0.68	0.43	0.38	0.27	0.27	0.003	0.24
0.73	0.44	0.39	0.27	0.26	0.005	0.25
0.78	0.45	0.40	0.27	0.26	0.007	0.27
0.83	0.46	0.40	0.28	0.26	0.009	0.28
0.87	0.46	0.41	0.28	0.26	0.011	0.29

Growth of Consumer Spending per Person per Hour

Year	Broadcast TV	Cable & Satellite TV	Total TV	Box Office	Home Video	Interactive TV & Wireless Content	Consumer Books
2000	—	–1.4%	2.6%	6.8%	–2.7%	—	7.0%
2001	—	–2.1	6.5	5.0	2.1	—	–0.3
2002	—	1.9	7.4	3.5	–3.1	—	0.9
2003	—	1.3	5.5	3.0	7.7	16.1%	2.5
2004	—	3.6	6.0	3.8	–8.4	12.6	1.0
2005	—	5.5	5.5	1.7	–2.4	6.8	3.3
2006	—	4.5	4.3	0.9	–1.1	5.7	0.2
2007	—	3.9	4.6	2.1	–1.4	–9.6	2.0
2008	—	2.6	3.5	2.3	1.6	–4.5	–0.1
2009	—	5.2	4.3	1.7	1.1	–16.2	0.9
Compound Annual Growth							
1999-2004	—	0.6	5.6	4.4	–1.1	—	2.2
2004-2009	—	4.4	4.5	1.7	–0.5	–4.0	1.3

Sources: Veronis Suhler Stevenson, PQ Media, Adams Media Research, Alexander & Associates, Arbitron, Audit Bureau of Circulations, Book Industry Study Group, Business 2.0, comScore Networks, Datamonitor, Digital Entertainment Group, DIRECTV, DSL Forum, EchoStar, *Editor & Publisher*, Entertainment Software Association, Federal Communications Commission, *The Financial Post*, The Gallup Organization, In Demand, Insight Research, In-Stat/MDR, Jupiter Media Metrix, Kagan Research, Kinetic Strategies, Leichtman Research Group, Lexis/Nexis, LodgeNet, Magazine Publishers of America, Motion Picture Association of America, National Cable & Telecommunications Association, Newspaper Association of America, Nielsen Media Research, NPDFunworld, Online Publishers Association, Recording Industry Association of America, Rentrak, Replay TV, Scarborough Research, Sirius Satellite Radio, Smith Travel Research, SRDS, Time Warner, Telecommunications Industry Association, TiVo, U.S. Census Bureau, *Video Business*, Video Software Dealers Association, XM Satellite Radio, Yankee Group

CABLE & SATELLITE TELEVISION

Total consumer end-user spending on cable and satellite television—the largest consumer end-user subsegment—including expenditures on basic, premium, pay-per-view (PPV) and VOD services, increased 7.5 percent to $56.28 billion in 2004. Consumer expenditures on cable and satellite TV grew at a compound annual rate of 8.6 percent from 1999 to 2004, outpacing nominal GDP, and accounting for 30.2 percent of all consumer spending on communications in 2004. Growth was fueled by several key drivers, including more original and local programming offered by cable and satellite providers, the rollout of additional bundled services by cable companies, greater availability of digital cable, rate hikes by cable operators, and discounts on hardware and installation by satellite providers. The total number of subscriptions to cable and satellite television increased 4.4 percent to 99.8 million in 2004, and multichannel penetration reached 92.1 percent of all television households, an increase of 2.5 percentage points over 2003.

The direct broadcast satellite sector has experienced dramatic subscriber growth over the past five years, due primarily to the ability of satellite providers to deliver local channels. However, DBS's subscriber growth is

Consumer Internet	Videogames	Consumer Magazines	Newspapers	Recorded Music	Broadcast & Satellite Radio	Total
–8.8%	–11.2%	–1.6%	1.5%	5.7%	—	2.2%
10.3	2.6	4.7	2.7	6.8	—	6.6
11.3	3.9	1.8	2.7	3.5	—	6.8
5.2	–6.0	1.1	0.6	1.2	423.2%	5.1
4.9	–1.5	–0.2	0.1	0.6	213.7	4.6
6.2	1.1	1.6	–0.5	–0.2	132.0	5.8
6.9	2.0	1.4	–0.1	–1.5	76.8	5.0
6.5	2.0	2.0	0.5	–1.0	47.8	4.9
6.6	1.6	1.4	1.1	–0.7	30.7	4.0
5.2	1.4	1.2	1.6	–0.2	22.3	4.0
4.3	–2.6	1.1	1.5	3.5	—	5.0
6.3	1.6	1.5	0.5	–0.7	57.5	4.7

expected to decelerate during the forecast period because most major TV markets are fully served by DBS. But in an effort to continue to drive subscriber growth and to compete with cable's bundling strategy, DBS providers are pursuing partnerships with telephone companies to offer comparable services through the integration of digital satellite and digital subscriber line telephony. Meanwhile, phone companies are entering into similar deals with satellite providers in order to compete with cable companies that are providing voice and data services in an attempt to pilfer their telephony and Internet access revenues.

Despite the surging growth of DBS in recent years, wired cable still dominates the overall industry, with 69.9 million subscribers in 2004. Due to the sheer size of its subscriber base, cable has achieved only single-digit growth since 1999. Total consumer spending on basic cable subscriptions increased 5.9 percent to $32.48 billion in 2004, due mainly to rate increases, and posted compound annual growth of 7.4 percent from 1999 to 2004. Total cable PPV spending increased only 3.1 percent in 2004 to $1.15 billion, as a result of slower-than-expected acceptance of digital cable and VOD, and the continuing popularity of adult programming. VOD showed spectacular growth of 123.9 percent to $318.0 million in 2004, but the installed base is still dwarfed by PPV. Spending on cable PPV achieved compound annual growth of 7.5 percent from 1999 to 2004. Expenditures on cable's premium channel services rose 3.4 percent to $5.37 billion in 2004, and expanded at a compound annual rate of 2.2 percent from 1999 to 2004.

In addition, cable subscriber numbers continue to be negatively affected by changes in accounting practices at some cable operators. This led to some overzealous subscriber counting in incidents that occurred in the 1998-2003 period. For example, Adelphia lowered its subscriber counts for basic cable, digital cable and high-speed Internet service in 2002, following a review of the company's accounting practices by the U.S. Government. Nevertheless, wired cable passed 98.8 percent of U.S. TV households in 2004, and 65.3 percent of homes passed subscribed to cable services. Cable operators hope to attract new subscribers and reduce subscriber churn by offering packages consisting of high-speed Internet access, cable telephony, digital video recorders, ITV, VOD and digital cable.

Total consumer end-user spending on cable and satellite television, including expenditures on basic, premium, PPV and VOD services, is projected to increase 6.8 percent to $60.12 billion in 2005, and grow at a compound annual rate of 5.9 percent in the 2004-2009 period to $74.83 billion. Growth will be spurred by cable rate hikes, the launch of more bundled services by cable and satellite providers, the rollout of new original and local programming, wider availability of digital cable and continued investment in new technology. The total number of multichannel subscriptions is projected to reach 110.5 million in 2009, rising at a compound annual rate of 2.1 percent from 2004 to 2009. The multichannel penetration rate in all TV households will increase to 96.6 percent in 2009 from 92.1 percent in 2004. Wired cable subscriptions are expected to advance at a compound annual rate of 0.7 percent from 2004 to 2009 to 72.5 million.

CONSUMER INTERNET

Consumer end-user spending on Internet access and content increased 14.1 percent to $27.93 billion in 2004, and although growth decelerated for the fourth consecutive year, Internet spending was still among the fastest-growing subsegments of the consumer end-user sector. Consumer Internet expenditures grew at a compound annual rate of 28.7 percent from 1999 to 2004, significantly outpacing GDP growth, and the subsegment accounted for 15.0 percent of all consumer end-user media spending in 2004. Among the important growth drivers of the Internet subsegment, which was the second-largest in the consumer end-user sector, were the continued transition from dial-up to broadband access and the launch of more rich content applications. These two key trends united to spur improvement in the time-efficient use of the medium, and they empowered more consumers to retrieve and utilize rich media, while at the same time providing for faster and more frequent searches.

Consumer Web access spending continued to account for the largest share of the overall market in 2004, with expenditures of $25.58 billion, a 13.0 percent increase compared with the previous year. The double-digit gain was due to the increasing penetration of broadband access, which includes both cable modem and digital subscriber line (DSL) installations. Household spending on cable modem access increased 35.1 percent to $9.30 billion in 2004, while DSL household spending climbed 35.8 percent to $6.56 billion for the year. Household spending on dial-up dropped 15.4 percent to $8.22 billion in 2004. Web access penetration among households with computers has already reached 95.1 percent, and is not expected to reach much higher going forward because not all computer owners need or desire the Internet.

On the content front, increased spending on Internet gaming and digital music drove overall growth of content expenditures, regardless of the continued threat from piracy and file sharing. Content spending increased 27.9 percent to $2.35 billion in 2004. Of the three content categories—general content, online games and digital music—general content accounted for the largest share with $1.36 billion in 2004 expenditures. However, general content spending—which includes news, personals, greeting cards and research—declined 3.6 percent for the year, as a result of consumers questioning the value of paid content in a heavily free content market. Digital music posted the strongest gain in the content segment, with spending up 312.5 percent to $330.0 million in 2004, fueled by strong sales of Apple's iPod and other digital media players. Online game spending also soared in 2004, rising 91.3 percent to $656.0 million for the year, driven by enthusiasts who have created community portals including bulletin boards, chat rooms, news, articles and events.

Total consumer spending on Internet access and content continued its double-digit growth during the first half of 2005 and is expected to do so for the remainder of the year. Many of the trends that drove 2004 spending are also spurring 2005 growth. Access spending is rising due to the migration away from dial-up to more expensive broadband and wireless services. Consumer expenditures on online games and downloaded music are also climbing. As a result, consumer spending on Internet access and content is expected to rise 11.7 percent in 2005 to $31.19 billion.

Fueled by double-digit upside in both spending categories, overall consumer expenditures on Internet access and content are projected to grow at a compound annual rate of 10.4 percent from 2004 to 2009, reaching $45.84 billion in 2009. Consumer spending on access will rise at a compound annual rate of 8.3 percent in the 2004-2009 period to $38.08 billion, driven by the continued transition to broadband services. Meanwhile, online content spending is expected to rise at a compound annual rate of 27.1 percent from 2004 to 2009, reaching $7.76 billion, propelled by strong growth in both digital music downloads and online gaming. As the market advances, the availability of digital music downloads will become more pervasive to the point where any retailer that sells entertainment merchandise will likely offer some form of download. Digital music downloads of albums will post compound annual growth of 46.6 percent in the 2004-2009 period. Spending on general content, however, will be sluggish in the forecast period as the market matures.

HOME VIDEO

Following three consecutive years of double-digit gains, consumer home video spending growth decelerated dramatically in 2004 due to the dearth of blockbuster box office releases the previous year, the continued transition from VHS to DVD players, and a significant slowdown in the buildup of DVD libraries. As a result, consumer expenditures on home video rose only 3.8 percent to $27.62 billion in 2004, as the subsegment dropped below consumer Internet to become the third-largest consumer end-user segment with a 14.8 percent share of all sector spending. Home video spending grew at a compound annual rate of 10.7 percent from 1999 to 2004, more than twice the rate of growth for the broader economy.

Strong growth in DVD sales and rentals in 2004, owing to falling prices and increased penetration of DVD players, was offset by plummeting sales and rentals in the VHS market. DVDs represented 78.9 percent of home video sales for the year, up from 61.6 percent in 2003. DVD spending grew to $21.79 billion in 2004, up from $16.39 billion in 2003. The installed base of DVD players also surpassed the 50 percent milestone in 2004, as a result of hardware prices falling below $30 in some cases, making this format the fastest-growing consumer electronics product of all time. DVD expenditures, however, showed signs of weakening in late 2004 and early 2005 because the format has grown so quickly. DVD players are already in 65.4 million households less than eight years after the format was launched.

The home video segment is projected to return to double-digit growth in 2005 on the strength of DVD sell-through, as the installed base of DVD players grows to 78.6 million by year's end. Total home video expenditures are expected to increase at an accelerated 11.8 percent in 2005 to $30.88 billion, driven by several new hot movie and television show releases, and a slower decline in the VHS market. Key releases in 2005 include *Meet the Fockers* (which sold 3.0 million copies in its first day of availability), *Ocean's Twelve* and *Lemony Snicket's A Series of Unfortunate Events*. Other drivers include the continued release of recent seasons of popular TV shows like *Friends* and *Seinfeld* on home video. DVD spending will grow 22.7 percent in 2005 to $26.73 billion.

Going forward, we expect consumer spending on home video will grow at a compound annual rate of 8.8 percent from 2004 to 2009, a deceleration from the 10.7 percent growth in the previous five-year period, with expenditures hitting $42.05 billion in 2009. The home video market will be challenged in the forecast period by the burgeoning VOD market and the pressure cable operators are applying to Hollywood studios in order to make movies available through VOD as soon as possible. In addition, the number of box office hits is anticipated to be relatively minimal in 2005 and 2006, and the slate of hot television programs entering the home video space is slowing. DVD rental spending will grow at a compound annual rate of 11.6 percent during the forecast period, compared to 130.6 percent upside from 1999 to 2004.

CONSUMER BOOKS

Consumer book spending inched up 1.2 percent to $19.76 billion in 2004, driven primarily by a 3.4 percent hike in prices, which offset a 2.1 percent decline in unit sales for the year. Strong growth in the first half of the year and a respectable holiday season counterbalanced the weak summer and fall seasons. Spending on political books drove growth in the first half of 2004, particularly books challenging the policies of the Bush Administration, in addition to former President Bill Clinton's autobiography, which sold 400,000 copies in its first day of sale and went on to sell nearly two million copies by the end of the year. Spending on political books began to ebb in the summer, and without any hot fiction titles, expenditures on consumer books slumped badly from July through October. The rebound in November was driven by nonfiction titles and political books, led by *America (The Book)*, the faux textbook by writers of *The Daily Show*, and *The 9/11 Commission Report*, the official investigative analysis of the 2001 terrorist attacks.

The fastest-growing consumer book segment in 2004 was religion, which posted a 10.7 percent increase in spending. *The Purpose-Driven Life* continued its phenomenal run, selling more than 7 million copies in 2004 after selling over 11 million in 2003. Growth in religious book spending was fueled by an aging American public that continues its shift toward spirituality and conservatism, a trend that became more pronounced after the 2001 terrorist attacks. To capitalize on the heightened interest in religious books, more mainstream bookstores have expanded their inventories of religious books, and these works are also among the top sellers at Wal-Mart. Online bookstore sales grew more rapidly than those of bricks-and-mortar stores in 2004, as Web spending rose 9.6 percent to $2.05 billion, led by Amazon.com. Online sales accounted for 10.4 percent of total spending on consumer books in 2004, a slight increase from the prior year.

Meanwhile, the growth of consumer book spending continued to be hampered by competition from other forms of media. A widely released study in July 2004, titled *Reading at Risk*, documented the decline in time spent reading books. The survey found that about 57 percent of adult Americans had read some type of book in 2003, down from approximately 61 percent in 1992. The percentage of Americans who had read any type of fiction title fell to about 47 percent, down from approximately 54 percent in 1992. The report also found that reading fell among the affluent and highly educated, the two groups most associated with reading books.

Consumer book spending was sluggish in the first quarter of 2005, due to the post-election decline in spending on political books coupled with the lack of a new fiction blockbuster. The U.S. Census Bureau reported that bookstore sales were down 4.6 percent in the first two months of 2005, while the Association of American Publishers reported sales down in all consumer book categories in the first two months of 2005, except juvenile hardcover. Despite the lethargic start to 2005, sales at traditional and online bookstores will undoubtedly receive a spark on July 16 with the release of *Harry Potter and the Half-Blood Prince*. The book immediately hit the number-one spot on Amazon.com in late 2004 after the on-sale date was announced. Virtually every bookstore in America has some sort of Potter-related event planned for July. As a result, we project consumer book spending to increase at an accelerated 3.0 percent in 2005 to $20.36 billion, driven by growth in the juvenile hardcover and religious categories, offset somewhat by a decline in the mass-market paperback and book club categories. We forecast consumer book expenditures to grow at an accelerated compound annual rate of 2.1 percent from 2004 to 2009, reaching $21.90 billion in 2009. The higher growth rate in the forecast period will be driven primarily by a minor increase in units and moderate price hikes. Unit sales are projected to rise at a 0.5 percent compound annual rate in the 2004-2009 timeframe, while prices are expected to hike up 1.4 percent on a compound annual basis in the period. The religious category will post the strongest compound annual growth over the next five years, rising 3.8 percent from 2004 to 2009. Spending in the juvenile trade category is also forecast to beat the 2.1 percent industry average, growing 3.1 percent on a compound basis over the next five years.

RECORDED MUSIC

Recorded music spending, excluding online music downloads, increased 2.5 percent to $12.15 billion in 2004, ending the industry's four-year slide. But spending declined at a compound annual rate of 3.6 percent from 1999 to 2004, the only consumer end-user subsegment to contract in the period. The record industry was bolstered by Usher's *Confessions* album in 2004, which sold 8.0 million copies, more than the year's second and third bestselling albums combined, and 1.5 million more than the top album of 2003. The first-ever decline in the average price of a CD also helped spark sales in 2004. The music industry is still a hit-driven business, and the top 10 albums of 2004 sold a combined 34.6 million copies, up from 33.3 million copies in 2003. Although spending on recorded music grew for the first time in four years in 2004, the market is expected to continue its struggles in the forecast period as a result of online music piracy and competition from other entertainment media, such as DVD movies and videogames.

CD sales, by far the largest recorded music format, were up 1.9 percent to $11.45 billion in 2004. The gain in sales was due in part to a 0.9 percent decrease in the average CD price to $14.93. CD net unit sales grew 2.8 percent to 766.9 million in 2004, up from 745.9 million units in 2003. Only music video units grew more, up 64.3 percent to 32.7 million. All six other categories experienced declines. CD sales represented more than 94 percent of all music spending in 2004.

While recorded music unit sales increased 3.5 percent in the first half of 2004, they declined 0.6 percent in the second half of the year, and the downtrend continued through the first half of 2005, indicating that the upswing in 2004 was more likely an aberration than a trend. First-quarter 2005 unit sales were down an estimated 8 percent compared with the same period in 2004, although industry executives were hopeful that key upcoming album releases—including those from Mariah Carey, The Dave Matthews Band, Bruce Springsteen and *American Idol*—would spur growth in the second half of the year. Despite these releases, we expect music expenditures, excluding online spending, to decline 2.5 percent to $11.85 billion for the full year of 2005, as unit sales slip 2.3 percent to 795.2 million for the year.

Piracy continues to be a key issue for the recorded music industry, costing the business an estimated $4.6 billion annually in the U.S. alone. The industry has been fighting back and appears to have made at least some headway by shutting down a number of illegal file-sharing Web sites, although it is unlikely the industry will ever stamp out piracy completely. On a positive note, both the industry and consumers are beginning to embrace legitimate Internet music downloading, as sales of portable digital audio players—most notably Apple's iPod—are strong and appear to be helping to drive sales of legitimate digital music, which grew 312.5 percent to $330.0 million in 2004. As traditional revenue streams continue to decline, the music industry is seeking other income sources to offset the losses, including cell phone ringtones and the licensing of music to other industries. For example, it is estimated that 30 million to 35 million cell phone mastertones were sold in the U.S. in 2004 at an average price of around $2.

Meanwhile, the lack of consumer interest in SACD and DVD-Audio, next-generation formats that were expected to challenge the CD, has further dampened market growth. We anticipate that both formats will struggle during the forecast period because consumers prefer online distribution. Total net unit shipments of recorded music are projected to fall 2.3 percent in 2005, and at a compound annual rate of 1.3 percent from 2004 to 2009 to 761.3 million. As the installed base of portable digital audio players increases, so will digital music spending. The installed base of iPods, the bestselling portable digital audio player on the market, is expected to more than triple to about 35 million by the end of 2005. Sony, Creative Labs, Yahoo! and Philips are among the companies trying to compete with Apple in this market, but have yet to come up with alternatives with wide consumer appeal. Spending on digital music downloads is expected to grow 131.7 percent to $765.0 million in 2005, and at a compound annual growth rate of 59.5 percent to $3.41 billion in the 2004-2009 period. Overall, recorded music spending will decline 2.5 percent to $11.85 billion in 2005, and decrease 2.1 percent on a compound annual basis from 2004 to 2009.

NEWSPAPERS

Total daily and weekly newspaper circulation spending was down 0.8 percent to $11.38 billion in 2004, due to declining unit circulation at major daily and weekly newspapers, and a downturn in prices of weekday and Sunday papers. Newspaper circulation expenditures grew a slim 1.0 percent on a compound annual basis in the 1999-2004 period. Aggregate newspaper unit circulation dropped 1.1 percent to 55.97 million in 2004, as readership of daily newspapers continued its decades-long decline among adults across different age groups, especially younger adults who prefer online news sources. Falling unit circulation, combined with price reductions, drove down daily circulation spending 0.9 percent to $10.99 billion in 2004, accounting for more than 95 percent of all newspaper circulation expenditures. The average price for a weekday newspaper was flat for the year, while that of Sunday editions rose 0.7 percent.

Aggravating this tenuous situation, reports surfaced in 2004 and 2005 that five major newspapers had misreported circulation in prior years. The Audit Bureau of Circulations (ABC) issued sanctions against four of the offending newspapers in 2004 (the fifth was pending in court as of May 2005), but news of the misstatements hurt the image of the newspaper industry and left advertisers demanding greater accountability from publishers. In an effort to address advertiser concerns about circulation quality, some publishers scaled back the number of bulk copies sold to third parties, removing them from paid circulation totals.

Publishers are looking to their Web sites as a means of increasing subscription spending. *The Wall Street Journal*'s online edition, the most successful of all online newspaper ventures, had more than 730,000 subscribers in the first quarter of 2005, each of whom pays $79 annually for the service ($39 if they are subscribers to the print version). In May 2005, *The New York Times* announced that it would charge visitors to its Web site an annual fee of $49.95 to read its Op-Ed and news columnists, archives and other features. In the future, more newspapers are expected to try to generate revenues from content on their Web sites, either through subscriptions or single-article pricing. Meanwhile, the cost of acquiring subscribers has soared in recent years. As a result of the Do Not Call Registry, which took effect in 2003, newspapers were forced to drastically reduce their use of telesales, and rely more on alternative means of reaching customers, such as advertising, direct mail and even door-to-door sales. As a result, the median cost per new subscriber has increased substantially, with the average price of newsprint climbing 9.3 percent in 2004.

Unit circulation of daily newspapers has been declining since 1991, as more potential readers have migrated to other news media, and more evening papers have shuttered. The younger demographics have reduced their consumption of daily newspapers by about 20 percentage points since 1982, while older audiences trimmed their readership as well, although not in as large numbers. Publishers have been trying to stem the slide of unit circulation by various means, including redesigning papers to make them more appealing, launching youth-oriented publications, including more entertainment features, and targeting the growing Hispanic population. Publishers are also trying to boost circulation by becoming more involved in their communities, sponsoring events and reaching out to their readers. The results of these measures are still uncertain, and we don't foresee them making a substantial dent going forward.

Therefore, we are projecting that daily unit circulation will decline 1.3 percent in 2005 to 55.21 million, and continue to fall in the 2004-2009 period at a compound annual rate of 1.8 percent. Daily circulation spending is expected to decrease 1.9 percent to $10.78 billion in 2005, due to falling unit circulation. Publishers will reduce weekday edition prices 0.7 percent and Sunday prices 0.3 percent. As unit circulation declines from 2004 to 2009, publishers will raise daily and Sunday prices. As a result, circulation spending will decrease at a lower compound annual rate of 1.1 percent, compared with the prior five-year period, reaching $10.42 billion in 2009. Total newspaper circulation spending, including daily and weekly, will decline 1.7 percent to $11.18 billion in 2005, and decrease at a compound annual rate of 1.0 percent from 2004 to 2009.

CONSUMER MAGAZINES

Consumer magazine circulation spending surged 3.0 percent to $10.33 billion in 2004—the largest increase in seven years—despite the lack of price growth, as an upswing in unit circulation spurred the overall gain. Circulation expenditures experienced an up-and-down period from 1999 to 2004 that resulted in compound annual growth of only 0.8 percent for the five-year timeframe. The average single-copy price increased 3.1 percent to $3.36 in 2004, as publishers found newsstand buyers more receptive to higher prices. The average annual subscription price decreased 0.7 percent to $23.06, while the average per-unit price was flat at $1.65 for the year.

Meanwhile, magazine publishers' intentional circulation cuts—more than 30 percent reduced rate bases from 1999 to 2004—were offset by unit gains at other magazines. The result was a per-issue circulation gain of 3.0 percent in 2004 to 363.1 million. Similar to circulation spending, this represented the first gain in units in seven years, driven by increases in both subscriptions and single copies. Much of the circulation declines of the past few years were spurred by publishers reducing their rate bases to increase profitability and give advertisers better quality circulation. As advertising spending grew in 2004, publishers reduced subscription prices to build and retain their subscriber bases. Maintaining circulation, however, remains challenging for most magazines. With annual subscription renewal rates averaging about 46 percent, retaining current subscribers and attracting new ones is critical to the industry's future health. Direct mail, telesales and third-party subscription agencies are not filling the void left by the demise of sweepstakes subscriptions. The decline of advertising and circulation revenues in recent years has resulted in further erosion of dollars available for circulation-building. And while the Internet has helped bring in new business, its growth is leveling off. Despite the difficulties, individual titles have had success acquiring and retaining readers through strategies such as limited sweepstakes, direct-to-publisher subscription sales, multiyear subscriptions, automatic renewals and retail tie-ins.

Magazines are also trying harder to forge stronger bonds with audiences by launching programs like community events. Magazine executives are also focusing on improving newsstand sales and revenues. Seeking to increase the number of outlets for single-copy sales, publishers and distributors are testing wholesale clubs, dollar stores and specialty stores like sporting goods retailers. Meanwhile, some magazines raised their cover prices in 2004 as an inexpensive way to boost revenues and combat circulation shortfalls. The tactic paid off, as single-copy unit circulation and spending rose. At the same time, some new magazines achieved successful launches by charging less than $2 at the newsstand. In addition, publishers continue to develop magazines to capitalize on emerging editorial and demographic trends, such as the burgeoning Hispanic market.

Subscription unit circulation is expected to grow 1.5 percent to 316.5 million in 2005, followed by a dip in 2006 when postal rates increase, causing publishers to cut back on direct mail. Improvements in database technology and cost management, and savings from postal reforms, such as the elimination of mail sacks, will help drive up subscription growth 1.0 percent in 2007. Compound annual growth in the forecast period will be 0.5 percent. Single-copy unit circulation will increase 1.3 percent to 52.0 million in 2005, due to rising newsstand sales, more retail outlets and better merchandising via end caps and other special display units. Over the forecast period, single-copy circulation will grow 1.3 percent compounded annually, hitting 54.8 million in 2009. Overall per-issue unit circulation will increase 1.5 percent to 368.5 million in 2005, and grow at a compound annual rate of 0.6 percent from 2004 to 2009.

To make the recent circulation turnaround stick, publishers will continue to hone their subscription and newsstand strategies, and look for unconventional means to reach buyers. In order to improve consumer targeting, magazine executives will develop titles for new demographic and editorial niches. With general economic conditions improving, we expect more publishers to raise prices, anticipating that consumers will absorb the hikes and increase spending. Prices will rise at a compound annual rate of 1.6 percent from 2004 to 2009. Driven by increases in unit price and circulation volume, total circulation expenditures will rise 3.1 percent in 2005 to $10.65 billion, and will grow at a compound annual rate of 2.3 percent from 2004 to 2009, reaching $11.56 billion.

BOX OFFICE

After a slight downturn in 2003, consumer box office spending increased 0.5 percent to $9.54 billion in 2004 as a result of higher ticket prices. Escalating prices suppressed admissions, which fell 2.4 percent to 1.54 billion for the year, a trend that began after a record-setting year in 2002. Instead of paying high ticket prices at theaters, consumers are spending more money to watch movies at home, taking advantage of new DVD and VOD services. Box office expenditures grew at a compound annual rate of 5.1 percent from 1999 to 2004.

While overall attendance was down in 2004, family movies and big-budget blockbusters continued to draw crowds. The two biggest box office draws in 2004 were the PG-rated films *Shrek 2* and *Spider-Man 2*, which grossed $437.0 million and $373.0 million, respectively. The top five movies of 2004 each grossed over $200 million, including three that surpassed the $300 million mark. However, there were only 21 movies that exceeded the $100 million threshold, compared to 26 in 2003, which suggests that audiences are gravitating toward bigger releases and dismissing marginal films. The box office success of *Spider-Man 2* propelled Sony to the top spot among distributors in 2004, with $872.0 million in domestic box office receipts. Total sales from the top 50 movies released in 2004 generated $6.04 billion.

The number of movie screens increased 1.3 percent to 36,660 in 2004, the second consecutive year of growth. Consolidation remains a growing trend in the movie theater business, as the total number of facilities shrank 1.0 percent to 6,012 in 2004. The number of multiplex (8 to 16 screens) and megaplex (16-plus screens) facilities rose 3.4 percent and 6.7 percent, respectively, while the number of single-screen and miniplex (2 to 7 screens) theaters fell 3.3 percent and 3.4 percent, correspondingly. Smaller theaters still control the bulk of the market with a 66.0 percent share; however, the increasing cost of real estate and pressure for greater yield per facility will ultimately favor the larger theater chains. The adoption of digital screens worldwide continued its meteoric rise in 2004, with the number of screens increasing 80.0 percent over the 328 in place the prior year.

Box office spending was tepid in the first quarter of 2005, with only four films topping the $100 million mark, led by *Hitch* at $176.0 million. Results were better than expected for the spring release of *Star Wars: Episode III: Revenge of the Sith*, the last installment of the successful science-fiction franchise, which broke box office records in its first four days. Other films anticipated to do well in 2005 include the latest caped crusader flick, *Batman Begins*; *Charlie and the Chocolate Factory*, a contemporary remake of the 1971 classic *Willy Wonka & the Chocolate Factory*; and a new take on the TV program, *The Dukes of Hazzard*. Whether or not these movies deliver on their potential will impact how major studios approach remakes in the future. In contrast, the success of lower-budget movies, such as Mel Gibson's *The Passion of the Christ* and Michael Moore's documentary *Fahrenheit 9/11* in 2004, will push production companies not only to niche genres, but also potentially controversial ones. Studios are also looking at product placement deals to help offset production costs, and advertisers have been more than happy to comply. The average cost of producing and marketing a film fell nearly 5 percent to $98.0 million in 2004, and this trend will continue in the forecast period as studios seek out high-yield genres like animated and family-oriented films, and they become more judicious about investing in high-budget projects.

Despite the decline in production costs, the average price of admission continues to climb, albeit at a decelerating rate, and is expected to reach $6.32 in 2005. As theaters continue to test the limits of consumer spending and push average ticket prices toward the $7 mark, repeat attendance will be adversely affected. The number of frequent and occasional moviegoers increased 2.0 percent in 2004 to 83.0 percent of total admissions. But the five-year trend reflects a drop of 3.0 percent among frequent and occasional moviegoers, and the continued growth of VOD and DVD offerings will also negatively impact attendance. Consumer box office expenditures are expected to rise 1.2 percent to $9.65 billion in 2005, and grow at a compound annual rate of 2.1 percent over the next five years to $10.60 billion in 2009.

VIDEOGAMES

Total videogame spending, including sell-through and rental of console and PC software, increased 2.1 percent to $8.11 billion in 2004. Growth was driven by a record 12 videogame titles surpassing the one-million-unit milestone for the year, but was tempered by the lack of new videogame console systems. Hardware and software sales are expected to rebound in the second half of 2005 and 2006 when Microsoft and Sony launch their new Xbox and PlayStation systems, respectively. Videogame spending, excluding advertising and online gaming, rose at a compound annual rate of 4.4 percent from 1999 to 2004.

In the absence of new console hardware systems, handheld games, including the recently launched Sony PSP and Nintendo DS, continue to sell well and helped boost hardware and software sales in late 2004 and early 2005. The PSP generated buzz among videogame enthusiasts because of its strong graphics and additional features; however, overall hardware and software expenditures will remain tempered until the new console hardware systems are released. Sales of videogame hardware fell to 10.8 million units in 2004 from 12.8 million in 2003, while the average console price fell to $138.21 in 2004 from $159.04 the previous year.

Halo 2, one of the bestselling titles of 2004, took in $125 million in its first day of release. It helped boost videogame sell-through 7.0 percent in 2004 to $6.22 billion, offsetting a 2.1 percent decline in videogame rentals to $682.0 million. A total of 203 million software units were sold in 2004, up 8.9 percent. Videogame software prices fell 1.8 percent during the year. Action games dominate videogames, representing 30.1 percent of purchases. Sports games are the second bestselling genre, with 17.8 percent of sales, followed by shooters at 9.6 percent, family and children titles at 9.5 percent, and racing games with 9.4 percent.

Spending on videogame console software will grow 5.3 percent to $7.27 billion in 2005. Growth for the year will be held back by the late arrival of Sony's and Microsoft's next-generation videogame systems. The segment will see a return to double-digit growth in 2006. Total videogame spending is projected to increase 2.7 percent to $8.33 billion in

2005, and grow at a compound annual rate of 7.1 percent in the forecast period.

INTERACTIVE TELEVISION & WIRELESS CONTENT

The evolution of mobile communication technology is greatly altering the way information is exchanged. Consumer consumption has been robust, and manufacturers have been aggressive in their efforts to develop new applications, such as instant messaging, text messaging, ringtones, gaming and picture downloading. As a result, consumer end-user spending on ITV and wireless content—excluding advertising expenditures—surged 82.1 percent to $2.93 billion in 2004, and grew at a compound annual rate of 234.5 percent from 1999 to 2004.

Cell phones, PDAs, Blackberrys, Blueberrys and other forms of pocket phones are among the catalog of products driving growth in this subsegment. Wireless communication is the backbone of this new technology, but devices are quickly evolving to accommodate music and picture downloading, gaming and TV viewing. While upfront costs will continue to drop as mobile technology advances and becomes more mainstream, manufacturers and service providers will have to address concerns about back-end service, subscriptions and contractual obligations that might leave first-time buyers wary about considering additional products. These customer service issues will become more important as vendors target older consumers, who tend to be more skeptical and value-conscious in their spending habits. Younger consumers, however, have readily bought into the technology.

Advertisers are keen on approaching the wireless market because the technology allows them to reach consumers beyond TV or movie screens. The variety of applications that these devices can hold has opened a window for marketers to send direct and concise messages to captive audiences. FOX, for example, has entered into an agreement with Vodafone to offer one-minute "mobisodes," or dramas based on its hit show *24*. The expectation is that the evolution of this service will allow FOX to eventually transmit trailers and clips of movies, as well.

On the ITV front, VOD households grew 61.0 percent in 2004 to 19.8 million, and the market is estimated to grow 39.0 percent to 27.5 million households in 2005, driven by continued efforts on the part of cable providers to upgrade their digital services. VOD technology is still in its infancy and hasn't penetrated the consumer market as quickly as expected. The increasing popularity of DVDs and competition from traditional and online rental companies have impeded growth. But the future of VOD is encouraging. The technology offers consumers greater convenience when watching movies at home, eliminating the need for DVD rentals, while offering flexibility in starting and stopping movies. The average cost of renting a movie using VOD was less than $4 in 2004, and the average price will likely drop going forward as the medium gains momentum. Growing availability of VOD to digital cable and satellite subscribers will also drive deeper market penetration.

Total spending on VOD in 2004 was $318.0 million, an increase of 123.9 percent over the prior year. Although still in its early stages, VOD spending per household will drop from $38.31 annually in 2004 to $35.91 in 2005, a 6.3 percent decline. The pace of ITV change has been rapid and some formats, such as stand-alone DVRs, are already showing signs of obsolescence as newer and cheaper technologies replace them. The growing popularity of DVDs has limited VOD traction and will continue to do so until VOD reaches the mainstream. Continuing innovation in the ITV sector, like interactive program guides, will expand the possibilities of digital recording and proactive program surfing. As these technologies continue to evolve, advertisers will attempt to find new ways to reach consumers. The potential for growth in the wireless content subsegment is strong, especially as high-speed wireless services progress. In the short-term, there are consumer security and privacy concerns that service providers have to address.

Nevertheless, overall consumer end-user spending on ITV and wireless content is projected to rise 52.7 percent in 2005 to $4.48 billion, and grow at a compound annual rate of 27.5 percent in the forecast period to $9.89 billion in 2009.

SATELLITE RADIO

Satellite radio is the fastest-growing medium of all time, outstripping even cable television's sharp rise in the 1980s, making satellite radio the darling of Wall Street and the media industry. Consumer spending on satellite radio subscriptions, the primary driver of the business, soared 212.5 percent in 2004 to $284.0 million, accounting for 96.8 percent of all expenditures on the medium, including advertising, which is not counted in this chapter. OEM, content and licensing deals are driving more subscribers to the medium, as satellite subscriptions grew 169.7 percent to 4.4 million in 2004, an addition of 2.8 million new subscribers in just one year. The triple-digit growth was spurred mainly by several new licensing deals closed by duopoly competitors XM Satellite Radio and Sirius Satellite Radio.

XM Satellite, which accounted for 73.9 percent of all satellite subscribers in 2004, has been at the forefront of the industry since its inception in 2001 by virtue of the fact that it raced out of the blocks first. The company has since inked OEM deals with General Motors, the world's largest auto maker, to provide XM's service as an option on most models and, more recently, with Hyundai to provide the service as standard equipment on all U.S. models. GM plans to produce more than 1.5 million XM-equipped vehicles in 2005, while Hyundai is scheduled to deliver more than 400,000 this year. As far as major licensing deals, XM holds the long-term rights to Major League Baseball.

Although it was slower to get started, Sirius Satellite—which accounts for the other 26.1 percent of satellite subscribers—has been moving at a frenetic pace to catch up with XM on all fronts. Since 2002, Sirius has penned OEM agreements with several car manufacturers to provide its service as an option on various models, including Ford, BMW, Mitsubishi and Volkswagen. On the licensing front, Sirius has become the premiere provider of sports programming by signing deals with the National Football League, NASCAR, National Basketball Association and the NCAA.

With many of the major content licensing deals already sealed up, we believe the future content battles will focus mainly on key on-air talent, although some of these deals have already been done. The most notable was Sirius's agreement to bring Howard Stern to the satellite landscape in 2006 through a five-year, $500 million deal. Both companies in 2004 decided to broaden their services beyond national programming by providing local traffic and weather data, a move they see as critical to their long-term growth. XM is also fending off competition from Web-based radio by partnering with America Online in 2005 to launch an Internet-based radio service that will be integrated into AOL's free AOL.com portal, making 130 of its radio stations and 20 XM stations available at no cost for unlimited listening. Meanwhile, XM and Sirius have also pursued arrangements with retailers to market their satellite radios for home and out-of-home use. XM rolled out its first wearable device in late 2004 called MyFi. The potential of combining satellite radio with handheld devices like mobile phones could lead to greater retail distribution since consumers won't need to carry an extra device to garner the satellite platform.

The subscriber churn rate is a data point that should be watched closely in the coming years. The average monthly churn for non-promotional subscribers in the fourth quarter of 2004 was between 1.0 percent and 1.5 percent, and most industry analysts expect that rate to increase only slightly in 2005, but forecast churn to approach 2.0 percent at maturity, assuming an average subscriber life of approximately four years. We expect total satellite radio subscriptions to grow 86.2 percent to 8.1 million by the end of 2005. With a cadre of OEM, licensing and retail deals on the books and a relatively low subscriber churn rate, we anticipate the number of satellite subscribers to grow at comparatively high rates throughout the forecast period. As a result, subscription spending will climb at triple- and double-digit rates over the next five years, outpacing all other media segments. Satellite radio subscription spending will grow at a compound annual rate of 59.0 percent from 2004 to 2009, reaching $2.88 billion.

The Outlook For Consumer End-User Spending

End-User Spending On Communications

In recent years, consumer media spending has been driven mainly by strong expansion in cable and satellite television, consumer Internet and home video content. While these segments will continue to provide solid growth during the forecast period, we anticipate an even stronger uptick in the satellite radio and ITV and wireless content markets, as well as notable expansion in the videogame segment once the new console platforms are released. As on-demand technology, such as VOD and DVRs, becomes more prevalent in consumer households, we also expect increased pressure on traditional media to branch out into new revenue streams, such as podcasting radio signals, digital box office releases and t-commerce during television programs.

The bullish outlook for consumer media spending is based on various industry trends, including lower price points for various hardware, such as videogame consoles; growing penetration rates of new technology like ITV and wireless content, satellite radio, VOD and DVRs; the continued investment in bundled services offered by both cable and satellite providers; and richer online content due to the continued migration from dial-up to broadband access.

Total consumer end-user spending on communications is forecast to grow at a compound annual rate of 6.3 percent from 2004 to 2009, reaching $252.80 billion. The sector's growth will outperform that of nominal GDP during the early stages of the forecast, but fall below nominal GDP by 2009 as new media penetration rates near saturation and double-digit growth rates will no longer be the norm. For example, although the three largest segments—cable and satellite television, consumer Internet, and home video—will all post relatively strong growth in the period, each market's growth will decelerate somewhat. This will be offset to some extent by accelerated expansion in the videogame, satellite radio, and ITV and wireless segments, currently the three smallest segments of consumer end-user spending. Consequently, the overall compound annual growth will come in a bit slower than in the 1999-2004 period.

Cable and satellite television will remain the largest consumer end-user segment through the forecast period, as compound annual growth slows but stays solid at 5.9 percent. Total spending will hit $74.83 billion in 2009. Spending on consumer Internet access and content will rise 10.4 percent on a compound annual basis in the period to $45.84 billion in 2009. Expenditures on home video, the third-largest segment, will escalate at a compound annual rate of 8.8 percent from 2004 to 2009, reaching $42.05 billion.

Satellite radio, the smallest segment, will grow the fastest in the period. By the end of 2004, there were approximately 4.4 million satellite radio subscribers, of which XM Satellite Radio controlled slightly fewer than 80 percent of the market. By the end of 2005, the subscriber count is expected to rise to 8.1 million, and subscription revenues are projected to increase 132.4 percent for the full year. Satellite radio providers will continue to sign additional OEM licensing agreements with carmakers, and satellite radio will increasingly become an option in almost all vehicles, including lower-end models. Consumer spending on subscriptions is expected to soar at a compound annual rate of 59.0 percent from 2004 to 2009. The second-fastest growing segment is expected to be ITV and wireless content, projected to climb 52.7 percent in 2005. Continued penetration increases in DVRs and the growing popularity of wireless content, such as ringtones and wireless games, will drive this market.

Increased time spent with new media, like the Internet, wireless content, and DVDs, will compensate for the lesser time consumers spend with traditional media, like recorded music, newspapers, consumer books and consumer magazines from 2004 to 2009. However, the companies hardest hit by the decline in time spent will also be the ones most likely to improve the current presentation of content while cross-branding services through newer media formats. Newspapers, magazines and broadcast television will provide content for the Internet, while recorded music will provide content for both the Internet and satellite radio, and broadcast radio will become available on the Internet and wireless devices, such as the iPods or handheld videogames like PSPs.

Spending on Internet access and content will continue to decelerate during the forecast period, falling below double-digit growth in 2009, as market penetration reaches saturation levels. The market has reached sufficient mass, however, that the decelerating growth still equates to a large consumer base of spending. Slower growth in dial-up access spending will be offset by significant gains in cable modem, DSL and Wi-Fi access spending. Consumer spending on content will grow steadily, driven by increases in online gaming and music.

The videogame market will struggle somewhat in the short term due to the lack of new video console platforms since 2002. However, after Microsoft, Sony, and Nintendo release the next generation of hardware and more titles become available to support the transition in the coming months, the videogame market will surge to post double-digit growth near the end of the forecast period. Meanwhile, home video usage will continue to increase due to the transition from VHS to DVD, where sell-through is more important than the rental market. Due to the increases in time spent with videogames, the Internet, home videos, and ITV and wireless content, the average consumer will increase time spent with all media at a compound annual rate of 0.4 percent to 3,555 hours in 2009.

The Institutional End-User Spending Market in 2004 and 2005

New technology, stronger ROI requirements, end-user empowerment and growing demand for customization are speeding the development and growth of alternative business, training and learning environments in the institutional sector, which drove the sector to outperform the other three media sectors in 2004 and in the 1999-2004 period. The key driver has been and will continue to be multimedia workflow and learning solutions that provide the tools necessary for executives, workers and students to execute their jobs and consumer assignments more efficiently. Institutional end-user spending on communications was trending upward in the first half of 2005, as the momentum that began in 2003 continued through the first half of 2005, although at a somewhat slower rate than in 2004. Institutional spending increased 8.8 percent to $171.08 billion in 2004, the highest growth rate in a decade, fueled by increased spending in the professional and business information services (PBIS) and television programming segments. Institutional spending is expected to increase at a slightly decelerated rate of 7.2 percent in 2005, as a number of subsegments in the professional and business information services segment are unable to sustain high growth and an expected drop in television programming spending due to the lack of Olympics or political election programming. However, institutional end-user spending will outpace nominal GDP for the second consecutive year.

The institutional end-user sector includes spending on professional and business information services; television programming; educational and training media; and business-to-business magazine circulation and trade show exhibition space. The institutional sector benefits from a varied spending pool of government agencies, corporations and professional firms, and has been one of the most consistently growing sectors of the U.S. economy for the past 30 years. Several key factors impact this sector on an annual basis, including economic growth, corporate earnings, government budgets, and demographics, while in more recent years, the aforementioned factors have played a more important role.

The largest segment of the institutional sector, PBIS, will post the best growth in 2005 with 8.1 percent, trailed by 7.2 percent expansion in educational and training media and 6.0 percent upside in television programming. Spending on business-to-business magazine circulation and trade show space will increase 4.2 percent, the slowest growth, but the highest growth for the segment since the recession. Overall institutional sector growth will be stimulated by products that provide end users with value, functionality and creativity, while improving productivity, efficiency and workflow.

The institutional sector's accelerated growth in 2004 was driven by stronger growth in PBIS, which also posted accelerated growth in 2003 after two consecutive years of slowing growth due to weaker economic conditions, slower corporate profit growth, institutional budget cutbacks and general caution related to world events. The outsourced training market was particularly hard hit by the economic downturn, as corporations with more control over their training budgets were quick to reduce them when the recession began. Similar to the b-to-b media segment, we anticipate the training segment will grow slowly in the first half of 2005, with better growth expected in the second half of the year as corporations hire more workers and ramp up training for them.

It is important to note here that, similar to other segments, a number of changes were implemented in the institutional end-user sector such as new exclusive methodologies. We believe that these additions have enhanced the value of this year's *Forecast*, providing our subscribers with what we hope will be an engaging and insightful communications industry analysis. Professional information was combined with business information services and a new proprietary methodology was developed to size the whole PBIS market. This change also led to a new chapter exclusively on the educational and training media seg-

HIGHLIGHTS

Institutional End-User Spending

Institutional end-user spending increased 8.8 percent to $171.08 billion in 2004, the highest growth rate during the decade, driven by increased spending in professional and business information services and television programming. Overall growth was stimulated by products that delivered improved ROI measurements, increased corporate confidence, a higher employment rate of knowledgeable workers, and demand for new custom services.

■

Institutional media spending grew at a compound annual rate of 5.6 percent from 1999 to 2004, slightly higher than nominal GDP, which grew 4.8 percent in the same period. Institutional end-user spending underperformed GDP each year from 2001 to 2003, but outperformed the broader economy in 1999, 2000 and 2004.

■

Spending on professional and business information services, which accounted for 57.2 percent of all institutional end-user spending, accelerated 9.7 percent to $97.82 billion in 2004. Professional and business information services was also the second-fastest-growing segment of the institutional sector for the year, spurred by solid gains in five of the eight subsegments of the industry. Expenditures on television programming, the second-largest and fastest-growing institutional market, were up 9.8 percent in 2004, to $45.54 billion, fueled by high growth in both of its subsegments.

■

Television programming was the fastest-growing institutional segment in the 1999-2004 period, as spending climbed 8.0 percent on a compound annual basis, outpacing GDP in every year of the period. The segment was spurred by double-digit growth in spending on cable and satellite television license fees, which grew at double-digit rates each year from 1999 to 2004. Expenditures on professional and business information services grew at a compound annual rate of 5.7 percent during the same five-year timeframe, slightly below the rate of the broader institutional sector. The segment's growth was driven by expansion in its three largest markets, which stimulated the development of new products and services that provided value-added components.

■

Institutional spending is expected to grow at a slightly decelerated rate of 7.2 percent in 2005, as a number of subsegments in the professional and business information services sector will be unable to sustain their 2004 double-digit growth, as well as the expected drop in spending in television programming due to the lack of spending on Olympics or political election programming. However, institutional end-user spending will outpace nominal GDP for the second consecutive year, fueled by solid growth in each of the four broad segments.

■

Institutional end-user spending is projected to expand at a compound annual rate of 7.0 percent in the forecast period to $239.82 billion in 2009, outpacing nominal GDP in each of the five forecast years. The key trends driving growth will be technology and products that deliver improved ROI metrics, solid economic expansion, stronger corporate profits, increased institutional budgets and innovations in the development, delivery and use of integrated information services. Professional and business information services will expand 7.8 percent, television programming expenditures will increase 6.5 percent, educational and training media will rise 5.2 percent and business-to-business media spending will climb 4.1 percent from 2004 to 2009.

Institutional End-User Spending on Communications

($ MILLIONS)

Year	*Professional & Business Information Services**	*Total Television Programming†‡*	*Educational & Training Media**	*Business-to-Business Media§*	*Total Institutional End-User Spending*
1999	$ 75,190	$30,970	$15,838	$ 8,438	$130,436
2000	80,846	34,525	17,106	8,906	141,383
2001	81,326	35,667	17,601	8,738	143,332
2002	84,156	38,964	17,553	8,683	149,356
2003	89,175	41,480	17,939	8,712	157,306
2004	97,822	45,535	18,694	9,031	171,082
2005	105,757	48,261	20,048	9,407	183,473
2006	113,662	51,921	20,914	9,762	196,259
2007	122,766	54,903	21,910	10,126	209,706
2008	132,049	59,086	22,955	10,566	224,656
2009	142,325	62,410	24,037	11,048	239,820

Sources: Veronis Suhler Stevenson, PQ Media, Book Industry Study Group, BPA International, Center for Exhibition Research, Kagan Research, Outsell, Simba Information, SRDS, Tradeshow Week, Training Magazine, World Airline Entertainment Association

*The professional information subsegment, including legal & regulatory, scientific & technical, and health & life science, was combined with the business information services subsegment, including, marketing, payroll & human resources, financial & economic, credit & risk, and general business news, to form two revised chapters, Professional and Business Information Services and Educational and Training Media, to coincide with broader trends in the overall professional and business information marketplace. Additionally, a new methodology was developed to size, structure and forecast the professional and business information services segment, as well as a new source was used to determine the size and structure of the outsourced training subsegment of the Educational and Training Media chapter, in order to provide a more accurate picture of those two marketplaces.

†Includes spending on cable & satellite television license fees and broadcast television, cable & satellite television and in-flight entertainment programming costs.

‡To avoid double counting, barter syndication spending from the Entertainment Media chapter is included in this chapter, but not in the Advertising, Specialty Media & Marketing Services chapter because of its inclusion in the Broadcast Television chapter.

§Includes spending on magazine circulation and trade show exhibition space.

ment, with a major revision to the outsourced training sector based on a new data source that we believe better structures this market.

The institutional end-user sector continued to rebound in 2004, following three of the slowest growth years in the last 30 years. Growth decelerated markedly in 2001 and 2002, and continued to lag in 2003 as the impact of several negative factors filtered through the sector one segment at a time. While b-to-b media and PBIS were hampered by economic recession, corporate budget cuts and government pullbacks in 2001, these same variables struck the educational and training media segment in 2002.

Institutional media spending grew at a compound annual rate of 5.6 percent from 1999 to 2004, slightly higher than nominal GDP, which grew 4.8 percent in the same period. Institutional end-user spending underperformed GDP each year from 2001 to 2003, but outperformed the broader economy in 1999 and 2000. Flat spending on professional and business information services and a decline in b-to-b spending held the institutional sector's growth below that of GDP in 2001. Spending declines in the educational and training segment and the b-to-b market caused the sector's underperformance in 2002. The same two segments hindered

Growth of Institutional End-User Spending on Communications

Year	*Professional & Business Information Services**	*Total Television Programming†‡*	*Educational & Training Media**	*Business-to-Business Media§*	*Total Institutional End-User Spending*
2000	7.5%	11.5%	8.0%	5.5%	8.4%
2001	0.6	3.3	2.9	–1.9	1.4
2002	3.5	9.2	–0.3	–0.6	4.2
2003	6.0	6.5	2.2	0.3	5.3
2004	9.7	9.8	4.2	3.7	8.8
2005	8.1	6.0	7.2	4.2	7.2
2006	7.5	7.6	4.3	3.8	7.0
2007	8.0	5.7	4.8	3.7	6.9
2008	7.6	7.6	4.8	4.3	7.1
2009	7.8	5.6	4.7	4.6	6.7
Compound Annual Growth					
1999-2004	5.4	8.0	3.4	1.4	5.6
2004-2009	7.8	6.5	5.2	4.1	7.0

Sources: Veronis Suhler Stevenson, PQ Media, Book Industry Study Group, BPA International, Center for Exhibition Research, Kagan Research, Outsell, Simba Information, SRDS, Tradeshow Week, Training Magazine, World Airline Entertainment Association

*The professional information subsegment, including legal & regulatory, scientific & technical, and health & life science, was combined with the business information services subsegment, including, marketing, payroll & human resources, financial & economic, credit & risk, and general business news, to form two revised chapters, Professional and Business Information Services and Educational and Training Media, to coincide with broader trends in the overall professional and business information marketplace. Additionally, a new methodology was developed to size, structure and forecast the professional and business information services segment, as well as a new source was used to determine the size and structure of the outsourced training subsegment of the Educational and Training Media chapter, in order to provide a more accurate picture of those two marketplaces.

†Includes spending on cable & satellite television license fees and broadcast television, cable & satellite television and in-flight entertainment programming costs.

‡To avoid double counting, barter syndication spending from the Entertainment Media chapter is included in this chapter, but not in the Advertising, Specialty Media & Marketing Services chapter because of its inclusion in the Broadcast Television chapter.

§Includes spending on magazine circulation and trade show exhibition space.

the overall institutional sector again in 2003. However, the growth engines in each of the four broad segments of the institutional sector revved up in 2004, and growth for the full year outpaced nominal GDP for the first time in four years. Sector growth is expected to outperform GDP over the next five years, as well.

Spending on PBIS, which accounted for 57.2 percent of all institutional end-user spending, accelerated 9.7 percent to $97.82 billion in 2004, the second-fastest-growing segment of the institutional sector for the year. Stronger growth in PBIS was driven by gains in spending on business information services in the marketing, credit and risk, and financial and economic markets, in addition to gains in the professional information categories of scientific and technical, and health and life science. Expenditures on PBIS services grew at a compound annual rate of 5.7 percent in the five-year timeframe, slightly below the rate of the broader institutional sector. The segment's growth in the period was driven by expansion in its three largest markets, which stimulated the development of new products and services that provided value-added components. These include digital interfaces and analytical capabilities that hasten corporate efficiency and increase

Shares of Institutional End-User Spending on Communications

Year	*Professional & Business Information Services**	*Total Television Programming†‡*	*Educational & Training Media**	*Business-to-Business Media§*
1999	57.6%	23.7%	12.1%	6.5%
2000	57.2	24.4	12.1	6.3
2001	56.7	24.9	12.3	6.1
2002	56.3	26.1	11.8	5.8
2003	56.7	26.4	11.4	5.5
2004	57.2	26.6	10.9	5.3
2005	57.6	26.3	10.9	5.1
2006	57.9	26.5	10.7	5.0
2007	58.5	26.2	10.4	4.8
2008	58.8	26.3	10.2	4.7
2009	59.3	26.0	10.0	4.6

Sources: Veronis Suhler Stevenson, PQ Media, Book Industry Study Group, BPA International, Center for Exhibition Research, Kagan Research, Outsell, Simba Information, SRDS, Tradeshow Week, Training Magazine, World Airline Entertainment Association

*The professional information subsegment, including legal & regulatory, scientific & technical, and health & life science, was combined with the business information services subsegment, including, marketing, payroll & human resources, financial & economic, credit & risk, and general business news, to form two revised chapters, Professional and Business Information Services and Educational and Training Media, to coincide with broader trends in the overall professional and business information marketplace. Additionally, a new methodology was developed to size, structure and forecast the professional and business information services segment, as well as a new source was used to determine the size and structure of the outsourced training subsegment of the Educational and Training Media chapter, in order to provide a more accurate picture of those two marketplaces.

†Includes spending on cable & satellite television license fees and broadcast television, cable & satellite television and in-flight entertainment programming costs.

‡To avoid double counting, barter syndication spending from the Entertainment Media chapter is included in this chapter, but not in the Advertising, Specialty Media & Marketing Services chapter because of its inclusion in the Broadcast Television chapter.

§Includes spending on magazine circulation and trade show exhibition space.

customer satisfaction. Spending on business information services is expected to grow at accelerated rates throughout the forecast period, outperforming nominal GDP in each of the five years.

Expenditures on television programming, the second-largest and fastest-growing institutional market, were up 9.8 percent in 2004, to $45.54 billion, fueled by high growth in both subsegments, as growth of cable and satellite television license fees remained in the double-digits and expenditures by broadcast and cable networks on original scripted programs climbed into the high-single-digit range. Television programming was the fastest-growing institutional segment in the 1999-2004 period, as spending climbed 8.0 percent on a compound annual basis, outpacing GDP every year of the period. The segment was spurred by double-digit growth in spending on cable and satellite television license fees, which grew at double-digit rates each year from 1999 to 2004. The television programming segment—which includes spending on television programs and cable network license fees—flourished in the five-year timeframe, with the exception of a minor decline in 2001, but rebounded quickly the following year. We expect growth in the overall television programming segment to fluctuate between even- and odd-numbered years, due to the increased programming costs associated with the Olympics and covering political campaigns.

Expenditures on educational and training media rose for the second consecutive year in 2004, mainly due to increased spending on outsourced training materials. Spending in this segment accelerated 4.2 percent to $18.69 billion in 2004, but grew only 3.4 percent on a compound annual basis from 1999 to 2004, largely due to the significant contractions in the outsourced training subsegment from 2001 to 2003. Corporations were quick to slash training, travel and conference budgets following the onset of the recession, and those budgets were not raised until 2004 when corporations finally felt comfortable with the economic recovery. The college instructional materials market grew 1.5 percent in 2004, while the K-12 instructional materials market was flat. As education budgets are increased, especially in the 2005 K-12 market, the overall educational and training segment will grow rapidly in 2005. However, growth will decelerate slightly due to a weak adoption schedule in 2006, but regain momentum in 2007 and beyond, as hiring picks up, training budgets are restored, enrollments grow and innovative new services are rolled out.

Business-to-business media expenditures climbed 3.7 percent to $9.03 billion in 2004, as growth in exhibit space spending was offset by the continuing decline in magazine circulation spending. The growth in business-to-business spending represented the highest growth rate on institutional spending since the recession, due to the strengthening economy and corporate budget increases that included more business travel to trade shows. The overall b-to-b segment was spurred upward by higher exhibit space expenditures that were driven up by price hikes among leading shows and additional space being rented as vendors upgraded exhibit layouts. Meanwhile, spending on magazine circulation dwindled for the fourth consecutive year, offsetting combined growth in this segment. Combined circulation and exhibit space spending grew at a compound annual rate of 1.4 percent from 1999 to 2004, well below GDP growth as circulation spending declined 1.2 percent during that time. Growth in this segment will quicken over the forecast period, fueled by trade show expansion.

KEY TRENDS IMPACTING THE INSTITUTIONAL END-USER SEGMENT

Parallel to the demands made by marketers, institutional end users have begun to request better ROI measurements from information vendors to justify expenditures. In the professional and business information services segment, professional publishers are migrating print products to online suites, while business information service providers are expanding integrated workflow suites that are able to combine internal proprietary databases with external data. Business-to-business media companies, using the e-media platform, are expanding their online capabilities from advertising support to include a number of subscription-based services running from community links to database directories. Outsourced training firms are upgrading online courses to include characteristics formerly found only in classroom settings. The educational markets are embracing supplemental materials and digital products ranging from online classrooms to Web-based course materials. Television producers are working more closely with marketers to integrate products into programs.

A common theme in most of the institutional end-user segments is that technology has hastened the growth of ROI measurement through the creative use of technology. Technological advances and the implementation of electronic services have helped to increase productivity, enhance tracking capabilities, support workflow solutions and improve efficiency in corporate and government institutions. For example, the ability to access information through wireless devices has become paramount to improve efficiency. The number of subscribers who access data, such as e-mail, through PDAs, Blackberrys and other wireless devices is expected to rise 118.2 percent in 2005 to 8.1 million subscribers. Approximately 80 percent surveyed stated that the number-one use of wireless data is e-mail or calendar updates. Mobile

Institutional Subscribers and Spending on Wireless Data Content*

Year	Subscribers (Millions)				Wireless Data Spending ($ Billions)
	Wireless E-mail	*Sales Force Automation*	*Field Force Automation*	*Total Wireless Subs*	
2004	4.4	2.6	2.1	9.1	$ 5.1
2005	9.6	3.7	3.0	16.3	8.0
2006	13.5	4.8	4.0	22.3	11.4
2007	17.4	5.8	4.8	28.0	15.3
2008	21.5	6.6	5.5	33.6	17.9
2009	25.1	7.5	6.2	38.8	21.4

Sources: Veronis Suhler Stevenson, PQ Media, Insight Research

*Includes spending on wireless business data only. Spending on wireless business voice, which is not considered communications content, was $40.1 billion in 2004.

End-User Spending On Communications

Growth of Institutional Subscribers and Spending on Wireless Data Content*

Year	Subscribers				Wireless Data Spending
	Wireless E-mail	*Sales Force Automation*	*Field Force Automation*	*Total Wireless Subs*	
2005	118.2%	42.3%	42.9%	79.1%	56.9%
2006	40.6	29.7	33.3	36.8	42.5
2007	28.9	20.8	20.0	25.6	34.2
2008	23.6	13.8	14.6	20.0	17.0
2009	16.7	13.6	12.7	15.5	19.6
Compound Annual Growth					
2004-2009	41.7	23.6	24.2	33.6	33.2

Sources: Veronis Suhler Stevenson, PQ Media, Insight Research

*Includes spending on wireless business data only. Spending on wireless business voice, which is not considered communications content, was $40.1 billion in 2004.

Top 5 Business Applications for Wireless Data

Application	*% Share*
Mobile Access to Enterprise	36%
Sales Force Communications	20
Data Entry from Field	18
Logistics Support	13
Manufacturing Floor Data Entry	9
All Others	4

Sources: Veronis Suhler Stevenson, PQ Media, Insight Research, AMR Research

Growth Opportunities versus Value-Added Opportunities in The Professional and Business Information Services Market

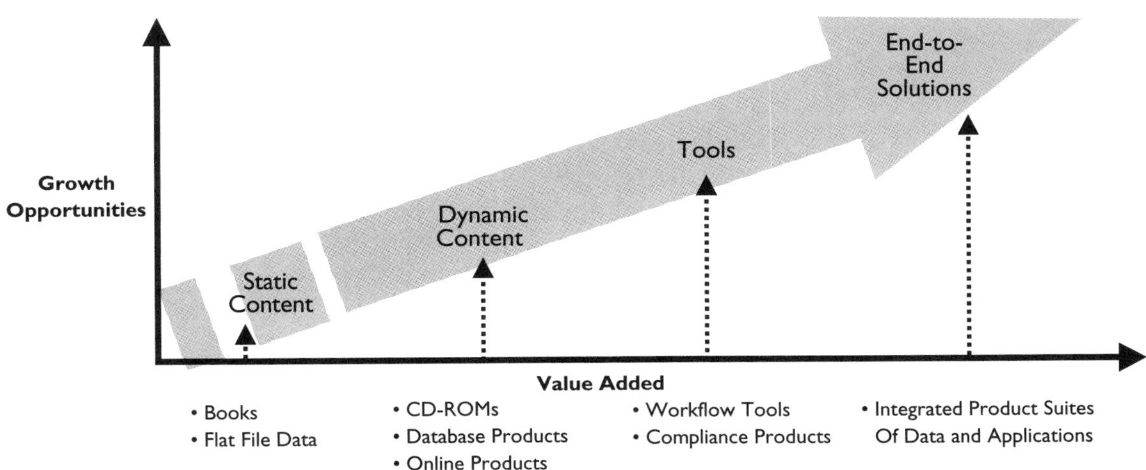

Sources: Veronis Suhler Stevenson, PQ Media

access to data and data entry from the field represent 54 percent of the deployment of enterprise wireless applications. In addition to accessing e-mail and other information, wireless applications have become very crucial for sales and field forces, with subscribers rising from 4.7 million in 2004 to 13.7 million by 2009.

Institutional end users have become more reliant on technology-related products and services, and as a result of corporate consolidation and downsizing, companies more than ever are seeking better tools to automate workflow and make more data actionable. The need for products accessible through the Internet continues to increase as more employees access the Web. Institutional information providers offering value-added products that combine flexible delivery with analytics are finding more growth opportunities than those firms delivering static data.

The migration from print to online products in recent years has been extraordinary. Spending on online professional information products has increased at double-digit rates each year since 1999, and when Veronis Suhler Stevenson was tracking distribution methods in previous years, it accounted for the largest share of overall professional market spending. In other segments of institutional spending, such as business information services and business-to-business media, customers are requesting and requiring more solutions-oriented products, and this has increasingly led to strategic consolidation by business information providers. These providers are acquiring specialized software tools and niche information companies to expand product offerings and functionality. Digital delivery of information is transforming the methods by which information is distributed to customers and by which end users provide feedback to the providers.

As part of the ROI measurement trend, institutional firms are closely monitoring how digital products are being used and how effectively. For example, when comparing business-to-business print magazines with their online counterparts, publishers are finding only a gradual decline in the actions taken when comparing how each is used. One study found that 70 percent of all archived end-user articles were in print versus 64 percent that were online. However, readers are more likely to discuss an article or advertisement with a colleague when they see

Reading Business-to-Business Magazines, Print vs. Online

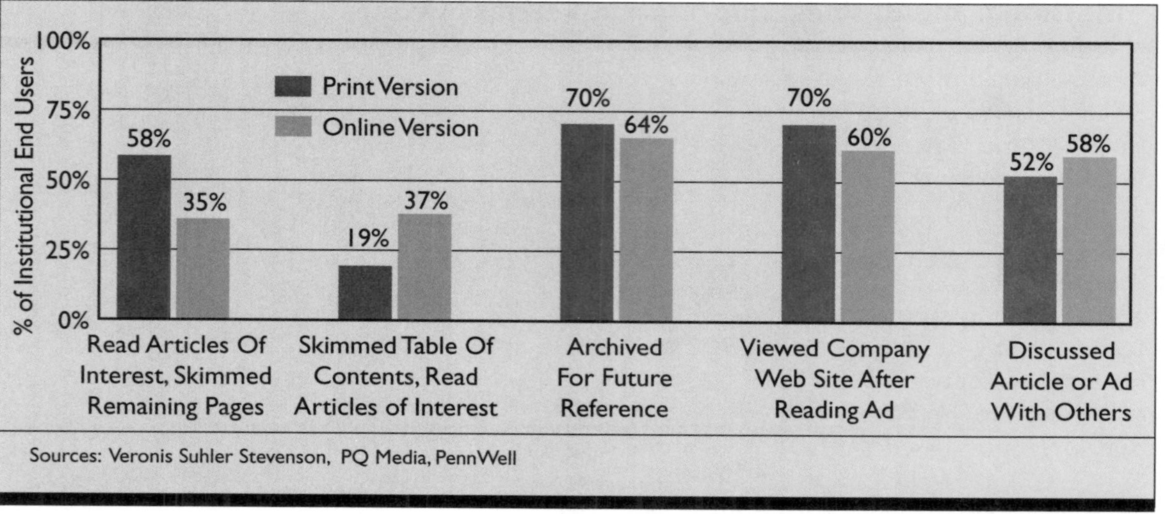

Sources: Veronis Suhler Stevenson, PQ Media, PennWell

it online (58 percent) versus those who view the print version (52 percent). Print readers skim pages more often than do online readers, while the latter tend to look at the table of contents before choosing an article to read. Another study found that the time needed to gather information online has increased from eight hours in 2004 to 11 hours in 2005. While the Internet is the primary source for this information, more companies are looking to intranets. Concurrently, as a result of the increased time required to find information, upper management is delegating more of the fact-finding to others, relying on updates, team members or their corporate libraries. Helping increase the efficiency of searching the Web, more than two-thirds of all corporations have broadband services.

Within each individual segment of the institutional sector, the impact of technology has been significant. In the professional and business information services segment, demand for scalable, enterprise-wide information products is increasing, especially those that marry internal proprietary databases with external data. Expenditures are rising due to the development of products that combine analytics, reporting and content so that end users reduce the number of information products they utilize. As a result of these expanded services, professional and business information service providers are developing sophisticated database products that require a substantial investment from the end user, while delivering a level of functionality that allows end users to create customized solutions for a fraction of the cost of custom data. The digitally enhanced products offer critical data and information, as well as search and workflow tools. When combined with expanded mission-critical content, these solutions-oriented services provide end users with manipulative analytics aimed at improving efficiency and productivity.

Technology has also impacted the competitive educational and training media segments, as these industries are using technology to add value to the end-user experience. In 2004, more K-12 students gained access to computers and the Internet, while teachers increased their use of the Web as a teaching tool, much of it linked to national movement towards standards, accountability and testing. At the college level, more dorm rooms, libraries and classrooms are wired, expanding e-learning platforms and digital coursework. The number of college-age students and working adults using distance learning has increased, leading to more emphasis on digital material. For example, online universities have become proactive in launching digital initiatives, such as electronic textbook programs and textbooks, emphasizing digital databases. In the outsourced training market, live e-learning and the LMS platform are the fastest-growing sectors of the industry, both increasing by double digits in 2004 and expected to continue doing so in 2005. Corporations are becoming more comfortable with computer-based and remote learning as they attempt to cut costs on items such as travel and lodging for training participants. The Internet has also been a catalyst in this area, allowing students to interact with instructors and to other students via streaming video and e-mail, making classroom learning characteristics interactive.

Business-to-business media companies are using digital technology to expand magazine brands, enhance the trade show experience, and increase the viability of their e-media experience. The use of the Web by many business-to-business media firms is transforming those companies from publishers to business intelligence providers, with access to databases and directories. Leading companies, such as Reed Elsevier and pure-play online business-to-business providers like CNET, are leading the charge into the digital marketplace by repackaging their vast supply of data and content in various ways. In addition to the Web version of magazines, many of these online sites offer e-newsletters and access to databases. A number of magazines such as *Business Week* and *Fortune* are finding that the Web is helping to shift the demographics of subscribers to a younger audience, often ready to pay more for customized digital information not available in print. The trade show sector continues to make online registration and detailed vendor and speaker information easier to access, proving to be a vital tool in managing costs and expanding attendance.

In the competitive war between cable multiple system operators (MSOs) and satellite providers, digital technology has been a major weapon. Wired cable providers are touting VOD services not available from satellite providers; meanwhile, satellite providers offered DVR services much earlier than their counterparts in cable. The issue of license fees will become prickly in the near future when broadcast stations and networks switch entirely to digital signals with the capability of transmitting multiple signals. Cable MSOs and satellite providers are seeking guidance from the FCC on must-carry rules regarding these additional services. For television programmers, the end result is an environment that has led cable and satellite networks to invest heavily in original programming to continue increasing their lead over broadcast television in the ratings. Broadcast network programmers have countered with more scripted programs, which are more expensive to produce, as well as continued to look for the next breakout reality program.

Information Gathering Techniques By Corporate End Users, 2001 vs. 2005

Action	*2001*	*2005*
Gathering Information		
Use Web	79%	67%
Use Corporate Intranets	5	15
Consult Colleagues	5	9
Share of Time Spent Seeking vs. Analyzing Information		
Seeking	42	53
Analyzing	58	47
Information Source		
Find Information Themselves	68	51
Rely on Updates, Team Members or Library	32	49

Sources: Veronis Suhler Stevenson, PQ Media, Outsell

PROFESSIONAL & BUSINESS INFORMATION SERVICES

Institutional end-user spending on professional and business information services (PBIS) rose 9.7 percent to $97.82 billion in 2004, stimulated by an expanding national economy that gave corporations more money to spend on coveted multimedia workflow solutions. While expenditures in both subsegments grew at healthy rates during the year, spending in the larger subsegment—business information services (BIS)—increased at a faster rate than expenditures in the other subsegment, professional information (PI). Growth in BIS was driven mainly by demand for solutions complete with real-time, analytical functionality, a trend that was accentuated by burgeoning corporate budgets. BIS spending rose 10.2 percent in 2004 to $78.09 billion. Meanwhile, the continued launch of online products and the introduction of services that complement new technology, such as wireless devices, spurred a gain of 7.9 percent in PI to $19.73 billion in 2004 as all three categories—legal and regulatory; scientific and technical; and health and life science—recorded relatively strong growth.

The overall PBIS market grew at a compound annual rate of 5.7 percent from 1999 to 2004, also surpassing the broader economy's growth, which was 4.8 percent in the five-year period. In addition, the PBIS market's growth in 2004 also exceeded its peak expansion pace of 9.0 percent in 2000, which was followed by a deceleration in growth to 0.6 percent during the recession year of 2001. The market, however, grew at an accelerated rate in each of the next three years. Overall growth of the PBIS market in 2004 outpaced that of nominal GDP for the second consecutive year—this time by almost 3 percentage points—a trend we expect to continue during the forecast period. Among the primary growth drivers going forward will be the continued demand for products and services that support more efficient and effective workflow and production capabilities utilizing the latest technology innovations, analytical tools and functionality offerings.

Spending growth over the next five years in the PBIS segment will be sparked by several key factors. First, providers of PBIS information will continue to transition their portfolios of product suites to be more heavily weighted with Internet-based products and services in lieu of traditional print publications and CD-ROMs. These Web-based products more effectively fit PBIS firms' overall strategy to become end-to-end multimedia service providers, in that these electronic products offer increased functionality and can be integrated into an end-user organization's other operations. The PBIS market's adaptability to Internet-based products and services will yield an abundance of opportunities through newer technologies, such as PDAs, Really Simple Syndication (RSS) feeds, and blogs. Customer demand for products that are supported by these technologies is growing and PBIS companies are positioning themselves to offer the tools that utilize them.

Additionally, there will be increased demand for the services that integrate in-house proprietary data with external databases. PBIS companies that can provide customers with flexible, customizable product offerings, which can amalgamate content, software and services, will be the most successful during the forecast period. One method many PBIS companies are using to expand their offerings is through the acquisition of organizations that offer complementary products. This will enable PBIS firms to build relationships with their customers by delivering products and services that meet every operational need.

The demand for such mission-critical content from end-user companies will only strengthen as the forecast period progresses, the economy expands, corporations increase their budgets for business information services and a robust job market yields an increased customer base. This new climate will offer business information vendors an expanded market in which to launch new products and services that provide end-to-end solutions for their customers. As a result, we expect aggressive growth from most PBIS subsegments over the next five years, especially from 2005 to 2007. This trending will be due, in part, to the ability of information providers to expand integrated software suites by upgrading technologies that provide institutional end users with workflow solutions that combine high-end content with analytical tools to help end users do their jobs more efficiently and effectively. As a result, we expect the PBIS segment to expand at an 8.1 percent pace in 2005, and to grow at a compound annual rate of 7.8 percent from 2004 to 2009, reaching $142.33 billion in 2009.

BROADCAST & CABLE TELEVISION PROGRAMMING

Total institutional spending on broadcast and cable television programming increased 9.8 percent to $45.54 billion in 2004, and grew at a compound annual rate of 8.0 percent from 1999 to 2004. Overall expenditures in this segment include spending on cable and satellite television license fees and filmed entertainment for broadcast and cable television.

Spending on cable and satellite TV license fees increased 10.4 percent to $18.18 billion in 2004, and grew at a compound annual rate of 14.0 percent from 1999 to 2004. Cable and satellite TV license fees have been an extremely contentious area in recent years, as cable and satellite TV providers have expressed their irritation to networks about the rate at which these fees have increased for much of the past five years, beginning in 2000. That year, Time Warner Cable yanked all ABC stations from its services for several days in response to a dispute with ESPN over the network's escalating fees. Cox Communications also clashed with ESPN in 2004, when the network proposed a deal that would raise its fees by more than 20 percent annually. Following weeks of dispute, a deal was finally struck that included a sliding scale of rate increases, which reportedly averaged 7.0 percent a year, versus the originally proposed 20.0 percent. Also in 2004, EchoStar Communications pulled all Viacom-owned CBS stations and cable networks off its DISH Network, and blacked out local CBS programming to 1.6 million subscribers in 16 cities, while also precluding 9.5 million subscribers nationwide from accessing 10 Viacom cable channels, including MTV and Nickelodeon. That dispute, too, was eventually settled. Retransmission rights are also becoming an area of contention for cable and satellite operators. Traditionally, over-the-air broadcasters who were part of larger multimedia groups had supplied retransmission consent to cable operators gratis, in exchange for operators carrying their cable networks. However, stand-alone television broadcasters, or individual stations, have no such bargaining option, and have been pushing cable operators for cash in exchange for retransmission consent. As this *Forecast* went to press, Cox and Cable One were battling Nexstar over retransmission rights in four southwestern TV markets, and were not carrying local ABC, CBS and NBC programming as a result. This is being viewed as a test case by many in the industry, as the resolution may well establish precedent.

These ongoing challenges to increased license fees will likely suppress growth rates going forward. Consequently, we project spending on cable and satellite TV license fees to increase at a decelerated 8.6 percent in 2005 to $19.74 billion. Expenditures will grow only 7.4 percent on a compound annual basis in the 2004-2009 period to $26.03 billion in 2009.

Spending on filmed entertainment for broadcast and cable TV rose 9.3 percent to $27.36 billion in 2004, and grew at a compound annual rate of 4.9 percent from 1999 to 2004, as broadcast and cable networks increased their investments in original program development and off-network syndicated content. To better compete with cable, broadcast TV networks increased spending to develop more scripted shows and fewer low-budget reality shows. Meanwhile, television stations increased spending at a double-digit rate in 2004, while in-flight entertainment expenditures also grew at a double-digit pace and barter syndication remained strong. Encouraged by the success of new shows, such as *Lost, The OC* and *Desperate Housewives*, networks are looking to develop inventive new scripted dramas, as well as resurrect the struggling sitcom genre. The failure of a string of copycat reality shows has prompted networks to reconsider the prospects of unscripted programming.

While networks are still exercising some restraint in their programming ideas, they have been willing to take more chances in recent years on creative new programs that can better compete with edgy cable content. ABC's two new offbeat dramas in 2004, *Lost* and *Desperate Housewives*, instantly found large audiences. ABC's success in 2004 bolstered the network's confidence in its programming, prompting it to relinquish the rights to *Monday Night Football* in April 2005 to ESPN after a 35-year run. Unlike the short-term ratings boost reality-based shows provide, scripted programming has a much longer shelf life. While the characters on most reality shows come and go each season, audiences become attached to the characters on scripted shows and loyally follow their experiences from week to week and season to season. For the 2005-06 television season, networks are developing creative new scripted dramas that they hope will follow the success of *Lost* and *Desperate Housewives*. In addition, with the only top 10 comedy—*Everybody Loves Raymond*—ending in 2005, networks are searching for new comedies to infuse life into the ailing sitcom genre.

Meanwhile, premium cable networks, such as HBO, are forging ahead with successful original programs like *The Sopranos, Curb Your Enthusiasm* and *Deadwood*, and the highly anticipated debut of the new series, *Rome*, in the second half of 2005. While network stations may be hesitant to rely more heavily on reality-based shows, cable networks have much greater flexibility in developing new programs and rerunning them to build viewer interest.

Overall expenditures on broadcast and cable television programming will rise 6.0 percent in 2005 to $48.26 billion, and will grow at a compound annual rate of 6.5 percent from 2004 to 2009, reaching $62.41 billion. Growth will be driven primarily by increased investments in new programming as broadcast and cable networks grapple for audiences.

EDUCATIONAL & TRAINING MEDIA

Total spending on educational and training media rose 4.2 percent in 2004 to $18.69 billion, the market's fastest growth since 2000. The gain was driven by the outsourced corporate training subsegment, which benefited from the robust economy and improved job market as companies invested more capital in training new employees and developing existing ones. The rebound in spending on outsourced corporate training, however, was offset somewhat by a more sluggish gain in the educational subsegment, resulting in combined spending growth that trailed that of nominal GDP for the fourth consecutive year.

The K-12 instructional materials market, including spending on basal, supplemental and electronic learning materials, turned in the worst performance of the three subsegments included in this chapter—K-12, college, and outsourced corporate training—with spending flat at $4.06 billion in 2004. A decline of about 29 percent in spending by textbook adoption states in 2004 to approximately $530 million was offset by higher spending in open territories, strong funding from the federal government and higher expenditures on supplementary materials. The K-12 market's growth in 2004 lagged GDP expansion for the third consecutive year.

Spending on college instructional materials, which includes textbooks, coursepacks, software and online services, grew 1.5 percent to $4.71 billion in 2004, due to students' reluctance to pay for expensive new textbooks. High tuition costs and negative publicity about college textbook prices spurred students to find alternatives to buying new texts.

After a three-year slump, spending on outsourced corporate training increased 7.4 percent to $9.92 billion in 2004, driven by growth in the information technology (IT) subsegment, the largest sector of the corporate training market. The gain in the IT sector offset spending declines in the other three training subsegments.

Total spending on educational and training media grew at a compound annual rate of 3.4 percent from 1999 to 2004, trailing nominal GDP growth by more than one percentage point in the period. Following the recession of 2001, corporations trimmed their corporate training budgets, while state budget cuts and a lack of textbook adoptions limited spending gains in the K-12 instructional materials sector. Rising enrollments and moderate price increases drove spending gains in the college instructional materials market early in the 1999-2004 period, but high prices curbed spending and hindered growth in 2003 and 2004.

We project the growth of spending on educational and training media will accelerate in 2005, rising 7.2 percent to $20.05 billion. The strong economy and robust job market will drive another gain in the outsourced corporate training subsegment in 2005, while healthier state budgets and more adoption opportunities will spur double-digit upside in the K-12 market for the year. Meanwhile, high prices and a slow transition from the use of print materials to electronic learning materials will limit growth in the college market in 2005. Mid-single-digit gains are projected for the remainder of the forecast period for the overall educational and training media segment, resulting in a compound annual growth rate of 5.2 percent from 2004 to 2009. Total segment spending will reach $24.04 billion in 2009.

BUSINESS-TO-BUSINESS MEDIA

Total business-to-business media spending, including magazine circulation and trade show exhibition space, increased 3.7 percent to $9.03 billion in 2004, and grew at a compound annual rate of 1.4 percent from 1999 to 2004. Growth in 2004 was the highest in four years and accelerated notably from a relatively flat 2003, driven mainly by expansion in the trade show market.

Spending on exhibit space increased 5.6 percent to $7.11 billion in 2004, fueled by price hikes and additional exhibit space rented. Growth was driven partly by gains in the healthcare industry, which has benefited from advances in medical technology. Also, a 15.7 percent gain in corporate profits allowed show organizers to substantially increase prices on exhibit space for the first time in years without much backlash from exhibitors. Average price per square foot rose 4.0 percent to $19.15, bolstered by enthusiasm related to the industry's long-awaited recovery. However, the market will not be able to sustain such high price hikes going forward, as vendors become less willing to absorb large annual increases. The healthcare category was largely responsible for the increase in professional attendance in 2004, and demand for new technology, equipment and pharmaceuticals, along with increased specialization, has led several healthcare associations to develop new trade shows focusing on education. Spending on continuing medical education continues to rise in relation to new medical discoveries.

Contrary to prior concerns that the growing use of the Internet would stifle attendance at in-person events, the medium has actually helped trade show companies in terms of gathering attendee and marketing registration information in advance. New product offerings, especially those that are technology-based, continue to support the need for face-to-face trade shows. An increase in business-related travel also accentuated trade show growth in 2004. Since September 11, 2001, the vast majority of high technology events has suffered, but 2004 signaled a slow resurgence in that market. Technology companies are attempting to drive growth by channeling event marketing resources into private events, utilizing custom programs, or marketing smaller, invitation-only, face-to-face events. Indications in the first half of 2005 signaled that transaction-focused retail events in fragmented industries will continue to grow. We expect the trade show market to grow at an accelerated pace during the forecast period, driven by an increase in exhibitors and attendees. For exhibitors, the high costs associated with exhibiting, including travel expenses, are being offset by the upswing in integrated marketing packages for exhibitors. Although these new packages are offered at a premium price, the additional exposure they provide helps to boost ROI due to the number of deals made at trade shows. Spending on trade shows is expected to recover more rapidly than spending on b-to-b magazines, and we expect it will accelerate at a growth rate in the single digits for the next five years, driven by prosperity in the healthcare and retail industries.

B-to-b magazine circulation expenditures actually declined in 2004, as paid unit circulation decreased in all but three of the 15 leading categories. Titles in the business, banking, insurance, financial and legal category posted the largest decline in unit circulation for the year, followed by the retail segment. Circulation spending is expected to drop again in 2005, as b-to-b magazine readers have become more accustomed to receiving free information, forcing publishers to transition more circulation to controlled. In an effort to justify the move to controlled circulation, publishers have been creating more sophisticated databases that have demographic-sensitive circulation data. To recoup some of the revenues that were lost in the transition to controlled circulation, price hikes have been applied to remaining subscriptions. In the past, these hikes have been met with resistance, but in 2004, increased corporate spending in numerous markets caused publishers to be more aggressive with their pricing. In 2004, only three of the top 15 categories experienced paid circulation unit gains, including home design and furnishing; agriculture; and architecture, engineering and construction titles. Controlled circulation represented 67.0 percent of total distribution in 2004, while paid circulation accounted for 33.0 percent, down from 33.9 percent five years ago.

The increase in paid circulation for health and life science publications in 2004 pushed the segment to the top spot among the 15 categories, surpassing business, banking, insurance, financial and legal. Controlled circulation also expanded in the healthcare segment. Nevertheless, paid circulation is expected to continue to decline throughout the forecast period, causing overall spending to drop on a compound annual basis. While paid circulation continues to diminish, publishers will increasingly focus on Internet distribution, custom publishing efforts and demographic targeting, which often provides better insight into the makeup of readers than simply reviewing job titles.

B-to-b media expenditures, including exhibition space and circulation, will increase at an accelerated 4.2 percent in 2005 to $9.41 billion, driven by upside in the trade show segment. Total spending will grow at a compound annual rate of 4.1 percent in the forecast period to $11.05 billion in 2009.

The Outlook For Institutional End-User Spending

The momentum that began in the second half of 2003 took hold in full force in 2004 in institutional end-user spending, as each of the four broad segments trended upward during the year. The aggressive growth of 2004 translated well into the first part of 2005, though some subsegments, such as marketing information in the business information services segment, were unable to sustain their double-digit growth rates for the full year. Overall institutional spending growth in 2005 is projected to outpace nominal GDP upside for the second consecutive year and is expected to outperform the broader economy over the remaining four years of the *Forecast*. The institutional sector is projected to expand at a compound annual rate of 7.0 percent in the forecast period to $239.82 billion in 2009. Professional and business information services will be the largest segment of institutional end-user spending, expanding 7.8 percent from 2004 to 2009, reaching $142.33 billion. Television programming expenditures will increase 6.5 percent in the five-year timeframe to $62.41 billion, and educational and training media will rise 5.2 percent to $24.04 billion. Business-to-business media spending, including circulation and exhibit space, will climb at a compound annual rate of 4.1 percent in the forecast period, reaching $11.05 billion. The key trends driving growth over the next five years will be technology and products that deliver ROI metrics, the solid economic expansion, stronger corporate profits, increased institutional budgets and innovations in the development, delivery and use of integrated information services.

4

BROADCAST TELEVISION

Television Networks, page 217

Television Stations, page 226

Broadcast Television

Broadcast Television Advertising Spending and Nominal GDP Growth, 2000-2009

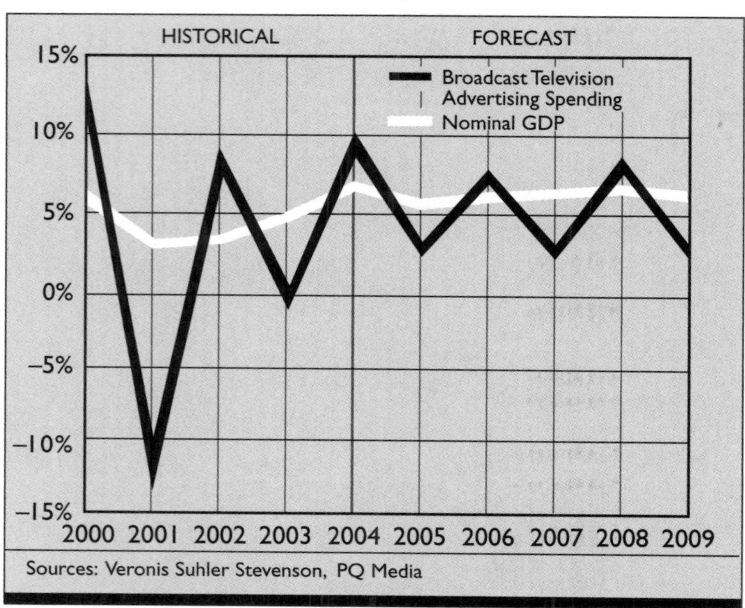

Sources: Veronis Suhler Stevenson, PQ Media

Growth of U.S. Broadcast Television Spending

	Television Networks	*Television Stations*	*Barter Syndication*	*Total*
2004 Expenditures ($ Millions)	$17,563	$25,613	$2,844	$46,020
1999-2004 Compound Annual Growth (%)	3.8%	2.0%	4.7%	2.8%
2004-2009 Projected Compound Annual Growth (%)	4.4%	4.2%	4.9%	4.3%
2009 Projected Expenditures ($ Millions)	$21,799	$31,452	$3,610	$56,861

Sources: Veronis Suhler Stevenson, PQ Media, Universal McCann

THE BROADCAST TELEVISION MARKET IN 2004 AND 2005

The broadcast television industry closed 2004 emboldened by spending growth that approached double digits, thanks to record presidential election spending and Olympics-related advertising. But heading into 2005, the industry faced a number of challenges that threatened to chip away at broadcast television advertising expenditures in the near term. Among them, the emergence of ad-skipping technology and less reliance on the 30-second spot, increased competition with cable television and the Internet for consumer attention, and heightened interest among advertisers in non-traditional marketing vehicles.

Recognizing these looming obstacles to sustained sales growth, television executives have departed from their recent strategy of relying on low-budget copycat reality shows and took chances on some innovative new scripted shows. The gamble paid off in the 2004-05 season, as several new shows scored with viewers, encouraging producers and network executives to seek out potential hits for 2005-06 that stray from traditional formulas.

The industry's efforts to win back viewers and maintain their loyalty are critical in today's fragmented media environment in which consumers and advertisers have a cornucopia of options. Despite declining ratings for the past 10 years, advertisers have stuck with broadcast television because of its ability to deliver mass audiences. However, the rising cost of traditional television advertising, coupled with concerns that more viewers are bypassing ads, has prompted marketers to re-evaluate their investments in broadcast television advertising. Automobile advertisers, for example, have been experimenting with new concepts in Internet advertising. At the same time, direct-to-consumer drug advertising—a big source of broadcast TV spending in recent years—is beginning to fade amidst a Food and Drug Administration (FDA) crackdown.

Indeed, the broadcast television market has reached a crossroads. Viewers have been migrating from broadcast to cable television for years; now advertisers may follow. The question for broadcast television executives is whether they can muster a crop of compelling new shows that will excite viewers and advertisers, restoring their loyalty to broadcast television.

Advertisers were asking the same question as this *Forecast* went to press and networks were preparing for the upfront buying season. Heading into this year's upfront market, advertisers once again were balking at the upfront buying process in which prices consistently escalate despite declining ratings. Although broadcast networks are expected to raise rates once again, they are experiencing some pressure on pricing. Scatter market prices were actually below 2004 upfront prices in the first and fourth buying periods since then, and they were level with the 2004 upfront prices in the second period. (Scatter market prices are typically about 10 percent above upfront prices.) Upfront prices were expected to be up in the low single digits in 2005, compared with an 11.5 percent gain in the 2004 upfront market. However, pricing will depend largely on the volume the networks offer for sale. Last year they sold about 80 percent of their ad time, but this year they are expected to sell in the 70 percent range, and the limited supply may help boost prices. Manufacturers of drugs and remedies are expected to spend less on television advertising in the 2005 upfront market, due to crackdowns on advertising by the FDA, stemming from the well-publicized concerns over prescription and non-prescription pain relievers. However, automakers are expected to spend big, despite increased interest in Web advertising.

While networks are experiencing pricing pressure on commercial inventory, it should be noted that hit prime-time shows and special events, such as the Super Bowl and the Academy Awards, will continue to command lofty rates. The cost for a 30-second spot during the 2005 Super Bowl increased 6.7 percent to $2.4 million, while ratings were up only 1.7 percent in 2004. Ratings increased 0.7 percent in 2003, and the cost for a 30-second spot rose

HIGHLIGHTS

Television Networks

Broadcast television advertising spending increased 9.7 percent to $46.02 billion in 2004, bolstered by record spending on election campaigns and Olympics-related advertising. Compound annual growth was 2.8 percent from 1999 to 2004.

■

Network advertising spending grew 9.1 percent to $17.56 billion in 2004, due primarily to record spending on the presidential campaign, as well as advertising during the summer Olympics.

■

Networks continued to lose audiences to cable and satellite television in the 2003-04 season, as prime-time network ratings slid 0.7 of a point to 28.9. However, a renewed interest in scripted series, sparked by the introduction of compelling new dramas such as *Desperate Housewives* and *Lost*, is boosting prime-time network ratings in 2004-05.

■

We anticipate network advertising spending growth will slow to 2.3 percent in 2005, due to pressure on pricing, diminished spending on direct-to-consumer drug ads, and the absence of political and Olympics advertising. Spending will reach $17.97 billion in 2005. Spending is expected to grow at a compound annual rate of 4.4 percent in the 2004-2009 period, reaching $21.80 billion in 2009.

■

Total spending on broadcast television advertising, including networks, stations and barter syndication, is projected to grow 2.0 percent to $46.93 billion in 2005. Growth during even years in the forecast period is expected to be slower than in the previous five-year period due to a number of challenges facing the broadcast television industry, such as the emergence of ad-skipping technology, increased competition with cable television and the Internet for consumer attention, and heightened interest among advertisers in alternative marketing vehicles.

■

Spending is projected to rise at a compound annual rate of 4.3 percent from 2004 to 2009 to $56.86 billion, an improvement compared to 2.8 percent compound annual growth in the previous five-year period. However, a large decline in spending during the recession of 2001 negatively affected compound annual growth in the 1999-2004 period.

7.1 percent to $2.3 million in 2004. The cost for a 30-second spot during the Academy Awards increased 10.9 percent to $1.5 million in 2004, compared to an increase of 5.0 percent to $1.4 million in 2003.

The networks will have to rely on their programming to draw audiences and advertisers in 2005, because they will not have political advertising and the Olympics to prop up sales. Record spending on the presidential election campaign, coupled with Olympics-related advertising, boosted broadcast television advertising spending 9.7 percent to $46.02 billion in 2004. The solid gain in 2004 lifted compound annual growth to 2.8 percent for the 1999-2004 period, despite setbacks in 2001 and 2003.

Political spending on advertising media reached $1.85 billion in 2004, an increase of 58.9 percent from 2002 spending levels, and a gain of 112.1 percent from 2000 levels, according to PQ Media. However, PQ Media's research shows that broadcast's share of this important spending source is dwindling. While broadcast television accounted for the largest share of political media spending in 2004 with 52.8 percent, its share declined from 56.4 percent in 2002 and 56.1 percent in 2000. Spending on Internet political advertising grew the fastest since 2000, up 998.1 percent, followed by cable television, which rose 432.5 percent, and public relations/promotions, which climbed 149.7 percent.

National spot spending benefited the most from political advertising in 2004, growing 10.0 percent to $10.94 billion. Compound annual growth was 0.8 percent in the 1999-2004 period, due primarily to a 24.8 percent drop during the recession of 2001. Network advertising expenditures rose 9.1 percent to $17.56 billion, driven primarily by presidential election spending and Olympics-related advertising. Compound annual growth was 3.8 percent from 1999 to 2004. Local advertising spending increased 8.5 percent to $14.67 billion, fueled in part by strong gains in the largest advertising category, automotive, as manufacturers sought to promote a slew of new car launches. Automakers boosted spending 11.5 percent in the television station market overall, including local and national spot. The financial and insurance/real estate categories also achieved strong gains of better than 20 percent each. Compound annual growth in the local market was 3.0 percent in the 1999-2004 period, due to a substantial decline during the recession of 2001.

Broadcast television advertising, including barter syndication, is expected to grow only 2.0 percent to $46.93 billion in 2005, driven mainly by the absence of political and Olympics advertising, as well as the erosion of drug advertising and pricing pressures. Broadcast television advertising typically surpasses nominal GDP growth in even years due to political and Olympics advertising, and lags GDP growth in odd years due to the lack of such spending. The gap between GDP and broadcast television growth is starting to shrink, and this trend is expected to continue in the forecast period as advertisers re-evaluate their TV ad budgets and seek non-traditional media options. Broadcast television advertising spending rose 9.7 percent in 2004, exceeding nominal GDP growth by 3.1 percentage points, the slimmest margin in the past three even years. In 2002, broadcast television growth was 4.7 percentage points ahead of GDP growth because the market rebounded sharply after plunging during the recession of 2001. In 2000, heavy dot-com spending combined with political and Olympics advertising sparked a double-digit gain in broadcast television spending, beating GDP by 6.1 percentage points.

During the forecast period, the margin between GDP growth and broadcast television advertising growth is expected to contract further in even years. As noted earlier, television's share of political advertising is shrinking as candidates employ alternative advertising vehicles, such as the Internet and public relations, pursuing a strategy similar to that of other TV advertisers. The prospects for Olympics advertising are also weaker in the forecast period than in the previous five-year timeframe. In 2002, advertisers boosted spending due to high hopes for winter Olympics ratings because of the games' domestic location in Salt Lake City. Prospects for the summer Olympics in 2004 were not as strong, given the seven-hour time difference between the U.S. East Coast and Athens, Greece. The same will be true for the 2006 Winter Olympics in Turin, Italy. The potential for good U.S. TV audiences is even weaker for the 2008 summer Olympics because they will be held in Beijing, a 12-hour time difference.

The news on the programming front was positive in the 2004-05 season. Television networks won back audiences thanks to breakout hits *Desperate Housewives* and *Lost* on ABC, and the enduring success of *CSI* and reality favorites *Survivor*, *American Idol* and *The Apprentice*. Prime-time network ratings increased 2.3 points to 31.2 through January 2005. However, the increase is not expected to be as pronounced when the full-year results are tabulated because the networks always enjoy an initial boost at the start of the TV season and during the winter when people tend to stay indoors.

On the strength of *CSI* and *Survivor*, CBS maintained its 8.4 rating through December of the 2004-05 season, leading the four major networks. *Desperate Housewives* and *Lost* lifted ABC's ratings nearly a point to 6.8 in 2004-05 (through December 2004) from 5.9 in 2003-04. The loss of *Friends* and *Frasier*, and the declining popularity of *ER*, caused NBC's ratings to slip 0.3 of a point to 7.0. FOX had a 4.2 rating at the beginning of the 2004-05 season because *American Idol*, the highest-rated show in America aside from *CSI*, did not debut until January. FOX had a 6.1 rating in the 2003-04 season.

Among other developments in the broadcast television market, the Federal Communications Commission (FCC) in June 2003 raised the limit on the percentage of U.S. households station owners could reach, capping penetration at 45 percent, up from 35 percent. Congress later passed legislation directing the FCC to reduce the cap to 39 percent. The FCC also loosened restrictions on cross-ownership of television stations and newspapers in the same market, and on ownership of two television stations in the same market. Various parties challenged the FCC's order in federal courts; the cases were combined and assigned by lottery to the Third Circuit Court of Appeals in Philadelphia. In June 2004, the Third Circuit Court overturned the FCC's ruling and directed the commission to further review the ownership regulations.

Broadcasters received another legal blow in February 2005 when the FCC ruled that cable operators are not required to carry a broadcaster's analog and digital signals simultaneously, nor are they required to carry multiple digital programming streams from an individual broadcaster. Broadcasters are concerned that the decision could hinder their efforts to transition from analog to digital programming, as they await a decision from Congress on the deadline for completing the conversion. Meanwhile, sales of digital television sets are on the rise. Factory-to-dealer sales of digital TV products reached 927,000 units in December 2004, a 45.0 percent gain over December 2003. Full-year 2004 sales hit 7.2 million units, up 75.0 percent from 2003.

Television Networks

The Television Network Market in 2004 and 2005

Network advertising spending increased 9.1 percent to $17.56 billion in 2004, mainly as a result of the influx of political and Olympics-related advertising. Network advertising growth outpaced nominal GDP growth by 2.5 percentage points. Strong spending growth in the leading advertising category, automobiles, contributed to the gains, as did double-digit gains in drugs/remedies, due to direct-to-consumer advertising.

Viewing Trends

Prompted by the huge success of reality TV forerunners *Who Wants to Be a Millionaire?* and *Survivor* in the 1999-00 television season (*Survivor* actually debuted in the summer of 2000 after the season ended), television networks have relied on low-cost unscripted shows to fill much of their schedules for the past three seasons. However, in the 2004-05 season, scripted shows made a comeback. ABC introduced two new dramas, *Desperate Housewives* and *Lost*, which broke into the Nielsen top 10. NBC's *Medium*, introduced at mid-season, also scored with audiences. Meanwhile, the *CSI* franchise has become so popular with viewers that it holds three positions in the Nielsen top 20 for the 2004-05 season through April 3, 2005. The original

CSI is still the top-rated show in America, while *CSI: Miami* ranks number seven and *CSI: New York* ranks number 19. *Desperate Housewives* holds the number-four spot, and *Without a Trace* ranks number six.

The instant success of ABC's *Desperate Housewives* and *Lost*, coupled with the enduring popularity of *CSI* and *Without a Trace* on CBS, has rejuvenated scripted dramatic programming. The success of *Desperate Housewives* and *Lost* is expected to encourage producers to introduce more scripted shows to networks. However, at least a few of the new shows being considered for 2005-06 draw on elements of *Desperate Housewives* and *Lost*, which owe much of their success to their originality. For instance, shades of *Lost* are evident in *Triangle* (UPN) and *Invasion* (ABC), while *Soccer Moms* (ABC) and *The Commuters* (CBS) have similarities to *Desperate Housewives*. In *Triangle*, a young doctor searches the Caribbean islands for his new wife after she disappears from their yacht during their honeymoon. *Invasion* is set in a Florida town where something strange happens during a hurricane. *Soccer Moms* follows two housewives-turned-private investigators, and *The Commuters* centers on suburban characters harboring secrets.

The networks are also attempting to capitalize on the popularity of religious stories in pop culture, such as Mel Gibson's blockbuster film *The Passion of the Christ* and Dan Brown's bestselling book *The Da Vinci Code*. NBC is creating a drama called *Book of Daniel* about a drug-addicted priest who converses with Jesus, and CBS is developing a supernatural thriller about a religious physicist. NBC was first out of the gate with the mini-series *Revelations* in the spring of 2005, which managed to draw 15.6 million viewers in its first week.

Although scripted dramatic shows are making a comeback, sitcoms struggled in 2004-05, with only *Everybody Loves Raymond* in the top 10. The networks' other reliable performers, such as *The Simpsons* and *Will & Grace*, failed to live up to their past records, while all of the season's new entries floundered. CBS's *Two and a Half Men*, which debuted during the 2003-04 season, is the only sitcom to achieve growth in 2004-05; it stood at number 12 in the season-to-date ratings through April 3, 2005. The state of the network sitcom is unsettling to network executives because the genre has been the mainstay of prime-time schedules for many years. The last time networks experienced such a dearth of comedy hits was in the 1983-84 season when CBS's *Kate & Allie* was the only sitcom in a top 10 populated by night-time soaps and news programs (*Dallas*, *60 Minutes*, *Dynasty*). However, comedy was resurrected in the following season with the debut of *The Cosby Show* and the emerging success of *Cheers* and *Family Ties*. A host of hits debuted in the years to follow including *The Golden Girls*, *Married . . . With Children*, *Coach*, *Murphy Brown* and *Seinfeld*.

It is evident that the networks are attempting to resuscitate the sitcom yet again. The news out of network development meetings in Los Angeles in March 2005 was that programming executives are focused on the search for breakout sitcom hits for the 2005-06 season. Furthermore, they have become willing to take chances on non-traditional formats and themes, a strategy reminiscent of *Seinfeld*, the self-proclaimed "show about nothing." NBC is reportedly looking at one show that takes place in a retirement community and another set in a trailer park, while FOX is considering a show depicting Jesus as a teenage slacker. Shows are being centered around rock stars, such as the Barenaked Ladies and Melissa Etheridge. The emphasis on the offbeat stems from the success of such cable shows as *Curb Your Enthusiasm*, developed for HBO by *Seinfeld* co-creator Larry David, and *Chappelle's Show* on Comedy Central. The networks have gotten a jump-start on the 2005-06 season by introducing new comedies late in 2004-05, including FOX's *Stacked*, starring Pamela Anderson, and NBC's take on the BBC hit *The Office*.

Despite the shortcomings of the networks' comedy line-up, scripted shows remain the lifeblood of prime-time network television. Only three of the scores of new reality programs that have been introduced over the past few years have retained their top 20 positions—*American Idol*, *Survivor* and *The Apprentice*. For the 2004-05 season through April 3, 2005, *American Idol* holds the number-two and number-three spots because it airs two shows a week, while *Survivor: Palau* (introduced mid-season) ranks number five, *Survivor: Vanuatu* (aired in the fall) ranks number eight, and the second installment of *The Apprentice* ranks number 14. Overall, however, the popularity of reality TV is dissipating, as the overabundance of sub-par copycat shows that followed the original *Survivor* and *American Idol* turned off audiences. Even *The Apprentice* franchise has dropped in the ratings with its third installment, but *Survivor* and *American Idol* continue to hold strong.

While the networks have had some high-profile hits, reality TV continues to be dogged by embarrassing scandals and major flops. FOX has come under fire from other networks for purportedly copying their programs. Producers of *The Contender* on NBC took FOX to court, claiming FOX stole its concept to create *The Next Great Champ*. ABC accused FOX of copying *Wife Swap* with its *Trading Spouses* and copying *Supernanny* with its *Nanny 911*. FOX's *Who's Your Daddy* failed to muster an audience even before news broke that the woman trying to identify her biological father on the show appeared in a pornographic film in 1995. CBS cancelled *The Will* after one broadcast because the premiere attracted only 4.3 million viewers, placing it at the bottom of CBS's ratings that week.

As the networks execute their programming strategies for the 2005-06 season, they must consider that the way viewers are counted may change. Nielsen has faced concerns over the past two years that its ratings may not be fully counting African Americans. As a result, an independent task force chaired by former Illinois Congresswoman Cardiss Collins was established in April 2004, on the recommendation of New York Congressman Charles Rangel, to counsel Nielsen on how it can more accurately measure diverse television audiences. Nielsen made the task force's report public in March 2005 and announced it would implement many of the recommendations. The report noted that while Nielsen can improve its measurement service, the quality of its data has been vital to the TV industry's success.

New breakout hits are only part of the reason for broadcast network television's improvement in the ratings in 2004-05. Pay cable viewership took a hit in the 2004-05 season, with the absence of *Sex and the City*, which aired its final episode on HBO in 2003-04, and *The Sopranos,* which is on hiatus until the 2005-06 season. While the absence of HBO's two biggest series and the emergence of new hits on broadcast television have allowed networks to regain some ground in the ratings wars, the networks must still contend with ad-supported cable, which continues to expand programming choices and boost overall ratings.

As the penetration of multichannel cable and satellite services in U.S. households increased over the past 20 years, the networks' share of the television audience has dwindled. In 2000, when 86.9 percent of television households had multichannel services, broadcast networks captured 59 percent of the prime-time audience. In 2004, multichannel services were in 90.3 percent of television homes, and prime-time network's share dropped to 49. Network television managed to gain a point to 50 through January of the 2004-05 season, despite the rise in multichannel penetration to 91.8 percent; however, we expect network television's share to drop back down a point to 49 by year-end. But cable's overall share still exceeds that of broadcast television. Cable

Broadcast Television

Network Prime-Time Audience Share vs. Multichannel TV Household Penetration

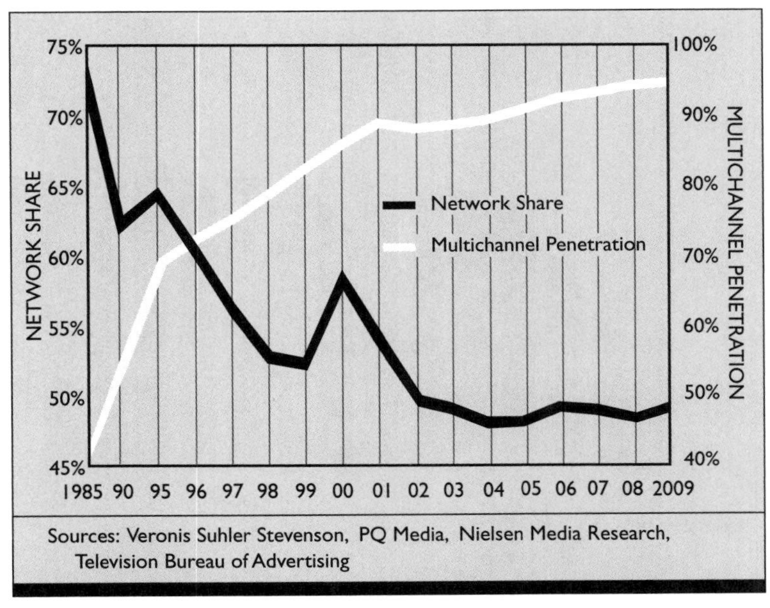

Sources: Veronis Suhler Stevenson, PQ Media, Nielsen Media Research, Television Bureau of Advertising

Impact of Additional Channels

Number of Channels Received	Average Number of Channels Received	Average Number of Channels Viewed	Percent of Channels Viewed
11-20	15.4	5.5	35.7%
21-30	24.7	6.8	27.5
31-40	35.4	10.2	28.8
41-50	45.7	12.6	27.6
51-60	55.9	15.2	27.2
61-70	66.4	15.3	23.0
71-80	75.9	15.4	20.3
81-90	84.5	15.5	18.3
91-100	95.1	16.6	17.5
101-110	105.2	18.4	17.5
111-120	115.9	16.5	14.2
120+	183.2	19.2	10.5

Sources: Veronis Suhler Stevenson, PQ Media, Nielsen Media Research, Television Bureau of Advertising

Household Hours of Television Viewing

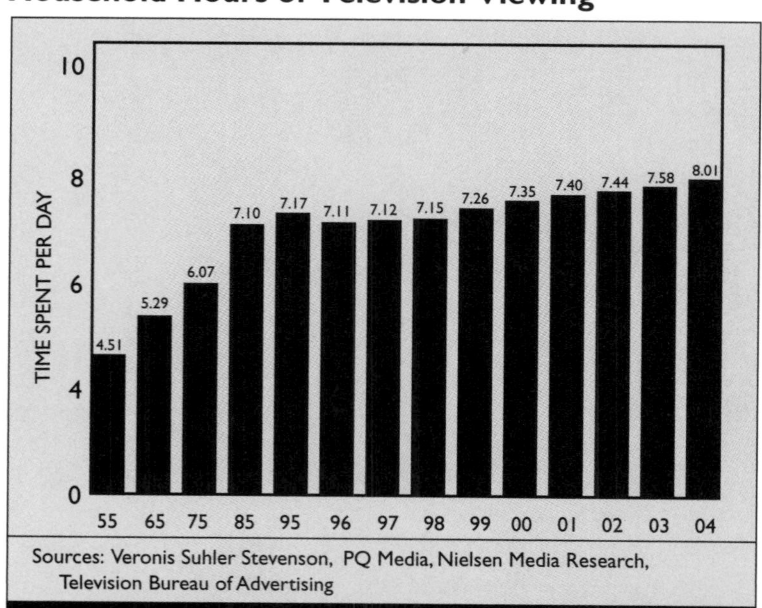

Sources: Veronis Suhler Stevenson, PQ Media, Nielsen Media Research, Television Bureau of Advertising

surpassed broadcast television viewership for the first time in 2002-03, with a 60 share, compared to a 57 share for broadcast. Broadcast TV's share remained at 57 in 2003-04, while cable climbed to 63. During 2004-05 February sweeps, more households tuned in to cable than to broadcast TV for the first time. Cable's sports programming and original scripted shows, such as A&E's *Growing Up Gotti*, are helping to propel its viewership ahead of broadcast TV's. Reruns of popular network shows have also contributed to cable's gains, including *Law & Order* on TNT and *CSI* on Spike TV.

While multichannel services pose a competitive threat to networks because of the wide variety of programming options available, more choices do not necessarily lead to increased viewing. In homes with 51-60 channels received, an average of 15.2 channels, or 27.2 percent of all available channels, are viewed. As the number of available channels grows, the number viewed increases only minimally. For example, in homes that receive 101-110 channels, only 18.4, or 17.5 percent of the total number received, are viewed. But households are increasing their overall television viewing time. In 2003, households spent 7 hours and 58 minutes watching television, and an estimated 8 hours and 1 minute in 2004. In addition, the average number of television sets per household increased to 2.47 in 2004 from 2.44 in 2003.

Not only are networks facing competition from cable, but they are also contending with the rising popularity of digital video recorders (DVRs), such as TiVo. The DVR is even more versatile than its predecessor, the VCR, because it can be programmed to record a user's favorite shows on a regular basis, and it allows the user to rewind and pause live television. A study in late 2004 showed that more than three-quarters of advertising leaders believe that DVRs will have a significant impact on television advertising and spark growth of non-traditional advertising formats. However, there is evidence that ad-skipping technology has not led consumers to bypass commercials any more frequently than they did with their remote controls in hand. And industry pundits had predicted the VCR would precipitate the demise of commercials, which has not happened.

Another issue concerning network executives and advertisers is the growing practice of Internet piracy of TV shows. Users of peer-to-peer networks are not only pirating and disseminating popular TV shows, but they are removing commercials before doing so. The proliferation of broadband access is making digital piracy of TV shows easier and more frequent.

To grab the viewer's attention and avoid ad zapping, advertisers are striving to create more entertaining commercials. For example, Cingular Wireless' symbol of five vertical lines appears in almost every scene of its commercials—as lanes of taxis or as lines of people—to turn the spot into a game. The company has held a contest for employees and is considering one for customers. Advertisers are even running promotions for their commercials. Radio ads launched in March 2005 prompted listeners to tune into Comedy Central to view commercials for Sierra Mist that featured an improvisational comedy troupe.

Advertisers are also becoming more flexible in how they approach the standard commercial spot, choosing to make them longer or shorter than the traditional 30 seconds or to create different configurations. For example, Puma ran duos of 15-second spots back-to-back in 30-second time slots. And Cadillac ran five-second spots to promote three cars that can go from zero to 60 in less than five seconds.

Marketers are striving to develop broader advertising and marketing packages that include not only 30-second spots during popular programs, but also sponsorships and product placements. Spending on product placement is increasing significantly as advertisers move toward integrating their products into television programs, rather than merely placing them as props. Spending on product placement and product integration has been climbing since the late 1990s, when marketers aimed to reach 18- to 34-year-olds, who were spending more time with the Internet and videogames. Also at this time, TiVo came on the scene, and cable ratings were on the rise. Spending on product placement in television, including cable, grew at a compound annual rate of 21.5 percent from 1999 to 2004, according to PQ Media. Product placement spending surged in 2004, increasing 46.4 percent to $1.88 billion. Broadcast television accounts for the overwhelming majority of product placement spending because individual network shows receive higher ratings than do individual cable shows.

Television Sets

Year	*In Home (Thousands)*	*Average Sets Per Household*
1997	228,740	2.36
1998	235,010	2.40
1999	240,320	2.42
2000	244,990	2.43
2001	248,160	2.43
2002	254,360	2.41
2003	260,230	2.44
2004	268,260	2.47

Sources: Veronis Suhler Stevenson, PQ Media, Nielsen Media Research, Television Bureau of Advertising

However, broadcast TV's share has diminished over the past 30 years because of cable television. Scripted shows, including comedies and dramas, accounted for the highest product placement spending on television in 2004. Scripted dramas have been the most aggressive in pursuing product placement deals because they can offset their costs through barter arrangements with products used on the show. Spending on reality and game shows is growing the fastest. PQ Media forecasts that broadcast television product placement spending will grow at a compound annual rate of 11.3 percent from 2004 to 2009, due to rising costs for scripted dramas and continued growth of spending on reality shows. Spending is expected to reach $3.20 billion in 2009.

Advertisers are hoping that interactive television (ITV) will engage consumers in commercials, as well as track the effectiveness of ads. EchoStar Communications' DISH Network has already introduced ITV advertising capabilities, and rival DIRECTV is preparing to roll out such a service. Mercedes-Benz has tested ITV ads in the U.S., and Hewlett-Packard (HP) plans to launch ITV ads by the end of 2005 after testing a campaign in the

U.K., where half of households have ITV. The HP ads would allow viewers to access a coupon from their remote controls during spots for its digital photography and printing products. Consumers can also click through to an HP screen to view demonstrations of the company's products and short films.

NETWORK RATINGS

CBS continued to lead the big four networks in the ratings in the 2003-04 season, due primarily to the unwavering success of *CSI* and *Survivor*. CBS had an 8.4 rating and 14 share in the 2003-04 season. Through December 5 of the 2004-05 season, CBS retained its 8.4 rating, but lost a share point. Through April 3, 2005, CBS had six shows in the Nielsen top 10, including *CSI*, *Survivor: Palau* (introduced mid-season), *Without a Trace*, *CSI: Miami*, *Survivor: Vanuatu* (aired in the fall), and *Everybody Loves Raymond*.

NBC followed CBS in the 2003-04 season with a 7.3 rating and a 12 share, bolstered by the long-running sitcoms *Friends* and *Frasier*, as well as the hit medical drama *ER*. With *Friends* and *Frasier* off the air and the popularity of *ER* diminishing, NBC had slipped to a 7.0 rating and an 11 share through December 5 of the 2004-05 season. NBC had no shows in the Nielsen top 10 through April 3, 2005, with *ER* at number 11 and the second installment of *The Apprentice*—its popular contribution to the reality genre—at number 14. *The Apprentice* dropped to number 19 with its third installment, introduced mid-season. However, NBC's new psychic drama—*Medium*, introduced late in the season—was showing promise.

Without any major hits in either the reality or scripted genre, ABC trailed the other big four networks in the 2003-04 season, with a 5.9 rating and a 10 share. However, the breakout success of *Desperate Housewives* and *Lost* in the 2004-05 season has led ABC out of the ratings doldrums. Through December 2004, ABC gained nearly a point, increasing its rating to 6.8 and its share to 11. *Desperate Housewives* was ranked number four through April 3, 2005, behind *CSI* and both weekly episodes of *American Idol. Lost* is at number 15 for the overall season, but had been in the weekly top 10. The network followed up on the success of *Desperate Housewives* and *Lost* with the new medical series *Grey's Anatomy*, which was introduced late in the television season. But as a result of its cushy time slot after *Desperate Housewives* (in place of *Boston Legal*), the show was number 12 through April 3, 2005. Because the program was launched late in the year, it was too early at press time to determine whether it would be able to hold on to the *Desperate Housewives* audience for the remainder of the season.

Aside from the immense success of *American Idol*, FOX is struggling. The network had a 6.1 rating in the 2003-04 season, but only a 4.2 rating through December of the 2004-05

U.S. Population (THOUSANDS)

Category	*1994*	*2004*	*Percent Change*
Age 18-49	126,642	135,508	7.0%
Age 50+	67,852	84,869	25.1
TV Households	211,443	268,260	26.9

Sources: Veronis Suhler Stevenson, PQ Media, Nielsen Media Research, Television Bureau of Advertising, U.S. Census Bureau

Prime-Time Network Ratings

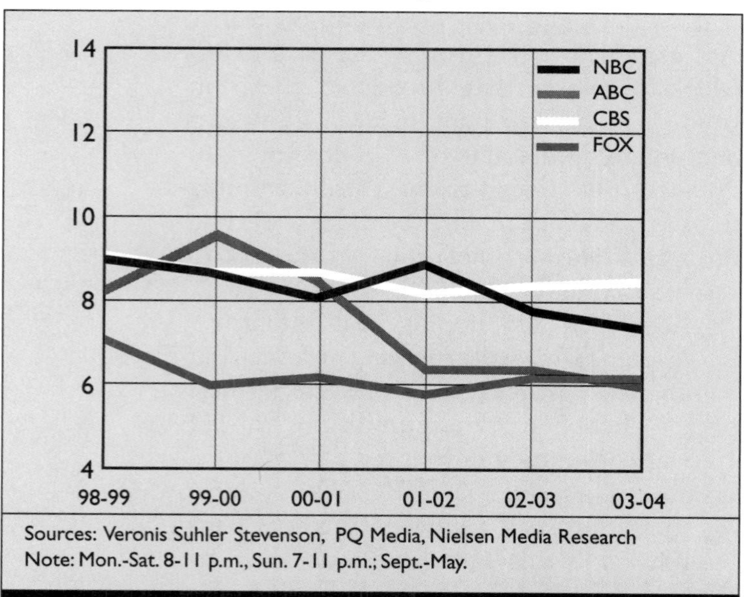

Sources: Veronis Suhler Stevenson, PQ Media, Nielsen Media Research
Note: Mon.-Sat. 8-11 p.m., Sun. 7-11 p.m.; Sept.-May.

Network Prime-Time Television Viewing

Year	*Network Prime-Time Rating*	*Network Prime-Time Audience Share*	*Total U.S. TV Households (Millions)*	*Percent of Households With TV*	*Prime-Time Households (Millions)*
1998-99	31.3	53	99.4	95.7%	31.1
1999-00*	34.7	59	100.8	96.3	35.0
2000-01	32.6	55	102.2	94.4	33.3
2001-02	30.3	51	105.5	96.5	32.0
2002-03	29.6	50	106.7	95.9	31.6
2003-04	28.9	49	108.4	96.4	31.3
2004-05	29.1	49	109.6	96.5	31.9
2005-06	29.2	50	110.8	96.5	32.4
2006-07	29.2	50	112.0	96.5	32.7
2007-08	29.1	49	113.2	96.5	32.9
2008-09	29.2	50	114.4	96.5	33.4

Sources: Veronis Suhler Stevenson, PQ Media, Nielsen Media Research, Television Bureau of Advertising
Note: Ratings are for Mon.-Sat. 8-11 p.m., Sun. 7-11 p.m.
*UPN, WB and PAX included beginning in 1999.

season because the latest installment of *American Idol* did not debut until mid-season. The Tuesday edition of *American Idol*, which features performances by the contestants, ranked number two in the Nielsen ratings through April 3, 2005, and the Wednesday edition, which reveals the results of the audience's call-in votes on Tuesday, ranked number three. *American Idol* has become a powerhouse, generating $908 million in revenues in 2004, including national and local sales, merchandise, recordings, concerts and overseas sales. But other than *American Idol*, FOX does not have another show in the Nielsen top 20, although *24* and *House* have periodically broken into the top 20 shows in certain weeks.

Overall, the networks had a prime-time rating of 28.9 in the 2003-04 season and a 49 share. The success of *Desperate Housewives* and *Lost* helped lift the networks' rating to 31.2 for the 2004-05 season through January 30, 2005. However, that figure is expected to slide by the end of the year because networks typically receive an initial bump in the ratings when new shows debut in the fall. In addition, viewership is higher in the winter when people spend more time indoors.

UPN, WB and PAX Prime-Time Ratings

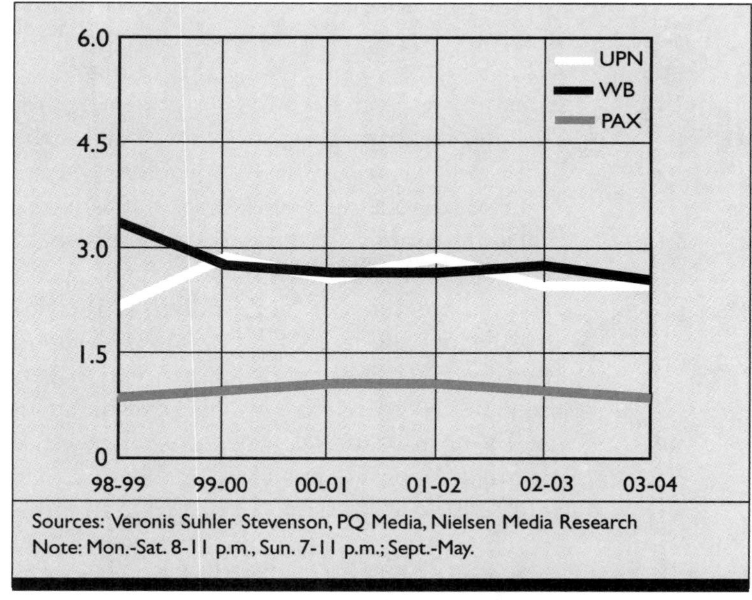

Sources: Veronis Suhler Stevenson, PQ Media, Nielsen Media Research
Note: Mon.-Sat. 8-11 p.m., Sun. 7-11 p.m.; Sept.-May.

Top Product Category Spending Growth, 2004 vs. 2003*

Category	*Network TV*†	*Spot TV*	*Consumer Magazines*	*Total*
Automobiles	11.0%	11.0%	3.0%	10.0%
Food	4.0	–6.0	15.0	7.0
Movies	8.0	–11.0	17.0	8.0
Toiletries & Cosmetics	9.0	–7.0	4.0	7.0
Drugs & Remedies	29.0	–1.0	3.0	21.0
Beverages & Snacks	12.0	–16.0	9.0	11.0
Restaurants	5.0	–2.0	92.0	6.0

Sources: Veronis Suhler Stevenson, PQ Media, Universal McCann
*January to August.
†ABC, CBS, NBC, FOX, UPN, WB, PAX, cable TV networks and national TV syndication.

Broadcast Television

NETWORK ADVERTISING

As consumers slice up their time among an expanding array of media options—particularly the coveted 18- to 34-year-old demographic—advertisers are increasingly pursuing alternatives to traditional vehicles in an effort to reach them. For example, automobile manufacturers, the biggest spenders on network television advertising, are turning to the Internet with increasing frequency. In early 2005, for example, Volvo Cars of North America signed on as a sponsor of Microsoft's new Internet feature MSN Spaces, which allows users to start personal Web logs, better known as blogs. About 4.5 million users signed up for the free feature as of mid-April. Meanwhile, Toyota Motor Sales USA in April introduced its first interactive game on its Spanish-language Web site in an effort to target the Hispanic market by extending its reach beyond television and print. Another factor that does not bode well for the automobile category is the problems facing General Motors, the world's largest automaker. The company has shaken up its management ranks to stem declining market share, and it reported a net loss of $839 million in the first quarter of 2005. Despite GM's woes and its rivals' Web advertising efforts, car makers are expected to make a sizable investment in the TV upfront market. Spending to advertise automobiles on TV was strong in 2004, as well, up 11.0 percent through the first eight months.

The drugs and remedies category is not expected to fare as well in the upfront market due to FDA crackdowns on direct-to-consumer advertising stemming from new data on the potential side effects of popular pain relievers. In December 2004, the FDA asked Pfizer to suspend direct-to-consumer advertising for the anti-inflammatory drug Celebrex while the agency reviewed new data on adverse side effects. While Celebrex remains on the market, the FDA told Pfizer in April 2005 to remove another arthritis medication, Bextra, from the market. Pain medication is not the only class of drugs to come under fire from the FDA. Also in April, the FDA ordered Bayer, Schering-Plough and GlaxoSmithKline to stop TV advertising for Levitra, a drug for erectile dysfunction. The agency also told Pfizer to cease print advertising for Zyrtec, an allergy medication. The FDA told Bayer and its co-marketers that the TV ads don't disclose the drug's indications or include information on side effects, and they suggest that the drug is better than its competitors in the absence of clinical proof. Pfizer was also told it was making unsubstantiated claims that Zyrtec was superior to competitors on the market. Other drug manufacturers are expected to voluntarily pull ads to avoid a conflict with the FDA. TAP Pharmaceutical Products has already decided to pull TV commercials for heartburn medication Prevacid in favor of print ads, which allow for a more detailed description of the drug and more time for consumers to comprehend it. The loss from drug advertising will be a blow to TV, which experienced a 29.0 percent gain in the category through the first eight months of 2004, the strongest gain among the top product categories.

Secondary Product Category Spending Growth, 2004 vs. 2003*

Category	*Network TV*†	*Spot TV*	*Consumer Magazines*	*Total*
Telecommunications	7.0%	2.0%	42.0%	9.0%
Computers	13.0	44.0	–8.0	5.0
Apparel	–13.0	–19.0	11.0	5.0
Beer & Wine	7.0	–26.0	25.0	9.0
Resorts & Tours	19.0	8.0	16.0	17.0
Airlines	35.0	35.0	81.0	47.0
Insurance	41.0	38.0	57.0	43.0

Sources: Veronis Suhler Stevenson, PQ Media, Universal McCann
*January to August.
†ABC, CBS, NBC, FOX, UPN, WB, PAX, cable TV networks and national TV syndication.

Broadcast Television

FORECAST ASSUMPTIONS

- The broadcast television industry faces a number of challenges that threaten to chip away at advertising expenditures, such as the emergence of ad-skipping technology, audience fragmentation and heightened advertiser interest in non-traditional marketing vehicles.
- Political campaign spending and Olympics-related advertising will fuel spending growth in even-numbered years during the forecast period, followed by slow-downs in growth in odd-numbered years. However, television's share of political advertising is diminishing, and Olympics viewership in the U.S. may be dampened by time differences.
- A renewed interest in scripted shows among audiences and network executives—sparked by the breakout hits *Desperate Housewives* and *Lost*—are expected to stem the decline in network ratings. While the most popular reality shows will endure, scripted shows will replace the overabundance of reality shows that have characterized the past three television seasons.
- The strength of the U.S. economy during the forecast period will also contribute to sustained growth for television advertising spending.

Network Television Advertising Spending And Nominal GDP Growth, 2000-2009

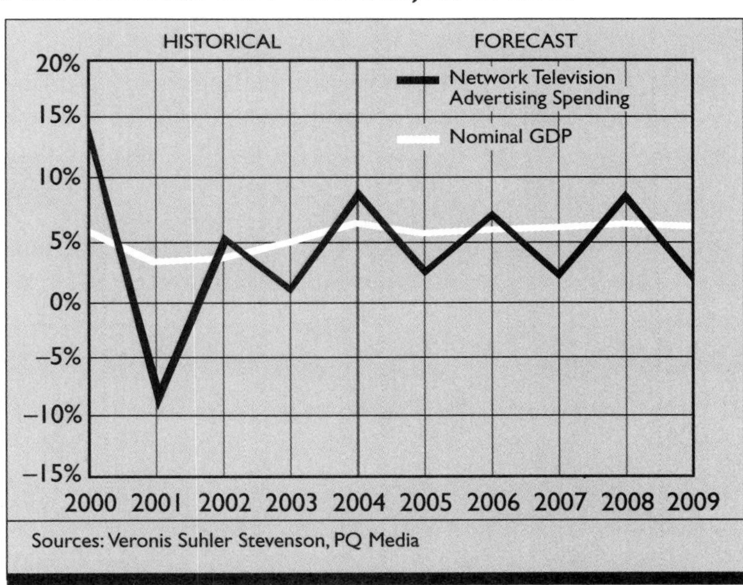

Sources: Veronis Suhler Stevenson, PQ Media

Television Stations

THE TELEVISION STATIONS MARKET IN 2004 AND 2005

Advertising spending at television stations grew 9.1 percent to $25.61 billion in 2004, due primarily to record political advertising for congressional races, and local issues and referendums. Automotive, financial and insurance/real estate advertisers also contributed to the gains. Television station advertising grew at a compound annual rate of 2.0 percent from 1999 to 2004.

National spot advertising climbed 10.0 percent in 2004 to $10.94 billion, and grew at a compound annual rate of 0.8 percent from 1999 to 2004. Local advertising increased 8.5 percent to $14.67 billion in 2004, and rose at a compound annual rate of 3.0 percent from 1999 to 2004.

Television stations, like networks, experience accelerated growth in even years because of political advertising. Television stations experienced spending gains of 11.3 percent in 2000, 11.9 percent in 2002 and 9.1 percent in 2004. By comparison, spending dropped 16.8 percent in 2001 and declined 2.4 percent in 2003, owing to the absence of political advertising. Spending is expected to increase only 1.6 percent in 2005 compared with 9.1 percent in 2004.

VIEWING TRENDS

Total-day ratings at network affiliates dropped to 14.2 points in the 2003-04 season from 14.5 points in the 2002-03 season. Independent stations experienced a minor gain, increasing from 1.3 to 1.4 points. For the 2004-05 season through January 30, network affiliates experienced an 0.8 of a point increase to 15.0, due to the new hit shows *Desperate Housewives* and *Lost.* However, by year's end, ratings should drop to 14.4 as a result of decreased viewership during the spring and summer. Independent stations also experienced a gain, increasing from 1.4 to 1.8. We expect network ratings to inch up again in 2005 and remain steady during the forecast period, as a result of the resurgence in scripted programming, which has brought audiences back to network television. The enduring strength of a few reality shows, such as *Survivor*, *American Idol* and *The Apprentice*, will also help networks maintain audiences.

Hampering daytime ratings growth is the lack of successful syndicated programs.

Television Station and Network Advertising Growth In Even-Numbered Years vs. Odd-Numbered Years

	Even-Numbered Years				*Odd-Numbered Years*		
Year	*Broadcast Networks*	*Television Stations*	*Differential*	*Year*	*Broadcast Networks*	*Television Stations*	*Differential*
2000	14.0%	11.3%	–2.7%	2001	–8.7%	–16.8%	–8.0%
2002	5.2	11.9	6.6	2003	0.8	–2.4	–3.2
2004	9.1	9.1	0.0	2005	2.3	1.6	–0.7
Wgt. Average	9.4	10.8	1.4	Wgt. Average	–1.8	–6.0	–4.2

Sources: Veronis Suhler Stevenson, PQ Media, Universal McCann

Highlights

Television Stations

Television station advertising increased 9.1 percent to $25.61 billion in 2004, fueled by unprecedented political advertising spending, particularly in congressional races. The market grew at a compound annual rate of 2.0 percent from 1999 to 2004.

■

The national spot market benefited the most from political advertising, expanding 10.0 percent to $10.94 billion in 2004. Compound annual growth was 0.8 percent from 1999 to 2004, due primarily to a sharp decline in 2001 resulting from the recession and the aftermath of the September 11 terrorist attacks.

■

Local advertising increased 8.5 percent to $14.67 billion in 2004, fueled by growth in the automotive, financial, and insurance/real estate categories. Spending grew at a compound annual rate of 3.0 percent in the 1999-2004 period.

■

Total-day ratings at network affiliates slipped 0.3 of a point to 14.2 in the 2003-04 television season, but began to pick up in the 2004-05 season as a result of new hit scripted shows, such as *Desperate Housewives* and *Lost*, and the absence of popular HBO series, such as *Sex and the City* and *The Sopranos*.

■

Spending on television station advertising is expected to grow at a moderate pace of 1.6 percent to $26.02 billion in 2005, owing to the lack of political and Olympics advertising and some of the same factors affecting network television spending. The market will grow at a compound annual rate of 4.2 percent in the 2004-2009 period, reaching $31.45 billion in 2009.

Local and National Spot Advertising Growth In Even-Numbered Years vs. Odd-Numbered Years

	Even-Numbered Years				*Odd-Numbered Years*		
Year	*National Spot*	*Local*	*Differential*	*Year*	*National Spot*	*Local*	*Differential*
2000	16.8%	6.8%	–10.0%	2001	–24.8%	–9.5%	15.3%
2002	18.4	7.0	–11.4	2003	–8.9	3.1	12.0
2004	10.0	8.5	–1.5	2005	1.8	1.4	–0.4
Wgt. Average	15.0	7.5	–7.5	Wgt. Average	–11.2	–1.6	9.6

Sources: Veronis Suhler Stevenson, PQ Media, Universal McCann

Prime-Time Ratings

Year	*Network-Affiliated TV Stations*	*Independent TV Stations **	*Public TV Stations*	*All TV Stations*	*Ad-Supported Cable†*	*Premium Pay Cable*	*All Other Cable‡*	*All Cable*	*All TV*
1999-00	34.7	2.1	2.0	38.8	24.0	3.5	1.9	29.4	68.2
2000-01	32.6	2.4	1.9	36.9	26.0	3.5	2.1	31.6	68.5
2001-02	30.3	2.5	1.6	34.4	28.2	3.5	2.1	33.8	68.2
2002-03	29.6	2.6	1.7	33.9	29.4	3.6	2.4	35.4	69.3
2003-04	28.9	2.9	1.6	33.4	30.9	3.4	2.9	37.2	70.6

Sources: Veronis Suhler Stevenson, PQ Media, Nielsen Media Research
Note: Ratings are for Mon.-Sat., 8-11 p.m., Sun 7-11 p.m.
*Includes Telemundo and Univision.
†Includes TBS and WGN.
‡Includes pay-per-view, interactive channels, home shopping channels, and audio-only feeds.

Broadcast Television

Total-Day Ratings

Year	*Network-Affiliated TV Stations*	*Independent TV Stations**	*PBS Stations*	*All TV Stations*	*Ad-Supported Cable†*	*Premium Pay Cable*	*All Other Cable‡*	*All Cable*	*All TV*
1999-00	16.5	1.1	1.0	18.6	13.3	1.9	1.0	16.2	34.8
2000-01	15.7	1.2	1.0	17.9	14.6	1.9	1.2	17.7	35.6
2001-02	14.6	1.2	0.9	16.7	15.8	2.0	1.2	19.0	35.7
2002-03	14.5	1.3	0.9	16.7	16.9	2.1	1.5	20.5	37.2
2003-04	14.2	1.4	0.8	16.4	17.7	2.1	1.8	21.6	38.0
2004-05	14.4	1.8	0.9	17.1	18.8	1.9	1.9	22.6	39.7
2005-06	14.5	1.8	0.9	17.2	19.1	1.9	2.0	23.0	40.2
2006-07	14.5	1.8	0.9	17.2	19.5	2.0	2.0	23.5	40.7
2007-08	14.4	1.8	0.9	17.1	19.8	2.0	2.1	23.9	41.0
2008-09	14.5	1.8	0.9	17.2	20.0	1.9	2.1	24.0	41.2

Sources: Veronis Suhler Stevenson, PQ Media, Nielsen Media Research
Note: Ratings are for Mon.-Sat., 8-11 p.m., Sun 7-11 p.m.
*Includes Telemundo and Univision.
†Includes TBS and WGN.
‡Includes pay-per-view, interactive channels, home shopping channels, and audio-only feeds.

Prime-Time Audience Shares

Year	Network-Affiliated TV Stations	Independent TV Stations*	Public TV Stations	All TV Stations	Ad-Supported Cable†	Premium Pay Cable	All Other Cable‡	All Cable
1999-00	59%	4%	3%	66%	41%	6%	3%	50%
2000-01	55	4	3	62	44	6	4	54
2001-02	51	4	3	58	48	6	4	58
2002-03	50	4	3	57	50	6	4	60
2003-04	49	5	3	57	52	6	5	63

Sources: Veronis Suhler Stevenson, PQ Media, Nielsen Media Research

Note: Shares are for Mon.-Sat., 8-11 p.m., Sun. 7-11 p.m. Total shares exceed 100% because Nielsen double-counts multiple-set households and multiple channels viewed during the quarter-hour.

*Includes Telemundo and Univision.

†Includes TBS and WGN.

‡Includes pay-per-view, interactive channels, home shopping channels, and audio-only feeds.

Broadcast Television

Shares of Total-Day Television Viewing

Year	Network-Affiliated TV Stations	Independent TV Stations*	PBS Stations	All TV Stations	Ad-Supported Cable†	Premium Pay Cable	All Other Cable‡	All Cable
1999-00	53%	4%	3%	60%	42%	6%	3%	51%
2000-01	49	4	3	56	46	6	4	56
2001-02	46	4	3	53	49	6	4	59
2002-03	44	4	3	51	51	6	5	62
2003-04	43	4	3	50	53	6	5	64
2004-05	43	5	2	50	54	5	5	64
2005-06	44	5	2	51	55	5	5	65
2006-07	44	5	2	51	55	6	5	66
2007-08	43	5	2	50	55	6	5	66
2008-09	44	5	2	51	56	5	5	66

Sources: Veronis Suhler Stevenson, PQ Media, Nielsen Media Research

Note: Shares are for Mon.-Sat., 8-11 p.m., Sun. 7-11 p.m. Total shares exceed 100% because Nielsen double-counts multiple-set households and multiple channels viewed during the quarter-hour.

*Includes Telemundo and Univision.

†Includes TBS and WGN.

‡Includes pay-per-view, interactive channels, home shopping channels, and audio-only feeds.

Top 15 Local Broadcast TV Advertisers*

($ THOUSANDS)

Category	2003 Spending	2004 Spending	Percent Change
DaimlerChrysler	$ 596,171	$ 604,577	1.4%
Ford Motor Co. Dlr. Assn.	428,324	465,860	8.8
General Motors Corp.	393,010	444,599	13.1
General Motors Corp. Dlr. Assn.	385,771	419,841	8.8
Nissan Motor Co. Ltd.	320,141	389,701	21.7
Honda Motor Co. Ltd.	330,932	384,141	16.1
Toyota Motor Corp. Dlr. Assn.	277,175	327,526	18.2
Ford Motor Co.	277,789	285,447	2.8
Toyota Motor Corp.	201,345	236,281	17.4
Verizon Communications	153,364	214,007	39.5
SBC Communications	266,040	213,714	–19.7
General Mills Inc.	219,797	213,180	–3.0
Yum Brands Inc.	197,293	208,612	5.7
Hyundai Corp.	146,239	162,356	11.0
McDonalds Corp.	143,969	158,281	9.9
Total	4,337,360	4,728,123	9.0

Sources: Veronis Suhler Stevenson, PQ Media, Television Bureau of Advertising, TNS Media Intelligence
*Includes local and national spot spending.

Television has not had a breakout hit in syndication since *Dr. Phil*, but even the popular self-help guru for the masses is losing some of his audience. While *The Oprah Winfrey Show* and *The Ellen DeGeneres Show* increased their 2004-05 ratings through January 2, 2005 (13.0 percent and 33.0 percent, respectively), *Dr. Phil* was down 2.0 percent. Among the new talk show hosts who debuted in the 2004-05, only Tony Danza is expected to return next season. In the game show genre, *Wheel of Fortune* and *Jeopardy* still top the syndicated ratings charts, but no new game shows are planned for 2005-06. The Nielsen list of the top 10 syndicated shows is devoid of original scripted programs with the absence of *Baywatch*, *Hercules* and *Xena: Warrior Princess*. Networks are also facing tough competition from cable networks for off-network scripted shows, with cable networks willing to pay top dollar for a *CSI* (SpikeTV) or *Law & Order* (TNT).

Total-day ratings for ad-supported cable, or basic cable, continued to rise in 2003-04, growing to 17.7 points from 16.9 points. Basic cable's popularity can be attributed to niche programming for enthusiasts in particular areas, such as food and home decorating, as well as acclaimed original series, such as *Monk* on the USA Network. Basic cable has also delved into the reality genre, achieving a measure of success with certain shows that have caught on with audiences, such as *Queer Eye for the Straight Guy*. While basic

FORECAST ASSUMPTIONS

- Television stations will benefit from congressional and gubernatorial campaign spending, particularly in the national spot market, in even-numbered years.
- Television stations are expected to maintain their ratings during the forecast period on the strength of new scripted shows, as well as the continued success of reality shows that have developed followings, such as *American Idol* and *Survivor.*
- The nation's economic growth will fuel television station advertising increases throughout the forecast period.

Television Station Advertising Spending And Nominal GDP Growth, 2000-2009

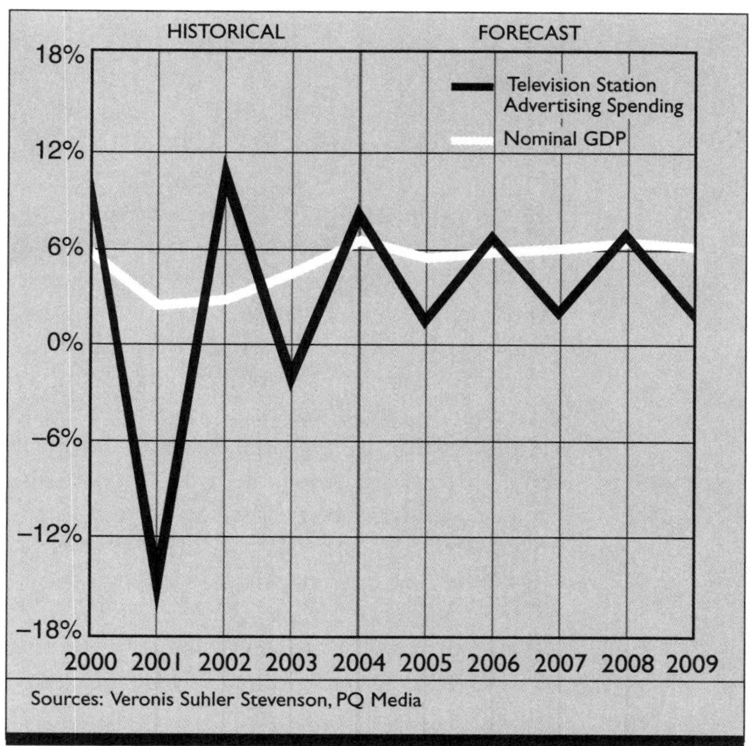

Sources: Veronis Suhler Stevenson, PQ Media

Broadcast Television

cable ratings continue to rise, pay cable was flat at 2.1 points in 2003-04. Pay cable dropped to 1.9 points in 2004-05 through January 30, due to the absence of HBO's *Sex and the City* and *The Sopranos.*

Increasing competition with cable television has made it critical for broadcast TV stations to air quality local programming, particularly local news shows, to maintain audiences and grow revenues. A solid news operation allows a station to develop a strong identity and generate a loyal following among audiences, allowing it to become a better distribution vehicle for network programming. Local news programs are not only an important source of revenues for local stations, but also serve as lead-ins for prime-time network shows.

TELEVISION STATION ADVERTISING

All but two of the top 15 local television advertisers, including national spot, increased spending in 2004. Total spending among the top 15 increased 9.0 percent to $4.73 billion for the year. DaimlerChrysler was the biggest spender at $604.6 million, up 1.4 percent in 2004. The Ford Motor's dealer association followed with $465.9 million in spending, up 8.8 percent. General Motors rounded out the top three with $444.6 million in spending in 2004, an increase of 13.1 percent. Verizon Communications posted the largest gain in spending, up 39.5 percent to $214.0 million for the year. Only SBC Communications and General Mills cut spending on television station advertising in 2004.

The Outlook for Broadcast Television

Broadcast television advertising growth is expected to decelerate to 2.0 percent in 2005, due to pricing pressures on commercial inventory, the lack of direct-to-consumer drug advertising, and the absence of political and Olympics-related advertising. Spending is expected to reach $46.93 billion in 2005. Spending is expected to accelerate in even years during the forecast period, but growth will be slower than in the past because television's share of political advertising is diminishing, and international Olympic locations will suppress viewership because of time zone differences. But the overarching issue facing broadcasters in the long-term is the efforts among advertisers to seek out alternatives to traditional media and advertising—such as the Internet, videogames, product placements and sponsorships—as they attempt to reach fragmented audiences who are dividing their time among an expanding array of options. While broadcast TV ratings have been on the decline for 10 years, advertisers have continued to boost spending. The emergence of DVRs, however, has caused advertisers to question the value of their investments in traditional television advertising and to seek out alternatives, such as product placement.

To retain audiences and appease advertisers, networks are investing in program development, and they hope to churn out new shows that duplicate the success of *Desperate Housewives* and *Lost* in the 2004-05 season. We expect these efforts to allow networks to maintain ratings during the forecast period and continue to grow advertising expenditures. However, annual growth will be slower than in the past. Compound annual growth from 2004 to 2009 will be 4.3 percent, with spending reaching $56.86 billion in 2009.

Television Advertising Expenditures*

Year	*Network*	*National Spot*	*Local*	*Total Station*	*Total Network and Station*	*Barter Syndication*
1999	$14,571	$10,500	$12,680	$23,180	$37,751	$2,260
2000	16,614	12,264	13,542	25,806	42,420	2,382
2001	15,163	9,223	12,256	21,479	36,642	2,239
2002	15,959	10,920	13,114	24,034	39,993	2,075
2003	16,091	9,948	13,520	23,468	39,559	2,373
2004	17,563	10,943	14,670	25,613	43,176	2,844
2005	17,967	11,140	14,875	26,015	43,982	2,952
2006	19,279	12,165	15,797	27,963	47,241	3,123
2007	19,664	12,372	16,208	28,580	48,244	3,236
2008	21,414	13,460	17,311	30,771	52,185	3,501
2009	21,799	13,743	17,709	31,452	53,251	3,610

Sources: Veronis Suhler Stevenson, PQ Media, Universal McCann, Television Bureau of Advertising

*To avoid double counting, barter syndication spending is counted in the TV programming section of the Entertainment Media chapter.

2004 Communications Industry Forecast Compared with Actual Growth

Advertising Category	*2004 Forecasted Growth**	*Actual 2004 Growth*†
Television Networks	10.0%	9.1%
Television Stations	7.5	9.1
National Spot	8.5	10.0
Local	6.8	8.5
Barter Syndication	7.6	19.8
Total Television Broadcasting	8.5	9.7

*Veronis Suhler Stevenson 2004 Communications Industry Forecast & Report
†Veronis Suhler Stevenson, PQ Media

Broadcast Television

($ MILLIONS)

Total Broadcasting	*National Cable*	*Local/ Regional Cable*	*Total Cable*	*Total National*	*Total Local*	*Total TV*
$40,011	$ 8,598	$3,026	$11,624	$35,929	$15,706	$51,635
44,802	10,281	3,507	13,788	41,541	17,049	58,590
38,881	10,532	3,682	14,214	37,157	15,938	53,095
42,068	10,944	3,792	14,736	39,898	16,906	56,804
41,932	12,224	4,080	16,304	40,636	17,600	58,236
46,020	14,043	4,882	18,925	45,393	19,552	64,945
46,934	16,060	5,626	21,686	48,119	20,501	68,620
50,364	17,717	6,541	24,258	52,283	22,339	74,622
51,480	19,408	7,480	26,888	54,679	23,689	78,368
55,686	21,191	8,555	29,746	59,567	25,865	85,432
56,861	23,644	9,717	33,361	62,796	27,426	90,222

Growth of Television Advertising Expenditures*

Year	*Network*	*National Spot*	*Local*	*Total Station*	*Total Network and Station*	*Barter Syndication*
2000	14.0%	16.8%	6.8%	11.3%	12.4%	5.4%
2001	–8.7	–24.8	–9.5	–16.8	–13.6	–6.0
2002	5.2	18.4	7.0	11.9	9.1	–7.3
2003	0.8	–8.9	3.1	–2.4	–1.1	14.4
2004	9.1	10.0	8.5	9.1	9.1	19.8
2005	2.3	1.8	1.4	1.6	1.9	3.8
2006	7.3	9.2	6.2	7.5	7.4	5.8
2007	2.0	1.7	2.6	2.2	2.1	3.6
2008	8.9	8.8	6.8	7.7	8.2	8.2
2009	1.8	2.1	2.3	2.2	2.0	3.1
Compound Annual Growth						
1999-2004	3.8	0.8	3.0	2.0	2.7	4.7
2004-2009	4.4	4.7	3.8	4.2	4.3	4.9

Sources: Veronis Suhler Stevenson, PQ Media, Universal McCann

*To avoid double counting, barter syndication spending is counted in the TV programming section of the Entertainment Media chapter.

Broadcast Television

Total Broadcasting	*National Cable*	*Local/ Regional Cable*	*Total Cable*	*Total National*	*Total Local*	*Total TV*
12.0%	19.6%	15.9%	18.6%	15.6%	8.6%	13.5%
–13.2	2.4	5.0	3.1	–10.6	–6.5	–9.4
8.2	3.9	3.0	3.7	7.4	6.1	7.0
–0.3	11.7	7.6	10.6	1.8	4.1	2.5
9.7	14.9	19.6	16.1	11.7	11.1	11.5
2.0	14.4	15.2	14.6	6.0	4.9	5.7
7.3	10.3	16.3	11.9	8.7	9.0	8.7
2.2	9.5	14.4	10.8	4.6	6.0	5.0
8.2	9.2	14.4	10.6	8.9	9.2	9.0
2.1	11.6	13.6	12.2	5.4	6.0	5.6
2.8	10.3	10.0	10.2	4.8	4.5	4.7
4.3	11.0	14.8	12.0	6.7	7.0	6.8

Recent Fund III Portfolio Exit

a portfolio company of
VS&A Communications Partners III, L.P.

has been sold to

Global Signal

for

$63,100,000

We acted as financial advisor to and assisted in the negotiations as the representative of GoldenState Towers.

November 2004

Business Overview

GoldenState Towers L.L.C. was a wireless communications tower company based in San Ramon, CA. GST was focused on the western portion of the United States and owned over 200 towers in Arizona, California, Idaho, Iowa, Missouri, Oregon and Washington. The Company built a tower portfolio focused on the western region through acquisition and development of tower sites. All of GST's tenants were all telephonic in nature with 36.8% of such tenants consisting of the "Big 7" carriers.

The Company was led by John F. Ricci (CEO) and employed 8 individuals with extensive experience in the wireless tower sector.

Background

Having successfully sold Spectrum Resources Towers L.P. (Fund II platform), VSS's Fund III formed GoldenState Towers in November 2002 in partnership with John F. Ricci, former Vice President of West Coast Operations for SpectraSite. Along with John Ricci, GST's senior management team is experienced in acquisitions, new tower development and integration of assets, having been associated with four public tower companies over the past ten years. The company was sold to Global Signal in November 2004.

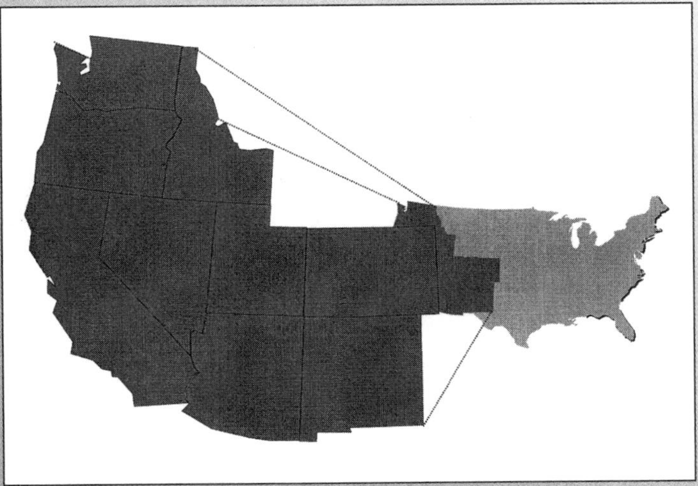

Strategy & Rationale

- Invest $30-$50 million of equity in a leveraged roll-up aggregating over 500 towers in the western United States.
- Seasoned management team well suited to execute a buy and build strategy.
- Strong industry fundamentals and growth prospects, high cash flow margins, long-term customer contracts.
- Valuations supported by business fundamentals, attractive acquisition and build-to-suit opportunities.

Add-on Acquisition Activities

GST completed numerous acquisitions :

- 11/02—Acquired 37 towers from **TowerCom Inc.** located in Idaho and Arizona
- 12/02—Acquired 7 towers from **Northwest Towers** located in Idaho and Washington
- 12/02—Acquired 6 towers and 25 entitlements from **Fidelity Towers** located in California, Washington and Idaho
- 2/03—Acquired 2 towers and 4 entitlements from **Alaris Towers** in California and Washington
- 2/03—Acquired 3 towers from **Alpine Towers** located in California
- 4/03—Acquired 7 towers from **Global Towers L.L.C.** located in Arizona, Oregon and Missouri
- 8/03—Acquired 98 towers from **UbiquiTel** located in the central valley of California
- 3/04—Acquired 8 towers from **Northwest Towers** located around Spokane, Washington
- 10/04—Acquired 38 towers from **Master Towers** in Portland, Oregon

Exit

In November 2004, VSS completed the sale of GoldenState Towers to Global Signal with a gross IRR of 50.5% or 2.2x the original investment.

350 Park Avenue, New York, NY 10022
212-935-4990 212-381-8168 fax
www.vss.com

5

CABLE & SATELLITE TELEVISION

Total Cable & Satellite Television Spending and Nominal GDP Growth, 2000-2009

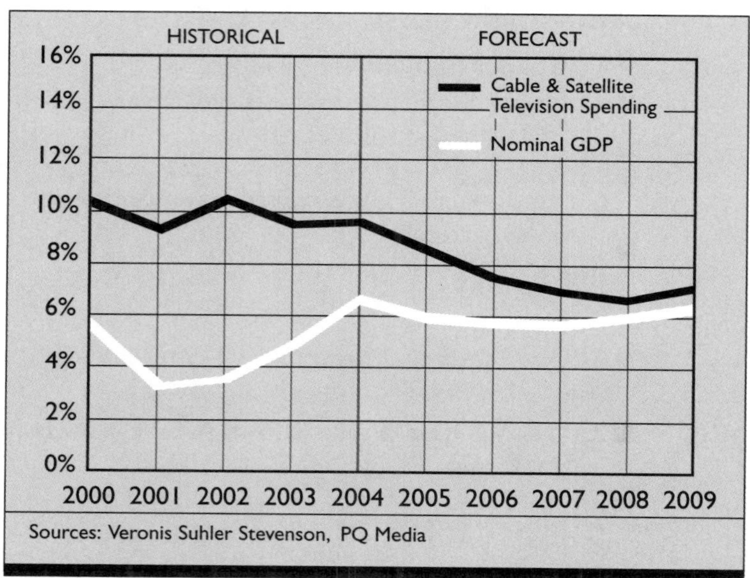

Sources: Veronis Suhler Stevenson, PQ Media

THE CABLE & SATELLITE TELEVISION MARKET IN 2004 AND 2005

Total expenditures on cable and satellite television reached $93.38 billion in 2004, a 9.7 percent increase over the prior year, driven by growth in national and local advertising revenues, expansion of the direct broadcast satellite (DBS) subscriber base, subscription rate hikes for both cable and DBS, and increased spending on license fees. After two years of sluggish advertising spending growth in 2001 and 2002, the market rebounded in 2003 and continued to expand in 2004, posting compound annual growth of 10.2 percent for the 1999-2004 period. Growth in 2004 and in the five-year period easily outpaced that of GDP, a trend we expect to continue in the forecast period.

While the wired cable television and the satellite television are two distinct competitive businesses, there are some trends and drivers that are affecting both industries. Competitive factors particular to each segment will be discussed in more detail in the respective cable and satellite television market sections found later in the chapter.

The DBS subsegment has experienced dramatic subscriber growth over the past five years, due primarily to the ability of satellite providers to deliver local channels. However, DBS's subscriber growth is expected to decelerate during the forecast period because most major television markets are now fully served by DBS. In addition, cable operators have stepped up their game to fend off the DBS

Growth of U.S. Spending on Cable & Satellite Television

	Subscription Spending	*Advertising*	*License Fees*	*Total*
2004 Expenditures ($ Millions)	$56,276	$18,925	$18,175	$93,376
1999-2004 Compound Annual Growth (%)	8.6%	10.2%	14.0%	9.9%
2004-2009 Projected Compound Annual Growth (%)	5.9%	12.0%	7.4%	7.5%
2009 Projected Expenditures ($ Millions)	$74,829	$33,361	$26,030	$134,220

Sources: Veronis Suhler Stevenson, PQ Media, Universal McCann, Kagan Research
Federal Communications Commission, Nielsen Media Research, National Cable and Telecommunications Association
*Includes basic service, premium services, pay-per-view and video-on-demand.

threat and stem the migration of subscribers. Cable companies are increasing their investment in original and syndicated programming to maintain subscriber loyalty, grow ratings and attract advertisers. Cable providers are also investing in new technology to offer advanced services such as telephony, Internet access and video-on-demand (VOD). Not to be outdone, DBS providers are also pursuing partnerships with telephone companies in an effort to offer similar services.

The rivalry between cable and satellite companies has taken center stage in the multichannel services market, as most other competitors are fading away. We expect the penetration rates for all other segments to decrease at a steady pace throughout the forecast period. Wireless cable penetration is projected to drop to 0.5 percent in 2009, SMATV to 0.6 percent in 2009, local telephone video services to 0.7 percent, and C-band to 0.1 percent. We expect subscription growth for local telephone companies will decline at a compound annual rate of 0.7 percent from 2004 to 2009 compared with 14.9 percent growth in the 1999-2004 period. While SMATV and C-band are essentially obsolete technologies, the frequencies used for wireless cable will be devoted primarily to high-speed data transfer by the end of the forecast period.

Overall, the number of subscriptions to cable and satellite television increased 4.4 percent to 99.8 million in 2004, driven by the increased availability of local programming on DBS, investments by cable and satellite networks in original programming, added channel capacity by both DBS and cable providers, increases in the number of bundled services offered by all providers, and greater availability of digital cable, as well as continued discounts on hardware and installation for DBS. Multichannel penetration reached 92.1 percent of all television households in 2004, an increase of 2.5 percentage points over 2003.

The total number of multichannel subscriptions is projected to reach 110.5 million in 2009, rising at a compound annual rate of 2.1 percent from 2004 to 2009 compared with 3.8 percent in the 1999-2004 period. The multichannel penetration rate in all television households will increase to 96.6 percent in 2009. Wired cable subscriptions are expected to advance at a compound annual rate of 0.7 percent from 2004 to 2009 to 72.5 million, slightly less than the 1.0 percent compound annual rate achieved in the 1999-2004 period. Cable subscription growth has been limited because of the large size of the customer base, but upside potential is strong given the increasing demand for cable modem

Cable & Satellite Television

Multichannel Penetration of TV Households

Year	*Wired Cable*	*DBS*	*SMATV*	*Wireless Cable*	*Local Telephone Companies*	*C-Band Satellite Dishes*	*Total**
1999	66.9%	11.6%	1.4%	1.5%	0.4%	1.7%	83.5%
2000	67.7	14.2	1.5	1.6	0.8	1.2	86.9
2001	67.5	17.3	1.6	1.7	0.9	1.0	89.9
2002	66.0	18.5	1.4	1.5	0.9	0.8	89.1
2003	64.8	21.1	1.3	1.1	0.8	0.5	89.6
2004	64.5	24.5	1.1	0.9	0.7	0.3	92.1
2005	64.5	26.9	0.9	0.8	0.7	0.2	94.0
2006	64.3	28.5	0.8	0.7	0.6	0.1	95.1
2007	64.0	29.7	0.7	0.6	0.6	0.1	95.8
2008	63.7	30.6	0.6	0.5	0.7	0.1	96.2
2009	63.4	31.4	0.6	0.5	0.7	0.1	96.6

Sources: Veronis Suhler Stevenson, PQ Media, Cabletelevision Advertising Bureau, Federal Communications Commission, Nielsen Media Research
*Households that subscribe to more than one type of service are counted separately.

Highlights

Total expenditures on cable and satellite television reached $93.38 billion in 2004, a 9.7 percent increase over the prior year, driven by growth in national and local advertising revenues and in license fees. Total subscription spending grew 7.5 percent to $56.28 billion, as the number of subscriptions to cable and satellite television increased 4.4 percent to 99.8 million. Subscription growth was driven by the increased availability of local programming on DBS, investments in original programming, added channel capacity, greater availability of digital cable and bundled services, as well as continued discounts on hardware and installation for DBS.

■

Double-digit growth in cable and satellite television advertising in 2004 was spurred by the increasing availability of interconnects, strong growth in local cable markets and increased network ratings. Advertising spending increased 16.1 percent to $18.93 billion in 2004, as expenditures on cable network advertising advanced 14.6 percent to $13.89 billion and local cable advertising rose 20.5 percent to $4.32 billion. Advertising on regional sports networks grew 13.4 percent to $559.0 million in 2004.

■

Driven by strong increases in local advertising revenues and video-on-demand fees, total spending on wired cable television reached $44.20 billion in 2004, a 7.3 percent increase over the prior year. The growing availability of cable interconnects drove a 19.6 percent gain in local cable advertising in 2004 to $4.88 billion, as the medium continues its assault on radio's dominance of the local advertising market.

■

Wired cable subscribers spent an additional $11.04 billion on cable modems and telephony services in 2004, that were often bundled with basic and premium services, an increase of 31.2 percent from 2003. Multiple-system operators (MSOs) are rolling out bundled services in more markets to combat growing satellite television penetration.

■

Total spending on local cable television advertising grew at a 10.0 percent compound annual rate from 1999 to 2004, while household spending on subscription services rose at a rate of 6.7 percent during the same period. Overall, the annual growth of spending on wired cable has outpaced that of nominal GDP since 1999 and the industry has been one of the fastest-growing media segments for the past six years.

■

Total spending on satellite television grew at a double-digit rate for the fourth consecutive year in 2004, posting a gain of 11.8 percent to $16.17 billion for the year. Spending was driven by a surge in subscribers, rate hikes and spending on DBS avail advertising.

access to the Internet and the gradual adoption of other new services. (Usage and spending figures for cable modem access are included in the Consumer Internet chapter.) The cable and satellite advertising market is also expected to achieve considerable growth during the forecast period due to an expanding subscriber base and growing ratings.

THE CABLE TELEVISION MARKET IN 2004 AND 2005

Driven by strong increases in local advertising revenues and license fees, total spending on cable television reached $44.20 billion in 2004, a 7.3 percent increase over the prior year. The growing availability of cable inter-

■

Total spending on DBS grew at a 15.0 percent compound annual rate in the 1999-2004 period, driven primarily by a 14.8 percent gain in subscription spending. Overall, the annual growth of subscriber and advertiser spending on DBS has almost tripled that of nominal GDP since 1999.

■

Total cable and satellite television spending grew at a compound annual rate of 9.9 percent from 1999 to 2004. Growth in 2004 and in the five-year period grew at double the rate of nominal GDP, a trend we expect to continue in the forecast period. Overall spending on cable and satellite television subscriptions, advertising and license fees will increase 8.7 percent to $101.54 billion in 2005.

■

Cable's prime-time audience share grew 3.0 percentage points to 63.0 percent in the 2003-2004 season, with 52.0 percent coming from ad-supported cable programming and 6.0 percent derived from pay cable programs. Ad-supported cable fueled the gain as a result of the expanding array of niche channels.

■

Consumer spending on premium services increased 6.7 percent to $9.66 billion in 2004, with wired cable subscribers accounting for $5.37 billion of the total, and satellite comprising the other $4.29 billion. Spending is expected to rise at a compound annual rate of 4.8 percent from 2004 to 2009, reaching $12.23 billion in 2009.

■

Overall household expenditures on subscription services, including basic, premium, pay-per-view and video-on-demand, will grow at a compound annual rate of 5.9 percent from 2004 to 2009, reaching $74.83 billion in 2009, fueled by rate hikes, increased acceptance of digital cable and continued investment in original programming. Subscription spending on wired cable will grow at a compound annual rate of 5.1 percent to $50.50 billion in 2009, while DBS subscriber spending will grow at a slightly higher rate of 7.4 percent to $22.94 billion.

■

Total cable and satellite television advertising expenditures are expected to expand at a compound annual rate of 12.0 percent from 2004 to 2009, hitting $33.36 billion in 2009. Growth will be driven by increased ratings and audience share, continued investment in technology and programming, economic expansion and lower CPMs compared with broadcast television.

■

Overall spending on cable and satellite television will grow at a compound annual rate of 7.5 percent from 2004 to 2009, reaching $134.22 billion in 2009, propelled by a strong increase in advertising expenditures, and more moderate growth in license fees and subscription spending.

connects drove a 19.6 percent gain in local cable advertising in 2004 to $4.88 billion, as the medium continues to make inroads on local television advertising expenditures and on radio's dominance of the local advertising market. Total spending on cable television advertising grew at a 10.0 percent compound annual rate in the 1999-2004 period, driven by a healthier local ad market during 2003 and 2004. Household spending increased 5.9 percent to $39.32 billion in 2004, and achieved a compound annual growth rate of 6.7 percent from 1999 to 2004. Overall, the annual growth of subscriber and advertiser spending on cable television has outpaced that of nominal GDP since 1999, and the

Multichannel Subscriptions

(MILLIONS)

Year	TV Households	Wired Cable	DBS	SMATV	Wireless Cable	Local Telephone Companies	C-Band Satellite Dishes	Total
1999	99.4	66.5	11.5	1.4	1.5	0.4	1.7	83.0
2000	100.8	68.2	14.3	1.5	1.6	0.8	1.2	87.6
2001	102.2	69.0	17.7	1.6	1.7	0.9	1.0	91.9
2002	105.5	69.6	19.5	1.5	1.6	1.0	0.8	94.0
2003	106.7	69.1	22.5	1.4	1.2	0.9	0.5	95.6
2004	108.4	69.9	26.6	1.2	1.0	0.8	0.3	99.8
2005	109.6	70.7	29.5	1.0	0.9	0.7	0.2	103.3
2006	110.8	71.2	31.6	0.9	0.8	0.7	0.2	105.4
2007	112.0	71.7	33.3	0.8	0.7	0.7	0.1	107.3
2008	113.2	72.1	34.7	0.7	0.6	0.7	0.1	108.9
2009	114.4	72.5	35.9	0.7	0.6	0.8	0.1	110.5

Sources: Veronis Suhler Stevenson, PQ Media, Federal Communications Commission, Nielsen Media Research, National Cable and Telecommunications Association

Cable & Satellite Television

Growth of Multichannel Subscriptions

Year	Wired Cable	DBS	SMATV	Wireless Cable	Local Telephone Companies	C-Band Satellite Dishes	Total
2000	2.6%	24.3%	7.1%	6.7%	100.0%	–29.4%	5.5%
2001	1.2	23.8	6.7	6.3	12.5	–16.7	4.9
2002	0.9	10.2	–6.3	–5.9	11.1	–20.0	2.3
2003	–0.7	15.4	–6.7	–25.0	–10.0	–37.5	1.7
2004	1.2	18.2	–14.3	–16.7	–11.1	–40.0	4.4
2005	1.1	11.0	–16.7	–9.7	–9.1	–34.3	3.2
2006	0.8	7.0	–9.0	–10.3	–1.5	–22.1	2.3
2007	0.7	5.3	–13.1	–14.2	1.2	–19.6	1.8
2008	0.5	4.2	–10.3	–11.0	2.5	–13.3	1.5
2009	0.6	3.5	–8.2	–7.0	4.2	–11.3	1.5
Compound Annual Growth							
1999-2004	1.0	18.3	–3.0	–7.8	14.9	–29.3	3.8
2004-2009	0.7	6.2	–11.5	–10.5	–0.7	–20.6	2.1

Sources: Veronis Suhler Stevenson, PQ Media, Federal Communications Commission, Nielsen Media Research, National Cable and Telecommunications Association

industry has been one of the fastest-growing media segments for the past six years.

Wired cable passes 98.8 percent of U.S. television households, and 65.3 percent of homes passed subscribe to these services. Cable operators hope to attract new subscribers and reduce the churn of existing subscribers by offering packages consisting of high-speed Internet access, cable telephony, digital video recorders (DVRs), interactive

Homes Passed by Cable and Incidence of Subscription

Year	*TV Households (Millions)*	*Homes Passed by Wired Cable (Millions)*	*Homes Passed as a % of TV Households*	*Number of Wired Cable Households (Millions)*	*Wired Cable Subscribers as a % of Homes Passed*	*Wired Cable Penetration of TV Households*
1999	99.4	97.6	98.2%	66.5	68.1%	66.9%
2000	100.8	98.9	98.1	68.2	69.0	67.7
2001	102.2	100.6	98.4	69.0	68.6	67.5
2002	105.5	103.4	98.0	69.6	67.3	66.0
2003	106.7	106.0	99.3	69.1	65.2	64.8
2004	108.4	107.1	98.8	69.9	65.3	64.5
2005	109.6	108.2	98.7	70.7	65.3	64.5
2006	110.8	108.6	98.0	71.2	65.6	64.3
2007	112.0	110.2	98.4	71.7	65.1	64.0
2008	113.2	111.4	98.4	72.1	64.7	63.7
2009	114.4	112.8	98.6	72.5	64.3	63.4

Sources: Veronis Suhler Stevenson, PQ Media, Federal Communications Commission, Kagan Research, Nielsen Media Research

television (ITV), VOD and digital cable. Cable operators offer the average customer 70 analog video channels and 120 digital video channels.

Cable subscriber numbers continue to be negatively affected by changes in accounting practices at some cable operators. Wall Street values cable companies based on subscription numbers, which led to overzealous subscriber counting in isolated incidents in the 1998-2003 period. For example, Adelphia lowered its subscriber counts for basic cable, digital cable and high-speed Internet service in 2002, following a review of the company's accounting practices by the Securities and Exchange Commission (SEC). Charter Communications also reduced the number of subscribers counted in its 2003 base as a result of an SEC investigation of the company's method for counting subscribers.

Despite the surging growth of DBS over the past two years, wired cable still dominates the industry, with 69.9 million subscribers in 2004. Due to the sheer size of its subscriber base, cable has achieved only single-digit growth since 1999. Total consumer spending on basic cable subscriptions increased 5.9 percent to $32.48 billion in 2004, due mainly to rate increases, and posted compound annual growth of 7.4 percent from 1999 to 2004. Total cable pay-per-view (PPV) spending increased 3.1 percent in 2004 to $1.15 billion, as a result of slower-than-expected acceptance of digital cable and VOD, and the continuing popularity of adult programming. VOD showed spectacular growth of 123.9 percent to $318.0 million in 2004, but the installed base is still dwarfed by PPV. Spending on cable PPV achieved compound annual growth of 7.5 percent from 1999 to 2004. Expenditures on premium channel services rose 3.4 percent to $5.37 billion in 2004, and expanded at a compound annual rate of 2.2 percent from 1999 to 2004.

Double-digit growth in local cable advertising in 2004 was spurred by the growing availability of interconnects, strong growth in local markets and increased ratings. Interconnects link two or more cable systems to distribute ads across a wider geographic region, such as the entire Denver market. Cable operators are acting cooperatively to enable advertisers to make a single ad buy and select specific time slots in that region over multiple systems in more than half of the major U.S. television markets. An expanding array

Total Spending on Wired Cable Television

Year	Subscription Spending: Basic Service Spending	Premium Service Spending	Pay-Per-View Spending	Video-on-Demand Spending*	Total Subscription Spending	Local Cable Advertising Spending	Total Wired Cable Content Spending†	Other Cable Spending: Cable Modem Spending	Cable Telephony Spending	Total Other & Content Spending†
1999	$22,772	$4,822	$ 800	$ 0.3	$28,394	$3,026	$31,420	$ 422	—	$31,842
2000	24,445	5,001	751	6	30,203	3,507	33,710	1,072	—	34,782
2001	26,027	5,059	875	26	31,987	3,682	35,669	2,348	$ 831	38,848
2002	28,452	5,226	1,143	56	34,877	3,792	38,669	4,494	1,107	44,270
2003	30,671	5,192	1,114	142	37,119	4,081	41,200	6,888	1,524	49,612
2004	32,481	5,369	1,148	318	39,316	4,882	44,198	9,303	1,732	55,233
2005	34,300	5,530	1,169	495	41,494	5,626	47,120	11,052	2,279	60,451
2006	36,118	5,704	1,180	678	43,680	6,541	50,221	12,588	3,536	66,346
2007	37,960	5,933	1,191	880	45,964	7,480	53,444	14,124	5,346	72,913
2008	39,820	6,134	1,197	1,079	48,230	8,554	56,784	15,579	7,031	79,394
2009	41,731	6,330	1,199	1,237	50,497	9,717	60,215	17,059	8,187	85,460

Sources: Veronis Suhler Stevenson, PQ Media, Sanford C. Bernstein, Cabletelevision Advertising Bureau, Federal Communications Commission Annual Report, Forrester Research, In-Stat, Kagan Research, Leichtman Group, LodgeNet, Merrill Lynch, National Cable & Telecommunications Association, Smith Travel Research, U.S. Department of Commerce

*Does not include pay-per-view or video-on-demand spending available through hotels and motels.

†Only wired cable content spending is included in overall Cable & Satellite TV spending to avoid double counting and non-communications spending.

Cable & Satellite Television

of channels featuring niche programming, meanwhile, allows advertisers to target consumers by demographic segment or special interest. Spending on local cable advertising increased at a rate of 19.6 percent for the year to $4.88 billion. Of all 210 U.S. television markets, 110 were interconnected by the end of 2004. We project local advertising will grow at a compound annual rate of 14.8 percent in the forecast period, reaching $9.72 billion in 2009.

In an effort to maintain and grow its subscriber base in the face of competition from satellite television, wired cable operators have invested more than $85 billion since 1996 in systems upgrades, including $9.54 billion in 2004. Such upgrades allow cable operators to offer advanced services, including high-speed cable modems; digital video; high definition television (HDTV); voice over Internet protocol (VoIP), also known as cable telephony; PPV; VOD; and DVRs. Cable operators are bundling advanced services and offering package deals to subscribers in an effort to reduce churn. The current hypothesis is that subscribers who make the initial investment in specialized equipment will be less susceptible to churn. Additionally, the convenience and perceived cost-reduction of one-stop shopping for voice, data and programming may increase subscriber loyalty. Evidence of churn reduction or suppression through bundled offerings is mostly anecdotal, yet virtually all cable providers are pursuing this strategy.

Satellite operators also offer PPV and DVRs, but must partner with telephone companies to offer phone services, and they cannot yet offer VOD due to the constraints of their delivery systems. Consumer adoption of advanced cable services is gradually rising. In 2004, 97.0 percent of all cable subscribers were offered digital video service, and 95.0 percent of all subscribers were served by systems that offered Internet access. In addition, 28.5 percent of subscribers were offered telephone service by their cable operators.

While dial-up Internet access remained

Growth of Total Spending on Wired Cable Television

Year	Subscription Spending: Basic Service Spending	Premium Service Spending	Pay-Per-View Spending	Video-on-Demand Spending*	Total Subscription Spending	Local Cable Advertising Spending	Total Wired Cable Content Spending†	Other Cable Spending: Cable Modem Spending	Cable Telephony Spending	Total Other & Content Spending†
2000	7.3%	3.7%	–6.1%	1,704.0%	6.4%	15.9%	7.3%	154.0%	—	9.2%
2001	6.5	1.2	16.5	315.3	5.9	5.0	5.8	119.0	—	11.7
2002	9.3	3.3	30.6	115.4	9.0	3.0	8.4	91.4	33.2%	14.0
2003	7.8	–0.7	–2.5	153.6	6.4	7.6	6.5	53.3	37.7	12.1
2004	5.9	3.4	3.1	123.9	5.9	19.6	7.3	35.1	13.6	11.3
2005	5.6	3.0	1.8	55.6	5.5	15.2	6.6	18.8	31.6	9.4
2006	5.3	3.2	1.0	37.1	5.3	16.3	6.6	13.9	55.1	9.8
2007	5.1	4.0	0.9	29.7	5.2	14.4	6.4	12.2	51.2	9.9
2008	4.9	3.4	0.5	22.6	4.9	14.4	6.3	10.3	31.5	8.9
2009	4.8	3.2	0.2	14.7	4.7	13.6	6.0	9.5	16.4	7.6
Compound Annual Growth										
1999-2004	7.4	2.2	7.5	291.2	6.7	10.0	7.1	85.6	—	11.6
2004-2009	5.1	3.3	0.9	31.2	5.1	14.8	6.4	12.9	36.4	9.1

Sources: Veronis Suhler Stevenson, PQ Media, Sanford C. Bernstein, Cabletelevision Advertising Bureau, Federal Communications Commission Annual Report, Forrester Research, In-Stat, Kagan Research, Leichtman Group, LodgeNet, Merrill Lynch, National Cable & Telecommunications Association, Smith Travel Research, U.S. Department of Commerce

*Does not include pay-per-view or video-on-demand spending available through hotels and motels.

†Only wired cable content spending is included in overall Cable & Satellite TV spending to avoid double counting and non-communications spending.

the most widely used mode of accessing the Internet in 2004, cable modem access is gaining ground quickly. By the end of 2004, 33.5 million of all Internet households were accessing the Internet through dial-up modems. Cable modem households, however, grew 27.7 percent in 2004, accounting for 21.0 million of the total 71.0 million Internet households. Cable modems are currently available to over 98 million TV households, and by year-end 2005, industry investments should put that figure closer to 102 million homes, indicating an enormous untapped market for cable modems.

In addition to investing in new technologies, cable operators have also stepped up their investment in programming, having spent $14.6 billion in 2004 to develop and acquire original programs. In 2005, ESPN won the rights to ABC's *Monday Night Football* for eight years beginning in 2006, indicating that cable networks' dedication to investment in quality programming will continue in the forecast period. Investments in original and acquired programming have paid off for cable operators, many of whom own major shares in the programs they carry. Ad-supported cable achieved a 52 share in prime time, on average, during the 2004-05 season through April, coming in under combined totals of the seven broadcast networks—ABC, CBS, NBC, FOX, UPN, WB, and PAX—by 2.0 share points. However, when the 6.0 share achieved by pay cable is added to the total, all cable viewing represents an impressive 58.0 share in prime time.

One of the cable industry's key competitive strengths is the ownership of programming networks by cable operators. In 2004, there were more than 388 national non-broadcast programming networks, an increase of 49 networks over the 2003 total of 339. Twenty-three percent of these networks are owned, in varying degrees, by four of the top six cable operators (Comcast, Time Warner, Cox and Cablevision).

Household Spending on Basic Cable & Satellite Television

	Basic Subscriptions (Millions)			*Average Monthly Spending Per Household*		*Total Spending ($ Millions)*		
Year	*Wired Cable*	*Satellite & Other Multichannel Services*	*Total*	*Wired Cable*	*Satellite & Other Multichannel Services*	*Wired Cable*	*Satellite & Other Multichannel Services*	*Total*
1999	66.5	16.5	83.0	$28.54	$23.68	$22,772	$ 4,688	$27,460
2000	68.2	19.4	87.6	29.87	24.57	24,445	5,719	30,164
2001	69.0	22.9	91.9	31.43	25.13	26,027	6,905	32,932
2002	69.6	24.4	94.0	34.07	27.69	28,452	8,108	36,560
2003	69.1	26.5	95.6	36.99	29.53	30,671	9,391	40,062
2004	69.9	29.9	99.8	38.72	29.29	32,481	10,509	42,990
2005	70.7	32.4	103.0	40.45	29.83	34,300	11,581	45,881
2006	71.2	34.2	105.4	42.25	30.52	36,118	12,519	48,637
2007	71.7	35.6	107.3	44.10	31.54	37,960	13,470	51,430
2008	72.1	36.8	108.9	46.03	32.64	39,820	14,427	54,247
2009	72.5	38.0	110.5	47.95	33.92	41,731	15,451	57,182

Sources: Veronis Suhler Stevenson, PQ Media, Federal Communications Commission Annual Report, Kagan Research, National Cable & Telecommunications Association

Growth of Household Spending on Basic Cable & Satellite Television

	Basic Subscriptions			*Average Monthly Spending Per Household*		*Total Spending*		
Year	*Wired Cable*	*Satellite & Other Multichannel Services*	*Total*	*Wired Cable*	*Satellite & Other Multichannel Services*	*Wired Cable*	*Satellite & Other Multichannel Services*	*Total*
2000	2.6%	17.6%	5.5%	4.7%	3.8%	7.3%	22.0%	9.8%
2001	1.2	18.0	4.9	5.2	2.3	6.5	20.7	9.2
2002	0.9	6.6	2.3	8.4	10.2	9.3	17.4	11.0
2003	–0.7	8.6	1.7	8.6	6.6	7.8	15.8	9.6
2004	1.2	12.8	4.4	4.7	–0.8	5.9	11.9	7.3
2005	1.1	8.2	3.2	4.5	1.8	5.6	10.2	6.7
2006	0.8	5.7	2.3	4.5	2.3	5.3	8.1	6.0
2007	0.7	4.1	1.8	4.4	3.3	5.1	7.6	5.7
2008	0.5	3.5	1.5	4.4	3.5	4.9	7.4	5.5
2009	0.6	3.1	1.4	4.2	3.9	4.8	7.1	5.4
Compound Annual Growth								
1999-2004	1.0	12.6	3.8	6.3	4.3	7.4	17.5	9.4
2004-2009	0.7	4.9	2.1	4.4	3.0	5.1	8.0	5.9

Sources: Veronis Suhler Stevenson, PQ Media, Federal Communications Commission Annual Report, Kagan Research, National Cable & Telecommunications Association

Household Spending on Premium Cable & Satellite Television

	Premium Subscriptions (Millions)*			*Average Monthly Spending Per Household*		*Total Spending ($ Millions)*		
Year	*Wired Cable*	*Satellite & Other Multichannel Services*	*Total*	*Wired Cable*	*Satellite & Other Multichannel Services*	*Wired Cable*	*Satellite & Other Multichannel Services*	*Total*
1999	48.5	19.4	67.9	$8.29	$10.27	$4,822	$2,390	$ 7,212
2000	49.4	22.4	71.8	8.44	8.60	5,001	2,313	7,314
2001	50.5	24.9	75.4	8.35	9.75	5,059	2,912	7,971
2002	51.3	27.2	78.5	8.49	10.49	5,226	3,423	8,649
2003	52.0	29.1	81.1	8.32	11.04	5,192	3,856	9,048
2004	52.6	30.0	82.6	8.51	11.91	5,369	4,288	9,657
2005	53.3	30.8	84.2	8.64	12.69	5,530	4,695	10,225
2006	54.2	31.5	85.7	8.77	13.35	5,704	5,048	10,752
2007	54.9	32.2	87.1	9.01	13.86	5,933	5,350	11,283
2008	55.6	32.8	88.4	9.20	14.26	6,134	5,618	11,752
2009	56.3	33.5	89.9	9.36	14.65	6,330	5,899	12,229

Sources: Veronis Suhler Stevenson, PQ Media, Federal Communications Commission Annual Report, Kagan Research, National Cable & Telecommunications Association

*Households may subscribe to more than one premium channel.

Cable & Satellite Television

Growth of Household Spending on Premium Cable & Satellite Television

	Premium Subscriptions			*Average Monthly Spending Per Household*		*Total Spending*		
Year	*Wired Cable*	*Satellite & Other Multichannel Services*	*Total*	*Wired Cable*	*Satellite & Other Multichannel Services*	*Wired Cable*	*Satellite & Other Multichannel Services*	*Total*
2000	1.9%	15.5%	5.7%	1.8%	–16.2%	3.7%	–3.2%	1.4%
2001	2.2	11.2	5.0	–1.0	13.3	1.2	25.9	9.0
2002	1.6	9.2	4.1	1.7	7.6	3.3	17.5	8.5
2003	1.4	7.0	3.3	–2.0	5.3	–0.7	12.6	4.6
2004	1.2	3.1	1.8	2.2	7.9	3.4	11.2	6.7
2005	1.4	2.8	1.9	1.6	6.5	3.0	9.5	5.9
2006	1.6	2.2	1.8	1.5	5.2	3.2	7.5	5.1
2007	1.3	2.1	1.6	2.7	3.8	4.0	6.0	4.9
2008	1.2	2.0	1.5	2.2	2.9	3.4	5.0	4.2
2009	1.4	2.2	1.7	1.8	2.7	3.2	5.0	4.1
Compound Annual Growth								
1999-2004	1.6	9.1	4.0	0.5	3.0	2.2	12.4	6.0
2004-2009	1.4	2.3	1.7	1.9	4.2	3.3	6.6	4.8

Source: Veronis Suhler Stevenson, PQ Media, Federal Communications Commission, Kagan Research, National Cable & Telecommunications Association

The Overall Pay-Per-View Market* ($ MILLIONS)

Year	Movies	Events	Hotels/Motels	Total
1999	$1,185	$570	$368	$2,123
2000	1,057	398	369	1,824
2001	1,458	297	370	2,125
2002	1,724	407	376	2,507
2003	1,826	398	391	2,615
2004	1,951	416	404	2,771
2005	2,050	433	431	2,914
2006	2,136	451	448	3,035
2007	2,204	467	459	3,130
2008	2,247	481	468	3,196
2009	2,290	493	474	3,257

Sources: Veronis Suhler Stevenson, PQ Media, Federal Communications Commission, National Cable & Telecommunications Association, Kagan Research, LodgeNet, Smith Travel Research

*Includes spending on pay-per-view on satellite television.

Growth of the Overall Pay-Per-View Market*

Year	Movies	Events	Hotels/Motels	Total
2000	–10.8%	–30.2%	0.3%	–14.1%
2001	37.9	–25.4	0.3	16.5
2002	18.2	37.0	1.7	18.0
2003	5.9	–2.2	4.0	4.3
2004	6.8	4.5	3.5	6.0
2005	5.1	4.1	6.5	5.1
2006	4.2	4.2	4.0	4.2
2007	3.2	3.5	2.5	3.1
2008	2.0	2.9	1.9	2.1
2009	1.9	2.6	1.2	1.9
Compound Annual Growth				
1999-2004	10.5	–6.1	1.9	5.5
2004-2009	3.3	3.5	3.2	3.3

Sources: Veronis Suhler Stevenson, PQ Media, Federal Communications Commission, National Cable & Telecommunications Association, Kagan Research, LodgeNet, Smith Travel Research

*Includes spending on pay-per-view on satellite television.

To offset the impact of greater technology, programming and marketing costs, cable companies are looking to increase their economies of scale through acquisitions. At press time of this *Forecast,* several cable companies were angling to acquire the troubled Adelphia, the seventh-largest multichannel provider in the country with 5.9 million subscribers. The cable operator that acquires Adelphia will not only reduce costs per subscriber, but will also wield more power in increasingly contentious license fee negotiations. At press time, it was widely reported that the winning bid for Adelphia would be from the team of Time Warner and Comcast, in a deal that would be worth an estimated $12.5 billion in cash and $5.1 billion in stock. The acquisition would combine cable systems in Los Angeles, Cleveland and Buffalo for Time Warner, and Florida and Pennsylvania for Comcast. Cablevision was also rumored to be bidding on Adelphia, but the advantages of such a deal were not as apparent because the combined company would have none of the geographical advantages of the Time Warner/Comcast deal, and the combined Cablevision/Adelphia subscriber base would not be large enough to make a significant change in programming costs per subscriber.

HOUSEHOLD SPENDING ON CABLE TELEVISION

Basic Services

Total household spending on basic cable television services rose 5.9 percent in 2004 to $32.48 billion, driven by rate hikes, increases in average revenue per unit (ARPU) due to growing acceptance of bundled services, and slight advances in subscriber growth. With a 1.2 percent gain in subscribers to 69.9 million, the average household spent $38.72 per month on average for basic wired cable in 2004. Monthly spending on basic services was up 4.7 percent, marking the ninth consecutive year of spending increases for wired cable.

Digital cable households accounted for 23.3 million cable subscribers in 2004, an increase of 8.4 percent over the prior year. By

2009, 43.7 million households will have been upgraded to digital cable services. Industry analysts point to the need for cable operators to more aggressively market digital cable, as consumers do not yet see how the benefit of digital services outweighs the additional cost.

We expect the average monthly spending per household for basic wired cable to climb at a steady pace throughout the forecast period, growing at a compound annual rate of 3.7 percent from 2004 to 2009, reaching $46.46 billion. Growth will be driven primarily by the rollout of advanced services, rate increases and increased investment in programming. Total spending on basic cable will increase at a compound annual rate of 5.1 percent during the forecast period, a deceleration from the 7.4 percent growth rate posted during the 1999-2004 period. By 2009, spending on basic wired cable is projected to reach $41.73 billion. The disparity between the average monthly spending per household and total spending growth rates is due to the increasing number of households that subscribe to various bundled services, but are counted just once.

Premium Channels

Premium cable television services had 52.6 million subscribers in 2004, an increase of 1.2 percent over 2003. Cable operators are offering tiers of premium networks at reduced costs to encourage subscribers to upgrade from analog to digital. Digital tiers often package network lineups by genre, such as sports, music, movies, family and Spanish-language programming. Cable companies are using the economies achieved by digital compression to challenge DBS directly on price and breadth of service. A tier simply describes a level of service, most often referring to channel line-up. Most cable operators offer at least three tiers of digital service. For example, Cox digital cable is available to all of its basic cable subscribers, and subscribers may select from four digital tiers arranged along lines of content, such as movies, sports and information; family and variety; and Tele-Latina. Cox also offers a series of multiplexed premium digital tiers, including HBO, Showtime and international premium services,

Wired Cable Digital Households

Year	*Wired Cable Digital Households (Millions)*	*Growth in Wired Cable Digital Households*
2000	9.7	—
2001	15.2	56.7%
2002	19.2	26.3
2003	21.5	12.0
2004	23.3	8.4
2005	26.5	13.7
2006	30.9	16.6
2007	34.5	11.7
2008	39.4	14.2
2009	43.7	10.9

Sources: Veronis Suhler Stevenson, PQ Media, National Cable & Telecommunications Association

such as TV Asia and Washington Korean TV, totaling over 300 channels. Time Warner's digital cable service offers up to 200 video and audio channels.

Despite growth in digital cable, the overall rate of growth in spending on premium cable services is expected to be modest during the forecast period, due to discounted rates stemming from multiplexing and competition. Industry concerns that increasing penetration of VOD and growing sell-through rates of DVDs would affect premium channel spending have not borne out. In 2004, spending grew 3.4 percent compared with a drop of 0.7 percent in 2003. Spending on premium cable services reached $5.37 billion in 2004.

Growth in subscribers to cable services, increased investment in programming and more attractive pricing based on the use of digital tiers are expected to fuel 3.3 percent compound annual growth in spending on premium services from 2004 to 2009. Spending is projected to reach $6.33 billion in 2009.

Pay-Per-View

Spending on cable PPV rose 3.1 percent to $1.15 billion in 2004, due mainly to slower-than-anticipated consumer acceptance of digital cable, which is necessary for VOD usage. However, growth in PPV spending is expected to decelerate over the next five years as DVD sell-through rises and VOD penetration increases. VOD is more user-friendly than PPV, allowing viewers to pause, rewind and select their own start times. In addition, movies are being released more quickly on DVD, which will spur sales growth and cut into PPV spending. Major movies are available on DVD 35 to 45 days sooner than on PPV, and DVDs offer added features. Household penetration of DVD players has expanded rapidly since their introduction and sales continue to rise.

Cable households spent an aggregate of $230.0 million on events in 2004, up 1.3 percent from the prior year. Cable household spending on PPV movies grew 3.5 percent to $918.0 million in 2004, despite increased sell-through of DVD titles. However, the growing accessibility of VOD will severely curtail growth in the PPV cable segment during the forecast period. Spending on PPV will grow only 0.9 percent on a compound annual basis from 2004 to 2009 to $1.20 billion in 2009, compared with a compound annual growth rate of 7.5 percent in the 1999-2004 period.

Spending in the hotel/motel PPV market increased 3.5 percent to $404.0 million in 2004. Growth was due primarily to an increase in the number of rooms with PPV availability. The hotel/motel video industry was expected to undergo a major overhaul in which PPV would be replaced or supplemented by VOD technology, but this initiative never materialized. As a result, the hotel/motel PPV market is expected to continue to grow in the forecast period, albeit at slower rates, because the technology has not yet been eclipsed by VOD. Growth will begin to trail off in the latter portion of the forecast period as more rooms are furnished with VOD. Spending on hotel/motel PPV will continue to grow at a compound annual rate of 3.2 percent from 2004 to 2009 to $474.0 million.

Video-on-Demand

VOD is one of cable's trump cards in its battle against further DBS encroachment on its subscriber base. Because satellite operators can offer only a watered-down version of VOD, this service is emerging as a major marketing differentiator. Total residential cable VOD spending increased a hefty 123.9 percent to $318.0 million in 2004 compared with $142.0 million in 2003. With just 8.3 million subscribers in 2004, the average VOD household spent $16.06, translating into a nice boost for the increasingly important ARPU numbers. The number of VOD subscribers is projected to rise 29.7 percent from 2004 to 2009, reaching 30.4 million in

Pay-Per-View: Cable

Year	Addressable Households* (Millions)		Annual Spending Per Household			Aggregate Spending ($ Millions)		
	Households	Penetration	Movies	Events	Total	Movies	Events	Total
1999	45.0	45.3%	$10.56	$7.22	$17.78	$475	$325	$ 800
2000	78.6	78.0	6.28	3.27	9.55	494	257	751
2001	84.2	82.4	8.25	2.14	10.39	695	180	875
2002	91.9	87.1	9.56	2.87	12.43	879	264	1,143
2003	95.9	89.9	9.25	2.37	11.62	887	227	1,114
2004	100.9	93.1	9.10	2.28	11.38	918	230	1,148
2005	104.2	95.1	8.98	2.23	11.21	937	232	1,169
2006	107.5	97.0	8.80	2.18	10.98	946	234	1,180
2007	109.6	97.9	8.71	2.15	10.86	955	236	1,191
2008	110.7	97.8	8.67	2.14	10.81	960	237	1,197
2009	111.8	97.7	8.60	2.12	10.72	962	237	1,199

Source: Veronis Suhler Stevenson, PQ Media, Federal Communications Commission, Kagan Research, National Cable & Telecommunications Association
*Though a household may have multiple pay-per-view capability, many choose not to subscribe to it or the wired cable services necessary to access it.

Growth of Pay-Per-View: Cable

Year	Addressable Households	Annual Spending Per Household			Aggregate Spending		
		Movies	Events	Total	Movies	Events	Total
2000	74.7%	–40.5%	–54.7%	–46.3%	4.0%	–20.9%	–6.1%
2001	7.1	31.3	–34.6	8.8	40.7	–30.0	16.5
2002	9.1	15.9	34.4	19.7	26.5	46.7	30.6
2003	4.4	–3.3	–17.6	–6.6	0.9	–14.0	–2.5
2004	5.2	–1.6	–3.7	–2.1	3.5	1.3	3.1
2005	3.3	–1.3	–2.2	–1.5	2.0	1.0	1.8
2006	3.1	–2.0	–2.2	–2.1	1.0	0.8	1.0
2007	2.0	–1.0	–1.3	–1.0	1.0	0.7	0.9
2008	1.0	–0.5	–0.7	–0.5	0.5	0.3	0.5
2009	1.0	–0.5	–0.8	–0.8	0.2	0.2	0.2
Compound Annual Growth							
1999-2004	17.5	–2.9	–20.6	–8.5	14.1	–6.7	7.5
2004-2009	2.1	–1.1	–1.4	–1.2	0.9	0.6	0.9

Source: Veronis Suhler Stevenson, PQ Media, Federal Communications Commission, Kagan Research, National Cable & Telecommunications Association

Pay-Per-View: Hotels/Motels

Year	*Total Hotel/Motel Rooms in United States (Thousands)*	*Total Pay-Per-View Rooms* (Thousands)*	*Penetration of Hotel/Motel Rooms With Pay-Per-View*	*Annual Revenue Per Pay-Per-View Hotel/Motel Room*	*Total Hotel/Motel Pay-Per-View Spending ($ Millions)*
1999	3,900	2,873	73.7%	$128	$368
2000	4,100	2,963	72.3	124	369
2001	4,200	3,018	71.9	123	370
2002	4,284	3,099	72.3	121	376
2003	4,371	3,285	75.2	119	391
2004	4,414	3,458	78.3	117	404
2005	4,542	3,634	80.0	118	431
2006	4,678	3,740	79.9	120	448
2007	4,823	3,796	78.7	121	459
2008	4,954	3,834	77.4	122	468
2009	5,082	3,861	76.0	123	474

Sources: Veronis Suhler Stevenson, PQ Media, Kagan Research, LodgeNet, Smith Travel Research
*A number of pay-per-view rooms also have VOD capabilities.

Growth of Pay-Per-View: Hotels/Motels

Year	*Total Hotel/Motel Rooms in United States*	*Total Pay-Per-View Rooms*	*Annual Revenue Per Pay-Per-View Hotel/Motel Room*	*Total Hotel/Motel Pay-Per-View Spending*
2000	5.1%	3.1%	–2.8%	0.3%
2001	2.4	1.9	–1.6	0.3
2002	2.0	2.7	–1.0	1.7
2003	2.0	6.0	–1.9	4.0
2004	1.0	5.3	–1.7	3.5
2005	2.9	5.1	1.3	6.5
2006	3.0	2.9	1.1	4.0
2007	3.1	1.5	1.0	2.5
2008	2.7	1.0	0.9	1.9
2009	2.6	0.7	0.5	1.2
Compound Annual Growth				
1999-2004	2.5	3.8	–1.8	1.9
2004-2009	2.9	2.2	1.0	3.2

Sources: Veronis Suhler Stevenson, PQ Media, Kagan Research, LodgeNet, Smith Travel Research

Spending on Video-on-Demand: Residential*

Year	Total VOD Residential Households (Millions)	Total VOD Residential Subscribers (Millions)	Annual VOD Spending Per Subscriber	Total VOD Residential Spending ($ Millions)
1999	0.30	0.02	$23.13	$ 0.3
2000	1.6	0.2	25.87	6
2001	4.0	0.9	28.89	26
2002	7.0	2.0	28.00	56
2003	12.3	4.7	30.21	142
2004	19.8	8.3	38.31	318
2005	27.5	13.8	35.91	495
2006	33.5	20.1	33.68	678
2007	38.1	24.4	36.07	880
2008	42.0	28.1	38.39	1,079
2009	44.9	30.4	40.69	1,237

Sources: Veronis Suhler Stevenson, PQ Media, Leichtman Group, In-Stat, Kagan Research, Forrester Research
*Wired cable homes only. Satellite providers currently do not have the technology to offer VOD.

Cable & Satellite Television

Growth of Spending on Video-on-Demand: Residential

Year	Total VOD Households	Total VOD Subscribers	Annual VOD Spending Per Household	Total VOD Spending
2000	433.3%	1,513.3%	11.8%	1,704.0%
2001	150.0	271.9	11.7	315.3
2002	75.0	122.2	–3.1	115.4
2003	75.7	135.0	7.9	153.6
2004	61.0	76.6	26.8	123.9
2005	39.0	66.0	–6.3	55.6
2006	21.6	46.2	–6.2	37.1
2007	13.9	21.1	7.1	29.7
2008	10.1	15.2	6.4	22.6
2009	6.9	8.2	6.0	14.7
Compound Annual Growth				
1999-2004	131.2	253.7	10.6	291.2
2004-2009	17.8	29.7	1.2	31.2

Sources: Veronis Suhler Stevenson, PQ Media, Federal Communications Commission, National Cable & Telecommunications Association, Kagan Research, LodgeNet, Smith Travel Research

Spending on Video-on-Demand: Hotels/Motels

Year	Total Hotel/Motel Rooms in United States (Thousands)	Total Rooms With VOD Capacity (Thousands)	Percent of Hotel/Motel Rooms with VOD	VOD Revenue Per Hotel/Motel Room	Total Hotel/Motel VOD Spending ($ Millions)
1999	3,900	1,852	47.5%	$232	$430
2000	4,100	1,964	47.9	226	444
2001	4,200	2,025	48.2	223	452
2002	4,284	2,126	49.6	221	470
2003	4,371	2,312	52.9	219	506
2004	4,414	2,436	55.2	222	540
2005	4,502	2,699	59.9	223	601
2006	4,592	2,958	64.4	225	665
2007	4,684	3,281	70.0	227	744
2008	4,778	3,619	75.7	230	832
2009	4,864	3,948	81.2	234	924

Sources: Veronis Suhler Stevenson, PQ Media, Kagan Research, LodgeNet, Smith Travel Research

Growth of Spending on Video-on-Demand: Hotels/Motels

Year	Total Hotel/Motel Rooms in United States	Total Rooms With VOD Capacity	VOD Revenue Per Hotel/Motel Room	Total Hotel/Motel VOD Spending
2000	5.1%	6.0%	–2.6%	3.3%
2001	2.4	3.1	–1.3	1.7
2002	2.0	5.0	–0.9	4.0
2003	2.0	8.7	–0.9	7.7
2004	1.0	5.4	1.2	6.7
2005	2.0	10.8	0.5	11.4
2006	2.0	9.6	0.9	10.6
2007	2.0	10.9	0.9	11.9
2008	2.0	10.3	1.4	11.8
2009	1.8	9.1	1.7	11.0
Compound Annual Growth				
1999-2004	2.5	5.6	–0.9	4.7
2004-2009	2.0	10.1	1.1	11.3

Sources: Veronis Suhler Stevenson, PQ Media, Kagan Research, LodgeNet, Smith Travel Research

Subscription Spending on Digital Video Recorders (DVRs)*

Year	Stand-Alone DVR Households (Thousands)†	DBS DVR Households (Thousands)‡	Cable DVR Households (Thousands)§	Total DVR Households (Thousands)	DVR Subscription Rates Per Year Per Household	Total DVR Spending ($ Millions)
1999	95	88	—	183	$38.25	$ 7
2000	236	172	50	458	43.67	20
2001	435	402	180	1,017	46.21	47
2002	626	968	330	1,924	49.90	96
2003	906	1,716	830	3,452	53.30	184
2004	1,137	2,641	1,096	4,874	55.80	272
2005	1,389	3,691	1,594	6,673	57.55	384
2006	1,547	4,661	2,247	8,455	58.91	498
2007	1,619	5,397	2,977	9,994	61.31	613
2008	1,646	5,809	3,793	11,248	63.95	719
2009	1,670	6,082	4,746	12,497	66.48	831

Sources: Veronis Suhler Stevenson, PQ Media, Leichtman Research Group, TiVo, ReplayTV, DIRECTV, EchoStar, Business 2.0, Lexis/Nexis

*To avoid double counting, digital video recorder (DVR) spending will be found in the Entertainment Media chapter.

†Services provided by TiVo, ReplayTV, and UltimateTV.

‡Services provided by DIRECTV, EchoStar and other DBS providers, often in alliance with TiVo or UltimateTV.

§Various MSO cable providers signed alliances with TiVo, ReplayTV or UltimateTV from 1999 to 2002. In 2003, most MSOs began using separate stand-alone set-top DVR boxes, though Comcast announced a planned alliance with TiVo in 2005.

Growth of Subscription Spending on Digital Video Recorders (DVRs)*

Year	Stand-Alone DVR Households†	DBS DVR Households‡	Cable DVR Households§	Total DVR Households	DVR Subscription Rates Per Year Per Household	Total DVR Spending
2000	148.4%	95.5%	—	150.3%	14.2%	185.7%
2001	84.3	133.7	260.0%	122.1	5.8	135.0
2002	43.9	140.8	83.3	89.2	8.0	104.3
2003	44.7	77.3	151.5	79.4	6.8	91.7
2004	25.5	53.9	32.0	41.2	4.7	47.8
2005	22.1	39.7	45.4	36.9	3.1	41.2
2006	11.4	26.3	41.0	26.7	2.4	29.7
2007	4.7	15.8	32.5	18.2	4.1	23.0
2008	1.6	7.6	27.4	12.5	4.3	17.4
2009	1.4	4.7	25.1	11.1	4.0	15.5
Compound Annual Growth						
1999-2004	64.3	97.5	—	92.8	7.8	107.9
2004-2009	8.0	18.2	34.1	20.7	3.6	25.0

Sources: Veronis Suhler Stevenson, PQ Media, Leichtman Research Group, TiVo, ReplayTV, DIRECTV, EchoStar, Business 2.0, Lexis/Nexis

*To avoid double counting, digital video recorder (DVR) spending will be found in the Entertainment Media chapter.

†Services provided by TiVo, ReplayTV, and UltimateTV.

‡Services provided by DIRECTV, EchoStar and other DBS providers, often in alliance with TiVo or UltimateTV.

§Various MSO cable providers signed alliances with TiVo, ReplayTV or UltimateTV from 1999 to 2002. In 2003, most MSOs began using separate stand-alone set-top DVR boxes, though Comcast announced a planned alliance with TiVo in 2005.

Total Spending on Video-on-Demand ($MILLIONS)

Year	Residential VOD Spending	Hotel/Motel VOD Spending	Total VOD Spending
1999	$ 0.3	$430	$ 430
2000	6	444	450
2001	26	452	478
2002	56	470	526
2003	142	506	648
2004	318	540	858
2005	495	601	1,096
2006	678	665	1,343
2007	880	744	1,624
2008	1,079	832	1,911
2009	1,237	924	2,161

Sources: Veronis Suhler Stevenson, PQ Media, Federal Communications Commission, National Cable & Telecommunications Association, Kagan Research, LodgeNet, Smith Travel Research

Cable & Satellite Television

2009, pushing up spending 31.2 percent to $1.24 billion.

In the hotel/motel market, VOD growth will be strong, as well. After posting a 6.7 percent increase to $540.0 million in 2004, the market is expected to advance at double-digit rates throughout the forecast period. As the market continues its overhaul of video services, rooms with VOD capacity will increase a brisk 10.1 percent over the forecast period, allowing the sector to attain an estimated 11.3 percent compound annual increase in spending to $924.0 million in 2009.

THE SATELLITE TELEVISION MARKET IN 2004 AND 2005

Total spending on satellite television grew at a double-digit rate for the fourth year in a row in 2004, posting a gain of 11.8 percent to $16.17 billion for the year. Spending was driven by a surge in subscribers, rate hikes and spending on DBS local avails advertising. DBS local avails are not truly local, but are technically national buys. However, the DBS industry is attempting to tailor the ads to local communities as a way of promoting its expanded local footprint and to battle the increased spending on wired cable's local interconnects.

Total spending on DBS grew at a 15.0 percent compound annual rate in the 1999-2004 period, driven primarily by a 14.8 percent gain in subscription spending. Overall, the annual growth of subscription spending on DBS has almost tripled that of nominal GDP since 1999.

To combat cable's success in upgrading subscribers to bundled service packages, DBS has been inking strategic marketing alliances to explore the integration of digital satellite and digital subscriber line (DSL) telephony.

EchoStar has agreements with SBC, Sprint and CenturyTel, in addition to Internet service provider EarthLink. DIRECTV has agreements with SBC, Verizon, BellSouth and Cincinnati Bell. SBC and EchoStar's joint venture, known as SBC DISH Network, features satellite services starting at $29.99 per month for SBC phone customers. This service provides a quadruple-play bundle of high-speed Internet, local and long distance telephone, wireless telephone and video service. By year-end 2004, the service had nearly 250,000 subscribers. Phone companies are entering into such deals with satellite providers in an effort to offer direct competition to cable companies that are offering voice and data and taking telephony and broadband Internet access revenues away from the RBOCs. Additionally, both phone and satellite companies are banking on the same theory under which cable operators are operating, that subscribers to bundled packages are less susceptible to churn. Similar to the SBC venture, BellSouth and DIRECTV launched a joint service delivering the same bundle. As of September 2004, BellSouth served over 90,000 DIRECTV customers. Verizon and DIRECTV offer a similar bundle in New England, New York and the Mid-Atlantic region.

DIRECTV announced in 2004 that it would spend about $1 billion to launch four new satellites capable of providing local-into-local service, national high-definition channels and interactive programming. The satellites are being converted to provide 500 local HD channels, as well as broadband Internet service. One major driver behind DBS's ability to grow its market share is that operators have been able to deliver many local broadcast stations since 2000. As of December 2004, local stations

Growth of Spending on Total Video-on-Demand

Year	*Residential VOD Spending*	*Hotel/Motel VOD Spending*	*Total VOD Spending*
2000	1,704.0%	3.3%	4.7%
2001	315.3	1.7	6.1
2002	115.4	4.0	10.1
2003	153.6	7.7	23.3
2004	123.9	6.7	32.4
2005	55.6	11.4	27.8
2006	37.1	10.6	22.6
2007	29.7	11.9	20.9
2008	22.6	11.8	17.7
2009	14.7	11.0	13.1
Compound Annual Growth			
1999-2004	291.2	4.7	14.8
2004-2009	31.2	11.3	20.3

Sources: Veronis Suhler Stevenson, PQ Media, Federal Communications Commission, National Cable & Telecommunications Association, Kagan Research, LodgeNet, Smith Travel Research

Cable Modem Spending*

Year	Cable Modem Households (Millions)	Average Annual Spending Per Cable Modem Household	Total Cable Modem Spending ($ Millions)
1999	1.8	$234	$ 422
2000	3.7	290	1,072
2001	7.2	326	2,348
2002	11.6	387	4,494
2003	16.4	419	6,888
2004	21.0	443	9,303
2005	24.3	454	11,052
2006	27.0	466	12,588
2007	29.5	478	14,124
2008	31.5	495	15,579
2009	33.1	516	17,059

Sources: Veronis Suhler Stevenson, PQ Media, Federal Communications Commission, National Cable & Telecommunications Association, US Department of Commerce

*To avoid double counting, cable modem spending found in the Consumer Internet chapter will be added to overall spending data.

Growth of Cable Modem Spending*

Year	Cable Modem Households (Millions)	Average Annual Spending Per Cable Modem Household	Total Cable Modem Spending ($ Millions)
2000	105.6%	23.6%	154.0%
2001	94.6	12.6	119.0
2002	61.1	18.8	91.4
2003	41.8	8.1	53.3
2004	27.7	5.8	35.1
2005	15.9	2.5	18.8
2006	11.1	2.5	13.9
2007	9.2	2.7	12.2
2008	6.6	3.5	10.3
2009	5.0	4.3	9.5
Compound Annual Growth			
1999-2004	63.5	13.6	85.6
2004-2009	9.5	3.1	12.9

Sources: Veronis Suhler Stevenson, PQ Media, Federal Communications Commission, National Cable & Telecommunications Association, US Department of Commerce

*To avoid double counting, cable modem spending found in the Consumer Internet chapter will be added to overall spending data.

were offered by at least one DBS operator in 155 of the 210 television markets, or designated market areas (DMAs), which cover about 95 percent of all U.S. television households. EchoStar offered subscribers in 150 DMAs a package of local broadcast stations, including commercial and noncommercial stations, up from 101 DMAs in 2004. DIRECTV offers local-into-local service in 130 DMAs, more than double its 2004 total of 64. As a cautionary note, it is likely that the days of huge subscriber increases are winding down, as the number of local markets not yet served by satellite is dwindling.

Growth in the forecast period will continue to come primarily from new subscribers, although the rate of growth will decelerate. DBS has made significant inroads in the market for multichannel services over the past decade. Ten years ago, cable companies served almost 100 percent of multichannel subscribers; today, cable accounts for only 71.6 percent of all subscribers, while DBS claims 25.1 percent. While cable TV was once the only game in town, almost all TV households can now choose between cable and at least two DBS providers.

DBS operates at a disadvantage to cable when it comes to network ownership. News Corporation, which holds an approximate 34 percent interest in DIRECTV, has ownership interests in only 12 national networks through its Fox subsidiary, which also operates the FOX television network. As noted earlier, about 23 percent of non-broadcast networks are owned, in varying degrees, by four of the top six cable operators (Comcast, Time Warner, Cox and Cablevision).

Although it remains a distant second to cable, with 26.6 million subscribers in 2004, the DBS sector has continually posted stellar gains in household subscriptions since entering the market in 1994. DBS has posed a formidable challenge to cable because of its ability in the last few years to offer local programming combined with expanded channel offerings, early adoption of DVRs, exclusive national sports packages, such as *NFL Sunday Ticket*, and its market positioning as the alternative for dissatisfied cable customers.

DBS subscription growth accelerated to 18.2 percent in 2004 from 15.4 percent in

Residential Cable Telephony Spending*

	Circuit Switched Cablephone			VoIP Cablephone			Total Residential		
	Subs (Millions)	Avg. Monthly Rate per Sub	Total Spending ($ Millions)	Subs (Millions)	Avg. Monthly Rate per Sub	Total Spending ($ Millions)	Subs (Millions)	Avg. Monthly Rate per Sub	Total Spending ($ Millions)
2001	1.4	$50.94	$ 831	0.0	$41.74	$ 0.02	1.4	$50.94	$ 831
2002	1.9	49.32	1,107	0.0	41.25	0.5	1.9	49.31	1,107
2003	2.6	47.72	1,513	0.0	40.26	11	2.7	47.66	1,524
2004	2.9	46.19	1,622	0.2	40.30	110	3.2	45.77	1,732
2005	3.2	44.74	1,728	1.2	39.78	552	4.4	43.42	2,279
2006	3.5	43.35	1,811	3.7	39.30	1,725	7.1	41.27	3,536
2007	3.7	42.03	1,868	7.4	38.91	3,478	11.2	39.94	5,346
2008	3.8	40.93	1,851	11.2	38.63	5,180	14.9	39.21	7,031
2009	3.7	39.91	1,790	13.9	38.44	6,397	17.6	38.75	8,187

Sources: Veronis Suhler Stevenson, PQ Media, Kagan Research, Merrill Lynch, Sanford C. Bernstein

*Cable telephony is not considered communications spending as it does not pertain to communications content. Therefore, total spending data from this table are not added to overall Cable & Satellite TV spending.

Cable & Satellite Television

Growth of Residential Cable Telephony Spending*

	Circuit Switched Cablephone			VoIP Cablephone			Total		
	Subs (Millions)	Avg. Monthly Rate per Sub	Total Spending ($ Millions)	Subs (Millions)	Avg. Monthly Rate per Sub	Total Spending ($ Millions)	Subs (Millions)	Avg. Monthly Rate per Sub	Total Spending ($ Millions)
2002	37.5%	–3.2%	33.1%	3,233.3%	–1.2%	3,194.2%	37.6%	–3.2%	33.2%
2003	41.3	–3.2	36.7	2,150.0	–2.4	2,096.0	42.4	–3.4	37.7
2004	10.7	–3.2	7.2	911.1	0.1	912.1	18.3	–4.0	13.6
2005	10.0	–3.2	6.5	407.9	–1.3	401.3	38.7	–5.1	31.6
2006	8.2	–3.1	4.8	216.5	–1.2	212.7	63.2	–5.0	55.1
2007	6.4	–3.1	3.2	103.7	–1.0	101.7	56.2	–3.2	51.2
2008	1.7	–2.6	–0.9	50.0	–0.7	49.0	34.0	–1.8	31.5
2009	–0.8	–2.5	–3.3	24.1	–0.5	23.5	17.8	–1.2	16.4
Compound Annual Growth									
2004-2009	5.0	–2.9	2.0	127.5	–0.9	125.4	41.1	–3.3	36.4

Sources: Veronis Suhler Stevenson, PQ Media, Kagan Research, Merrill Lynch, Sanford C. Bernstein

*Cable telephony is not considered communications spending as it does not pertain to communications content. Therefore, total spending data from this table are not added to overall Cable & Satellite TV spending.

Total Spending on Satellite Television

Year	Subscription Spending: Basic Service Spending	Premium Service Spending	Pay-Per-View Spending	Total Subscription Spending	DBS Local Avails Advertising Spending	Total Satellite Television Content Spending
1999	$ 4,688	$2,390	$ 955	$ 8,033	$ 5	$ 8,038
2000	5,719	2,313	704	8,736	22	8,758
2001	6,905	2,912	880	10,697	38	10,735
2002	8,108	3,423	988	12,519	63	12,582
2003	9,391	3,856	1,110	14,357	102	14,459
2004	10,509	4,288	1,219	16,016	152	16,168
2005	11,581	4,695	1,314	17,590	196	17,786
2006	12,519	5,047	1,407	18,973	251	19,224
2007	13,470	5,350	1,480	20,300	300	20,600
2008	14,427	5,618	1,531	21,576	364	21,940
2009	15,451	5,899	1,585	22,935	442	23,377

Sources: Veronis Suhler Stevenson, PQ Media, Federal Communications Commission Annual Report, Kagan Research, National Cable & Telecommunications Association

Growth of Total Spending on Satellite Television

Year	Subscription Spending: Basic Service Spending	Premium Service Spending	Pay-Per-View Spending	Total Subscription Spending	DBS Local Avails Advertising Spending	Total Satellite Cable Content Spending
2000	22.0%	–3.2%	–26.3%	8.8%	340.0%	9.0%
2001	20.7	25.9	25.0	22.4	72.7	22.6
2002	17.4	17.5	12.3	17.0	65.8	17.2
2003	15.8	12.6	12.3	14.7	61.3	14.9
2004	11.9	11.2	9.8	11.6	49.3	11.8
2005	10.2	9.5	7.8	9.8	29.5	10.0
2006	8.1	7.5	7.1	7.9	27.6	8.1
2007	7.6	6.0	5.2	7.0	19.5	7.2
2008	7.1	5.0	3.5	6.3	21.5	6.5
2009	7.1	5.0	3.5	6.3	21.5	6.5
Compound Annual Growth						
1999-2004	17.5	12.4	5.0	14.8	97.9	15.0
2004-2009	8.0	6.6	5.4	7.4	23.9	7.7

Sources: Veronis Suhler Stevenson, PQ Media, Federal Communications Commission Annual Report, Kagan Research, National Cable & Telecommunications Association

2004, driven by the churn of disgruntled cable customers and expansion into previously underserved television markets. DBS's rapid gains have continued to hasten the decline of competing technologies, as noted earlier.

Due to higher programming costs for channels, both of the nation's largest satellite television providers are planning to increase prices for many of their popular packages. DIRECTV raised prices for its consumer packages in March 2005, as the basic tier rose 5.0 percent to $41.99 a month, the middle tier climbed 7.0 percent to $45.99, and the premium package—Total Choice Premier—jumped 3.3 percent to $93.99. EchoStar's DISH Network, citing a 7.0 percent increase in programming costs, boosted various package prices by between $2 and $4 per month.

HOUSEHOLD SPENDING ON SATELLITE TELEVISION

Basic Services

Driven by an 18.2 percent increase in subscribers in 2004, spending on DBS basic services notched its fifth straight year of double-digit growth, rising 11.9 percent to $10.51 billion in 2004. Gains were driven by the increased availability of local programming on DBS and continuing discounts on hardware and installation for DBS.

We expect growth in the average monthly spending per household on DBS to slow slightly to the high-single-digit range throughout the forecast period. At $29.29 per month in 2004, average monthly spending will advance only 2.4 percent compounded annually to $32.93 in 2009. The main growth drivers are expected to be increased investment in promotional spending and technology, such as DVRs. Spending on basic satellite services will reach $15.45 billion in 2009, increasing at a compound annual rate of 8.0 percent from 2004 to 2009.

Premium Services

Spending on premium satellite services rose 11.2 percent to $4.29 billion in 2004. Although cable still accounts for the majority of premium service subscribers at 52.6 million, satellite showed slightly stronger growth in 2004, with subscriptions up 3.1 percent to 30.0 million.

DBS continues to attract higher spending per household on premium subscriptions because of its strength in urban markets, where viewers tend to demand more channel choices. This represents a change from DBS's traditional strength in rural areas, as this is where DBS had originally staked a claim, due to the historical dearth of cable service in less populated areas. As cable has become more available to most TV homes, DBS has lost this rural advantage. Satellite subscribers are expected to continue to spend more on premium services than are cable subscribers because of the economies cable operators achieve through digital delivery. DBS has traditionally been purchased by a higher economic demographic than wired cable; as a result, more discretionary income is available in these households for premium channel subscriptions.

The satellite subsegment will experience a faster compound annual growth rate in the forecast period, rising 6.6 percent to $5.90 billion, compared to the cable subsegment's 3.3 percent gain. Individual DBS households have spent significantly more for premium services than cable users since 1999, due to the demographic factors discussed above, and we expect this trend to continue throughout the forecast period.

Pay-Per-View

Due in large part to DBS's expanding subscriber base and limited penetration of VOD, the satellite PPV market grew 9.8 percent to $1.22 billion in 2004. The average satellite household spent $38.83 on movies and $6.99 on events, far exceeding cable households, which spent $9.10 on movies and $2.28 on events. Satellite viewers spent a total of $1.03 billion on PPV movies, up 10.0 percent over 2003, and $186.0 million on events. From 2004 to 2009, we project satellite PPV spending will increase at a compound annual rate of 5.4 percent to $1.59 billion in 2009.

Pay-Per-View: Satellite

Year	Addressable Households* (Millions) Households	Penetration	Annual Spending Per Household Movies	Events	Total	Aggregate Spending ($ Millions) Movies	Events	Total
1999	11.5	11.6%	$61.74	$21.30	$83.04	$ 710	$245	$ 955
2000	14.3	14.2	39.37	9.86	49.23	563	141	704
2001	17.7	17.3	43.11	6.61	49.72	763	117	880
2002	19.5	18.5	43.33	7.33	50.66	845	143	988
2003	22.5	21.1	41.73	7.60	49.33	939	171	1,110
2004	26.6	24.5	38.83	6.99	45.82	1,033	186	1,219
2005	29.8	27.2	37.38	6.74	44.12	1,113	201	1,314
2006	32.2	29.0	37.00	6.75	43.75	1,190	217	1,407
2007	33.9	30.2	36.87	6.83	43.70	1,249	231	1,480
2008	35.6	31.5	36.13	6.85	42.98	1,287	244	1,531
2009	37.4	32.7	35.48	6.84	42.32	1,329	256	1,585

Source: Veronis Suhler Stevenson, PQ Media, Federal Communications Commission, Kagan Research, National Cable & Telecommunications Association
*Though a household may have pay-per-view capability through its satellite provider, it may choose not to subscribe to it.

Cable & Satellite Television

Growth of Pay-Per-View: Satellite

Year	Addressable Households	Annual Spending Per Household Movies	Events	Total	Aggregate Spending ($ Millions) Movies	Events	Total
2000	24.3%	–36.2%	–53.7%	–40.7%	–20.7%	–42.4%	–26.3%
2001	23.8	9.5	–33.0	1.0	35.5	–17.0	25.0
2002	10.2	0.5	10.9	1.9	10.7	22.2	12.3
2003	15.4	–3.7	3.6	–2.6	11.1	19.5	12.3
2004	18.2	–6.9	–7.9	–7.1	10.0	8.8	9.8
2005	12.0	–3.7	–3.6	–3.7	7.8	8.0	7.8
2006	8.0	–1.0	0.1	–0.8	6.9	8.1	7.1
2007	5.3	–0.4	1.2	–0.1	4.9	6.5	5.2
2008	5.2	–2.0	0.3	–1.6	3.1	5.5	3.5
2009	5.1	–1.8	–0.1	–1.5	3.2	5.0	3.5
Compound Annual Growth							
1999-2004	18.3	–8.9	–20.0	–11.2	7.8	–5.4	5.0
2004-2009	7.1	–1.8	–0.4	–1.6	5.2	6.6	5.4

Source: Veronis Suhler Stevenson, PQ Media, Federal Communications Commission, Kagan Research, National Cable & Telecommunications Association

Prime-Time Ratings

Year	*Network-Affiliated TV Stations*	*Independent TV Stations**	*Public TV Stations*	*All TV Stations*	*Ad-Supported Cable†*	*Premium Pay Cable*	*All Other Cable‡*	*All Cable*	*All TV*
1999-00	34.7	2.1	2.0	38.8	24.0	3.5	1.9	29.4	68.2
2000-01	32.6	2.4	1.9	36.9	26.0	3.5	2.1	31.6	68.5
2001-02	30.3	2.5	1.6	34.4	28.2	3.5	2.1	33.8	68.2
2002-03	29.6	2.6	1.7	33.9	29.4	3.6	2.4	35.4	69.3
2003-04	28.9	2.9	1.6	33.4	30.9	3.4	2.9	37.2	70.6

Sources: Veronis Suhler Stevenson, PQ Media, Nielsen Media Research
Note: Ratings are for Mon.-Sat., 8-11 p.m., Sun 7-11 p.m.
*Includes Telemundo and Univision.
†Includes TBS and WGN.
‡Includes pay-per-view, interactive channels, home shopping channels, and audio-only feeds.

Prime-Time Audience Shares

Year	*Network-Affiliated TV Stations*	*Independent TV Stations**	*Public TV Stations*	*All TV Stations*	*Ad-Supported Cable†*	*Premium Pay Cable*	*All Other Cable‡*	*All Cable*
1999-00	59%	4%	3%	66%	41%	6%	3%	50%
2000-01	55	4	3	62	44	6	4	54
2001-02	51	4	3	58	44	6	4	58
2002-03	50	4	3	57	44	6	4	60
2003-04	49	5	3	57	44	6	5	63

Sources: Veronis Suhler Stevenson, PQ Media, Nielsen Media Research
Note: Shares are for Mon.-Sat., 8-11 p.m., Sun. 7-11 p.m. Total shares exceed 100% because Nielsen double-counts multiple-set households and multiple channels viewed during the quarter-hour.
*Includes Telemundo and Univision.
†Includes TBS and WGN.
‡Includes pay-per-view, interactive channels, home shopping channels, and audio-only feeds.

CABLE & SATELLITE TELEVISION PROGRAMMING

Programming differentiation for cable versus satellite television is virtually indistinguishable, as providers in both industries carry most of the same networks. Although there are a very few networks exclusive to DBS, this has more to do with cable systems lacking channel capacity to add them rather than the networks' choice to be primarily on satellite. Because of the lower subscriber numbers of DBS, the few networks available only on satellite are not as profitable as other networks that are carried by both providers.

Total-Day Ratings

Year	*Network-Affiliated TV Stations*	*Independent TV Stations**	*Public TV Stations*	*All TV Stations*	*Ad-Supported Cable*†	*Premium Pay Cable*	*All Other Cable*‡	*All Cable*	*All TV*
1999-00	16.5	1.1	1.0	18.6	13.3	1.9	1.0	16.2	34.8
2000-01	15.7	1.2	1.0	17.9	14.6	1.9	1.2	17.7	35.6
2001-02	14.6	1.2	0.9	16.7	15.8	2.0	1.2	19.0	35.7
2002-03	14.5	1.3	0.9	16.7	16.9	2.1	1.5	20.5	37.2
2003-04	14.2	1.4	0.8	16.4	17.7	2.1	1.8	21.6	38.0
2004-05	14.4	1.8	0.9	17.1	18.8	1.9	1.9	22.6	39.7
2005-06	14.5	1.8	0.9	17.2	19.1	1.9	2.0	23.0	40.2
2006-07	14.5	1.8	0.9	17.2	19.5	2.0	2.0	23.5	40.7
2007-08	14.4	1.8	0.9	17.1	19.8	2.0	2.1	23.9	41.0
2008-09	14.5	1.8	0.9	17.2	20.0	1.9	2.1	24.0	41.2

Sources: Veronis Suhler Stevenson, PQ Media, Nielsen Media Research
Note: Ratings are for Mon.-Sat., 8-11 p.m., Sun 7-11 p.m.
*Includes Telemundo and Univision.
†Includes TBS and WGN.
‡Includes pay-per-view, interactive channels, home shopping channels, and audio-only feeds.

Shares of Total-Day Television Viewing

Year	*Network-Affiliated TV Stations*	*Independent TV Stations**	*Public TV Stations*	*All TV Stations*	*Ad-Supported Cable*†	*Premium Pay Cable*	*All Other Cable*‡	*All Cable*
1999-00	53%	4%	3%	60%	42%	6%	3%	51%
2000-01	49	4	3	56	46	6	4	56
2001-02	46	4	3	53	49	6	4	59
2002-03	44	4	3	51	51	6	5	62
2003-04	43	4	3	50	53	6	5	64
2004-05	43	5	2	50	54	5	5	64
2005-06	44	5	2	51	55	5	5	65
2006-07	44	5	2	51	55	6	5	66
2007-08	43	5	2	50	55	6	5	66
2008-09	44	5	2	51	56	5	5	66

Sources: Veronis Suhler Stevenson, PQ Media, Nielsen Media Research
Note: Shares are for Mon.-Sat., 8-11 p.m., Sun. 7-11 p.m. Total shares exceed 100% because Nielsen double-counts multiple-set households and multiple channels viewed during the quarter-hour.
*Includes Telemundo and Univision.
†Includes TBS and WGN.
‡Includes pay-per-view, interactive channels, home shopping channels, and audio-only feeds.

Prime-time ratings for ad-supported (basic) cable programs rose 1.5 points to 30.9 in the 2003-04 season, primarily as a result of the industry's continuing investment in original programming. For the same period, prime-time ratings for pay cable programs dropped 0.2 of a point to 3.4, due to the absence of HBO hits *Sex and the City* and *The Sopranos*. Combined, cable ratings rose 1.3 points to 34.3 in the 2003-04 season. Cable's prime-time audience share grew 3.0 percentage points to 63.0 in the 2003-04 season, with basic cable accounting for 52.0 percent and pay cable representing 6.0 percent.

The total-day rating for ad-supported cable was 17.7 for the 2003-04 season, up from 16.9 the previous season. Pay cable was flat at 2.1 points. Ad-supported cable had a 53 audience share in 2003-04, up from 51 in 2002-03.

Six of the top 10 cable networks experienced an increase in viewers in 2004 compared with the previous year, including TNT, Cartoon Network, Lifetime, Fox News Channel, ESPN and Spike TV. TNT was the leading cable network, and achieved its fifth consecutive year of growth in the key 18- to 49-year-old demographic.

Of the shows that are driving ratings growth for cable, only two are syndicated: *CSI* and *Law & Order*. A&E has fueled growth with original shows like *Dog the Bounty Hunter, Growing Up Gotti, The First 48* and *Intervention*. Cartoon Network announced 400 hours of new programming for 2005. Comedy Central scored big with its original series, *Blue Collar TV*, and spin-offs of that show such as Comedy Central's roast of Jeff Foxworthy, which drew 6.2 million viewers.

As cable networks continue to invest in programming, ad-supported cable's share of total viewing is projected to reach 56 in the 2008-09 television season, while pay cable's share will drop to 5. In total, cable's share will reach 66 in the 2008-09 season.

Meanwhile, cable and satellite television companies are incorporating DVRs into their offerings. Spending on DVR subscriptions grew 47.8 percent to $272.0 million in 2004, as total DVR households increased 41.2 percent to 4.9 million. DBS accounts for 2.6 million DVR users, while cable claimed 1.1 million in 2004.

Spending on DVRs is projected to accelerate at a compound annual rate of 25.0 percent in the forecast period, reaching $831.0 million in 2009. By that time, however, growing acceptance of advanced capabilities by cable subscribers will have resulted in compound annual growth of 34.1 percent to 4.7 million cable subscribers, as opposed to growth of 18.2 percent to 6.1 million DVR subscribers through DBS.

CABLE & SATELLITE TELEVISION NETWORK ADVERTISING

Cable and satellite television network advertising spending increased 14.6 percent to $13.89 billion in 2004, while regional sports advertising grew 13.4 percent to $559.0 million and DBS local avails increased 49.3 percent to $152.0 million. Double-digit growth in cable and satellite television advertising in 2004 was spurred by the growing availability of interconnects, increased ratings and audience share, continued investment in technology

Cable & Satellite Television

Cable & Satellite Television Advertising ($ MILLIONS)

Year	*Network*	*Local*	*Regional Sports*	*DBS Local Avails**	*Total*
1999	$ 8,593	$2,685	$341	$ 5	$11,624
2000	10,259	3,128	379	22	13,788
2001	10,494	3,240	442	38	14,214
2002	10,881	3,337	455	63	14,736
2003	12,122	3,587	493	102	16,304
2004	13,891	4,323	559	152	18,925
2005	15,864	4,997	629	196	21,686
2006	17,466	5,851	690	251	24,258
2007	19,108	6,735	745	300	26,888
2008	20,827	7,739	816	364	29,746
2009	23,202	8,822	895	442	33,361

Sources: Veronis Suhler Stevenson, PQ Media, Cabletelevision Advertising Bureau, Kagan Research

*The equivalent of cable's local avails, although they are sold as national time on DBS.

Growth of Cable & Satellite Television Advertising

Year	Network	Local	Regional Sports	DBS Local Avails*	Total
2000	19.4%	16.5%	11.1%	340.0%	18.6%
2001	2.3	3.6	16.6	72.7	3.1
2002	3.7	3.0	2.9	65.8	3.7
2003	11.4	7.5	8.4	61.3	10.6
2004	14.6	20.5	13.4	49.3	16.1
2005	14.2	15.6	12.5	29.5	14.6
2006	10.1	17.1	9.6	27.6	11.9
2007	9.4	15.1	8.0	19.5	10.8
2008	9.0	14.9	9.5	21.5	10.6
2009	11.4	14.0	9.7	21.5	12.2
Compound Annual Growth					
1999-2004	10.1	10.0	10.4	97.9	10.2
2004-2009	10.8	15.3	9.9	23.9	12.0

Sources: Veronis Suhler Stevenson, PQ Media, Cabletelevision Advertising Bureau, Kagan Research

*The equivalent of cable's local avails, although they are sold as national time on DBS.

and programming, and favorable CPMs when compared with broadcast television.

We expect the market for cable and satellite TV advertising to grow 14.6 percent to $21.69 billion in 2005. Annual ad spending throughout the remainder of the forecast period will be robust. Comcast, Time Warner, Cox and Charter are touting technology that will eventually enable them to target advertising as precisely as direct mail, segregating ads that send different messages to different neighborhoods within their viewing areas. Time Warner and Charter Communications are currently testing services that target ads to homes based on subscriber spending patterns.

Advertising spending on networks is forecast to rise at a compound annual rate of 10.8 percent from 2004 to 2009, reaching $23.20 billion in 2009. Advertising expenditures on regional sports is expected to advance at a compound annual rate of 9.9 percent over the next five years to $895.0 million in 2009. DBS local avails are forecast to grow at a compound annual rate of 23.9 percent in the 2004-2009 period to $442.0 million in 2009.

Top 10 National Cable Advertisers

Advertiser	10/02-9/03 ($ Thousands)	10/03-9/04 ($ Thousands)	$ Change	Percent Change
Procter & Gamble	$ 474,736	$ 694,098	$219,362	46.2%
General Motors	391,779	306,123	–85,656	–21.9
GlaxoSmithKline	140,383	204,664	64,281	45.8
Altria Group	177,639	190,484	12,845	7.2
Walt Disney Co.	160,900	188,955	28,055	17.4
Time Warner	252,784	182,101	–70,683	–28.0
Sony	152,067	168,975	16,908	11.1
Dell Computer	125,454	167,474	42,020	33.5
Johnson & Johnson	163,218	165,386	2,168	1.3
Pfizer	143,732	148,285	4,553	3.2
Top 10 Total	2,182,692	2,416,545	233,853	10.7

Sources: Veronis Suhler Stevenson, PQ Media, Cabletelevision Advertising Bureau

Procter & Gamble and General Motors remained the top two cable advertisers in 2004, but Time Warner tumbled into sixth place from third. Five of the 10 largest national advertisers on cable increased their spending at double-digit rates in 2004, with Procter & Gamble and GlaxoSmithKline increasing their expenditures by 46.2 percent and 45.8 percent, respectively. General Motors dropped 21.9 percent and Time Warner cut spending 28.0 percent. Overall, major advertisers increased spending 10.7 percent in 2004, and they are expected to continue to increase spending on cable advertising in the forecast period as a result of the projected rise in viewership.

As of September 2004, the top 10 cable and DBS operators controlled 84.7 percent of the subscriber market. The dominant player, Comcast, accounted for 23.4 percent of all multichannel subscribers. Following Comcast are DIRECTV with 12.1 percent of the market, Time Warner Cable with 11.9 percent and EchoStar with 10.6 percent. If the Adelphia acquisition by Time Warner and Comcast is consummated, Time Warner would vault into the number-two spot.

Top 10 Cable and DBS Operators, July 2004

Operator	*Percentage of Overall Subscribers*
Comcast Cable Communications	23.4%
DIRECTV (News Corporation)	12.1
Time Warner Cable	11.9
EchoStar	10.6
Cox Communications	6.9
Charter Communications	6.7
Adelphia	5.9
Cablevision	3.2
Bright House (Advance)	2.4
Mediacom	1.7
Total Percent of Market	84.7

Sources: Veronis Suhler Stevenson, PQ Media, Federal Communications Commission

Cable & Satellite Television

Top 8 Cable Advertising Categories

Category	*10/02-9/03 ($ Thousands)*	*10/03-9/04 ($ Thousands)*	*$ Change*	*Percent Change*
Automotive, Automotive Accessories & Equipment	$1,096,519	$1,201,864	$105,345	9.6%
Medicines & Proprietary Remedies	743,647	1,034,839	291,192	39.2
Financial	781,245	880,795	99,550	12.7
Retail	551,750	716,766	165,016	29.9
Media & Advertising	613,224	576,399	–36,825	–6.0
Restaurants	460,491	534,964	74,473	20.7
Games & Toys	403,499	487,058	83,559	20.7
Telecommunications	510,226	484,709	–25,517	–5.0
Top 8 Total	5,160,601	5,917,394	756,793	14.7

Sources: Veronis Suhler Stevenson, PQ Media, Cabletelevision Advertising Bureau

Spending by Operators and Advertisers on Basic Network and Premium Channels

($ MILLIONS)

	Basic Networks			Premium Channels	
Year	*License Fees*	*Advertising*	*Total*	*License Fees*	*Total*
1999	$ 6,091	$ 8,593	$14,684	$3,351	$18,035
2000	7,139	10,259	17,398	3,609	21,007
2001	8,630	10,494	19,124	3,979	23,103
2002	10,471	10,881	21,352	4,260	25,612
2003	12,098	12,122	24,220	4,361	28,581
2004	13,630	13,891	27,521	4,545	32,066
2005	14,979	15,864	30,843	4,758	35,601
2006	16,358	17,466	33,824	4,963	38,787
2007	17,702	19,108	36,810	5,147	41,957
2008	19,135	20,827	39,962	5,327	45,289
2009	20,533	23,202	43,735	5,497	49,232

Sources: Veronis Suhler Stevenson, PQ Media, Cabletelevision Advertising Bureau, Kagan Research

Cable & Satellite Television

Growth of Spending by Operators and Advertisers on Basic Network and Premium Channels

	Basic Networks			Premium Channels	
Year	*License Fees*	*Advertising*	*Total*	*License Fees*	*Total*
2000	17.2%	19.4%	18.5%	7.7%	16.5%
2001	20.9	2.3	9.9	10.3	10.0
2002	21.3	3.7	11.6	7.1	10.9
2003	15.5	11.4	13.4	2.4	11.6
2004	12.7	14.6	13.6	4.2	12.2
2005	9.9	14.2	12.1	4.7	11.0
2006	9.2	10.1	9.7	4.3	8.9
2007	8.2	9.4	8.8	3.7	8.2
2008	8.1	9.0	8.6	3.5	7.9
2009	7.3	11.4	9.4	3.2	8.7
Compound Annual Growth					
1999-2004	17.5	10.1	13.4	6.3	12.2
2004-2009	8.5	10.8	9.7	3.9	9.0

Sources: Veronis Suhler Stevenson, PQ Media, Cabletelevision Advertising Bureau, Kagan Research

LICENSE FEES FOR CABLE & SATELLITE TELEVISION NETWORKS

License fees for basic networks grew 12.7 percent to $13.63 billion in 2004, while license fees for premium channels rose 4.2 percent to $4.55 billion. Total spending by both operators and advertisers on basic network and premium channels increased 12.2 percent to $32.07 billion in 2004.

With both DBS companies pointing to license fees as the reason for rate increases in 2005, attention has increasingly focused on the rate at which license fees have increased. Multichannel providers have griped about license fees at least since 2000, when Time Warner Cable yanked all ABC stations for a few days as a ploy in their battle with ESPN over escalating fees. Cox Communications battled with ESPN in 2004 in an effort to keep ESPN from raising its fees by more than 20 percent annually. A deal was finally struck, with sliding scales of rate increases that reportedly averaged 7.0 percent a year, versus 20.0 percent in the previous contract. The license deal slides from a 13.0 percent annual rise at the beginning of the contract to a 5.0 percent increase in the final year. Also in 2004, EchoStar Communications pulled all Viacom-owned CBS stations and cable networks off its DISH Network, and blacked out local CBS programming to 1.6 million subscribers in 16 cities, while also blacking out 9.5 million subscribers nationwide from 10 Viacom cable channels, including MTV and Nickelodeon. That dispute, too, was eventually settled. The average license fees for sports networks are substantially higher than the average license fees for non-sports networks.

Retransmission rights are also becoming an area of contention for cable and satellite operators. Traditionally, over-the-air broadcasters who were part of larger multimedia groups had supplied retransmission consent to cable operators gratis, in exchange for operators carrying their cable networks. However, stand-alone television broadcaster groups or individual stations have no such bargaining option, and have been pushing cable operators for cash in exchange for retransmission consent. Satellite providers typically pay local television stations 15 to 20 cents per subscriber to rebroadcast these analog signals. As this *Forecast* went to press, Cox and Cable One were battling Nexstar over retransmission rights in four southwestern television markets, and are not currently carrying several local ABC, CBS and NBC affiliates in those markets. Nexstar is holding out for 25 to 30 cents per viewer per month for retransmission rights; the cable operators are refusing to pay. This is being viewed as a test case by many in the industry, as the eventual resolution may well establish a precedent for many retransmission consent contracts that are up for renewal in 2006.

We expect basic network license fees to rise 9.9 percent in 2005 to $14.98 billion. In the face of fierce resistance, compound annual growth will slow to 8.5 percent from 2004 to 2009, with expenditures reaching $20.53 billion in 2009. Compound annual growth was 17.5 percent in the 1999-2004 timeframe. Ongoing challenges to increased license fees will suppress growth rates going forward. Spending on basic network advertising and license fees will post compound annual growth of 9.0 percent from 2004 to 2009 to $49.23 billion in 2009. Compound annual growth in license fees for premium channels will decelerate from 6.3 percent in the 1999-2004 period to 3.9 percent in the forecast period, with spending of $5.50 billion in 2009.

The Outlook For Spending on Cable & Satellite Television

Overall spending on cable and satellite television subscriptions, advertising and license fees will increase 8.7 percent to $101.54 billion in 2005, fueled by growth in license fee and advertising rates. Growth in the forecast period will be driven by increased ratings and audience share, continued investment in technology and programming, economic expansion and lower CPMs compared with broadcast television.

Total spending on wired cable will grow at a compound annual rate of 6.4 percent to $60.22 billion due mainly to increased spending on local advertising and increased use of video-on-demand services. When cable modem and telephony services are included, spending on wired cable will rise 9.1 percent during this period to $85.46 billion. Meanwhile, spending on satellite television will increase at a compound annual rate of 7.7 percent to $23.38 billion as satellite providers seek to increase their subscription base, add more DBS avail inventory and upgrade technology in order to offer more bundled services.

Total spending on cable and satellite television will grow at a compound annual rate of 7.5 percent from 2004 to 2009, reaching $134.22 billion in 2009, driven by strong increases in advertising spending and more moderate growth in license fees.

Overall subscription spending will be driven by bundling of interactive services with cable, extended channel capacity due to digital cable and new investments in the DBS market. Subscriber spending on basic, premium and PPV services will grow at a compound annual rate of 5.9 percent from 2004 to 2009 to $74.83 billion in 2009. Expenditures on basic services will rise at a compound annual rate of 5.9 percent in the forecast period to $57.18 billion in 2009, while spending on premium services will advance at a compound annual rate of 4.8 percent to $12.23 billion, expenditures on PPV services will expand 3.3 percent to $3.26 billion, and VOD spending will grow 20.3 percent to $2.16 billion. Cable subscriber spending on basic, premium, PPV

Cable & Satellite Television

2004 Communications Industry Forecast Compared with Actual Growth

Category	*2004 Forecasted Growth**	*Actual 2004 Growth†*
Wired Cable	—	3.4%
Satellite Cable	—	11.8
Basic Services	7.5%	7.3
Premium Services	5.1	6.7
Pay-Per-View	3.4	6.0
VOD	19.3	32.4
Advertising	13.5	16.1
License Fees	10.5	10.4
Total	8.8	9.7

*Veronis Suhler 2004 Communications Industry Forecast & Report
†Veronis Suhler Stevenson, PQ Media

and VOD services will grow at a compound annual rate of 5.1 percent to $50.50 billion, while satellite subscriptions for these services will grow at a slightly higher rate of 7.4 percent to $22.94 billion.

Total cable and satellite television advertising expenditures are expected to expand at a compound annual rate of 12.0 percent from 2004 to 2009, reaching $33.36 billion in 2009. Investments in programming will drive increased ratings and audience share, while a continuation of overall industry investment in technology and favorable CPMs compared with broadcast television will bolster advertising spending in the forecast period. In the local advertising arena, new demographic targeting services will help to drive growth. The continued expansion of regional sports networks will spur investment and growth in this sector. As digital cable develops a larger installed base, its proven ability to deliver vastly increased channel offerings and programming will come into play, and the continued success of original programming on both analog and digital services will attract advertising spending in the cable network sector.

FORECAST ASSUMPTIONS

- In an attempt to sell more bundled services and reduce subscriber churn, cable providers will ramp up marketing spending to better educate consumers on the benefits of newer products such as digital video recorders (DVRs), cable modems, high-definition television (HDTV) and voice over Internet protocol (VoIP).
- The growth of cable and satellite television advertising in the forecast period will be bolstered by the increased availability of interconnects, the ability of cable and satellite television to deliver advertisers tightly targeted demographics, and increased ratings and audience share.
- With multichannel penetration at 92.1 percent of all available U.S. television households, the cable and satellite TV sector is becoming mature and will no longer be able to drive revenue growth through new subscriber acquisitions. As a result, cable providers will have to shift their focus to improving average revenue per unit (ARPU) by investing in new technology—or for the satellite sector, strategic partnerships—and developing new or improved services such as VOD and VoIP that can be offered in bundled packages. DBS providers will seek to roll out local service in more markets, as well as provide services that are currently available only on wired cable systems, such as video-on-demand.
- In the face of ongoing challenges and fierce cable and satellite operator resistance to previous increases, the growth rate of license fees will slow in the forecast period.
- Although telephone service providers are attempting to move into the cable and satellite market, they will not be a major factor in the forecast period because they cannot currently compete with cable operators' investments in original programming and their ownership of cable networks.

Household, Advertiser & License Fee Spending On Cable & Satellite Television*

($ MILLIONS)

Year	Basic Services	Premium Services	Pay-Per-View	VOD	Total End-User Spending	Advertising	License Fees	Total Spending
1999	$27,460	$ 7,212	$2,123	$ 430	$37,225	$11,624	$ 9,441	$ 58,290
2000	30,164	7,314	1,824	450	39,752	13,788	10,748	64,288
2001	32,932	7,971	2,125	478	43,506	14,214	12,609	70,329
2002	36,560	8,649	2,507	526	48,242	14,736	14,730	77,708
2003	40,062	9,048	2,615	648	52,373	16,304	16,459	85,136
2004	42,990	9,657	2,771	858	56,276	18,925	18,175	93,376
2005	45,881	10,225	2,914	1,096	60,116	21,686	19,737	101,539
2006	48,637	10,752	3,035	1,343	63,767	24,258	21,321	109,346
2007	51,430	11,283	3,130	1,624	67,467	26,888	22,849	117,204
2008	54,247	11,752	3,196	1,911	71,106	29,746	24,462	125,314
2009	57,182	12,229	3,257	2,161	74,829	33,361	26,030	134,220

Sources: Veronis Suhler Stevenson, PQ Media, Sanford C. Bernstein, Cabletelevision Advertising Bureau, Federal Communications Commission Annual Report, Forrester Research, In-Stat, Kagan Research, Leichtman Group, LodgeNet, National Cable & Telecommunications Association, Merrill Lynch, Smith Travel Research, U.S. Department of Commerce

*To avoid double counting, cable modem and digital video recorder (DVR) spending are not included here. Spending is included in the Consumer Internet and Entertainment Media chapters, respectively.

Growth of Household, Advertiser & License Fee Spending On Cable & Satellite Television*

Year	*Basic Services*	*Premium Services*	*Pay-Per-View*	*VOD*	*Total End-User Spending*	*Advertising*	*License Fees*	*Total Spending*
2000	9.8%	1.4%	−14.1%	4.7%	6.8%	18.6%	13.8%	10.3%
2001	9.2	9.0	16.5	6.1	9.4	3.1	17.3	9.4
2002	11.0	8.5	18.0	10.1	10.9	3.7	16.8	10.5
2003	9.6	4.6	4.3	23.3	8.6	10.6	11.7	9.6
2004	7.3	6.7	6.0	32.4	7.5	16.1	10.4	9.7
2005	6.7	5.9	5.1	27.8	6.8	14.6	8.6	8.7
2006	6.0	5.1	4.2	22.6	6.1	11.9	8.0	7.7
2007	5.7	4.9	3.1	20.9	5.8	10.8	7.2	7.2
2008	5.5	4.2	2.1	17.7	5.4	10.6	7.1	6.9
2009	5.4	4.1	1.9	13.1	5.2	12.2	6.4	7.1
Compound Annual Growth								
1999-2004	9.4	6.0	5.5	14.8	8.6	10.2	14.0	9.9
2004-2009	5.9	4.8	3.3	20.3	5.9	12.0	7.4	7.5

Sources: Veronis Suhler Stevenson, PQ Media, Sanford C. Bernstein, Cabletelevision Advertising Bureau, Federal Communications Commission Annual Report, Forrester Research, In-Stat, Kagan Research, Leichtman Group, LodgeNet, National Cable & Telecommunications Association, Merrill Lynch, Smith Travel Research, U.S. Department of Commerce

*To avoid double counting, cable modem and digital video recorder (DVR) spending are not included here. Spending is included in the Consumer Internet and Entertainment Media chapters, respectively.

6

BROADCAST & SATELLITE RADIO

Total Radio Spending and Nominal GDP Growth, 2000-2009

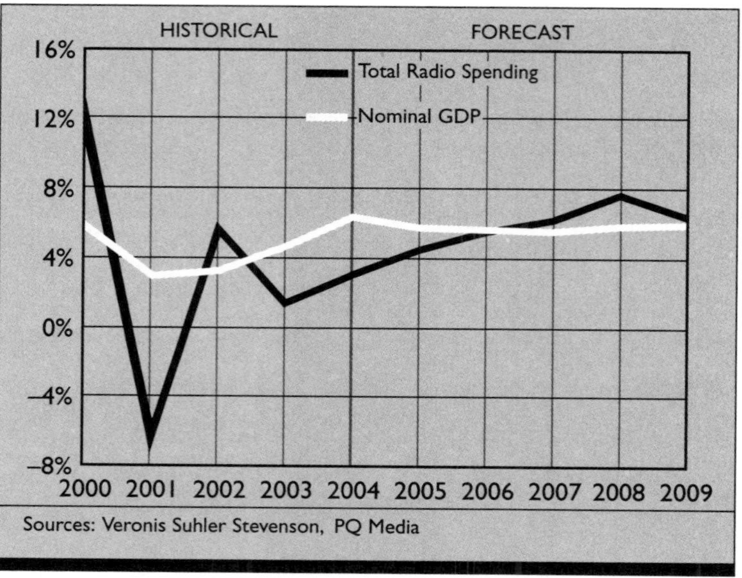

Sources: Veronis Suhler Stevenson, PQ Media

Growth of U.S. Broadcast & Satellite Radio Spending

	Local Advertising	*National Advertising*	*Satellite Radio*	*Total*
2004 Expenditures ($ Millions)	$15,479	$4,534	$293	$20,306
1999-2004 Compound Annual Growth (%)	2.6%	2.1%	—	2.8%
2004-2009 Projected Compound Annual Growth (%)	4.0%	4.1%	60.3%	6.2%
2009 Projected Expenditures ($ Millions)	$18,809	$5,534	$3,106	$27,449

Sources: Veronis Suhler Stevenson, PQ Media, Radio Advertising Bureau, Merrill Lynch, Harris Nesbitt, XM Satellite Radio, Sirius Satellite Radio

THE BROADCAST RADIO ADVERTISING MARKET IN 2004 AND 2005

The broadcast radio sector entered 2004 with optimism following a year in which advertising spending posted meager and decelerating growth, as spending rose just 1.0 percent in 2003 and lagged nominal GDP expansion for only the second time in more than a decade. The industry's confidence was bolstered in the first quarter of 2004, when broadcast radio advertising grew at an accelerated pace in each of the first three months of the year, capped by a 10.0 percent surge in March, often the annual inflection point for the market. In addition, advertising was pacing up in the mid-single digits in April, with local outperforming national spot, appearing to lend credence to the assumption that many advertisers wrote off the last couple of months of 2003 in an effort to drive sales in 2004.

While the year-over-year comparisons in March and April 2004 were easy due to the Iraq war's impact in 2003, many industry analysts at the time believed the positive signals emerging pointed to upward momentum that could have accelerated in the second half of the year. Some of these encouraging trends included the strengthening economy, the effect of campaign finance reform and the expected influx of advertising related to new car launches. Unfortunately, these sanguine views evaporated in the second half of 2004 and turned downright bearish on the industry's long-term outlook by the end of the year.

From a statistical standpoint, broadcast radio advertising growth peaked at 10.0 percent in March, decelerated to 4.0 percent in April, slowed even further to 1.0 percent in May and never pushed past 4.0 percent for the rest of 2004, including three months of negative growth. A look behind the numbers reveals that the 10.0 percent rise in March and the lofty forecasts for the second quarter of 2004 were misleading. Inventory sellout levels were low in March 2003 due to the effect of the Gulf War. As a result, even normal sellouts in March 2004 appeared extraordinarily improved; however, the true test of recovery—unit price increases—did not happen. In fact, the opposite occurred. Advertising rates were flat to down in March and

April 2004, masked by increased sellout levels that produced revenue gains. As the rest of the year unfolded, pricing was flat to down with little change in sellouts, which underpinned the anemic growth rates that characterized much of the rest of the year.

The result was a 2.1 percent increase to $20.01 billion in total broadcast radio advertising spending for 2004, despite accelerated GDP growth, a record year of political and Olympics advertising expenditures, and additional advertising dollars associated with an unprecedented number of new car launches for 2005. Local advertising, which accounted for 77.3 percent of all broadcast radio spending in 2004, grew 2.5 percent to $15.48 billion for the year, while national spot expenditures declined 0.5 percent to $3.45 billion and network spending increased 4.6 percent to $1.08 billion. National spot, which accounted for 17.3 percent of total broadcast radio spending, and network, which comprised 5.4 percent, combined for the other 22.7 percent of overall broadcast radio expenditures in 2004. While the 2.1 percent increase in total advertising represented accelerated growth over the 1.0 percent rise in 2003, it also signified the second consecutive year in which terrestrial radio advertising lagged annual GDP growth.

Despite the sector's relatively lackluster performances in 2003 and 2004, broadcast

Compound Annual Growth in Local And National Spot Advertising, 1999-2004

Medium	*Local*	*National*	*Total*
Radio Stations	2.6%	1.5%	2.4%
Cable Systems*	10.0	NA	10.0
Consumer Internet*	44.6	NA	44.6
Daily Newspapers†	1.0	3.7	1.7
Magazines*	3.5	NA	3.5
Out-of-Home	3.9	3.7	3.8
Television Stations	3.0	0.8	2.0
Weekly Newspapers*	4.4	NA	4.4
Yellow Pages‡	4.0	3.1	3.8

Sources: Veronis Suhler Stevenson, PQ Media, Borrell Associates, Harris Nesbitt, Kagan Research, Merrill Lynch, MNI, Newspaper Association of America, Outdoor Advertising Association of America, Radio Advertising Bureau, Simba Information, Universal McCann

*Data on national advertising sold by weekly newspapers, cable MSOs, local magazines, or local Internet sites are not available.

†Local includes retail only, not classified advertising.

‡Local includes Internet yellow pages.

Shares of Local and National Advertising

	Local		*National*		*Total*	
Medium	*1999*	*2004*	*1999*	*2004*	*1999*	*2004*
Radio Stations	19.2%	18.4%	13.1%	12.7%	17.6%	17.0%
Cable Systems*	4.3	5.8	NA	NA	3.2	4.4
Consumer Internet*	0.6	3.1	NA	NA	0.4	2.3
Daily Newspapers†	29.5	26.1	27.5	29.7	29.0	27.0
Magazines*	2.5	2.5	NA	NA	1.9	1.9
Out-of-Home	4.1	4.2	7.9	8.6	5.1	5.2
Television Stations	17.9	17.4	43.0	40.2	24.3	23.0
Weekly Newspapers*	6.2	6.5	NA	NA	4.6	4.9
Yellow Pages‡	15.7	16.1	8.4	8.8	13.9	14.3

Sources: Veronis Suhler Stevenson, PQ Media, Borrell Associates, Harris Nesbitt, Kagan Research, Merrill Lynch, MNI, Newspaper Association of America, Outdoor Advertising Association of America, Radio Advertising Bureau, Simba Information, Universal McCann

*Data on national advertising sold by weekly newspapers, cable MSOs, local magazines and local Internet sites are not available.

†Local includes retail only, not classified advertising.

‡Local includes Internet yellow pages.

Highlights

Broadcast radio advertising increased 2.1 percent to $20.01 billion in 2004, accelerating only slightly over 2003 despite faster GDP growth, record spending on political and Olympics advertising, and additional advertising related to a plethora of new car launches. Local advertising, which accounted for 77.3 percent of all broadcast radio spending, grew 2.5 percent to $15.48 billion in 2004, while national spot expenditures declined 0.5 percent to $3.45 billion and network spending increased 4.6 percent to $1.08 billion. Broadcast radio growth lagged GDP growth for the second consecutive year.

■

Broadcast radio advertising growth peaked at 10.0 percent in March 2004, but decelerated in April and May, and never pushed past 4.0 percent for the rest of the year, including three months of negative growth. Going behind the numbers shows that the surge in March and the lofty forecasts for the rest of the year were misleading due to low inventory sellout levels in 2003 as a result of the Gulf War. Unit price increases—the true test of recovery—did not happen, and actually were flat to down in March and April 2004, shrouded by increased sellout levels. As the year unfolded, pricing was flat to down with little change in sellouts, resulting in anemic growth for the rest of 2004.

■

Despite terrestrial radio's lackluster performances in 2003 and 2004, this sector has maintained its share of total advertising spending over the past five years. Broadcast radio expenditures grew at a compound annual rate of 2.5 percent from 1999 to 2004, accounting for about 10.6 percent of all advertising spending in 2004, virtually the same share as in 1999.

■

We believe the broadcast radio sector is transitioning from a growth business to a mature one, as a result of near-term pricing issues due to overcapacity, the lack of a sophisticated local sales management system and increased competition from local cable and satellite radio. Additionally, we don't foresee a significant event similar to the Internet advertising boom of the late 1990s. Therefore, we expect the growth of broadcast radio advertising to be more in line with, if not trailing, that of GDP over the next five years. As a result, broadcast radio will perform only slightly better in 2005 versus 2004, with advertising increasing 2.7 percent to $20.55 billion. We project spending on terrestrial radio advertising to grow at a compound annual rate of 4.0 percent from 2004 to 2009, reaching $24.34 billion in 2009, driven by 4.0 percent compound annual growth in local ad spending, 3.8 percent growth in national spot and 4.8 percent growth in network.

radio has maintained its share of total advertising industry spending over the past five years. And this segment is still considered a leading indicator of the traditional advertising industry's health. Broadcast radio expenditures grew at a compound annual rate of 2.5 percent from 1999 to 2004, and accounted for approximately 10.6 percent of all advertising spending in 2004, virtually the same share as in 1999. By the same token, local radio expenditures grew at a compound annual rate of 2.6 percent in the 1999-2004 period, and comprised about 15.1 percent of total local advertising spending in 2004, also nearly the same share as in 1999. But if radio is a leading indicator of the traditional advertising industry's health, the prognosis at the outset of 2005 was neutral.

The reasons for this outlook are rather simple but crucial to an advertising industry that is undergoing a rapid transition in this era of ad-skipping technologies and accelerating audience fragmentation. With near-term pricing issues due to overcapacity, the lack of sophisticated local sales management systems and increasing competition from the likes of local cable and satellite radio, the terrestrial radio sector is transitioning from a

Satellite radio spending, including subscriptions and advertising, rose 208.6 percent in 2004 to $293.4 million, as subscription expenditures grew 212.5 percent to $284.0 million and advertising spending increased 124.8 percent to $9.4 million for the year. Subscriptions, which accounted for 96.8 percent of all spending, are the primary driver of the satellite radio business, and OEM, content and licensing deals are driving more subscribers to the medium.

■

With a cadre of OEM, licensing and retail deals already completed or in negotiation, and a subscriber churn rate in the low single digits, we anticipate the number of subscribers to satellite radio will continue to grow at strong rates in 2005 and throughout the forecast period. Driven by this trend, subscription and advertising expenditures will again climb at triple-digit rates in 2005, and while growth will decelerate over the next five years, the expansion will outpace all other media segments. Satellite radio subscription spending will grow at a compound annual rate of 59.0 percent from 2004 to 2009, reaching $2.88 billion, while advertising expenditures will increase at a compound annual rate of 88.2 percent in the period to $222.2 million in 2009. Total satellite radio spending will grow 60.3 percent on a compound annual basis from 2004 to 2009, reaching $3.11 billion.

■

Radio listenership declined for the first time in a decade in 2004, as the total number of people listening to radio in the average quarter-hour declined 0.8 percent to 27.6 million. Radio listenership grew at a compound annual rate of 2.2 percent from 1999 to 2004, driven primarily by increased listening to the AM band, a departure from earlier trending, and the expansion of the at-home and automobile listening audiences.

■

Several developments, including Clear Channel's advertising reduction program, the continued rollout of HD radio and the emergence of Internet podcasts, will hasten a minor rebound in radio listening in 2005 and beyond. In addition, satellite radio is expected to have a positive impact on the growth of automobile listenership in the forecast period, while we anticipate commuting times to either level or increase going forward. As a result, the total number of people listening to radio in the average quarter-hour will grow at a compound annual rate of 1.0 percent from 2004 to 2009, reaching 29.0 million.

growth business to a mature one. In addition, we don't foresee a seminal event in the forecast period akin to the Internet advertising boom of the late 1990s and, as a result, we anticipate the growth of broadcast radio advertising will be more in line with, if not lagging, that of GDP over the next five years.

Nevertheless, there are several factors that hold potential for broadcast radio to exceed these expectations, although only time will tell if these factors grow into positive trends in the coming years. Among them, Clear Channel's inventory tightening initiative called "Less Is More," the rollout of digital radio technologies and the launch of Internet "podcasts," which will allow listeners to download exclusive radio programs and live concert performances.

Not surprisingly, optimism among industry executives and Wall Street analysts was more tempered at the beginning of 2005 than a year earlier, and this bearish outlook was fortified in the first quarter of the year. Broadcast radio advertising growth was up 3.0 percent in January, but was flat in February despite relatively easy comparisons with 2004. Nonetheless, these are the two least lucrative months of the year for terrestrial

Broadcast Radio Advertising Expenditures*

($ MILLIONS)

	Radio Stations						
Year	*Local*	*National Spot*	*Total Radio Station Advertising*	*Network Radio Advertising*	*National*[†] *Radio Advertising*	*Local Radio Advertising*	*Total Radio Advertising*
1999	$13,592	$3,211	$16,803	$ 878	$4,089	$13,592	$17,681
2000	15,223	3,596	18,819	1,029	4,625	15,223	19,848
2001	14,552	2,898	17,450	919	3,817	14,552	18,369
2002	15,134	3,275	18,409	1,000	4,275	15,134	19,409
2003	15,100	3,470	18,570	1,033	4,503	15,100	19,603
2004	15,479	3,453	18,932	1,081	4,534	15,479	20,013
2005	15,912	3,522	19,434	1,117	4,639	15,912	20,551
2006	16,436	3,610	20,046	1,161	4,771	16,436	21,207
2007	17,061	3,747	20,808	1,214	4,961	17,061	22,022
2008	17,999	3,972	21,971	1,292	5,264	17,999	23,263
2009	18,809	4,171	22,980	1,363	5,534	18,809	24,343

Sources: Veronis Suhler Stevenson, PQ Media, Radio Advertising Bureau, Merrill Lynch, Harris Nesbitt

*Not including satellite radio advertising.

[†]Network and national spot.

radio, representing only about 6 percent to 7 percent of annual spending apiece, compared to 8 percent to 9 percent for each of the remaining months. Advertising in March, the first month of the year with typical radio demand, increased 3.0 percent, with local growth up 3.0 percent and national up 5.0 percent. The March pacing was somewhat encouraging, given the unusual 10.0 percent surge in the same month of 2004, but we don't expect growth in any given month for the remainder of 2005 to exceed 4.0 percent. April spending is forecast to increase 3.0 percent, followed by 2.0 percent growth in May and 4.0 percent in June, and this is the pattern we expect for the rest of the year.

The interval from March through June tends to be a benchmark for broadcast radio because of the relatively large amount of advertising committed in this period. Accordingly, we expect broadcast radio to turn in a slightly better performance for the full year 2005 with 2.7 percent growth, compared with the 2.1 percent increase in 2004. As mentioned previously, however, there are several emerging developments that could alter the outlook for broadcast radio positively, albeit slightly, in 2005, but perhaps more so in the years that follow.

In response to complaints of increasing advertising clutter and amateurish 60-second spots that seemed to drone on forever, Clear

Growth of Broadcast Radio Advertising Expenditures*

Year	Radio Stations: Local	Radio Stations: National Spot	Radio Stations: Total Radio Station Advertising	Network Radio Advertising	National† Radio Advertising	Local Radio Advertising	Total Radio Advertising
2000	12.0%	12.0%	12.0%	17.2%	13.1%	12.0%	12.3%
2001	–4.4	–19.4	–7.3	–10.7	–17.5	–4.4	–7.5
2002	4.0	13.0	5.5	8.8	12.0	4.0	5.7
2003	–0.2	6.0	0.9	3.3	5.3	–0.2	1.0
2004	2.5	–0.5	1.9	4.6	0.7	2.5	2.1
2005	2.8	2.0	2.7	3.3	2.3	2.8	2.7
2006	3.3	2.5	3.2	4.0	2.9	3.3	3.2
2007	3.8	3.8	3.8	4.5	4.0	3.8	3.8
2008	5.5	6.0	5.6	6.5	6.1	5.5	5.6
2009	4.5	5.0	4.6	5.5	5.1	4.5	4.6
Compound Annual Growth							
1999-2004	2.6	1.5	2.4	4.2	2.1	2.6	2.5
2004-2009	4.0	3.8	4.0	4.8	4.1	4.0	4.0

Sources: Veronis Suhler Stevenson, PQ Media, Radio Advertising Bureau, Merrill Lynch, Harris Nesbitt
*Not including satellite radio advertising.
†Network and national spot.

Broadcast & Satellite Radio

Shares of Broadcast Radio Advertising Expenditures*

Year	Radio Stations: Local	Radio Stations: National Spot	Radio Stations: Total Radio Station Advertising	Network Radio Advertising	National† Radio Advertising	Local Radio Advertising
1999	76.9%	18.2%	95.0%	5.0%	23.1%	76.9%
2000	76.7	18.1	94.8	5.2	23.3	76.7
2001	79.2	15.8	95.0	5.0	20.8	79.2
2002	78.0	16.9	94.8	5.2	22.0	78.0
2003	77.0	17.7	94.7	5.3	23.0	77.0
2004	77.3	17.3	94.6	5.4	22.7	77.3
2005	77.4	17.1	94.6	5.4	22.6	77.4
2006	77.5	17.0	94.5	5.5	22.5	77.5
2007	77.5	17.0	94.5	5.5	22.5	77.5
2008	77.4	17.1	94.4	5.6	22.6	77.4
2009	77.3	17.1	94.4	5.6	22.7	77.3

Sources: Veronis Suhler Stevenson, PQ Media, Radio Advertising Bureau, Merrill Lynch, Harris Nesbitt
*Not including satellite radio advertising.
†Network and national spot.

Channel—the nation's largest broadcast radio station owner—announced an inventory tightening initiative in the second half of 2004 dubbed "Less Is More." The plan was aimed at appeasing radio listeners who data showed were increasingly switching channels or turning off their radios altogether as a result of a sharp rise in commercial minutes per hour in recent years. In some cases, stations were airing almost 20 minutes of commercials per hour. Accordingly, Clear Channel said it would reduce available advertising time to no more than 15 minutes of ads per hour and no more than six ads in a row. In addition, Clear Channel was hoping to get advertisers hooked on 30-second spots and increase revenues by charging more for two 30-second spots than for one 60-second ad.

Not surprisingly, some advertisers balked initially, but by March 2005 total commercial air time had declined 4.3 percent to 11 minutes per hour versus the same period the previous year. Also led by Clear Channel, which owns 1,200 or about 40 percent of the local stations nationwide, the percentage of commercial air time dedicated to 30-second spots soared 40.7 percent year-over-year in March 2005, compared with a 4.7 percent decline in 60-second spots. The result of this initiative in the first quarter of 2005 was a shortage of 60-second spots, which drove up sellouts and increased unit prices; however, 30-second spots remained undersold, indicating a shortage of demand. The net effect is that we believe the full impact of "Less Is More" won't be felt until later in the year, and the resultant benefits in spending growth likely will not materialize until 2006.

Another development that holds promise for terrestrial radio in the forecast period is the rollout of new digital technologies, particularly HD radio, which allows stations to broadcast their programs digitally, providing listeners with improved reception and audio quality, and new data services. These data services include displayed song and artist information, traffic and weather alerts, surround sound, multicasting (multiple audio sources at the same dial position) and on-demand audio services, such as store and replay of programs. We see this new technology as essential to the future of broadcast radio as the medium looks to expand beyond just ad-based music programming in an effort to compete with its emerging satellite radio competitors. But while 2,500 stations have committed to upgrading to digital quality, only 250 had done so by the end of 2004. Additionally, it may take at least several more years before even 1,000 stations nationwide have upgraded using this important new technology.

One more event that we see as having a potential positive impact on the future of broadcast radio is Clear Channel's launch in the first quarter of 2005 of a new Internet podcast program, in which the station owner will start broadcasting clips from its radio shows and hosting exclusive online concerts in an attempt to draw more traffic to its radio Web sites. Clear Channel's goal is to build listener relationships with local stations and increase ad revenues by selling online spots that will run with the concerts or podcasts, which are programs that listeners can download and listen to on their computers or digital audio players. Some industry analysts see the move as the first step toward radio station owners transitioning from simply broadcast radio companies to multifaceted music companies. Although we agree with this assessment to a certain extent, it will be many years before such a major transformation comes full circle.

While these positive developments hold potential for the future of broadcast radio, there are several negative trends that may offset this promise in 2005 and beyond. On the local front, terrestrial radio has come under increasing pressure in recent years from other media, particularly cable television. Radio for many years was seen as the low-cost alternative to other media, particularly in recessionary periods, offering advertisers a relatively inexpensive and efficient way to reach local consumers. But over the past few years, the establishment of the cable interconnect—which allows cable providers to offer advertisers efficient audience targeting—and the rise of local Internet advertising options have combined to put more pressure on local broadcast radio stations. The primary reason for this is that local stations lack a sophisticated

Percent Change in Spotload at Major Radio Groups in Top 9 Markets, 1Q 05 vs. 1Q 04

Owner	*YoY Change in :30 Inventory*	*YoY Change in :60 Inventory*	*YoY Total Change In Inventory*
Clear Channel	153.6%	−17.2%	−19.1%
Infinity	−3.3	0.4	1.1
Cox	21.5	−0.4	0.9
Emmis	5.0	−0.3	13.5
Salem	−28.7	1.2	−17.8
Beasley	−5.0	0.4	−13.5
Univision	−13.6	1.3	5.5
ABC/Disney	24.1	−3.7	−2.4
Radio One	45.7	−4.8	−10.7
Susquehanna	53.5	−3.3	3.1
Mount Wilson	27.6	−1.3	−4.3
Bonneville	−7.4	0.5	0.4
Total	40.7	−4.7	−4.3

Sources: Veronis Suhler Stevenson, PQ Media, Harris Nesbitt, Media Monitors

sales management system to track inventory levels and return on investment. While broadcast radio has managed to maintain its local market share in recent years, this could very well change in the coming years if such a system is not put in place.

Another troubling trend is the three-year slowdown in national spot advertising, which declined 0.5 percent in 2004. National spot advertising increased at double-digit rates for four consecutive years from 1997 to 2000 before the recession and dot-com meltdown sent this category into a double-digit tailspin in 2001. Following passage of the Telecommunications Act of 1996, which created three large station groups that controlled one-third of the market, these station giants touted their ability to increase bottom-line growth through back-office efficiencies, sales force consolidation and innovative national marketing campaigns using their new station clusters. For several years it appeared that they were correct as they melded their low-cost inventory with one-stop shopping packages that stimulated national growth. Following the one-two punch of the recession and dot-com downturn, however, national spot advertising came back strong in 2002, only to see growth decelerate each year since. Some of the reasons for the slowdown are the same as those impacting local radio, such as the cable interconnect and Internet advertising that provides immediate return on investment data. But in 2004 and 2005 another disturbing development emerged when the nation's largest national radio sales rep firm reported several negative events, including poor financials, and Wall Street analysts said they expected disruption in the sales force as a result, further clouding national spot advertising in 2005.

On the network front, the departure of Howard Stern from Infinity to Sirius Satellite Radio could have a substantial impact on network advertising in the second half of 2005 and particularly in 2006. Stern was one

Top 10 Radio Groups by Stations, 1999-2004*

Owner	*2004*	*2003*	*2002*	*2001*	*2000*	*1999*
Clear Channel	1,203	1,207	1,212	1,201	1,020	485
Cumulus	292	268	258	222	270	245
Citadel	214	218	205	205	207	122
Infinity	185	185	183	183	187	162
Entercom	105	105	102	96	97	87
Salem	94	92	84	82	72	50
Saga	78	71	67	56	—	—
Cox	76	76	75	79	82	60
Regent	75	76	—	—	—	—
Univision	72	—	—	—	—	—
ABC-Radio	—	74	65	—	—	43
Radio One	—	—	62	62	—	—
NextMedia	—	—	—	57	55	—
Marathon Media	—	—	—	—	83	92
Entravision	—	—	—	—	66	—
AMFM	—	—	—	—	—	458
Total	2,394	2,372	2,313	2,243	2,139	1,804
Increase	22	59	70	104	335	—
Growth	5.0%	2.6%	3.1%	4.9%	18.6%	—

Sources: Veronis Suhler Stevenson, PQ Media, *Who Owns What*

*Number of radio stations are listed only for the top 10 owners in a given year.

of the most high-profile targets of the federal indecency crackdown that swept the broadcast television and radio industries in the wake of Janet Jackson's breast-baring Super Bowl performance in 2004. Federal regulators pursued broadcast indecency with a vengeance in 2004, doling out large fines to stations carrying programs featuring shock jocks and sexually explicit themes. Stations carrying Stern were rapped with almost $500,000 in various fines for allegedly airing indecent comments and themes, a move that led Clear Channel to drop Stern permanently from six of its stations. In response, Stern decided to take his popular show to satellite radio beginning in January 2006. Stern's show is syndicated nationally and reaches about 15 million listeners a day, generating approximately $100 million in revenues for Infinity. Total network ad spending was $1.08 billion in 2004. With the controversial personality scheduled to leave Infinity in January 2006, Stern's network distribution is expected to begin drying up, possibly by as much as two-thirds by the end of the third quarter of 2005.

The Outlook For Broadcast Radio Advertising

As mentioned previously, we believe the broadcast radio sector is transitioning from a growth business to a mature one, as a result of near-term pricing issues due to overcapacity, the lack of sophisticated local sales management systems and increasing competition from other media such as local cable and satellite radio. Additionally, we don't foresee a significant event in the forecast period similar to the Internet advertising boom of the late 1990s. Therefore, we expect the growth of broadcast radio advertising to be more in line with, if not trailing, that of GDP over the next five years.

There are several factors, however, that hold potential for broadcast radio to surpass this outlook. In the near term, Clear Channel's inventory tightening initiative had begun to show results by March 2005, as commercial air time declined and the percentage of air time dedicated to 30-second spots surged. But despite a shortage of 60-second spots, which drove up sellouts and increased unit prices, 30-second spots remained undersold, indicating a shortage of demand. As a result, we believe the full impact of "Less Is More" won't be felt until later in the year, and the associated top-line benefits likely won't materialize until 2006.

We see digital radio as the key for broadcast radio to grow beyond just ad-based music programming, and we don't view satellite radio and other digital technologies as a near-term threat to terrestrial radio growth in 2005. But these technologies could have a long-term impact if broadcast radio does not move swiftly to implement its digital strategy. It likely will take satellite radio at least a decade to accumulate 40 million subscribers, which equates to only about 15 percent of broadcast radio's audience base. By comparison, the rapid growth of cable television has not put broadcast television out of business. In fact, total broadcast television advertising grew at a compound annual rate of about 4 percent from 1985 to 2004, despite a decline in the audiences of the three major networks to approximately 27 percent of U.S. households in 2004 from about 63 percent in 1985. Nevertheless, while 2,500 radio stations have committed to upgrading to digital quality, only 250 had done so by the end of 2004, and it may take at least several more years before even 1,000 stations nationwide have upgraded to the new technology.

Potentially offsetting the effects of these more upbeat trends, there are several more troubling developments broadcast radio must deal with in the forecast period. On the local front, terrestrial radio's lack of a sophisticated sales management system has left it vulnerable to losing market share to competitors such as cable television and the Internet. In addition, the slowdown in national spot advertising after several years of double-digit growth and the potential sales force disruptions as a result have hung another cloud over broadcast radio in 2005 and beyond. Finally, the departure of Howard Stern from Infinity to Sirius Satellite Radio could have a substantial impact on network advertising in 2005 and 2006, given that Stern's show reaches about 15 million listeners a day and generates approximately $100 million in revenues annually.

Taking these trends into account, the 3.0 percent increase in terrestrial radio advertising in March 2005 was relatively encouraging, but we don't expect growth in any given month for the rest of the year to exceed 4.0 percent. Accordingly, we expect broadcast radio to perform only slightly better for the full year 2005 compared with 2004. Total broadcast radio advertising is forecast to increase 2.7 percent to $20.55 billion in 2005. Local advertising is expected to rise 2.8 percent to $15.91 billion in 2005, while national spot will grow 2.0 percent to $3.52 billion and network will post decelerated growth at 3.3 percent to $1.12 billion for the year.

For the remainder of the forecast period, we project spending on total broadcast radio advertising will grow at a compound annual rate of 4.0 percent from 2004 to 2009, reaching $24.34 billion, driven by 4.0 percent compound annual growth in local ad spending to $18.81 billion in 2009. National spot advertising will rise at a compound annual rate of

Satellite Radio Subscriber Growth

	XM			Sirius			Total Satellite Radio Subscribers		
Year	*New Subscribers*	*Total Subscribers Year-End*	*Percent Change Year To Year*	*New Subscribers*	*Total Subscribers Year-End*	*Percent Change Year To Year*	*New Subscribers*	*Total Subscribers Year-End*	*Percent Change Year To Year*
2001	—	27,773	—	—	—	—	—	27,773	—
2002	319,386	347,159	1,150.0%	—	29,947	—	349,333	377,106	1,257.8%
2003	1,013,069	1,360,228	291.8	231,114	261,061	771.7%	1,244,183	1,621,289	329.9
2004	1,868,896	3,229,124	137.4	882,197	1,143,258	337.9	2,751,093	4,372,382	169.7
2005	2,361,811	5,590,935	73.1	1,408,870	2,552,128	123.2	3,770,681	8,143,063	86.2

Sources: Veronis Suhler Stevenson, PQ Media, XM Satellite Radio, Sirius Satellite Radio, Merrill Lynch

3.8 percent in the 2004-2009 period, reaching $4.17 billion, and network advertising will increase at a compound annual rate of 4.8 percent in the period to $1.36 billion in 2009.

THE SATELLITE RADIO MARKET IN 2004 AND 2005

While satellite radio accounted for a relatively small share of overall broadcast and satellite radio spending in 2004, the medium's share is growing quickly and it has become the darling of Wall Street and the media industry. Indeed, satellite radio has become the fastest-growing medium of all time, outstripping even cable television's sharp rise in the 1980s. The satellite radio segment accounted for only 0.4 percent of total broadcast and satellite radio spending in 2003, but that share jumped to 1.4 percent at the conclusion of 2004, and we expect the medium's share to continue its quick rise in 2005 and beyond. Satellite radio's share of all radio spending will reach 3.2 percent at year end 2005 and the medium is forecast to command 11.3 percent of total radio expenditures by the end of 2009.

Satellite radio spending, including subscriptions and advertising, rose 208.6 percent in 2004 to $293.4 million, as subscription expenditures grew 212.5 percent to $284.0 million and advertising spending increased 124.8 percent to $9.0 million for the year. Subscriptions, which accounted for 96.8 percent of all spending, are the primary driver of the satellite radio business, and OEM, content and licensing deals are driving more subscribers to the medium. Satellite subscriptions grew 169.7 percent in 2004 to 4.4 million, an addition of 2.8 million new subscribers in just one year. The triple-digit growth was spurred mainly by several new licensing deals closed by duopoly competitors XM Satellite Radio and Sirius Satellite Radio.

XM Satellite, which accounted for 73.9 percent of all satellite subscribers in 2004, has been at the forefront of the industry since its inception in 2001 by virtue of the fact that it raced out of the blocks first. The company has since inked OEM deals with General Motors, the world's largest auto maker, to provide XM's service as an option on most models and, more recently, with Hyundai to provide the service as standard equipment on all U.S. models. GM plans to produce more than 1.5 million XM-equipped vehicles in 2005, while Hyundai is scheduled to deliver more than 400,000 this year. As far as major licensing deals, XM holds the long-term rights to Major League Baseball.

Although it was slower to get started, Sirius Satellite—which accounts for the other 26.1 percent of satellite subscribers—has been moving at a frenetic pace to catch up with XM on all fronts. Since 2002, Sirius has penned OEM agreements with several car manufacturers to provide its service as an

Satellite Radio Spending

($ MILLIONS)

Year	*Subscription**	*Advertising*	*Total*
2001	$ 0.2	$ 0.3	$ 0.5
2002	17	3	20
2003	91	4	95
2004	284	9	293
2005	660	20	680
2006	1,176	51	1,227
2007	1,754	98	1,852
2008	2,337	156	2,493
2009	2,884	222	3,106

Sources: Veronis Suhler Stevenson, PQ Media, XM Satellite Radio, Sirius Satellite Radio, Merrill Lynch
*Less rebates and other costs.

Growth of Satellite Radio Spending

Year	*Subscription**	*Advertising*	*Total*
2002	8,385.0%	888.0%	4,212.6%
2003	435.6	68.6	388.8
2004	212.5	124.8	208.6
2005	132.4	112.8	131.8
2006	78.2	152.5	80.4
2007	49.1	94.7	51.0
2008	33.2	58.2	34.6
2009	23.4	42.9	24.6
Compound Annual Growth			
2004-2009	59.0	88.2	60.3

Sources: Veronis Suhler Stevenson, PQ Media, XM Satellite Radio, Sirius Satellite Radio, Merrill Lynch
*Less rebates and other costs.

option on various models, including Ford, BMW, Mitsubishi and Volkswagen. On the licensing front, Sirius has become the premiere provider of sports programming by signing deals with the National Football League, NASCAR, the National Basketball Association and the NCAA.

With many of the major content licensing deals already sealed up, we believe the future content battles will focus mainly on key on-air talent, although some of these deals have already been done. The most notable was Sirius's agreement to bring Howard Stern to the satellite landscape in 2006 through a five-year, $500 million deal. Meanwhile, XM signed on Opie & Anthony, another pair of shock jocks who fell victim to the federal indecency crackdown.

Both companies in 2004 decided to broaden their services beyond national programming by providing local traffic and weather data, a move that agitated traditional broadcasters into urging the FCC to investigate. But the FCC responded that limiting satellite radio to national programming was not necessarily its intention when it proposed a set of rules related to satellite radio in 1997. The issue is similar to that of the dispute over cable operators' right to offer local television programming, which led to the right-to-carry rules that remain a contentious subject today for broadcast, cable and satellite television operators. Satellite radio operators see this matter as critical to their long-term growth, much the way cable providers did, in that they believe local services are the added value their subscribers will increasingly demand. As a result, XM announced in 2004 that it would provide an instant traffic and weather service in 21 major markets, while Sirius began streaming regional Weather Channel reports to its listeners.

XM also has attempted to fend off emerging competition from Web-based radio by reaching an arrangement with America Online in the first quarter of 2005 to launch an Internet-based radio service that will be integrated into AOL's free AOL.com portal. AOL through AOL.com will make 130 of its radio stations and 20 XM stations available at no cost for unlimited listening throughout the Internet. An enhanced subscription-based version will feature 70 XM stations and more than 130 original and third-party AOL radio stations.

Meanwhile, XM and Sirius have also pursued arrangements with retailers to market their satellite radios for home and out-of-home use. XM rolled out its first wearable device in late 2004 called MyFi. While we believe OEM distribution will continue to be the primary driver of satellite radio penetration, given the various other portable music devices such as MP3 and iPod players, the potential of combining satellite radio with handheld devices like mobile phones could lead to greater retail distribution since consumers won't need to carry an extra device to garner the satellite platform.

But even with all the OEM, licensing and retail deals that have been done, the subscriber churn rate is a data point that should be watched closely in the coming years. The average monthly churn for non-promotional subscribers in the fourth quarter of 2004 was between 1.0 percent and 1.5 percent, depending upon the data source. Most industry analysts expect that rate to increase only slightly in 2005, but forecast churn to approach 2.0 percent at maturity, assuming an average subscriber life of approximately four years (similar to the length of a car lease). We project that between 55 percent and 60 percent of all promotional subscribers will convert to regular fee-paying subscribers in the near future. We expect total satellite radio subscriptions to grow 86.2 percent to 8.1 million by the end of 2005, with XM accounting for 68.6 percent of that total and Sirius the other 31.4 percent.

While advertising spending accounted for only 3.2 percent of total satellite radio expenditures in 2004, we expect ad spending to increase at a higher compound annual rate than subscription spending in the forecast period, and account for 7.2 percent of all expenditures at the conclusion of 2009. The main driver of this outlook was Sirius's hiring of former Viacom executive and radio advertising guru Mel Karmazin as CEO in the second half of 2004. Although Karmazin has been tight-lipped about his exact plans for Sirius on the advertising front, he has made it clear that advertising will become a major revenue stream for the company in the future. The addition of more advertising to a medium that touts itself as commercial-free presents a sticky situation for the duopoly, leading industry analysts to speculate about possible creative ways in which Karmazin may introduce new advertising programs. One idea is that of a two-tier system, one with advertising and one without. Another is the use of "mentions" melded directly into programs, something Howard Stern is known for on his Infinity show. Either way, satellite radio's affluent older male demographic is too attractive to completely pass up for the fledgling medium.

The Outlook For Satellite Radio

With a cadre of OEM, licensing and retail deals already bagged or in the works, and a subscriber churn rate in the low single digits, we anticipate that the number of subscribers to satellite radio will continue to grow at high rates in 2005 and throughout the forecast period. As a result, subscription spending and advertising expenditures will again climb at triple-digit rates in 2005, and although growth will decelerate as the base expands in the forecast period, the expansion will still outpace all other media segments. Satellite radio subscription spending will grow at a compound annual rate of 59.0 percent from 2004 to 2009, reaching $2.88 billion, while advertising expenditures will increase at a compound annual rate of 88.2 percent in the period to $222.0 million in 2009. Total satellite radio spending will grow 60.3 percent on a compound annual basis from 2004 to 2009, reaching $3.11 billion.

BROADCAST & SATELLITE RADIO LISTENING TRENDS

Radio listenership declined for the first time in a decade in 2004 due to several factors, not the least of which was the broadcast audience's frustration with the increase in commercial time per hour. Data in the first half

Listeners in the Average Quarter-Hour* (THOUSANDS)

	By Station Band		*By Location*					
Year	*AM Stations*	*FM Stations*	*At Home*	*In Automobiles*†	*Other Than Home or Auto*‡	*Total Out of Home*	*Radio Stations Affiliated With Radio Networks*	*All Radio Stations*
1986	6,715	17,472	12,644	5,275	6,160	11,435	15,575	24,187
1989	5,618	18,380	11,166	5,929	6,778	12,707	13,828	23,998
1994	4,904	19,050	9,816	7,067	6,944	14,011	11,784	23,954
1999	4,347	20,424	9,069	7,885	7,262	15,147	14,918	24,771
2000	4,648	20,476	10,137	8,286	7,097	15,383	17,350	25,124
2001	4,833	20,921	10,276	8,673	6,683	15,356	18,833	25,754
2002	4,987	22,170	11,056	8,752	7,321	16,073	19,364	27,157
2003	5,353	22,430	11,378	8,930	7,478	16,408	20,959	27,783
2004	5,237	22,328	11,361	9,037	7,167	16,204	20,971	27,565
2005	5,253	22,440	11,361	9,191	7,239	16,429	21,139	27,692
2006	5,284	22,619	11,395	9,402	7,347	16,749	21,414	27,903
2007	5,311	22,845	11,486	9,684	7,502	17,186	21,735	28,156
2008	5,374	23,257	11,636	10,052	7,712	17,764	21,952	28,631
2009	5,412	23,559	11,752	10,484	7,966	18,450	22,062	28,971

Sources: Veronis Suhler Stevenson, PQ Media, RADAR®, Copyright © Arbitron Inc., 2004

*Persons 12 and older reached in the average quarter-hour.

†Includes some satellite radio listening.

‡Includes work, portable radios and entertainment venues.

Growth of Radio Listening*

	By Station Band		By Location					
Year	AM Stations	FM Stations	At Home	In Automobiles†	Other Than Home Or Auto‡	Total Out Of Home	Radio Stations Affiliated With Radio Networks	All Radio Stations
1987	–10.8%	0.0%	–10.5%	5.9%	5.0%	5.4%	–6.3%	–3.0%
1990	–2.1	–0.3	–4.0	2.9	1.8	2.3	–1.7	–0.7
1995	3.2	–0.9	–1.8	3.1	–0.6	1.3	–5.4	–0.1
2000	6.9	0.3	11.8	5.1	–2.3	1.6	16.3	1.4
2001	4.0	2.2	1.4	4.7	–5.8	–0.2	8.5	2.5
2002	3.2	6.0	7.6	0.9	9.5	4.7	2.8	5.4
2003	7.3	1.2	2.9	2.0	2.1	2.1	8.2	2.3
2004	–2.2	–0.5	–0.1	1.2	–4.2	–1.2	0.1	–0.8
2005	0.3	0.5	0.0	1.7	1.0	1.4	0.8	0.5
2006	0.6	0.8	0.3	2.3	1.5	1.9	1.3	0.8
2007	0.5	1.0	0.8	3.0	2.1	2.6	1.5	0.9
2008	1.2	1.8	1.3	3.8	2.8	3.4	1.0	1.7
2009	0.7	1.3	1.0	4.3	3.3	3.9	0.5	1.2
Compound Annual Growth								
1999-2004	3.8	1.8	4.6	2.8	–0.3	1.4	7.0	2.2
2004-2009	0.7	1.1	0.7	3.0	2.1	2.6	1.0	1.0

Sources: Veronis Suhler Stevenson, PQ Media, RADAR®, Copyright © Arbitron Inc., 2004
*Persons 12 and older reached in the average quarter-hour.
†Includes some satellite radio listening.
‡Includes work, portable radios and entertainment venues.

of 2004 showed that terrestrial radio listeners increasingly were switching channels or turning their radios off altogether as a result of the sharp rise in commercial minutes per hour. Some stations were airing almost 20 minutes of advertisements in a given hour, leading to a host of complaints from listeners nationwide. Accordingly, Clear Channel in the second half of the year announced a plan to reduce available advertising time to no more than 15 minutes per hour and no more than six ads in a row.

But Clear Channel's plan had little impact on the dismal listening results that came in at the end of 2004, as the total number of people listening to radio in the average quarter-hour declined 0.8 percent to 27.6 million. Radio listenership grew at a compound annual rate of 2.2 percent from 1999 to 2004, driven primarily by increased listening to the AM band, a departure from earlier trending, and the expansion of the at-home and automobile listening audiences.

The largest decline in 2004 was registered by the other-than-home-or-auto category, which includes listening at work and through portable devices such as walkmans. The number of people listening to radio in the average quarter-hour at work and through portable devices dropped 4.2 percent in 2004 to 7.2 million, as this audience was more apt to listen to Web radio at work

Shares of Radio Listening*

	By Station Band		By Location			
Year	*AM Stations*	*FM Stations*	*At Home*	*In Automobiles*†	*Other Than Home or Auto*‡	*Total Out of Home*
1986	27.8%	72.2%	52.5%	21.9%	25.6%	47.5%
1989	23.4	76.6	46.8	24.8	28.4	53.2
1994	20.5	79.5	41.2	29.7	29.1	58.8
1999	17.5	82.5	37.5	32.6	30.0	62.5
2000	18.5	81.5	39.7	32.5	27.8	60.3
2001	18.8	81.2	40.1	33.8	26.1	59.9
2002	18.4	81.6	40.8	32.3	27.0	59.2
2003	19.3	80.7	40.9	32.1	26.9	59.1
2004	19.0	81.0	41.2	32.8	26.0	58.8
2005	19.0	81.0	40.9	33.1	26.0	59.1
2006	18.9	81.1	40.5	33.4	26.1	59.5
2007	18.9	81.1	40.1	33.8	26.2	59.9
2008	18.8	81.2	39.6	34.2	26.2	60.4
2009	18.7	81.3	38.9	34.7	26.4	61.1

Sources: Veronis Suhler Stevenson, PQ Media, RADAR®, Copyright © Arbitron Inc., 2004
*Persons 12 and older reached in the average quarter-hour.
†Includes some satellite radio listening.
‡Includes work, portable radios and entertainment venues.

and CDs on their mobile music players. Listeners via other out-of-home outlets declined 0.3 percent on a compound annual basis from 1999 to 2004. The largest audience category, at home, remained essentially flat in 2004 at 11.4 million people in the average quarter-hour, but grew at a compound annual rate of 4.6 percent from 1999 to 2004, mostly as a result of two unusually large upswings in listening data in 2000 and 2002.

The only category to post an increase in listenership in 2004 was the automobile audience. This category for the first time included some satellite radio listening data, which had a positive impact on the segment's overall performance as did the continued increase in traffic and commuting times. One study released in 2004 found that the average commuter in major cities such as New York, Los Angeles and Chicago spent between 50 and 93 hours annually traveling to and from work, which is double the number of hours spent commuting 20 years ago. As a result of these factors, automobile listeners increased 1.2 percent to 9.0 million in 2004. In the 1999-2004 period, the automobile audience grew at a compound annual rate of 2.8 percent.

The number of listeners to the AM band declined in 2004 for the first time in more than five years, following a relatively steady

Index of Radio Listening*

(1986=100.0)

	By Station Band		By Location					
Year	AM Stations	FM Stations	At Home	In Automobiles†	Other Than Home Or Auto‡	Total Out Of Home	Radio Stations Affiliated With Radio Networks	All Radio Stations
1986	100.0	100.0	100.0	100.0	100.0	100.0	100.0	100.0
1989	83.7	105.2	88.3	112.4	110.0	111.1	88.8	99.2
1994	73.0	109.0	77.6	134.0	112.7	122.5	75.7	99.0
1999	64.7	116.9	71.7	149.5	117.9	132.5	95.8	102.4
2000	69.2	117.2	80.2	157.1	115.2	134.5	111.4	103.9
2001	72.0	119.7	81.3	164.4	108.5	134.3	120.9	106.5
2002	74.3	126.9	87.4	165.9	118.8	140.6	124.3	112.3
2003	79.7	128.4	90.0	169.3	121.4	143.5	134.6	114.9
2004	78.0	127.8	89.9	171.3	116.3	141.7	134.6	114.0
2005	78.2	128.4	89.9	174.2	117.5	143.7	135.7	114.5
2006	78.7	129.5	90.1	178.2	119.3	146.5	137.5	115.4
2007	79.1	130.8	90.8	183.6	121.8	150.3	139.5	116.4
2008	80.0	133.1	92.0	190.6	125.2	155.3	140.9	118.4
2009	80.6	134.8	92.9	198.8	129.3	161.4	141.6	119.8

Sources: Veronis Suhler Stevenson, PQ Media, RADAR®, Copyright © Arbitron Inc., 2004

*Persons 12 and older reached in the average quarter-hour.

†Includes some satellite radio listening.

‡Includes work, portable radios and entertainment venues.

growth pattern from 1999 to 2003, a period that featured significant news events such as the 2000 presidential election, the 2001 terror attacks, the 2001 Afghanistan invasion and the 2003 Iraq war. The AM band most likely could not continue such strong growth, as the news/talk/sports format matures and listeners migrate to any one of a number of newer technologies for this information. AM listening grew at a compound annual rate of 3.8 percent from 1999 to 2004.

The migration of listeners from AM to FM in the 1980s and 1990s boosted FM's audience share to 82.5 percent in 1999; however, that share dropped two percentage points by 2003 as a result of the aforementioned factors. The number of people reached through the FM band in the average quarter-hour also decreased in 2004, but at a slower 0.5 percent rate to 22.3 million. FM listenership grew at a compound annual rate of 1.8 percent from 1999 to 2004.

The Outlook For Broadcast & Satellite Radio Listening

While overall radio listening declined in 2004, there are several developments that we believe foreshadow a rebound in 2005 and beyond. Among them, Clear Channel's commitment to reduce advertising clutter, the continued rollout of HD radio and the emergence of Internet podcasts, all of which have the potential not only to re-engage traditional listeners who have been displeased with broadcast radio in recent years, but also to attract new listeners. In addition, satellite radio is expected to have a positive impact on the growth of the automobile listening audience going forward, and there is no sign that commuting times will shorten anytime soon. Finally, we anticipate that an increase in sales of new satellite radios at retail, as well as the delivery of satellite radio content to various mobile devices, will bode well for the growth of the at-home and other-than-home-or-auto audiences in the forecast period. As a result, we project the total number of people listening to radio in the average quarter-hour will grow at a compound annual rate of 1.0 percent from 2004 to 2009, reaching 29.0 million. Automobile listening will outpace all other categories in the forecast period, increasing at a compound annual rate of 3.0 percent from 2004 to 2009, while listening through venues other than home or auto will rise 2.1 percent on a compound annual basis over the next five years.

Number of Radio Stations, by Format

Format	*1999*	*2000*	*2001*	*2002*	*2003*	*2004*	*2003-2004 Percent Change*	*1999-2004 Percent Change*
Country	2,253	2,189	2,132	2,084	2,041	2,021	–1.0%	–10.3%
News/Talk/Sports	1,350	1,393	1,471	1,517	1,579	1,686	6.8	24.9
Adult Contemporary	1,351	1,327	1,286	1,245	1,213	1,197	–1.3	–11.4
Religious	1,003	1,034	1,025	999	1,019	1,012	–0.7	0.9
Golden Oldies	848	846	827	804	822	816	–0.7	–3.8
Spanish	409	442	486	591	625	659	5.4	61.1
Classic Rock	546	580	599	622	639	641	0.3	17.4
Top-40	388	440	445	453	444	453	2.0	16.8
Standard/Big Band	544	536	520	474	448	424	–5.4	–22.1
Alternative/Modern Rock	240	294	344	332	334	335	0.3	39.6
Urban Contemporary	260	275	287	299	312	310	–0.6	19.2
Soft Contemporary	201	232	259	273	307	309	0.7	53.7
Album-Oriented Rock	163	146	141	156	162	171	5.6	4.9
Variety/Children/Full Service	95	103	91	93	97	111	14.4	16.8
Ethnic	64	65	77	80	82	83	1.2	29.7
Black/Rhythm & Blues	59	62	63	70	72	69	–4.2	16.9
All News	64	62	67	64	69	61	–11.6	–4.7
Easy Listening	78	69	49	42	38	33	–13.2	–57.7
Classical	35	36	30	32	33	28	–15.2	–20.0
Business News	26	29	37	32	36	26	–27.8	0.0
Jazz	48	19	20	13	8	4	–50.0	–91.7
Total	10,025	10,179	10,256	10,275	10,380	10,449	0.7	4.2

Sources: Veronis Suhler Stevenson, PQ Media, Center for Radio Information

Distribution of Radio Station Programming, By Format

Format	1999 Share Of Stations	2004 Share Of Stations	Point Change
Country	22.5%	19.3%	–3.1
News/Talk/Sports	13.5	16.1	2.7
Adult Contemporary	13.5	11.5	–2.0
Religious	10.0	9.7	–0.3
Golden Oldies	8.5	7.8	–0.6
Spanish	4.1	6.3	2.2
Classic Rock	5.4	6.1	0.7
Top-40	3.9	4.3	0.5
Standard/Big Band	5.4	4.1	–1.4
Alternative/Modern Rock	2.4	3.2	0.8
Urban Contemporary	2.6	3.0	0.4
Soft Contemporary	2.0	3.0	1.0
Album-Oriented Rock	1.6	1.6	0.0
Variety/Children/Full Service	0.9	1.1	0.1
Ethnic	0.6	0.8	0.2
Black/Rhythm & Blues	0.6	0.7	0.1
All News	0.6	0.6	–0.1
Easy Listening	0.8	0.3	–0.5
Classical	0.3	0.3	–0.1
Business News	0.3	0.2	0.0
Jazz	0.5	0.0	–0.4

Sources: Veronis Suhler Stevenson, PQ Media, Center for Radio Information

BROADCAST RADIO FORMATS

The foremost trend in broadcast radio formatting today is the proliferation of Spanish-language stations across the country. Once relegated to a few stations located near the borders with Mexico in states like Texas and California, as well as a handful of stations in large cities such as New York, Spanish-language programming has swept the nation with no attention paid to the compass dial. This trend, which reflects the shifting demographics of the U.S., has led to a 61.1 percent increase to 659 stations formatted for various Spanish-language programming in 2004 compared with only 409 stations in 1999. Also, the number of Spanish-language radio stations has nearly doubled over the past 10 years. The Spanish-language audience has grown about 37 percent since 1998, and in 2004 this audience represented approximately 9 percent of all radio listeners.

The Spanish format is by far the fastest-growing and shows no signs of abating, as the number of Spanish-language stations grew another 5.4 percent in 2004. Latin America has a heritage of small town radio stations where the radio serves as the community voice in many ways, providing message boards and information exchanges on issues ranging from employment and healthcare to child care and immigration. This tradition appears to have been replicated in the U.S. The Spanish format accounted for 6.3 percent of all stations in 2004 compared with 4.1 percent in 1999.

Meanwhile, news/talk/sports continues to expand as a programming choice, remaining the second most popular format in terms of number of stations behind only country, which continues to lose stations. News/talk/sports was the format of choice at 1,686 stations in 2004, a 6.8 percent increase over the previous year and a 24.9 percent rise since 1999. News/talk/sports was programmed at 16.1 percent of all stations in 2004. This format received a strong jolt in recent years as major news events filled the airwaves, including the 2000 election, the 2001 terrorist attacks, and the wars in Afghanistan and Iraq in 2001 and 2003, respectively. While country remains the most programmed format in America with a 19.3 percent market share, or 2,021 stations, this format continues to lose share, declining another 1.0 percent in 2004. Adult contemporary placed third with 1,197 stations, or 11.5 percent of the market, but the number of stations carrying this format has dropped 11.4 percent since 1999. Among the big format losers in 2004 was jazz, which plunged 91.7 percent since 1999, and easy listening, which cratered 57.7 percent in the five-year period.

Format Gainers and Losers, 1999-2004

Format Gainers	*Number of Stations Gained*	*Format Losers*	*Number of Stations Lost*
News/Talk/Sports	336	Country	–232
Spanish	250	Adult Contemporary	–154
Soft Contemporary	108	Standard/Big Band	–120
Classic Rock	95	Easy Listening	–45
Alternative/Modern Rock	95	Jazz	–44
Top-40	65	Golden Oldies	–32
Urban Contemporary	50	Classical	–7
Ethnic	19	All News	–3
Variety/Children/Full Service	16		
Black/Rhythm & Blues	10		
Religious	9		
Album-Oriented Rock	8		
Business News	0		

Sources: Veronis Suhler Stevenson, PQ Media, Center for Radio Information

The Outlook For Broadcast & Satellite Radio

Total broadcast and satellite radio spending, including broadcast advertising, satellite subscriptions and satellite advertising, is projected to increase 4.6 percent to $21.23 billion in 2005, as the low-single-digit growth in broadcast advertising expenditures is augmented by triple-digit expansion in both satellite subscription and advertising spending. Broadcast radio advertising expenditures are expected to rise 2.7 percent to $20.55 billion in 2005, while satellite radio subscription spending will climb 132.4 percent to $660.0 million and satellite radio advertising expenditures will increase 112.8 percent to $20.0 million for the year. Total satellite radio spending will rise 131.8 percent to $680.0 million in 2005.

Going forward, we project overall broadcast and satellite radio spending will grow at a compound annual rate of 6.2 percent from 2004 to 2009, reaching $27.45 billion, as the unprecedented expansion of satellite radio accentuates the relatively tempered growth of broadcast radio advertising. Spending on broadcast radio advertising will grow at a compound annual rate of 4.0 percent from 2004 to 2009, reaching $24.35 billion, driven by comparatively similar growth across all three ad segments, which will experience some acceleration in the latter part of the forecast period due to the various aforementioned trends. Meanwhile, satellite radio subscription spending will grow at a compound annual rate of 59.0 percent from 2004 to 2009, reaching $2.88 billion, while satellite radio advertising expenditures will increase at a compound annual rate of 88.2 percent in the period to $222.2 million in 2009. Total satellite radio spending will grow 60.3 percent on a compound annual basis from 2004 to 2009, reaching $3.11 billion, bolstered by various OEM, licensing and retail deals, and a low subscriber churn rate.

The total number of people listening to radio in the average quarter-hour will grow at a compound annual rate of 1.0 percent from 2004 to 2009, reaching 29.0 million, paced by an increase in automobile listening, as well as new technologies and content programs.

Total Radio Spending

($ MILLIONS)

Year	Broadcast Advertising*	Satellite Radio†	Total
1999	$17,681	—	$17,681
2000	19,848	—	19,848
2001	18,369	$ 0.5	18,369
2002	19,409	19	19,428
2003	19,603	95	19,698
2004	20,013	293	20,306
2005	20,551	680	21,231
2006	21,207	1,227	22,434
2007	23,022	1,852	23,874
2008	23,263	2,493	25,756
2009	24,343	3,106	27,449

Sources: Veronis Suhler Stevenson, PQ Media, Radio Advertising Bureau, Merrill Lynch, Harris Nesbitt, XM Satellite Radio, Sirius Satellite Radio
*Includes only broadcast radio advertising spending.
†Includes satellite radio subscription and advertising spending.

Broadcast & Satellite Radio

Growth of Total Radio Spending

Year	Broadcast Advertising*	Satellite Radio†	Total
2000	12.3%	—	12.3%
2001	–7.5	—	–7.4
2002	5.7	4,212.6%	5.8
2003	1.0	388.8	1.4
2004	2.1	208.6	3.1
2005	2.7	131.8	4.6
2006	3.2	80.4	5.7
2007	3.8	51.0	6.4
2008	5.6	34.6	7.9
2009	4.6	24.6	6.6
Compound Annual Growth			
1999-2004	2.5	—	2.8
2004-2009	4.0	60.3	6.2

Sources: Veronis Suhler Stevenson, PQ Media, Radio Advertising Bureau, Merrill Lynch, Harris Nesbitt, XM Satellite Radio, Sirius Satellite Radio
*Includes only broadcast radio advertising spending.
†Includes satellite radio subscription and advertising spending.

FORECAST ASSUMPTIONS

- The broadcast radio sector is transitioning from a growth business to a mature one as a result of several factors, including near-term pricing issues due to overcapacity, the lack of a sophisticated local sales management system and increasing competition from local cable and satellite radio. In addition, no seminal event is expected to emerge in the forecast period akin to the Internet advertising boom of the late 1990s. Accordingly, the growth of broadcast radio advertising is projected to be more in line with, if not trailing, that of GDP over the next five years.
- Several factors, however, hold potential for broadcast radio to exceed these expectations in the coming years, including Clear Channel's inventory tightening initiative, the rollout of digital radio and the launch of Internet podcasts, allowing listeners to download radio programs and live concerts.
- Nevertheless, there are several more troubling developments that terrestrial radio must deal with in the forecast period that may offset these positive trends, such as the lack of an effective local sales management system, the slowdown in national spot advertising and the departure of Howard Stern from broadcast to satellite radio, which could have a substantial impact on network advertising in 2005 and 2006.
- The number of subscribers to satellite radio will continue to grow at high rates in 2005 and throughout the forecast period, driven by a spate of OEM, licensing and retail deals, and a subscriber churn rate in the low single digits. As a result, subscription and advertising spending will again climb at triple-digit rates in 2005, and although growth will decelerate somewhat in the forecast period, the expansion will still outpace all other media segments.
- Several developments emerged in 2005 that foreshadow a rebound in radio listening, following the first decline in a decade in 2004. Among them, Clear Channel's commitment to reduce advertising clutter, the continued rollout of HD radio and the emergence of Internet podcasts. In addition, satellite radio is expected to have a positive impact on the growth of automobile listenership going forward, and there is no sign that commuting times will shorten anytime soon. Finally, the anticipated increase in satellite radio sales at retail and the delivery of satellite radio content to mobile devices bodes well for future listenership.

2004 Communications Industry Forecast Compared with Actual Growth

Category	*2004 Forecasted Growth**	*Actual 2004 Growth†*
Radio Stations	6.6%	1.9%
Local	6.7	2.5
National Spot	6.3	−0.5
Radio Networks	7.2	4.6
Satellite Radio	252.9	208.6
Total Radio	7.8	3.1

*Veronis Suhler Stevenson 2004 Communications Industry Forecast & Report
†Veronis Suhler Stevenson, PQ Media

Recent Fund IV Portfolio Investment

7

ENTERTAINMENT MEDIA

Entertainment Media

Total Entertainment Media Spending and Nominal GDP Growth, 2000-2009

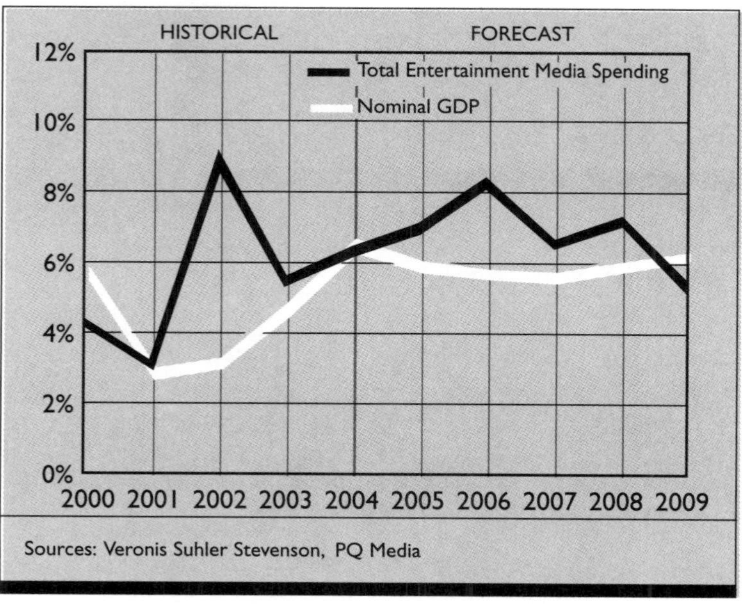

Sources: Veronis Suhler Stevenson, PQ Media

SUMMARY OF THE ENTERTAINMENT MEDIA MARKET IN 2004 AND 2005

Spending on entertainment media grew 6.5 percent to $88.56 billion in 2004, fueled by strong growth in the filmed entertainment segment due to investments in broadcast and cable television programming, and strong consumer spending on DVD rentals and sales. The burgeoning market for interactive television (ITV) and wireless content also contributed to the filmed entertainment segment's growth. While expenditures on in-home filmed entertainment posted solid growth in 2004, box office spending was sluggish. Meanwhile, spending on recorded music rebounded in 2004, driven by successful album releases, attractive CD pricing and growing demand for legal online music downloads. Spending on interactive entertainment, however, was hampered by the lack of a new console system launch during the year.

Although the entertainment market's growth in 2004 accelerated from the 5.8 percent performance the previous year, it trailed nominal GDP slightly—a minor disappointment considering the market's growth exceeded that of GDP in three of the previous four years. Nevertheless, strong growth in filmed entertainment in the first half of 2005 foreshadowed accelerated growth in the overall entertainment media market for the full year, as the market is expected to outpace GDP once again. Deeper ITV penetration, growing demand for wireless content and increased spending on new scripted programs by television networks were driving the gains in filmed entertainment in the first half of 2005. The growth of interactive entertainment spending is also expected to quicken in 2005 when new console systems are released later in the year, as well as when new titles are developed for the new PlayStation Portable (PSP), but recorded music's 2004 rebound will be short-lived, as spending will decline again in 2005. Overall expenditures on entertainment media are projected to increase 7.1 percent to $94.86 billion for the full-year 2005.

The largest segment of the entertainment industry, filmed entertainment, grew 7.7 percent to $68.18 billion in 2004, due primarily to increased household penetration of DVD players, falling DVD software prices and growth in the television programming sector. The number of DVD households grew 40.0 percent to 65.4 million in 2004. The growing popularity of DVDs somewhat suppressed box office spending in 2004, as consumers waited for films to come out on DVD rather than view them in theaters. Box office expenditures grew only 0.5 percent to $9.54 billion in 2004, due to a decline in attendance. Rising ticket prices helped offset the drop in attendance and pushed 21 movies past the $100 million revenue mark, while five exceeded $200 million, and three were among the 10 highest-grossing movies of all time. Box office spending is expected to show modest growth in 2005, due in part to the release of *Star Wars: Episode III: Revenge of the Sith* and new versions of *The Pink Panther*, *The Dukes of Hazzard*, and *Charlie and the Chocolate Factory*, a remake of *Willy Wonka & the Chocolate Factory*.

The television programming subsegment of filmed entertainment expanded 9.3 percent to $27.36 billion in 2004, as networks invested more money in expensive scripted dramas and relied less on low-budget reality shows. This trend will continue in 2005, when we expect television and cable broadcasters to boost spending 4.3 percent to $28.52 billion. Though broadcast television's share of programming is declining slightly as cable networks invest in more original shows, the broadcast networks represent approximately 45 percent of the market. This investment in Hollywood production keeps the pipeline filled and the system sustained. Meanwhile, the growing adoption of ITV and wireless content services fueled a 78.0 percent

Total Entertainment Media Spending ($ MILLIONS)

Year	*Filmed Entertainment*	*Recorded Music*	*Interactive Entertainment*	*Total*
1999	$ 45,723	$14,585	$ 6,540	$ 66,848
2000	48,779	14,327	6,555	69,661
2001	51,494	13,745	6,953	72,192
2002	58,197	12,615	7,819	78,631
2003	63,292	11,855	8,022	83,169
2004	68,183	12,154	8,227	88,564
2005	74,508	11,849	8,505	94,862
2006	81,845	11,502	9,346	102,693
2007	87,943	11,505	10,264	109,712
2008	95,138	11,135	11,510	117,783
2009	101,150	10,953	12,246	124,349

Sources: Veronis Suhler Stevenson, PQ Media, Adams Media Research, Alexander & Associates, Business 2.0, Cinema Advertising Council, Digital Entertainment Group, DIRECTV, EchoStar, Entertainment Software Association, In Demand, Insight Research, InStat/MDR, Kagan Research, Leichtman Research Group, Lexis/Nexis, LodgeNet, Motion Picture Association of America, Myers Mediaenomics, National Cable & Telecommunications Association, NPD FunWorld, Recording Industry Association of America, Rentrak, ReplayTV, Screenvision, Smith Travel Research, SoundScan, Universal McCann, U.S. Bureau of the Census, *Variety*, *Video Business*, Video Software Dealers Association, World Airline Entertainment Association, Yankee Group

Growth of U.S. Spending on Entertainment Media

	Filmed Entertainment	*Recorded Music*	*Interactive Entertainment*	*Total*
2004 Expenditures ($ Millions)	$68,183	$12,154	$8,227	$88,564
1999-2004 Compound Annual Growth (%)	8.3%	–3.6%	4.7%	5.8%
2004-2009 Projected Compound Annual Growth (%)	8.2%	–2.1%	8.3%	7.0%
2009 Projected Expenditures ($ Millions)	$101,150	$10,953	$12,246	$124,349

Sources: Veronis Suhler Stevenson, PQ Media, Adams Media Research, Alexander & Associates, Business 2.0, Cinema Advertising Council, Digital Entertainment Group, DIRECTV, EchoStar, Entertainment Software Association, In Demand, Insight Research, InStat/MDR, Kagan Research, Leichtman Research Group, Lexis/Nexis, LodgeNet, Motion Picture Association of America, Myers Mediaenomics, National Cable & Telecommunications Association, NPD FunWorld, Recording Industry Association of America, Rentrak, ReplayTV, Screenvision, Smith Travel Research, SoundScan, Universal McCann, U.S. Bureau of the Census, *Variety*, *Video Business*, Video Software Dealers Association, World Airline Entertainment Association, Yankee Group

Growth of Total Entertainment Media Spending

Year	*Filmed Entertainment*	*Recorded Music*	*Interactive Entertainment*	*Total*
2000	6.7%	–1.8%	0.2%	4.2%
2001	5.6	–4.1	6.1	3.6
2002	13.0	–8.2	12.5	8.9
2003	8.8	–6.0	2.6	5.8
2004	7.7	2.5	2.5	6.5
2005	9.3	–2.5	3.4	7.1
2006	9.8	–2.9	9.9	8.3
2007	7.5	0.0	9.8	6.8
2008	8.2	–3.2	12.1	7.4
2009	6.3	–1.6	6.4	5.6
Compound Annual Growth				
1999-2004	8.3	–3.6	4.7	5.8
2004-2009	8.2	–2.1	8.3	7.0

Sources: Veronis Suhler Stevenson, PQ Media, Adams Media Research, Alexander & Associates, Business 2.0, Cinema Advertising Council, Digital Entertainment Group, DIRECTV, EchoStar, Entertainment Software Association, In Demand, Insight Research, InStat/MDR, Kagan Research, Leichtman Research Group, Lexis/Nexis, LodgeNet, Motion Picture Association of America, Myers Mediaenomics, National Cable & Telecommunications Association, NPD FunWorld, Recording Industry Association of America, Rentrak, ReplayTV, Screenvision, Smith Travel Research, SoundScan, Universal McCann, U.S. Bureau of the Census, *Variety*, *Video Business*, Video Software Dealers Association, World Airline Entertainment Association, Yankee Group

Shares of Total Entertainment Media Spending

Year	*Filmed Entertainment*	*Recorded Music*	*Interactive Entertainment*
1999	68.4%	21.8%	9.8%
2000	70.0	20.6	9.4
2001	71.3	19.0	9.6
2002	74.0	16.0	9.9
2003	76.1	14.3	9.6
2004	77.0	13.7	9.3
2005	78.5	12.5	9.0
2006	79.7	11.2	9.1
2007	80.2	10.5	9.4
2008	80.8	9.5	9.8
2009	81.3	8.8	9.8

Sources: Veronis Suhler Stevenson, PQ Media, Adams Media Research, Alexander & Associates, Business 2.0, Cinema Advertising Council, Digital Entertainment Group, DIRECTV, EchoStar, Entertainment Software Association, In Demand, Insight Research, InStat/MDR, Kagan Research, Leichtman Research Group, Lexis/Nexis, LodgeNet, Motion Picture Association of America, Myers Mediaenomics, National Cable & Telecommunications Association, NPD FunWorld, Recording Industry Association of America, Rentrak, ReplayTV, Screenvision, Smith Travel Research, SoundScan, Universal McCann, U.S. Bureau of the Census, *Variety*, *Video Business*, Video Software Dealers Association, World Airline Entertainment Association, Yankee Group

gain in spending on these services to $3.23 billion in 2004, not including video-on-demand (VOD). The pace of growth in this sector is projected to remain in the double digits throughout the forecast period as household penetration of ITV technology expands and more consumers download wireless content.

Meanwhile, recorded music spending rebounded in 2004 to post a gain of 2.5 percent to $12.15 billion, the market's first gain in five years. The music business continues to be driven by hit titles, as the top 10 albums of 2004 outsold the 10 bestselling albums of the previous year, spurring growth in the market. CD sales rose partly as a result of a 0.9 percent decrease in the average price of a music album to $14.93. CD sales represented more than 94 percent of all music revenues in 2004. Despite the music industry's 2004 recovery, we expect recorded music expenditures to decline during the forecast period, owing to the heavy reliance on blockbusters to drive growth and continued losses to digital piracy.

The interactive entertainment segment continues to draw consumer attention and dollars away from other entertainment media, such as the box office and music. The typical gamer plays for nearly seven hours a week and no longer fits the stereotype of being a teenage boy; in contrast, 40.0 percent of gamers are women, and the average age of a gamer is now 26. Interactive entertainment spending, which includes expenditures on console videogames, computer game and entertainment software, and videogame advertising, increased 2.5 percent to $8.23 billion in 2004. Growth was tempered by the lack of a new major videogame console release, which typically fuels new hardware and software sales. New videogame consoles from Sony and Microsoft will not be released until the second half of 2005, but will help drive a 3.4 percent increase in spending to $8.51 billion in 2005.

Total expenditures on entertainment media are expected to grow at a compound annual rate of 7.0 percent from 2004-2009, reaching $124.35 billion in 2009. Continued expansion in the ITV, wireless and home video sectors, and renewed spending on TV programming and video console games will drive growth.

Filmed Entertainment

Theatrical Films

The Theatrical Films Market in 2004 and 2005

Total box office expenditures grew a modest 1.3 percent to $9.98 billion in 2004, due primarily to strong movie screen advertising growth. After a slight downturn in 2003, consumer box office spending increased 0.5 percent to $9.54 billion in 2004 as a result of higher ticket prices. Escalating prices suppressed admissions, which fell 2.4 percent to 1.54 billion for the year, a trend that began after a record-setting year in 2002. Instead of paying high ticket prices at theaters, consumers are spending more money to watch movies at home, taking advantage of DVDs and VOD.

While overall attendance was down in 2004, family movies and big-budget blockbusters continued to draw crowds. The two biggest box office draws in 2004 were PG-rated *Shrek 2* and PG-13-rated *Spider-Man 2*, which grossed $437.0 million and $373.0 million, respectively. The top five movies of 2004 all grossed over $200 million, including three that surpassed the $300 million mark. However, there were only 21 movies that exceeded the $100 million mark, compared to 26 in 2003, which suggests that audiences are gravitating toward bigger releases and dismissing marginal films.

The box office success of *Spider-Man 2* propelled Sony to the top spot among distributors in 2004, with $872.0 million in domestic box office receipts. DreamWorks, which appealed to audiences with *Shrek 2* and *Shark Tale*, followed with $859.0 million, while Buena Vista ranked third with $823.0 million. These numbers reflect total sales from the top 50 movies released in 2004. Overall, distributors generated $6.04 billion from the top 50 films of the year.

Lackluster growth in consumer spending at the box office was offset by strong growth in advertising, as marketers continue to explore this emerging ad medium that offers them a captive audience. Advertising on

Top 13 Titles versus Other Releases

Category	*2003 ($ Millions)*	*2004 ($ Millions)*	*Percent Change*
Top 13	$2,706	$2,973	9.9%
Others	6,783	6,566	–3.2
Total	9,489	9,539	0.5

Sources: Veronis Suhler Stevenson, PQ Media, AC Nielsen EDI, Motion Picture Association of America, *Variety*

Top Box Office Titles Grossing More Than $100 Million in 2004

Film	*Distributor*	*2004 Domestic Box Office Gross ($ Millions)*
Shrek 2	DreamWorks	$ 437
Spider-Man 2	Sony	373
The Passion of the Christ	New Market	370
The Incredibles	Buena Vista	253
Harry Potter and the Prisoner of Azkaban	Warner Brothers	249
The Day After Tomorrow	Fox	187
The Bourne Supremacy	Universal	176
Meet The Fockers	Universal	176
Shark Tale	DreamWorks	161
The Polar Express	Warner Brothers	157
National Treasure	Buena Vista	156
I, Robot	Fox	145
Troy	Warner Brothers	133
50 First Dates	Sony	121
Van Helsing	Universal	120
Fahrenheit 9/11	Lions Gate	119
DodgeBall: A True Underdog Story	Fox	114
The Village	Buena Vista	114
The Grudge	Sony	110
Ocean's Twelve	Warner Brothers	110
Collateral	DreamWorks	100
Total		3,881

Sources: Veronis Suhler Stevenson, PQ Media, *Variety*

HIGHLIGHTS

Filmed Entertainment

Total expenditures on filmed entertainment—including box office, home video, interactive television (ITV) and wireless content, and television programming—increased 7.7 percent to $68.18 billion in 2004. Continued growth in ITV and wireless content, as well as in-home video spending, fueled the gain. Compound annual growth during the forecast period is projected to be 8.2 percent, compared with 8.3 percent in the 1999-2004 period, reaching $101.15 billion in 2009.

■

Box office spending grew only 0.5 percent to $9.54 billion in 2004, due to a 2.4 percent decline in admissions to $1.54 billion. Ticket price increases and double-digit growth in movie screen advertising helped offset the drop in admissions, leading to overall growth of 1.3 percent in 2004 to $9.98 billion. Compound annual growth from 1999 to 2004 was 5.7 percent, driven by steady double-digit growth in 2001 and 2002.

■

Spending to rent and buy DVDs grew 32.9 percent to $21.79 billion in 2004, owing to the rapidly growing installed base of DVD players and attractive retail prices on DVDs. Sales of DVDs grew 30.8 percent to $16.05 billion in 2004, as the average retail price of a DVD dropped $1.80 to $16.04. Spending on videocassettes continued to decline.

■

Total ITV spending surged 78.0 percent in 2004 to $3.23 billion, fueled by continued growth in the digital video recorder (DVR) sector and wireless content use. DVR households grew 41.2 percent in 2004 to 4.9 million, with more than 2.6 million of those households subscribing through direct broadcast satellite. Stand-alone and cable services accounted for 1.1 million subscribers each.

■

Broadcast television networks and stations boosted spending on programming 9.3 percent to $27.36 billion in 2004, as they relied less on low-budget reality shows and developed more expensive scripted programs. The cable and satellite television segment increased its investment in original and syndicated programs in an effort to draw subscribers and bolster ratings; expenditures rose 9.9 percent to nearly $7.86 billion for the year.

movie screens increased 21.3 percent to $438.0 million in 2004.

The number of theatrical screens increased 1.3 percent to 36,660 in 2004, marking the second consecutive year of growth. Consolidation remains a growing trend in the movie theater business, as the total number of facilities shrank 1.0 percent to 6,012 in 2004. The number of multiplex (8 to 16 screens) and megaplex (16-plus screens) facilities rose 3.4 percent and 6.7 percent, respectively, while single-screen and miniplex (2 to 7 screens) theaters fell 3.3 and 3.4 percent, correspondingly. Smaller theaters still control the bulk of the market with a 66.0 percent share; however, the increasing cost of real estate and pressure for greater yield per facility will ultimately favor the larger theater chains. The adoption of digital screens worldwide continued its meteoric rise in 2004, with the number of screens increasing 80.0 percent over the 328 in place the prior year. Nearly one-fifth of those screens are in the U.S., where digital screens increased 10.0 percent to 66 in 2004.

THE OUTLOOK FOR THEATRICAL FILMS

Driven by several major film releases, continued growth in cinema advertising and slightly higher ticket prices, we project total box office spending will increase 2.0 percent to $10.18 billion in 2005. Overall box office expenditures will grow at a compound annual rate of 2.8 percent from 2004 to 2009, reaching $11.47 billion in 2009.

Box office spending was tepid in the first quarter of 2005, with only four films topping the $100 million mark, led by *Hitch* with

Leading Distributors of Top 50 Films, 2004

Distributor	*Domestic Box Office Gross ($ Millions)*
Sony	$ 872
DreamWorks	859
Buena Vista	823
Warner Bros.	821
Universal	752
Fox	679
Paramount	450
Newmarket	370
New Line	160
Lions Gate	119
Miramax	66
MGM/UA	65
Total	6,036

Sources: Veronis Suhler Stevenson, PQ Media, *Variety*

Number of Box Office Screens

Year	*Indoor*	*Digital*	*Drive-In*	*Total*
1999	33,440	5	737	34,182
2000	36,679	18	717	37,414
2001	36,110	30	654	36,794
2002	34,630	50	650	35,330
2003	35,499	60	647	36,206
2004	35,993	66	601	36,660

Sources: Veronis Suhler Stevenson, PQ Media, Motion Picture Association of America, dlp.com

Growth in the Number of Box Office Screens

Year	*Indoor*	*Digital*	*Drive-In*	*Total*
2000	9.7%	260.0%	–2.7%	9.5%
2001	–1.6	66.7	–8.8	–1.7
2002	–4.1	66.7	–0.6	–4.0
2003	2.5	20.0	–0.5	2.5
2004	1.4	10.0	–7.1	1.3

Sources: Veronis Suhler Stevenson, PQ Media, Motion Picture Association of America, dlp.com

Box Office Admissions, Average Prices, Box Office Advertising And Total Spending

Year	*Admissions (Millions)*	*Average Price*	*Box Office Spending ($ Millions)*	*Movie Screen Advertising ($ Millions)*	*Total Box Office Spending ($ Millions)*
1999	1,465	$5.08	$ 7,448	$129	$ 7,577
2000	1,421	5.39	7,661	194	7,855
2001	1,487	5.66	8,413	246	8,659
2002	1,639	5.81	9,520	301	9,821
2003	1,574	6.03	9,489	361	9,850
2004	1,536	6.21	9,539	438	9,977
2005	1,528	6.32	9,653	522	10,175
2006	1,542	6.37	9,827	608	10,435
2007	1,548	6.51	10,074	694	10,768
2008	1,545	6.66	10,285	782	11,067
2009	1,567	6.77	10,604	863	11,467

Sources: Veronis Suhler Stevenson, PQ Media, Motion Picture Association of America, Cinema Advertising Council, Screenvision

$176.0 million in total receipts. But expectations were more than met for the spring release of *Star Wars: Episode III: Revenge of the Sith*, the last installment of the highly successful and profitable science-fiction franchise, which grossed more in its first four days than any film in history. Other films anticipated to attract audiences to the box office in 2005 include the newest caped crusader flick, *Batman Begins*; *Charlie and the Chocolate Factory*, a contemporary remake of the 1971 classic *Willy Wonka & the Chocolate Factory*; and new takes on *The Pink Panther* and *The Dukes of Hazzard*. Whether or not these movies deliver on their potential or fall short—as did *Starsky & Hutch* in 2004—will impact how major studios approach remakes in the future.

In contrast, the success of lower-budget movies, such as Mel Gibson's *The Passion of the Christ* and Michael Moore's documentary *Fahrenheit 9/11*, will push production companies toward not only niche genres, but also potentially controversial ones. Controversy attracts publicity, and for studios and distributors that are cutting back on marketing expenditures—to the tune of 12.0 percent according to one industry source—these types of films are worth consideration. Studios are also looking at product placement deals to help offset production costs, and advertisers have been more than happy to comply. The average cost of producing and marketing a film fell nearly 5 percent to $98.0 million in 2004, and this trend will likely

Growth of Box Office Admissions, Average Prices, Box Office Advertising And Total Spending

Year	*Admissions*	*Average Price*	*Box Office Spending*	*Movie Screen Advertising*	*Total Box Office Spending*
2000	–3.0%	6.0%	2.9%	50.4%	3.7%
2001	4.6	4.9	9.8	26.8	10.2
2002	10.2	2.7	13.2	22.4	13.4
2003	–4.0	3.8	–0.3	19.9	0.3
2004	–2.4	3.0	0.5	21.3	1.3
2005	–0.5	1.7	1.2	19.3	2.0
2006	0.9	0.9	1.8	16.4	2.6
2007	0.4	2.1	2.5	14.1	3.2
2008	–0.2	2.3	2.1	12.7	2.8
2009	1.4	1.7	3.1	10.3	3.6
Compound Annual Growth					
1999-2004	1.0	4.1	5.1	27.7	5.7
2004-2009	0.4	1.7	2.1	14.5	2.8

Sources: Veronis Suhler Stevenson, PQ Media, Motion Picture Association of America, Cinema Advertising Council, Screenvision

continue in the forecast period as studios seek out high-yield genres like animated and family-oriented films, and they become more judicious about investing in high-budget projects. In addition, studios are expected to implement more cost-cutting measures and revenue-generating marketing tactics, such as product placement, to maximize profits.

Despite the decline in production costs, the average price of admission continues to climb, albeit at a decelerating rate, and is expected to reach $6.32 in 2005. As theaters continue to test the limits of consumer box office spending and push average ticket prices toward the $7 mark, repeat attendance will be adversely affected. The number of frequent (once a month) and occasional (at least one visit per six months) moviegoers increased 2.0 percent in 2004 to 83.0 percent of total admissions. But the five-year trend reflects a drop of 3.0 percent among frequent and occasional moviegoers, and an increase of 3.0 percent among infrequent (less than one visit per six months) viewers. Continuing growth of VOD offerings and DVD rental services will also negatively impact attendance.

Additionally, theaters and distributors are contending with the growth of movie pirating. One major Hollywood trade organization estimates that its member companies lose in excess of $3.5 billion in potential revenues annually from pirating, but recent high-profile arrests of bootleggers indicate the industry is cracking down on copyright infringement.

HOME VIDEO

THE HOME VIDEO MARKET IN 2004 AND 2005

Strong growth in DVD sales and rentals, due to falling prices and increased penetration of players, was offset by plummeting sales and rentals in the VHS market in 2004. Overall, the home video segment expanded only 3.8 percent to $27.62 billion in 2004 after three straight years of double-digit gains. DVDs now represent 78.9 percent of home video sales, up from 61.6 percent in 2003 and 47.2 percent in 2002. DVD spending grew to $21.79 billion in 2004, up from $16.39 billion in 2003. The installed base of DVD players surpassed the 50 percent milestone in 2004, as a result of hardware prices falling below $30 in some cases, making the format the fastest-growing consumer electronics product ever.

DVD expenditures began to show signs of weakening in late 2004 and early 2005 because the format has grown so quickly. DVD players are already in 65.4 million households less than eight years after the format was launched.

Fox's *The Day After Tomorrow* was the top overall rental title in the home video market in 2004, generating $67.4 million in spending for the year. Warner's *Mystic River* finished a close second, garnering $66.9 million, while Fox's *Man on Fire* was third with $65.2 million.

THE VIDEOCASSETTE MARKET

Videocassette sales and rentals have been plummeting at an accelerated pace for the past three years, as the household penetration of DVD players increases and more consumers are attracted to the higher quality and additional features the DVD format offers. The only reason the videocassette market remains viable is that the current generation of home DVD players lacks the ability to record. As a result, some consumers are putting off purchases of DVD players until they offer this feature, while others purchase DVD players but retain their VHS devices. Spending on videocassettes fell 42.9 percent to $5.83 billion in 2004, following a 16.9 percent decline in 2003 and a 13.8 percent drop in 2002.

THE DVD MARKET

In sharp contrast to the VHS market, DVD spending grew 32.9 percent to $21.79 billion in 2004. DVD growth is attributable to a fast-growing installed base of hardware, and attractive retail prices on DVDs. Sales of DVDs grew 30.8 percent to $16.05 billion as the average retail price of a DVD dropped $1.80 to $16.04. New owners of DVD players are taking advantage of low prices on old DVDs—less than $5 in some cases—to build their movie libraries. More than one-third of all DVD movies sold are bought at Wal-Mart, which uses attractive DVD pricing to get customers into the store to purchase higher-margin items.

The sale of television shows on DVD is also contributing to the growth of DVD spending. Although purchasing television shows on VHS never caught on, consumers are drawn to the bonus material on DVDs, such as interviews with the actors, outtakes and other special features. Spending on television shows on DVD generated more than $2 billion in revenues in 2004, and was on track in the first half of 2005 to surpass $2.5 billion for the year. Top rated TV shows, such as *Seinfeld*, have also experienced success in the DVD market. Within a few months of being released on DVD, *Seinfeld* sold more than 4 million copies. Even marginally successful shows are selling on DVD; for example, *What's Happening!*, sold more than 100,000 units of a season in just a few months. The sale of TV programs on DVD kicks off strong profits for producers, networks and distributors because the shows have already been created and the DVDs are relatively inexpensive to produce.

DVD rental sales grew 39.2 percent to $5.73 billion in 2004, spurred by the success of rent-by-mail services, such as Netflix, and the increased marketing efforts of traditional movie rental chains, such as Blockbuster.

The future of next-generation DVD formats is still cloudy. At press time of this *Forecast*, two competing formats—HD-DVD and Blu-ray—were slated to launch their products in late 2005, although the respective developers were discussing the possibility of joining forces.

VCR and DVD Households

Year	Television Households (Millions)	VCR Households (Millions)	VCR Penetration Of TV Households %	DVD Households (Millions)	DVD Penetration Of TV Households %
1999	99.4	86.3	86.8%	4.9	4.9%
2000	100.8	88.1	87.4	13.0	12.9
2001	102.2	96.2	94.1	24.8	24.3
2002	105.5	97.6	92.5	38.8	36.8
2003	106.7	98.4	92.2	46.7	43.8
2004	108.4	98.9	91.2	65.4	60.3
2005	109.6	98.6	90.0	78.6	71.7
2006	110.8	97.9	88.4	88.1	79.5
2007	111.9	96.7	86.4	94.5	84.5
2008	113.2	94.9	83.8	97.1	85.8
2009	114.4	92.2	80.6	99.2	86.7

Sources: Veronis Suhler Stevenson, PQ Media, Nielsen Media Research, U.S. Census Bureau

Growth of VCR and DVD Households

Year	Television Households	VCR Households	Point Change In VCR Penetration Of TV Households	DVD Households	Point Change In DVD Penetration Of TV Households
2000	1.4%	2.1%	0.6	165.3%	8.0
2001	1.4	9.2	6.7	90.8	11.4
2002	3.2	1.5	–1.6	56.5	12.5
2003	1.1	0.8	–0.3	20.4	7.0
2004	1.6	0.5	–1.0	40.0	16.6
2005	1.1	–0.3	–1.3	20.2	11.4
2006	1.1	–0.7	–1.6	12.1	7.8
2007	1.0	–1.2	–1.9	7.3	4.9
2008	1.2	–1.9	–2.6	2.8	1.3
2009	1.1	–2.8	–3.2	2.2	0.9
Compound Annual Growth					
1999-2004	1.7	2.8	—	67.9	—
2004-2009	1.1	–1.4	—	8.7	—

Sources: Veronis Suhler Stevenson, PQ Media, Nielsen Media Research, U.S. Census Bureau

Entertainment Media

Top 10 Rental Titles in 2004*

Title	*Video Label*	*Rental Spending ($ Millions)*
The Day After Tomorrow	Fox	$67.4
Mystic River	Warner	66.9
Man on Fire	Fox	65.2
50 First Dates	Sony	65.0
The Butterfly Effect	New Line/Warner	60.1
The Last Samurai	Warner	58.5
Radio	Sony	58.1
Out of Time	MGM	57.5
Along Came Polly	Universal	57.4
Something's Gotta Give	Sony	56.6

Sources: Veronis Suhler Stevenson, PQ Media, *Variety*
*VHS and DVD rentals combined.

Entertainment Media

Top 10 Sell-Through Titles in 2004*

Title	*Studio*	*Consumer Spending ($ Millions)*
Shrek 2	DreamWorks/Universal	$341
Lord of the Rings: Return of the King	New Line/Warner, all editions	274
Passion of the Christ	Fox	218
Star Wars Trilogy	Warner	215
Harry Potter Azkaban	Warner	185
Spider-Man 2	Sony	173
Lion King 1½	Buena Vista	141
Brother Bear	Buena Vista	140
Elf	Warner	123
Matrix Revolutions	Warner	116

Sources: Veronis Suhler Stevenson, PQ Media, *Variety*
*VHS and DVD sell-through combined.

Home Videocassette Spending

		Rentals				Retail Sales				
Year	*VCR Households (Millions)*	*Rentals Per VCR Household*	*Rental Transactions (Millions)*	*Average Rental Price*	*Rental End-User Spending ($ Millions)*	*Cassette Unit Sales Per VCR Household*	*Cassette Unit Sales (Millions)*	*Average Retail Price*	*Cassette End-User Spending ($ Millions)*	*Total Cassette Spending ($ Millions)*
1999	86.3	31.8	2,741	$2.70	$7,398	6.9	593	$13.74	$8,145	$15,543
2000	88.1	30.9	2,725	2.61	7,125	6.5	576	13.22	7,620	14,745
2001	96.2	25.2	2,425	2.74	6,636	6.2	601	12.67	7,611	14,247
2002	97.6	20.3	1,984	2.66	5,286	6.0	583	12.01	6,997	12,283
2003	98.4	14.3	1,412	2.81	3,973	4.5	440	14.17	6,239	10,212
2004	98.9	8.5	842	2.76	2,328	2.9	283	12.37	3,501	5,829
2005	98.6	6.1	601	2.70	1,623	2.1	211	11.96	2,524	4,147
2006	97.9	4.6	453	2.68	1,214	1.7	164	11.71	1,918	3,132
2007	96.7	3.7	358	2.63	943	1.4	131	11.31	1,485	2,428
2008	94.9	3.1	293	2.61	764	1.1	107	11.16	1,191	1,955
2009	92.2	2.7	250	2.58	645	0.9	87	11.05	963	1,608

Sources: Veronis Suhler Stevenson, PQ Media, Adams Media Research, Alexander & Associates, Digital Entertainment Group, Rentrak, Kagan Research, Video Software Dealers Association

Growth of Home Videocassette Spending

		Rentals				Retail Sales				
Year	*VCR Households*	*Rentals Per VCR Household*	*Rental Transactions*	*Average Rental Price*	*Rental End-User Spending*	*Cassette Unit Sales Per VCR Household*	*Cassette Unit Sales*	*Average Retail Price*	*Cassette End-User Spending*	*Total Cassette Spending*
2000	2.1%	–2.6%	–0.6%	–3.1%	–3.7%	–4.8%	–2.8%	–3.8%	–6.4%	–5.1%
2001	9.2	–18.5	–11.0	4.7	–6.9	–4.6	4.2	–4.2	–0.1	–3.4
2002	1.5	–19.4	–18.2	–2.6	–20.3	–4.4	–3.0	–5.2	–8.1	–13.8
2003	0.8	–29.4	–28.8	5.6	–24.8	–25.1	–24.4	18.0	–10.8	–16.9
2004	0.5	–40.7	–40.4	–1.7	–41.4	–36.0	–35.7	–12.7	–43.9	–42.9
2005	–0.3	–28.4	–28.6	–2.4	–30.3	–25.2	–25.4	–3.4	–27.9	–28.9
2006	–0.7	–24.1	–24.6	–0.8	–25.2	–21.8	–22.4	–2.1	–24.0	–24.5
2007	–1.2	–20.0	–21.0	–1.6	–22.3	–18.9	–19.9	–3.4	–22.6	–22.5
2008	–1.9	–16.8	–18.3	–0.9	–19.0	–17.2	–18.7	–1.4	–19.8	–19.5
2009	–2.8	–12.0	–14.5	–1.2	–15.5	–15.9	–18.3	–1.0	–19.1	–17.7
Compound Annual Growth										
1999-2004	2.8	–23.2	–21.0	0.5	–20.6	–16.1	–13.7	–2.1	–15.5	–17.8
2004-2009	–1.4	–20.4	–21.6	–1.4	–22.6	–19.9	–21.0	–2.2	–22.8	–22.7

Sources: Veronis Suhler Stevenson, PQ Media, Adams Media Research, Alexander & Associates, Digital Entertainment Group, Rentrak, Kagan Research, Video Software Dealers Association

Home Video DVD Spending*

Year	DVD Households (Millions)	Rentals Per DVD Household	Rental Transactions (Millions)	Average Rental Price	Rental End-User Spending ($ Millions)	Unit Sales Per DVD Household	DVD Unit Sales (Millions)	Average Retail Price	DVD End-User Spending ($ Millions)	Total DVD Spending ($ Millions)
		Rentals				*Retail Sales*				
1999	4.9	4.9	24	$3.67	$ 88	9.6	47	$20.83	$ 979	$ 1,067
2000	13.0	11.8	153	3.41	521	7.5	97	18.91	1,834	2,355
2001	24.8	15.4	382	3.30	1,259	8.9	220	18.86	4,150	5,409
2002	38.8	19.8	768	3.35	2,575	12.7	493	17.08	8,418	10,993
2003	46.7	26.4	1,235	3.33	4,118	14.7	688	17.84	12,276	16,394
2004	65.4	26.8	1,753	3.27	5,734	15.3	1,001	16.04	16,052	21,786
2005	78.6	27.2	2,140	3.24	6,938	16.1	1,266	15.63	19,792	26,730
2006	88.1	27.8	2,446	3.19	7,805	16.9	1,489	15.52	23,117	30,922
2007	94.5	28.8	2,720	3.16	8,593	17.8	1,680	15.30	25,706	34,299
2008	97.1	29.7	2,886	3.23	9,315	18.8	1,821	15.54	28,302	37,617
2009	99.2	30.6	3,031	3.28	9,930	19.6	1,941	15.72	30,510	40,440

Sources: Veronis Suhler Stevenson, PQ Media, Adams Media Research, Alexander & Associates, Digital Entertainment Group, Rentrak, Kagan Research, Video Software Dealers Association

*DVD-Video players only.

Entertainment Media

Growth of Home Video DVD Spending*

Year	DVD Households	Rentals Per DVD Household	Rental Transactions	Average Rental Price	Rental End-User Spending	Unit Sales Per DVD Household	DVD Unit Sales	Average Retail Price	DVD End-User Spending	Total DVD Spending
		Rentals				*Retail Sales*				
2000	165.3%	140.3%	537.5%	–7.1%	492.0%	–22.2%	106.4%	–9.2%	87.3%	120.7%
2001	90.8	30.9	149.7	–3.2	141.7	18.9	126.8	–0.2	126.3	129.7
2002	56.5	28.5	101.0	1.7	104.5	43.2	124.1	–9.5	102.8	103.2
2003	20.4	33.6	60.8	–0.6	59.9	15.9	39.6	4.5	45.8	49.1
2004	40.0	1.4	41.9	–1.9	39.2	3.9	45.5	–10.1	30.8	32.9
2005	20.2	1.6	22.1	–0.9	21.0	5.3	26.5	–2.5	23.3	22.7
2006	12.1	2.0	14.3	–1.6	12.5	4.9	17.6	–0.7	16.8	15.7
2007	7.3	3.7	11.2	–1.0	10.1	5.2	12.8	–1.4	11.2	10.9
2008	2.8	3.3	6.1	2.2	8.4	5.5	8.4	1.6	10.1	9.7
2009	2.2	2.8	5.0	1.5	6.6	4.3	6.6	1.1	7.8	7.5
Compound Annual Growth										
1999-2004	67.9	40.5	135.9	–2.3	130.6	9.8	84.4	–5.1	75.0	82.8
2004-2009	8.7	2.7	11.6	0.0	11.6	5.0	14.2	–0.4	13.7	13.2

Sources: Veronis Suhler Stevenson, PQ Media, Adams Media Research, Alexander & Associates, Digital Entertainment Group, Rentrak, Kagan Research, Video Software Dealers Association

*DVD-Video players only.

THE OUTLOOK FOR HOME VIDEO

The home video segment is projected to return to a double-digit growth track in 2005 on the strength of DVD software sell-through, as the installed base of DVD players grows to 78.6 million by year's end. Key releases in 2005 include *Meet the Fockers* (which sold 3.0 million copies in its first day of availability), *Ocean's Twelve* and *Lemony Snicket's A Series of Unfortunate Events*. Additionally, other drivers include the continued release of recent seasons of popular television shows such as *Friends* and *Seinfeld* onto home video. DVD expenditures will grow 22.7 percent to $26.73 billion in 2005. VHS sales will continue to decline in 2005, but at a significantly slower rate than in the previous year.

Rental spending is coming under fire due to the growth of VOD, as well as the pressure multiple system operator (MSO) cable providers are putting on studios to get movies to VOD as soon as possible. DVD rental spending will grow at a compound annual rate of just 11.6 percent during the forecast period, compared to 130.6 percent for the 1999-2004 period. VHS rental revenues will decline 22.7 percent during the forecast period, as the number of VOD households more than doubles from an installed base of just 19.8 million homes in 2004. Overall, we project the home video market will grow at a compound annual rate of 8.8 percent from 2004 to 2009, with sales reaching $42.05 billion in 2009.

The Home Video Market

($ MILLIONS)

Year	*Videocassette Spending*	*DVD Spending*	*Total Home Video Spending*
1999	$15,543	$ 1,067	$16,610
2000	14,745	2,355	17,100
2001	14,247	5,409	19,656
2002	12,283	10,993	23,276
2003	10,212	16,394	26,606
2004	5,829	21,786	27,615
2005	4,147	26,730	30,877
2006	3,132	30,922	34,054
2007	2,428	34,299	36,727
2008	1,955	37,617	39,572
2009	1,608	40,440	42,048

Sources: Veronis Suhler Stevenson, PQ Media, Adams Media Research, Alexander & Associates, Digital Entertainment Group, Rentrak, Kagan Research, Video Software Dealers Association, U.S. Census Bureau

Growth of the Home Video Market

Year	*Videocassette Spending*	*DVD Spending*	*Total Home Video Spending*
2000	–5.1%	120.7%	3.0%
2001	–3.4	129.7	14.9
2002	–13.8	103.2	18.4
2003	–16.9	49.1	14.3
2004	–42.9	32.9	3.8
2005	–28.9	22.7	11.8
2006	–24.5	15.7	10.3
2007	–22.5	10.9	7.8
2008	–19.5	9.7	7.7
2009	–17.7	7.5	6.3
Compound Annual Growth			
1999-2004	–17.8	82.8	10.7
2004-2009	–22.7	13.2	8.8

Sources: Veronis Suhler Stevenson, PQ Media, Adams Media Research, Alexander & Associates, Digital Entertainment Group, Rentrak, Kagan Research, Video Software Dealers Association, U.S. Census Bureau

INTERACTIVE TELEVISION & WIRELESS CONTENT

THE INTERACTIVE TELEVISION & WIRELESS MARKET IN 2004 AND 2005

The trend toward more proactive entertainment viewing, in which consumers essentially watch programs on their own time, has fueled growth in the ITV and wireless segment. Consumers are beginning to embrace digital video recorder (DVR) technologies, such as TiVo and DIRECTV-DVR, and to a lesser extent, VOD services. T-commerce still remains largely untapped and has seen much slower growth than originally anticipated. Additionally, cell phone technology has become more sophisticated, allowing consumers to download various wireless content, from instant messages to videos.

For the past two years, stand-alone provider TiVo has been the face of ITV, reaching the mainstream market of television viewers and shedding light on an industry niche designed to enhance the television viewing experience. But with a potential buyout of TiVo imminent, its demise could turn the industry in a new direction, as consumers migrate away from stand-alone DVR applications and move toward satellite and cable subscription services that offer competitive DVR services.

As DVR penetration expands, advertisers are becoming increasingly concerned that consumers will bypass commercials more frequently. In response, advertisers are looking at alternatives to the traditional 30-second commercial spot, such as varying the lengths and formats of commercials and integrating products directly into a television show's content.

Total ITV and wireless content spending surged 78.0 percent in 2004 to $3.23 billion, fueled mainly by rapid growth in the DVR market. Overall spending on ITV and wireless content is projected to grow another 52.6 percent in 2005 to $4.93 billion, due to stronger growth in the cable and satellite DVR sectors. To avoid double counting, VOD spending is not included in the ITV figures in this chapter because the spending data is incorporated in the Cable & Satellite Television chapter.

DIGITAL VIDEO RECORDERS

With approximately 10 percent penetration in U.S. households to date, the DVR market is quickly gaining traction among consumers who value convenient and efficient television viewing. In the past few years, stand-alone DVR products and direct broadcast satellite (DBS) have been the most popular formats, achieving steady double-digit growth. But TiVo is currently in a state of flux, as speculation of a potential buyout clouds its future and the prospects for other stand-alone vendors, as well. Increasing competition from cable and satellite companies that offer DVR capabilities as part of their subscription packages, which virtually eliminates the need for consumers to buy hardware, is stifling growth. These providers are also better able to reduce digital recording costs because of their subscription volume. In addition, they will likely drive the price of DVR hardware down as stand-alone sellers try to gain as much consumer buy-in as possible.

DVR households grew 41.2 percent in 2004 to 4.9 million, with more than 2.6 million of those households subscribing through DBS. Stand-alone and cable services accounted for 1.1 million subscribers each. The number of DVR households is projected to grow at a compound annual rate of 20.7 percent from 2004 to 2009, reaching nearly 12.5 million households. DBS and cable DVR households are expected to grow at a compound annual rate of 18.2 percent and 34.1 percent, respectively, in the forecast period, while stand-alone households will increase 8.0 percent through 2009, with much of the growth coming in the next two years.

Subscription spending on DVRs climbed 47.8 percent in 2004 to $272.0 million. Spending is forecast to rise another 41.2 percent in 2005 to $384.0 million, and will grow at a compound annual rate of 25.0 percent from 2004 and 2009 to $831.0 million.

VIDEO-ON-DEMAND

VOD technology is still in its formative years and hasn't penetrated the consumer market as quickly as expected. As a result of its

Subscription Spending on Digital Video Recorders (DVRs)

Year	Stand-Alone DVR Households (Thousands)*	DBS DVR Households (Thousands)†	Cable DVR Households (Thousands)‡	Total DVR Households (Thousands)	DVR Subscription Rates Per Year Per Household	Total DVR Spending ($ Millions)
1999	95	88	—	183	$38.25	$ 7
2000	236	172	50	458	43.67	20
2001	435	402	180	1,017	46.21	47
2002	626	968	330	1,924	49.90	96
2003	906	1,716	830	3,452	53.30	184
2004	1,137	2,641	1,096	4,874	55.80	272
2005	1,389	3,691	1,594	6,673	57.55	384
2006	1,547	4,661	2,247	8,455	58.91	498
2007	1,619	5,397	2,977	9,994	61.31	613
2008	1,646	5,809	3,793	11,248	63.95	719
2009	1,670	6,082	4,746	12,497	66.48	831

Sources: Veronis Suhler Stevenson, PQ Media, Leichtman Research Group, TiVo, ReplayTV, DIRECTV, EchoStar, Business 2.0, Lexis/Nexis

*Services provided by TiVo, ReplayTV, and UltimateTV.

†Services provided by DIRECTV, EchoStar and other DBS providers, often in alliance with TiVo or UltimateTV.

‡Various MSO cable providers signed alliances with TiVo, ReplayTV or UltimateTV from 1999 to 2002. In 2003, most MSOs began using separate stand-alone set-top DVR boxes.

Growth of Subscription Spending on Digital Video Recorders (DVRs)

Year	Stand-Alone DVR Households	DBS DVR Households	Cable DVR Households	Total DVR Households	DVR Subscription Rates Per Year Per Household	Total DVR Spending
2000	148.4%	95.5%	—	150.3%	14.2%	185.7%
2001	84.3	133.7	260.0%	122.1	5.8	135.0
2002	43.9	140.8	83.3	89.2	8.0	104.3
2003	44.7	77.3	151.5	79.4	6.8	91.7
2004	25.5	53.9	32.0	41.2	4.7	47.8
2005	22.1	39.7	45.4	36.9	3.1	41.2
2006	11.4	26.3	41.0	26.7	2.4	29.7
2007	4.7	15.8	32.5	18.2	4.1	23.0
2008	1.6	7.6	27.4	12.5	4.3	17.4
2009	1.4	4.7	25.1	11.1	4.0	15.5
Compound Annual Growth						
1999-2004	64.3	97.5	—	92.8	7.8	107.9
2004-2009	8.0	18.2	34.1	20.7	3.6	25.0

Sources: Veronis Suhler Stevenson, PQ Media, Leichtman Research Group, TiVo, ReplayTV, DIRECTV, EchoStar, Business 2.0, Lexis/Nexis

Spending on Video-on-Demand: Residential

Year	Total VOD Residential Households (Millions)	Total VOD Residential Subscribers (Millions)	Annual VOD Spending Per Household	Total VOD Residential Spending ($ Millions)
1999	0.30	0.02	$23.13	$ 0.3
2000	1.6	0.2	25.87	6
2001	4.0	0.9	28.89	26
2002	7.0	2.0	28.00	56
2003	12.3	4.7	30.21	142
2004	19.8	8.3	38.31	318
2005	27.5	13.8	35.91	495
2006	33.5	20.1	33.68	678
2007	38.1	24.4	36.07	880
2008	42.0	28.1	38.39	1,079
2009	44.9	30.4	40.69	1,237

Sources: Veronis Suhler Stevenson, PQ Media, Leichtman Group, In-Stat, Kagan Research, Forrester Research

*To avoid double counting, VOD spending from the Entertainment Media chapter will not be included in overall spending. VOD spending from the Cable & Satellite TV chapter will be included in overall communications spending.

Growth of Spending on Video-on-Demand: Residential

Year	Total VOD Households	Total VOD Subscribers	Annual VOD Spending Per Household	Total VOD Spending
2000	433.3%	1,513.3%	11.8%	1,704.0%
2001	150.0	271.9	11.7	315.3
2002	75.0	122.2	–3.1	115.4
2003	75.7	135.0	7.9	153.6
2004	61.0	76.6	26.8	123.9
2005	39.0	66.0	–6.3	55.6
2006	21.6	46.2	–6.2	37.1
2007	13.9	21.1	7.1	29.7
2008	10.1	15.2	6.4	22.6
2009	6.9	8.2	6.0	14.7
Compound Annual Growth				
1999-2004	131.2	253.7	10.6	291.2
2004-2009	17.8	29.7	1.2	31.2

Sources: Veronis Suhler Stevenson, PQ Media, Federal Communications Commission, National Cable & Telecommunications Association, Kagan Research, LodgeNet, Smith Travel Research

*To avoid double counting, VOD spending from the Entertainment Media chapter will not be included in overall spending. VOD spending from the Cable & Satellite TV chapter will be included in overall communications. spending.

impact on ITV expenditures, VOD spending is referenced in this chapter as well as in the Cable & Satellite Television chapter. The increasing popularity of DVDs and competition from online rental companies such as Netflix and bricks-and-mortar retailers like Blockbuster clearly have impeded growth. But the future of VOD services remains encouraging. The technology offers consumers greater convenience when watching movies at home, eliminating the need for renting DVDs, while offering similar flexibility in starting and stopping a movie. In 2004, the average cost of renting a movie using VOD was less than $4, and the prices will likely drop significantly as the market matures. Growing availability of VOD services from digital cable and satellite subscribers will accelerate market penetration and acceptance from consumers going forward.

VOD households grew 61.0 percent in 2004 to 19.8 million. The market is estimated to grow 39.0 percent in 2005 to 27.5 million households, driven by continued efforts on the part of cable providers to upgrade their digital services. Total spending on VOD in 2004 was $318.0 million, an increase of 123.9 percent over 2003. Still in its early stages, VOD spending per household will drop from $38.31 per year in 2004, to $35.91 in 2005, a 6.3 percent decrease. Total spending will expand 55.6 percent in 2005 to $495.0 million. On a compound annual basis, VOD will grow 31.2 percent in the 2004-2009 period to $1.24 billion.

HOTEL/MOTEL VIDEO-ON-DEMAND

Hotel/motel VOD has grown much faster than in the residential sector due to the convenience and practicality it offers traveling guests who prefer this format over pay-per-view (PPV) because it offers user-directed start and stop times. The industry has been an appropriate testing ground for VOD technology, as well as a good marketing channel because it allows prospective buyers to sample its potential. VOD penetration in the hotel/motel market is expected to increase as the technology replaces outdated PPV services.

Spending on hotel/motel VOD services grew 6.7 percent in 2004 to $540.0 million, and the market is projected to rise 11.4 per-

Spending on Video-on-Demand: Hotels/Motels*

Year	*Total Hotel/Motel Rooms In United States (Thousands)*	*Total Rooms With VOD Capacity (Thousands)*	*Percent Of Hotel/Motel Rooms With VOD*	*VOD Revenue Per Hotel/Motel Room*	*Total Hotel/Motel VOD Spending ($ Millions)*
1999	3,900	1,852	47.5%	$232	$430
2000	4,100	1,964	47.9	226	444
2001	4,200	2,025	48.2	223	452
2002	4,284	2,126	49.6	221	470
2003	4,371	2,312	52.9	219	506
2004	4,414	2,436	55.2	222	540
2005	4,502	2,699	59.9	223	601
2006	4,592	2,958	64.4	225	665
2007	4,684	3,281	70.0	227	744
2008	4,778	3,619	75.7	230	832
2009	4,864	3,948	81.2	234	924

Sources: Veronis Suhler Stevenson, PQ Media, Kagan Research, LodgeNet, Smith Travel Research
*To avoid double counting, VOD spending from the Entertainment Media chapter will not be included in overall spending. VOD spending from the Cable & Satellite TV chapter will be included in overall communications spending.

Growth of Spending on Video-on-Demand: Hotels/Motels*

Year	*Total Hotel/Motel Rooms In United States*	*Total Rooms With VOD Capacity*	*VOD Revenue Per Hotel/Motel Room*	*Total Hotel/Motel VOD Spending*
2000	5.1%	6.0%	–2.6%	3.3%
2001	2.4	3.1	–1.3	1.7
2002	2.0	5.0	–0.9	4.0
2003	2.0	8.7	–0.9	7.7
2004	1.0	5.4	1.2	6.7
2005	2.0	10.8	0.5	11.4
2006	2.0	9.6	0.9	10.6
2007	2.0	10.9	0.9	11.9
2008	2.0	10.3	1.4	11.8
2009	1.8	9.1	1.7	11.0
Compound Annual Growth				
1999-2004	2.5	5.6	–0.9	4.7
2004-2009	2.0	10.1	1.1	11.3

Sources: Veronis Suhler Stevenson, PQ Media, Kagan Research, LodgeNet, Smith Travel Research
*To avoid double counting, VOD spending from the Entertainment Media chapter will not be included in overall spending. VOD spending from the Cable & Satellite TV chapter will be included in overall communications spending.

Spending on Interactive Television Promotions/Advertising

Year	*Total Digital Households (Millions)*	*Total ITV Promotions/Ad Spending ($ Millions)*
2000	9.7	$ 27
2001	15.2	74
2002	19.2	134
2003	21.5	161
2004	23.3	193
2005	26.5	253
2006	30.9	364
2007	34.5	458
2008	39.4	611
2009	43.7	759

Sources: Veronis Suhler Stevenson, PQ Media, National Cable & Telecommunications Association

Entertainment Media

Growth of Spending on Interactive Television Promotions/Advertising

Year	*Total Digital Households*	*Total ITV Promotions/Ad Spending*
2001	56.7%	174.1%
2002	26.3	80.4
2003	12.0	20.6
2004	8.4	19.9
2005	13.7	31.3
2006	16.6	43.6
2007	11.7	25.9
2008	14.2	33.3
2009	10.9	24.3
Compound Annual Growth		
2004-2009	12.9	30.6

Sources: Veronis Suhler Stevenson, PQ Media, National Cable & Telecommunications Association

cent to $601.0 million in 2005. The number of rooms with VOD services continues to expand, reaching 55.2 percent penetration in 2004, up 2.3 percentage points from the prior year. By 2009, an estimated 81.2 percent of hotel rooms will have VOD capabilities. Hotel/motel VOD is expected to become available in more rooms across the U.S. in the forecast period, as spending grows at a compound annual rate of 11.3 percent from 2004 to 2009 to $924.0 million.

INTERACTIVE TELEVISION PROMOTIONS AND ADVERTISING

ITV promotions and advertising spending increased 19.9 percent to $193.0 million in 2004, driven by greater consumer interest in ITV products and services. Expenditures are expected to grow 31.3 percent to $253.0 million in 2005 and advance at a compound annual rate of 30.6 percent in the forecast period to $759.0 million in 2009.

The growing popularity of DVRs continues to be a major concern for advertisers because the technology allows viewers to fast-forward through commercials. However, the same concern arose when VHS came on the market a quarter-century ago. As a result of television viewing being a passive activity, viewers may not even invest the effort to skip many commercials. Viewers appear to be interested in DVRs primarily because the technology allows them to watch programs at their convenience, not because they can bypass commercials.

It is still too early to determine the ultimate effect DVRs will have on television advertising. But ITV providers, television producers and advertisers are already addressing the problem. TiVo is using pop-ups to flash advertising messages as users fast-forward through commercials. Advertisers are experimenting with variations on the traditional 30-second spot, and they are increasing spending to integrate their products directly into program content, rather than just placing their products as props.

T-COMMERCE

T-commerce is ITV's answer to shopping on the Web, but because such services can capture a user's personal information before he or she makes a purchase, it is faster and more convenient than e-commerce. T-commerce spending reached $48.4 million in 2004, up 44.5 percent from the previous year. Like e-commerce, t-commerce is not considered communications spending and is included in this discussion because of its impact on the use of DVR and VOD.

The primary difficulty with t-commerce is that prospective shoppers cannot consult objective resources when watching ITV, like they do when they are on the Internet. One application that has raised interest is the use of t-commerce to facilitate real-time betting on horse races and other sporting events. While there is some potential synergy in tying channel changing to Web surfing, marketers and advertisers have yet to demonstrate a compelling value proposition for consumers to buy into.

Despite these issues, spending on t-commerce is projected to post strong growth in 2005, rising 16.1 percent to $56.2 million. The market is expected to grow at a compound annual rate of 20.7 percent from 2004 to 2009, reaching $98.5 million.

Spending on T-commerce*

Year	*Total Spending on T-commerce ($ Millions)*	*Growth of Spending on T-commerce*
2000	$ 8.1	—
2001	18.4	127.2%
2002	28.2	53.3
2003	33.5	18.8
2004	48.4	44.5
2005	56.2	16.1
2006	65.8	17.1
2007	73.2	11.2
2008	85.8	17.2
2009	98.5	14.8
Compound Annual Growth		
2004-2009		20.7

Sources: Veronis Suhler Stevenson, PQ Media, Lexis/Nexis, Myers Mediaenomics
*Spending on t-commerce is not considered communications spending; therefore, t-commerce is not included in entertainment media spending.

WIRELESS CONTENT

The evolution of mobile computing and communication technologies is greatly altering the way people exchange information, if for no other reason than the convenience they offer. Consumer consumption has been robust, and manufacturers and advertisers have been aggressive in their efforts to develop new applications and formats, such as instant messaging, text messaging, ringtones, gaming and picture downloading. In addition to consumers, corporations have been adopting the technology because it increases the speed and efficiency of doing business.

Cell phones, PDAs, Blackberrys, Blueberrys and other forms of pocket phones are among the catalog of products that are driving growth in this segment. Wireless communications is the backbone of these technologies, but devices are quickly evolving to accommodate music and picture downloading, gaming and television viewing. While upfront costs will continue to drop as mobile technology evolves and becomes more mainstream, manufacturers and service providers will have to address consumer concern about back-end service, subscriptions and contractual obligations that might leave first-time buyers wary about considering other products. This customer service effort will become more apparent as vendors and advertisers target older consumers, who tend to be more skeptical and value-conscious in their spending habits. Younger consumers, however, have readily bought into the technology.

Advertisers are keen to approach the market for wireless devices because the technology allows them to reach consumers beyond the confines of the television or movie screen. The variety of applications that these devices can hold has opened a window for marketers to send direct and concise messages to consumers. FOX, for example, has entered into an agreement with UK-based Vodafone to offer one-minute "mobisodes," or dramas based on its hit show *24*. The expectation is that as this service evolves, FOX will be able to transmit trailers and clips of movies, as well.

As a result of these trends, overall wireless content spending grew 88.1 percent in 2004, totaling $2.77 billion. Instant messaging accounted for the greatest portion of spending in this subgroup at $1.77 billion, followed by e-mail and information alerts ($433.0 million) and ringtones ($307.0 million). Mobile advertising and spending grew 143.0 percent to $105.0 million in 2004 and is expected to reach $201.0 million in 2005.

Spending on Wireless Content ($ MILLIONS)

Year	*Instant Messaging*	*E-mail & Information Alerts*	*Ringtones*	*Wireless Games*	*Picture & Video Downloads*	*Mobile Advertising & Marketing*	*Total Wireless Content Spending*
2002	$ 515	$ 80	$ 22	$ 2	$ 5	$ 12	$ 636
2003	1,081	222	82	20	22	43	1,470
2004	1,769	433	307	82	70	105	2,766
2005	2,355	683	681	224	151	201	4,295
2006	2,852	945	1,099	430	250	318	5,894
2007	3,302	1,155	1,436	634	371	425	7,323
2008	3,751	1,322	1,716	791	449	516	8,545
2009	4,190	1,488	1,958	912	513	604	9,665

Sources: Veronis Suhler Stevenson, PQ Media, Insight Research, eMarketer, Kagan Research

Total wireless content spending is projected to rise 55.3 percent in 2005 to $4.30 billion, and grow at a compound annual rate of 28.4 percent in the forecast period to $9.67 billion in 2009.

THE OUTLOOK FOR INTERACTIVE TELEVISION AND WIRELESS CONTENT

Overall spending on ITV and wireless content is projected to rise 52.6 percent in 2005 to $4.93 billion, and grow at a compound annual rate of 28.4 percent in the forecast period to $11.26 billion in 2009.

The pace of change for ITV has been rapid, and some formats such as stand-alone DVRs are already showing signs of obsolescence as newer and cheaper technologies replace them. The growing popularity of DVDs has limited VOD traction thus far and will continue to do so until VOD reaches the mainstream. Continuing innovation in the ITV sector with new applications like interactive program guides—a format that will offer television viewers a digital database of viewing options broken down by genre—will expand the possibilities of digital recording and proactive program surfing. As these technologies continue to evolve, advertisers will attempt to find new ways to reach consumers.

The potential for growth in the wireless content segment is strong, especially as high-speed wireless services become more evolved. In the short-term, there are security and privacy concerns that service providers and advertisers will have to address to appease potential buyers. Advertisers will also need to ensure that they do not inundate potential consumers with too much information too quickly, or else they could face a similar problem as telemarketers—people will refrain from answering their phones. But with permission-based marketing on the rise, the upside to delivering practical, tightly controlled messages to accessible consumers on their wireless devices is difficult to ignore.

Growth of Spending on Wireless Content

Year	*Instant Messaging*	*E-mail & Information Alerts*	*Ringtones*	*Wireless Games*	*Picture & Video Downloads*	*Mobile Advertising & Marketing*	*Total Wireless Content Spending*
2003	109.8%	177.1%	281.9%	778.3%	377.8%	249.2%	131.2%
2004	63.6	94.9	274.3	303.5	224.7	143.0	88.1
2005	33.1	57.7	121.5	175.4	116.0	91.1	55.3
2006	21.1	38.4	61.4	91.6	65.7	58.4	37.2
2007	15.8	22.2	30.7	47.4	48.7	33.4	24.3
2008	13.6	14.5	19.5	24.7	20.8	21.5	16.7
2009	11.7	12.5	14.1	15.4	14.4	17.1	13.1
Compound Annual Growth							
1999-2004	—	—	—	—	—	—	—
2004-2009	18.8	28.0	44.8	62.1	49.0	41.9	28.4

Sources: Veronis Suhler Stevenson, PQ Media, Insight Research, eMarketer, Kagan Research

Spending on Interactive Television and Wireless Content* ($ MILLIONS)

Year	Total DVR Spending	Interactive Television Promo/Ad Spending	Wireless Content Spending	Total ITV & Wireless Spending	VOD Residential Spending	VOD Hotel/ Motel Spending	Total ITV & Wireless Spending Including VOD
1999	$ 7	—	—	$ 7	$ 0.3	$430	$ 437
2000	20	$ 27	—	47	6	444	497
2001	47	74	—	121	26	452	599
2002	96	134	$ 636	866	56	470	1,391
2003	184	161	1,470	1,815	142	506	2,464
2004	272	193	2,766	3,231	318	540	4,089
2005	384	253	4,295	4,932	495	601	6,028
2006	498	364	5,894	6,756	678	665	8,099
2007	613	458	7,323	8,394	880	744	10,018
2008	719	611	8,545	9,875	1,079	832	11,786
2009	831	759	9,665	11,255	1,237	924	13,416

Sources: Veronis Suhler Stevenson, PQ Media, Business 2.0, DIRECTV, EchoStar, eMarketer, In Demand, Insight Research, InStat/MDR, Kagan Research, Leichtman Research Group, Lexis/Nexis, LodgeNet, Myers Mediaenomics, National Cable & Telecommunications Association, ReplayTV, Yankee Group

*To avoid double counting, VOD spending from the Entertainment Media chapter will not be included in overall spending. VOD spending from the Cable & Satellite TV chapter will be included in overall communications spending.

FILMED ENTERTAINMENT PROGRAMS

THE FILMED ENTERTAINMENT PROGRAM MARKET IN 2004 AND 2005

Total spending on television programming grew 9.3 percent to $27.36 billion in 2004, as broadcast and cable networks invested in developing new programs to drive ratings. Cable and satellite television posted a 9.9 percent gain to $7.86 billion, due to increased investment in developing original programming and in purchasing off-network syndicated programming. To better compete with cable, television networks increased spending 7.9 percent in 2004 to $12.20 billion to develop more scripted shows and fewer low-budget reality shows. Meanwhile, television stations increased spending 11.5 percent to $5.51 billion and in-flight entertainment spending grew 10.1 percent to $1.79 billion. Barter syndication remained strong, with spending up 19.8 percent to $2.84 billion in 2004.

Encouraged by the success of new shows such as *Lost*, *The OC* and *Desperate Housewives*, networks are looking to develop inventive new scripted dramas, as well as resurrect the struggling sitcom genre. The failure of a string of copycat reality shows has prompted networks to reconsider the prospects of unscripted programming, despite the low cost.

BROADCAST NETWORKS

While networks are still exercising some restraint in their programming ideas—they continue to rely on standbys like police and medical dramas—they have been willing to take more chances on creative new programs that can better compete with cable, despite the higher price tag. Spending on television network programming increased 7.9 percent to $12.20 billion in 2004, accounting for 44.6 percent of television programming expenditures. ABC's two offbeat new dramas, *Lost* and *Desperate Housewives*, instantly found audiences. ABC's success in 2004 boosted the network's confidence in its programming, prompting it to relinquish the rights to *Monday Night Football* in April 2005 to ESPN after 35 years.

Growth of Spending on Interactive Television and Wireless Content*

Year	Total DVR Spending	Interactive Television Promo/Ad Spending	Wireless Content Spending	Total ITV & Wireless Spending	VOD Residential Spending	VOD Hotel/ Motel Spending	Total ITV & Wireless Spending Including VOD
2000	185.7%	—	—	571.4%	1,704.0%	3.3%	13.8%
2001	135.0	—	—	157.4	315.3	1.7	20.4
2002	104.3	174.1%	—	615.4	115.4	4.0	132.5
2003	91.7	80.4	131.2%	109.7	153.6	7.7	77.1
2004	47.8	20.6	88.1	78.0	123.9	6.6	66.0
2005	41.2	19.9	55.3	52.6	55.6	11.4	47.4
2006	29.7	31.3	37.2	37.0	37.1	10.6	34.4
2007	23.0	43.6	24.3	24.3	29.7	11.9	23.7
2008	17.4	25.9	16.7	17.6	22.6	11.8	17.6
2009	15.5	33.3	13.1	14.0	14.7	11.0	13.8
Compound Annual Growth							
1999-2004	107.9	—	—	241.1	291.2	4.7	56.4
2004-2009	25.0	30.6	28.4	28.4	31.2	11.3	26.8

Sources: Veronis Suhler Stevenson, PQ Media, Business 2.0, DIRECTV, EchoStar, eMarketer, In Demand, Insight Research, InStat/MDR, Kagan Research, Leichtman Research Group, Lexis/Nexis, LodgeNet, Myers Mediaenomics, National Cable & Telecommunications Association, ReplayTV, Yankee Group

*To avoid double counting, VOD spending from the Entertainment Media chapter will not be included in overall spending. VOD spending from the Cable & Satellite TV chapter will be included in overall communications spending.

Unlike the short-term ratings boost reality-based shows provide, scripted programming has a much longer shelf life. While the characters on most reality shows come and go each season, audiences become attached to the characters on scripted shows and loyally follow their experiences from week to week and season to season. For the 2005-06 television season, networks are developing creative new scripted dramas that they hope will follow the success of *Lost* and *Desperate Housewives*. In addition, with the only top 10 comedy—*Everybody Loves Raymond*—drawing to a close in 2004-05, networks are searching for new comedies to infuse life into the sitcom, once a hallmark of prime-time television. Television network programming spending is expected to increase 1.4 percent in 2005 to $12.37 billion. Expenditures will rise 3.6 percent from 2004 to 2009 to $14.55 billion.

TELEVISION STATIONS

The off-network syndicated television market continues to face strong competition from cable networks that have the financial clout to outbid TV stations for programs. The Syndicated Network Television Association, which was formed a few years ago to represent television program syndicators, has given TV stations much greater leverage in negotiating for syndicated shows, and stations are doing their part to grow market share. Television station spending rose 11.5 percent to $5.51 billion in 2004. Compound annual growth in the segment was 3.3 percent from 1999 to 2004. The upside for off-network stations is that they are now better able to tap into a $2.66 billion advertising marketplace because syndication airs more hours of programming each week than the six major networks combined. The downside is that the quality of recently syndicated programs, a result of production cost-cutting and the abundance of reality shows on networks, has been declining, causing advertiser interest to diminish. Still, syndicated programming includes a wide range of genres, including game shows,

Expenditures, by Outlet, on Filmed Entertainment Programs

Year	Total TV Network Programming Spending	*Television Stations* Affiliated Station's Syndicated* Programming Spending	Independent Station's Syndicated* Programming Spending†	Barter Syndication Programming	Total Station Programming Spending
1999	$ 9,674	$1,047	$1,368	$2,260	$4,675
2000	11,203	1,098	1,426	2,382	4,906
2001	10,586	1,141	1,481	2,239	4,861
2002	11,444	1,201	1,548	2,075	4,824
2003	11,306	1,136	1,429	2,373	4,938
2004	12,203	1,186	1,477	2,844	5,507
2005	12,374	1,204	1,502	2,918	5,624
2006	13,067	1,262	1,566	3,087	5,915
2007	13,354	1,283	1,587	3,198	6,068
2008	14,209	1,353	1,668	3,461	6,482
2009	14,550	1,383	1,699	3,568	6,650

Sources: Veronis Suhler Stevenson, PQ Media, Universal McCann, Kagan Research, World Airline Entertainment Association
*Off-network and first-run syndicated licensing.
†Includes WB, UPN, and PAX affiliates.

Entertainment Media

Growth of Expenditures, by Outlet, on Filmed Entertainment Programs

Year	Total TV Network Programming Spending	*Television Stations* Affiliated Station's Syndicated* Programming Spending	Independent Station's Syndicated* Programming Spending†	Barter Syndication Programming	Total Station Programming Spending
2000	15.8%	4.9%	4.2%	5.4%	4.9%
2001	–5.5	3.9	3.9	–6.0	–0.9
2002	8.1	5.3	4.5	–7.3	–0.8
2003	–1.2	–5.4	–7.7	14.4	2.4
2004	7.9	4.4	3.4	19.8	11.5
2005	1.4	1.5	1.7	2.6	2.1
2006	5.6	4.8	4.3	5.8	5.2
2007	2.2	1.7	1.3	3.6	2.6
2008	6.4	5.5	5.1	8.2	6.8
2009	2.4	2.2	1.9	3.1	2.6
Compound Annual Growth					
1999-2004	4.8	2.5	1.5	4.7	3.3
2004-2009	3.6	3.1	2.8	4.6	3.8

Sources: Veronis Suhler Stevenson, PQ Media, Universal McCann, Kagan Research, World Airline Entertainment Association
*Off-network and first-run syndicated licensing.
†Includes WB, UPN, and PAX affiliates.

($ MILLIONS)

Cable & Satellite Television				
Basic Cable Network Programming	*Pay TV Programming*	*Total Cable & Satellite Programming Spending*	*Total In-Flight Entertainment Spending*	*Total Programming & Entertainment Spending*
$3,413	$1,745	$ 5,158	$2,022	$21,529
3,717	1,846	5,563	2,105	23,777
4,051	1,989	6,040	1,571	23,058
4,476	2,092	6,568	1,398	24,234
5,002	2,153	7,155	1,622	25,021
5,448	2,416	7,864	1,786	27,360
5,982	2,587	8,569	1,957	28,524
6,616	2,864	9,480	2,138	30,600
7,218	3,090	10,308	2,324	32,054
7,998	3,393	11,391	2,542	34,624
8,781	3,648	12,429	2,751	36,380

Cable & Satellite Television				
Basic Cable Network Programming	*Pay TV Programming*	*Total Cable & Satellite Programming Spending*	*Total In-Flight Entertainment Spending*	*Total Programming & Entertainment Spending*
8.9%	5.8%	7.9%	4.1%	10.4%
9.0	7.7	8.6	–25.4	–3.0
10.5	5.2	8.7	–11.0	5.1
11.8	2.9	8.9	16.0	3.2
8.9	12.2	9.9	10.1	9.3
9.8	7.1	9.0	9.6	4.3
10.6	10.7	10.6	9.2	7.3
9.1	7.9	8.7	8.7	4.8
10.8	9.8	10.5	9.4	8.0
9.8	7.5	9.1	8.2	5.1
9.8	6.7	8.8	–2.5	4.9
10.0	8.6	9.6	9.0	5.9

Entertainment Media

Shares of Expenditures, by Outlet, On Filmed Entertainment Programs

Year	TV Networks	TV Stations	Cable Networks	In-Flight Entertainment
1999	44.9%	21.7%	24.0%	9.4%
2000	47.1	20.6	23.4	8.9
2001	45.9	21.1	26.2	6.8
2002	47.2	19.9	27.1	5.8
2003	45.2	19.7	28.6	6.5
2004	44.6	20.1	28.7	6.5
2005	43.4	19.7	30.0	6.9
2006	42.7	19.3	31.0	7.0
2007	41.7	18.9	32.2	7.2
2008	41.0	18.7	32.9	7.3
2009	40.0	18.3	34.2	7.6

Sources: Veronis Suhler Stevenson, PQ Media, Universal McCann, Kagan Research, World Airline Entertainment Association

reality shows, entertainment news programs, talk shows and off-network runs of popular sitcoms like *Friends*, *Frasier* and *ER*. As a result, spending on barter syndication programming increased 19.8 percent in 2004 to $2.84 billion, and is expected to rise another 2.6 percent in 2005. Projections through 2009 look promising with 4.6 percent compound annual growth.

CABLE NETWORKS

Cable networks increased spending 9.9 percent to $7.86 billion in 2004, driven by increased investments in original and syndicated programming. Compound annual growth was 8.8 percent from 1999 to 2004.

Premium cable networks, such as HBO, are leading the way with successful programs including *The Sopranos*, *Curb Your Enthusiasm* and *Deadwood*, and the highly anticipated debut of its new series, *Rome*, later this year. Reality programming also continues to hook cable viewers: ESPN (*Dream Job*), MTV (*Meet the Barkers* and *Viva La Bam*), The Discovery Channel (*American Chopper* and *Monster Garage*) and VH1 (*The Surreal Life*) have all taken advantage of viewer demographics to build successful niche shows. While network stations may be hesitant about relying more heavily on reality-based shows, cable networks have much greater flexibility in developing new programs and then rerunning them to build viewer interest.

One of the potential consequences of increased ratings among cable networks, however, is that original programming is no longer a novel concept. Viewers are becoming considerably more judicious about programs they watch—given the sheer volume of options—and networks are, therefore, compelled to enhance their offerings by developing new shows and enhancing existing ones. TLC's *Trading Spaces*, for example, changed its format by bringing in a new cast of designers and changing the way it approaches redesigns in an effort to keep the show fresh and new. HBO has taken a different approach by giving its subscribers more flexibility in watching shows. Its on-demand service allows viewers to watch programs whenever they choose, in much the same way as VOD and ITV. Other networks are similarly injecting new ideas and capital into existing programs to retain and build consumer interest. This trend has been further impacted by new cable and satellite channels that keep cropping up, which will likely further dilute audiences and require networks to be even more aggressive and innovative in their approach to developing new and existing programs.

Because of the strength of cable's original programming, cable ratings continue to expand and total expenditures for cable and satellite programming are gradually closing the gap with network stations. We expect progressive spending growth over the forecast period for cable and satellite television programming, which will rise at a compound annual rate of 9.6 percent from 2004 to 2009, reaching $12.43 billion in 2009.

IN-FLIGHT ENTERTAINMENT

In-flight entertainment spending continues to show positive growth following the drastic decline in 2001 and 2002 when airlines significantly cut operating budgets. Expenditures grew 10.1 percent in 2004 to $1.79 billion. Still reeling from the terrorist attacks in 2001, the segment shrank at a compound annual rate of 2.5 percent from 1999 to 2004. Competition among airlines to lure

Total Spending on Filmed Entertainment

($ MILLIONS)

Year	Box Office	Home Video	Interactive TV & Wireless Content	Television Programming	Total
1999	$ 7,577	$16,610	$ 7	$21,529	$ 45,723
2000	7,855	17,100	47	23,777	48,779
2001	8,659	19,656	121	23,058	51,494
2002	9,821	23,276	866	24,234	58,197
2003	9,850	26,606	1,815	25,021	63,292
2004	9,977	27,615	3,231	27,360	68,183
2005	10,175	30,877	4,932	28,524	74,508
2006	10,435	34,054	6,756	30,600	81,845
2007	10,768	36,727	8,394	32,054	87,943
2008	11,067	39,572	9,875	34,624	95,138
2009	11,467	42,048	11,255	36,380	101,150

Sources: Veronis Suhler Stevenson, PQ Media, Adams Media Research, Alexander & Associates, Business 2.0, Cinema Advertising Council, Digital Entertainment Group, DIRECTV, EchoStar, In Demand, Insight Research, InStat/MDR, Kagan Research, Leichtman Research Group, Lexis/Nexis, Motion Picture Association of America, Myers Mediaenomics, National Cable & Telecommunications Association, Nielsen Media Research, Rentrak, ReplayTV, Screenvision, TiVo, Universal McCann, Video Business, Video Software Dealers Association, World Airline Entertainment Association, Yankee Group

travelers with innovative technologies, including digital touch-screen monitors, satellite radio and pay-per-view movies, bodes well for investment in the in-flight entertainment segment. Growth during the forecast period is expected to rise at a compound annual rate of 9.0 percent to $2.75 billion by 2009.

We predict in-flight entertainment will experience continued growth due to investment in new and innovative technologies, such as VOD, enhanced videogame modules, in-flight gambling, broadcast television, real-time video broadcast via satellite and outlets for laptop computer use.

THE OUTLOOK FOR FILMED ENTERTAINMENT PROGRAM SPENDING

Spending on filmed entertainment programs is projected to grow at a compound annual rate of 5.9 percent from 2004 to 2009, reaching $36.38 billion by 2009, compared with 4.9 percent compound annual growth in the 1999-2004 period. Growth will be driven primarily by increased investments in new programming as broadcast and cable networks continue their battle for audiences.

Growth of Total Spending On Filmed Entertainment

Year	Box Office	Home Video	Interactive TV & Wireless Content	Television Programming	Total
2000	3.7%	3.0%	571.4%	10.4%	6.7%
2001	10.2	14.9	157.4	–3.0	5.6
2002	13.4	18.4	615.4	5.1	13.0
2003	0.3	14.3	109.7	3.2	8.8
2004	1.3	3.8	78.0	9.3	7.7
2005	2.0	11.8	52.6	4.3	9.3
2006	2.6	10.3	37.0	7.3	9.8
2007	3.2	7.8	24.3	4.8	7.5
2008	2.8	7.7	17.6	8.0	8.2
2009	3.6	6.3	14.0	5.1	6.3
Compound Annual Growth					
1999-2004	5.7	10.7	241.1	4.9	8.3
2004-2009	2.8	8.8	28.4	5.9	8.2

Sources: Veronis Suhler Stevenson, PQ Media, Adams Media Research, Alexander & Associates, Business 2.0, Cinema Advertising Council, Digital Entertainment Group, DIRECTV, EchoStar, In Demand, Insight Research, InStat/MDR, Kagan Research, Leichtman Research Group, Lexis/Nexis, Motion Picture Association of America, Myers Mediaenomics, National Cable & Telecommunications Association, Nielsen Media Research, Rentrak, ReplayTV, Screenvision, TiVo, Universal McCann, Video Business, Video Software Dealers Association, World Airline Entertainment Association, Yankee Group

FORECAST ASSUMPTIONS

- Growth of box office spending is expected to accelerate in 2005, driven by the highly successful release of *Star Wars: Episode III: Revenge of the Sith* during the important summer box office season, as well as *Charlie and the Chocolate Factory*, a contemporary remake of the 1971 classic *Willy Wonka & the Chocolate Factory*, and new takes on *The Pink Panther* and *The Dukes of Hazzard*. Declining admissions and stabilizing ticket prices, however, will hinder growth.
- DVD sales will continue to be strong, but growth will decelerate in the forecast period because the expansion of DVD households is tapering off. The DVD market will be adversely affected by the emergence of two competing, next-generation formats, HD-DVD and Blu-ray, which will be launched in late 2005.
- The pace of change in the interactive television and wireless content segment has been rapid and some formats, such as stand-alone digital video recorders, are already showing signs of obsolescence as newer and cheaper technologies replace them. The introduction of new applications like interactive program guides will expand the possibilities of digital recording and attract greater advertising interest.
- Building on the success of scripted shows, such as *Lost* and *Desperate Housewives*, television networks will try to outdo cable channels by developing stronger dramas and sitcoms while relying less on low-cost reality programs.

The Outlook for Total Filmed Entertainment Spending

Total expenditures on filmed entertainment, including box office, home video, ITV and television programming, are expected to hit $101.15 billion in 2009, up from $68.18 billion in 2004. Compound annual growth during the forecast period is projected to be 8.2 percent, compared with 8.3 percent in the 1999-2004 period. Continued double-digit growth in the ITV, wireless content and home video sectors, and renewed spending among television networks, will drive the filmed entertainment market over the next five years.

Recorded Music

THE RECORDED MUSIC MARKET IN 2004 AND 2005

Recorded music spending grew 2.5 percent to $12.15 billion in 2004, ending the industry's four-year slide. The record industry was bolstered by Usher's *Confessions* album in 2004, which sold 8.0 million copies, more than the year's second and third bestselling albums combined, and 1.5 million more than the top album of 2003, *Get Rich or Die Tryin'* by 50 Cent. A decrease for the first time in the average price of a CD also helped spark sales. The recorded music industry is still largely driven by hits, and it comes as no surprise that the top 10 albums of 2004 sold 34.6 million copies combined, up from 33.3 million copies in 2003.

Recorded music unit sales grew in the first half of 2004 by 3.5 percent, but decreased 0.6 percent in the second half of the year. Early 2005 data indicated that the growth achieved in 2004 was more likely an aberration than a trend, as first-quarter 2005 unit sales were down approximately 8.0 percent compared to 2004. Music industry executives were hopeful that some key second-quarter 2005 album releases—from artists including Mariah Carey, the Dave Matthews Band, Bruce Springsteen and American Idol—would help the industry perpetuate growth. Despite these releases, we expect music expenditures, excluding online spending, to decrease 2.5 percent to $11.85 billion for the full-year 2005, and unit sales to fall 2.3 percent to 795.2 million.

Piracy continues to be a key issue for the recorded music industry, costing the business an estimated $4.6 billion annually in the U.S. alone. The Recording Industry Association of America (RIAA) is fighting back against illegal music downloads, and is making some headway by shutting down many illegal file sharing Web sites, although it will never be able to stamp out piracy completely.

On the positive side, both the recorded music industry and more importantly, consumers, are beginning to embrace legitimate music downloading. Sales of portable digital audio players—most notably, Apple's iPod—

HIGHLIGHTS

Recorded Music

Recorded music spending grew 2.5 percent to $12.15 billion in 2004, ending the industry's four-year slide. Successful album releases and falling CD prices drove the gain.

■

Digital music spending increased 312.5 percent to $330.0 million in 2004, as consumers began to pay for legitimate music downloads.

■

CDs, by far the largest recorded music format, enjoyed a 1.9 percent increase in spending to $11.45 billion in 2004 after three straight years of decline. CD sales rose in part due to a 0.9 percent decrease in the average price to $14.93. CD sales represented more than 94 percent of all music revenues in 2004.

■

Most disappointing for the music industry was the fall in sales of next-generation formats Super Audio CDs (SACD) and DVD-Audio of 36.9 percent and 20.0 percent, respectively. SACD and DVD-Audio were expected to compete to replace the CD, but consumers prefer digital music downloading to either SACD or DVD-Audio, primarily because it costs less.

■

The average price of LPs, CD singles and SACD all grew in 2004, 2.1 percent, 11.1 percent and 3.9 percent, respectively. The average price of vinyl singles remained flat, while CDs, cassettes, music videos and DVD-Audios all declined.

■

Recorded music expenditures will continue to dip during most of the forecast period, with industry spending falling to $10.95 billion in 2009. Recorded music spending will decline at a compound annual rate of 2.1 percent from 2004 to 2009, compared with a compound annual decrease of 3.6 percent in the 1999-2004 period. As a result, the share of recorded music spending within entertainment media will drop from 13.7 percent in 2004 to 8.8 percent in 2009.

Recorded Music Expenditures, by Format*

($ MILLIONS)

Year	Vinyl Singles	LPs	CDs	Cassettes	Cassette Singles	CD Singles	Music Videos†	DVD-Audios	SACDs	Total
1999	$28	$32	$12,816	$1,062	$48	$222	$377	—	—	$14,585
2000	26	28	13,214	626	5	143	282	$3	—	14,327
2001	31	27	12,909	363	—	79	329	6	—	13,745
2002	25	20	12,044	210	—	20	288	9	—	12,615
2003	22	22	11,233	108	—	36	400	8	$26	11,855
2004	20	19	11,446	24	—	15	607	6	17	12,154
2005	18	18	11,205	21	—	12	551	7	17	11,849
2006	17	17	10,814	18	—	11	601	7	17	11,502
2007	15	15	10,782	17	—	9	642	8	17	11,505
2008	14	14	10,394	16	—	8	667	7	16	11,135
2009	13	13	10,196	13	—	6	690	7	15	10,953

Sources: Veronis Suhler Stevenson, PQ Media, Recording Industry Association of America
*At suggested list prices.
†The Recording Industry Association of America includes DVD music videos in music videos.

Entertainment Media

Growth of Recorded Music Expenditures, by Format*

Year	Vinyl Singles	LPs	CDs	Cassettes	Cassette Singles	CD Singles	Music Videos†	DVD-Audios	SACDs	Total
2000	–6.1%	–13.2%	3.1%	–41.0%	–90.4%	–35.9%	–25.2%	—	—	–1.8%
2001	19.1	–2.2	–2.3	–42.0	—	–44.5	16.7	81.8%	—	–4.1
2002	–20.5	–25.2	–6.7	–42.2	—	–75.3	–12.3	41.7	—	–8.2
2003	–14.0	7.4	–6.7	–48.5	—	83.2	38.7	–5.9	—	–6.0
2004	–8.3	–11.5	1.9	–78.2	—	–58.5	51.8	–20.0	–36.9%	2.5
2005	–7.6	–7.3	–2.1	–13.1	—	–18.1	–9.3	6.3	1.8	–2.5
2006	–7.7	–7.3	–3.5	–10.2	—	–11.5	9.1	8.8	1.2	–2.9
2007	–8.3	–7.3	–0.3	–9.8	—	–14.8	6.8	4.1	–2.3	0.0
2008	–7.8	–9.8	–3.6	–5.4	—	–16.3	3.9	–2.8	–4.2	–3.2
2009	–11.9	–4.4	–1.9	–15.0	—	–18.2	3.5	–10.7	–5.0	–1.6
Compound Annual Change										
1999-2004	–6.6	–9.6	–2.2	–53.3	—	–41.8	10.0	—	—	–3.6
2004-2009	–8.7	–7.2	–2.3	–10.8	—	–15.8	2.6	0.9	–1.7	–2.1

Sources: Veronis Suhler Stevenson, PQ Media, Recording Industry Association of America
*At suggested list prices.
†The Recording Industry Association of America includes DVD music videos in music videos.

are strong and are helping drive sales of legitimate digital music, which grew 312.5 percent to $330.0 million in 2004.

As traditional revenue streams continue to decline, the music industry is finding other income sources to offset the losses, including cell phone ringtones and the licensing of music to other industries. For example, it is estimated that 30 to 35 million cell phone mastertones were sold in the U.S. in 2004, at an average price of more than $2.00 each.

CDs, by far the largest recorded music format, enjoyed a 1.9 percent increase in spending to $11.45 billion in 2004. The gain in sales was due in part to a 0.9 percent decrease in the average price to $14.93. CD net unit sales grew 2.8 percent to 766.9 million in 2004, up from 745.9 million units in 2003. Only music video units grew more, up 64.3 percent to 32.7 million. All six other categories experienced declines. CD sales represented more than 94 percent of all music spending in 2004. Music video spending, (which includes DVD music videos), the second-largest category after CDs, was the only other category to increase, with a 51.8 percent gain to $607.0 million.

Bestselling Albums in 2004

Artist	*Album*	*Units Sold (Millions)*
Usher	Confessions	8.0
Norah Jones	Feels Like Home	3.8
Eminem	Encore	3.5
Kenny Chesney	When The Sun Goes Down	3.1
Gretchen Wilson	Here for the Party	2.9
Tim McGraw	Live Like You Were Dying	2.8
Maroon	Songs About Jane	2.7
Evanescence	Fallen	2.6
Ashlee Simpson	Autobiography	2.6
Now 16	Now That's What I Call Music!	2.6

Sources: Veronis Suhler Stevenson, PQ Media, SoundScan, Recording Industry Association of America

Online Music Spending*

Year	*Digital Singles Downloaded (Millions)†*	*Growth Of Digital Singles Downloaded*	*Digital Albums Downloaded (Millions)†*	*Growth Of Digital Albums Downloaded*	*Digital Music Spending ($ Millions)*	*Growth Of Digital Music Spending*
2001	—	—	—	—	$ 13	—
2002	—	—	—	—	25	92.3%
2003	—	—	—	—	80	220.0
2004	139.4	—	4.5	—	330	312.5
2005	257.1	84.4%	6.8	51.5%	765	131.7
2006	420.0	63.4	9.2	35.4	1,387	81.4
2007	623.7	48.5	11.9	29.3	2,125	53.2
2008	825.8	32.4	14.1	18.4	2,875	35.3
2009	943.9	14.3	15.7	11.4	3,407	18.5
Compound Annual Growth						
1999-2004	—	—	—	—	—	—
2004-2009	—	46.6	—	28.5	—	59.5

Sources: Veronis Suhler Stevenson, PQ Media, Jupiter Media Metrix, comScore, International Federation of Phonographic Industry, Recording Industry Association of America

*The RIAA did not begin analyzing downloaded units until 2004.

Average Prices of Recorded Music, by Format

Year	*Vinyl Singles*	*LPs*	*CDs*	*Cassettes*	*Cassette Singles*	*CD Singles*	*Music Videos**	*DVD-Audios*	*SACDs*	*Total*
1999	$5.26	$10.97	$13.65	$8.59	$3.38	$3.98	$19.03	—	—	$12.57
2000	5.46	12.55	14.02	8.24	3.54	4.17	15.48	$22.00	—	13.27
2001	5.67	11.74	14.64	8.07	—	4.58	18.59	20.00	—	14.17
2002	5.64	11.88	14.99	6.77	—	4.36	19.62	21.25	—	14.67
2003	5.68	14.47	15.06	6.28	—	4.33	20.10	20.00	$20.23	14.85
2004	5.66	14.77	14.93	4.54	—	4.81	18.57	18.29	21.01	14.93
2005	5.38	12.71	14.90	4.10	—	3.70	19.12	17.90	21.12	14.90
2006	5.28	12.69	14.65	4.00	—	3.60	18.77	18.50	20.85	14.68
2007	5.16	11.77	14.48	3.96	—	3.29	18.49	18.34	21.98	14.53
2008	4.93	11.50	14.44	4.14	—	3.50	16.14	19.20	21.34	14.41
2009	4.66	11.00	14.52	4.05	—	3.32	14.13	19.11	21.72	14.39

Sources: Veronis Suhler Stevenson, PQ Media, Recording Industry Association of America
*The Recording Industry Association of America includes DVD music videos in music videos.

Growth of Average Prices of Recorded Music, by Format

Year	*Vinyl Singles*	*LPs*	*CDs*	*Cassettes*	*Cassette Singles*	*CD Singles*	*Music Videos**	*DVD-Audios*	*SACDs*	*Total*
2000	3.7%	14.4%	2.7%	−4.1%	4.7%	4.8%	−18.6%	—	—	5.6%
2001	3.9	−6.4	4.4	−2.0	—	9.8	20.0	−9.1%	—	6.8
2002	−0.6	1.2	2.4	−16.1	—	−4.9	5.5	6.3	—	3.5
2003	0.8	21.7	0.4	−7.1	—	−0.7	2.4	−5.9	—	1.2
2004	−0.5	2.1	−0.9	−27.8	—	11.1	−7.6	−8.6	3.9%	0.6
2005	−4.9	−13.9	−0.2	−9.6	—	−23.1	3.0	−2.1	0.5	−0.2
2006	−1.9	−0.2	−1.7	−2.4	—	−2.7	−1.8	3.3	−1.3	−1.5
2007	−2.2	−7.3	−1.2	−1.2	—	−8.7	−1.5	−0.9	5.4	−1.0
2008	−4.6	−2.3	−0.3	4.6	—	6.5	−12.7	4.7	−2.9	−0.8
2009	−5.4	−4.3	0.6	−2.1	—	−5.3	−12.4	−0.5	1.8	−0.2
Compound Annual Change										
1999-2004	1.5	6.1	1.8	−12.0	—	3.9	−0.5	—	—	3.5
2004-2009	−3.8	−5.7	−0.6	−2.3	—	−7.2	−5.3	0.9	0.7	−0.7

Sources: Veronis Suhler Stevenson, PQ Media, Recording Industry Association of America
*The Recording Industry Association of America includes DVD music videos in music videos.

Net Unit Shipments of Recorded Music, by Format*

(MILLIONS)

Year	Vinyl Singles	LPs	CDs	Cassettes	Cassette Singles	CD Singles	Music Videos†	DVD-Audios	SACDs	Total
1999	5.3	2.9	938.9	123.6	14.2	55.9	19.8	—	—	1,160.6
2000	4.8	2.2	942.5	76.0	1.3	34.2	18.2	0.2	—	1,079.4
2001	5.5	2.3	881.9	45.0	—	17.3	17.7	0.3	—	970.0
2002	4.4	1.7	803.3	31.0	—	4.5	14.7	0.4	—	860.0
2003	3.8	1.5	745.9	17.2	—	8.3	19.9	0.4	1.3	798.3
2004	3.5	1.3	766.9	5.2	—	3.1	32.7	0.4	0.8	813.8
2005	3.4	1.4	752.1	5.0	—	3.3	28.8	0.4	0.8	795.2
2006	3.2	1.3	738.2	4.6	—	3.0	32.0	0.4	0.8	783.5
2007	3.0	1.3	744.8	4.2	—	2.8	34.7	0.4	0.8	792.0
2008	2.9	1.2	720.0	3.8	—	2.2	41.3	0.4	0.8	772.5
2009	2.7	1.2	702.3	3.3	—	1.9	48.8	0.4	0.7	761.3

Sources: Veronis Suhler Stevenson, PQ Media, Recording Industry Association of America
*Shipments less returns.
†The Recording Industry Association of America includes DVD music videos in music videos.

Growth of Net Unit Shipments of Recorded Music, by Format*

Year	Vinyl Singles	LPs	CDs	Cassettes	Cassette Singles	CD Singles	Music Videos†	DVD-Audios	SACDs	Total
2000	–9.4%	–24.1%	0.4%	–38.5%	–90.8%	–38.8%	–8.1%	—	—	–7.0%
2001	14.6	4.5	–6.4	–40.8	—	–49.4	–2.7	100.0%	—	–10.1
2002	–20.0	–26.1	–8.9	–31.1	—	–74.0	–16.9	33.3	—	–11.3
2003	–13.6	–11.8	–7.1	–44.5	—	84.4	35.4	0.0	—	–7.2
2004	–7.9	–13.3	2.8	–69.8	—	–62.7	64.3	–12.5	–39.2%	1.9
2005	–2.9	7.7	–1.9	–3.8	—	6.5	–11.9	8.6	1.3	–2.3
2006	–5.9	–7.1	–1.8	–8.0	—	–9.1	11.1	5.3	2.5	–1.5
2007	–6.3	0.0	0.9	–8.7	—	–6.7	8.4	5.0	–7.3	1.1
2008	–3.3	–7.7	–3.3	–9.5	—	–21.4	19.0	–7.1	–1.3	–2.5
2009	–6.9	0.0	–2.5	–13.2	—	–13.6	18.2	–10.3	–6.7	–1.5
Compound Annual Change										
1999-2004	–8.0	–14.8	–4.0	–46.9	—	–43.9	10.6	—	—	–6.9
2004-2009	–5.1	–1.6	–1.7	–8.7	—	–9.3	8.3	0.0	–2.4	–1.3

Sources: Veronis Suhler Stevenson, PQ Media, Recording Industry Association of America
*Shipments less returns.
†The Recording Industry Association of America includes DVD music videos in music videos.

Most disappointing for the music industry was the fall in sales of next-generation formats Super Audio CDs (SACD) and DVD-Audio: 36.9 percent and 20.0 percent, respectively. The two competing formats were originally expected to fight to displace the CD as the primary distribution media for music sales, but consumers have not bought into either. Revenues declined in 2004 for vinyl singles (8.3 percent), LPs (11.5 percent), cassettes

Entertainment Media

(78.2 percent) and CD singles (58.5 percent). Cassettes fell well below the $100 million mark, and are all but extinct outside of audio book sales.

Overall, the average prices across all seven formats increased a scant 0.6 percent to $14.93 in 2004. The average price of LPs, CD singles and SACD all grew in 2004, 2.1 percent, 11.1 percent, and 3.9 percent, respectively. The average price of vinyl singles remained flat, while CDs (0.9 percent), cassettes (27.8 percent), music videos (7.6 percent) and DVD-Audios (8.6 percent) all declined. Net unit shipments of recorded music by format increased 1.9 percent to 813.8 million in 2004, despite the fact that only CD and music video unit shipments increased.

FORECAST ASSUMPTIONS

- The music business continues to be a hit-driven industry, as the top 10 albums of 2004 outsold the 10 best-selling albums of 2003, resulting in an overall spending gain. The heavy reliance on blockbusters to drive growth, along with continued losses to digital piracy, will cause spending to decline in the forecast period.
- The DVD-Audio and Super Audio CD formats will fail to find acceptance during the forecast period, as consumers prefer lower-quality, but less expensive digital downloads than the higher-priced next-generation formats.
- The market for digital downloading will continue to thrive, driven by Apple's iPod and other mobile electronic devices, such as cell phones, as well as consumers' increasing willingness to pay for legitimate music downloads.

The Outlook For Recorded Music

Although the recorded music industry experienced a boost in 2004 spending, the market will continue to struggle in the forecast period due to online piracy and competition from other entertainment media, including DVD movies and videogames.

Not including online music spending (which is included in the Consumer Internet chapter), recorded music expenditures are projected to fall 2.5 percent to $11.85 billion in 2005. The compound annual rate of decline for recorded music spending is projected to fall 2.1 percent from 2004 to 2009. The lack of consumer interest in SACD and DVD-Audio is dampening growth. Both formats are expected to struggle during the forecast period because consumers prefer electronic distribution. Total net unit shipments of recorded music are projected to fall 2.3 percent in 2005, and at a compound annual rate of 1.3 percent from 2004 to 2009 to 761.3 million.

As the installed base of portable digital audio players increases, so will digital music spending. The installed base of iPods, the bestselling portable digital audio player on the market, is expected to more than triple to 35 million by year-end 2005. Sony, Creative Labs, Yahoo! and Philips are among the companies trying to compete with Apple in the market, but have yet to come up with alternatives with wide appeal to consumers. Spending on digital music downloads are expected to grow 131.7 percent to $765.0 million in 2005, and at a compound annual growth rate of 59.5 percent to $3.41 billion.

Interactive Entertainment

CONSOLE VIDEOGAMES

THE CONSOLE VIDEOGAMES MARKET IN 2004 AND 2005

The total videogame console software business—including sell-through and rental—grew 6.0 percent to $6.91 billion in 2004, thanks to a record 12 videogames surpassing the 1 million-unit milestone during the year. Handheld games, including the recently launched Sony PlayStation Portable (PSP) and Nintendo DS, continue to sell well and helped boost hardware and software sales in late 2004 and early 2005. The PSP has generated a buzz among videogame enthusiasts because of its strong graphics and additional features; however, overall spending on software has been tempered by the limited availability of new titles, most of which are duplicates of PlayStation 2 titles.

Sales of console videogame hardware fell to 10.8 million units in 2004, from 12.8 million in 2003. The average console price fell to $138.21 in 2004, from $159.04 in 2003. The drop in unit sales and prices resulted in a 27.0 percent decrease in videogame console spending to $1.49 billion for the year.

Hardware sales are expected to rebound in the second half of 2005 when Microsoft and Sony launch their respective new Xbox and PlayStation systems. Hardware sales should rise significantly in 2006, when the production of the latest new systems catches up with demand, and hardware prices start to fall.

Halo 2, one of the bestselling titles of 2004, took in $125 million in its first day of sales alone. It helped boost videogame console software sell-through 7.0 percent in 2004 to $6.22 billion, offsetting a 2.1 percent decline in videogame rentals to $682.0 million. A total of 203.0 million software units were sold in 2004, up 8.9 percent. Videogame software prices fell 1.8 percent during the year.

Movie studios and advertisers are converging on the videogame market to capital-

Highlights

Interactive Entertainment

Sales of console videogame hardware fell to 10.8 million units in 2004, from 12.8 million in 2003. The average console price fell to $138.21 in 2004, from $159.04 in 2003. The drop in unit sales and prices resulted in a 27.0 percent decrease in videogame console spending to $1.49 billion for the year.

■

The videogame console software market rose 6.0 percent to $6.91 billion in 2004. It was the second straight year of single-digit growth due mainly to consumers waiting for the next generation of console hardware before investing in new game titles.

■

The PC entertainment software market fell 15.9 percent to $1.20 billion in 2004, as educational software sales continued to plummet due to competition from online sources.

■

Online gaming and in-game advertising represent two new revenue streams for the videogame industry. Online gaming nearly doubled to $656.0 million in 2004, and is expected to grow to $2.89 billion by 2009. In-game advertising grew 51.9 percent to $120.0 million in 2004, and will increase at a compound annual rate of 46.1 percent to $800.0 million during the forecast period.

ize on what has become one of the entertainment industry's strongest growth areas. Some movie studios have actively been searching for videogame company acquisitions, particularly as videogames are cutting into the time consumers spend viewing movies and television shows. Advertisers have already begun to recognize the potential of videogames as advertising vehicles, as some games sell as many as 5 million units. Videogame advertising grew 51.9 percent to $120.0 million, with such companies as McDonald's, Coca-Cola and Nokia incorporating advertising messages in videogames. In-game advertising typically ranges from a few cents to more than 50 cents per unit sold, depending on the product placement and overall sales of the game.

Action games dominate videogame software, representing 30.1 percent of purchases. Sports games are the next bestselling genre, with 17.8 percent of sales, followed by shooter (9.6 percent), family and children (9.5 percent) and racing (9.4 percent) games.

THE OUTLOOK FOR CONSOLE VIDEOGAMES

The interactive entertainment segment is drawing more consumer attention and dollars away from the other entertainment segments, such as box office and music. The typical gamer plays videogames nearly seven hours a week. Spending on videogame console software will grow 5.3 percent to $7.27 billion in 2005. Growth for the year will be held back due to the late arrival of Sony and Microsoft's next-generation videogame systems. The segment will see a return to double-digit growth in 2006, fueled by strong hardware and software sales of the new systems. Spending growth is expected to remain strong during the forecast period, with compound annual growth increasing to 9.2 percent in the 2004-2009 period to $10.74 billion, from 8.2 percent in the previous five-year period. Growth will be fueled by online gaming, particularly as the industry and consumers become more comfortable with the format. Online gaming expenditures are expected to grow to $2.89 billion by 2009.

The Videogame Console Market

Year	*Unit Sales (Thousands)*	*Average System Price**	*Spending ($ Millions)*	*Percent Change In Spending*
1999	11,800	$118.64	$1,400	8.4%
2000	8,200	134.15	1,100	–21.4
2001	11,400	216.67	2,470	124.5
2002	14,153	169.29	2,396	–3.0
2003	12,821	159.04	2,039	–14.9
2004	10,770	138.21	1,488	–27.0

Sources: Veronis Suhler Stevenson, PQ Media, NPDFunworld
*Including peripherals.

The Videogame Console Software Market*

Year	Sell-Through			Rental			Total Videogame Console Software Spending ($ Millions)
	Units Sold (Millions)	Average Price	Sell-Through Console Software Spending ($ Millions)	Units Rented (Millions)	Average Price Per Rental	Rental Console Software Spending ($ Millions)	
1999	112.6	$37.41	$4,212	113.8	$3.82	$435	$ 4,647
2000	131.6	31.50	4,145	124.4	3.92	488	4,633
2001	141.5	32.75	4,634	132.0	4.16	549	5,183
2002	162.8	33.58	5,467	138.5	4.70	651	6,118
2003	186.4	31.22	5,819	139.3	5.00	697	6,516
2004	203.0	30.66	6,224	127.1	5.36	682	6,906
2005	211.1	31.18	6,583	124.6	5.53	689	7,272
2006	230.8	32.09	7,404	130.6	5.62	734	8,138
2007	250.2	32.89	8,227	135.4	5.74	777	9,004
2008	277.2	33.58	9,307	142.5	5.85	834	10,141
2009	290.2	34.12	9,901	138.6	6.03	836	10,737

Sources: Veronis Suhler Stevenson, PQ Media LLC, NPDFunworld, Entertainment Software Association, Rentrak
*Includes portable game units.

Growth of the Videogame Console Software Market*

Year	Sell-Through			Rental			Total Videogame Console Software Spending
	Units Sold	Average Price	Sell-Through Console Software Spending	Console Software Units Rented	Average Price Per Rental	Rental Console Software Spending	
2000	16.9%	–15.8%	–1.6%	9.3%	2.6%	12.2%	–0.3%
2001	7.5	4.0	11.8	6.1	6.0	12.5	11.9
2002	15.1	2.5	18.0	4.9	13.1	18.6	18.0
2003	14.5	–7.0	6.4	0.6	6.4	7.0	6.5
2004	8.9	–1.8	7.0	–8.8	7.3	–2.1	6.0
2005	4.0	1.7	5.8	–2.0	3.0	1.0	5.3
2006	9.3	2.9	12.5	4.8	1.7	6.6	11.9
2007	8.4	2.5	11.1	3.7	2.0	5.8	10.6
2008	10.8	2.1	13.1	5.2	2.0	7.3	12.6
2009	4.7	1.6	6.4	–2.7	3.1	0.3	5.9
Compound Annual Growth							
1999-2004	12.5	–3.9	8.1	2.2	7.0	9.4	8.2
2004-2009	7.4	2.2	9.7	1.7	2.4	4.2	9.2

Sources: Veronis Suhler Stevenson, PQ Media LLC, NPDFunworld, Entertainment Software Association, Rentrak
*Includes portable game units.

The PC Entertainment Software Market*

Year	Computer Households (Millions)	Unit Sales Per Computer Household	Aggregate Units Sold (Millions)	Average Price	Aggregate Software Spending ($ Millions)
1999	43.7	1.91	83.4	$22.66	$1,890
2000	53.4	1.66	88.6	21.59	1,913
2001	61.1	1.33	81.3	21.50	1,748
2002	65.7	1.10	72.4	22.89	1,657
2003	70.6	0.92	64.8	22.03	1,427
2004	74.8	0.74	55.1	21.79	1,201
2005	78.0	0.63	48.8	21.62	1,055
2006	80.9	0.54	44.1	21.35	941
2007	83.2	0.48	40.3	21.27	858
2008	85.0	0.44	37.2	20.84	775
2009	86.4	0.40	34.5	20.55	709

Sources: Veronis Suhler Stevenson, PQ Media, NPDFunworld, Entertainment Software Association, U.S. Bureau of the Census
*Includes educational software.

Entertainment Media

Growth of the PC Entertainment Software Market*

Year	Computer Households	Unit Sales Per Computer Household	Aggregate Units Sold	Average Price	Aggregate Software Spending
2000	22.2%	–13.1%	6.2%	–4.7%	1.2%
2001	14.4	–19.8	–8.2	–0.4	–8.6
2002	7.5	–17.2	–10.9	6.5	–5.2
2003	7.5	–16.7	–10.5	–3.8	–13.9
2004	5.9	–19.7	–15.0	–1.1	–15.9
2005	4.3	–15.1	–11.4	–0.8	–12.1
2006	3.7	–12.9	–9.7	–1.2	–10.8
2007	2.8	–11.0	–8.5	–0.4	–8.9
2008	2.2	–9.8	–7.8	–2.0	–9.7
2009	1.7	–8.8	–7.2	–1.4	–8.5
Compound Annual Growth					
1999-2004	11.3	–17.3	–8.0	–0.8	–8.7
2004-2009	2.9	–11.5	–8.9	–1.2	–10.0

Sources: Veronis Suhler Stevenson, PQ Media, NPDFunworld, Entertainment Software Association, U.S. Bureau of the Census
*Includes educational software.

PC ENTERTAINMENT SOFTWARE

THE PC ENTERTAINMENT SOFTWARE MARKET IN 2004 AND 2005

Spending on the PC entertainment software market fell 15.9 percent to $1.20 billion in 2004, as educational software sales continued to plummet. With the preponderance of higher-speed Internet connections, consumers are increasingly choosing to access content and games online, rather than on disc. PC entertainment software spending has declined at a compound annual rate of 8.7 percent in the period from 1999 to 2004.

Unit sales were 55.1 million in 2004, down 15.0 percent. Unit sales per household fell 19.7 percent to 0.74 units, marking the fifth straight year of double-digit declines. The average price for PC entertainment software fell 1.1 percent to $21.79 in 2004.

THE OUTLOOK FOR PC ENTERTAINMENT SOFTWARE

Without a killer application—strategy games are the business' closest thing to a killer application, representing 26.9 percent of all sales—PC entertainment software sales will continue to fall due to competition from better, and often cheaper, online options.

Computer household penetration rose 5.9 percent to 74.8 million, but PC entertainment software unit sales per household are projected to decline 11.5 percent on a compound annual basis. Unit sales are also expected to drop, falling at a compound annual rate of 8.9 percent. Spending on computer-game and entertainment software will fall 10.0 percent during the forecast period, to $709.0 million in 2009.

Shares of Videogame Purchases, by Genre

	Console Games		*PC Games*	
Rank	*Category*	*% Share*	*Category*	*% Share*
1	Action	30.1%	Strategy	26.9%
2	Sports	17.8	Family & Children	20.3
3	Shooter	9.6	Shooter	16.3
4	Family & Children	9.5	Role-Playing	10.0
5	Racing	9.4	Adventure	5.9
6	Role-Playing	9.0	Sports	5.4
7	Fighting	5.4	Action	3.9
	Other	9.2	Other	11.3

Sources: Veronis Suhler Stevenson, PQ Media, NPDFunworld, Entertainment Software Association

Interactive Entertainment Spending

($ MILLIONS)

Year	Videogame Software*	PC Entertainment Software†	Videogame Advertising‡	Total Console/ Computer Videogames	Online Games§	Total Videogames Including Online
1999	$ 4,647	$1,890	$ 3	$ 6,540	$ 71	$ 6,611
2000	4,633	1,913	9	6,555	127	6,682
2001	5,183	1,748	22	6,953	196	7,149
2002	6,118	1,657	44	7,819	274	8,093
2003	6,516	1,427	79	8,022	343	8,365
2004	6,906	1,201	120	8,227	656	8,883
2005	7,272	1,055	178	8,505	1,072	9,577
2006	8,138	941	267	9,346	1,563	10,909
2007	9,004	858	402	10,264	2,055	12,319
2008	10,141	775	594	11,510	2,532	14,042
2009	10,737	709	800	12,246	2,886	15,132

Sources: Veronis Suhler Stevenson, PQ Media, NPDFunworld, Rentrak, Yankee Group, Entertainment Software Association

*Includes portable games.

†Includes educational software.

‡Includes in-game advertising and advergaming.

§To avoid double counting in overall spending, online game spending is included in the Consumer Internet chapter.

Growth of Interactive Entertainment Spending

Year	Videogame Software*	PC Entertainment Software†	Videogame Advertising‡	Total Console/ Computer Videogames	Online Games§	Total Videogames Including Online
2000	–0.3%	1.2%	200.0%	0.2%	78.9%	1.1%
2001	11.9	–8.6	144.4	6.1	54.3	7.0
2002	18.0	–5.2	100.0	12.5	39.8	13.2
2003	6.5	–13.9	79.5	2.6	25.2	3.4
2004	6.0	–15.9	51.9	2.5	91.3	6.2
2005	5.3	–12.1	48.3	3.4	63.4	7.8
2006	11.9	–10.8	50.0	9.9	45.8	13.9
2007	10.6	–8.9	50.6	9.8	31.5	12.9
2008	12.6	–9.7	47.8	12.1	23.2	14.0
2009	5.9	-8.5	34.7	6.4	14.0	7.8
Compound Annual Growth						
1999-2004	8.2	–8.7	109.1	4.7	56.0	6.1
2004-2009	9.2	–10.0	46.1	8.3	34.5	11.2

Sources: Veronis Suhler Stevenson, PQ Media, NPDFunworld, Rentrak, Yankee Group, Entertainment Software Association

*Includes portable games.

†Includes educational software.

‡Includes in-game advertising and advergaming.

§To avoid double counting in overall spending, online game spending is included in the Consumer Internet chapter.

The Outlook For Total Interactive Entertainment

The late 2005 release of Sony's PlayStation and Microsoft's Xbox next-generation videogame consoles will help drive sales in 2006 and 2007, as gamers purchase new hardware and software.

The interactive entertainment industry will continue to move toward an online model during the forecast period. Online gaming expenditures are expected to grow at a compound annual rate of 34.5 percent during the forecast period. In-game advertising is the only segment that will outgrow online sales, at a compound annual rate of 46.1 percent.

Interactive entertainment expenditures, not including online games, are projected to grow from $8.23 billion in 2004 to $12.25 billion in 2009. Compound annual growth for the forecast period will be 8.3 percent, up from 4.7 percent from 1999 to 2004.

FORECAST ASSUMPTIONS

- Videogame console and software sales will struggle in 2005 until next-generation systems are rolled out by Sony and Microsoft late in the year. Sales of the two new, next-generation videogame systems, along with software, will take off in 2006, when prices fall and production catches up with demand.
- Online gaming and in-game advertising represent two new sources of revenues for the videogame industry, and will help boost spending during the forecast period. The industry must address challenges for both, including piracy and business models.
- PC gaming software revenues will continue to decline during the forecast period, as PC entertainment and edutainment lose users to online games, which offer lower prices and higher download speeds.

Entertainment Media

2004 Communications Industry Forecast Compared with Actual Growth

Category	*2004 Forecasted Growth**	*Actual 2004 Growth†*
Filmed Entertainment	9.7%	3.9%
Recorded Music	–1.2	2.5
Interactive Entertainment	5.2	6.1
Total	7.9	8.2

*Veronis Suhler Stevenson 2004 Communications Industry Forecast & Report
†Veronis Suhler Stevenson, PQ Media

8

Consumer Internet

Consumer Internet Spending And Nominal GDP Growth, 2000-2009

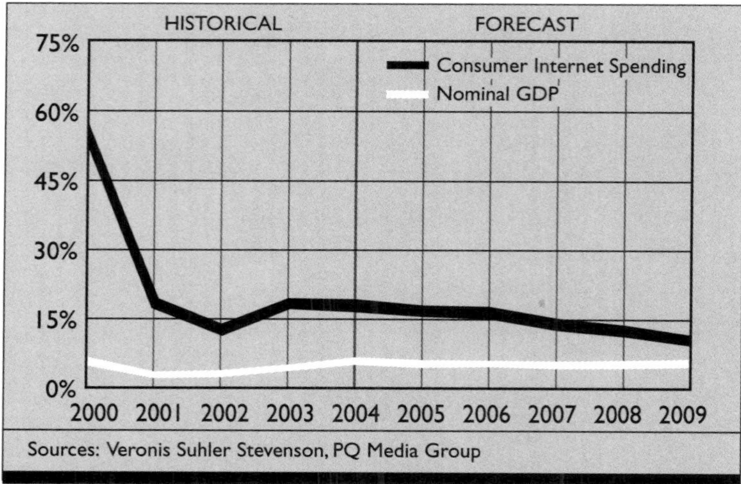

Sources: Veronis Suhler Stevenson, PQ Media Group

Growth of U.S. Consumer Internet Spending

	Internet Access	*Internet Content*	*Internet Advertising*	*Total*
2004 Expenditures ($ Millions)	$25,581	$2,345	$9,626	$37,552
1999-2004 Compound Annual Growth (%)	26.5%	—	15.8%	24.6%
2004-2009 Projected Compound Annual Growth (%)	8.3%	27.1%	24.0%	14.5%
2009 Projected Expenditures ($ Millions)	$38,076	$7,764	$28,198	$74,038

Sources: Veronis Suhler Stevenson, PQ Media, AOL Time Warner, Borrell Associates, CMR Interactive, comScore Networks, Corzen, DataMonitor, eMarketer, Jupiter Media Metrix, Kinetic Strategies, Interactive Advertising Bureau, National Cable & Telecommunications Assocation, Online Publishers Association, Simba Information

THE CONSUMER INTERNET MARKET IN 2004 AND 2005

Consumer Internet expenditures, including spending on Web access, advertising and content, rose at a double-digit rate for the fifth consecutive year in 2004, as total spending in this market surged 18.3 percent to $37.55 billion for the year. Driven by several key trends in the three major subsegments, consumer Internet spending growth significantly outpaced that of nominal GDP in 2004 and in the 1999-2004 period, when expenditures grew at a compound annual rate of 24.6 percent.

Among the important market drivers was the continued transition from dial-up to broadband access, a material improvement in speed and time-efficient use of the medium, which empowered more consumers to retrieve and utilize rich media advertising and content, as well as to conduct more frequent searches. In addition, marketers accelerated the shift of advertising dollars to the Internet in response to data that shows the coveted 18- to 34-year-old demographic is spending more time online and less with traditional media. The Internet's detailed and timely return on investment (ROI) data also allowed advertisers to optimize their spending, resulting in the attraction of new marketers to the medium and higher spending from existing ones. On the content front, increased spending on Web gaming and digital music contributed to the strong performance of the overall consumer Internet segment in 2004, regardless of the continued threat from piracy and file sharing.

Consumer Web access spending continued to account for the largest share of the overall market in 2004, with expenditures of $25.58 billion, a 13.0 percent increase compared with the previous year. The double-digit gain was due to the increasing penetration of broadband access, which includes both cable modem and digital subscriber line (DSL) installations. Household spending on cable modem access increased 35.1 percent to $9.30 billion in 2004, while DSL household spending climbed 35.8 percent to $6.56 billion for the year. Meanwhile, household spending on dial-up dropped 15.4 percent to

Internet Households and Household Penetration

Year	U.S. Households (Millions)	Computer Households (Millions)	Computer Penetration Of U.S. Households	Internet Households (Millions)	Internet Households As a % Of Computer Households	Internet Households As a % of U.S. Households
1999	103.9	43.7	42.1%	27.2	62.2%	26.2%
2000	104.7	53.4	51.0	43.6	81.6	41.6
2001	108.2	61.1	56.5	54.8	89.6	50.6
2002	109.3	65.7	60.1	60.9	92.7	55.7
2003	111.3	70.6	63.4	66.8	94.6	60.0
2004	112.4	74.8	66.5	71.1	95.1	63.3
2005	113.6	77.2	68.0	73.7	95.5	64.9
2006	114.8	79.5	69.3	76.2	95.8	66.4
2007	116.1	81.4	70.1	78.2	96.1	67.4
2008	117.3	83.1	70.8	80.0	96.3	68.2
2009	118.6	84.6	71.3	81.7	96.6	68.9

Sources: Veronis Suhler Stevenson, PQ Media, U.S. Census Bureau, U.S. Department of Commerce, Jupiter Research, Pew Internet & Life Project

$8.22 billion in 2004. Total spending on consumer Internet access grew at a compound annual rate of 26.5 percent from 1999 to 2004.

While Web access expenditures account for the largest share of the Internet market, they have posted the slowest growth among the three major subsegments over the past two years. Web access penetration among households with computers has already reached 95.1 percent, and is not expected to reach much higher going forward because not all computer owners need or desire to use the Internet. Access spending's 13.0 percent growth in 2004 was twice that of Internet households, which grew only 6.4 percent for the year. The continued migration from dial-up to broadband access drove the overall spending gain in 2004, due to higher prices for broadband access, which range from $25 to $45 per month compared with $10 to $25 for dial-up. DSL households grew the fastest in 2004, up 44.4 percent to 13.7 million, compared with cable modem households, which grew 27.7 percent to 21.0 million households. Total household spending on cable modem access increased 35.1 percent to $9.30 billion in 2004, while average annual household spending on cable modem access rose 5.8 percent to $443. Overall spending on DSL service increased 35.8 percent to $6.56 billion in 2004, while average annual household spending on DSL access declined 6.0 percent to $478, as a result of providers cutting their prices to attract new customers.

Meanwhile, the number of households using dial-up service decreased 13.2 percent to 33.5 million in 2004, the third consecutive annual decline. Average annual household spending on dial-up shrank 2.6 percent to $245 as the number of households accessing the Internet via other means, such as Wi-Fi and satellite services, increased 26.1 percent to 2.9 million in 2004, a direct result of consumers becoming increasingly more mobile. Rather than accessing the Internet at home, school or the library, more consumers—particularly the younger generation—are surfing the Internet, playing games, visiting chat rooms and/or sending e-mail on the fly from a variety of places, such as malls, parks and Internet cafés. This desire for mobility is expected to continue in the future, and will

Highlights

Consumer Internet spending, including expenditures on Web access, advertising and content, surged at a double-digit rate in 2004 for the fifth consecutive year. Total consumer Internet spending rose 18.3 percent to $37.55 billion for the year, vastly outpacing nominal GDP growth, driven by several major trends. Overall expenditures grew at a compound annual rate of 24.6 percent from 1999 to 2004.

■

Among these trends was the continued transition from dial-up to broadband access, which empowered more consumers to retrieve and utilize rich media advertising and content, as well as to conduct more frequent searches. In addition, marketers accelerated the shift of advertising dollars to the Internet in response to data that show the coveted 18- to 34-year-old demographic is spending more time online and less with traditional media. In addition, the Internet's granular return on investment (ROI) data allowed advertisers to optimize their spending, resulting in the attraction of new advertisers to the medium and higher spending from existing ones. Finally, increased spending on Web gaming and digital music also contributed to consumer Internet's strong performance in 2004.

■

Consumer Web access spending continued to account for the largest share of the overall market in 2004, with expenditures of $25.58 billion, a 13.0 percent increase compared with the previous year. The gain is attributable to the increasing penetration of broadband access, which includes both cable modem and digital subscriber line (DSL) installations. Household spending on cable modem access increased 35.1 percent to $9.30 billion in 2004, while DSL household spending climbed 35.8 percent to $6.56 billion for the year. Household spending on dial-up dropped 15.4 percent to $8.22 billion in 2004. Total spending on consumer Internet access grew at a compound annual rate of 26.5 percent from 1999 to 2004.

■

Consumer Internet advertising, the second-largest subsegment, grew at an accelerated rate of 32.5 percent to $9.63 billion in 2004, driven by increased demand for keyword search advertising, which pushed prices up, as well as an expanded amount of searchable content that generated more advertising opportunities. Greater broadband penetration drove up growth in rich media advertising, since it allowed more users to view these larger files more rapidly. Total spending on consumer Internet advertising grew at a compound annual rate of 15.8 percent from 1999 to 2004.

have a positive effect on the wireless access sector.

Consumer Internet advertising, the second-largest subsegment, grew the fastest in 2004 as spending surged at an accelerated rate of 32.5 percent to $9.63 billion for the year. The strong gain was driven by increased demand for keyword search advertising, which pushed prices up, as well as an expanded amount of searchable content that generated more advertising opportunities. Among the major drivers pushing continued double-digit growth in Internet advertising, and keyword search in particular, is demand from advertisers that media increasingly provide detailed and timely ROI data. Greater broadband penetration drove up growth in rich media advertising, since it allowed more users to view these larger files more rapidly. Total spending on consumer Internet advertising

Spending on keyword search advertising grew 51.0 percent in 2004 to $3.85 billion, while classifieds and rich media also showed strong growth for the year at 41.9 percent and 33.8 percent, respectively. Despite losing share to other formats, display ads grew 19.3 percent, after three consecutive years of double-digit declines. Referrals posted the strongest growth among all ad categories in 2004, up 140.8 percent, as more companies turned to referral marketing because it produced higher response and retention rates than did other forms of acquisition marketing.

■

Content spending, the smallest of the three consumer Internet subsegments, expanded 27.9 percent to $2.35 billion in 2004. Of the three content categories—general content, online games and digital music—general content accounted for the largest share with $1.36 billion in 2004 expenditures. However, general content spending—which includes news, personals, greeting cards and research—declined 3.6 percent for the year. Digital music posted the strongest gain in the content segment, with spending up 312.5 percent to $330.0 million in 2004.

■

Total consumer Internet spending is projected to increase 16.7 percent in 2005 to $43.82 billion, spurred by double-digit growth in Web advertising and content expenditures, while Internet access spending will post high-single-digit growth for the year. The expansion of the overall consumer Web market, which will again outpace that of the broader economy in 2005, will be fueled by several key drivers, but chief among them is the continued shift of ad dollars to media that provide marketers with detailed ROI data in a timely manner.

■

Overall consumer Internet expenditures are expected to maintain a double-digit growth pace throughout the forecast period, consistently beating nominal GDP, as advertisers move to more effectively reach target audiences and track the benefits of media buys, and consumers ratchet up their use of online games and digital downloads. Total consumer Internet spending will grow at a compound annual rate of 14.5 percent from 2004 to 2009, reaching $74.04 billion in 2009. Web advertising spending will increase at a compound annual rate of 24.0 percent in the forecast period, while access spending will rise 8.3 percent and content spending will grow 27.1 percent. The share of Internet spending on access will decline from 68.1 percent in 2004 to 51.4 percent by 2009, while advertising's share will rise from 25.6 percent to 38.1 percent during this period.

grew at a compound annual rate of 15.8 percent from 1999 to 2004.

Keyword search is the largest category of online advertising, and this category continued to post strong growth in 2004. Keyword search ad spending increased 51.0 percent to $3.85 billion in 2004, accounting for 40.0 percent of all online advertising expenditures for the year. Keyword search ads, which generate revenues based on the number of click-throughs they receive, are directly measurable and their value on the market has increased in recent years as advertisers seek ways in which to prove ROI in their media buys. In addition, the growing development of Web content has created additional keyword search opportunities, as search engines now trek through an estimated 8 billion documents, compared with about 1 billion just five years ago.

While keyword search advertising generated the most spending in 2004, referrals posted the strongest growth, up 140.8 percent to $193.0 million for the year. One of the major drivers of the referral category's growth has been the Federal Trade Commission's Do Not Call Registry, as well as requirements for consumers to opt-in to receive e-mail and the emerging capabilities for consumers to skip commercials altogether. Customer response and retention rates are generally higher for referral programs because they are sent by trusted associates. The strong job and real estate markets, as well as additional spending in the automotive category, helped to boost online classified spending 41.9 percent to $1.73 billion in 2004. Increasing broadband penetration prompted more advertisers to use rich media advertising, which rose 33.8 percent to $963.0 million for the year. Additionally, display or banner ads had positive growth for the first time since 2000, rising 19.3 percent to $1.83 billion in 2004.

Content spending, the smallest of the three consumer Internet subsegments, expanded 27.9 percent to $2.35 billion in 2004. Of the three content categories—general content, online games and digital music—general content accounted for the largest share with $1.36 billion in 2004 expenditures. However, general content spending—which includes news, personals, greeting cards and research—declined 3.6 percent for the year. Digital music posted the strongest gain in the content segment, with spending up 312.5 percent to $330.0 million in 2004.

The decline in general content spending came as a result of consumers questioning the value of paid content in a heavily free content market. Categories such as entertainment/lifestyle, community-made directories and credit help each declined at double-digit rates in 2004. Within general content, personals/dating remained the leading paid online content category in 2004 with $469.5 million in spending, but growth was relatively moderate at 4.4 percent. Spending growth in the personals/dating category is slowing as the market moves into a more stable and mature phase. The strongest growth was posted by the sports category, which was up 38.2 percent to $52.8 million in 2004, fueled by interest in various fantasy leagues.

The sharp rise in spending on digital music in 2004 was fueled by strong sales of Apple's iPod and other digital media players. More than 10 million iPods, which store up to 10,000 songs, were sold through the first quarter of 2005, despite the device's price point of between $249 and $399. The solid growth of digital music downloads is expected to continue in 2005, due in part to a new mid-priced iPod set to launch later in the year. Total digital music player sales are forecast to grow at more than 10 percent in each of the next five years and reach 18.2 million units by the end of 2009. Digital music downloads of albums will grow 84.4 percent in 2005 to 257.1 million units, and post compound annual growth of 46.6 percent in the 2004-2009 period.

Online game spending also soared in 2004, rising 91.3 percent to $656.0 million for the year. Online games are drawing enthusiasts through community-building portals that include bulletin boards, chat rooms, news, articles and events. Subscriptions to online games are forecast to double in 2005 as console game makers work to develop stronger online titles. Recent research shows less than 5 million U.S. online subscribers in 2004, but the online gaming audience will soar to more than 40 million players by 2009.

The overall consumer Internet market continued its double-digit growth during the first half of 2005 and is expected to do so for the remainder of the year. Many of the trends that drove 2004 spending are also spurring 2005 growth. Access spending is rising due to the migration away from dial-up to more expensive broadband and wireless services. Advertisers on traditional media are shifting their budgets to the online market in an attempt to more efficiently reach younger demographics. Consumer expenditures on online games and downloaded music are climbing. As a result, overall spending on consumer Internet is expected to grow 16.7 percent in 2005 to $43.82 billion.

Internet access spending will decelerate below double-digit growth for the first time in 2005, rising 9.3 percent to $27.97 billion during the year. The deceleration is mainly tied to fewer new households adding Internet service, parallel to overall U.S. household growth. DSL penetration will climb slightly higher than modem penetration mainly due to its availability in smaller and rural markets. While dial-up penetration will fall, lower income and ethnic demographics will be the main purchasers of this service because of its lower price points. Spending on access will remain the largest sector of the Internet, but its slower growth will result in its share of spending falling from 68.1 percent in 2004 to 51.4 percent by 2009. Consumer spending on access will rise at a compound annual rate of 8.3 percent during the 2004-2009 period to $38.08 billion.

In addition to the attractive demographic profile that the Internet offers to marketers, advertisers are embracing the Internet's ROI metrics that track usage. As a result, spending on Internet advertising will grow 31.2 percent in 2005 to $12.63 billion. During the forecast period, the development of more sophisticated local search engine technology will hasten the migration of advertisers from traditional local media, such as television and radio, to the Internet. Newspaper publishers, a major force in the local online market, are competing with pure-play providers to become the local search engine preference in many communities. Due to the burgeoning growth of keyword search ads, as well as the increased use of other online advertising options, such as rich media and referrals, Internet advertising will climb at a compound annual rate of 24.0 percent from 2004 to 2009, reaching $28.20 billion. Its share of Internet spending will climb from 25.6 percent in 2004 to 38.1 percent by 2009.

Spending on online games and music will rise substantially in 2005 and beyond mainly due to graphic upgrades in online games and increased memory in MP3 players. However, the general content area will see less boisterous increases in spending, in some instances decreases, as consumers become more selective in purchasing information. One trend that might aid online content will be increased pressure for blogs to generate a profit, resulting in subscription fees for content that is currently available free. Due to the rapid growth in online games and music, overall spending on online content will grow 37.3 percent in 2005, reaching $3.22 billion. During the forecast period, spending on online content will be the fastest-growing sector of the Internet market, rising at a compound annual rate of 27.1 percent from 2004 to 2009 to $7.76 billion. Its share of the market will climb from 6.2 percent in 2004 to 10.5 percent by 2009.

Overall spending on consumer Internet will grow at a compound annual rate of 14.5 percent during the 2004-2009 period, reaching $74.04 billion. High-speed technology will serve as the nucleus for this growth as consumers continue to migrate to broadband services, rich media advertising takes on more prominence and online content becomes more attractive because of the capability to download more quickly.

INTERNET ACCESS

Internet users continue to migrate from dial-up to broadband access to take advantage of higher connection speeds that allow them to retrieve, view and download rich media and other large files that require high-speed access. The number of households with broadband service, which includes cable modem and DSL access, increased 34.0 percent to 34.7 million U.S. households in 2004, or 48.8 percent of all Internet-enabled households. Rising penetration of broadband access is driving growth in both the advertising and content segments of the online market because of the increased capabilities it offers. Broadband's value as a facilitator of consumer Internet spending will increase further as the quality of voice over Internet protocol (VoIP)—the ability to talk over a broadband line—continues to improve and becomes more affordable. Dozens of broadband access providers are currently offering VoIP. (Note: Additional information on VoIP can be found in the Cable & Satellite Television chapter.)

While broadband access continues to grow, overall Internet access penetration is reaching a saturation point. Roughly 66.5 percent of all U.S. households have computers, and 95.1 percent of computer households

Consumer Internet Access Spending*

Year	Dial-up Access: Dial-up Households (Millions)	Dial-up Access: Average Annual Spending Per Dial-up Household	Dial-up Access: Total Dial-up Spending ($ Millions)	Cable Modem Access: Cable Modem Households (Millions)	Cable Modem Access: Average Annual Spending Per Cable Modem Household	Cable Modem Access: Total Cable Modem Spending ($ Millions)
1999	25.1	$291	$ 7,300	1.8	$234	$ 422
2000	38.4	256	9,812	3.7	290	1,072
2001	44.2	258	11,420	7.2	326	2,348
2002	43.4	263	11,422	11.6	387	4,494
2003	38.6	252	9,720	16.4	419	6,888
2004	33.5	245	8,221	21.0	443	9,303
2005	29.4	241	7,070	24.5	464	11,387
2006	25.6	235	6,024	27.7	487	13,493
2007	21.9	232	5,060	30.6	504	15,423
2008	18.5	228	4,220	33.1	526	17,428
2009	16.3	227	3,709	35.0	550	19,275

Sources: Veronis Suhler Stevenson, PQ Media, Federal Communications Commission, National Cable & Telecommunications Association, DSL Forum, Telecommunications Industry Association, Kagan Research

*Includes wireless and satellite access.

Consumer Internet

Growth of Consumer Internet Access Spending*

Year	Dial-up Access: Dial-up Households	Dial-up Access: Average Annual Spending Per Dial-up Household	Dial-up Access: Total Dial-up Spending	Cable Modem Access: Cable Modem Households	Cable Modem Access: Average Annual Spending Per Cable Modem Household	Cable Modem Access: Total Cable Modem Spending
2000	53.0%	–12.1%	34.4%	105.6%	23.6%	154.0%
2001	15.1	1.1	16.4	94.6	12.6	119.0
2002	–1.8	1.9	0.0	61.1	18.8	91.4
2003	–11.1	–4.3	–14.9	41.8	8.1	53.3
2004	–13.2	–2.6	–15.4	27.7	5.8	35.1
2005	–12.3	–1.9	–14.0	16.9	4.7	22.4
2006	–12.9	–2.2	–14.8	12.8	5.1	18.5
2007	–14.6	–1.7	–16.0	10.4	3.5	14.3
2008	–15.3	–1.5	–16.6	8.4	4.2	13.0
2009	–11.6	–0.5	–12.1	5.7	4.6	10.6
Compound Annual Growth						
1999-2004	5.9	–3.3	2.4	63.5	13.6	85.6
2004-2009	–13.4	–1.6	–14.7	10.8	4.4	15.7

Sources: Veronis Suhler Stevenson, PQ Media, Federal Communications Commission, National Cable & Telecommunications Association, DSL Forum, Telecommunications Industry Association, Kagan Research

*Includes wireless and satellite access.

DSL Access			Other Access*			Total Internet Access	
DSL Households (Millions)	Average Annual Spending Per DSL Household	Total DSL Spending ($ Millions)	Other Households (Millions)	Average Annual Spending Per Other Household	Total Other Spending ($Millions)	Total Internet Households (Millions)	Total Access Spending ($ Millions)
0.3	$611	$ 174	—	—	—	27.2	$ 7,896
1.4	498	677	0.1	$578	$ 52	43.6	11,613
3.2	522	1,671	0.2	529	90	54.8	15,529
5.1	547	2,807	0.8	503	402	60.9	19,125
9.5	508	4,833	2.3	524	1,205	66.8	22,646
13.7	478	6,563	2.9	515	1,494	71.1	25,581
16.3	474	7,731	3.5	513	1,779	73.7	27,968
18.9	474	8,968	4.0	511	2,036	76.2	30,521
21.3	476	10,161	4.4	516	2,288	78.2	32,932
23.5	482	11,329	4.9	525	2,551	80.0	35,529
25.0	490	12,270	5.3	535	2,822	81.7	38,076

DSL Access			Other Access*			Total Internet Access	
DSL Households	Average Annual Spending Per DSL Household	Total DSL Spending	Other Households	Average Annual Spending Per Other Household	Total Other Spending	Total Internet Households	Total Access Spending
377.2%	−18.5%	289.1%	—	—	—	60.1%	47.1%
135.3	4.9	146.8	88.9%	−8.4%	73.1%	25.8	33.7
60.3	4.8	68.0	370.6	−5.1	346.7	11.2	23.2
85.4	−7.1	72.2	187.5	4.3	199.8	9.7	18.4
44.4	−6.0	35.8	26.1	−1.7	24.0	6.4	13.0
18.8	−0.8	17.8	19.5	−0.3	19.1	3.7	9.3
16.1	−0.1	16.0	15.0	−0.5	14.4	3.4	9.1
12.7	0.5	13.3	11.2	1.1	12.4	2.6	7.9
10.1	1.3	11.5	9.7	1.6	11.5	2.3	7.9
6.6	1.6	8.3	8.5	1.9	10.6	2.1	7.2
117.1	−4.8	106.7	—	—	—	21.2	26.5
12.8	0.5	13.3	18.1	0.4	18.5	2.8	8.3

Consumer Internet

Shares of Consumer Internet Access Spending*

	Dial-up Access		*Cable Modem Access*		*DSL Access*		*Other Access**	
Year	*Dial-up Households*	*Total Dial-up Spending*	*Cable Modem Households*	*Total Cable Modem Spending*	*DSL Households*	*Total DSL Spending*	*Other Households*	*Total Other Spending*
1999	92.3%	92.5%	6.6%	5.3%	1.0%	2.2%	—	—
2000	88.2	84.5	8.5	9.2	3.1	5.8	0.2%	0.4%
2001	80.7	73.5	13.1	15.1	5.8	10.8	0.3	0.6
2002	71.3	59.7	19.0	23.5	8.4	14.7	1.3	2.1
2003	57.8	42.9	24.6	30.4	14.2	21.3	3.4	5.3
2004	47.1	32.1	29.5	36.4	19.3	25.7	4.1	5.8
2005	39.9	25.3	33.3	40.7	22.1	27.6	4.7	6.4
2006	33.6	19.7	36.3	44.2	24.9	29.4	5.2	6.7
2007	27.9	15.4	39.1	46.8	27.3	30.9	5.7	6.9
2008	23.1	11.9	41.4	49.1	29.4	31.9	6.1	7.2
2009	20.0	9.7	42.9	50.6	30.7	32.2	6.5	7.4

Sources: Veronis Suhler Stevenson, PQ Media, Federal Communications Commission, National Cable & Telecommunications Association, DSL Forum, Telecommunications Industry Association, Kagan Research

*Includes wireless and satellite access.

have Internet access. The growth of access spending is attributed to households adding or replacing computers and other access devices, such as Wi-Fi and satellite services. Future increases in the number of new households with Internet access will be generated mainly by growth in overall U.S. households, rather than by current households becoming first-time subscribers.

There are currently more cable modems installed (21.0 million) than DSL lines (13.7 million), but DSL penetration expanded more quickly in 2004. The number of DSL households grew 44.4 percent for the year, compared with 27.7 percent growth for cable. Total spending increased for both cable and DSL households: Cable modem spending increased 35.1 percent to $9.30 billion, while DSL spending increased 35.8 percent to $6.56 billion. Average annual household spending for cable modem access increased 5.8 percent to $443 in 2004, reflecting price hikes. Conversely, average household spending on DSL service declined 6.0 percent to $478, due to reduced rates. DSL providers, particularly telcos such as Verizon Wireless, have had to offer more attractive pricing to acquire new customers since they entered the market later than cable companies. Verizon reported 3.9 billion broadband connections as of March 2005. DSL has a limited advantage in small pockets of the U.S. where cable is not available. However, about 20 percent of the United States does not have access to any form of broadband, and the U.S. lags behind Canada and some other countries in broadband penetration. To help boost the economy through online channels, President

Bush made a public call last year for nationwide affordable, high-speed access by 2007.

Dial-up access is still the most popular way to get onto the Internet. It holds the largest share of households, with 33.5 million. Total dial-up spending continues to shrink, declining 15.4 percent to $8.22 billion in 2004, as more consumers grew impatient with slow connection speeds and long download times, and abandoned dial-up for broadband. To sustain their dial-up businesses, AOL, NetZero, Road Runner and other service providers spent much of 2004 in promotional price wars. As a result, AOL managed to turn in only a meager 1.1 percent increase in 2004 revenues to $8.7 billion, including advertising. Average annual household spending on dial-up access dropped 2.6 percent to $245 for the year. We anticipate that cable modem access will outpace dial-up access by 2006, and DSL will do so by 2008. However, dial-up access will never fully disappear, as there will always be a need for low-priced services among groups like college students and low-income households.

Other access, which includes Wi-Fi devices and satellite services, grew 26.1 percent to 2.9 million households in 2004, a substantial slowdown from the triple-digit growth it generated in the previous two years. Total spending for households with other access increased 24.0 percent to $1.49 billion in 2004, while average annual household spending declined 1.7 percent to $515, reflecting decreasing service prices. In 2004, monthly service prices averaged $36.92 for cable, $39.83 for DSL, $20.42 for dial-up and $42.92 for other access services. By mid-2005, the WiMax wireless communication standard, which promises a strong signal for wireless Internet access for a distance of three to five miles, should be finalized and could reach the vast majority of U.S. households. This event could pave the way for higher increases in consumer Internet spending through other devices. Cities such as Philadelphia have announced plans to be among the first to offer wireless access throughout their metropolitan areas.

Americans' desire for regular upgrades and their need for speed will continue to drive up subscriptions to broadband access in 2005 and beyond, despite the lower cost of dial-up. Consumer Internet access spending continued to account for the largest share of the overall Web market in 2004, as spending increased 13.0 percent to $25.58 billion, driven by expansion in high-speed access services. Total spending on consumer Internet access grew at a compound annual rate of 26.5 percent from 1999 to 2004, and we anticipate access expenditures will grow another 9.3 percent in 2005 to $27.97 billion.

INTERNET ADVERTISING

The advertising community was stunned in late 2004 when Nielsen Media Research released data that indicated certain key demographic groups, including the important 18- to 34-year-old demographic, were spending more time using the Internet than they were viewing television. Nielsen's announcement was quite controversial, and the magnitude of the response the firm received from various sectors of the media industry eventually led Nielsen to retract some of its findings. But despite the inevitable public relations scramble that took place immediately following the release of Nielsen's findings, it has become clear to many in the media business that a shift is under way, one that has the potential to seriously injure traditional advertising media going forward. While we have noted a gradual change in the way consumers use media in previous editions of this *Forecast*, this shift appears to be accelerating and advertisers only in recent years have begun to respond.

In essence, media and its consumers are becoming increasingly fragmented; at the same time, consumers are spending more time and money on non-traditional advertising media while multitasking with various forms of communications. The result is that time and money spent on ad-based media are not growing as quickly as those of consumer-supported media, and in some cases they are declining. In addition, the emergence of new ad-skipping technologies has thrown yet another scare into the traditional advertising industry. The upshot is those advertisers are progressively demanding proof of effectiveness and ROI data on their media buys, and they are ratcheting up the use of alternative

Consumer Internet Advertising* ($ MILLIONS)

Year	Local Internet Advertising	National Internet Advertising	Total Consumer Internet Advertising
1999	$ 409	$ 4,212	$ 4,621
2000	995	7,092	8,087
2001	1,095	6,039	7,134
2002	1,404	4,606	6,010
2003	1,681	5,586	7,267
2004	2,582	7,044	9,626
2005	3,689	8,940	12,629
2006	4,892	11,160	16,052
2007	6,360	13,642	20,002
2008	7,975	16,087	24,062
2009	9,602	18,597	28,198

Sources: Veronis Suhler Stevenson, PQ Media, Interactive Advertising Bureau, Borrell Associates, Corzen, Simba Information

*Does not include Internet yellow pages.

Growth of Consumer Internet Advertising*

Year	Local Internet Advertising	National Internet Advertising	Total Consumer Internet Advertising
2000	143.3%	68.4%	75.0%
2001	10.0	–14.8	–11.8
2002	28.2	–23.7	–15.8
2003	19.7	21.3	20.9
2004	53.6	26.1	32.5
2005	42.9	26.9	31.2
2006	32.6	24.8	27.1
2007	30.0	22.2	24.6
2008	25.4	17.9	20.3
2009	20.4	15.6	17.2
Compound Annual Growth			
1999-2004	44.6	10.8	15.8
2004-2009	30.0	21.4	24.0

Sources: Veronis Suhler Stevenson, PQ Media, Interactive Advertising Bureau, Borrell Associates, Corzen, Simba Information

*Does not include Internet yellow pages.

Consumer Internet

marketing methods, such as branded entertainment. While this has left traditional media segments, such as newspapers, magazines and broadcast television, scuttling to develop various measurements of effectiveness, the Internet sector already has these in place and, as a result, is benefiting greatly. The prime example, of course, is keyword search advertising, which provides proof of effectiveness with extreme granularity and at lower-than-traditional-media costs.

The Internet's ability to measure usage and deliver target audiences has prompted many advertisers to either shift dollars away from traditional media or funnel budget increases to online advertising instead. For example, Unilever announced in early 2005 that it would increase its online ad spending from 5 percent to 15 percent of its total budget, and Visa acknowledged that its Internet marketing budget had increased steadily for four consecutive years. In addition, Pepsi said that it would relaunch its PepsiOne cola without the use of any traditional advertising. Meanwhile, gaming and entertainment content firm IGN, which operates several community sites with millions of young male users, announced several new ad campaigns from first-time marketers Absolut Vodka and Tylenol, as well as increased activity from electronics retailers and automotive manufacturers.

It should be noted, however, that measurability can also be a curse for the Internet advertising market because when the Web doesn't deliver ROI, an outlet can be dropped like a hot potato, which is why banner ad use has been falling for several years and online pop-up media is in a steady decline.

These trends helped drive the growth of consumer Internet advertising up at an accelerated 32.5 percent to $9.63 billion in 2004. Web advertising grew at a compound annual rate of 15.8 percent from 1999 to 2004, hindered by the downturns in 2001 and 2002. The momentum from 2004 continued into the first quarter of 2005, when Internet advertising was expected to turn in another double-digit increase for the period at press time of this *Forecast*. The strong gains were fueled primarily by increased demand for keyword search advertising, which has driven prices up, and the increase in searchable con-

Advertising Growth by Quarter, 2003-2004

	2003 Advertising Spending ($ Millions)	*Percent Change Quarter To Quarter*	*2004 Advertising Spending ($ Millions)*	*Percent Change Quarter To Quarter*	*Percent Change 2004 vs. 2003*
1st Quarter	$1,632	—	$2,230	2.2%	36.6%
2nd Quarter	1,660	1.7%	2,369	6.2	42.7
3rd Quarter	1,793	8.0	2,333	–1.5	30.1
4th Quarter	2,182	21.7	2,694	15.5	23.5
Total	7,267		9,626		32.5

Sources: Veronis Suhler Stevenson, PQ Media, Interactive Advertising Bureau

tent, which has produced more advertising opportunities. The major driver pushing the gains in keyword search has been advertiser demand for detailed and timely ROI data.

Keyword search is the largest category of online advertising, and it continued to post strong growth in 2004. Keyword search ad spending increased 51.0 percent to $3.85 billion for the year, accounting for 40.0 percent of all online advertising expenditures. Keyword search ads, which generate revenues based on the number of click-throughs they receive, are directly measurable, and their value on the market has increased in recent years as advertisers seek ways in which to prove ROI in their media buys. In addition, the growing development of Web content has created additional keyword search opportunities, as search engines slog through some 8 billion documents today, compared with only about 1 billion five years ago. Demand for keywords also drove prices up in the first half of 2005, but pricing is expected to level off at least for larger companies with more clout, as they attempt to negotiate better deals. Both Yahoo! and its rival Google, which went public in August 2004, reported record keyword search revenues in 2004. Google announced in early 2005 that it would begin offering CPM advertising in an effort to further expand its ad revenues.

While keyword search advertising generated the most spending in 2004, referrals posted the strongest growth, up 140.8 percent to $193.0 million. This movement is also fueled by the growth of the Federal Trade Commission's Do Not Call Registry, which has more than 92 million phone numbers, the need to have consumers opt-in to receive e-mail, and the ability of consumers to skip over commercials, all of which limit advertisers' acquisition options. Customer response and retention rates are generally higher for referral programs than other forms of advertising because they are sent by a trusted associate.

The strong job market and robust real estate market helped boost online classified spending 41.9 percent to $1.73 billion in 2004. Auto dealers also contributed to the gain, nearly doubling their spending on Internet ads. Dealer associations increased online spending 20.2 percent for the year, while manufacturers spent an additional 38.8 percent. Meanwhile, increasing broadband penetration prompted more advertisers to use rich media, which rose 33.8 percent to $963.0 million. Display ads grew 19.3 percent after three consecutive years of double-digit declines as the format benefited from the general trend toward online advertising. However, display advertising's share of online media spending has declined for the last four years. E-mail spending dropped 54.3 percent to $96.0 million in 2004, reflecting the growing use of e-mail as a retention tool, allowing companies to interact with customers who already know them.

Of the five leading industry categories, consumer-related advertising maintained the largest share, with 49.0 percent in 2004. Computing followed with an 18.0 percent market share, and financial services rounded

Consumer Internet Advertising Spending, by Type

($ MILLIONS)

Year	Keyword Searches	Display Ads (Banner)	Classified	Sponsorship	Rich Media	Slotting Fees	E-mail	Referrals	Total
2000	$ 113	$3,793	$ 598	$2,289	$461	$251	$226	$356	$8,087
2001	300	2,554	1,149	1,848	364	549	221	150	7,134
2002	920	1,731	920	1,070	589	469	228	84	6,010
2003	2,551	1,533	1,221	727	719	225	211	80	7,267
2004	3,850	1,829	1,733	770	963	193	96	193	9,626

Sources: Veronis Suhler Stevenson, PQ Media, Interactive Advertising Bureau

Growth of Consumer Internet Advertising, by Type

Year	Keyword Searches	Display Ads (Banner)	Classified	Sponsorship	Rich Media	Slotting Fees	E-mail	Referrals	Total
2001	164.6%	–32.7%	91.9%	–19.3%	–21.1%	119.1%	–2.3%	–57.9%	–11.8%
2002	206.9	–32.2	–19.9	–42.1	61.9	–14.7	3.3	–43.8	–15.8
2003	177.4	–11.4	32.8	–32.1	22.1	–51.9	–7.7	–5.0	20.9
2004	51.0	19.3	41.9	6.0	33.8	–14.5	–54.3	140.8	32.5

Sources: Veronis Suhler Stevenson, PQ Media, Interactive Advertising Bureau

Shares of Consumer Internet Advertising, by Type

Year	Keyword Searches	Display Ads (Banner)	Classified	Sponsorship	Rich Media	Slotting Fees	E-mail	Referrals
2000	1.4%	46.9%	7.4%	28.3%	5.7%	3.1%	2.8%	4.4%
2001	4.2	35.8	16.1	25.9	5.1	7.7	3.1	2.1
2002	15.3	28.8	15.3	17.8	9.8	7.8	3.8	1.4
2003	35.1	21.1	16.8	10.0	9.9	3.1	2.9	1.1
2004	40.0	19.0	18.0	8.0	10.0	2.0	1.0	2.0

Sources: Veronis Suhler Stevenson, PQ Media, Interactive Advertising Bureau

Advertising Spending Concentration, 2004

	Percent of Advertising Spending
Top 10 Sites	71%
Top 25 Sites	85
Top 50 Sites	94

Sources: Veronis Suhler Stevenson, PQ Media, Interactive Advertising Bureau

out the top three with 17.0 percent. Pharmaceutical and healthcare (6.0 percent) and telecom (4.0 percent) entered the top five in 2004, reflecting increased marketing among drug and cellular phone advertisers. Among the top five consumer categories, retail captured the largest market share at 40.0 percent, followed by automotive with 19.0 percent and leisure with 16.0 percent. The Web appeals to auto advertisers because research shows that 80.0 percent of all new cars sold are first researched on the Internet. Also, readers of real estate ads like online listings because they are more robust than those in print. Since 1997, online spending per home sold went from $16 to $148. Meanwhile, with help wanted, users are able to search for the job of their choice across many markets, rather than having to manually scan print ads, which is a slow process.

The most prominent Web sites continue to garner the lion's share of advertising sales; however, the shares of smaller sites made significant gains in 2004. The top 10 ad-selling sites captured 71.0 percent of advertising spending for the year, while the top 50 Web sites captured 94.0 percent, compared with 97.0 percent in 2003. Yet while the remaining 6.0 percent—which is split among tens of thousands of smaller sites—seems like an insignificant amount, it is actually important for several reasons. First, this is the first time that majority revenues have fallen below 96.0 percent since Internet advertising data has been compiled. Furthermore, the non-top 50's spending increased from slightly under $300 million in 2003 to over $500 million in 2004, a sizeable jump.

Spending on local online advertising grew 53.6 percent to $2.58 billion, compared with 26.1 percent for national advertising in 2004, which finished the year with $7.04 billion. Local online growth can be attributed to a number of factors. Newspapers continue to be proactive in becoming the local online voice for many communities. Many publishers have created separate Internet sales divisions rather than bundling online ads with print ads as they have done in the past. The online classified business has grown faster than print versions. For example, careerbuilders .com, a cooperative among a number of newspaper publishers, has grown employment classifieds faster in recent years than its national competitors in a number of categories including the number of employment listings and end-users seeking employment. Newspapers are also embracing real simple syndication (RSS) technology and blogging in attempts to offer advertisers and consumers access to sources outside their communities. As a result, spending on local newspaper online advertising rose 47.1 percent in 2004 to $1.19 billion.

Pure-play online advertising sites that specialize in classifieds, such as Monster.com and RealEstate.com, as well as major national online leaders AOL, Yahoo! and Google,

Advertising Revenues in Top 5 Industry Categories

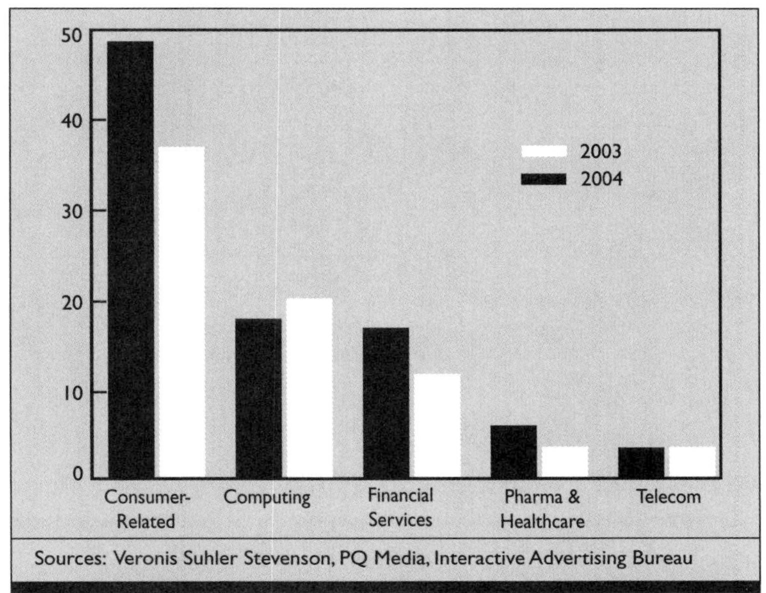

Sources: Veronis Suhler Stevenson, PQ Media, Interactive Advertising Bureau

Advertising Revenues in Top 5 Consumer Categories

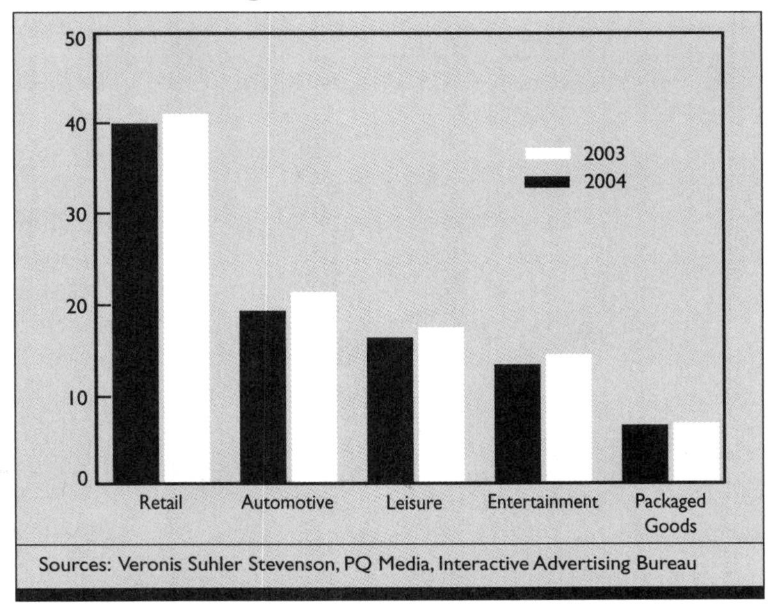

Sources: Veronis Suhler Stevenson, PQ Media, Interactive Advertising Bureau

Local Consumer Internet Advertising Spending*

($ MILLIONS)

Year	Newspaper Sites	Pure-Play†	Local Search	TV Sites	Radio Sites	Total	Internet Yellow Pages	Total With Yellow Pages
2001	$ 494.1	$ 538.6	$ 5.4	$ 42.5	$14.2	$1,094.8	$262.5	$1,419.4
2002	655.2	660.2	16.3	55.0	17.2	1,403.9	347.2	1,839.6
2003	811.4	734.8	41.7	75.0	18.0	1,680.9	596.8	2,412.4
2004	1,193.5	1,101.5	134.4	119.0	34.0	2,582.4	775.0	3,644.8
2005	1,522.3	1,578.6	329.7	196.4	62.4	3,689.4	966.0	5,243.9

Sources: Veronis Suhler Stevenson, PQ Media, Interactive Advertising Bureau, Borrell Associates, Simba Information

*To avoid double counting, Internet yellow pages spending is included in total yellow pages spending in the Advertising, Marketing Services and Specialty Media chapter. Newspapers, television and radio online advertising spending are not included in overall spending in those chapters.

†Local ads from national services, such as Hotjobs.com, Monster.com, Realtor.com and local regional portals from national services, such as MSN, Yahoo!, Google and Time Warner.

Growth of Local Consumer Internet Advertising Spending*

Year	Newspaper Sites	Pure-Play†	Local Search	TV Sites	Radio Sites	Total	Internet Yellow Pages	Total With Yellow Pages
2002	32.6%	22.6%	201.9%	29.4%	21.1%	28.2%	32.3%	29.6%
2003	23.8	11.3	155.8	36.4	4.7	19.7	71.9	31.1
2004	47.1	49.9	222.3	58.7	88.9	53.6	29.9	51.1
2005	27.5	43.3	145.3	65.0	83.5	42.9	24.6	43.9

Sources: Veronis Suhler Stevenson, PQ Media, Interactive Advertising Bureau, Borrell Associates, Simba Information

*To avoid double counting, Internet yellow pages spending is included in total yellow pages spending in the Advertising, Marketing Services and Specialty Media chapter. Newspapers, television and radio online advertising spending are not included in overall spending in those chapters.

†Local ads from national services, such as Hotjobs.com, Monster.com, Realtor.com and local regional portals from national services, such as MSN, Yahoo!, Google and Time Warner.

have become more aggressive in providing local online capabilities to advertisers. Google and Yahoo!, for example, provide advertising packages connected to such items as maps and zip codes. Spending on pure-play local advertising climbed 49.9 percent in 2004, reaching $1.10 billion. Concurrently, local keyword search capabilities are becoming more sophisticated. AOL has launched a local search service that compiles events, movies, business listings and other information into a single local search result. Local search is the fastest-growing online advertising sector, posting a gain of 222.3 percent to $134.4 million in 2004.

Internet yellow pages (IYP), the third-largest local online advertising category, grew 29.9 percent to $775.0 million in 2004. While more people use search engines to find what they're looking for, consumers who use IYP are more likely to be in buying mode, and therefore tend to have a higher conversion rate. IYP users are also attractive to high-end advertisers because the former are also reported to be a more affluent demographic, with incomes greater than $75,000, than the broader search audience. (Note: To avoid double counting, the total for Internet yellow pages is not included in overall Internet advertising spending, but is instead charted in the yellow pages section of the Advertising, Specialty Media and Marketing Services chapter.)

Other traditional media, such as local television and radio, have ramped up online advertising initiatives, but their online businesses pale in comparison to the newspaper and yellow pages online presence. Local online advertising at television sites grew 58.7 percent in 2004 to $119.0 million, and online radio advertising climbed 88.9 percent

Shares of Local Consumer Internet Advertising Spending

Year	*Newspaper Sites*	*Radio Sites*	*Pure-Play**	*Local Search*	*TV Sites*	*Internet Yellow Pages*
2001	45.1%	49.2%	0.5%	3.9%	1.3%	24.0%
2002	46.7	47.0	1.2	3.9	1.2	24.7
2003	48.3	43.7	2.5	4.5	1.1	35.5
2004	46.2	42.7	5.2	4.6	1.3	30.0
2005	41.3	42.8	8.9	5.3	1.7	26.2

Sources: Veronis Suhler Stevenson, PQ Media, Interactive Advertising Bureau, Borrell Associates, Simba Information

*Local ads from national services, such as Hotjobs.com, Monster.com, Realtor.com and local regional portals from national services, such as MSN, Yahoo!, Google and Time Warner.

to $34.0 million. Online radio usage is up—approximately 20 million listeners in 2004, more than double 2003—but it represents less than 10 percent of all radio listenership. However, due to the weakening over-the-air advertising market, as well as competition from satellite radio and pure-play online radio, more group owners are expanding the reach of their signals. Companies such as Clear Channel and Viacom have announced plans to podcast their music, hoping to generate more listeners to their Web sites. Additionally, some of the increase in radio's local Internet advertising growth can be tied to pure-play online radio, which is still in its infancy. There are over 13,500 over-the-air radio stations compared with an estimated 450 pure-play online stations. Lead players in the online radio market include Yahoo!, AOL and MSN. Yahoo!'s LAUNCHcast claims a 1.3 million average weekly audience, AOL Radio@Network reported 1.2 million listeners, and MSN Radio reported 481,200.

Advertising spending on Web logs ("blogs") are not measured in this chapter because data are unavailable and mainly anecdotal. An estimate of blog media spending, which also includes subscriptions, was projected to be between $5 million and $10 million in 2004. Evidence suggests that approximately a dozen blogs are generating $100,000 or more each in annual revenues, while thousands of blogs are generating anywhere from nothing to only a few thousand dollars a year. Though blogs have yet to generate significant spending, their influence has grown, as shown during the recent presidential election when certain blogs were instrumental in discrediting a major television news organization. However, their influence is limited to a small, but powerful, universe of Internet users. Just 7 percent of U.S. Internet households have created a blog, 27 percent report reading one, while 62 percent of online Americans say they don't even know what a blog is.

Furthermore, the blog technology market is fragmented. Not counting MSN, there were 15 distributors of blog technology in 2004, with a total of 5,049 customers who have downloaded blogging tools. Their aggregate sales—which is a typical measure of an industry's growth, but is not tracked here because it is not considered media spending—have been estimated at $12.2 million. However, in late 2004, MSN launched a free blogging tool, and in just five months garnered 4.5 million downloads, which suggests that this market will further splinter and growth will continue to be too small to track in the near future. Meanwhile, another 5 percent of Internet users say they use RSS feeds or XML readers to get news and other information delivered from blogs and other sites.

INTERNET CONTENT

Spurred by the increasing popularity of online gaming and the growing acceptance of paid online music downloads, content spending—the smallest of the three consumer Internet subsegments—advanced 27.9 percent to $2.35 billion in 2004. General content accounted for the largest share of the three

Internet Content Spending

($ MILLIONS)

Year	General Content	Online Games	Digital Music	Total
2001	$ 610	$ 196	$ 13	$ 819
2002	1,216	274	25	1,515
2003	1,410	343	80	1,833
2004	1,359	656	330	2,345
2005	1,382	1,072	765	3,219
2006	1,413	1,563	1,387	4,363
2007	1,427	2,055	2,125	5,607
2008	1,467	2,531	2,875	6,873
2009	1,471	2,886	3,407	7,764

Sources: Veronis Suhler Stevenson, PQ Media, Jupiter Media Metrix, International Federation of Phonographic Industry, comScore Networks, Online Publishers Association, DFC Intelligence, The Themis Group, IDC

Growth of Internet Content Spending

Year	General Content	Online Games	Digital Music	Total
2002	99.3%	39.8%	92.3%	85.0%
2003	16.0	25.2	220.0	21.0
2004	–3.6	91.3	312.5	27.9
2005	1.7	63.4	131.7	37.3
2006	2.2	45.8	81.4	35.5
2007	1.0	31.5	53.2	28.5
2008	2.8	23.2	35.3	22.6
2009	0.3	14.0	18.5	13.0
Compound Annual Growth				
2004-2009	1.6	34.5	59.5	27.1

Sources: Veronis Suhler Stevenson, PQ Media, Jupiter Media Metrix, comScore Networks, Online Publishers Association

content categories—general content, online games and digital music—with expenditures of $1.36 billion in 2004. However, general content spending, including news, personals, greeting cards and research, declined 3.6 percent for the year. Digital music, on the other hand, posted the strongest growth in the content segment, as spending rose 312.5 percent to $330.0 million for the year.

Going forward, we expect online content growth will get a boost from expanding broadband penetration, which will allow more users to access rich media content such as streaming video and audio. Web gaming will push content growth further as graphics become richer, and videogame makers increase the number of titles that include enhanced multiplayer platforms available online. Additionally, the growing popularity of iPod and competing MP3 players will drive more use of downloaded music by consumers in the forecast period. Total content spending, including general, music and games, is expected to grow 37.3 percent in 2005 to $3.22 billion, driven by 131.7 percent growth in digital music downloads and a 63.4 percent increase in online games. Web music and games will each surpass general content spending as the larger categories by 2007.

General content includes personals/dating, entertainment/lifestyles, business/investment, research, personal growth, general news, community-made directories, sports, greeting cards and credit help. This category's contraction in 2004 compares with its 99.3 percent growth in 2002 and 16.0 percent growth in 2003. Overall growth was stunted by declines in five subcategories: entertainment/lifestyles, credit help, community-made directories, business/investment and general news. Spending in the credit help and business/investment categories was stronger when the economy was weak. Meanwhile, other categories may be losing steam because they are no longer viewed as providing added value as they were in the past. For instance, personals/dating grew only 4.4 percent in 2004 after an increase of 48.8 percent in 2003 because individuals didn't hook up early on with the right person as they had expected, and many were hesitant to try again.

Within general content, the personals/

Online General Content Spending Pricing Models, by Category

Category	Subscriptions	Single Payment	Types of Subscriptions: Annual	Monthly	Other*
Personals/Dating	99%	1%	19%	65%	16%
Business/Investment	95	5	49	44	7
Personal Growth	94	6	27	64	10
Community-Made Directories	91	9	61	26	13
Greeting Cards	91	9	44	51	5
Sports	85	15	42	49	10
General News	85	15	20	79	6
Entertainment/Lifestyles	70	30	31	63	6
Games	64	36	36	60	4
Research	58	42	47	48	5
Credit Help	57	43	74	18	8
Total	85	15	33	58	10

Sources: Veronis Suhler Stevenson, PQ Media, comScore Networks, Online Publishers Association
*Other includes weekly, biweekly, quarterly, semiannually and other nonstandard subscription terms.

dating category holds the largest share, with $469.5 million in spending in 2004. The category is maturing, and is expected to grow at a slower pace in the forecast period. Companies in this category include Yahoo! Personals, Match.com and eHarmony. Match.com, which is owned by InterActiveCorp and has millions of members in 31 countries, experienced slower growth in 2004 than in 2003. The Web site was mired in legal costs as it pursued a claim against six former employees who left Match.com for True (formerly True Beginnings), a Texas-based relationship Web site, claiming breach of contract. eHarmony, a privately held firm with over 4.5 million members, received a $110.0 million investment in December 2004. In January 2005, wedding site TheKnot.com joined the personals category by acquiring GreatBoyfriends, which operates GreatBoyfriends.com and GreatGirlfriends.com—sites based on personal referrals from friends and family. Business/investment was the second-largest category with $312.9 million, a decline of 6.3 percent from the 2003 level, while research was ranked third at $115.1 million in spending in 2004, an increase of 4.9 percent.

The second-largest content category was

Online General Content Spending, By Category

Category	2004 ($ Millions)	2003 ($ Millions)	Percent Change
Personals/Dating	$ 469.5	$ 449.5	4.4%
Business/Investment	312.9	334.0	–6.3
Research	115.1	109.7	4.9
Personal Growth	96.5	91.1	5.9
General News	87.9	88.0	–0.1
Entertainment/Lifestyles*	83.5	135.0	–38.1
Community-Made Directories	70.5	87.1	–19.1
Sports	52.8	38.2	38.2
Greeting Cards	43.4	40.0	8.5
Credit Help	27.1	37.0	–26.8
Total	1,359.2	1,409.6	–3.6

Sources: Veronis Suhler Stevenson, PQ Media, comScore Networks, Online Publishers Association
*Does not include online music downloads.

Online Music Spending*

Year	Digital Singles Downloaded (Millions)	Growth Of Digital Singles Downloaded	Digital Albums Downloaded (Millions)	Growth Of Digital Albums Downloaded	Digital Music Spending ($ Millions)	Growth Of Digital Music Spending
2001	—	—	—	—	$ 13	—
2002	—	—	—	—	25	92.3%
2003	—	—	—	—	80	220.0
2004	139.4	—	4.5	—	330	312.5
2005	257.1	84.4%	6.8	51.5%	765	131.7
2006	420.0	63.4	9.2	35.4	1,387	81.4
2007	623.7	48.5	11.9	29.3	2,125	53.2
2008	825.8	32.4	14.1	18.4	2,875	35.3
2009	943.9	14.3	15.7	11.4	3,407	18.5
Compound Annual Growth						
1999-2004	—	—	—	—	—	—
2004-2009	—	46.6	—	28.5	—	59.5

Sources: Veronis Suhler Stevenson, PQ Media, Jupiter Media Metrix, comScore, International Federation of Phonographic Industry, Recording Industry Association of America

*The RIAA did not begin analyzing downloaded units until 2004.

Consumer Internet

online games in 2004, with $656.0 million in spending, up 91.3 percent. The category, which is still in its infancy as console game makers work to develop stronger online revenues, is projected to grow at double-digit rates throughout the forecast period. The online gaming industry owes its strength to the community model that has been built around it, which includes chats, bulletin boards and other forms of peer-to-peer communication. Reality TV shows featuring high-stakes poker games have also helped generate interest in online gaming.

While companies such as IGN Entertainment are generating growth, U.S. game manufacturers are struggling with the online model. IGN, which operates more than 70 gaming and entertainment community sites and online forums primarily for young male audiences, grew revenues by 40.0 percent in 2004. Yet Electronic Arts, the leading provider of traditional videogames, noted in its annual report that online gaming operations are still in their early development, and that 2004 online revenues were comparatively insignificant. The company recorded just 300,000 online subscribers in 2004. According to recent research, the online gaming audience will include 376.0 million players globally by 2009 and comprise 25.0 percent of total videogame spending.

In contrast to the typical U.S. videogame consumer, the online game sector is global and diversified. One segment, the so-called "massively multiplayer online games," or MMOGs, generated about 34 percent of its revenues from Korea in 2004, more revenues than it gleaned from North America, Europe and Japan combined (which made up approximately 32 percent). The rest of Asia accounted for the remaining 34 percent. Also, while the U.S. gaming market is predominantly 18- to 34-year-old males, the global market has a higher percentage of females and younger children. While the American videogame market will remain strong in the near future, growth in online gaming, in which other countries are more advanced, will be stronger outside the U.S.

Digital music was the third-largest category in 2004, but posted the strongest growth, stimulated by strong sales of Apple's iPod and

Spending on Wireless Content*

($ MILLIONS)

Year	Instant Messaging	E-mail & Information Alerts	Ringtones	Wireless Games	Picture & Video Downloads	Mobile Advertising & Marketing	Total Wireless Content Spending
2002	$ 515	$ 80	$ 22	$ 2	$ 5	$ 12	$ 636
2003	1,081	222	82	20	22	43	1,470
2004	1,769	433	307	82	70	105	2,766
2005	2,355	683	681	224	151	201	4,295
2006	2,852	945	1,099	430	250	318	5,894
2007	3,302	1,155	1,436	634	371	425	7,323
2008	3,751	1,322	1,716	791	449	516	8,545
2009	4,190	1,488	1,958	912	513	604	9,665

Sources: Veronis Suhler Stevenson, PQ Media, Insight Research, eMarketer, Kagan Research
*To avoid double counting, wireless communications spending on content found in the Entertainment Media chapter will be added to overall spending data.

Growth of Spending on Wireless Content*

Year	Instant Messaging	E-mail & Information Alerts	Ringtones	Wireless Games	Picture & Video Downloads	Mobile Advertising & Marketing	Total Wireless Content Spending
2003	109.8%	177.1%	281.9%	778.3%	377.8%	249.2%	131.2%
2004	63.6	94.9	274.3	303.5	224.7	143.0	88.1
2005	33.1	57.7	121.5	175.4	116.0	91.1	55.3
2006	21.1	38.4	61.4	91.6	65.7	58.4	37.2
2007	15.8	22.2	30.7	47.4	48.7	33.4	24.3
2008	13.6	14.5	19.5	24.7	20.8	21.5	16.7
2009	11.7	12.5	14.1	15.4	14.4	17.1	13.1
Compound Annual Growth							
1999-2004	—	—	—	—	—	—	—
2004-2009	18.8	28.0	44.8	62.1	49.0	41.9	28.4

Sources: Veronis Suhler Stevenson, PQ Media, Insight Research, eMarketer, Kagan Research
*To avoid double counting, wireless communications spending on content found in the Entertainment Media chapter will be added to overall spending data.

Consumer Internet

other MP3 players. Apple shipped 5.3 million iPods in its fiscal second quarter, ending March 26, 2005, a 558.0 percent increase over the same quarter the previous fiscal year. More than 16.2 million digital music players are now owned in the U.S. and growth is forecast to reach higher than 10 percent in each of the next few years. Apple's iPod holds roughly 50 percent of the market and a new mid-priced model is scheduled for release in 2005, a development that could expand the iPod beyond early adopters and into the mainstream. More

Consumer Internet Retail Spending*

Year	Internet Households (Millions)	Number Of Internet Households Shopping Online (Millions)	Percent Of Internet Households Shopping Online	Average Annual Spending Per Internet Household	Spending By Internet Households On Online Shopping ($ Millions)
1999	27.2	11.2	41.2%	$1,310	$ 14,667
2000	43.6	20.6	47.3	1,359	28,000
2001	54.8	27.9	50.9	1,228	34,263
2002	60.9	35.3	58.0	1,255	44,287
2003	66.8	45.7	68.4	1,176	53,766
2004	71.1	55.2	77.6	1,229	67,822
2005	73.7	62.0	84.1	1,259	78,063
2006	76.2	67.5	88.6	1,295	87,431
2007	78.2	71.4	91.2	1,320	94,163
2008	80.0	74.4	93.0	1,359	101,131
2009	81.7	76.7	93.9	1,396	107,098

Sources: Veronis Suhler Stevenson, PQ Media, U.S. Department of Commerce, eMarketer, *Wall Street Journal*

*Spending on consumer goods over the Internet is not considered communications spending; therefore, consumer expenditures are not included in total consumer Internet spending.

Consumer Internet

Growth of Consumer Internet Retail Spending*

Year	Internet Households	Number Of Internet Households Shopping Online	Average Annual Spending Per Internet Household	Spending By Internet Households On Online Shopping
2000	60.1%	83.9%	3.8%	90.9%
2001	25.8	35.4	–9.6	22.4
2002	11.2	26.5	2.2	29.3
2003	9.7	29.5	–6.2	21.4
2004	6.4	20.8	4.4	26.1
2005	3.7	12.3	2.5	15.1
2006	3.4	8.9	2.8	12.0
2007	2.6	5.7	1.9	7.7
2008	2.3	4.3	3.0	7.4
2009	2.1	3.1	2.7	5.9
Compound Annual Growth				
1999-2004	21.2	37.6	–1.3	35.8
2004-2009	2.8	6.8	2.6	9.6

Sources: Veronis Suhler Stevenson, PQ Media, U.S. Department of Commerce, eMarketer, *Wall Street Journal*

*Spending on consumer goods over the Internet is not considered communications spending; therefore, consumer expenditures are not included in total consumer Internet spending.

than 200 million online songs were purchased in the U.S. and Europe in 2004, due primarily to the popularity of the iPod. However, consumers who have bought iPods and MP3 players make up less than 20 percent of the market; the majority of people still prefer CDs over downloads and many have not given up their Walkmans and boom boxes.

In addition to iPods, the online community is watching the evolution of mobile computing and communication technologies that are greatly altering the way people exchange information. Consumers and institutional end users are migrating to wireless content as manufacturers and advertisers develop new applications and formats like text messaging, ringtones, gaming and picture downloading. Cell phones, PDAs, and Blackberrys are among the products that are driving growth in this segment, but other devices are evolving to accommodate music and picture downloading, gaming and television viewing. Of major concern, however, are back-end costs, like subscriptions and contractual obligations that have made older consumers skeptical and value-conscious in their spending habits. Younger consumers, however, have readily bought into the technology.

Advertisers are approaching the wireless market because the technology allows them to reach consumers beyond the confines of the television screen. The variety of applications that these devices can hold has opened a window for marketers to send direct and concise messages to consumers. As a result of these trends, overall wireless content spending rose 88.1 percent in 2004, reaching $2.77 billion. Instant messaging accounted for the greatest portion of spending at $1.77 billion, followed by e-mail and information alerts at $433.0 million. Total wireless content spending is forecasted to grow at a compound annual rate of 28.4 percent from 2004 to 2009 to $9.67 billion. (Note: To avoid double counting, wireless content spending found in the Entertainment Media chapter will be added to overall communications spending data.)

E-COMMERCE

E-commerce spending is not considered part of the Internet media category because it is not communications spending. However, it is discussed here because of its importance in the Internet market. Of the 71.1 million Internet households, 55.2 million, or 77.6 percent, shopped online in 2004. Online spending by Internet households in 2004 was $67.82 billion, a 26.1 percent increase over 2003. Compound annual growth for the last five years was 35.8 percent. Average annual household e-commerce spending increased 4.4 percent in 2004 to $1,229, after declining 6.2 percent in 2003. The recent spending increase resulted from growing broadband access; more than two-thirds of e-commerce transactions were conducted via high-speed connections in 2004. In addition, increasing gas prices and threats of terrorism have contributed somewhat to increased online shopping. Conversely, acts of identity theft, which filled the news in 2004 and early 2005, don't appear to have negatively impacted online shopping. In addition, companies that sell goods and services online are upgrading their infrastructures and customer service to improve the Internet

Domestic Business-to-Business E-commerce*

Year	*Internet Spending ($ Billions)*	*Percent Change*
1999	$ 210	—
2000	248	18.4%
2001	286	15.2
2002	320	11.7
2003	341	6.5
2004	494	45.2
2005	661	33.7
2006	802	21.3
2007	923	15.1
2008	1,022	10.7
2009	1,105	8.1
Compound Annual Growth		
1999-2004		18.7
2004-2009		17.4

Sources: Veronis Suhler Stevenson, PQ Media, U.S. Department of Commerce, Jupiter Media Metrix, eMarketer

*Spending on business goods over the Internet is not considered communications spending; therefore, business expenditures are not included in total consumer Internet spending.

Consumer Internet

Spending on Consumer Internet ($ MILLIONS)

Year	Internet Access	Internet Advertising	Internet Content	Total
1999	$ 7,896	$ 4,621	—	$12,517
2000	11,613	8,087	—	19,700
2001	15,529	7,134	$ 819	23,482
2002	19,125	6,010	1,515	26,650
2003	22,646	7,267	1,833	31,746
2004	25,581	9,626	2,345	37,552
2005	27,968	12,629	3,219	43,816
2006	30,521	16,052	4,363	50,936
2007	32,932	20,002	5,607	58,541
2008	35,529	24,062	6,873	66,464
2009	38,076	28,198	7,764	74,038

Sources: Veronis Suhler Stevenson, PQ Media, AOL Time Warner, Borrell Associates, CMR Interactive, comScore Networks, Corzen, DataMonitor, eMarketer, Jupiter Media Metrix, Kinetic Strategies, Interactive Advertising Bureau, National Cable & Telecommunications Assocation, Online Publishers Association, Simba Information

Growth of Spending on Consumer Internet

Year	Internet Access	Internet Advertising	Internet Content	Total
2000	47.1%	75.0%	—	57.4%
2001	33.7	−11.8	—	19.2
2002	23.2	−15.8	85.0%	13.5
2003	18.4	20.9	21.0	19.1
2004	13.0	32.5	27.9	18.3
2005	9.3	31.2	37.3	16.7
2006	9.1	27.1	35.5	16.2
2007	7.9	24.6	28.5	14.9
2008	7.9	20.3	22.6	13.5
2009	7.2	17.2	13.0	11.4
Compound Annual Growth				
1999-2004	26.5	15.8	—	24.6
2004-2009	8.3	24.0	27.1	14.5

Sources: Veronis Suhler Stevenson, PQ Media, AOL Time Warner, Borrell Associates, CMR Interactive, comScore Networks, Corzen, DataMonitor, eMarketer, Jupiter Media Metrix, Kinetic Strategies, Interactive Advertising Bureau, National Cable & Telecommunications Assocation, Online Publishers Association, Simba Information

shopping experience and encourage completed checkout and repeat purchases.

Non-travel-related sites generated twice as much revenues as travel sites (travel sites are not included in our spending data). At year-end, auction sites captured the most market share in number of visits, followed closely by retail stores. Six of the top 15 fastest-growing retail sites over the holiday season were affiliated with traditional offline department stores, such as Home Depot, Neiman Marcus, Nordstrom, Wal-Mart and May Department Stores. Blockbuster's online traffic quadrupled in 2004 after the launch of the store's new DVD delivery service (an attempt to combat its nimble online competitor Netflix). In addition, pure-plays such as Amazon, Dell and eBay saw visits peak last year, while several cellular phone sites, including T-Mobile, AT&T Wireless and LetsTalk.com, posted traffic gains of more than 80 percent. By comparison, domestic business-to-business e-commerce, a $494.0 billion market, which grew 45.2 percent in 2004, is seven times larger than business-to-consumer e-commerce.

Consumer e-commerce will continue to grow in the low double digits for the next two years, then slow down to single-digit growth for the rest of the forecast period, due to audience saturation. Average annual spending per consumer household will grow at a compound annual rate of 2.6 percent during the forecast period to $1,396, pushing up business-to-consumer e-commerce expenditures to $107.10 billion in 2009, a compound annual increase of 9.6 percent. Growth will be well below the 35.8 percent increase during the 1999-2004 period. Business-to-business e-commerce is projected to climb at a compound annual rate of 17.4 percent from 2004 to 2009, slightly lower than its 18.7 percent increase during the prior five-year period. Overall business-to-business e-commerce will reach $1.11 trillion by 2009, 10 times larger than business-to-consumer e-commerce.

The Outlook For Consumer Internet

Total consumer Internet spending is projected to increase 16.7 percent to $43.82 billion in 2005, driven by double-digit growth in advertising and content spending, while Internet access expenditures will post high-single-digit growth for the year. The expansion of the overall consumer Internet market, which will again outpace that of the broader economy in 2005, will be spurred by several critical drivers, including the shift of advertising dollars to media that provide marketers with detailed ROI data in a timely fashion. Overall consumer Internet expenditures are expected to maintain a double-digit growth rate throughout the 2004-2009 period, consistently beating nominal GDP, as advertisers move to more effectively reach target audiences and track the benefits of media buys, and consumers ratchet up their use of online games and digital music downloads. Total consumer Internet spending will grow at a compound annual rate of 14.5 percent from 2004 to 2009, reaching $74.04 billion in 2009.

While the growth in overall Internet households is expected to slow down over the next three years, cable modem and DSL installations will continue to increase in the low-double-digit range. Total spending on Internet access will increase 9.3 percent in 2005 to $27.97 billion, as a result of broadband's higher pricing compared with dial-up. Spending on broadband access will continue to drain spending from the dial-up market, causing steady declines in dial-up expenditures. By 2006, cable modem households' steady upward movement in market share will overtake dial-up households' continually shrinking share. The dial-up market will remain larger than the DSL market until 2008 because DSL customers tend to be more price-conscious, and prices are lower than cable service.

Internet advertising is expected to grow 31.2 percent in 2005, and post compound annual growth of 24.0 percent from 2004 to 2009, with spending reaching $28.20 billion.

Shares of Spending On Consumer Internet

Year	*Internet Access*	*Internet Advertising*	*Internet Content*
1999	63.1%	36.9%	—
2000	58.9	41.1	—
2001	66.1	30.4	3.5%
2002	71.8	22.6	5.7
2003	71.3	22.9	5.8
2004	68.1	25.6	6.2
2005	63.8	28.8	7.3
2006	59.9	31.5	8.6
2007	56.3	34.2	9.6
2008	53.5	36.2	10.3
2009	51.4	38.1	10.5

Sources: Veronis Suhler Stevenson, PQ Media, AOL Time Warner, Borrell Associates, CMR Interactive, comScore Networks, Corzen, DataMonitor, eMarketer, Jupiter Media Metrix, Kinetic Strategies, Interactive Advertising Bureau, National Cable & Telecommunications Assocation, Online Publishers Association, Simba Information

2004 Communications Industry Forecast Compared With Actual Growth

Category	*2004 Forecasted Growth**	*Actual 2004 Growth†*
Internet Access	10.4%	13.0%
Internet Content	33.2	27.9
Advertising	15.8	32.5
Total	13.1	18.3

*Veronis Suhler Stevenson 2004 Communications Industry Forecast & Report

†Veronis Suhler Stevenson, PQ Media

FORECAST ASSUMPTIONS

- Consumer Internet spending is expected to grow at rates much higher than nominal GDP growth, as well as most of the other media segments, over the next five years, primarily as a result of several key trends. Among these are the continued transition from dial-up to broadband access, the shift of advertising dollars to media that provide detailed and timely return on investment (ROI) data, and increased spending on Web gaming and digital music downloads.
- Despite low dial-up pricing, consumers' need for speed will continue to drive the move to broadband Internet access, such as cable modem service. Dial-up access, however, likely will never disappear entirely, as certain budget-conscious consumers who can't afford broadband prices, such as college students and low-income households, will seek out cheaper alternatives.
- The growing use of high-speed access will facilitate the development and use of more rich media applications by consumers who will also increase the frequency of their searches. In addition, the availability of more searchable content will create more keyword search advertising opportunities, while referral programs will continue to trend upward as well. Local advertising growth will outpace national advertising growth over the next five years as local businesses, which have been slow to embrace the Web, begin to accept that customers search for local service providers via the Internet's search and classified offerings.
- Online content growth will also be fueled by increasing broadband penetration, which will allow more users to view rich media content, primarily streaming audio and video. Web gaming will push content growth as graphics become richer, and videogame makers increase the number of titles that include enhanced multiplayer platforms available online. Additionally, the growing popularity of iPod and competing MP3 players will drive more use of downloaded music by consumers in the forecast period.
- As a result of higher growth rates for online advertising and content during the forecast period, the share of spending on access will account for only half of all consumer Internet expenditures in 2009. Internet advertising's share of overall consumer Web spending will rise faster than the content subsegment, due to online ads' stronger ROI measurements when compared with traditional media.
- While the number of visitors to web logs, commonly referred to as "blogs," has increased significantly in recent years, most blogs generate relatively minimal spending. During the forecast period, however, consumer usage of blogs will rise and blog owners will seek to increase advertising revenues, while shifting from free content offerings to subscription-based models.

Keyword search advertising and rich media will continue to fuel Internet advertising growth, while use of banner ads will drop, as advertisers increasingly look for ways of engaging consumers in an interactive experience that drives loyalty. As local search and classifieds continue to see strong results, these categories will see growth move steadily upward. As a result, local advertising will outpace national advertising growth over the next five years.

Internet content spending will increase in the double digits throughout the forecast period, generating compound annual growth of 27.1 percent. Spending will reach $7.76 billion in 2009. Growth will be driven by digital music downloads and online gaming. As the market advances, the availability of digital music downloads will become more pervasive to the point where any retailer that sells entertainment merchandise will likely offer some form of download. The online digital music market already includes traditional retailers such as Wal-Mart and Virgin Records, but some firms like Tower Records and Columbia Music Club have yet to join the fray. AOL's differentiation strategy may make it a formidable competitor in the market for digital music. The company has built a vast database of exclusive music content, including private concerts and downloadable songs available only to its subscribers. AOL is also adept at building communities around its products, and may use that strategy to draw in new digital downloader customers. Entertainment retailers will either partner with existing download technology firms or even acquire them to compete effectively.

While growth in online game spending is expected to be strong in the forecast period, the direction of the market remains unclear. Videogame makers have yet to determine the optimal online model. With millions of game cartridges being sold each year, cannibalization is a real threat, as manufacturers have not determined how to make online gaming a successful compliment to their growing core businesses. One option is to allow consumers to purchase online upgrades for games they purchase at a retail store, rather than offer the entire game online. Upgrades could include extra power, characters, tools or weapons. Gaming companies are also building advertising revenues through communities, where visitors can sign up for tournaments, interact with fellow gamers and purchase other gaming or entertainment-related products.

Spending on general content will be sluggish in the forecast period as the market matures. Players in the personals/dating category are expected to reinvigorate their businesses by building communities, using content, forums, chat rooms and events to keep visitors on their sites for longer periods of time and foster more peer-to-peer interaction. Additional spending on online content will be generated through blogs as more of these sites increasingly shift from free content to a subscription-based model.

9

NEWSPAPER PUBLISHING

Newspaper Publishing

Total Newspaper Spending And Nominal GDP Growth, 2000-2009

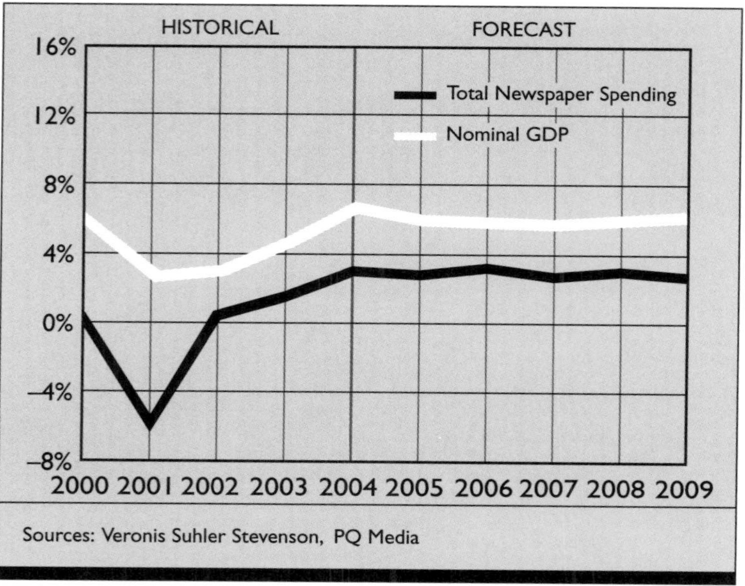

Sources: Veronis Suhler Stevenson, PQ Media

SUMMARY

Total newspaper spending, including daily and weekly advertising and circulation, posted accelerated growth for the third consecutive year in 2004, increasing 3.1 percent to $63.53 billion, driven by the fastest advertising growth in four years. Although still trailing nominal GDP growth, newspaper advertising expenditures advanced 4.0 percent to $52.15 billion in 2004, fueled by the strengthening economy, expanding job market and expansion in each of the three major ad categories. Retail advertising grew on the strength of several subcategories, including home supplies and furniture, financial, and the automotive aftermarket, while classified advertising was driven by double-digit gains in the employment category. Meanwhile, strong growth in the publishing and media, and political and government categories fueled upside in national advertising. The weekly newspaper subsegment also contributed to the overall newspaper segment's growth in 2004, as weeklies continue to deliver the attractive young and affluent demographic.

It is important to note here that advertising spending figures in this chapter are for print advertising only, and do not include expenditures on newspaper Web sites. However, we have provided data regarding online newspaper advertising as part of this chapter's tables, but the actual spending is not included in this segment's totals to avoid double counting. As a result, newspaper Web advertising expenditures are included in the Consumer Internet chapter's totals.

Overall newspaper spending grew at a paltry compound annual rate of 0.6 percent in the 1999-2004 period, driven down mainly by the 6.3 percent decline in the 2001 recession year, but also because of a slower-than-expected recovery in the ensuing years, a trend that affected most ad-based media. Going forward, we expect newspapers and other traditional media will be challenged like never before to prove their return on investment (ROI) to major advertisers, who are increasingly skeptical of the value of their conventional advertising buys, a development that will hamper ad growth in the forecast period.

On the circulation front, total spending

decreased 0.8 percent to $11.38 billion in 2004, due to declining unit circulation at major daily and weekly newspapers, and a downturn in prices of weekday and Sunday papers. Aggregate unit circulation of U.S. newspapers dropped 1.1 percent to 55.97 million in 2004, as readership of daily newspapers continued its decades-long decline among adults across different age groups, especially younger adults who prefer online news sources.

Reports surfaced in 2004 and early 2005 that five major newspapers had misreported circulation in prior years. The Audit Bureau of Circulations (ABC) issued sanctions against four of the offending newspapers in 2004 (the fifth was pending in court as of May 2005), but news of the misstatements hurt the image of the newspaper industry and left advertisers demanding greater accountability from publishers. In an effort to address advertiser concerns about the quality of newspaper circulation, some publishers scaled back the number of bulk copies sold to third parties, removing them from paid circulation totals.

Overall daily newspaper spending, including advertising and circulation, grew 3.0 percent to $57.69 billion in 2004, driven by an increase in all three major advertising categories, but tempered by a decrease in circulation spending. While each of the three key ad categories posted growth in 2004, upside was slower than in prior years during recovery intervals, another reason for the scanty overall expansion. Daily ad spending, which accounted for 79.1 percent of all newspaper expenditures in 2004, increased 3.9 percent to $46.70 billion. Circulation spending declined 0.9 percent to $10.99 billion, as both unit circulation and prices fell. Daily newspaper unit circulation has declined every year since 1994.

Weekly newspaper spending, including advertising and circulation at weekly and shopper publications, grew 4.9 percent to $5.84 billion in 2004, driven by the fourth straight year of accelerating gains in advertising expenditures. Ad spending increased 5.1 percent to $5.45 billion, outpacing daily growth, with most of the expansion coming from the entertainment and specialty mer-

Growth of U.S. Spending on Newspapers

	Daily Newspapers	*Weekly Newspapers*	*Total*
2004 Expenditures ($ Millions)	$57,687	$5,840	$63,527
1999-2004 Compound Annual Growth (%)	0.3%	4.2%	0.6%
2004-2009 Projected Compound Annual Growth (%)	2.5%	5.3%	2.8%
2009 Projected Expenditures ($ Millions)	$65,357	$7,569	$72,926

Sources: Veronis Suhler Stevenson, PQ Media, Newspaper Association of America, Kagan Research, *Editor & Publisher*

2004 Communications Industry Forecast Compared with Actual Growth

Category	*2004 Forecasted Growth**	*Actual 2004 Growth†*
Daily Newspapers	4.7%	3.0%
Advertising	5.8	3.9
Retail	3.7	3.1
National	8.6	3.7
Classified	7.2	5.1
Circulation Spending	0.3	–0.9
Weekly Newspapers	4.9	4.9
Advertising	5.1	5.1
Circulation Spending	1.9	1.8
Total Newspaper Spending	4.7	2.9

*Veronis Suhler Stevenson 2004 Communications Industry Forecast & Report
†Veronis Suhler Stevenson, PQ Media

Newspaper Publishing

Total Spending On Newspapers

($ MILLIONS)

Year	Daily Newspapers*	Weekly Newspapers	Total
1999	$56,759	$4,752	$61,511
2000	59,212	5,055	64,267
2001	55,086	5,142	60,228
2002	55,126	5,352	60,478
2003	56,027	5,569	61,596
2004	57,687	5,840	63,527
2005	59,104	6,162	65,266
2006	60,755	6,545	67,300
2007	62,258	6,796	69,054
2008	63,818	7,253	71,071
2009	65,357	7,569	72,926

Sources: Veronis Suhler Stevenson, PQ Media, Newspaper Association of America, Kagan Research, *Editor & Publisher*

*To avoid double counting, these figures do not include online advertising on newspaper Web sites. Online advertising is found in the Consumer Internet chapter.

Growth of Total Spending On Newspapers

Year	Daily Newspapers*	Weekly Newspapers	Total
2000	4.3%	6.4%	4.5%
2001	–7.0	1.7	–6.3
2002	0.1	4.1	0.4
2003	1.6	4.1	1.8
2004	3.0	4.9	3.1
2005	2.5	5.5	2.7
2006	2.8	6.2	3.1
2007	2.5	3.8	2.6
2008	2.5	6.7	2.9
2009	2.4	4.4	2.6
Compound Annual Growth			
1999-2004	0.3	4.2	0.6
2004-2009	2.5	5.3	2.8

Sources: Veronis Suhler Stevenson, PQ Media, Newspaper Association of America, Kagan Research, *Editor & Publisher*

*To avoid double counting, these figures do not include online advertising on newspaper Web sites. Online advertising is found in the Consumer Internet chapter.

chandise categories, accentuated by the trend of weeklies delivering a coveted younger and affluent demographic. Paid unit circulation declined 1.4 percent to 20.9 million in 2004, but an increase in prices led to growth in circulation spending. Total unit circulation, including free weeklies, rose 0.8 percent to 48.9 million. Paid circulation made up 42.0 percent of total unit circulation in 2004. Total weekly newspaper spending grew at a compound annual rate of 4.2 percent from 1999 to 2004.

Total spending on daily and weekly newspapers is expected to grow just 2.7 percent to $65.27 billion in 2005. The increase will be driven by the anticipated economic expansion and more robust job market during the year, tempered by a deceleration in growth of retail and national advertising. Both unit circulation and circulation spending are expected to decline over the forecast period, as consumers increasingly turn to electronic media, such as the Internet and cable television, for their news. The decline in circulation is expected to hinder advertising spending, as marketers perceive diminishing returns from shrinking audiences. As a result, even as the general advertising market expands, total newspaper spending will grow at a tepid compound annual rate of 2.8 percent in the 2004-2009 period, reaching $72.93 billion in 2009. By comparison, nominal GDP will grow 6.1 percent over the same period.

Advertising and Circulation Spending On Newspapers

($ MILLIONS)

Year	Advertising*	Circulation	Total
1999	$50,689	$10,822	$61,511
2000	53,371	10,896	64,267
2001	49,093	11,135	60,228
2002	49,079	11,399	60,478
2003	50,126	11,470	61,596
2004	52,152	11,375	63,527
2005	54,090	11,176	65,266
2006	56,262	11,038	67,300
2007	58,126	10,928	69,054
2008	60,204	10,867	71,071
2009	62,086	10,840	72,926

Sources: Veronis Suhler Stevenson, PQ Media, Newspaper Association of America, Kagan Research, *Editor & Publisher*

*To avoid double counting, these figures do not include online advertising on newspaper Web sites. Online advertising is found in the Consumer Internet chapter.

Growth of Advertising and Circulation Spending on Newspapers

Year	Advertising*	Circulation	Total
2000	5.3%	0.7%	4.5%
2001	–8.0	2.2	–6.3
2002	0.0	2.4	0.4
2003	2.1	0.6	1.8
2004	4.0	–0.8	3.1
2005	3.7	–1.7	2.7
2006	4.0	–1.2	3.1
2007	3.3	–1.0	2.6
2008	3.6	–0.6	2.9
2009	3.1	–0.2	2.6
Compound Annual Growth			
1999-2004	0.6	1.0	0.6
2004-2009	3.5	–1.0	2.8

Sources: Veronis Suhler Stevenson, PQ Media, Newspaper Association of America, Kagan Research, *Editor & Publisher*

*To avoid double counting, these figures do not include online advertising on newspaper Web sites. Online advertising is found in the Consumer Internet chapter.

HIGHLIGHTS

Daily Newspapers

Total spending on daily newspapers grew 3.0 percent to $57.69 billion in 2004, driven by gains in retail, classified and national advertising. Daily newspaper expenditures grew from 1999 to 2004 at a compound rate of only 0.3 percent, due primarily to a 7.0 percent drop in 2001 as a result of the broader economic and advertising market contractions.

■

Advertising spending on newspapers increased 3.9 percent to $46.70 billion in 2004, as economic growth and a strong job market fueled gains in advertising on employment, real estate, home supplies and furniture, and financial services. Spending on classifieds moved into positive territory after three years of declines, as a surging job market drove increases in help wanted linage. Advertising expenditures in the 1999-2004 period grew at a compound annual rate of 0.2 percent, as a result of a 9.0 percent plunge in 2001, followed by a 0.5 percent dip in 2002.

■

Circulation spending fell 0.9 percent to $10.99 billion in 2004—the first decline since 1988—as weekday and Sunday circulation declined 1.2 percent and 0.5 percent, respectively. Average prices of daily newspapers were flat, while Sunday prices rose 0.7 percent. Unit circulation decreased 1.1 percent, perpetuating a downward trend that began in 1994.

■

Four major newspapers overreported circulation in 2004, drawing sanctions from the Audit Bureau of Circulations (ABC), while a fifth case was pending in court as of May 2005. The ABC and individual newspaper publishers assured advertisers that the misstatements did not indicate widespread circulation irregularities throughout the industry. While few hard data exist on the impact of the circulation scandals, advertisers are paying more attention to the quality of newspaper circulation, which has led many publishers to stop counting bulk sales to third parties in their paid circulation. Anecdotal evidence from several papers in 2005 appeared to support claims of some advertiser defection and loss of loyalty, but the industry was quick to point out that only a handful of such cases have been reported out of 1,500 papers nationwide.

■

Newspaper advertising is expected to increase at a decelerated rate of 3.5 percent in 2005 to $48.32 billon, as retail and national advertising experience lower growth compared with 2004, resulting from consolidation among large advertisers and competition from electronic media. Newspaper ad spending will grow at a compound annual rate of 3.3 percent from 2004 to 2009, reaching $54.94 billion in 2009, due to slowing growth in classified and retail expenditures, which will be balanced somewhat by upswings in political advertising during election years.

■

Circulation spending will decrease 1.9 percent to $10.78 billion in 2005, driven by a decline in unit circulation as consumers increasingly look to the Internet for local and national news, and by efforts from publishers to reduce sales of bulk copies. Over the forecast period, as unit circulation falls, publishers will raise prices, but will not succeed in reversing the decline in circulation spending, which will decrease 1.1 percent on a compound annual basis from 2004 to 2009, dropping to $10.42 billion in 2009.

■

Total expenditures on daily newspapers are projected to increase at a decelerated rate of 2.5 percent in 2005 to $59.10 billion, as a result of slower ad growth, the increasing challenge to prove return on investment in the medium and a drop in circulation spending. Continued circulation spending declines and reduced advertising growth will temper compound annual growth at 2.5 percent over the forecast period, with spending reaching $65.36 billion in 2009.

Daily Newspapers

THE DAILY NEWSPAPER MARKET IN 2004 AND 2005

Daily newspaper advertising spending increased at a quicker pace for the third consecutive year in 2004, propelled by the rising economy, an expanding job market and record home sales. However, growth was hampered by mergers in the telecommunications and retailing industries, and by changes in the marketing strategies of some of the medium's largest advertisers. Circulation spending fell as aggregate newspaper circulation declined for the eleventh year in a row, while the discovery of exaggerated circulation numbers at four large newspapers marred the industry's image. Meanwhile, the Internet and cable TV continued to chip away at newspaper circulation, although newspapers have begun to derive growing revenues from their own Web sites.

Total spending on daily newspapers, including advertising and circulation, grew 3.0 percent to $57.69 billion in 2004, driven by an increase in advertising but hindered by a decline in circulation spending. Total expenditures advanced at a compound annual rate of 0.3 percent in the 1999-2004 period, trailing GDP growth by a wide margin, due to a significant decline in the 2001 recession year followed by a flat performance in 2002.

Daily newspaper advertising spending increased 3.9 percent to $46.70 billion in 2004, fueled by gains in the national, retail and classified categories. Nevertheless, the growth rate was among the weakest in the advertising-based media sector, as total ad market expenditures increased 7.6 percent for the year. National newspaper advertising, which surged in 2003 due to an increase in telecommunications spending, slowed down in 2004 as the telecommunications category contracted, while media and political and government advertising increased. Classified advertising grew, thanks to strong employment and real estate spending, turning positive for the first time since 2000, when the category expanded 5.1 percent. Retail advertising benefited from increases in the automotive aftermarket, home supplies and furniture, and apparel categories. The improvement in classified advertising spending continued into the first quarter of 2005. Several newspapers reported double-digit gains in employment advertising, along with continued strength in real estate listings. The strength in the real estate market, however, is not expected to last as the forecast period progresses, according to several studies released at press time of this *Forecast*.

Aggregate newspaper circulation, including weekday and Sunday editions, decreased 1.1 percent to 56.0 million in 2004. The numbers of deeply discounted copies, as well as "other paid" copies sold to third parties, increased. The increase in discounted copies led to lower average prices of daily and Sunday newspapers. As a result of the decline in unit circulation and price reductions, circulation spending fell 0.9 percent to $10.99 billion in 2004. The decline of unit circulation continued into the first quarter of 2005, when the average circulation of dailies fell 1.9 percent, and that of Sunday editions tumbled 2.5 percent. These were the largest declines in daily and Sunday circulations since 1996 and 1994, respectively.

Newspaper circulation has been adversely affected by a number of factors. More people are getting their news from other sources, particularly electronic media such as the Internet and cable TV news networks. Audiences across several age groups tend to avoid the medium: Only about 39 percent of adults between the ages of 18 and 34 read a daily newspaper in 2004, down from about 59 percent in 1982. In addition, the percentage of adults over the age of 55 who read a newspaper in 2004 declined to approximately 67 percent from 72 percent two decades earlier. Finally, the federal Do Not Call Registry, which took effect in 2003, has severely limited the ability of newspapers to sign up subscribers through telemarketing efforts.

The circulation practices of the industry came under intense scrutiny in 2004, after four major newspapers were found to have exaggerated their circulation figures. The *Dallas Morning News*, the *Chicago Sun-Times*, *Newsday* of Long Island, NY, and the Spanish-language *Hoy* overstated their circulations by amounts ranging from a few thousand copies to nearly 100,000 copies, over various periods of time going back one to several years. Following these revelations, advertisers demanded verification of all newspaper circulation claims, while the ABC and newspaper executives tried to restore confidence in circulation figures. The ABC issued sanctions against the four newspapers, prohibiting them from releasing ABC-audited circulation figures for two years, and requiring these publications to undergo biannual audits instead of annual ones. The ABC also expanded its use of "discovery sampling," a process by which it polls a sample of about 100 subscribers of a given newspaper and verifies that they have, in fact, paid for the publication and are receiving it. In addition, the ABC limited the number of days that a newspaper could omit from its circulation to 10 per year, and required that all publishers sign the publisher's statement that they submit to the ABC twice a year.

Federal regulators also took note of the circulation irregularities. In October 2004, the Securities and Exchange Commission asked at least five publishers of publicly held newspapers for information on the calculation of circulation figures. The request was part of an investigation into whether or not the circulation problems were localized to specific companies or systemic to the industry.

A new ABC rule went into effect in April 2005 that required newspapers to state circulation for each day of the week, in addition to a Monday-through-Friday weekly average. Some publishers expressed concern that reporting daily fluctuations in circulation would lead advertisers to press for different ad rates for different days of the week. Others believed the rule would help make newspaper circulation more transparent to advertisers and enable them to better plan their schedules, without any detrimental effects on ad rates. Publishers' statements for the period ending September 30, 2005, will be the first to report these figures.

Whether such measures have allayed the concerns of advertisers is still unclear. Several newspaper publishers, such as Gannett, the New York Times Co., Tribune Co. and A.H. Belo reported that the circulation scandals were not having an impact on advertising rates. Anecdotal evidence from the *Dallas Morning News* and *Newsday* supported claims of advertiser defection as well as loyalty. Meanwhile, a real estate firm sued Journal Sentinel Inc. in April 2005, alleging circulation fraud at the *Milwaukee Journal Sentinel*, Wisconsin's top-selling newspaper. The lawsuit filed by Shorewest Realtors contends the newspaper deliberately overstated circulation since 1996 and used the "artificially inflated rates to surreptitiously overcharge" the home-seller for advertising. The case was still pending at press time of this *Forecast*, and no other circulation irregularities had surfaced. Publishers, however, were quick to point out that only a handful of newspapers out of about 1,500 members of the ABC were found guilty of overstating circulation figures. Nevertheless, advertisers are paying more attention to the quality of newspaper circulation, which has led many publishers to stop counting bulk sales to third parties in their paid circulation.

Total spending on daily newspapers is expected to grow 2.5 percent in 2005 to $59.10 billion, due to a decline in circulation spending and deceleration in retail and national advertising expenditures. This slowdown in growth stands in stark contrast to the overall advertising market, which is projected to grow 6.1 percent in 2005.

In an effort to reverse the deceleration in ad spending, the industry's leading trade organization, the Newspaper Association of America (NAA), is planning to launch a newspaper marketing campaign later in 2005. The goal of the campaign will be to change perceptions among advertisers and to promote the image of newspapers as an effective medium to connect with younger audiences.

RETAIL ADVERTISING

The strength of retail advertising is a key measure of the newspaper industry's performance, as it accounts for between 44 percent and 48 percent of all newspaper advertising expenditures in a given year. In 2004, retail advertising grew only 3.1 percent to $22.01 billion, fueled by spending increases in the home supplies and furniture, financial and automotive aftermarket categories. Strong sales of new and existing homes boosted home supplies and furniture advertising,

Retail Newspaper Advertising Expenditures, by Category*

($ MILLIONS)

Category	*1999*	*2000*	*2001*	*2002*	*2003*	*2004*
General Merchandise	$ 7,995	$ 7,582	$ 7,586	$ 7,541	$ 6,976	$ 6,864
Financial	2,985	2,926	2,719	2,718	3,268	3,439
Home Supplies/Furniture	2,121	2,459	2,653	2,790	3,064	3,428
Computers/Electronics	3,468	3,927	3,103	2,885	2,434	2,505
Food	1,885	1,777	1,674	1,850	1,998	1,940
Hobbies/Toys/Sports	766	827	1,025	1,096	1,197	1,213
Building Materials	564	679	675	777	978	951
Apparel & Accessories	637	728	747	776	841	928
Automotive Aftermarket	316	325	301	369	396	537
Records/Books/Cards	168	179	195	190	187	203
Total	20,905	21,409	20,678	20,992	21,339	22,008

Sources: Veronis Suhler Stevenson, PQ Media, Newspaper Association of America

*Does not include spending from the "Other" category that normally represents approximately .01 percent share of retail advertising.

Growth of Retail Newspaper Advertising Expenditures, by Category*

Category	*2000*	*2001*	*2002*	*2003*	*2004*	*1999-2004 Compound Annual Growth*
General Merchandise	–5.2%	0.1%	–0.6%	–7.5%	–1.6%	–2.7%
Financial	–2.0	–7.1	0.0	20.2	5.2	1.8
Home Supplies/Furniture	15.9	7.9	5.2	9.8	11.9	7.6
Computers/Electronics	13.2	–21.0	–7.0	–15.6	2.9	–6.8
Food	–5.7	–5.8	10.5	8.0	–2.9	1.2
Hobbies/Toys/Sports	8.0	23.9	6.9	9.2	1.3	9.3
Building Materials	20.4	–0.6	15.1	25.9	–2.8	11.6
Apparel & Accessories	14.3	2.6	3.9	8.4	10.3	5.7
Automotive Aftermarket	2.8	–7.4	22.6	7.3	35.6	4.6
Records/Books/Cards	6.5	8.9	–2.6	–1.6	8.6	2.2
Total	2.4	–3.4	1.5	1.7	3.1	0.4

Sources: Veronis Suhler Stevenson, PQ Media, Newspaper Association of America

*Does not include spending from the "Other" category that normally represents approximately .01 percent share of retail advertising.

while the financial category was driven primarily by advertising from mortgage companies. However, most industry analysts believe that the housing market is ripe for a fall in the near future, although they disagree on the magnitude of the contraction and when it will happen. Nonetheless, we believe real estate advertising will not grow as quickly in the forecast period as it did in the prior five-year timeframe.

General merchandise, which includes department, discount and specialty stores, is the largest retail advertising category. In 2004, spending in the category fell for a third straight year, down 1.6 percent to $6.86 billion. Department store advertising has experienced spending declines for a variety of reasons. First, department store mergers, such as those between Federated and May, and between Sears and Kmart, will reduce the number of advertisers in the field, leading to a decrease in run-of-press ad spending. The mergers have also created larger entities that serve bigger markets and often find broadcast television more effective in reaching their customers. Second, shoppers have been deserting traditional department stores in favor of superstores and specialty retailers. Costco, the nation's fifth-largest retailer in 2003, does little or no newspaper advertising, except when announcing new store openings. Wal-Mart, the world's largest retailer, limits its advertising to preprint inserts a few times a year. Specialty stores, such as J. Jill, concentrate on custom publishing, direct mail and the Internet. And third, department stores are changing their marketing focus. For example, Macy's in 2005 stated that its advertising would not be as price-oriented as before because it was now targeting a different type of customer. The company said it would focus on building its brands, which will result in reduced reliance on newspaper advertising.

Although some department stores are cutting newspaper advertising, others such as Kohl's and J.C. Penney have stepped up their newspaper spending, albeit only slightly. These increases helped keep the ad spending decline relatively minor in what was a turbulent year for department stores. Meanwhile, consolidation is occurring in other industries, such as Procter & Gamble's recent acquisition of Gillette, but these mergers have had less of an impact on the newspaper industry because many of these industries tend to advertise through other media like broadcast TV and direct mail.

Newspapers, meanwhile, have been upgrading their preprint insertion technology in recent years to make their papers more flexible to meet advertiser demands. For example, the *Boston Globe* in 2005 began offering preprint advertisers the ability to reach their customers by zip code, which increased the number of clusters available to advertisers from 96 to 279.

Spending on retail preprints is estimated to have grown slightly in the first quarter of 2005, driving gains in the retail category. For the year, retail advertising spending is expected to grow at a slower 2.1 percent to $22.47 billion. Spending will grow at a reduced compound annual rate of 2.0 percent from 2004 to 2009, due to continued softness in general merchandise brought about by the aforementioned factors, coupled with smaller increases in the financial and furniture categories, as interest rates rise and the housing market cools down over the forecast period. To put the newspaper market's growth challenges in perspective, the broader advertising market is expected to grow at a compound annual rate of 6.8 percent in the 2004-2009 period.

CLASSIFIED ADVERTISING

Classified advertising spending declined every year from 2001 to 2003, due to decreases in employment ads as net jobs in the U.S. either declined or were flat. In 2004, spending rose 5.1 percent to $16.61 billion, driven by double-digit gains in help wanted advertising. The nation's employers increased net hiring in 2004 for the first time since 2000 and created almost 1.5 million new non-farm jobs. The pace of job creation continued through April 2005, foreshadowing the possibility of another good year for jobs in 2005.

Employment classified advertising spending increased 15.1 percent to $4.58 billion in 2004. Recognizing the threat from Monster and other online job boards, Knight Ridder

Classified Advertising, by Category

($ MILLIONS)

Category	*1999*	*2000*	*2001*	*2002*	*2003*	*2004*
Automotive	$ 4,912	$ 5,026	$ 4,889	$ 5,156	$ 5,192	$ 5,015
Employment	8,026	8,713	5,705	4,388	3,977	4,576
Real Estate	3,116	3,167	3,512	3,668	3,954	4,222
Other	2,596	2,703	2,515	2,686	2,678	2,795
Total	18,650	19,609	16,621	15,898	15,801	16,608

Sources: Veronis Suhler Stevenson, PQ Media, Newspaper Association of America

Growth of Classified Advertising, by Category

Category	*2000*	*2001*	*2002*	*2003*	*2004*	*1999-2004 Compound Annual Growth*
Automotive	2.3%	–2.7%	5.5%	0.7%	–3.4%	0.4%
Employment	8.6	–34.5	–23.1	–9.4	15.1	–10.6
Real Estate	1.6	10.9	4.4	7.8	6.8	6.3
Other	4.1	–7.0	6.8	–0.3	4.4	1.5
Total	5.1	–15.2	–4.3	–0.6	5.1	–2.3

Sources: Veronis Suhler Stevenson, PQ Media, Newspaper Association of America

Jobs Added in the United States

Year	*Employees on Nonfarm Payrolls* (Thousands)*	*Increase (Thousands)*	*Percent Change*
1999	128,993	—	—
2000	131,785	2,792	2.2%
2001	131,826	41	0.0
2002	130,341	–1,485	–1.1
2003	129,999	–342	–0.3
2004	131,480	1,481	1.1

Sources: Veronis Suhler Stevenson, PQ Media, Bureau of Labor Statistics
*Not seasonally adjusted.

and Tribune joined forces in 2000 to acquire CareerBuilder.com, a site that concentrates job listings from more than 130 newspapers, and offers career advice and resume-posting services. Gannett became an equal partner of CareerBuilder in 2002. By 2004, CareerBuilder had surpassed its rivals by drawing the most job search traffic of any site. The site claims to have superiority in the local jobs market, where national job sites like Monster and Yahoo! HotJobs are still weak.

Publishers are taking other innovative steps to protect their employment advertising turf. For example, the *Star* of Ventura County, CA, collaborates with the local county's Workforce Investment Board and co-sponsors community job fairs. The *Star* also places kiosks in government centers

National Advertising, by Leading Categories

($ MILLIONS)

Category	*1999*	*2000*	*2001*	*2002*	*2003*	*2004*
Utilities	$1,062	$1,391	$1,394	$1,498	$1,859	$1,823
Transportation/Travel	1,489	1,429	1,359	1,359	1,291	1,331
Motion Pictures	535	1,276	1,012	1,125	1,163	1,149
Coupon Marketing Organizations	1,048	964	886	899	924	987
Automotive	777	638	633	638	690	757
Publishing/Media	434	432	357	390	391	469
Political/Government	217	248	240	240	229	268
Computer Equipment	203	229	196	173	228	216
Miscellaneous	199	248	302	259	239	214
Mail Order	190	168	119	135	169	147
Top 10 Total	6,154	7,023	6,498	6,716	7,183	7,361
Other Categories	578	630	506	494	614	722
Total	6,732	7,653	7,004	7,210	7,797	8,083

Sources: Veronis Suhler Stevenson, PQ Media, Newspaper Association of America

where people can access the newspaper's employment classifieds.

Real estate and other classified advertising expenditures rose 6.8 percent and 4.4 percent, respectively, in 2004. Even though interest rates rose during 2004, mortgage rates were comparatively low. Consequently, home sales remained strong. However, real estate classifieds are expected to face competition in the forecast period from Web sites maintained by local real estate brokers and multiple listing services. A study released in the second quarter of 2005 projected that approximately half of all real estate classifieds will be online in 2009, compared to about 10 percent in 2004.

Meanwhile, the general merchandise category, which is the smallest ad category representing about 17 percent of classified spending, is estimated to have lost market share to eBay, a popular auction Web site, and craigslist.org, a community-based Web site. To combat further incursions by the online auction company, several newspapers have launched competing services on their own Web sites. For example, the *St. Petersburg Times* has a "Click and Buy" feature on its site that enables online transactions between buyers and sellers. Between 2003 and 2004, about 150 newspapers sold more than $46 million in online auctions lasting from eight to 10 days. While the amount is a small fraction of eBay's revenues ($3.27 billion in 2004), the auctions help newspapers build relationships with readers and retailers. In another effort to connect retailers with readers, CrossMedia Services, owned by Gannett, Tribune and Knight Ridder, launched an initiative called ShopLocal in August 2004, linking visitors to newspaper sites with sale circulars from national and local retailers.

Automotive classified advertising spending, essentially flat in 2003, decreased 3.4 percent in 2004, to $5.02 billion as car dealers cut back spending and relied more on national advertising from manufacturers to generate business. This trend likely will continue in the forecast period as the auto industry—from dealers to manufacturers—migrates its advertising to other media, including the Internet and direct marketing.

Growth of National Advertising, by Leading Categories

Category	*2000*	*2001*	*2002*	*2003*	*2004*	*1999-2004 Compound Annual Growth*
Utilities	31.0%	0.2%	7.5%	24.1%	−1.9%	11.4%
Transportation/Travel	−4.0	−4.9	0.0	−5.0	3.1	−2.2
Motion Pictures	138.5	−20.7	11.2	3.4	−1.2	16.5
Coupon Marketing Organizations	−8.0	−8.1	1.5	2.8	6.8	−1.2
Automotive	−17.9	−0.8	0.8	8.2	9.7	−0.5
Publishing/Media	−0.5	−17.4	9.2	0.3	19.9	1.6
Political/Government	14.3	−3.2	0.0	−4.6	17.0	4.3
Computer Equipment	12.8	−14.4	−11.7	31.8	−5.3	1.2
Miscellaneous	24.6	21.8	−14.2	−7.7	−10.5	1.5
Mail Order	−11.6	−29.2	13.4	25.2	−13.0	−5.0
Top 10 Total	14.1	−7.5	3.4	7.0	2.5	3.6
Other Categories	9.0	−19.7	−2.4	24.3	17.6	4.5
Total	13.7	−8.5	2.9	8.1	3.7	3.7

Sources: Veronis Suhler Stevenson, PQ Media, Newspaper Association of America

We expect spending on classifieds to increase 6.4 percent to $17.67 billion in 2005 on the strength of help wanted and real estate advertising. Several large newspaper companies with strong local newspapers reported double-digit classified ad gains in the first quarter of 2005, fueled by rising employment, real estate and automotive listings. The broader economy continued to grow in the first quarter of the year, keeping job growth robust. Sales of existing homes in the first quarter of 2005 set a record, although home sales are expected to slow down in the second half of the year. And despite higher gas prices, the automobile industry expects 2005 sales to match those of 2004, although a dealer push at the local level may be required to reach this sales target.

Classified advertising is expected to grow 5.4 percent on a compound annual basis over the next five years, reaching $21.60 billion in 2009. Growth will decelerate over the forecast period as the employment and real estate markets are expected to start running out of steam in 2006.

NATIONAL ADVERTISING

National advertising spending grew 3.7 percent in 2004 to $8.08 billion, despite a 26.0 percentage-point drop in telecommunications spending. Growth was fueled by double-digit gains in media, and political and government advertising, along with smaller increases in automotive and coupon marketing expenditures. Broadcast and cable TV networks find it advantageous to advertise in newspapers, as they can reach potential viewers on the day of a particular program's broadcast.

The political and government category, mainly comprising advertising the government has to run in newspapers under law, was helped by substantial increases in political advertising in 2004. Political advertising benefited from a Federal Elections Commission rule that prohibited advertising by so-called "Section 527" groups on television in the 60 days prior to the presidential election. The rule, however, did not prohibit Section 527 groups from advertising in newspapers during that time. As a result, newspaper publishers stepped up their sales efforts in 2003

Number of U.S. Daily Newspapers

Year	Morning	Evening	Total Newspapers*	Papers With Sunday Editions
1999	736	760	1,483	905
2000	766	727	1,480	917
2001	776	714	1,468	913
2002	777	692	1,457	913
2003	787	680	1,456	917
2004	813	653	1,456	914

Sources: Veronis Suhler Stevenson, PQ Media, Newspaper Association of America, *Editor & Publisher*

*All-day newspapers are counted in the morning column and in the evening column, but only once in the total column.

Growth of the Number Of U.S. Daily Newspapers

Year	Morning	Evening	Total Newspapers	Papers With Sunday Editions
2000	4.1%	−4.3%	−0.2%	1.3%
2001	1.3	−1.8	−0.8	−0.4
2002	0.1	−3.1	−0.7	0.0
2003	1.3	−1.7	−0.1	0.4
2004	3.3	−4.0	0.0	−0.3
Compound Annual Change				
1999-2004	2.0	−3.0	−0.4	0.2

Sources: Veronis Suhler Stevenson, PQ Media, Newspaper Association of America, *Editor & Publisher*

and 2004, meeting with political consultants and campaign managers, presenting research on reader attitudes toward political advertising and making it easier for candidates to advertise through group buys. Political campaigns spent an estimated $61.5 million on newspaper advertising in 2004, an increase of 81.5 percent from $33.8 million in 2002 and up 132.4 percent from $26.4 million in 2000, according to exclusive research from PQ Media. Newspapers also garnered a larger share of political advertising from other media in 2004, as the industry launched an aggressive marketing campaign aimed at political campaign managers and consultants, and local issue and referendum campaigns spent a record amount on their causes during the year, particularly in California. Newspapers accounted for 3.3 percent of all political ad spending in 2004, compared with 2.9 percent in 2002 and 3.0 percent in 2000, according to PQ Media.

Automobile manufacturers boosted their brand advertising 9.7 percent to about $757 million in 2004, driving buyers to local dealerships. Spending from coupon marketing firms grew 6.8 percent to about $987 million. Newspapers have taken various measures to make the medium more attractive to coupon producers, such as Valassis, and to obtain business that would have otherwise gone to competitors like ADVO. In 2005, for example, six newspapers from southern California joined one from Las Vegas to start a regional network for coupon preprint advertising. By using the network, advertisers could reach 7.2 million households with one buy.

Travel advertising grew in 2004 after being down or flat for five consecutive years. Spending in this category grew 3.1 percent to $1.33 billion, driven by a resurgence in the travel market as the number of people taking business and leisure trips has increased since 2000.

In 2003, spending by telecommunications companies, such as SBC Communications, AT&T Wireless and Sprint, drove up the utilities category, which accounted for 23.8 percent of all national advertising. Subsequent cutbacks in spending, brought about by the mergers of AT&T Wireless and Cingular Wireless, and Sprint and Nextel, led to a 1.9 percent decline in 2004 expenditures.

Spending on national advertising is expected to grow just 1.2 percent in 2005 to $8.18 billion, due to continued weakness and unpredictability in several sectors. Telecommunications will continue to be soft as a result of the aforementioned mergers. Although the market remains competitive, there are few remaining players, and spending is being diverted from newspapers to television and the Internet. Motion pictures

Aggregate Circulation of U.S. Daily Newspapers

(THOUSANDS)

Year	*Morning*	*Evening*	*Total Circulation For Weekday Editions*	*Sunday Editions*	*Overall Newspaper Circulation**
1999	45,997	9,981	55,978	59,894	57,656
2000	46,772	9,000	55,772	59,420	57,335
2001	46,821	8,757	55,578	59,090	57,083
2002	46,617	8,569	55,186	58,780	56,726
2003	46,930	8,255	55,185	58,495	56,604
2004	46,887	7,739	54,626	57,753	55,966
2005	46,512	7,445	53,957	56,887	55,213
2006	46,000	7,117	53,117	56,204	54,440
2007	45,310	6,768	52,078	55,305	53,461
2008	44,540	6,409	50,949	54,365	52,413
2009	43,605	6,037	49,642	53,332	51,223

Sources: Veronis Suhler Stevenson, PQ Media, Newspaper Association of America, *Editor & Publisher*

*Daily editions are given a weight of 4/7 and Sunday editions 3/7.

Growth of Aggregate Circulation of U.S. Daily Newspapers

Year	*Morning*	*Evening*	*Total Circulation For Weekday Editions*	*Sunday Editions*	*Overall Newspaper Circulation**
2000	1.7%	–9.8%	–0.4%	–0.8%	–0.6%
2001	0.1	–2.7	–0.3	–0.6	–0.4
2002	–0.4	–2.1	–0.7	–0.5	–0.6
2003	0.7	–3.7	0.0	–0.5	–0.2
2004	–0.1	–6.3	–1.0	–1.3	–1.1
2005	–0.8	–3.8	–1.2	–1.5	–1.3
2006	–1.1	–4.4	–1.6	–1.2	–1.4
2007	–1.5	–4.9	–2.0	–1.6	–1.8
2008	–1.7	–5.3	–2.2	–1.7	–2.0
2009	–2.1	–5.8	–2.6	–1.9	–2.3
Compound Annual Change					
1999-2004	0.4	–5.0	–0.5	–0.7	–0.6
2004-2009	–1.4	–4.8	–1.9	–1.6	–1.8

Sources: Veronis Suhler Stevenson, PQ Media, Newspaper Association of America, *Editor & Publisher*

*Daily editions are given a weight of 4/7 and Sunday editions 3/7.

suffered from two years of declining box office admissions, which continued into the first quarter of 2005. Political advertising is not expected to come back until 2006. However, travel advertising, one of the largest categories, is expected to increase as travel activity expands from that of 2004. Media, coupons and automotive advertising will also grow. The automobile industry predicts that 2005 sales will be on par with 2004, but will need a push from advertising to get there. While the housing market remained robust during the first quarter of 2005, this category is expected to decline for the full year, as the broader real estate market cools due to rising interest rates and several other factors.

Spending on national advertising will grow at a reduced compound annual rate of 2.4 percent from 2004 to 2009, reaching $9.09 billion in 2009, compared with 3.7 percent growth in the 1999-2004 period. Growth will be subdued as national advertisers, seeking better ROI from their advertising budgets, continue to redirect their spending away from newspapers and into electronic media such as the Internet.

CIRCULATION

Total daily newspaper circulation fell 1.1 percent in 2004 to 56.0 million, a total that was lower than overall newspaper circulation in 1970. Aggregate morning circulation declined 0.1 percent to 46.9 million, while evening circulation dropped 6.3 percent to 7.7 million, as 26 evening newspapers folded or merged with morning papers. Three Sunday newspapers ceased publication in 2004, contributing to an overall loss of 742,000 copies, as Sunday circulation fell 1.3 percent to 57.8 million.

Unit circulation of daily newspapers has been declining since 1991, as more potential readers have migrated to other media for their news and as more evening papers have shuttered, and evening subscribers have largely not switched over to the replacement morning papers. While people in the younger age groups have reduced their consumption of daily newspapers by about 20 percentage points since 1982, older audiences have trimmed their readership of dailies, too, though not in as large numbers. However, the latter decline may only have a minimal impact on overall newspaper readership because while the share of readers in the over-55 audience has declined in recent years, the number of readers over 55 has actually increased slightly due to the market's gain in share of the overall U.S. population. Nevertheless, the net number of newspaper readers is declining, and will continue to do so in the forecast period.

The decline in unit circulation in 2004 occurred despite recent ABC rule changes that allowed newspapers to count deeply discounted and bulk-delivered copies as paid circulation. In 2001, the ABC permitted copies sold for more than 25.0 percent of the base price to be included as paid circulation. Previously, only copies sold for 50.0 percent or more of the base price could be included. Then in 2002, publishers were allowed to regard "other paid" copies sold to third parties, not the end user, as part of paid circulation. In 2004, these two categories of copies accounted for about 9 percent of total circulation across the 50 largest newspapers. Without the allowances, unit circulations of many newspapers would have declined to present levels sooner. Under the assumption that readers of discounted and unpaid copies are not as engaged in newspapers as those who pay full price, advertisers are looking closer at the quality of circulation.

Publishers have been trying to stem the slide of unit circulation by various means, including redesigning papers to make them more appealing to readers. For example, *The New York Times* announced in 2005 that it would restrict the length of its stories to 1,800 words, and that longer stories would require prior approval from one of three top editors. The *Chicago Tribune*, after losing 6.6 percent of its weekday circulation in the six months ended in March 2005, launched three new entertainment features in May 2005. In addition, several large publishers have been proactive in their efforts to become the local online voice of authority. So, while overall print circulation is declining, some of the lost readers have become loyal to the online editions, which are not counted in the overall circulation figures.

To extend their reach beyond that of the

Percentage of Population Reading Newspapers, by Age Group

	Weekday Edition				Sunday Edition			
Age Group	*1982*	*1992*	*2003*	*2004*	*1982*	*1992*	*2003*	*2004*
18-24	59%	54%	40%	39%	64%	63%	49%	47%
25-34	61	57	41	39	64	66	52	50
35-54	72	67	54	53	71	71	64	63
55+	72	67	68	67	66	69	74	73

Sources: Veronis Suhler Stevenson, PQ Media, Newspaper Association of America, Scarborough Research, W.R. Simmons & Associates

Adult Population, by Age Group

(THOUSANDS)

Age Group	*1994*	*1999*	*1994-1999 Percent Change*	*2004*	*1999-2004 Percent Change*	*2009*	*2004-2009 Percent Change*
18-24	25,703	26,059	1.4%	26,685	2.4%	30,805	15.4%
25-34	42,330	40,757	–3.7	40,178	–1.4	41,629	3.6
35-44	41,819	44,748	7.0	45,077	0.7	41,838	–7.2
45-54	30,153	35,232	16.8	36,578	3.8	44,736	22.3
55-64	21,159	23,011	8.8	23,778	3.3	34,842	46.5
65+	33,331	34,619	3.9	34,798	0.5	39,399	13.2
Total	194,495	204,426	5.1	207,094	1.3	233,249	12.6
18-34	68,033	66,815	–1.8	66,863	0.1	72,434	8.3
35+	126,462	137,610	8.8	140,230	1.9	160,815	14.7
55+	54,490	57,630	5.8	58,576	1.6	74,241	26.7

Sources: Veronis Suhler Stevenson, PQ Media, U.S. Census Bureau

Newspaper Publishing

Percentage and Number of Adult Population Reading Newspapers*

Year	*Weekday Editions*	*Number Of Adult Readers (Millions)*	*Sunday Editions*	*Number Of Adult Readers (Millions)*
1999	56.9%	77.7	66.9%	91.4
2000	55.1	77.6	65.1	90.5
2001	54.3	76.4	63.7	89.5
2002	55.4	79.6	63.6	91.4
2003	54.1	79.1	62.5	91.5
2004	52.8	78.3	61.5	90.8

Sources: Veronis Suhler Stevenson, PQ Media, Newspaper Association of America Simmons Market Research Bureau, Scarborough Research

*Beginning in 1998, readership is based on top 50 markets only.

core print product, newspapers have added a host of special-interest publications. Several large publishing companies now own weekly tabloids targeting young readers. For example, the *South Florida Sun-Sentinel*, owned by Tribune, publishes *CityLink*, a tabloid aimed at the youth market.

Publishers are hoping that they will be able to graduate readers of their youth publications to their core newspapers. But the success of such efforts is difficult to predict, and it may be years before any results are realized. Anecdotal evidence from newspaper vendors suggests that, at least for now, free newspapers are pilfering readers from their parent publications.

In addition to the youth market, publishers are also targeting the growing Hispanic population. In 2004, about 29 percent of the NAA's members that did not have a Spanish-language publication were planning to start one. Meanwhile, several major publishers already own Hispanic newspapers. Tribune's *Hoy* is published in New York, Los Angeles and Chicago, while the Miami Herald's *El Nuevo Herald* is the country's second-largest Spanish-language newspaper. But some Hispanic newspapers are now experiencing circulation declines. *La Opinion* in Los Angeles and *El Nuevo Herald* both lost circulation in 2005. And while many Spanish-language newspapers are growing, they have not kept

Joint Operating Agreements

Market	*Paper*	*Type*	*Owner*	*Year Of Expiration*
Cincinnati	Enquirer Post	a.m. p.m.	Gannett E.W. Scripps	2007
Salt Lake City	Tribune Deseret News	a.m. p.m.	MediaNews Deseret News Publications	2012
Tucson	Arizona Daily Star Citizen	a.m. p.m.	Pulitzer Publishing Gannett	2015
Birmingham	News Post-Herald	a.m. p.m.	Advance Publications E.W. Scripps	2015
Albuquerque	Journal Tribune	a.m. p.m.	Albuquerque Publishing Company E.W. Scripps	2022
Charleston, WV	Gazette Daily Mail	a.m. p.m.	Daily Gazette Company MediaNews	2036
Las Vegas	Review-Journal Sun	a.m. p.m.	Donrey Media Group Las Vegas Sun Company	2049
Fort Wayne	Journal-Gazette News-Sentinel	a.m. p.m.	Journal Gazette Company Knight Ridder	2050
Denver	Post Rocky Mt. News	a.m. a.m.	MediaNews E.W. Scripps	2051
Seattle	Times Post-Intelligencer	a.m. a.m.	Seattle Times Company Hearst Corporation	2083
Detroit	Free Press News	a.m. p.m.	Knight Ridder Gannett	2086
York, PA	Daily Record Dispatch	a.m. p.m.	Buckner News Alliance MediaNews	2090

Sources: Veronis Suhler Stevenson, PQ Media, Newspaper Association of America

pace with Hispanic population growth, as the newspapers attract few new readers.

Publishers are also trying to boost circulation by becoming more involved with their communities, sponsoring events and reaching out to their readers. The Norfolk, NE, *Daily News*, for example, sends staffers out to area restaurants where they ask customers for comments, concerns, suggestions and questions about the paper. However, the results of these measures to shore up circulation are still uncertain, and we do not foresee them making a substantial dent in the downward trend of unit circulation in the forecast period. Therefore, we are projecting that unit circulation will decline 1.3 percent in 2005 to 55.21 million, and will continue to fall during the 2004-2009 period at a compound annual rate of 1.8 percent.

JOINT OPERATING AGREEMENTS

Joint operating agreements (JOAs) were created by the Newspaper Preservation Act of 1970. They allow the sharing of production and business operations between two competing newspapers in the same market without violating antitrust laws, but only if one paper states that it would otherwise go out of business. During the past 70 years, newspapers in 29 cities have formed JOAs.

In most markets, JOAs have not helped turn around the weaker newspaper's circulation.

Newsprint Prices: Annual Averages

Year	*Price Per Metric Ton*	*Percent Change*	*U.S. Newsprint Consumption (Millions of Metric Tons)*	*Percent Change*
1999	$514	—	12.061	—
2000	558	8.6%	12.039	–0.2%
2001	575	3.0	10.725	–10.9
2002	455	–20.9	10.395	–3.1
2003	493	8.4	10.299	–0.9
2004	539	9.3	10.123	–1.7
2005	555	3.0	10.050	–0.7
2006	560	0.9	10.012	–0.4
2007	545	–2.7	9.947	–0.6
2008	540	–0.9	9.931	–0.2
2009	565	4.6	9.870	–0.6
Compound Annual Growth				
1999-2004		1.0		–3.4
2004-2009		0.9		–0.5

Sources: Veronis Suhler Stevenson, PQ Media, Canadian Pulp & Paper Association, Pulp & Paper Products Council, Resource Information Systems, Newspaper Association of America

Newspaper Publishing

Average Daily Newspaper Prices*

Year	Weekday	Sunday
1999	$0.370	$1.283
2000	0.373	1.305
2001	0.385	1.332
2002	0.395	1.373
2003	0.400	1.374
2004	0.400	1.384
2005	0.397	1.380
2006	0.397	1.381
2007	0.400	1.391
2008	0.405	1.411
2009	0.413	1.439

Sources: Veronis Suhler Stevenson, PQ Media, Newspaper Association of America, *Editor & Publisher*
*Includes single-copy and subscription prices.

Growth of Average Daily Newspaper Prices*

Year	Weekday	Sunday
2000	0.8%	1.7%
2001	3.2	2.1
2002	2.6	3.1
2003	1.3	0.1
2004	0.0	0.7
2005	–0.7	–0.3
2006	0.0	0.1
2007	0.8	0.7
2008	1.3	1.4
2009	2.0	2.0
Compound Annual Growth		
1999-2004	1.6	1.5
2004-2009	0.6	0.8

Sources: Veronis Suhler Stevenson, PQ Media, Newspaper Association of America, *Editor & Publisher*
*Includes single-copy and subscription prices.

The circulation of the *Cincinnati Post* in Ohio accounts for only about 37,000 of the combined 301,000 circulation of the *Post* and the *Enquirer*. Gannett, the owner of the *Enquirer*, has told the *Post* that it will not renew the JOA when it expires at the end of 2007. And in Seattle, WA, the *Post-Intelligencer* lost about 3 percent of its circulation during the past year, while its partner, the *Seattle Times*, remained flat. In April 2003, the *Times* notified the *Post-Intelligencer* that it wished to end the JOA ahead of its scheduled expiration in 2083. Under the JOA's terms, the two sides have until late 2005 to work out an arrangement whereby both papers can continue to operate. If no agreement is reached, the JOA will end. The *Post-Intelligencer*'s publisher, Hearst Corp., sued the *Times* in a move to prevent the premature end of the JOA. The lawsuit was unresolved as of May 2005.

Many JOAs have terminated early because of mergers between the partners, or because one of the newspapers was bought by a third party. At present, newspapers in 12 markets have JOAs. Since 2000, there have been no new JOAs.

CIRCULATION SPENDING AND COSTS

Falling unit circulations, combined with a decrease in price, led circulation spending to decline 0.9 percent to $10.99 billion in 2004. The average price for a weekday newspaper was flat at 40.0 cents for the year, while that of Sunday editions rose 0.7 percent to $1.38. Circulation spending on weekday papers decreased 1.2 percent to $6.83 billion. Spending on Sunday papers fell 0.5 percent to $4.16 billion, compared with a 0.4 percent decline in 2003.

Publishers are looking to their Web sites as a means of increasing subscription spending. *The Wall Street Journal*'s online edition had more than 730,000 subscribers in the first quarter of 2005, each of whom pays $79 annually for the service ($39 if they are subscribers of the print version). At present, it is the only newspaper that is successfully charging customers for online content. In May 2005, *The New York Times* announced that it would charge visitors to its Web site an annual fee of $49.95 to read its Op-Ed and

Growth of Prices and Aggregate Daily Newspaper Circulation

	Weekday		*Sunday*	
Year	*Price*	*Unit Volume*	*Price*	*Unit Volume*
2000	0.8%	–0.4%	1.7%	–0.8%
2001	3.2	–0.3	2.1	–0.6
2002	2.6	–0.7	3.1	–0.5
2003	1.3	0.0	0.1	–0.5
2004	0.0	–1.0	0.7	–1.3
2005	–0.7	–1.2	–0.3	–1.5
2006	0.0	–1.6	0.1	–1.2
2007	0.8	–2.0	0.7	–1.6
2008	1.3	–2.2	1.4	–1.7
2009	2.0	–2.6	2.0	–1.9
Compound Annual Growth				
1999-2004	1.6	–0.5	1.5	–0.7
2004-2009	0.6	–1.9	0.8	–1.6

Sources: Veronis Suhler Stevenson, PQ Media, Newspaper Association of America, *Editor & Publisher*

news columnists, archives and other features. In the future, more newspapers are expected to try to generate revenues from content on their Web sites, either through subscriptions or single-article pricing.

Meanwhile, the cost of acquiring subscribers soared in the past two years. As a result of the Do Not Call Registry, which took effect in 2003, newspapers were forced to drastically reduce their use of telemarketing. It is estimated that telemarketing historically accounted for around 33 percent of new subscriptions. To make up for the loss, newspapers have increased their reliance on alternate methods of reaching their customers, such as advertising, direct mail and even door-to-door sales. The *Los Angeles Times*, for example, will spend approximately $10 million through the end of 2005 on advertising and direct marketing to win new subscribers. The newspaper had lost 6.5 percent of its daily circulation in the six months ended in March 2005. According to the NAA, the median direct cost per new order increased about 25 percent in the past two years, from $13.04 in 2002 to $16.36 in 2004.

Cost pressures increased further in 2004 when the average price of newsprint climbed 9.3 percent to $539 per metric ton. Prices increased for the second year in a row, despite falling consumption, due to a combination of higher fiber and fuel costs, a strong Canadian dollar and a decrease in newsprint production. North American newsprint production declined about 6 percent in 2004, as manufacturers such as Abitibi-Consolidated and NorskeCanada permanently closed plants or converted them for the production of higher-grade white paper, leading to a tightening of supply. This tightening was balanced somewhat by lower demand from U.S.

Daily Newspaper Spending, by Source

($ MILLIONS)

	Print Newspapers								Online Newspaper Advertising*			
	Advertising Spending				Circulation Spending							
Year	Retail	Classified	National	Total	Weekday	Sunday	Total	Total Print	National	Local	Total	Total Print & Online
1999	$20,905	$18,650	$6,732	$46,287	$6,475	$3,997	$10,472	$56,759	$162	$ 143	$ 305	$57,064
2000	21,409	19,609	7,653	48,671	6,508	4,033	10,541	59,212	318	348	666	59,878
2001	20,678	16,621	7,004	44,303	6,690	4,093	10,783	55,086	291	494	785	55,871
2002	20,992	15,898	7,210	44,100	6,830	4,196	11,026	55,126	256	655	911	56,037
2003	21,339	15,801	7,797	44,937	6,912	4,178	11,090	56,027	305	811	1,116	57,143
2004	22,008	16,608	8,083	46,699	6,832	4,156	10,988	57,687	348	1,194	1,542	59,229
2005	22,470	17,671	8,180	48,321	6,702	4,081	10,783	59,104	429	1,524	1,953	61,057
2006	22,964	18,696	8,458	50,118	6,601	4,036	10,637	60,755	526	1,989	2,515	63,270
2007	23,377	19,706	8,653	51,736	6,522	4,000	10,522	62,258	635	2,496	3,131	65,389
2008	23,774	20,672	8,921	53,367	6,463	3,988	10,451	63,818	733	3,053	3,786	67,604
2009	24,249	21,602	9,090	54,941	6,424	3,992	10,416	65,357	835	3,587	4,422	69,779

Sources: Veronis Suhler Stevenson, PQ Media, Newspaper Association of America, Borrell, Interactive Advertising Bureau

*To avoid double counting, online advertising spending is represented in the Consumer Internet chapter. Online advertising in weekly newspapers is included.

Growth of Daily Newspaper Spending, by Source

	Print Newspapers								Online Newspaper Advertising*			
	Advertising Spending				Circulation Spending							
Year	Retail	Classified	National	Total	Weekday	Sunday	Total	Total Print	National	Local	Total	Total Print & Online
2000	2.4%	5.1%	13.7%	5.2%	0.5%	0.9%	0.7%	4.3%	96.3%	143.4%	118.4%	4.9%
2001	–3.4	–15.2	–8.5	–9.0	2.8	1.5	2.3	–7.0	–8.5	42.0	17.9	–6.7
2002	1.5	–4.3	2.9	–0.5	2.1	2.5	2.3	0.1	–12.0	32.6	16.1	0.3
2003	1.7	–0.6	8.1	1.9	1.2	–0.4	0.6	1.6	19.1	23.8	22.5	2.0
2004	3.1	5.1	3.7	3.9	–1.2	–0.5	–0.9	3.0	14.1	47.2	38.2	3.7
2005	2.1	6.4	1.2	3.5	–1.9	–1.8	–1.9	2.5	23.4	27.6	26.7	3.1
2006	2.2	5.8	3.4	3.7	–1.5	–1.1	–1.4	2.8	22.5	30.5	28.8	3.6
2007	1.8	5.4	2.3	3.2	–1.2	–0.9	–1.1	2.5	20.7	25.5	24.5	3.4
2008	1.7	4.9	3.1	3.2	–0.9	–0.3	–0.7	2.5	15.5	22.3	20.9	3.4
2009	2.0	4.5	1.9	2.9	–0.6	0.1	–0.3	2.4	13.9	17.5	16.8	3.2
Compound Annual Growth												
1999-2004	1.0	–2.3	3.7	0.2	1.1	0.8	1.0	0.3	16.5	52.9	38.3	0.7
2004-2009	2.0	5.4	2.4	3.3	–1.2	–0.8	–1.1	2.5	19.1	24.6	23.5	3.3

Sources: Veronis Suhler Stevenson, PQ Media, Newspaper Association of America, Borrell, Interactive Advertising Bureau

*To avoid double counting, online advertising spending is represented in the Consumer Internet chapter. Online advertising in weekly newspapers is included.

Shares of Daily Newspaper Spending, by Source

	Print Newspapers								Online Newspaper Advertising*		
	Advertising Spending				Circulation Spending						
Year	Retail	Classified	National	Total	Weekday	Sunday	Total	Total Print	National	Local	Total
1999	36.6%	32.7%	11.8%	81.1%	11.3%	7.0%	18.4%	99.5%	0.3%	0.3%	0.5%
2000	35.8	32.7	12.8	81.3	10.9	6.7	17.6	98.9	0.5	0.6	1.1
2001	37.0	29.7	12.5	79.3	12.0	7.3	19.3	98.6	0.5	0.9	1.4
2002	37.5	28.4	12.9	78.7	12.2	7.5	19.7	98.4	0.5	1.2	1.6
2003	37.3	27.7	13.6	78.6	12.1	7.3	19.4	98.0	0.5	1.4	2.0
2004	37.2	28.0	13.6	78.8	11.5	7.0	18.6	97.4	0.6	2.0	2.6
2005	36.8	28.9	13.4	79.1	11.0	6.7	17.7	96.8	0.7	2.5	3.2
2006	36.3	29.5	13.4	79.2	10.4	6.4	16.8	96.0	0.8	3.1	4.0
2007	35.8	30.1	13.2	79.1	10.0	6.1	16.1	95.2	1.0	3.8	4.8
2008	35.2	30.6	13.2	78.9	9.6	5.9	15.5	94.4	1.1	4.5	5.6
2009	34.8	31.0	13.0	78.7	9.2	5.7	14.9	93.7	1.2	5.1	6.3

Sources: Veronis Suhler Stevenson, PQ Media, Newspaper Association of America, Borrell, Interactive Advertising Bureau
*To avoid double counting, online advertising spending is represented in the Consumer Internet chapter. Online advertising in weekly newspapers is included in this data.

newspapers due to declining circulations and less-than-stellar advertising page growth.

At the end of April 2005, it was expected that a price increase announced for the spring would meet with resistance from the newspaper industry. However, growing demand from China may help newsprint producers make the price increase stick. We expect supply to fall faster than demand, leading to a modest price increase of 3.0 percent to $555 per metric ton in 2005. Over the forecast period, costs will grow slowly or decline because of continued weak demand as the aggregate circulation of U.S. newspapers falls and advertising growth remains muted. The average price will increase 0.9 percent on a compound annual basis from 2004 to 2009.

Demand for newsprint will also be reduced by the expected conversions of some newspapers from broadsheet size to tabloid. In March 2005, Knight Ridder announced that it would proceed with such conversions for many of its newspapers, raising speculation that the *Miami Herald* would eventually become a tabloid. In May 2005, *The Wall Street Journal* announced that it would transform its European and Asian editions to tabloids in October the same year, a move that will be closely followed by newspaper publishers for its potential ramifications in the U.S.

Circulation spending is expected to decrease 1.9 percent to $10.78 billion in 2005, due to falling unit circulation. Publishers will reduce weekday edition prices 0.7 percent and Sunday prices 0.3 percent. As unit circulation declines from 2004 to 2009, publishers will raise daily and Sunday prices. As a result, circulation spending will decrease at a lower compound annual rate of 1.1 percent, compared with the prior five-year period, reaching $10.42 billion in 2009.

FORECAST ASSUMPTIONS

- Similar to the trend in other traditional media, advertisers will challenge newspapers in the forecast period to prove the return on investment (ROI) in this medium versus that of electronic media, such as the Internet and cable television. As a result, marketers will continue to shift advertising dollars out of traditional media, which will hamper spending growth in all newspaper ad categories going forward. Consequently, growth will lag nominal GDP by 3 to 4 percentage points over the next five years.
- Consolidation among retailers will have two major effects on the newspaper market. First, as stores get converted into a new post-merger brand, they will cut back on their combined run-of-press and preprint insertions. As a result, the amount of retail newspaper advertising will decrease in the 2004-2009 timeframe. Second, as the customer base and geographic coverage of merged retailers become larger, retailers will increase their usage of broadcast television, because of its wider reach. In addition, the trend toward consumers shopping more frequently at superstores and specialty retailers will also hinder retail advertising during the next five years. Superstores advertise in newspapers far less than do traditional department stores, and specialty retailers often rely on alternative marketing, such as custom publishing, direct mail and the Internet, to reach their customers.
- The percentage of young audiences reading daily newspapers has dropped approximately 20 percentage points since 1982, and will continue to fall over the forecast period. Older audiences, traditionally considered the strongest demographic for newspaper readership, are also scaling back their daily newspaper consumption, though at a smaller rate. Finally, print newspaper circulation will continue to decline as consumers get more local news free through Web sites, which include newspaper sites. The result of these trends will be an irreversible decline in total newspaper circulation going forward.
- The decline in circulation will lead national advertisers to increase spending on other forms of media, including the Internet and cable TV, at the expense of newspapers, as they seek to maximize ROI. Newspapers in major metro markets that rely heavily on national advertising will see slower growth than those in secondary markets, which are driven more by retail and classified ads.

The Outlook For Daily Newspapers

Total spending on daily newspapers will increase only 2.5 percent to $59.10 billion in 2005, driven by accelerated classified ad spending, along with smaller upticks in the retail and national categories. Continued unit circulation declines over the next five years will lead more advertisers to be skeptical of their ROI in newspapers as compared with that of electronic media. In the wake of the 2004 circulation scandals, the increased scrutiny of circulation quality by advertisers indicates that they are aware of deeper, long-term issues that newspapers face about their declining readership.

Mergers in the retailing industry, combined with changes in shopping habits as consumers bypass traditional department stores in favor of superstores and specialty retailers, will curtail the growth of ad spending in the retail category over the forecast period. National advertisers will find that other media, such as the Internet and cable TV, deliver better ROI as newspaper audiences shrink. On the bright side, the classified category will prove to be the most resilient, and is expected to post faster growth in 2005. In most secondary markets, newspapers are often a more effective vehicle for local advertising, which makes them somewhat immune to competition in comparison to major-market dailies. We expect advertising spending to grow 3.5 percent in 2005, compared with 3.9 percent upside in 2004. Advertising expenditures will increase at a compound annual rate of 3.3 percent in the 2004-2009 period, as spending in all advertising categories decelerates. Expenditures will hit $54.94 billion in 2009.

Total daily newspaper expenditures will be tempered by weaker ad growth and declining circulation over the forecast period, and will grow at a compound annual rate of 2.5 percent from 2004 to 2009, reaching $65.36 billion in 2009.

Weekly Newspapers

THE WEEKLY NEWSPAPER MARKET IN 2004 AND 2005

Total expenditures on weekly newspapers grew 4.9 percent to $5.84 billion in 2004 on the strength of both advertising and circulation spending. Advertising expenditures climbed 5.1 percent to $5.45 billion, driven by the highly targeted nature of the publications and their relatively low advertising rates. Advertising spending in weeklies has grown every year since 1999, even rising 1.9 percent during the 2001 recession. Despite a drop in paid unit circulation in 2004, circulation spending grew 1.8 percent to $387.0 million as the average price per newspaper rose.

Weekly newspapers consist of paid and free papers that are published less than three times a week. They deliver editorial content that is focused to specific demographic and/or psychographic groups, such as youth and ethnic markets, or are distributed to a limited geographic area. Included among weeklies are community newspapers, shoppers and the so-called alternative newsweeklies, such as the *L.A. Weekly*. Alternative weeklies appeal to narrow niches defined by age, gender or lifestyle. Shoppers typically focus on reaching the broadest possible audience within a specific region, and account for the bulk of advertising spending. In 2004, shoppers received $4.92 billion in advertising spending, while alternative weeklies garnered about $530 million. Most weekly papers thrive on advertising from local restaurants, nightclubs, specialty retailers, car dealerships and real estate agents. Tobacco and liquor advertising targeting young adults had declined between 2001 and 2003 with the general advertising slump, but both are now growing categories.

Weekly papers were traditionally owned and operated by small independent publishers, but mergers and acquisitions over the years have created newspaper chains that stretch over broader areas. For example, Philip Anschutz's Clarity Media Group bought *The San Francisco Examiner* and other free newspapers in the Washington, DC, area in 2004. By the first quarter of 2005, Clarity Media Group had

Highlights

Weekly Newspapers

Total spending on weekly newspapers grew 4.9 percent to $5.84 billion in 2004, driven by gains in both advertising and circulation expenditures. The compound annual growth rate from 1999 to 2004 was 4.2 percent.

■

Advertising spending increased 5.1 percent to $5.45 billion in 2004, on the strength of local advertising. Over the 1999-2004 period, advertising expenditures grew at a compound annual rate of 4.4 percent.

■

Circulation spending rose 1.8 percent to $387.0 million in 2004, driven by a price hike of 3.2 percent to 35.6 cents for the average weekly. Paid unit circulation fell 1.4 percent to 20.9 million, while free circulation rose 2.5 percent to 28.9 million.

■

Total spending on weekly newspapers is expected to increase 5.5 percent in 2005 to $6.16 billion, due to continued gains in advertising and circulation expenditures. Spending will increase at a compound annual rate of 5.3 percent over the next five years, reaching $7.57 billion in 2009.

Circulation and Advertising In Alternative Newsweeklies*

Year	*Unit Circulation (Millions)*	*Advertising ($ Millions)*
1999	28.6	$503
2000	27.4	515
2001	27.3	510
2002	27.5	512
2003	28.2	520
2004	28.9	530

Sources: Veronis Suhler Stevenson, PQ Media, Association of Alternative Newsweeklies, *Editor & Publisher*

*Advertising figures available for AAN members only.

Growth of Circulation and Advertising In Alternative Newsweeklies*

Year	*Unit Circulation*	*Advertising*
2000	−4.2%	2.4%
2001	−0.4	−1.0
2002	0.7	0.4
2003	2.5	1.6
2004	2.5	1.9
Compound Annual Growth		
1999-2004	0.2	1.1

Sources: Veronis Suhler Stevenson, PQ Media, Association of Alternative Newsweeklies, *Editor & Publisher*

*Advertising figures available for AAN members only.

Aggregate Circulation Of Weekly Newspapers (MILLIONS)

Year	*Paid*	*Free*	*Total*
1999	20.6	28.6	49.2
2000	20.6	27.4	48.0
2001	20.2	27.3	47.5
2002	21.1	27.5	48.6
2003	21.2	28.2	49.4
2004	20.9	28.9	49.8
2005	20.7	28.8	49.5
2006	20.8	29.1	49.9
2007	20.9	29.3	50.2
2008	21.2	29.7	50.9
2009	21.3	29.9	51.2

Sources: Veronis Suhler Stevenson, PQ Media, *Editor & Publisher*, Association of Free Community Newspapers

trademarked the *Examiner* name in 60 markets, suggesting that the company may start a new chain of free dailies.

Alternative weeklies focus on investigative journalism, culture and entertainment. Their readers tend to be young, active and affluent, making them desirable targets for advertisers. The combination of local news stories and entertainment listings creates a loyal reader following, which in turn insulates the weeklies to some extent from advertising downswings that affect general-editorial newspapers. As a result, while daily newspaper advertising declined in 2001 and 2002, the alternative weekly market attracted the attention of large publishers. Gannett, for instance, launched a free alternative weekly called *Noise* in Lansing, MI, in 2002, and now owns youth-oriented weekly newspapers in nine cities.

Major publishers are also entering the free-publication market to inculcate the newspaper readership habit in young readers. For example, The New York Times Co. owns the youth-oriented *Boston Metro*, and other publishing companies, such as Tribune Co. and Washington Post Co., own *RedEye* and *Express* in Chicago and Washington, DC, respectively, free tabloids that are also written for young readers. The *Express* promotes the parent company's flagship paper by putting its logo on the *Express*'s front page, along with a small box on one of the inside pages labeled, "Today in the *Washington Post*."

ADVERTISING

In 2004, advertising spending in weekly papers increased 5.1 percent to $5.45 billion, and grew at a compound annual rate of 4.4 percent from 1999 to 2004. Most of the growth occurred in smaller markets such as Burlington, VT, and Missoula, MT, where publications are about five to 10 years old and are still expanding their reader base.

To help increase spending from regional and national advertisers, a number of organizations have set up networks of weekly papers to facilitate the buying of space in multiple markets simultaneously. The Association of Free Community Newspapers' National Advertising Network represents more than 3,000 free community papers nationwide, reaching

Growth of Aggregate Circulation Of Weekly Newspapers

Year	Paid	Free	Total
2000	0.0%	–4.2%	–2.4%
2001	–1.9	–0.4	–1.0
2002	4.3	0.7	2.3
2003	0.6	2.5	1.6
2004	–1.4	2.5	0.8
2005	–1.0	–0.4	–0.6
2006	0.7	1.0	0.8
2007	0.5	0.7	0.6
2008	1.2	1.2	1.4
2009	0.5	0.8	0.6
Compound Annual Growth			
1999-2004	0.3	0.2	0.2
2004-2009	0.4	0.7	0.6

Sources: Veronis Suhler Stevenson, PQ Media, *Editor & Publisher*, Association of Free Community Newspapers

Shares of Aggregate Weekly Newspaper Circulation

Year	Paid	Free
1999	41.9%	58.1%
2000	42.9	57.1
2001	42.5	57.5
2002	43.4	56.6
2003	42.9	57.1
2004	42.0	58.0
2005	41.8	58.2
2006	41.7	58.3
2007	41.6	58.4
2008	41.7	58.3
2009	41.6	58.4

Sources: Veronis Suhler Stevenson, PQ Media, *Editor & Publisher*, Association of Free Community Newspapers

approximately 40 million homes. The Alternative Weekly Network comprises 106 weekly papers with a combined circulation of about 7 million. The Ruxton Media Group offers weeklies in 28 markets. And the Association of Alternative Newsweeklies Classified Advertising Network enables clients to place classified ads in all of its 123 weekly papers with one buy.

We expect weekly newspaper ad spending to grow 5.8 percent in 2005 to $5.77 billion, due to the papers' highly focused targeting and reasonable advertising pricing. As many of these publications regularly carry political investigative stories, we expect spikes in advertising during the 2006 and 2008 election years. Aided by these increases, advertising spending will grow at a compound annual rate of 5.6 percent in the forecast period, reaching $7.15 billion in 2009.

CIRCULATION

Total unit circulation of weekly newspapers increased 0.8 percent to 49.8 million in 2004. Circulation of free weeklies grew 2.5 percent to 28.9 million, while the circulation of paid weeklies fell 1.4 percent to 20.9 million, as the price per copy increased 3.2 percent to an average of 35.6 cents. More newspapers are switching from paid to free as a means of increasing circulation. For example, the free San Francisco *Examiner* expanded its circulation from approximately 67,000 in 2003 to an estimated 160,000 in 2005.

While readers are typically loyal to weekly newspapers, the cultural forces that drive circulation declines in daily newspapers also apply to weeklies. The alternative weeklies specifically target young audiences, who are also the most likely to turn to the Internet for news, entertainment and shopping. But while weekly papers are vulnerable to the Internet, local Internet search is much weaker at this point than on the national level.

We expect unit circulation to decline 0.6 percent to 49.5 million in 2005, but in 2006 and 2008—both election years—we expect increases in circulation as readers turn to the papers for their investigative journalism, leading unit circulation to grow at a compound annual rate of 0.6 percent from 2004 to 2009. Continued price increases will drive a 1.8 percent compound annual increase in circulation spending in the 2004-2009 timeframe.

Spending on Weekly Newspapers

Year	Paid Circulation (Millions)	Average Price Of Paid Weeklies (Cents)	Total End-User Spending ($ Millions)	Total Advertising Spending ($ Millions)	Total Spending ($ Millions)
1999	20.6	32.7	$350	$4,402	$4,752
2000	20.6	33.1	355	4,700	5,055
2001	20.2	33.5	352	4,790	5,142
2002	21.1	34.0	373	4,979	5,352
2003	21.2	34.5	380	5,189	5,569
2004	20.9	35.6	387	5,453	5,840
2005	20.8	36.3	393	5,769	6,162
2006	21.0	36.7	401	6,144	6,545
2007	20.9	37.4	406	6,390	6,796
2008	21.2	37.7	416	6,837	7,253
2009	21.5	37.9	424	7,145	7,569

Sources: Veronis Suhler Stevenson, PQ Media, *Editor & Publisher*

Growth of Spending on Weekly Newspapers

Year	Paid Circulation	Average Price Of Paid Weeklies	Total End-User Spending	Total Advertising Spending	Total Spending
2000	0.0%	1.2%	1.4%	6.8%	6.4%
2001	–1.9	1.2	–0.8	1.9	1.7
2002	4.5	1.5	6.0	3.9	4.1
2003	0.5	1.5	1.9	4.2	4.1
2004	–1.4	3.2	1.8	5.1	4.9
2005	–0.5	2.0	1.5	5.8	5.5
2006	1.0	1.1	2.0	6.5	6.2
2007	–0.5	1.9	1.2	4.0	3.8
2008	1.4	0.8	2.5	7.0	3.8
2009	1.2	0.5	1.9	4.5	6.7
Compound Annual Growth					
1999-2004	0.3	1.7	2.0	4.4	4.2
2004-2009	0.6	1.3	1.8	5.6	5.3

Sources: Veronis Suhler Stevenson, PQ Media, *Editor & Publisher*

The Outlook For Weekly Newspapers

Total spending on weekly newspapers will rise 5.5 percent to $6.16 billion in 2005, fueled by increases in both advertising and circulation expenditures. The precise audience targeting of weekly newspapers and their near-monopoly positions in their respective markets are expected to drive continued growth over the forecast period. As weeklies are relatively less subject to the competitive pressures that dailies face from other media, advertising and circulation spending in these papers will show healthier growth rates. We project that total spending will advance at a compound annual rate of 5.3 percent from 2004 to 2009, with expenditures hitting $7.57 billion in 2009.

FORECAST ASSUMPTIONS

- Advertising spending will continue to increase in the forecast period, driven by the relatively low advertising rates of weekly papers, their near-monopoly positions in their markets, and their focused demographic, psychographic and geographic targeting.
- Major publishers, capitalizing on the ability of weeklies to deliver younger audiences to advertisers, will increase their acquisitions of youth-oriented free publications.
- Online auction and dating sites will continue to erode merchandise and personal classified ad spending in weeklies and alternative papers.
- While unit circulation will decline in 2005, price increases among paid weeklies will result in higher circulation spending going forward.

Business Overview

Facts On File is one of the leading independent publishers of print and online reference materials for the school and library markets. The company, based in New York City, was founded in 1940 and publishes high-quality encyclopedias, dictionaries, atlases, chronologies, almanacs and biographies in a variety of platforms, including print and online databases. The Company's 1,800 titles span a multitude of topics such as U.S. and world history, language and literature, science and technology, careers and social issues.

Background

On April 22, 2005, VSS's Fund IV, along with management, acquired the stock of Facts On File, Inc.

Fund IV believes Facts On File is an attractive platform opportunity from which to gain a meaningful presence within the U.S. educational publishing market. The Company will continue to grow through a combination of continued print product sales, expansion of online databases, and add-on acquisitions within both its core public and school library reference markets and in adjacent educational markets.

Strategy & Rationale

- **Strong management team**—the management team led by CEO Mark McDonnell is experienced and has worked together for eight years.
- **Products**—established reputation within the education sector with strong brand identity, quality products, growing front list, significant backlist; market share opportunity is real.
- **Electronic publishing**—well positioned with content brands, and systems to take advantage of the ongoing transition from print to electronic in the reference sector.
- **Customers**—Although schools and libraries often face budget constraints, they represent a relatively stable, broad, viable customer base with little concentration risk.

Add-on Acquisition Activities

Within the first two months following the acquisition, VSS has worked with Facts On File management to identify and approach several acquisition candidates. VSS and Management are currently in active discussions with multiple parties.

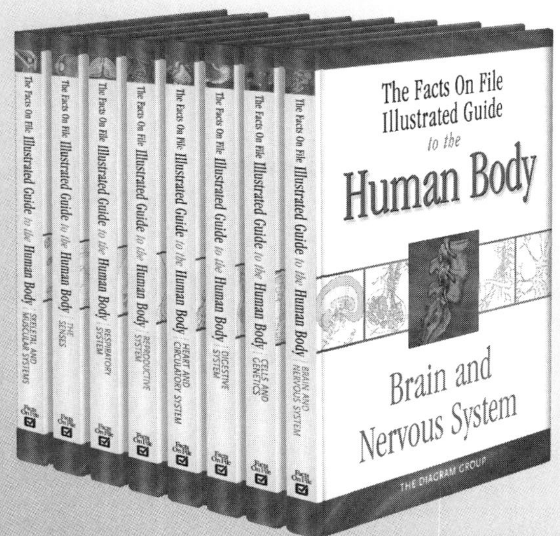

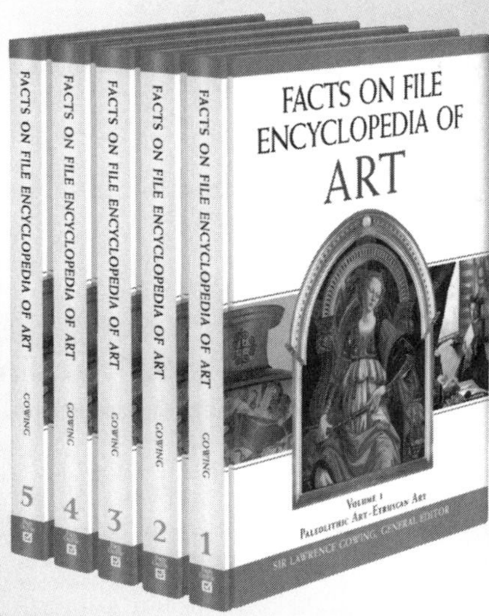

Private Equity Capital / Mezzanine Capital / Industry Research and Forecasts

Veronis Suhler Stevenson
MEDIA • COMMUNICATIONS • INFORMATION

350 Park Avenue, New York, NY 10022
212-935-4990 212-381-8168 fax
www.vss.com

10

Consumer Book Publishing

Consumer Book Spending and Nominal GDP Growth, 2000-2009

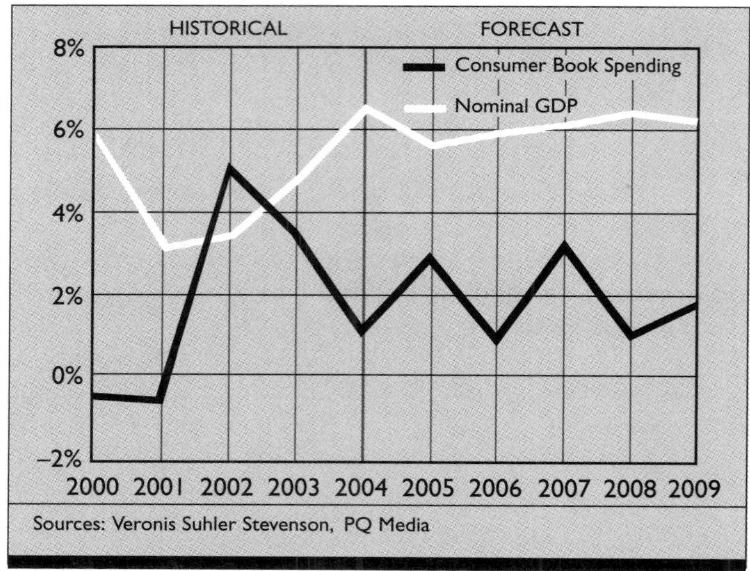

Sources: Veronis Suhler Stevenson, PQ Media

Growth of U.S. Spending on Consumer Books

	Consumer Book Expenditures
2004 Expenditures ($ Millions)	$19,761
1999-2004 Compound Annual Growth (%)	1.8%
2004-2009 Projected Compound Annual Growth (%)	2.1%
2009 Projected Expenditures ($ Millions)	$21,903

Sources: Veronis Suhler Stevenson, PQ Media, Book Industry Study Group

THE CONSUMER BOOK PUBLISHING MARKET IN 2004 AND 2005

Strong consumer book sales at the start of the year and a respectable holiday season offset a weak summer and fall, resulting in a 1.2 percent increase in spending in 2004 to $19.76 billion. Spending growth was driven primarily by a 3.4 percent hike in prices, which offset a 2.1 percent decline in unit sales for the year.

Spending on political books drove sales growth in the first half of 2004. Books challenging the policies of the Bush Administration, such as *The Price of Loyalty* and *Against All Enemies*, and titles about the Gulf War, headed by Bob Woodward's *Plan of Attack*, were popular early in the year. The biggest political bestseller in 2004 was *My Life*, the autobiography of former President Bill Clinton, which sold 400,000 copies on its first day of sale in June and went on to sell nearly 2 million copies for full-year 2004. Spending on political books began to ebb in the summer, and without any hot fiction titles, spending on consumer books slumped badly in the period from July through October.

The rebound in spending in November was driven by nonfiction titles, led by *America (The Book)*, the faux textbook by Jon Stewart and writers of *The Daily Show*, and another politically-oriented title, *The 9/11 Commission Report*, the official book of the committee that investigated the terrorist attacks on September 11, 2001, which sold about 1.4 million copies.

Consumer book spending was sluggish in the first quarter of 2005, due to the post-election decline in spending on political books coupled with the lack of a new fiction blockbuster. The U.S. Census Bureau reported that bookstore sales were down 4.6 percent in the first two months of 2005. Monthly estimates from the Association of American Publishers showed sales down in all consumer book categories in the first two months of 2005, with the exception of juvenile hardcover. A modest rebound is expected to occur toward mid-year, although spending growth is expected to increase only 3.0 percent for full-year 2005.

The fastest-growing consumer book segment in 2004 was religion, which posted a 10.7 percent increase in spending. *The*

Highlights

Spending on consumer books rose 1.2 percent in 2004 to $19.76 billion, driven by a strong gain in the religious category and, to a lesser degree, by an upswing in the adult trade segment. *The Purpose-Driven Life,* published by religious book publisher Zondervan, was the fastest-selling nonfiction book in 2004.

■

Spending on religious books grew at a 6.2 percent compound annual rate in the 1999-2004 period, the largest increase among all consumer book segments. The increase was driven by double-digit spending growth in 2003 and 2004, which was driven, in part, by increased interest in spiritual issues by the American public.

■

Nominal GDP growth traditionally has had only a marginal impact on the growth of consumer book spending. Consumer book expenditures rose 1.2 percent in 2004, compared to a 6.6 percent increase in nominal GDP, and GDP growth in 2005 is expected to be almost double that of the increase in consumer book spending.

■

Expenditures in four consumer book categories fell in 2004, with the largest decline coming in the juvenile trade segment, as the lack of a new Harry Potter hardcover drove down spending in the juvenile hardcover segment for the year.

■

Political books, ranging from titles on the Gulf War to Senator John Kerry's fitness to be president, enjoyed widespread media exposure in a contentious election year in 2004. The tremendous increase in publicity resulted in record demand for political books, which placed an unprecedented 35 books on *Publishers Weekly*'s bestseller list.

■

Total spending on consumer books is expected to increase 3.0 percent to a projected $20.36 billion in 2005, driven primarily by the juvenile hardcover segment, which will post a 14.6 percent gain to $1.67 billion due to the release of the sixth volume in the Harry Potter series. Consumer expenditures on mass-market paperbacks are expected to decline in 2005, partly as a result of a loss of shelf space, while spending on book clubs will slip due to a decline in membership.

■

Total spending on consumer books is projected to grow at a compound annual rate of 2.1 percent from 2004 to 2009, compared with compound annual growth of 1.8 percent in the 1999-2004 period. While unit sales growth in the forecast period will outperform growth during the previous five-year period, prices will increase at a slower pace as publishers moderate price hikes to focus on unit gains. Overall consumer book expenditures are forecast to reach $21.90 billion in 2009.

Online Book Sales

Year	Consumer Online Households (Millions)	Spending on Books Per Online Household	Total Online Spending on Consumer Books ($ Millions)
1999	27.2	$41.54	$1,130
2000	43.6	33.49	1,460
2001	54.8	28.83	1,580
2002	60.9	28.33	1,725
2003	66.8	27.99	1,870
2004	71.1	28.83	2,050
2005	72.0	30.76	2,215
2006	72.5	32.90	2,385
2007	73.5	34.90	2,565
2008	75.0	36.80	2,760
2009	76.0	38.82	2,950

Sources: Veronis Suhler Stevenson, PQ Media, U.S. Census Bureau, Kagan Research

Growth of Online Book Sales

Year	Consumer Online Households	Spending on Books Per Online Household	Total Online Spending on Consumer Books
2000	60.3%	–19.4%	29.2%
2001	25.7	–13.9	8.2
2002	11.1	–1.8	9.2
2003	9.7	–1.2	8.4
2004	6.4	3.0	9.6
2005	1.3	6.7	8.0
2006	0.7	6.9	7.7
2007	1.4	6.1	7.5
2008	2.0	5.5	7.6
2009	1.3	5.5	6.9
Compound Annual Growth			
2004-2009	1.3	6.1	7.6

Sources: Veronis Suhler Stevenson, PQ Media, U.S. Census Bureau, Kagan Research

Purpose-Driven Life continued to be a phenomenon in 2004, selling more than 7 million copies after selling more than 11 million in 2003. Growth in religious book spending was fueled by an aging American public that continues its shift toward spirituality and conservatism, a trend that became more pronounced after the terrorist attacks of September 2001. To capitalize on the public's heightened interest in religious books, more mainstream bookstores have expanded their inventories of religious books, and religious books are also among the top sellers at superstores such as Wal-Mart.

The only other consumer book segment to achieve a meaningful increase in spending in 2004 was the adult trade category, which posted an increase of 4.3 percent for the full year. Spending in the university press segment rose 1.3 percent, but expenditures fell in the juvenile, mass-market paperback, book club and mail order categories.

Without any new hot fiction titles, it was the breadth of offerings, particularly in nonfiction, that provided the increase in spending in 2004. Barnes & Noble, for example, reported that it sold more than 1 million different titles in 2004 and that bestsellers represented only 3 percent to 5 percent of its total sales. Overall sales for the nation's major chains, including Barnes & Noble, Borders and Books-A-Million, rose 5.1 percent in 2004 to $8.80 billion. The chains did better than expected in the first half of the year, slumped in the third quarter due in part to three major hurricanes in the Southeast, and rebounded in the critical fourth quarter when sales increased 4.2 percent. The major chains continued to augment their book offerings with other entertainment products in 2004. Barnes & Noble has had success with its music offerings, while Borders has offset soft demand for music in its stores with solid gains for DVDs and stationery items.

Independent bookstores managed to boost sales an estimated 2 percent in 2004, as a result of good gains in the holiday season and strong sales in the juvenile book category. While the rate of decline in the number of independent bookstores has slowed considerably, independents are still faced with increased competition from the major bookstore chains, online retailers and mass merchandisers, which heavily discount bestsellers.

Online sales grew at a faster rate than bricks-and-mortar bookstore sales in 2004. Led by Amazon.com, online book spending rose 9.6 percent in 2004 to $2.05 billion. Sales in Amazon's North American media segment—which includes books, music, DVDs, magazines and software—rose 14.0 percent in the year to $2.6 billion. Books are estimated to account for approximately half of the overall media segment's sales, but grew at a slower rate than did the media segment as a whole. Sales of used books continue to account for a higher percentage of consumer books sold through e-tailers, angering publishers and authors who do not benefit from the sales. But publishers are loath to challenge Amazon over the used book issue since Amazon is now the third-largest account for many publishers. Sales at the country's second-largest online bookstore, Barnes&Noble.com, fell to $420.0 million from $428.0 million in 2003. B&N.com executives attributed the decline to the termination of unprofitable marketing deals, which hurt sales but cut losses. Despite the cancellations, B&N.com failed to turn a profit in 2004.

Meanwhile, publishers are delving into the online book market. While scores of small and mid-size publishers already sell directly to consumers from their Web sites, Penguin was the first major house to add a direct sales component to its Web site early in 2004. Although sales were modest in 2004, estimated at about $1 million, the company plans to move ahead with the initiative. In early 2005, Simon & Schuster announced that it planned to begin selling directly to consumers from its Web site by the 2005 holiday season, and there were indications that Random House would also begin selling direct to consumers before the end of the year. Unless publishers find a way to drive consumers to their sites, however, their online sales are unlikely to give a significant boost to overall consumer book spending during the forecast period.

Online sales accounted for about 10.4 percent of total spending on consumer books in 2004, a slight increase over 2003. Indeed, there was only a minimal shift in the sales of books through the different market channels. Bookstores accounted for about 40 percent of spending in 2004, even with 2003. Non-traditional channels, such as price clubs and mass merchandisers that feature bestsellers registered a slight decline in market share, falling from approximately 13 percent in 2003 to about 12 percent in 2004. The absence of new fiction bestsellers—a staple of price clubs—hindered price club spending during the year. No other market channel accounted for more than 10 percent of consumer book expenditures in 2004. Sales through the multimedia channel fell last year as some of the largest retailers in the segment, such as FAO Inc. and Musicland, experienced severe operating problems.

The growth of consumer book spending in 2004 continued to be hampered by competition from other forms of media. The National Endowment for the Arts released a study in July 2004 that documented the decline in the amount of time Americans spend reading. The survey, titled *Reading at Risk*, found that about 57 percent of adult Americans had read some type of book in the previous year, down from approximately 61 percent in 1992. The percentage of Americans who read any type of fiction title fell to about 47 percent in 2002, down from approximately 54 percent in 1992 and about 57 percent in 1982. The report also found that reading fell among nearly all groups surveyed, including the affluent and highly educated, the two groups most associated with buying and reading books. The study did not detail reasons for the decline, but it noted the explosive growth in the use of electronic media by Americans, ranging from the Internet to cell phones.

To try to take advantage of the growth in the public's use of electronic media, and the Internet in particular, many publishers are now taking part in Google Print, a program launched by the giant search engine company in the fall of 2004. Under the initiative, Google scans a book into its search engines. When a search turns up the book's content, a link directs users to e-tailers and bookstores that sell the book.

Despite the sluggish start to 2005, consumer book spending is expected to post a

Number of Books Selling over 100,000 Copies

Category	2000	2001	2002	2003	2004
Adult Hardbound Fiction	112	110	125	128	131
Adult Hardbound Nonfiction	117	123	130	121	132

Sources: Veronis Suhler Stevenson, PQ Media, *Publishers Weekly*

modest spending gain for the full year. Borders Group projects that its sales will increase by about 7 percent in 2005, driven by double-digit gains from its international stores, low-single-digit same-store gains in its domestic superstores, and the opening of 15 to 20 new superstores. Barnes & Noble projects that same-store sales will increase by about 3 percent, and the company will open 30 to 35 new superstores, a formula that should result in a 6 percent to 7 percent sales gain.

Barnes & Noble has more modest expectations for Barnes&Noble.com, projecting that sales will increase about 3 percent in 2005. Amazon offered no specific growth forecast for books, but is expecting solid gains for its entire media group. To spur product sales, Amazon introduced a new shipping option in February 2005 that gives customers who pay a $79 annual fee the option to receive unlimited two-day free shipping. Based on projections from the two major online book retailers, online spending for consumer books will grow at a slightly slower rate in 2005 than in the prior year, increasing 8.0 percent to $2.22 billion. Growth in online spending is expected to remain solid throughout the forecast period, rising at a compound annual growth rate of 7.6 percent to $2.95 billion in 2009.

Sales at both traditional retail outlets and online bookstores will undoubtedly receive a spark on July 16, 2005, when Scholastic releases *Harry Potter and the Half-Blood Prince*, the sixth volume in the wildly popular Harry Potter series. The book immediately hit the number-one spot on Amazon.com when the announcement of the book's on-sale date was made in late 2004. Virtually every bookstore in America will have some sort of Potter-related event in July, with many hoping that the sales momentum created by Potter will continue into the fall.

TRADE BOOKS

Total spending on trade books rose 1.2 percent to $11.75 billion in 2004, marking the third consecutive year of spending growth. Unit sales, however, declined 2.3 percent to 819.0 million, ending a two-year string of gains. The increase in spending was driven primarily by the 5.5 percent increase in expenditures in the adult hardcover segment. Spending on trade paperbacks rose 2.9 percent for the year, while spending in the juvenile paperback segment rose 2.8 percent. Juvenile hardcover was the poorest performer of the year, with expenditures tumbling 15.7 percent.

In the adult trade books segment, the nonfiction category drove the spending gains, particularly political books. Although only two political books were among *Publishers Weekly*'s top 10 nonfiction sellers in 2004—*My Life* and *America (The Book)*—35 political books hit the magazine's bestseller list in 2004, a record number. Among the political books that sold in big numbers in 2004, but didn't make the top 10, were *Unfit for Command* (814,015 units sold); Kitty Kelley's look at the Bushes, *The Family* (715,000 units); *Deliver Us from Evil* (527,364); and *How to Talk to a Liberal* (445,792). In addition to politics, the public once again exhibited its bipolar attitude toward food in 2004, buying diet books and cookbooks in large quantities; 10 cookbooks had sales of more than 100,000 in 2004, compared with only four titles in 2003.

The strength in the nonfiction segment was somewhat offset by softness in fiction. The top 10 fiction bestsellers in 2004 sold a total of 17.9 million units, down from 19.4 million units in 2003. Moreover, the two top-selling books in 2004—*The Da Vinci Code* and *The Five People You Meet in Heaven*—were also the top sellers in 2003, highlighting the dearth of strong new blockbuster novels in 2004. The lack of exciting new fiction titles in 2004 is underscored by the appearance of three Dan Brown books in the list of bestselling fiction titles. The illustrated edition of *The Da Vinci Code* sold 905,000 units, while a Brown book written before *Da Vinci*, *Angels & Demons*, sold nearly 1.3 million copies. Spending on fiction titles was also curtailed by the slowing rate of sales among a number of bestselling authors whose books did not sell in the same quantities in 2004 as they had in the past.

Despite the weakness in the fiction segment, the strength in nonfiction was enough to drive up adult hardcover sales 5.5 percent in 2004 to $4.98 billion. Unit sales rose a healthy 4.4 percent to 227.0 million units.

Unlike the hardcover segment, in which the nonfiction category drove the spending gain, expenditures in the trade paperback segment were led by fiction. Eighteen of the 25 trade paperbacks that had sales of more than 500,000 copies in 2004 were novels, with nine coming from new authors. The popularity of fiction in the trade paperback format reflects the growing willingness among publishers to break out new authors in trade paperback rather than in hardcover. Publishers hope that the lower prices of trade paperbacks will attract a wider audience than higher-priced hardcovers. As authors become more established, publishers can then move them into the higher-priced hardcover format.

Although the top 10 bestselling trade paperbacks in 2003 outsold the top 10 bestsellers of 2004 by about 4 million units, frontlist titles still performed better than backlist books for the year. The chronic weakness in backlist, due in part to the unwillingness of retailers to keep slow-moving titles on the shelves for a long period of time, limited spending gains on trade paperbacks to 2.9 percent in 2004 to $4.02 billion. Units rose 0.9 percent to 223.5 million for the year.

Without a new hardcover edition to the Harry Potter series, a drop in spending in the juvenile hardcover segment was expected. However, the 15.7 percent decline to $1.46 billion was larger than expected. Unit sales fell a hefty 18.1 percent to 147.5 million. Sales of the top 10 juvenile bestsellers in 2004 totaled just under 8 million units compared with the 18 million units sold in 2003 when *Harry Potter and the Order of the Phoenix* sold more than 12 million units alone. In addition to the lack of a new Harry Potter title, continued softness in library funding contributed to the weakness in the

Top 10 Hardcover Adult Fiction Trade Books, 2004

Book	*Author*	*Unit Sales*
The Da Vinci Code	Dan Brown	4,290,000
The Five People You Meet in Heaven	Mitch Albom	3,287,722
The Last Juror	John Grisham	2,290,000
Glorious Appearing	Tim LaHaye/ Jerry B. Jenkins	1,600,318
Angels & Demons	Dan Brown	1,285,000
State of Fear	Michael Crichton	1,249,277
London Bridges	James Patterson	1,064,378
Trace	Patricia Cornwell	1,033,573
The Rule of Four	Ian Caldwell/ Dustin Thomason	945,000
The Da Vinci Code: Illustrated Ed.	Dan Brown	905,000
Total		17,950,268

Sources: Veronis Suhler Stevenson, PQ Media, *Publishers Weekly*

Top 10 Hardcover Adult Nonfiction Trade Books, 2004

Book	*Author*	*Unit Sales*
The Purpose-Driven Life	Rick Warren	7,340,000
The South Beach Diet	Arthur Agatston	3,002,597
My Life	Bill Clinton	2,000,000
America (The Book)	Jon Stewart	1,519,027
The South Beach Diet Cookbook	Arthur Agatston	1,490,898
Family First	Phil McGraw	1,355,000
He's Just Not That into You	Greg Behrendt/ Liz Tuccillo	1,261,055
Eats, Shoots & Leaves	Lynne Truss	1,092,128
Your Best Life Now	Joel Osteen	974,645
Guinness World Records 2005	Guinness World Records Ltd.	970,000
Total		21,005,350

Sources: Veronis Suhler Stevenson, PQ Media, *Publishers Weekly*

Top 10 Adult Trade Paperbacks, 2004

Book	*Author*	*Unit Sales*
The South Beach Diet Good Fats/Good Carbs Guide	Arthur Agatston	2,419,332
The 9/11 Commission Report	The 9/11 Commission	1,430,000
The Secret Life of Bees	Sue Monk Kidd	1,117,738
The Wedding	Nicholas Sparks	965,338
Anna Karenina	Leo Tolstoy	937,408
Reading Lolita in Tehran	Azar Nafisi	883,715
1,000 Places to See Before You Die	Patricia Schultz	873,797
One Hundred Years of Solitude	Gabriel Garcia Marquez	849,337
The Curious Incident of the Dog in the Night-Time	Mark Haddon	834,790
The Kite Runner	Khaled Hosseini	808,391
Total		11,119,846

Sources: Veronis Suhler Stevenson, PQ Media, *Publishers Weekly*

Top 10 Hardcover Juvenile Trade Books, 2004

Book	*Publisher*	*Unit Sales*
The Grim Grotto (A Series of Unfortunate Events #11)	HarperCollins	1,404,367
The Polar Express	Houghton Mifflin	1,305,367
The Bad Beginning (A Series of Unfortunate Events #1)	HarperCollins	986,085
The Reptile Room (A Series of Unfortunate Events #2)	HarperCollins	753,693
Eragon	Knopf	753,002
The Wide Window (A Series of Unfortunate Events #3)	HarperCollins	642,627
Goodnight Moon	HarperCollins	616,414
Green Eggs and Ham	Random House	560,573
Oh, The Places You'll Go!	Random House	483,064
The Miserable Mill (A Series of Unfortunate Events #4)	HarperCollins	473,241
Total		7,978,433

Sources: Veronis Suhler Stevenson, PQ Media, *Publishers Weekly*

juvenile hardcover segment. High-priced picture books have been hurt the most by cuts in library funding, and spending on this format was soft in 2004. A bright spot in 2004 was the success of the *A Series of Unfortunate Events* books that placed five titles on the bestseller list, driven by the holiday release of the first *Lemony Snicket's A Series of Unfortunate Events* film. *The Polar Express*, a strong seller annually, did better than usual because of the release of *The Polar Express* movie.

Harry Potter does not have as much of a dominating role in the spending patterns in the juvenile paperback segment as it does in the hardcover category. Nevertheless, the paperback edition of *Harry Potter and the Order of*

Top 10 Paperback Juvenile Trade Books, 2004

Book	*Publisher*	*Unit Sales*
Harry Potter and the Order of the Phoenix	Scholastic	1,488,503
Disney/Pixar's The Incredibles	Random/Disney	1,122,281
Spider-Man 2: Spider-Man Versus Doc Ock	HarperFestival	666,010
Shark Tale Movie Storybook	Scholastic	596,983
My Little Pony	HarperFestival	490,837
Holes	Dell	489,887
The Giver	Dell	450,892
Spider-Man 2: Everyday Hero	HarperFestival	430,208
The Outsiders	Puffin	407,954
Dinosaurs Before Dark	Random House	407,854
Total		6,551,409

Sources: Veronis Suhler Stevenson, PQ Media, *Publishers Weekly*

Consumer Book Publishing

the Phoenix was the bestselling juvenile paperback in 2004, selling nearly 1.5 million copies. The presence of a Potter title, however, was not enough to keep the total number of top 10 bestselling juvenile titles from falling from more than 8 million copies in 2003 to 6.6 million in 2004. While sales of bestsellers slowed, a wider number of titles generated strong sales, leading to an overall gain in juvenile paperbacks of 2.8 percent in 2004 to $1.30 billion. Unit sales inched up 0.7 percent to 221.0 million. Movie tie-ins, a staple of the juvenile paperback market, enjoyed a particularly strong year in 2004, led by tie-ins to such movies as *The Incredibles*, *Spider-Man 2*, *The Polar Express*, *Shark Tale* and *Shrek 2*.

Trade Book Net Unit Shipments

(MILLIONS)

Year	*Adult Hard-bound*	*Juvenile Hard-bound*	*Total Hard-bound*	*Adult Paper-bound*	*Juvenile Paper-bound*	*Total Paper-bound*	*Total Adult*	*Total Juvenile*	*Total Trade*
1999	249.0	206.6	455.6	258.1	188.8	446.9	507.1	395.4	902.5
2000	216.7	223.3	440.0	208.7	212.2	420.9	425.4	435.5	860.9
2001	205.9	167.2	373.1	218.1	226.4	444.5	424.0	393.6	817.6
2002	218.5	163.7	382.2	227.1	225.0	452.1	445.6	388.7	834.3
2003	217.5	180.2	397.7	221.6	219.4	441.0	439.1	399.6	838.7
2004	227.0	147.5	374.5	223.5	221.0	444.5	450.5	368.5	819.0
2005	225.0	165.0	390.0	223.0	224.5	447.5	448.0	389.5	837.5
2006	225.0	150.0	375.0	225.0	229.5	454.5	450.0	379.5	829.5
2007	226.0	168.5	394.5	229.5	232.5	462.0	455.5	401.0	856.5
2008	226.5	159.0	385.5	231.5	233.0	464.5	458.0	392.0	850.0
2009	227.0	165.0	392.0	230.5	233.0	463.5	457.5	398.0	855.5

Sources: Veronis Suhler Stevenson, PQ Media, Book Industry Study Group

Total spending on trade books is projected to increase 4.1 percent to $12.24 billion in 2005, while units are expected to increase 2.3 percent to 837.5 million. Gains will be led by the juvenile hardcover category, with spending projected to jump 14.6 percent to $1.67 billion for the year, while units will increase 11.9 percent to 165.0 million. The impact of a new Harry Potter title on spending in the juvenile hardcover segment cannot be overstated. Publication of the last two hardcover editions, in 2000 and 2003, resulted in spending increases of 13.2 percent and 14.1 percent, respectively, and there is every reason to believe spending in the segment will increase at a double-digit rate with the July release of *Harry Potter and the Half-Blood Prince*. Scholastic has set a record 10.8 million-copy first printing for the book, which will be priced at $29.95, although many retailers will discount the title, limiting growth in spending. Neither Amazon.com nor B&N.com has disclosed figures, but pre-orders of *Half-Blood* kept the title atop both companies' bestseller lists for most of the first half of 2005. Spending on *Half-Blood* will easily top $200 million in 2005, and account for at least 12 percent of spending in the segment.

Other trends that point toward solid gains in the juvenile hardcover segment in 2005 include a gradual recovery in library

Growth of Trade Book Net Unit Shipments

Year	*Adult Hard-bound*	*Juvenile Hard-bound*	*Total Hard-bound*	*Adult Paper-bound*	*Juvenile Paper-bound*	*Total Paper-bound*	*Total Adult*	*Total Juvenile*	*Total Trade*
2000	–13.0%	8.1%	–3.4%	–19.1%	12.4%	–5.8%	–16.1%	10.1%	–4.6%
2001	–5.0	–25.1	–15.2	4.5	6.7	5.6	–0.3	–9.6	–5.0
2002	6.1	–2.1	2.4	4.1	–0.6	1.7	5.1	–1.2	2.0
2003	–0.5	10.1	4.1	–2.4	–2.5	–2.5	–1.5	2.8	0.5
2004	4.4	–18.1	–5.8	0.9	0.7	0.8	2.6	–7.8	–2.3
2005	–0.9	11.9	4.1	–0.2	1.6	0.7	–0.6	5.7	2.3
2006	0.0	–9.1	–3.8	0.9	2.2	1.6	0.4	–2.6	–1.0
2007	0.4	12.3	5.2	2.0	1.3	1.7	1.2	5.7	3.3
2008	0.2	–5.6	–2.3	0.9	0.2	0.5	0.5	–2.2	–0.8
2009	0.2	3.8	1.7	–0.4	0.0	–0.2	–0.1	1.5	0.6
Compound Annual Growth									
1999-2004	–1.8	–6.5	–3.8	–2.8	3.2	–0.1	–2.3	–1.4	–1.9
2004-2009	0.0	2.3	0.9	0.6	1.1	0.8	0.3	1.6	0.9

Sources: Veronis Suhler Stevenson, PQ Media, Book Industry Study Group

funding and the growing market for children's books written by popular writers of adult books. Among the adult authors with children's books set to be released in 2005 are Ridley Pearson, Joyce Carol Oates, Neil Gaiman, James Patterson, John Feinstein and Peter Benchley.

The release of a hardcover edition of the Harry Potter series historically has not resulted in big gains in spending for juvenile paperbacks, and no significant increase is projected for 2005. The segment should benefit from increased library funding and by higher school funding. Movie tie-ins will also remain popular. The juvenile paperback segment is expected to experience another 2.8 percent increase in spending in 2005 to $1.34 billion, and is forecast to increase unit sales 1.6 percent to 224.5 million for the year.

The combination of a big jump in hardcover spending and modest gains in spending on paperbacks is projected to result in a total spending increase in the juvenile segment of 9.0 percent to $3.01 billion in 2005. Unit sales will increase 5.7 percent to 389.5 million for the year.

Aided by the release of two Harry Potter titles in the forecast period, total spending in the juvenile segment is projected to achieve a compound annual growth rate of 3.1 percent

Average Trade Book Prices

Year	*Adult Hard-bound*	*Juvenile Hard-bound*	*Total Hard-bound*	*Adult Paper-bound*	*Juvenile Paper-bound*	*Total Paper-bound*	*Total Adult*	*Total Juvenile*	*Total Trade*
1999	$19.66	$ 8.36	$14.54	$13.92	$5.38	$10.31	$16.74	$6.94	$12.44
2000	19.97	8.75	14.28	16.77	5.11	10.89	18.40	6.98	12.62
2001	20.88	8.91	15.52	16.28	5.67	10.87	18.51	7.05	12.99
2002	21.26	9.25	16.12	17.00	5.56	11.30	19.09	7.11	13.51
2003	21.68	9.59	16.20	17.62	5.76	11.72	19.63	7.49	13.85
2004	21.92	9.88	17.17	17.98	5.88	11.96	19.96	7.48	14.35
2005	22.62	10.12	17.33	18.57	5.95	12.23	20.60	7.72	14.61
2006	23.04	10.17	17.89	18.82	6.03	12.37	20.93	7.67	14.86
2007	23.43	10.39	17.86	18.91	6.13	12.48	21.15	7.92	14.96
2008	23.75	10.35	18.22	19.05	6.24	12.63	21.38	7.91	15.16
2009	24.01	10.48	18.32	19.48	6.33	12.87	21.73	8.05	15.37

Sources: Veronis Suhler Stevenson, PQ Media, Book Industry Study Group

from 2004 to 2009. Spending on juvenile books will reach $3.21 billion. Unit sales are projected to grow at a compound annual rate of 1.6 percent in the forecast period to 398.0 million units in 2009. The juvenile hardcover segment is expected to grow at a slightly faster rate than the paperback category from 2004 to 2009. Spending on juvenile hardcovers is projected to grow at a 3.5 percent compound annual rate over the next five years, reaching $1.73 billion in 2009. Consumer expenditures in the paperback segment are forecast to grow at a compound annual rate of 2.6 percent from 2004 to 2009 to $1.48 billion in 2009.

Spending in the adult segment in 2005 will reflect a decline in spending on political titles and an increase in spending on fiction. With the presidential election over, political books are not expected to capture the interest level they did in 2004. However, the division of the country into "blue states" and "red states" should propel some political titles into the bestseller list, but not in 2004's quantities. A couple of surprise bestsellers in early 2005 were *God's Politics*, aimed at liberals, and *Men In Black: How the Supreme Court Is Destroying America*, targeted at conservatives.

With spending on political books returning to historic levels in 2005, interest in diet, health and financial planning is expected to increase as the aging baby boomers look for ways to live healthier lives while enjoying a prosperous retirement. Among the books

Growth of Average Trade Book Prices

Year	*Adult Hard-bound*	*Juvenile Hard-bound*	*Total Hard-bound*	*Adult Paper-bound*	*Juvenile Paper-bound*	*Total Paper-bound*	*Total Adult*	*Total Juvenile*	*Total Trade*
2000	1.6%	4.7%	–1.8%	20.5%	–5.0%	5.6%	9.9%	0.6%	1.4%
2001	4.6	1.8	8.7	–2.9	10.9	–0.2	0.6	0.9	2.9
2002	1.8	3.9	3.9	4.4	–2.0	3.9	3.1	1.0	4.0
2003	2.0	3.7	0.5	3.7	3.7	3.7	2.8	5.3	2.5
2004	1.1	3.0	6.0	2.0	2.0	2.1	1.7	–0.1	3.6
2005	3.2	2.5	0.9	3.3	1.2	2.3	3.2	3.2	1.8
2006	1.9	0.4	3.2	1.4	1.5	1.1	1.6	–0.6	1.7
2007	1.7	2.2	–0.2	0.5	1.6	0.9	1.0	3.3	0.6
2008	1.4	–0.4	2.0	0.7	1.9	1.2	1.1	–0.1	1.4
2009	1.1	1.3	0.5	2.3	1.4	1.9	1.6	1.8	1.3
Compound Annual Growth									
1999-2004	2.2	3.4	3.4	5.3	1.8	3.0	3.6	1.5	2.9
2004-2009	1.8	1.2	1.3	1.6	1.5	1.5	1.7	1.5	1.4

Sources: Veronis Suhler Stevenson, PQ Media, Book Industry Study Group

with high expectations and big first printings are Suzanne Somers' *Slim and Sexy Forever*, *The 3-Hour Diet* and *Jim Cramer's Real Money*. Spending on business books, which has been soft in recent years, is also expected to have a mild recovery in 2005. *Conspiracy of Fools*, about the Enron scandal, was a bestseller in early 2005, and Jack Welch's *Winning* had a 750,000-copy first printing when it was released in April. The biggest nonfiction book of 2005, however, could be David McCullough's *1776*, which had a first printing of 1.2 million copies. Another title that could surpass expectations is Priscilla and Lisa Marie Presley's *Elvis by the Presleys*, which had a 400,000-copy first printing.

Among the new fiction titles that publishers hope will overcome the slump of 2004 are John Grisham's *The Broker*, *Conviction* by Richard North Patterson, *Honeymoon* by James Patterson and Howard Roughan, Danielle Steel's *Impossible*, *Ya-Yas in Bloom* by Rebecca Wells, *Star Wars: Episode III: Revenge of the Sith*, *4th of July* by James Patterson and Maxine Paetro, Dean Koontz's *Velocity*, *Eleven on Top* by Janet Evanovich, and *No Place Like Home* by Mary Higgins Clark. The novel that stood atop the fiction bestsellers in early 2005, however, remained *The Da Vinci Code*.

Given the likelihood that some interest in political books will shift to more escapist fare in 2005, spending in the adult hardcover segment is projected to increase 2.3 percent

Consumer Spending on Trade Books

($ MILLIONS)

Year	Adult Hard-bound	Juvenile Hard-bound	Total Hard-bound	Adult Paper-bound	Juvenile Paper-bound	Total Paper-bound	Total Adult	Total Juvenile	Total Trade
1999	$4,896	$1,727	$6,623	$3,592	$1,016	$4,608	$8,488	$2,743	$11,231
2000	4,328	1,955	6,283	3,500	1,085	4,585	7,828	3,040	10,868
2001	4,300	1,490	5,790	3,550	1,283	4,833	7,850	2,773	10,623
2002	4,645	1,515	6,160	3,860	1,250	5,110	8,505	2,765	11,270
2003	4,715	1,729	6,444	3,904	1,264	5,168	8,619	2,993	11,612
2004	4,975	1,457	6,432	4,018	1,299	5,317	8,993	2,756	11,749
2005	5,090	1,670	6,760	4,140	1,335	5,475	9,230	3,005	12,235
2006	5,185	1,525	6,710	4,235	1,385	5,620	9,420	2,910	12,330
2007	5,295	1,750	7,045	4,340	1,425	5,765	9,635	3,175	12,810
2008	5,380	1,645	7,025	4,410	1,455	5,865	9,790	3,100	12,890
2009	5,450	1,730	7,180	4,490	1,475	5,965	9,940	3,205	13,145

Sources: Veronis Suhler Stevenson, PQ Media, Book Industry Study Group

in 2005 to $5.09 billion. Price increases will fuel the gain as unit shipments are expected to dip 0.9 percent to 225.0 million. Spending in the 2004-2009 period is projected to rise at a compound annual rate of 1.8 percent, reaching $5.45 billion in 2009. Unit sales are projected to reach 227.0 million in 2009, the same level as in 2004.

Spending on trade paperbacks should increase at a slightly faster rate than spending in the hardcover segment in the forecast period, fueled in part by a projected 3.3 percent increase in prices. The trend toward releasing more fiction works as original trade paperbacks should continue in 2005, while growth is expected to come from such traditional trade paperback strengths as cookbooks, travel and humor. Spending is also expected to remain strong in a relatively new area, videogame guidebooks. Similar to 2004, spending growth in the trade paperback segment in 2005 will be curbed by sluggish spending on backlist titles. Consumer expenditures in the adult paperback segment are projected to increase 3.0 percent to $4.14 billion in 2005. Unit sales are forecast to slip 0.2 percent to 223.0 million. Spending on adult paperbacks is projected to grow at a compound annual rate of 2.2 percent in the forecast period to $4.49 billion in 2009.

MASS-MARKET PAPERBACKS

Spending in the mass-market paperback segment fell 4.2 percent to $2.81 billion in 2004, and the segment remained soft in early 2005. The prolonged slump caused some publishing executives to express concern in the beginning of the year about the segment's future. The format has lost shelf space to trade paperbacks and hardcovers in nearly all outlets in recent years, and other market channels that were major supporters of paper-

Growth of Consumer Spending on Trade Books

Year	*Adult Hard-bound*	*Juvenile Hard-bound*	*Total Hard-bound*	*Adult Paper-bound*	*Juvenile Paper-bound*	*Total Paper-bound*	*Total Adult*	*Total Juvenile*	*Total Trade*
2000	–11.6%	13.2%	–5.1%	–2.6%	6.7%	–0.5%	–7.8%	10.8%	–3.2%
2001	–0.6	–23.8	–7.8	1.4	18.3	5.4	0.3	–8.8	–2.2
2002	8.0	1.7	6.4	8.7	–2.6	5.7	8.3	–0.3	6.1
2003	1.5	14.1	4.6	1.1	1.1	1.1	1.3	8.2	3.0
2004	5.5	–15.7	–0.2	2.9	2.8	2.9	4.3	–7.9	1.2
2005	2.3	14.6	5.1	3.0	2.8	3.0	2.6	9.0	4.1
2006	1.9	–8.7	–0.7	2.3	3.7	2.6	2.1	–3.2	0.8
2007	2.1	14.8	5.0	2.5	2.9	2.6	2.3	9.1	3.9
2008	1.6	–6.0	–0.3	1.6	2.1	1.7	1.6	–2.4	0.6
2009	1.3	5.2	2.2	1.8	1.4	1.7	1.5	3.4	2.0
Compound Annual Growth									
1999-2004	0.3	–3.3	–0.6	2.3	5.0	2.9	1.2	0.1	0.9
2004-2009	1.8	3.5	2.2	2.2	2.6	2.3	2.0	3.1	2.3

Sources: Veronis Suhler Stevenson, PQ Media, Book Industry Study Group

backs, such as discount stores, now have fewer stores. The format's most important advantage in the past, affordability, has also been eroded by the greater availability of used books and deeper discounting of hardcovers. In addition, mass-market publishers are confronted with the reality that the paperback's small type may be a turnoff to sight-impaired baby boomers, the largest audience for mass-market paperbacks.

In a move to address the latter issue in early 2005, several mass-market paperback publishers introduced "premium paperbacks," a slightly larger version of mass-market paperbacks that features bigger type. The new format also carries a $9.99 price point, higher than the $7.99 price point that had been the most expensive for mass-market paperbacks. Publishers are betting that they can offset a decline in units with higher prices.

Despite these negative factors, mass-market paperbacks still sell an abundance of units. The top 10 bestselling paperbacks in 2004 sold 24.5 million copies combined, a slight decline from the 25.1 million units sold in 2003. Despite a 4.3 percent drop in units in 2004, the segment still sold a total of 429.5 million copies for the year. The bestselling mass-market title in 2004 was Dan Brown's *Angels & Demons*, which sold 3.8 million units. Brown's *Deception Point* was also among the year's biggest sellers, and other familiar fiction writers, such as John Grisham, Nora Roberts and Danielle Steel, dotted the bestseller list.

The mass-market paperback segment has reached a crossroads in 2005. Publishers are looking to stem the loss of shelf space by making book designs more appealing and by raising prices. It is unlikely these efforts will halt the slide in unit sales, as units are projected to fall 2.8 percent in 2005 to 417.5 million.

Top 10 Mass-Market Paperbacks, 2004

Book	*Author*	*Unit Sales*
Angels & Demons	Dan Brown	3,800,000
Bleachers	John Grisham	2,850,000
The Last Juror	John Grisham	2,792,483
Deception Point	Dan Brown	2,500,000
Skipping Christmas	John Grisham	2,400,000
Safe Harbor	Danielle Steel	2,250,000
Blue Dahlia	Nora Roberts	2,177,030
Digital Fortress	Dan Brown	2,000,000
Dr. Atkins New Diet Revolution	Robert C. Atkins	1,900,000
The Notebook	Nicholas Sparks	1,875,589
Total		24,545,102

Sources: Veronis Suhler Stevenson, PQ Media, *Publishers Weekly*

Spending is also forecast to slip in 2005, although the projected decline of 0.9 percent would represent a decelerated drop compared with the 4.2 percent decline in 2004. Total spending will dip to $2.79 billion in 2005. We expect spending on mass-market paperbacks to increase at a compound annual rate of 0.5 percent from 2004 to 2009, reaching $2.88 billion in 2009. Units will fall at a 0.5 percent compound annual rate in the forecast period, dipping to 419.5 million in 2009.

RELIGIOUS BOOKS

Religious book spending recorded a double-digit gain for the second consecutive year in 2004, increasing 10.7 percent to $2.90 billion. Unit sales rose a solid 7.8 percent to 186.2 million. *The Purpose-Driven Life* was once again the top-selling nonfiction book, either religious or mainstream, in 2004, selling 7.3 million units. But *Purpose-Driven* was not the only reason for the continued surge in religious book spending in 2004. *Your Best Life Now* sold just under 1 million copies in 2004, despite being released late in the year. The success of both *Purpose-Driven* and *Your Best Life Now* point to broader trends that will continue to bolster spending on religious books in the forecast period.

Terrorism, unrest abroad and the aging baby boomer generation have helped to bring religious and spiritual issues to the forefront of American culture. The increased interest in religious and spiritual matters has prompted mainstream retailers to carry more titles related to these areas, helping to fuel the boom in spending. Heightened interest in religious subjects has not only resulted in an unprecedented number of blockbusters, but has also driven sales of books below the bestseller list; books that previously may have sold in the tens of thousands are now selling hundreds of thousands of copies, benefiting from exposure in mainstream stores and more publicity from the general media.

The success of *Purpose-Driven* has not been lost on general publishers; indeed, *Your Best Life Now* is published by Time Warner Book Group's Warner Faith division. The move by general publishers to broaden their religious lists will only serve to expand the penetration of religious books into secular retail outlets. The only looming threat to sustained growth in religious book spending is the steady decline in the number of independent Christian booksellers. As more sales move to mainstream bookstores and price clubs, sales at independent religious stores

Net Unit Shipments of Consumer Books

(MILLIONS)

Year	Adult Trade	Juvenile Trade	Total Trade	Mass-Market Paperbacks	Religious	Book Clubs	Mail Order	University Press	Total
1999	507.1	395.4	902.5	430.1	164.1	142.3	63.3	32.0	1,734.3
2000	425.4	435.5	860.9	418.0	161.2	139.8	63.1	31.0	1,674.0
2001	424.0	393.6	817.6	416.0	168.3	140.5	51.1	29.5	1,623.0
2002	445.6	388.7	834.3	451.0	158.5	145.2	46.5	28.5	1,664.0
2003	439.1	399.6	838.7	448.7	172.7	143.7	47.7	28.1	1,679.6
2004	450.5	368.5	819.0	429.5	186.2	135.5	46.5	27.7	1,644.4
2005	448.0	389.5	837.5	417.5	193.0	133.0	46.0	28.0	1,655.0
2006	450.0	379.5	829.5	415.0	197.5	132.0	45.7	28.4	1,648.1
2007	455.5	401.0	856.5	415.0	201.0	132.0	45.0	29.0	1,678.5
2008	458.0	392.0	850.0	417.0	204.0	132.5	45.0	29.2	1,677.7
2009	457.5	398.0	855.5	419.5	206.5	133.5	44.8	29.3	1,689.1

Sources: Veronis Suhler Stevenson, PQ Media, Book Industry Study Group

Growth of Net Unit Shipments of Consumer Books

Year	Adult Trade	Juvenile Trade	Total Trade	Mass-Market Paperbacks	Religious	Book Clubs	Mail Order	University Press	Total
2000	–16.1%	10.1%	–4.6%	–2.8%	–1.8%	–1.8%	–0.3%	–3.1%	–3.5%
2001	–0.3	–9.6	–5.0	–0.5	4.4	0.5	–19.0	–4.8	–3.0
2002	5.1	–1.2	2.0	8.4	–5.8	3.3	–9.0	–3.4	2.5
2003	–1.5	2.8	0.5	–0.5	9.0	–1.0	2.6	–1.4	0.9
2004	2.6	–7.8	–2.3	–4.3	7.8	–5.7	–2.5	–1.4	–2.1
2005	–0.6	5.7	2.3	–2.8	3.7	–1.8	–1.1	1.1	0.6
2006	0.4	–2.6	–1.0	–0.6	2.3	–0.8	–0.7	1.4	–0.4
2007	1.2	5.7	3.3	0.0	1.8	0.0	–1.5	2.1	1.8
2008	0.5	–2.2	–0.8	0.5	1.5	0.4	0.0	0.7	0.0
2009	–0.1	1.5	0.6	0.6	1.2	0.8	–0.4	0.3	0.7
Compound Annual Growth									
1999-2004	–2.3	–1.4	–1.9	0.0	2.6	–1.0	–6.0	–2.8	–1.1
2004-2009	0.3	1.6	0.9	–0.5	2.1	–0.3	–0.7	1.1	0.5

Sources: Veronis Suhler Stevenson, PQ Media, Book Industry Study Group

Shares of Net Unit Shipments of Consumer Books

Year	*Adult Trade*	*Juvenile Trade*	*Total Trade*	*Mass-Market Paperbacks*	*Religious*	*Book Clubs*	*Mail Order*	*University Press*
1999	29.2%	22.8%	52.0%	24.8%	9.5%	8.2%	3.6%	1.8%
2000	25.4	26.0	51.4	25.0	9.6	8.4	3.8	1.9
2001	26.1	24.3	50.4	25.6	10.4	8.7	3.1	1.8
2002	26.8	23.4	50.1	27.1	9.5	8.7	2.8	1.7
2003	26.1	23.8	49.9	26.7	10.3	8.6	2.8	1.7
2004	27.4	22.4	49.8	26.1	11.3	8.2	2.8	1.7
2005	27.1	23.5	50.6	25.2	11.7	8.0	2.8	1.7
2006	27.3	23.0	50.3	25.2	12.0	8.0	2.8	1.7
2007	27.1	23.9	51.0	24.7	12.0	7.9	2.7	1.7
2008	27.3	23.4	50.7	24.9	12.2	7.9	2.7	1.7
2009	27.1	23.6	50.6	24.8	12.2	7.9	2.7	1.7

Sources: Veronis Suhler Stevenson, PQ Media, Book Industry Study Group

have fallen, forcing about 200 Christian bookstores to close over the last two years. Fewer independent Christian bookstores could hurt sales of new and midlist authors.

The broader spending trend for religious books, however, is positive, although spending will grow at a somewhat decelerated rate in 2005 than in the previous two years. Spending is projected to increase 5.0 percent to $3.05 billion in 2005, with units rising 3.7 percent to 193.0 million. We anticipate relatively steady spending growth in this segment during the forecast period. Spending is projected to grow at a compound annual rate of 3.8 percent from 2004 to 2009 to $3.50 billion in 2009.

BOOK CLUBS

The growth of online bookstores and the spread of superstores have been impinging on the book club industry for years, and those forces were major factors in the 4.5 percent drop in book club spending in 2004, which fell to $1.39 billion.

Bookspan, the major adult book club business in the U.S., has suffered from membership erosion for years in its main general interest clubs, Book-of-the-Month Club (BOMC) and Literary Guild, and membership declines occurred again in 2004. In order to reverse the membership slide, Bookspan has initiated a number of new programs. Its most ambitious endeavor in 2004 was the launch of Smart Reader Rewards, which permits new members to order the book of their choice, rather than having a book selected for them by BOMC. Late in 2004, Bookspan reached a deal with Little, Brown to offer James Patterson's new book, *Honeymoon*, to its members a month before it was available to stores.

While Bookspan struggled in the adult book club segment in 2004, Scholastic was dealing with sluggish growth in the school book club market, a segment where it is the dominant player. Scholastic said it expected book club sales to be flat for the fiscal year ended May 31, 2005.

The best hope for book clubs to maintain their share of consumer book spending is the development of niche clubs. Bookspan has pursued this strategy for several years with mixed results. Among its newest efforts were the 2004 launches of Circulo, its second

Average End-User Prices of Consumer Books

Year	Adult Trade	Juvenile Trade	Total Trade	Mass-Market Paperbacks	Religious	Book Clubs	Mail Order	University Press	Total
1999	$16.74	$6.94	$12.44	$5.81	$13.10	$ 8.94	$6.74	$15.85	$10.43
2000	18.40	6.98	12.62	6.22	14.24	9.24	7.13	16.36	10.76
2001	18.51	7.05	12.99	6.25	14.34	9.74	7.73	17.69	11.04
2002	19.09	7.11	13.51	6.43	14.78	9.91	8.04	18.35	11.33
2003	19.63	7.49	13.85	6.54	15.19	10.12	7.84	18.93	11.63
2004	19.96	7.48	14.35	6.54	15.60	10.25	7.94	19.46	12.02
2005	20.60	7.72	14.61	6.67	15.80	10.34	8.02	19.46	12.30
2006	20.93	7.67	14.86	6.66	16.08	10.42	7.99	19.72	12.48
2007	21.15	7.92	14.96	6.78	16.44	10.53	8.02	19.83	12.66
2008	21.38	7.91	15.16	6.83	16.69	10.57	8.00	20.21	12.81
2009	21.73	8.05	15.37	6.87	16.95	10.64	7.99	20.48	12.97

Sources: Veronis Suhler Stevenson, PQ Media, Book Industry Study Group

Spanish-language book club, and American Compass, a club aimed at conservatives. But while Bookspan has had success with developing some specialized clubs, it has found it difficult to replace the loss of membership in its large clubs with new membership from smaller clubs.

The outlook for the book club segment over the next five years is for comparatively slow growth as increased membership in niche clubs offsets declines in membership in general clubs. Spending in 2005 is projected to decline 1.0 percent to $1.38 billion. The future of the book club business is in niche clubs. Many publishing companies, for example, have small clubs tied to their publishing efforts. The conservative book publisher Regnery has approximately 75,000 members in its affiliated Conservative Book Club, while romance publishers Kensington and Leisure Books both have several different clubs aimed at romance readers. It is unlikely, however, that niche clubs will be able to drive significant spending gains in the forecast period, in which we project compound annual growth of 0.4 percent, with spending of $1.42 billion in 2009.

MAIL ORDER

Mail order spending slipped 1.3 percent in 2004 to $369.0 million as more companies moved their direct-to-consumer efforts to the Web and away from traditional catalog and other mail promotions.

The future of mail order is that of an adjunct business to book publishers that also operate significant magazine divisions. The mail order publishers that remain successful, such as Rodale, Taunton Press and Oxmoor House (part of Time Inc.), are all part of companies that have magazine divisions. By working with the magazine units, mail order book publishers have been able to keep costs down while improving sell-through.

Although it is unlikely that the mail order segment will experience a revival—there are only a few companies that possess the combination of book and magazine publishing that makes the format economically viable—the category should be able to maintain spending at a fairly even level. Spending in 2005 is projected to be level with 2004 at $369.0 million, while spending in the 2004-2009 period is projected to decline at a

Growth of Average End-User Prices of Consumer Books

Year	*Adult Trade*	*Juvenile Trade*	*Total Trade*	*Mass-Market Paperbacks*	*Religious*	*Book Clubs*	*Mail Order*	*University Press*	*Total*
2000	9.9%	0.6%	1.4%	7.0%	8.7%	3.4%	5.9%	3.2%	3.2%
2001	0.6	0.9	2.9	0.6	0.7	5.4	8.4	8.2	2.6
2002	3.1	1.0	4.0	2.8	3.1	1.7	4.1	3.7	2.6
2003	2.8	5.3	2.5	1.7	2.7	2.1	–2.5	3.2	2.6
2004	1.7	–0.1	3.6	0.1	2.7	1.3	1.2	2.8	3.4
2005	3.2	3.2	1.8	1.9	1.3	0.9	1.1	0.0	2.4
2006	1.6	–0.6	1.7	–0.1	1.7	0.8	–0.4	1.3	1.5
2007	1.0	3.3	0.6	1.8	2.3	1.1	0.4	0.6	1.5
2008	1.1	–0.1	1.4	0.8	1.5	0.3	–0.3	1.9	1.2
2009	1.6	1.8	1.3	0.5	1.5	0.7	–0.1	1.3	1.2
Compound Annual Growth									
1999-2004	3.6	1.5	2.9	2.4	3.5	2.8	3.3	4.2	2.9
2004-2009	1.7	1.5	1.4	1.0	1.7	0.7	0.1	1.0	1.5

Sources: Veronis Suhler Stevenson, PQ Media, Book Industry Study Group

Consumer Book Publishing

0.6 percent compound annual rate to $358.0 million in 2009.

UNIVERSITY PRESSES

Spending in the university press segment rose 1.3 percent to $539.0 million in 2004, marking the third consecutive year of relatively marginal growth. The segment continues to be confronted by cuts in public and academic library funding, which reduces budgets of university presses' most important customers. Meanwhile, reductions in subsidies from their own universities often result in the cutting of title output.

Despite the lackluster spending performance in 2004, and predictions for more marginal gains in 2005, the long-term outlook for university presses is more favorable than it has been for some time. Print-on-demand technology has taken hold in the sector, allowing presses to take some costs out of their bottom lines, while also permitting them to keep slow-selling books in print longer, adding incremental sales to their top line. Library funding is expected to gradually improve over the next few years, giving a nudge to spending on the presses' core academic titles. Many university presses are also moving deeper into electronic publishing, either by developing e-books, particularly for the library market, or entirely new products that can be sold via the Internet. And after several years of experimenting with trade publishing, most university presses have found the mix of trade and scholarly publishing that works best for them.

Although the most difficult times for university presses appear to have past, it is unlikely that big spending gains lie ahead in a market where funding is tight in the best of times. Still, the 2.2 percent compound annual growth projected for the 2004-2009 period is higher than the 1.2 percent compound annual increase recorded over the last five years. Spending in 2005 is projected to rise 1.1 percent to $545.0 million with unit sales also increasing 1.1 percent to 28.0 million. Spending in 2009 will reach $600.0 million.

End-User Spending on Consumer Books

($ MILLIONS)

Year	Adult Trade	Juvenile Trade	Total Trade	Mass-Market Paperbacks	Religious	Book Clubs	Mail Order	University Press	Total
1999	$8,488	$2,743	$11,231	$2,500	$2,151	$1,272	$426	$507	$18,087
2000	7,828	3,040	10,868	2,600	2,295	1,292	450	507	18,012
2001	7,850	2,773	10,623	2,602	2,413	1,369	395	522	17,924
2002	8,505	2,765	11,270	2,900	2,343	1,439	374	523	18,849
2003	8,619	2,993	11,612	2,934	2,623	1,454	374	532	19,529
2004	8,993	2,756	11,749	2,811	2,904	1,389	369	539	19,761
2005	9,230	3,005	12,235	2,785	3,050	1,375	369	545	20,359
2006	9,420	2,910	12,330	2,765	3,175	1,375	365	560	20,570
2007	9,635	3,175	12,810	2,815	3,305	1,390	361	575	21,256
2008	9,790	3,100	12,890	2,850	3,405	1,400	360	590	21,495
2009	9,940	3,205	13,145	2,880	3,500	1,420	358	600	21,903

Sources: Veronis Suhler Stevenson, PQ Media, Book Industry Study Group

Growth of End-User Spending on Consumer Books

Year	Adult Trade	Juvenile Trade	Total Trade	Mass-Market Paperbacks	Religious	Book Clubs	Mail Order	University Press	Total
2000	–7.8%	10.8%	–3.2%	4.0%	6.7%	1.5%	5.5%	0.0%	–0.4%
2001	0.3	–8.8	–2.2	0.1	5.1	6.0	–12.2	2.9	–0.5
2002	8.3	–0.3	6.1	11.5	–2.9	5.1	–5.3	0.2	5.2
2003	1.3	8.2	3.0	1.2	12.0	1.0	0.0	1.7	3.6
2004	4.3	–7.9	1.2	–4.2	10.7	–4.5	–1.3	1.3	1.2
2005	2.6	9.0	4.1	–0.9	5.0	–1.0	0.0	1.1	3.0
2006	2.1	–3.2	0.8	–0.7	4.1	0.0	–1.1	2.8	1.0
2007	2.3	9.1	3.9	1.8	4.1	1.1	–1.1	2.7	3.3
2008	1.6	–2.4	0.6	1.2	3.0	0.7	–0.3	2.6	1.1
2009	1.5	3.4	2.0	1.1	2.8	1.4	–0.6	1.7	1.9
Compound Annual Growth									
1999-2004	1.2	0.1	0.9	2.4	6.2	1.8	–2.9	1.2	1.8
2004-2009	2.0	3.1	2.3	0.5	3.8	0.4	–0.6	2.2	2.1

Sources: Veronis Suhler Stevenson, PQ Media, Book Industry Study Group

Shares of End-User Spending on Consumer Books

Year	Adult Trade	Juvenile Trade	Total Trade	Mass-Market Paperbacks	Religious	Book Clubs	Mail Order	University Press
1999	46.9%	15.2%	62.1%	13.8%	11.9%	7.0%	2.4%	2.8%
2000	43.5	16.9	60.3	14.4	12.7	7.2	2.5	2.8
2001	43.8	15.5	59.3	14.5	13.5	7.6	2.2	2.9
2002	45.1	14.7	59.8	15.4	12.4	7.6	2.0	2.8
2003	44.1	15.3	59.5	15.0	13.4	7.4	1.9	2.7
2004	45.5	13.9	59.5	14.2	14.7	7.0	1.9	2.7
2005	45.3	14.8	60.1	13.7	15.0	6.8	1.8	2.7
2006	45.8	14.1	59.9	13.4	15.4	6.7	1.8	2.7
2007	45.3	14.9	60.3	13.2	15.5	6.5	1.7	2.7
2008	45.5	14.4	60.0	13.3	15.8	6.5	1.7	2.7
2009	45.4	14.6	60.0	13.1	16.0	6.5	1.6	2.7

Sources: Veronis Suhler Stevenson, PQ Media, Book Industry Study Group

The Outlook for Consumer Books

Spending on consumer books is expected to increase 3.0 percent in 2005 to $20.36 billion, driven by growth in the juvenile hardcover and religious book segments, which will be somewhat offset by a decline in the mass-market paperback and book club categories. Spending in the adult hardcover segment, the industry's largest category, will increase 2.3 percent. Total units will be flat with 2004 at 1.66 billion.

We project total spending on consumer books will grow at a 2.1 percent compound annual rate from 2004 to 2009, a slight acceleration from the 1999-2004 period. Expenditures are expected to reach $21.90 billion in 2009, compared with $19.76 billion in 2004. The higher growth rate in the forecast period will be driven primarily by a minor increase in units and moderate price hikes. Unit sales are projected to rise at a 0.5 percent compound annual rate in the forecast period, compared to a 1.1 percent decline in the 1999-2004 timeframe. Price increases are projected to rise at a compound annual rate of 1.4 percent from 2004 to 2009, slower than the 2.9 percent increase in the previous five years.

The strongest growth in spending in the forecast period is expected to be in the religious segment, with expenditures projected to increase 3.8 percent on a compound annual basis from 2004 to 2009. Spending in the juvenile trade category is also forecast to beat the 2.1 percent industry average, growing at a compound annual rate of 3.1 percent from 2004 to 2009. The weakest performing segments will be book clubs and mail order.

FORECAST ASSUMPTIONS

- The consumer book market is a mature one that often exhibits marginal annual increases in spending, driven largely by price increases with an occasional spike in spending as a result of blockbuster bestsellers. These trends are expected to continue in the forecast period.
- Consumer books continue to compete with other media segments for the average consumers' time and dollars, thereby softening overall demand for books. This trend will continue in the forecast period. Demand over the next five years will also be dampened by the continued decline in the reading habits of Americans, as documented in a report released by the National Endowment for the Arts in July 2004, which found that only about 57 percent of Americans had read a book in the previous year.
- Although the release of fiction titles is stronger in 2005 than in 2004, the lack of a new franchise author will limit spending growth in the fiction category in the forecast period.
- The July 2005 publication of *Harry Potter and the Half-Blood Prince*, which had a record first printing of 10.8 million copies, will drive a double-digit increase in spending in the juvenile hardcover segment, ratcheting up total consumer book spending by 3.0 percent in 2005. The final edition of the Harry Potter series is likely due out in 2007, and will again boost spending.
- The religious book segment will continue to experience spending gains in the forecast period as the aging American public continues its shift toward spirituality and conservatism.

2004 Communications Industry Forecast Compared with Actual Growth

Category	*2004 Forecasted Growth**	*Actual 2004 Growth*[†]
Trade	1.1%	4.1%
Mass-Market Paperbacks	1.2	–4.2
Religious	5.9	10.7
Book Clubs	1.4	–4.5
Mail Order	1.1	–1.3
University Press	0.0	1.3
Total	1.8	1.2

*Veronis Suhler Stevenson 2004 Communications Industry Forecast & Report
[†]Veronis Suhler Stevenson, PQ Media

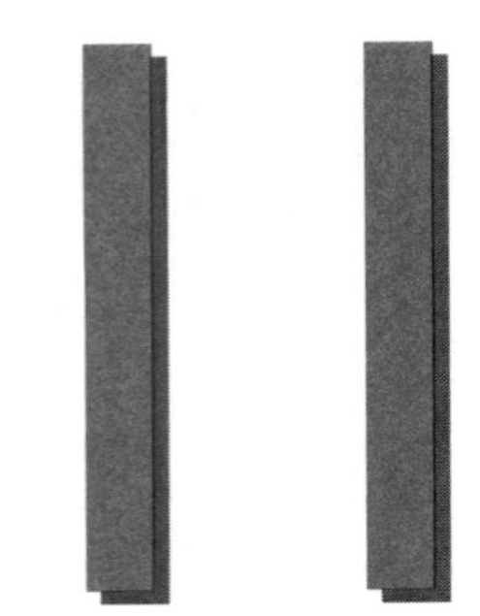

Consumer Magazine Publishing

Consumer Magazine Spending And Nominal GDP Growth, 2000-2009

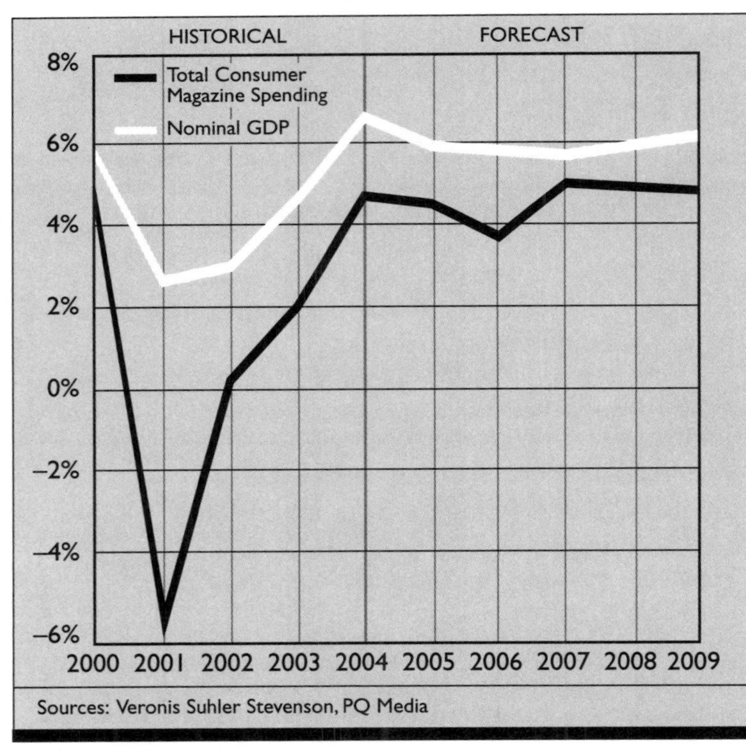

Sources: Veronis Suhler Stevenson, PQ Media

Consumer Magazine Publishing

THE CONSUMER MAGAZINE MARKET IN 2004 AND 2005

The consumer magazine market continued its recovery in 2004 as total spending increased at an accelerated 4.6 percent rate to $22.45 billion for the year, driven by gains in both advertising and circulation. Overall consumer magazine spending grew at a compound annual rate of 1.0 percent from 1999 to 2004, lagging nominal GDP by almost 4 percentage points, primarily as a result of the significant downturn in 2001 and the relatively flat performance in 2002.

Advertising expenditures, which accounted for 54.0 percent of total segment spending, rose 6.0 percent to $12.12 billion in 2004, fueled by the improving economy and strong gains in the retail, financial and travel categories. Comparatively strong advertising growth in 2004 offset the declines in 2001 and 2002, resulting in compound annual growth of 1.2 percent for the 1999-2004 period. The accelerated upswing in ad spending was the fastest growth posted by consumer magazines in four years and followed a 4.0 percent rise in 2003. Improving retail sales and higher personal incomes drove double-digit spending gains in the three aforementioned categories, combined with increases, albeit smaller ones, in six other major ad categories. General business and regional magazines also notched strong growth, as consumers once again started paying attention to financial markets, and many local economies revitalized.

Circulation spending, which comprised 46.0 percent of total segment expenditures, surged 3.0 percent to $10.33 billion in 2004, the largest increase in seven years. Circulation spending increased despite the lack of price growth, as an upswing in unit circulation spurred the overall gain. Circulation expenditures experienced an up-and-down period from 1999 to 2004 that resulted in compound annual growth of only 0.8 percent for the five-year timeframe. The average single-copy price increased 3.1 percent to $3.36 in 2004, as publishers found newsstand buyers more receptive to higher prices. The average annual subscription price decreased

0.7 percent to $23.06, while the average per-unit price was flat at $1.56 for the year.

While several other traditional media segments appeared to be struggling in the first three months of 2005, consumer magazines continued on its recovery track. Spending on consumer magazine advertising was up an estimated 4.3 percent for the first quarter of the year compared with the same period in 2004. In contrast, magazine ad spending in the first quarter of 2004 declined an estimated 0.3 percent compared with the same period the previous year, which tempered the growth outlooks of many industry analysts at that time. First-quarter growth in 2005 was driven by gains in seven of the 12 major ad categories, including food and food products, financial, insurance and real estate, and direct response. Advertising growth is expected to accelerate somewhat in the second half of 2005, fueled by gains in categories such as toiletries and cosmetics, while upside in major categories like automotive, and food and food products will be more tempered. Food and food products advertising increased sharply in the first quarter, but leveled off in April, and we anticipate gains going forward will be in the single-digit range. Meanwhile, the automotive category got off to a very slow start, but this segment is expected to rebound slightly in the second half of the year when manufacturers, particularly those of foreign vehicles, launch ad campaigns to support 2006 models. This growth, however, will be offset somewhat by slower growth among American car makers, which announced reductions in magazine advertising in the first half of the year, and are expected to continue to delay buys until the last minute in the second half of 2005.

As GDP growth slows a bit in 2005, consumer magazine advertising growth also is expected to decelerate somewhat to 5.5 percent, with expenditures reaching $12.79 billion for the year. Growth will be driven primarily by the continued expansion of the economy and the overall ad market, although at a slower pace than in 2004, as well as by the magazine industry's extensive marketing and research campaigns designed to tout consumer magazines as the engaging alternative to other media.

Growth of U.S. Consumer Magazine Spending

	Advertising	*Circulation*	*Total*
2004 Expenditures ($ Millions)	$12,121	$10,331	$22,452
1999-2004 Compound Annual Growth (%)	1.2%	0.8%	1.0%
2004-2009 Projected Compound Annual Growth (%)	6.2%	2.3%	4.5%
2009 Projected Expenditures ($ Millions)	$16,374	$11,562	$27,936

Sources: Veronis Suhler Stevenson, PQ Media, Universal McCann, Magazine Publishers of America, Audit Bureau of Circulations

The magazine industry continues to promote the value of magazines in the media mix through advertising campaigns and research studies. The industry's primary trade organization, the Magazine Publishers of America (MPA), released a number of research reports in 2004, highlighting the trust that readers put in magazines, their acceptance of ads in magazines as opposed to other media, the impact of magazines on buying behavior and the return on investment (ROI) from magazine advertising. In early 2005, the MPA kicked off a three-year, $40.0 million marketing campaign targeting advertisers and advertising agencies. The campaign is an effort to improve the attitudes of advertisers and media buyers toward magazines, with the expectation that an attitudinal shift will ultimately result in higher advertising spending for magazines.

The industry hopes that such marketing efforts will mitigate the increasing skepticism of many marketers about their ROI in traditional media advertising. While it remains to be seen how effective the industry's marketing campaign will be, we still anticipate that going forward at least some advertisers will progressively shift more ad dollars out of print media, such as consumer magazines, and into electronic media and alternative marketing methods. This shift will moderate spending growth in consumer magazine advertising, which will grow more in line with that of nominal GDP over the next five years, instead of exceeding economic growth by 2 to 3 percentage points as in previous expansion periods.

Highlights

Total spending on consumer magazines grew 4.6 percent to $22.45 billion in 2004, driven by gains in both advertising and circulation. Overall consumer magazine spending grew at a compound annual rate of 1.0 percent from 1999 to 2004, trailing nominal GDP by nearly 4 percentage points, mainly due to the notable downturn in 2001 and the relatively flat performance in 2002.

■

Advertising spending grew 6.0 percent to $12.12 billion in 2004, fueled by the improving economy and strong gains in the retail, financial and travel segments. Solid advertising growth in 2004 helped offset declines in 2001 and 2002, resulting in compound annual growth of 1.2 percent for the 1999-2004 period.

■

Total per-issue unit circulation climbed 3.0 percent to 363.1 million in 2004, following three consecutive down years, due to gains in celebrity, lifestyle and health titles. Subscription circulation rose 3.3 percent to 311.8 million for the year. Single-copy circulation increased 1.0 percent to 51.3 million, reversing a six-year downward trend. Overall, per-issue unit circulation declined at a compound annual rate of 0.5 percent from 1999 to 2004.

■

Circulation spending rose 3.0 percent to $10.33 billion in 2004, the largest increase in seven years. Circulation expenditures increased despite the lack of price growth, as an upswing in unit circulation drove the overall gain. Circulation spending grew at a compound annual rate of 0.8 percent from 1999 to 2004. The average single-copy price increased 3.1 percent to $3.36 in 2004, as publishers found newsstand buyers more receptive to higher prices. The average annual subscription price decreased 0.7 percent to $23.06, while the average per-unit price was flat at $1.56 for the year.

■

Spending on consumer magazine advertising is expected to increase 5.5 percent to $12.79 billion in 2005. Advertising expenditures will grow at a compound annual rate of 6.2 percent from 2004 to 2009, reaching $16.37 billion in 2009, driven mainly by economic expansion and growth in the overall advertising market, as well as the industry's marketing and research initiatives.

■

Circulation spending is projected to increase 3.1 percent to $10.65 billion in 2005, and will grow at a compound annual rate of 2.3 percent from 2004 to 2009, reaching $11.56 billion in 2009. Growth will be fueled primarily by increases in cover and subscription prices, improved circulation acquisition and renewal practices, and a stronger emphasis on newsstand sales; however, growth will be tempered in 2006 by a scheduled postal rate hike.

■

Total spending on consumer magazines will increase 4.4 percent to $23.44 billion in 2005, and will grow 4.5 percent on a compound annual basis from 2004 to 2009, hitting $27.94 billion in 2009.

Nevertheless, we expect magazine advertising growth to outpace nominal GDP growth in 2006 for the first time in six years, although it will do so by only a slim margin. Overall, we expect spending on consumer magazine advertising to grow at an accelerated pace during the forecast period, compared with the 1999-2004 timeframe, but level with the broader economic expansion. Magazine ad expenditures will grow at a compound annual rate of 6.2 percent from 2004 to 2009, exceeding the 1.2 percent compound annual growth in the previous five-year period, but very close to the 6.1 percent expansion in nominal GDP.

Meanwhile, some publishers' intentional circulation cuts—more than 30 percent of consumer magazines have reduced their rate bases over the last five years—were offset by unit gains at other magazines. The result was a per-issue circulation gain of 3.0 percent in 2004 to 363.1 million. Similar to circulation spending, this represented the first gain in circulation units in seven years, driven by increases in both subscriptions and single copies. The circulation unit drops of the past few years were spurred by publishers voluntarily reducing their rate bases to increase profitability and give advertisers better quality circulation. As advertising spending revived in 2004, publishers reduced subscription prices to build and retain their subscriber bases.

Maintaining circulation, however, remains challenging for most magazines. With annual subscription renewal rates averaging about 46 percent, retaining current subscribers and attracting new ones is critical to the magazine industry's future health. Direct mail, telemarketing and third-party subscription agencies are not filling the void left by the demise of sweepstakes-driven subscriptions. The decline of advertising and circulation revenues in recent years has resulted in further erosion of dollars available for circulation-building. And while the Internet has helped bring in new business, its growth is leveling off.

In spite of these difficulties, individual magazines have had success in acquiring and retaining readers through strategies such as sweepstakes, direct-to-publisher subscription solicitations that don't involve third-party subscription agents, multiyear subscriptions with automatic renewals and tie-ins with retailers. For example, *Elle* participated in DKNY's spring fashion shows in 2005 at selected Macy's stores in California, presenting *Elle*-branded gifts to customers who bought DKNY products. These so-called "below the line" marketing costs are expected to surpass "above the line" brand advertising costs for the first time in 2005. Magazines are also trying harder to forge stronger bonds with their audiences. Meredith's *American Baby*, for example, makes use of baby fairs to better connect with its target market. Magazine executives are also focusing their energies on improving newsstand unit sales and revenues. Seeking to increase the number of outlets for single-copy sales, publishers and distributors are testing wholesale clubs, dollar stores, and specialty stores such as sporting goods retailers.

Meanwhile, a number of magazines raised their cover prices in 2004, as an inexpensive way to boost revenues and to combat shortfalls if circulation were to slip. The tactic paid off, as single-copy unit circulation and spending rose. At the same time, some new magazines achieved successful launches by charging less than $2 at the newsstand. Time Inc. launched *All You* amid skepticism in the industry about its announcement that it would sell 500,000 copies monthly at a cover price of $1.47 exclusively in Wal-Mart stores. The magazine had consistently met its rate base through the first quarter of 2005. Other newsstand-driven launches in 2004, such as Bauer Publishing's *Life & Style Weekly* and Hachette Filipacchi's *For Me*, were also priced under $2. These two magazines, with circulations of 350,000 and 480,000, respectively, are further proof that high circulation numbers can be achieved through newsstand sales. In late 2004, American Media and Hearst both announced new magazines that would be sold exclusively, or largely, through newsstands.

Publishers continue to develop magazines aimed at emerging editorial and demographic trends. Magazines targeting young Hispanic women showed large circulation gains in 2004. The circulation of *Latina* rose 36.0 percent, while circulation of *Cosmopolitan en Espanol* soared 88.0 percent for the

New Magazine Launches in the United States

Year	*Total*	*4+ Frequency*	*Percent Of Total*
1988	509	300	58.9%
1989	608	284	46.7
1990	557	325	58.3
1991	553	363	65.6
1992	679	443	65.2
1993	789	417	52.9
1994	832	458	55.0
1995	838	510	60.9
1996	933	535	57.3
1997	852	459	53.9
1998	1,065	518	48.6
1999	864	360	41.7
2000	874	333	38.1
2001	702	301	42.9
2002	745	290	38.9
2003	955	450	47.1
2004	1,006	473	47.0
1988-2004 Total	13,361	6,819	51.0

Sources: Veronis Suhler Stevenson, PQ Media, Samir Husni (www.mrmagazine.com)

year. The increasing economic clout of Hispanic women prompted Meredith to announce that it will launch a new lifestyle/shelter magazine aimed at this segment in 2005. The magazine catalog niche enjoyed continued growth in 2004, as well. Condé Nast scored a hit with *Lucky*, which saw circulation grow from 605,000 in 2001 to more than 1 million in 2004. That success led the publisher to introduce *Cargo* in 2004, a shopping title for men. Fairchild Publications entered the fray in 2004 with a competing title called *Vitals*, and followed up with a women's version in 2005 called *Vitals Woman*.

Encouraged by the increasing number of audience niches, a host of publishers introduced new magazines geared to them in 2004. New magazine launches grew for a third straight year in 2004, when a total of 1,006 magazines were introduced. Of these, 473, or 47.0 percent, had quarterly frequency or more. Almost every major magazine publisher announced new titles for the year.

Most new magazines catered to home-based interests such as crafts, hobbies and food, reflecting the nesting inclinations of the baby boom generation. *Cottage Living*, which doubled its rate base within six months of its introduction, and *Cargo*, Condé Nast's aforementioned shopping "magalog" for men, are notable examples. *Cargo* debuted in March 2004, and by September was guaranteeing a rate base of 350,000. Reader's Digest will introduce a food and lifestyle magazine, *Every Day with Rachael Ray*, in September 2005. Celebrity magazines make up an estimated 25 percent of newsstand sales, and the market for these magazines shows no signs of slowing down. After the successful launch of *Life & Style Weekly*, this year will see the launches of TV Guide spin-off *Inside TV*,

Consumer Magazine Publishing

Adult Population, by Age Group

Age Group	*Population (Thousands)* 1999	2004	2009	*Percent Change* 1999-2004	2004-2009
18-44	111,940	113,386	114,272	1.3%	0.8%
45+	95,154	106,992	118,977	12.4	11.2

Sources: Veronis Suhler Stevenson, PQ Media, U.S. Census Bureau

with a first-year budget of about $30 million, and American Media's *Celebrity Living*.

The pace of magazine launches in early 2005 indicated that the total number of new titles may exceed that of 2004. Time Inc., which introduced six magazines in 2004, is set to launch six more in 2005. Condé Nast extended its magalog concept to the home decorating field with the April 2005 launch of *Domino*.

Ironically, publishers of new magazines have overlooked a large and growing demographic group: older Americans. The number of adults aged 45 and older increased 12.4 percent from 1999 to 2004, and this population is projected to grow another 11.2 percent in the 2004-2009 period. In contrast, the number of adults aged 18 to 44 rose just 1.3 percent from 1999 to 2004, and will rise only a slim 0.8 percent over the next five years. Yet only a handful of major magazines, such as the two AARP titles and *More* from Meredith are written for the over-45 demographic.

Meanwhile, publishers continue to try to boost revenues derived from Internet operations. Magazine Web sites are currently used to bring in subscribers, offer free content and build relationships with subscribers. The prelaunch Web site for *Domino*, for example, asked visitors what they would like to see in the magazine. Many magazine sites, such as *Forbes.com*, sell advertising space on their pages.

The Internet accounts for an estimated 8 percent to 10 percent of new consumer magazine subscribers, but this percentage is leveling off. The next challenge for publishers is converting free Web content to paid. Visitors to the *Time* Web site who wish to read archived and selected new articles are given access to the articles only if they subscribe to the magazine. *Newsweek*, in contrast, offers all of its Web content free.

The Internet side of the consumer magazine business is still comparatively small. For example, *Business Week's* annual revenues from its Web site were estimated at between $10 million and $15 million in 2004. By comparison, its print advertising revenues in 2004 were estimated at $144.5 million. However, the profit margins from Web sites are better than those from print, due to lower costs, and the numbers are growing faster.

For now, publishers are preparing for higher expenses due to an almost-certain postal rate hike in 2006. Postage rates are expected to increase 5.4 percent across the board beginning in January 2006. While this increase is much lower than the 15 percent to 18 percent increase that was previously anticipated, it represents a substantial cost to the magazine industry. The MPA estimates that every percentage point increase in postal rates costs the industry an estimated $20 million. The U.S. Postal Service (USPS) has also stated that it will seek small price increases going forward every 12 to 18 months, and that another 4 to 5 percent hike may be imposed in mid-2007. Such frequent changes in postal pricing will mean that circulation directors will be under continuous pressure to find new approaches to reduce mailing and distribution costs. On the bright side, the USPS is seeking input from the magazine industry on cost-reduction measures, such as the elimination of mail sacks.

Consumer Magazine Advertising and Growth

Year	*Advertising ($ Millions)*	*Growth*
1999	$11,433	—
2000	12,370	8.2%
2001	11,095	−10.3
2002	10,995	−0.9
2003	11,435	4.0
2004	12,121	6.0
2005	12,788	5.5
2006	13,555	6.0
2007	14,409	6.3
2008	15,346	6.5
2009	16,374	6.7
Compound Annual Growth		
1999-2004		1.2
2004-2009		6.2

Sources: Veronis Suhler Stevenson, PQ Media, Veronis Suhler Stevenson Consumer Magazine Database, Universal McCann

ADVERTISING

After a precipitous 10.3 percent drop in 2001 and a 0.9 percent decline in 2002, consumer magazine advertising expenditures rebounded in 2003, posting a 4.0 percent gain. Spending growth accelerated in 2004, rising 6.0 percent to $12.12 billion, bolstered by gains in women's, business, news and regional titles. Spending in the retail, financial and travel categories surged at double-digit rates for the year, contributing to the overall gain.

Like several other traditional advertising segments, the consumer magazine sector rebounded from the 2001 recession at a slower pace than past recoveries due to several factors. Among these were the longer-than-expected caution in the marketplace, multiple worldwide events that negatively impacted the advertising market, the lack of a new ad-based media catalyst and the relatively long lead time between magazine advertising sales and publication. In contrast, spending on network television advertising—a strong competitor to magazine advertising in the national market—has been more resilient following the most recent recession. Spending on network television advertising declined 8.7 percent in 2001, but rebounded with a solid 5.2 percent increase in 2002, as magazine advertising dropped for the second consecutive year. In 2004, network TV ad expenditures outpaced consumer magazines again with a 9.1 percent gain.

In efforts to improve advertising spending, the MPA and individual publishers released various research studies in 2004 pointing to the effectiveness and value of magazines versus other media. One study found that magazine advertising delivered higher return on investment than did television, radio, outdoor and newspaper advertising to marketers in the financial services, personal care products and OTC/healthcare product fields. Another research company launched a new syndicated service that gives advertisers the ability to rank magazines based on their audiences' potential to buy certain product categories and brands. And a

Advertising Spending on Consumer Magazines and Network Television

	Advertising Spending ($ Millions)		*Growth of Advertising Spending*		
Year	*Consumer Magazine Advertising*	*Network Television Advertising*	*Consumer Magazine Advertising*	*Network Television Advertising*	*Percentage Point Difference*
1999	$11,433	$14,571	—	—	—
2000	12,370	16,614	8.2%	14.0%	–5.8
2001	11,095	15,163	–10.3	–8.7	–1.6
2002	10,995	15,959	-0.9	5.2	–6.1
2003	11,435	16,091	4.0	0.8	3.2
2004	12,121	17,563	6.0	9.1	–3.1
2005	12,788	17,967	5.5	2.3	3.2
2006	13,555	19,279	6.0	7.3	–1.3
2007	14,409	19,664	6.3	2.0	4.3
2008	15,346	21,414	6.5	8.9	–2.4
2009	16,374	21,799	6.7	1.8	4.9
Compound Annual Growth					
1999-2004			1.2	3.8	
2004-2009			6.2	4.4	

Sources: Veronis Suhler Stevenson, PQ Media, Veronis Suhler Stevenson Consumer Magazine Database, Universal McCann

Local and National Consumer Magazine Advertising

($ MILLIONS)

Year	Spot Print Market-Specific	Regional & Split-Run National Magazines	City & State Regional Magazines	Total Local Advertising	Total National Advertising	Total Consumer Magazine Advertising
1999	$ 86	$ 834	$ 855	$1,775	$ 9,658	$11,433
2000	95	858	887	1,840	10,530	12,370
2001	90	791	847	1,728	9,367	11,095
2002	95	834	877	1,806	9,189	10,995
2003	105	888	935	1,928	9,507	11,435
2004	116	959	1,030	2,105	10,016	12,121
2005	128	1,029	1,144	2,301	10,487	12,788
2006	139	1,102	1,240	2,481	11,074	13,555
2007	151	1,182	1,349	2,682	11,727	14,409
2008	165	1,272	1,473	2,910	12,436	15,346
2009	179	1,357	1,588	3,124	13,250	16,374

Sources: Veronis Suhler Stevenson, PQ Media, Universal McCann, TNS Media Intelligence/CMR, Media Networks

Growth of Local and National Consumer Magazine Advertising

Year	Spot Print Market-Specific	Regional & Split-Run National Magazines	City & State Regional Magazines	Total Local Advertising	Total National Advertising	Total Consumer Magazine Advertising
2000	10.0%	2.9%	3.7%	3.7%	9.0%	8.2%
2001	–5.2	–7.8	–4.5	–6.1	–11.0	–10.3
2002	6.0	5.4	3.5	4.5	–1.9	–0.9
2003	10.2	6.5	6.6	6.8	3.5	4.0
2004	11.1	7.9	10.2	9.2	5.4	6.0
2005	10.1	7.3	11.0	9.3	4.7	5.5
2006	8.7	7.1	8.4	7.8	5.6	6.0
2007	8.9	7.3	8.8	8.1	5.9	6.3
2008	9.3	7.6	9.2	8.5	6.0	6.5
2009	8.3	6.7	7.8	7.4	6.5	6.7
Compound Annual Growth						
1999-2004	6.2	2.8	3.8	3.5	0.7	1.2
2004-2009	9.0	7.2	9.0	8.2	5.8	6.2

Sources: Veronis Suhler Stevenson, PQ Media, Universal McCann, TNS Media Intelligence/CMR, Media Networks

Advertising in General- and Special-Interest Magazines

Year	Advertising Spending ($ Millions)			Percent Change			
	General-Interest Magazines	Special-Interest Magazines	Total Magazines	General-Interest Magazines	Special-Interest Magazines	Total Magazines	Nominal GDP Growth
1999	$8,060	$3,373	$11,433	—	—	—	—
2000	8,758	3,612	12,370	8.7%	7.1%	8.2%	5.9%
2001	7,744	3,351	11,095	−11.6	−7.2	−10.3	3.2
2002	7,653	3,342	10,995	−1.2	−0.3	−0.9	3.5
2003	7,936	3,499	11,435	3.7	4.7	4.0	4.9
2004	8,400	3,721	12,121	5.8	6.3	6.0	6.6
Compound Annual Growth							
1999-2004				0.8	2.0	1.2	4.8

Sources: Veronis Suhler Stevenson, PQ Media, Veronis Suhler Stevenson Consumer Magazine Database, Universal McCann

third report found that consumers labeled "influentials"—those who are twice as likely to be sought out for their opinions on goods and services—read 44.0 percent more magazine titles per month than did the general public.

The MPA's previously mentioned three-year, $40.0 million marketing campaign aimed at the advertising industry is another attempt to drive ad spending. As part of the campaign, about 30 MPA members will publish magazines with fictional covers bearing dates 100 years into the future. These issues will be delivered to advertiser and agency personnel who are on the magazines' "complimentary copy" lists. The campaign's objective is to convince advertisers and agencies that readers enjoy and value their magazines, feel engaged by them and will continue to do so in the future. By shifting advertisers' perceptions about magazines, the MPA hopes to ensure that marketers do not exclude magazines from their media buys, and hopefully will increase their use of the medium.

However, larger advertising trends are moving against the magazine industry. Since 1999, consumers have progressively reduced the time they spend with magazines while dramatically increasing their consumption of the Internet, videogames, DVDs, VHS and cable TV. Advertisers have reacted by increasing their expenditures on electronic media, as well as alternative marketing vehicles, often at the expense of traditional media. For example, total spending on product placement, particularly in television and films, grew at a compound annual rate of 16.3 percent from 1999 to 2004, according to PQ Media, while consumer magazine advertising expenditures grew only 1.2 percent on a compound annual basis in the same period.

The consumer magazine industry is responding aggressively to these trends by trying to prove that magazines can be an effective advertising medium, either by themselves or in combination with other media. While we expect the magazine industry's marketing and research initiatives to generate some positive "buzz" and perhaps help the medium defend its market share in the near future, the broader current of the communications industry is flowing against traditional media. As a result, we believe magazine ad spending will be hampered during the forecast period by the increased use of non-traditional media, with annual growth rates remaining within 0.5 of a percentage point of nominal GDP growth.

Looking for other means of increasing effectiveness for advertisers and generating additional revenues, some magazines have launched initiatives that are blurring the lines

Advertising in Major General-Interest Magazine Categories*

($ MILLIONS)

Category	2000	2001	2002	2003	2004
Women	$1,499	$1,484	$1,590	$1,767	$1,893
News	653	496	522	540	601
Business	915	578	529	484	547
General Editorial	580	509	523	516	527
Entertainment	444	377	371	393	419
Sports	369	314	365	374	406
Men	273	283	330	338	384
Regional	248	234	238	248	297
Lifestyle	124	118	137	152	184
Consumer	130	104	94	96	104
Top 10 Categories	5,235	4,497	4,699	4,908	5,362
Other	218	218	265	267	276
Total, Selected Magazines	5,453	4,715	4,964	5,175	5,638
Total, All General-Interest	8,758	7,744	7,653	7,936	8,400

Sources: Veronis Suhler Stevenson, PQ Media, Veronis Suhler Stevenson Consumer Magazine Database
*Reflects a sample of 111 general-interest magazines.

Growth in Major General-Interest Magazine Categories*

Category	2001	2002	2003	2004	Compound Annual Growth 2000-2004
Women	–1.0%	7.1%	11.1%	7.1%	6.0%
News	–24.0	5.2	3.4	11.3	–2.1
Business	–36.8	–8.5	–8.5	13.0	–12.1
General Editorial	–12.2	2.8	–1.3	2.1	–2.4
Entertainment	–15.1	–1.6	5.9	6.6	–1.4
Sports	–14.9	16.2	2.5	8.6	2.4
Men	3.7	16.6	2.4	13.6	8.9
Regional	–5.6	1.7	4.2	19.8	4.6
Lifestyle	–4.8	16.1	10.9	21.1	10.4
Consumer	–20.0	–9.6	2.1	8.3	–5.4
Top 10 Categories	–14.1	4.5	4.4	9.3	0.6
Other	0.0	21.6	0.8	3.4	6.1
Total, Selected Magazines	–13.5	5.3	4.3	8.9	0.8
Total, All General-Interest	–11.6	–1.2	3.7	5.8	–1.0

Sources: Veronis Suhler Stevenson, PQ Media, Veronis Suhler Stevenson Consumer Magazine Database
*Reflects a sample of 111 general-interest magazines.

Advertising in Major Special-Interest Magazine Categories*

($ MILLIONS)

Category	2000	2001	2002	2003	2004
Home	$ 418	$ 386	$ 450	$ 444	$ 457
Women	290	265	302	317	328
Health & Fitness	202	200	240	257	299
Sports	246	225	213	231	260
Automotive	203	184	202	219	251
Epicurean	123	120	132	152	170
Travel	111	103	101	118	133
Boating	92	88	87	92	128
Computers	164	123	105	104	101
Hunting	87	65	61	67	74
Top 10 Categories	1,936	1,759	1,893	2,001	2,201
Other	315	278	271	278	298
Total, Selected Magazines	2,251	2,037	2,164	2,279	2,499
Total, All Special-Interest	3,612	3,351	3,342	3,499	3,721

Sources: Veronis Suhler Stevenson, PQ Media, Veronis Suhler Stevenson Consumer Magazine Database
*Reflects a sample of 134 special-interest magazines.

between advertising and editorial. In some cases, certain titles are running ads that refer to stories in the same issue, and in others, magazines have taken a cautious step toward embracing product placement. For instance, a 2004 issue of *Country Living* carried an eight-page insert from Home Depot's EXPO Design Center facing a story about the benefits of EXPO Design Center's help in kitchen renovation. The June 2005 cover of *Marie Claire* featured pop singer Gwen Stefani wearing a T-shirt, along with information on how readers could buy that T-shirt. And *Modern Bride* made space on the spine of its June/July 2004 issue for a small ad from Target's bridal registry.

To better compete in today's fragmented media market, in which advertisers are increasingly turning to non-traditional marketing vehicles, magazines are extending their brands into such venues as business conferences, television, the Internet, content licensing, book spin-offs and custom publishing. For example, *Business Week* regularly holds "Small Business Breakfasts" in cities around the country. *Sports Illustrated* launched the *Swimsuit Model Search* reality television show on NBC in 2005. Meanwhile, custom publishing spending continues to rise, although growth figures, the size of the market and the definitions of what is included in custom publishing vary widely from source to source. It's safe to say, however, that custom publishing as part of the overall media market is a multibillion-dollar business with double-digit growth in recent years. A number of other magazines create Web site content that is not available in print, such as *Fortune's* various company lists that can be downloaded as spreadsheets.

In addition to brand extension opportunities, prospects for growth in the local market are strong. Local advertising is defined as advertising in local, state or regional publications, along with advertising in state, market, regional and split-run editions of national magazines. For advertisers that have geographically limited customer bases, such as banks,

Growth in Major Special-Interest Magazine Categories*

Category	*2001*	*2002*	*2003*	*2004*	*Compound Annual Growth 2000-2004*
Home	–7.7%	16.6%	–1.3%	2.9%	2.3%
Women	–8.6	14.0	5.0	3.5	3.1
Health & Fitness	–1.0	20.0	7.1	16.3	10.3
Sports	–8.5	–5.3	8.5	12.6	1.4
Automotive	–9.4	9.8	8.4	14.6	5.4
Epicurean	–2.4	10.0	15.2	11.8	8.4
Travel	–7.2	–1.9	16.8	12.7	4.6
Boating	–4.3	–1.1	5.7	39.1	8.6
Computers	–25.0	–14.6	–1.0	–2.9	–11.4
Hunting	–25.3	–6.2	9.8	10.4	–4.0
Top 10 Categories	–9.1	7.6	5.7	10.0	3.3
Other	–11.7	–2.5	2.6	7.2	–1.4
Total, Selected Magazines	–9.5	6.2	5.3	9.7	2.6
Total, All Special-Interest	–7.2	–0.3	4.7	6.3	0.7

Sources: Veronis Suhler Stevenson, PQ Media, Veronis Suhler Stevenson Consumer Magazine Database
*Reflects a sample of 134 special-interest magazines.

retailers and hospitals, local magazine advertising is a cost-effective and efficient means of targeting that customer base. In 2004, local magazine advertising climbed 9.2 percent to $2.11 billion, compared to 5.4 percent to $10.02 billion for national advertising.

Besides targeting readers geographically, advertisers have also demonstrated an interest in targeting consumers based on their specific interests. In the 1999-2004 period, advertising spending on special-interest publications increased at a compound annual rate of 2.0 percent compared with 0.8 percent for general-interest publications. In 2004 alone, spending on special-interest magazines rose 6.3 percent to $3.72 billion compared with a gain of 5.8 percent to $8.40 billion for general interest magazines.

Among general-interest magazines, women's titles generated $1.89 billion in advertising spending in 2004, an increase of 7.1 percent over 2003. Women's magazines garnered more dollars than the next three categories (news, business and general editorial) combined. Among the titles tracked, *Better Homes and Gardens* generated the most spending, eclipsing such mainstays as *Good Housekeeping, Cosmopolitan* and *Woman's Day*. Spending on news magazines increased 11.3 percent in 2004 to $601.0 million. *Time* had the highest ad spending at an estimated $277 million in 2004, a gain of 9.9 percent over the prior year. Business titles ranked third with a 13.0 percent increase to $547.0 million. Titles in this group include *Forbes, Fortune* and *Business Week*. The increase in advertising in this category is an outcome of the general improvement of the business climate.

Among special-interest magazines, publications in the home category generated the most revenues, rising 2.9 percent to $457.0 million in 2004. Magazines in this category include *Architectural Digest, Country Home* and *Country Living*. Many well-established titles, such as *Southern Accents* and *Metropolitan Home*, realized double-digit rev-

Consumer Magazine Advertising Spending, by Top 12 Categories

Category	*2003 ($ Millions)*	*2004 ($ Millions)*	*Percent Change 2003-2004*
Automotive	$ 890	$ 937	5.3%
Toiletries & Cosmetics	735	757	3.0
Apparel & Accessories	663	708	6.8
Drugs & Remedies	716	708	–1.1
Home Furnishings & Supplies	686	685	–0.1
Food & Food Products	586	622	6.1
Direct Response Companies	540	580	7.4
Media & Advertising	490	538	9.8
Retail	447	496	11.0
Technology	491	444	–9.6
Financial, Insurance & Real Estate	384	436	13.5
Public Transportation, Hotels & Resorts	321	368	14.6
Top 12 Total	6,949	7,279	4.7

Sources: Veronis Suhler Stevenson, PQ Media, Magazine Publishers of America, Publishers Information Bureau

Shares of Consumer Magazine Advertising Spending, by Top 12 Categories

Category	*2003*	*2004*
Automotive	12.8%	12.9%
Toiletries & Cosmetics	10.6	10.4
Apparel & Accessories	9.5	9.7
Drugs & Remedies	10.3	9.7
Home Furnishings & Supplies	9.9	9.4
Food & Food Products	8.4	8.5
Direct Response Companies	7.8	8.0
Media & Advertising	7.1	7.4
Retail	6.4	6.8
Technology	7.1	6.1
Financial, Insurance & Real Estate	5.5	6.0
Public Transportation, Hotels & Resorts	4.6	5.1

Sources: Veronis Suhler Stevenson, PQ Media, Magazine Publishers of America, Publishers Information Bureau

enue gains, although *Martha Stewart Living* reported a drop of 58.0 percent in 2004. With home sales and refinancings at historic highs, consumers have both the inclination and money to spend on renovating and decorating their homes. As an illustration of the continued bull market for home improvement, Home Depot's fiscal 2004 sales grew 12.8 percent, with the company projecting another 9 percent to 12 percent sales increase for fiscal 2005. Women's magazines, which include titles such as *Parenting*, *Parents* and *Bride's*, ranked second with ad revenues of $328.0 million in 2004, a gain of 3.5 percent. The health and fitness category was third at $298.0 million, an impressive 16.3 percent growth over 2003. Titles in this category include *Shape*, *Prevention* and *Men's Health*, and their popularity reflects the increasing health consciousness of Americans.

Spending in the 12 leading advertising categories increased 4.7 percent to $7.28 billion in 2004. Automotive remained the largest category, with $937.0 million in spending, up 5.3 percent. Toiletries and cosmetics ranked second, with spending totaling $757.0 million in 2004, up 3.0 percent. Apparel and accessories grew 6.8 percent to $708.0 million for the year. The drugs and remedies category dipped 1.1 percent, after posting the strongest gain in 2003. During 2004, several highly-publicized prescription drugs drew warnings from, or were banned by, the Food & Drug Administration. As a result, advertising in this category was severely curtailed. Public transportation, hotels and resorts posted the strongest gain, up 14.6 percent to $368.0 million. According to the Travel Industry Association of America, all travel industry sectors showed strong demand in 2004 and the number of people taking business and leisure trips has increased steadily since 2000. The only category with a major decline during the year was technology. Technology advertising has shrunk every year since 2001, with spending increasingly being diverted to the Internet.

Primarily as a result of slower economic growth and increased competition from electronic media, we project consumer magazine ad growth to decelerate in 2005 to 5.5 percent, with spending of $12.79 billion for the year. Magazine advertising growth is forecast to outpace nominal GDP growth in 2006 for the first time in six years, albeit by a slim margin. Going forward, we expect spending on consumer magazine advertising to grow at an accelerated rate in the 2004-2009 period, compared with the previous five-year timeframe, but growth will be relatively even with that of the broader economy. Magazine ad expenditures will grow at a compound annual rate of 6.2 percent from 2004 to 2009, surpassing the 1.2 percent increase in the 1999-2004 period, but comparatively even with the 6.1 percent advance in GDP.

CIRCULATION

Circulation managers also had a recovery story to tell at the end of 2004. Total per-issue unit circulation grew 3.0 percent to 363.1 million for the year, reversing three straight years of declines. Among magazines measured by the Audit Bureau of Circulation (ABC), the average unit circulation per title rose 2.1 percent to 626,096. Overall growth was driven by increases in both single-copy and subscription unit circulation. Single copies rose 1.0 percent to 51.3 million, while subscription units grew

Per-Issue Unit Circulation Of Consumer Magazines

Year	*Single-Copy (Millions)*	*Subscription (Millions)*	*Total (Millions)*	*Magazines Per Adult*
1999	62.0	310.1	372.1	1.80
2000	60.2	318.7	378.9	1.81
2001	56.1	305.3	361.4	1.70
2002	52.9	305.4	358.3	1.67
2003	50.8	301.8	352.6	1.62
2004	51.3	311.8	363.1	1.65
2005	52.0	316.5	368.5	1.65
2006	52.9	312.1	365.0	1.62
2007	53.6	315.2	368.8	1.62
2008	54.3	318.0	372.3	1.61
2009	54.8	320.2	375.0	1.61

Sources: Veronis Suhler Stevenson, PQ Media, Magazine Publishers of America, Audit Bureau of Circulations, U.S. Census Bureau

Growth of per-Issue Unit Circulation Of Consumer Magazines

Year	*Single-Copy*	*Subscription*	*Total*
2000	–2.9%	2.8%	1.8%
2001	–6.8	–4.2	–4.6
2002	–5.7	0.0	–0.9
2003	–4.0	–1.2	–1.6
2004	1.0	3.3	3.0
2005	1.3	1.5	1.5
2006	1.7	–1.4	–0.9
2007	1.4	1.0	1.0
2008	1.3	0.9	0.9
2009	1.0	0.7	0.7
Compound Annual Change			
1999-2004	–3.7	0.1	–0.5
2004-2009	1.3	0.5	0.6

Sources: Veronis Suhler Stevenson, PQ Media, Magazine Publishers of America, Audit Bureau of Circulations

Shares of Consumer Magazine Per-Issue Unit Circulation

Year	Single-Copy	Subscription
1999	16.7%	83.3%
2000	15.9	84.1
2001	15.5	84.5
2002	14.8	85.2
2003	14.4	85.6
2004	14.1	85.9
2005	14.1	85.9
2006	14.5	85.5
2007	14.5	85.5
2008	14.6	85.4
2009	14.6	85.4

Sources: Veronis Suhler Stevenson, PQ Media, Magazine Publishers of America, Audit Bureau of Circulations

Average Single-Copy And Annual Subscription Prices

Year	Single-Copy	Subscription
1999	$2.71	$22.18
2000	2.79	21.70
2001	2.98	22.67
2002	3.13	23.14
2003	3.26	23.23
2004	3.36	23.06

Sources: Veronis Suhler Stevenson, PQ Media, Magazine Publishers of America, Audit Bureau of Circulations

Consumer Magazine Publishing

Growth of Average Single-Copy And Annual Subscription Prices

Year	Single-Copy	Subscription
2000	3.0%	–2.2%
2001	6.8	4.5
2002	5.0	2.1
2003	4.2	0.4
2004	3.1	–0.7
Compound Annual Growth		
1999-2004	4.4	0.8

Sources: Veronis Suhler Stevenson, PQ Media, Magazine Publishers of America, Audit Bureau of Circulations

3.3 percent to 311.8 million. The growth in single-copy units was a welcome development, as it possibly signaled the end of a long downward trend. The top 100 magazines have reportedly lost more than one-third of their newsstand circulation over the last 10 years.

Magazines focusing on celebrities, lifestyle and health generally reported larger circulation gains than magazines in other categories. Among ABC-measured titles, *AARP The Magazine* had the highest circulation gain, rising 7.8 percent, or 1.6 million copies, from 2003 to 2004. Its sister publication, the monthly *AARP Bulletin*, was close behind with an increase of 481,526 copies in 2004. Other magazines with substantial circulation hikes were *Game Informer*, *In Touch*, and *Everyday Food*. These magazines grew 40.1 percent, 80.0 percent (almost entirely on newsstands) and 71.3 percent, respectively.

A number of successful new launches, which relied wholly or predominantly on newsstand distribution, helped boost single-copy sales in 2004. Time Inc.'s *All You* and Hachette's *For Me*, both introduced in 2004, are sold only on newsstands. *All You* has a rate base of 500,000, and *For Me* had an initial distribution of 480,000. Bauer Publishing USA, a unit of Germany-based H. Bauer Publishing, launched *Life & Style Weekly* in 2004 with a rate base of 350,000. In 2005, Condé Nast debuted *Domino*, a home decorating-shopping title with a rate base of 400,000, of which 150,000 will be sold via newsstands.

Although publishers have been raising single-copy cover prices steadily since 1999, the average increase in 2004 was lower than in past years. Also, in previous years single-copy spending declined despite cover price hikes. But in 2004, the average single-copy cover price rose only 3.1 percent to $3.36, and single-copy circulation spending increased 3.9 percent to $3.14 billion. Average subscription prices grew between 2001 and 2003, but at decelerating rates. In 2004, subscription prices fell 0.7 percent to $23.06, as publishers attempted to regain lost circulation by lowering prices. As a result, subscription spending grew 2.6 percent to $7.19 billion. Consumers who buy magazines at newsstands appear to be more willing to accept price increases, according to recent research, which

Average Price per Copy, Average Issue Circulation and Circulation Spending Of General- and Special-Interest Magazines*

	Average Price Per Copy		*Average Issue Circulation (Millions)*		*Circulation Spending ($ Millions)*	
Year	*General-Interest Magazines*	*Special-Interest Magazines*	*General-Interest Magazines*	*Special-Interest Magazines*	*General-Interest Magazines*	*Special-Interest Magazines*
1999	$1.38	$1.79	242.2	129.9	$7,373	$2,564
2000	1.37	1.76	246.7	132.2	7,411	2,564
2001	1.43	1.85	235.2	126.1	7,395	2,571
2002	1.46	1.87	233.7	124.7	7,509	2,570
2003	1.47	1.91	229.5	123.1	7,445	2,589
2004	1.47	1.93	237.1	126.0	7,655	2,676

Sources: Veronis Suhler Stevenson, PQ Media, Veronis Suhler Stevenson Consumer Magazine Database, Audit Bureau of Circulations
*Based on a sample of 111 general-interest magazines and 134 special-interest magazines.

Growth of Average Price per Copy, Average Issue Circulation and Circulation Spending Of General- and Special-Interest Magazines*

	Average Price Per Copy		*Average Issue Circulation*		*Circulation Spending*	
Year	*General-Interest Magazines*	*Special-Interest Magazines*	*General-Interest Magazines*	*Special-Interest Magazines*	*General-Interest Magazines*	*Special-Interest Magazines*
2000	–0.7%	–1.7%	1.9%	1.8%	0.5%	0.0%
2001	4.4	5.1	–4.7	–4.6	–0.2	0.3
2002	2.1	1.1	–0.6	–1.1	1.5	0.0
2003	0.7	2.1	–1.8	–1.3	–0.9	0.7
2004	0.0	1.0	3.3	2.4	2.8	3.4
Compound Annual Growth						
1999-2004	1.3	1.5	–0.4	–0.6	0.8	0.9

Sources: Veronis Suhler Stevenson, PQ Media, Veronis Suhler Stevenson Consumer Magazine Database, Audit Bureau of Circulations
*Based on a sample of 111 general-interest magazines and 134 special-interest magazines.

showed that newsstand readers are younger, more interested in ads and are twice as likely to be employed compared with subscribers.

Subscriptions made up the larger share of per-issue unit circulation, accounting for 85.9 percent of the total. We expect subscriptions' share to decline during the forecast period, reaching 85.4 percent by 2009. The share of single copies is expected to increase as publishers continue to improve distribution strategies and tactics. For example, research shows that shoppers are making more trips to dollar stores, supercenters and warehouse clubs, while reducing the number of trips to grocery stores. Accordingly, 6,000 to 7,000 dollar stores are testing magazine sales programs. Sam's and Costco warehouse stores are testing certain magazine sales, while BJ's Wholesale has been selling single copies for years. Bookstores and specialty retailers are

Consumer Magazine Circulation: Price, Volume and Spending

Year	*Price Per Copy*	*Unit Circulation (Millions)*	*Circulation Spending ($ Millions)*
1999	$1.47	372.1	$ 9,936
2000	1.45	378.9	9,975
2001	1.52	361.4	9,966
2002	1.55	358.3	10,079
2003	1.56	352.6	10,033
2004	1.56	363.1	10,331
2005	1.59	368.5	10,654
2006	1.61	365.0	10,726
2007	1.65	368.8	11,053
2008	1.67	372.3	11,341
2009	1.69	375.0	11,562

Sources: Veronis Suhler Stevenson, PQ Media, Magazine Publishers of America, Audit Bureau of Circulations

Growth of Consumer Magazine Circulation: Price, Volume and Spending

Year	*Price Per Copy*	*Unit Circulation*	*Circulation Spending*
2000	–1.4%	1.8%	0.4%
2001	4.8	–4.6	–0.1
2002	2.0	–0.9	1.1
2003	0.6	–1.6	–0.5
2004	0.0	3.0	3.0
2005	1.9	1.5	3.1
2006	1.3	–0.9	0.7
2007	2.5	1.0	3.0
2008	1.2	0.9	2.6
2009	1.2	0.7	1.9
Compound Annual Growth			
1999-2004	1.2	–0.5	0.8
2004-2009	1.6	0.6	2.3

Sources: Veronis Suhler Stevenson, PQ Media, Magazine Publishers of America, Audit Bureau of Circulations

additional promising outlets for magazines, as such stores understand their customers and are experts at merchandising printed matter. Barnes & Noble, for example, receives 6 percent to 7 percent of its revenues from magazine sales. And the world's largest bookseller, Amazon.com, announced it would launch an enhanced magazine subscription service by the end of 2005.

Magazine publishers are also improving the way they manage subscription acquisitions and renewals. More publishers are implementing direct-to-publisher circulation models, reducing their reliance on subscription agencies and thereby gaining better quality subscribers and prospect lists. Magazines are increasing their reliance on multi-year subscriptions and automatic renewals, which lower costs and reduce subscriber churn. To improve results, publishers have also been investing in technology for direct mail efforts. Over the past three years, for instance, Meredith has invested about $10 million in consumer database technology.

In addition, publishers are exerting more control over circulation because of the intensified scrutiny that advertisers and auditors are placing on subscription numbers. While the industry would like to put news of circulation irregularities behind it, issues continue to arise. As recently as January 2005, Gruner + Jahr announced that it had overreported circulation for several titles because of errors by third-party subscription agents.

Per-issue unit circulation declined 0.5 percent on a compound annual basis from 1999 to 2004, due largely to falling sales from 2001 to 2003. Circulation spending, however, advanced at a compound annual rate of 0.8 percent during the same period, driven by a 3.0 percent gain in 2004. Of note is that while single copies made up 14.1 percent of total circulation units, they accounted for 30.4 percent of total circulation spending, indicating that they are more than twice as efficient at delivering revenues as subscription copies.

General-interest titles have higher total circulation than special-interest titles, but publishers are able to charge more for special-interest titles because they are aimed at enthusiasts. For example, among women's magazines, *Ladies' Home Journal*, a general-interest title, has a cover price of $2.49, while the cover price of *Parenting*, a special-interest title, is $3.50. In 2004, special-interest magazines charged an average price per copy of $1.93 compared to the $1.47 average price for general-interest magazines, a 31.3 percent difference. Average issue circulation of special-interest magazines grew 2.4 percent in 2004, while that of general-interest magazines grew slightly faster, at 3.3 percent. As general-interest magazines generate higher circulation spending than special-interest magazines, they have more funds available to invest in building circulation.

Subscription unit circulation is expected to grow 1.5 percent to 316.5 million in 2005, followed by a dip in 2006 when postal rates increase, causing a tightening in subscriptions as publishers cut back on direct mail. Improvements in database technology and cost management, along with savings from postal reforms, such as the eventual elimination of mail sacks, will help drive subscription growth up 1.0 percent in 2007. Compound annual growth over the forecast period will be 0.5 percent. Single-copy unit circulation will increase 1.3 percent to 52.0 million in 2005, due to a renewed interest in newsstand sales, more retail outlets and better merchandising of the product via end caps and other special display units. Over the forecast period, single-copy circulation will grow 1.3 percent compounded annually, compared to a 3.7 percent decline from 1999 to 2004. Single-copy circulation will be 54.8 million in 2009. Overall per-issue unit circulation will increase 1.5 percent to 368.5 million in 2005. In the 2004-2009 period, circulation will grow at a compound annual rate of 0.6 percent.

The average price per copy remained flat during 2004. With general economic conditions improving, we expect that more publishers will raise prices, anticipating that consumers will absorb the hikes and increase spending. Prices will rise at a 1.6 percent compound annual rate from 2004 to 2009. Total circulation spending, driven by increases in both unit price and circulation volume, will rise 3.1 percent in 2005 to $10.65 billion. Spending will grow at a compound annual rate of 2.3 percent from 2004 to 2009, reaching $11.56 billion in 2009.

Spending on Consumer Magazines ($ MILLIONS)

Year	*Advertising*	*Circulation*	*Total*
1999	$11,433	$ 9,936	$21,369
2000	12,370	9,975	22,345
2001	11,095	9,966	21,061
2002	10,995	10,079	21,074
2003	11,435	10,033	21,468
2004	12,121	10,331	22,452
2005	12,788	10,654	23,442
2006	13,555	10,726	24,281
2007	14,409	11,053	25,462
2008	15,346	11,341	26,687
2009	16,374	11,562	27,936

Sources: Veronis Suhler Stevenson, PQ Media, Veronis Suhler Stevenson Consumer Magazine Database, Universal McCann, Magazine Publishers of America, Audit Bureau of Circulations

Growth of Spending on Consumer Magazines

Year	*Advertising*	*Circulation*	*Total*
2000	8.2%	0.4%	4.6%
2001	–10.3	–0.1	–5.7
2002	–0.9	1.1	0.1
2003	4.0	–0.5	1.9
2004	6.0	3.0	4.6
2005	5.5	3.1	4.4
2006	6.0	0.7	3.6
2007	6.3	3.0	4.9
2008	6.5	2.6	4.8
2009	6.7	1.9	4.7
Compound Annual Growth			
1999-2004	1.2	0.8	1.0
2004-2009	6.2	2.3	4.5

Sources: Veronis Suhler Stevenson, PQ Media, Veronis Suhler Stevenson Consumer Magazine Database, Universal McCann, Magazine Publishers of America, Audit Bureau of Circulations

Shares of Spending on Consumer Magazines

Year	*Advertising*	*Circulation*
1999	53.5%	46.5%
2000	55.4	44.6
2001	52.7	47.3
2002	52.2	47.8
2003	53.3	46.7
2004	54.0	46.0
2005	54.6	45.4
2006	55.8	44.2
2007	56.6	43.4
2008	57.5	42.5
2009	58.6	41.4

Sources: Veronis Suhler Stevenson, PQ Media, Veronis Suhler Stevenson Consumer Magazine Database, Universal McCann, Magazine Publishers of America, Audit Bureau of Circulations

The Outlook For Consumer Magazines

As non-traditional media invade advertisers' budgets and consumers' leisure time, magazines will fight back on several fronts. To increase ad spending, the industry will aggressively market itself to advertisers and try to raise the market share of magazines in general. To make the circulation turnaround stick, publishers will continue to hone their subscription and newsstand strategies, and look for unconventional venues in which to reach buyers. Finally, to improve consumer targeting, magazine executives will seek new demographic and editorial niches, to create magazines that resonate with, and provide value to, their readers.

Along with these three drivers, the strength of the economy will play a role in the industry's performance. With the economy cooling somewhat in 2005, total spending on consumer magazines is expected to increase 4.4 percent to $23.44 billion, slightly less than the 2004 pace of 4.6 percent. Advertising expenditures will grow 5.5 percent to $12.79 billion, fueled by a resurgence in the food, finance, media, direct response and automotive categories. Circulation spending will grow at a slower rate in 2005, increasing 3.1 percent to $10.65 billion.

Over the forecast period, we expect magazine advertising spending to come under further pressure from newer media. As a result, compound annual growth will be 6.2 percent from 2004 to 2009, barely higher than the 6.1 percent rate for nominal GDP. Advertising expenditures will reach $16.37 billion in 2009. Circulation spending over the forecast period will be slowed by a contraction in 2006. As a result, the compound annual growth rate will be 2.3 percent. Total consumer magazine expenditures are projected to increase at a compound annual rate of 4.5 percent from 2004 to 2009, reaching $27.94 billon in 2009.

FORECAST ASSUMPTIONS

- Consumer magazines, as well as other traditional ad-based media, will be increasingly challenged in the forecast period to prove their return on investment (ROI) to major advertisers. As a result, we believe some marketers, skeptical of their ROI in traditional media, will progressively shift more ad dollars out of print media, such as consumer magazines, and into electronic media and alternative marketing methods. This will temper spending growth in consumer magazine advertising, which will grow more in line with that of nominal GDP over the next five years, instead of exceeding economic growth by 2 to 3 percentage points as in previous expansion periods.
- The consumer magazine industry, led by its major trade organization, will combat this challenge by aggressively promoting the effectiveness of the medium to advertisers through various marketing and research programs highlighting consumer engagement with magazines, which has created a strong bond between readers and the medium.
- Magazine publishers plan to capitalize on the circulation recovery in 2004 by improving subscription and single-copy sales strategies, and by developing magazines that cater to emerging niche audiences. Subscriptions and single-copy sales will continue to grow throughout the forecast period, although at levels below the rate of advertising spending.
- The average price per magazine will continue to rise from 2005 to 2009, as publishers seek to push through price increases to drive spending. This strategy will, to some extent, help the industry maintain circulation spending growth.

2004 Communications Industry Forecast Compared with Actual Growth

Category	*2004 Forecasted Growth**	*Actual 2004 Growth†*
Advertising	4.3%	6.0%
Circulation Spending	0.4	3.0
Total	2.5	4.6

*Veronis Suhler Stevenson 2004 Communications Industry Forecast & Report
†Veronis Suhler Stevenson, PQ Media

Consumer Magazine Publishing

hanley wood

Business Overview

Hanley Wood, L.L.C. is the leading business media company serving the building and construction industry. The Company's market-leading products and diverse media channels target customers in-print, in-person and interactively.

Background

VSS's Fund III, together with management and co-investors, provided $150 million in equity to acquire HanleyWood, Inc. for approximately $260 million on September 15, 1999. The balance of the purchase price was provided by a $130 million senior credit facility.

Strategy & Rationale

- VSS was attracted to the Company's served market dominance, profitability as evidenced through both high EBITDA margins and superior free cash flow conversion, and experienced management team.
- Together, these attributes created an ideal "platform" company to pursue new product launches and add-on acquisitions.
- Market opportunities to aggressively pursue add-on acquisitions that complement existing products and produce cross-marketing opportunities in privately negotiated sales.

Add-on Acquisition Activities

During the six years of VSS ownership, Hanley Wood completed 23 add-on acquisitions and investments including the following:

- January 2000—Acquired the **Surfaces Show**, the leading trade show serving the floor covering industry.
- October 2000—Acquired the **Journal of Light Construction** and the **JLC Live!** trade shows.
- March 2001—Acquired **Pool & Spa Expo**, the leading trade show serving the pool & spa industry.
- June 2001—Acquired **Pool & Spa News** and **Aquatics International**, the leading business magazines serving the pool & spa industry.
- November 2001—Entered into an agreement to manage the **Remodelers' Show** for the **National Association of Home Builders**.
- August 2002—Acquired **Multifamily Executive Magazine and Conference**, the leading magazine and conference for the apartment market.
- November 2002—Acquired **AEC Systems**, a tradeshow serving the commercial architectural market.
- April 2003:
  - Acquired **Public Works** magazine, the leading business magazine for the public works sector of commercial construction.
  - Acquired the **Luxury Kitchen & Bath Collection** trade shows.
- December 2003—Acquired **Dream Home Source, Inc** one of the leading Internet-based providers of home plans.
- May 2004—Acquired the **National Roofing Contractors'** annual trade show, North America's largest roofing exhibition.
- June 2004—Acquired the **Meyers Group**, the housing industry's leading provider of residential real estate data and consulting services.

Exit

On May 26, 2005, VSS announced that it had entered into a definitive agreement to sell Hanley Wood to an investment group led by JPMorgan Partners. This resulted in a 2.2x return of capital and a 16% IRR.

12

Business-to-Business Media

Business-to-Business Magazines, page 446

Trade Shows and Exhibitions, page 462

Business-to-Business Media Spending And Nominal GDP Growth, 2000-2009

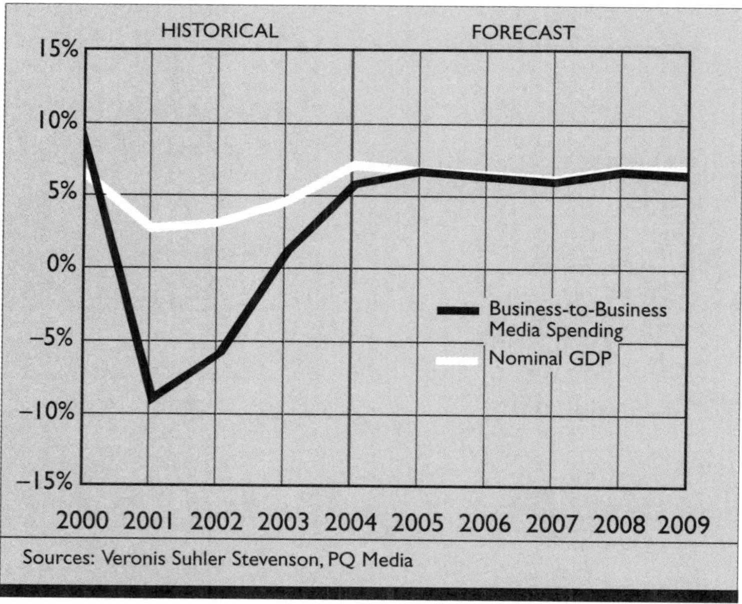

Sources: Veronis Suhler Stevenson, PQ Media

Summary

Total business-to-business media spending, including expenditures on magazines, electronic media and trade shows, grew at an accelerated rate for the third consecutive year in 2004, as spending in all three market subsegments increased. Overall b-to-b media expenditures climbed 5.2 percent to $20.91 billion in 2004, driven by surging e-media spending—the smallest subsegment—which grew 25.9 percent to $1.47 billion, and trade show expenditures, which escalated 5.8 percent to $9.15 billion for the year. Solid growth in these two subsegments, however, was tempered by only a 2.2 percent expansion in the largest subsegment—b-to-b magazine spending, including expenditures on advertising and circulation—which combined to produce spending of $10.29 billion in 2004.

Spending on b-to-b magazine advertising, which was the hardest hit media sector during the 2001 recession, continued to rebound in 2004, posting growth of 3.4 percent to $8.37 billion, the sector's first positive growth in four years and its fastest expansion since 2000. Circulation spending, however, declined 2.9 percent for the year, with some solace taken in the fact that this represented a decelerated decline from the 2003 downturn.

Total business-to-business media spending was essentially flat on a compound annual basis from 1999 to 2004, as this segment took a frightening blow from the economic recession in 2001, declined for the second consecutive year in 2002 and posted relatively meager growth in 2003, mostly due to two straight years of double-digit declines in magazine advertising in 2001 and 2002. Similar to past recessions, marketers cut magazine advertising budgets as profits began to fall and waited more than a year to ensure profits returned before spending on b-to-b magazine advertising. By comparison, nominal GDP grew at a compound annual rate of 4.8 percent in the 1999-2004 period, while total advertising market spending increased 3.0 percent in the period.

Overall spending generated by b-to-b magazine advertising in 2004 was the highest total in three years. Growth was fueled primarily by solid expansion in five of Veronis Suhler Stevenson's (VSS) 15 leading ad categories. Among these key categories was the second-largest, business and financial, which grew 5.9 percent in 2004, in addition to an 8.0 percent increase in the health and life sciences category, a 7.5 percent rise in retail advertising, an 8.7 percent climb in architecture and construction, and a 19.8 percent surge in automotive advertising for the year. Of the 15 top categories, only four reported spending declines in 2004. Despite the increase in 2004, b-to-b ad spending declined at a compound annual rate of 3.9 percent from 1999 to 2004, driven down by the double-digit contractions in 2001 and 2002.

Circulation expenditures dropped 2.9 percent for the year to $1.92 billion, as paid unit circulation decreased in all but three of VSS's 15 leading categories. Titles in the business, banking, insurance, financial and legal category posted the largest decline in unit circulation in 2004, down 6.9 percent, followed by the retail segment, down 5.8 percent. Paid unit circulation slipped 0.5 percent on a compound annual basis from 1999 to 2004, leading to a 1.2 percent compound annual decline for spending in the period. Overall spending on business-to-business magazines, including advertising and circulation, grew 2.2 percent to $10.29 billion in 2004, but declined 3.4 percent on a compound annual basis from 1999 to 2004.

It is important to note here that this year, VSS changed our methodology that we use to size, structure and forecast the business-to-business media market, in order to provide a more accurate picture of this media segment. As part of this change in methodology, we are using a new primary source for historical b-to-b magazine advertising data, which served as the basis for a proprietary regression analysis used to develop the 1999-2004 spending and growth figures. VSS also developed a proprietary forecast analysis to create the spending and growth figures for the 2004-2009 timeframe. In addition, VSS, in collaboration with PQ Media, developed a proprietary methodology to determine what we believe are the first ever spending and growth figures for business-to-business electronic media, or e-media. VSS defines this subsegment as online spending generated by b-to-b media companies through advertising, including online search and recruitment sites; via subscriptions to online content, such as Webzines; and through digital data services and directories. E-media spending was by far the fastest-growing subsegment of the b-to-b media sector in the 1999-2004 period, a trend we expect to continue in the forecast period.

E-media expenditures raced up 25.9 percent in 2004 to $1.47 billion, and grew at a compound annual rate of 40.0 percent from 1999 to 2004. Growth was spurred by a surfeit of new online advertising and content initiatives launched by b-to-b publishers, such as Reed Elsevier and Hanley-Wood, over the past five years, as they scrambled to provide end users with comprehensive electronic

Growth of U.S. Spending On Business-to-Business Media

	Business-to-Business Magazines	*E-media*	*Trade Shows And Exhibitions*	*Total*
2004 Expenditures ($ Millions)	$10,290	$1,472	$9,149	$20,911
1999-2004 Compound Annual Growth	–3.4%	40.0%	1.4%	–0.1%
2004-2009 Projected Compound Annual Growth	3.3%	18.7%	5.8%	5.8%
2009 Projected Expenditures ($ Millions)	$12,117	$3,466	$12,101	$27,684

Sources: Veronis Suhler Stevenson, PQ Media, IMS/The Auditor, AdScope, Agricom, American Business Media, BPA International, Center for Exhibition Research, PERQ, SRDS, TNS Media Intelligence/CMR, *Tradeshow Week*

Business-to-Business Media Spending

($ MILLIONS)

Year	Business-to-Business Magazines	E–media	Trade Shows And Exhibitions	Total
1999	$12,251	$ 274	$ 8,538	$21,063
2000	13,338	544	8,908	22,790
2001	11,465	724	8,621	20,810
2002	10,165	913	8,521	19,599
2003	10,068	1,169	8,649	19,886
2004	10,290	1,472	9,149	20,911
2005	10,571	1,862	9,710	22,143
2006	10,897	2,274	10,240	23,411
2007	11,269	2,667	10,792	24,728
2008	11,670	3,089	11,417	26,176
2009	12,117	3,466	12,101	27,684

Sources: Veronis Suhler Stevenson, PQ Media, IMS/The Auditor, AdScope, Agricom, American Business Media, BPA International, Center for Exhibition Research, PERQ, SRDS, TNS Media Intelligence/CMR, *Tradeshow Week*

Growth of Business-to-Business Media Spending

Year	Business-to-Business Magazines	E-media	Trade Shows And Exhibitions	Total
2000	8.9%	98.5%	4.3%	8.2%
2001	–14.0	33.1	–3.2	–8.7
2002	–11.3	26.1	–1.2	–5.8
2003	–0.9	28.0	1.5	1.5
2004	2.2	25.9	5.8	5.2
2005	2.7	26.5	6.1	5.9
2006	3.1	22.1	5.5	5.7
2007	3.4	17.3	5.4	5.6
2008	3.6	15.8	5.8	5.9
2009	3.8	12.2	6.0	5.8
Compound Annual Growth				
1999-2004	–3.4	40.0	1.4	–0.1
2004-2009	3.3	18.7	5.8	5.8

Sources: Veronis Suhler Stevenson, PQ Media, IMS/The Auditor, AdScope, Agricom, American Business Media, BPA International, Center for Exhibition Research, PERQ, SRDS, TNS Media Intelligence/CMR, *Tradeshow Week*

alternatives to help them do their jobs more efficiently. Also contributing to this growth were technological developments at pure-play e-media companies like CNET Networks, which have helped shape the evolution of the online advertising market. While the majority of spending during the early stages of the migration to e-media involved advertising, additional tools have been added in more recent years as leading b-to-b media companies steadily transform their businesses from simply magazine publishers to multimedia business information providers. Looking to take advantage of broader economic trends toward corporations demanding effective electronic workflow tools to make their operations more efficient and profitable, b-to-b media firms have gradually rolled out online search and recruitment services, as well as digital content and other data services. As a result, e-media spending grew to account for 7.0 percent of all b-to-b media spending at the conclusion of 2004. We expect e-media to continue to be the fastest-growing subsegment in 2005 and throughout the forecast period, as b-to-b media companies continually attempt to add search capabilities and other tools to aid in the measurement of return on investment (ROI) as it pertains to online advertising. The more often e-media provides better ROI data results than print, the more advertising dollars will migrate from print to online b-to-b services, as ROI measurement has become critical for companies to compete in this evolving market. E-media's primary impact on the size and structure of the b-to-b media market will be on print magazine advertising and circulation expenditures. Similar to the trends in other traditional ad-based media segments, we anticipate that the increased use of e-media advertising and content will siphon dollars away from print products at an accelerating rate over the next five years. However, in contrast to some other ad-based segments, this will prove to be a positive trend for b-to-b media companies, as they progressively acclimate to their evolving role as multimedia information providers.

Meanwhile, on the trade show front, spending growth outpaced that of b-to-b magazines in 2004 and in the 1999-2004 period by several percentage points, fueled by the expansion in corporate travel budgets and the availability of low-cost airlines that don't charge additional fees for last-minute bookings. As travel budgets and overall business information budgets increased over the past two years, trade show organizers have been able to amplify vendor-related costs without much backlash. Trade show spending grew 5.8 percent to $9.15 billion for the year, as exhibit space spending rose 5.6 percent to $7.11 billion, driven by price hikes among leading shows. Expanded travel budgets allowed companies to send additional executives to shows in 2004, leading to a 2.7 percent increase in professional attendance that propelled a 6.5 percent gain in spending on fees and sponsorships to $2.04 billion. Spending on trade shows increased at a compound annual rate of 1.4 percent from 1999 to 2004.

Going forward, we expect the growth of the overall business-to-business media segment to accelerate in 2005, fueled by solid gains in the trade show subsegment and a double-digit increase in e-media spending. Growth in business-to-business magazine expenditures will be modest, as falling circulation spending offsets gains in advertising spending. Total b-to-b media spending growth is expected to match GDP expansion in 2005 for the first time since 2000.

In the business-to-business magazine market, increased advertising in healthcare, banking, automotive and construction publications is expected to drive an overall spending gain of 2.7 percent in 2005 to $10.57 billion. We expect business-to-business magazine advertising to increase 3.8 percent to $8.70 billion in 2005, driven partially by increased advertising expenditures in automotive titles, as manufacturers promote overstocks to the fleet and trucking industries. Through the first quarter of 2005, concern that higher interest rates would drive down spending in the housing market was unproven, and the strength of this market will actually drive spending gains in the architecture, engineering and construction segments, as well as in the home design and furnishings category. Healthcare will continue to post strong gains in 2005 due to

Shares of Business-to-Business Media Spending

Year	*Business-to-Business Magazines*	*E-media*	*Trade Shows And Exhibitions*
1999	58.2%	1.3%	40.5%
2000	58.5	2.4	39.1
2001	55.1	3.5	41.4
2002	51.9	4.7	43.5
2003	50.6	5.9	43.5
2004	49.2	7.0	43.8
2005	47.7	8.4	43.9
2006	46.5	9.7	43.7
2007	45.6	10.8	43.6
2008	44.6	11.8	43.6
2009	43.8	12.5	43.7

Sources: Veronis Suhler Stevenson, PQ Media, IMS/The Auditor, AdScope, Agricom, American Business Media, BPA International, Center for Exhibition Research, PERQ, SRDS, TNS Media Intelligence/CMR, *Tradeshow Week*

Comparative Growth Rates: Corporate Profits And Business-to-Business Magazine Advertising

Year	*Corporate Profit*	*Business-to-Business Magazine Advertising*
2000	−3.9%	8.8%
2001	−6.2	−15.8
2002	14.0	−13.3
2003	16.8	−0.2
2004	15.7	3.4

Sources: Veronis Suhler Stevenson, PQ Media, IMS/The Auditor, AdScope, Agricom, PERQ, TNS Media Intelligence/CMR, U.S. Department of Commerce

2004 Communications Industry Forecast Compared with Actual Growth

Category	*2004 Forecasted Growth**	*Actual 2004 Growth†*
Business-to-Business Magazines	1.3%	2.2%
Advertising	1.8	3.4
Circulation Spending	–1.2	–2.9
E-media	—	25.9
Trade Shows	2.4	5.8
Total	1.7	5.2

*Veronis Suhler Stevenson 2004 Communications Industry Forecast & Report
†Sources: Veronis Suhler Stevenson, PQ Media

Business-to-Business E-media Spending and Growth

Year	*E-media Spending ($ Millions)*	*Percent Change*
1999	$ 274	—
2000	544	98.5%
2001	724	33.1
2002	913	26.1
2003	1,169	28.0
2004	1,472	25.9
2005	1,862	26.5
2006	2,274	22.1
2007	2,667	17.3
2008	3,089	15.8
2009	3,466	12.2
Compound Annual Growth		
1999-2004		40.0
2004-2009		18.7

Source: Veronis Suhler Stevenson, PQ Media

advertising to promote new medical technology and new trade shows launched by healthcare-related associations. Spending by pharmaceutical companies is expected to decelerate in 2005 as a result of the Food and Drug Administration (FDA) crackdown on drug-related advertising, and this category will remain threatened by the potential shift of dollars to consumer magazines and other media such as television. Declines in the largest category, information technology (IT) and telecommunications, will slow in 2005, posting the slowest decline since 2000. While we expect automotive titles to post year-end growth in excess of 10 percent, four of the top 15 magazine categories also recorded double-digit growth in the first four months of 2005, including automotive; energy and natural resources; government, education and defense; and home design and furnishing. The automotive category's double-digit increase compares favorably to the decline in the same consumer magazine ad category in the first four months, illustrating that spending on b-to-b magazine advertising is less cyclical than that of consumer magazines.

Overall b-to-b magazine spending will reach $12.12 billion in 2009, growing 3.3 percent on a compound annual basis from 2004 to 2009. This growth will be driven by a compound annual increase of 4.3 percent in advertising, which will offset a 1.5 percent decline in circulation spending during the five-year period.

In the trade show segment, an increase in business-related travel in the first half of 2005 led to record gains in attendance and exhibitors at several shows, and we expect this trend to continue through the rest of the year. Trade show spending growth will continue to surpass magazine expenditure growth in 2005, with an accelerated increase of 6.1 percent to $9.71 billion, as corporate profits continue upward and show organizers attract more attendees and exhibitors through exclusive, invitation-only events. With rising exhibit space costs, organizers are offering packages that include supplementary brand marketing opportunities, such as prominent placement in marketing brochures, in order to meet ROI needs for attendees. To generate excitement and draw attendees, exhibitors will feature more introductions of new products. Spending on trade shows and exhibitions will increase 5.8 percent on a compound annual basis from 2004 to 2009, reaching $12.10 billion in 2009, spurred by escalating spending on fees, sponsorships and advertising.

Circulation spending is expected to drop 2.2 percent to $1.88 billion for the year. Accelerated advertising spending growth will partially offset the decline in circulation expenditures in 2005, as subscribers increasingly take advantage of more cost-effective, Web-based methods of obtaining information.

Spending on e-media will continue to be the fastest-growing subsegment of the b-to-b media market in 2005, with a projected increase of 26.5 percent to $1.86 billion for the year. The gain will result from the efforts of traditional publishers to build their e-media operations in order to meet the growing demand for faster delivery and more targeted information. Total b-to-b media spending, including expenditures on magazines, trade shows and e-media, is expected to increase 5.9 percent to $22.14 billion in 2005, the market's best gain in five years. Although the increasing use of e-media will continue to pilfer dollars from traditional print-based advertising and circulation, b-to-b publishers will benefit as they become more accustomed to their new roles as providers of mission-critical multimedia information. Spending on paid circulation will continue to be absorbed by e-media initiatives in 2005, as the lower costs and immediacy of Web-based information make it an attractive alternative to traditional print products. In particular, e-media is impacting the operations of technology publishers, such as Ziff Davis Media and 101communications, which both reported that e-media accounted for more than 10 percent of total revenues in the first quarter of 2005, higher than the industry average. Historically, the majority of spending on e-media has been generated through advertising, but companies will continue to expand their portfolios of Internet-based tools like search engines. In addition to efforts by traditional publishers, pure-play e-media companies, such as TechTarget and CNET, also reported accelerated growth in the first half of 2005.

Growth in the overall business-to-business media market over the next five years will surpass the gain in the 1999-2004 interval, as traditional publishers continue to create new revenue streams through the Internet. Online offerings, such as e-newsletters, weekly e-mail blasts and Webcasts, will increasingly become part of the basic subscription model, as publishers address reader demand for instant access to information. The ability to more accurately measure ROI with the help of online tools will also fuel the market's growth in the forecast period. Overall business-to-business media spending growth will match that of nominal GDP for much of the forecast period, but will not be as strong as it had been during previous economic recoveries due to the accelerating absorption of dollars by the Internet and consumer-based media. Key categories, such as IT and telecommunications; business, banking, insurance, financial and legal; and health and life sciences—the three largest categories—are projected to expand in the 2004-2009 timeframe, driven by advances in technology, stronger related economic sectors, online start-up technologies that need to introduce products with funding from venture capital firms, and progression in drug therapies. As b-to-b media companies take a more customized and consultative approach to selling advertising and trade show space—drawing on the success of outsourced and internal custom publishing operations—overall b-to-b spending will speed up during the forecast period. The total market is projected to grow at a compound annual rate of 5.8 percent from 2004 to 2009 to $27.68 billion, compared to a 0.1 percent decline in the previous five-year period.

Highlights

Business-to-Business Magazines

Total spending on business-to-business magazines, including advertising and circulation, increased 2.2 percent to $10.29 billion in 2004, representing a marked improvement over the decline of 0.9 percent the previous year. Advertising expenditures rose 3.4 percent to $8.37 billion, driven largely by healthy growth among healthcare, banking, automotive, and home design and furnishing titles.

■

E-media has become the fastest-growing subsegment of b-to-b media operations, growing at a rate of 25.9 percent to $1.47 billion in 2004. E-media accounted for about 7 percent of total revenues at leading b-to-b companies in 2004, spurred by new online initiatives launched by traditional magazine publishers as they transition to multimedia business information providers.

■

Circulation spending dropped for the fourth consecutive year, declining 2.9 percent to $1.92 billion in 2004, driven down by a 3.4 percent decline in paid circulation. The steady migration toward controlled circulation has led to price increases at the remaining paid titles.

■

We expect growth in b-to-b magazine expenditures to be modest going forward, as falling circulation is offset by gains in advertising spending. Increased advertising in automotive, healthcare, banking, and home design and furnishing titles will drive an overall spending gain of 2.7 percent in 2005 to $10.57 billion. This would be the largest increase in four years.

■

Total magazine expenditures will grow at a compound annual rate of 3.3 percent from 2004 to 2009, reaching $12.12 billion in 2009, fueled by compound annual growth of 4.3 percent in advertising spending during the period. The growth in advertising will offset a compound annual decline of 1.5 percent in circulation spending, which will fall to $1.78 billion in 2009.

Business-to-Business Magazines and E-media

THE BUSINESS-TO-BUSINESS MAGAZINES AND E-MEDIA MARKETS IN 2004 AND 2005

Driven by spending gains in several key advertising categories, total spending on business-to-business magazines, including advertising and circulation, increased for the first time in four years in 2004, growing 2.2 percent to $10.29 billion. By comparison, overall b-to-b magazine expenditures declined 0.9 percent the previous year. A decrease of 2.9 percent in circulation spending in 2004 was offset by an increase of 3.4 percent in magazine advertising, which was fueled by upside in four of the five largest advertising categories, particularly in the third-largest category—health and life sciences—which expanded 8.0 percent for the year. Circulation spending declines in 2001, 2002 and 2003, however, led to a compound annual decrease of 3.4 percent in total b-to-b magazine spending from 1999 to 2004. In contrast, nominal GDP grew at a compound annual rate of 4.8 percent in the five-year period.

Spending in the largest category, IT and telecommunications, declined 0.8 percent to $1.32 billion in 2004, after posting declines of 4.5 percent in 2003 and a devastating 29.8 percent plunge in 2002. The category's turnaround is being driven by renewed corporate and venture capital investments in computer hardware, software and networking. The category is also still recovering from the implosion of the much-hyped dot-com market that paralleled the recession in 2001.

Publications serving the automotive and recreational vehicle market experienced the strongest advertising gains in 2004 among VSS's top 15 magazine categories, growing 19.8 percent to $377.0 million for the year. Growth was spurred mainly by auto makers that launched an unprecedented number of new models for 2005, and supported these introductions with aggressive advertising spending in the second half of 2004. This resulted in higher participation in auto-related trade shows, as well as an increase in advertising targeted at fleet buyers and the trucking industry. Titles within the agriculture category experienced the slowest growth in 2004, with spending rising a mere 0.4 percent to $194.0 million.

Data from the first four months of 2005 indicate another year of moderate recovery via single-digit growth in the b-to-b magazine market. Overall spending on b-to-b magazines was up 4.0 percent year-to-date through April 2005, bolstered by double-digit growth in four of the 15 leading categories, including home design and furnishing; government, education and defense; automotive and recreational vehicles; and energy and natural resources. Spending in the largest category, IT and telecommunications, was still on the downswing, albeit decelerating, through April 2005, as was spending in electronic engineering and manufacturing, and media and entertainment. Overall, 12 of the 15 ad categories were showing upside in the first four months of 2005.

Recent consolidation among large companies in several key b-to-b magazine categories has resulted in the reduction of many major corporate advertising accounts. The retail market received its most recent jolt in January 2005 when Procter & Gamble announced plans to acquire Gillette, signaling the likely potential for consolidation of two major ad budgets. Fortunately, traditional b-to-b magazine publishers have been able to recover from these losses by increasingly capitalizing on technological advancements in order to cultivate new e-media-based revenues.

Most publishers have acknowledged that the Internet must play a prominent role in their business models if they want to remain competitive. They are incorporating online advertising into their marketing programs to meet the demands of advertisers for faster and more measurable return on investment. In the first quarter of 2005, leading b-to-b publishers in various markets, such as Reed Elsevier, reported that e-media accounted for between 7 percent and 10 percent of their total revenues, including advertising, circulation and trade shows. Going forward, spending on e-media will increasingly represent a larger share, but as b-to-b publishers con-

Spending On Business-to-Business Magazines

($ MILLIONS)

Year	*Advertising**	*Circulation*	*Total*
1999	$10,218	$2,033	$12,251
2000	11,115	2,223	13,338
2001	9,361	2,104	11,465
2002	8,115	2,050	10,165
2003	8,094	1,974	10,068
2004	8,373	1,917	10,290
2005	8,696	1,875	10,571
2006	9,056	1,841	10,897
2007	9,448	1,821	11,269
2008	9,873	1,797	11,670
2009	10,336	1,781	12,117

Sources: Veronis Suhler Stevenson, PQ Media, IMS/The Auditor, AdScope, Agricom, American Business Media, BPA International, IMS, PERQ, SRDS, TNS Media Intelligence/CMR

*The methodology used to size, structure and forecast the business-to-business magazine advertising market was changed in order to provide a more accurate picture of this marketplace. As part of this change, a new primary source for historical data was used, coupled with a secondary source for certain market subsegments and categories, which served as the basis for a proprietary regression analysis.

Growth of Spending On Business-to-Business Magazines

Year	*Advertising**	*Circulation*	*Total*
2000	8.8%	9.3%	8.9%
2001	−15.8	−5.4	−14.0
2002	−13.3	−2.6	−11.3
2003	−0.2	−3.7	−0.9
2004	3.4	−2.9	2.2
2005	3.8	−2.2	2.7
2006	4.1	−1.8	3.1
2007	4.3	−1.1	3.4
2008	4.5	−1.3	3.6
2009	4.7	−0.9	3.8
Compound Annual Growth			
1999-2004	−3.9	−1.2	−3.4
2004-2009	4.3	−1.5	3.3

Sources: Veronis Suhler Stevenson, PQ Media, IMS/The Auditor, AdScope, Agricom, American Business Media, BPA International, IMS, PERQ, SRDS, TNS Media Intelligence/CMR

*The methodology used to size, structure and forecast the business-to-business magazine advertising market was changed in order to provide a more accurate picture of this marketplace. As part of this change, a new primary source for historical data was used, coupled with a secondary source for certain market subsegments and categories, which served as the basis for a proprietary regression analysis.

Business-to-Business Magazine Advertising, by Industry*

Industry	*1999*	*2000*	*2001*	*2002*
Information Technology & Telecommunications	$ 2,748	$ 2,756	$1,985	$1,393
Business, Banking, Insurance, Financial & Legal	901	1,080	966	823
Health & Life Sciences	752	790	703	716
Media & Entertainment	740	886	684	653
Retail	576	719	655	614
Manufacturing & Processing	957	961	815	699
Architecture, Engineering & Construction	507	581	616	573
Travel & Hospitality	821	909	779	742
Electronic Engineering & Manufacturing	476	589	580	433
Automotive & Recreational Vehicles	346	391	291	291
Government, Education & Defense	348	407	366	356
Home Design & Furnishing	260	303	289	279
Transportation, Logistics & Aviation	342	303	263	217
Agriculture	252	258	220	189
Energy & Natural Resources	192	183	151	138
Total	10,218	11,115	9,361	8,115

Sources: Veronis Suhler Stevenson, PQ Media, IMS/The Auditor, AdScope, Agricom, American Business Media, BPA International, PERQ, TNS Media Intelligence/CMR

*The methodology used to size, structure and forecast the business-to-business magazine advertising market was changed in order to provide a more accurate picture of this marketplace. As part of this change, a new primary source for historical data was used, coupled with a secondary source for certain market subsegments and categories, which served as the basis for a proprietary regression analysis.

Business-to-Business Media

tinue to reposition themselves as providers of business information, they will rely less on e-media advertising revenues.

Print advertising will take longer to recover in certain markets like IT, as that industry continues to struggle with losses incurred during the dot-com meltdown and increasing competition from Internet keyword search advertising. However, b-to-b publishers are successfully rallying against sluggish print-based sales by developing more customized programs for clients and using the Internet for lead generation, given the strength of e-media's ROI measurements.

Subscription spending dropped 2.9 percent to $1.92 billion in 2004, driven down by a 3.4 percent decline in paid unit circulation, with 12 of 15 magazine categories posting losses, including the five largest: health and life sciences; business, banking, insurance, financial and legal; government; manufacturing and processing; and IT and telecommunications.

Circulation will continue to shift from paid to controlled, leading publishers to develop more sophisticated databases of demographic-based circulation that is attractive to advertisers. Spending on paid circulation will also continue to be absorbed by e-media initiatives in 2005, as the lower costs and immediacy of Web-based information make it an attractive alternative to tradi-

(MILLIONS)

2003	2004	2005	2006	2007	2008	2009
$1,331	$1,319	$1,310	$1,313	$1,323	$1,339	$ 1,358
866	918	974	1,035	1,104	1,183	1,270
775	837	905	980	1,061	1,142	1,234
656	678	691	706	718	731	741
628	675	705	738	775	813	854
663	642	660	680	698	717	739
572	622	651	683	718	754	788
676	641	661	684	710	740	772
407	420	425	430	438	448	461
315	377	417	447	475	506	541
372	377	394	414	435	455	477
291	313	337	365	397	429	465
209	218	224	231	240	248	258
193	194	196	199	202	207	212
141	141	146	150	155	160	166
8,094	8,373	8,696	9,056	9,448	9,873	10,336

tional print products. In particular, e-media is impacting the operations of technology publishers such as Ziff Davis Media and 101communications, both of which reported that e-media accounted for more than 10 percent of total revenues in the first quarter of 2005, higher than the industry average. In addition to efforts by traditional publishers, pure-play e-media companies, like TechTarget and CNET, have also reported accelerating growth.

Spending on circulation is expected to decline 2.2 percent to $1.88 billion in 2005, as subscribers continue to migrate to other information sources, such as the Internet, and publishers increase controlled circulation's share of the mix. A 3.8 percent increase in advertising spending to $8.70 billion will offset the circulation spending decline, leading to a gain of 2.7 percent to $10.57 billion in total b-to-b magazine spending for the year.

ADVERTISING

B-to-b magazine advertising was the hardest hit media segment during the 2001 recession, and the doldrums continued for two more years as b-to-b publishers struggled to regain some of the traction they had lost in the early part of the decade. The b-to-b market, however, turned the corner in 2004, posting its first growth year since 2000, and the market's performance in the first half of

Growth of Business-to-Business Magazine Advertising, by Industry*

Industry	*2000*	*2001*	*2002*	*2003*
Information Technology & Telecommunications	0.3%	–28.0%	–29.8%	–4.5%
Business, Banking, Insurance, Financial & Legal	19.9	–10.6	–14.7	5.2
Health & Life Sciences	5.0	–11.0	1.9	8.2
Media & Entertainment	19.7	–22.8	–4.5	0.5
Retail	24.9	–8.9	–6.3	2.3
Manufacturing & Processing	0.4	–15.2	–14.3	–5.2
Architecture, Engineering & Construction	14.6	5.9	–7.0	–0.1
Travel & Hospitality	10.7	–14.4	–4.8	–8.9
Electronic Engineering & Manufacturing	23.7	–1.5	–25.3	–6.2
Automotive & Recreational Vehicles	12.9	–25.6	0.0	8.2
Government, Education & Defense	17.1	–10.0	–2.9	4.4
Home Design & Furnishing	16.7	–4.6	–3.5	4.4
Transportation, Logistics & Aviation	–11.6	–13.0	–17.6	–3.8
Agriculture	2.3	–14.8	–14.0	2.0
Energy & Natural Resources	–4.5	–17.8	–8.2	1.8
Total	8.8	–15.8	–13.3	–0.2

Sources: Veronis Suhler Stevenson, PQ Media, IMS/The Auditor, AdScope, Agricom, American Business Media, BPA International, PERQ, TNS Media Intelligence/CMR

*The methodology used to size, structure and forecast the business-to-business magazine advertising market was changed in order to provide a more accurate picture of this marketplace. As part of this change, a new primary source for historical data was used, coupled with a secondary source for certain market subsegments and categories, which served as the basis for a proprietary regression analysis.

2005 indicates that b-to-b advertising may be recovering and is on track to record its best performance of the past five years. The industry's leading trade association, American Business Media (ABM), reported that it experienced the most upbeat annual meeting in recent memory in May 2005, with industry veterans exuding optimism about all aspects of the industry. In addition, talk swirled around the uptick in merger and acquisition activity in recent months, with major industry players recently sold, such as Hanley-Wood and Canon, or put on the block like Primedia Business Information, expecting to fetch solid double-digit EBITDA multiples when deals are finalized.

Total spending on b-to-b magazine advertising grew 3.4 percent to $8.37 billion in 2004, driven by gains in 11 of the 15 leading ad categories. Despite these gains in 2004, b-to-b magazine advertising posted a compound annual decline of 3.9 percent from 1999 to 2004, due mainly to the market's decline from 2001 through 2003.

Spending in three of VSS's top 15 categories rebounded into positive territory in 2004 following declines in 2003. Architecture, engineering and construction achieved an 8.7 percent gain to $622.0 million in 2004, after declining 0.1 percent in 2003 and 7.0 percent in 2002. The continued strong housing market and gains in corporate earn-

2004	*CAGR 1999-2004*	*2005*	*2006*	*2007*	*2008*	*2009*	*CAGR 2004-2009*
-0.8%	-13.6%	-0.7%	0.2%	0.8%	1.2%	1.4%	0.6%
5.9	0.4	6.1	6.3	6.7	7.1	7.4	6.7
8.0	2.2	8.1	8.3	8.2	7.7	8.0	8.1
3.3	-1.7	1.9	2.2	1.6	1.8	1.4	1.8
7.5	3.2	4.4	4.7	5.1	4.9	5.0	4.8
-3.1	-7.7	2.8	3.1	2.5	2.8	3.1	2.9
8.7	4.2	4.6	5.0	5.1	5.0	4.5	4.8
-5.1	-4.8	3.1	3.4	3.8	4.2	4.4	3.8
3.4	-2.4	1.0	1.3	1.8	2.4	2.7	1.8
19.8	1.7	10.5	7.1	6.3	6.6	6.9	7.5
1.6	1.6	4.5	4.9	5.2	4.6	4.9	4.8
7.3	3.8	7.8	8.4	8.6	8.2	8.4	8.3
4.6	-8.6	2.8	3.2	3.7	3.5	3.8	3.4
0.4	-5.1	1.2	1.5	1.8	2.2	2.5	1.8
-0.1	-6.0	3.6	3.0	3.2	3.4	3.8	3.4
3.4	-3.9	3.8	4.1	4.3	4.5	4.7	4.3

ings fueled growth in this segment. The electronic engineering and manufacturing, and transportation, logistics and aviation segments also posted gains in 2004 after experiencing declines in 2003. Spending in the largest segment, IT and telecommunications, declined 0.8 percent to $1.32 billion in 2004, but this decrease compared favorably with declines of 4.5 percent in 2003 and the 29.8 percent plunge in 2002. The category's turnaround is being driven by renewed corporate and venture capital investments in computer hardware, software and networking.

Health and life sciences, the third-largest segment, sustained robust growth for the second consecutive year in 2004, posting an increase of 8.0 percent to $837.0 million, driven by the introduction of new drugs in the first half of 2004. During the latter part of 2004, new data emerged that linked several popular pain relievers to an increased risk of heart attack, which caused the FDA to crack down on direct-to-consumer advertising. While this action immediately impacted advertising expenditures in consumer healthcare titles, it could potentially benefit b-to-b publishers if dollars eventually shift toward the creation of more qualified professional educational programs, which would spark additional advertising.

In the first quarter of 2005, 12 of VSS's 15 categories posted overall advertising growth,

Shares of Business-to-Business Magazine Advertising, by Industry*

Industry	*1999*	*2000*	*2001*	*2002*
Information Technology & Telecommunications	26.9%	24.8%	21.2%	17.2%
Business, Banking, Insurance, Financial & Legal	8.8	9.7	10.3	10.1
Health & Life Sciences	7.4	7.1	7.5	8.8
Media & Entertainment	7.2	8.0	7.3	8.0
Retail	5.6	6.5	7.0	7.6
Manufacturing & Processing	9.4	8.6	8.7	8.6
Architecture, Engineering & Construction	5.0	5.2	6.6	7.1
Travel & Hospitality	8.0	8.2	8.3	9.1
Electronic Engineering & Manufacturing	4.7	5.3	6.2	5.3
Automotive & Recreational Vehicles	3.4	3.5	3.1	3.6
Government, Education & Defense	3.4	3.7	3.9	4.4
Home Design & Furnishing	2.5	2.7	3.1	3.4
Transportation, Logistics & Aviation	3.3	2.7	2.8	2.7
Agriculture	2.5	2.3	2.3	2.3
Energy & Natural Resources	1.9	1.6	1.6	1.7

Sources: Veronis Suhler Stevenson, PQ Media, IMS/The Auditor, AdScope, Agricom, American Business Media, BPA International, PERQ, TNS Media Intelligence/CMR

*The methodology used to size, structure and forecast the business-to-business magazine advertising market was changed in order to provide a more accurate picture of this marketplace. As part of this change, a new primary source for historical data was used, coupled with a secondary source for certain market subsegments and categories, which served as the basis for a proprietary regression analysis.

regulated by increases and declines in each industry's subcategory. For example, overall advertising growth of 4.4 percent in the architecture, engineering and construction category was driven by an 11.7 percent increase in the engineering and construction subcategory, which offset a decline of 0.6 percent in building spending. The health and life sciences category posted total advertising growth of 8.2 percent in the first quarter of 2005, fueled by an 8.6 percent increase in science, research and development, which offset a 4.4 percent drop in pharmaceuticals and pharmacology.

For the first time in more than five years, we expect all categories except for IT and telecommunications to post gains in 2005. Overall ad pages are expected to increase 2.5 percent in 2005, which will boost ad spending during the second half of 2005, leading to a 3.8 percent increase for the year. Spending will reach $8.70 billion in 2005, compared with $8.37 billion in 2004. The increase would be the largest since 2000. Total ad expenditures are forecast to grow at a compound annual rate of 4.3 percent from 2004 to 2009, driven by positive reaction to integrated marketing packages featuring Web-related advertising, compared with a 3.9 percent decline in the previous five-year period. Spending will reach $10.34 billion in 2009, surpassing the level of 1999.

The automotive and recreational vehicles category is the only one expected to experience double-digit growth in 2005, as the onslaught of new vehicles released over the preceding two years continues to upset the balance of supply and demand, and forces advertisers to

2003	2004	2005	2006	2007	2008	2009
16.4%	15.8%	15.1%	14.5%	14.0%	13.6%	13.1%
10.7	11.0	11.2	11.4	11.7	12.0	12.3
9.6	10.0	10.4	10.8	11.2	11.6	11.9
8.1	8.1	7.9	7.8	7.6	7.4	7.2
7.8	8.1	8.1	8.1	8.2	8.2	8.3
8.2	7.7	7.6	7.5	7.4	7.3	7.2
7.1	7.4	7.5	7.5	7.6	7.6	7.6
8.3	7.7	7.6	7.6	7.5	7.5	7.5
5.0	5.0	4.9	4.8	4.6	4.5	4.5
3.9	4.5	4.8	4.9	5.0	5.1	5.2
4.6	4.5	4.5	4.6	4.6	4.6	4.6
3.6	3.7	3.9	4.0	4.2	4.3	4.5
2.6	2.6	2.6	2.6	2.5	2.5	2.5
2.4	2.3	2.3	2.2	2.1	2.1	2.1
1.7	1.7	1.7	1.7	1.6	1.6	1.6

target fleet buyers and trucking companies more aggressively. Advertising spending in this category will grow 10.5 percent to $417.0 million in 2005. The slowest growth will come from the electronic engineering and manufacturing category, which will grow 1.0 percent to $425.0 million, compared with a 3.4 percent increase in 2004.

The IT and telecommunications category is still recovering from the dot-com implosion that paralleled the recession in 2001, and more recently has been hurt by a loss of ad dollars to online pure-plays. We expect the decline in spending in this category to decelerate in 2005, dropping 0.7 percent, compared to a 0.8 percent drop in 2004. The anticipated growth in this category over the forecast period will be driven by an uptick in equipment purchases that were postponed when the economy slowed. Print advertising growth in technology markets, however, is not expected to return to double-digit levels, and will continue to lag growth in the overall category as companies shift more marketing resources to search engine marketing, e-media and customized, face-to-face programs.

We expect the health and life sciences category to increase 8.1 percent in 2005 to $905.0 million, fueled primarily by consistent efforts to promote new drugs, medical devices and diagnostics to healthcare professionals; however, expansion will fluctuate during the forecast period as the direct-to-consumer market recovers.

Custom publishing is also becoming a larger part of the b-to-b spending mix, as publishers increase their use of Web-based

Unit Circulation of Business-to-Business Magazines, by Categories

	Controlled					
Category	*1999*	*2000*	*2001*	*2002*	*2003*	*2004*
Health & Life Sciences	20,397	20,247	20,873	21,754	22,407	22,595
Business, Banking, Insurance, Financial & Legal	16,148	16,496	17,574	17,182	16,563	15,354
Government, Education & Defense	4,840	4,810	4,668	4,970	4,961	5,543
Manufacturing & Processing	11,616	11,640	11,536	11,794	11,346	10,992
Information Technology & Telecommunications	8,263	8,487	9,422	8,866	8,887	8,394
Architecture, Engineering & Construction	7,661	7,693	8,062	7,718	7,709	7,869
Agriculture	5,600	5,594	5,641	5,517	5,656	5,363
Travel & Hospitality	5,559	5,728	5,618	5,414	5,427	5,681
Automotive & Recreational Vehicles	5,298	4,850	4,832	4,868	4,764	4,798
Retail	4,300	4,397	4,327	4,682	4,909	4,659
Media & Entertainment	2,833	2,938	2,993	2,879	2,993	3,000
Electronic Engineering & Manufacturing	3,716	3,710	3,862	3,606	3,449	3,342
Energy & Natural Resources	2,154	2,186	2,120	2,263	2,294	2,372
Home Design & Furnishing	2,463	2,464	2,448	2,428	2,307	2,425
Transportation, Logistics & Aviation	1,931	1,948	1,958	2,017	2,031	2,157
Total	102,779	103,188	105,934	105,958	105,703	104,544

Sources: Veronis Suhler Stevenson, PQ Media, BPA International, SRDS

services to meet client demands. Custom publishing tends to act as an alternative marketing tool and, therefore, is covered in more detail in the Advertising, Specialty Media & Marketing Services chapter. Spending on custom publishing—consumer and business-to-business—grew 20.4 percent to $22.1 billion in 2004, based on data from the Custom Publishing Council. The major shift impacting custom publishing in 2004 was the increasing migration away from printed newsletters to more magazines and e-media. The latter market has grown its share of the custom publishing market to 19.0 percent in 2004, up from only 3.0 percent in 1999.

CIRCULATION

As b-to-b magazine readers have become more accustomed to receiving free information, publishers have been forced to transition more circulation to controlled in recent years, causing overall circulation to steadily dwindle. In an effort to justify the move to controlled circulation, publishers have been creating more sophisticated databases that have demographic-sensitive circulation data. In 2004, paid fell 3.4 percent to 53.2 million units, following a 0.3 percent decline in 2003, and controlled dropped 1.1 percent to 104.5 million units, following a decline of 0.2 percent in 2003. To recoup some of the

(THOUSANDS)

Paid						Total					
1999	*2000*	*2001*	*2002*	*2003*	*2004*	*1999*	*2000*	*2001*	*2002*	*2003*	*2004*
10,243	10,514	10,474	10,512	11,054	10,988	30,640	30,761	31,347	32,266	33,461	33,583
11,807	11,986	11,850	11,702	11,051	10,349	27,955	28,482	29,424	28,884	27,614	25,703
9,177	9,310	9,725	9,220	9,263	8,727	14,017	14,120	14,393	14,190	14,224	14,270
1,361	1,344	1,330	1,388	1,466	1,367	12,977	12,984	12,866	13,182	12,812	12,359
5,018	5,088	5,108	5,132	5,023	4,746	13,281	13,575	14,530	13,998	13,910	13,140
2,882	2,894	3,280	3,186	3,278	3,317	10,543	10,587	11,342	10,904	10,987	11,186
4,267	4,147	4,114	4,193	4,140	4,205	9,867	9,741	9,755	9,710	9,796	9,568
1,068	1,050	1,068	1,076	1,031	986	6,627	6,778	6,686	6,490	6,458	6,667
1,353	1,209	1,202	1,227	1,261	1,232	6,651	6,059	6,034	6,095	6,025	6,030
1,183	1,172	1,192	1,289	1,401	1,285	5,483	5,569	5,519	5,971	6,310	5,944
1,870	1,916	1,946	1,940	1,799	1,790	4,703	4,854	4,939	4,819	4,792	4,790
460	413	428	359	365	330	4,176	4,123	4,290	3,965	3,814	3,672
979	993	1,038	1,017	988	951	3,133	3,179	3,158	3,280	3,282	3,323
487	485	486	464	436	464	2,950	2,949	2,934	2,892	2,743	2,889
632	640	668	651	658	643	2,563	2,588	2,626	2,668	2,689	2,800
52,787	53,161	53,909	53,356	53,214	51,380	155,566	156,349	159,843	159,314	158,917	155,924

revenues that were lost in the transition to more controlled circulation, price hikes have been applied to the remaining subscriptions. In the past, these hikes have been met with resistance, but in 2004 increased corporate spending in numerous markets caused publishers to be more aggressive with their pricing. However, many of the largest titles, including those in the business, banking, insurance, financial and legal category, saw paid circulation slide, as well as significant declines in the manufacturing and processing; retail; and electrical engineering and manufacturing categories.

The growing influence of the Internet on b-to-b media is also strengthening as b-to-b publishers reposition themselves to provide business-critical information through multiple platforms. The speed at which information is disseminated has taken on a new level of importance, and the Internet has forced publishers of both monthly and weekly titles, like *Advertising Age* and *Official Board Markets* (OBM), to offer digital editions that arrive on subscribers' desktops before being published in print. Users are charged fees for online access to complete articles. In the case of OBM, an Advanstar publication covering the paperboard industry, digital subscribers receive news on Fridays, while print subscriptions

Growth of Unit Circulation of Business-to-Business Magazines, by Categories

	Controlled					
Category	*2000*	*2001*	*2002*	*2003*	*2004*	*CAGR 1999-2004*
Health & Life Sciences	–0.7%	3.1%	4.2%	3.0%	0.8%	2.1%
Business, Banking, Insurance, Financial & Legal	2.2	6.5	–2.2	–3.6	–7.3	–1.0
Government, Education & Defense	–0.6	–3.0	6.5	–0.2	11.7	2.7
Manufacturing & Processing	0.2	–0.9	2.2	–3.8	–3.1	–1.1
Information Technology & Telecommunications	2.7	11.0	–5.9	0.2	–5.5	0.3
Architecture, Engineering & Construction	0.4	4.8	–4.3	–0.1	2.1	0.5
Agriculture	–0.1	0.8	–2.2	2.5	–5.2	–0.9
Travel & Hospitality	3.0	–1.9	–3.6	0.2	4.7	0.4
Automotive & Recreational Vehicles	–8.5	–0.4	0.7	–2.1	0.7	–2.0
Retail	2.3	–1.6	8.2	4.8	–5.1	1.6
Media & Entertainment	3.7	1.9	–3.8	4.0	0.2	1.2
Electronic Engineering & Manufacturing	–0.2	4.1	–6.6	–4.4	–3.1	–2.1
Energy & Natural Resources	1.5	–3.0	6.7	1.4	3.4	1.9
Home Design & Furnishing	0.1	–0.6	–0.8	–5.0	5.1	–0.3
Transportation, Logistics & Aviation	0.9	0.5	3.0	0.7	6.2	2.2
Total	0.4	2.7	0.0	–0.2	–1.1	0.3

Sources: Veronis Suhler Stevenson, PQ Media, BPA International, SRDS

publish the following Monday. Out of an initial base of 4,000 print subscribers in 2002, 27.0 percent had converted to digital subscriptions by January 2005.

In 2004, only three of the top 15 categories experienced paid circulation unit gains. Paid circulation among home design and furnishing rose 6.4 percent to 464,000 units. Agriculture, and architecture, engineering and construction titles experienced increases in paid unit circulation of 1.6 percent to 4.2 million units and 1.2 percent to 3.3 million units, respectively, in 2004.

The drop in unit circulation led to a 2.9 percent decline in circulation spending to $1.92 billion for the year. Paid unit circulation declined 0.5 percent on a compound annual basis from 1999 to 2004, while overall circulation spending dipped 1.2 percent on a compound annual basis in the five-year period.

Controlled circulation remained relatively flat on a compound annual basis from 1999 to 2004, rising only 0.3 percent. Controlled circulation represented about 67.0 percent of total distribution in 2004, up from 66.1 percent in 1999. Paid circulation accounted for 33.0 percent, down from 33.9 percent five years ago.

The increase in controlled circulation for health and life sciences publications in 2004

Paid						*Total*					
2000	*2001*	*2002*	*2003*	*2004*	*CAGR 1999-2004*	*2000*	*2001*	*2002*	*2003*	*2004*	*CAGR 1999-2004*
2.6%	−0.4%	0.4%	5.2%	−0.6%	1.4%	0.4%	1.9%	2.9%	3.7%	0.4%	1.9%
1.5	−1.1	−1.2	−5.6	−6.4	−2.6	1.9	3.3	−1.8	−4.4	−6.9	−1.7
1.4	4.5	−5.2	0.5	−5.8	−1.0	0.7	1.9	−1.4	0.2	0.3	0.4
−1.2	−1.0	4.4	5.6	−6.8	0.1	0.1	−0.9	2.5	−2.8	−3.5	−1.0
1.4	0.4	0.5	−2.1	−5.5	−1.1	2.2	7.0	−3.7	−0.6	−5.5	−0.2
0.4	13.3	−2.9	2.9	1.2	2.9	0.4	7.1	−3.9	0.8	1.8	1.2
−2.8	−0.8	1.9	−1.3	1.6	−0.3	−1.3	0.1	−0.5	0.9	−2.3	−0.6
−1.7	1.7	0.7	−4.2	−4.4	−1.6	2.3	−1.4	−2.9	−0.5	3.2	0.1
−10.6	−0.6	2.1	2.8	−2.3	−1.9	−8.9	−0.4	1.0	−1.1	0.1	−1.9
−0.9	1.7	8.1	8.7	−8.3	1.7	1.6	−0.9	8.2	5.7	−5.8	1.6
2.5	1.6	−0.3	−7.3	−0.5	−0.9	3.2	1.8	−2.4	−0.6	0.0	0.4
−10.2	3.6	−16.1	1.7	−9.6	−6.4	−1.3	4.1	−7.6	−3.8	−3.7	−2.5
1.4	4.5	−2.0	−2.9	−3.7	−0.6	1.5	−0.7	3.9	0.1	1.2	1.2
−0.4	0.2	−4.5	−6.0	6.4	−1.0	0.0	−0.5	−1.4	−5.2	5.3	−0.4
1.3	4.4	−2.5	1.1	−2.3	0.3	1.0	1.5	1.6	0.8	4.1	1.8
0.7	1.4	−1.0	−0.3	−3.4	−0.5	0.5	2.2	−0.3	−0.2	−1.9	0.0

pushed the segment to the top spot among the 15 categories, surpassing business, banking, insurance, financial and legal. Controlled circulation in the healthcare segment rose 0.8 percent to 22.6 million units. Total circulation in this category increased 0.4 percent to 33.6 million. The business category pulled in 10.3 million units in paid circulation in 2004, down 6.3 percent. Controlled circulation was 15.4 million units, down 7.3 percent, and total circulation for the segment declined 6.9 percent to 25.7 million in 2004. Government, education and defense titles round out the top three, with 8.7 million units in paid circulation, down 5.8 percent. An increase of 11.7 percent in controlled circulation to 5.5 million units led to a 0.3 percent increase in total circulation to 14.3 million units for the category.

Paid circulation is expected to continue to decline throughout the forecast period, causing spending to drop at a compound annual rate of 1.5 percent to $1.8 million from 2004 to 2009. While paid circulation continues to diminish, publishers will increasingly focus on Internet distribution, custom publishing efforts and demographic targeting, which often provides better insight into the makeup of readers than just reviewing job titles.

Distribution of Unit Circulation of Business-to-Business Magazines, by Categories

Category	Controlled					
	1999	*2000*	*2001*	*2002*	*2003*	*2004*
Health & Life Sciences	66.6%	65.8%	66.6%	67.4%	67.0%	67.3%
Business, Banking, Insurance, Financial & Legal	57.8	57.9	59.7	59.5	60.0	59.7
Government, Education & Defense	34.5	34.1	32.4	35.0	34.9	38.8
Manufacturing & Processing	89.5	89.6	89.7	89.5	88.6	88.9
Information Technology & Telecommunications	62.2	62.5	64.8	63.3	63.9	63.9
Architecture, Engineering & Construction	72.7	72.7	71.1	70.8	70.2	70.3
Agriculture	56.8	57.4	57.8	56.8	57.7	56.1
Travel & Hospitality	83.9	84.5	84.0	83.4	84.0	85.2
Automotive & Recreational Vehicles	79.7	80.0	80.1	79.9	79.1	79.6
Retail	78.4	79.0	78.4	78.4	77.8	78.4
Media & Entertainment	60.2	60.5	60.6	59.7	62.5	62.6
Electronic Engineering & Manufacturing	89.0	90.0	90.0	90.9	90.4	91.0
Energy & Natural Resources	68.8	68.8	67.1	69.0	69.9	71.4
Home Design & Furnishing	83.5	83.6	83.4	84.0	84.1	83.9
Transportation, Logistics & Aviation	75.3	75.3	74.6	75.6	75.5	77.0
Total	66.1	66.0	66.3	66.5	66.5	67.0

Sources: Veronis Suhler Stevenson, PQ Media, BPA International, SRDS

Paid					
1999	*2000*	*2001*	*2002*	*2003*	*2004*
33.4%	34.2%	33.4%	32.6%	33.0%	32.7%
42.2	42.1	40.3	40.5	40.0	40.3
65.5	65.9	67.6	65.0	65.1	61.2
10.5	10.4	10.3	10.5	11.4	11.1
37.8	37.5	35.2	36.7	36.1	36.1
27.3	27.3	28.9	29.2	29.8	29.7
43.2	42.6	42.2	43.2	42.3	43.9
16.1	15.5	16.0	16.6	16.0	14.8
20.3	20.0	19.9	20.1	20.9	20.4
21.6	21.0	21.6	21.6	22.2	21.6
39.8	39.5	39.4	40.3	37.5	37.4
11.0	10.0	10.0	9.1	9.6	9.0
31.2	31.2	32.9	31.0	30.1	28.6
16.5	16.4	16.6	16.0	15.9	16.1
24.7	24.7	25.4	24.4	24.5	23.0
33.9	34.0	33.7	33.5	33.5	33.0

E-MEDIA

Real-time data and information are rapidly becoming a larger part of the b-to-b business model, as traditional b-to-b publishers continue to reposition themselves as business information providers. As a result, there has been a steady shift from print to online products and services in this market. The advertising recovery of the past two years also allowed smaller publishers to increase investments in online technology, which is often more cost-efficient in reaching target audiences due to increasing postage, paper and print production costs. The proliferation of pure-play e-media companies like CNET and TechTarget has also infused new life into the e-media market, which has become the fastest-growing category of the b-to-b segment, growing 25.9 percent to $1.47 billion in 2004.

The original e-media model of the late 1990s focused mostly on advertising, but has since grown into a more comprehensive model that includes content, and databases that serve as directories, in addition to advertising models that have expanded from banner to search ads and classifieds. Reed Business Information, for example, has expanded its advertising base from banners to search, and also tweaked the model to include classifieds, such as online employment ads specific to industries. Furthermore, to remain a key b-to-b information provider, Reed has weighed alternative models including selling more research and databases over the Internet.

In early 2005, e-media continued to represent the fastest-growing portion of many businesses and is said to account for between 7 percent and 10 percent of total corporate revenues, compared to 3 percent to 5 percent a few years ago. E-media will continue to be strong going forward as more b-to-b media companies add additional paid services to their online offerings, rather than maintain a simple advertising-based model. The growth will remain in double-digits during the forecast period due to the continued migration to online products and services, although it is expected to decelerate as the online model becomes more established and requires less manipulation during the latter part of the forecast period.

Marketing dollars will continue to increase throughout the forecast period, driven by an increase in print advertising among automotive and construction titles. As marketers become more selective in how they spend their dollars, e-media will become an increasingly attractive alternative to print advertising due to the higher level of ROI measurement the medium provides. The Internet will become an important part of the traditional b-to-b business model, as publishers look to stem the flow of spending to search-engine marketing by launching similar businesses. Reed also recently built upon the kellysearch .com manufacturing search engine to create Reed Link, which allows for online product searches.

Editorial blogs are not as advanced in the b-to-b media space as they are in the consumer market, and have not contributed significantly to revenues. A revenue stream model has yet to be developed to justify some of the costs of blogs, especially as the technology becomes more sophisticated and, consequently, financially prohibitive to some of the smaller b-to-b media companies. Currently in the b-to-b media space, blogs are more of an extension of a company's public relations initiatives than a separate entity. However, blogs could potentially become more essential going forward as they relate to the growing trend toward publishing in real time. During a recent trade show, *Millimeter* and *Mix*, two Primedia Business titles, launched blogs spun off of the trade show daily from the tradeshow floor. A branded blogging station led to increased traffic at the company's booth, and traffic to both blog sites was up about 30 percent over the three-day event. *Millimeter's* blog was sponsored by Intel, and revenues generated by the blogs were said to be greater than most ad page sells but less than a large Webinar.

The Outlook For Business-to-Business Magazines and E-media

We expect total business-to-business magazine spending, including advertising and circulation, to accelerate in 2005, growing 2.7 percent to $10.57 billion, as a 3.8 percent increase in advertising spending offsets a 2.2 percent decline in circulation. Growth in the segment will lag GDP growth over the next five years. Business-to-business magazine advertising is expected to reach $8.70 billion in 2005, due in part to increased spending on automotive; healthcare; and home design and furnishing publications, as well as a gradual recovery among technology titles. The solid economy will also drive growth in retail and banking titles.

The b-to-b magazine market will grow at a compound annual rate of 3.3 percent from 2004 to 2009, reaching $12.12 billion in 2009. Advertising expenditures will grow at a compound annual rate of 4.3 percent, reaching $10.34 billion in 2009, and circulation spending will decline at a compound annual rate of 1.5 percent over the next five years, dropping to $1.78 billion by 2009.

We project e-media spending will grow 26.5 percent to $1.86 billion in 2005, as b-to-b publishers transition their operations into a multimedia mix of content and advertising, and e-media becomes an increasingly utilized alternative to print advertising as a result of providing a higher level of ROI assurance to clients. Spending on e-media is forecast to grow at a compound annual rate of 18.7 percent from 2004 to 2009, reaching $3.47 billion, as b-to-b publishers transform into b-to-b media information providers.

FORECAST ASSUMPTIONS

- Spending on business-to-business magazine advertising expanded at an accelerated rate in the first half of 2005, a trend we expect to continue during the forecast period, Growth will be driven by more integrated marketing packages featuring Web-related advertising. Spending will continue to shift to e-media as b-to-b publishers reposition themselves as providers of mission-critical business information.
- The automotive and recreational vehicles category will experience double-digit growth in 2005, as an inventory glut forces advertisers to target fleet buyers and trucking companies more aggressively. The health and life sciences category will experience healthy single-digit growth, driven by consistent efforts to promote new medical devices and diagnostics to healthcare professionals. The information technology and telecommunications category will recover from the recession and begin to post slow growth in the forecast period, spurred by an uptick in equipment purchases that were postponed when the economy slowed.
- Circulation will continue to migrate from paid to controlled because end users have become accustomed to receiving free information, and publishers are seeking to mine and track demographic circulation data more efficiently. With the decline in paid subscriptions, end users will increasingly turn to the Internet as their preferred distribution channel, while publishers will be turning to custom publishing projects to reach their target audiences.
- E-media spending will continue to be the fastest-growing subsegment of the market in the forecast period, growing at a double-digit pace, driven by continued online advertising and content initiatives at traditional b-to-b publishers. Spending on e-media will negatively impact spending on print products, forcing b-to-b publishers to speed up their transformation into multimedia information providers.

Highlights

Trade Shows and Exhibitions

Total spending on trade shows, including expenditures on exhibit space and fees, sponsorships and advertising, grew 5.8 percent to $9.15 billion in 2004, driven by healthy corporate profits and an increase in business-related travel. Healthcare-related shows were the most profitable due to an upswing in continued medical education. Growth in 2004 was an improvement over growth of 1.5 percent in 2003 and a 1.2 percent decline in 2002.

■

Exhibit space rented increased 1.5 percent to 371.5 million square feet, after declining 0.4 percent in 2003 and 1.0 percent in 2002. The average price per square foot jumped 4.0 percent to $19.15, as organizers took advantage of the fading recession and increased prices with little resistance from vendors. These price hikes fueled a 5.6 percent increase in total exhibit space spending to $7.11 billion

■

Trade show organizers are continuing to offer exhibitors multifaceted packages that increase brand exposure by prominently featuring logos on marketing materials, which led to an increase in fees, sponsorships and advertising of 6.5 percent to $2.04 billion in 2004. Trade show organizers are also increasingly offering higher-quality education sessions and invitation-only events to boost attendance, which led to a 2.7 percent increase in professional attendance to 40.9 million in 2004.

■

In the first half of 2005, many corporations reported that they were increasing funding for business-related travel, and we believe this will drive trade show expenditures up 6.1 percent to $9.71 billion for the year.

■

Spending on trade shows is expected to rise 5.8 percent on a compound annual basis from 2004 to 2009, driven by a 6.8 percent rise in fees, sponsorships and advertising and a 5.4 percent gain in total exhibit space spending. Overall spending will reach $12.10 billion in 2009.

Trade Shows and Exhibitions

THE TRADE SHOWS AND EXHIBITIONS MARKET IN 2004 AND 2005

The trade shows and exhibitions market also continued to recover in 2004 and shows signs of expansion for the next five years as across-the-board increases in spending by exhibitors and attendees last year propelled growth and spending at a rate not seen since 2000. The market posted a 5.8 percent increase in overall spending to $9.15 billion in 2004, following growth of 1.5 percent in 2003 and a decline of 1.2 percent in 2002. Growth was driven partly by gains in the healthcare industry, which has benefited from advances in medical technology. Also, a 15.7 percent gain in corporate profits allowed show organizers to substantially increase prices on exhibit space for the first time in years without much backlash from exhibitors.

An increase in business-related travel drove growth in most shows in 2004. The International Consumer Electronics Show, the largest trade show in 2004 based on 1.3 million net square feet of paid exhibit space, saw a 13.2 percent increase in professional attendance last year, according to *Tradeshow Week 200*. On the opposite end of the spectrum, The International Boston Seafood Show, the 200th-largest show in 2004 at 130,455 net square feet of paid exhibit space, saw a 34.6 percent increase in attendance.

Since September 11, the vast majority of high technology events have suffered, but 2004 signaled a slow resurgence in that market. While some of the large, horizontal, technology-focused trade shows like COMDEX and Internet World no longer exist, smaller shows serving vertical markets and association-sponsored events experienced an increased number of exhibitors and attendees in 2004. For example, SUPERCOMM, managed by the Telecommunications Industry Association, reported an increase of 28.4 percent in exhibitors in 2004, along with an increase of 2.4 percent in professional attendance. Concurrently, Interop (formerly NetWorld) has recovered somewhat as revenues, attendees and exhibitors were all up about 10 percent

The Trade Show and Exhibition Market

Year	*Exhibit Space (Millions Of Square Feet)*	*Average Price Per Square Foot*	*Total Spending On Exhibit Space ($ Millions)*	*Fees, Sponsorships And Advertising ($ Millions)*	*Total Trade Show Spending ($ Millions)*
1999	366.0	$17.50	$6,405	$2,133	$ 8,538
2000	376.5	17.75	6,683	2,225	8,908
2001	371.2	17.87	6,634	1,987	8,621
2002	367.5	18.05	6,633	1,888	8,521
2003	366.0	18.41	6,738	1,911	8,649
2004	371.5	19.15	7,114	2,035	9,149
2005	378.2	19.92	7,532	2,178	9,710
2006	386.1	20.51	7,921	2,319	10,240
2007	395.0	21.03	8,306	2,486	10,792
2008	406.1	21.59	8,769	2,648	11,417
2009	419.1	22.11	9,267	2,834	12,101

Source: Veronis Suhler Stevenson, PQ Media, *Tradeshow Week 200*, Center for Exhibition Research

Growth of the Trade Show and Exhibition Market

Year	*Exhibit Space*	*Average Price Per Square Foot*	*Total Spending On Exhibit Space*	*Fees, Sponsorships And Advertising*	*Total Trade Show Spending*
2000	2.9%	1.4%	4.3%	4.3%	4.3%
2001	–1.4	0.7	–0.7	–10.7	–3.2
2002	–1.0	1.0	0.0	–5.0	–1.2
2003	–0.4	2.0	1.6	1.2	1.5
2004	1.5	4.0	5.6	6.5	5.8
2005	1.8	4.0	5.9	7.0	6.1
2006	2.1	3.0	5.2	6.5	5.5
2007	2.3	2.5	4.9	7.2	5.4
2008	2.8	2.7	5.6	6.5	5.8
2009	3.2	2.4	5.7	7.0	6.0
Compound Annual Growth					
1999-2004	0.3	1.8	2.1	–0.9	1.4
2004-2009	2.4	2.9	5.4	6.8	5.8

Source: Veronis Suhler Stevenson, PQ Media, *Tradeshow Week 200*, Center for Exhibition Research

Trade Show Professional Attendance

Year	*Professional Attendance (Thousands)*	*Percent Change*
1999	39,450	—
2000	41,225	4.5%
2001	39,370	–4.5
2002	38,400	–2.5
2003	39,782	3.6
2004	40,856	2.7
Compound Annual Growth		
1999-2004		0.7

Sources: Veronis Suhler Stevenson, PQ Media, *Tradeshow Week 200*

in 2004. Nevertheless, they have not yet made up for lost revenues during the recession. Technology companies are attempting to drive growth by channeling event marketing resources to private events, utilizing custom programs, or marketing smaller, invitation-only, face-to-face events.

Early signs in the first half of 2005 indicated that transaction-focused retail events in fragmented industries will continue to grow. We expect the overall trade show market to grow at an accelerated pace throughout the forecast period, driven equally by an increase in exhibitors and attendees. For exhibitors, the high costs associated with exhibiting, including travel expenses—such as airfare, hotels and meals—are being offset by the upswing in integrated marketing packages for exhibitors. Although these new packages are offered at a premium price, the additional exposure they provide, such as prominent brand placement on all marketing materials related to the show, helps to boost ROI due to the number of deals made at trade shows.

Total spending on exhibit space increased 5.6 percent to $7.11 billion in 2004, and was fueled by price hikes and additional exhibit space rented. Average price per square foot rose 4.0 percent to $19.15, bolstered by enthusiasm related to the industry's long-awaited recovery. However, the market will not be able to sustain such massive price hikes going forward, as vendors become less willing to absorb large annual increases as the market levels off. Exhibit space was up by 1.5 percent to 371.5 million square feet in 2004.

The healthcare category was also largely responsible for a 2.7 percent increase in professional attendance to 40.9 million in 2004. The demand for new technologies, equipment and pharmaceuticals, along with increased specialization, has led several healthcare-related associations to develop new trade shows that focus more on education than on selling. Spending on continuing medical education continues to rise in relation to new medical discoveries, as does the number of new companies entering the market. The overall increase in attendance sparked growth in spending on fees, sponsorships and advertising, which rose 6.5 percent to $2.04 billion, after climbing 1.2 percent in 2003 and dipping 0.5 percent in 2002. Total spending on trade shows grew at a compound annual rate of 1.4 percent from 1999 to 2004, with exhibit space increasing 0.3 percent, and fees and sponsorships down 0.9 percent.

Contrary to prior concerns that the growing use of the Internet would stifle attendance at in-person events, the medium has actually helped trade show companies in terms of gathering attendee and marketing registration information in advance. New product offerings, especially those that are technology-based, continue to support the need for face-to-face trade shows.

The Outlook For Trade Shows And Exhibitions

Spending on trade shows and exhibitions is expected to recover faster than spending on b-to-b magazines, and we expect it will accelerate at a growth rate in the single digits for the next five years, driven by the prosperity of the healthcare and retail industries. Spending will increase 6.1 percent to $9.71 billion in 2005, as trade show marketers continue to apply ROI measurements to trade show spending and develop marketing tools that help define the quality, not only quantity, of attendees. The market will also benefit from an uptick in business-related travel and the planned expansion and addition of several major exhibit halls in key cities across the nation. The increasing use of third-party audits of the trade shows will help to demonstrate value to exhibitors.

As trade show organizers continue to host more invitation-only events that allow booth holders to get closer to their top customers, total spending on exhibit space will grow 5.9 percent to $7.53 billion in 2005. Exhibit space sold will rise 1.8 percent to 378.2 million square feet, and prices will increase 4.0 percent to $19.92 on average.

An increasingly higher caliber of keynote speakers and educational sessions will lead to an increase in attendance, boosting fees, sponsorships and advertising 7.0 percent to $2.18 billion in 2005. Trade show spending will grow at a compound annual rate of 5.8 percent from 2004 to 2009, reaching $12.10 billion in 2009.

FORECAST ASSUMPTIONS

- The trade show industry will experience moderate single-digit growth over the next five years as the economy, corporate profits and travel budgets strengthen, and dominant industries like healthcare and technology launch new events in line with continuing education efforts.
- Spending on exhibit space will remain relatively strong throughout the forecast period, driven by value-added marketing packages that promise to deliver a good return on investment to offset increasing booth rental fees.
- Prices for exhibit space will decelerate over the next five years as the market's recovery levels off and vendors become less inclined to absorb major price hikes.
- Trade show organizers, as part of the e-media initiatives, have continued to provide more content on Web-specific trade show sites, ranging from program highlights to vendor directories. Efforts are being made to provide live feeds, such as blogs developed at the trade show events.

Business Overview

Established in 1999, Schofield Publishing Ltd. ("Schofield" or the "Company") is a publisher of business-to-business controlled circulation magazines in the US and the UK. With a focus on "best practices", its magazines cover industry areas such as manufacturing and services, general business, food and drink, construction, design and healthcare. Schofield's model is to produce editorial profiles of successful companies and then target the subject's vendors and suppliers for advertising sales. With its recent acquisition of four titles from VNU, the Company also operates business-to-business magazines and tradeshows that derive revenue from traditional contract advertisers in the food retail and beverage industries.

Background

Andrew Schofield founded Schofield Publishing Ltd. in the UK in 1999 using a model of selling advertisements around profiled businesses in trade magazines. In 2000, Schofield Media, the US operation was launched, recognizing the potential for growth in the US market.

Excellent organic growth was supplemented with VSS Mezzanine Partners committing $7.0 million of Subordinated Debt to fund the acquisition of four business-to-business magazines from VNU and cash for working capital.

Strategy & Rationale

- Leverage first mover advantage in the US by continuing to launch new magazine titles within verticals that will attract advertising from the suppliers and business partners of profiled companies.
- Continue to seek the acquisition of underperforming magazine titles within select verticals of both profile magazine and traditional business-to-business magazine titles.
- Expand the scope of the Company's trade show operations through acquisition and new launches and continue to leverage the cross promotional opportunities if its shows with its associated magazines.

Add-on Acquisition Activities

- In December, prior to VSS's investment in the Company, Schofiled acquired **Red Coat Publishing**, adding two additional profile0style magazine title that focus on business and healthcare sectors.
- In March, the Company acquired four business-to-business magazine titles from VNU Inc., *Restaurant Business, Food Service Network, Retail Merchandiser* and *Beverage World.* Accompanying the titles are tradeshows, conferences and a leading website.

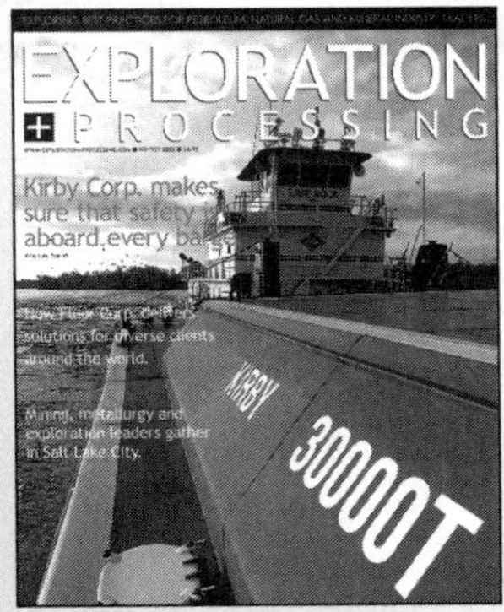

13

EDUCATIONAL AND TRAINING MEDIA

SUMMARY

Total spending on educational and training media rose 4.2 percent in 2004 to $18.69 billion, the market's largest increase since 2000. The gain was driven by the outsourced corporate training subsegment, which benefited from the robust economy and improved job market, as companies invested more capital in training new employees and developing existing ones. The rebound in spending on outsourced corporate training, however, was offset somewhat by a more sluggish gain in the educational segment, resulting in combined spending growth that trailed that of nominal GDP for the fourth consecutive year.

The K-12 instructional materials market, including spending on basal, supplemental and electronic learning materials, turned in the worst performance of the three subsegments included in this chapter—K-12, college and outsourced corporate training—with spending flat at $4.06 billion in 2004. A decline of about 29 percent to approximately $530 million in spending by textbook adoption states in 2004 was offset by higher spending in open territories, strong funding from the federal government and higher expenditures on supplementary materials. The K-12 market's growth in 2004 lagged GDP expansion for the third consecutive year.

Growth of U.S. Spending on Educational and Training Media

	K-12 Instructional Materials	*College Instructional Materials*	*Outsourced Corporate Training*	*Total*
2004 Expenditures ($ Millions)	$4,063	$4,708	$9,923	$18,694
1999-2004 Compound Annual Growth (%)	4.2%	5.2%	2.2%	3.4%
2004-2009 Projected Compound Annual Growth (%)	5.4%	2.7%	6.2%	5.2%
2009 Projected Expenditures ($ Millions)	$5,279	$5,378	$13,380	$24,037

Sources: Veronis Suhler Stevenson, PQ Media, Book Industry Study Group, Simba Information, *Training Magazine*

Spending on college instructional materials, which includes textbooks, coursepacks, software and online services, grew 1.5 percent to $4.71 billion in 2004, due to students' reluctance to pay for expensive new textbooks. High tuition costs and negative publicity about college textbook prices spurred students to find alternatives to buying new texts.

After a three-year slump, spending on outsourced corporate training increased 7.4 percent to $9.92 billion in 2004, driven by growth in the information technology (IT) subsegment, the largest sector of the corporate training market. The gain in the IT sector offset spending declines in the other three training subsegments.

Total spending on educational and training media grew at a compound annual rate of 3.4 percent from 1999 to 2004, trailing nominal GDP growth by more than 1 percentage point in the period. Following the recession of 2001, corporations trimmed their corporate training budgets, while state budget cuts and a lack of textbook adoptions limited spending gains in the K-12 instructional materials sector. Rising enrollments and moderate price increases drove spending gains in the college instructional materials market early in the 1999-2004 period, but high prices curbed spending and hindered growth in 2003 and 2004.

We project the growth of spending on educational and training media will accelerate in 2005, rising 7.2 percent to $20.05 billion. The strong economy and robust job market will drive another gain in the outsourced corporate training subsegment in 2005, while healthier state budgets and more adoption opportunities will spur double-digit upside in the K-12 market for the year. Meanwhile, high prices and a slow transition from the use of print materials to electronic learning materials will limit growth in the college market in 2005. Mid-single-digit gains are projected for the remainder of the forecast period for the overall educational and training media segment, resulting in a compound annual growth rate of 5.2 percent from 2004 to 2009. Total segment spending will reach $24.04 billion in 2009.

Spending on Educational and Training Media And Nominal GDP Growth, 2000-2009

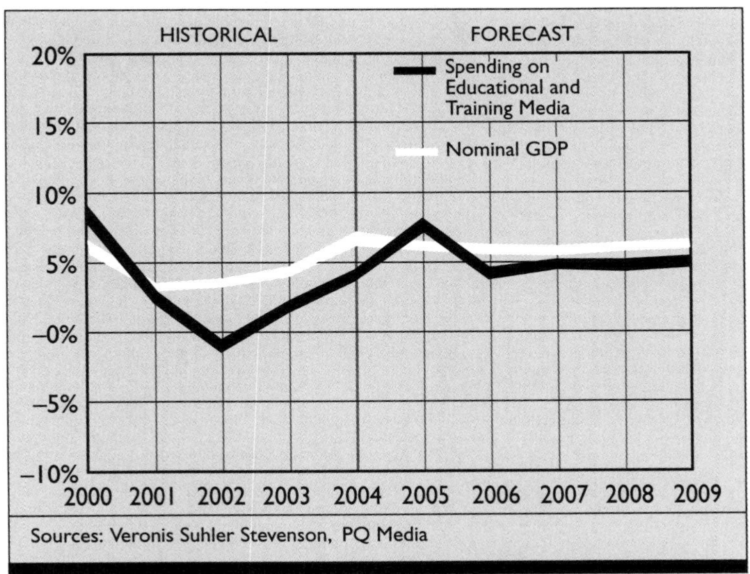

Sources: Veronis Suhler Stevenson, PQ Media

2004 Communications Industry Forecast Compared with Actual Growth

Category	*2004 Forecasted Growth**	*Actual 2004 Growth*†
K-12 Instructional Materials	3.0%	0.0%
College Instructional Materials	5.5	1.5
Outsourced Corporate Training	2.2	7.4
Total	4.4	4.2

*Veronis Suhler Stevenson 2004 Communications Industry Forecast & Report
†Veronis Suhler Stevenson, PQ Media

Spending on Educational and Training Media

($ MILLIONS)

Year	*K-12 Instructional Materials*	*College Instructional Materials*	*Outsourced Corporate Training**	*Total*
1999	$3,314	$3,645	$ 8,880	$15,838
2000	3,754	3,772	9,580	17,106
2001	4,047	4,044	9,510	17,601
2002	3,926	4,469	9,158	17,553
2003	4,063	4,638	9,237	17,939
2004	4,063	4,708	9,923	18,694
2005	4,531	4,802	10,716	20,048
2006	4,671	4,907	11,336	20,914
2007	4,905	5,045	11,961	21,910
2008	5,125	5,196	12,634	22,955
2009	5,279	5,378	13,380	24,037

Sources: Veronis Suhler Stevenson, PQ Media, Book Industry Study Group, Simba Information, *Training Magazine*

*The methodology used to size, structure and forecast the outsourced corporate training market was changed in order to provide a more accurate picture of this marketplace. As part of this change, a new primary source for historical data was used, coupled with a secondary source for certain market subsegments and categories, which served as the basis for a proprietary regression analysis.

Growth of Spending on Educational and Training Media

Year	*K-12 Instructional Materials*	*College Instructional Materials*	*Outsourced Corporate Training**	*Total*
2000	13.3%	3.5%	7.9%	8.0%
2001	7.8	6.7	–0.7	2.9
2002	–5.0	9.5	–3.7	–0.3
2003	3.5	3.6	0.9	2.2
2004	0.0	1.5	7.4	4.2
2005	11.5	2.0	8.0	7.2
2006	3.1	2.2	5.8	4.3
2007	5.0	2.8	5.5	4.8
2008	4.5	3.0	5.6	4.8
2009	3.0	3.5	5.9	4.7
Compound Annual Growth				
1999-2004	4.2	5.2	2.2	3.4
2004-2009	5.4	2.7	6.2	5.2

Sources: Veronis Suhler Stevenson, PQ Media, Book Industry Study Group, Simba Information, *Training Magazine*

*The methodology used to size, structure and forecast the outsourced corporate training market was changed in order to provide a more accurate picture of this marketplace. As part of this change, a new primary source for historical data was used, coupled with a secondary source for certain market subsegments and categories, which served as the basis for a proprietary regression analysis.

K-12 Instructional Materials

THE K-12 INSTRUCTIONAL MATERIALS MARKET IN 2004 AND 2005

The lack of major new adoptions and tight state funding combined to give publishers low expectations heading into 2004. And while spending on basal programs in adoption states fell in 2004, this decline was offset by an increase in spending in non-adoption states and growth in expenditures on supplementary materials. The result was flat spending in 2004 of $4.06 billion on K-12 instructional materials, including basal, supplemental and electronic resources. Weakness in state funding was countered in part by nearly $1 billion in funds from the federal government to support its hallmark program, No Child Left Behind (NCLB).

Growth in the K-12 learning materials market in 2004 trailed that of nominal GDP for the third consecutive year, but this trend is expected to change in 2005. A jump in the number of state adoptions, coupled with improvement in the economies of most states, will fuel an 11.5 percent increase in spending on K-12 instructional materials in 2005 to $4.53 billion. Funding for state adoptions in 2005 is estimated to be approximately $900 million, up some 70 percent from about $530 million in 2004, primarily due to increased allocations in Texas. Indications in the first half of 2005 suggest that spending on K-12 instructional materials is on track to post the largest annual gain since 2000. McGraw-Hill, one of the nation's three largest K-12 publishers, reported that sales in its school group were up 12.6 percent in the first quarter of the year, and the company told investors that it expects strong gains in K-12 spending for several years to come. Monthly estimates from the Association of American Publishers (AAP) showed school sales up 14.2 percent in the first quarter of 2005, driven by the strong growth of basal textbooks.

After an extended period of relatively strong expansion, the K-12 instructional materials market hit a trough in the 2002-2004 interval. In that three-year span, annual spending rose only in 2003, and the $4.06 billion in 2004 expenditures was only slightly higher than the $4.05 billion in spending recorded for 2001. Spending during most of the three-year period was depressed because of a sluggish economy, state budget cuts and few adoption opportunities. Weak expenditures on school learning materials in 2002 and 2004 offset stronger gains in 2000 and 2001, resulting in compound annual growth of 4.2 percent from 1999 to 2004.

Following a 3.5 percent spending increase in 2003, expenditures on K-12 instructional courseware leveled off in 2004 due to an estimated 30 percent decline in adoption funds, which fell to approximately $530 million. The decline in adoption funding was offset in part by higher-than-expected spending on instructional materials in open territories, as well as increased outlays on supplemental materials and federal funding of about $1 billion to support NCLB. Spending gains were strongest in the core disciplines of reading and math. The positive trends in 2004—strong spending in open territories, the expansion of the supplemental market and increased federal funding—will continue in 2005, augmented by more adoptions and even higher overall funding.

MAJOR TRENDS IN THE K-12 INSTRUCTIONAL MATERIALS MARKET

The K-12 market is driven primarily by state funding, textbook adoptions and school enrollments on an annual basis. In 2004, state funding was down, the textbook adoption market was weak and school enrollments experienced only a minimal gain. In 2005, state funding is expected to rise, adoption opportunities will increase significantly and enrollment will grow 0.3 percent. Another trend spurred by the implementation of NCLB—more standards-based testing—is expected to accelerate in 2005, driving funding growth for learning courseware to help students pass required tests.

The most important factor driving the spending gains on K-12 instructional materials in 2005 is an estimated 70 percent increase in adoption funding to about $900 million. Major adoptions are planned in key subject areas such as math, social studies and

Highlights

K-12 Instructional Materials

Spending on K-12 instructional materials, including basal, supplemental and electronic resources, was flat in 2004 at $4.06 billion, trailing the expansion of the broader economy for the third consecutive year. A decline in spending on basal textbooks in adoption states was offset by an increase in spending in open territories, higher expenditures on supplementary materials and strong funding from the federal government.

■

The K-12 instructional materials market grew at a compound annual rate of 4.2 percent in the 1999-2004 period, as strong spending gains in 2000 and 2001 countered weaker expenditure growth in the 2002-2004 timeframe.

■

Total K-12 enrollment will increase at a 0.3 percent compound annual rate in the forecast period, reaching 55.2 million in 2009. Enrollment in secondary schools will grow by more than 1 percent in 2005 and 2006, but will decline at the end of the forecast period as the last of the baby boomlet generation graduates. Elementary school enrollment will turn upward in 2006 and increase at a relatively slow pace throughout the rest of the forecast period.

■

Spending on K-12 instructional materials will post the strongest gain in five years in 2005, jumping 11.5 percent to $4.53 billion. A total increase in funding of about 70 percent in adoption states will be the primary driver of spending growth for the year. Improved state economies, continued growth in open territories and the expansion of the supplementary materials market will also contribute to the market's growth.

■

We anticipate steady single-digit growth during the forecast period as adoption opportunities even out, open territories continue to fund textbook purchases and the supplemental market expands. K-12 materials spending will grow at a compound annual rate of 5.4 percent in the 2004-2009 period, with total expenditures reaching $5.28 billion in 2009.

science. Several major adoption states, particularly Texas, plan to increase textbook purchases in 2005, and opportunities in open territories will also expand during the year compared with 2004.

Texas will provide publishers with their best adoption opportunities in 2005. Although the final budget had not been passed at press time, the Texas State Board of Education was asking for $714.3 million in instructional materials aid for the 2005-06 school year, a 134.1 percent increase over the $305.1 million allocated in 2004-05. If approved by the state legislature, about $145 million of the new funds will be used to pay for purchases of learning materials that were postponed from 2004-05 in English as a second language (ESL), computer science and vocational education. New funding will be put toward acquiring materials in health, foreign languages, fine arts and music. Among some of the other key adoption states, Florida is adopting in social studies and speech, and Georgia is adopting for social studies, as is Oregon. North Carolina is adopting in science and foreign languages, while Illinois is adopting in all subjects for grades K-4. The only reading adoption set for 2005 is in Arkansas.

Meanwhile, Texas lawmakers are also considering a drastic overhaul in the adoption process that would move buying to the school level from the state level. State aid in the other four largest textbook markets in 2005—including adoption and non-adoption states—including California, Florida, New York and Illinois, is expected to be relatively stable. That is particularly good news in the volatile California market, where aid is expected to increase 1.9 percent to $380.0 million in 2005.

The strength of the adoption market in 2005 will be augmented by several other positive factors. First, state economies are in much better condition this year than in 2004. As this *Forecast* went to press, it was estimated that only three states were planning to cut their state budgets in 2005, compared to 15 in 2004 and more than 30 in 2003. NCLB is expected to add another $1 billion in federal funds in 2005 to support initiatives such as Reading First. Stricter

Elementary and Secondary School Fall Enrollment

(THOUSANDS)

Year	*Elementary*	*Secondary*	*Total*
1999	38,253	14,623	52,876
2000	38,584	14,801	53,385
2001	38,832	15,058	53,890
2002	38,827	15,331	54,158
2003	38,719	15,577	54,296
2004	38,541	15,914	54,455
2005	38,412	16,203	54,615
2006	38,522	16,385	54,907
2007	38,605	16,445	55,050
2008	38,766	16,358	55,124
2009	38,995	16,228	55,223

Sources: Veronis Suhler Stevenson, PQ Media, National Center for Educational Statistics

Growth of Elementary and Secondary School Fall Enrollment

Year	*Elementary*	*Secondary*	*Total*
2000	0.9%	1.2%	1.0%
2001	0.6	1.7	0.9
2002	0.0	1.8	0.5
2003	–0.3	1.6	0.3
2004	–0.5	2.2	0.3
2005	–0.3	1.8	0.3
2006	0.3	1.1	0.5
2007	0.2	0.4	0.3
2008	0.4	–0.5	0.1
2009	0.6	–0.8	0.2
Compound Annual Growth			
1999-2004	0.2	1.7	0.6
2004-2009	0.2	0.4	0.3

Sources: Veronis Suhler Stevenson, PQ Media, National Center for Educational Statistics

State Instructional Materials Aid in Largest Markets*

State	*2003 ($ Millions)*	*2004 ($ Millions)*	*2005 ($ Millions)*	*2003-04 Growth*	*2004-05 Growth*
California	$297.0	$ 373.0	$ 380.0	25.6%	1.9%
Texas†	248.4	305.1	714.3	22.8	134.1%
Florida	227.8	235.4	226.0	3.3	−4.0
New York	190.7	255.0	254.0	33.7	−0.4
Illinois	29.1	29.1	29.1	0.0	0.0
Total	993.0	1,197.6	1,603.4	20.6	33.9

Sources: Veronis Suhler Stevenson, PQ Media, State Budget Offices

*Note: State instructional materials aid does not include special line items for technology products or funds derived from federal technology programs that are distributed by the state.

†The Texas legislature was still debating textbook funding at press time; therefore, data are subject to change.

accountability standards on student performance demanded by NCLB will also serve as an incentive for state and local governments to increase their aid for educational materials. NCLB requires schools to meet so-called Adequate Yearly Progress standards for the entire student body.

While NCLB has put a spotlight on accountability in education, the act has sparked some controversy. In mid-2005, the National Education Association (NEA), along with state attorneys general from several different states, filed a lawsuit against the federal government, charging that NCLB does not provide enough funding to meet all the requirements mandated by the government. In addition to the NEA suit, which was just beginning to wend its way through the courts in the first quarter of 2005, a number of other self-styled "adequacy" lawsuits had been filed by teachers and parents against states demanding that schools receive sufficient funding to allow students to meet testing goals. Plaintiffs have prevailed in the vast majority of decisions so far, resulting in more school funding.

Meanwhile, total K-12 enrollment growth, including elementary and secondary schools, is expected to increase 0.3 percent in 2005, the same rate of growth as in the previous two years. Enrollment increases will be the strongest in secondary schools in 2005 and 2006, but will fall off toward the end of the forecast period as the last children of the baby boomlet generation move on to college. After falling in 2005 for the third consecutive year, elementary school enrollment will begin to increase again in 2006, with growth accelerating later in the 2004-2009 period. Total K-12 enrollment, however, is expected to grow at a slower compound annual rate in the forecast period than in the 1999-2004 timeframe. Overall enrollment rose at a compound annual rate of 0.6 percent from 1999 to 2004, driven largely by growth in the secondary school segment. Total enrollment will increase by only 0.3 percent on a compound annual basis from 2004 to 2009.

An important trend within school enrollment is the continuing shift in the composition of the student population. Minorities now account for approximately one-third of all students, and approximately 5.5 million students in public schools don't speak English. By far, the largest group of minorities is Hispanic, with the fastest growth in this segment of the population coming from Florida, California and Texas. The increase in the U.S. population over the next 20 years will be driven in part by immigrants from Mexico, Central America, the Caribbean and China, many of whose children will not speak English. The result of the increase in non-English-speaking students is creating a growing demand for ESL and ELL (English Language Learners) materials.

The use of technology in classrooms has been well-established over the last decade, but penetration has slowed in recent years, an indication that most schools that can afford technology have already acquired the necessary hardware. The total number of computers in the K-12 market dropped slightly to 12.3 million in the 2004-05 school year from 12.9 million in the prior academic year. While the research firm that compiled the data reported that the decline was likely due to a change in the survey's methodology, the lack of growth supports the theory that growth in the installed base of computers in schools has slowed significantly. The increase in student access to the Internet also slowed in the 2004-05 school year. The ratio of students per Internet-access computer was 3.9 in 2004-05, only a slight improvement over the 4.0 ratio in the 2003-04 academic year. As recently as 1997-98, student per Internet-access computer stood as high as 19.7.

The recent technology trends suggest that the drive to bring technology into the K-12 market has largely been successful. But that also means spending on electronic instructional materials, such as computer software, multimedia packages and online services, already has been factored into school budgets. Most state adoption boards already require that all textbooks submitted for adoptions include electronic components.

The use of technology in schools will continue upward in the forecast period, but most of the growth will be directed at upgrading instructional management and student information systems as school districts work to comply with stricter accountability and testing requirements. While outlays for management systems are expected to increase significantly in 2005, spending on electronic courseware will increase at more modest levels. (The spending figures in this *Forecast* include only expenditures on instructional materials, not hardware or networking systems.) In New York, for example, the state plans to reduce its funding for the purchase of educational software from $47.0 million to $46.0 million in the 2005-06 school year. Textbook aid, however, will remain at $189.0 million for the year. A battle has been raging in Texas over whether to increase the annual per-pupil technology allotment from $30 to $300 per student. As in the case of most political issues in the Lone Star State, it was not clear at press time how such an increase in electronic courseware funding would impact textbook financing. We project that spending on electronic instructional materials will increase at about the same 11.5 percent rate projected for the entire K-12 market in 2005.

Computers in the K-12 Market

	2001-02	*2002-03*	*2003-04*	*2004-05*
Total Computers (Thousands)	11,200	12,200	12,950	12,300
Students Per Computer	4.3	4.0	3.8	3.8
Students Per Internet Access Computer	7.9	5.5	4.0	3.9

Sources: Veronis Suhler Stevenson, PQ Media, Market Data Retrieval

While technology has garnered big headlines over the past decade, the supplementary materials market quietly has been one of the most consistently fast-growing areas of the K-12 courseware subsegment. Supplementary publishers produce everything from workbooks and storybooks to manipulatives and software. Reading/language arts/English is by far the largest market for supplementary materials, followed by social science and math, which have been the fastest-growing subject areas in recent years. Many supplemental publishers are owned by entrepreneurial former teachers, but the segment has experienced increasing consolidation in recent years. Saxon Publishers, a leading publisher of math and phonics alternative textbooks, was acquired in June 2004 by Harcourt, which integrated Saxon into its supplementary division. In early 2005, EMC/Paradigm Publishing, which produces supplementals for the K-12 and college markets, was acquired by private equity firm Wicks Group. EMC

K-12 Instructional Materials Market

Year	Unit Sales (Millions)	Average Price	End-User Spending ($ Millions)
1999	139	$23.84	$3,314
2000	152	24.70	3,754
2001	159	25.45	4,047
2002	153	25.66	3,926
2003	155	26.17	4,063
2004	154	26.43	4,063
2005	168	27.04	4,531
2006	169	27.60	4,671
2007	173	28.27	4,905
2008	178	28.82	5,125
2009	180	29.39	5,279

Sources: Veronis Suhler Stevenson, PQ Media, Book Industry Study Group

Growth of K-12 Instructional Materials Market

Year	Unit Sales	Average Price	End-User Spending
2000	9.4%	3.6%	13.3%
2001	4.6	3.1	7.8
2002	–3.8	0.8	–5.0
2003	1.5	2.0	3.5
2004	–1.0	1.0	0.0
2005	9.0	2.3	11.5
2006	1.0	2.1	3.1
2007	2.5	2.4	5.0
2008	2.5	2.0	4.5
2009	1.0	2.0	3.0
Compound Annual Growth			
1999-2004	2.0	2.1	4.2
2004-2009	3.2	2.1	5.4

Sources: Veronis Suhler Stevenson, PQ Media, Book Industry Study Group

was added to Wicks's other publishing properties, including supplemental producer Delta Publishing.

Each of the leading basal publishers operates a substantial supplemental publishing business, either one created internally or one formed through acquisitions. Nevertheless, the supplemental materials market is highly fragmented, making it difficult to track. The AAP reported that sales of supplementary materials rose by more than 11 percent in 2004, but that figure includes only AAP members, which are estimated to represent only one-third of the market. Other estimates indicate that supplementary publishing increased in the high single digits in 2004 to approximately $1.6 billion, with similar growth projected for the next couple of years. The majority of spending is captured in our overall K-12 figures, but there is a sizeable minority that is not, since most supplemental producers are small companies with sales hard to quantify.

An important sales channel for supplementary publishers is the home school market, which is estimated to include between 1 million and 2 million children educated at home. Anecdotal evidence further suggests that spending on instructional materials in this market per child ranges from $450 to $1,200 annually. The home school market is even more difficult to track than the supplemental industry because much of the spending comes from parents who purchase materials through various retail, online and publishing outlets. We believe that some of this spending is captured in our overall figures, but most is not for this reason.

The Outlook for K-12 Instructional Materials

Spending on K-12 instructional materials is expected to surge 11.5 percent in 2005 to $4.53 billion, representing the largest spending increase in five years. Growth will be driven by a substantial increase in funding for textbook adoptions, improved state and local economies, and strong funding from the federal government.

For the rest of the forecast period, we anticipate low- to mid-single-digit growth with less pronounced spikes, as adoption opportunities spread out, open territories become more important, and demand for supplemental materials remains strong. Expenditures on K-12 learning materials will grow at a compound annual rate of 5.4 percent from 2004 to 2009, reaching $5.28 billion in 2009.

Total K-12 enrollment growth will increase at a slower rate in the forecast period compared with the 1999-2004 timeframe, although the slowdown is not expected to have an effect on instructional materials spending. The decelerating growth rate will be most noticeable in the secondary school market, which is forecast to have a decline in enrollment at the tail end of the forecast period, following enrollment gains of more than 1 percent in 2005 and 2006. A slight upswing in elementary enrollment is expected to begin in 2006, and small gains are projected through 2009. Total enrollment will inch up at a compound annual rate of 0.3 percent in the forecast period to 55.2 million in 2009.

Spending on school technology is expected to pick up in 2005, as districts scramble to meet federal reporting guidelines. The emphasis, however, will be on management and assessment tools, not on digital courseware. Expenditures on items like educational software are projected to increase in line with the 11.5 percent growth projected for all K-12 instructional materials.

FORECAST ASSUMPTIONS

- Growth in the K-12 instructional materials market is projected to increase significantly in 2005. An increase in total state adoption funding of about 70 percent, stronger state and local economies, and continued funding for major federal programs such as No Child Left Behind will drive the gains in 2005.
- The double-digit spending increase in 2005 is expected to begin a string of moderate annual spending gains that will last through the forecast period. A robust adoption schedule, improved state economies and the high priority placed on education by national and state leaders will drive spending gains through 2009.
- Total K-12 enrollment growth will increase slowly during the forecast period. Growth in secondary school enrollment will be relatively strong in 2005 and 2006, but will trail off toward the end of the forecast period. After declining in 2005, expansion in elementary school enrollment will accelerate slightly toward the end of the 2004-2009 timeframe.
- The use of technology in schools will continue to increase during the next five years as this trend becomes more intertwined with the national movement toward standards, accountability, testing and remediation. To qualify for major federal programs, school districts are required to produce specialized student data reports. These requirements will drive schools to spend additional money on performance management systems and less on instructional materials.

College Instructional Materials

THE COLLEGE INSTRUCTIONAL MATERIALS MARKET IN 2004 AND 2005

Spending on college instructional materials, including textbooks, coursepacks, software and online services, rose a disappointing 1.5 percent to $4.71 billion in 2004, marking the second consecutive year in which college courseware growth lagged that of nominal GDP. The deceleration in spending growth was tied to a 0.3 percent dip in unit sales that was offset by a 1.8 percent increase in prices. The price increase was the smallest in more than five years and reflected the growing resistance among college students to pay full price for new college textbooks.

Many college publishers are bracing for low-single-digit growth over the next several years. While the perceived high price of textbooks has been a concern of students for some time, the issue exploded in early 2004 with the release of *Ripoff 101*, a research study conducted by the California Public Interest Research Group (CPIRG). The report, which asserted that textbook prices are artificially high because of the monopoly held by a few large college publishers, sparked widespread media coverage questioning the college textbook pricing model. With the cost of college tuition soaring and student aid declining, the negative publicity generated by the CPIRG study gave students added incentive to cut costs by buying used textbooks, sharing textbooks, or not buying course books at all.

In addition to high prices, other issues that limited growth in spending on college instructional materials in 2005 included the growing sophistication of the used book network and the transition to electronic media. Although college enrollment rose again in 2004, the 0.7 percent increase was the slowest gain in at least five years as the increase in part-time enrollment slowed to 0.3 percent from 1.2 percent in 2003.

The negative news continued through the first quarter of 2005, when spending on college instructional materials declined an estimated 6 percent for the period. While we expect spending to rebound somewhat in the third quarter, when students return to campus in August to start the fall semester, expenditures on college courseware are projected to increase only 2.0 percent in 2005 to $4.80 billion. This lethargic performance will result from modest enrollment gains that will be only slightly accentuated by minimal price increases from publishers.

MAJOR TRENDS IN THE COLLEGE INSTRUCTIONAL MATERIALS MARKET

The college instructional materials market is in transition. The negative trends that plagued the college market in 2004—questions over pricing, used books and the use of technology in classrooms—are not expected to be resolved in 2005. College publishers confessed to being "sideswiped" by the negative publicity generated by textbook pricing in 2004, following the release of the CPIRG report and accompanying bad press, and executives were forced to devote a significant amount of time to dealing with the crisis. The pricing issue, however, is unlikely to fade away in 2005. In February of this year, a second study released by the CPIRG claimed that publishing practices were unnecessarily driving up the price of college textbooks. Publishers responded with a study of their own that cited widespread support among college faculty for the use of textbooks in university courses. At the request of Congress, the General Accountability Office (GAO) in July 2004 launched a study of textbook pricing that is expected to reveal findings by July 2005, an event sure to generate more media coverage about textbook prices. In addition to the GAO study, approximately 25 states have introduced bills dealing with the college textbook pricing question. The bills range in scope from providing sales tax exemptions for textbooks to measures related to bundling print and electronic components.

To help counter the increasing resistance to price hikes—both perceived and real—a number of publishers have developed less expensive editions of some of their most popular textbooks. For the fall semester of 2004, Thomson Corporation's higher education group developed the Advantage Program,

HIGHLIGHTS

College Instructional Materials

Spending on college instructional materials, which include textbooks, coursepacks, software and online services, grew 1.5 percent to $4.71 billion in 2004, the second consecutive year in which growth trailed the pace of nominal GDP. Negative publicity about high textbook prices stiffened student resistance to paying full price for new textbooks during the year, which limited spending gains. Increases in expenditures were also curbed by the inability of publishers to charge for stand-alone electronic materials.

■

Total enrollment grew 0.7 percent in 2004, the slowest increase in more than five years, as the growth in part-time students decelerated to 0.3 percent from 1.2 percent in 2003. Most students were enrolled full-time, that is, 9.9 million compared with 6.6 million part-time students.

■

Despite soft spending gains in 2003 and 2004, expenditures on college instructional materials increased at a compound annual rate of 5.2 percent in the 1999-2004 period, driven by sharp gains in 2001 and 2002 that were fueled by price increases and enrollment growth.

■

We project spending on college instructional materials to increase 2.0 percent to $4.80 billion in 2005. The soaring cost of tuition and continued media attention regarding high textbook prices will reinforce students' resistance to paying full prices for textbooks. Weak spending on electronic materials will also limit gains.

■

Total college enrollment will rise at a compound annual rate of 1.1 percent from 2004 to 2009, reaching 17.4 million. Enrollment increases will be strongest for full-time students, rising at a compound annual rate of 1.4 percent in the forecast period. Enrollment in distance learning programs, particularly Web-based courses, will continue to expand over the next five years due to growth in adult education.

■

We project spending on college instructional materials will increase at a compound annual rate of 2.7 percent from 2004 to 2009, reaching $5.38 billion in 2009. Growth could exceed this expectation if the transition from print-based instructional materials to digitally focused learning environments progresses faster than expected during the forecast period. This trend would be stimulated forward by a newer generation of instructors embracing electronic teaching tools and improving the user experience.

College Enrollment

Year	Full-Time Students (Thousands)	Part-Time Students (Thousands)	Total Enrollment (Thousands)	Full-Time Equivalents (Thousands)	Unit Sales (Millions)	Unit Sales Per Full-Time Equivalent
1999	8,786	6,005	14,791	11,789	93.5	7.9
2000	9,010	6,303	15,313	12,162	94.5	7.8
2001	9,146	6,338	15,484	12,315	98.0	8.0
2002	9,590	6,512	16,102	12,846	106.0	8.3
2003	9,774	6,587	16,361	13,068	107.5	8.2
2004	9,860	6,608	16,468	13,164	107.2	8.1
2005	10,008	6,671	16,679	13,344	107.7	8.1
2006	10,160	6,727	16,887	13,524	108.6	8.0
2007	10,272	6,749	17,021	13,647	109.7	8.0
2008	10,400	6,767	17,167	13,784	111.3	8.1
2009	10,560	6,815	17,375	13,968	113.0	8.1

Sources: Veronis Suhler Stevenson, PQ Media, National Center for Educational Statistics, Book Industry Study Group

Growth of College Enrollment

Year	Full-Time Students	Part-Time Students	Total Enrollment	Full-Time Equivalents	Unit Sales	Unit Sales Per Full-Time Equivalent
2000	2.5%	5.0%	3.5%	3.2%	1.1%	–2.0%
2001	1.5	0.6	1.1	1.3	3.7	2.4
2002	4.9	2.7	4.0	4.3	8.2	3.7
2003	1.9	1.2	1.6	1.7	1.4	–0.3
2004	0.9	0.3	0.7	0.7	–0.3	–1.0
2005	1.5	1.0	1.3	1.4	0.5	–0.9
2006	1.5	0.8	1.2	1.3	0.8	–0.5
2007	1.1	0.3	0.8	0.9	1.0	0.1
2008	1.2	0.3	0.9	1.0	1.5	0.5
2009	1.5	0.7	1.2	1.3	1.5	0.2
Compound Annual Growth						
1999-2004	2.3	1.9	2.2	2.2	2.8	0.5
2004-2009	1.4	0.6	1.1	1.2	1.1	–0.1

Sources: Veronis Suhler Stevenson, PQ Media, National Center for Educational Statistics, Book Industry Study Group

which offered about 150 titles in scaled down paperback editions that sold for about half the price of the regular textbooks. Other publishers are using technology to help lower prices. Pearson Education, the nation's largest college publisher, added SafariX.com to its Safari.com operation in 2004, which is an online joint venture between Pearson and computer book publisher O'Reilly Media. The service offers students as much as 50 percent off the price of the 300 textbooks that are part of the online service. SafariX Web books offer the same content as the print edition and are enhanced by full-text search, a Web browser and other digital functionality. SafariX is part of PearsonChoices, which offers students a suite of lower-cost alternatives to full-price print textbooks.

Another publisher hoping technology will help lower textbook prices and spur sales is John Wiley, which has made 32 of its major frontlist titles available through eGrade Plus. The online product provides students with a print and/or online textbook, as well as online study guides and self-testing products that students can purchase at different price points. Morgan Kaufmann, the computer book imprint of Harcourt, has created a new edition of its popular *Computer Organization and Design* title, which can be sold around the world for the same price, $64.95. By designing a smaller paperback edition of the hardcover and moving some content from print to CD-ROM, Morgan Kaufmann was able to lower the cost of this title from $84.95, the price of the textbook in the U.S. The one-price edition is designed to fight another problem that has plagued college publishers in recent years—the re-importation into the U.S. of cheaper editions of foreign textbooks, many of which are sold over the Internet. It is common practice among publishers to price international editions of textbooks lower than the American versions to make them more affordable for local students in foreign countries. Re-importation of textbooks is illegal, but the Web has spurred the practice's growth.

Greater use of the Internet has also changed the complexion of the used textbook market, which has been estimated to siphon off more than $1.5 billion in potential sales annually from college publishers. Efforts to combat used textbook sales, either by issuing new textbook editions more quickly or bundling digital courseware with texts, were somewhat successful over the past decade in blunting the growth of used books. But the Internet has made it easier than ever to sell used textbooks, particularly for students. Indeed, the most significant change in the used textbook market in recent years has been the growth of student-to-student sales through such online stores as Amazon.com and eBay, sales that bypass not only publishers but college bookstores, as well. The major deterrent to the growth of used book sales is lack of supply, not lack of demand, and greater use of the Web as a sales channel for used books has made the market even more efficient, giving a boost to sales.

The popularity of used textbooks is another factor driving publishers to use technology to develop entirely new products. Thomson, which derives about 30 percent of its college sales from electronic publishing, reorganized its higher education operation in 2004 to generate more sales from electronic publishing. Thomson's goal is to move away from selling electronic products that are bundled with textbooks to selling software learning tools, such as course modules and electronic assessment devices, which can be sold separately, generating a new revenue stream. McGraw-Hill, which was one of the first publishers to publish custom textbooks, has created more than 50 online courses that can be delivered over Cisco Systems' global learning network. The company is also creating courses that can be used by the for-profit University of Phoenix Online (UOP). McGraw-Hill's online courses complement UOP's so-called rEsource program that allows online professors to either assign print textbooks from major college publishers or build virtual textbooks from a digital database of various content sources. The digital database, which includes content from the large textbook houses, can be accessed through subscription by any UOP student. Each course that is part of the program has its own online portal through which students pay set fees per course for a collection of materials.

Internet Access, by College Location

Location	*2003*	*2004*	*Point Change*
Computer Lab	97%	95%	–2
Library	87	90	3
Classroom	69	64	–5
Student Center	49	52	3
Residence Hall	54	50	–4

Sources: Veronis Suhler Stevenson, PQ Media, Market Data Retrieval

College Distance Learning Programs, 2004

Colleges Offering Programs		64%
Most Popular Programs	Business	20
	Social Science	16
	Science	7
	Education	7
	Vocational Education	7

Sources: Veronis Suhler Stevenson, PQ Media, Market Data Retrieval

Creating courses for distance learning classes is viewed as a major potential growth area for publishers. Distance learning is now offered at about 64 percent of all colleges and universities, with the most popular degree-granting disciplines being business, social sciences and education. Distance learning is a win-win situation for college publishers. Not only can publishers develop content for online courses, but many online courses require the use of a textbook. Distance learning also holds the potential of attracting more adults who don't have the time to attend classes on campuses, giving college publishers access to new consumers. UOP's distance learning program, one of the nation's largest, had 120,400 students enrolled in 2004, up from 99,000 in 2003. UOP's distance learning services, like its other programs offered through small campuses and learning centers, are aimed at providing continuing education classes for adults over 24.

Another new area being explored by publishers is course management systems. Virtually all colleges and universities now use course management systems, which allow professors to build Web sites for their courses where they can post syllabi, schedules, grades, assignments and quizzes. The most popular systems are developed by Blackboard and WebCT. By partnering with course management companies, publishers can package assessment tools to help college instructors better manage their teaching loads.

Despite the gains made by publishers in introducing technology into the college marketplace, the strategy has not proven to be a panacea to alleviate the industry's ills. While college students are typically among the first to adopt new technology—Internet access is available in nearly all college computer labs and libraries—faculty members have been slow to fully integrate electronic teaching materials into the classroom. In 2005, college instruction is still rooted in print-based materials, the preferred format of many college instructors. Even students have been reluctant to use some new technologies. McGraw-Hill, for example, reports that it sold only 10,000 e-books in 2004 to college students.

With all the questions surrounding the college instructional materials market, the key driver of spending, enrollment, remains generally favorable. But while enrollment is projected to increase throughout the forecast period, the rate of growth will decelerate compared with that of the 1999-2004 period. Projections call for total higher education enrollments to grow at a compound annual rate of 1.1 percent from 2004 to 2009, reaching 17.4 million. Total enrollment in the 1999-2004 interval rose at a compound annual rate of 2.2 percent. Enrollment of full-time students is expected to post the strongest growth in the forecast period, up 1.4 percent on a compound annual basis through 2009, compared to 0.6 percent growth for part-time students.

The Outlook For College Instructional Materials

We project spending on college instructional materials will increase at a compound annual rate of 2.7 percent from 2004 to 2009, reaching $5.38 billion in 2009. The inability of publishers to raise prices at historic levels will be the primary driver limiting spending gains over the next five years. Average prices are projected to increase at a compound annual rate of 1.6 percent in the 2004-2009 timeframe, compared with compound annual growth of 2.4 percent in the previous five-year period. Unit sales will not compensate for the slow growth in prices. Unit sales are projected to increase at a 1.1 percent compound annual rate during the forecast period, compared with a 2.8 percent increase in the 1999-2004 span.

The rate of spending growth could exceed our forecasts if college instruction moves from a primarily print-based learning structure to a digitally-driven teaching environment. That shift may or may not occur as a younger generation of professors, more comfortable with digital media, replaces older faculty who are generally more bound to print texts. A better online learning experience for students, including acceptable digital courseware, would also be needed before pupils more fully embrace the electronic learning environment.

College publishers control a tremendous amount of content, but student resistance to buying textbooks will hamper growth going forward. Spending growth will return to the high-double-digit range only when publishers can create and charge for stand-alone electronic products. Publishers have engaged in the practice of bundling electronic products with textbooks primarily to add value to the print products, but also to blunt the growth of the used textbook market. To develop a new revenue stream, publishers must focus on the development of strong stand-alone digital courseware that students will want to buy and use regularly.

College publishers have been frustrated in recent years by the slow transition to the

FORECAST ASSUMPTIONS

- As tuitions rise and financial aid falls, students will cut costs by refusing to buy new textbooks in 2005, forcing publishers to limit price increases. A minimal price increase, combined with sluggish unit gains, will limit spending gains in 2005 and beyond. The increased use of the Internet, which facilitates student-to-student sales, will give a slight boost to sales of used books.
- Enrollment will not increase quickly enough to counter the effects of student reluctance to buy high-priced new textbooks, with students turning to more affordable alternatives. Total college enrollment will grow at a compound annual rate of 1.1 percent from 2004 to 2009, a substantial deceleration from the 2.2 percent expansion in the 1999-2004 period, while unit growth will slow to 1.4 percent over the next five years, down from the 2.3 percent compound annual increase from 1999 to 2004.
- Spending on electronic courseware by students will not advance notably until college faculties fully embrace the use of technology in classroom instruction and more user-friendly products are developed.

College Instructional Materials Market

Year	Unit Sales (Millions)	Average Price	End-User Spending ($ Millions)
1999	94	$38.98	$3,645
2000	95	39.92	3,772
2001	98	41.27	4,044
2002	106	42.16	4,469
2003	108	43.14	4,638
2004	107	43.92	4,708
2005	108	44.58	4,802
2006	109	45.20	4,907
2007	110	46.00	5,045
2008	111	46.68	5,196
2009	113	47.60	5,378

Sources: Veronis Suhler Stevenson, PQ Media, Book Industry Study Group

Growth of College Instructional Materials Market

Year	Unit Sales	Average Price	End-User Spending
2000	1.1%	2.4%	3.5%
2001	3.7	3.4	6.7
2002	8.2	2.2	9.5
2003	1.4	2.3	3.6
2004	−0.3	1.8	1.5
2005	0.5	1.5	2.0
2006	0.8	1.4	2.2
2007	1.0	1.8	2.8
2008	1.5	1.5	3.0
2009	1.5	2.0	3.5
Compound Annual Growth			
1999-2004	2.8	2.4	5.2
2004-2009	1.1	1.6	2.7

Sources: Veronis Suhler Stevenson, PQ Media, Book Industry Study Group

use of new media in university lecture halls. The Zogby college faculty member survey released by the AAP in January 2005 found overwhelming support for the importance of textbooks in classroom instruction. But while publishers were heartened that college faculty value textbooks, the survey also pointed out that professors still see print materials, not digital alternatives, as their core teaching tools. A dramatic change in instruction, which would shift the emphasis to electronic materials, is not likely to take place until after the forecast period when new instructors are in place, and more user-friendly materials are developed. While publishers wait for that shift to occur, they will continue to explore ways to leverage their content by developing courses that can be sold through non-traditional outlets such as distance learning providers.

Outsourced Corporate Training

THE OUTSOURCED CORPORATE TRAINING MARKET IN 2004 AND 2005

Spending on outsourced corporate training rebounded in 2004 to post the market's fastest growth in four years, following the economic downturn in 2001 and lingering weakness in the job market that caused many corporations to slash training budgets. Confidence in the strength of the nation's economy, the growth of corporate profits and continued job market expansion combined to reverse the sluggish growth trend that had plagued the corporate training market for three consecutive years. Total spending on outsourced corporate training, which ranges from individual training projects performed by outside firms to the complete takeover of a corporation's training department, increased 7.4 percent to $9.92 billion in 2004. This gain followed declines in 2001 and 2002 and a meager increase in 2003. Compound annual growth from 1999 to 2004 was 2.2 percent, which trailed nominal GDP expansion by nearly 3 percentage points in the period.

It is important to note here that Veronis Suhler Stevenson (VSS) this year decided to change the methodology we use to size, structure and forecast the outsourced corporate training market in order to provide what we believe is a more accurate picture of this marketplace. As part of this change in methodology, we are using a new primary source for historical data, coupled with a secondary source for certain market subsegments and categories, which served as the basis for a proprietary regression analysis used to develop the 1999-2004 period figures. VSS also developed a proprietary forecast analysis to create the 2005-2009 period figures.

Although corporations were willing to expand their training budgets in 2004, the lack of an industry-wide method for measuring return on investment forced them to remain cautious when selecting a training partner. As a result, many suppliers enhanced their programs by incorporating simulations of real-life events and by tacking on additional follow-up sessions in an effort to improve employee retention and

Highlights

Outsourced Corporate Training

Total spending on outsourced corporate training materials and services rose at an accelerated 7.4 percent rate in 2004 to $9.92 billion, outpacing nominal GDP growth and representing the market's fastest expansion in four years. Key growth drivers in 2004 were the stronger economy and improved job market, which led corporations to increase their investments in new and current employee training to capitalize on expanding opportunities created by the economic recovery.

■

Increased spending on disciplines such as security training boosted spending in the information technology segment 3.9 percent in 2004 to $4.86 billion, while demand for strong leaders lifted the soft skills training segment by 10.0 percent to $4.38 billion. Although it still remains the smallest segment, Web-based training delivered through learning management systems, virtual classrooms and Web conferencing collectively accounted for a total of $684.0 million in spending in 2004, up 17.9 percent from the prior year and representing the fastest growth of all segments.

■

Total spending on outsourced corporate training grew at a compound annual rate of 2.2 percent from 1999 to 2004, lagging economic growth in the period by almost 2 percentage points as a result of the contractions in 2001 and 2002. Training budgets are typically among the first to be cut by corporations during economic downturns; therefore, recovery in this market usually trails the broader economy by six to 12 months.

■

We expect outsourced corporate training expenditures to increase another 8.0 percent in 2005 to $10.72 billion, driven by a healthy economy and an expanding job market that will incite employees to switch jobs and cause companies to spend more on employee training. Spending on outsourced corporate training is projected to grow at a compound annual rate of 6.2 percent from 2004 to 2009, reaching $13.38 billion, fueled by an uptick in leadership and security training, as well as technological advances in Web-based delivery platforms.

Spending on Outsourced Training, by Category*

($ MILLIONS)

Year	*IT Training*	*Soft Skills*	*LMS Platform*	*Live E-learning*	*Total*
1999	$5,429	$3,451	—	—	$ 8,880
2000	5,836	3,744	—	—	9,580
2001	5,100	3,788	$464	$159	9,510
2002	4,630	3,904	453	171	9,158
2003	4,676	3,982	382	198	9,237
2004	4,859	4,380	427	257	9,923
2005	5,072	4,818	491	334	10,716
2006	5,357	5,059	519	401	11,336
2007	5,603	5,362	530	465	11,961
2008	5,883	5,684	541	526	12,634
2009	6,207	6,042	548	584	13,380

Sources: Veronis Suhler Stevenson, PQ Media, Simba Information

*The methodology used to size, structure and forecast the outsourced corporate training market was changed in order to provide a more accurate picture of this marketplace. As part of this change, a new primary source for historical data was used, coupled with a secondary source for certain market subsegments and categories, which served as the basis for a proprietary regression analysis.

Growth of Spending on Outsourced Training, by Category*

Year	*IT Training*	*Soft Skills*	*LMS Platform*	*Live E-learning*	*Total*
2000	7.5%	8.5%	—	—	7.9%
2001	–12.6	1.2	—	—	–0.7
2002	–9.2	3.1	–2.2%	7.5%	–3.7
2003	1.0	2.0	–15.9	15.9	0.9
2004	3.9	10.0	12.0	30.0	7.4
2005	4.4	10.0	15.0	30.0	8.0
2006	5.6	5.0	5.7	20.0	5.8
2007	4.6	6.0	2.1	16.0	5.5
2008	5.0	6.0	2.0	13.0	5.6
2009	5.5	6.3	1.3	11.0	5.9
Compound Annual Growth					
1999-2004	–2.2	4.9	—	—	2.2
2004-2009	5.0	6.6	5.1	17.8	6.2

Sources: Veronis Suhler Stevenson, PQ Media, Simba Information

*The methodology used to size, structure and forecast the outsourced corporate training market was changed in order to provide a more accurate picture of this marketplace. As part of this change, a new primary source for historical data was used, coupled with a secondary source for certain market subsegments and categories, which served as the basis for a proprietary regression analysis.

increase productivity. A high customer renewal rate remained the best barometer by which to measure a vendor's worth.

The information technology (IT) training segment, which accounts for the largest portion of overall outsourced training expenditures, underwent fundamental changes in 2004. Vendors are no longer able to rely on revenues generated by new technology introductions, which have slowed down in recent years. In addition, there has been less of a need for training in standard IT courses, like Word and Excel, and more of an interest in specialty IT categories, causing large players like New Horizons Computer Learning Centers to add courses on topics such as Helpdesk and Wireless Network to their portfolios. To create new revenue streams, many of the leading vendors have also beefed up their certification programs, particularly in the high-demand areas of project management and security training, which accounted for most of the growth in 2004. Several vendors have also added more soft skills courses on topics like effective leadership and executive coaching to meet the increased demand for these skills within the IT department. Spending on IT training grew 3.9 percent to $4.86 billion in 2004, following a mere 1.0 percent gain in 2003.

The soft skills segment was also redefined in 2004, largely by merger and acquisition activity that changed the position of some of the leading players in this space. But the market is also being transformed by an anticipated shift in leadership. The segment's 10.0 percent growth to $4.38 billion in 2004, following growth of only 2.0 percent in 2003, reflects the beginning of a wave of turnovers in top management posts. Long-term leaders born during the baby boom era from 1946 to 1964 are gearing up for retirement and vacating the top executive posts that many have held for decades. The entrance of newcomers to these leadership positions is expected to be the key driver of soft skills training expenditures during the forecast period. Vendors are also expecting an increase in spending on soft skills training for retirees who are returning to the workforce after the economic recession devastated their retirement plans. And, in light of recent corporate accounting scandals that were traced directly back to company leaders, such as those at Enron and WorldCom, CEOs are being held more accountable and are at greater risk of being forced out of their roles. For example, Centra Software made adjustments to its management staff in late April 2005, when the company's board of directors and its CEO mutually agreed that he resign after the board indicated it was unhappy with the slow pace at which the company was increasing shareholder value.

In terms of the delivery of training content, companies that provide learning management systems (LMS), increasingly used as the backbone of enterprise-wide training deployments, experienced a 12.0 percent increase in expenditures to $427.0 million in 2004. The improved content authoring tools offered by the leading players in this space remain one of the more attractive features of LMS, and they feed off of the growth in demand for customized training. In addition, the allowance for interoperability among many of the newer systems affords users more freedom when selecting various training partners.

Corporations are also shifting more of their budgets to delivery platforms that allow for live e-learning, making it the fastest-growing platform in 2004. However, despite its rapid growth rate, the category still only accounts for 2.5 percent of all outsourced training spending. Many corporate cultures continue to gravitate to the face-to-face instruction provided in traditional bricks-and-mortar classrooms, but the attractive cost savings associated with live e-learning are driving growth in this category, which experienced a 30.0 percent increase in expenditures to $257.0 million in 2004. Providers of live online delivery, which consists mainly of virtual classrooms and Web conferencing, can help companies trim training costs by up to 50 percent through the addition of new services

Training Delivery Mode Breakdown, 2004

Platform	*Spending ($ Millions)*	*Percent of Total*
Instructor-Led (Classroom)	$6,946	70%
Computer-Based (No Instructor)	1,687	17
Instructor-Led (Remote)	794	8
Other	496	5
Total	9,923	

Sources: Veronis Suhler Stevenson, PQ Media, *Training Magazine*, Simba Information

like voice-activated conferencing technology. Today, computers can take the place of the telephone and become the only medium necessary for all forms of conferencing. Although this platform is in its infancy, several new companies have emerged that could potentially move to the forefront of this burgeoning market.

MAJOR TRENDS IN OUTSOURCED CORPORATE TRAINING

As the economy continues to grow and the job market maintains a healthy level of expansion, workers will explore new employment opportunities. As corporations continue to expand their workforces, they will likely encounter newcomers to their fields, who will require skill-set overhauls. This trend, which is expected to occur in the latter part of the forecast period after the supply of qualified new hires has been exhausted, will fuel accelerated growth in outsourced corporate training expenditures.

As companies expand globally, implement more training programs and extend existing programs to a wider group of employees, they will increasingly turn to Web-based training because of its greater efficiency and lower cost compared to instructor-led courses. Although traditional classroom-based training remains the preferred delivery method because it has been proven to result in the highest level of knowledge retention on the part of the learner, the Web has become a more efficient delivery channel as it causes less disruption to daily productivity by eliminating the need to uproot employees from their workstations. We anticipate that Web-based training will consistently gain market share throughout the forecast period. Instructor-led training accounted for 70.0 percent of all outsourced corporate training in 2004, while virtual classroom training captured about 8.0 percent of overall training expenditures. We expect Web-based training's share of the total market will reach about 8.5 percent in 2009.

While corporations are attempting to improve efficiency and contain costs through Web-based training programs, investments in customized training materials appeal mostly to large organizations that can easily absorb the high premiums associated with tailored content. Smaller organizations with tighter budgets are more drawn to the affordable, albeit more general in nature, content offered at seminars and in off-the-shelf materials. Spending on customized training materials accounted for 22.0 percent of spending in 2004, compared to 25.8 percent in 2003. Growth in spending on custom materials, including videos, lesson plans and computer courseware, is mostly driven by industry-specific needs that cannot be satisfied by off-the-shelf content or public seminars. The government and military, for example, require specialized courses designed around topics like emergency management systems and fire training. Despite this heightened need for customized materials in some pockets, materials provided by sponsors of seminars and conferences accounted for the most spending in 2004, 40.0 percent, compared with 40.5 percent in 2003. Off-the-shelf materials, including CD-ROMs, videos and paper-based workbooks, accounted for 22.0 percent of spending in 2004, compared to 24.4 percent in 2003.

While the opportunities for corporate training vendors have increased, they are facing more competition from academic institutions, such as New York University, which continue to expand their presence in the corporate training market as a way to establish new revenue streams in the face of rising tuition costs and state budget cuts. One example is Duke University's Office of Continuing Studies, in which professors conduct customized corporate training programs for clients. Colleges are also beginning to offer content from training vendors as part of their curricula, and credits upon course completion are being applied to undergraduate degree programs. The University of Phoenix recently approved 400 business skills and 1,000 IT skills courses from SkillSoft, an e-learning content firm, for such an arrangement.

Training Materials Breakdown, 2004

Category	*Spending ($ Millions)*	*Percent of Total*
Seminars/Conferences	$4,026	40%
Custom	2,168	22
Off-the-Shelf	2,162	22
Other	1,567	16
Total	9,923	

Sources: Veronis Suhler Stevenson, PQ Media, *Training Magazine*, Simba Information

The Outlook For Outsourced Corporate Training

Spending on outsourced corporate training will accelerate in 2005 as the economy and job market continue to improve and companies expand their investments in training new employees and developing the skills of existing ones. Total spending on outsourced corporate training will increase 8.0 percent to $10.72 billion in 2005, and grow at a compound annual rate of 6.2 percent from 2004 to 2009, reaching $13.38 billion. Growth over the next five years will be fueled mainly by the expansion of the soft skills, e-learning and Web-based categories, which will be spurred by a need for more accountable corporate leaders and more cost-effective training solutions that can be delivered to a plethora of employees at once.

Spending on IT training will grow at a moderate rate during the forecast period, expanding 4.4 percent to $5.07 billion in 2005, and rising at a compound annual rate of 5.0 percent from 2004 to 2009, reaching $6.21 billion. Growth will be driven by increased demand for project management and security certification programs, but will moderate as the software applications that are in high demand now become more commonplace and new technologies need to be developed.

E-learning will post the fastest growth among the four training categories, rising 30.0 percent to $334.0 million in 2005 and growing at a compound annual rate of 17.8 percent from 2004 to 2009 to $584.0 million. The market for soft skills training will increase 10.0 percent to $4.82 billion in 2005 as corporations hire new leaders. Spending on soft skills training will grow at a compound annual rate of 6.6 percent in the 2004-2009 period, reaching $6.04 billion.

Expenditures on LMS will be strong in 2005, increasing 15.0 percent to $491.0 million, but growth will decelerate during the forecast period. Once a company licenses an LMS, the only real investment needed is in upgrades as more features become available. Therefore, the LMS segment will grow at a compound annual rate of only 5.1 percent in the forecast period to $548.0 million in 2009.

FORECAST ASSUMPTIONS

- The strong economy and improved job market will fuel steady single-digit growth in outsourced corporate training expenditures throughout the forecast period. Growth in the information technology segment will be driven by the increasing importance placed on certification, while the soft skills market will be boosted by the influx of newcomers to top management posts, as many current leaders prepare for retirement.
- The rollout of training programs that increasingly encourage practice and follow-up sessions will drive growth in the corporate training market over the next five years, as corporations look for more measurable ways to track return on investment. In addition, components of training programs will be integrated into daily job performance, and will more frequently become part of the pre-employment process.
- The relatively low cost and convenience of Web-based training will prompt more employers to integrate this platform into training programs. By the end of the forecast period, most training programs will be delivered via a blended solution that features at least one component of e-learning, such as Web conferencing or virtual classrooms.

FUND III INVESTMENTS: Hemscott Add-ons and Transactions

CenterPoint Data
a portfolio company of
VS&A Communications Partners III, L.P.

has merged its
wholly owned subsidiary

with

HEMSCOTT

We acted as financial advisor to, and assisted in the negotiations as the representative of CenterPoint Data.

August 2004

CenterPoint Data
a portfolio company of
VS&A Communications Partners III, L.P.

has completed a partial tender for

10 million ordinary shares of

HEMSCOTT

CenterPoint Data has acquired
majority stockholding in Hemscott plc.

We acted as financial advisor to, and assisted in the negotiations as the representative of CenterPoint Data.

October 2004

HEMSCOTT
a portfolio company of
VS&A Communications Partners III, L.P.

has acquired

for

$38,000,000

We acted as financial advisor to, and assisted in the negotiations as the representative of Hemscott plc.

November 2004

Private Equity Capital / Mezzanine Capital / Industry Research and Forecasts

Veronis Suhler Stevenson
MEDIA • COMMUNICATIONS • INFORMATION

350 Park Avenue, New York, NY 10022
212-935-4990 212-381-8168 fax
www.vss.com

14

Professional & Business Information Services

Professional and Business Information Services Spending and Nominal GDP Growth, 2000-2009

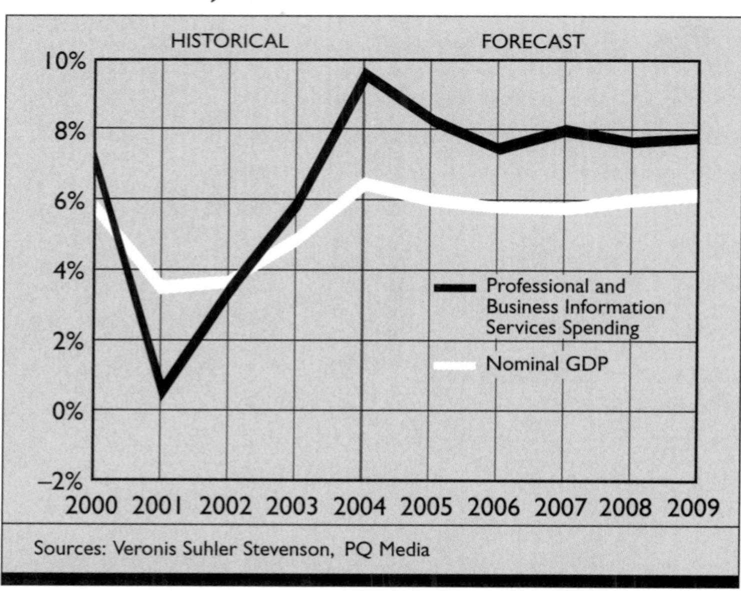

Sources: Veronis Suhler Stevenson, PQ Media

THE PROFESSIONAL & BUSINESS INFORMATION SERVICES MARKET IN 2004 AND 2005

Driven by strong demand for workflow solutions, creative online delivery options and a growing national economy, spending on professional and business information services (PBIS) surged 9.7 percent to $97.82 billion in 2004, as expenditures in both subsegments expanded at healthy rates during the year. Spending in the largest subsegment, business information services (BIS), grew at a faster rate than expenditures in the other subsegment, professional information (PI), as solutions complete with real-time, analytical functionality were purchased at a faster rate, due in part to increased corporate budgets. This trend drove up spending on BIS 10.2 percent to $78.09 billion in 2004. Meanwhile, the continued launch of online products and the introduction of services that complement new technology, such as wireless devices, spurred a gain of 7.9 percent in PI to $19.73 billion in 2004 as all three categories—legal and regulatory; scientific and technical; and health and life science—recorded relatively strong growth.

Overall growth of the PBIS market in 2004 outpaced that of nominal GDP for the second consecutive year—this time by almost 3 percentage points—a trend we expect to repeat in each of the next five years. Among the primary future growth drivers will be the continued focus on creating products and services that utilize the latest technological innovations.

The overall PBIS market outgrew nominal GDP by 3.1 percentage points in 2004, and the market grew at a compound annual rate of 5.4 percent from 1999 to 2004, also surpassing the broader economy's growth, which was 4.8 percent in the five-year period. The PBIS market's growth rate in 2004 also surpassed its peak 2000 expansion pace of 7.5 percent, which was followed by a deceleration in growth to 0.6 percent in the 2001 recession year. The market grew at an accelerated rate in each of the next three years.

Total spending on PI increased 7.9 percent in 2004 to $19.73 billion, and grew at a compound annual rate of 6.4 percent from 1999 to 2004. Key growth drivers were the

Highlights

Motivated by a demand for multimedia workflow tools and increased interest in the online delivery of information, total professional and business information services (PBIS) spending grew 9.7 percent to $97.82 billion in 2004, as both the professional and business information services subsegments posted solid gains. The PBIS market grew at a compound annual rate of 5.4 percent from 1999 to 2004, one of the few communications segments to outpace nominal GDP in the period.

■

The business information services (BIS) subsegment grew 10.2 percent in 2004 to $78.09 billion, driven by double-digit gains in spending on marketing information services, financial and economic information, and credit and risk information. BIS spending grew at a compound annual rate of 5.2 percent from 1999 to 2004.

■

The largest spending category in the BIS subsegment, marketing information services, also posted the strongest growth in 2004, up 14.7 percent to $23.55 billion, fueled by demand for research services in areas such as information technology, pharmaceuticals and healthcare. Expenditures on marketing information services expanded at a compound annual rate of 6.5 percent in the 1999-2004 period.

■

The professional information (PI) subsegment expanded 7.9 percent to $19.73 billion in 2004, due primarily to gains in the scientific and technical, and health and life science categories. Compound annual growth from 1999 to 2004 was 6.4 percent.

■

Spending in the scientific and technical category of the PI subsegment increased 8.5 percent to $6.71 billion in 2004, driven by increased demand for online delivery of content, as well as searchable Web databases. Meanwhile, spending in the health and life science category rose 8.5 percent to $4.31 billion for the year, spurred by further development of online products and services, and content delivered through wireless devices. The legal and regulatory category remained the largest in the PI subsegment, but posted the slowest growth, as spending rose 7.2 percent to $8.71 billion in 2004.

■

As the U.S. economy has advanced from recession to recovery to expansion over the past three years, corporations have begun to expand their workforces and operating budgets, creating a growing market for PBIS. As a result, demand has strengthened for mission-critical information and services that help workers be more efficient and effective on the job. In addition, the desire for more multimedia workflow devices has led providers to develop new products that deliver enhanced features, functionality and analytical tools.

■

Total spending on PBIS is projected to increase 8.1 percent to $105.78 billion in 2005, and grow at a compound annual rate of 7.8 percent in the forecast period to $142.33 billion in 2009. The market's expansion will be driven by a strong economy, growing demand for multimedia information products and services that enable workers to be more productive, and the rollout of more digital end-to-end workflow solutions.

Growth of U.S. Spending on Professional and Business Information Services

	Business Information Services Expenditures	*Professional Information Expenditures*	*Professional & Business Information Services Expenditures*
2004 Expenditures ($ Millions)	$78,093	$19,729	$97,822
1999-2004 Compound Annual Growth (%)	5.2%	6.4%	5.4%
2004-2009 Projected Compound Annual Growth (%)	7.7%	8.1%	7.8%
2009 Projected Expenditures ($ Millions)	$113,159	$29,166	$142,325

Sources: Veronis Suhler Stevenson, PQ Media, Outsell

Spending on Professional and Business Information Services, by Category*

	Business Information Services					
Year	*Marketing Information Services*	*Payroll & Human Resource Services*	*Financial & Economic Information*	*Credit & Risk Information*	*General Business Industry News*	*Total Business Information Services*
1999	$17,179	$16,347	$13,032	$10,422	$3,714	$ 60,694
2000	18,342	17,617	14,012	11,154	3,980	65,105
2001	18,691	17,425	13,802	11,344	3,880	65,142
2002	19,307	18,018	13,677	11,821	4,023	66,846
2003	20,543	19,117	14,608	12,424	4,205	70,895
2004	23,554	20,264	16,068	13,666	4,541	78,093
2005	25,226	21,297	18,093	14,951	4,818	84,385
2006	26,840	22,831	19,631	16,027	5,165	90,494
2007	28,907	24,406	21,417	17,486	5,532	97,748
2008	30,988	26,041	23,302	18,832	5,908	105,071
2009	33,096	27,968	25,446	20,263	6,386	113,159

Sources: Veronis Suhler Stevenson, PQ Media, Outsell

*The methodology used to size, structure and forecast the professional and business information services segment was changed in this year's *Forecast* in order to provide a more accurate picture of this marketplace. As part of this change, a new proprietary methodology was developed for historical data that provided a more detailed analysis of this segment, and served as the basis for our regression analysis. In addition, the professional information subsegment, including legal & regulatory, scientific & technical, and health & life science, has been melded into this chapter with the business information services subsegment, including, marketing, payroll & human resources, financial & economic, credit & risk, and general business news, to coincide with broader trends in the overall professional and business information marketplace.

expanded use of digital content delivery and the development of solutions compatible with the latest technological advances. Spending on legal and regulatory information increased 7.2 percent to $8.71 billion in 2004, driven by the rollout of new online delivery options, acquisitions that created larger customer bases and the integration of popular PDA-supported products into providers' slate of offerings. Content delivery via PDAs is quickly supplanting CD-ROM delivery in this market, and we expect spending on legal and regulatory information to grow another 6.2 percent to $9.25 billion in 2005. One of the chief growth drivers will be the launch of more online tools that promote increased functionality supporting an array of Internet-based products and services.

Spending on scientific and technical information increased 8.5 percent to $6.71 billion in 2004, as demand for more accessible and searchable information led to the rollout of improvements to online database products. Additional research and development funding also led scientific and technical information providers to focus on the needs of scientists eager to promote their innovations via publications covering this market. Total spending in the scientific and technical category will increase 10.4 percent to $7.41 billion in 2005. Expenditures in the health and life science category—the smallest in the PI subsegment—increased 8.5 percent to $4.31 billion in 2004, spurred by rising demand for portable information in real time. In particular, this category's growth is being sparked by the creation of Web-based products and services that healthcare professionals can use at the point of care.

One challenge PI providers face, however, is the threat of a shrinking customer base. The current and potential user markets have been posting relatively slow growth as fewer people are entering and remaining

($ MILLIONS)

Professional Information				
Legal & Regulatory Information	*Scientific & Technical Information*	*Health & Life Science Information*	*Total Professional Information*	*Total Professional & Business Information Services*
$ 6,307	$ 4,943	$3,246	$14,496	$ 75,190
7,013	5,279	3,449	15,741	80,846
7,273	5,379	3,532	16,184	81,326
7,716	5,815	3,779	17,310	84,156
8,125	6,187	3,968	18,280	89,175
8,711	6,713	4,305	19,729	97,822
9,251	7,411	4,710	21,372	105,757
9,881	8,092	5,195	23,168	113,662
10,602	8,780	5,636	25,018	122,766
11,355	9,553	6,070	26,978	132,049
12,252	10,346	6,568	29,166	142,325

Growth of Spending on Professional and Business Information Services, by Category*

	Business Information Services					
Year	*Marketing Information Services*	*Payroll & Human Resource Services*	*Financial & Economic Information*	*Credit & Risk Information*	*General Business Industry News*	*Total Business Information Services*
2000	6.8%	7.8%	7.5%	7.0%	7.2%	7.3%
2001	1.9	−1.1	−1.5	1.7	−2.5	0.1
2002	3.3	3.4	−0.9	4.2	3.7	2.6
2003	6.4	6.1	6.8	5.1	4.5	6.1
2004	14.7	6.0	10.0	10.0	8.0	10.2
2005	7.1	5.1	12.6	9.4	6.1	8.1
2006	6.4	7.2	8.5	7.2	7.2	7.2
2007	7.7	6.9	9.1	9.1	7.1	8.0
2008	7.2	6.7	8.8	7.7	6.8	7.5
2009	6.8	7.4	9.2	7.6	8.1	7.7
Compound Annual Growth						
1999-2004	6.5	4.4	4.3	5.6	4.1	5.2
2004-2009	7.0	6.7	9.6	8.2	7.1	7.7

Sources: Veronis Suhler Stevenson, PQ Media, Outsell

*The methodology used to size, structure and forecast the professional and business information services segment was changed in this year's *Forecast* in order to provide a more accurate picture of this marketplace. As part of this change, a new proprietary methodology was developed for historical data that provided a more detailed analysis of this segment, and served as the basis for our regression analysis. In addition, the professional information subsegment, including legal & regulatory, scientific & technical, and health & life science, has been melded into this chapter with the business information services subsegment, including, marketing, payroll & human resources, financial & economic, credit & risk, and general business news, to coincide with broader trends in the overall professional and business information marketplace.

active in these professional fields. The total number of graduate school majors by professional discipline (legal and regulatory, scientific and technical, health and life science) increased 3.7 percent to 244,820 in 2004, and rose at a compound annual rate of 2.3 percent from 1999 to 2004. In addition, the total number of practicing professionals (which includes lawyers, scientists and engineers, and healthcare practitioners) increased only 1.2 percent in 2004 to 6.95 million, and grew at a compound annual rate of 3.1 percent from 1999 to 2004. The comparatively minimal growth of practicing professionals in the U.S. can be attributed to several factors. Among them, healthcare professionals have been faced with rising malpractice insurance costs for years, making the expense of providing these services prohibitive for many in the field. For legal professionals, there has been a steady loss of job opportunities as U.S. companies are outsourcing many legal functions abroad to countries including Australia, India and South Korea as a cost-saving measure.

Growth in the BIS subsegment in 2004 was driven primarily by the marketing information services category, which expanded more rapidly than all other categories for the year, growing 14.7 percent to $23.55 billion. Key growth drivers in this category included escalating demand for real-time, analytical

Professional Information				
Legal & Regulatory Information	*Scientific & Technical Information*	*Health & Life Science Information*	*Total Professional Information*	*Total Professional & Business Information Services*
11.2%	6.8%	6.3%	8.6%	7.5%
3.7	1.9	2.4	2.8	0.6
6.1	8.1	7.0	7.0	3.5
5.3	6.4	5.0	5.6	6.0
7.2	8.5	8.5	7.9	9.7
6.2	10.4	9.4	8.3	8.1
6.8	9.2	10.3	8.4	7.5
7.3	8.5	8.5	8.0	8.0
7.1	8.8	7.7	7.8	7.6
7.9	8.3	8.2	8.1	7.8
6.7	6.3	5.8	6.4	5.4
7.1	9.0	8.8	8.1	7.8

information and research services. At the same time, content providers have had to address the changing nature by which users find and analyze their information. Research suggests that professionals are relying less on Internet searches and more on colleagues and peers, as well as various alerting services. In 2001, 79 percent of the professionals surveyed relied on the Web for information, compared to only 67 percent in 2005. The time spent on gathering and analyzing information has also shifted: In 2005, professionals complained that they were spending more time gathering information rather than analyzing it, a reversal of the trend in 2001, when more time was spent analyzing information.

Time Spent by Professional and Business Information End Users on Gathering And Analyzing Information

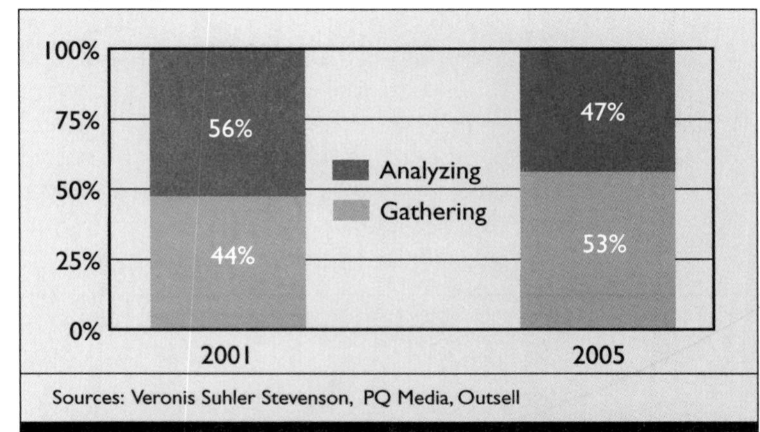

Sources: Veronis Suhler Stevenson, PQ Media, Outsell

Shares of Spending on Professional and Business Information Services, by Category*

	Business Information Services					
Year	*Marketing Information Services*	*Payroll & Human Resource Services*	*Financial & Economic Information*	*Credit & Risk Information*	*General Business Industry News*	*Total Business Information Services*
1999	22.8%	21.7%	17.3%	13.9%	4.9%	80.7%
2000	22.7	21.8	17.3	13.8	4.9	80.5
2001	23.0	21.4	17.0	13.9	4.8	80.1
2002	22.9	21.4	16.3	14.0	4.8	79.4
2003	23.0	21.4	16.4	13.9	4.7	79.5
2004	24.1	20.7	16.4	14.0	4.6	79.8
2005	23.9	20.1	17.1	14.1	4.6	79.8
2006	23.6	20.1	17.3	14.1	4.5	79.6
2007	23.5	19.9	17.4	14.2	4.5	79.6
2008	23.5	19.7	17.6	14.3	4.5	79.6
2009	23.3	19.7	17.9	14.2	4.5	79.5

Sources: Veronis Suhler Stevenson, PQ Media, Outsell

*The methodology used to size, structure and forecast the professional and business information services segment was changed in this year's *Forecast* in order to provide a more accurate picture of this marketplace. As part of this change, a new proprietary methodology was developed for historical data that provided a more detailed analysis of this segment, and served as the basis for our regression analysis. In addition, the professional information subsegment, including legal & regulatory, scientific & technical, and health & life science, has been melded into this chapter with the business information services subsegment, including, marketing, payroll & human resources, financial & economic, credit & risk, and general business news, to coincide with broader trends in the overall professional and business information marketplace.

The financial and economic information category, and the credit and risk information category, also posted solid gains, up 10.0 percent each in 2004, driven by a strong economy that has yielded an increase in equities trading and debt issuance, as well as the need for research to assist in regulatory compliance. The payroll and human resource information category posted 6.0 percent growth to $20.26 billion in 2004, led by organizations' continued interest in outsourcing and an increase in the hiring of new employees. The general business industry news category grew 8.0 percent to $4.54 billion in 2004, led by these providers' various offerings of real-time information to users.

Professional Information

MAJOR TRENDS AND DRIVERS

PI providers are striving to become complete information sources. Publishers are accomplishing this goal, in part, by increasing their investment and commitment to their electronic publishing initiatives. While publishers began their forays into electronic publishing by simply offering online versions of their print publications, they are now taking steps to improve the features and functionality of their online products.

Professional Information			
Legal & Regulatory Information	*Scientific & Technical Information*	*Health & Life Science Information*	*Total Professional Information Services*
8.4%	6.6%	4.3%	19.3%
8.7	6.5	4.3	19.5
8.9	6.6	4.3	19.9
9.2	6.9	4.5	20.6
9.1	6.9	4.4	20.5
8.9	6.9	4.4	20.2
8.7	7.0	4.5	20.2
8.7	7.1	4.6	20.4
8.6	7.2	4.6	20.4
8.6	7.2	4.6	20.4
8.6	7.3	4.6	20.5

Publishers are even enhancing their online products by incorporating publications from other publishers to make all of the materials a customer requires accessible via one service.

PI providers have been migrating from print to online services for years. John Wiley & Sons delivers online content through its Wiley InterScience product. Reed Elsevier launched its new online abstracting and indexing database, Scopus, in 2004. Wolters Kluwer, through its Ovid Technologies unit, offers content online through its SilverPlatter database. In addition, PI providers have also embraced PDA technology and have created products to support this latest application. McGraw-Hill formed an alliance with Unbound Medicine in 2004 to make a collection of McGraw-Hill titles available in PDA format. Ovid Technologies has its own PDA program in Ovid@Hand and Reed Elsevier's MD Consult subsidiary launched a PDA product in 2003. There is also a PDA version available of Thomson's *Physicians' Desk Reference.*

Technological advances, such as RSS (Really Simple Syndication) feeds and Weblogs, or blogs, also present opportunities. RSS allows publishers to syndicate their content. Blogs can be created at a relatively low

Number of Graduate School Majors, By Professional Discipline

Year	Law	Scientific/ Technical	Health Science	Total
1999	42,533	80,795	95,180	218,508
2000	41,976	82,496	99,270	223,742
2001	41,209	85,058	102,756	229,023
2002	43,113	84,558	102,691	230,362
2003	44,265	85,708	106,056	236,029
2004	43,901	87,168	113,751	244,820
2005	38,786	92,814	117,618	249,218
2006	38,825	94,577	121,147	254,549
2007	39,058	97,036	124,902	260,996
2008	39,409	99,171	128,899	267,479
2009	40,020	101,310	131,585	272,915

Sources: Veronis Suhler Stevenson, PQ Media, National Center for Educational Statistics

Growth of the Number of Graduate School Majors, By Professional Discipline

Year	Law	Scientific/ Technical	Health Science	Total
2000	–1.3%	2.1%	4.3%	2.4%
2001	–1.8	3.1	3.5	2.4
2002	4.6	–0.6	–0.1	0.6
2003	2.7	1.4	3.3	2.5
2004	–0.8	1.7	2.3	3.7
2005	–0.7	6.5	3.4	1.8
2006	0.1	1.9	3.0	2.1
2007	0.6	2.6	3.1	2.5
2008	0.9	2.2	3.2	2.5
2009	1.6	2.2	2.1	2.0
Compound Annual Growth				
1999-2004	–1.7	1.5	3.6	2.3
2004-2009	0.5	3.1	3.0	2.2

Sources: Veronis Suhler Stevenson, PQ Media, National Center for Educational Statistics

cost and can provide another way in which publishers (through site editors) can build relationships with their customers. However, publishers are still working to find a workable revenue-generating model for blogs, which will likely include some form of advertising.

LEGAL AND REGULATORY

Spending on legal and regulatory information increased 7.2 percent to $8.71 billion in 2004, and this category expanded at a compound annual rate of 6.7 percent from 1999 to 2004, driven by the continued development of more sophisticated online products and services and greater demand for the reception of up-to-date information about legislative and regulatory issues. But the number of future attorneys is diminishing. The number of graduate students majoring in law decreased 0.8 percent to 43,901 in 2004, and fell 1.7 percent on a compound annual basis from 1999 to 2004. Similarly, the number of practicing lawyers decreased 0.2 percent to 970,000 in 2004, as more organizations chose to outsource their legal needs. The number of lawyers increased at a minimal compound annual rate of 0.1 percent from 1999 to 2004.

Legal and regulatory publishers have always seemed to be a step ahead of other professional publishing segments in terms of technological advances. With complete online offerings already in place, they are now promoting wireless services. For West, Thomson's legal unit, this meant forming a relationship with technology provider Blackberry to tout West's wireless capabilities. As a result, West will appear in Blackberry newsletters and on the technology company's Web site. West first entered the wireless market in 2000. LexisNexis began working with Blackberry on a wireless option for business users (not legal professionals) in April 2004.

The breadth of content offerings on these electronic formats as well as traditional print (such as books and journals) has also spurred spending growth in this segment. As law becomes more complex, legal and regulatory publishers have a substantial opportunity to expand their content portfolio to include new and emerging legal information needs. For example, publishers have most recently deepened their suite of products to address compliance issues such as the Sarbanes-Oxley Act.

Legal and regulatory publishers of all sizes are pursuing aggressive acquisition strategies to advance their efforts to become complete solutions providers. In 2004, Thomson West acquired legal marketing services developer Hubbard One. This acquisition was intended to improve the organization's marketing function. Meanwhile, in late 2004, Dolan Media acquired 14 newspapers and related Web sites from Lawyers Weekly.

In addition, legal publishers are expanding globally to achieve further growth. Wolters Kluwer acquired Verlag Praktisches, a German online legal publication, in 2004. At the same time, LexisNexis bolstered its Chinese operations in Beijing. These acquisitions of international companies and their products emphasize the ultimate goal of professional publishers to offer clients complete suites of products and services, and it allows them to expand their product line beyond U.S.-based legislation. Customers of professional information rely on these publishers for global information, and they will likely continue to make strategic acquisitions to further broaden their reach and scope in the forecast period. This strategy is not unlike that of their business information counterparts, who already have an international customer base.

SCIENTIFIC AND TECHNICAL

Spending on scientific and technical information increased 8.5 percent to $6.71 billion in 2004, and grew at a compound annual rate of 6.3 percent from 1999 to 2004, due in part to increased research and development funding. This additional funding is supporting the need for scientists and engineers to release new findings, and PI leaders are positioned to create new products around their innovations. This highest rate of growth in five years can also be attributed to a successful evolution of online products that appeal to scientific and technical customers because of their functionality. The leading scientific and technical publishers have online database products that provide customers access to publications, mostly journals, of the hosting publisher as well as competitive publishers.

Number of Practicing Professionals (THOUSANDS)

Year	*Lawyers*	*Scientists and Engineers*	*Healthcare Practitioners**	*Total*
1999	964	3,928	1,071	5,963
2000	934	4,229	1,066	6,229
2001	969	4,836	1,115	6,920
2002	963	4,603	1,176	6,742
2003	972	4,682	1,211	6,865
2004	970	4,724	1,254	6,948
2005	969	4,842	1,352	7,163
2006	973	4,953	1,405	7,331
2007	980	5,013	1,496	7,489
2008	985	5,063	1,509	7,557
2009	991	5,124	1,544	7,659

Sources: Veronis Suhler Stevenson, PQ Media, Bureau of Labor Statistics

*Healthcare practitioners include medical doctors, dentists, optometrists, podiatrists, osteopathic physicians and veterinarians. Scientists and engineers include natural scientists, mathematical and computer scientists, and aerospace, chemical, civil, electrical, industrial and mechanical engineers.

Growth in the Number Of Practicing Professionals

Year	*Lawyers*	*Scientists and Engineers*	*Healthcare Practitioners*	*Total*
2000	–3.1%	7.7%	–0.5%	4.5%
2001	3.7	14.4	4.6	11.1
2002	–0.6	–4.8	5.5	–2.6
2003	0.9	1.7	3.0	1.8
2004	–0.2	0.9	3.6	1.2
2005	–0.1	2.5	7.8	3.1
2006	0.4	2.3	3.9	2.3
2007	0.7	1.2	6.5	2.2
2008	0.5	1.0	0.9	0.9
2009	0.6	1.2	2.3	1.2
Compound Annual Growth				
1999-2004	0.1	3.8	3.2	3.1
2004-2009	0.4	1.6	4.2	2.0

Sources: Veronis Suhler Stevenson, PQ Media, Bureau of Labor Statistics

While the number of graduate school students majoring in scientific/technical fields rose only 1.7 percent to 87,168 in 2004, a rebound of 6.5 percent to 92,814 is expected for 2005. The number of students grew at a compound annual rate of 1.5 percent from 1999 to 2004. The number of practicing scientists and engineers, meanwhile, increased just 0.9 percent to 4.72 million in 2004, and rose at a compound annual rate of 3.8 percent from 1999 to 2004.

The scientific and technical segment faces a unique challenge—increased competition from non-paid start-up publications. One such entity, the Public Library of Science, is producing its own journals and offering them free online. But scientific and technical publishers continue to fight these battles and defend their prices by touting the quality of their information. In addition, scientific and technical information providers are currently battling open access to scholarly and scientific publications. In 2004, professional publishers were taken aback when the National Institutes of Health (NIH) proposed that biomedical research funded by taxpayers should be available to the general public. Such a move would jeopardize potential revenues generated by journal subscriptions. The NIH also proposed that any research the institute funds should be available free within six months, and immediately if funded with NIH grants.

On the pricing front, the battle of rising journal prices waged between professional publishers and librarians continues, as publishers keep raising prices on these products. A late 2004 study commissioned by Oxford University Press subsidiary Oxford Journals revealed that journal pricing is extremely inconsistent. According to the study, subscription prices increased in the past four years from 27.0 percent to 94.0 percent. Regardless of the increase, library budgets continue to shrink at a steady pace and libraries are being forced to cancel their subscriptions due to lack of funding. Just a few years ago, librarians dealt with this issue by forming consortia that had stronger buying power than did each individual library. But now they have some potentially stronger ammunition with the open source initiative. This would provide libraries with the scholarly information they demand at little or no cost. As a result, open access initiatives have been given a great deal of momentum.

Publishers are certainly not sitting idle as the open source debate continues. For example, in 2004, Springer Science + Business Media launched a program with a similar model, Open Choice. Through Open Choice, journal authors can either select a traditional publishing model or allow free public access to their articles. Publishers such as Springer Science + Business Media believe that if an open access model gains widespread acceptance, they must be prepared to compete in such an environment. Programs such as Open Choice will allow professional information services providers the opportunity to determine if such models are viable for them.

Scientific and technical information providers are continuing to expand and promote their own proprietary online services, and they are turning to third-party services to expand their reach. One such example is the strengthened alliance between MetaPress, a content host provider, and Springer Science + Business Media. The result is more than 650 titles added to SpringerLink (Springer's online delivery service). As of January 2005, the number of journal titles available through SpringerLink increased from 500 to 1,250 as the service showcases articles from Kluwer Academic Publishers and BertelsmannSpringer that were published before 1997.

John Wiley & Sons enjoys steady growth with its online delivery service, as well, known as Wiley InterScience. But Wiley is also working with a third party. In late 2004, the publisher signed on with content management provider Infotrieve in an agreement that enables Infotrieve to distribute Wiley publications, including journals, books and articles. Another PI provider, Reed Elsevier, made news in 2004 with the launch of its abstracting and indexing database, Scopus. The University of Toronto, which worked with Reed on development of the database, signed a three-year license before Scopus even launched. At the onset, Scopus offered users access to publications from more than 4,000 scientific, technical and medical publishers.

These online databases serve as a platform for customers that encourages increased usage and spending on such services. Because the databases provide access to a publisher's complete slate of works, as well as articles from other publications in some instances, customers are able to find the exact content they seek without the need to rely on a variety of different products. Online searchable databases are also a prominent and profitable product within this category, as demonstrated by the leading publishers' entries in this area, as well as their well-noted commitment to these products. Reed Elsevier boasts a wide range of content contained in its Scopus database, which includes articles that date back to the mid-1960s. Scopus was created as a competitive product to Thomson's ISI Web of Knowledge, as well as Chemical Abstracts Service's SciFinder database. Chemical Abstracts Service is a division of the American Chemical Society. In April 2005, the Institute of Electrical and Electronics Engineers (IEEE) launched the IEEE Xplore 2.0 database with increased functionality. Xplore offers access to IEEE's 1.1 million documents.

Organizations with consumer-based roots, such as Google, are now beginning to enter the online scientific content market, as well. Google's entrance into the market was marked by the launch of Google Scholar, which helps researchers find the tools and information they desire on demand. While these databases focus mainly on journal content, Ovid Technologies (a subsidiary of Wolters Kluwer) offers an online database of book titles through its Books@Ovid product. The further success and development of these online products is expected to help spending in the scientific and technical category increase at a compound annual rate of 9.0 percent from 2004 to 2009.

HEALTH AND LIFE SCIENCE

Health and life science is the smallest of the professional information segments in terms of spending, which increased 8.5 percent to $4.31 billion in 2004, and grew at a 5.8 percent compound annual rate from 1999 to 2004. The expansion was fueled, in part, by an increased commitment to digitally delivered products and services, such as those via PDAs. PI providers have shown a strong interest in providing content solutions to all facets of their customer bases, and the PDA is being used to offer physicians access to data from the point of care.

The health and life science segment maintains a steady base of potential customers who will likely demand more technology-based solutions in the future. The number of graduate students majoring in health science increased 2.3 percent in 2004 to 113,751, and rose at a compound annual rate of 3.6 percent from 1999 to 2004. The number of practicing healthcare professionals increased 3.6 percent to 1.25 million in 2004, growing at a 3.2 percent compound annual rate in the 1999-2004 period.

Health science publishers, including professional publishing powerhouses Reed Elsevier, Wolters Kluwer and Thomson, as well as several smaller players, continue to enjoy steady growth. While this category has served its customers in recent years through a variety of online tools, such as extensive searchable databases, it is further building on its electronic-based offerings with the continual launch of PDA-based products and services. For example, an April 2005 deal between McGraw-Hill and Unbound Medicine called for the development of a PDA version of McGraw-Hill's *Harrison's Manual of Medicine.* Ovid Technologies, a unit of Wolters Kluwer, has its own PDA program in Ovid@Hand, and Reed Elsevier's MD Consult subsidiary launched a PDA product in 2003.

PROFESSIONAL INFORMATION: END USERS BY PROFESSION

The major categories of professional information are legal and regulatory; scientific and technical; and health and life science. The information created for these categories is produced to assist customers in performing their various job responsibilities in their specific industries. While professional information is published in traditional print formats such as books, journals and newsletters, much of the growth is attributable to Internet-based products and services.

Legal and regulatory information is the

largest PI category with spending of $8.71 billion in 2004, or an 8.9 percent share of the total PBIS market. The category includes publishers of various sizes that produce content and services mainly for attorneys and other practitioners who perform duties for the legal profession. The leading publishers of legal and regulatory information are Thomson (through its legal and regulatory division that includes West and FindLaw), LexisNexis (the legal division of Reed Elsevier), Wolters Kluwer and the Bureau of National Affairs.

Technological advances have presented multiple opportunities for professional publishers as they attempt to serve the varied informational and functional needs of this customer base. In addition to providing new content related to the legal field, publishers have ventured into new areas such as marketing services, software development and knowledge management to provide customers with full-service solutions. Online content is the fastest-growing piece of this category in terms of spending, as customers prefer the searchability of these products. They also enjoy the portability of these products, and publishers are responding with launches of PDA versions of their trademark offerings and continuing to expand the breadth and depth of their online services. LexisNexis recently expanded its Martindale-Hubbell database to attract smaller law firms to coincide with its database of larger customers. Journals, while a prominent medium in other professional publishing segments, are not responsible for much of the legal segment's overall growth. Spending in this category is expected to increase at a compound annual rate of 7.1 percent from 2004 to 2009.

Scientific and technical information is the second-largest PI category with spending of $6.71 billion in 2004 and a 6.9 percent PBIS market share. This group, which has experienced change among the top players in recent years, focuses its attention on a customer base of scientists and technical professionals that demand the most up-to-date information available in the most accessible formats. In addition, their customers are also the authors of their scientific and technical publications, specifically journals. Internet-based content and services continue to yield growth in this category. The top publishers of scientific and technical content include Reed Elsevier, Thomson and Springer Science + Business. The last entry is new to the top three, following its formation in April 2004 as a result of the merger between Bertelsmann-Springer and Kluwer Academic Publishing.

Health and life science information (or medical) is the third-largest category of the PI subsegment with a 4.4 percent share of overall PBIS spending. Expenditures in this category—which mainly comprises several large publishers, plus several smaller niche firms—increased 8.5 percent to $4.31 billion in 2004. The top three publishers are Reed Elsevier, Wolters Kluwer and Thomson. The main customers for this information are physicians and other medical professionals. This segment will continue to post solid growth as the demand for health science information remains steady. Because of the changing nature of this type of information, new products and services are constantly in demand. In addition, this segment is gradually embracing online content and tools, potentially opening up more opportunities for publishers in the health science space. Nevertheless, journals represent the largest medium in this category.

Thomson, which is represented in the health science segment with its Thomson Healthcare unit, is focused on bolstering its online offerings and is continuing its development of PDA technology tools. Thomson emphasized its commitment to online products when it divested its *Medical Economics* print magazines in 2003. Thomson Healthcare has also demonstrated a devotion to the pharmaceutical space with its December 2004 launch of Thomson Pharma, a research aggregation tool. Thomson's growth in healthcare, however, has also been aided by its January 2004 acquisition of life science database publisher BIOSIS. Another player in the segment, McGraw-Hill, continues to enjoy success with electronic products, from Diagnosaurus (a PDA product) to Harrison's Online and AccessMedicine. Market leader Reed Elsevier's growth can be attributed to revenues generated by books and journals.

Spending in this segment is expected to grow at a compound annual rate of 8.8 percent from 2004 to 2009.

PROFESSIONAL INFORMATION: PURCHASERS BY INDUSTRY

Demand for PI from customers in a variety of industries and market segments has contributed greatly to the continued growth in spending on this information. Intermediary and professional services were the largest purchasers of professional information in 2004 at $5.90 billion. The total spending was divided among three segments: legal, financial and business data services. Wall Street was the largest spender at $2.30 billion.

The consumer goods industry was the second-largest purchaser of professional information in 2004, with spending of $4.60 billion. This category includes the following segments: food and beverage, health and beauty aids, drugs and medical supplies, automobiles, and general merchandise. The largest spender of these segments was food and beverage at $1.62 billion in 2004.

THE OUTLOOK FOR PROFESSIONAL INFORMATION

Spending on PI was steady throughout 2004 as the changing nature of this type of information requires a constant investment over time. This has never been the type of content that can be classified as a one-time purchase. For example, in the legal and regulatory category, lawyers and other legal professionals must be kept current on the latest legislation and regulations, and they rely on professional information to keep them up-to-date. This gains further importance as the law increases in complexity. This segment has also shown a strong proclivity toward the ability to access information remotely (from a courtroom or other meeting venue, for instance) and the industry has been quick to respond with a slate of online and wireless applications. In both the scientific and technical, and health and life science categories, similar trends apply as information in these fields is constantly changing and PI providers are increasingly challenged to develop solutions that can be implemented at the point of care.

Professional information print products, such as journals, books and directories that have been a staple of the industry for many years, have struggled to grow in more recent times and will continue to do so during the forecast period. As a result, professional publishers will continue to transform their products and services into integrated multimedia suites in an effort to meet the demands of their clients. The companies that are able to integrate internal proprietary data with their external databases will be the most successful going forward.

PI providers have typically responded to this unquenched need for up-to-date information by launching new complementary products that help them solidify their relationships with current customers while attracting new customers to their portfolios of offerings. As a result, we expect PI spending to increase 8.3 percent in 2005 to $21.37 billion, and grow at a compound annual rate of 8.1 percent from 2004 to 2009, reaching $29.17 billion in 2009.

BUSINESS INFORMATION SERVICES

MAJOR TRENDS AND DRIVERS

As the job market strengthens, and demand for accurate, up-to-date business and professional information grows, we expect total spending on BIS to increase 8.1 percent to $84.39 billion in 2005. Business information solutions that can be integrated into in-house operations will increase in popularity and spark growth. Yet, outsourcing and data security are also expected to yield positive results for segments such as payroll and human resource business information.

Both the PI and BIS markets have been successful in developing content in various formats over the years. From static content, such as books, these markets have evolved greatly in a relatively short period of time with the introduction of dynamic content, such as CD-ROMs, and later with database and online products and services. The next step was to move from the role of content provider to complete solution provider. This began with the addition of workflow tools and compliance products, and has shifted to end-to-end solutions, such as integrated product suites of data and applications.

Outsourcing also continues to drive growth, especially for organizations operating in the BIS subsegment, such as marketing information services, payroll and human resource services, and credit information. One area of opportunity is organizations' continued need to deal with compliance issues, such as the Sarbanes-Oxley Act. Another is the potential cost savings that outsourcing functions such as human resources can achieve. As outsourcing becomes more popular among end-user organizations, business information companies are responding with formats that can be integrated into their proprietary operations. Despite recent security breaches by credit and risk information providers, outsourcing continues to grow as end-user companies become more comfortable sharing sensitive consumer data with outsourcers.

Spending on marketing information services, the largest BIS category, posted the strongest growth rate in 2004, up 14.7 percent to $23.55 billion. Spending in the segment grew at a 6.5 percent compound annual rate from 1999 to 2004 in large part because of increased interest in market research in areas such as information technology, pharmaceuticals and healthcare. Steady growth will continue because product and price information changes so frequently and customers will be forced to continue their steady purchases of this data in order to compete in their respective marketplaces. Spending will also increase as customers are more likely to pay premiums for integrated, end-to-end solutions that marketing information providers are launching with increasing frequency.

The marketing and information services category demands products that allow easy measurement of results, and clients want these tools directly accessible via their desktop so analysis can be accomplished in near real-time fashion. This category offers BIS providers a willing market for Internet-based offerings as their customers demand tools that help them create a 360-degree view of each of their own clients. And they are expanding that view across borders. In 2004, Acxiom Corporation expanded into China, as part of the company's international growth strategy. Acxiom increased its presence outside the U.S. with its purchase of ChinaLOOP, an organization providing business intelligence, as well as customer relationship and data management.

The marketing and information category in recent years has become more tightly focused on the delivery of real-time data. This trend comes in response to a customer base that is used to receiving real-time information generated through the Internet. Information providers are also offering analytical tools, in addition to content, for customers who demand an end-to-end solution.

Payroll and human resource expenditures increased 6.0 percent to $20.26 billion in 2004, as organizations continued to outsource these services for a variety of reasons. Many organizations deem outsourcing a cost-saving measure since it eliminates the need for a full-time staff dedicated to these functions. From 1999 to 2004, spending on payroll and human resource services grew at a 4.4 percent compound annual rate. Spending in this segment is expected to increase as the outsourcing trend continues. In addition, an increased investment in technology is also driving growth for payroll and human resource information providers. Customers are readily adopting solutions that provide self-service functions to employees (for example, employees can access their benefits information and pay stubs online without contacting an HR representative). To capitalize on this development, payroll and human resource service providers will likely launch more services to provide end users with complete solutions that they can meld into their back-office operations.

Spending in this segment increased during poor economic times because staff layoffs involved a large amount of paperwork. Yet, spending activity remains robust in a strong economic climate, in part because of a more active hiring environment, which was the case in 2004.

Payroll and human resource information providers are benefiting from a customer base of corporations under pressure to reduce costs and increase productivity. In addition, regulatory compliance is a time-consuming issue that many companies don't have the time or expertise to properly address. The players in this market are focusing on needs and increasing spending by offering customers end-to-end solutions that meet all facets of the payroll and human resource function. Paychex, for example, offers Paychex Major Market Services, a solution geared toward its medium- and large-sized businesses. In late 2004, Paychex announced that this product served more than 25,000 U.S.-based customers. Also in 2004, Hewitt Associates acquired Exult, which enabled Hewitt to expand the suite of services it offered to customers—from benefits, payroll, information system, recruiting and learning to consulting services.

Spending in the financial and economic segment increased 10.0 percent in 2004 to $16.07 billion and grew at a 4.3 percent compound annual rate from 1999 to 2004. Demand for this type of information naturally began to increase in the second half of 2003 and the upward trend continued through 2004. While a recovering economy has helped fuel spending growth in financial and economic information, providers are also leading the charge with solutions that allow users to receive both content and analytical instruments in the same product. These providers are also spurring growth with a commitment to provide users with the real-time data they demand.

Companies are responding in a variety of ways—through both the launch of these new products and services, and acquisitions that will provide such solutions for their customers. For example, Standard and Poor's acquisition of Capital IQ gave them their own distribution platform on which to deliver their proprietary data, rather than rely on partnerships to deliver their content. Reuters, in late 2004, acquired real-time information provider Moneyline Telerate in order to improve the dissemination of financial content to its end users. Now that financial and economic information customers are able to purchase more content, they will likely begin to seek out the best price. So, in order to yield the benefits of increased spending in this area, these providers will have to create packages of information available at a variety of price points.

Spending on credit and risk information increased 10.0 percent in 2004 to $13.67 billion. The nation's economic expansion has enabled corporations to invest in the acquisition of new customers, creating an increased need for credit checks. In addition, the growing frequency of identity theft in the U.S. has led to an increased demand for credit and risk information in the professional and consumer markets. The ADP Employer Services' Hiring Index noted that the number of background checks performed in 2004 tripled from the 1997 level, while another survey revealed a 16.0 percent increase in credit checks in 2004 compared with the previous year. Spending in this category increased at a 5.6 percent compound annual rate from 1999 to 2004 as consumer confidence led to an increase in large purchases, such as homes, which require extensive checks. In addition, companies that were hiring more staff than in prior years had a larger volume of background checks to perform.

Credit and risk information providers may have the largest challenge of any BIS category. New products and services notwithstanding, these organizations must first address trust issues among their customers before they can consider traditional growth strategies. Companies such as LexisNexis and ChoicePoint are just two examples of prominent firms caught in security breaches in 2004 and 2005 with customers' personal information. Because of these events, credit information providers will have to invest in improving their security measures. Once those issues are addressed, they can return their focus to providing customers with the information and tools necessary to perform their risk management and credit dimensioning capabilities.

Equifax, a leader in this category, has launched products to ease processes for business customers. In mid-2004, the company launched Equifax InterConnect, a product line designed to help business customers make their credit and lending processes more efficient. Yet, risk mitigation and business solution provider First Advantage Corporation was perhaps the most acquisitive provider in this segment during 2004—utilizing each deal to expand its slate of products and services. Among those deals was its acquisition of CompuNet Credit Services, a proprietary database provider of payment practice records of transportation brokers and shippers. Other acquisitions included the purchase of Alameda, a business and tax credits and incentives consulting organization, as well as National Background Data, a criminal records aggregator and reseller.

The smallest category in the BIS subsegment, general business industry news, posted an 8.0 percent increase in spending in 2004 to $4.54 billion. From 1999 to 2004, spending grew at a 4.1 percent compound annual rate, the lowest of all the PBIS categories. However, we anticipate a rebound in growth in this category beginning in 2005 and during the remainder of the forecast period. This trend is expected to result from the emergence of key players that will have the resources to bolster their offerings organically and, more so, through acquisitions. Examples of such acquisitions include MarketWatch to Dow Jones, About.com to The New York Times and Slate to the Washington Post. In addition, many customers of the PBIS segment prefer more targeted and niche (such as industry-specific) news sources to general business news. As a result, the demand for general business industry news will lag other BIS categories. However, we expect spending growth in the general business industry news segment to rebound by 2009 because we believe these providers will respond to their free news competitors by augmenting their offerings to make them more appealing to existing and potential customers. Companies in this category will likely investigate the integration of RSS feeds and blogs into their offerings. In addition, these providers will likely receive interest from consumers and business professionals alike.

BUSINESS INFORMATION SERVICES: END USERS BY PROFESSION

BIS categories include marketing information services, payroll and human resource services, economic and financial, credit and risk, and general business industry news.

Marketing information services is the largest BIS category and includes companies such as AC Nielsen, Acxiom and Experian. It includes primarily market research organizations, monitoring services and other companies that are focused on tracking usage, product and price trends. Marketing information services spending totaled $23.55 billion in 2004, a 14.7 percent increase from spending of $20.54 billion in 2003. From 1999 to 2004, spending on marketing information services increased at a 6.5 percent compound annual rate. The largest purchaser of marketing information is the consumer goods industry, with expenditures of $5.91 billion in 2004. Consumer goods include food and beverage, health and beauty aids, drugs and medical supplies, automobiles, and general merchandise. The marketing information services category represented a 24.1 percent share of all PBIS expenditures in 2004.

Marketing information services firms continue to work to add value to their offerings, and some are pursuing acquisitions to accomplish this goal. In 2004, Acxiom announced plans to acquire Digital Impact, an integrated digital marketing solutions provider, and purchased SmartDM, a full-service direct marketing firm. Experian acquired Simmons Market Research Bureau in 2004. Experian management noted that the deal would help Experian further develop its offerings for users, from more extensive databases (of customer and prospect information) to other strategic services. Marketing information services firms are also positioned to address customer demand for more tools that allow them to measure the effectiveness of marketing techniques.

Spending in this category is expected to grow at a compound annual rate of 7.0 percent from 2004 to 2009 to $33.10 billion as marketing information services companies continue to add new products and services in order to maintain and strengthen relationships with current customers. In addition, they hope to encourage further spending and engage new clients.

Payroll and human resource information is the second-largest business information category, with a 6.0 percent increase in spending to $20.26 billion in 2004. Spending in this category also grew at a compound annual rate of 4.4 percent from 1999 to 2004. This segment controls a 20.7 percent share of spending among all PBIS categories. The top companies in the payroll and human resource information segment provide payroll and human resource content and services, and include such well-known entities as Automatic Data Processing, Paychex and Ceridian.

The main driver of growth in this segment is the trend toward outsourcing of such functions as payroll and human resources. Companies are outsourcing human resource functions to achieve cost savings. Benefits administration is emerging as a strong growth opportunity because of the unabated rise in healthcare costs. As workforces are expanded due to the strong economy, the need for such services will naturally increase. The top performers in this segment will respond with new products that make these processes even more efficient for their end users.

Human resource firms are also striving to become complete service providers for their customers. Paychex in early 2005 noted that it experienced strong growth in its full-service offerings, reflecting high demand. ADP has also recognized the growing demand for full-service solutions and has expanded its sales force to accommodate this demand. ADP acquired more than 10,000 new clients in the first half of 2005.

Led by continued growth in outsourcing, as well as customer demand for complete suites of products, the payroll and human resource information category is expected to grow at a 6.7 percent compound annual rate from 2004 to 2009. In 2009, spending in this segment is expected to top $27.97 billion. Customers in this category are continually seeking ways in which to strengthen the relationship between employers and employees, and will likely turn to payroll and human resource information providers to offer new services that will help make the communication between these two groups more efficient. In addition, the creation of new jobs through the nation's economic expansion will increase demand for human resource and payroll solutions.

The financial and economic category is the third-largest business information category. The leading companies in this category are Thomson, Reuters, Bloomberg and Dow Jones, which have a core customer base whose spending is perhaps more closely tied to economic conditions than any other in the PBIS sector. Investment banks, accounting firms, brokerage houses and research companies are just some of the entities that use financial and economic business information. After two consecutive years of spending declines (2001 and 2002), this category pulled out of the recession to post growth in 2003, with spending up 6.8 percent. Expenditures rose 10.0 percent to $16.07 billion in 2004. From 1999 to 2004, spending in the financial and economic category grew at a compound annual rate of 4.3 percent. The financial and economic category accounted for a 16.4 percent share of all PBIS spending in 2004.

Buyers of financial and economic information have the greatest demand for up-to-date, real-time content and solutions. For this reason, this user base is perhaps one of the most Web-savvy of the BIS subsegment. Providers continue to respond by offering packages that provide such information. Such organizations, like Reuters, claim to offer end users a strong combination of content and analytics that provide solutions for the day-to-day responsibilities of those users right at their desktops. As a result, Reuters expects to record strong growth in 2005 in many areas including front-, mid- and back-office automation.

Dow Jones is expanding its breadth of offerings to end users, as well. The company's online division, WSJ.com, was one of the first successful paid online content ventures, and the company plans to build on that success with its purchase of MarketWatch, another online financial information provider. Expenditures in the financial and economic information category are projected to increase at a compound annual rate of 9.6 percent from 2004 to 2009 to $25.45 billion as demand for real-time content leads to the launch of additional online content offerings for customers in this market.

Spending on credit and risk information was $13.67 billion in 2004, a 10.0 percent increase over spending totals from 2003. Credit information spending rose at a compound annual rate of 5.6 percent from 1999 to 2004. Of all professional and business information expenditures, credit information comprised a 14.0 percent share in 2004. The largest and most well-known of credit data providers are ChoicePoint, Moody's and Equifax. Their primary offerings usually include credit reports and other detailed credit information. These providers serve a variety of customers, but the main buyers of credit information typically include banks and insurance companies.

Demand and spending for credit information hit a peak in 2003, as low interest rates precipitated a boon in home refinancing and debt consolidation. As a result, more jobs were necessary to handle this influx of paperwork and credit information requests. We expect this segment to post substantial growth during the forecast period if the economy continues its expansion. Credit information providers will likely respond with new products and services that will assist end customers in assessing information more quickly and easily, as well as enable them to manipulate the data in any desired manner. Providers will also likely launch products and services that complement these credit information-based products. For example, LexisNexis formed two alliances in early 2005 to improve the offerings of its Risk Management unit, which assists the financial services sector in identity theft prevention, fraud prevention and Patriot Act compliance solutions. A partnership with Verid will enable LexisNexis customers to better detect fraud. A partnership with Quova, a Web geography service provider, will help LexisNexis users prevent credit card deception. Moody's has been working to achieve growth through the expansion of its international operations, as well.

While the aforementioned security breaches have generated much interest and press, they do not represent the only activity generated by credit information providers. In light of another consumer-based issue, identity theft, credit checks are becoming more prevalent. As customers demand solutions to deal with this issue, spending on credit information products and services increased in 2004.

However, we caution that these service providers have more to accomplish than launching the next generation of products and services for their end users. Because of the well-publicized security breaches involving prominent firms such as LexisNexis and ChoicePoint, these organizations will have to spend time on damage control to maintain current customers and attract prospective clients, as well as put safeguards in place to prevent future violations.

Credit and risk information spending is projected to increase at a compound annual rate of 8.2 percent in the 2004-2009 period to $20.26 billion, as the prevalence of credit checks climbs and the threat of identity theft continues, but is diligently addressed.

General business industry news spending rose 8.0 percent to $4.54 billion in 2004, and accounted for 4.6 percent of the overall PBIS segment. Spending on general business industry news increased at a compound annual rate of 4.1 percent in the 1999-2004 period. The general business industry news includes organizations that produce a variety of more generic information. Topics they typically cover include real estate, farming, energy and weather.

Spending in the general business industry news category, which includes companies such as MapInfo and Comtex, is shrinking because many large information providers prefer to aggregate their own content. In addition, PBIS customers prefer niche offerings meeting their particular needs. Perhaps one of the greatest challenges is the abundance of free general business information available over the Internet. It is difficult to maintain a pay-for-content business model in the general business information segment when there are a variety of sources that provide the same information with no fee or commitment.

Spending in the general business industry news segment is expected to increase 6.1 percent in 2005 to $4.82 billion. The category is anticipated to grow at a compound annual rate of 7.1 percent in the forecast period to $6.39 billion in 2009. But these general business industry news sources provide a quality of information to which we believe customers will return. And many business customers demand the real-time information that these providers offer. However, further growth will likely be achieved if these organizations can incorporate analytical tools to add value to their content and create an end-to-end solution for customers.

BUSINESS INFORMATION SERVICES: PURCHASERS BY INDUSTRY

As mentioned previously, the recovering economy along with consistent demand for BIS fueled healthy spending increases in all categories in 2004. That spending was distributed among a variety of industries.

Intermediary and professional services firms were the largest purchasers of business information in 2004 at $22.12 billion. Though other economic sectors grew faster in 2004 than this industry, such as energy, end users at intermediary and professional services firms require access to more real-time information than most other industries. Of the segments included in this category, the largest was banks with expenditures of $6.26 billion in 2004.

Distribution services firms were the second-largest purchasers of business information in 2004, with total spending of $13.69 billion. This category comprises retail (supermarkets, department stores, drugstores and specialty stores), wholesale, utilities, communications and transportation. Specialty stores, at $2.91 billion, were the largest spenders among these industries.

In the professional and business information industries combined, three categories of spenders—intermediary and professional services, consumer goods, and distribution services—account for more than 60 percent of all PBIS spending. Intermediary and professional services were the largest spenders at $28.02 billion in 2004, a 28.6 percent share of PBIS spending. Second-largest was consumer goods at $18.02 billion (18.4 percent) and the third-largest was distribution services at $16.88 billion (17.3 percent). We expect intermediary and professional services to remain the top category in terms of PBIS spending as the economy continues to rebound. As consumer confidence increases, more spending will likely be generated by the consumer goods segment. Thus, providers of business and professional information will likely maintain this segment as a strong customer base in 2005 and for the rest of the forecast period.

THE OUTLOOK FOR BUSINESS INFORMATION SERVICES

We foresee potential growth opportunities for BIS providers in emerging electronic formats, in addition to the growing use of Internet applications in the forecast period. Information providers are expected to substantially ratchet up their use of wireless technologies, such as PDAs and cell phones, which have already become a major focus in consumer markets. We believe this is a natural and necessary extension of publishers' business models because their future is in a younger, technology-oriented customer base, which prefers to receive its content via electronic means. This is evident in the proliferation of technological devices, such as digital cameras, cell phones and iPods, which are expected to expand as alternative media outlets from the consumer market to the professional market in the coming years.

Overall BIS market spending is projected to increase 8.1 percent to $84.39 billion in 2005, and to escalate at a compound annual rate of 7.7 percent from 2004 to 2009, reaching $113.16 billion.

Shares of Spending on Professional & Business Information,

CORPORATE

INDUSTRY FOCUS	*Business Information Services* Marketing Information Services	Payroll & Human Resource Services	Financial & Economic Information	Credit & Risk Information	General Business Industry News	Total Business Information Services
Consumer Goods						
Food & Beverage	2.9%	0.9%	0.7%	0.2%	0.1%	4.8%
Health & Beauty Aids	0.8	0.3	0.2	0.1	0.0	1.5
Drugs & Medical Supplies	1.3	0.3	0.3	0.2	0.1	2.1
Automobiles	0.7	1.2	0.7	1.2	0.1	3.9
General Merchandise	0.4	0.5	0.2	0.4	0.1	1.5
Total	*6.0*	*3.2*	*2.1*	*1.9*	*0.4*	*13.7*
Consumer Services						
Healthcare	1.0	2.6	0.4	0.5	0.3	4.8
Media	1.6	0.5	0.4	0.3	0.2	3.0
Leisure & Restaurants	0.5	2.2	0.2	0.2	0.1	3.2
Total	*3.1*	*5.4*	*1.0*	*0.9*	*0.7*	*11.1*
Construction	*0.8*	*0.5*	*0.3*	*0.4*	*0.2*	*2.2*
Industrial						
Energy	0.5	0.5	0.5	0.5	0.1	2.1
Process Goods	0.6	0.5	0.4	0.4	0.1	2.0
Manufacturing	1.0	0.6	0.5	0.4	0.3	2.8
Technology	1.9	0.9	0.6	0.5	0.4	4.2
Total	*4.0*	*2.5*	*2.0*	*1.7*	*0.9*	*11.1*
Agriculture	*0.2*	*0.2*	*0.1*	*0.1*	*0.1*	*0.7*
Distribution Services						
Retail						
*Supermarkets	0.4	0.5	0.1	0.1	0.1	1.1
*Department Stores	0.6	0.4	0.1	0.4	0.1	1.6
*Drugstores	0.3	0.3	0.1	0.1	0.1	0.8
*Specialty Stores	1.2	1.1	0.1	0.4	0.2	3.0
Wholesale	0.4	0.7	0.2	0.5	0.1	1.9
Utilities	0.3	0.3	0.2	0.3	0.1	1.1
Communications	0.9	0.4	0.7	0.5	0.2	2.8
Transportation	0.3	0.4	0.3	0.5	0.1	1.7
Total	*4.4*	*4.1*	*1.7*	*2.8*	*1.0*	*14.0*
Intermediary & Professional Services						
Legal	0.1	0.6	0.0	0.2	0.1	1.0
Financial						
*Wall Street	0.4	0.3	4.9	0.4	0.1	6.1
*Banks	1.2	0.7	1.6	2.7	0.2	6.4
*Insurance	1.2	0.7	1.2	2.0	0.2	5.2
Business Data Services	1.2	1.1	0.8	0.5	0.3	3.9
Total	*4.1*	*3.3*	*8.6*	*5.8*	*0.9*	*22.6*
Government & Nonprofit	*1.6*	*1.6*	*0.5*	*0.3*	*0.4*	*4.4*
TOTAL	**24.1**	**20.7**	**16.4**	**14.0**	**4.6**	**79.8**

Sources: Veronis Suhler Stevenson, PQ Media, Outsell

by Corporate Function and Industry Focus

FUNCTION

Legal & Regulatory Information	Scientific & Technical Information	Health & Life Science Information	Total Professional Information	Total Professional & Business Information Services
Professional Information				
0.7%	0.6%	0.4%	1.7%	6.4%
0.3	0.2	0.1	0.6	2.1
0.4	0.3	0.2	0.9	3.0
0.5	0.4	0.3	1.2	5.1
0.2	0.1	0.1	0.4	1.8
2.1	*1.6*	*1.0*	*4.7*	*18.4*
0.5	0.4	0.2	1.0	5.8
0.2	0.2	0.1	0.6	3.6
0.4	0.3	0.2	1.0	4.2
1.1	*0.9*	*0.6*	*2.5*	*13.6*
0.2	*0.1*	*0.1*	*0.4*	*2.6*
0.3	0.2	0.1	0.6	2.7
0.2	0.1	0.1	0.4	2.4
0.1	0.1	0.1	0.3	3.1
0.5	0.4	0.2	1.1	5.3
1.1	*0.8*	*0.5*	*2.4*	*13.6*
0.1	*0.1*	*0.0*	*0.2*	*0.9*
0.1	0.1	0.0	0.2	1.2
0.2	0.1	0.1	0.4	2.0
0.0	0.0	0.0	0.1	0.9
0.3	0.3	0.2	0.8	3.7
0.2	0.1	0.1	0.4	2.3
0.1	0.1	0.1	0.3	1.5
0.3	0.2	0.2	0.7	3.5
0.2	0.2	0.1	0.5	2.1
1.4	*1.1*	*0.7*	*3.3*	*17.3*
0.1	0.1	0.1	0.3	1.3
1.0	0.8	0.5	2.4	8.5
0.6	0.4	0.3	1.3	7.7
0.6	0.4	0.3	1.3	6.5
0.4	0.3	0.2	0.8	4.7
2.7	*2.1*	*1.3*	*6.0*	*28.6*
0.3	*0.2*	*0.1*	*0.6*	*5.1*
8.9	**6.9**	**4.4**	**20.2**	**100.0**

Professional & Business Information Services Map

CORPORATE FUNCTION

All Dollar Amounts in Millions

INDUSTRY FOCUS	Business Information Services						Professional Information				
	Marketing Information Services	Payroll & Human Resource Services	Financial & Economic Information	Credit & Risk Information	General Business Industry News	Total Business Information Services	Legal & Regulatory Information	Scientific & Technical Information	Health & Life Science Information	Total Professional Information	Total Professional & Business Information Services
Consumer Goods											
Food & Beverage	$ 2,836	$ 868	$ 693	$ 169	$ 122	$ 4,688	$ 714	$ 550	$ 352	$ 1,616	$ 6,304
Health & Beauty Aids	821	289	231	78	26	1,445	268	206	132	606	2,051
Drugs & Medical Supplies	1,242	299	289	149	59	2,038	377	291	187	855	2,893
Automobiles	667	1,200	673	1,163	124	3,827	518	399	256	1,173	5,000
General Merchandise	347	492	156	345	81	1,421	154	119	76	349	1,770
Total	*5,913*	*3,148*	*2,042*	*1,904*	*412*	*13,419*	*2,031*	*1,565*	*1,003*	*4,599*	*18,018*
Consumer Services											
Healthcare	952	2,539	408	460	340	4,699	447	344	221	1,012	5,711
Media	1,583	509	389	246	231	2,958	239	184	118	541	3,499
Leisure & Restaurants	482	2,188	177	197	131	3,175	412	317	204	933	4,108
Total	*3,017*	*5,236*	*974*	*903*	*702*	*10,832*	*1,098*	*845*	*543*	*2,486*	*13,318*
Construction	*760*	*511*	*333*	*357*	*193*	*2,154*	*164*	*126*	*81*	*371*	*2,525*
Industrial											
Energy	463	508	532	465	116	2,084	266	205	131	602	2,686
Process Goods	603	476	384	383	146	1,992	171	132	85	388	2,380
Manufacturing	992	613	459	383	266	2,713	136	105	67	308	3,021
Technology	1,857	838	598	450	354	4,097	479	369	237	1,085	5,182
Total	*3,915*	*2,435*	*1,973*	*1,681*	*882*	*10,886*	*1,052*	*811*	*520*	*2,383*	*13,269*
Agriculture	*187*	*155*	*120*	*80*	*130*	*672*	*73*	*57*	*36*	*166*	*838*
Distribution Services											
Retail											
*Supermarkets	356	446	73	93	91	1,059	66	51	32	149	1,208
*Department Stores	619	386	79	397	90	1,571	154	118	76	348	1,919
*Drugstores	268	300	59	79	72	778	43	33	21	97	875
*Specialty Stores	1,134	1,119	132	362	162	2,909	333	257	164	754	3,663
Wholesale	432	671	185	473	122	1,883	162	125	80	367	2,250
Utilities	256	256	192	323	93	1,120	145	112	72	329	1,449
Communications	896	431	682	516	225	2,750	305	235	151	691	3,441
Transportation	302	427	309	477	107	1,622	201	155	99	455	2,077
Total	*4,263*	*4,036*	*1,711*	*2,720*	*962*	*13,692*	*1,409*	*1,086*	*695*	*3,190*	*16,882*
Intermediary & Professional Services											
Legal	99	584	30	188	76	977	129	100	64	293	1,270
Financial											
*Wall Street	425	286	4,806	361	104	5,982	1,015	782	502	2,299	8,281
*Banks	1,145	652	1,609	2,652	198	6,256	550	424	272	1,246	7,502
*Insurance	1,148	658	1,179	1,978	156	5,119	563	434	278	1,275	6,394
Business Data Services	1,162	1,042	762	501	314	3,781	349	269	173	791	4,572
Total	*3,979*	*3,222*	*8,386*	*5,680*	*848*	*22,115*	*2,606*	*2,009*	*1,289*	*5,904*	*28,019*
Government & Nonprofit	*1,520*	*1,521*	*529*	*341*	*412*	*4,323*	*278*	*214*	*138*	*630*	*4,953*
TOTAL	**23,554**	**20,264**	**16,068**	**13,666**	**4,541**	**78,093**	**8,711**	**6,713**	**4,305**	**19,729**	**97,822**

Sources: Veronis Suhler Stevenson, PQ Media, Outsell

Professional & Business Information Services

The Outlook For Professional And Business Information Services

Spending growth over the next five years in the PBIS segment will be sparked by several key factors. First, providers of PBIS information will continue to transition their portfolios of product suites to be more heavily weighted with Internet-based products and services in lieu of traditional print publications and CD-ROMs. These Web-based products more effectively fit PBIS firms' overall strategy to become end-to-end multimedia service providers, in that these electronic products offer increased functionality and can be integrated into an end-user organization's other operations.

The PBIS market's adaptability to Internet-based products and services will yield an abundance of opportunities through newer technologies, such as PDAs, RSS feeds and blogs. Customer demand for products that are supported by these technologies is growing and PBIS companies are positioning themselves to offer the tools that utilize them.

Additionally, there will be increased demand for the services that integrate in-house proprietary data with external databases. PBIS companies that can provide customers with flexible, customizable product offerings, which can amalgamate content, software and services, will be the most successful during the forecast period. One method many PBIS companies are using to expand their offerings is through the acquisition of organizations that offer complementary products. This will enable PBIS firms to build relationships with their customers by delivering products and services that meet every operational need.

The forecast period for PBIS is projected to be one of strong, sustained growth, with many opportunities emerging. Perhaps most important will be the surfacing of new customers with more money to spend and higher demands, which will drive the research and development of creative multimedia workflow solutions that transform this market at a brisker rate than even that of the past five years. The demand for such mission-critical content from end-user companies is traditionally steady, and will only strengthen as the economy expands and corporations increase

Growth Opportunities versus Value-Added Opportunities In the Professional and Business Information Services Market

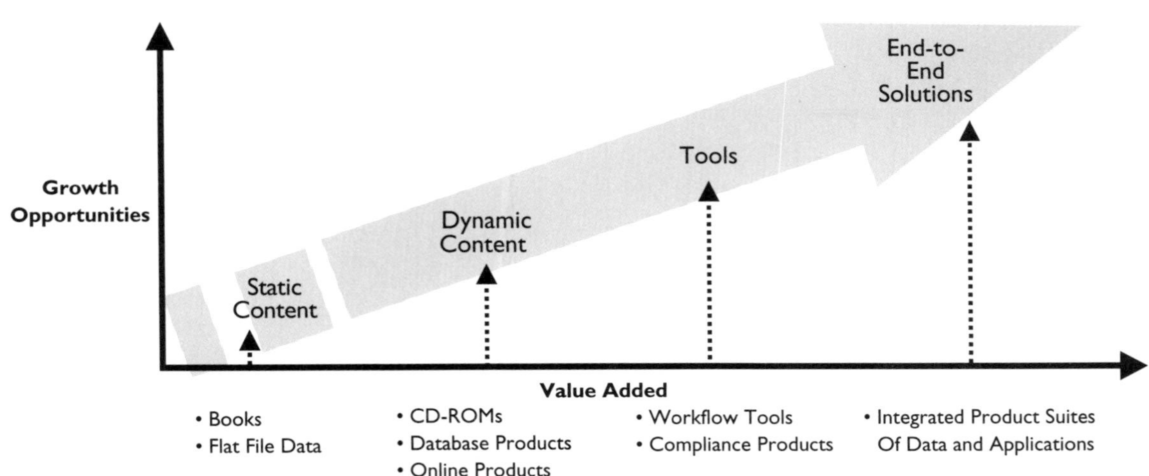

Sources: Veronis Suhler Stevenson, PQ Media

Professional & Business Information Services

2004 Communications Industry Forecast Compared with Actual Growth

Category	*2004 Forecasted Growth**	*Actual 2004 Growth†*
Business Information Services	6.5%	10.2%
Marketing Information Services	6.7	14.7
Payroll & Human Resource Services	6.4	6.0
Financial & Economic Information	7.0	10.0
Credit & Risk Information	5.3	10.0
General Business Industry News	5.0	8.0
Professional Information	6.6	7.9
Legal & Regulatory Information	6.2	7.2
Scientific & Technical Information	6.2	8.5
Health & Life Science Information	7.8	8.5
Total	6.5	9.7

*Veronis Suhler Stevenson 2004 Communications Industry Forecast & Report
†Veronis Suhler Stevenson, PQ Media

their budgets for business information services. A robust job market will yield an increase in customers that need this content, as well. Growth in the labor market has and will continue to correlate with growth in PBIS spending. Anecdotal evidence, based on 2002 data, suggests that PBIS spending fell during the recession, along with related labor segments, as well as the spending recovery corresponding with an increase in hiring the following year. For example, in the financial services sector, spending in financial and economic information fell 1.5 percent in 2001 and 0.9 percent in 2002, analogous to the 5.2 percent decline in financial management and sales positions during the recession. Spending climbed 6.8 percent in this market in 2003 after a 3.5 percent rebound in financial management positions in 2002. As mentioned previously, this new climate will offer business information vendors an expanded market in which to launch new products and services that provide end-to-end solutions for their customers.

As a result, we expect aggressive growth from most PBIS subsegments over the next five years, especially from 2005 to 2007. This trending will be due, in part, to the ability of information providers to expand integrated software suites by upgrading technologies that provide institutional end users with workflow solutions that do a better job of combining high-end content with analytical tools. This demand, however, will begin to soften in the latter part of the forecast period as the cost to expand these tools will be amortized, in addition to the projected slower growth of potential users of this information, such as college graduates and practicing professionals.

We expect the PBIS segment to post an 8.1 percent spending increase in 2005, outpacing GDP growth of 6.0 percent. This trend is expected to continue over the next five years, as GDP is projected to rise at a compound annual rate of 6.1 percent in the period compared with 7.8 percent upside for PBIS from 2004 to 2009, with expenditures reaching $142.33 billion in 2009.

FORECAST ASSUMPTIONS

- The continued migration of professional and business information services (PBIS) customers from traditional print products to Internet-based products and services will be the primary driver of growth in the forecast period. Increased demand for improved search functionality and analytical tools that allow for intense data manipulation will lead to the rollout of more sophisticated digital workflow tools that better meet the changing needs of PBIS customers.
- Growth over the next five years will also be spurred by the PBIS industry's commitment to develop products and services that utilize the latest technological advances. PBIS growth opportunities abound through some of the newest formats and processes, such as PDAs, RSS (Really Simple Syndication) feeds and Web logs, popularly known as blogs.
- Mergers and acquisitions in the PBIS market will yield expansion potential as well in the forecast period. Deals of various size and scope are expected to transform the industry as major players seek to bolster their slate of offerings in an effort to become full-service PBIS providers.
- In the professional information subsegment, scientific and technical publishers will be challenged by competition from non-paid start-up electronic publications. These entities are producing proprietary journals and offering them free online. In response, scientific and technical publishers are defending their content and pricing by touting their information's superior quality, in addition to launching their own programs allowing authors to select from either a traditional publishing model or offering free access to their articles.
- In the business information services (BIS) subsegment, growth in the marketing information, payroll and human resource services, and credit information services categories will be driven by more outsourcing, particularly with respect to compliance issues such as the Sarbanes-Oxley Act. Outsourcing also provides potential cost savings. At the same time, BIS firms will develop content formats that integrate customers' proprietary databases with external data sources.

Business Overview

Formed by VSS in 1997 with the acquisition of Multi-Local Media Information Group, Yellow Book USA, L.P. ("Yellow Book" or the "Company") became the largest independent competitive publisher of yellow page directories in the U.S. publishing over 250 directories with a combined circulation of 13 million in New York, New Jersey, Pennsylvania, Florida, Delaware, Maryland, Virginia, and Washington, D.C. Yellow Book publishes two core products: Community Directories (Yellow Pages) and two editions of the Business-to-Business Directories.

Background

VSS's Fund II developed this opportunity internally. Joseph A. Walsh, President, had been with Yellow Book since 1987 and had served as President since 1993. Prior to joining Yellow Book, he was Executive Vice President - Sales and Marketing of Data National, a directory publishing company.

In September 1997, Fund II formed Yellow Book as part of the purchase of the assets of Multi-Local Media Information Group ("MLMIG") from Acadia/Oak Hill Partners and Cigna Investments.

Two months following the acquisition of MLMIG, Yellow Book signed a definitive agreement to acquire Reuben H. Donnelley's (a division of Dun & Bradstreet) Proprietary East division ("RHPDE"), an independent publisher of yellow page directories in Pennsylvania, Delaware, New Jersey, Maryland, Washington, D.C. and Northern Virginia.

Strategy & Rationale

- Continue to compete against regional phone company wide-area yellow pages by creating directories which take into account the buying behavior and shopping patterns of local residents in order to better serve the advertiser.
- Launch new directories in contiguous attractive markets to capitalize on Yellow Book's well established franchise positions, clustered network of directories, and seasoned sales force.
- Acquire underperforming independent yellow page companies in similar contiguous geographical markets and utilize Yellow Book's sales methodology and business approach to bring these properties up to Yellow Books' operating performance.

Add-on Acquisition Activities

- In addition to completing four add-on acquisitions, Yellow Book actively launched a significant number of new directories in new markets including Manhattan. At the time of the first acquisition in 1997, Yellow Book published 175 directories with circulation of 5,000,000 and revenues of $60 million. At exit, Yellow Book published 260 directories with circulation of 18,000,000 and revenues of $210 million.

Exit

In August 1999, VSS completed the sale of Yellow Book USA to British Telecommunications. This resulted in a 4.5x return of capital and a 122% IRR.

APPENDIX

Changes in Methodology

Veronis Suhler Stevenson (VSS), and its editorial partner, PQ Media, instituted relatively substantial changes to the historical and forecast methodologies of several chapters of the 2005 edition of the *Veronis Suhler Stevenson Communications Industry Forecast*. In some cases, the changes in methodology involved using new sources or those with more updated information, while in other cases, changes were made to reflect the emergence of many new trends and drivers in the media industry over the past several years. We also developed a number of exclusive methodologies, as well as new subsegments and data tables, for this edition of the *Forecast*. In addition, we partnered with research firm PQ Media to license exclusive original content on two emerging media segments that is not available from any other source. We believe that these additions have provided significantly enhanced value to this year's *Forecast*, giving our subscribers what we hope will be a very engaging and insightful communications industry analysis.

Additionally, some data were placed in two chapters due to the cross-branding that has become common in the communications industry. However, to avoid double counting, the data were included in the overall spending data from only one chapter. These additions are mentioned below in the original chapter in which they appeared. Finally, in most instances except where stated, new data were historical in nature, except for several areas in which PQ Media and/or VSS developed historical and forecast data, such as in the product placement subsegment. Below is a detailed explanation of the changes made in each chapter.

FORECAST SUMMARY

- Data were included on economic cycles based on information from the Bureau of Economic Analysis.

EXECUTIVE SUMMARY

- The Executive Summary pertaining to operating performance of publicly reporting companies that appeared in prior editions of the *Forecast*, as well as summary tables and text that followed each segment chapter, was deleted from this year's edition of the report.

CHAPTER 1: COMMUNICATIONS IN THE U.S. ECONOMY

- Data were included on the consumer price index to better reflect inflation trends based on information from the Bureau of Labor Statistics.

CHAPTER 2: ADVERTISING, SPECIALTY MEDIA & MARKETING SERVICES

- Exclusive data and forecasts were included on political media buying across all nine media used for this purpose, based on new information from PQ Media.

Advertising

- Data were included on the Top 100 advertisers, reflecting consolidations of marketers based on information from *Advertising Age*.
- The outdoor advertising segment was changed to out-of-home advertising to better reflect changes in the industry. As such, data were included on non-traditional out-of-home advertising based on new information from the Outdoor Advertising Association of America.
- New tables were developed on traditional ad media spending versus new ad media spending. These tables replaced tables found in previous editions on electronic media ad spending versus print/outdoor media ad spending.

Specialty Media & Marketing Services

- Data on the direct mail segment were expanded to include communications spending on all direct marketing subsegments based on data available from the Direct Marketing Association and other data providers in this segment.
- Data on custom publishing were included based on new information from the Custom Publishing Council.
- A new segment, branded entertainment, was developed to reflect spending in alternative media. Information on event sponsorships was combined with promotional licensing data, formerly included with consumer promotions, as well as exclusive data and forecasts on product placement licensed exclusively from PQ Media.

CHAPTER 3: END USER SPENDING ON COMMUNICATIONS

Consumer End-User Spending

- Data were included on consumer media penetration, including adoption cycles, based on data from multiple sources.
- The time spent data pertaining to television was revised to include teenage viewing habits, which reflected fewer hours spent with television than found in previous editions of the *Forecast*.
- The time spent data related to newspapers were revised to include weekly newspapers based on new readership data available from the Newspaper Association of America and Northwestern University.
- Information was included on time spent in various activities on the Internet derived from new information available from the Online Publishers Association and Nielsen/Net Ratings.
- Data were included on the U.S. demographic shifts based on revised information from the U.S. Census Bureau.
- New information was included on various time spent metrics, in order to enhance VSS's proprietary data on the subject. New data derived from demographic information were available from the U.S. Department of Labor, Mendelsohn Media, Mediamark Research, Starcom Worldwide, BIGResearch and the International Digital Media & Arts Association.

Institutional End-User Spending

- Data were included on institutional subscribers' use of wireless data based on new information from Insight Research.
- Data were included on time spent by institutional end users on information-gathering and business-to-business magazine reading habits based on new information from PennWell and Outsell.

CHAPTER 4: BROADCAST TELEVISION

- Ratings and share data were expanded to include viewing on public broadcast stations, as well as "other" cable networks, as a result of new information released by Nielsen Media Research. These revised tables are also found in the Cable & Satellite Television chapter.

CHAPTER 5: CABLE & SATELLITE TELEVISION

- New tables were developed with separate spending data for wired cable television versus satellite television in order to reflect the competitive nature of the industry.
- Data were included on video-on-demand (VOD), previously found only in the Entertainment Media chapter, to better reflect the medium's increased penetration in cable households. To avoid double counting, the spending data were only included in this chapter.
- Data were included on cable modems, previously found only in the Consumer Internet chapter, in order to reflect the impact on cable penetration. To avoid double counting, the spending data are included in the Consumer Internet chapter along with other access spending data.
- Data were included on digital video recorders (DVRs), found previously only in the Entertainment Media chapter, in order to reflect its impact on cable & satellite TV penetration rates. To avoid double counting, spending is included in the Entertainment Media chapter because some DVR spending occurs outside of cable and satellite television.

CHAPTER 6: BROADCAST & SATELLITE RADIO

- The table of Top 10 Radio Groups was revised to include a ranking based on the number of stations owned instead of by revenues, as a result of information from *Who Owns What.*
- Data were included on radio spotloads to reflect industry concerns over ad clutter, based on new information available from Harris Nesbitt and Media Monitors.

CHAPTER 7: ENTERTAINMENT MEDIA

- The tables on home video rental spending, both VHS and DVD, were revised to include information from Rentrak.
- Data on VOD, formerly found only in this chapter, were also included in the Cable & Satellite Television chapter. To avoid double counting and to better reflect VOD penetration, the data were included in the Cable & Satellite Television chapter, rather than in this chapter.
- Information was included on wireless content spending based on new information available from Insight Research. The data were also included in the Consumer Internet chapter, but to avoid double counting, data were only included in this chapter.
- Data were included on online music downloads, formerly found only in the Consumer Internet chapter, derived from information released by the Recording Industry of America Association. To avoid double counting, the data were only included in the Consumer Internet chapter, along with other online content data.
- The table on videogame console spending was expanded to include videogame rentals based on new information from Rentrak.
- Data were included on online games, formerly found only in the Consumer Internet chapter, to better reflect current videogame trends. To avoid double counting, the data were only included in the Consumer Internet chapter along with other online content data.
- The table on overall interactive entertainment spending was expanded to include videogame advertising based on new information available from the Yankee Group.

CHAPTER 8: CONSUMER INTERNET

- Information on music downloads was included as a result of data made available for the first time by the Recording Industry of America Association. The data were also included in the Entertainment Media chapter, but to avoid double counting, the data were counted only in this chapter along with other online content spending.
- Data were included on wireless content spending based on new information available from Insight Research. The data were also included in the Entertainment Media chapter, but to avoid double counting, were only included in the total spending in that chapter.

CHAPTER 9: NEWSPAPER PUBLISHING

- Data on online newspaper advertising, found previously only in the Consumer Internet chapter, were included with daily newspaper expenditures, based on new information available from the Newspaper Association of America. To avoid double counting, the data were only included in the Consumer Internet chapter totals for other online advertising data.

CHAPTER 10: CONSUMER BOOK PUBLISHING

- No changes.

CHAPTER 11: CONSUMER MAGAZINE PUBLISHING

- The tables on local consumer magazine advertising were revised to better reflect the local ad market and were based on new information from MNI.

CHAPTER 12: BUSINESS-TO-BUSINESS MEDIA

- A new proprietary methodology was developed to size and structure spending on business-to-business magazine advertising, including new categories, based on assistance and data from IMS/The Auditor, which replaced data from TNS Media Intelligence/CMR.
- The tables on b-to-b magazine circulation were revised to better reflect industry trends and were based on the new categories adopted for the magazine advertising tables.
- A new proprietary methodology was developed to size and structure spending on e-media, in collaboration with PQ Media. These are the first-ever data on this sector of the b-to-b market.

CHAPTER 13: EDUCATIONAL & TRAINING MEDIA

- This chapter was revised and given a new title as a result of moving the professional information data out of this chapter and combining it with business information services data in the newly formed Professional & Business Information Services chapter.
- Of the remaining segments in the chapter, data on outsourced training were revised, including new categories, to better reflect industry trends based on the use of a new source, Simba Information, which is now supplemented by information from the previous source, *Training Magazine.*

CHAPTER 14: PROFESSIONAL & BUSINESS INFORMATION SERVICES

- The chapter was revised and given a new title as a result of the inclusion of professional information data that were formerly found in the Professional, Educational & Training Media chapter, which no longer exists in this form.
- A new proprietary methodology was developed to better reflect the size and structure of the industry, with assistance and data from Outsell.
- Information was included on time spent to gather and analyze professional and business data and was based on new information from Outsell.

About PQ Media

PQ Media LLC is a market research and strategic consulting firm delivering custom media intelligence to corporations, law firms, financial institutions and trade organizations serving the media, entertainment and information industries. PQ Media's analysts cover the 12 key segments of the media industry, as well as dozens of subsegments and new media, while providing expertise on the critical trends that are driving the media and entertainment industries today. These include, among others, media usage and multitasking, the impact of ad-skipping technology, alternative media such as branded entertainment and product placement, the future of traditional media and advertising, and determining return on investment and media engagement parameters. We provide to our clients custom market research and analysis in any one of multiple formats, including print and digital reports, newsletters, white papers and presentations.

PQ Media's practice areas include:

Strategic Consulting

- Custom research on demand
- Multitude of markets covered
- Derived from PQ Media's global databases

Research Publications

- Original: *Product Placement Spending in Media 2005*
- Collaborative: *Communications Industry Forecast*
- Extensive news coverage: CNN, *The New York Times*, *Advertising Age*

Instant Media Analysis

- Custom media briefs—concise, detailed segment analyses
- Telephone and e-mail consultation
- Quick response time

Legal & Regulatory

- Declarations and other supporting materials
- Depositions
- Expert court testimony

PQ Media's clients are some of the most respected names in the media, entertainment and information industries. They include, among others, the Associated Press, News Corporation, GE Commercial Finance, Skadden Arps, Veronis Suhler Stevenson, Hill & Knowlton, Gerson Lehrman Group, American Business Media, and Association of American Publishers.

PQ MEDIA
Two Stamford Landing, Suite 100
Stamford, CT 06902
Phone: 203-921-0368
Fax: 203-921-0367
E-mail: info@pqmedia.com
Website: www.pqmedia.com

Notes

Early Reading: Strategies and Resources

As adults, and fluent readers, we tend to take the complex process of reading for granted. Yet for many of the children described in this book, learning to read is the greatest challenge of their school lives. Mary K. Fitzsimmons (1998) writes:

> The truth is that learning to read is anything but natural. In fact, it does not develop incidentally; it requires human intervention and context. While skillful readers look quite natural in their reading, the act of reading is complex and intentional; it requires bringing together a number of complex actions involving the eyes, the brain, and the psychology of the mind (e.g., motivation, interest, past experience) that do not occur naturally. (p.1)

Teachers must become the engineers of this complex process for all children. Fortunately, today we have an accumulating body of research that provides us with compelling evidence that structured, consistent instruction in the foundation skills of reading can lead to fluency. We discuss reading in several places in this book, particularly in Chapter 4. Reading problems are common to students receiving special education services—and to many who are not.

The basic components of sound early reading instruction are phonological awareness, or "awareness of the sound structure of words and the ability to manipulate sounds in words" (Smith, Simmons, & Kameenui, 1995, p. 2) and knowledge of the alphabetic principle, the idea that letters, or groups of letters, represent phonemes (Burns, Griffin, & Snow, 1999).

Some examples of phonological awareness activities include asking a child to respond to the following (Stanovich, 1994):

1. What would be left if the /k/ sound were taken away from *cat*?
2. What do you have if you put these sounds together: /s/, /a/, /t/?
3. What is the first sound in *rose*?

Teaching Tips: Phonological Awareness and Alphabetic Understanding

Make phonological awareness instruction explicit. Use conspicuous strategies and make phonemes prominent to students by modeling specific sounds and asking students to reproduce the sounds.

Ease into the complexities of phonological awareness. Begin with easy skills, such as rhyming and blending, and progress to more difficult ones, such as segmenting and substitution.

Provide support and assistance for learning the alphabetic code. The following research-based instructional sequence summarizes the kind of scaffolding beginning readers need:

(a) Model the sound or the strategy for making the sound. (b) Have students use the strategy to produce the sound. (c) Repeat steps (a) and (b) using several sounds for each type and level of difficulty. (d) Prompt students to use the strategy during guided practice. (e) Use steps (a) through (d) to introduce more difficult examples.

Develop a sequence and schedule, tailored to each child's needs, for opportunities to apply and develop facility with sounds. Give this schedule top priority among all classroom activities.

Learning to read does not simply require the acquisition of specific skills—children must also become enthusiastic about deriving meaning from print. Reading programs must be balanced between the introduction and practice of skills, and activities and experiences that promote a love of reading.

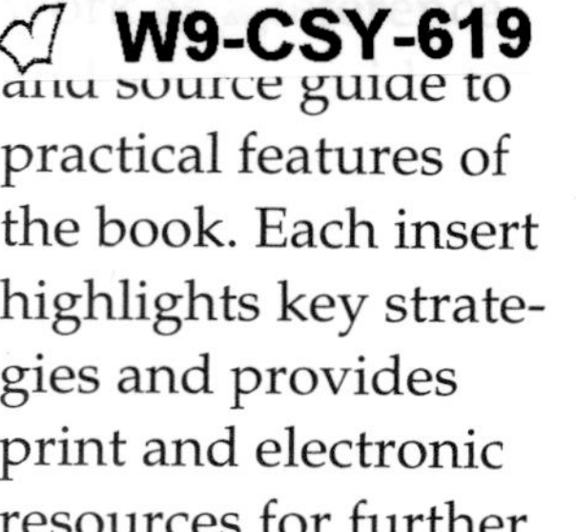

and source guide to practical features of the book. Each insert highlights key strategies and provides print and electronic resources for further investigation.

Popular First Person features let readers experience the topic of the chapter through the story of someone who has "been there."

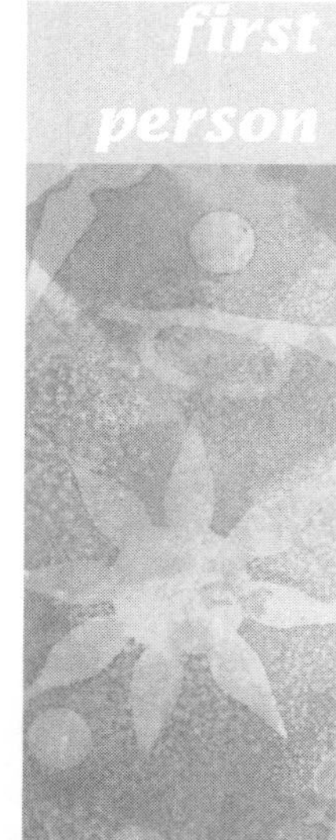

first person

It is said that beauty is in the eye of the beholder. In Carolyn's eyes, everything is beautiful. She is always so happy that beauty seems to generate into the hearts of everyone around her.

Carolyn Dadd, 15, has moyamoya disease. She cannot walk, talk or feed herself, and she requires total care. She knows the people around her, though. I only wish more people could realize how capable she is.

I am 19 years old, and I have been Carolyn's sitter for the past seven years. I first met Carolyn when I was 12 and she was 9. I had never seen anyone quite like her. She was very small then, barely 60 pounds. Her smile was deep as if it sank back into her soul. When we met she raised her hand in a gentle motion to touch my face and laughed as if there was a joke beween us. Soon I found myself laughing, too. That day started our friendship—one that I will cherish the rest of my life. It was obvious that Carolyn was different from anyone I had ever met, and that is exactly what I liked about her.

Jessica Morgan

Moyamoya disease is a progressive disease that affects the blood vessels in the brain. It is characterized by narrowing and/or closing of the carotid artery. This lack of blood may cause paralysis of the feet, legs or upper extremities. Headaches, various vision problems, mental retardation, and psychiatric problems may also occur.

Source: "Good Things Come in Small Packages" by Jessica Morgan, *Exceptional Parent*, July, 2000.

Exceptional Children and Youth

An Introduction to Special Education

THIRD EDITION

NANCY HUNT

California State University Los Angeles

KATHLEEN MARSHALL

University of South Carolina

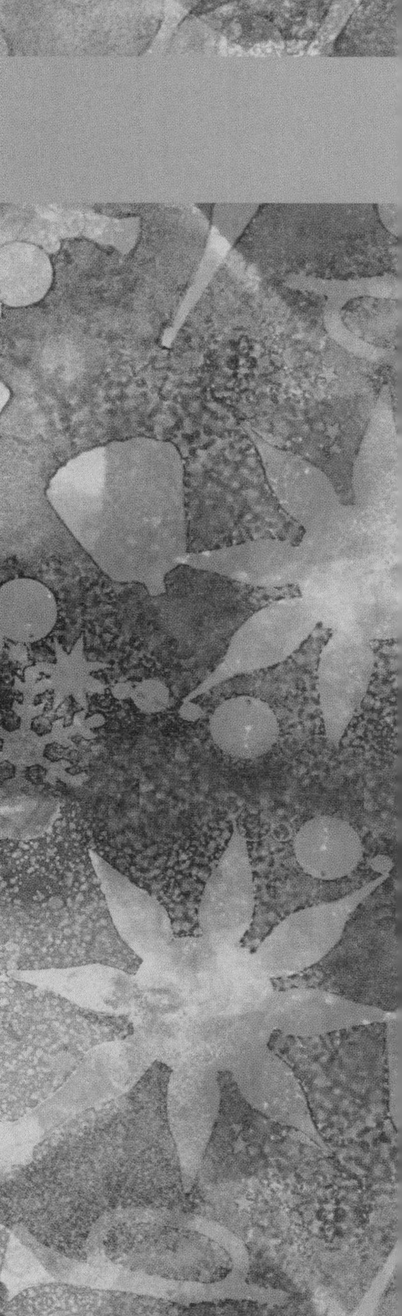

Houghton Mifflin Company BOSTON NEW YORK

Senior sponsoring editor: *Sue Pulvermacher-Alt*
Senior development editor: *Lisa Mafrici*
Senior project editor: *Bob Greiner*
Senior production/design coordinator: *Jill Haber*
Senior designer: *Henry Rachlin*
Manufacturing manager: *Florence Cadran*

Printed in the U.S.A.

Library of Congress Catalog Card Number: 2001131509

ISBN: 0-61811650-8

4 5 6 7 8 9 DW 05 04 03

Contents

Preface

In a time when most advocates believe in the importance of seeing children with disabilities first as children, and as children who will benefit from schooling and experiences that are as normal as possible, this book attempts to accomplish a difficult goal. We expect that our readers—teachers, future teachers, and professionals in related fields—will come to appreciate both the commonalities between children with disability labels and their age peers *and* the unique learning characteristics they may have as a result of their disabilities.

The emphasis on *commonalities* is important for several reasons. For too long, an "us" and "them" attitude relative to children receiving special education services has prevailed in schools, and it has resulted in children and their teachers, parents, and programs being segregated from the normal experiences of a school community. In addition, focusing on differences may lead teachers to believe that they do not have the skills to teach children with disability labels, or that such children are not their responsibility, rather than emphasizing that *all* children are *our* children. Both assumptions are, at best, counterproductive and, at worst, destructive.

Yet learning about uniqueness is important, too. Children who are deaf or blind *will* learn more efficiently with specific teaching strategies adapted to their disabilities that have been developed over years of teachers' experiences. Children identified as having learning disabilities *do* need a focused, deliberate, and individualized emphasis on learning to read and write. And the field of special education has developed such a focus, such strategies, over the last decades. Furthermore, these strategies may improve learning for many children who are *not* eligible for special education services.

The goal of this book has evolved from a commitment to both commonalities and uniqueness. We hope that our readers will recognize the need to work with other professionals in the schools to improve educational achievement for *all* students—those who learn without struggle and those who need a specialized and individualized focus. And in the third edition of this textbook, our goal is that our readers will have the attitudes, the knowledge, and the skills needed to do just that.

Approach of the Text

As a teacher (and we believe all professionals who work in schools are teachers, at one level or another), your classes will reflect all of the injustices, strengths, and questions faced by individuals with disabilities in our society: they are mirrors of our communities. Your voice, behavior, and example will set the stage for how individual students are treated, whether differences are appreciated and respected, and whether students learn to work together.

Because of this, we believe that the most important characteristic you can acquire as a teacher is the ability to be a good problem-solver within cooperative and supportive contexts. The desire and ability to identify learning problems, find the best teaching strategy for a situation, or discover the best way to break down a social barrier is the strength of the most effective teachers. As we present the many puzzles, challenges, and opportunities in the field of special education, we hope you will experience the desire to investigate and grow as individuals and educators.

We want to share our commitment to individuals with disabilities and do our part to help you become effective and confident teachers. Our goal is to communicate our feelings of optimism and determination to our readers.

To help you develop an interactive and effective approach to teaching based on cooperation, support, and problem solving, the text often presents information that draws on our personal experiences. And to help you understand the bases of our philosophy, we have identified three themes that underlie all the book's content and are addressed throughout the text:

- **Theme 1** *Commonalities* unite all students more than differences separate them. We hope that our book helps teachers recognize the commonalities among all students. Seeing the similarities among all individuals breaks down the barriers that set people apart.
- **Theme 2** *Collaborative relationships* enhance student learning and make the job of teaching richer and more enjoyable. This book says, "You are not alone." It emphasizes the importance of the links among professionals and the links between professionals and families.
- **Theme 3** You *"can do"* the work that will make a difference. You may feel uncertain or nervous about working with students who are exceptional. This book demonstrates how you and other professionals can make a significant difference in helping *all* students reach their potential.

These themes play an important role in bringing together all the parts of the book and provide an integrated approach for the introductory course in special education. We expect that through this book you will see and feel differently about yourself and your future students and act on these new understandings as a teacher.

Organization of the Text

Exceptional Children and Youth is presented in three major parts:

- **Part One,** "Building Blocks for Working with Exceptional Children and Youth," introduces the major topics in special education. Chapters 1 through 3 address the history, development, and current status of special education, factors that put children at risk for disability, early intervention, and the role of the child's family and culture in the educational process. In the third edition, we have decided that cultural issues must assume greater importance and appear "up front" in the book. This emphasis provides a starting point from which issues of cultural and linguistic diversity can be infused throughout the remaining chapters. These first three chapters are grouped together because they address critical elements for all areas of special education—and for all individuals with disabilities.
- **Part Two,** "Learning About the Potential of Exceptional Children," discusses students with specific types of disabilities within the context of early life experiences and schooling. We continually point out the similarities in learning characteristics among students with different categorical labels and the similarities in most effective instructional procedures. When you work with individuals with disabilities, we encourage you to

focus on the level of support a student needs to learn critical skills, to identify the most effective way to present those skills, and to recognize that categories and labels have limited value. Chapters 4 through 13 provide a basic background on the definition and prevalence of each exceptionality. Each chapter is mainly devoted to understanding the effects of the exceptionality on the child and family and to educational issues such as placement, assessment, and appropriate teaching strategies.

- **Part Three,** "Looking at Special Education Programs," includes Chapter 14, "Inside Special Education Classes." As you finish the book, reflection about the practice of special education seems appropriate. Therefore, after describing two excellent programs for exceptional children, we take time to reexamine our themes and discuss ways in which you can become a lifelong learner.

Revisions in This Edition

The third edition of *Exceptional Children and Youth* has been updated to reflect changes in the field and in the literature of special education. We would like to draw your attention to some significant changes in the organization and content of the book:

- **A new Chapter 3, "Families and Culture,"** brings issues of cultural and linguistic diversity to the front of the book, giving them the emphasis they demand for those who will work in our demographically changing schools. The chapter covers the ways in which exceptionalities affect families, how their cultural backgrounds and experiences may color their perception of their child's characteristics, and how families and professionals can collaborate in the interests of the child despite cultural differences.
- **A new Chapter 8, "Autism and Related Syndromes,"** discusses the rapid growth in the number of young children being identified with autism and related syndromes. The needs expressed by our students for information and strategies suggest a need for expanded emphasis on the characteristics and educational needs of children with autism. We think this new chapter will begin to meet teachers' needs for information about children with autism and related syndromes.
- **A new Chapter 14, "Inside Special Education Classes,"** asks the reader to think about "best practices" in special education, especially those validated by research. We do this by examining two programs that serve students with disabilities "up close," in the words of the teachers who work with them.

In addition, each categorical chapter (Chapters 4 through 13) continues to have a clear emphasis on strategies for inclusive classrooms, and each chapter has been revised and updated to reflect changes in the field. Here is a listing of the major changes in this edition in addition to those mentioned above:

Chapter 1, "The Context of Special Education: Focus on the Individual," has been updated, and the topic of disproportionate representation of students from culturally diverse backgrounds is newly introduced here.

Chapter 2, "Risk Factors and Early Intervention," contains new and up-to-date material on the latest research concerning biological and environmental factors that place a child at risk.

Chapter 4, "Children with Learning Disabilities," has been updated and now includes even more information on instruction and technology.

Chapter 5, "Children with Mental Retardation," has been updated and includes expanded coverage on teaching strategies.

Chapter 6, "Children with Severe Disabilities," has been updated to include new information on effective instruction and successful transition.

Chapter 7, "Children with Behavioral and Emotional Disorders," now includes new material on academic as well as behavioral interventions and has been updated to reflect current legislation.

Chapter 9, "Children with Communication Disorders," now focuses on collaboration between the classroom teacher and the speech pathologist in inclusive settings.

Chapter 10, "Children Who Are Deaf and Hard of Hearing," includes a new emphasis on elements of curriculum for students with hearing loss.

Chapter 11, " Children Who Are Blind and Have Low Vision," also focuses on curricular issues; in this case it is the expanded core curriculum for students with vision loss.

Chapter 12, "Children with Physical Disabilities and Health Impairments," has been updated, particularly in the areas of technology and transition.

Chapter 13, "Children Who Are Gifted and Talented," retains its emphasis on strategies for students identified as gifted and adds new ideas to benefit all students.

Special Learning Features of the Text

In the third edition we have continued to emphasize teaching *strategies* that our readers can use in their work with individuals with disabilities. The strategies are based on both research and practice, and they are infused into the narrative of the textbook and also presented in boxes set apart from the narrative. While an introductory course in special education is not generally considered a methods course, we think we offer the groundwork here for successful teaching strategies:

- **The First Person** section in each chapter lets the reader experience the topic of the chapter through the story of someone who has "been there."
- **A Closer Look** sections examine subjects of special interest to the topic at hand—model programs, treatments, or professionals who work with specific groups of children.
- **What You Can Do Now** sections at the end of each chapter provide the reader with specific suggestions exemplifying our *can-do* theme: ideas for learning more about a topic, volunteering with a group, or putting new learning into action through an activity.
- **New full-color inserts** on key strategies and resources important to general and special education teachers. Topics include early reading strategies, applied behavior analysis, assisted communication, and technology.

Other Learning and Study Features

In addition to the special features, *Exceptional Children and Youth* contains useful learning tools such as

- **Orientations.** Chapter-opening overviews that provide both a coherent narrative and focusing questions to point readers to key material.
- **Chapter summaries.** Comprehensive summaries of major points for review.
- **Margin notes.** Main ideas and definitions for easy reference.
- **Key terms.** For review at the end of the chapter.
- **Teaching tips and strategies.** Set apart from the text for easy reference.
- **Multimedia resources.** Contain lists and descriptions of organizations, books, journal articles, and web sites on the Internet related to each chapter topic that are relevant for personal interests and professional development.

Accompanying Teaching and Learning Resources

New Companion Website

This new website (college.hmco.com) contains many valuable resources for both students and instructors using the text. Highlights include an updated version of the "Story of Lucy and Nell" (case study), additional IEP examples, relevant web links, self-testing opportunities, and more.

Epilogue

On our website you will find an *Epilogue* in which the authors provide additional thoughts on the future of speical education.

Special Education Resource Center

Find extensive professional resources in the "Special Education Resource Center" website (college.hmco.com). This site features print and electronic resources, assistive technology resources, links to professional organizations, school reform and standards content, current legislation, teaching tools and supports, and a Discussion Forum.

Instructor's Resource Guide

This extensive print guide offers one convenient publication that includes Model Syllabi, Chapter Instructional Resources, Major Reference Works and Data Banks, Case Studies, and a complete Test Bank.

Computerized Test Bank

The same test items as the printed Test Bank, enhanced with an editing capability that allows professors to create customized exams by editing or adding questions.

Transparencies

Numerous colorful transparencies including graphic "What You Can Do" maps, ideas, charts, and additional material to support classroom instruction.

Acknowledgments

We would like to acknowledge once more the contributions of the authors who contributed either complete or partial chapters in the first edition: Dr. Elaine Silliman and Janet Stack, University of South Florida, "Children with Communication Disorders"; Dr. Cay Holbrook and Dr. Mary Scott Healy, University of Arkansas, Little Rock, "Children Who Are Blind or Have Low Vision"; Dr. Emma Guilarte, University of South Carolina, "Children with Physical Disabilities and Health Impairments"; Dr. James Delisle, Kent State University, "Children Who Are Gifted and Talented"; and Dr. Philip Chinn, California State University, Los Angeles, "Exceptional Children from Diverse Cultural Backgrounds."

We also appreciate the many constructive suggestions and feedback provided by the reviews of the text, including the following:

Meg Carroll, Saint Xavier University

Vinni M. Hall, Chicago State University

Vicki Jean Hartley, Delta State University

Clyde Shepherd, Keen State College

Janna Siegel Robertson, University of Memphis

Colleen A. Thoma, University of Nevada, Las Vegas

Mary E. Ulrich, Miami University

It is only right that a book with the theme of collaboration be built on a strong collaborative process. We greatly value our partnership with our editors at Houghton Mifflin. This revision began under the guidance of our friend and mentor Loretta Wolozin, then Senior Sponsoring Editor in Education. When Loretta decided to go back to school, Sue Pulvermacher-Alt assumed her responsibilities with grace and patience, and we are grateful for her skill. As always, Lisa Mafrici has kept it all together for us with unfailing kindness, and we have been lucky enough to work with our able Developmental Editor Elaine Silverstein for the second time. Bob Greiner shepherded us through the book's production with efficiency, humor, and kindness. The class is theirs, and the bloopers, should any be found, are ours.

Away from the computer monitor, Nancy Hunt would like to express her gratitude to her wonderful colleagues in the Division of Special Education at California State University, Los Angeles for their hallway consultations and professional inspiration, and especially to Maria Gutierrez and Margie Moennich for their friendship and support. Thanks also to Dewey Gram for his understanding as a member of the fellowship of writers. I hope my daughters, Maggie, Lucy, and Nell, see my commitment to this book as a model of industriousness rather than a crazed obsession. They make it all worthwhile for me.

Kathleen Marshall expresses appreciation to her colleagues at the University of South Carolina for their professional generosity and great humor. I would like to thank my graduate assistant, Christy Lockhart, for her many significant contributions to the manuscript. Finally, thanks to my family, and especially my husband Richard Sribnick, for their continuous support and encouragement.

Nancy Hunt
Kathleen J. Marshall

Building Blocks for Working with Exceptional Children and Youth

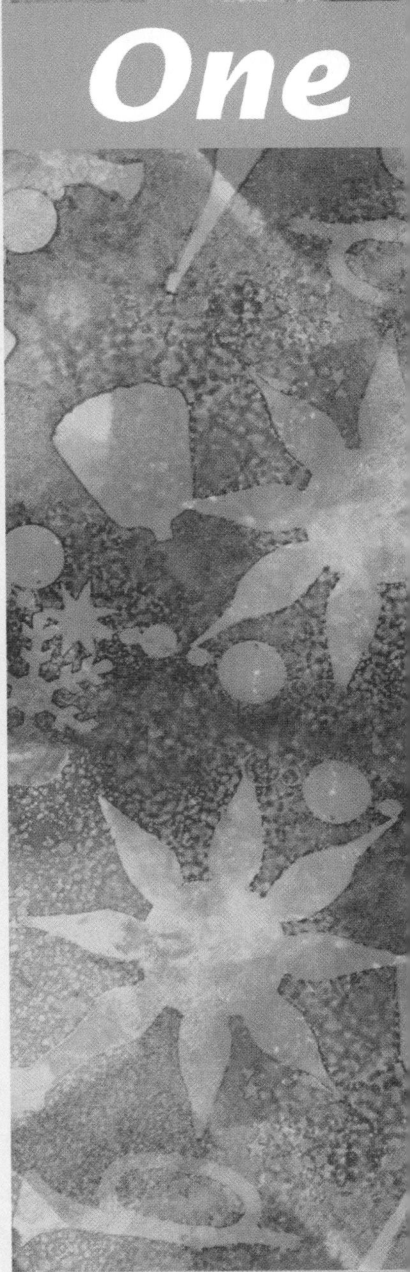

PART ONE introduces you to the major topics in the field of special education. You'll learn how special education has evolved during the past three decades and its implications for your future classroom. You'll learn about the factors that may affect individual students' educational experiences: their individual strengths, their families, their cultural backgrounds, and their exposure to risk. In your role as a teacher, you will need to take all of these factors into account. As you will see, the building blocks we discuss here are a vital foundation for your work with exceptional individuals.

PART OUTLINE

The Context of Special Education: Focus on the Individual

1

THE GOAL of this chapter is to introduce you to the context of special education—the rewards and challenges; the diversity of students' needs, backgrounds, and abilities; the historical and legal roots from which contemporary special education has developed; and the ongoing questions of how and where we can best help exceptional students reach their potential. As you read, look for answers to these questions:

What is special education?

How have legislation and litigation opened doors for exceptional individuals?

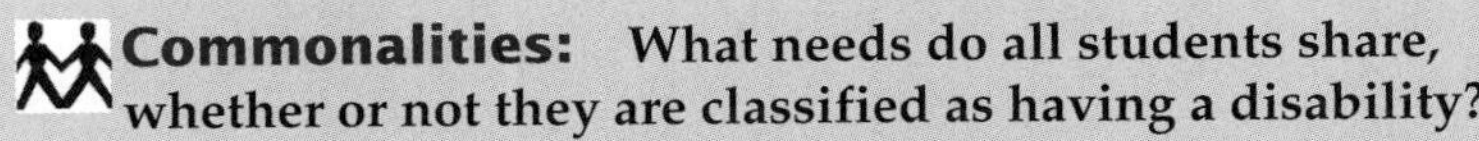

Commonalities: **What needs do all students share, whether or not they are classified as having a disability?**

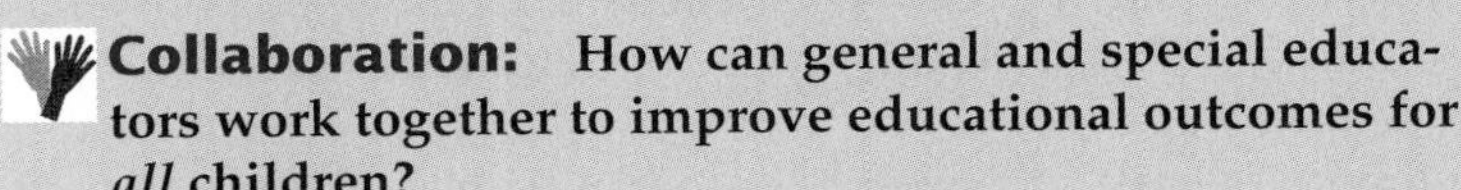

Collaboration: **How can general and special educators work together to improve educational outcomes for *all* children?**

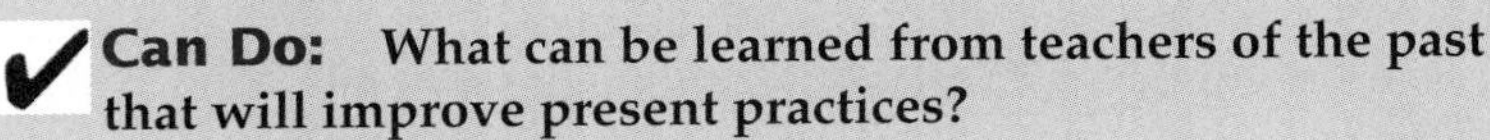

Can Do: **What can be learned from teachers of the past that will improve present practices?**

Schools are filled with children—dark and light, quiet and loud, happy and sad—with special needs. For some it's the need for warmth, patience, and support to weather a tough emotional time; for others it's the need for someone to take time to find out what really interests and motivates them. We are about to embark on the study of some of those children who present special challenges to their teachers by virtue of their disabilities and their special gifts and talents. But each child in school will challenge you, and we hope to show you that the differences among children are simply variations on a theme of *commonalities.* You can reach and teach every one of them.

The Context of Special Education: Focus on the Individual

Disability should not stop a child from being totally involved in school life. (© 2001Lydia Gans.)

More and more, American schools are becoming places of great student diversity. The changes that result from this diversity are sometimes unsettling to us. If you cannot speak Korean, can you teach a child who does? If the new child in your class cannot speak, will you be able to communicate? How can you best *collaborate* with other professionals in your school to meet the needs of these children? With so much expected of teachers, so much responsibility resting on your shoulders, will you be able to respond, to teach, to see progress in each of your students?

We think you will. We hope to help you to get to know some of the characteristics of your students who are considered exceptional. We believe that our teachers are up to the challenge of teaching all students—you *can do* it, and do it well.

Definitions and Terms

Exceptional students are all those who receive special education services in the school.

Like other fields of study, special education has its own terminology. We use several terms to describe the group of students we work with. Among them is **exceptional,** used in the title of this book. We use this word to describe the range of students—those who are called blind, gifted, deaf—who receive special education services in the school. It does not simply refer to students who are gifted but to any student who may be an "exception" to the rule.

Some of these students have a **disability** (students who are gifted do not fall into this category). A disability is a limitation, such as a difficulty in learning to read or an inability to hear, walk, or see. A **handicap** is not the same as a disability; a handicap results from the limitations imposed by the environment and by attitudes toward a person with disabilities.

A disability is a limitation; a handicap is the limitations imposed by the environment and by people's attitudes.

Some examples will help here. Some adults who are deaf, for example, admit that they are disabled—they hear very little. But they do not consider themselves handicapped. Their disability does not limit them in ways that they consider significant. They associate with a community of other deaf people with whom they can communicate freely; they do not often encounter people who manifest prejudice against them. They are satisfied with their lives, their abilities and limitations. The deaf schoolchild, however, may be considered handicapped; she may not yet have learned how to communicate efficiently or to read English well, which considerably limits her ability to communicate with others and to achieve in school.

A young person who has experienced a spinal cord injury may emerge from the hospital unable to walk—a serious disability and perhaps a handicap. Through physical therapy and rehabilitation, however, that person can often learn strategies to cope with the handicap associated with the disability. Use of a wheelchair and adaptive devices in the car will enable him to become mobile again; modifications of work space and the home may make those places accessible to him using a wheelchair. Nowadays, a physical limitation does not prevent a person from participating in sports, from wheelchair racing to mountain climbing.

Overcoming the attitudes of others toward a disability may be a more difficult fight. Will the behavior of friends and family change? Will job opportunities be there? Will new acquaintances think of him as a disabled person, or as a person who happens to have a disability?

You will notice that we try to use **people-first language** in this book; first we describe the person, then the disability (see the box "People-First Language"). This is so that we can think about individuals who have disabilities, such as the young person just described, as *people* who happen to have a disability.

People-first language focuses on the person, not the disability.

Naturally, within special education there is an emphasis on prevention of disabilities and on starting services as early as possible. **Early intervention** is the provision of services for children from birth to age 3 and their families. It has the goal of optimizing each child's learning potential and daily well-being and increasing the child's opportunities for functioning effectively in the community (Cook, Tessier, & Klein, 2000). We use the term **at risk** to describe those infants and young children who have a greater-than-average likelihood of developing a disability because of factors such as extreme prematurity, chronic poverty, or early medical problems. Some educators also use the term to describe older students who may be more likely to drop out of school; however, in this book we use it to describe infants and young children only.

Early intervention helps reduce the impact of disabilities on young children.

What *is* special education, you may wonder, and what is so special about it? **Special education** is the educational program designed to meet the unique learning and developmental needs of a student who is exceptional. What is special about special education is the recognition of the unique nature of each individual and the accompanying design of an educational program specifically planned to meet that person's needs. Special education is not limited to a particular "special" place; most special educators believe that it should take place in the most normal, natural environment possible. That may be in a baby's home, in a general education classroom, or in the Pizza Hut in the student's community; sometimes it may be in a hospital or a special school designed for a

Special education is the education program designed to meet the unique needs of exceptional children.

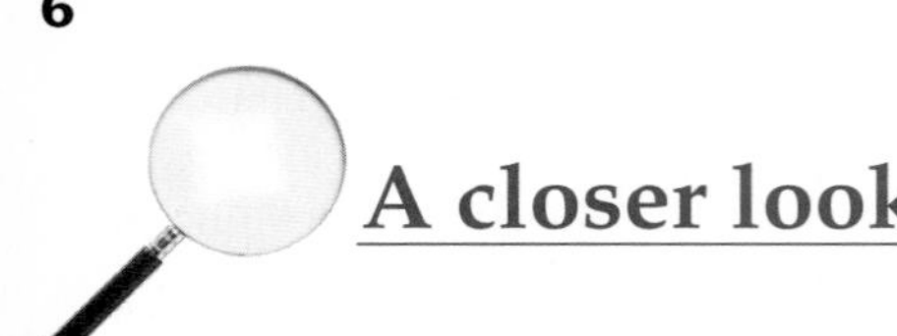

A closer look

People-First Language

In speaking or writing, remember that children and adults with disabilities are like everyone else—except that they happen to have a disability. Here are a few tips for improving your language related to disabilities and handicaps.

1. Speak of the person first, then the disability.
2. Emphasize abilities, not limitations.
3. Do not label people as part of a disability group.
4. Don't give excessive praise or attention to a person with a disability; don't patronize.
5. Choice and independence are important; let the person do or speak for himself or herself as much as possible.
6. A disability is a functional limitation that interferes with a person's ability to walk, hear, talk, learn, etc.; use the word *handicap* to describe a situation or barrier imposed by society, the environment, or oneself.

Say	**Instead of**
child with a disability	disabled or handicapped child
person with cerebral palsy	palsied, CP, or spastic person
person who has	afflicted, suffers from, victim of
developmental delay	slow
emotional disorder, mental illness	crazy, insane
uses a wheelchair	confined to a wheelchair
person with Down syndrome	mongoloid
has a physical disability	crippled
condition	disease (unless it *is* a disease)
seizures	fits
paralyzed	invalid
chronic illness	sickly
has paraplegia, semiplegia, quadraplegia	paraplegic, semiplegic, quadraplegic

Source: "It's the 'Person First'—Then the Disability," *Pacesetter* (September 1989), p. 13. Reprinted by permission from *Pacesetter*. *Pacesetter* is published by the PACER Center, Minneapolis, Minnesota.

particular group of students, such as a school for students who are deaf. This book is designed to help you learn more about special education; we hope that it will help you find your own role in serving students who are exceptional.

Prevalence of Exceptional Children

Prevalence figures reflect how many students within a given category need special services.

Every year the Office of Special Education and Rehabilitative Services (OSERS) in the U.S. Department of Education prepares a report for Congress that describes the prevalence, or number, of students with disabilities receiving special education services. Chapters 4 through 12 will give you more information on some of the issues surrounding how we identify and count individuals within categories. What's important to note here is that prevalence figures reflect how many students need special services. These figures are used to allocate funds, to determine whether there are enough teachers, and for many other purposes.

Table 1.1 Students Age 6–21 Served Under IDEA, by Disability Category: 1998-1999

Disability	Number	Percentage
Specific learning disabilities	2,817,148	50.8
Speech and language impairments	1,074,548	19.4
Mental retardation	611,076	11.0
Emotional disturbance	463,262	8.4
Multiple disabilities	107,763	1.9
Hearing impairments	70,883	1.4
Orthopedic impairments	69,495	1.1
Other health impairments	220,831	1.2
Visual impairments	26,132	0.5
Autism	53,576	1.0
Deaf-blindness	1,609	>0.1
Traumatic brain injury	12,933	0.2
Developmental delay	11,910	0.2
All disabilities	5,541,166	

Source: U.S. Department of Education, Office of Special Education Programs, Data Analysis System (DANS), cited in the *Twenty-second Annual Report to Congress on the Implementation of the Individuals with Disabilities Education Act* (2000), pp. II-21.

The *Twenty-second Annual Report to Congress on the Implementation of the Individuals with Disabilities Education Act* (2000) reported that there were 6,114,803 children from ages 3 to 21 receiving special education services during the 1998–1999 school year. Table 1.1 shows the breakdown of students between ages 6 and 21 by disability group. Notice that almost 51 percent of the total number of school-age students being served are classified as learning disabled, and about 90 percent of the total number fall into the four largest categories: learning disabilities, speech or language impairments, mental retardation, and serious emotional disturbance. Overall, about 12 percent of elementary and secondary students in the United States receive special education services.

Foundations of Special Education

Although there have always been exceptional children, documented attempts to teach them are relatively recent. As Hewett and Forness (1984) put it, "Throughout recorded history, perhaps the only categories that mattered were the *weak*, the *odd*, and the *poor*" (p. 3). Present-day concepts of disability are a reflection of the values and beliefs of contemporary culture, which emphasizes verbal and intellectual achievement. The first known attempts to teach children with disabilities came in the sixteenth and seventeenth centuries, when priests and other religious men and women taught small groups of deaf and blind children, usually the offspring of the aristocracy (Moores, 2001).

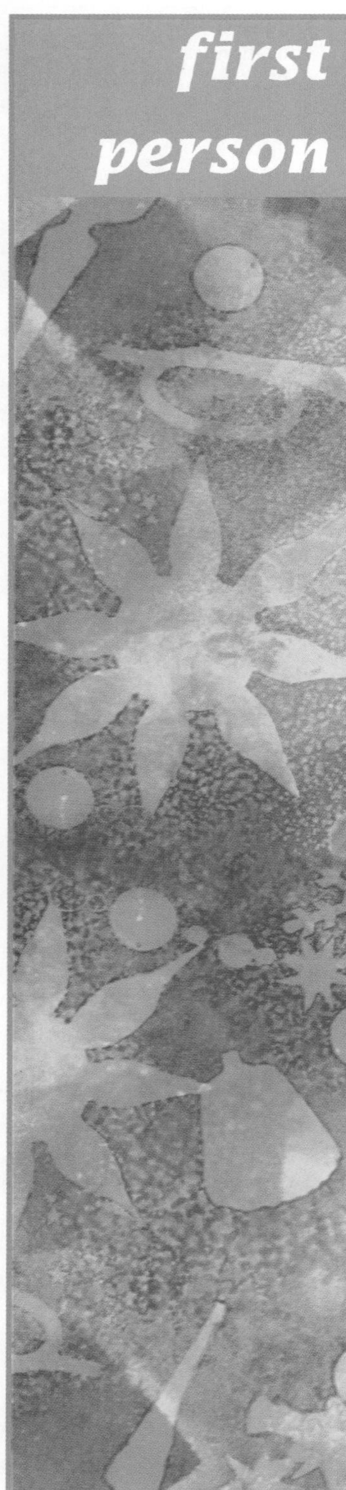

David learned to jump rope last week.

It may not seem like much of an accomplishment for a strapping fourth-grader. By the time kids reach the fourth grade, haven't they mastered rope jumping, and soccer, and dodge ball and capture the flag?

Not all of them.

Jumping rope can be a source of pride for an awkward boy who has spent most of his time on the sidelines, watching other children . . . and for my daughter and her friends, who taught him how to play.

I don't know much about David. Only the stories my daughter tells.

He sits near the teacher, in the front row, and struggles through even the most basic tasks. He giggles when nothing's funny, speaks out when he hasn't been called upon, mumbles to himself. He has a distracting habit of constantly wringing his hands. He spends part of each day away from class, with a special teacher.

"I think he's handicapped," my daughter says, not as judgment but as explanation.

It takes me back to my days as a reporter and all the stories I wrote on "mainstreaming"—the practice of teaching disabled students alongside other children, instead of isolating them in classes labeled "special ed."

Over the years I'd duly noted the pros and cons: the advocates' claims that disabled kids benefit by making friends and learning social skills from other children, and the critics' concerns that handicapped kids might be shunned or belittled or take up too much of a teacher's time.

What neither argument acknowledges is what I see: that the benefits of this social experiment flow not just one way, but back from the disabled child to mine.

Because, while David might be struggling to learn, he is teaching without effort—providing his classmates with new opportunities each day to learn and practice patience, tolerance, kindness, ingenuity.

I know it's not always easy, for him or for them. He is annoying at times, tagging along, interrupting conversations. I'm sure he tries the teacher's patience.

He fails, it seems, as often as he succeeds. That hurts, and he doesn't know how not to let it show. He cries sometimes. And on the playground, the older kids tease him.

But his classmates comfort him and rise to his defense. They encourage him when he's afraid to try something new. They teach him songs, tell him jokes . . . even if it means explaining the punch line over and over, until he understands it well enough to laugh.

And every day at recess, my daughter and her friends take out the long, red jump rope that David likes. They station him at one end, put the rope in his hand, take his arm and start it turning. Then as they jump, they swing their arms in big, wide circles, so David can keep pace by mimicking them.

Then it is his turn to stand alongside the rope and jump.

My daughter laughs with glee as she tells the story. I can imagine the grin on David's face, his fists clenched in determination, his pride as he launches himself airborne. And I can almost hear the shouts of his cheering section, yelling at him to lift his feet: *"Jump! . . . jump! . . . jump!"*

It has taken my daughter days longer than her classmates, but she finally has completed her computer lesson. Now everyone in class has finished and has received an award . . . everyone but David.

My daughter's sense of accomplishment is tinged by a tender sort of pity. "I wish everything wasn't so hard for David," she says, putting her award aside. "It's just not fair."

And I have to fight back tears . . . but not for David. You see, my daughter is no stranger to struggle. School has never come easy for her. She knows how it feels to be last, to be wrong . . . to miss the joke's punch line, to jump at the wrong time.

Fourth grade has been a good year for her. She has earned A's and B's, learned long division, won a solo in the school's musical, become a standout on her soccer team.

But if you ask her now what she's proudest of, she's liable to tell you that it's teaching David that he can jump rope.

Because she has learned how one small achievement can lift you up, make you believe that big things are possible. And she wants David to learn that too.

Sandy Banks

Sandy Banks is a columnist for the *Los Angeles Times.* This column appeared on February 21, 1999.

The Context of Special Education: Focus on the Individual

Early History: Great Teachers and Their Legacy

Jean-Marc-Gaspard Itard tried to teach the "wild boy of Aveyron" to speak.

A series of curious, innovative, and dedicated men and women in Europe and the United States pioneered the teaching techniques that are the foundation of special education. First among them was **Jean-Marc-Gaspard Itard.** In 1799, Itard was a 25-year-old physician in Paris when an 11- or 12-year-old boy emerged from the woods near the French town of Aveyron. The boy was unclothed, scarred, and covered with dirt; he did not walk, but ran; he knew none of the conventions of human civilization and did not speak. This boy became the focus of a great controversy in France between the "nativists," who believed that a person's potential was determined by genetic heritage and was therefore unalterable, and the "sensationalists," who believed that environmental input in the form of sensory experience could change a person's intellectual development. Who would venture to teach this "wild boy"—to civilize him?

Itard, who bore within him the optimistic legacy of the French Revolution, volunteered for the task. For five years, he and the boy, whom he named Victor, lived at the school for deaf children in Paris while he attempted to teach him. His greatest hope was that the boy would learn language, which Itard considered the hallmark of civilized society. Through daily, painstaking lessons, Itard rewarded Victor with small amounts of food when he accomplished a task. After nine months, Victor had accomplished Itard's first goals for him: He had developed normal eating, sleeping, and personal hygiene routines (Lane, 1976).

After five years, however, Itard considered his work a failure; although Victor could recognize some words in print and had acquired many of the behaviors of "civilization," his only words were *lait* and *oh Dieu* (French for "milk" and "oh God"). With great disappointment, Itard abandoned his work with Victor, who was cared for by the wife of a groundskeeper at the school for deaf children until his death at around the age of 40.

Edouard Seguin and Maria Montessori applied Itard's methods to the teaching of children with mental retardation.

Although Itard felt he had failed because he had not made Victor "normal," others found both teaching techniques and encouragement in the changes that had occurred in Victor. Among those was **Edouard Seguin,** who became a student of Itard; he built on Itard's methods to form his own approach to teaching children that we would now say have mental retardation. **Maria Montessori** translated a book that Seguin wrote about his own methods and materials and made them the foundation of the Montessori method, first used with children with mental retardation. Montessori's teaching methods involve the development of the child's natural curiosity and the training of the senses through materials that are manipulable, three-dimensional, and concrete (Cook, Tessier, & Klein, 2000).

Samuel Gridley Howe developed methods of teaching students who were both deaf and blind.

The ideas and methods of these great European teachers reached several Americans who were influential in setting up special education services in the United States. **Samuel Gridley Howe** (1801–1876) was a graduate of Harvard Medical School and a political reformer. He taught Laura Bridgeman, a young deaf and blind woman, and his teaching techniques became the foundation for the methods used at the Perkins School for the Blind in Watertown, Massachusetts, the first school for students with disabilities in this country, which Howe helped to found.

Thomas Hopkins Gallaudet (1787–1851) was a graduate of Yale and Andover Theological Seminary when he attempted to teach 9-year-old Alice Cogswell, the deaf daughter of a neighbor, some simple words and sentences (Moores, 2001). Gallaudet traveled to Europe to learn from teachers there and returned home with a teacher who was deaf himself, **Laurent Clerc.** Gallaudet

Alexander Graham Bell was a mentor and friend to Helen Keller and her teacher, Anne Sullivan Macy. (© Bettmann/ CORBIS)

then became the principal at the first school for deaf children in the United States, founded by Alice Cogswell's father and others. The first teacher at the school was Laurent Clerc. Clerc trained many of the teachers at the early schools for deaf children in this country. Gallaudet University in Washington, D.C., was named for T.H. Gallaudet. The Laurent Clerc National Deaf Education Center at Gallaudet University has been named to acknowledge the early role of a deaf teacher in the education of deaf children.

Gallaudet, Clerc, and Bell pioneered methods of teaching children who were deaf.

Alexander Graham Bell (1847–1922) did not think of himself as the inventor of the telephone but as a teacher of children who were deaf. Bell came from a family of speech teachers, and his mother was deaf, so it was natural for him to use his skills to teach deaf children to speak. Bell's views on enhancing speech and residual hearing in deaf children are still alive today, exemplified by members of the Alexander Graham Bell Association for the Deaf, headquartered in Washington, D.C.

Anne Sullivan Macy (1866–1936), Helen Keller's beloved "Teacher," has been an inspiration to many entering the teaching profession. Sullivan, who had a serious vision impairment until her teenage years, attended the Perkins School for the Blind and was recommended to Helen Keller's mother through Alexander Graham Bell. Annie Sullivan carefully studied Dr. Howe's records from teaching Laura Bridgeman before she went to work for the Keller family. Those methods, and Annie Sullivan's intelligence, dedication, and ingenuity, helped Helen Keller to become the person that she was. The intricate and remarkable relationship between this teacher and her student is detailed in Joseph Lash's fascinating book, *Helen and Teacher* (1980).

The dedication and ingenuity of Annie Sullivan, Helen Keller's teacher, have inspired many to become teachers.

The Context of Special Education: Focus on the Individual

Later History: Advocates for Social Change

After the initial surge of interest in the education of children who were deaf and blind and had mental retardation in the United States, school services for children with disabilities plateaued for many years. It was not until the 1960s that two events converged to reignite national interest in the needs of children with disabilities. The first of these was the election of John F. Kennedy as president in 1960. Kennedy had a sister, Rosemary, with mental retardation, and he was openly committed to improving the quality of life for people with mental retardation. He did two concrete things to accomplish this goal: He set up the President's Commission on Mental Retardation, a group of expert researchers and practitioners who identified the issues and priorities in the field, and he supported the use of federal funds to educate teachers of children with disabilities. Kennedy's greatest contribution was less concrete. His acknowledgment of mental retardation in his family and his dedication to improving services for people with disabilities played a large part in lessening the stigma of mental retardation and added prestige to the career of teaching children with disabilities.

The Kennedy family's commitment to improving services for people with disabilities helped lessen the stigma of mental retardation.

The other event of the 1960s that influenced families and other advocates of children with disabilities was the civil rights movement. The political and social demands of African Americans for equal rights and access to opportunities at all levels of society provided an example to families and groups working with children with disabilities of what could be accomplished on behalf of disenfranchised groups.

In 1972, Wolf Wolfensberger articulated the principle of **normalization**—that people with disabilities should have the opportunity to lead as close to a normal life as possible. This philosophy implies that no matter how severe an individual's disability, he or she should have the opportunity to participate in all aspects of society. The normalization principle, which is "deeply embedded in services to individuals with disabilities" (Harry, Rueda, & Kalyanpur, 1999, p. 123), implied that special institutions for people with mental retardation, which tended to be segregated from the community, should be deemphasized. This movement, known as **deinstitutionalization,** has led to the establishment of many small group homes and other community residential facilities in towns and cities.

With normalization, people with disabilities have the opportunity to lead typical lives.

Deinstitutionalization has helped end the segregation of people with mental retardation from the community.

In schools, the application of the concept of normalization has also led away from segregation—the education of exceptional children in special schools or separate buildings—and toward the goal of education in the least restrictive environment (see the next section). After the landmark special education legislation P.L. 94-142 (now known as IDEA—The Individuals with Disabilities Education Act) was passed in 1975, educators used the term **mainstreaming** to describe the participation of children with disabilities in the general education classroom. Today, the word **inclusion** is used. Inclusion refers to placement of the child with disabilities in the general education classroom, with the supports the child needs also provided there. A report on the 1997 amendments to IDEA reminds us of the purposes of inclusion:

Inclusion refers to placement of the child with disabilities in the general education classroom, with the supports the child needs also provided in the classroom.

> The 1997 amendments to the Individuals with Disabilities Education Act (IDEA) placed renewed emphasis on educating students with disabilities in less restrictive environments. In particular, the law encourages opportunities for children with disabilities to participate in general education settings and in the general education curriculum. Inclusion of children with disabili-

ties in such settings is important because **it raises expectations for student performance, provides opportunities for children with disabilities to learn alongside their nondisabled peers, improves coordination between regular and special educators, and increases school-level accountability for educational results** (National Center for Education Statistics, 1999).

The practice of inclusion requires collaboration between the general educator and the special educator, as well as time, patience, and willingness.

In practice, there appears to be a continuum of inclusion, ranging from full-time, complete membership of the student with disabilities in the general education classroom to part-time participation for nonacademic subjects and activities. The practice of inclusion makes considerable demands on both the general educator and the special educator. The collaboration that must occur is often new to both, and it is a skill that requires time, patience, and willingness. Certainly, not everyone is in support of inclusion—in fact, the practice can be quite controversial. Many special educators strongly believe that inclusion should simply be one option in the continuum of program options and that the individual needs of the child, rather than a "one-size-fits-all" philosophy, should determine the child's placement (see Figure 1.1). Court decisions over

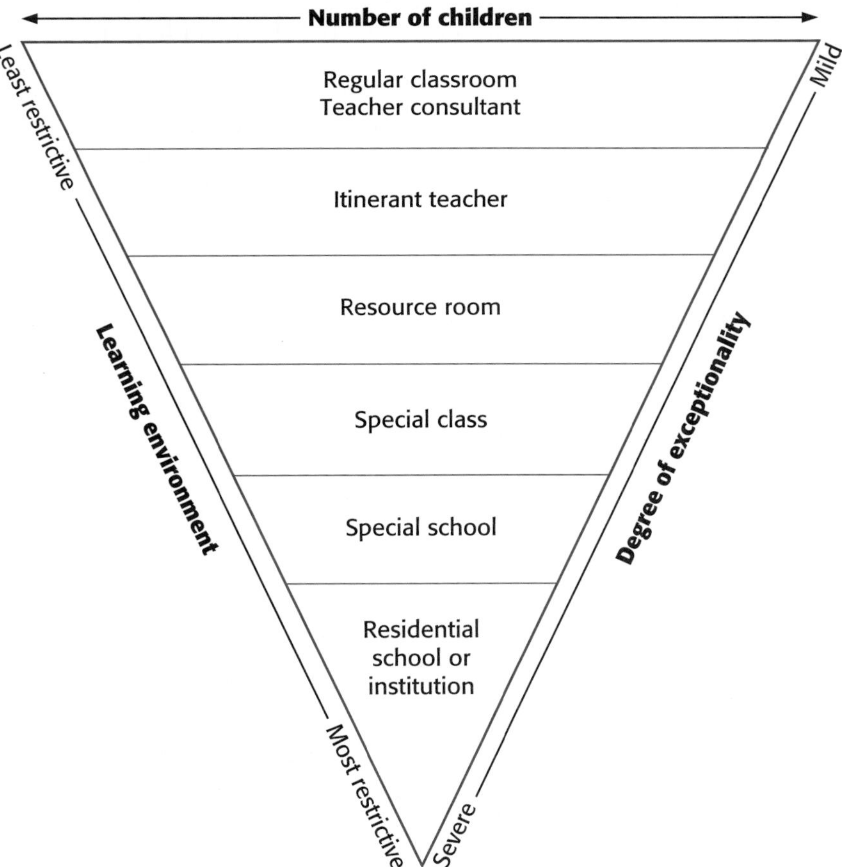

Figure 1.1
Learning Environments for Exceptional Children

Source: E. Deno, "Special Education as Developmental Capital," *Exceptional Children* 37 (1970), 229–237. Copyright 1970 by the Council for Exceptional Children. Reprinted with permission.

the past several years have affirmed the need for the continuum of program options (U.S. courts affirm, 1996). Between the 1985–1986 and 1996–1997 school years, however, the number of students with disabilities served in the general education classroom increased from 25.5 to 45.7 percent—a 20 percent rise in eleven years. Along with that change has come a downward trend in the percentage of students with disabilities educated in resource rooms and special classes (except for children with the most severe disabilities) (National Center for Education Statistics, 1999).

General educators have sometimes objected to inclusive practices, maintaining that they are not prepared to meet the individual needs of children with disabilities, that the practice is too time-consuming, and that it takes time from other children. But many special educators believe that placement in segregated settings like a special school or even a special day class has interfered with the social and academic growth of children with disabilities and has also limited the opportunities of children who are not disabled to learn from those who are. Research suggests that the majority of general educators and administrators support the idea of inclusion, given the appropriate supports and collaborative practices (Scruggs & Mastropieri, 1996; Villa, Thousand, Meyers, & Nevin, 1996) (see the accompanying box, "Supports for General Education Teachers").

Regardless of your personal experiences or beliefs about inclusion, it is important to understand what the "best practices" for including children with disabilities in general education classrooms are. They rest on three assumptions: first, that all teachers receive appropriate preparation and education about meeting the needs of children with disabilities; second, that children with disabilities are productive learners in the general education classroom; and third, that the appropriate supports are provided to both the student with disabilities and the teacher.

Legislation

Federal law now mandates that children with disabilities be educated in the **"least restrictive environment"**—that setting which gives the child the greatest number of options for interactions with nondisabled peers and the same opportunities as those peers.

P.L. 94-142, now known as IDEA, requires that children 3 to 21 with a disability be provided a free, appropriate, public education in the least restrictive environment.

■ ***Public Law 94-142*** The law that has had the most profound impact on children with disabilities is Public Law 94-142, formerly known as the Education for All Handicapped Children Act (1975) and now known as the **Individuals with Disabilities Education Act (IDEA).** It requires that every child between the ages of 3 and 21 with a disability be provided a free, appropriate public education in the least restrictive environment.

Before P.L. 94-142 was passed, only one-fifth of the children with disabilities in the United States were enrolled in school programs at all (U.S. Department of Education, 1995); the remainder were excluded from school, received inappropriate education, or were housed in institutions that did not provide educational programs at all. Now we are much closer to enrolling all children with disabilities, although that is still an elusive goal. Congress has amended the law several times (see Table 1.2); as a result of the 1975 law and its amendments, children with disabilities and their families have well-defined rights. See the accompanying box for the key components of IDEA.

~ Supports for General Education Teachers

A synthesis of research studies on inclusion has determined that the following supports are needed by general education teachers who are including students with disabilities in their classrooms:

- Time: Teachers report a need for one hour or more per day to plan for students with disabilities.
- Training: Teachers need systematic, intensive training—as part of their certification programs, as intensive and well-planned inservices, or as an ongoing process with consultants.
- Personnel resources: Teachers report a need for additional personnel assistance to carry out objectives. This could include a half time aide and daily contact with special education teachers.
- Materials resources: Teachers need adequate curriculum materials and other classroom equipment appropriate to the needs of students with disabilities.
- Class size: Teachers agree that their class size should be reduced to fewer than twenty students if students with disabilities are included.
- Consideration of severity of disability: Teachers are more willing to include students with mild disabilities than students with more severe disabilities, apparently because of teachers' perceived ability to carry on their teaching mission for the entire classroom. By implication, the more severe the disabilities in the inclusive setting, the more the previously mentioned sources of support would be needed.

These needs may be greater for secondary teachers than for elementary teachers. Overall, it seems clear that many teachers have reservations or concerns about mainstreaming and inclusion and believe that substantial supports are necessary to enable these efforts to succeed. The ultimate success of mainstreaming or inclusion efforts, then, may well depend on the extent to which such supports are made available.

Source: T.E. Scruggs & M.A. Mastropieri, "Teacher Perceptions of Mainstreaming/Inclusion, 1958–1995: A Research Synthesis," *Exceptional Children, 63*(1) (1996), 72. Copyright © 1996 by the Council for Exceptional Children. Reprinted by permission.

IDEA identifies specific categories that qualify a student for special education and related services. Under the law, the term "child with a disability" means a child:

- with mental retardation, hearing impairments (including deafness), speech or language impairments, visual impairments (including blindness), serious emotional disturbance, orthopedic impairments, autism,

Table 1.2 Selected Foundations of Special Education Law

1973	P.L. 93-112	Section 504 of the Rehabilitation Act
1975	P.L. 94-142	Education for All Handicapped Children Act (now known as IDEA)
1986	P.L. 99-457	IDEA amendments
1990	P.L. 101-336	Americans with Disabilities Act
1990	P.L. 101-476	IDEA amendments
1997	P.L. 105-17	IDEA amendments

A good day at school means having fun with friends. (Evan Johnson/Jeroboam)

Key Components of IDEA

- **Zero reject.** No child, no matter how severely disabled, shall be refused an appropriate education by the schools.
- **Free appropriate public education.** Each student is entitled to special education and related services in public school at no cost. At the heart of this component of the law is the Individualized Education Plan (IEP). We describe the IEP further on page 29 of this chapter, and refer to its use in the classroom throughout this book.
- **Least restrictive environment.** Each child must be educated with nondisabled peers to the maximum extent appropriate. We discuss the differing perspectives on this concept later in the chapter (see p. 29).
- **Nondiscriminatory evaluation.** Evaluation procedures must be conducted with fairness in the child's native language, using multiple measures.
- **Due process and procedural safeguards.** Families and school districts can exercise their Fourteenth Amendment rights to due process under the law; that is, they may resort to mediation and appeal procedures when they do not agree with one another over issues such as the child's placement.
- **Technology-related assistance.** IEP teams must consider whether students with disabilities need assistive technology devices and services in order to benefit from special education and related services.

Source: Adapted from M. Yell, *The law and special education* (Columbus, OH: Merrill, 1998).

traumatic brain injury, other health impairments, or specific learning disabilities; and

- who, by reason thereof, needs special education and related services (Knoblauch & Sorenson, 1998).

In addition to these categories, the 1997 amendments to IDEA allow states to classify children age 3–9 as "developmentally delayed."

A child must meet two criteria to qualify for special education services under IDEA: he or she must have one of the disabilities listed above, and he or she must require special education and related services. Not all children with disabilities do require services; many attend school without any modifications to their program (Knoblauch & Sorenson, 1998).

You can see that under federal law a great deal of emphasis is placed on what is called "categorical special education": providing services to children as if they fall into neat boxes, or categories. You may know from your own experience that this isn't the case in "real life"; children are much more complicated than that. You may find that, as you read through this book, you will find characteristics of a child you know in several different chapters. Keep in mind that the categories we use are for the convenience of lawmakers and educators; they are not iron-clad descriptors of the way children really learn and function.

■ ***Categorical and Noncategorical Special Education*** When the term *category* is used in the context of special education today, it refers to one of the types of disabilities described and defined in IDEA. According to federal regulations, students must fit into one of these categories before they are considered eligible for special education services and before states can receive federal funding for the students' needs. Other groups of students (for example, students who are gifted and students with attention deficit disorder) may receive services through other federal or state funds, but they do not belong to the categorical groups described in IDEA. Although, as you will see, there are many proposed reasons for categorical identification, we must always address first and foremost the individual and specific needs of each student, whatever name or label we give to a specific disability a student might have.

Categories of eligibility for special education services have changed somewhat since the advent of IDEA.

The number of categories in special education and the definitions of the disability areas have changed considerably over the years. Categories were developed because of the assumed differences in the causes of learning difficulties and the perceived differences in the types of educational programs needed by students in each group. The number and nature of categories change as professionals in medical, psychological, and educational fields learn more about disabilities, develop opinions about educational strategies, and identify desired educational outcomes for students.

Some of the information gathered over the past few years, however, has caused a number of professionals in the field of special education to question the need for categories. Some of their concerns relate to philosophical issues. For example, must we label children in order to serve their educational needs? Another area of concern relates to practical issues, such as educational programming. If the same instructional strategies are used to teach most children with disabilities, why should we categorize them? Another practical concern focuses on the selection of only certain children to receive special education services. Other children, who do not meet the federal definition, may "slip through the cracks" and fail to receive special services even though they are not succeeding in the school environment.

In a categorical framework, students receive instruction from a teacher who is certified in their eligibility category.

These, and related concerns, have resulted in changes in the way special education services are delivered in approximately half of the states in this country. In some states, students with disabilities are served according to categorical label, whereas in other states, they are not. If students are served on the basis of their category, it means that they are grouped together and served by a teacher who is certified in that particular area. For example, students with learning disabilities would receive specialized services by a teacher who is certified in learning disabilities. If those students receive services outside of the general education classroom, only students with learning disabilities will be in that educational setting. States that provide categorical programming adhere to the philosophy that students with different types of disabilities require different specialized services and/or learning environments.

Some individuals agree with the categorical model for service delivery, because they believe it increases the probability that the students in a class will have similar needs. They feel that teaching procedures, or at least the primary emphasis of instruction, is different for students with, for example, mental retardation, than for students with learning disabilities or behavior disorders. Others, however, disagree with the emphasis that categorical special education places on labels, as opposed to services. They argue that often the differences among students within a category are as great or greater than the differences among students with different categorical labels. This philosophical disagreement has led to other types of identification practices for service delivery.

In a noncategorical framework, students are grouped according to the services they need.

Although students must be identified according to category to meet federal regulations, a school does not have to use categories as a guideline for providing services. In many states, for example, special education services are provided using a *noncategorical* approach. Students are grouped according to the level or amount of services needed rather than a specific category. For example, if a number of students who have been identified as needing special education all are experiencing reading difficulties and require specialized reading instruction, a teacher may provide instruction for all of those children together, even though one may have a behavior disorder, one may have a learning disability, and two may have mild mental retardation. In some instances, students may be grouped according to the level of service required, for example, in-class support, pullout support, or separate curriculum. In other settings, students may simply be identified as having mild or significant disabilities. Teachers in states that use a noncategorical approach to special education may be certified according to general level of disability rather than category. For example, certification may be in the area of mild disabilities rather than learning disabilities.

Individuals who support noncategorical special education believe that this approach is based more on instructional needs and prevents having an arbitrary label dictate instructional setting or services. Others feel that noncategorical special education makes incorrect assumptions about the similarities of educational programming required by teachers and for students. They are also concerned about the range of skills and disabilities teachers may be required to address in a specific setting.

Is it better to use a categorical or noncategorical service delivery approach? This is one question we hope you will keep in mind as you read the following chapters. Consider the points we've discussed and how they relate to your own ideas about categories of special education and teaching. You can also expect your ideas and opinions to adjust at least a little once you enter the school setting.

■ *Major Amendments to IDEA*

Public Law 99-457 In 1986, Congress amended P.L. 94-142 with P.L. 99-457. This amendment extended the provisions of P.L. 94-142 to all children between the ages of 3 and 5 through the Preschool Grants Program. Now states receiving federal funds under these laws *must* provide a free and appropriate public education to preschoolers as well. In addition, under the Handicapped Infants and Toddlers Program, states are provided incentives to develop early intervention programs for infants with disabilities and those who are at risk for developing disabilities from birth through age 3. We will learn more about these provisions in Chapter 2.

P.L. 99-457 extended the provisions of P.L. 94-142 to children between the ages of 3 and 5.

Public Law 101-476 These 1990 amendments used "people-first" language to rename the Education of the Handicapped Act the Individuals with Disabilities Education Act (IDEA). This law also recognized the importance of preparing students for life and work after school. It mandated the creation of an individualized transition plan (ITP) for each adolescent student receiving special education services.

IDEA now mandates an individualized transition plan (ITP) for each student receiving special education from the age of 14.

Public Law 105-17 The 1997 amendments to IDEA provided the most substantial revision of the law relating to the education of children with disabilities since P.L. 94-142 was passed in 1975. The accompanying box, "The 1997 Amendments to IDEA," lists some of the most recent changes in the law.

■ ***Section 504*** Are you taking class in a building that has ramps leading up to it? Are there elevators as well as stairs and escalators? In the elevators are there Braille cells next to the numerals indicating each floor? Is there a wide stall, a low sink, and a low mirror in the restroom? Is one of the public telephones set low on the wall? Are there plenty of special parking places for people with disabilities outside?

Let us hope that all these adaptations make your school building accessible to students, faculty, and staff with disabilities. Most public facilities have not become accessible out of the goodness of anyone's heart. They are accessible because of Section 504 of the Rehabilitation Act of 1973, a civil rights law that requires that institutions not discriminate against people with disabilities in any way if they wish to receive any federal funds.

Section 504 of the Rehabilitation Act of 1973 requires that public facilities be accessible to people with disabilities.

Section 504 has had considerable impact on architecture and construction in the United States, since it requires changes in building design for physical access. It has also been used to prohibit discrimination against a person simply because he or she is disabled. For example, if you had a newborn baby who needed corrective surgery to open a blocked trachea, would you hesitate about having it performed? Well, that surgery cannot be denied to a baby with Down syndrome either, simply because she will have mental retardation. Section 504 prohibits discrimination on the basis of disability.

Students who may not qualify for services in the schools under the thirteen definitions in IDEA but still have a significant learning problem that affects their ability to perform in school may qualify for services under Section 504. Although there is no funding available under Section 504, it requires that the school create a special plan to accommodate the student's learning needs and create an accessible environment (Mastropieri & Scruggs, 2000). Figure 1.2 outlines the steps for consideration of IDEA and Section 504 eligibility.

~ The 1997 Amendments to IDEA

Changes That Affect Practice:

Students with disabilities will participate in state and district-wide assessment (testing) programs, with accommodations where necessary.

The IEP process will place increased emphasis on participation of students with disabilities in the general education curriculum.

General education teachers will be involved in developing, reviewing, and revising the IEP.

Each state will establish a voluntary mediation process to resolve parent-school differences. Mediation must be available when a parent or school district requests a due process hearing.

States will be able to identify children age 3–9 as developmentally delayed, if they so choose.

Changes Related to Discipline:

Schools may suspend students with disabilities for up to ten school days, if such alternatives are used with students without disabilities, BUT . . .

Schools must continue to provide educational services for students with disabilities whose suspension or expulsion constitutes a change of placement (usually more than ten days in a school year).

Schools may remove students with disabilities to appropriate interim alternative educational settings (IAES) for behavior related to drugs, guns, and other dangerous weapons for up to forty-five days.

The law now requires the IEP team to conduct a "manifestation determination" once a disciplinary action for a student with a disability is contemplated. The IEP team must determine—within ten calendar days after the school decides to discipline a student—whether the student's behavior is related to the disability. If the behavior *is not* related to the disability, the student may be disciplined in the same way as a student without a disability, but the appropriate educational services must continue.

Source: Adapted from *ERICEC Digest E576,* June 1999, "An Overview of the Individuals with Disabilities Education Act Amendments of 1997 (P.L. 105-17): Update 1999," by Bernadette Knoblauch and Kathleen McLane. (E576; EDO-99-4)

The ADA protects the civil rights of people with disabilities in four major areas: private-sector employment, public services, public accommodations, and telecommunications.

■ ***The Americans with Disabilities Act*** On July 26, 1990, President George Bush signed into law Public Law 101-336, the Americans with Disabilities Act (ADA), with these words: "Today, America welcomes into the mainstream of life all people with disabilities. Let the shameful wall of exclusion finally come tumbling down." The ADA is civil rights legislation for people with disabilities, and it is patterned on Section 504 of the Rehabilitation Act of 1973. The provisions of the ADA cover four major areas: *private-sector employment; public services,* including public facilities, buses, and trains; *public accommodations,* including restaurants, hotels, theaters, doctors' offices, retail stores, museums, libraries, parks, private schools, and day-care centers; and *telecommunications,* making telephone relay services available twenty-four hours a day to people with speech and hearing impairments. Table 1.2 presents a summary of key legislation in special education.

Litigation

Behind the laws pertaining to the education of exceptional children and youth is a series of court cases initiated by parent and advocacy groups to improve services for children. Two important state court cases preceded the passage of

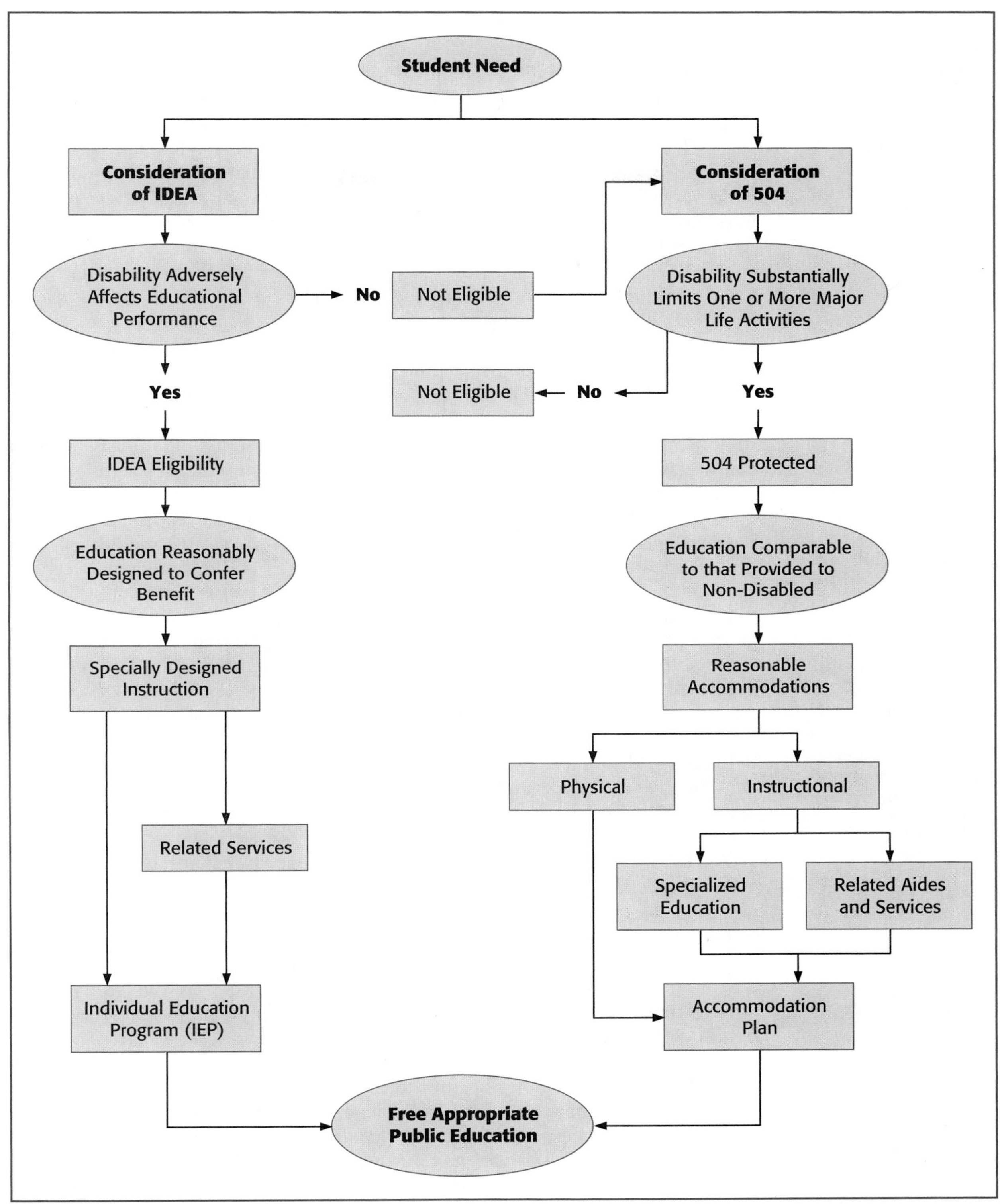

Figure 1.2
IDEA/504 Flow Chart

Note: Reprinted with permission from "Student Access: A Resource Guide for Educators," by Council of Administrators of Special Education, 1992, Council for Exceptional Children.

IDEA and addressed the need for schooling for children with disabilities who at the time were not provided with any education at all. In *Pennsylvania Association for Retarded Citizens (PARC) v. Commonwealth of Pennsylvania* (1972), parents of children with mental retardation sued to procure an education for their children. The courts decided in their favor and required Pennsylvania to provide a free, appropriate public education for students with mental retardation. In *Mills v. the Washington, D.C., Board of Education* (1972), a similar decision was reached in regard to all children with disabilities in the District of Columbia.

PARC required Pennsylvania schools to provide a free and appropriate education to students with mental retardation.

Since the passage of P.L. 94-142, there have been several cases in which the courts have interpreted various aspects of the law. The first case to reach the U.S. Supreme Court, *Board of Education of Hendrick Hudson School District v. Rowley* (1982), concerned the question of what constitutes an "appropriate" education. The parents of Amy Rowley, a deaf child, requested that she have a sign language interpreter so that she could benefit fully from her placement in a regular class. The court wrote that an "appropriate" education did not mean that the student must reach her maximum potential, but that she have a reasonable opportunity to learn. Since there was evidence presented that Amy Rowley could derive some benefit from regular class placement without a sign language interpreter, she was denied that additional service.

In *Irving Independent School District v. Tatro* (1984), the Supreme Court explored the school's responsibility to provide catheterization, a medical service, to a child with spina bifida who needed this service in order to remain in school. The Court decided that since this procedure could be performed by a school nurse and the child needed it to remain in school, it should be considered a related service rather than a medical service, and the schools must provide it.

The *Rowley* and *Tatro* cases concerned the schools' responsibilities to provide "related services."

In 1988, the Supreme Court, in *Honig v. Doe,* ruled that a student receiving special education services cannot be excluded indefinitely from school and from receiving the services specified in the IEP (see next major section). In addition, the student cannot be expelled from school if the behavior in question is related to his or her disability.

In *Honig v. Doe* the Supreme Court ruled that a student receiving special education services cannot be expelled if the behavior in question is related to his or her disability.

The 1999 *Garret F.* ruling by the U.S. Supreme Court ensures that any and all services necessary for a student with complex health-care needs are covered by IDEA, as long as a physician does not provide the services (Maag & Katsiyannis, 2000). Table 1.3 summarizes these and other court cases that have significantly affected special education.

■ ***Disproportionate Representation of Minority Children*** The next three court cases we will discuss addressed the overrepresentation of children from minority backgrounds in special education classes. The issue of disproportionate representation of minority children remains an important one in our field today. Let's review the background on this issue.

What would you expect the racial breakdown of students receiving special education services to look like? In the United States, where 66.2 percent of the school-age population is white, 14.8 percent African American, 14.2 percent Latino, and 3.8 percent Asian and Pacific Islander (*Twenty-second Annual Report to Congress on the Implementation of the Individuals with Disabilities Education Act,* 2000), shouldn't the representation in special education be approximately the same? In both the past and the present, this has not been the case, and the disparities from our expectations have presented a significant problem for our field.

In an often-cited article in *Exceptional Children,* Lloyd Dunn (1968) reported that a disproportionately high number of African American, American Indian,

Table 1.3 Important Litigation Involving Special Education

1954 *Brown v. Board of Education* In this case, the U.S. Supreme Court decided that the concept of "separate but equal" schools was unconstitutional and declared that all children must have equal opportunity for education.

1970 *Diana v. Board of Education* (California) This state case established that California schools could not place students in special education on the basis of culturally biased tests or tests given in the student's nonprimary language.

1972 *Pennsylvania Association for Retarded Citizens v. Pennsylvania* This state case established the right of children with mental retardation to a public education in Pennsylvania.

1972 *Mills v. Washington, D.C. Board of Education* This state case established that all students with disabilities were entitled to a public education in the District of Columbia.

1979 *Larry P. v. Riles* (California) In this state case, it was decided that IQ tests could not be used to identify African American students with mental retardation.

1982 *Board of Education of the Hendrick Hudson Central School District v. Rowley* The U.S. Supreme Court, in its first decision interpreting P.L. 94-142, defined an "appropriate" education as one that provides a child with a reasonable opportunity to learn.

1984 *Irving Independent School District v. Tatro* The U.S. Supreme Court decided that procedures that could be performed by a nonphysician (such as catheterization) qualified as related services, not medical services, and must be provided by the school district, so that a child can attend school and benefit from special education.

1988 *Honig v. Doe* The U.S. Supreme Court ruled that a student receiving special education services cannot be excluded from school indefinitely (expelled), particularly if the behavior is related to the student's disability.

1999 *Cedar Rapids Community School District v. Garret F.* The U.S. Supreme Court ruled that services related to a student's complex health-care needs are covered under IDEA as long as a physician does not provide them.

Mexican, and Puerto Rican children from low socioeconomic backgrounds were being placed in special education classes for students with mild mental retardation. Jane Mercer (1973) provided support for Dunn's findings when she reported that three times as many African American and four times as many Mexican-American children were being placed in classes for students with mild mental retardation as compared to their numbers in the general school population. This situation is referred to as **overrepresentation,** or a representation greater than would be expected based on the actual number of students in that group in school.

Overrepresentation occurs when there are more students in a group than would be expected from the population.

Those findings are nearly thirty years old. But the overrepresentation and underrepresentation of individuals from certain ethnic cultures in categories of special education persist today. Black students account for 14.8 percent of the school-aged population but 20.2 percent of the special education population in all disabilities. American Indian students remain overrepresented in special education services as well (*Twenty-second Annual Report to Congress on the Implementation of the Individuals with Disabilities Act,* 2000). This suggests that we, as educators, must continue to examine this issue and ourselves.

Underrepresentation occurs when fewer students are receiving services than would be expected based on their representation in the general school population. African American, Hispanic, and American Indian students, for example, are underrepresented in gifted and talented programs.

Underrepresentation occurs when there are fewer students in a group than would be expected from the population.

Factors Contributing to Over- and Underrepresentation Why are some culturally diverse groups overrepresented in classes for children with disabilities and others not? Do the statistics accurately reflect the incidence of exceptionalities among culturally diverse students? In addressing these questions, we must consider the referral, assessment, and placement process. We must also concern ourselves with the access these children have to educational services, along with environmental and poverty factors.

One factor in overrepresentation may be overreferral of culturally diverse children to special education. Who makes referrals? Primarily teachers, and most teachers are white, middle-class women. Most referrals to special education involve males from culturally diverse lower socioeconomic backgrounds. Even if the teachers themselves are from culturally diverse backgrounds, they are still typically from a different gender group and a different socioeconomic background. Different backgrounds may result in incongruent values, and a lack of tolerance or understanding may lead to a predisposition toward referrals.

Fair assessment of children from diverse backgrounds is challenging and complex.

Another variable contributing to the overrepresentation of culturally diverse children in classes for students with mild mental retardation has been the use of culturally biased assessment instruments. These assessment tools are often used by psychologists, psychometrists, or diagnosticians who are inadequately trained and unprepared to test culturally and linguistically diverse children. The problem becomes even more acute when bias enters into the interpretation of test results and the placement process.

Poverty is a third factor that affects representation rates in special education classes. When you have your own classroom, you will find that poverty tends to affect some ethnic groups more than others. In 1995, 29.3 percent of African Americans and 30.3 percent of Hispanics in this country were poor (U.S. Bureau of the Census, 1995). Poverty contributes to poor nutrition, poor quality of medical care, and poor living conditions. Poor women must often work even when a pregnancy is at risk. These factors can contribute to children being born preterm or at risk. As you will learn in Chapter 2, children born at risk are more likely to develop learning problems and disabilities. In addition, poverty often contributes to stress, which affects the overall mental health of a family. Finally, studies have demonstrated that children from poor environments are more likely to be exposed to lead and other environmental toxins.

Reasons for underrepresentation are as varied as the reasons for overrepresentation and may differ according to the type of cultural diversity. The low national prevalence figures for Hispanics in classes for students with mental retardation and emotional disturbance, for example, may be related in part to the advent of bilingual education programs. These programs were only in their infancy at the time of the Dunn (1968) and Mercer (1973) studies but now provide an alternative to special education programs. School districts with bilingual education programs have fewer problems with disproportionate representation of students than those without bilingual programs (Finn, 1982). Aware that the language of instruction in special education is primarily English, bilingual teachers are sometimes reluctant to refer their students to special education, believing that their needs can better be met in a bilingual setting (Dew, 1984).

As with Latinos, there are several reasons why Asians may be underrepresented in classes for children with disabilities. First, some Asian parents are reluctant to seek external assistance for their child with disabilities (Chan, 1986). Parents may be hesitant to grant permission to school personnel to test their child or to consider special education placement. A second variable is the fact that, as a group (with some exceptions), Asians in the United States enjoy a relatively high standard of living. With the exception of the second wave of Southeast Asian immigrants beginning in 1978, most of the Asian immigrants entering the country have middle- or upper-middle-class backgrounds with a relatively high educational level. The children from these families are at less risk of special education placement than many of the children from other culturally diverse groups, who come from backgrounds of poverty. In addition, educators may also have a tendency to stereotype Asian children as being very quiet. Thus children who are seriously withdrawn may be passed off as having typical Asian behaviors and are not referred for possible special education placement.

The disproportionately low placement of American Indian, African American, and Latino children in classes for students labeled gifted and talented is also an important issue. For a child to be placed in such a class, the child's potential must be recognized by someone, usually a teacher. He or she must then be referred, tested, and ultimately placed. A child will not be placed, however, if no one recognizes his or her abilities and makes a referral. Gifted children from culturally diverse backgrounds may go unnoticed because they express their talents in ways different from some white children (Kitano & Kirby, 1986). Negative teacher attitudes toward culturally diverse students may also affect their referral rates. In addition, parents from culturally diverse low-income backgrounds may be less likely to recognize their child's giftedness and less likely to nominate their child for gifted class placement.

Since teachers often unwittingly contribute to the problems of disproportionate placement of culturally diverse children in special education classes, it is important for you as a teacher to be aware of your own attitudes toward diverse students and to develop greater insight and sensitivity toward cultural diversity. You can make a difference.

Litigation Relating to Over- and Underrepresentation A number of critical court cases have addressed the issues of overrepresentation in special education and the appropriate assessment and placement of students from culturally diverse backgrounds. The landmark *Brown v. Board of Education of Topeka, Kansas* (1954) decision set the stage for several important court cases concerning children with disabilities. In the *Brown* decision, the U.S. Supreme Court ruled that separate schools for African American and white students cannot be considered equal and are therefore unconstitutional. This ruling provided the precedent for parents and advocates who maintained that children with disabilities were being unfairly denied equal educational opportunities.

In *Brown v. Board of Education*, the Supreme Court ruled that "separate but equal" schools were unconstitutional.

Diana v. Board of Education (1970) was a state class-action suit that addressed the overrepresentation of children from non–English-speaking backgrounds in special classes in California. It was filed on behalf of nine Mexican-American children who had been placed in classes for students with mental retardation based on results of IQ tests given in English. Advocates for the children argued that their assessment had been unfair, since it was not conducted in Spanish,

Diana v. Board of Education mandated that children be tested in their primary language for special education services.

their native language. The case was settled with the agreement that children must be tested in both their primary language and in English when special education placement is being considered. When the children involved in the case were retested more appropriately, seven of the nine were no longer eligible for special education.

Larry P. v. Riles dealt with the fairness of IQ testing for African American children.

In *Larry P. v. Riles* (1979) the issue was the disproportionate number of African American students in classes for students with educable mental retardation in California. The plaintiffs maintained that standardized IQ tests, which were used as the basis for placement of these students, were culturally biased against African American children. The *Larry P.* ruling eliminated the use of IQ tests to place African American students in classes for students with mental retardation in California. The overrepresentation of African American children in special education remains a cause of great concern, despite changes in assessment practices spurred by the *Larry P.* decision.

These cases are a small sample of the numerous court decisions rendered on behalf of culturally and linguistically diverse students. They illustrate the inequities inherent in our educational system, many of which are so institutionalized that it often requires the threat of litigation to inspire changes.

IDEA reflects many of the decisions handed down by the courts through the years. The provisions in IDEA require testing in the native language by trained professionals, nondiscriminatory assessment, due process, least restrictive environment, appropriate education, individualization, and confidentiality. In addition, IDEA provides certain procedural safeguards for language minority students by requiring written or verbal communication to be provided to parents or guardians in the language of the home. All meetings or hearings must have a qualified translator.

Table 1.3 summarizes the court cases that have significantly affected both law and special education practice.

Individualized Education

With individualized education, each student has a program tailored to his or her unique needs.

At the core of the laws pertaining to the education of exceptional children is the concept of individualized education: Each student should have a program tailored to his or her unique needs. IDEA and its amendments have instituted a system of planning that can now extend from birth to the postschool years. Table 1.4 describes the components of individualized education. In the following sections we'll look at each of these individualized programs.

The Individualized Family Service Plan (IFSP)

The IFSP ensures that the youngest children and their families receive the services they need.

Exceptional children and their families can first receive individualized services through the IFSP. Congress, recognizing the importance of early intervention for young children in the context of the family, mandated that an **individualized family service plan (IFSP)** be drawn up by an interdisciplinary team that includes family members. The major components of the IFSP are listed in Table 1.4. The IFSP is meant to ensure that young children from birth to age 3 who are identified as having disabilities or developmental delay or who are at risk receive the services they need to develop skills and prevent additional disabilities. Chapter 2 will provide more detail on the IFSP.

Table 1.4 Key Components of Individualized Education

Relevant Ages	Description
	The IFSP: The individualized family service plan must include the following components:
Children birth to age 3 and their families	▪ A statement of the infant's or toddler's present levels of development (physical, cognitive, speech/language, psychosocial, motor, and self-help) ▪ A statement of family's strengths, needs, resources, and priorities related to enhancing the child's development ▪ A statement of major outcomes expected to be achieved for the child and the family ▪ The criteria, procedures, and time lines for determining progress ▪ The specific early intervention services necessary to meet the unique needs of the child and family, including the frequency, intensity, and method of delivering services ▪ The projected dates for the initiation of services and expected duration of those services ▪ The name of the case manager (service coordinator) ▪ The procedures for transition from early intervention into the preschool program
	The IEP: The Individualized Education Program must include the following components:
Students age 3 through 21	▪ A statement of the child's current educational performance levels ▪ Annual goals and benchmarks or short-term objectives ▪ A description of the special education and related services provided ▪ A statement describing the program modifications and supports the child needs to benefit from the general education curriculum ▪ A statement of the extent to which the child will be able to participate in general education programs ▪ The date on which services begin and their anticipated duration ▪ Appropriate objective evaluation criteria and evaluation procedures and schedules for determining, at least annually, whether the short-term objectives are being achieved ▪ A statement of transition services (ITP) needed by students who are 14 and over

Table 1.4 Key Components of Individualized Education (cont.)

Relevant Ages	Description
	The ITP: Individualized transition plan might include the following components:
Students age 14 through 21	▪ A statement of transition services needed (career planning, self-advocacy, social life, community participation, postsecondary education, leisure services, advocacy/legal services, daily living, physical care) ▪ Annual goals in each service area, accompanied by objectives designed to meet those goals ▪ Statements of educational and related services needed to enable the student to meet the goals and objectives ▪ Statement of interagency responsibilities and linkages, including the agency, purpose, contact persons, and the time by which the reponsibility or linkage must be established

Source: Adapted from "Legal Foundations: The Individuals with Disabilities Education Act (IDEA)," *Teaching Exceptional Children* (Winter 1993), pp. 85–87. Copyright © 1993 by The Council for Exceptional Children. Reprinted with permission. Updated by authors, 2000.

The Individualized Education Program (IEP)

The IEP outlines the educational plan for each student.

The **individualized education program (IEP)** is the basis for special education programming in preschool, elementary, middle, and high school. IDEA calls for a team of people to draw up a written IEP at a meeting called for that purpose. The team is typically made up of the parent(s), the special education teacher, the regular education teacher, and the school principal. When it is appropriate, the student is also present at the IEP meeting. Other school professionals become involved, too, when the student needs supportive services: The school nurse, speech-language specialist, adaptive physical education teacher, and other school professionals may participate in the IEP process. According to the law, the IEP must have the components listed in Table 1.4. Figure 1.3 provides more information on the IEP.

The Individualized Transition Plan (ITP)

The ITP helps prepare students for life and work after school.

As noted earlier, the Individuals with Disabilities Education Act mandated transition services for all students receiving special education services. Transition plans are now required from the age of 14. The **individualized transition plan (ITP)** includes the components listed in Table 1.4.

The Pros and Cons of Labeling

We use terms that we call "labels" to describe groups of exceptional children. In this book, you will read about students with mental retardation, learning disabilities, physical and health impairments, speech and language impairments, and emotional disturbance, as well as students who are deaf and hard of hearing, visually handicapped, or gifted and talented.

Guide to the Individualized Education Program

Introduction

Each public school child who receives special education and related services must have an Individualized Education Program (IEP). Each IEP must be designed for one student and must be a truly *individualized* document. The IEP is the cornerstone of a quality education for each child with a disability.

To create an effective IEP, parents, teachers, other school staff—and often the student—must come together to look closely at the student's unique needs. These individuals pool knowledge, experience, and commitment to design an educational program that will help the student be involved in, and progress in, *the general curriculum.* The IEP guides the delivery of special education supports and services for the student with a disability. Without a doubt, writing—and implementing—an effective IEP requires teamwork.

The information in this guide is based on what is required by our nation's special education law—the Individuals with Disabilities Education Act, or IDEA.

The Basic Special Education Process Under IDEA

The writing of each student's IEP takes place within the larger picture of the special education process under IDEA. Before taking a detailed look at the IEP, it may be helpful to look briefly at how a student is identified as having a disability and needing special education and related services and, thus, an IEP.

Step 1. Child is identified as possibly needing special education and related services.
The state must identify, locate, and evaluate all children with disabilities in the state who need special education and related services. To do so, states conduct "Child Find" activities.

Step 2. Child is evaluated.
The evaluation must assess the child in all areas related to the child's suspected disability. The evaluation results will be used to decide the child's eligibility for special education and related services and to make decisions about an appropriate educational program for the child.

Step 3. Eligibility is decided.
A group of qualified professionals and the parents look at the child's evaluation results. Together, they decide if the child is a "child with a disability," as defined by IDEA.

Step 4. Child is found eligible for services.
If the child is found to be a "child with a disability," as defined by IDEA, he or she is eligible for special education and related services. Within 30 calendar days after a child is determined eligible, the IEP team must meet to write an IEP for the child.

Step 5. IEP meeting is scheduled.
The school system schedules and conducts the IEP meeting.

Step 6. IEP meeting is held and the IEP is written.
The IEP team gathers to talk about the child's needs and write the student's IEP. Parents and the student (when appropriate) are part of the team.

Figure 1.3
The Office of Special Education and Rehabilitation Services in the U.S. Department of Education has put together a very specific, helpful guide to the IEP and the IEP process. What follows is excerpts from that guide.

Step 7. Services are provided.
The school makes sure that the child's IEP is being carried out as it was written. Parents are given a copy of the IEP. Each of the child's teachers and service providers has access to the IEP and knows his or her specific responsibilities for carrying out the IEP. This includes the accommodations, modifications, and supports that must be provided to the child, in keeping with the IEP.

Step 8. Progress is measured and reported to parents.
The child's progress toward the annual goals is measured, as stated in the IEP. His or her parents are regularly informed of their child's progress and whether that progress is enough for the child to achieve the goals by the end of the year.

Step 9. IEP is reviewed.
The child's IEP is reviewed by the IEP team at least once a year, or more often if the parents or school ask for a review.

Step 10. Child is re-evaluated.
At least every three years the child must be re-evaluated. This evaluation is often called a "triennial." Its purpose is to find out if the child continues to be a "child with a disability," as defined by IDEA, and what the child's educational needs are.

A Closer Look at the IEP

Clearly, the IEP is a very important document for children with disabilities and for those who are involved in educating them. Done correctly, the IEP should improve teaching, learning, and results. Each child's IEP describes, among other things, the educational program that has been designed to meet that child's unique needs.

Contents of the IEP
By law, the IEP must include certain information about the child and the educational program designed to meet his or her unique needs. In a nutshell, this information is:

- **Current performance.** The IEP must state how the child is currently doing in school (known as present levels of educational performance). This information usually comes from the evaluation results such as classroom tests and assignments, individual tests given to decide eligibility for services or during reevaluation, and observations made by parents, teachers, related service providers, and other school staff. The statement about "current performance" includes how the child's disability affects his or her involvement and progress in the general curriculum.
- **Annual goals.** These are goals that the child can reasonably accomplish in a year. The goals are broken down into short-term objectives or benchmarks. Goals may be academic, address social or behavioral needs, relate to physical needs, or address other educational needs. The goals must be measurable—meaning that it must be possible to measure whether the student has achieved the goals.
- **Special education and related services.** The IEP must list the special education and related services to be provided to the child or on behalf of the child. This includes supplementary aids and services that the child needs. It also includes modifications (changes) to the program or supports for school personnel—such as training or professional development—that will be provided to assist the child.
- **Participation with nondisabled children.** The IEP must explain the extent (if any) to which the child will not participate with nondisabled children in the regular class and other school activities.

Figure 1.3 (continued)

- **Participation in state and district-wide tests.** Most states and districts give achievement tests to children in certain grades or age groups. The IEP must state what modifications in the administration of these tests the child will need. If a test is not appropriate for the child, the IEP must state why the test is not appropriate and how the child will be tested instead.
- **Dates and places.** The IEP must state when services will begin, how often they will be provided, where they will be provided, and how long they will last.
- **Transition service needs.** Beginning when the child is age 14 (or younger, if appropriate), the IEP must address (within the applicable parts of the IEP) the courses he or she needs to take to reach his or her post-school goals. A statement of transition services needs must also be included in each of the child's subsequent IEPs.
  - **Needed transition services.** Beginning when the child is age 16 (or younger, if appropriate), the IEP must state what transition services are needed to help the child prepare for leaving school.
  - **Age of majority.** Beginning at least one year before the child reaches the age of majority, the IEP must include a statement that the student has been told of any rights that will transfer to him or her at the age of majority. (This statement would be needed only in states that transfer rights at the age of majority.)
- **Measuring progress.** The IEP must state how the child's progress will be measured and how parents will be informed of that progress.

It is useful to understand that each child's IEP is different. The document is prepared for that child only. It describes the individualized education program designed to meet that child's needs

Special Factors To Consider

Depending on the needs of the child, the IEP team needs to consider what the law calls special factors. These include:

- If the child's *behavior* interferes with his or her learning or the learning of others, the IEP team will consider strategies and supports to address the child's behavior.
- If the child has *limited proficiency in English,* the IEP team will consider the child's language needs as these needs relate to his or her IEP.
- If the child is *blind or visually impaired,* the IEP team must provide for instruction in Braille or the use of Braille, unless it determines after an appropriate evaluation that the child does not need this instruction.
- If the child has *communication needs,* the IEP team must consider those needs.
- If the child is *deaf or hard of hearing,* the IEP team will consider his or her language and communication needs. This includes the child's opportunities to communicate directly with classmates and school staff in his or her usual method of communication (for example, sign language).
- The IEP team must always consider the child's need for *assistive technology* devices or services.

There is much more information available in the complete *Guide.* Copies are available online from: *http://www.ed.gov/offices/OSERS/.*

To obtain this publication in an alternate format (braille, large print, audio cassette, or disk), please contact Katie Mincey, Director of the Alternate Format Center, at (202) 260-9895, or via e-mail at *Katie_Mincey@ed.gov.*

Figure 1.3 (continued)

The Context of Special Education: Focus on the Individual

Think of the labels that could be applied to you. Are you a Caucasian female? A Latino male? A Catholic, Protestant, Jew, Muslim? Would you want those labels to be the first piece of information other people learn about you? People with disabilities and their families and advocates have worked very hard to erase the "disability-first" perception that has often pursued them.

Why use labels at all? Many people feel that we should not. But labels do serve some useful purposes. First, they help us count individuals with exceptionalities. Just as the United States government wants to know your sex, race, and age in order to provide representation and services to your community, the federal government and the states count the numbers of students with disabilities in order to plan for and provide educational and supportive services.

Labels also help professionals differentiate methods of instruction and support services to different groups. Children who have visual disabilities learn to read with materials that are quite different from those used by children who have learning disabilities. Children who are deaf or hard of hearing need the support services of an audiologist and possibly a speech-language specialist. Gifted and talented students may learn more from a differentiated curriculum tailored to their learning strengths and needs (Clark, 1997). Many special educators would argue, however, that instructional methods do not vary significantly for students who are identified as having learning disabilities, mild mental retardation, or severe emotional disturbance, although the emphasis of instruction might vary from student to student, depending on individual student learning needs.

Labels can lead to prejudging and stereotyping.

Labels enable professionals to communicate efficiently about children and their needs. But they are frequently misused and can carry an enormous stigma. Words like *hyperactive, autistic,* and *dyslexic* are often used freely to describe children who are having academic or behavioral difficulties in school. Using such terms may make a professional sound knowledgeable, but labels like these may alter the perceptions of others about the learning potential of such children. Moreover, labels often obscure individual differences among children (Hobbs, 1975); we assume that all children identified as "learning disabled" are somehow the same. (Table 1.5 shows how labels have changed over time.)

Special education professionals would like to replace current labels with terminology directly related to instruction.

Many professionals within special education see categorical labels as a necessary evil and would like to replace current labels with terminology that is directly related to instruction and that minimizes negative connotations (Adelman, 1996).

Educational Setting

The least restrictive environment, which may be different for each child, allows the most interaction with nondisabled peers.

IDEA requires that each school district provide a range of program options for students with disabilities. As you saw in Figure 1.1, these programs range from what is considered the least restrictive to the most restrictive environment. Remember that the concept of "least restrictive environment" is based on the opportunities available for interaction between the student with a disability and nondisabled peers. In practical terms, this means that a family attending an IEP meeting must have the option of choosing from this range of programs in order to obtain the most appropriate education for the child. The family and the school district must come to an agreement about the setting in which the child's educational needs can most appropriately be met.

The concept of the least restrictive environment was originally envisioned as a relative one—that is, one that must be interpreted anew for each student on

Table 1.5 Terms Reflecting Social Changes

Areas of Disability	Past	Present
Mental Retardation	idiots, feebleminded, cretin, mentally deficient, educably retarded or trainably retarded, morons, high level or low level	mild, moderate, severe retardation and intermittent, pervasive, extensive, and limited retardation
Learning Disabilities	dyslexia, minimal cerebral dysfunction, specific learning disabilities, learning disabilities	learning disabilities
Emotional Disturbance	unsocialized, dementia, emotionally disturbed, acting out, withdrawn	emotional/behavioral disorders (E/BD)
Attention Deficit Disorder (with or without hyperactivity)	hyperactivity, specific learning disabilities	ADD (Attention Deficit Disorder without hyperactivity) or ADHD (with hyperactivity) and combined
Head Injuries	strephosymbolia, brain-crippled children, brain-injured, closed head injury	traumatic brain injury
Deafness	deaf and dumb, deaf mute	severely/profoundly hearing impaired
Persons with Orthopedic Disabilities	crippled children, physically handicapped	physical disabilities
Learning Disability in Reading	dyslexia, minimal cerebral dysfunction, specific learning disabilities	dyslexia
Autism	childhood schizophrenia, children with refrigerator parents, Kanner's Syndrome, autoid	autism (high functioning or low functioning)
Placements for Individuals with More Severe Disabilities	Asylums, institutions, residential schools, group homes	community living, assistive living, and supportive employment
Placements for Individuals with Mild Disabilities	normalization, mainstreaming, Regular Education Initiative, integration	inclusion
Assessment	testing, measurement	assessment, norm-referenced or authentic/performance based assessment
Preassessment	diagnosis, child study teacher assistance teams	prereferral teams, student support teams

Source: G. Vergason and M.L. Anderegg, "The Ins and Outs of Special Education Terminology," *Teaching Exceptional Children*, 29(5) May/June (1997), p. 36. Copyright © 1996 by The Council for Exceptional Children. Reprinted with permission.

the basis of his or her unique learning characteristics. Some professionals today, however, interpret the least restrictive environment in a more general fashion and argue for the inclusion of students with disabilities in the general education classroom, along with curricular adaptations and the collaboration and teaming of professionals from special and general education (Stainback, Stainback, & Ayres, 1996). Others call for maintaining the continuum of educational services (Council for Exceptional Children, 1997; Leiberman, 1996) as represented in Figure 1.1.

Let's consider an example. Ana is a student who has engaged in violent and self-destructive behavior. These behaviors have decreased in the special school for students labeled seriously emotionally disturbed that she has been attending, but this is considered a relatively restrictive setting for Ana, since she has no opportunity there to interact with her nondisabled peers. At her IEP meeting, her family and teachers decide that Ana's educational goals could best be reached in a less restrictive setting: a special class for students labeled severely emotionally disturbed on an elementary school campus. There she will have opportunities to participate in social and academic activities with her peers, with her special-class teacher planning and overseeing those experiences. With success she will have the opportunity for more and more of those experiences.

Advocates of inclusion might suggest that Ana be placed at her grade level in her neighborhood school, with a special education teacher or instructional aide available to monitor her behavior and make curricular adaptations as they are needed. They would argue that only with the models of appropriate behavior available in the regular class and the opportunities for meaningful social interaction provided there can Ana be motivated to change her behavior. This picture of inclusion can succeed only if professionals from special and regular education team up to provide individualized educational services for Ana and each included student.

Most exceptional students receive the majority of their instruction in the general education classroom.

The majority of students identified as exceptional *are receiving their instruction primarily in the regular classroom.* A number of different kinds of programs have been developed to ensure that these students and their teachers receive the support they need. Many involve **collaboration** between the special educator and the regular educator—the foundation for successful inclusive practices. Marilyn Friend and Lynne Cook (2000) define collaboration as " a style for direct interaction between at least two coequal parties voluntarily engaged in shared decision making as they work toward a common goal" (p. 6). The accompanying box describes key characteristics of collaboration.

Defining Characteristics of Collaboration

- Collaboration is *voluntary.* People cannot be forced to use a particular style in their interactions with others.
- Collaboration requires *parity* among participants. Each person's contribution is equally valued, and each person has equal power in decision-making.
- Collaboration is based on *mutual goals.* Professionals do not have to share all goals in order to collaborate, just one that is specific and important enough to maintain their shared attention.
- Collaboration depends on *shared responsibility* for participation and decision-making. Collaborators must assume the responsibility of actively engaging in the activity and in the decision-making it entails.
- Individuals who collaborate *share their resources.* Sharing resources of time, knowledge, and materials can enhance the sense of ownership among professionals.
- Individuals who collaborate *share responsibility for outcomes.* Whether the results of collaboration are positive or negative, all participating individuals are responsible for the outcomes.

Source: Adapted from M. Friend & L. Cook, *Interactions: Collaboration Skills for School Professionals* (White Plains, NY: Longman, 2000), pp. 6–11.

In inclusive settings, special and regular educators also work together in **team-teaching** situations. Team teaching, also called co-teaching, can involve shared instruction of a lesson, a subject area, or an entire instructional program. At the TRIPOD-Burbank program in southern California, for example, teachers of deaf students pair with elementary teachers in classrooms with three to six deaf students and twenty-two hearing peers. Both teachers sign and speak at all times, and many of the hearing students learn to understand and use sign language quite well. According to Vaughn, Schumm, and Arguelles (1997), co-teaching is "a bit like a marriage" (p. 5); it can be very rewarding once some of the common issues are worked out.

Team teaching can involve shared instruction of a lesson, a subject area, or an entire instructional program.

Another arrangement is the **student support team** (also known by many other names, such as the *teacher assistance team*). This is a group of teachers and other school professionals who work together to assist the regular classroom teacher. Under some circumstances, a team concentrates on keeping children in the regular classroom instead of referring them to special education; a team like this is sometimes known as a **prereferral intervention team** (Graden, 1989; Safran & Safran, 1996). In other situations, team members provide consultation to teachers or direct services to students who are identified with special needs but who are in the regular classroom.

The prereferral intervention team works to keep students in the general education classroom.

These arrangements are designed to maintain the student's instruction within the regular classroom. Other kinds of services for students with special needs are called **pullout programs,** since they involve the student leaving the classroom to receive specialized instruction. The traditional organization of the resource room, for example, involves students leaving the regular classroom for specialized instruction in academic areas of need. In many parts of the country, however, this practice is changing, and the resource teacher is operating on the **consultation model**—meeting with teachers to plan instructional adaptations for students as well as providing direct instructional services within the regular classroom. Some other examples of traditional pullout programs are speech and language services, orientation and mobility for students with visual handicaps, and physical therapy for students with physical disabilities. Table 1.6 describes the settings in which special education is provided.

In today's schools, the great majority of students with disabilities are receiving their education in a regular school building: The *Twenty-second Annual Report* (2000) put that number at more than 95 percent of students aged 3 to 21. At the classroom level, 46 percent were served in regular classrooms, 27 percent were served in resource rooms, and 22 percent were served in separate classes. The remaining students received their educational services in public and private separate school facilities (3 percent), public and private residential facilities (0.7 percent), and homebound or hospital settings (0.7 percent) (see Figure 1.4).

Measuring Progress and Identifying Ongoing Challenges

You can see from what you have read so far in this chapter that the last twenty-five years have been a very rich period in the United States for people with disabilities and their families and advocates. New laws and new attitudes have opened up many opportunities for learning, growth, health, and friendships.

Table 1.6 Settings for Delivery of Special Education

General education classroom	With supports as needed.
Resource room	A special education teacher provides instruction or support to identified students, either in the general education classroom or in a separate room.
Special classes in elementary or secondary schools	These classes group children by exceptionality—gifted, deaf, learning disabled—and a specialist teacher instructs them together. Individual students may leave the special class for part of the day to receive instruction in the general education classroom, but the majority of their time is usually spent in the special class.
Special schools	Designed exclusively for students with exceptionality. The related services that the students need are usually housed under the same roof. Special schools may be public or private.
Residential schools	Special schools where the students live during the school year. This is considered the most restrictive educational environment for exceptional students, since they have no opportunity to interact with their nondisabled peers.
Home- or hospital-based instruction	Provided by a special education teacher to students who, because of chronic illness or other needs, are taught at home or while they are hospitalized.

Students educated since IDEA was passed are more likely to have completed school and found employment than their predecessors.

We are beginning to see documentation of the improvements in outcomes for students with disabilities as a result of IDEA and its amendments. Those who have been educated under IDEA are more likely to complete high school than those who came before them and more likely to be competitively employed. Today, a record 55 percent of America's students with disabilities are graduating from high school. Employment rates of high school graduates who have been educated under IDEA are twice that of the overall population of people with disabilities. Today, 44 percent of all adults with a disability have completed some college or received a degree, compared to 29 percent in 1986 (U.S. Department of Education, 1995), and more students with disabilities are attending regular classes alongside nondisabled students than ever before.

Progress in Community Settings

Many believe that adults with disabilities should be permitted to live in the least restrictive, most "normal" environment.

The philosophy of normalization has had a significant effect on the residential options available to people with disabilities. Through the deinstitutionalization movement, over the last twenty-five years a large number of individuals with disabilities have successfully moved from institutions to community settings such as group homes and apartments. At present, only about 1 percent of children with disabilities live in expensive and isolated institutions (U.S. Depart-

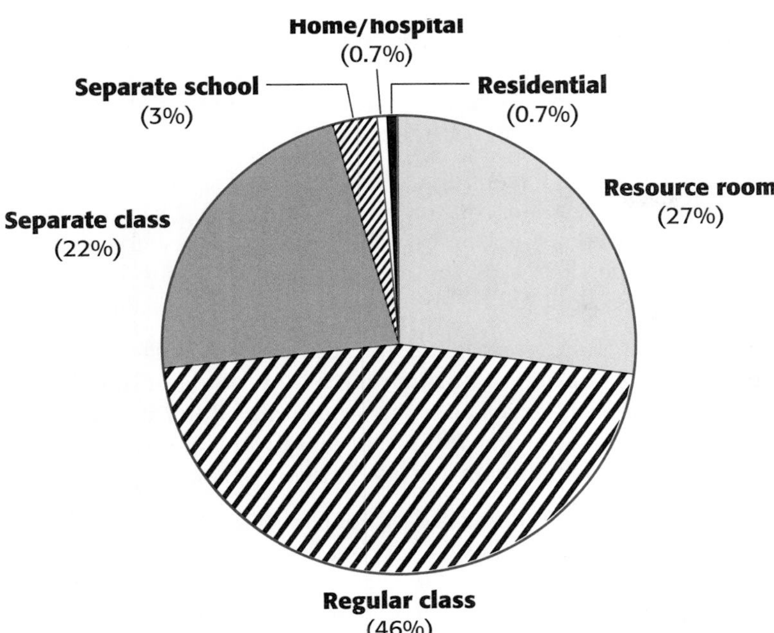

Figure 1.4
Percentage of All Students with Disabilities Age 3–21 Served in Six Educational Placements; 1997–1998 School Year

Source: Twenty-second Annual Report to Congress on the Implementation of the Individuals with Disabilities Education Act, U.S. Department of Education, Office of Special Education Programs, Data Analysis System (DANS).

Notes: Includes data from 50 states, the District of Columbia, and outlying areas. Separate school includes both public and private separate school facilities. Residential includes both public and private residential facilities.

ment of Education, 1995). The concept of the least restrictive environment can also be applied to housing; many feel that the least restrictive community settings—that is, those that allow greatest access to normal daily life experiences and interaction with one's neighbors—are the most desirable for adults with disabilities (Walsh, Rice, & Rosen, 1996).

Schools must work to improve the educational achievement of students with disabilities.

Although impressive improvements have been made, challenges still remain. Too many children are being served without the supports they need to succeed; too many young people, particularly those identified with learning disabilities and emotional disturbance, are dropping out of school. Children of color, and those from non–English-speaking backgrounds, are still being over-identified, stigmatized, and misserved. Too many teachers are inadequately prepared to serve children with complex teaching and learning needs. Our problems in special education remain daunting, despite our progress.

But we cannot become discouraged. The hoped-for result of the changes and trends within special education and its related fields is not simply to extend opportunities and access to people with disabilities. It is to provide an improved overall quality of life. We have come a long way toward providing the rights guaranteed by our Constitution and Bill of Rights to people with disabilities, but there are still many goals we have yet to attain. Through reading this book and working with students with disabilities, we hope you will join us in our quest to reach those goals.

Summary

- Special education can be understood as providing an individualized educational program to meet a student's unique learning needs.
- When describing exceptional students, we distinguish between a disability (which refers to a student's condition) and a handicap (which refers to a limitation imposed by his or her environment). We also use people-first language, which decreases the negative impact of the labels that are used to categorize exceptional children in school.
- Exceptional children make up about 12 percent of the school-age population, but advances in their education have been made only recently. Despite pioneering work by early advocates and educators, it was not until the civil rights movement of the 1960s that significant movement toward full acceptance and participation in society by people with disabilities began.
- In 1975 Congress passed a law that revolutionized education for students with disabilities: that law is now known as IDEA, the Individuals with Disabilities Education Act. IDEA and the Americans with Disabilities Act, passed in 1990, guarantee people with disabilities specific educational and civil rights. Among the most important are the individualized education program and the continuum of educational settings ranging from the least to the most restrictive environment.
- Progress has also been made through litigation. Cases such as *Diana v. Board of Education* and *Larry P. v. Riles* challenged the disproportionate representation of students from minority groups in special education.
- Special education professionals continue to be concerned about the disproportionate representation of students from culturally diverse backgrounds in special education services.
- The options for educational settings for students with disabilities include regular classrooms, resource rooms, special classes, special schools, residential schools, or other placements such as home or hospital.

Key Terms

exceptional
disability
handicap
people-first language
early intervention
at risk
special education
Jean-Marc-Gaspard Itard
Edouard Seguin
Maria Montessori
Samuel Gridley Howe
Thomas Hopkins Gallaudet
Laurent Clerc
Alexander Graham Bell
Anne Sullivan Macy
normalization
deinstitutionalization
mainstreaming
inclusion
least restrictive environment
Individuals with Disabilities Education Act (IDEA)
overrepresentation
underrepresentation
individualized family service plan (IFSP)
individualized education program (IEP)
individualized transition plan (ITP)
collaboration
team teaching
student support team
prereferral intervention team
pullout programs
consultation model

Multimedia Resources

Anderson, W., S. Chitwood, and D. Hayden. *Negotiating the Special Education Maze* (3rd ed.) (Bethesda, MD: Woodbine House, 1997). A guide to help parents and teachers understand the special education system.

Carballo, Julie B., et al. *Survival Guide for the First-Year Special Education Teacher, Revised* (Reston, VA: Council for Exceptional Children, 1994). Developed by special education teachers who survived their first five years, this guide offers tips on many aspects of teaching, from organizing your classroom to managing stress.

Council for Exceptional Children (CEC) website: http://www.cec.org. CEC is the major professional organization in special education, serving children with disabilities through their families, teachers, and other advocates.

Council for Exceptional Children. *IEP Team Guide, 1999.* This book reviews federal mandates for the IEP and walks the participant through the IEP process.

Getskow, Veronica, and Dee Konczal. *Kids with Special Needs: Information and Activities to Promote Awareness and Understanding* (Santa Barbara, CA: The Learning Works, 1996). This is a guide to promoting awareness and knowledge of childhood disability among children, teachers, and parents. It contains valuable suggestions for classroom activities aimed at nondisabled children.

IDEA Practices is a website that provides information and support for implementing IDEA. Visit http://www.ideapractices.org/.

"Lessons for All." To commemorate the twenty-fifth anniversary of the 1975 passage of IDEA, the federal Office of Special Education and Rehabilitation Services (OSERS) launched its new "Lessons for All" IDEA twenty-fifth anniversary site. It offers information on the history of the act and its impact on improving results for infants, toddlers, children, and youth with disabilities; links to IDEA-funded resources; stories from students and community members who have benefited from IDEA; and related news and events. Visit http://www.ed.gov/offices/OSERS/IDEA25th or http://www.ed.gov/offices/OSERS/OSEP/index.html#Publications/.

National Information Center for Handicapped Children and Youth (NICHCY) website: http://www.nichcy.org. NICHCY is a treasure trove of information about children with disabilities and their educational needs, for teachers and families.

The Office of Special Education and Rehabilitation Services (OSERS) within the U.S. Department of Education has published *A Guide to the Individualized Education Program.* Its purpose is to assist educators, parents, and state and local educational agencies in implementing the requirements of IDEA regarding individualized education programs (IEPs) for children with disabilities, including preschool-aged children. Visit http://www.ed.gov/offices/OSERS/OSEP/IEP_Guide/.

Special Ed News is an online newspaper that covers breaking news in grades Pre-K through 12. Visit http://www.specialednews.com/.

Teaching Exceptional Children, 29(5) (May/June 1997) (Seventy-fifth Anniversary Issue). This journal, published by the Council for Exceptional Children, has useful and timely articles for all teachers six times a year. This particular issue focuses on the history of special education in the United States.

What You Can Do

1. Begin a journal in which you reflect on your own attitudes and feelings toward people with disabilities. Which of your feelings are based on experiences, and which on media reports or stereotypes? What do you hope to learn from this course that might change your attitudes?

2. Visit a classroom setting where students with disabilities are served. How is it different from what you are used to? How is it similar? Perhaps you could spend time as a volunteer in such a setting.

3. Volunteer at a service agency that serves children with disabilities in the age range that interests you. Call your local United Way, March of Dimes, or children's hospital, and ask about volunteering opportunities.

4. How do people in your community refer to exceptional individuals? During the first few weeks of this semester, keep a file of newspaper clippings of articles that relate to exceptional individuals, special education, or related services. What types of issues are discussed? What types of language are used? What conclusions can you draw about the role of exceptional individuals in the community, their acceptance, and their visibility?

5. Observe media coverage of people with disabilities or issues important to them. Do newspapers and television newscasts cover these topics in a fair and unbiased manner? Write a letter to the editor suggesting more coverage or more positive coverage, perhaps concerning access, bias, aging, employment, or medical advances.

6. Invite a person with a disability to visit your class (with your instructor's permission) and tell his or her story.

Risk Factors and Early Intervention

2

IN THIS chapter, we introduce you to the factors and conditions that put children at risk for developmental disabilities. These factors can result in any of the specific disabilities that are discussed in later chapters, but a child may also have the experiences and resilience to overcome a risk without developmental delay. You will also learn what *early intervention* can do for young children and families. As you read, look for the answers to these questions:

Why is it important to identify children at risk?

How does early intervention work to prevent disability or to lessen its impact?

Commonalities: **Why is it important for all of us to value prevention and prenatal care?**

Collaboration: **How can teachers and early intervention specialists work with other professionals to minimize the effects of a child's risk status?**

Can Do: **What can be done to prevent disabilities?**

Happily, the great majority of pregnancies result in healthy babies. Yet each woman, each couple conceiving a child, also takes a chance that the child will develop differently from "the norm" and as a result have special needs that will require extra help and support at home and at school.

Many factors can place a child at risk for the development of a disability.

Why do some pregnancies produce children with special needs? Why do some children who have difficult starts in life do just fine, while others who begin life under ideal circumstances develop problems? The answers are complicated—many times no medical or psychological expert can answer them for

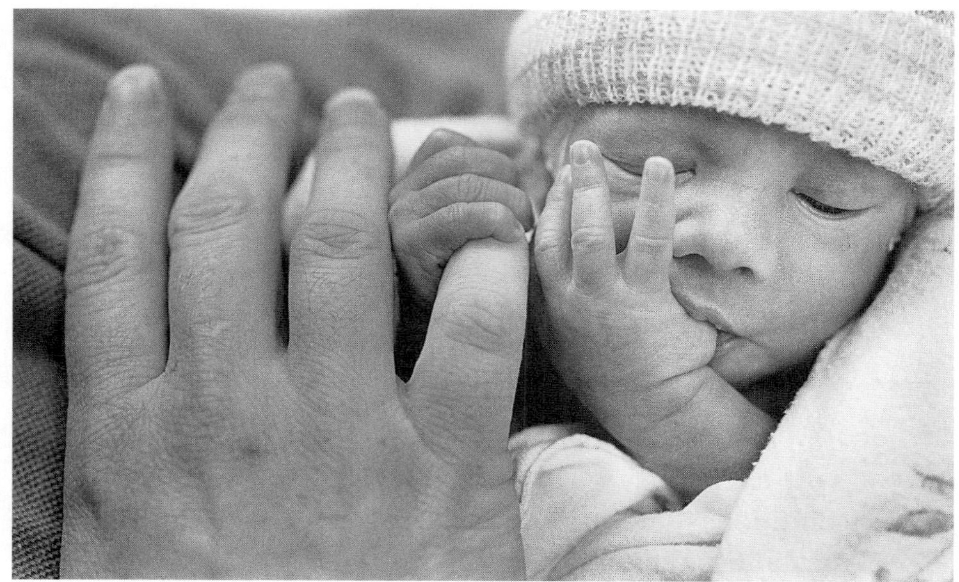

The great majority of pregnancies result in healthy babies, yet each woman who conceives a child takes a risk that her child will be different from the norm. (John Schoenwalter/ Jeroboam)

bewildered parents. But in this chapter we will describe some of the circumstances that place a child at risk for the development of a disability.

The information in this chapter should have meaning for you as a teacher or other professional working with exceptional children. First, it should help you decide whether the cause of a student's disability has any bearing on the kind of instruction or support you will provide. Second, it should help you give more complete information to family members who come to you for advice and counsel. This information will be relevant to each of the specific disabilities discussed later in the book. We encourage you to review this chapter as you learn about children with specific disabilities.

We must all help prevent disabilities in children.

We also expect that this information will have personal meaning for each reader. Some of you may be making decisions about whether or when to begin a family. Others may be watching your own children have children. We hope that the information presented here will help you to plan for a healthy family and to make intelligent, well-informed decisions that can enhance the possibilities for a healthy baby. Ultimately, the message of this chapter is that we can all have an impact on the prevention of disabilities in children. Each one of us has a responsibility to do whatever is within our power to *prevent* disabilities in the children of our country—and that is part of what this chapter is all about.

Definitions and Terms

The Individuals with Disabilities Education Act (IDEA) identifies three groups of children aged birth to 3 who may be eligible for early intervention services. They are:

- Children with developmental delay
- Children with a physical or mental condition that carries a high probability of developmental delay

- Children who are medically or environmentally *at risk* for developmental delay if early intervention is not provided

Let us look at how the term *risk* is used.

Psychologist and researcher Claire Kopp (1983) defined **risk factors** as "a wide range of *biological and environmental conditions* [emphasis added] that are associated with increased probability for cognitive, social, affective, and physical problems" (p. 1). Biological conditions generally arise from factors related to pregnancy or maternal and child health, such as low birthweight, exposure to drugs or toxic substances, or a chromosomal abnormality. Environmental conditions include negative influences in the child's physical or social surroundings after birth, such as extreme poverty, child abuse, or neglect.

Risk factors are biological or environmental conditions associated with cognitive, social, affective, and physical problems.

The second part of Kopp's definition contains a crucial concept. These conditions are *associated with increased probability* for a variety of later problems. It is more probable that these adverse outcomes will occur if there are risk factors present—but the presence of one or more risk factors *does not guarantee* developmental problems in children. Children may be at risk for developmental problems, but they will not necessarily have them. The severity of the risk factor as well as the nature of the environment in which each child grows will determine whether developmental problems will occur.

Some children overcome both biological and environmental hurdles and, because of their own characteristics and the outside support that they receive, emerge as strong and productive adults. We refer to these children as especially *resilient.* You will see, however, that the existence of clusters or combinations of risk factors makes it more likely that developmental problems will occur and that *early intervention*—comprehensive, individualized services provided to children from birth to age 3 and their families—can have a significant impact on a child's development.

The presence of risk factors increases the probability of adverse outcomes but does not guarantee them.

Types of Risk

Since the concept of risk is wide-ranging, it is helpful to have a framework within which categories of vulnerable infants can be described. We will use the categories of **biological risk** and **environmental risk** to describe the potential impact of specific factors on young children (see Fig. 2.1).

Biological Risk

Biological risk exists when events occur before, during, or after birth that may be associated with damage to the child's developing systems, increasing the likelihood that he or she will experience developmental problems. Biological risk factors can be divided into three categories that correspond with the earliest periods of development (Kopp, 1983): the **prenatal** period, from conception to birth; the **perinatal period** (which overlaps the prenatal period somewhat), from the twelfth week of pregnancy through the twenty-eighth day of life (Gorski & VandenBerg, 1996); and the **postnatal** period, covering events of early childhood that occur after the twenty-eighth day of life.

Biological risk exists when prenatal, perinatal, or postnatal events increase the likelihood that the child will experience developmental problems.

■ ***Prenatal Factors*** Prenatal factors are those that affect embryologic and fetal development before birth. Adverse prenatal events often account for the most severe developmental outcomes among the infants who survive them. If

Risk Factors and Early Intervention

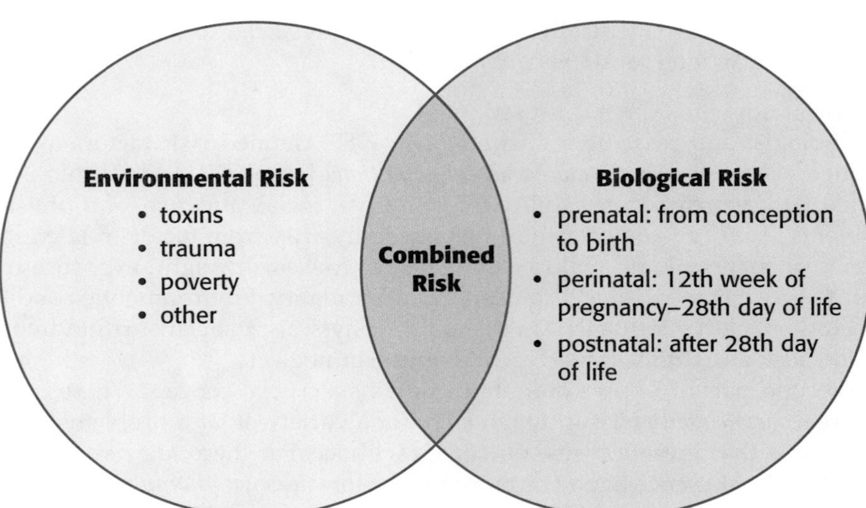

Figure 2.1
Types of Risk

they have their impact during the **first trimester** (first three months) of pregnancy, they may compromise the organs and body parts developing at that time; if they occur later in pregnancy, they may affect the growth and differentiation of those organs that are still developing, such as the brain and central nervous system. Prenatal factors include maternal illnesses and maternal use and abuse of substances, including drugs and alcohol. These factors—alcohol, drugs, illnesses, infections, and so on—are often called **teratogens,** substances that can cause birth defects. We will discuss some of the most common factors that research tells us can affect embryologic and fetal development during pregnancy (see Fig. 2.2). The accompanying box, "Newborn Screening," discusses the benefits of routine screening of newborns for genetic diseases.

Teratogens are substances that can cause birth defects.

Maternal Illness and Infection Not every illness of the pregnant mother will affect her unborn child, but some illnesses and infections are known to have a devastating impact on embryologic and fetal development. **Rubella,** for example, sometimes called "German measles," is a highly contagious virus. Rubella is particularly damaging if contracted by a woman during the first sixteen weeks of pregnancy. It can result in blindness, deafness, heart malformation, and/or mental retardation in surviving infants, depending on the fetal organ developing at the time the rubella virus strikes. Moores (2001, p. 106) describes the impact of the virus:

Illness of the mother during pregnancy can cause damage to the developing fetus.

> If a pregnant woman contracts rubella, particularly during the first trimester (three months) of pregnancy, the virus may cross the placental barrier and attack the developing cells and structures of the fetus, killing or crippling the unborn child. The virus can kill growing cells, and it attacks tissues of the eye, ear, and other organs.

Fortunately, immunization against rubella (see the section of this chapter that discusses prevention) has virtually eliminated this disease as a cause of disability in the United States.

Cytomegalovirus (CMV) is currently the most common congenital infection in the United States (**congenital** refers to a condition the child is born with). Approximately 1–2 percent of all newborns are infected at birth. The virus can re-

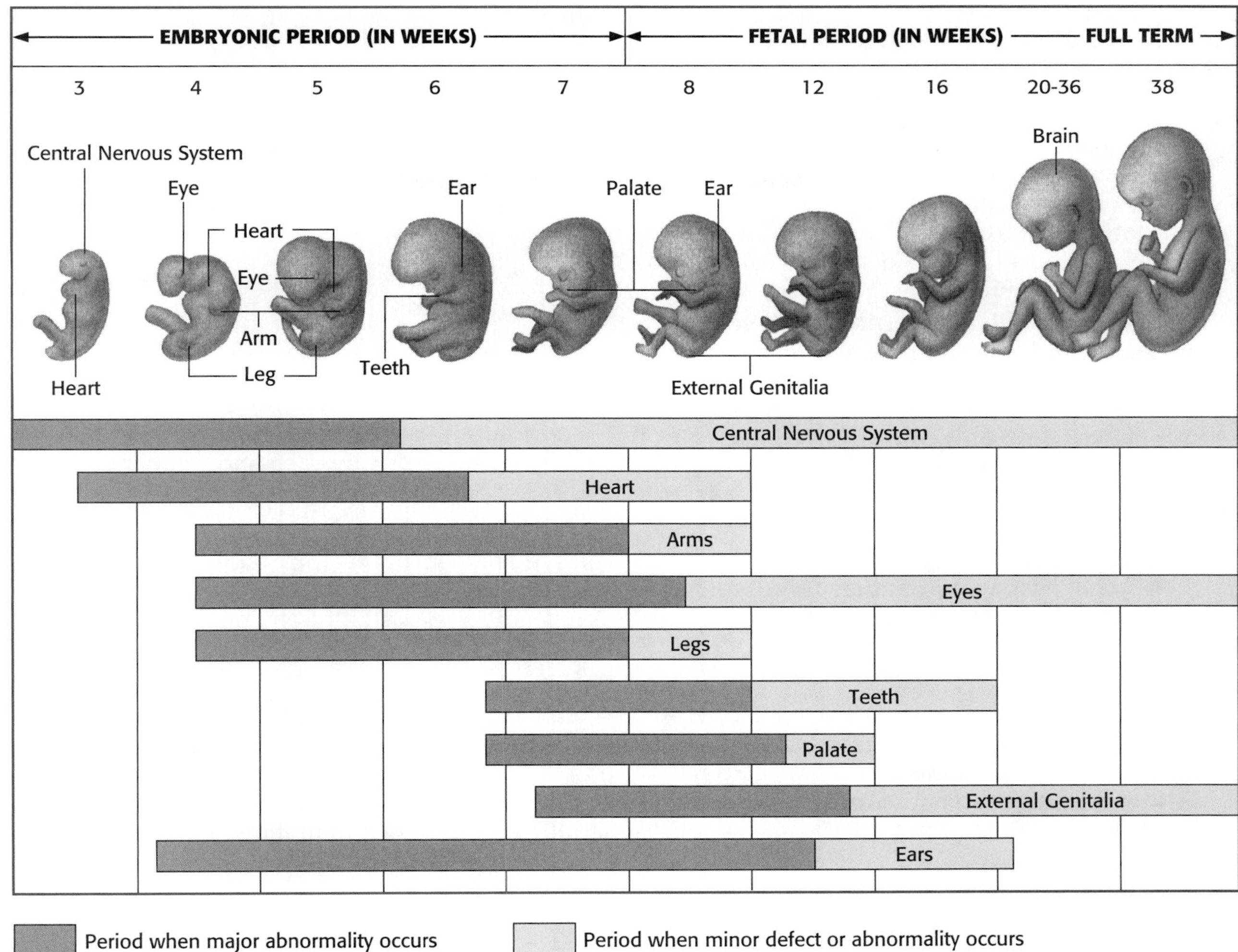

Figure 2.2
Sensitive Periods in Prenatal Development
Source: Adapted from *Before We Are Born,* Fifth Edition by K. L. Moore. Copyright © 1998. Used by permission of W. B. Saunders.

sult in the infant's death or in aftereffects such as mental retardation, vision and hearing loss, and learning disabilities, which may not manifest themselves until later in the child's life (Hutchinson & Sandall, 1995).

When STDs are identified and treated during the first trimester of pregnancy, harm to the fetus can be avoided.

Sexually transmitted diseases (STDs) affect a mother and her partner and can have serious implications for the child. The term "STD" denotes the more than twenty-five infectious organisms that are transmitted through sexual activity. Active infection with STDs during pregnancy may result in a range of serious health problems among infected infants, including severe central nervous system damage and death (Eng & Butler, 1997). For example, a mother with syphilis may have a child with congenital syphilis, which can result in death or severe mental retardation, deafness, and blindness. If the illness is identified during the first trimester of pregnancy, harm to the fetus can be avoided, but many infants with congenital syphilis are born to women who receive no

~ Newborn Screening

Hospitals across the United States take a blood sample from the heel of each newborn baby and test the blood for the presence of phenylketonuria (PKU), a metabolic disorder which, when left untreated, can cause mental retardation. More than forty states also screen for sickle cell disease, forty-eight screen for galactosemia, and over half the states require all newborns to be screened for hearing loss. Now there is the possibility of identifying an even wider range of potentially treatable diseases and genetic and metabolic disorders at birth—toxoplasmosis, maple syrup urine disease, propionic academia, cystic fibrosis, HIV, and many others—but hospitals and states are arguing over the necessity for such programs.

Why not just screen babies for all identifiable disorders at birth? Fern Potvin in *Exceptional Parent* lists the reasons:

- *Problems with the testing methodology.* Although there are still issues with screening methodologies, *tandem mass spectrometry* is an extremely sensitive new tool that can test for many disorders.
- *Difficulty providing necessary follow-up and counseling.* Once a disorder has been identified, families must be located for counseling and treatment.
- *No available treatment.* Not every disorder can be treated or cured.
- *Limited resources.* Testing is expensive, as is training and hiring new personnel.
- *Rarity of the diseases.* The incidence of these conditions is very low (for example, homocystinuria, a metabolic disorder, occurs about once in every 150,000 live births) and varies by race and ethnicity.

The inconsistency of screening procedures from state to state can cause problems for families. For example, Mubashir Younis was identified with propionic academia (PA) at birth in Massachusetts; he is now receiving treatment and is doing quite well. But Jordan Franks was born in Illinois, where PA is not screened for; he had a metabolic crisis at four days of age that might have been avoided had PA been identified at birth (Stagni, 2000).

The *Newborn Screening Task Force* report (2000) recommends that families should be

prenatal care. Herpes, another STD, has symptoms such as cold sores and vaginal infections. Although the risk of transmitting herpes to an unborn child is relatively low, if transmission does occur during a vaginal delivery it can have severe consequences for the infant, such as neurological, vision, and hearing impairment (Hutchinson & Sandall, 1995). Other STDs, including chlamydia, can also affect fetal development and the health of the newborn. STDs are a particular risk for adolescents (Eng & Butler, 1997).

AIDS and HIV can be transmitted during pregnancy, birth, and breastfeeding.

About 25 percent of U.S. women who have **acquired immune deficiency syndrome (AIDS),** or those who test positive for the human immunodeficiency virus (HIV) transmit HIV infection to their offspring during pregnancy, birth, or breastfeeding. Treatment with drug therapy during pregnancy can reduce the transmission rate to 8 percent (Lindegren, Steinberg, & Byers, 2000), so prenatal care is crucial for women with HIV/AIDS and their children. AIDS weakens the immune system and ultimately results in death. Since HIV infection can cause central nervous system damage in children, children who are HIV positive may experience significant developmental difficulties. Improvements in treatments for infants and children with HIV appear to be lessening the severity of early appearing symptoms (Abuzaitoun & Hanson, 2000), but children with HIV or AIDS in its more severe forms will qualify for special education services. Those

educated about newborn screening and be involved in informed decision-making from the outset. Once a condition has been diagnosed, they should be made aware of the short- and long-term characteristics of the condition, treatment goals, and the health-care and social service resources that are available. Newborn screening can save lives and prevent illness and disability, but it comes with the responsibility of education and follow-up treatment.

Some recommendations:

- Families should be educated about newborn screening. Information should be provided before birth or after birth. Information should be provided during the follow-up process if the initial screening test is positive.
- The family should be involved in informed decision-making beginning with the initiation of newborn screening through the initial screening test, the confirmatory testing, and the enrollment in therapeutic interventions.
- Patient educational materials should be developed and reviewed in conjunction with families, be assessed for literacy levels, and reflect cultural competency.
- Families should receive information and counseling so that they are aware of the diagnosed condition, the potential associated co-morbidities, the short- and long-range treatment goals and interventions, and the availability of health-care resources, including primary care health professionals, pediatric subspecialty consultants, genetic counselors, and state financial case management and assistance programs.
- Affected individuals and families should be involved in newborn screening program oversight advisory boards, and review committees.

Sources: Newborn Screening Task Force (2000), Newborn screening: A blueprint for the future. *Exceptional Parent,* October, pp. 69–73; F.R. Potvin (2000), Newborn screening: Testing for disorders at birth. *Exceptional Parent,* October, pp. 90–93; and K. Stagni (2000). Newborn screening and parent support groups. *Exceptional Parent,* October, pp. 66–68.

services should focus on enhancing the quality of life for eligible children and their caregiving families (Boland, 2000).

The incidence of AIDS is rapidly increasing among women and children all over the world. In the United States, women infected with HIV are more likely to be young, poor, and urban (Lindegren, Steinberg, & Byers, 2000), and therefore their children may be subject to multiple biological and environmental risk factors. Black and Hispanic women have particularly high rates of the disease. Lindegren and her colleagues warn that "despite encouraging evidence of increased survival because of effective therapies, transmission is ongoing, and young women are especially at risk" (p. 2). The accompanying box, "Education of Children with HIV Infection," provides recommendations. You will read more about HIV/AIDS in Chapter 12.

Maternal Substance Abuse Maternal drug use during pregnancy continues to generate great concern among professionals, politicians, and the general public. Doctors recommend that even the most common legal drugs, whether they are over-the-counter or prescription, should not be taken by pregnant women or be taken only with a doctor's recommendation. Many over-the-counter or prescription drugs have been associated with birth defects, particularly congenital

~ Education of Children with HIV Infection

As treatment for children with HIV improves, they are more likely to attend school and participate in school activities. The majority of children with HIV reaching school age will have normal cognitive function. The American Academy of Pediatrics makes the following recommendations for the education of children with HIV.

Recommendations

1. All children and youths with HIV infection should have the same right as those without infection to attend school and receive high-quality educational services.
2. Children and youths with HIV infection should have access to special education and other related services in accord with their needs as the disease progresses.
3. Mechanisms for administration of medications, including confidential methods for HIV infection, should be in place in all schools. This includes appropriate facilitation of specific needs for fluids or bathroom privileges.
4. Continuity of education must be ensured for children and adolescents with HIV infection and encompasses the spectrum of traditional school, medical day treatment programs, and home schooling.
5. Confidentiality of HIV infection status should be respected and maintained, with disclosure given only with the consent of the parent(s) or legal guardian(s) and age-appropriate assent of the student.
6. The pediatrician/medical home providers should maintain appropriate communication with the school to facilitate the education of children in their care.

For the complete Policy Statement, see http://www.aap.org/policy/re9950.html.

malformations such as heart defects, ear damage, and cleft lip and palate (Dixson, 1989); the effects of others on the developing fetus have not been adequately investigated by researchers.

The thalidomide tragedy of the 1950s demonstrated that great care must be taken with all drugs during pregnancy.

The caution of medical professionals about over-the-counter and prescription drugs comes in part from the experience of many Europeans with **thalidomide** in the late 1950s. Thalidomide was prescribed to pregnant women for nausea; over time it was learned that taking it during the first trimester of pregnancy caused shortened or missing arms and legs in the child (Graham & Morgan, 1997). The thalidomide experience taught medical researchers and practitioners that great care is needed with drug ingestion during pregnancy.

Polysubstance abusers are those who use a combination of drugs as well as alcohol.

The long-term effects of illegal drug use during pregnancy are only beginning to be known. Babies of mothers who have used cocaine, heroin or methadone, marijuana, PCP, or amphetamines (substance-abusing mothers who use combinations of drugs as well as alcohol are referred to as **polysubstance abusers**) appear to be at significant short-term risk and may be particularly vulnerable to the effects of an unstable environment.

Cocaine and marijuana are currently the drugs most commonly used by women of childbearing age (Widerstrom & Nickel, 1997). Babies prenatally exposed to cocaine are more likely to be born early and to have a low birthweight and a smaller head circumference. Some research indicates that they are also more likely to have congenital malformations, to die during the perinatal period, and to die of sudden infant death syndrome (SIDS) during the first year of life (Myers, Olson, & Kaltenbach, 1992).

The long-term effects of exposure to illicit drugs on development remain unclear, but most researchers agree that preschool and school-aged children who were exposed to drugs in utero are at risk for developmental lags, language disorders, and emotional, behavioral, and attentional difficulties (Jansson & Velez, 1999). In addition, substance abuse significantly affects the family environment; more than half the women who are dependent on cocaine, for example, will experience physical abuse, STDs, or separation from their children by imprisonment (Richardson & Day, 1994). Mothers who continue as substance abusers may neglect the most basic needs of their infants (Jansson & Velez, 1999). It appears that the substance-exposed children who are most likely to develop problems in life are those who also experience additional risk factors, such as family instability and absence of medical care. Since these outcomes are so variable, we can do these children and their families a service by avoiding the use of sensationalized labels that may become self-fulfilling prophecies. Think next time you hear the term *drug baby*—is it fair to the child to make assumptions about what that will mean?

The long-term effects of illicit drug exposure on the child are difficult to predict.

Maternal alcohol intake during pregnancy can have grave effects on the developing fetus. Most seriously for surviving children, it can result in **fetal alcohol syndrome (FAS).** The child with FAS has altered facial features, such as a small head, widely spaced eyes, upturned nose, large ears, and a small chin; he or she will also have developmental delays in language and cognition and may have behavior problems such as oppositional and defiant behavior, poor judgment, and social withdrawal (Batshaw & Conlon, 1997). Some children have the cognitive and behavioral characteristics associated with FAS but not the physical abnormalities; they are said to have **fetal alcohol effects (FAE).** Alcohol-related birth defects (FAS and FAE) occur in about 1 in 200 births worldwide, making them one of the leading causes of mental retardation today (Batshaw & Conlon,

Maternal alcohol use during pregnancy can result in fetal alcohol syndrome or fetal alcohol effects.

Fetal alcohol syndrome results in specific physical characteristics along with behavioral and cognitive deficits. (George Steinmetz)

1997). Although not all offspring of women who drink alcohol experience these significant aftereffects, researchers have not identified a "safe" level of alcohol intake during pregnancy. As a result, doctors now recommend that pregnant women drink no alcohol at all.

Smoking can result in pregnancy complications as well as low birthweight and physical abnormalities in the infant.

Prenatal exposure to tobacco also has a serious impact on the developing fetus. Maternal cigarette smoking during pregnancy is the single most important cause of low birthweight (Shiono & Behrman, 1995); pregnant women who smoke have a relatively high number of pregnancy complications that can result in perinatal loss, premature delivery, and physical abnormalities. Studies of the long-term effects of smoking during pregnancy on child development are inconclusive, but it is clear that maternal smoking results in more colds, asthma, other respiratory problems, and middle-ear infections for children (Cook, Petersen, & Moore, 1990).

Young mothers and older mothers are at risk for different pregnancy complications.

Extremes of Maternal Age Mothers at the beginning and at the end of their reproductive span are at the greatest risk for potential pregnancy problems. Young mothers, particularly those in the earliest teenage years, are more likely to have pregnancy complications resulting in prematurity or low birthweight, as well as other medical complications that could endanger the life and health of their babies (Smith, 1994). Among the biological factors that place the infants of adolescent mothers at risk are poor maternal nutrition, small maternal size, and, most important, limited access to prenatal care (Meisels & Wasik, 1990). The children of very young mothers are also considered at risk because of characteristics of their caregiving environment.

Older mothers may present a different set of problems. They are more likely to have a child with **Down syndrome,** a condition caused by an extra twenty-first chromosome that results in mental retardation and physical anomalies in the child (see Table 2.1). Since the older a mother is, the more likely she is to have a baby with Down syndrome, the American Medical Association recommends that pregnant women aged 35 and older undergo amniocentesis or other prenatal testing. We will discuss prenatal testing procedures later in the chapter in the section on prevention of disabilities.

Women over 35 are also more likely to have health problems such as diabetes and high blood pressure, which can complicate a pregnancy. Older mothers, however, are also more likely to have access to early and consistent prenatal

Table 2.1 Maternal Age and the Risk of Having a Baby with Down Syndrome

Age of Mother	At any Pregnancy	After a Previous Baby with Down Syndrome
29 or below	1 in 1,000	1 in 100
30–34	1 in 600	1 in 100
35–39	1 in 200	1 in 100
40–44	1 in 65	1 in 25
45–49	1 in 25	1 in 15

Source: From Matson, J. L. and Mulick, J. A., *Handbook of Mental Retardation*, Second Edition. Copyright © 1991 by Allyn & Bacon. Reprinted/adapted by permission.

medical care, and, given such care, many potential pregnancy complications can be managed, and a healthy baby is born. Early and ongoing prenatal care can minimize the effects of maternal age.

The perinatal period ranges from the twelfth week of pregnancy to the twenty-eighth day of life.

■ ***Perinatal Factors*** Perinatal factors are those that occur from the twelfth week of pregnancy to the twenty-eighth day of infant life. It is here that medical research and technology have had a profound impact on both the survival and the quality of life of small and sick babies. Nevertheless, perinatal stresses still increase the risk status and, at times, call for special treatment and follow-up (Keogh, Wilcoxen, & Bernheimer, 1986).

Oxygen Deprivation For a variety of reasons during pregnancy, labor, delivery, and newborn life, the infant can experience **hypoxia,** or a decreased availability of oxygen in the body tissues. Hypoxia can cause cells in the brain to die, resulting in brain damage and sometimes death. The long-term effects of oxygen deprivation can be severe or minimal, but among the disabling conditions associated with prolonged hypoxia are cerebral palsy, mental retardation, seizures, visual and auditory deficits, and behavior problems. Most affected infants, however, experience mild episodes of hypoxia and therefore do not develop disabilities (Robertson & Finer, 1993).

Premature babies are born before thirty-seven weeks' gestation; low birthweight babies weigh less than five and a half pounds.

Prematurity and Low Birthweight The average length of pregnancy, or gestation, is forty weeks. Babies born before thirty-seven weeks' gestation are called **premature,** or **preterm.** Although the timing of a birth is important, the baby's weight may be even more crucial. Babies born weighing less than about five and a half pounds (2500 grams) are said to be **low birthweight.** Even full-term babies can be low birthweight; thus, prematurity and low birthweight can be independent of one another. Think of it this way: A premature baby, born at thirty-four weeks' gestation, might already weigh six pounds; a baby born on her "due date" might weigh only four pounds.

Some of the conditions that have been associated with prematurity in the research literature are lack of prenatal care, the mother's prepregnancy health and illness during pregnancy, her nutritional status before pregnancy and weight gain during pregnancy, her age, height, and weight, smoking, use of drugs, uterine and cervical problems, social class, ethnic group membership, multiple births, and geography (Bernbaum & Batshaw, 1997; Kopp, 1983). Women who are poor and young are in particular danger of delivering prematurely; they are also more likely to receive little or no prenatal care and to be undernourished (Paneth, 1995; Scholl, Hediger, & Belsky, 1994).

What are the dangers of premature birth? Premature babies are more likely to be low birthweight, and the lower the birthweight, the more likely a baby will have serious complications or die. Premature babies' systems are sometimes not ready to function independently; the babies need to gain weight but often have not developed the ability to coordinate sucking and swallowing, and their intestines are not yet ready to digest food normally, so feeding and weight gain are complicated; and their immature immune systems make them very vulnerable to infection. In addition, the lower the birthweight, the more likely it is that the baby will develop complications of prematurity, such as respiratory distress syndrome (extreme difficulty in breathing), brain hemorrhage (bleeding), and retinopathy of prematurity (an eye condition that can lead to blindness), which place their long-term development at risk.

Risk Factors and Early Intervention

Advances in neonatology and high-risk infant care have ensured the survival of many low birthweight babies.

Advances in **neonatology,** the study of newborns, have dramatically changed the prognosis for even the tiniest surviving premature babies. The specialized care given to these fragile infants in the **neonatal intensive care unit,** the area of the hospital that provides care for sick and premature newborns, has ensured the survival of many babies who, even a few years ago, would have died. Until recently, babies weighing three and a half pounds and under (now called very low birthweight) routinely died; now most are routinely saved. The limits of survival have changed dramatically over the last few years; currently, the majority of infants born at twenty-four or more weeks' gestational age survive. Most of those babies weigh less than two pounds; the smallest survivors weigh around one pound. New drugs that successfully treat respiratory distress syndrome are helping to increase those numbers (Shiono & Behrman, 1995). However, premature babies are much more likely than full-term babies to have conditions such as cerebral palsy, mental retardation, seizures, and vision and hearing impairments.

The number of premature survivors with disabling conditions increases as the birthweight drops. Current research suggests that from 10 to 30 percent of very low birthweight babies who survive are chronically ill or disabled. Their disabilities range from school learning problems, particularly those related to hyperactivity and attention, to severe disabilities (Hack & Fanaroff, 2000; Saigal, 2000).

Diseases like meningitis and conditions like chronic otitis media can result in disabilities that affect school performance.

■ ***Postnatal Factors*** Among the postnatal biological factors of early childhood that place a child at risk for school learning problems are *chronic diseases and infections* and *severe nutritional deficiencies.* Chronic diseases like asthma or juvenile arthritis may cause the child to miss too many school days or may have more serious consequences, as we will discuss in Chapter 10. Infections of childhood like **meningitis** that are accompanied by a high fever can also cause damage to the brain, resulting in a range of disabling conditions such as hearing and vision loss and mental retardation. Conditions like **chronic otitis media,** the most serious form of the middle-ear infections so common in early childhood, can have subtle but important effects on language learning and later school performance (Medley, Roberts, & Zeisel, 1995).

In the United States, nutritional deprivation is usually associated with extreme poverty, and it is difficult to separate the effects of poor nutrition from the other deprivations of poverty (Kopp, 1983). In many Third World countries, however, there is dramatic evidence that malnutrition alters brain development in children. There is little doubt that chronic poor nutrition can cause learning problems in school.

Environmental Risk

Environmental risk includes all the risk factors related to the environment in which the child develops.

The second risk category that we will examine, environmental risk, includes risk factors related to the environment in which the child develops (Garbarino, 1990; Sameroff & Chandler, 1975). Environmental factors can influence development at any stage; our discussion will first refer to prenatal events that may affect the environment of the mother before birth.

■ ***Environmental Factors That Influence Prenatal Development*** Studies from Hiroshima and Nagasaki, as well as ongoing observation of the aftereffects of the fire at the nuclear reactor at Chernobyl, suggest a strong relationship between exposure to radiation in pregnant women and such birth defects in their offspring as mental and growth retardation and congenital malformations (Dixson, 1989). The effects of radiation depend on the distance from the source, the intensity of the source, and the time during pregnancy of the exposure (Graham & Morgan, 1997). Although the diagnostic x-rays that would most commonly be experienced by pregnant women are rarely strong enough to harm the fetus, exposure to any form of radiation during pregnancy should be avoided because of the increased risk of childhood cancer for the fetus (Dixson, 1989).

Since many women today continue to work during pregnancy, they must consider the **occupational hazards** associated with some workplaces. Some occupations expose workers to low levels of radiation, and others expose them to low levels of lead and mercury. Exposure to these and other substances has been linked to reproductive loss and birth defects (Sparks, 1984).

Traditionally, physicians and researchers have looked to mothers as the source of risk in their children, but some recent research has attempted to identify the role of the father in contributing to biological risk (American College of Medical Genetics, 1996). Older fathers account for a small percentage of all cases of Down syndrome (Skinner, 1990). Also, investigations of exposure to toxic substances in the environment have intensified because of the conviction of many veterans of the Vietnam War that their exposure to the defoliant Agent Orange increased the number of birth defects such as spina bifida and the incidence of childhood cancer in their offspring. See the "First Person" box later in the chapter for more on this.

■ ***Postnatal Environmental Factors*** The characteristics of the child's immediate caregiving environment are vital to optimal development. That environment must provide protection from exposure to dangerous toxins and disease as well as opportunities for learning and social growth and a stable home and family. We'll look at each of these areas.

Most researchers agree that the results of adverse biological risk events can be exaggerated or improved upon by the characteristics of the environment. For example, although AIDS is classified as a biological risk factor and occurs in all sectors of our population, it is more likely to occur among those living in poverty. Children who are "at risk" develop as they do because of a complex interaction between their risk history and their caregiving environments.

Other agents within our environment can cause problems for children that may affect their school learning. Some of these, such as exposure to radiation and toxic chemicals, we are aware of, although hard data verifying the effects of these substances on the developing nervous system in children are difficult to come by.

Lead One substance scientists are learning more about is lead. There are at least 2 million homes in the United States where lead-paint-covered surfaces are chalking and flaking, and almost every child in such a home has elevated levels of lead in the blood (Needleman, 1992). Although poverty significantly increases the risk of lead exposure, excessively high levels of lead are found in children of all social classes and racial backgrounds. African American children living in poverty are at greatest risk: 55 percent have elevated lead levels (Agency for Toxic Substances and Disease Registry, 1995).

Early exposure to lead is associated with a greater likelihood of school problems.

Children with high lead levels have decreased IQ scores and poorer language and attention skills; their teachers find them more distractible and less well organized and persistent (Needleman et al., 1979). Long-term follow-

Dao My and His Family: Environmental Risk in Vietnam

Hanoi—Not until he was dying did Dao My tell his family his secret of the war. His voice was faint and raspy, and the gaunt face bore little resemblance to that of the smiling man who, in a photograph on the bedside table, wore the uniform of a North Vietnamese colonel and a chestful of medals.

"There is Agent Orange in my body," his wife remembers him saying.

"And in yours," he added, nodding to his two handicapped sons. "I have seen doctors. There are no drugs, no cures. It is time you understand this, and perhaps I should not have waited so many years to tell you."

My was 62 when he died two years ago. He had diabetes, a bad heart, itchy skin, respiratory problems—the result, his wife believes, of his exposure to chemical defoliants sprayed by the United States over Vietnam's southern jungles, where he fought for six years. She cites their five children as evidence: The three born before My went south are normal; the two after Agent Orange entered his blood are severely disabled, mentally and physically.

His wife, Nguyen Thi Nhan, 67, who lives on a $14-a-month pension and cares for her two sons, now 29 and 27, smiles today, remembering the joy she felt when My, home from the war, appeared unexpectedly at her door in 1975. She had not seen him or heard a word about him in three years.

"He said, 'Get some food for a party,'" she recalled. "But all I could manage was crab chowder. No beer. No wine. It was wartime." She sighed quietly. "In Hanoi, it was always wartime."

up of these children indicates that early lead exposure is associated with a substantially elevated likelihood of having a reading disability and dropping out of school (Needleman et al., 1991).

There are, no doubt, other substances within our environment that cause damage to the developing nervous system in children that have not yet been identified. Many of the causes of childhood learning problems, as we shall see in future chapters, are unknown.

Accidents Accidents of all kinds are examples of environmental risks. Car accidents are the most common, but accidents may also happen on bikes, in swimming pools, and anywhere else that active, curious young children play and

Hanoi, basking in a generation of peace, is now a prosperous place, its markets bountifully supplied. But the legacy of war lingers.

Families in Vietnam search for 300,000 soldiers still listed as missing in action. Mines laid three decades ago still explode, killing farmers and children. Deformed, disabled kids known as "Agent Orange babies" are still born in large numbers. And studies on the people most affected by chemical defoliants used in the war lag far behind those done on U.S. servicemen who became victims.

"Agent Orange is our most important problem remaining from the war," said Nguyen Van Hoi, director of the state's War Aftermath Division. "It is a bigger problem than the mines, bigger than the number of handicapped from the war. It is getting more and more serious, and it is something we need scientific and financial support to solve."

For a long time Vietnam remained relatively silent about the problems created by Agent Orange, a defoliant named for the color of the band around the barrels in which the chemical was stored. Though Hanoi did study its effects and hold seminars on the use of herbicides in war, it never directly raised the issue with visiting groups of U.S. officials or veterans.

"I asked the foreign affairs ministry a couple of years ago why," a U.S. veteran said, "and their reply was that relations with the United States were slowly normalizing, and it wouldn't have been constructive."

But in the last several months, with normal relations realized and a U.S. ambassador now in residence, Vietnam has taken Agent Orange out of the closet.

Articles about its continuing effects are printed almost daily in state-run newspapers, and officials never miss an opportunity to raise the issue with visiting U.S. delegations—partly as a counterweight to Americans who always bring up U.S. MIAs. Vietnam has kept discussions free of political rhetoric and has not mentioned compensation.

explore. Accidents that involve head trauma, oxygen deprivation, or spinal cord injury can cause severe physical disability as well as learning and behavior problems. Caregivers must be extremely watchful and observant of their children's play areas and their risks.

Accidents are the most common postnatal risk factor.

The characteristics of the social environment are also crucial for optimal development: the nature of the medical technology available to support a sick newborn or child, the availability of public health services in the community, and the emphasis on educational achievement within the society as a whole. The next part of our discussion of environmental risk concentrates on the social aspects of poverty and family issues. You will see, however, that there is a great deal of overlap among these areas, and they are often interrelated.

What it wants, the government says, is scientific help to research the precise depth of the problem and to find a solution.

Tran Van Dieu, 47, who served as an artillery gunner near Da Nang and has two mentally disabled sons, remembers the U.S. C-123 cargo planes that used to sweep low over the jungle-covered hills, trailing misty plumes of defoliants. Within a day or two the canopy of leaves would disappear, and in a few weeks a swath of jungle would be stripped bare of all living things.

"We thought of it as more a nuisance than a danger," Dieu said. "Our commanders gave us gas masks, but usually we threw them away. We'd just put wet scarves over our nose and mouth when the planes came.

"When you are a soldier, you expect to suffer. Soldiers on both sides suffered. So I don't hold the Americans responsible, but I wish someone would help solve my difficulties. My wife and I have to do everything for our boys, and that means I am home all day and cannot work."

Operation Ranch Hand, carried out from 1962 to 1971, was designed to destroy the camouflage jungle provided Communist supply routes and base camps—not to kill or maim. During that period, the U.S. dumped 12 million gallons of chemicals on South Vietnam, said to be the most used in any war. The chemicals destroyed 14 percent of South Vietnam's forests, according to official U.S. reports.

Generally the herbicides—the most prominent of which was Agent Orange—dissipated within weeks but left behind a toxic contaminant, dioxin, that was inadvertently created during the manufacturing process. Dioxin, Vietnamese officials say, remains to this day in the soil of regions that were heavily sprayed—and in the blood of soldiers and civilians who spent long periods in the areas.

Vietnam, which runs eleven hospices called "peace villages" for "Agent Orange babies," estimates that half a million people have died

Poverty—which can include both economic and social factors—is a major cause of environmental risk.

Poverty Biologically normal infants who live in poverty may be at risk for problems of development because of characteristics of their caregiving environment. Vonnie McLloyd (1998) identifies some of the risk factors associated with persistent poverty: higher rates of perinatal complications, reduced access to resources that might buffer the effects of those complications, increased exposure to lead, and less home-based cognitive stimulation. These inadequacies are more likely to exist in impoverished families—money *does* buy health care, food, and quality day care for working or absent parents—but they are by no means exclusive to poor families. The accompanying box, "Child Poverty in the United States," provides basic information.

or contracted serious illnesses over the years because of the chemical campaign. It says about 70,000 are still affected.

The United States has no official position on the effects of Agent Orange on the Vietnamese, with its diplomats saying only that more evidence is needed to prove a link between the chemicals and the birth of deformed babies. Vietnam believes that it has established the link beyond a reasonable doubt but acknowledges that its findings may fall short of what the international scientific community would accept as conclusive evidence.

Dioxin is found in people everywhere, in proportion to the industrialization in their countries, and scientists say it would be expensive and difficult at this late date to establish that Agent Orange—not the chemicals that farmers spray on their crops, or other factors—was responsible for deformities.

"To be frank, some American scientists question our findings," said Dr. Hoan Dinh Cau, chairman of the national committee researching the effects of Agent Orange. "But they don't say what we have found is not true. They just say more research is needed."

In 1978, Washington told Hanoi during talks aimed at mending relations that there were two subjects that would end the discussion immediately if they were even brought up. One was compensation to rebuild the North. The other was Agent Orange.

American servicemen—whose exposure to dioxin was measured in months, as opposed to years for many North Vietnamese soldiers—reached an out-of-court settlement in 1984 in their liability suit over generic effects and illnesses associated with Agent Orange. The seven manufacturers paid $180 million to establish a fund for the veterans, who number at least 180,000.

Source: David Lamb, "Vietnam Ends Silence on Issue of Wartime Exposure to Agent Orange." *Los Angeles Times,* September 26, 1998.

In the United States today one out of six children lives in poverty; a baby is born into poverty every 35 seconds, and child poverty rates are two to nine times as high as those in other industrialized nations (Children's Defense Fund, 2000). The children of poverty are more likely to die in childhood, to be in special education programs, and to drop out of school; the girls are more likely to become pregnant during adolescence and the boys to engage in criminal behavior. Figure 2.3 demonstrates that children who live below the poverty level are less likely to be in good health than those above the poverty line; they are also more likely to have limitations in their activity because of a chronic health condition (e.g., asthma or diabetes) (Health Indicators, 2000). Problems with physical health can affect the child's cognitive status (McLloyd, 1998).

~ Child Poverty in the United States

How many U.S. children are poor?

12.1 million in 1999—or one in six (16.9 percent).

Are there poor children in working families?

Yes, more than three out of four poor children (78 percent) live with a family member who worked at least part of the year, up from 61 percent just six years ago. One out of three poor children (3.8 million) lives in a household where someone is employed full-time year round. The proportion of poor families with children that were poor despite being headed by somebody who worked during the year 1999 is *the highest in the 25 years for which data exist.*

Are non-White children more likely to be poor?

Yes. More than one in three Black children (33.1 percent) and Hispanic children (30.3 percent) are poor in America, compared to 13.5 percent of White children and 11.8 percent of Asian and Pacific Islander children.

Are children in single-parent families more likely to be poor?

Yes. More than two out of five children in families headed by single women (42 percent) were poor in 1999. Only eight percent of children in married families were poor.

How many children get food stamps?

9.3 million in FY 1999. More than half of the people who get food stamps are children.

How many children get free or reduced-price school lunches?

15.4 million in FY 2000.

Source: Children's Defense Fund website, http://www.childrensdefense.org/fair-start-faqs.htm, February 1, 2001.

What is it about living in poverty that leads to poor outcomes for children? The obvious answer, lack of access to good medical care and nutrition, as well as to experiences and opportunities, is only partly right. Most of us can cite several examples of people who grew up in such circumstances who have reached significant levels of achievement in our society. Garbarino (1990) made the point that some families are economically impoverished but have a "socially rich family environment": family members, neighbors, and friends who provide support for both children and parents—the "informal helping relationships" that are the foundation of some communities. Other families are both economically and socially impoverished. According to Garbarino (1990, p. 90),

> These are the environments in which prenatal care is inadequate, intervals between births are often too short, beliefs about child care too often dysfunctional, access to and utilization of well-baby care inadequate, early intervention for child disabilities inadequate, and thus in which child mortality and morbidity are rampant.

These conditions are more likely to occur in our inner cities, where families must also live with the reality of frequent violence that respects no target—not even a small child. The stresses in such communities can become unbearable; neighbors may be afraid and distrustful of one another, and little sense of community may exist.

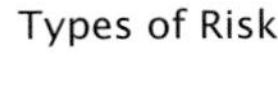

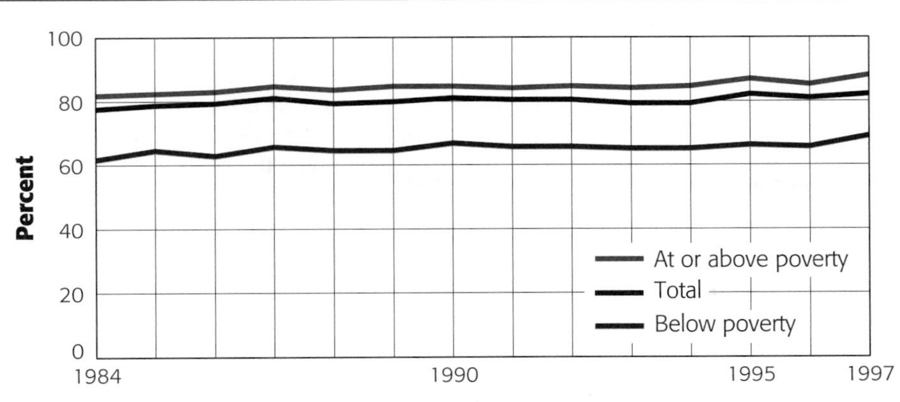

SOURCE: Centers for Disease Control and Prevention, National Center for Health Statistics, National Health Interview Survey.

- In 1997, about 81 percent of children were reported by their parents to be in very good or excellent health.
- Child health varies by family income. Children living below the poverty line are less likely than children in higher-income families to be in very good or excellent health. In 1997, about 68 percent of children in families below the poverty line were in very good or excellent health, compared with 86 percent of children in families living at or above the poverty line.
- The percentage of children in very good or excellent health remained stable between 1984 and 1997. The health gap between children below and those at or above the poverty line also did not change during the time period. Each year, children at or above the poverty line were about 20 percentage points more likely to be in very good or excellent health than children whose families were below poverty.

Figure 2.3
Percentage of Children under Age 19 in Very Good or Excellent Health, by Poverty Status, 1984 to 1987

Social impoverishment can occur at every economic level, but more affluent families can pay for supportive services when they are not available through friends and family. Many poor families, frequently headed by single mothers, are left with few resources to help with the considerable stresses of child-rearing.

Families come in all shapes, sizes, and configurations. We can no longer assume that a child will grow up in a traditional nuclear family, nor do we insist that there is one "right" way to raise children. We do know, however, that certain characteristics of the caregiving environment appear to help children develop optimally. Emotional and physical safety, responsive and sensitive caregivers, and stability of family members are all tied to the healthy development of children.

We will discuss issues related to families in the next chapter. But here it is important to describe two characteristics of families that place the child at risk: maltreatment and family instability.

Child abuse may be responsible for some cases of mental retardation, physical disability, and emotional disturbance in the United States today.

Child Maltreatment Child abuse and child neglect are grouped together under the term *maltreatment,* and reports of both are abundant in the United States today. Although hard economic times and high rates of unemployment no doubt increase the likelihood of child maltreatment (Garbarino, 1990), reports of the murder, abuse, and neglect of children are as old as recorded history and appear in all cultures.

Children with disabilities are overrepresented in samples of abused children, but it is difficult to determine how many children with disabilities are abused (Turnbull, Buchele-Ash, & Mitchell, 1994). Professionals suspect, however, that child abuse is responsible for a proportion of the cases of mental retardation, physical disability, and emotional disturbance in the United States today: One group estimates that over 18,000 children are seriously disabled every year as a result of abuse or neglect by parents or caregivers (U.S. Advisory Board on Child Abuse and Neglect, 1995).

Family Instability Although we now know that the two-parent family is not a necessary condition for optimal child growth and development, it does seem clear that children need at least one stable caregiver throughout their childhood in order to develop well (Werner & Smith, 1982). That caregiver may not be a parent; often, a grandmother or other relative can provide the ongoing stability a child needs. As developmental psychologist Urie Bronfenbrenner reminds us in his often-quoted statement, "The critical factor in a child's development is the active involvement of at least one adult who is simply crazy about the child" (1993, p. 47). Children who experience many changes in the adult makeup of the household appear to do less well in school (Hunt, 1982) and may be at greater risk for dropping out of school and engaging in criminal behavior.

Developmental problems most often stem from a combination of biological and environmental risk factors.

It is important to emphasize that the existence of one risk factor alone does not ensure developmental problems. Rather, those problems occur because of multiple risk factors, most often a combination of biological and environmental events.

Research on risk factors has shown us that children with some of the previously described biological risks, such as prematurity, are more vulnerable to environmental stresses than other children are. It is the combination of biological and environmental risk factors that places that developing child in jeopardy for future school problems.

Prevention

Fortunately, many steps can be taken to prevent or minimize the occurrence of risk factors and developmental problems in infants and children. Some of these steps can be taken for our children; some we can take ourselves; some are questions of public policy, and we can work within our political system to advocate for important changes (Simeonsson, 1994).

Major Strategies for Prevention

Inoculation, or vaccination against infectious diseases, is a prevention strategy that should be available to every child.

■ ***Inoculation*** **Inoculation**—vaccination against infectious diseases—starts in the first year of life and should continue through early childhood. Children are inoculated against diphtheria, tetanus, pertussis (whooping cough), measles, mumps, rubella, and polio, among other diseases. An effective, wide-reaching immunization program can virtually eliminate these diseases, many of which can also harm pregnant women. Many adults have not been immunized against rubella. Administration of a rubella titer test can determine whether you have had the disease, which can be easily confused with other common illnesses. If you have not had rubella, you will be doing a service to your community by be-

Not everyone enjoys inoculations, but they do prevent illnesses that historically led to disability and death. (Andy Levin/Photo Researchers, Inc.)

coming immunized against it, so you will not contribute to the spread of this destructive virus. It is not only women thinking of having children who should be immunized—men can spread this virus too!

■ ***Genetic Counseling*** Couples who have reason to be concerned that they might have a child with a disabling condition will find that **genetic counseling** can provide them with helpful information. With information from a couple's family and personal health history, a genetic counselor can often discuss the likelihood that their child will inherit a genetic condition (see the accompanying Closer Look box, "Genetic Counseling: 'The Science Is the Easy Part'").

Genetic counseling can also be a step in preventing disability.

The role of the genetic counselor is a neutral one; the counselor provides prospective parents with information and possible options, but the parents are then left to make their own decision about whether or not to have a child (Chedd, 1995). The prospective parents must often make difficult choices, since rarely can a genetic counselor guarantee what the outcome of a pregnancy will be.

■ ***Early Prenatal Care*** The easiest, most routine step a pregnant woman can take to reduce the risk for her baby may also be the most effective. Early **prenatal care,** the care an expectant mother receives from her physician during pregnancy, can provide a prospective mother with crucial but routine tests and observations that can drastically affect her baby's health. Blood tests that rule out the presence of sexually transmitted and other diseases, information about proper nutrition and activity level during pregnancy, and counseling and

Early and consistent prenatal care is the most effective way to prevent many disabilities.

A closer look

Genetic Counseling: "The Science Is the Easy Part"

What is genetic counseling? The mother of a 6-year-old with Down syndrome put it well when she said, "In two one-hour sessions, our counselor taught me everything I wished I had remembered from Biology 101, Psychology 101, and Philosophy 101." Genetic counseling draws on knowledge from these fields and others in an effort to provide the most accurate, up-to-date information on the causes and treatment of genetic disorders, the tests available for identifying them, a possible prognosis for a child with a genetic condition, and the prospects for future pregnancies.

A good genetic counselor should have first-rate knowledge of genetics. But he or she should also be able to communicate that knowledge in easy-to-understand language. And, according to Barbara Bowles Biesecker, genetic counselor and section head at the National Center for Human Genome Research, National Institutes of Health, genetic counselors must be able to listen as well as talk. "People are terrified when they get a diagnosis," she explains. "They often ask, 'Why did this happen?' They already know the scientific explanation; what they are really asking are the more soul-searching questions: How will I cope? Will I be able to love and accept this child?' Genetic counseling is much more complicated than explaining percentages. Actually, the science is the easy part."

Possibly the most important thing families can get from a genetic counselor is time—time to process a lot of information, time to grieve the considerable losses they may experience.

A genetic counselor can provide a tremendous amount of information about local and national resources. He or she may also be able to explain the practical implications of recent research results.

Genetic counselors are also familiar and comfortable with conditions other medical professionals rarely see. Whereas your pediatrician might see two children a year with your child's disability, a genetic counselor may see two a week. "One of the best things our counselor did was hook us up with other parents. Nobody can understand what we're going through except other CF parents," says the mother of a child with cystic fibrosis.

Different families seek genetic counseling for different reasons. A couple with a newly diagnosed infant or young child, for example, will probably want a comprehensive explanation of the child's condition and likely prognosis. They

treatment based on the prospective mother's needs significantly lower the level of risk in each pregnancy.

Despite the effectiveness of early prenatal care as a preventive measure, thousands of women give birth each year without ever seeing a doctor or visiting a clinic. Many of them are young, and most of them are poor. Babies born to women who do not receive prenatal medical care are more likely to be premature or sick at birth. There is also a higher likelihood of miscarriage, stillbirth, and early infant death in these pregnancies (Mechaty & Thompson, 1990).

The availability of free or low-cost prenatal care varies from state to state. Federal and state governments have, for the most part, failed to implement policy that would make these services available to all women, despite persuasive data that document the cost-effectiveness of such action. In countries where free prenatal care is routinely available, infant mortality and morbidity are considerably lower (Garbarino, 1990).

may also want to know the chances of this or another birth defect occurring in future pregnancies.

According to Phillip R. Reilly, M.D., clinical geneticist, lawyer, and president of the Shriver Center for Mental Retardation, the following people may benefit from consulting a genetic counselor:

- Families in which there is a known genetic disorder, such as cystic fibrosis, Huntington's disease, or hemophilia.
- Couples that come from the same ethnic group, when that group is known to have a high incidence of certain disorders. For example, Tay-Sachs disease is common among some ethnic groups, such as Ashkenazi Jews, and one in twelve African Americans carries the gene for sickle cell anemia.
- Families in which there have been multiple miscarriages, stillbirths, or a childhood death from unknown causes.
- Women older than 34 who are pregnant or planning a pregnancy.
- Relatives—especially siblings—of a child with a genetically transmitted disorder.

How do you find a genetic counselor?

A pediatrician or the geneticist at your HMO or local hospital may be able to refer you to a qualified genetic counselor. Or contact one of the following organizations:

National Society of Genetic Counselors
233 Canterbury Drive
Wallingford, PA 19086-6617
http://www.nsgc.org/

Genetic Alliance
4301 Connecticut Avenue, NW, #404
Washington, DC 20008-2304
(202) 966-5557 FAX: (202) 966-8553
(800) 336-GENE—Helpline only
e-mail: info@geneticalliance.org
http://www.geneticalliance.org/

Source: Adapted from "Genetic Counseling—The science is the easy part" by Naomi Angoff Chedd, *Exceptional Parent,* August 1995, pp. 26–27. Copyright © 1995. Reprinted with the expressed consent and approval of *Exceptional Parent,* a monthly magazine for parents and families of children with disabilities and special health care needs. Subscription cost is $32 per year for 12 issues; call 1-800-562-1973. Offices at 555 Kinderkarnack Rd., Oradell, NJ 07649.

■ ***Prenatal Testing*** For those who have received genetic counseling or are concerned about the health of their growing fetus, two procedures can provide more information: **amniocentesis** and **chorionic villous sampling (CVS).**

Amniocentesis and chorionic villous sampling can provide information on the health of the fetus.

Amniocentesis was the first technique developed for prenatal diagnosis (Batshaw & Rose, 1997). It is performed between the fourteenth and eighteenth weeks of pregnancy by inserting a needle through the mother's abdomen into the amniotic sac and withdrawing less than one ounce of amniotic fluid. The amniotic fluid contains cells shed by the fetus, and these are cultured. A karyotype (a study of the number and description of the fetal chromosomes) is generally available in two weeks or less. Examination of the fetal chromosomes can lead to identification of chromosomal abnormalities like Down syndrome. Evidence of neural tube defects like spina bifida can be seen in the analysis of the amniotic fluid cells. The risk to the fetus and the mother from amniocentesis is quite low.

In chorionic villous sampling (CVS), which is performed between the eighth and tenth weeks of pregnancy, a thin catheter is inserted through the vagina into the uterus and used to remove a small portion of the cells from the chorion, part of the developing placenta (Batshaw & Rose, 1997). Those cells, which contain genetic material from the fetus, are cultured. In two to three days a karyotype is obtained. Evidence of Down syndrome and other relatively common genetic abnormalities can then be determined. CVS is slightly less safe than amniocentesis; there is an approximately 1 percent greater risk of miscarriage following CVS than following amniocentesis (Burton, Schulz, & Burd, 1992), but with further research and refinement it may be used more frequently than amniocentesis.

One mother who had prenatal testing before the birth of her daughter, who has spina bifida, reminds us that prenatal testing is often helpful no matter what a couple's views are on the termination of pregnancy:

> I will always be grateful that when I finally gave birth to my daughter, it was in a setting where she could get the best of care from the moment of her first breath, and that my husband and I were fully prepared to welcome her into our lives with open arms. At the time of a prenatal diagnosis, it may be hard for families to see the value of the opportunity they have been given, but ultimately I believe families and their children benefit most by knowing about problems as early as possible. (Reichard, 1995, p. 131)

Early Intervention as Prevention

Early intervention is the set of services provided to children from birth to age 3 and their families that is designed for their unique characteristics and needs.

As we have emphasized, the presence of risk factors does not guarantee a developmental delay or disability. **Early intervention** plays an important role in preventing additional deficits in children who are at risk. Early intervention programs may lessen the effects of risk factors on a child by enlisting the support of a team of professionals and family members in the child's care and development.

■ ***Early Intervention Programs*** What is early intervention? What are its goals? These are vital concerns for the parents or caregivers of a child with a disability or a child at risk for developing a disability. Hanson, Ellis, and Deppe (1989) define early intervention as "a comprehensive set of services that are provided to children from birth to age three and their families" (p. 211). The basic component of this intervention is a teacher (often called an early intervention specialist) who works collaboratively with other professionals, the family, and the child to provide information, support, activities, and strategies designed to minimize the effects of the child's risk status or disability on his or her development.

Research documents the effectiveness of early intervention services.

As you learned in Chapter 1, early intervention services for infants and toddlers and their families are authorized by IDEA. Early intervention includes efforts to improve the child's performance in all major functional areas—language, cognition, fine and gross motor skills, and social-emotional development. And because research shows that early intervention yields significant results (Guralnick, 1997), the availability and comprehensiveness of early intervention programs can have a great impact on the lives of children who are at risk and those with disabilities.

Hanson (1996) describes the defining characteristics of early intervention:

- Services are individualized, based on the varying needs of children and their families, and the individualized family service plan (IFSP) is the document that outlines these services.
- Services are provided in varying locations, either the child's home, a center, or a combination of home- and center-based settings.
- Services should be cross-disciplinary and coordinated with one another.
- Depending on child and family needs, disciplines represented may be education, medicine, nursing, nutrition and dietetics, social work, speech-language pathology and audiology, occupational therapy, physical therapy, and psychology.
- Since no one agency can provide all those services, an interagency, collaborative approach is necessary.
- A continuum of services must be available, from comprehensive and intensive services to those that may be short-term and limited.
- Services must be enmeshed in the broad range of community services available to young children, also referred to as "natural environments."

■ ***Models for Early Intervention Programs*** Early intervention services are generally delivered through either a home-based program, in which the early intervention specialist provides services to the family in its own home, a center-based program, in which the family brings the child to an early intervention center, or another program for young children within their community. Often, services to infants and medically fragile toddlers are provided in the home; as children grow older and stronger, they are more likely to attend a program in the community.

Early intervention can be provided in the family home, at an early intervention center, or in the community.

Cook, Tessier, and Klein (2000) identified eleven elements in the early intervention literature that are associated with effective early intervention programs. Among them are:

- A well-defined program model and philosophy with staff commitment to the approach being implemented
- A consistent system that promotes a high level of family involvement and support with an emphasis on caregiver-child interaction
- Extensive and cooperative team planning and program implementation
- Facilitation of functional skills to enable children to cope with environmental expectations as determined through individualized program and service planning
- Flexible adaptation of intervention techniques to determine those most effective in meeting child- and family-focused outcomes and objectives
- Strong emphasis on language and social skill development
- Incorporation of "best practices" as they are continually determined through practice and research in the field
- A well-designed system for staff and parent training and development

The best early intervention programs will reflect these elements, as well as the practices identified in the Closer Look box, "Commonalities: Best Practices in Early Childhood Education."

A closer look

Commonalities: Best Practices in Early Childhood Education

The best practices for the field of early childhood special education must be built on those well-established principles of practice that are best for all young children. These are perhaps best stated in the position statements offered by the National Association for the Education of Young Children (Bredekamp, 1987; Bredekamp & Copple, 1997) and the Division of Early Childhood of the Council for Exceptional Children (Sandall, McLean, & Smith, 2000). Two major themes have guided the development of these best practices: (1) that early education must meet the individual developmental needs of each child, and (2) that the best medium through which to do this is children's play.

Several key recommendations emerge within these frameworks related to curriculum, adult-child interactions, family involvement, and evaluation that are essential to high-quality early intervention programs. These are summarized below. The field of early childhood special education is built on best practices from the fields of both early childhood and special education.

Curriculum

- Educational goals are incorporated into all daily activities. Objectives are not taught in isolation but are integrated into meaningful activities and events.
- Curriculum planning and intervention are based on the teacher's specific observations of each child in natural contexts.
- Learning is an interactive process. Children's interactions with adults, peers, and the physical environment are all important.
- Learning activities and materials must be concrete and relevant to children's lives. Teachers should make use of real-life objects and activities (e.g., make a trip to the fire station, not just read a story about fire engines).
- Programs must be able to meet a wide range of interests and abilities. Teachers are expected to individualize instructional programs.
- Teachers must increase the difficulty and challenge of activities gradually and skillfully.
- Teachers must be able to facilitate engagement of each child by offering choices, making suggestions, asking questions, and describing events in ways that are meaningful and interesting to the child.
- Children should be given opportunities for self-initiation, self-direction, and repeated practice.
- Teachers must accept and appreciate cultural differences in children and families and avoid ethnic and gender stereotypes.
- Programs must provide a balance between rest and activity, and they should include outdoor activities each day.
- Outdoor activities should be planned, not simply opportunities to release pent-up energy.
- Programs must create careful transitions from one activity to the next. Children should not be rushed, and schedules should be flexible enough to take advantage of impromptu experiences.

Adult-Child Interaction

- Adults should respond quickly and directly to children's needs and attempts to communicate. Whenever possible, adults should be at eye level with children.
- Children must be provided with a variety of opportunities to communicate. Interaction is best facilitated on a one-to-one basis, or in groups of two to three children. Large-

group instruction is less effective in facilitating communication.

- Professionals must be alert to signs of stress and provide sensitive, appropriate assistance to children.
- Adults must facilitate the development of self-esteem by "expressing respect, acceptance, and comfort for children, regardless of the child's behavior" (NAEYC, 1986, p. 14).
- Adults must use disciplinary techniques that enhance the development of self-control. These include setting clear, consistent limits; redirecting inappropriate behavior; valuing mistakes; listening to children's concerns and frustrations; helping children solve conflicts; and patiently reminding children of rules as needed.
- Adults must be responsible for all children at all times. Health and safety issues must be addressed constantly.
- Adults must plan for gradually increasing children's independence.

Family Involvement

- Parents have the right and responsibility to share in decision making regarding their children's care and education. Professionals must maintain frequent contact, and parents should be encouraged to participate.
- Professionals must regularly share information and resources with parents, including information regarding stages of child development. They must also obtain and respect parents' views of individual children's behavior and development.

Evaluation

- Child evaluations should not rely on a single instrument.
- Evaluations should identify children with special needs and provide information that will lead to meaningful educational modifications.
- Evaluations must be culturally appropriate.

Additional Best Practices for Children with Special Needs

In addition to the recommendations just summarized, certain other recommendations are particularly important for young children with special needs. McDonnell and Hardman (1988) have suggested the following:

- Services for young children with disabilities should be provided in integrated settings within the local community.
- A transdisciplinary model of service delivery should be utilized; isolated therapies should be minimized.
- Artificial reinforcement and aversive control techniques should be avoided.
- Training should emphasize function rather than form of response.
- Program planning should include planned enhancement of the child's skill development within daily family routines.
- Curriculum should be developed with reference to the individual child, as well as to family, peers, and the community.
- Program evaluation and child assessment should be accomplished using a variety of outcome measures.
- Transitions from one educational setting to the next should be planned carefully.

Source: *Adapting Early Childhood Curricula for Children, in Inclusive Settings.* Fifth Edition by Cook et al., © 2000. Reprinted by permission of Prentice-Hall, Inc., Upper Saddle River, NJ.

Risk Factors and Early Intervention

Family involvement and family support are the foundation of effective early intervention.

The Role of the Family in Early Intervention With the growing appreciation of the importance of viewing the child within the context of the family, the focus of early intervention has shifted from the child to the entire family system. This broadened focus is reflected in the law, which mandates that each family receive an **Individualized Family Service Plan (IFSP)**, a written account of the personal and social services needed to promote and support each family member for the first three years of the child's life.

Each IFSP must include:

The IFSP must describe the family's strengths as well as its needs.

- A statement of the family's strengths, as well as needs related to the child;
- A description of the major outcomes to be achieved by the child and the family;
- A description of the family's current resources, priorities, and concerns; and
- A list of the specific services needed to meet the unique requirements of each child and family. These services may include family training, counseling, respite care, and home visits, as well as physical, occupational, and speech therapy, audiological services, and so on (Sandall, 1997a, 1997b).

Most families need information related to their child's condition, assistance in learning to identify their child's unique cues, guidance in handling the child in a more therapeutic and easy manner, and referrals for other services. The focus of early intervention is typically on facilitating and coordinating this range of activities so that the family may experience more satisfying and rewarding relationships with the child and the child may develop more fully (Chen, 1999).

Remember that three groups of young children (from birth to age 3) are eligible for early intervention services:

Three groups of infants and toddlers are eligible for early intervention services under the law.

- Those with an identified condition related to developmental disability, such as hearing or vision loss or Down syndrome
- Those who are experiencing developmental delay in motor, cognitive, communication, psychosocial, or self-help skills
- Those who are at risk for significant developmental delay because of biological and/or environmental events in their lives

Let's look at a hypothetical baby, Sarah, who has Down syndrome. Down syndrome carries with it an extremely high probability of mental retardation, and often involves physical abnormalities (such as organ defects) as well. Sarah is 8 months old and is recovering from heart surgery that successfully repaired a congenital heart defect. In the next year, Sarah's physical health must be monitored closely to ensure her complete and successful recovery. Her family will need help facilitating Sarah's speech and language development, which is usually delayed in children with mental retardation. Sarah is not sitting or crawling, which suggests a delay in her motor development, and we know that her cognitive development is likely to be delayed. Because of Sarah's varied needs, the design of her intervention program, or the outcomes on her IFSP, will benefit from the input of a team consisting of health-care professionals, a speech-language specialist, a physical therapist, and a teacher skilled in activities that will facilitate cognitive development. And we haven't even mentioned her parents' needs!

The IFSP outcomes for Sarah and her family might look like this:

1. Sarah's parents will learn more about Down syndrome and meet other parents of children with Down syndrome through participation in a parent-to-parent support group.
2. Sarah's parents will feel confident in their ability to facilitate their daughter's healthy growth and development, particularly in the area of communication skills.
3. Sarah will begin to use pointing and vocalizations to indicate her needs.
4. Sarah's parents will learn more about the impact of her surgery and recovery on Sarah's overall development, particularly her motor development.
5. Sarah will sit and crawl independently. (Cook, Tessier, & Klein, 2000)

According to the IFSP, Sarah will receive weekly home visits from an early intervention specialist and a speech-language pathologist, and her parents will take her to physical therapy twice weekly. Sarah's parents will be given the name of their local Down syndrome parent group, and respite care will be provided so that they can attend the meetings. The team expects that Sarah will be attending a center-based early intervention program by the time she is 18 months old, with one or both of her parents attending with her.

With the help of an **interdisciplinary team** of professionals, Sarah's parents will make sure that she is off to a healthy start in life.

Identification and Assessment of Infants at Risk

Since most states have developed early intervention programs for infants and young children under IDEA, criteria must be designed to identify children who are eligible for these services. Clearly, young children with identified disabilities are eligible. Also eligible are those children described as developmentally delayed. It is the group of children we discuss in this chapter, those who are categorized as biologically and environmentally "at risk," who have presented the most significant problems to the state teams working on eligibility criteria, and, based on our previous discussions in this chapter, we can begin to see why. We have developed a considerable list of biological and environmental risk factors, and there are many others we have not had the space to present. Deciding which risk factors or how many factors will qualify a child for services has presented a major challenge to the states. Many states require that multiple risk factors be used to qualify children for programs, since we know that as risk factors multiply, their combined effect is likely to be greater than that of any single factor.

Techniques for Identification and Assessment

We obtain information about a child's risk status from a number of sources: hospital and health records, family interviews, observation of the child, developmental and health screenings, and diagnostic assessment. **Screening** refers to quick and efficient procedures whereby large numbers of children can be evaluated to determine whether more in-depth assessment is required; screenings of young children's development, hearing, vision, and overall health can identify children with a high probability of delayed development. **Diagnostic assessment,** a more in-depth look at the child's development, provides a more definitive picture of whether the child has special needs; in diagnostic assessment, formal assessment tools are used by a multidisciplinary team, with considerable input from the child's family (Meisels & Provence, 1989).

"Best practices" in assessment demand that multiple types of data from multiple sources, especially the family, be used for good decision-making.

No one source of information should be used to make any decisions concerning a child's eligibility for services; "best practices" in assessment demand that multiple types of data from multiple sources be used for good decision-making. Foremost among these sources is the family. Meisels and Provence (1989) put it this way:

> One should not try to screen or assess young children without the active participation of those most expert about them—their parents. All parents know a great deal about their children, and the task of those conducting the screening and assessment is to enable parents to transmit that information productively. (p. 15)

The Problems of Predicting Disabilities from Risk Factors

Despite the large number of studies that identify biologically at-risk infants and follow their development over time, researchers have found that their ability to predict which children will develop disabilities is relatively poor. Children with severe disabilities, often caused by massive central nervous system insult, are an exception to this rule, but they are the very small minority. Fortunately, many of the early complications of biological risk status are transient; that is, they disappear over time. Many infants can and do recover from the trauma of premature birth and early medical complications.

But, once again, the child's ability to recover from these early experiences appears to be mediated by the caregiving characteristics in his or her environment. Cohen and Parmalee (1983), for example, found that for most of their premature subjects, neonatal complications did not necessarily predict scores on the Stanford-Binet IQ test at age 5. But children whose developmental performance improved the most had caregiving that was more responsive and more reciprocal and that encouraged more autonomy than those children whose performance did not improve. We can begin to see why early intervention for infants at risk must focus on the infant within the context of the family.

Children with responsive and consistent caregiving have the best chance of recovering from the effects of risk factors.

The Resilient Child

The impact of risk factors varies a great deal in different children, families, and environments. For example, there are many healthy young children doing well in school today who were born at very low weight; other low birthweight children are striving to overcome disabilities ranging from mild learning disabilities to severe mental retardation. Many children grow up in poverty and go on to lead productive adult lives; others develop school problems that lead to dropping out of school or to special educational programming. On the other hand, few children born with serious chromosomal abnormalities grow up without developmental delays (although many of them can, as we shall see, become productive citizens).

So far in this chapter, we have identified a large number of biological and environmental risk factors that increase the likelihood of poor developmental outcomes in children. No single risk factor satisfactorily predicts or explains what will happen to a child, but the accuracy of our predictions increases with the number of risk factors that the child experiences, and the most vulnerable children of all are those who experience both biological and environmental risk factors. In fact, most children who experience a series of biological risk factors (with the exception of those that clearly damage the central nervous system) but grow up in a stable, supportive environment develop very well.

There are also the remarkable children who, despite a multitude of adverse biological and environmental events, overcome the odds and become healthy, productive adults (Masten & Coatsworth, 1998). See Table 2.2. Werner and Smith (1982) called them "vulnerable but invincible." What is it about these children that protects them from the school failure, emotional distress, early parenthood, and criminal behavior demonstrated by other children from similar backgrounds?

To find these protective factors, we look first within the child. Werner (1986, p. 16) defined the characteristics shared by the **resilient,** or "stress-resistant," children of several studies:

Resilient children can overcome the odds and become healthy, productive adults.

> (1) An active, evocative approach toward solving their developmental tasks, enabling them to negotiate successfully an abundance of emotionally hazardous experiences; (2) the ability, from infancy on, to gain other people's positive attention, and to recruit "surrogate parents" when necessary; (3) a tendency to perceive and interpret their experiences constructively, even if they caused pain and suffering; and (4) a strong "sense of coherence," a belief that their lives had meaning.

Werner described the most resilient subjects of her longitudinal study of the children of Kauai: One out of three grew up in chronic poverty, had experienced

Table 2.2 Characteristics of Resilient Children

Source	Characteristic
Individual	Good intellectual functioning
	Appealing, sociable, easygoing disposition
	Self-efficacy, self-confidence, good self-esteem
	Talents
Family	Faith
	Close relationship to caring parent figure
	Authoritative parenting: warmth, structure, high expectations
Extrafamilial context	Socioeconomic advantages
	Connections to extended supportive family networks
	Bonds to prosocial adults outside the family
	Connections to prosocial organizations
	Attending effective schools

Source: From A. S. Masten and J. D. Coatsworth, "The development of competence in favorable and unfavorable environments: Lessons from research on successful children." *American Psychologist, 53*, p.212. Copyright 1998 by the American Psychological Association.

perinatal stresses or had congenital defects, was raised by mothers with little formal education, and lived in families with serious instability, discord, or parental mental illness. But one out of four of these children "escaped the ill effects of such multiple risks and developed into stable, mature, and competent young adults who 'worked well, played well, loved well, and expected well'" (Werner, 1986, p. 13). There were ameliorative personal factors within these children and protective factors within their caregiving environments, among them a close bond with a primary caregiver and emotional support provided by other family members (such as siblings and grandparents) during early and middle childhood (Werner, 1999).

Personal factors and a close bond with a primary caregiver may help resilient children overcome early risk factors.

As Werner's research indicates, risk factors are not the only significant variables capable of influencing the course of children's development. Dunst (1993) suggests that it is not simply the absence of risk factors that helps us predict which children develop well; there are also "opportunity factors" that can occur within a family and community and that may enhance and strengthen a child's development. According to Dunst, research demonstrates that positive development outcomes are influenced by the power of factors such as high education level of parents, stimulating and warm caregiver-child interaction, and a supportive extended family. The influence of these opportunity factors increases when multiple factors are present.

The fact that there are children who can experience many stressful biological and environmental events and emerge as healthy, competent adults provides us with hope and encouragement. We must use the results of this research to support other at-risk children and families so that they, too, can develop protective personal characteristics despite stressful caregiving environments.

Summary

- Risk factors include a wide range of biological and environmental conditions associated with increased probability of developmental problems in young children.
- Risk factors can be categorized as biological risks and environmental risks. Biological risks are a threat to a child's developing systems and can include diseases, maternal substance abuse, and oxygen deprivation. Environmental risk stems from damaging physical and social surroundings of the child and his or her caretakers, such as exposure to lead, accidents, or limited access to health care.
- Some steps that help prevent risk status and disability include inoculation, genetic counseling, prenatal care, and prenatal testing. Early intervention is another means of preventing the negative impact of risk factors.
- Early intervention consists of a comprehensive set of services for infants and toddlers aged birth to 3 and their families that is designed for the unique needs and built on the unique strengths of each child and family. Early intervention has a strong family focus and can consist of services offered by a range of professionals across disciplines.
- At-risk children can pose a challenge for early intervention personnel because the range of possible risk factors is so great and because the presence of one or more risk factors does not guarantee a developmental delay. Tech-

niques used to identify children for early intervention include screening and diagnostic assessment.

- It must be remembered that no absolute predictions can be made regarding at-risk children. Some children are exceptionally resilient and succeed despite seemingly large odds. A strong bond with a caregiving adult and emotional support from other family members can help a child overcome biological and environmental stresses.

Key Terms

risk factors
biological risk
environmental risk
prenatal
perinatal
postnatal
first trimester
teratogens
rubella
cytomegalovirus (CMV)
congenital
sexually transmitted diseases (STDs)
acquired immune deficiency syndrome (AIDS)
thalidomide
polysubstance abusers
fetal alcohol syndrome (FAS)
fetal alcohol effects (FAE)
Down syndrome
hypoxia
premature (preterm)
low birthweight
neonatology
neonatal intensive care unit
meningitis
chronic otitis media
occupational hazards
inoculation
genetic counseling
prenatal care
amniocentesis
chorionic villous sampling (CVS)
early intervention
Individualized Family Service Plan (IFSP)
interdisciplinary team
screening
diagnostic assessment
resiliency

Multimedia Resources

The American Academy of Pediatrics has a website that provides information about childhood diseases and psychosocial risk factors in children. Visit www.aap.org/.

"America's Children: Key National Indicators of Well-Being, 2000" provides figures on national poverty and violent crime among young people. This annual report, compiled by the Federal Interagency Forum on Child and Family Statistics, looks at economic security, health, behavior and social environment, and education. Visit http://childstats.gov.

The Centers for Disease Control (CDC) has developed the CDC National Prevention Information Network (NPIN), devoted to disseminating information about the prevention of HIV/AIDS, sexually transmitted diseases, and tuberculosis. The web address is http://www.cdcnpin.org/. The site has separate sections on children and youth; many resources are available in Spanish.

ComeUnity has a website for families of children born premature. It's at http://www.comeunity.com/premature/.

The National Association for the Education of Young Children (NAEYC) leads and consolidates the efforts of individuals and groups working to achieve healthy development and constructive education for all young children.

Primary attention is devoted to ensuring high-quality early childhood programs for young children. Visit http://www.naeyc.org/.

The National Maternal and Child Health Clearinghouse website is at http://wwnmchc.org/. This clearinghouse gathers and disseminates material on topics related to the health of mothers and children, such as prenatal care and nutrition, in the form of pamphlets, bibliographies, and other resources. The clearinghouse has a toll-free telephone number: (888) 434-4MCH. Available at this site is a booklet titled *Lead Poisoning. . . . still an environmental problem for children and families,* which contains information on lead poisoning in children of all ages. It informs the public about lead poisoning, its causes and problems. It also suggests steps to help protect children from lead poisoning in school and at home.

The National Early Childhood Technical Assistance System (NECTAS) is a consortium of six organizations providing assistance to early childhood specialists. Visit their website at http://www.nectas.unc.edu/default.html.

Streissguth, Ann. *Fetal Alcohol Syndrome: A Guide for Families and Communities* (Baltimore: Brookes, 1997). This book, by one of the foremost researchers on FAS, reviews the research and interventions for a popular and professional audience.

Zero to Three is an organization devoted to the healthy development of infants and toddlers. The website has good information for both parents and professionals. Visit at www.zerotothree.org/ or write to the organization at 734 15th St. NW, Washington, DC 20005.

What You Can Do

Each of us has a personal and a social responsibility to help prevent disability in our communities. Here are some ways for you to help.

1. Participate in fundraising and awareness campaigns.

- Pledge or organize a team of volunteers for a fundraising event. Major fundraising organizations like the March of Dimes, the United Way, UNICEF, the United Cerebral Palsy Association, or the Cystic Fibrosis Foundation would love to have your help.
- Working as a class, design posters illustrating risk factors and related prevention strategies for display in a community education program.
- Hold a "risk awareness" education day at your local high school or community center.

2. Promote early prenatal care and early recognition of risk and disability.

- Invite a genetic counselor from a local hospital to come and speak to your class or your parent group.
- Find out about the low-cost prenatal care services in your community and, in a small group, devise a plan to publicize them.
- Find out where you can refer parents who are concerned about their child's early development in your town or city. Make a list for your school and local pediatricians.
- Visit a neonatal intensive care unit. Write a narrative report of what you observed and present it to your classmates.

3. Take care of yourself and the people you care about.

- Avoid alcohol use when considering pregnancy.
- Advocate for early and consistent prenatal care.
- Remember that modeling of responsible behavior for others can be a powerful influence.

Families and Culture

3

SPECIAL EDUCATION professionals have increasingly based their decisions about services to children on the knowledge that the family's involvement can make their work much more effective. In this chapter, you will learn how exceptionalities affect families, how the family's cultural background and experiences may color their perception of their child's characteristics, and how families and professionals can collaborate in the interests of the child despite cultural differences. As you read, look for answers to these questions:

What is the legal basis for family involvement in special education?

How does a family's cultural background color their perception of "disability"?

How does the birth of an exceptional child affect the family?

Commonalities: **Are there common issues for families of exceptional children across cultures?**

Collaboration: **How can family members and professionals learn to work together as partners?**

Can Do: **What are some ways in which exceptional children contribute to the strength and richness of a family?**

Defining a family today can be more difficult than it used to be. Although for many of us the family unit still consists of two or more blood relatives residing together, there are plenty of exceptions: foster families (those created by the courts) and adoptive families are two that come to mind. For those of us living far away from relatives, close friends can create the kind of company and support that an extended family might.

Each family's cultural background—its combination of values, beliefs, history, traditions, and language—helps determine its response to the birth and raising of children, and to the birth and raising of a child with a disability. In the United States, a nation formed of the melding of thousands of groups from all over the world, the possibilities for variation in beliefs and traditions about child-rearing are nearly endless. And it is within this context that most of our readers will work, often with families whose values, beliefs, history, traditions, and language will be very different from their own. This chapter is designed to help you begin to learn about families of children with disabilities and to reflect on how their traditions and beliefs form their responses to their children and to you, the teacher. Without such reflection, there is no foundation for real partnership with families.

Definitions and Terms

> Teachers will encounter families with many or few family members. Housing and community opportunities will vary. Families represent all walks of life, from indigent families without homes to those families with multiple residences. Family members may or may not hold educational degrees. Primary languages will vary. Families may practice daily religious traditions, or may hold little or no religious affiliation. (p. 31)

How would *you* define family? How would *you* define culture? Your own experiences and your cultural *milieu* will color your ideas about both these terms. Families of exceptional children have their ideas about child-rearing, relations with the school, and disability colored by similar experiences. In this book, we broadly define **family** as two or more people who live together and who are related by blood or marriage (O'Shea, O'Shea, Algozzine, & Hammitte, 2001). Beyond this, you can expect to encounter many variations. A **household** is one or more people, including members of a family and others, who live under the same roof. An **extended family** consists of relatives across generations who may or may not live together. Many African American families report having "a wide network of kin and community" (O'Shea et al., 2001, p. 53) that provides them with support.

We define *family* as people living together who are related by blood or marriage.

Clearly it is not always the biological parent who raises the exceptional child. It may be one biological parent, a grandparent, a foster parent, another relative, or a family friend. Acknowledging these diverse possibilities, many professionals prefer to use the term **caregiver** to refer to the person who assumes that role. That term seems relatively impersonal to us, so in this chapter we use the word *parent* generically, to include all those caregivers who take the responsibilities traditionally associated with being a parent.

Culture refers to the shared values, traditions, and beliefs of a group of people.

Culture means different things to different people. Most anthropologists define culture broadly, as ways of perceiving, believing, evaluating, and behaving

(Goodenough, 1987). Culture can be seen as a series of norms or tendencies that are shared, interpreted, and adapted by a group of people. The characteristics of a given culture may be described as specific behaviors or life patterns; however, every person is an individual, and groups of individuals within a culture represent a *range* of characteristics (Hanson, 1998). Culture, therefore, may guide the way you think, feel, behave, dress, and eat, but it does not ensure that every member of a culture will do things in the same way. The word *culture* can also be used to describe many of the shared behaviors we experience in a number of different parts of our lives. For example, the shared language, dress, communication patterns, and food preferences of our ethnic background, as well as the behavioral, ethical, social, and dietary guidelines of our religion, reflect two aspects of culture.

The cultural backgrounds of our own families and the families we work with will influence beliefs about child-rearing, education, and family life, as well as attitudes toward an exceptional family member. In one useful definition, *culture* is a framework that guides life practices (Hanson, 1998). The term does not refer to a rigid or prescribed set of characteristics but "a set of tendencies or possibilities from which to choose" (Anderson & Fenichel, 1989, p. 8). The practices and traditions that arise from family culture may provide a source of pride and comfort to family members—and may sometimes be a source of misunderstanding or confusion for the professionals who work with them.

One component of culture that is very much related to school learning is the *language* of the family. Whether it be Spanish (the most common language spoken in American homes after English), American Sign Language, Cantonese, Swahili, Gujerati, or another language, the child's home language will affect both your ability to communicate with family members and the child's ability to profit from instruction in English. In 2000, the Los Angeles Unified School District's Home Language Survey identified eighty-three different home languages or dialects used by pupils in the district, which is the second largest in the United States (approximately 722,727 pupils in kindergarten through twelfth grade). Although your area may not be quite as diverse, you can be sure that it is becoming more so!

Macroculture

Have you noticed how your classmates, roommates, and friends from different ethnic groups seem to have quite a lot in common with you? If so, it is because you all belong to the **macroculture,** the core, or universal, culture of this country. Our macroculture evolved from Western European traditions. No longer limited to white Anglo-Saxon Protestants, the macroculture comprises many different ethnic groups, primarily middle class, that have a shared core of values and beliefs (see the accompanying box, "Shared Values of the American Macroculture"). Most educators, regardless of their ethnic background, belong to the middle class and subscribe to the values of the macroculture.

The *macroculture* is the core culture of a country or area.

Microcultures

The macroculture alone does not define our pluralistic society, however. In your classroom you will find that all of your students belong to subcultures, or **microcultures,** that have their own distinctive cultural patterns while at the same time sharing core values with the macroculture. There are many microcultures, and each of your students will belong to several. All of your students and their

Microcultures have their own norms while they share core values with the macroculture.

~ Shared Values of the American Macroculture

- Individualism and privacy
- Equality and equity
- Industriousness
- Ambition
- Competition
- Self-reliance
- Independence
- Appreciation of "the good life"
- Perception that humans are separate and superior in nature
- Freedom of speech
- Freedom of choice
- Expert knowledge
- Social mobility
- Importance of education and learning

Think about how these shared values effect our common perception of disability.

Sources: Klein & Chen, 2001; Gollnick & Chinn, 1998; Chan, 1998; Zuniga, 1998; Kalyanpur & Harry, 1999; Harry, Kalyanpur, & Day, 1999).

families will belong to a microculture related to ethnicity. Some will be Chinese, Vietnamese, Cuban, or Haitian in national origin. All will also belong to a microculture related to socioeconomic status. Some may be middle class, others poor. All will belong to a language group. Probably all speak English to some extent. Some, however, may speak Spanish or Korean as their primary language. All will belong to a microculture related to gender. You will find that the boys are socialized to behave differently than the girls. All will belong to a microculture related to geographic region. If you live and teach in the Midwest, it is likely that your students are socialized differently than American children living in Hawaii. Consequently, the way an African American gifted female in your classroom thinks, feels, perceives, and behaves may be related to the fact that she is African American, or it may be directly related to her middle-class background, her close relationship to and beliefs in the Roman Catholic church, or the fact that she is a female.

Minority and Ethnic Groups

A *minority group* may be a numerical minority, or its members may hold a less powerful position in society.

Ethnicity refers to membership in a racial or national group.

Minority and *minority group* are terms often used in discussions about certain groups in this country. Although **minority** usually denotes a numerical minority, it may also suggest a subordinate power position in society (Gollnick & Chinn, 1998). **Minority groups** may be categorized according to ethnicity, gender, language, religion, disability, or socioeconomic status.

Ethnicity refers to membership in a particular racial or national group. It denotes the common history, values, attitudes, and behaviors that bind such a group of people together (Yetman, 1985). Examples of ethnic groups in this country include Irish Americans, Native Americans, Chinese Americans, Latinos, and German Americans. Ethnic groups may be *ethnocentric:* they may view their own traits as natural, correct, and superior to that of other ethnic groups, whom they tend to view as odd, amusing, inferior, or immoral (Yetman, 1985). Used in a broader context, the term *ethnocentrism* describes the narrow perspective of individuals from various microcultures. An example of this might include the ethnocentric, or intolerant, view of a particular Protestant group toward Roman Catholics. Although ethnicity is often the benchmark factor we think of when we use the term *culture*, culture and ethnicity are not the same, and many different microcultures interact with a person's ethnicity to form his or her cultural heritage (Keogh, Gallimore, & Weisner, 1997).

Culture and Disability

The recent work of Maya Kalyanpur and Beth Harry (1999) identifies some of the basic assumptions of the U.S. macroculture that influence our nation's response to disability, which is reflected in the special education system. The social construction of disability in the United States depends on a set of embedded beliefs. Among these beliefs is what is called the "reification" of disability—that is, we make disability into a *thing* that someone *has*. Disability is perceived as "a feature of the individual's constitution and exists as objective reality" (Kalyanpur & Harry, 1999, p. 10). Moreover, our perception of disability is rooted in our values. If reading and speaking well are highly valued, not being able to do those things becomes a mark of failure.

The perception of disability is rooted in the values of the culture.

Special education practices also have been influenced by the "medical model," which suggests that disability is physical, chronic, individually owned, and fixable. However, families from linguistically and culturally diverse backgrounds may have very different embedded values based on those of the microculture with which they were raised. They may see disability as having spiritual rather than physical causes; as a group phenomenon, shared by the family, rather than an individual one; and as temporary rather than fixed (Kalyanpur & Harry, 1999).

Beth Harry and her colleagues (Harry, Kalyanpur, & Day, 1999; Kalyanpur & Harry, 1999) urge school professionals to build bridges between the values and experiences of families and those of the special education system by operating within a framework of **cultural reciprocity**—a two-way process of information sharing and understanding which can be truly reciprocal and which can lead to genuine mutual understanding and cooperation. See the accompanying box to learn more about establishing such a framework for working with families.

Cultural reciprocity is built on mutual respect and information sharing.

Cultural Diversity

For the remainder of this book, we will refer to ethnic minority groups as *culturally diverse groups*. This designation is primarily a recognition of the pluralistic nature of the United States and the numerous contributions that diverse groups have made to the development of this country. Using the term **cultural diversity** does not place or rank groups in relation to one another; rather, it acknowledges that a wide range of cultural characteristics and norms affects families within our society.

As you read the following sections, think about your own cultural identity. Reflect on your participation in the macroculture and microcultures. Why is this important to you as a prospective teacher? A thorough knowledge of who you are, how your beliefs and actions are influenced, and how you relate to students and family members who have different life experiences can lead not only to self-growth, but also to your ability to teach all children effectively.

~ Four Essential Steps for Developing a Posture of Cultural Reciprocity

Step 1: Identify the cultural values that are embedded in your interpretation of a student's difficulties or in the recommendation for service.

Step 2: Find out whether the family being served recognizes and values these assumptions, and, if not, how their view differs from yours.

Step 3: Acknowledge and give explicit respect to any cultural differences identified, and fully explain the cultural basis of your assumptions.

Step 4: Through discussion and collaboration, set about determining the most effective way of adapting your professional interpretations or recommendations to the value system of this family.

Source: Harry, B., Kalyanpur, M., & Day, M. (1999). *Building cultural reciprocity with families: Case studies in special education* (pp. 7–11). Baltimore: Paul H. Brookes.

Approaches to Studying Families

The Family Systems Approach

The *family systems approach* provides a useful framework for understanding the diversity among families.

Professionals writing about families with exceptional members have borrowed and expanded on a framework used by sociologists to understand family life; that framework is known as the **family systems approach.** Family systems theory is a framework for understanding the family as an interrelated social system with unique characteristics and needs. It is based on the assumption that an experience that affects one family member will affect all family members (Turnbull & Turnbull, 1997).

The family systems approach, mapped out in Figure 3.1, suggests that each family has its own characteristics, interactions, functions, and life cycle, and interaction within each family is unique. Family characteristics include the characteristics of the exceptional child, such as the nature, degree, and demands of the child's exceptionality, as well as the family itself—its size, socioeconomic status, ethnicity, religion, and so on. Family interactions are the relationships between and among family members, which are often very much affected by a child's exceptionality. Family functions include all the tasks and responsibilities of family members. The family life cycle is the experiences of the family over time.

The family systems approach provides a helpful framework for viewing the child in the context of his or her family, in all its uniqueness and complexity, including the components related to traditions, values, and belief systems that we call culture.

Ecocultural Theory

Ecocultural theory requires that we respect each family's daily routines and activities.

Another framework through which the home environment can be studied is **ecocultural theory**, which is based on two fundamental premises. First, families are in the process of adapting to the environment in which they live. This adaptation is based on the family's goals, dreams, and beliefs, as well as on the physical, material, and sociocultural environment in which they live. The interaction of these two forces make up the "ecocultural niche" of the family. The second premise is that to understand the influence of this ecocultural niche on the individuals within the family system, one must look at the family's daily routines and activities. Activities are defined and analyzed by the following five dimensions: the people present; the

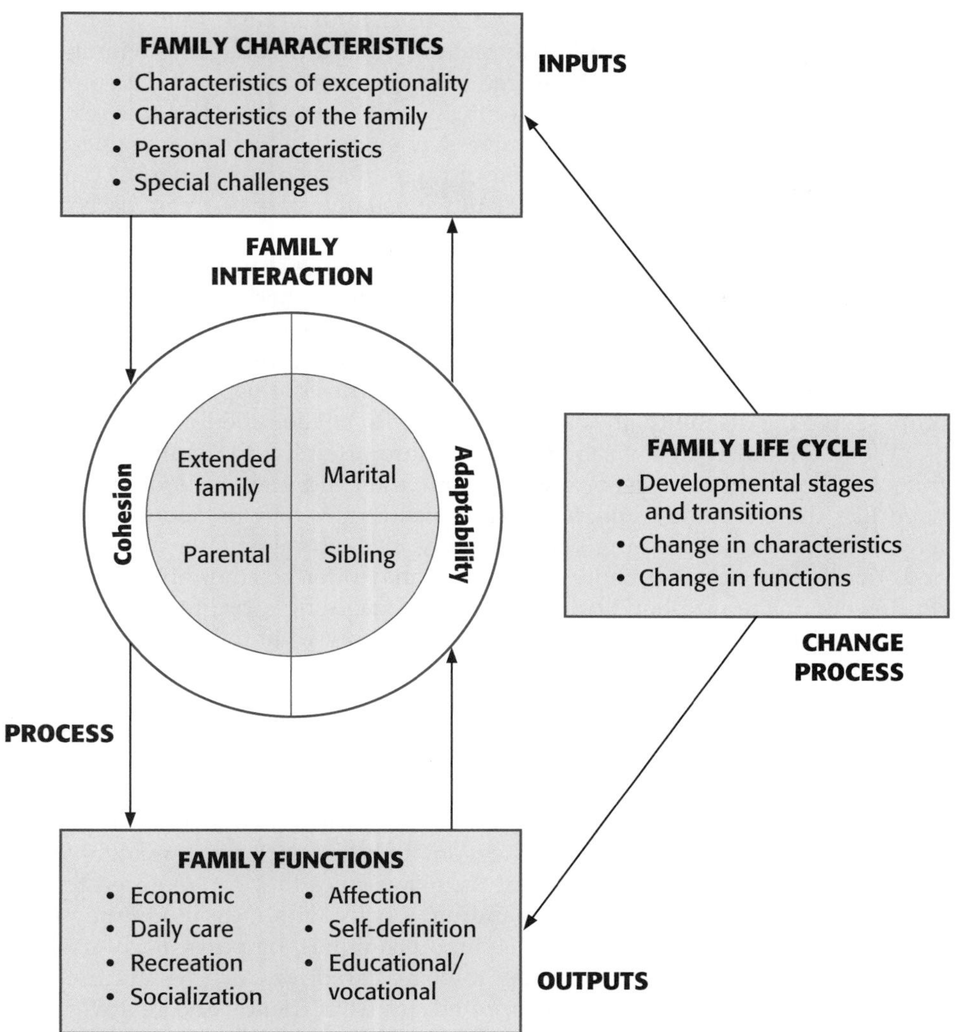

Figure 3.1
Family Systems Conceptual Framework

Source: A. P. Turnbull, J. A. Summers, and M.J. Brotherson. *Woring with Families with Disabled Members: A Family Systems Approach* (Lawrence: University of Kansas, Beach Center on Families and Disabilities, 1984), p. 60. Adapted by permission.

cultural goals, values, and beliefs of the participants; the motives, purposes, and intentions that guide the activities; the nature of the tasks; and the scripts, routines, and patterns of behavior used during the activities (Bernheimer, Gallimore, & Weisner, 1990; Dingle & Hunt, 2001). It is through these activity variables that early experiences are created and shaped (Reese, Goldenberg, Loucky, & Gallimore, 1995). Analysis of these family activities and routines can help us "weave interventions into the fabric of everyday life" (Bernheimer & Keogh, 1995).

Family Reactions to Disability Across Cultures

We all have fantasies about our unborn children—which the experience of having a real child soon erases. We may think of an adorable toddler holding our hand and walking contentedly by our side. We may look at other people's children behaving irritably or having a temper tantrum and think, "*My* child will never behave like that." We may picture our future offspring winning the science fair, writing the Great American Novel, or competing in the Olympics.

Most of the time, our children don't fit those fantasies. They may excel in ways that surprise us and show no interest in areas in which we imagined they would achieve. We seldom live up to our own dreams of being perfect parents, either. Our children love us anyway, and we usually come to accept each other, imperfect as we all are.

The discovery that a child is exceptional may come at birth or soon after, or it may come later in a child's life—perhaps, as with giftedness or learning disabilities, at school age. Although parents may experience similar feelings at either point, the age of the child does appear to make a difference in the family's initial response. First we will discuss early diagnosis. Keep in mind that the more severe the disability, the earlier it is likely to be identified.

When a child with a disability is born into a family, the family's expectations are violated in at least two ways. First, the child may not look like or behave like the child they imagined. The doctor's predictions about the future may be dour and depressing or frightening in their vagueness. Grandparents and friends may not know how to react and may offer no congratulations, send no flowers, make no phone calls. Instead of imagining a bright future for the child, the parents imagine the worst—or don't know what to imagine. The family's cultural background may also influence how grandparents and extended family respond to the birth of a child with a disability. For some it may bring dishonor, with the sense that the parents have done something wrong for such a thing to happen; others accept disability as something that "just happens" (Klein & Chen, 2001).

Second, the parents' expectations for caring for the child may not match with reality. Nearly all families underestimate how much work is involved in having a new baby and how much of their own lives they are required to give up. Although all newborns are demanding, a baby with a disability may have special equipment, require special feeding techniques, be particularly irritable or fussy, and not respond predictably to being cared for. As a result, first-time parents may not be able to benefit from advice from friends and relatives, and experienced parents may not be able to rely on their experiences with their other children for some aspects of caregiving.

Families who have access to parent support groups when their children are identified with a disability are fortunate: Other parents of children with disabilities can often provide both emotional support and specific ideas for easing the burdens of child care. Organizations founded by parents of children with a specific disability, like the Association for Retarded Citizens–United States (ARC-US), the Cystic Fibrosis Foundation, or the Down Syndrome Congress, are often a great help to families with newly identified young children. (See our website for a list of useful organizations.)

National and local organizations can provide both information and support to families.

When parents of exceptional children look to the future, their dreams and expectations may also be violated. During childhood, the parents may be required to advocate for their child to ensure that he or she receives an appropriate educational program. As an adult, their child may still need their care. Parents must prepare for what will happen to that child—no matter what age—when they die.

This is not what we bargain for when we begin to dream about having a child. But it is not the catastrophe that it might seem to be at first glance, either. Many families become stronger and wiser for the experience of having an exceptional member. As usual, those virtues do not arrive without pain and struggle.

As an illustration, let us observe a hypothetical family:

> Tranh and Thu Le's baby is whisked away from them the minute she is born and soon surrounded by green-coated medical personnel who work over her quietly but urgently for many minutes. Returning from the huddle, their ashen-faced obstetrician tells them that their baby appears to have Down syndrome and is having difficulty breathing. The doctors suspect that she has a heart problem, and she is being taken to the neonatal intensive care unit, where she will undergo tests and be evaluated.
>
> Before they can think about what questions to ask, Tranh and Thu Le are in the recovery room, looking at each other. Down syndrome? Doesn't that mean mental retardation? And a heart problem? Will she survive? Do we want her to survive? Will she need surgery? Why is this happening to us?

In describing the experience of learning that their child had a disability, many parents remember the initial feeling as one of *shock*. Parents sometimes describe themselves as standing over the situation, looking down on it and watching themselves. These feelings can be short-lived or persist for some time. Because of this, professionals are encouraged to repeat the information they have about the baby or child at another time, or in a different way, as often as possible over the first few days. It is crucial for professionals to be available to parents as they ask questions and as the import of the news slowly dawns on them.

As the shock diminishes, parents may begin to feel a deep *grief*. Their "dream child" is gone, and they don't know what they are left with. This is a feeling that many parents continue to feel for a long time, although it is not a constant feeling. For many, this grief is alleviated by the beginnings of attachment to their child. Let's go back to our hypothetical situation . . .

> Late that night, Tranh and Thu Le are able to visit their new daughter in the neonatal intensive care unit. The doctors have told them that their baby has a congenital heart defect that will require open-heart surgery. Although the baby is wearing a heart monitor and receiving some oxygen through a nasal tube, the nurse takes her out of her incubator and places her in Thu Le's arms. She's adorable! Tranh and Thu Le exclaim with surprise as they notice her fuzzy hair, her smooth skin, her tiny hands. Tranh notices that her nose is small and her eyes appear to have an upward slant. She opens those eyes, and suddenly the baby and her parents are looking at each other for the first time. Despite the sadness and anxiety in their hearts, Tranh and Thu Le fall in love with their new daughter. They decide to name her Angelica.

Another feeling that parents must often struggle with is *anger*. They look at friends and family members with normal, healthy babies and wonder why their baby couldn't have been that way. They look for someone to blame for their dilemma, and if they find no one, they may turn the anger inward and blame themselves, often without reason.

Feelings of shock, grief, and anger may recur throughout child-rearing, but most parents ultimately accept and adjust to their child's disability.

Despite the pain, most parents eventually reach a point at which they accept the fact that their child has a disability, which Jan Blacher (1984a) describes as *adjustment and acceptance:* "a constructive adaptation to the child's handicap and realistic expectations of his or her progress" (p. 28). Although feelings of anger, guilt, and sadness do not disappear, the parents are able to recognize and rejoice in their child's progress and to act as advocates for their child.

Our story of Tranh and Thu Le depicts a hypothetical example of a family learning shortly after birth that their child will have a disability. In some instances, early diagnoses like these do occur. Some disabilities are present at birth and are identified immediately or in the first few days of life. For many other families, however, the knowledge that their child has a disability comes later. Parents may suspect that something is wrong, but they sometimes have difficulty getting professionals to confirm their suspicions. Parents typically suspect hearing loss in their child, for example, before the age of 12 months, yet the average age at which the diagnosis is confirmed is 2½ years (Northern & Downs, 1991). Learning disabilities typically do not appear until the child is in school and must begin to learn to read; children with autism may develop normally for the first months of life. The worry that something is wrong with their child is very stressful for parents; they often veer back and forth between reassurance and deep anxiety. See the accompanying box, "Samples of Developmental Tasks for Families with Young Children."

Factors Affecting Families' Reaction

We know a great deal about families and how they work from our own experiences, and the components of the family systems approach provide us with a conceptual framework for discussion. Foremost among these is the first component, **family characteristics,** which includes the characteristics of the exceptional child as well as the family itself. Let us examine how this information has specific implications for families with a child with a disability.

~ Samples of Developmental Tasks for Families with Young Children

- Coming to terms with a diagnosis and violation of expectations for a "perfect" child
- Negotiating the maze of fragmented services
- Becoming an advocate for the child
- Ensuring time for sustained positive interactions with the child
- Nurturing a positive and pleasurable relationship with the child
- Developing synchronous parent-child interaction
- Maintaining relationships with other family members (e.g., siblings, partner, or extended family)
- Managing contextual challenges (e.g., housing, nutrition)
- Clarifying a personal view of early childhood and family services within one's cultural paradigm
- Adopting flexible family roles
- Building informal network of support
- Balancing work and caregiving demands
- Maintaining self-esteem and building sense of competence as parents

Source: S. Epps & B.J. Jackson (2000). *Empowered families, successful children*, p. 34. Washington, DC: American Psychological Association.

■ ***Characteristics of the Child's Exceptionality*** Clearly, various abilities and disabilities will have differing effects on family life. For one thing, the *nature* of the exceptionality will determine the family reaction. The child who is deaf challenges the family to alter their communication system; will family members use sign language or speech for communication? If the choice is sign language, is each family member willing to take on the commitment of attending sign language classes? The child who is chronically ill places financial as well as emotional stress on the family; the child with a learning disability requires extra academic support and may cause a family to examine the emphasis they place on school achievement.

The nature of the child's disability has an influence on family life.

The *degree* of exceptionality may also have an impact on the family reaction. Children with more severe disabilities may look and behave quite differently than other children. Although on one hand these factors might stigmatize a family, on the other they clearly communicate that the child has a disability, relieving the family of the need to explain. Some disabilities, like deafness and learning disabilities, are "invisible"; they are less likely to be apparent from looking at the child. Families of children with disabilities often describe the stress and frustration that accompany the constant explanations of their child's disability that are expected by family, friends, and strangers. Berry and Hardman (1998) provide a poignant example of family stress in their excerpt from Kathryn Morton's description of going grocery shopping with her daughter, Beckie: "I took her shopping with me only if I felt up to looking groomed, cheerful, competent, and in command of any situation. . . . to look tired and preoccupied with surviving . . . would have turned both of us into objects of pity" (Morton, 1985, p. 144).

Parents often spend time explaining their child's disability to others.

The *demands* of the exceptionality will also affect the family's ability to respond. Children who are medically fragile, needing special equipment such as ventilators, oxygen, or gastrointestinal tubes, present great caregiving demands on a family. Children in wheelchairs or who use other equipment require special accommodations in their homes. Children with behavioral and emotional disorders may be destructive of themselves, of others, or of objects within the home. Each exceptionality places its own unique constraints on family life. Even giftedness is no exception; the needs of the talented child for lessons, tutoring, or special attention may create difficulties for other children in the family.

Disabilities place varying demands on family members.

■ ***Characteristics of the Family*** In addition to the nature and demands of the child's exceptionality, each family has qualities and characteristics that make it unique. Among these characteristics are family configuration and family size. Family configuration refers to the adults present in the family. These can include one or both parents, stepparents, or foster parents, and extended family members such as grandparents, aunts, uncles, cousins, or family friends. There may be one adult living with the child or many. For children of working parents, the caregiver during the parents' work hours may also be essential to the family configuration. Children who experience many changes in family configuration (such as several foster placements) appear to be particularly vulnerable to school problems later in life (Baker, Mednick, & Hunt, 1987; Werner & Smith, 1982). Related to family configuration is family size, which usually refers to the number of children in the family. Issues for only-child families may be quite different from those of larger families. Where brothers and sisters are involved, we must consider their needs in light of their exceptional sibling.

The word *family* has a unique meaning for the Giraldis, who have adopted 17 children with disabilities. (Andy Levin/ Photo Researchers, Inc.)

Socioeconomic status is determined by family income, education, and employment.

Another important family characteristic, one determined by income, education, and employment, is its **socioeconomic status** (SES), which may affect the family's ability to participate in the child's educational program. Although most families have periods of financial strain, for some it is a more chronic problem than others. As this is being written, more than one in six of all urban children in the United States live in families whose income is below the poverty line (Children's Defense Fund, 2001). As we noted in Chapter 2, poverty can affect a child's health and nutrition as well as access to experiences.

As we have seen, a family's culture has a profound effect on its world view and on its attitudes toward an exceptional child. A child with a disability may be perceived quite differently from culture to culture. Many Native American groups, for example, believe in accepting all events as they are; this value is based on the Indian belief that these events occur as part of the nature of life, and one must learn to live with the good and the bad in life (Coles, 1977; Joe & Malach, 1998). As the result of these values, attitudes toward children with disabilities are often open and accepting; difference and disability may be viewed as a natural part of life (Dorris, 1989). Other groups define a broad spectrum for "normal" behavior, and therefore have difficulty with a school label such as "mental retardation" for their child (Harry, 1992a). In some Latino cultures, strong beliefs in the powers of good and evil, reinforced by religious beliefs, may lead a family to believe that the birth of a child with a disability has resulted from a curse put on the child or the effects of an evil spirit (Zuniga, 1998). Families with Anglo-European roots are more likely to use the tradition of scientific explanation to understand the cause of a child's disability. But each of us must take care not to make blanket assumptions about families' beliefs and practices based on their cultural background. According to Zuniga, "The central principle is to view each family as an individual unit to ascertain what meaning they ascribe to the illness or disability. Assumptions should not be made without first getting to know the family since so many variables contribute to views on causation and disability, particularly related to children" (p. 235).

A family's religious beliefs can provide them with comfort and support.

Religious background is another family characteristic that will affect the perception of disability. Churches, temples, and other religious communities often provide a significant source of support for families, and religious beliefs can shape a family's strategies for coping with a disability.

Impact of Exceptionality on Family Functions

Think about the list you may currently have—either in your head or written down—of "things to do." Going to the bank, shopping for groceries, registering for a class, buying a book, calling a friend to arrange an outing, having your eyes examined—all of these tasks are related to personal needs. If you are a parent, your own list is probably at the bottom of an infinite list of things to do for other family members.

Family functions include all the life tasks the family performs to meet its needs.

Families with exceptional children are often responsible for complex **family functions,** which include all the tasks the family performs to meet its needs. Family finances can be strained by the need for ongoing professional evaluation and services. Taking care of the everyday needs of an exceptional child can be a full-time job in itself: Feeding, dressing, toileting, and transporting a child with a severe disability is labor-intensive. The socialization and self-definition needs of parents are often sacrificed to the needs of children, and families are expected to devote a great deal of time and energy to the educational and vocational needs of their exceptional child. When needs of family members are not met, stress may result.

When you work with the family of an exceptional child, you must take into account the needs of the entire family and the responsibilities for fulfilling family functions that parents already carry. These responsibilities are challenging for any parent, and sometimes feel overwhelming in economically secure two-parent families; they are compounded in single-parent families and in those families where economic strains are real. Your expectations for families of children who are exceptional must be tempered by your appreciation for the responsibilities involved in meeting their overall needs. Your most useful suggestions to parents will help them incorporate effective strategies for facilitating their child's development into their daily routines; there will also be times when you can offer families additional means to cope with the demands of their family life and the stress that results from unmet needs.

Exceptionality and Family Interactions

All the relationships within families can be touched by the presence of a child with exceptionality. Traditionally, conventional wisdom assumed that relationships would be affected negatively. More recently, researchers have begun to examine the possibility that the presence of such a child can affect **family interactions** in positive as well as negative ways, and we have begun to alter many of our long-held assumptions and views.

Family interaction addresses the relationships among family members.

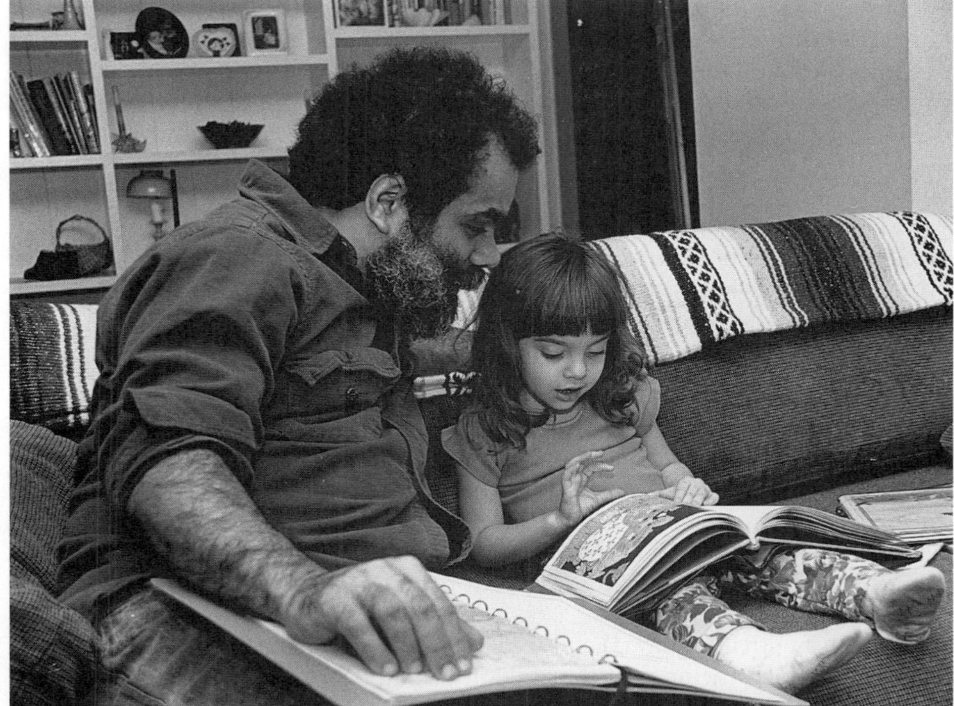

Family support for people with disabilities can take many forms. Here a father and daughter read together from a book that has typed words for her and a braille overlay for him. (Linda Eber/Impact Visuals)

■ ***Within the Family*** Research on the lifespan of a typical marriage suggests that most marital partners report a decrease in satisfaction with marriage in the years following the birth of children (Belsky, Lang, & Rovine, 1985). With the presence of any child adding to strain in a marriage, some researchers have assumed that the presence in a family of a child with a disability would lead to increased stress and family breakdown. A large-scale study done in England by Pahl and Quine (1987) described a complex situation in which a number of specific factors led to unusually high levels of stress in parents of children with severe handicaps. Some factors were related to the child's disability, such as the child's behavior problems, and some to general family problems, such as parents' money worries. The highest levels of stress were reported by the families of children with the most severe disabilities. Breslau, Staruch, and Mortimer (1982) found that the best predictor of mothers' distress was the intensity of the child's daily needs—the amount of help, for example, that the child needed with eating, dressing, grooming, and so on. You can see that the weight of these factors within each family would vary depending on the nature of the child's disability and other family characteristics, and on the coping strategies and sources of support available to each family. While having a child with a disability can increase family stress, most families remain together despite those strains. In fact, some couples report that their marriage is strengthened by the presence of their child with a disability (Turnbull & Turnbull, 2001).

■ ***Between Parents and Children*** Researchers have identified some differences in parent-child interaction when the child has a disability or is at risk for the development of a disability. (The interaction between mothers and their children is studied much more frequently than that of fathers and their children.) These differences vary according to the characteristics of each mother and each child and appear to change somewhat over time, particularly during the first year of life. In general, it appears that mothers of young children with disabilities dominate the communication interactions with their children more than mothers of children without disabilities, perhaps because it is more difficult to interpret infant cues and responses (Barnard & Kelly, 1990). Mothers may talk more simply because their children talk less—so many children with disabilities have delayed language development. Klein and Briggs (1987) demonstrated through their Mother-Infant Communication Project that effective communication techniques could be facilitated through indirect modeling in a group of mothers and high-risk infants.

■ ***Among Siblings*** What happens to the brothers and sisters of children with exceptionalities? Do they suffer from lack of parental attention? Are they given too much responsibility for caregiving? The impact of a sibling with a disability on brothers and sisters seems to depend on a number of factors, such as the attitudes and expectations of parents, family size, family resources, religion, the severity of the disability, and the pattern of interactions between siblings (Powell & Gallagher, 1993). Some studies have cited the negative aspects of the experience. Increased need for child care, for example, may make particular demands on older sisters (Stoneman, Brody, Davis, & Crapps, 1988). Brothers and sisters of children with disabilities may also react to related stress with changes in their behavior or feelings of loneliness, insecurity, or incompetence (Milstead, 1988).

Most professionals today believe that it is important to invite siblings to participate in decisions concerning their brother or sister with a disability, and sometimes to help with the exceptional child's educational programs. Swenson-Pierce, Kohl, and Egle (1987) taught siblings to instruct their brothers and sisters with severe handicaps and found that they were successful teachers: Their siblings with severe handicaps increased their independent performance of the skills taught. Of course, teaching is not appropriate for every sibling; some will enjoy the process and some will not. But many brothers and sisters are natural teachers of their exceptional siblings, and the family benefits from these positive interactions.

Brothers and sisters of children with disabilities can participate in their siblings' care.

■ ***The Extended Family*** Families with effective support systems seem to cope better with the stresses of daily life (Garbarino, 1990). For many, this group includes extended family members who provide help and support. The extended family includes grandparents, aunts, uncles, nieces, nephews, and other relatives. Extended family members may live with parents and child or apart from them. They can be respite caregivers as well as sources of emotional (and sometimes economic) support to overstressed parents. Family support programs should consider the impact of a child with a disability on grandparents as well as on more immediate family members; many parents of children with disabilities worry about how their own parents will accept their grandchild (Seligman & Darling, 1989).

■ ***Families Under Stress*** Raising children today presents special challenges to families in environments that Garbarino (1997) calls "socially toxic." Garbarino believes that elements of children's social world—violence, poverty, disruption of family relationships, substance use, the proliferation of guns, the threat of AIDS—have become poisonous to their development and undermine

Families under stress may have less time in which to interact with their children.

their sense of security. In addition, researchers tell us that adults are spending less time with children, and "the lack of adult supervision and time spent doing constructive, cooperative activities compounds the effects of other negative influences in the social environment for kids" (Garbarino, 1997, p. 14). The children who may be most vulnerable to the "social toxins" are those who already have the most developmental risk factors (see Chapter 2), especially those who live in poverty.

Some families have difficulty withstanding these social stresses. Hanson and Carta (1996) call them "**families with multiple risks**" and suggest strategies for educators working with them (see the accompanying box, "Principles of Support and Intervention for Children and Their Families").

Families with children with HIV infection, for example, must deal with many stressful issues (Lesar, Gerber, & Semmel, 1995). The negative social climate and stigma still associated with HIV and AIDS caused 70 percent of the families in the Lesar study not to disclose the cause of their child's illness to anyone outside their immediate families. The amount and nature of the social support they received were therefore diminished, leaving them isolated, and the intense caregiving demands of the child's illness isolated them further.

~ Principles of Support and Intervention for Children and Their Families

1. *Providing opportunities for positive caregiving transactions.* Providing support at the earliest point for children and parents or caregivers in establishing positive and mutually satisfying relationships with one another holds promise for preventing or relieving sources of stress.
2. *Shifting focus from deficits to emphasis on individual and family strengths.* Services to children and families will be best served by identifying and supporting strengths, rather than by fault-finding and blaming.
3. *Recognizing and encouraging informal sources of support.* Friends, community members, teachers, and others may be natural supports for families.
4. *Becoming cross-culturally competent.* Professionals must be sensitive, respectful, and knowledgeable about the family culture .
5. *Providing comprehensive, coordinated services.* Services to families must be community-based, appropriate, and valued by families; agencies must work together to provide coordinated services to families.
6. *Recognizing the need to offer families a broad spectrum of services.* Schools and other agencies must recognize that families with multiple challenges may require assistance in numerous areas before they can make use of other interventions that address specific child needs.
7. *Delivering flexible, usable services.* Service providers must individualize services based on family needs.
8. *Crossing professional boundaries and overcoming bureaucratic limitations.* Agencies and professionals must break through bureaucratic boundaries to work together on behalf of families.

Adapted from Hanson, M. J., & Carta, J. J. (1996). "Addressing the challenges of families with multiple risks," *Exceptional Children, 62*(3), 201–212.

Coping Strategies and Sources of Support

Despite the responsibilities and strains we have described, many families of children with disabilities survive and thrive:

> These are the families who roll up their sleeves and get on with the task of finding the best available services for their child; who both accept the reality of the disability and are able to love the child for who he or she is; who manage to have successful marriages and emotionally well-adjusted children, both with and without disabilities. Many of them have enough energy left over from coping with the demands of their own lives to provide support to other families, and even to give encouragement now and again to weary educators and service providers. These families are said to have made a positive adaptation to their child with a disability. We meet these parents every day in the course of our educational or health practices. (Summers, Behr, & Turnbull, 1989, p. 27)

Recently researchers have begun to study how people cope with stress and adversity. **Coping strategies** are the things people do to enhance a sense of well-being in their lives and to avoid being harmed by stressful demands (Turnbull & Turnbull, 1993).

Coping strategies help people avoid the harmful effects of high levels of stress.

Some of the resources that have been found to assist families in successful coping include problem-solving and behavior-management skills; negotiation and communication skills in working with professionals; informal social support, including other family members; and community support. In addition, Summers, Behr, and Turnbull (1989) note that a family's coping strategies have

Family dinners provide structure and support for all family members. (Jeff Dunn/Index Stock Imagery)

a great impact on how well they adapt to their child's disability. Families that cope successfully tend to use three key coping strategies:

- They attribute a cause to the event in order to establish a sense of personal control.
- They acquire mastery, or a feeling of control, in order to keep the adverse events from occurring again.
- They enhance self-esteem by finding the benefits or positive experiences that can result from adverse events. (Taylor, 1983)

Turnbull and Turnbull (1993) describe these strategies as "cognitive coping"—"thinking about a particular situation in ways that enhance well-being" (p. 1). Thus, successful support of families incorporates strategies that increase not only the families' understanding of the causes of disability but also their sense of control over the events of their lives and their self-esteem related to the presence of their children with disabilities (Summers, Behr, & Turnbull, 1989).

■ ***Parent Support Groups*** At times, organizations, school programs, or agencies offer support groups for parents of children with similar disabilities or ages. These groups may have a specific goal, such as teaching advocacy skills, or they may be formed to provide parents with an opportunity to get to know other parents who have similar concerns. Parents often feel most comfortable among a group of peers and can discuss their very private fears and worries about their children with other parents who may have shared their experiences and feelings. Participation in support groups appears to help many parents feel less isolated; often parents report that until they participated in a group they felt they were the only people in the world with their problems. Participation in groups can also help parents form a network of new and understanding friends, and this helps families fulfill the often-neglected socialization function previously mentioned.

Support groups can provide comfort and information for parents.

One effective model for parent support is the **parent-to-parent model,** which links experienced parents of young children with disabilities to parents who are new to the programs and processes. Through phone conversations and group meetings, experienced parents listen, comfort, and share their experiences with others just beginning to learn about their children. Parents who have had similar experiences are often the most empathic and knowledgeable source of support for new parents.

Turnbull and Turnbull (1997) point out that support groups are common in early intervention programs, somewhat less so in school-age programs, and almost nonexistent for parents of older children and adults. Parents of older children and adults with disabilities often need information, communication, and sharing as well, and programs designed to meet their needs could fill a void that leaves many parents isolated.

■ ***Respite Care*** For many families, the constant vigilance and caregiving required by a son or daughter with a disability can become overwhelming. A young child with intensive medical requirements, for example, may need to have equipment cleaned, adjusted, and monitored throughout the day; parents may even sleep lightly, perhaps with an intercom to the child's room next to them, in order to be able to hear if equipment "beeps," indicating that the child (or the equipment) is having a problem. The child may be on several different medications or require special treatments that must be administered day and night. The child's care can be so complex that parents cannot simply leave the child with a babysitter. Children with unusual or demanding behavioral characteristics, such as those typical of some children with autism, for example, can also be particularly difficult to care for.

Most parents benefit from spending some time without their children in order to build up their spirits for the relentless requirements of being a parent. This is the case for parents of *all* children. For some families of children with very intensive caregiving needs, this time is much more difficult to obtain, and single-parent families are especially hard-hit. It is for families like this that the concept of **respite care** was developed. In respite care, trained substitute caregivers take over the care of the family member with a disability for a period of time that can range from an hour to a weekend. Respite care is usually provided in the family home, but it can also occur in the caregiver's home or in another facility such as a day-care center or a group home. Families from culturally diverse backgrounds may not be comfortable with the notion of respite care or may prefer to have extended family members provide it. In those cases, the wishes of the family should be respected; some states allow family members to be paid for providing respite care.

Respite care is not yet widely available all over the country for families of children with disabilities; when it is provided, however, families report that it positively benefits their families and helps reduce stress levels (Abelson, 1999).

The Role of the Family in Special Education Services

As we saw in Chapter 1, the laws pertaining to the education of children with disabilities (IDEA and its amendments) allow for parent partnership in every stage of the educational process. Parents choose to collaborate with professionals to varying degrees—some participate a great deal, some not at all.

The concerns of families with exceptional children change as their children grow and develop, moving from infancy through the school years. Sometimes their children receive special education services from the first year of life through age 21. Let us take a look at the programs available for children with disabilities throughout the school years, and the provisions and expectations for parent involvement within those programs.

The Parents' Rights

Parents have the right to be informed and to consent, and to participate in placement and program decisions.

Built into IDEA (see Chapter 1) is an acknowledgment of the parents' *right to be informed and to consent*. Before a child can be evaluated to determine whether he or she is eligible for special education services at all, parents must receive a written assessment plan that thoroughly describes, in clear, everyday language, what kind of evaluation will be conducted and for what purpose. They must sign and return the assessment plan before an evaluation can take place. In fact, parents' right to an informed consent must be considered at every educational decision point for their child. Ask yourself these questions when considering how this operates in the school in which you teach:

- Are the written materials that explain procedures and alternatives available in the parents' native language? Verbally translating or paraphrasing this information may not constitute informed consent.

- Are the explanations on those written documents suitably simple and straightforward enough for a layperson to comprehend? Educators, like many other professionals, are notorious for their use of jargon; sometimes we are so immersed in it that we assume that everyone else understands it, too.
- Do parents understand that they have the option *not* to consent? Sometimes this information is not emphasized by professionals who talk with parents, or it is "buried" in consent forms.

Parents also have *the right to participate in placement and program decisions* through the individualized education program (IEP) process. Parents are equal members of the IEP team, as discussed in Chapter 1. They can express preferences for where their child will attend school and what the primary goals and objectives of their child's educational program will be. If parents do not agree with the IEP team's recommendations, no change in placement or program can be made until the disagreement has been settled.

Due process procedures help parents and schools resolve disagreements about the child's schooling.

When parents and school personnel disagree about a child's evaluation, placement, or program, parents must be informed of their **right to due process.** Either the parents or the school may call for a hearing (usually called a **due process hearing**) in order to resolve the conflict. Under the 1997 amendments to IDEA, **mediation** must be available to families and the school district before they go to a due process hearing, although participation in mediation in order to resolve disputes is voluntary. At the due process hearing, both parties may be represented by lawyers and have the opportunity to call witnesses who will testify for their point of view. The decision is made by an impartial hearing officer. Usually both parties accept the decision of the hearing officer, but if either side still strongly disagrees, the decision can be appealed to the state educational agency and to state and federal courts.

Because of the many opportunities for parent participation that IDEA provides, some professionals come to believe that parents are under an obligation to play a part in this process. This assumption is not correct. Parents also have the *right not to participate* in this educational decision-making. Some parents are not comfortable in such a situation; others are not able to take part, and so they waive their rights. Cultural considerations come into play here, too. Parents from some cultural groups may prefer to leave educational decision-making to the schools. When parents choose not to become involved in the IEP process, you must be sure that they understand all their options. Perhaps transportation is difficult for them, and telephone participation would be easier. Has it been made clear to them that an interpreter will be available?

Parents who are not involved in their child's education may have barriers to participation that school professionals do not understand.

Teachers sometimes equate parents' noninvolvement in schooling with noninvolvement with the child who has a disability (MacMillan & Turnbull, 1983). This is usually an inaccurate perception. Parents of children with disabilities, especially those with more severe conditions, have strenuous demands on their time and energy; they may see the time the child is in school as their only respite. In addition, family factors such as lack of child care, lack of a support system, or an inflexible work schedule may make participation in the child's educational programming nearly impossible for some families (Shea & Bauer, 1991). The cultural disconnect between the family and the school may also contribute to the family's lack of participation in school activities.

As part of a study of Latino families of Puerto Rican and Mexican descent, Bailey, Skinner, Rodriguez, Gut, and Correa (1999) asked parents whether they were aware of the range of services available to their young children with disabilities. While the great majority of families were aware of services, they reported only a moderate level of satisfaction with them. The parents who were most dissatisfied had several reasons, among them feelings that they had been discriminated against, and the lack of spoken or written communication in Spanish. Those families who were most satisfied reported that there was one key professional who helped them navigate the system, as well as professionals who took time with them and were able to explain their child's condition and treatment.

The earlier work of Beth Harry and her colleagues (1992b, 1995) identified some of the factors that may contribute to the relatively low level of participation in special education procedures on the part of African American families. Harry's longitudinal study identified several factors that discouraged the parents' participation and advocacy for their children:

- *Late notices and inflexible scheduling of conferences.* Despite mandated timelines, parents did not always receive notices of meetings in a timely manner.
- *Limited time for conferences.* Meetings averaged twenty to thirty minutes in length unless parents expressed many concerns.
- *Emphasis on documents rather than participation.* According to Harry and her colleagues:

  > When parents were asked how they perceived their role in the conferences, the majority consistently replied that their main role was to receive information about their child's progress and to sign the documents. . . . Observations revealed that parents' participation in conferences usually consisted of listening, perhaps asking a question (usually regarding logistical issues such as transportation), and signing papers. A typical view, expressed by one mother, was: "They lay it out [the IEP]. If you have questions, you can ask them. Then you sign it." (p. 371)

- *The use of jargon.* The use of unexplained technical terms by professionals can have a silencing effect on parents and can cloud their understanding of information and decision-making.
- *The structure of power.* When conferences are structured so that professionals report and parents listen, there is an implication that power is in the hands of the professionals.

Practices like these violate the spirit of the law when they diminish parents' incentive to participate as partners in assessment, planning, and placement issues regarding their children.

Before Formal Schooling: The Early Years

In Chapter 2 we described the **early intervention** services that can be provided when a child under the age of 3 is identified with a specific disability or developmental delay or is considered at risk for the development of a disability. Parents of young children in early intervention services are typically concerned with meeting the day-to-day needs of their child and learning more about the implications of their child's developmental status or disability. As we discussed in Chapter 1, the strengths and needs of the family are identified in the **individ-**

IDEA allows parents to stay actively involved in the education of their children with disabilities through participation on the IFSP team.

ualized family service plan (IFSP), which is developed cooperatively by the family and the family service team (Sandall, 1997a, 1997b).

During the School Years

Starting school is an important event in every child's life, and it means adjustments for every family. For parents of typically developing children, school entry usually means that they will play less of a role in their child's education. Although they will help with homework, confer with teachers, and possibly attend school meetings, the decisions about what their child will learn, how he or she will learn it, and where learning will take place are all made by the school.

This process is quite different for parents of a child with a disability. Under the provisions of IDEA, educational decisions, including those relative to program planning and placement, are made by a team that includes one or both parents. This process may begin as early as age 3, when a child who has been in an early intervention program or who has been recently identified with a disability transitions into a preschool program.

■ ***The Parent-Teacher Relationship*** The laws mandating educational programs for exceptional children require that parents and professionals work together, or collaborate, to meet the best interests of the child. Although most teachers see the importance of this collaboration, some may not have the skills or the persistence needed to help parents become involved. The "Closer Look" box provides teachers with *Ideas for Involving Families at School,* which may be helpful in this regard.

New roles for parents can increase the possibility of true partnership.

Beth Harry (1992b) suggests that new roles for parents need to be developed to restructure parent-teacher communication:

- *Parents as assessors.* Parents' participation in the assessment processes that occur before the IEP meeting legitimizes their roles as providers of meaningful information about their children.
- *Parents as presenters of reports.* A parent report could be a formal part of the process, signaling to parents that their input is valued and necessary.
- *Parents as policymakers.* Harry recommends school-based, advisory parent bodies for special education programs, as well as active recruitment of parents as teacher's aides.
- *Parents as advocates and peer supports.* Parents serving in policymaking and support roles within schools may be more inclined to share their learning with other parents.

Despite gains, most schools and school districts have a great deal of readjustment to do before parents feel like true partners in their children's education.

Leaving School

When the young person with a disability has completed school or reached age 22 (IDEA allows for schooling through age 21), the family must face a new bureaucracy and new issues. How will the child, now a young adult, spend his or her time? Is he or she prepared for employment? Can he or she find a job? How will he or she spend leisure time? What kinds of friendships and relationships will he or she have? Will there be a place for him or her in the community?

Where will he or she live? Most of these issues confront any young adult seeking to separate from the family and achieve a sense of personal identity and independence, but they often assume a special degree of intensity and poignancy when faced by young adults with disabilities. Whitney-Thomas and Hanley-Maxwell (1996) found that parents of students with disabilities have less optimistic visions about their son or daughter's future than do parents of students without disabilities. They suggest that parents' feelings may realistically reflect the more narrow range of choices in adult life for students with disabilities.

Transitions to Work and Higher Education

Transition planning helps parents plan for their exceptional child as an adult.

Although many in special education equate **transition** with employment opportunities, Halvorsen et al. (1989) broaden the concept of transition to include the needs of the whole person across all life areas. Transition planning helps parents understand how their exceptional child will live as an adult.

In the past, many families had to make the difficult decisions about the needs of their young adult child with little help. To compound the problem, few alternatives were available for quality residential and employment opportunities for young adults with disabilities. Over the past fifteen years, however, the federal government has turned its attention to postschool choices for individuals with disabilities (Will, 1984), and since 1990, special education professionals have been required to focus on providing transition services to families at times of change. Preparation for the transition from school to work must begin long before school ends. In fact, many experienced parents and professionals believe that for some students, particularly those with severe disabilities, preparation should begin very early in the child's schooling (Falvey, 1995). (See the accompanying "First Person" box.)

The services for students with disabilities that have been provided since the passage of IDEA in 1975 have led to an increased number of those students attending higher education programs (U.S. Office of Special Education: http://www.ed.gov/offices/OSERS/IDEA/overview.html/). Section 504 of the Rehabilitation Act of 1973 and the Americans with Disabilities Act (1990) require that higher education opportunities be extended to all qualified individuals with disabilities. You will read more about transition planning in the chapters to follow.

Family Concerns for the Future

The future of their children with disabilities is often a source of great concern for parents. Many parents, recognizing that they are not immortal, worry about what will happen to their child when they are no longer able to take responsibility for his or her care. Participation in the process of transition planning can allay some of the natural anxiety about future options (Clark & Patton, 1997). Along the way, the parents become aware of the resources available to help plan for the long-term future of their son or daughter. Families need information and support to confront the intricacies of financial planning and government benefits, guardianship, making a will, and finding and evaluating residential options for their son or daughter. Decisions relating to these crucial areas should be made, whenever possible, with the input of the son or daughter with a disability and should be based on his or her personal preferences (Turnbull et al., 1989). Even individuals with the most severe disabilities have ways of communicating

A closer look

Ideas for Involving Families at School

Many families, particularly those from culturally and linguistically diverse backgrounds, are hesitant to become involved in school activities. Here are some steps school professionals can take to meet the needs of families of children receiving special education services, and further the likelihood that families will participate at school.

- *Establish an advisory committee* composed of parents and professionals to outline and monitor the "family-professional" goals of the school.
- *Gather extensive information on the families' concerns, priorities, strengths, and needs.* Use a variety of informal and formal assessment instruments to gather information, emphasizing family interviews.
- *Identify family needs and preferences for school involvement.* The Family Information Preference Inventory (Turnbull & Turnbull, 1997) can be adapted to provide school professionals with information on the needs of families in the areas of teaching the child at home, advocacy, working with professionals on planning for the future, coping with family stress, and using resources.
- *Develop school manuals on policies and procedures, curriculum, and transition planning.* "User-friendly" materials that describe school practices, available in the parents' home language, can be a starting point for understanding and involvement.
- *Provide parents with videotapes, films, and slide presentations that focus on instruction and support.* See the list at the end of this chapter for resources.
- *Establish a materials lending library for parents and a toy lending library for their children.*
- *Invite parents to help with classroom projects.* Publish family recipe books or calendars in which every family contributes a recipe; write a class newsletter with and for families; begin home-school diaries; ask for parent help when the class is doing a special project.
- *Develop a system for providing regular feedback on the child's progress in school.* Notes are the standard, but think about phone calls, email, a classroom web page, or videotapes.
- *Develop survival vocabulary lists in the native languages of your classroom families.* Include greetings, special education terms, body parts, action words, calendar words, etc.
- *Provide parents with a current list of respite providers and babysitters who are experienced with children with disabilities.*

personal preferences, and family members are most likely to be able to interpret their signals.

Working with Culturally Diverse Families

Knowing Yourself

Self-examination is the first step to becoming culturally competent.

One of the first steps to cultural awareness should be self-examination. Self-examination is not particularly difficult, but doing it honestly and objectively may be a little harder than you think. Begin by asking yourself who you are. Get a sheet of paper and provide information on your:

- *Post a bulletin board specifically for families, with photographs and announcements that might interest them.*
- *Include parents in transition planning,* discussing the expectations of the next environment (whether it be kindergarten or the workplace), issues of inclusion, or whatever the parents seem to need. Have parents visit potential receiving classrooms. Provide team meetings including family members and school professionals from the old and new environments.
- *Make extra efforts to include hard-to-reach families.* Provide single parents, fathers, and parents who live a long way from the school or do not have transportation an opportunity to share in their child's learning by organizing activities that do not require them to come to the school building.
- *Organize a telephone tree for the families in your classroom.* Use the telephone tree to remind parents of upcoming events including classroom learning units, field trips, celebrations, and open-house meetings.
- *Communicate personally with the family as frequently as possible.*
- *When you do communicate with the family, be a good listener.* Don't monopolize the conversation with school news—provide parents with a chance to share home news, too.
- *Consider making a home visit for families who cannot come to school.* If your school administrator and the family are comfortable with home visiting, it can be an invaluable link between home and school.
- *Provide a competent interpreter for conversations with families who do not speak English.* Don't use the child or someone pulled in from the hallway to interpret, except in an emergency. Having trained interpreters available lets parents know that the school is committed to successful communication with them.

All these ideas assume that resources AND a considerable amount of energy are available to improve home-school relationships. But research tells us that children whose parents are involved in school perform at a higher level (Edwards, Pleasants, & Franklin, 1999)—so your efforts are very much worthwhile!

Source: Adapted from C.C. Thomas, V. I. Correa, and C. V. Morsink (2001), *Interactive teaming: Enhancing programs for children with special needs* (third ed.), pp. 295–296. Upper Saddle River, NJ: Merrill/Prentice-Hall.

- ethnicity
- social class
- gender
- geographical background
- language background
- age
- religion
- teaching style

After you have completed the initial exercise, examine the importance you place on each of these items. Now go down your class roll and ask yourself where

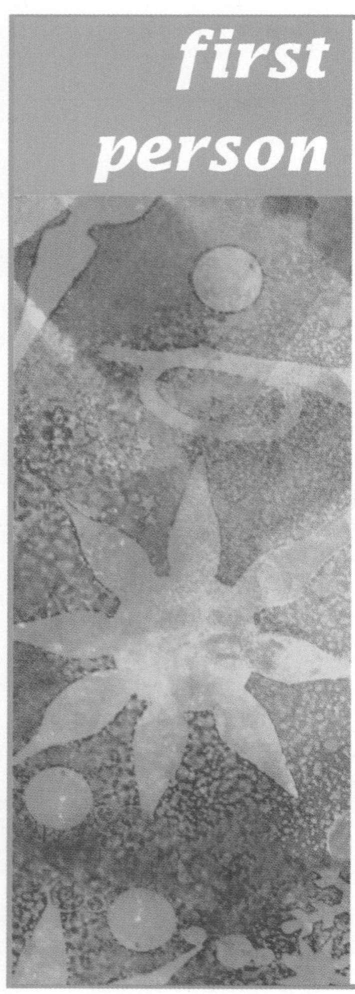

I believe that as professionals you can make a difference in our lives as parents of children with special needs.

You have the opportunity not to be intimidated when we blow off steam. You should not personalize these angry negative feelings. The great challenge for you is to give us the opportunity to fall apart once in a while.

You have the opportunity to decrease our profound sense of loneliness. . . . So often we want to talk about "it," but few people appear to want us to talk. You will often be the ONE person who will say: Tell me more. And then what happened? And how did that feel?

You have the opportunity to help us know our child. In the beginning, most of us know very little about their special needs. . . . You can model for us how to say the words, how to tell others. You can take us into our children's lives.

You have the opportunity to share books, pamphlets, and resources. Take the articles out of your file cabinets and off the shelves and spread them to the parents who have no idea where to find the stories and facts about our children.

You have the opportunity to help us recognize and celebrate our victories. They are often small for the "normal" population to appreciate. You know that awful-sounding "grunt" made by our child is truly a miracle. Often it is only you that knows that a new movement is significant and indicates a renewed sense of hope.

You have the opportunity to remind us how far we have come and how much we have accomplished. You, often more than our clos-

each of your students fits in each of these areas. How important is ethnicity to them? How important is language and dialect? How congruent are your values with those of your students? Your values don't have to be congruent, but it is important to know who you are with respect to your students. Do you have biases and prejudices? Almost everyone does. You should be suspicious of the teacher who says, "I don't have a prejudiced bone in my body!" What is important is that we recognize these biases and not let them cause us to be unfair or insensitive to students, their parents, our colleagues, and others who are associated with the school.

Developing Cultural Competence

To be able to work effectively with culturally diverse parents, it is important for teachers to be aware of their own attitudes toward people from diverse groups. Because of their different backgrounds, parents will often look different, speak differently, and dress differently than you do. Thus, you must begin to develop **cultural competence,** "respect for difference, eagerness to learn, and a willingness to accept that there are many ways of viewing the world" (Hanson, 1998, p. 493).

Cultural competence involves respect, willingness to learn, and appreciation of the many different ways of viewing the world.

est friends, know the details of our successes. Over and over, you can highlight those changes and celebrate the growth.

You have the opportunity to allow us those moments when our souls fall into deep despair. We will, at times, feel that we cannot and don't want to continue for another moment.

You can give us the space to be in that dark place. It is one of the greatest "interventions" you can give us.

If at times you can do some of these suggested activities, then you will have the opportunity to help us feel hope. We must feel hope if we are to get to our next appointment, or to face the next birthday party or to use the words *special needs.*

Partnership is a collaboration. Plopped right in the middle of that word you will find the word *labor.* Partnership is labor. It is hard work. You are the midwives helping us to give birth to a new relationship. Let us begin.

Janice Fialka

Source: Excerpted and adapted from "You Can Make a Difference in Our Lives," *DEC Communicator,* November 1996 23 (1), p. 8. Reprinted by permission of the author. Janice Fialka is the mother of two children, Micah (who has developmental disabilities) and Emma. This excerpt is published in a collection of her writings called "It Matters: Lessons from my son." To obtain a copy or receive information about her speaking engagements, contact her at 10474 LaSalle Boulevard, Huntington Woods, ME 48070 or by email: ruaw@aol.com.

Cultural competence is based on two key skills: awareness and communication. These skills become especially important when working with exceptional students and their families. See the accompanying box, "Questions About Cultural Competence," for questions that can be used to develop your awareness and communication skills and, ideally, to establish trust and rapport between you and the family.

> Our cultural and ethnic identities help to shape our beliefs and practices, and who we are as individuals and family members. These identities are not the script for our behavior, but they do provide a texture and a richness—and they can bind us together in groups or separate us from one another. Knowledge and understanding, sensitivity, and respect for these cultural differences can significantly enhance the effectiveness of service providers in the helping professions. (Hanson, 1998, p. 21)

Regardless of their economic status, language skills, or educational level, parents are greatly concerned about the welfare of their children. They, better than anyone else, know the child's characteristics, strengths and weaknesses, and perceptions of the school. Cultivating a working relationship with

~ Questions About Culturally Diverse Families

- How is the family organized (extended or nuclear)? Who are the primary caregivers? What language is spoken at home? What is the family pattern of decision-making? Does the family wish to include traditional practitioners or other members of the community in program planning and/or implementation?
- What values are shared with the Anglo mainstream? What aspects of working with the Anglo mainstream may be difficult?
- What is the most comfortable way for the family to work with the service provision system?
- Is there any other information that is important for personnel to know regarding the family and child and/or that is important to the family to relate or to question?

Source: P.P. Anderson & E.S. Fenichel, *Serving Culturally Diverse Families of Infants and Toddlers with Disabilities* (Arlington, VA: National Center for Clinical Infant Programs, 1989), p. 16.

culturally diverse parents requires respect for these understandings. See the box, "Building Blocks for Partnership with Families."

Good communication with the family, despite cultural and language differences, is key to the child's learning.

In special education, our work with families begins early, particularly if a disability is discovered when the child is quite young. As we discussed in Chapter 2, the development of the Individualized Family Service Plan involves planning not only for the child but for the family as well. Therefore, our ability to communicate and relate to the family, to identify the information parents need, and to integrate our educational and social interventions with the participation preferences of the family are critical aspects of service delivery (Sontag & Schacht, 1994). Our knowledge of how a family perceives not only a disability but also special services can affect the type of programming permitted and the extent to which services such as assistive technology are used (Hourcade, Parette, & Huer, 1997). Linan-Thompson and Jean (1997) suggest that when communicating with linguistically diverse parents of students with disabilities, it is important to use the method of communication preferred by the parent, to have interpreters who are knowledgeable about special education as well as bilingual, and to provide information to the family in a variety of formats (videos, text, etc.).

~ Building Blocks for Partnership with Families

The personal attributes and attitudes of the professional can be at the crux of forming a partnership with families. Among the important personal attributes are:

- Respect for families. Respect is based on the belief that the family is the most important element in a child's life, and that the family is managing their situation to the best of their ability (Beckman et al., 1996). Families sense when respect is lacking, and lack of respect makes it very difficult to build rapport between the professional and family member.
- A nonjudgmental attitude.
- Empathy.

Positive Aspects of Disabilities for Families

The ties that bind family members usually persist throughout a lifetime. When a son or daughter has a disability, those ties may involve more responsibility for decision-making and caregiving than a family anticipates. But despite these responsibilities, and despite the stresses and strains that can accompany them, many family members describe the benefits gained by living with a son or daughter or brother or sister with a disability. According to Ann and Rud Turnbull (1990) and their colleagues, families have identified six ways in which young people with disabilities can make positive contributions:

- Being a source of joy
- Providing a means of learning life's lessons
- Giving and receiving love
- Supplying a sense of blessing or fulfillment
- Contributing a sense of pride
- Strengthening the family (p. 115)

An exceptional child can affect family relationships in positive ways, too.

Although it is important to stress that the journey isn't easy and families must be supported through their very real times of crisis, professionals in special education are finding that, given support, information, and strategies from professionals and other parents, most families can come to recognize and experience the positive contributions made by their family member with a disability. Our role is to support and inform families in that process.

SUMMARY

- Professionals in schools are increasingly called upon to work with families and students from a variety of cultures. It is crucial that we begin to examine our own cultural experiences and attitudes so that we can respectfully engage family members with diverse backgrounds and experiences in a framework of cultural reciprocity.
- Theories of family life like the family systems approach and ecocultural theory shape our understanding of families and the demands of family life.
- The family systems approach uses the characteristics, interaction, function, and life cycle of each family to describe its unique dynamics, including the initial reaction to the child who is exceptional, the child's impact on the family, and the family's ability to cope and find support.
- The initial reaction to a child with a disability may be influenced by the nature and degree of the disability, family size and socioeconomic status, and cultural and religious background.
- Some of the most important sources of support for parents are parent-to-parent support groups, respite care, and early intervention and special education services.
- IDEA provides a series of rights and opportunities so that parents can participate in decisions related to their child's schooling.

- Parents continue to play a key role through the school years. They have the right to be informed and to consent to evaluation of their child, and to participate in placement and program decisions through the IEP process. Families are the focus of transition services and resources for planning for their child's future needs.
- Each school professional must develop self-knowledge as the cornerstone of cultural competence, which will enhance our ability to work effectively with families from culturally and linguistically diverse backgrounds.

Key Terms

family
household
extended family
caregiver
culture
ethnicity
macroculture
microculture
minority
minority groups
cultural reciprocity
cultural diversity
family systems approach
ecocultural theory
family characteristics
socioeconomic status
family functions
family interactions
families with multiple risks
coping strategies
parent-to-parent model
respite care
right to due process
due process hearing
mediation
early intervention
individualized family service plan
transition
cultural competence

Multimedia Resources

Anderson, Winifred, Stephen Chitwood, and Deirdre Hayden. *Negotiating the Special Education Maze: A Guide for Parents and Teachers*. 3rd ed. (Rockville, MD: Woodbine House, 1997). This book is a step-by-step guide for parents of exceptional children as well as teachers and other professionals. Its emphasis on the collaborative relationships among special education providers is highlighted by many practical checklists, examples, and guidelines.

Beckman, P.J., Frank, N., & Newcomb, S. (1996). Qualities and skills for communicating with families. In P.J. Beckman (Ed.), *Strategies for working with young children with disabilities,* pp.31–46. Baltimore: Paul H. Brookes.

Children's Defense Fund—Parent Resource Network (PRN).

Website: http:// www.childrensdefense.org/prn.html.

Provides access to a variety of national websites offering parents information on caring for their own children and on getting involved in group efforts to help children in their own communities or states.

Coalition for Asian-American Children and Families.

Website: http://www. cacf.org/.

The coalition advocates for social policies and programs that support Asian American children and families.

"Conversations for Three: Communicating Through Interpreters" is a new video and booklet published by Paul H. Brookes that is an invaluable tool for training interpreters (who translate or interpret one language into another in a signed or spoken form) and those who work with them.

Exceptional Parent magazine.

Website: http://www.eparent.com/news/resource/eparent/eparent.htm/.

This magazine publishes articles especially for families of children with disabilities and provides a forum for the exchange of information by families with children with rare or unusual conditions. Its address is

Exceptional Parent Magazine

555 Kinderkamack Road,

Oradell, NJ 07649

Telephone: 201-634-6550

Fax: 201-634-6599

Family Village is a web-based organization that integrates information, resources, and communication opportunities on the Internet for persons with cognitive and other disabilities.

Family Voices is an organization composed of families and others interested in children with special health care needs.

Their website is http://www.familyvoices.org/.

Featherstone, Helen. *A Difference in the Family: Life with a Disabled Child* (New York: Basic Books, 1980). The author, a parent and educator, discusses openly and honestly how it feels to raise a child with a disability. This remains one of the most powerful books on the topic.

Federal Interagency Coordinating Council (FICC).

Website: http://www.fed-icc.org.

This new website for parents and families of children with disabilities identifies people throughout government who can help answer parents' questions about children and disability issues.

Harry, Beth, Maya Kalyanpur, and Monimalika Day. *Building Cultural Reciprocity with Families: Case Studies in Special Education* (Baltimore: Paul H. Brookes, 1999); Kalyanpur, Maya, and Beth Harry. *Culture in Special Education: Building Reciprocal Family-Professional Relationships* (Baltimore: Paul H. Brookes, 1999). The work of Beth Harry and her colleagues has provided a voice for families who have not traditionally been heard in the special education system.

Kaufman, Sandra Z. *Retarded Isn't Stupid, Mom!* (Baltimore: Paul H. Brookes, 1999). Sandra Z. Kaufman's well-regarded book about her experiences with her daughter, Nicole, has been updated to include descriptions of Nicole's experiences as an adult.

The National Information Center for Children and Youth with Disabilities has put together *Parenting a Child with Special Needs: A Guide to Readings and Resources* at http://www.kidsource.com/popup.html/.

Seligman, Martin. *Conducting Effective Conferences with Parents of Children with Disabilities* (New York, NY: Guilford Press, 2000). A good book for teachers.

Organizations Providing Useful Resources for Families

National Parent Network on Disabilities
1130 17th Street N.W., Suite 400
Washington, DC 20036
(202) 463-2299 (V/TTY)

E-Mail: npnd@cs.com
Web: www.npnd.org

National Parent to Parent Support and Information System, Inc.
P.O. Box 907
Blue Ridge, GA 30513
(800) 651-1151
(706) 374-3822
E-mail: nppsis@ellijay.com
Web: www.nppsis.org

Parents Helping Parents:
The Parent-Directed Family Resource Center
for Children with Special Needs
3041 Olcott St.
Santa Clara, CA 95054
(408) 727-5775
Publications available in Spanish
Spanish speaker on staff
E-mail: info@php.com
Web: www.php.com

Sibling Information Network
A.J. Pappanikou Center
University of Connecticut
249 Glenbrook Road, U64
Storrs, CT 06269-2064
(860) 486-4985

National Council on Independent Living
1916 Wilson Boulevard, Suite 209
Arlington, VA 22201
(703) 525-3406
(703) 525-4153 (TTY)
E-mail: ncil@ncil.org
Web: www.ncil.org

Clearinghouse on Disability Information
Office of Special Education and Rehabilitative Services
Room 3132, Switzer Building
330 C Street S.W.
Washington, DC 20202-2524
(202) 205-8241 (Voice/TTY)

Visit our website for a more comprehensive list of organizations.

What You Can Do

1. Interview the parent or parents of a child with a disability. How much of the caregiving role does the parent currently undertake? Have the demands of caregiving increased or decreased during the past ten years? Have the parents sought support services, or do they rely on informal support from other family members, volunteers, and so forth? After complet-

ing the interview, summarize your results and present them to your classmates. Brainstorm some possible resources for the family.

2. What are the cultural groups (other than your own) represented in the area in which you live? Draw up a list of things you could do, based on what you have read in this chapter, to become more familiar with the values, traditions, and beliefs of those cultures.

3. Are you acquainted with the family of an exceptional child? If so, how do the components of the family systems approach apply to this family? Are they useful in identifying areas where services might be provided? Do they help you recognize the family's specific strengths and needs? Use the family systems framework to write a brief description of this family. If you're not familiar with a family yourself, read a book written by the parent of an exceptional child and apply these questions to that family. Some good choices might be Michael Berube's *Life As We Know It* (Pantheon Books, 1996) or *A Slant of Sun* by Beth Kephart (W.W. Norton, 1998).

4. Think about the way you communicate with parents. Do you:

- Use the primary language of the family, or have an experienced interpreter present?
- Avoid jargon?
- Allow time for questions and unexpected concerns to be addressed?
- Provide complete, unbiased information about the child's strengths and needs?
- Know how to relax and listen attentively? Many family members need and enjoy an opportunity to talk about their child.

Learning About the Potential of Exceptional Children

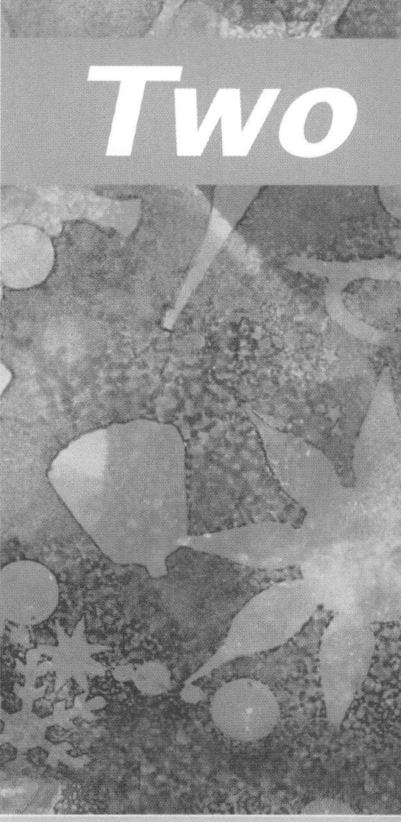

THE CHAPTERS in Part Two emphasize learning about the characteristics of individuals with specific disabilities. In addition to information on each category of exceptionality, Chapters 4 through 12 focus on helping you to understand the educational programs for each group of students. These chapters address several aspects of educational programs, including placement, assessment, and the selection and use of appropriate teaching strategies.

PART OUTLINE

Children with Learning Disabilities

4

IN THIS chapter we discuss students with learning disabilities, the largest group of children served in special education and the group most likely to be included in general education classes. Although these students require special education services, their learning needs are often balanced by excellence in other areas of life, and their ability to reach their potential can be dramatically enhanced by appropriate teaching and learning strategies. As you read about students with learning disabilities, think about the following questions:

What are learning disabilities? What distinguishes a learning disability from underachievement?

What do we know about the causes of learning disabilities?

What specific strategies are most helpful for teaching students with learning disabilities?

Commonalities: What interventions or adaptations presented in this chapter might be used to help all students learn?

Collaboration: What kinds of professional support are available to help classroom teachers work with students with learning disabilities?

Can Do: What specific adaptations will enable students with learning disabilities to achieve in the classroom setting?

Do you remember having to read aloud in school as a kid? Or sitting in a difficult math class, afraid of being called on to work a problem at the board? Many of us remember vividly the feelings of panic, fear, and anxiety that those situations evoked, particularly if we were not good readers or if we were not confident in our understanding of geometry. Even now we can remember what it is like to feel inadequate in school.

Some students feel this way in school every day. The most ordinary classroom tasks may be problematic for them. These students feel, as you would, frustrated and confused about their inability to understand and perform in the classroom. Although they have average intelligence, they do not do well in school. Many students with learning disabilities read very poorly, and reading competently is the keystone of school success. You know some of these students; let's find out more about them.

Definitions and Terms

Children with learning disabilities have probably always existed, but for many years educators failed to recognize their unique problems and characteristics. In 1963, a group of parents met in Chicago and invited the noted special educator Dr. Samuel Kirk to address them. When Kirk described the "specific learning disabilities" that their children shared, the parents seized on that term to describe and unite their children (Lerner, 1993). Although the term was adopted by educators, professionals from other disciplines used other labels and terminology, based on their beliefs about the causes of the specific disabilities. To physicians, these children were *neurologically impaired* or had *minimal brain dysfunction;* to speech and language pathologists, the same children might be called *aphasic* or *dyslexic;* and psychologists might call them *perceptually handicapped* or *hyperactive*. Various definitions of learning disabilities reflect the input of the variety of disciplines involved in the field over the years.

The Federal Definition

A number of definitions of learning disabilities have been put forth over the years; most of them are quite general in order to accommodate the wide range of beliefs related to learning disabilities. The most widely used definition of **learning disabilities** was originally written in 1968 by the National Advisory Committee on Handicapped Children. It was slightly adapted for inclusion in Public Law 94-142 (1975), now Public Law 101-476, the Individuals with Disabilities Education Act (1990). This definition attempts to unify this group of students by including some of the earlier labels used to describe students with learning disabilities, such as perceptual handicaps, brain damage, and so on. It reads:

The current federal definition of learning disabilities refers to a disorder in one or more of the basic psychological processes of understanding and using language.

> "Specific learning disabilities" means a disorder in one or more of the basic psychological processes involved in understanding or using language spoken or written, which may manifest itself in an imperfect ability to listen, think, read, write, spell, or to do mathematical calculations. The term includes such conditions as perceptual handicaps, brain injury, minimal brain dysfunction, and developmental aphasia. The term does not include learn-

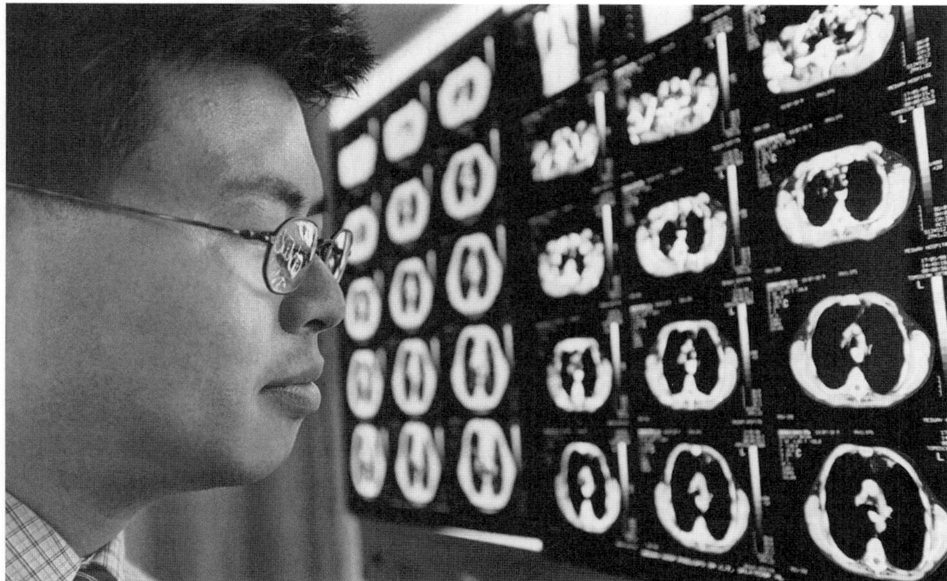

New techniques such as magnetic resonance imaging may soon help us discover the physical causes of learning disabilities. (© ER Productions/CORBIS)

> ing problems which are primarily the result of visual, hearing, or motor handicaps, of mental retardation, of emotional disturbance, or of environmental, cultural, or economic disadvantage. (USOE, 1977, p. 65083)

The federal law goes on to state that a student has a learning disability if he or she (1) does not achieve at the proper age and ability levels in one or more of several specific areas when provided with appropriate learning experiences, and (2) has a severe discrepancy between achievement and intellectual ability in one or more of the following areas: (a) oral expression, (b) listening comprehension, (c) written expression, (d) basic reading skill, (e) reading comprehension, (f) mathematics calculation, and (g) mathematics reasoning.

Key Elements in the Federal Definition

The federal definition emphasizes that the performance of students with learning disabilities is often tied to their ability to receive or express information. Reading, writing, listening, and speaking are some of the ways we take in information or communicate what we know. The academic areas listed in the definition illustrate how this disability can be manifested. It is important to note that a child may have a learning disability in all of the skill areas mentioned or just in one area. For example, a student may find it difficult to learn to read and spell, yet do quite well in math. Some individuals can speak and write in an organized and effective manner, yet become quite confused when dealing with number concepts and algorithms. Knowing that a child has a learning disability tells you only that the child is experiencing some difficulty processing information. You must learn much more about the child before you can tell how much difficulty he or she is experiencing or what impact the disability has on specific academic subjects or tasks.

Students with learning disabilities do not achieve at their age and ability levels in one or more specific areas.

Another key element of the federal definition is that the students demonstrate a severe **discrepancy** between achievement, or their performance in school, and their intellectual ability or potential. For example, a 9-year-old child with an average IQ who reads on the first-grade level would be exhibiting a discrepancy between what we expect (reading on the third-grade level) and the way he or she performs (reading on the first-grade level). A discrepancy is determined by examining the differences between scores on intelligence and achievement tests.

A diagnosis of learning disabilities calls for a discrepancy between achievement and ability.

All that really is needed in most states to obtain a diagnosis of learning disabilities is a discrepancy between achievement and ability. The extent of the discrepancy necessary for identification varies from state to state because the size of the discrepancy is not spelled out in the federal definition. A significant discrepancy is usually equal to one or two years below expected performance level or two standard deviations below average performance. Although most states identify this discrepancy by comparing scores on standardized achievement tests with scores on intelligence tests, some states use a formula that takes into account factors such as IQ, achievement level, and age, whereas others use simple differences in grade-level performance. It is important to remember that this discrepancy has only to occur in *one* of the areas listed in the definition for identification to be made.

The definition also outlines what learning disabilities are *not*, in an element of the definition that has come to be known as the **exclusion clause:** "The term does not include learning problems which are primarily the result of visual, hearing, or motor handicaps, of mental retardation, of emotional disturbance, or of environmental, cultural, or economic disadvantage." This sentence, which has caused a great deal of disagreement among professionals in the field, has important implications for identifying students with learning disabilities.

Because a number of other disabilities or life situations may also cause problems in learning, some professionals feel that it is important to ensure that the difficulties a child is experiencing cannot be attributed to the fact that he or she comes from a deprived family or suffers from another disability. As you might imagine, it is difficult to tease out the effects of a socially or economically deprived environment on a student's performance. Consequently, you may find few psychologists or child study teams who will deprive a child of the opportunity to receive special education services because they suspect that the environment contributed to her learning problems. On the other hand, this clause can be used to help prevent the improper labeling of children from distinct cultures who have acquired learning styles, language, or behaviors that are not compatible with the academic requirements of schools in the dominant culture.

The exclusion clause also reflects the opinion of some professionals that learning disabilities cannot exist in children with other disabilities. Other experts, however, do feel that there are children with sensory disabilities or cognitive disabilities who do not achieve up to the level of their ability and that they, too, can be considered to have learning disabilities.

The criteria for learning disabilities allow large numbers of children to be classified.

Because many children achieve below grade level, and it is often difficult to determine *why* a child is underachieving, the criteria for learning disabilities allow large numbers of children to be classified. As you might expect, this results in great diversity among the children identified as having a learning disability. Some children are one year behind in one subject whereas others are four years behind in three subjects. Although all of these children are identified as having a learning disability, their educational needs and programs may be very different.

Causes of Learning Disabilities

In most cases, the cause of a child's learning disability cannot be determined.

In a great majority of cases, the cause of an individual's learning disability is unknown. This is true despite a vast amount of research investigating the possible causes of these disabilities. Many educators and researchers caution us about placing too much emphasis on finding the cause or causes of learning disabilities (Hallahan, Kauffman, & Lloyd, 1999). Knowing the cause of the disability does not necessarily tell us how to teach a student; in fact, some people believe that it may hinder the teaching process, particularly in the case of vague and poorly defined terms like *brain damage*. Nevertheless, the search for the causes of learning disabilities continues to occupy many researchers in language, psychology, and medicine, and there is at least one good reason why this should be so. If we can identify the factors that cause learning disabilities, we may learn to prevent them.

The speculation and research about the causes of learning disabilities can be grouped into two categories: internal factors, such as organic, biological, or genetic factors, and external factors, sometimes referred to as environmental factors. Keep in mind, however, that when we are talking about possible causes of learning disabilities, we are referring mainly to hypotheses rather than facts.

Internal Factors

■ ***Brain Damage/Neurological Differences*** Since the brain is the center of learning, many professionals have assumed that students with serious learning problems have some type of brain damage. Although this explanation makes sense intuitively, there has been very little clear historical evidence. If brain damage exists, it has been too negligible to be identified through available technology, such as an electroencephalograph (EEG), a test used to measure brain activity. Today, however, there is renewed interest in neurological evaluations and brain research in the area of learning disabilities. One reason for this interest is advanced technology, which has allowed us to get more detailed information. Although there have been no definitive breakthroughs in identifying causes for learning disabilities, some researchers have reported interesting findings. For example, some findings suggest that there are differences in the structure, symmetry, or activity levels of at least one hemisphere of the brain for individuals with and without learning disabilities. Bigler (1992) used a procedure called magnetic resonance imaging (MRI) to get a picture (similar to an x-ray) of the brains of individuals who had severe reading disabilities and also of some people who did not have learning disabilities. He found that some of the individuals with learning disabilities had structural irregularities in the left hemisphere of their brains. This structural difference was not present in all of the individuals with disabilities, so Bigler could not draw any definitive conclusions. As technology advances, neurobiology certainly will provide more information and possibly some answers about the causes of learning disabilities.

■ ***Other Physiological Factors*** Medical researchers have suggested that other physiological factors have a role in causing learning disabilities. Many possible causes have been proposed over the years, including malnutrition and biochemical imbalances such as allergies or the inability of the blood to synthesize a normal supply of vitamins (Cott, 1972; 1977; Feingold, 1975). None of these theories, however, stood up to scientific experimentation (Arnold, Christopher, & Huestis, 1978; Kavale & Forness, 1983).

When we look back on the birth histories of students with learning disabilities, we do see that many of them experienced more **perinatal stress** than other babies. That is, during the perinatal period (from labor and delivery through the age of twenty-eight days) there were more traumatic events in their lives, such as difficult or prolonged labor and delivery, hypoxia during the birth process, low birthweight, or illness. Many babies with those same problems, however, do not have learning difficulties later in life, so perinatal stresses cannot be the sole cause of learning disabilities.

Several researchers have postulated that learning disabilities are inherited. As a teacher, you will often hear the parent of a child with learning disabilities say, "I had that same problem when I was in school—we just didn't have a name for it then." Although you may discover a lot of anecdotal evidence for inheritance, the empirical evidence is in dispute. The strongest evidence for a genetic basis for learning disabilities comes from studies of identical twins reared apart, which showed that both twins were likely to have a learning disability (De Fries, Gillis, & Wadsworth, 1993) if one twin had a learning disability, and studies of the rate of disability occurrence within families (Lewis, 1992). Much more conclusive research needs to be done, however, before a link between heredity and learning disabilities can be established.

No link between heredity and learning disabilities has yet been proved.

External Factors

If we look at learning disabilities as differences in **learning style,** or the way a student approaches learning, we may see the interaction between the student and the environment as a cause of learning disabilities. Some people believe that children identified as having a learning disability are really those children whose learning style is not compatible with the learning requirements of most school settings. In other words, rather than experiencing a deficit or disability, the students simply don't fit the mold. If teaching procedures and task requirements were different, the students wouldn't have a disability at all. Students with learning disabilities do often demonstrate a disorganized approach to learning; however, this may be a characteristic of the disability rather than a cause.

The learning styles of children with learning disabilities may be incompatible with school requirements.

Today, some educators believe that other external factors are the major cause of learning disabilities (Morsink, 1984). Those factors most frequently implicated are lack of motivation; inappropriate methods, materials, and curricula (Wallace & McLoughlin, 1988); and, simply, poor teaching. This theory is attractive to many people because many students with learning disabilities *can* learn when they receive direct, systematic instruction. Although skills that are missing or weak can be taught, a learning disability remains a lifelong problem.

Perhaps someday we will learn that some children, because of internal factors, are more vulnerable to external events and as a result develop what we now call learning disabilities. But since these learning disabilities range along a continuum from mild to severe and consist of many different types, it is probably foolhardy to search for *one* cause of a complicated group of learning problems (see the accompanying box, "Possible Causes of Learning Disabilities").

Prevalence

In 1963 the term *learning disabilities* was newly coined; twenty years later it described the largest group of children served in special education. Learning disabilities was first included in public law as a disability area in 1975. Since that

~ Possible Causes of Learning Disabilities

Internal Factors

The following causes have been suggested, but little hard data are available:

- Brain damage
- Malnutrition and biochemical imbalances
- Perinatal stress
- Genetics

External Factors

Many educators believe that external factors are major causes; others believe that they predispose children to learning disabilities. Major external factors include:

- Learning style
- Classroom factors (lack of motivation; inappropriate materials, methods, and curriculum)
- Environmental stressors (personal pain, family instability, poverty)

time the number of students identified as having a learning disability has grown by almost 250 percent, from approximately 800,000 students to about 2,750,000 students (U.S. Department of Education, 1991; 1999).

A number of reasons have been suggested for the enormous growth in the identification of students with learning disabilities. The following are some of the most frequently suggested:

1. Children who are underachieving are incorrectly identified as learning disabled. The evaluation and identification criteria are too subjective and unreliable, and there are few, if any, alternative programs for many of these students (Frankenberger & Fronzaglio, 1991; Henley, Ramsey, & Algozzine, 1993).
2. The classification of learning disabilities is more socially acceptable than many other special education classifications, particularly mild mental retardation and behavior disorders. Consequently, parents and teachers advocate for this classification (Frankenberger & Fronzaglio, 1991; Lerner, 1993).
3. Greater general awareness of learning disabilities has resulted in more appropriate referrals and diagnoses. Teachers and parents are more aware of the types of services that are available (Lerner, 1993).
4. The number of students identified as learning disabled parallels the increased social and cultural risks that have arisen during the past two decades. Biological and psychosocial stressors may place more children at risk for acquiring learning disabilities, and therefore more children are identified (Hallahan, 1992).

Although we have no way of knowing the extent to which any of these reasons are accurate, it is likely that they all have contributed to the expansion of the population.

Effects on the Developing Person

In this section we will examine some of the ways learning disabilities can affect individuals. We will focus on how people with learning disabilities receive, process, and produce information—in other words, how they learn. We will

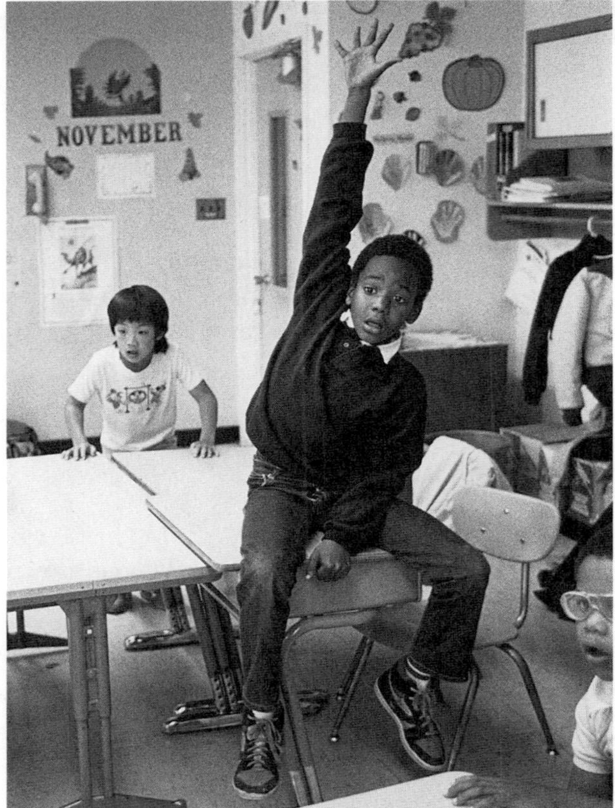

Class participation by students with learning disabilities depends on interest, confidence, and the ability to attend to the information being presented. (Elizabeth Crews/The Image Works, Inc.)

also look at the potential effects of learning disabilities on academic performance and social behavior.

Learning Disabilities and Cognition: Approaches to Learning

Learning disabilities can affect cognitive processes—thinking skills used to process information.

As you remember, the federal definition of learning disabilities specifies that it is "a disorder in one or more of the basic psychological processes involved in understanding or using language." In this definition, *language* refers to the symbols of communication—spoken, written, or even behavioral. Although *psychological processes* is a vague term, think of it as referring to all the things we do when we take in information (listen, read, observe), try to learn information (classify, remember, evaluate, imitate), and produce information (speak, write, calculate, behave). These psychological processes are aspects of *cognition*, the wide range of thinking skills we use to process and learn information (Henley, Ramsey, & Algozzine, 1993).

In this section, we will look at five cognitive processes: perception, attention, memory, metacognition, and organization. These processes are vital to our ability to understand and use language. All students who have difficulty learning are probably experiencing a problem in one or more of them. Although everyone uses the same basic processes to learn information, we don't always use them the same way or with the same degree of efficiency.

■ ***Perception*** **Perception,** as defined here, is the ability to organize and interpret the information we experience through our senses, such as visual or auditory abilities. Perception is important to learning because it provides us with our first sensory impressions about something we see or hear. When we hear a note or a sound, we are able to identify and appreciate its uniqueness. When we see the letter *B*, we identify its structure (overall shape), orientation (direction of the letter), and component parts (one straight line and two curved lines). Later, if we see the letter *D*, we are able to see that *D* has its own set of properties, and some are similar to *B* and some are different.

A student relies on his or her perceptual abilities to recognize, compare, and discriminate information. The ability to hold the image of a letter, word, or sound is necessary before information can be recognized, recalled, or applied. Let's look at an example of a young child who is just learning to read. If this child has difficulty discriminating sounds, she may confuse similar sounds, such as those made by the letters *m* and *n*. This confusion may make it difficult for the child to decode words by "sounding them out" and to make the connection between written letters and spoken sounds. In her mind, the relationship seems to change; sometimes she sees *m* and hears *mmm*; other times she sees *n* and hears *mmm*. This means she may begin guessing when asked to read a word such as *man*. (Is it *man, nam, nan*, or *mam*?)

Right away you can see the importance of two essential teaching approaches for a child with difficulty in perception; first, do not present pieces of information that are perceptually confusing (for example, that sound alike or look alike) together or right after each other. Second, point out the important characteristics of information. The student must be encouraged to attend to and recognize the identifying aspects, since she may have difficulty picking them out herself (see the accompanying box, "Teaching Strategies for Students with Perceptual Difficulties").

Some children with learning disabilities reverse letters, words, or whole passages during reading or writing. Occasional letter or word reversal is typical of all young children. Children with learning disabilities, however, may continue to have difficulty with letter and word orientation and therefore continue to reverse letters and words throughout elementary school. Children who reverse words while reading typically reverse words that can be read in either direction (*saw* and *was*). You will seldom see a child try to read *firetruck* as *kcurterif*. The most common letter reversals are also those that are letters in either direction (*b* and *d*). If we think about how close these two letters are in the alphabet and recognize that often they are taught close together, we can understand why children often reverse them. The child hasn't had time to learn one completely before he is introduced to the other.

~ Teaching Strategies for Students with Perceptual Difficulties

- If two pieces of information are perceptually confusing, do not present them together. For example, do not teach the spelling of *ie* words (*believe*) and *ei* words (*perceive*) on the same day.
- Highlight the important characteristics of new material. For example, underline or use bold letters to draw a student's attention to the same sound pattern presented in a group of reading or spelling words (*mouse, house, round*).

■ *Attention* The importance of attention to learning seems fairly obvious to most of us. It is the underlying factor in our ability to receive and process information. How can you take notes on a lecture if you can't tell what's important? How can you work a long division problem if you can't stay on task? **Attention** is a broad term that refers to the ability to focus on information. Students who experience attention difficulties to a considerable degree may be identified as having **attention deficit disorder (ADD)** or **attention deficit with hyperactivity disorder (ADHD),** in addition to having learning disabilities.

Attention deficits are frequently associated with individuals with learning disabilities.

Students with learning disabilities quite often experience difficulties in attention. In fact, attention deficits are probably the disorder most frequently associated with individuals with learning disabilities. Many teachers describe their students with learning disabilities as "distractible" or "in his own world." These teachers are talking about kids who have trouble coming to attention and maintaining attention; something appears to be interfering with their ability to get on task and stay focused. Sometimes they are distracted by things in the classroom; other times they are subject to internal distractions, such as random thoughts or ideas.

Teachers are also perplexed or frustrated because a child seems to be paying attention but doesn't follow directions or can't summarize the main idea of a story. These problems may be a result of difficulties with **selective attention**, the ability to zero in on the most important part of a piece of information. For example, given the directions "Circle the correct answer," Linda focuses on the fact that the word *circle* is underlined and proceeds to underline her answer. She attends to an inappropriate cue.

Again, once we understand the types of difficulties that can result from attention deficits, we can begin to restructure our teaching presentations to circumvent some of these problems or to teach some new attention skills. When children have difficulty attending to a task for a long period of time, it helps to break down the task into smaller segments. If Tom has difficulty maintaining attention, his assignment might be modified so he has to read two pages each night instead of twelve pages on Thursday evening. By gradually requiring a little more work each day, we can sometimes help children increase their attention span.

Problems with selective attention can first be addressed by making sure that the student attends to the *important* information. One can use a variety of prompts and cues—written, verbal, and instructional—as shown in the accompanying box, "Teaching Strategies for Students with Attention Difficulties."

Another technique is to teach students how to identify the important information in a task. As students become older, they are expected to do increasing amounts of independent work, including reading and writing. It is critical that they learn how to identify key material on their own.

■ *Memory* If perception and attention are the skills that form a foundation for learning, then memory is the major vehicle for acquiring and recalling information. **Memory** involves many different skills and processes. Some of these processes are used to organize information for learning; these are called **encoding processes.** When individuals encode information, they use visual, auditory, or verbal cues to arrange material; thus encoding relies heavily on skills such as perception and selective attention. Students with learning disabilities who experience difficulty in perception and attention are also likely to have problems remembering correctly, because they may be encoding partial, incorrect, or unimportant information.

Encoding processes organize information so it can be learned.

~ Teaching Strategies for Students with Attention Difficulties

Maintaining Attention

- Break long tasks or assignments into smaller segments. Administer the smaller segments throughout the day, if a shorter assignment isn't acceptable.
- Present limited amounts of information on a page.
- Gradually increase the amount of time a student must attend to a task or lecture.

Selective Attention

- Use prompts and cues to draw attention to important information. Types of cues include:
  1. Written cues, such as highlighting directions on tests or activity sheets
  2. Verbal cues, such as using signal words to let students know they are about to hear important information
  3. Instructional cues, such as having students paraphrase directions or other information to you
- Teach students a plan for identifying and highlighting important information themselves.

Students with learning disabilities may experience deficits in **working memory**—the ability to store new information and to retrieve previously processed information from long-term memory (Swanson, Cochran, & Ewers, 1990). Deficits in working memory translate into difficulties in the classroom. Students who don't use memory strategies try to learn information that is not broken down into manageable parts or that is unconnected to any previous knowledge. This makes it difficult for them to transfer the information into long-term memory and to retrieve it later on.

Students with learning disabilities often show deficits in working memory—the ability to store and retrieve information.

It is important to teach students memory strategies. Sometimes teachers try to associate materials with pictures, key words, or context clues to help students remember a number of facts or the relationships between them. Although many students with learning disabilities do not use tools for remembering, you can teach them some of these tools (see the accompanying box, "Memory Strategies").

■ ***Metacognition*** **Metacognition**, the ability to monitor and evaluate performance, is another area in which students with learning disabilities often experience difficulty (Wong, 1991). Metacognition requires the ability to identify and select learning skills and techniques to facilitate the acquisition of information; to choose or create the setting in which you are most likely to receive material accurately; to identify the most effective and efficient way to process and present information; and to evaluate and adapt your techniques for different materials and situations. Thus metacognitive skills are critical to all aspects of learning. These skills supply many of the keys to learning from experience, generalizing information and strategies, and applying what you have learned.

Lack of metacognitive skills may hinder competent learning.

The student who does not demonstrate metacognitive skills may experience difficulty developing into a competent learner (Kluwe, 1987). Because most of these skills focus on planning, monitoring, and evaluation, students who do not have them may appear to plunge into tasks without thinking about them and never look back once they're done. Practicing a book report before delivering it

~ Memory Strategies

Remember this number: 380741529

Look quickly at the number written above, then cover it completely with your finger. Wait one minute, and try to say the number out loud. Check your accuracy, but then ask yourself a more important question: What did I do to try to remember that long string of digits?

If that experiment didn't work, think of this situation. You are in a telephone booth, without a pencil and paper. You call Directory Assistance to get the number you need to call. How do you remember the number?

In either one of those situations, you probably used one of the following memory strategies:

- Chunking is the grouping of large strings of information into smaller, more manageable "chunks." Telephone numbers, for example, are "chunked" into small segments for easier recall; remembering 2125060595 is much harder than remembering (212) 506-0595.
- Rehearsal is the repetition, either oral or silent, of the information to be remembered.
- Elaboration is the weaving of the material to be remembered into a meaningful context. The numbers above, for example, could be related to birthdays, ages, or other telephone numbers.
- Another useful memory strategy is categorization, in which the information to be remembered is organized by the category to which it belongs. All the animals in a list, for example, could be grouped together for remembering.

to the class, making an outline of a paper before you begin writing, and jotting down the key points you want to make on an essay question before you begin writing all illustrate how metacognition can affect performance. As you probably know from personal experience, the students who practice, outline, and make notes are more likely to have coherent presentations or answers.

Self-monitoring teaches students to evaluate and record their own performance.

Fortunately, metacognitive skills can be taught. One technique that helps students plan, monitor, and evaluate—**self-monitoring**—is described in the accompanying box, "Teaching Self-Monitoring." Self-monitoring teaches students to evaluate and record their own performance periodically. Written or auditory cues are provided for students, which prompt them to check their behavior.

■ ***Organization*** If we look at the many behaviors we consider to be characteristic of individuals with learning disabilities and examine the processes we have just discussed, we can see that the underlying thread is difficulty in **organization.** Because *organization* is a term we all use often, it is a useful and familiar framework to apply to learning disabilities.

Difficulties in organization can affect the most superficial tasks or the most complex cognitive activities. The simple acts required to come to class with a paper, pencil, and books; to get a homework assignment home and then back to school; and to copy math problems on a piece of notebook paper all rely on organizational skills. These may seem minor problems that can be easily addressed. Next to attention deficits, however, these simple organization problems are mentioned most often by classroom teachers as sources of difficulty. Teachers often become frustrated at what appears to be a student's careless and thoughtless approach to class preparation. It is important to recognize,

~ Teaching Self-Monitoring

The following procedure teaches self-monitoring of attention, defined as attention to task. The same technique can be used for a variety of skills.

- Teach students the difference between on-task and off-task behavior. Model the different behaviors and have students demonstrate them to you.
- Provide students with written or auditory cues (a timer, an audiotape with a tone or beep) that prompt them to check their behavior.
- Have students stop what they are doing when they hear the cue, ask themselves if they are paying attention, and record their response.
- Gradually fade the cues, then the recording sheets, as students learn to self-monitor independently.

however, that many students with learning disabilities cannot plan effectively. To some extent, metacognitive skills play a role in organization. Students must be able to understand the need to have a system of organization and develop a plan for carrying it out.

Another factor that may interact with metacognitive activity to produce organizational problems is **cognitive style,** the cognitive activity that takes place between the time a student recognizes the need to respond to something and the time she actually does respond. Students are often categorized along a continuum that ranges from impulsive to reflective. A child with an *impulsive* cognitive style responds rapidly, without considering alternatives, consequences, or accuracy. A *reflective* cognitive style describes a slower rate of response that includes an examination of the response and its alternatives or consequences. Many students with learning disabilities possess an impulsive cognitive style (Walker, 1985). This means that they are likely to respond without thinking. A student with an impulsive cognitive style may wave her hand vigorously to answer a question before you have even finished asking it. The tendency to jump the gun precludes the opportunity for engaging in organizational activity regardless of the type of task or its complexity.

Individuals with learning disabilities are also often described as inactive or passive learners (Torgesen, 1977). This characterization reflects behavior rather than the attitude we usually ascribe to the word *passive*. It suggests that students with learning disabilities often do not take the initiative in the learning process. This passive role may contribute to deficits in organizational skills, since organization requires the individual to recognize the need to take action and to develop and carry out a plan.

Individuals with learning disabilities often are described as passive learners; they don't take the initiative in the learning process.

Classroom interventions designed to improve organizational skills usually provide students with specific actions or guidelines for organized behavior. Examples include having a single notebook with designated places for homework, paper, and pencils; developing a list for students' lockers that identifies what is needed for each class; and preparing a standard end-of-the-day checklist for students to use to ensure they have all required materials. Strategies like these have helped counteract the day-to-day organizational problems of many students with learning disabilities. We will look more closely at complex organizational problems involving writing and thinking skills when we discuss academic interventions.

Learning Disabilities and Academic Performance

Before we look at the effects of learning disabilities on academic performance, let's review the key processes involved in cognition. Perception, attention, memory, metacognition, and organization are the five key processes. Together, they enable us to receive information correctly, arrange it for easier learning, identify similarities and differences with other knowledge we have, select a way to learn the information effectively, and evaluate the effectiveness of our learning process. If a student has problems doing any or all of these things, it is easy to see how all learning can be affected. We will look at three basic skill areas—reading, language arts, and math—and give some ideas about how difficulties in these areas can affect other types of learning as well.

Reading

Reading is the most difficult skill area for most students with learning disabilities.

Reading is the most difficult skill area for most students with learning disabilities. Because reading is necessary for almost all learning, the student with a reading disability often experiences difficulty in many other subjects as well. In addition, the emphasis on oral reading in the early school years may make the child with a reading disability reluctant to read, so he or she may fall progressively further behind in reading skills. Teachers are often faced not only with the challenge of trying to teach a child *to* read but also with motivating the child to *try* to read. The term *dyslexia* is often associated with reading difficulties in students with learning disabilities. Although this term was initially used many years ago to refer to a severe reading disability caused by neurological impairment, the word is often used today, by some educators, to refer to the more general reading problems of students with learning disabilities (Wallace & McLoughlin, 1988).

If you think about everything you do when you read, you realize that it is a very complex process. To examine the potential effects of learning disabilities on reading, let's look at two of the major skills involved in the reading process: word analysis (identifying a word) and comprehension (understanding what is read).

■ ***Word Analysis*** In order to identify written words, we use a number of different skills. Some of the most important **word-analysis** skills include the ability to associate sounds with the various letters and letter combinations used to write them (phonic analysis), to immediately recognize and remember words (sight-word reading), and to use the surrounding text to help figure out a specific word (context clues). These skills rely heavily on perception, selective attention, memory, and metacognitive skills. Thus, word analysis is dependent almost entirely on the cognitive skills that are most problematic for individuals with learning disabilities.

In order to use phonic analysis, for example, the student must be able to remember all of the different associations between letters and sounds, learn the rules that govern different letter and sound patterns, remember the many exceptions to each rule, and blend sounds together. This process is the basic stumbling block for most students who have difficulty reading. The extensive and rapid presentation of memory requirements simply overloads children with learning disabilities, especially those who have difficulty identifying and discriminating specific sounds and letters.

Without basic phonics skills, students are very limited in the number of words they can read. This is particularly true given that many of these same skills are required in other word-analysis strategies, such as reading sight words. Recent research suggests the importance of assessing and teaching very young children skills in the areas of phonological and phonemic awareness (Foorman, Francis, Fletcher, Schatschneider, & Mehta, 1998). There appears to be an important relationship between a young child's ability to hear and distinguish among sounds and his or her later ability to read. Researchers and teachers are investigating the most effective way to teach young children these important skills (Torgesen, 2000).

Teaching reading to students with learning disabilities involves a structured presentation of phonics skills and rules.

The most frequently recommended approaches to teaching reading to elementary students with learning disabilities include a structured presentation of phonics skills and rules (Carnine, Silbert & Kameenui, 1990). These approaches are called *code-emphasis approaches.* Because the students cannot identify sound/letter associations and patterns on their own, it is necessary to present these associations in a very clear way and provide students with lots of opportunities to practice and remember them.

Many students with learning disabilities also run into obstacles when they try to use the sight-word approach to word analysis. Teachers often report spending an entire period working on a few sight words, only to find, the next day, that the child behaves as if he's never seen the words before. Learning most sight words, unless they are always in a specific context (such as the word *stop* on a stop sign), requires being able to identify and recall the aspects of the word that make it unique and to associate the correct sounds with the word. Children with learning disabilities may focus on only part of the characteristics of a letter or word, therefore increasing the probability of poor recall and confusion. In addition, active memory strategies are required for students to transfer words into their long-term memory, and we have seen that many students with learning disabilities do not use those strategies. There are many specific strategies for teaching sight words (see the accompanying box, "Teaching Word-Analysis Skills").

Many students with learning disabilities depend heavily on context clues for guessing words.

Poor readers tend to use context clues as their major word-analysis strategy. Although context can be helpful when you come across one or two words that are difficult to decode, using context to figure out 50 or 60 percent of the words in a passage is ineffective. At the early elementary level, children may achieve some success with this method because of the many pictures in the story, and because they may hear the story read several times. Many students, therefore, develop patterns of guessing words. Of course, as stories become more complex and students are required to read the words in other contexts, this strategy becomes useless. Yet, because students feel that their guessing method helps them read faster—more like other students—they continue to use it. This is the most common reading pattern we see in students with learning disabilities, and it is the most difficult to break. Some students try to guess their way through an entire story. Reading programs used for students with learning disabilities often try to prevent or eliminate this pattern by controlling the words students are expected to read so that only words the child knows how to decode are presented in stories; they also eliminate pictures and other cues from initial reading passages. Once the child gains confidence in her ability to use other word-attack skills and uses them effectively, then the use of context clues—which will become quite valuable when the student begins reading complex material—can be encouraged.

~ Teaching Word-Analysis Skills

Phonics

Use structured phonics programs that:

- Teach most common sounds first
- Stress specific phonics rules and patterns
- Expose the beginning reader only to words that contain sounds he or she has already learned

Sight Words

During instruction:

- Require the student to focus on all important aspects of the word (all letters, not just the first and last ones).
- Have the student discriminate between the new word and frequently confused words. For example, if you are introducing the word *what* as a sight word, make sure the child can read the word when it is presented with words such as *that*, *which*, and *wait*.
- Help the student devise strategies for remembering a particular word.

Context Clues

- Control the reading level of materials used so that students are presented with few unfamiliar words.
- For beginning readers, present illustrations after the text selection has been read.
- Teach students to use context clues as a decoding strategy after they are adept at beginning phonics analysis.

■ ***Reading Comprehension*** Students with learning disabilities may experience difficulties in **reading comprehension** because they lack the skills required for understanding text and have poor word-analysis skills. The child who has difficulty reading words will have trouble understanding the gist of sentences and passages. It is important to adjust your expectations for comprehension if the child has difficulty in the actual reading of material. It is better to teach or assess reading comprehension skills on material the students can decode fluently or that is presented orally.

In addition to word-analysis skills, a number of other factors can affect a child's ability to comprehend text. Literal comprehension of material—the ability to identify specifically stated information—requires the ability to select important information from unimportant details, to organize or sequence this information, and to recall it. Again, you can see the need for cognitive skills that frequently pose problems for students with learning disabilities. The ability to select and categorize information is also necessary for organizational comprehension, which includes identifying main ideas.

For more advanced comprehension activities, such as interpreting text, evaluating actions in a story, predicting consequences, and relating text to personal experience, students with learning disabilities can experience difficulty because of the role-taking skills required in some of these tasks and a reluctance to go beyond what is specifically stated in the text. Being able to put yourself in another's place (Why was hitting Joe a poor choice? What would you do if that happened to you?) requires seeing the similarities and differences between yourself and the character. Some students with learning disabilities cannot put themselves in another person's shoes and see things from another perspective, and this can interfere with projective or evaluative types of comprehension activities.

Many difficulties in reading comprehension can also be traced to the lack of specific strategies used to help remember material or to self-check understanding (Malone & Mastropieri, 1992). If you are reading a book that is not particularly interesting, you may find, after you've read a few pages, that you haven't actually taken in anything you've read. If you are reading this book to prepare for a test, you may go back and reread the material, perhaps stopping every so often to paraphrase what you've read, rehearse the important points, or ask yourself questions to see if you really do understand it. All of these learning strategies, which are essentially memory and metacognitive skills, help you to comprehend the text, and they become increasingly important as reading material becomes denser and more complex. Because students with learning disabilities do not use these active strategies, they are unlikely to have good comprehension.

Students need to develop strategies that will help them remember material and self-check their understanding of it.

Many teaching strategies that focus on reading comprehension emphasize the use of specific plans or behaviors to help students review material and check their comprehension periodically (Gajira & Salvia, 1992). Other techniques involve identifying and highlighting key information in the text, or recording the information using story maps (Gardill & Jitendra, 1999). Usually the teacher will model these skills initially and then teach the student how to pull out the key information necessary for good comprehension. Similar techniques are used to help students at the secondary level identify important information from textbooks, which are frequently several grade levels above their reading level. By using specific comprehension strategies and the conventions of the text (headings, vocabulary words, questions in text), students can find and retrieve essential information.

Reading continues to be the biggest obstacle faced by most students with learning disabilities. For this reason, the type of reading instruction used is critical. Snider (1997) found that students with learning disabilities who received thirty to forty-five minutes of instruction in the vocabulary-controlled,

~ Suggestions for Teaching Reading Comprehension

- *Predictions*: Predictions can be based on pictures, headings, subtitles, or graphs. They can be used to activate students' prior knowledge before reading and to increase attention to sequencing during reading, and they can be evaluated after reading to help summarize content.
- *Questions*: Questions can be asked before reading to help students attend to important information, or students can be taught to transform subtitles or headings into questions to ask themselves as they read. Having students make up questions to ask each other after reading is a good alternative to the typical question-answer period and helps students develop study skills as well.
- *Advance organizers or outlines*: You can prepare an advance organizer on the text to help focus students' attention on key material in the text. Students can review the organizer before reading and take notes on it while reading. When it is completed, the students have a study sheet to review.
- *Self-monitoring or self-evaluation*: When students begin reading longer text selections, they can learn to stop periodically and paraphrase the text or check their understanding. This can be done by using an auditory self-monitoring tape or by randomly placing stickers or other markers throughout the text. When the student reaches the sticker, it is time to think about what he or she has just read.

code-emphasis reading programs Reading Mastery Fast Cycle (Englemann & Bruner, 1988) and Corrective Reading Decoding B1 (Englemann, Carnine, & Johnson, 1988) acquired necessary decoding skills and transferred those skills to the material they read in their classrooms. Because more and more students with learning disabilities are served in general education classrooms, teachers must investigate ways to provide reading skill instruction, particularly for young children, in the classroom setting (see the accompanying box, "Suggestions for Teaching Reading Comprehension").

Language Arts

In this section, we will look at three general areas: spelling, spoken language, and written language. Because of the close ties of some of these skills to reading ability, they tend to be areas of great difficulty for many students with learning disabilities.

■ ***Spelling*** Spelling requires all of the essential skills used in the word-analysis strategies of phonics and sight-word reading. The student must either know specific sound and letter relationships or be able to memorize words. Spelling, for some students, may be even more difficult than reading because there are no context cues and because spelling requires recall rather than the simpler recognition skills used in reading. The difficulty students with learning disabilities have in learning and applying rules of phonics, visualizing the word correctly, and evaluating spellings results in frequent misspellings, even as they become more adept at reading. It is not uncommon to find the same word spelled five or six different ways on the same paper, regardless of whether the student is in the fifth grade or in college (for example, *ther, there, thare,* and *theyre* for *their*).

This pattern illustrates the procedure used by many students with learning disabilities when spelling a word: each word is spelled as if it were being approached for the first time, without reference to an image of the word held in memory or the consistent use of a most probable spelling. The majority of errors are phonetically acceptable, meaning that a reader can sound them out to read the word (Hom, O'Donnell, & Leicht, 1988). Other common errors include errors made in the middle of the word (vowel combinations are the most variable and confusing), scrambled words, and, in younger children, carryover from just-learned letter combinations. An example of carryover would be a child who has been spelling words such as *cake* and *late* correctly until she has a spelling lesson that contains the words *rain* and *pain.* The next time the child writes *cake* she may spell it *caik,* and *rain* may sometimes turn into *rane.* When a number of spelling patterns are presented to a child at one time, or if she doesn't have enough time to practice and recall individual patterns, the likelihood of confusion increases.

It is best to combine spelling lessons with reading lessons.

Many students with learning disabilities are in spelling programs that contain many words they cannot yet read. When this occurs, the students cannot be expected to succeed. If at all possible, it is best to combine spelling lessons with reading lessons. Use the sounds and words involved in reading as the sounds and words studied in spelling lessons. This will increase the probability that students will learn to spell with more confidence, because they will have the necessary prior knowledge to apply to spelling, and because of the repeated opportunities to practice sounds and words. For students of all ages, learning to evaluate spellings and developing a consistent mental representation of the word are critical skills. Recommended spelling strategies include teaching students to visualize the whole word while studying. Common spelling activities used by many classroom teachers, such as writing the words five times each, are useless if the student is copying the word one letter at a time. If students are encouraged to write the word, spell the word out loud, visualize the word, spell the word aloud without looking at it, check the word's spelling, write the word without looking, and then compare their word to the original, the task will help develop needed memory and metacognitive skills.

■ ***Spoken Language*** Many students with learning disabilities experience difficulties in spoken or oral language, which can affect academic as well as social performance. These may include problems identifying and using appropriate speech sounds, using appropriate words and understanding word meanings, using and understanding various sentence structures, and using appropriate grammar and language conventions. Other problem areas include understanding underlying meanings, such as irony or figurative language, and adjusting language for different uses and purposes, called **pragmatic language skills** (Gibbs & Cooper, 1989; Henley, Ramsey, & Algozzine, 1993).

Although you may not think of oral language as an academic skill, the effects of language difficulties on academic as well as social performance can be significant. For example, a student who has difficulty identifying and discriminating speech sounds may have difficulty reading and spelling. Many other difficulties with oral language may translate into problems understanding not only spoken directions or lectures but also written language. A student who can only use or understand simple sentences (for example, "The dog licked the cat") will interpret the information incorrectly if given a more complex sentence ("The cat was licked by the dog"). Instead of realizing that these two sentences mean the same thing, the child may impose the simple subject-verb-object order on the second sentence and be convinced that the cat licked the dog.

Pragmatic language skills enable the child to use language effectively in different settings and for different purposes. This includes **functional flexibility,** or the ability to move easily from one form of language to another to accommodate various settings or audiences (Simon, 1991). Functional flexibility requires the individual to identify the type of language appropriate to the setting, to anticipate the needs of the audience, and then to adjust language structure, content, and vocabulary to meet these needs. It also requires an understanding that different types of language are used for different purposes. Individuals with learning disabilities may have difficulty with pragmatic language because they have difficulty attending to the cues of various settings—the expected tone or type of language used by others, for example. In addition, anticipating an audience's needs requires putting yourself in other people's positions and being aware of, for example, their prior knowledge about a subject or their desire for clarity or brevity when asking for directions or making a request. Students with learning disabilities may not monitor their effectiveness in communicating and therefore may not adjust their language to the setting.

It is important to provide students with many models of different language structures; however, it also is important to understand that using and interpreting oral language require instruction. Interpreting oral language correctly involves reading nonverbal cues, such as raised eyebrows or posture, and understanding vocal cues, such as inflection and emphasis. The sentence "Just

Interpreting oral language correctly involves reading nonverbal cues, which can be difficult for students with learning disabilities.

turn in your paper whenever you feel like it" can mean two entirely different things, depending on the emphasis and inflection used. Because the identification and use of these conventions requires good perceptive and selective attention skills, many students with learning disabilities miss them.

Students with learning disabilities may have difficulty planning, organizing, and writing their papers.

■ ***Written language*** Students with learning disabilities often have great difficulty in written language or composition. Specific problems include inadequate planning, structure, and organization; immature or limited sentence structure; limited and repetitive vocabulary; limited consideration of audience; unnecessary or unrelated information or details; and errors in spelling, punctuation, grammar, and handwriting (Carnine, 1991; Mercer & Mercer, 1993a; Newcomer & Barenbaum, 1991). Students with learning disabilities also lack the motivation and the monitoring and evaluation skills often considered necessary for good writing (Newcomer & Barenbaum, 1991). When we look at the skills necessary for good writing and consider the characteristics of students with learning disabilities, the types of difficulties we have identified are not surprising.

Some students who are adept in oral language may show restricted syntax and vocabulary in written language. If a student has difficulty reading and spelling and is fearful of making errors, these written language problems may reflect fear of failure rather than actual limitations in language ability. It is important to encourage these students to work on transferring oral to written language, to have plenty of opportunities to write without fear of failing, and to have access to word or vocabulary banks if necessary, in order to encourage and broaden written language skills.

For most students with learning disabilities, the educational emphasis for written language is on the development and use of organizational and metacognitive skills. From the first paragraph a child writes to a major paper written by a college student, the ability to organize and sequence thoughts, present a logical, cohesive text, and review and edit writing is critical. Word processors and spell-check programs are used often by students with learning disabilities to address mechanical and handwriting problems, but the words chosen and the structure of the writing still must come from the students themselves.

Because many students with learning disabilities approach writing tasks without a plan, instructional techniques often include providing students with a series of steps to follow as guidelines for writing. Some techniques may be quite specific; for example, students may be taught to develop a graphic representation of their thoughts and ideas to help them organize material before they begin writing. One example is an activity called *webbing*. In this activity, students write their main topic in the middle of their paper—for example, cats. They then draw lines from the main topic that represent different subtopics (what cats look like, what they like to eat, and how they move). Under each subtopic, the student writes notes or words related directly to it (for example, soft, furry, long or short hair, different colors). Now the student can use this web to help write the paper: Each subtopic can represent a paragraph, and only related information will be included in the text (see Fig. 4.1). Other techniques may be more general so that they can be used in a variety of writing contexts, and they may include steps for planning, checking, and revising writing. As we will see when we discuss strategy instruction, a number of commercial strategies have been developed specifically to address the organizational skills of students with learning disabilities.

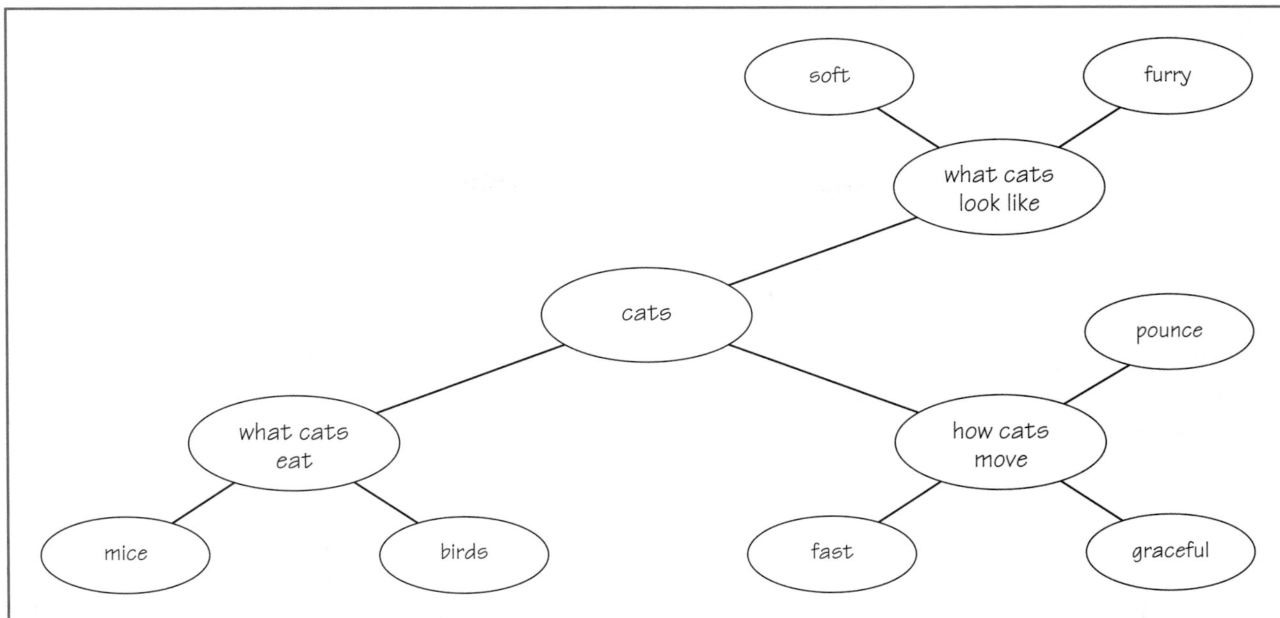

Figure 4.1
Webbing

Mathematics

Although, in general, difficulties in math do not receive the same attention as problems in reading and language arts, students with learning disabilities often have a number of problems in this area. Specific problem areas include difficulty understanding size and spatial relationships and concepts related to direction, place value, decimals, fractions, and time and difficulty remembering math facts (Lerner, 1993). Remembering and correctly applying the steps to mathematical algorithms (for example, how to divide) and reading and solving word problems are significant problem areas (Cawley et al., 1996; Harris, Miller, & Mercer, 1995). Students with learning disabilities, like all students, may also make simple computational errors because of inattention to the operation sign, incorrect alignment of problems, omission of steps in the algorithm, or not checking or reviewing work.

Many students with learning disabilities approach math skills as a series of unrelated memory tasks (Engelmann, Carnine, & Steely, 1991). Because of the rapid presentation of skills in most math curricula and the early and extensive memory requirements, students who have difficulty conceptualizing the process or learning the facts just try to get through whatever skill is being worked on at the time. We are not suggesting that the rate of presentation results in the disability, only that if sufficient and appropriate instruction is not provided, these students probably will not absorb the material they need on their own.

Let's look at an elementary classroom for a typical example of a problem a student with learning disabilities might have in math. The teacher, Mr. Hernandez, has been teaching the students single-digit subtraction for two weeks. Jimmy, the little boy with a learning disability, knows what they are doing—

they are putting out markers for the big number and then taking away the same number of markers as the smaller number. Mr. Hernandez gives a test, and Jimmy completes only five of the twenty problems, but he gets them correct. Now Mr. Hernandez decides it's time for review, and he gives the students a worksheet with addition and subtraction facts on it. What do you think Jimmy does with all of his problems? He puts out markers for the big numbers and takes away the same number of markers as the smaller numbers. Perhaps Jimmy didn't attend to the signs. Mr. Hernandez points out to Jimmy that some of the signs are addition signs. Jimmy looks at him in confusion. Addition? What is that?

It is important to review and assess math concepts and strategies constantly so that students can build on previous skills.

Many students, like Jimmy, are just following the pattern of the week. It is important to constantly review and assess concepts and strategies for students with learning disabilities. It is likely that unless Mr. Hernandez reviews, has Jimmy practice, and encourages him to discriminate between operations, subtraction will become as vague a concept to Jimmy as addition is now. Even more important, teachers must actually instruct children in the concept behind the procedure they are doing. Without this connecting knowledge, math will become increasingly difficult because students will not be able to build on previous skills.

When teaching students with learning disabilities, teachers should always keep in mind the learning characteristics of their students and try to tailor instruction accordingly. Instruction in word problems, for example, should begin early with very simple problems; key words or information should be highlighted to help students identify what they need to solve the problem. Later, students can be taught to identify this information themselves. Consider also the importance of certain memory tasks. Students may be able to remember some math facts and may learn all of them if they are not forced into a time frame—most students with learning disabilities aren't going to be able to learn the first three multiplication tables overnight.

For a number of years, researchers and teachers have investigated various alternative ways to help students with learning disabilities remember math facts. One strategy, the use of **pegwords**, has become popular for teaching multiplication facts and has a body of supporting research (Greene, 1999; Mas-

Using Pegwords to Teach Multiplication Facts

Facts	Pegword Associations	Visual Associations	Elaborations
$3 \times 3 = 9$	Tree and tree on a line		Remember the 2 trees sitting on a line.
$3 \times 4 = 12$	Tree with a door for an elf		Who would live in a tree with a door? An elf who bakes cookies, of course, as in the TV commercial.

Source: Wood, D.K., & Frank, A.R. (2000). "Using memory-enhancing strategies to learn multiplication facts," *Teaching Exceptional Children, 32*(5), 78–82.

tropieri & Scruggs, 1991; Wood, Frank, & Wacker, 1998). A pegword is a word that rhymes with a number and that is used in association with a picture to assist in remembering. For example, the number three has the pegword *tree,* which is presented with a picture of a tree. The multiplication fact "3 × 3 = 9" is represented by the pegword phrase "Tree and tree on a line" and by a picture of two trees with a line underneath. Students must first learn the pegwords and visual symbols associated with each number. Then flashcards containing the math facts and pegword symbols are presented to the students (Wood & Frank, 2000). The accompanying box, "Using Pegwords to Teach Multiplication Facts," presents some examples.

Current recommendations for instruction in mathematics include beginning your teaching, even of complex concepts, at the concrete level (materials that can be held and moved), then gradually moving to the semiconcrete level (pictures or graphics), and finally moving to the abstract level (numbers only) (Harris, Miller, & Mercer, 1995; Mercer & Mercer, 1993b). It is important for teachers to realize that advanced mathematical concepts, such as decimals, may take much more time to teach than they anticipate (Woodward, Baxter, & Robinson, 1999). For instruction in algorithms, word problems, and complex functions, the

Mathematics instruction for students with learning disabilities should move from concrete, to semiconcrete, to abstract levels.

STAR Strategy

1. **S**earch the word problem.
   a) Read the problem carefully.
   b) Ask yourself questions: "What facts do I know?" "What do I need to find?"
   c) Write down facts.

2. **T**ranslate the words into an equation in picture form.
   a) Choose a variable.
   b) Identify the operation(s).
   c) Represent the problem with the Algebra Lab Gear (CONCRETE APPLICATION).
      Draw a picture of the representation (SEMICONCRETE APPLICATION).
      Write an algebraic equation (ABSTRACT APPLICATION).

3. **A**nswer the problem.

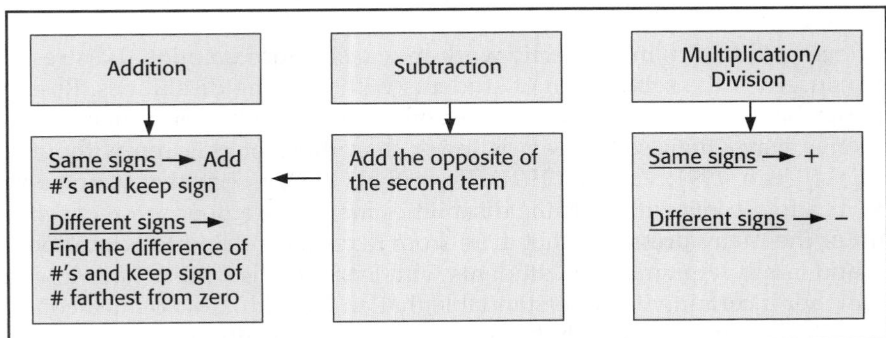

4. **R**eview the solution.
   a) Reread the problem.
   b) Ask question, "Does the answer make sense? Why?"
   c) Check answer.

Figure 4.2
Star Strategy

Source: Maccini, P., & Hughes, C.A. "Effects of a Problem-Solving Strategy on the Introductory Algebra Performance of Secondary Students with Learning Disabilities," *Learning Disabilities and Practice, 15,* 10–21.

use of step-by-step written plans, or strategies for students to follow, helps them in organization, memory, and evaluation skills. Instruction in mathemathics can move from presenting simple algorithms for addition or subtraction to presenting more complex skills, such as solving algebraic equations (Maccini & Hughes, 2000; Mercer & Miller, 1992; Montague, Warger, & Morgan, 2000). Figure 4.2 presents one strategy for teaching mathematics.

Learning Disabilities and Social and Emotional Development

Students with learning disabilities may have difficulty acquiring and interpreting social behaviors.

Although you may typically think of students with learning disabilities as individuals who have difficulty in academic tasks, it is important to realize that most social behaviors also involve learning. The characteristics that interfere with a student's acquisition of reading or writing skills can also interfere with his or her ability to acquire or interpret social behaviors (Carlson, 1987). Often these problems are related to difficulties in correctly interpreting or responding to social situations and in reading social cues, including nonverbal cues, and to acting impulsively without identifying the consequences of behavior or recognizing the feelings and concerns of others (Bryan, 1991; Carlson, 1987; Schumaker & Hazel, 1984). The individual who has difficulty identifying important information in academic work may also experience difficulty identifying important information in social situations. If a student has problems monitoring and evaluating his performance in spelling, he may also experience problems evaluating and adjusting his behavior on a date, in the classroom, or in the library.

Certainly, not *all* students with learning disabilities have problems with social behavior; however, many students with learning disabilities have problems relating to others and behaving acceptably at school. It is important to note that although some difficulties in social behavior may be related to learning characteristics, still others may be tied more directly to academic failure. The 16-year-old reading on the second-grade level may search for attention, acceptance, and control by engaging in inappropriate or even antisocial behavior. The search for a peer group, susceptibility to peer pressure, and problems anticipating consequences of actions may all contribute to the fact that adolescents with learning disabilities are often considered at risk for juvenile delinquency (Larson & Gerber, 1987).

Having difficulty in academic work may also cause emotional distress. Of most concern is the self-esteem of students with learning disabilities. Research suggests that students with learning disabilities may not perceive themselves in a positive way—their self-esteem is lower than those of children without disabilities (Bryan, 1991; Vaughn, 1991). Rosenthal (1992) asserts that young adults and late adolescents with learning disabilities may have a poor sense of self as a result of the many pressures that arise from decisions related to education, career, and family. Again, not all students with learning disabilities have low self-esteem, but it certainly is understandable that an individual who must confront his or her disability on a daily basis would have difficulty feeling good about himself or herself, particularly in the area of personal competence.

Think for a moment about something you do not do well. Perhaps it is singing. If you really don't sing well, you may just avoid singing in public and it may present no real problem for you. What if, however, you had to sing every day, in front of all your friends? Not only do you have to sing in front of them, but you will receive a grade in singing. You've really tried, but you just can't carry a tune. Soon, all of your friends are singing Mozart and you are still trying to get the scales right. Can you imagine how you would behave or feel in that situation? Perhaps you would begin to look for ways to avoid singing (lots of sore throats) or skip school altogether. You also might think of ways to avoid interacting with your friends, since you are so obviously different, and try to find other, nonsinging friends. Or, maybe, you would say you just didn't care—you never really wanted to sing anyway.

If we substitute reading or math for singing in the preceding story, you may understand how students with learning disabilities often feel. As a teacher, it may also help you recognize the need to identify and develop your students' strengths as well as work on remediating their skill deficits. It also may inspire you to think of ways to make school a positive experience for students, including ways to facilitate enjoyable and constructive interactions between the student or students with a learning disability and other students in the class. Seidel and Vaughn (1991) found that students with learning disabilities who had dropped out of school reported strong feelings of social alienation and an absence of attachment to either teachers or classmates. By demonstrating positive attitudes and encouraging positive interaction in the classroom, teachers may not only be helping students with learning disabilities feel better about themselves, they may be helping to keep them in school as well.

It is important to make school a positive experience for students with learning disabilities.

Effects on the Family

Most families do not realize that their child has a learning disability until he or she reaches school age and begins to fail at a school-related task. For these families, the major challenge may be finding the appropriate special education services for their child and helping the child deal with any stigma associated with the label *learning disabled* or with placement in special education services.

Learning that their child has a learning disability can have a number of different effects on a family, including increased family stress and conflict (Ehrlich, 1983). With all children with disabilities, parents are often put in the position of making educational decisions based on very little information, and this can result in conflicts between parents, and between parents and the child. Extra time may now need to be devoted to tutoring, homework, or conferences, which may mean taking time away from other children in the family. Usually, competition exists between children in a family, and this natural interaction may be either exacerbated or extinguished when one sibling has a learning disability. The child without a disability may be anxious for attention and promote his skills as a way of obtaining it. Parents, on the other hand, may want to protect the child with the disability and forbid overt competition. Any unnatural structuring of normal sibling interaction may serve only to add stress within the family.

Observing the difficulties that a student with learning disabilities may have in academic skills and in social relationships with others can be very painful for parents; they may tend to be overprotective of the child to try to save him or her from pain. Ideally, parents will help the child develop strategies to cope with rejection from peers, but doing so may tax the emotional strength of even the strongest parent. Parents of learning-disabled students can derive both practical suggestions and emotional support from belonging to groups that include other parents of children with similar problems.

Support groups can help parents of children with learning disabilities by providing both suggestions and support.

In spite of the many challenges they face, some families are relieved to find there is a reason for their child's poor school performance. As we mentioned

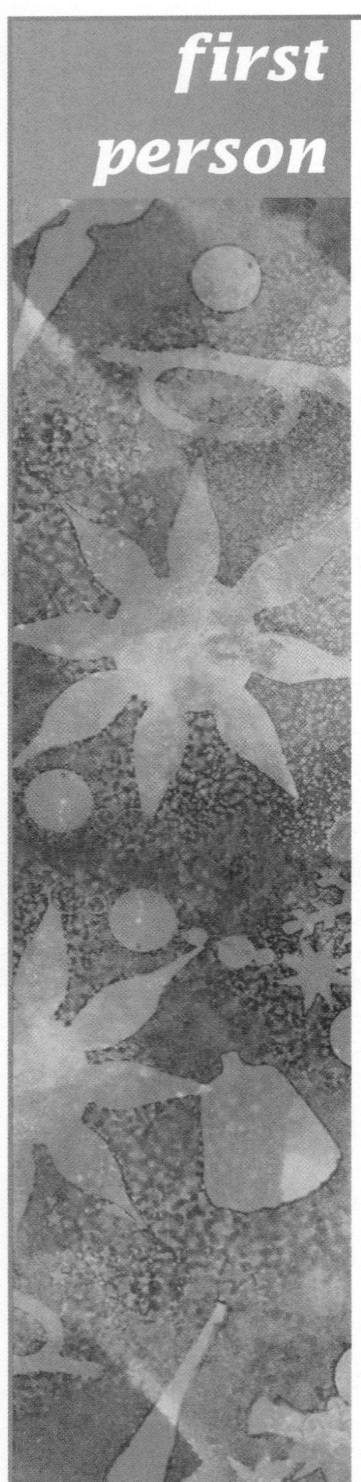

For any student with a learning disability, school often provides overwhelming challenges, which must be faced. The struggles come from both internal and external sources. The impacts of the disability vary and evolve, compounding the student's difficulty. Teachers, friends, and parents often add to the stress, in spite of their best intentions. Although as a student with a learning disability, I myself have experienced a great deal of pain and frustration, there are several survival techniques that help me cope. To be a student with a learning disability is to be a member of a minority, and as such, each of us should share our experiences so that others may develop strategies to help them through their struggles.

I believe one key idea is to find one's own definition of the dual identity within oneself as a learner and as a student. The learner is the one who makes an effort to be curious, involved, and motivated. The student is the one who determines how you cope in school. Not all knowledge is taught in school. It is the student identity that gets labeled as disabled. The "learning disability" should not be allowed to overwhelm one's desire to attain knowledge. The learner in you must prevent it.

Another piece of advice besides developing a personal definition is developing one's self-esteem, to learn to have no fear of oneself. I felt like there was something wrong with me before I found out I had a disability; when I finally was diagnosed, it took me years to believe that I was not stupid or limited. However, I now understand that "to be categorized is, simply, to be enslaved," as Gore Vidal expressed. The label of *learning disability* should not be allowed to determine one's identity, character, or self-image, nor one's potential.

Support from friends who can be trusted is crucial. It is destructive to believe that if you have a learning disability and your friends do not, you are too different from them to talk about your problems. I know from experience that the only result is self-imposed isolation. Asking for support from friends with whom you are comfortable will help maintain your self-esteem. Everyone wants to feel normal, not different, not disabled. The challenge is to accept yourself as who you are and believe in your own self-definition. Although there may be differences on some levels, you may also find friendships with those with whom you have something else in common. I have come to trust and value those similarities.

Getting help or asking for support in the areas that present hurdles is essential. What is equally important is choosing carefully which voices or people have influence over you, your goals, your self-esteem, and your successes. Well-meaning or good-intentioned professionals or teachers can be just as hurtful to you as those who speak with prejudice and ignorance about learning disabilities. It is not a kindness to limit opportunities in education when a student experiences difficulty. As a member of a minority group that frequently cannot be detected from behavior or external clues, a student with a "hidden" learning disability ought to be able to acknowledge his or her vulnerability without being overpowered by negative and condescending opinions. No one should determine what you can and cannot do because he or she thinks that having a learning disability automatically makes you less capable. "The power to exceed is not the same as the desire to exceed" (T.P. Gore). A student with a learning disability can have just as much desire for success as a student without a disability.

But most of all, a student with a learning disability should always ask questions—of herself, teachers, evaluators, and tutors. The reason is that only when there is knowledge about your disability can there be the opportunity for self-advocacy. Being able to speak for yourself is crucial for getting the accommodations needed for your education and for full inclusion in the class by the teacher. The children's storybook character Winnie the Pooh said appropriately that "rivers know this. There is no hurry. We shall get there someday." The fact is that every student can learn in school, even with a learning disability; we all will get there someday.

Caitlin Norah Callahan

Source: Caitlin Norah Callahan, "Advice About Being an LD Student." Reprinted by permission. LD OnLine is a service of the Learning Disabilities Project at WETA, Washington, D.C., in association with the Coordinated Campaign for Learning Disabilities. School partners include the Lab School of Washington and Arlington (VA) Public Schools. 1997 WETA.

earlier in the chapter, the label *learning disability* is much more acceptable to parents than some other labels. Some parents, however, may be ashamed or deny the existence of a disability.

Educational Issues and Teaching Strategies

How to assess and teach students with learning disabilities is a question that has been asked and debated for the past three decades. Many different philosophies can be found in the variety of educational programs for students with learning disabilities. In this section, we present assessment and teaching procedures that reflect what research has suggested to be best practice in the field.

Early Identification

By virtue of the definition, a learning disability does not exist until a student has experienced an academic problem in school. Typically, that happens in the early elementary years. Some preschool-aged children, though, seem more likely than others to develop learning disabilities at a later age; they are generally considered to be "at risk" for the development of school problems. Some of the factors that place a child at risk are medical in nature, such as low birthweight. Other factors are related to the child's parent or environment—for example, a mother who drinks during pregnancy. Remember, though, that no one of these factors is enough to qualify a child for special services; it is more likely that children who have a *cluster* of risk factors will be candidates for evaluation for special programming.

There are many problems for professionals in deciding whether or not a child is at risk for learning problems in school. Those of you who have young children or work with them will know that there is tremendous variation in the characteristics of 2-, 3-, and 4-year-olds. In any class of "normal" preschoolers there will be those who are talkative and articulate and those who are relatively silent, some who are daring and able climbers and runners and some who are hesitant and awkward with those skills. How different must a child be before we become concerned? There are no concrete answers to that question. Many of the relative "weaknesses" of these children will have disappeared by the time they reach elementary school.

Even when a cluster of risk factors can be identified in a child, it is often difficult to determine what the precise nature of the child's problem will be. Will the child have mental retardation, or will the profile change to the point where he or she will ultimately have learning disabilities or a language disorder? Or is the child's behavior or emotional status the primary problem? Sorting these issues out at later ages is difficult enough; at 2, 3, or 4, there are simply too many possibilities for error.

Another difficulty in determining whether a young child needs special services lies with the assessment process. It is possible that many of the assessment instruments used with young children have poor **predictive validity** (McLoughlin & Lewis, 1986). That simply means that these tests may not predict accurately whether or not a young child actually *will* have later problems in school. With poor predictive validity, there will be too many "false positives"—children who will be targeted as having potential learning problems who will not end up having them—and too many "false negatives"—children who actually *will* have problems who will not be identified.

It is also important to ask whether the benefits of early identification and intervention outweigh the possible liabilities. An early label, or even a nonlabeled special class placement, may have stigmatizing effects on a child and set up a "self-fulfilling prophecy" for the child in which teachers' expectations for performance are lowered (Lerner, 1993).

Because of these problems, there are few, if any, preschool programs specifically for children with suspected learning disabilities. The programs that do exist serve children who have been given the generic descriptor of developmental disabilities and those with a variety of problems. Most professionals believe strongly in the effectiveness of early intervention, and their beliefs are backed up by research findings (see Chapter 2). Their hope would be that children who are identified early and who participate in early intervention programs could avoid the need for special education by the time they reach elementary school.

Assessment for Teaching

There are two major purposes for assessment of students with learning disabilities. First, we assess in order to *identify* students who need special services and to determine the placement that best suits each child. Recall that we discussed this process in Chapter 1. Next we assess in order to *plan* the student's instructional program—to answer the question "What do I teach?" Assessment can also help us evaluate the effectiveness of the program and the progress that the student is making; in fact, it can serve a variety of purposes.

■ ***Formal Assessment*** **Formal assessment** involves the use of standardized tests, the results of which can be used to compare the student's performance with that of his or her same-age peers. Three tests commonly used at schools and diagnostic clinics are the Keymath Diagnostic Arithmetic Test, the Woodcock Reading Mastery Test—Revised, and the Peabody Individual Achievement Test—Revised (PIAT-R). These tests assess the student's performance in math, reading, and several basic skill areas, respectively, and provide scores that reveal grade level and standing relative to other students. The tests are examples of those used to document the grade of academic performance so that one can determine if a discrepancy exists between achievement and ability.

Although the information yielded by these tests may be useful in diagnostic contexts, it is not detailed or specific enough to provide a foundation for instructional planning. For that purpose, many teachers rely on informal measures.

■ ***Informal Assessment*** **Informal assessment** refers to direct measures of student performance and student progress in academic or behavioral tasks. These measures are the tools used to help the teacher identify what needs to be taught and how it should best be presented (McLoughlin & Lewis, 1986).

There are many ways for a teacher to get information using informal assessment. Among them are *observations* of the student's work habits—for example, identifying the amount of time a child is able to pay attention to a task or activity. Observing how a child performs his work can be very helpful to the teacher because of the particular difficulties experienced by many students with learning disabilities. Observations can provide some information about why the child is unable to do well in certain tasks. For example, you might notice that a child works very rapidly on certain tasks and never reflects on or checks his work. You may notice that the child spends large amounts of time playing with the buttons on his shirt, or writing, erasing, and rewriting his words. This information may help you target specific areas for intervention.

Observations can also help prepare students to move into regular classroom settings. Because classroom teachers may have specific behavioral or learning requirements, the special education teacher or another professional can conduct an informal observation of the regular classroom into which the child will be placed. By noting specific requirements, such as length of seatwork time, types of tests, and behavior rules and requirements, the special education teacher can prepare the student for his move in a more effective manner. If Les is used to sitting in his seat for a maximum of five minutes, and the classroom teacher usually has the students doing twenty minutes of seatwork at a time, it may be important to target longer in-seat behavior and increased sustained attention for instruction before Les makes the move. Figure 4.3 provides an example of an interview form used by a special education resource teacher to help her plan instruction for one of her students. Teachers can also use an observation form like this to target suggestions for the regular classroom teacher to use. Once differences between the classroom requirements and the abilities of the student have been identified, the special education teacher can suggest modifications to the classroom teacher to help the student gradually learn the behaviors necessary for successful classroom performance.

Using informal inventories, teachers observe how children approach classroom tasks.

A teacher can also analyze a student's work for error patterns by using **informal inventories** of reading and mathematics skills and teacher-made tests based on the classroom curriculum (Lerner, 1993). Informal inventories consist of a series of sequential passages or excerpts, on different grade levels, that are usually taken from several curricula (Wallace, Larsen, & Elksnin, 1992). Students are evaluated on reading accuracy and asked a series of comprehension questions after each passage. Research supports the importance of this type of assessment, also called **curriculum-based measurement (CBM)**, for student performance. Stecker and Fuchs (2000), found that when teachers used students' own curriculum-based measures to plan instruction, students performed significantly better than if more general informal measures were used. By using the informal curriculum-based assessment to assess a child's reading, writing, or math skills, the teacher can observe how the child approaches the task as well as the specific types of difficulties he or she is experiencing. For example, the teacher may note that a child misreads all words with a double vowel combination in the middle or never regroups when a zero is in the subtrahend. If teachers construct their own informal inventories, they can determine how well the child interacts with the curriculum in specific areas such as vocabulary and sentence structure.

Approaches and Strategies

Ideas about how to teach students with learning disabilities are usually based on a professional's beliefs, explicit or assumed, about causes of learning disabilities and characteristics of students with learning disabilities. Thus a wide variety of approaches for teaching students with learning disabilities has been presented over the years. Many of these approaches have been based on a hypothesized cause of learning disabilities (for example, brain damage, diet) and have been influenced by the professional affiliation and orientation of the developer (for example, physician, language therapist, optometrist). In our section on instructional approaches, we will focus on the most current and often-used procedures for teaching students with learning disabilities. Realize, however, that

ASSESSMENT OF MAINSTREAMED ENVIRONMENT
TEACHER INTERVIEW

Teacher Sara Walker

Class Science 6th Grade

How much time are students required to listen to lecture or general instruction?
Generally the first 10-15 minutes of class is lecture or instruction.

How much in-class reading is required? What is the nature of the reading material?
A textbook is not used. In class reading would consist of worksheets, dictionary, and encyclopedias (research materials). This is done daily for most of the class period—around 30 minutes.

What is the nature of classroom activities? (cooperative learning, independent work, discussion, pairs)
Mainly independent work and some discussion. Once a week there is a special speaker—students are required to take notes on speakers. Definitions or notes for science are often given during Lang. Arts period. Question: How much assistance do you give? Whatever is needed—I can meet with students at recess and before school.

How much homework is required and what is the nature of it?
At the beginning of the 4-week unit, a packet of assignments is given to students with a list of due dates. What is not completed in class should be completed for homework. Assignments are explained all on the first day of the 4 weeks. Assignments consist of wordfinds with unit vocab, research projects, essays or papers, labeling diagrams, answering questions. Students find answers from resources in room.

Do you assign projects or long-term assignments, and if so, how much structure or guidance is given?
(see above) In the beginning, teacher gives dates and explains expectations. Students are left on their own to complete them throughout the 4 weeks. (Some time is spent working in class.) On the day the assignment is done, students present them in class or teacher leads a discussion.

Do you give a final test at the end of the four-week unit?
No – grades are based on accuracy, punctuality, etc. of all assignments.

What are your behavioral expectations?
That students are responsible and can work independently. Students should turn in assignments on time. Students work on tasks during class and participate in discussion. Students can move freely about the room without disrupting others.

Figure 4.3
Assessment of Mainstreamed Environment: Teacher Interview

Source: Kim Phillips, "Assessment of Mainstreamed Environment" (Columbia, SC: Rosewood Elementary School, 1993) unpublished materials). Used by permission of the author.

the field virtually abounds with instructional approaches and techniques, many of which are here today and gone tomorrow.

We will look at two major instructional approaches to academic skills: direct instruction of specific skills, and strategy instruction. A teaching model combining both direct instruction and strategy instruction was found to be the most effective model for students with learning disabilities (Swanson, 1999). These approaches are integrated to a certain extent and reflect a similar philosophy about how students with learning disabilities should be taught as well as what types of skills should be taught. We also will review some of the approaches used to teach specialized skill areas, such as social or study skills.

In direct instruction, specific academic skills are taught using proven techniques.

■ ***Direct Instruction*** The term **direct instruction** may be interpreted several ways; however, as a philosophy and approach to teaching students with learning disabilities, direct instruction commonly refers to (1) the identification and instruction of specific academic skills and (2) the use of teaching techniques that have been empirically demonstrated to be effective with students with learning difficulties. The identification and instruction of specific skills may seem to be a fairly obvious approach to teaching, but it represents a departure from some of the instructional procedures used in the past for students with learning disabilities, in which the emphasis was on training sensory-processing abilities, such as visual or auditory discrimination. The philosophy behind direct instruction is that any specific processing disabilities the child demonstrates can be managed through effective teaching procedures and that the most efficient use of instructional time is to focus on the academic skills in need of remediation (see the accompanying box, "Designing Direct Instruction Programs in Reading").

~ Designing Direct Instruction Programs in Reading

The following six steps may be used for designing direct instruction programs in reading:

1. Identify specific objectives based on importance of skills.
2. Whenever possible, develop strategies or plans for students to follow to accomplish specific objectives (such as a strategy for decoding specific types of words).
3. Develop teaching formats and procedures before instruction begins; present only one concept at a time during each lesson.
4. Select examples for instruction; the role of examples is critical in direct instruction. If a concept is being taught, examples are used to teach students the critical attributes of the concept (for example, what makes a sentence a sentence); if a skill or strategy is being taught, examples are used to teach when and how to use the skill and to provide practice and demonstration of skill application.
5. Sequence skills carefully before instruction; when presented with a new skill, students must know needed preskills. Other sequencing guidelines are based on the importance of the skill and the difficulty of the skill and on reducing the potential for confusion between the new skill and other skills.
6. Provide sufficient opportunities for skill practice, and continually review previous learning.

Source: *Direct Instruction Reading,* Third Edition, by Carnine/Silbert/Kameenui. Copyright © 1990. Adapted by permission of Prentice-Hall, Inc. Upper Saddle River, NJ.

The teaching techniques commonly identified in the direct instruction approach address the organization and presentation of instruction. The approach is very teacher-directed and includes an initial presentation based on the teacher first *modeling* the skill or response, then providing guided practice (*leading*), and, finally, eliciting independent student responses (*testing*). This process is designed to provide students with positive examples of the response or strategy. Exposure to positive examples promotes the probability of correct responding and helps to eliminate the possibility of confusion related to poor directions or student misinterpretation of the task. The modeling and leading steps of the process are part of initial instruction and are eliminated as instruction in a specific skill progresses (Engelmann & Hanner, 1982).

Presentation Techniques for Direct Instruction The direct instruction approach includes a number of presentation techniques designed to maximize student attention and involvement in learning (Lewis, 1993). Some of these presentation techniques include:

1. *Small-group instruction* Recommendations include seating students in a small semicircle, facing the teacher.
2. *Using response signals* The teacher chooses a signal that indicates it is time to respond (this could be a slight tap on the board or table or a snap of the fingers). The signal allows the teacher to delay the students' responses for a few seconds to encourage time to think about or reflect on the response. This delay or pause is called *wait time.*
3. *Choral or unison responding* When using the model–lead–test format, the teacher can have the whole group answer together during guided practice and independent student response time. Individuals' responses would then follow unison responses. Unison responding helps to maintain students' attention, allows for more opportunities for practice, and provides numerous models of correct responding.
4. *Providing corrective feedback* During instruction, errors are corrected immediately by modeling and then retesting responses; students also are praised when they have made correct responses.
5. *Pacing* Lessons are presented at a fairly rapid pace to maintain students' attention and interest in the lesson (Carnine, Silbert, & Kameenui, 1990; Engelmann & Carnine, 1982; Engelmann & Hanner, 1982).

Evidence from research studies supports the effectiveness of direct instruction. Right now, it appears to be the most effective means of teaching students with learning disabilities (Adams & Engelmann, 1996; Rosenshine & Stevens, 1986). Some of the commercial programs based on this approach include Corrective Reading: Decoding Strategies (Engelmann, Carnine, & Johnson, 1988), Corrective Mathematics (Engelmann & Carnine, 1982), and Reading Mastery (Engelmann & Bruner, 1988). Figure 4.4 is an excerpt from Word Attack Basics, a direct instruction program (Engelmann, Carnine, & Johnson, 1988). All of the commercial direct instruction programs contain specific scripted lessons for teachers and incorporate the teaching techniques just described. Other materials that contain direct instruction techniques include a variety of computer software and multimedia and videodisk programs. These programs use direct instruction to involve students in more active learning (Hayden, Gersten, & Carnine, 1992).

Lesson 51

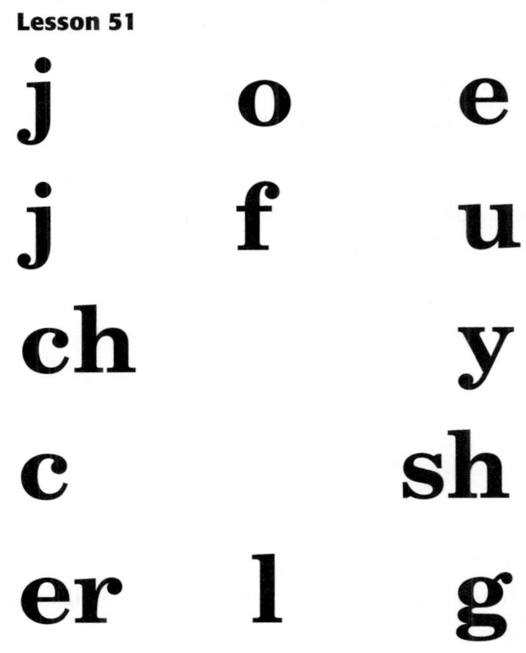

EXERCISE 1: Sound Introduction

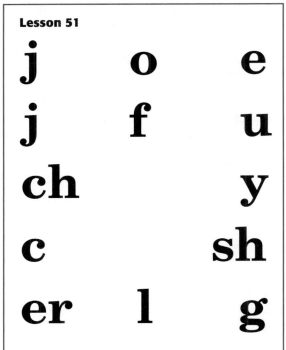

1. Point to **j. This letter makes the sound j. What sound?** Touch. j.
2. Point to **o. One sound you learned for this letter is the same as the letter name. Everybody, what's that sound?** Touch. ōōō. **Yes, ōōō.** **What's the other sound?** Touch. ŏŏŏ. **Yes, ŏŏŏ.**
3. Point to **e. One sound you learned for this letter is the same as the letter name. Everybody, what's that sound?** Touch. ēēē. **Yes, ēēē.** **What's the other sound?** Touch ĕĕĕ. **Yes, ĕĕĕ.**
4. Point to **j. What sound?** Touch. j. **Yes, j.**
5. Repeat step 4 for **f, u, ch, y, c, sh, er, l, g.**

Individual Test

Call on two or three students. Touch under each sound. Each student says all the sounds.

Figure 4.4
Word Attack Basics

Source: From S. Engelmann, L. Carnine, and G. Johnson, *Word-Attack Basics: Decoding A,* p. 225, 251.

■ ***Strategy Instruction*** A strategy can be defined as a set of responses that are organized to perform an activity or solve a problem (Swanson, 1993). Although the current knowledge base about the relationship between learning disabilities, strategy deficits, and strategy instruction consists of contributions from a number of psychological and educational theories and research, in this section we will focus primarily on the strategy approaches used most often by teachers of students with learning disabilities. In addition to academic skills instruction, we will see that strategies are also used to teach specialized skills, adaptive skills, and life skills.

Strategy instruction teaches specific skills by organizing steps, providing prompts, and focusing on metacognitive skills.

A **strategy instruction** approach to teaching students with learning disabilities involves first breaking down the skills involved in a task or problem—usually a procedure such as writing a paper—into a set of sequential steps. The steps are prepared so that the student may read or, later, memorize them in order to perform the skill correctly. Some strategies are developed so that the first letters of all the steps form an acronym to help students remember the purpose of the strategy and the steps involved (recall Fig. 4.2). Many strategies also include decision-making or evaluative components designed to help students use metacognitive skills (Deshler et al., 1983).

Strategy training involves more than just the presentation of steps, however. Careful assessment and direct instruction, including sufficient opportunities to practice the strategy, are considered essential in most strategy instruction. Students should see how to use the strategy, practice, and receive feedback before attempting to use it on their own. Deshler et al. (1983) suggest that it is very important for students to be interested in learning the strategy. Consequently, instruction often begins by establishing a need for the strategy and getting a commitment from students to learn.

Strategies have been developed to address the needs of students with learning disabilities in a wide range of areas. Test-taking skills, study skills, reading comprehension, written composition, anger control, and math problem solving are all possible target areas for strategies. Some research suggests that the use of strategy instruction can be an important learning tool for students with learning disabilities. For example, elementary and secondary students with learning disabilities are found to write more reflective, complex, and well-written essays when using writing strategies (De La Paz & Graham, 1997; De La Paz, Owen, Harris, & Graham, 2000). Learning strategies have even been integrated successfully with some computer software to assist in the decision-making and problem-solving skills of older students with reading disabilities (Hollingsworth & Woodward, 1993).

Given what you have read about the learning characteristics of students with learning disabilities, you may be able to see why the strategy instruction approach is intuitively appealing to educators. It teaches specific skills in a manner that controls for potential problems in a student's ability to identify important information or steps, organizes the steps for the student, provides a continual prompt for remembering, breaks the task into its component parts, and often focuses on metacognitive skills. In addition, we know that many students with learning disabilities do not use strategies or plans when approaching academic tasks. An important question, however, is whether or not students with disabilities can learn and apply strategies in general education classrooms. Concerns about the students' abilities to generalize learning from one classroom to the next and the general education teacher's willingness to devote time to teaching learning strategies suggest the need for continued research on effective implementation of strategy instruction in general education classrooms (Scanlon, Deshler, & Schumaker, 1996).

Although teachers often develop their own strategies, a number of commercially developed strategies and curricula based on strategies are available. One of the most well-known curricula designed for students with learning disabilities is the Learning Strategies Curriculum, which was developed at the University of Kansas Institute for Research in Learning Disabilities. This curriculum, which continues to expand, contains elaborate strategies and comprehensive procedures for teaching students ways to acquire information through skills such as paraphrasing, ways to store information through skills such as listening and notetaking, and ways to demonstrate knowledge through skills such as writing paragraphs and taking tests (Schumaker & Lyerla, 1991). Each component of the Learning Strategies Curriculum contains a sequence of steps for learners to follow and practice so they can perform the tasks. Teachers are provided with a series of specific guidelines for teaching students how to perform these strategies. As we usually see with strategy instruction, students are taught not only specific behaviors but also how to evaluate and monitor their performance.

■ ***Special Skills Instruction*** Many students with learning disabilities, especially older ones, may receive instruction in specialized skills such as study skills or social skills. Instruction in these skills may be the only type of service required by some students with learning disabilities; for others it may be one component of a more comprehensive set of support services. Sometimes special skills instruction is incorporated into the regular classroom curriculum; other times, these skills are taught in special education settings—for example, in a resource class. This section gives an overview of instructional approaches to teaching study and social skills.

Study Skills As we have seen throughout this chapter, the difficulties experienced by many students with learning disabilities revolve around the ability to receive, process, and express information effectively. Study skills instruction addresses these areas as they relate directly to classroom activities. The purpose of teaching study skills is to give the student a set of tools for performing required classroom activities, not to teach the content of a specific course. Because of the need for students to apply these skills in high school and college coursework, study skills instruction is increasingly considered a necessary component of the educational program for students with learning disabilities at both secondary and postsecondary levels (Ellis, Sabornie, & Marshall, 1989; Smith & Dowdy, 1989).

Study skills instruction for students with learning disabilities might include teaching techniques for reading and remembering material in content-area texts, taking and reviewing notes, taking essay or multiple-choice tests, and preparing reports or projects. Students learn and practice these skills on materials from a variety of content areas. Study skills are frequently taught through the use of strategy training. The strategies are usually general enough so that they can be applied to many different types of tasks and content areas. For example, a strategy taught for taking an essay exam should work in any type of essay exam (English, history, science, or psychology). Other instructional techniques include teaching students to use graphic aids, such as semantic mapping; to apply time management and general organization aids to study behavior; to use struc-

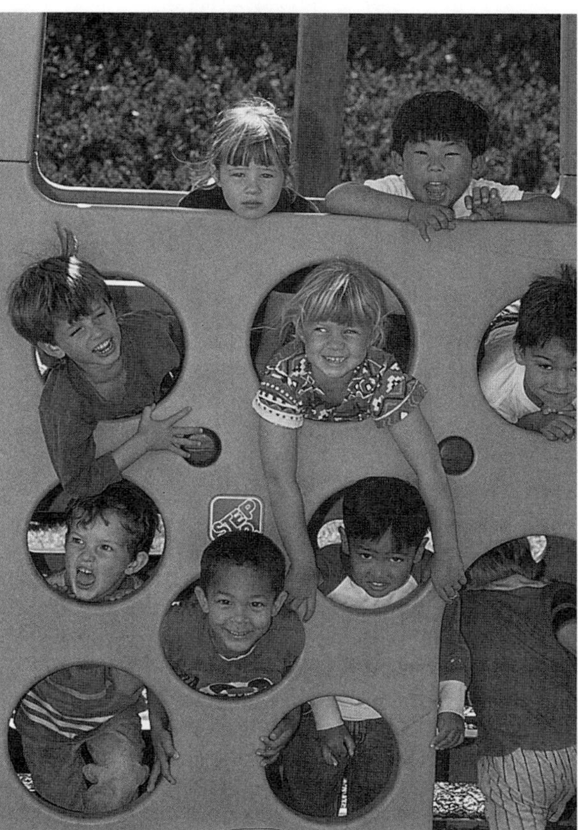

Normal variation makes it hard to tell which children will develop learning disabilities. (Tom Prettyman/ PHOTO EDIT)

ture or content outlines for taking notes; and to use alternative tools, such as tape recorders and computers (Smith, Finn, & Dowdy, 1993).

As you learned in the previous section, curricula such as the Learning Strategies Curriculum include strategies for teaching study skills. In addition, curricula designed specifically to teach study skills are currently available, such as Independent Strategies for Efficient Study (Rooney, 1988). Of course, a commercial curriculum is not necessary to teach study skills. If students are receiving a special course or series of classes in study skills, however, it is definitely helpful for the teacher to have an organized plan of instruction. Many teachers of students with learning disabilities develop original study skills curricula by drawing on existing programs and research and then adapting and applying those objectives and instructional techniques to the specific needs of their students. One of the most important goals of study skills instruction, regardless of the specific technique being taught, is to provide extensive practice on different types of work and to prompt the students to use the skills in other classes (Smith, Finn, & Dowdy, 1993). These activities help to ensure that students will actually use the skills to do their coursework, which, of course, is the purpose of study skills instruction.

Study skills instruction provides practice on different types of work so that students can use the skills in many classes.

Social Skills As we've seen, some students with learning disabilities experience difficulties in emotional and social adjustment. Educators are concerned about the effects of these difficulties on the behavior and adjustment of young adults with learning disabilities.

Although differences in the social behavior and social skills of students with learning disabilities have been documented over the years, instruction or training in social skills is often neglected. It is hard enough to find time to provide academic instruction, and it may be difficult to justify teaching social skills in lieu of reading or biology. Another barrier to social skills instruction is the equivocal empirical support for its effectiveness. Reviews of social skills training programs suggest that few programs have resulted in any positive change in students' social performance or social acceptance (McIntosh, Vaughn, & Zaragoza, 1991). Because of the perceived need to teach social skills to students with learning disabilities, however, research continues in two major areas: what skills should be taught and how to teach the skills so students will generalize them to real-life situations.

Teachers must tailor the social skills curriculum to their students' particular environment.

Many commercial curricula include or focus on social skills. It is important, however, for teachers to observe the student and his or her surroundings carefully before selecting skills for instruction. Skills necessary for success in a certain peer group or work setting may not be identified in a certain curriculum. For example, certain terms, forms of address, postures, and verbal skills will differ across regions, ages, and settings. If these particular skills are not identified and incorporated into the curriculum, the program may not be as successful as anticipated. It is helpful to conduct informal observations that allow a comparison to be made between the skills required in the target setting and the skills displayed by the students. The differences can then be identified and additional skills or adaptations integrated into the curriculum selected. The accompanying box, "Social Skills and Their Components," contains a list of possible social skills for instruction.

Social skills may be taught in a separate class, as you would teach history or math, or integrated into the regular curriculum as needed. For example, a teacher may notice that Antonio is always standing by the fence during recess and may decide that he might benefit from learning to play with other children. Another teacher might learn through experience that Sheila becomes very sullen and noncompliant whenever she receives any negative feedback or correction. The teacher may decide to teach Sheila some alternative ways to deal with criticism.

Generally, social skills programs involving multiple aspects of peer and adult interaction are taught in the classroom setting. However, social skills are difficult to transfer or generalize to other settings, and there is concern that the child who learns how to take turns and respond to questions in the classroom will not perform those behaviors in other classes or in the home and community. Nonetheless, Clement-Heist, Siegel, and Gaylord-Ross (1992) found that teaching job-related social skills in the classroom environment (for example, conversation skills, giving instructions) did result in behavior change in the actual work setting; even more change was noted when students were given additional instruction on the work site. The results of this study support the importance of teaching in the actual setting, yet also provide evidence that change can be achieved even when community-based instruction is not possible. The social skills program, like many others, includes a "homework" component that encourages students to practice the skills in real situations or settings. Most homework activities involve a recording sheet for students to identify when and how they use the skill.

Effective social skills training programs have a number of components in common, including small-group or individual instruction, long-term training programs, and procedures that show students how to guide, monitor, or evalu-

~ Social Skills and Their Components

Social Skill	Component Skills	Social Skill	Component Skills
Conversation skills	Joining a conversation Interrupting a conversation Starting a conversation Maintaining a conversation Ending a conversation Use of appropriate tone of voice Use of appropriate distance and eye contact	Self-help skills	Good grooming (clean, neat) Good dressing (wearing clothes that fit) Good table manners Good eating behaviors
Assertiveness skills	Asking for clarifications Making requests Denying requests Negotiating requests Exhibiting politeness	Classroom task-related behaviors	On-task behavior Attending to tasks Completing tasks Following directions Trying your best
"Play" interaction skills (e.g., making friends)	Sharing with others Inviting others to play Encouraging others Praising others	Self-related behaviors	Giving positive feedback to self Expressing feelings Accepting negative feedback Accepting consequences
Problem-solving and coping skills	Staying calm and relaxed Listing possible solutions Choosing the best solution Taking responsibility for self Handling name calling and teasing Staying out of trouble	Job interview skills	Being prepared (dress, attitude, etc.) Being attentive Listening skills Asking for clarification Thinking prior to speaking

Source: M.A. Mastropieri and T.E. Scruggs, *Effective Instruction for Special Education* (Boston: MIT Press, 1987), p. 319. Copyright © 1987. Used by permission of PRO-ED, Austin, TX.

ate their own behavior (McIntosh, Vaughn, & Zaragoza, 1991). A number of social skills training programs are available commercially. One respected curriculum is the Walker Social Skills Curriculum: The ACCESS Program (Walker, Todis, Holmes, & Horton, 1988). The procedures used in this curriculum to teach social skills related to peers, adults, and self are based on principles of direct instruction and include training in a general learning strategy. This program, like many others, also includes extensive role-playing opportunities, feedback sessions, and self-evaluation or assessment activities. As you can see, social skills are taught essentially the same way as academic skills: students are taught the skills directly; when appropriate, they learn a problem-solving or learning strategy; and numerous opportunities are provided for them to practice and evaluate their performance.

Instructional Considerations for Culturally Diverse Learners

If students in your classroom are not native English speakers, they may speak and understand English at different levels of proficiency. Obviously, it is important for you to know each child's level of English proficiency in both receptive and expressive language. The way you present information to students can help to facilitate their understanding of both directions and content. Many of the teaching techniques we have just described, such as using clear, simple instructions, providing examples, and using response signals or cues, are quite helpful. Holding and pointing to the material and demonstrating the response format provide a context by giving the listener cues about what is required (Fueyo, 1997). The specific difficulties encountered in reading and writing by students who are learning two languages may also require adjustments in how we teach these basic skills. In fact, many bilingual special educators advocate the use of the whole-language method of instruction, or direct instruction in a literature-based context, for students who are not native English speakers. These types of instruction allow students to use relevant books in their native language and helps the teacher evaluate the student's performance in higher-level thinking, planning, and conversational skills (Lopez-Reyna, 1996).

Many educators suggest supplementing direct instruction with motivating literature when teaching reading for bilingual students.

Recent research suggests that the direct instruction approach to teaching phonological awareness and other reading skills may be quite important for bilingual children (McKinney, Hocutt, Giambo, & Schumm, 2000). Gunn, Biglan, Smolkowski, and Ary (2000) found that a structured direct instruction reading program resulted in significant gains in skills such as word attack, vocabulary, and comprehension for young Hispanic children, even those who spoke little or no English, when compared to children who did not receive the intervention. The specific skill instruction characteristic of most special education programs appears to be quite important; however, any instructional method needs to be supported with motivating literature and with extensive opportunities to read, write, and discuss content in both native and new languages to facilitate development in both (Gersten & Woodward, 1994).

Adapting Classroom Materials

One of the best ways for teachers to address the needs of students with learning disabilities is to adapt instruction and materials. Although the way a textbook or worksheet looks may seem relatively inconsequential, students with learning disabilities face many unnecessary obstacles because of the way material is presented—in terms of both content and format. Adaptation of materials may entail something as simple as redoing a skill sheet or as complex as restructuring a curriculum. An understanding of the basic approaches to learning by students with learning disabilities is necessary, as are time, motivation, and a knowledge of course content. As we look at some basic guidelines, remember that you can make a number of different adaptations. If you keep in mind that students with learning disabilities often have difficulty perceiving, attending to, and organizing important information, you can go a long way in identifying what adaptations are needed. Couple this knowledge with the basic concepts of direct instruction discussed earlier, and you will be able to teach students with learning disabilities in a more effective manner. Our focus in this section is mainly on adapting written materials typically used in regular class instruction, which are not developed with students with learning disabilities in mind. We will look at organizing lessons from textbooks, preparations for lecture and reading activities in content areas, and general ideas for worksheet and test construction.

Lesson plans from a teacher's manual often have to be modified.

■ ***Modifications for Lesson Planning*** Many textbooks include teachers' manuals to assist in the presentation of instruction. Too often, however, the lessons in the manuals are brief and potentially confusing because of the amount and structure of the content. You may need to modify these lessons before you present them to the class.

The accompanying box, "Strategies for Lesson Planning," offers specific suggestions for modifying your lessons for students with learning disabilities. Keep them in mind as you review manuals before planning your lessons.

■ ***Modifications for Lectures and Reading Assignments*** In many content courses, particularly at the middle and high school level, the teaching format may be limited to lecturing by the teacher and independent reading by the student. Even if projects or other activities are a regular part of the class, much of the material essential for tests and passing the course comes from the student's ability to identify and organize important information from what is presented orally or in the textbook. Adaptations, therefore, focus on clarifying important information and providing a clear organizational structure.

Lectures Adaptations for lectures involve helping students with learning disabilities identify important information and take notes in an organized way. Some ways to help students do this include:

Advance organizers or outlines can help students identify important information in lectures and take organized notes.

- Providing students with an advanced organizer, such as an outline of the lecture, or with some questions to read before the lecture begins. The students can review the organizer and be better prepared to listen for key information.
- Preparing a simple outline that includes major topics but has room for the students to take notes under the different headings. This will help students organize and see the relationship between various pieces of information.
- Reviewing key vocabulary before the lecture begins or writing critical information on the board or on an overhead. Tell students specifically that information written on the board is important.
- Teaching students to recognize and identify the clues used most frequently to identify important information.
- Stopping every so often and asking students to paraphrase or talk about the topic.

Reading Assignments Adaptations for written texts include many of the same ideas just listed. Suggestions include:

- Providing advance organizers before reading, including both outlines and questions about the materials to help students read for important content. A number of content textbooks present questions or "what you will learn" guidelines at the beginning of chapters. If these exist in your text, remember to show students how to use them.
- Reviewing, highlighting, or boxing critical vocabulary or facts prior to reading.

~ Strategies for Lesson Planning

1. *Identify all of the new skills being taught in the lesson.* More than one is too many. Sequence the skills according to the hierarchy of content, and choose the first one in the sequence.
2. *Identify the preskills the student needs.* If the text does not provide a review of the preskills, prepare one.
3. *Review the introduction and actual teaching part of the lesson.* A surprising number of textbooks include very little instruction.
   - Is the skill or concept clearly identified and described at the beginning of the lesson? In most cases, you should avoid open-ended questions at the beginning of the lesson (for example, "Who thinks they know what a pronoun is?"). You are likely to get incorrect answers and guesses that will create confusion.
   - Are there plenty of positive examples of the skill or concept being taught? Are there negative or incorrect examples that require the student to discriminate and actually identify the fundamental parts of the skill? If not, prepare additional examples in advance. Try to begin all instruction with positive or correct examples—too many texts begin with examples of errors. The first example students see is the one they will remember!
   - Think of a rule or cue to help the student learn the skill more efficiently.
4. *Look at the opportunities for practice presented in the manual and student text.*
   - Is there a lot of guided practice and opportunity for response before the student has to work alone? Practice with the teacher gives the student a chance to learn the skill and allows the teacher to correct any errors right away. You may have to develop some practice examples.
5. *Examine application exercises or "written practice" activities.*
   - Do the independent activities reflect the skill that was taught? Sometimes the independent activities require students to perform tasks that were not done during oral practice. Do not assume the student will know how to do this task, just because he or she could do the oral practice tasks. For example, if a language arts lesson revolves around identifying the parts of a sentence, the student should be expected only to identify the parts of a sentence, not write a complete sentence.
   - Are the language and reading requirements appropriate for your student? If the purpose of the activity is to assess the acquisition of a new skill, make sure other skills aren't interfering. You can always rewrite a practice sentence or substitute an alternative example.
   - Is the right amount of independent work provided? Is there enough practice to show you the student has mastered the skill, but not so much that the amount is overwhelming? No one needs to find the least common denominator for a hundred pairs of fractions to show that she knows how to do it.

- Cueing students to stop reading after every paragraph or every few paragraphs to review the material. The review could consist of written or oral paraphrasing or answering questions prepared for the different sections of the text.
- Teaching students to develop questions about the text themselves for use during or after reading.

- Having students answer questions reviewed at the beginning of the passage, having them paraphrase, and fill in outlines or other advance organizers after they finish reading the text.
- Using other activities, such as the webbing technique discussed in the section on written language, or developing pictures or other graphic representations of content.

For students who are able to understand grade-level content but who read at a far lower grade level, interaction with the regular classroom text may be quite difficult. For these students, adaptations of content area texts may include simplifying instructional content so that the reading requirements are reduced and only key information is presented. Classroom teachers or special education consultants or resource teachers may want to prepare annotated outlines that present only essential information. In some instances, this technique may be very difficult because of the density of the test (U.S. history or chemistry, for example). Alternatives include taping the lectures, persuading someone to record the text on tape, attempting to find a simpler version of the text (some programs have two levels of textbooks), or using a peer or adult tutor to read the text.

Figures 4.5–4.7 show how one teacher adapted some material from an upper-elementary-level textbook. Figure 4.5 is an excerpt from the textbook, Figure 4.6 shows the material adapted as a review, and Figure 4.7 shows how the material has been adapted yet again for use as an advance organizer.

■ ***Modifications of Worksheets and Tests*** Much evaluation and practice in the classroom takes place through written performance. The content, structure, and appearance of worksheets and tests are important because they affect the ability of students with learning disabilities to perform as well as they can. The guidelines we provide in this section are simple ones designed to call

Directions on tests and worksheets should be simple and clear.

THE IMPORTANCE OF PLACE IN HISTORY

History contains four elements: place, time, people, and story. Place comes first. Place is the scene of the action, like the scenery for a play or a movie. But place is more than scenery. Place also shapes the story. Place changes over time, and it interacts with the people who create the story. The planet Earth is the major place of our history, though the Earth is affected by other parts of the solar system. The weather and the seasons affect all of history, and more recently, outer space and space travel are a part of the story.

Most of our attention will focus on the Western Hemisphere and on North America, in particular. The two areas we will study most thoroughly are the United States and the state of South Carolina.

Source: Archive Vernon Huff, Jr., "The History of South Carolina," in *The Building of the Nation* (Greenville, SC: Furma, 1991). Copyright © 1991. Reprinted by permission.

Figure 4.5
Modifications of Material from an Elementary Textbook

South Carolina History
Chapter 1: The Land
Lesson 1A

Name: ______________________

Date: ______________________

1. The importance of place in history

   A. History contains four elements. ____________, time, ____________, and story.

Elements of History

place | **time** | **people** | **story**

1. **Place.** Place tells where the action or event happened. Place is important because it can affect how the action or event occurs. Place is also important because it changes over time and it can affect the people who are a part of the event.
2. **Time.** Time tells when something happened.
3. **People.** The people are involved in the action or event.
4. **Story.** The story tells about the action or event and sometimes what caused it to occur.

Review what you have learned

1. What are the four elements that make up history? (1A)

   a. ____________________ b. ____________________

   c. ____________________ d. ____________________

2. Name one way that place is important when we learn about history. (A1)

   ____

Figure 4.6
Textbook excerpt adapted as an advance organizer.

Source: Archive Vernon Huff, Jr., "The History of South Carolina," in *The Building of the Nation* (Greenville, SC: Furma, 1991). Copyright © 1991. Reprinted by permission.

the student's attention to relevant information and to remove confusing or distracting information. They may be used when creating your own material or when adapting existing material.

Directions should be simple and clear.

- Use bold print, capital letters, or other means of highlighting important words in the directions.
- If more than one type of direction is necessary for different sections on the worksheet or test, make certain the sections are clearly separated from

South Carolina History
Chapter 1: The Land
Lesson 1A

Name: ____________________

Date: ____________________

1. The importance of place in history

   A. History contains four elements: ____________ , time, ____________ , and story.

Elements of History

time — story

1. **Place.** Place tells where the action or event happened. Place is important because it can affect how the action or event occurs. Place is also important because it changes over time and it can affect the people who are a part of the event.
2. ________________ tells when something happened.
3. **People.** The people are involved in the action or event.
4. ________________ tells about the action or event and sometimes what caused it to occur.

WORLD BANK: Lesson 1A

continental drift story people time place

Figure 4.7
Textbook excerpt adapted as a review

Source: Archive Vernon Huff, Jr., "The History of South Carolina," in *The Building of the Nation* (Greenville, SC: Furma, 1991). Copyright © 1991. Reprinted by permission.

each other. Each set of directions should be clearly identifiable and immediately precede the related section.

The *appearance* of the material should be organized and uncluttered.

- Avoid unnecessary pictures. If a picture or graphic is necessary to answer a question (for example, a map or a graph), make sure that the questions related to the graphic are on the same page and adjacent to the questions if possible.
- Make sure all writing is clear and legible and that adequate space is provided for responses.
- Break up long tests or exams into different sections to help students organize responses (and possibly to prevent them from skipping or omitting questions). If possible, allow room for answers directly under the questions. Try to minimize the amount of page flipping the students have to do. Students do need experience in standardized test formats (for

minimum competency tests, basic skills tests, or SAT exams), so specific practice in these types of tests must be provided. Understand, however, that these formats are difficult for students with learning disabilities and may need to be introduced carefully.

Although types of questions or written activities will vary depending on grade level or subject area, the *format* of the presentation is always important.

- Avoid long columns of matching items—the ones that require drawing all of those lines between the items on both sides of the paper. Either use another format or break the list into sections.
- Essay questions will create problems for many students with disabilities, and some guidelines may be necessary (outline, approximate number of sentences, strategy for answering essay questions).
- Some students with poor reading and writing skills may need to have the test read to them or have the whole test or worksheet on tape so that reading and writing are not necessary.

When preparing tests or other written assignments, it is important to remember that the goal of the assessment is to evaluate the students' knowledge of the subject matter. You don't want other skill difficulties to interfere with your understanding of what each student has actually learned.

■ ***Curriculum and Technology*** It is beyond the scope of this chapter to discuss curriculum in any detail; however, many educators have suggested the need to restructure curricula to present content effectively to students with learning disabilities and to encourage the development of higher-order thinking skills (Carnine, 1991). Curriculum, whether you select or develop it, should reflect the components of effective instruction, as well as sequential presentation of content. Researchers have found that organizing curriculum around the concept of "sameness" helps students learn more effectively (Engelmann, Carnine, & Steely, 1991). The underlying principle is using the same strategy or conceptual model for approaching all tasks in a skill or content area. For example, Kinder and Bursuck (1991) suggest that a model based on organizing knowledge into a "problem–solution–effect" structure should be applied to all social studies content. The box "Summary of Sameness Analysis" shows examples of how this sameness concept can be applied in various content areas.

Educational software should incorporate best teaching practices and match a student's instructional goals.

Swanson (1999) found that the integration of technology was one of eight instructional components that helped improve instructional outcomes for students with learning disabilities. As with curriculum, the selection or creation of technological options should be based on the extent to which the content and instructional style reflect best practices in the field of learning disabilities. Increasingly, technological options are becoming complex and are incorporating multimedia, and teachers may be confused about making selections for instruction. Is this program too distracting? Is actual instruction involved? Will the student be able to follow the format? Does the software address this student's instructional goals? All of these questions, and many more, need to be addressed before specific programs are selected. Research does suggest that teachers must serve as mediators of instruction to increase the probability of a program's success (Wissick & Gardner, 2000). The accompanying box presents a chart that associates instructional strategies and content with specific multimedia programs.

Placement and Program Options

Mercer (1987) reminds us there is a range of abilities and disabilities within the group of students with learning disabilities. Consequently, the range of program options discussed in Chapter 1 should be available within most school districts so that the unique needs of each student can be met. Decisions about how best to serve a student with a learning disability involve considerations related to more than just where those services will be received. The type of instruction the student requires, as well as the eventual academic and professional goals of the student, must be considered as well.

Although some students with learning disabilities have always received all their instruction in regular classroom settings, students with learning disabilities are increasingly being served in inclusive environments, although there are some differences among states (McLeskey, Henry, & Axelrod, 1999). The national education reforms of the early 1990s calling for a restructuring and reorganization of educational programs, an increased emphasis on inclusion of all students in the regular classroom, and ongoing controversy about the effectiveness of resource or pullout programs have contributed to this movement. Although these factors are strongly disputed by a number of professionals, the overall effect has been an emphasis on serving students with learning disabilities in the general education classroom (Kauffman, 1989; Reynolds, Wang, & Walberg, 1987; Wood, 1993).

Increasing numbers of students with learning disabilities are being taught in the general education classroom.

In-Class Options

■ ***Teacher-Directed*** Students with learning disabilities who are served in regular classroom settings receive the same basic curriculum as other students in the classroom. However, this type of program does not imply that special services are not provided. As we've mentioned earlier, regular curricula may present obstacles for students with learning disabilities and make service in the regular classroom more challenging (Pugach & Warger, 1993). A number of alternatives have been developed to allow these students to receive specialized services and still remain in the classroom setting. Chief among them are consultation, collaboration, co-teaching, and classroom tutoring, all of which provide for the teacher who has expertise in special education or learning disabilities to come into the regular classroom and work with the regular classroom teacher or the student. Some schools employ all of these models, whereas others select one or two depending on the needs of the students and regular classroom teacher.

In **consultation,** the special education teacher observes the student in the regular classroom and provides suggestions concerning how the regular classroom teacher can adapt instruction or materials to meet the specific needs of the student with learning disabilities in her class. "A Closer Look: Collaboration: Setting Them Up for Success" shows the first two pages of a manual on instructional adaptations developed by a consulting teacher for the regular classroom. **Collaboration** describes the process in which both regular and special education teachers identify the problems or difficulties a child is experiencing and work together to find intervention strategies (Dettmer, Thurston, & Dyck, 1993). Sometimes the special education teacher will come into the regular classroom and provide instruction. This method, called **co-teaching,** has many different forms. Co-teaching could involve the special educator teaching a specific subject area to the entire class (math, social skills) or teaching a specific group of

~ Summary of Sameness Analysis

Topic	Greatly Different Examples	Surface Features	Structural Sameness
Earth science	a. Pot of boiling water: When heated, molecules of water flow in roughly a circular pattern.	Small-scale example—stove; element, water	Convection cell: The circular movement of heat is away from a hot object, and the flow of cooler air is toward the object.
	b. Earthquake: Molten sections between earth's crust and core move in constant circulation.	Large-scale example—earth's core, molten rock	
Social studies	a. Invention of cotton gin: It was difficult to remove seeds from short staple cotton. The cotton gin removed the seeds efficiently and created a greater market for cotton.	Economic context—cotton, demands of market	Problem-solution-effects analysis: The sameness is not in the events but in the nature and sequence of events that involve identifying a social, political, economical problem, its solution, and the effects of the solution.
	b. Mormon practice of polygamy: Because of persecution over practice of polygamy, the Mormons moved west to Salt Lake and developed a successful farm community.	Human rights context—Mormons, Salt Lake, development of a community	
Spelling	a. Three morphographs: re (prefix) cover (base) -ed (suffix) recovered, recover, covered	Three different morphemes	Morphonemics: By using the same morphemes in selected combinations, the following words are spelled: recoverable, repute, reputable, reputed, disreputable, disrepute, coverable, discover, discoverable, discovered, undiscoverable, undiscovered, disputed.
	b. Four morphographs: un/dis (prefix) -pute (base) -able (suffix)	Four different morphemes	

students that includes the student with a learning disability (often a subject such as reading or a content area requiring reading skills). See the accompanying box, "Co-Teaching Models," for a description of the various co-teaching formats. A final alternative is individual tutoring of the student with a learning disability by a teacher, peer, or older student within the classroom setting.

■ ***Peer-Focused.*** Although several models of peer-tutoring and cooperative learning strategies have been suggested as means of integrating students with disabilities into general education classes, few have strong research supporting

Topic	Greatly Different Examples	Surface Features	Structural Sameness
Mathematics: word-problem solving	a. Subtraction word problem: Mark can get some money from his mother to help pay for a school trip. He has earned $57. He needs $112. How much more money will his mother give him?	Subtraction—linguistic features, numerical features, syntactic structure	Number-family analyses: The sameness is in mapping what is known and not known in a problem by determining if the "big" number and a "small" number are given, or if just the small numbers are given.
	b. Multiplication word problem: If each shirt requires 2 yards of material, how much material will be needed to make 5 shirts?	Multiplication—different linguistic features, numerical features, syntactic structure	
Writing: text structure	a. Writing stories: Develop the setting of the story (characters, time, place), problem, response, outcome, and conclusion.	Story grammar—characters, setting, problem, actions	Text structure analysis: Elements are used to map ideas.
	b. Writing expositions: Identify what is being compared/contrasted, on what, and how they are alike and different.	Topic—compare and contrast	

Source: From "Toward a Scientific Pedagogy of Learning Disabilities: A Sameness in the Message," by E.J. Kameenui, *Journal of Learning Disabilities* 24 (1991), pp. 364–372. Copyright © 1991 by PRO-ED, Inc. Reprinted by permission of the McGraw-Hill Companies, Inc.

their effectiveness. Teachers believe there is much potential in these types of interventions, however, and they also report that cooperative learning and peer tutoring are the most useful approaches for working with multicultural students with disabilities (Utley, Delquadri, Obiakor, & Mims, 2000). One peer-tutoring program that has been well researched and found to be effective for many students with learning disabilities is Peer-Assisted Learning Strategies (PALS) (Fuchs, Fuchs, Mathes, & Simmons, 1997). PALS, outlined in the accompanying box, is based on the Classwide Peer Tutoring Program (Greenwood, Delquadri, & Hall, 1989) and is designed to focus on reading instruction in

~ Multimedia Programs and Web Site That Complement Instructional Principles

Instructional Principles	Implementation with Multimedia: Multimedia Context	Programs and Web Sites
Automaticity and Overlearning	Provides a context for application of basic facts, anchors instruction in visual context, uses auditory feedback.	Spell It Deluxe, Davidson (Grades 1-5) Simon Sounds it Out, Don Johnston (Grades K-4) Simon Spells, Don Johnston (Grades K-4) SuperSonic Phonics, Curriculum Associates (Grades 1-12) Wild World of Words Challenge, Web Page
Mastery Learning	Arranges instruction so that all students learn objectives to mastery.	Net Frog: Web Page (high school) WebQuests, Matrix of Examples, Web Page
Mnemonics	Uses visual and auditory stimuli to assist the memorization and retention of important information and skills.	Curious Creatures, Curriculum Associates (Grades 2-8) BioSci, Videodiscovery (Grades 3-12) A World Alive, St. Louis Zoo (all grades) Inspiration, Inspiration Software (Grades 3-12)
Direct Instruction	Structures educational environment with specific objectives, rapid pacing, frequent feedback, and opportunities to answer.	Mastering Series Systems Impact (Grades 5-12) Windows on Science, Optical Data (Grades 1-8) Windows on Math, Optical Data (Grades 1-8) Earobics, Cognitive Concepts (Grades K-6)
Situated Cognition	Provides situations from which students can generate their own questions within authentic situations.	Adventures of Jasper Woodbury, Optical Data (Grades 4-8) Science Sleuths, Videodiscovery (Grades 3-9) The Real Scoop on Tobacco, WebQuest

Wissik, Cheryl A., and Gardner J. Emmett (2000). "Multimedia or Not to Multimedia?," *Teaching Exceptional Children,* 32, 34–43.

Instructional	Implementation with Multimedia	
Principles	**Multimedia Context**	**Programs and Web Sites**
Cooperative Learning	Provides students opportunities to work together to solve problems and assist one another in learning new information.	Decisions, Decisions, Tom Snyder (Grades 5-10) Choices, Choices, Tom Snyder (Grades K-6) Cultural Debates, Tom Snyder (Grades 6-12) Great Solar System and Ocean Rescue (Grades 5-8)
Writing Instruction	Incorporates visual and auditory prompts to assist with creating writing.	Write OutLoud & Co: Writer, Don Johnston (Grades K-12) Imagination Express, Edmark (Grades 2-8) Student Writing Center, Learning Company (Grades 5-12) Storybook Weaver, Learning Company (Grades 1-6) Postcards, Curriculum Associates (Grades 5-8) The Read to Write Project, Web Page
Reading Comprehension	Presents text with visual and auditory clues to enhance comprehension.	Living Books, Broderbund (Grades K-3) Little Planet, Little Planet Software (Grades K-3) Start-to-Finish Books, Don Johnston (Grades 5-8) Rainbow, Curriculum Associates (Grades 1-3) Online Story, Web Page
Study Skills	Encourages student research, provides models for management and searching of data.	TrackStar, Web Page Yahooligans, Web Directory & Search Engine The Traveling Tutor from the Alphabet Superhighway, Web Inspiration, Inspiration Software (Grades 3-12) My First Amazing Incredible Dictionary, DK (Grades K-4) Multimedia Encyclopedias

A closer look

Collaboration: Setting Them Up for Success

Here are some basic instructional adaptations for special needs students, prepared by a special educator who collaborates frequently in inclusion classrooms.

A. Adjust type, difficulty, amount, or sequence of material.
   1. Break assignments into short tasks.
   2. Give fewer problems.
   3. Assign only necessary material.
   4. Underline text passages for important facts or organization.
   5. Give specific questions to guide reading.
   6. Make sure the child's desk is free of unnecessary materials.
   7. Establish a small number of realistic goals.
   8. Take up the student's work as soon as it is completed.
   9. Provide a written copy of notes and/or a study guide.
   10. Provide a textbook that has important information highlighted.
   11. Have frequent individual conferences with students to ensure mutual understanding of goals and to assess progress.

B. Adjust space.
   1. Place the student close to you.
   2. Place the student next to another student who can provide assistance.
   3. Separate the student from others likely to distract him or her.
   4. Let the student choose the area of the room where he or she can concentrate best.
   5. Permit him or her to work alone, but do not isolate him or her against his or her will.

C. Adjust work time.
   1. Give extra time to complete assignments.
   2. Allow short breaks after fifteen minutes of on-task reading or writing.
   3. Set up a specific schedule so the student knows what to expect.
   4. Alternate quiet and active time.
   5. Give shorter assignments and more frequent tests.
   6. For long-term assignments, provide structured short-term deadlines.
   7. Provide extra time for teaching a new skill.

D. Adjust grouping.
   1. Match a special needs student with a peer helper who can help by:
      a. making certain directions are understood;
      b. reading important directions and essential material;
      c. drilling orally on various skills;
      d. summarizing orally important textbook passages;
      e. writing down answers to tests and assignments;
      f. working on a joint assignment;
      g. making suggestions for improvement.
   2. Formulate a small work group of three or four students, including one special needs student. Hold all members of the group responsible for making certain that each group member completes assignments successfully.

Source: Kim Phillips, "Setting Them Up for Success: Instructional and Behavioral Adaptations for Special Education Students in Regular Classrooms" (Columbia, SC: Rosewood Elementary School, 1993) (unpublished materials, pp. 1–11). Reprinted by permission of the author.

general education classrooms. What distinguishes PALS from other classroom tutorial programs is the use of structured peer interactions, including specific task strategies, and the incorporation of effective instructional practices. The PALS program was created for students in grades 2 through 6, but it has since been adapted for use with kindergarten children, first-graders, and high school students (Fuchs, Fuchs, & Burish, 2000; Mathes, Grek, Howard, Babyak, & Allen, 1999).

~ Co-Teaching Models

One Person Teaching in Classroom

1. One teacher prepares materials and offers strategies but does not actually teach in the classroom. This model frequently coexists with all of the other models.
2. One teach–one observe: One teacher observes a student in the classroom and perhaps takes data, evaluates student responses to instruction, etc. One teacher provides classroom instruction. Could be occasional or structured.

Two Teachers in Classroom—One Supplementing General Instruction

1. One teach–one drift: One teacher circulates around the room helping students with particular needs, and the co-teacher instructs the whole group. Can be most beneficial when roles are reversed regularly.
2. Alternative teaching: One teacher provides remediation, enrichment, or specialized instruction for students who need it while the other provides instruction for the rest of the group. This may be done occasionally, on an as-needed basis, or regularly—alternative reading instruction, for example.

Two Teachers in Classroom—Both Delivering General Instruction

1. Station teaching: Curriculum content is broken into components; each teacher teaches one part of content to a group of children, then students switch. Could also include a cooperative learning or independent group station.
2. Parallel teaching: Class is broken into two groups of students; each teacher teaches the same content material to one group of students. (Don't put all special education students in one group.)
3. Team teaching: Both teachers deliver the instruction together at the same time—share leadership in the classroom. This may be done for one class a day or more, but it should be consistent across time so that students perceive both teachers as the teachers.

Source: Adapted from M. Friend, *The Power of 2: Making a Difference Through Co-Teaching* (Bloomington, IN: Indiana University Press, 1996).

Resource or Pullout Programs

The resource room may include three types of instruction—remedial academic, adaptive, and special skills instruction.

In spite of the emphasis on serving students with learning disabilities in the classroom, the resource room continues to be used. The resource model allows students to receive the special instruction and support that they need but still maintain both academic and social contact with their nondisabled peers and continue, for the most part, in the general education curriculum. Generally, three types of instruction are provided in the resource setting: remedial academic, adaptive, or specialized skills instruction. Academic instruction is often provided in reading or math, because these skills are so important and will be used in other subject areas throughout students' academic careers. Adaptive skills instruction may include studying for or taking tests, preparing reports, or reviewing textbook material. Finally, some resource classes are used to teach specialized skills, such as study skills or social skills.

Self-Contained or Alternative Placements

Students who have severe learning disabilities may receive instruction in self-contained classes or alternative programs. Young children in self-contained

~ Peer-Assisted Learning Strategies (PALS)

Preparation

PALS involves preparation of students: teachers prepare students with a series of scripted lessons. Students are grouped into dyads—typically one student is a stronger reader than the other. Reading material is selected that is at the lower reader's level.

Implementation

PALS sessions are implemented three times a week, for 35 minutes each session. Students receive points for correct performance and appropriate tutoring behavior. Both students participate in tutoring activities, but the stronger reader begins the session. No answer keys are provided.

Activities

- *Partner reading:* The peer tutor, and then the other student, each read text for 5 minutes. The peer tutor stops the reader when an error occurs and asks the student to try to figure it out. If the reader cannot do this in 4 seconds, the tutor supplies the word. Then the sentence is reread by the student who made the error.
- *Paragraph shrinking:* The students read the text aloud, stopping at the end of each paragraph to state the main idea and eventually presenting the main idea in no more than ten words. The tutor prompts the identification of the main idea by asking questions. The tutor asks the other student to try again if the response is incorrect and to "shrink" the response if it is too long.
- *Prediction relay:* The reader makes predictions about the content of a half page of text, and then reads the text. While this student is reading, the tutor corrects errors, evaluates predictions, and presents the main idea of the text. The correction procedures used in the first two activities are included in this activity, and the tutor solicits new predictions if he or she deems the initial ones unreasonable.

For more program information, see D. Fuchs, L. S. Fuchs, P.G. Mathes, & D.C. Simmons, *Peer-Assisted Learning Strategies in Reading: A Manual* (1996) (available from Box 328 Peabody, Vanderbilt University, Nashville, TN 37203).

Fuchs, D., Fuchs, L. S., & Burish, P. (2000) "Peer-Assisted Learning Strategies: An evidence-based practice to promote reading achievement," *Learning Disabilities Research and Practice, 15,* 85–91.

programs may receive intensive remedial academic instruction in an attempt to bring them to grade level and eventually reintegrate them into the general education classroom. Because evidence suggests that many students with severe learning disabilities have postschool adjustment difficulties, the content of the curriculum for older students is often more functional in nature, emphasizing career and vocational instruction (Cline & Billingsley, 1991). A functional curriculum for students with learning disabilities is likely to be found at the middle school or high school level. For many students, this includes training and preparation for work activities, as well as training in social interaction skills and exposure to adult activities such as managing money, making major purchases (cars), and identifying community and legal resources.

Adult Life

Learning disabilities usually persist into adulthood.

Because learning disabilities are defined within the context of school, some people wonder if they persist into adulthood. Current research supports the conclusion that learning disabilities do continue throughout life. This is not surprising if we view learning disabilities as different ways of learning. Although a learning disability can be a significant challenge, it is not necessarily an obstacle to success and accomplishments in adult life.

Many students with learning disabilities graduate from high school with a diploma and go on to postsecondary education. As you might predict, however, far fewer students with learning disabilities attend community colleges or training programs than students without disabilities; even fewer attend four-year colleges (Murray, Goldstein, Nourse, & Edgar, 2000). The adaptive and social skills addressed throughout elementary and secondary school are important for those students who plan to continue their education. Social and interpersonal skills training, college preparatory coursework, and the use of accommodations such as taped lectures or untimed tests are examples of approaches that should be used before and after students begin postsecondary school (Aune, 1991; Gajar, 1992). Recent research suggests that students with learning disabilities who held two or more jobs in high school are almost twice as likely to be working or participating in postsecondary education after graduation as those who did not work (Berry, Lindstrom, & Vovanoff, 2000). Perhaps early work experience allows students to develop skills that help promote success later in life.

Why are some individuals with learning disabilities highly successful in their professional and personal lives? Gerber, Ginsberg, and Reiff (1992) talked to people with learning disabilities themselves to get the answers. The researchers interviewed a large number of adults who were considered highly or moderately successful (success was defined in terms of income, education level, prominence in field, job classification, and job satisfaction). Through their interviews, they tried to see if any factors were common to the individuals who achieved high degrees of success. Although they did find a number of self-described factors among successful adults, the one that was most strongly represented was the desire to take control of one's life. At one point or another, the successful adults with learning disabilities decided that they needed to take control of what was happening to them—and then they began to look for ways to achieve some control. This study suggests that showing students how to use learning tools to create change and facilitate self-reliance may increase their probability for success. Others support the idea that related attributes, including self-awareness, proactivity, and perseverance, are critical factors in achieving adult success (Raskind, Goldberg, Higgins, & Herman, 1999).

Highly successful individuals with learning disabilities credit their desire to take control of their lives for their success.

Summary

- Students with learning disabilities demonstrate a discrepancy between potential and achievement that cannot be attributed to other disabilities or to environmental or cultural factors. Although there is no single known cause of learning disabilities, internal and external factors may be involved.
- Learning disabilities affect five major cognitive processes: perception, attention, memory, metacognition, and organization. Difficulties with each of these processes can lead to problems in academic areas such as reading, language arts, and mathematics.
- The social difficulties often caused by learning disabilities may stem from problems in learning appropriate behavior or from repeated failures in school that lead to low self-esteem, helplessness, or acting out. Families are a vital source of support, encouragement, and motivation for these students.

- Students with learning disabilities are assessed formally and informally to determine their academic skills.
- The most widely used instructional techniques for students with learning disabilities are direct instruction, strategy instruction, and special instruction in study and social skills.
- Many classroom materials and presentations can be modified for students with learning disabilities. When these students are included in regular classrooms, general and special educators must collaborate in making the necessary modifications and providing instruction.

Key Terms

learning disabilities
discrepancy
exclusion clause
perinatal stress
learning style
perception
attention
attention deficit disorder (ADD)
attention deficit with hyperactivity disorder (ADHD)
selective attention
memory
encoding processes
working memory
metacognition
self-monitoring
organization
cognitive style
word analysis
reading comprehension
pragmatic language skills
functional flexibility
pegwords
predictive validity
formal assessment
informal assessment
informal inventories
curriculum-based measurement (CBM)
direct instruction
strategy instruction
consultation
collaboration
co-teaching

Multimedia Resources

Assis-TECH Inc.: http://www.irsc.org/learn_db.htm. This site is a source for assistive technology devices for students with learning disabilities.

Association for Direct Instruction: http://darkwing.uoregon.edu/~adiep/. This organization provides information, assistance, and support for educators interested in using direct instruction and/or ordering related materials.

National Center for Learning Disabilities (NCLD): 381 Park Avenue South, New York, NY 10016, (212) 545-7510.

Clayton, Lawrence. *Coping with a Learning Disability* (New York: Rosen Publishing Group, 1992). A book for families and teens that demonstrates that being a teen with a learning disability can be a positive experience. It discusses family, personal, and peer emotional reactions and provides biographies of famous people with learning disabilities as positive role models.

Farnham-Diggory, Sylvia. *The Learning-Disabled Child* (Cambridge, MA: Harvard University Press, 1992). This is an intelligent, easy-to-read introduction to characteristics of students with learning disabilities.

The Gram. Newsletter of the Learning Disabilities Association (formerly ACLD), 4156 Library Road, Pittsburgh, PA 15234, (412) 341-1515. This newsletter provides information about current legislation, educational programs, and research in the area of learning disabilities.

LDOnLine: www.LDOnLine.org. This is a comprehensive website on learning disabilities, and the official website of the Coordinated Campaign for learning disabilities.

Learning Disability Resources: http://www.as.wvu.edu/~scidis/ld_resources.html. This site has information and resources from the Research and Training Division of the Learning Disabilities Center at the University of Georgia.

National Center to Improve the Tools of Educators (NCITE): 805 Lincoln Street, Eugene, OR 97403-1211, (541) 346-1646, http: darkwing.uoregon.edu/~ncite/index.html. This site offers numerous publications on academic skill instruction, a curriculum, and related research.

National Institute of Child Health and Human Development (NICHD). Contact: Dr. G. Reid Lyon, National Institutes of Health, 6100 Executive Boulevard, Room 4B05, Bethesda, MD 20892, (301) 496-6591. Publications related to understanding learning disabilities, reading and learning disabilities, and other research areas are available at this location.

Reading and Learning Disabilities, NICHCY briefing paper, National Information Center for Youth with Disabilities, 1995, (800) 695-0285. This paper includes a look at learning disabilities in children and youth, suggestions for parents on how to help their school-age children learn, and issues for adults with reading and learning problems.

What You Can Do

1. Talk to a school psychologist in a local school district or to the consultant in the area of learning disabilities at your state department of education. Identify the state criteria for identifying students with learning disabilities. Ask if and how these criteria can be interpreted by school districts across your state.

2. Select a lesson from a textbook in your content area. Adapt the material along the lines suggested in the text. What specific changes did you make? Who is the intended audience for your revised version of the lesson? Can you envision making these types of modifications in your classroom?

3. Can-Do. How do successful adults with learning disabilities cope with the demands of their jobs and lives? Interview an adult with a learning disability. Invite him or her to talk to your class about the strategies he or she has used to succeed in life. What types of strategies are described? How might they be used by your future students?

4. Collaboration. How do the different types of co-teaching models work? Would you be interested in co-teaching? Visit some classes in a local school district that employ co-teaching. Discuss benefits and concerns of the models with the teachers. Develop some strategies for co-teaching in your own classroom.

5. Commonalities. Why are content, presentation, and classroom placement all vital to consider when planning a class that welcomes a student with learning disabilities? Based on what you've read in this chapter and your own experience, list classroom modifications in each of these areas that would be effective for all students. Be sure to consider social aspects of the class as well as academic ones.

Children with Mental Retardation

5

STUDENTS WITH mental retardation demonstrate a range of abilities and increasingly are included in the general education classroom. In this chapter we will look at how curriculum and teaching strategies are modified to help these students reach their potential in academic and life skills. We will also focus on the community as a source of instructional materials, employment, and independent living arrangements both during and after the school years. As you read, think about the following questions:

What are the criteria for classifying a student as having mental retardation?

What is adaptive behavior, and why is it significant?

How does mental retardation affect a student's learning patterns?

Commonalities: **How are the educational goals of individuals with mental retardation similar to the educational goals of all students?**

Collaboration: **How can educators work with businesses within the community to plan effective instruction?**

Can Do: **What teaching methods can you use in your class to help students with mental retardation achieve their learning potential?**

Children with Mental Retardation

Perhaps more than any other term used in the field of special education, the term *mental retardation* conjures up specific images of individuals or groups of individuals. We ask you to keep two basic things in mind as you begin this chapter. First, each individual with mental retardation is just that—and individual; you must let go of any negative preconceptions you may have. Second, each and every child has a promise; thus you must identify the specific skills and interests that need to be encouraged and strengthened.

Definitions and Terms

The definition of **mental retardation** has been revised numerous times to reflect our evolving understanding and philosophy. Currently, the most widely accepted definition comes from the American Association on Mental Retardation (AAMR). It was accepted as the federal definition in 1993:

Mental retardation is characterized by subaverage intellectual functioning and deficits in adaptive behavior.

> Mental retardation refers to substantial limitations in present functioning. It is characterized by significantly subaverage intellectual functioning, existing concurrently with related limitations in two or more of the following applicable adaptive skill areas: communication, self-care, home living, social skills, community use, self-direction, health and safety, functional academics, leisure, and work. Mental retardation manifests before age 18.

The four following assumptions are essential to the application of the definition:

1. Valid assessment considers cultural and linguistic diversity as well as differences in communication and behavioral factors.
2. The identification of limitations in adaptive skills occurs within the context of community environments typical of the individual's age peers and is indexed to the person's individualized needs for supports.
3. Specific adaptive limitations often coexist with strengths in other adaptive skills or other personal capabilities.
4. With appropriate supports over a sustained period, the life functioning of the person with mental retardation will generally improve.

Intelligence and General Cognitive Functioning

The concept of intelligence is critical to the definition of mental retardation and to our characterization of all individuals. Each reader of this book will have different ideas about what constitutes intelligence. Researchers, too, have difficulty agreeing on a definition of intelligence. Salvia and Ysseldyke (1991) wrote that "no one . . . has seen a thing called intelligence" (p. 145). It is what psychologists call a *construct*, defined by theorists and test makers and determined by their ideas, beliefs, and cultural values.

Even though no universal agreement exists on what constitutes intelligence, a number of tests have been developed to measure it. The **Stanford-Binet Intelligence Scale** and the **Wechsler Intelligence Scale for Children, Third Edition (WISC-III)** are the two tests most widely used by American psychologists to assess intelligence. These tests include a number of subtests and yield a composite score, the score we typically refer to when we state a student's IQ. The WISC-III also yields two major subscores, one for verbal ability and one for performance ability.

The intelligence test scores for the population at large can be represented in what is often described as a bell-shaped curve (see Figure 5.1). This distribution, also known as the normal curve, illustrates the range of scores that can be expected in any representative population. An average intelligence test score of 100 represents equivalence between mental age and chronological age.

The phrase *subaverage intellectual functioning* in the AAMR definition refers to performance on one or more intelligence tests resulting in an IQ score of about 70 or below. It is possible, however, for a student with an IQ score higher than 70 to qualify as having mental retardation if there are clear deficits in adaptive behavior. Conversely, it is possible for a student with an IQ score of 65 not to be identified as having mental retardation if he or she has good adaptive behavior. A critical point to remember is that the word *significantly*, which is used in the 1993 definition ("significantly subaverage intellectual functioning"), is subjective.

Adaptive Behavior

Adaptive behavior, the other key element of the AAMR definition, includes those social, maturational, self-help, and communicative acts that help each individual adapt to the demands of his or her environment (Patton, Beirne-Smith, & Payne, 1990). They are *age-appropriate* and *situation-appropriate*; that is, they are different at each age and in each situation. Adaptive behaviors present a more comprehensive picture of a child's abilities than do IQ scores alone. Let us examine some examples of adaptive behaviors found in different developmental periods to see how they vary.

The most rapid and dramatic changes in adaptive behavior occur during the infancy and preschool period. The infant learns to reach, roll over, sit, stand, walk, and run; to finger-feed and then to use a spoon and drink from a cup; to draw others into close social relationships; and to communicate—first through vocalizing, and then, gradually, through understanding and repeating single

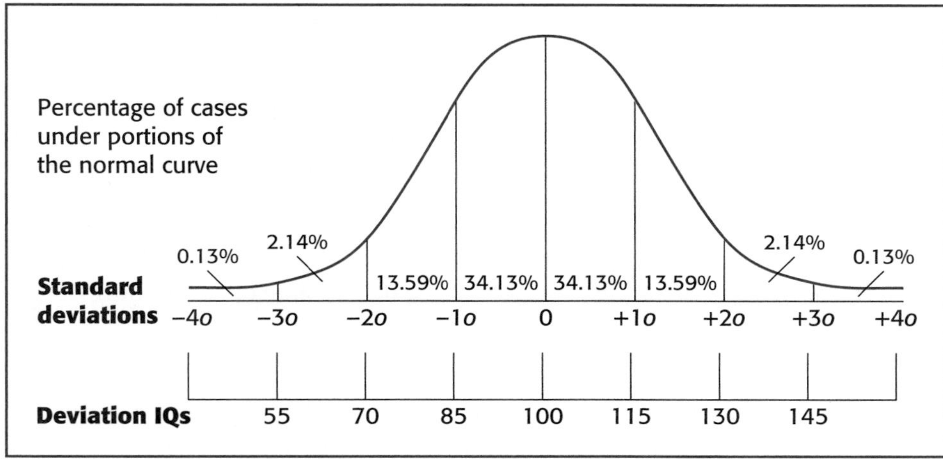

Figure 5.1
The Theoretical Distribution of IQ Scores

Source: S. A. Kirk and J. J. Gallagher, *Educating Exceptional Children*, 6th ed. (Boston: Houghton Mifflin, 1988), p. 11. Copyright © 1988. Used with permission.

words, two words together, short phrases, and finally sentences that increase in length and complexity. By preschool, many of these milestones have been mastered. The child becomes toilet-trained, and then many of the adaptive behaviors focus on social goals: learning to play and interact successfully with other children and with new adults, sharing, and making friends.

In the elementary school years the child must become socialized to the expectations of school and learn to adapt to those demands: to sit quietly until spoken to, to raise a hand to be recognized, and to follow the teacher's directions. Other adaptive behaviors are refinements of earlier milestones in motor, social, and language development; also included are academic skills that apply to everyday functioning in the environment, such as reading danger and warning signs.

Expectations for appropriate behavior may differ from place to place and culture to culture.

Adaptive behavior is not easy to measure. Expectations for age-appropriate and situation-appropriate behavior may differ from city to city, state to state, and culture to culture. Geography, local behavior norms, and cultural differences all interact to determine if a child's behavior is appropriate in a particular locale. These factors contribute to the variability of classification status from one school district to the next.

In order for a child to be classified as having mental retardation, he or she must demonstrate deficits in adaptive behavior that are comparable to the child's measured IQ. By incorporating the measure of adaptive behavior, the definition acknowledges that the child functions in various environments and potentially possesses many types of skills.

Adaptive behavior is usually measured through observation and interviews with the child's parents, guardians, or teachers. Two of the most widely used instruments are the **AAMR Adaptive Behavior Scale** (Nihara, Leland, & Lambert 1993) and the **Vineland Adaptive Behavior Scales** (Sparrow, Balla, & Cicchetti, 1984). Adaptive behavior scales enable the teacher, parent, or observer to determine the child's competence in a wide range of functional behaviors. The AAMR Adaptive Behavior Scale measures two major areas—independent performance of daily living skills and inappropriate or maladaptive behaviors, such as self-abuse or destructive behavior. The Vineland Adaptive Behavior Scales, Interview Editions, measure the domains of communication, daily living skills, socialization, motor skills, and maladaptive behavior. Figure 5.2 shows a section from one of these scales.

Manifestation During the Developmental Period

Mental retardation must be identified before age 18, but a child can show gains in adaptive behavior or measured intelligence.

Mental retardation must be present before the age of 18. This criterion is included in the AAMR definition to distinguish mental retardation from conditions in which adults suffer from impairment of brain functioning, such as from a head injury or a stroke. A child with an IQ test score of 70 or lower might not be identified until he or she reaches school age and deficits in adaptive behavior become apparent. It can also be decided that a child no longer has mental retardation if gains are made in adaptive behavior or in measured intelligence level. The term *mental retardation* can thus refer to a current state of functioning or performance rather than a permanent condition.

Classification Issues

Scientists and educational professionals differentiate among individuals with varying degrees of mental retardation. Scientists study the effects of degrees of

DOMAIN 1: Independent Functioning

A. Eating Subdomain

Item 1: Use of Table Utensils (circle highest level)

Uses table knife for cutting or spreading	6
Feeds self neatly with spoon and fork (or appropriate alternate utensils, e.g., chopsticks)	5
Feeds self causing considerable spilling with spoon and fork (or appropriate alternate utensil, e.g. chopsticks)	4
Feeds self with spoon—neatly	3
Feeds self with spoon—considerable spilling	2
Feeds self with fingers	1
Does not feed self or must be fed	0

Item 2: Eating in Public (circle highest level)

Orders complete meals in restaurants	3
Orders simple meals like hamburgers and hot dogs	2
Orders single items, e.g. soft drinks, ice cream, donuts, etc. at soda fountains or canteens	1
Does not order in public eating places	0

Item 3: Drinking (circle highest level)

Drinks without spilling, holding glass in one hand	3
Drinks from a cup or glass unassisted—neatly	2
Drinks from a cup or glass unassisted—considerable spilling	1
Does not drink from a cup or glass unassisted	0

Item 4: Table Manners (circle all answers)

If these items do not apply to the individual, e.g., because he or she is bedfast and/or has liquid food only, place a check in the blank and mark "Yes" for all statements.	Yes	No
Throws food	0	1
Swallows food without chewing	0	1
Chews food with mouth open	0	1
Drops food on table or floor	0	1
Does not use napkin	0	1
Talks with mouth full	0	1
Takes food off others' plates	0	1
Eats too fast or too slow	0	1
Plays in food with fingers	0	1

Subdomain total (add items 1–4)

Source: K. Nihira, H. Leland, and N. Lambert, *AAMR Adaptive Behavior Scale: Residential and Community,* 2d ed. (Austin, TX: PRO-ED, 1993). Copyright © 1993 by The American Association on Mental Retardation. Reprinted by permission.

Figure 5.2
AAMR Adaptive Behavior Scale

severity on the characteristics and behavior of people with mental retardation; administrators must determine which students need special programs; teachers plan educational programs for students based on their levels of functioning. As with most categories, or groups of exceptional individuals who share a common label, there is tremendous variety within the group of people identified as having mental retardation.

The American Association on Mental Retardation uses the terms *mild, moderate, severe,* and *profound* to denote degrees of mental retardation. People with mild mental retardation may require support services to enable them to graduate from high school, get appropriate job training, and get married and raise a family. Most individuals with mild mental retardation easily blend in to school and work environments. People with moderate mental retardation typically require support services and often supervision to enable them to live and work in independent or semi-independent community settings. People with moderate mental retardation have characteristics that are probably the ones you think of when you hear the phrase *mental retardation.*

There are varying degrees of mental retardation.

Individuals identified as having severe or profound mental retardation require more extensive educational services. In this chapter, we will discuss the needs of students with mild and moderate levels of mental retardation. You will learn about individuals with severe and profound mental retardation in Chapter 6.

An ongoing classification issue in the area of mental retardation is the overrepresentation of students from minority populations among those classified as having mental retardation, particularly mild mental retardation. As you learned in Chapter 1, representatives from minority groups have objected to the use of IQ tests with children from both racial and language minority backgrounds (*Larry P. v. Riles, Diana v. State Board of Education*) because they believe that these children do not have equal access to the middle-class American cultural experiences that may be measured by norm-referenced IQ tests. Both the law and good practice dictate that no one test should ever be the sole grounds for diagnosis of a disability or for special class placement. Other attempts to stem the overrepresentation of minority students in classes for children with mental retardation involve increasing the cultural awareness and cultural competence of all teachers before actual testing takes place. For example, Craig, Hull, Haggart, and Perez-Selles (2000) suggest the use of teacher assistance teams. Such teams are trained to recognize cultural differences and evaluate instruction in an attempt to stem the rate of minority overrepresentation at the referral stage. Figure 5.3 lists guidelines for teacher assistance teams.

Increasing cultural awareness in teachers may help address overrepresentation of minority students in classes for students with mental retardation.

Many children who used to be served under the classification of mild mental retardation are no longer being identified as having mental retardation (MacMillan, 1989). Although most states have used the same procedural guidelines to classify individuals with mental retardation for about twenty years (Denning, Chamberlain, & Polloway, 2000), increasingly stringent application of the adaptive behavior criterion has resulted in fewer children receiving the label of mild mental retardation. Those children who are identified are increasingly exposed to a curriculum that stresses preparation for life skills rather than the traditional remedial academic program. The expanded curriculum of life skills, vocational instruction, and basic academics now offered to many students with moderate mental retardation is often suitable to students in both groups and may make the distinction between moderate and mild mental retardation less important from an educational perspective.

With fewer children classified as having mild mental retardation, the mild and moderate categories are merging.

Now that we've made these comments, we would like to caution you about making assumptions about the ability levels of students identified as having mild mental retardation. As a teacher, you will always need to make your own careful assessments about what and how to teach an individual child. In addition, keep in mind that the purpose behind labels and categorical grouping is to provide better educational services to children.

Early Reading: Strategies and Resources

As adults, and fluent readers, we tend to take the complex process of reading for granted. Yet for many of the children described in this book, learning to read is the greatest challenge of their school lives. Mary K. Fitzsimmons (1998) writes:

> The truth is that learning to read is anything but natural. In fact, it does not develop incidentally; it requires human intervention and context. While skillful readers look quite natural in their reading, the act of reading is complex and intentional; it requires bringing together a number of complex actions involving the eyes, the brain, and the psychology of the mind (e.g., motivation, interest, past experience) that do not occur naturally. (p.1)

Teachers must become the engineers of this complex process for all children. Fortunately, today we have an accumulating body of research that provides us with compelling evidence that structured, consistent instruction in the foundation skills of reading can lead to fluency. We discuss reading in several places in this book, particularly in Chapter 4. Reading problems are common to students receiving special education services—and to many who are not.

The basic components of sound early reading instruction are phonological awareness, or "awareness of the sound structure of words and the ability to manipulate sounds in words" (Smith, Simmons, & Kameenui, 1995, p. 2) and knowledge of the alphabetic principle, the idea that letters, or groups of letters, represent phonemes (Burns, Griffin, & Snow, 1999).

Some examples of phonological awareness activities include asking a child to respond to the following (Stanovich, 1994):

1. What would be left if the /k/ sound were taken away from *cat*?
2. What do you have if you put these sounds together: /s/, /a/, /t/?
3. What is the first sound in *rose*?

Teaching Tips: Phonological Awareness and Alphabetic Understanding

Make phonological awareness instruction explicit. Use conspicuous strategies and make phonemes prominent to students by modeling specific sounds and asking students to reproduce the sounds.

Ease into the complexities of phonological awareness. Begin with easy skills, such as rhyming and blending, and progress to more difficult ones, such as segmenting and substitution.

Provide support and assistance for learning the alphabetic code. The following research-based instructional sequence summarizes the kind of scaffolding beginning readers need:

(a) Model the sound or the strategy for making the sound. (b) Have students use the strategy to produce the sound. (c) Repeat steps (a) and (b) using several sounds for each type and level of difficulty. (d) Prompt students to use the strategy during guided practice. (e) Use steps (a) through (d) to introduce more difficult examples.

Develop a sequence and schedule, tailored to each child's needs, for opportunities to apply and develop facility with sounds. Give this schedule top priority among all classroom activities.

Learning to read does not simply require the acquisition of specific skills—children must also become enthusiastic about deriving meaning from print. Reading programs must be balanced between the introduction and practice of skills, and activities and experiences that promote a love of reading.

Knowledge about and love for literacy can develop only through experience. Children should own books, should have access to books in their preschool and primary classrooms, should be read to often, and should see others reading and writing. Understanding the value of literacy as a means of communication, as well as coming to love book-reading as a time for emotional closeness, are accomplishments typical of the good future reader. (Burns, S.M., Griffin, P., Snow, C.E., 1999, p.9)

Those of you who have read aloud to children know that reading can be a social process as well as a cognitive one. Reading together, sharing the enjoyment of a good book is a very special pleasure. You are an important figure in the development of that shared enthusiasm in your students.

Source: Adapted from Mary K. Fitzsimmons, February 1998, *Beginning Reading*. ERIC/OSEP Digest #E565. Reston, VA: ERIC Clearinghouse for Disabilities and Gifted Education, Council for Exceptional Children.

MULTIMEDIA RESOURCES

Burns, S.M., Griffin, P., Snow, C.E. (1999), (Eds.). *Starting Out Right: A Guide to Promoting Children's Reading Success.* Washington, D.C.: Committee on the Prevention of Reading Difficulties in Young Children, National Research Council.

You can read this book online at: **http://books.nap.edu/books/0309064104/html/index.html**

Snow, C.E., Burns, M.S., & Griffin, P. (1998). *Preventing Reading Difficulties in Young Children.* Washington, D.C.: Committee on the Prevention of Reading Difficulties in Young Children, National Research Council.

This one is available online at **http://books.nap.edu/books/030906418X/html/index.html**

The ERIC Clearinghouse on Disabilities and Gifted Education has many resources on teaching reading. Start at: **http://ericec.org/**

LD Resources is also a good source of information. Go to: **http://www.ldresources.com/index.html**

Professional journals that address reading are *The Reading Teacher*, the *Journal of Learning Disabilities*, and *Learning Disabilities: Research and Practice.*

References

Burns, S.M., Griffin, P., Snow, C.E. (1999), (Eds.). *Starting Out Right: A Guide to Promoting Children's Reading Success.* Washington, D.C.: Committee on the Prevention of Reading Difficulties in Young Children, National Research Council.

Smith, S.B., Simmons, D.C. & Kameenui, E.J. (February 1995). *Synthesis of Research on Phonological Awareness: Principles and Implications for Reading Acquisition.* (Technical Report No. 21). Eugene: National Center to Improve the Tools of Educators, University of Oregon.

Stanovich, K.E. (1994). Romance and Reality. *The Reading Teacher*, 47, 280–290.

Applied Behavior Analysis: Strategies and Resources

Inevitably, new teachers perceive as their greatest challenge their ability to manage their classroom and to teach appropriate behavior. Nothing can undermine the potential of a learning community like a disruptive child or an out-of-control class. A good working knowledge of behavior management is critical, whether you are a general education teacher or a special education teacher (Schloss & Smith, 1998).

In special education, and often in general education as well, the term behavior management is synonymous with the term behavior modification. Behavior modification refers to behavior change programs based on the philosophy that behavior can be altered through new learning experiences (Kazdin, 2001). Applied behavior analysis, a process we refer to explicitly or implicitly in Chapters 6, 7, and 8, is a specific area within behavior modification.

Applied behavior analysis is a discipline technique devoted to the understanding and prediction of human behavior (Alberto & Troutman, 1999). Applied behavior analysis is based on the tenet that behavior follows laws—once you recognize the rules or laws that govern a particular behavior, you can predict that behavior. This belief implies that we can observe, describe, and identify the interactions between a child and his or her environment. We can see the purpose a behavior has by observing what comes before and seems to prompt the behavior, and what maintains it in various environments (Pierce & Epling, 1995). This sequence of events—what precedes a behavior, the display of the behavior, and what follows the behavior—is referred to as ABC, or antecedent, behavior, and consequence.

© Richard Hutchings / Photo Edit

Applied behavior analysis interventions explore and assess the ways that the antecedents and/or consequences of behavior can be changed or arranged, so that behavior change can occur (Kazdin, 2001).

Teachers require a lot of preparation in order to use applied behavior analysis correctly and effectively. Therefore, the guidelines provided below should be used only to guide practice after you have had more in-depth instruction. These guidelines or characteristics of applied behavior analysis were identified by Kazdin (2001). We provide some additional information, when necessary, to help you relate the guidelines to your classroom.

Guidelines for Applied Behavior Analysis

1. Focus on overt behaviors. Overt behaviors are those you can observe and measure.
2. Focus on behaviors of applied (social or clinical) significance. These are behaviors that are important to success in the classroom environment, and may range from physical aggression, to inappropriate verbalization, to turn taking.
3. Assess behavior through direct observation, such as counting the frequency of responses. There are many different ways to assess behavior, including how often a behavior occurs in a given period of time; or how long a behavior, such as a tantrum, occurs. We discussed several additional ways to assess, or measure, behavior in Chapter 7.
4. Assess behavior continuously over time (e.g., several days per week) to identify patterns of behavior that occur with and without interventions

in place or under various environmental or stimulus conditions (e.g., presence of another person, different situations). This step will help you to determine the purpose or function of the behavior, as well as identify any preceding event or consequence that appears to be clearly associated with the performance of the behavior. (See the section on Functional Behavior Assessment in Chapter 7.)

5. Search for marked intervention effects that make a clear difference to the everyday functioning of the individual. This guideline is here to remind us that we want change to be meaningful. Behavior change programs should only be used if you see important change occurring.

6. Focus on one or a small number of individuals over time. Because of the detailed and careful observation required in applied behavior analysis, typically only a few children participate in a given behavior change project at the same time.

7. Use environmental (and observable) events to influence the frequency of behavior. Carr et al. (1998) suggests that interventions should involve changing the social system around the individual. The environment and the people in it can encourage the occurrence and maintenance of a behavior, once a student learns it.

8. Identify, evaluate, and demonstrate the factors (e.g., events) that are responsible for behavior change. Part of the science of applied behavior analysis is an experimental component that is designed to demonstrate a functional relationship between an intervention and a behavior (Cooper, Heron, & Heard, 1987). For example, one can demonstrate experimentally that William's increased use of socially inappropriate words when he becomes frustrated clearly is due to the contract system you put into place with William, his parents, and you. The relationship is not assumed, but is demonstrated using data and an experimental design (Kazdin, 2001; p.29).

Applied behavior analysis, while always a component of preparation for teaching in special education, traditionally was associated with instructional programs for students with more severe cognitive disabilities and autism. Increasingly, the importance of data-based decision making is creating an emphasis on applied behavior analysis for all students with disabilities.

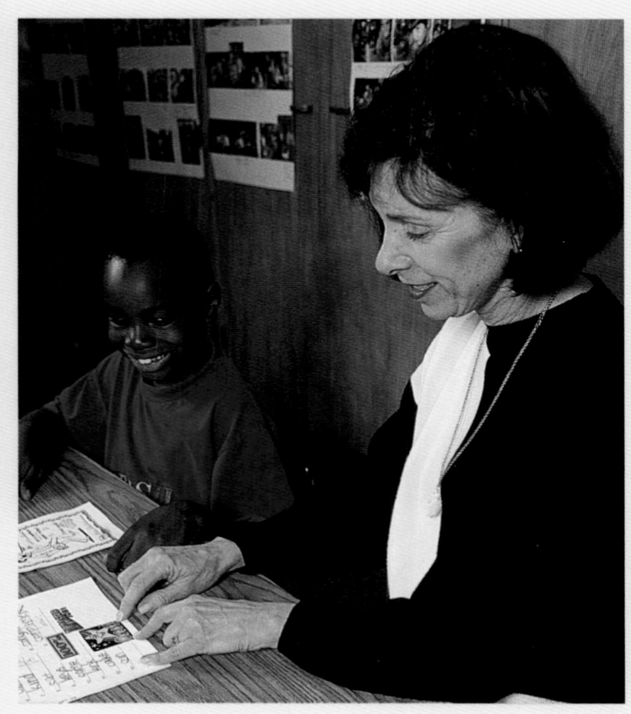

Multimedia Resources

Alberto, P.A., & Troutman, A.C. (1999). *Applied Behavior Analysis for Teachers* (5th ed.). Columbus, OH: Merrill.

Kazdin, A.E. (2001). *Behavior Modification* (6th ed.). Belmont, CA: Wadsworth/Thomson Learning.

Journal of Applied Behavior Analysis: The journal of the Society for the Experimental Analysis of Behavior: the home page for the journal is:
http://www.envmed.rochester.edu/wwwrap/behavior/jaba/jabahome.htm

The Association for Behavioral Analysis is an organization devoted to the applied and experimental study of behavior.
http://www.wmich.edu/aba

Fitzgerald, G., & Semrau, L. (1999). VRCbd - *First Step Kid Tools.* This CD for Macintosh and Windows contains reproducible material to use with students when developing behavior management plans.
http://www.coe.missouri.edu/~vrcbd

Questions About Cultural Context

1. What do we know about this student's linguistic, ethnic, and cultural background?
2. How would this child's family explain the student's behavior which is in question?
3. Do we notice the same or similar behaviors in other students with similar cultural backgrounds?
4. Is there any indication that the student's behavior has a cultural explanation?

Questions About Classroom Rules/Expectations

1. In what ways are students expected to respond to questions and directions?
2. In what ways are children expected to signal attention?
3. In what ways are students expected to behave toward authority?

Questions About Classroom Practices

1. In what ways is the teacher using flexible grouping?
2. In what ways is the teacher compacting curriculum?
3. In what ways is the teacher promoting interdependence?
4. In what ways is the teacher differentiating instruction?
5. In what ways is the teacher celebrating diversity?

Questions to Promote Culturally Competent Recommendations

1. Are there rules, expectations, and response behaviors that need to be explicitly taught to this student?
2. Are there classroom practices that need to be added, refined, or eliminated to more effectively support this student?
3. Do we need more information about this student's background and sociocultural context before we make recommendations for classroom adaptations?

Figure 5.3
Questions That Guide Culturally Competent Teacher Assistance Teams

Source: Craig, S., Hull, K., Haggart, A.G., & Perez-Selles, M. (2000). "Promoting cultural competence through teacher assistance teams," *Teaching Exceptional Children, 32,* 6–12.

Prevalence

A strict interpretation of the normal curve (see Figure 5.1) would suggest a prevalence rate for mental retardation of about 3 percent; that is, 3 percent of the total population would be identified as having mental retardation. According to the *Twenty-first Annual Report to Congress on the Implementation of the Individuals with Disabilities Act* (1999), however, the U.S. Department of Education reported that 0.96 percent of the school-age population, or 11.2 percent of all students with disabilities, was identified as having mental retardation. Factors affecting the prevalence rate include the procedures and recommendations used in school referral processes, changes over time in federal and state regulations, and the identification and elimination of potential risk factors through early intervention.

Approximately 1 percent of school-age children have mental retardation; most are classified with mild mental retardation.

The great majority of people with mental retardation—about 80 to 85 percent—are "invisible": They do not look "different." These individuals have mild mental retardation, and most of them are integrated naturally into the community. This fact adds to the difficulty of determining accurate prevalence rates

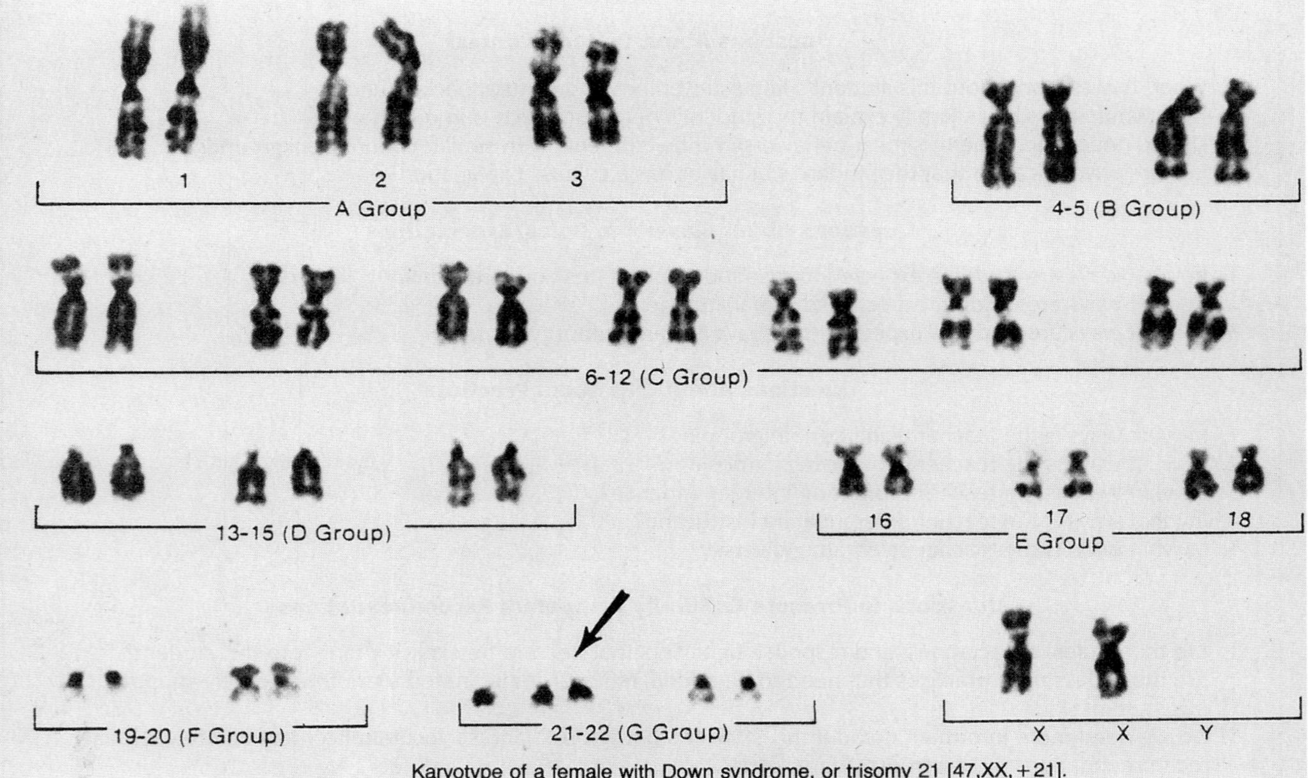

Karyotype of a female with Down syndrome, or trisomy 21 [47,XX,+21].

An extra chromosome can result from an incomplete division of the 23 pairs of chromosomes during the formation of an egg cell. The extra chromosome at the 21st position results in trisomy 21—the most common form of Down syndrome. (From "The Child with Down Syndrome," by S. Pueschel. In *Developmental Behavior Pediatrics* by Mel Levine, W. Carey, A. Crocker, and R. Gross, eds. (Philadelphia: Saunders, 1983. Copyright 1983 by W.B. Saunders and Company. Reprinted by permission)

and reveals one of the reasons many children aren't identified until they reach school. Children with moderate mental retardation, however, are more likely to exhibit distinguishing physical or developmental characteristics and therefore are more likely to be identified at an early age or at birth. Often the delay of certain developmental milestones, such as walking, the onset of speech, and the acquisition of self-help skills, alerts the parents and physician. Only about 7 to 10 percent of the people with mental retardation fall into this category.

Causes

There are a number of possible causes of mental retardation, many of which can be linked to the risk factors described in Chapter 2. Table 5.1 lists ten potential causes. The list includes causes for all levels of mental retardation. With the exception of category 9 (associated almost exclusively with mild mental retardation), the conditions listed can result in any level of mental retardation.

Table 5.1 Causes of Mental Retardation

1. *Infections and intoxications* Examples include rubella, syphilis, meningitis, and exposure to drugs, alcohol, or lead. The child may be exposed through the mother during pregnancy or may contract infections after birth. Unfortunately, fetal alcohol syndrome and drug addiction are major causes of mental retardation.
2. *Trauma or physical agents* Injuries to the child that occur before, during, or after birth fall into this category. Hypoxia (deprivation of oxygen) and injuries received through child abuse are examples.
3. *Metabolic or nutritional disorders* Examples of these disorders include phenylketonuria (PKU), Tay-Sachs disease, and galactosemia. In disorders of this type, the child's inability to metabolize or tolerate certain elements in food results in brain injury.
4. *Postnatal gross brain disease* This refers to tumors that occur after birth.
5. *Prenatal diseases or conditions of unknown origin* Examples of conditions found in this category include hydrocephalus and microcephaly. Hydrocephalus refers to the presence of cerebrospinal fluid in the skull, which increases the size of the skull while causing pressure on the brain; microcephaly describes a condition in which the skull is significantly smaller than normal.
6. *Chromosomal abnormality* Chromosomal abnormalities refer to an unusual pattern of genetic material on one or more of the child's chromosomes. Two of the more well-known syndromes associated with chromosomal abnormalities are Down syndrome and fragile-X syndrome. Both of these syndromes usually result in distinct physical characteristics and mental retardation. Fragile-X syndrome is found mostly in males (because of the defective X chromosome). Females carry the chromosome and some may experience mild mental retardation. In some instances, these syndromes appear as recessive genetic traits; in others (such as the most frequently occurring type of Down syndrome), the abnormality is associated with other factors, such as the age of the mother.
7. *Other perinatal/gestational conditions* Two prominent examples in this category are prematurity and low birthweight. Although many infants do not suffer negative effects from these conditions, both prematurity and low birthweight are risk factors for mental retardation. As you might expect, the more extreme these conditions are, the higher the level of risk.
8. *Presence of psychiatric disorders* A few psychiatric disorders may be associated with mental retardation. The most prominent example of this category used to be autism; however, autism is no longer considered a psychiatric disorder.
9. *Environmental influences* This category includes causes that are described as cultural-familial. We will describe this category in greater detail later in this section.
10. *Other unknown causes* Because it is difficult to identify the causes of mental retardation in many children, we suspect that there are causes that have yet to be discovered.

Source: H. J. Grossman, *Classification in Mental Retardation* (Washington, DC: American Association on Mental Deficiency, 1983).

Many causes of mental retardation appear to be related to biological factors, but cause is uncertain in over 50 percent of cases.

Biological Factors

Table 5.1 shows that many causes of mental retardation appear to be tied to biological factors. The more severe the level of mental retardation, the more likely it is that a cause can be pinpointed. For persons with moderate or severe mental retardation, biological causes can be pinpointed in 60 to 75 percent of the cases (McLaren & Bryson, 1987).

As we mentioned in Chapter 2, prenatal care, genetic counseling, and appropriate immunizations can help prevent many disabilities, including mental retardation. The medical community continues to identify ways to prevent or ameliorate mental retardation through genetic research or very early (often prenatal) treatment. For example, the effects of hydrocephalus can be greatly minimized by surgery in which a shunt is implanted in the head of the infant prior to birth, allowing the fluid to drain away before brain damage occurs. Another example involves the identification of phenylketonuria (PKU), a metabolic disorder. All hospitals now require a test for PKU at birth. If the condition is present, the child is put on a specific diet and mental retardation can be avoided.

Despite these advances, however, Patton, Beirne-Smith, and Payne (1990) point out that there is no certain cause in at least 50 percent of cases of mental retardation. This is particularly true for individuals with mild mental retardation.

Environmental Factors

It is difficult to pinpoint specific causal relationships between mental retardation and environmental factors such as cultural differences and socioeconomic conditions. Some relationships appear to be correlational in nature. For example, although poverty alone does not imply poor nutrition, poor health care, or a poor social environment, many of these risk factors do tend to occur together.

You may have heard about the ongoing debate over the role of environment versus the role of heredity in determining intelligence. Do smart parents have smart children because the children inherit intellectual ability, or do their surroundings encourage the fullest possible development of their intelligence? Could students with mild mental retardation inherit low intellectual ability from their parents, or could a bright child be affected by adverse environmental conditions? The relative importance of heredity and the environment in intellectual development has been discussed, debated, and researched for many years.

The relative importance of heredity and the environment in intellectual development has been debated for years.

The current thinking in this area represents a compromise. Each child probably comes into the world with a potential range of intellectual ability, and the environment in which the child is reared helps to determine the extent to which that ability is expressed (MacMillan, Semmel, & Gerber, 1994). In other words, it is likely that heredity and environment *interact* to result in the demonstrated intellectual ability of most children. Certainly the environment (including teaching) can affect how any child's cognitive, behavioral, and physical skills develop throughout his or her lifetime.

Effects on the Developing Person

Mental retardation is a developmental disability; that is, it affects a child's overall development in a relatively uniform manner. When we look at the effects of mental retardation on any individual, we must keep in mind not only the obvi-

Participation in exercise and competitive sports can result in high spirits and self-confidence as well as better physical conditioning. (T.L. Litt/Impact Visuals)

ous things, such as severity and complicating factors, but also the child's own personality and determination. The effects of mental retardation may be perceived as limiting by some and as challenging by others.

Cognitive Development

By definition, mental retardation can be interpreted to mean a low level of cognitive ability. Intelligence tests are used to provide an overall measure of cognitive ability, and persons with mental retardation are identified as having deficits in the ability to learn.

The ability to learn can be described in many ways. One aspect of learning is capacity—how much information can be processed at one time. Typically, children with mental retardation process smaller amounts of information than their average classmates. Another aspect of learning is the ability to engage in problem solving. Individuals with mental retardation may rely on a limited set of problem-solving strategies, which can cause difficulty when new, different, or complex problems arise (Wehmeyer & Kelchner, 1994). Students with mental retardation may also have difficulty using such cognitive skills as metacognition, memory, and attention.

■ ***Metacognition and Memory*** Most students with learning problems, including mental retardation, have difficulty in the areas of metacognition and memory, particularly short-term memory. *Metacognition* refers to the ability to identify how one learns and to evaluate, monitor, and adapt the learning process. These difficulties in metacognition and memory, therefore, translate into problems in planning, evaluating, and organizing information.

Let's look at a student learning to use a calculator for multiplication. The student will say and practice the steps involved in pushing the calculator buttons several times (rehearsal—a memory strategy). He will determine if he needs more practice (performance evaluation—a metacognitive strategy). He will say the problem aloud as he enters it into his calculator (rehearsal—a memory strategy). He may then work the problem by hand to double-check his answer and his ability to use the calculator correctly (awareness of need to evaluate performance and method of evaluating performance—a metacognitive strategy). If he has done the procedure incorrectly, he might rehearse the skill some more or create some type of mnemonic device to help him remember the procedure (metacognitive awareness and memory strategy.)

A student with mental retardation is more likely to have difficulty realizing the conditions or actions that will help her learn or retain the material. Given the calculator activity, the student might not think to practice or rehearse the process first, not think to evaluate her performance or know how to do it, and not realize that more practice or a new memory approach might be helpful. Because of these cognitive effects, we must focus instruction on *how* to learn as well as on *what* to learn so that the student can achieve the greatest possible level of independence.

Teachers must focus instruction on how as well as what students learn.

Memory and metacognitive skills are sometimes closely related. Before students can use strategies for aiding memory, they must be aware that such strategies are needed. Consequently, a very important way to improve the learning abilities of students with mental retardation is to teach when specific strategies for remembering need to be used.

■ ***Attention*** Mental retardation is often characterized by attentional deficits—the child has difficulty coming to attention, maintaining attention, and paying selective attention (Brooks & McCauley, 1984; Zeaman & House, 1963, 1979). In many instances, the problem is not that the child *won't* pay attention, but that he or she *can't* pay attention or doesn't know how to attend. It is possible, however, to minimize the effects of attentional deficits on learning.

A student with a deficit in coming to attention will experience difficulty focusing on the task at hand and, in the case of independent work, will have problems getting started. For some students this may be a result of having difficulty breaking their attention away from distractions or previous activities. Other students may have difficulty recognizing the signs, directions, or task requirements for a new activity. It is often helpful for teachers to use clear and unambiguous signals that indicate the beginning or ending of activities and that specify task requirements. These signals may be phrases, like "Eyes on me," or actions, like clapping the hands.

Many students with mental retardation have a shorter attention span than other children their age. A child experiencing difficulty maintaining attention will do much better on long tasks (such as practicing problems in arithmetic) if the task is broken into shorter segments that can be done throughout the day rather than all at once. Sometimes, gradually increasing the amount of time a child is required to pay attention will help to lengthen a child's attention span. Children with mental retardation, like all children, will be able to attend longer to material that is interesting and attractive.

A student with problems maintaining attention may need frequent direction to reorient him or her back to the task at hand. One way teachers try to deal with this problem is to establish a signal that can be used instead of constant verbal direction. A clap, or a tap on the board or desk, can be used to remind the child to refocus. Teachers also try different types of written cues, including colored marks, underlining, arrows, and so on, to help children focus on starting points in written material.

In the area of selective attention—attending to the key issues—students with mental retardation often have difficulty identifying the critical aspects or content of information. A young child might not be able to identify the distinguishing characteristics or dimensions of a letter or word. An older student might miss the key words in the directions for a test.

Some ways you can accentuate important information for students include:

- Underlining key words, using color or exaggeration to help draw attention to the words
- Using key words to cue the student that what you are about to say is important
- Presenting less extraneous information during initial teaching
- Teaching the student to recognize and use the cues you have provided

■ ***Generalization*** Most students with mental retardation experience difficulty transferring skills from one context to another. In other words, once a student has learned a specific skill in the classroom using certain materials, he or she may have difficulty performing that skill another way, in another setting, or with other materials. Sometimes the problem of **skill transfer**, or **generalization**, can be relatively minor and easy to remedy. Some children simply become confused by a change in format or materials and just need to be told that they can use the same skill or strategy in the new situation.

Teachers thus need to anticipate the possibility that students will need an explanation before performing the skill in the new format. For example, a student who can work single-digit addition problems successfully but has only been presented with problems in a vertical format may not realize that the same process applies to problems in a horizontal format (2 + 3 = __). This child will need additional instruction and demonstration.

Generalizing, or transferring skills from one setting to another, is often difficult for students with mental retardation.

You can maximize the potential for generalization by incorporating real-world materials into your instruction. For example, a student who has learned all of the basic addition and subtraction skills may not realize that those same skills can be used to balance a checkbook, so you can have students practice using real checkbooks. Use real materials whenever they are readily available—it makes learning more meaningful for all students and helps to address the problem of poor skill transfer.

The child with moderate mental retardation may experience a great deal of difficulty understanding that the pencil-and-paper addition he or she does in the classroom is the same basic skill used in counting money or adding up points in a board game. For students with moderate mental retardation, the use of actual materials to teach needed or desired skills has even more importance. Teachers should never assume that a generalization of responses will occur without specific instruction. See the box "Strategies for Enhancing Cognitive Skills" for a summary of instructional strategies.

Language Development

One early sign of mild or moderate mental retardation is a delay in the acquisition of communication skills. Children with mental retardation acquire language at a slower rate than other children, usually have limited vocabularies, and tend to use a restricted number of sentence constructions. Their language is

Children with mental retardation may experience a delay in language development.

~ Strategies for Enhancing Cognitive Skills

Metacognition and Memory

- Teach memory strategies, such as rehearsing and chunking information, if students are not using them.
- Teach students when to use memory strategies or provide cues for using them.

Attention

- Establish clear signals to orient students to the task or lesson.
- Break up long instructional segments or tasks into several short sessions.
- Gradually increase the amount of time you expect children to attend to a task.
- Accentuate key content and directions for the students through the use of response prompts or cues.

Generalization

- Teach students to use the skills they have learned in one class in other classes or settings.
- Use real-world materials to help students generalize basic skills to realistic situations.

structurally similar, however, to the language of other children, and it develops in the same way (Polloway, Patton, Payne, & Payne, 1989).

Speech problems are also found more frequently in children with mental retardation. A survey of services provided to elementary-age students with mild mental retardation found that 90 percent of the population surveyed had been identified as needing speech or language services, especially in the area of articulation (Epstein, Polloway, Patton, & Foley, 1989). Structural differences, such as tongue size or facial musculature, can affect the way some individuals pronounce certain sounds.

Individuals with mental retardation also may experience difficulty in nonverbal communication skills. Many children with mental retardation demonstrate appropriate nonverbal skills (proximity, gestures, eye contact), yet may display inappropriate skills or engage in appropriate skills at an unusual level (Bufkin & Altman, 1995). For example, a pat on the shoulder is appropriate during most interpersonal conversations. If someone were giving you a pat on the shoulder every few seconds, however, you would probably view the behavior as inappropriate. Nonverbal communication skills can be as important as verbal language in communication with peers.

Physical Development

People with mild retardation may, as a group, be less physically fit than others—they may weigh somewhat less and be of smaller stature, have poorer motor skills, and have more health-related problems than their peers (Drew, Logan, & Hardman, 1992).

The physical health and motor skills of individuals with mental retardation are more likely to be impaired as the degree of mental retardation increases. Thus, people with moderate mental retardation are more likely to have noticeable physical differences than are those with mild mental retardation. The same rule holds true when we consider the existence of additional disabling conditions, many of which, like cerebral palsy and epilepsy, involve physical ability and overall health. The greater the degree of mental retardation, the more likely it is that another disabling condition will accompany it.

Some of the specific syndromes that cause mental retardation result in accompanying physical impairments. The most common of these, Down syndrome, frequently results in structural heart defects, which in most cases can be corrected surgically. Individuals with Down syndrome are also prone to lung abnormalities, which makes them susceptible to upper respiratory infections (Patterson, 1987). The incidence of hearing and visual impairments in children with Down syndrome is also considerably higher than in the general population. Although at one time these physical disabilities greatly shortened the prospective life span of people with Down syndrome, medical technology has enabled most individuals to live well into adulthood.

People with mental retardation may have physical health problems.

Many students with mild retardation require no extra programs or assistance to participate in sports or physical education activities. Other students, however, require more specialized physical activities, such as adaptive physical education, that include specific activities designed to improve strength and coordination. There are also organized activities designed specifically for persons with mental retardation or other disabilities, such as the Special Olympics. These programs provide opportunities for persons with mental and physical disabilities to compete in adapted track and field events.

Social and Emotional Development

Research has indicated some variability in the extent to which students with mild mental retardation are accepted and liked by their peers (Sabornie, Kauffman, & Cullinan, 1990; Siperstein, Leffert, & Widaman, 1996). It is important to remember that every child or adolescent, with or without mental retardation, has personal and physical characteristics that can assist or detract from that individual's popularity and acceptance.

Students with mental retardation may display delays in the development of communication, self-help, and problem-solving skills (Wehmeyer & Kelchner, 1994). As we suggested earlier, children with mental retardation also may have difficulty interpreting social cues, particularly if multiple cues are presented at once, or if incongruent cues and behaviors are present (Leffert, Siperstein, & Millikan, 2000). All of these characteristics can contribute to ineffective interaction with others, but they can be addressed, in part, through specific training in communication and social skills.

Students with mental retardation may have difficulty interpreting social cues.

Most social behaviors are learned, just as other skills are learned. Sometimes students with mild and moderate mental retardation display **immature behaviors**, which generally reflect an inability to control emotions and delay gratification. Students with immature behaviors may have a low tolerance for frustration, cry easily, and do socially inappropriate things (Epstein, Polloway, Patton, & Foley, 1989). These behaviors may indicate a lack of appropriate social learning. A student with a problem in the area of selective attention, for example, may not have learned or may have difficulty identifying the relevant cues in a social situation, such as the nonverbal signals many of us use to judge how other people are reacting to us. When you enter a library, for example, you notice the low volume of speech and adjust your level of speech accordingly. If you don't, you probably notice the looks other people give you and then make the adjustment; if you do not, your behavior is interpreted as disruptive or inappropriate.

Studies have demonstrated that the behavior of students with mild and moderate mental retardation can be changed through behavior modification

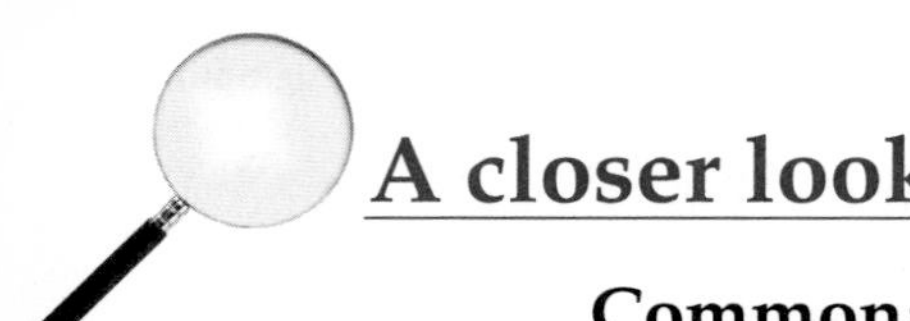

A closer look

Commonalities: Working Toward Tolerance

Diana Zernone's new doll is the first she's ever had that looks like her: The 14-year-old New York City girl has Down syndrome, and so does Dolly Downs, a pigtailed blonde who went on the market in 1992, assembled by workers with mental retardation and developmental disabilities at Camp Venture Inc.

The idea for a doll resembling a child with Down syndrome came from a Rockland County couple who have a 31-year-old son with autism and have run programs for people with mental retardation for twenty-three years. Dr. John Lukens, a child psychologist, and Kathleen Lukens, the executive director of Camp Venture, said their inspiration was a former client who once asked her parents why she did not look like them.

Seeing people with Down syndrome on television's "Life Goes On" and in advertisements convinced the Lukenses that the public might be ready for the doll, which is also intended to teach children who do not have a handicap to be more tolerant of those who do.

The building where the doll is assembled is off a country lane. The workshop itself is a huge open room. A number of those seated around long tables wave and shout greetings to visitors before returning to their work, but the hall was surprisingly quiet on a recent afternoon, with most people concentrating on putting together pens, packaging cameras, and in one corner assembling the dolls.

The job has been divided into fifteen steps, not including the stitching, which is done by several seamstresses who work at machines along the workshop's back wall. And after the last worker on the assembly line ties the red ribbons into Dolly's hair, all of those who have participated in making the doll take turns signing the cards attached to the finished product, which say, "I made this doll."

So far they have made about 100 of the dolls, which are sold for $24.95 and shipped directly from the workshop. The information numbers are 914-624-5330 and 800-682-3714. Eventually, Camp Venture directors hope that their new product will help secure steady employment for the 150 adults with disabilities in the sheltered workshop.

Source: Melinda Henneberger, "Doll Gives Identity to Down Syndrome Children," *New York Times*, December 12, 1992.

techniques and social skill instruction. With instruction, students can learn appropriate behaviors by modeling the behavior of peers in the classroom. This can pay off in improved social relations with others and an improved perception of self.

Effects on the Family

The realization that a child has mental retardation may be either sudden or gradual, as you learned in Chapter 3. Sometimes, when the child is very ill at birth or when recognizable physical signs are present, the parents know about their child's disability before they leave the hospital. More often, however, the clues come slowly. The child may not sit, stand, and walk at the expected ages and may not understand language or use words at the expected times. But there are many differences in the way children develop, and parents often postpone acknowledging that their child is different from others.

It is in the school environment that most children with mild mental retardation are identified and the effects on the family are fully realized. Parents may confer with their child's teacher or receive a letter from the school administrator requesting permission to assess their child for possible provision of special education services. A discussion with the school psychologist after testing, or the IEP meeting, may be the first place that the parents hear the words *mental retardation* applied to their child.

Most children with mild mental retardation are first diagnosed at school.

For some parents, diagnosis, labeling, and the provision of special services will come as a relief; they usually are the ones who have suspected that their child has learning difficulties. Others will react negatively to the term *mental retardation*. These words evoke a special set of reactions from parents, perhaps because most people have little knowledge of mental retardation or of persons with mental retardation. Skinner, Bailey, Correa, and Rodriguez (1999) found that a majority of Latino mothers who wrote narratives about their relationship with their children with mental retardation reported that the children brought about positive change in their lives and were also viewed as a blessing from God. Although both cultural and religious background may influence a parent's reaction to a child with a disability, ultimately, each parent reacts in his or her own way.

Another possible cause of negative reactions by parents is that their concept of mental retardation includes an inability to learn and limited potential for a fulfilling life. It can be particularly difficult for parents who have perceptions of this type to attach the label of mental retardation to their child—a child who seemed just like all of the other children until he or she reached school. Accepting mental retardation, for many parents, involves a significant adjustment in their expectations and hopes for the child. Of course, these adjustments are often based on the parents' perceptions of mental retardation rather than their knowledge. Once parents acquire a more realistic concept of mental retardation, they are often able to raise their expectations and focus on the strengths and abilities of their child.

Parents of children with mental retardation, like most parents of children with disabilities, often seek support from parent groups, gain knowledge from classes, books, and journals, and become aware of available services through contact with schools, associations, and service agencies (see the Multimedia Resources section at the end of this chapter). Balancing parenting roles and responsibilities and using resources effectively are effective life-management strategies used by parents of children with disabilities (Scorgie, Wilgosh, & McDonald, 1999).

Many parents of children with mental retardation find that support groups help them manage stress and access resources.

The presence of a child with mental retardation can affect family interactions and relationships. Although a common concern has been that children with mental retardation monopolize their parents' attention and disrupt sibling relationships, research indicates that the effects are minimal when children have mild or moderate mental retardation. Stoneman, Brody, Davis, and Crapps (1987) compared pairs of same-sex siblings and found no evidence that mothers attended to children with mental retardation at the expense of their siblings. Nonetheless, individuals with moderate mental retardation may demand more time of their parents than do other children.

Overall, the research in this area seems to suggest that siblings of children with mental retardation find ways to get the attention and social interaction they need (Stoneman, Brody, Davis, & Crapps, 1988). The interactions of siblings within families reflect the added child-care responsibilities of older siblings, and the sibling relationships are often characterized by a strong caregiving or dominant role on the part of the sibling without mental retardation. As individuals with mental retardation continue to receive educations that increasingly stress independent activities and functional skills, it will be interesting to see how sibling relationships change.

In Classrooms and Other Educational Settings

Because of our improved knowledge of effective educational technology, our changing philosophy toward inclusion, and a greater awareness of the rights of all individuals, educators are now rethinking the way we should educate individuals with mental retardation. As teachers, we now expect to provide meaningful educational experiences—experiences that will help prepare the students for life on their own—and to do it in the most inclusive setting possible. In many educational settings, the classroom teacher is responsible for the majority of service delivery to students with mental retardation. Interaction, communication, and professional cooperation between the special education teacher and classroom teacher are becoming the most important factors in the successful educational experience of students with mental retardation. Many current and upcoming educational issues, therefore, focus on the cooperative nature of educational programming and the development of challenging educational environments for full inclusion.

Early Intervention

Although diagnosis of severe mental retardation is typically made at birth or within the first year of life, children with moderate or mild mental retardation are more likely to be identified at a somewhat later age. The advent of Public Law 99-457, however, stresses early identification of children with disabilities and provision of appropriate services.

P.L. 99-457 (see Chapter 1) states that children identified as developmentally delayed, at risk, or having an identified disability between birth and the age of 3 are eligible to receive services. Most students in this age range receive services from the agency designated by the state to handle infant programs. Identified 3- and 4-year-olds are eligible for preschool programs through the local educational agency. As you might expect, one of the goals of early intervention is to reduce the effects of mental retardation on learning and basic skill acquisition.

Curriculum

Educational programs for many students with mental retardation emphasize preparing students for life after school.

Curriculum options for students with mild and moderate mental retardation include the basic skills (reading and math) and content-area skills (science and social studies) taught in the regular classroom, as well as functional life-skills content designed to help students learn the work, domestic, or leisure skills needed for independent living.

Curriculum decisions should be based on the anticipated outcomes, or expected goals, of education. For example, the anticipated outcome for a student who is capable of doing classwork in the regular class and has a high level of basic skills is to receive a high school diploma. This student may be best served by taking basic academic courses in the regular curriculum, which might also include some vocational classes and training. The anticipated outcome for another student might be to live and work in a supervised community setting. This student would follow a full-time curriculum devoted to life skills, which might include training in social skills; interpersonal communication skills; domestic skills such as cooking, managing finances, and cleaning; using community transportation; and prevocational and vocational preparation, including on-the-job training.

A functional or **life-skills curriculum** is intended to provide the skills necessary to maximize a student's ability to live and work independently. Curricula for students with mild mental retardation generally include instruction in basic academic areas with a focus on functional academics. **Functional academics** are basic academic skills, such as reading, writing, and arithmetic, taught in the context of real-life or community activities. For example, reading skills might be presented in the context of reading menus, clothing labels, signs, and directions; and arithmetic skills in the context of paying for food in restaurants or grocery stores, planning a weekly budget, or balancing a checkbook.

A functional or life-skills curriculum provides the skills necessary for students to live and work independently.

Other functional curriculum components considered important for students with mild disabilities include health, sexuality, and family care; job preparation; science and social studies—again with a functional emphasis; social skills; using community resources; and independent living skills (Drew, Logan, & Hardman, 1992; Morgan, Moore, McSweyn, & Salzberg, 1992; Patton, Beirne-Smith, & Payne, 1990).

Students with moderate mental retardation may require more support and have more difficulty in transfer or skill generalization. These students can benefit from a more comprehensive curriculum that includes self-care skills, community access skills, social interaction and communication skills, physical and motor development (including recreation and leisure skills), and specific job training (Drew, Logan, & Hardman, 1992; Patton, Beirne-Smith, & Payne, 1990). In the next section, we will discuss how the student's future goals affect his or her class placement.

The curriculum for students with moderate mental retardation encompasses the essential areas of everyday life. These areas are referred to as *domains*. Although you may see different terms used to describe these areas, they can be identified as domestic, recreation and leisure, vocational, and community living. The development of the curriculum involves:

The curriculum for students with moderate mental retardation emphasizes self-care skills, social interaction, recreation and leisure skills, and job training.

- Looking at the specific skills that the student needs in these areas
- Identifying the specific skills in which the student needs instruction
- Providing that instruction in the context of the particular domain

In other words, the curriculum is generated by the student's environment rather than by a list of skills found in basal texts or regular curriculum guides. Instruction involves presenting the skill in a naturally occurring context and integrating it with other skills found in that setting (Browder & Snell, 1987; Snell & Brown, 2000). Instead of teaching students a list of sight words or a few arithmetic operations or a series of social skills, one would identify a targeted activity, such as grocery shopping, going to a movie, applying for a job, or going to a fast-food restaurant. Then, one would teach the needed skills in reading, math, social behavior, transportation, communication, and organization related to the specific activity in conjunction with practicing and performing that activity. All instruction is therefore useful, meaningful, and motivating to the student; teaching is focused on usable skills that can be practiced often. (See the accompanying

~ Environmental Assessment of Skills for Instruction

Student: Patricia Kelly, age 16

Environment: Home

Domains: Domestic/Vocational

Rationale: Patricia is responsible for watching her two younger siblings (ages 8 and 10) every day from 3:30 to 5:30. Many of the skills required can also be used as a basis for employment in child-care fields. All of the skills can be used to address future parenting needs.

Area 1: **Recreation**—Skills for instruction

Suggest activities appropriate for indoor play.

Check toys and play materials to make sure they are safe and age-appropriate.

Check on children playing indoors every 15–20 minutes if they are not in sight.

Keep children in sight or hearing distance at all times when they are playing outside.

Recognize and prohibit rough or dangerous outside play.

Guide children in their selection of after-school snacks or prepare suitable snacks for them.

Play with children.

Area 2: **Child Management**—Skills for instruction

Know household rules for indoor/outdoor play.

Remind children of rules when they return from school.

Enforce rules.

Know and use only management strategies suggested by parents.

Know and use a few plans or "tricks" for diverting children's attention.

Give accurate report of children's behavior to parents.

Area 3: **Safety**—Skills for instruction

Identify and clear away unsafe debris, broken toys, etc., both inside and outside.

Check premises to ensure that potentially harmful materials are out of children's reach (matches, firearms, cleaning materials).

Be familiar with and experienced in administering emergency first aid procedures.

Know how to administer emergency procedures when a child is choking.

Distinguish between a mild incident and an emergency, and act according to plan.

Read labels to determine if substance is poisonous.

Locate and use fire extinguisher and know fire evacuation plan.

Locate and call appropriate persons in case of concern or emergency (includes neighbor, parents, local emergency number).

box, "Environmental Assessment of Skills for Instruction," for an example of curriculum planning.)

Community-based instruction allows students to receive instruction in meaningful and motivating settings.

The community itself is playing an ever-increasing role in curriculum content for students with mental retardation. One goal of **community-based instruction** is placing students in job settings that are found in their local community. In addition, the community provides opportunities for the functional application of basic skills. For example, teachers can use menus, job applications, store names, movie theater marquees, bank books, bowling scorecards, and city maps (to name a few items) from the local community to assist in developing skills that can be used immediately and practiced repeatedly in the student's home environment. The regular classroom teacher should find that using these resources facilitates learning and provides motivation for all the students in the class. A third role for the community is to serve as a source of activities. A series of local activities—using the post office, visiting the doctor and dentist, applying for a job, using the public recreation center, and eating at a favorite restaurant—could be the basic curriculum components for the school year, and all of the academic, social, communication, and self-care skills needed for each activity could be taught as the class participated in that activity.

Educational Setting

Students with mild and moderate levels of mental retardation attend school in a variety of settings, ranging from the regular classroom to the special school. These options should be considered in relation to the future goals or desired outcomes of education, because the setting for instruction is closely related to the curriculum. For example, the regular classroom may be the best setting for a student in a diploma-track program, whereas a special classroom or community setting might be the most appropriate primary instructional site for a student receiving instruction in social or vocational skills.

The focus of a student's instruction will often determine his or her educational setting.

Professional disagreement exists over the most appropriate instructional setting for students with mild mental retardation. This conflict involves questions about the efficacy of programs offered in special education classes, the current emphasis on maximizing integration of students into regular education classes, and the need to provide a specialized curriculum (MacMillan & Hendrick, 1993). Many schools emphasize including students with mental retardation as much as possible. Thus, students with mild mental retardation may spend most of the day in regular classes and receive special education services during one or two class periods in a resource class.

Sometimes, students with mild mental retardation remain in the resource class for several class periods, and some may be served in self-contained classes. In these instances, inclusion is often limited to nonacademic periods such as gym, music, lunch, and study hall. A curriculum that focuses more on functional or life skills can then be delivered in the special education class. Students also may receive related services, such as adaptive physical education, speech and language therapy, or counseling. If your school has a program for students with mild mental retardation, you should expect anything, from a child who is in your class for the entire school day, with consultation provided by the resource teacher, to a child you see only during nonacademic periods.

Students with moderate mental retardation are more likely to be placed in full-time or self-contained special education classes than are students with mild disabilities. Keep in mind, however, that many schools do have programs that include systematic inclusion of students with moderate disabilities, particularly, but not exclusively, in nonacademic subjects. These programs emphasize the importance of socialization and friendships between students with moderate mental retardation and those in the general education classroom. Research emphasizes the importance of the special educator's presence in the general education classroom to support the general education teacher when students with moderate to severe mental retardation are served in inclusive settings (Snell & Janney, 2000).

On the other hand, the rationale often used for placing students with moderate mental retardation in self-contained classes is that the teacher is able to develop and deliver an alternative curriculum. For example, the students can receive more intensive programming in life-skill activities or in community-based training when they are in a self-contained program.

Nonetheless, interaction with peers is a major focus of education—an important consideration for successful community integration in later years as well as during school. Students in self-contained programs may be mainstreamed into lunch or arts classes in order to provide at least minimal interactions with peers. Many educators, however, feel that more complete assimilation in regular classes is necessary. Sometimes the need for special instruction and training must be weighed against the philosophy of integration and the need for social interaction as educators and parents try to decide on the most appropriate program for an individual child.

The need for specialized instruction must be weighed against the need for inclusion.

Because of the current emphasis on community-based instruction, many secondary students with moderate mental retardation are receiving instruction outside of the school setting for part of the school day (Nietupski, Hamre-Nietupski, Donder, Houselog, & Anderson, 1988). As we discussed earlier, community-based instruction can provide students with appropriate educational experiences and also maximize opportunities for social and physical integration.

Teaching Strategies

■ ***Methods*** We see many commonalities in the instructional procedures used for students with mild and moderate mental retardation. A basic instructional technique focuses on the clear and straightforward presentation of tasks that have been carefully analyzed and sequenced. The process of breaking down a task or skill into its component parts is called **task analysis** (Alberto & Troutman, 1990). Teachers must be able to identify the skills required to complete a certain task (from preparing a sandwich to reading a newspaper article) and to develop an appropriate instructional sequence to teach them. The steps of a task analysis can be taught using a variety of techniques, ranging from physical guidance, to the use of verbal prompts, to observational learning. The level, or intensity, of instruction is directly related to the level of support required by the student. Researchers are constantly evaluating the most effective, most efficient, and least intrusive way to teach specific skills. For example, Biederman, Fairhall, Raven, and Davey (1998) found that children's simple observations of behavior was more effective than more intensive forms of instruction involving physical prompts when teaching children with mental retardation activities such as buttoning and putting puzzles together.

Teaching students with mental retardation includes focusing on task analysis, a clear presentation of carefully sequenced tasks.

Prompts are clues or guides that maximize the probability that a student will answer correctly or attend to the appropriate material. Prompts are an important aspect of instruction in special education and are used extensively during initial instruction. If you underline the key word in a series of directions, you are prompting the student to attend to that key word. If you model the correct way to sound out a word, you are providing a prompt for the correct response. Prompts are then faded, or eliminated, over time. Prompts for teaching students with mental retardation may begin as physical prompts and then gradually move to verbal or visual prompts. They may occur before or during skill performance; the timing of the prompt may have implications for skill acquisition and generalization. For example, Singleton, Schuster, Morse, and Collins (1999) found that prompts occurring before skill performance resulted in quicker skill acquisition, and prompts occurring during skill performance facilitated maintenance and generalization.

Prompting techniques are important strategies for teaching.

Many teachers focus on prompting students' awareness of their learning. Students with moderate mental retardation may need content-specific prompts, such as a series of pictures or photographs to remind them of what needs to be done. Browder and Minarovic (2000) found that nonreading students with moderate mental retardation were able to use sight word prompts and self-instruction to initiate work tasks in competitive employment settings. In another interesting study, Le Grice and Blampied (1994) taught students with moderate mental retardation to operate a video recorder and personal computer using color videotapes of a familiar staff member doing the steps of the skill. The videotape served as a sequenced series of prompts corresponding to the task analysis. We are only touching on the types of prompts that can be used in the classroom. The important thing to remember is that prompts can be easily integrated into regular classroom instruction.

Cooperative learning is a strategy that provides children of various skill levels with a task to complete together. The teacher must structure the activity to allow each child to make a significant contribution to the task. Cooperative learning is a good strategy to keep in mind when teaching students with mental retardation in an integrated classroom. Peer tutoring is a related strategy for teaching students with mental retardation in general education settings. When teachers provide structured activities for peer tutoring groups, all students can increase their amount of academic engaged time during a classroom period and can improve their academic performance (Mortweet, 1999).

Students receiving instruction in a functional curriculum also have many learning experiences that require attention, remembering, and organizing. These activities can range from something as simple as learning a telephone number and address to remembering the steps involved in following a recipe, writing a check, or going shopping for groceries. Instruction also needs to be sequenced and structured carefully, with reliance on prompts to illustrate how to do the task as well as when to do it (see the box "Simple Strategies for Teaching Students with Mental Retardation").

■ ***Materials*** Because of the issue of skill transfer and generalization, the types of materials used in instruction can be very important, particularly when life skills or vocational skills are being taught. Both simulated materials and real-life materials have their uses. If you were teaching sight words found in the environment, an example of a simulated material would be the word *exit* printed in red capital letters on a rectangular card placed over the doorway of the classroom. An alternative would be to use the real thing and conduct your lesson using the actual exit sign over the door at the end of the hallway. Because not all teachers are able to take their students into the community for training on a daily basis, teachers and researchers have looked at ways to combine the use of simulated materials with real materials in natural environments. For example, Morse and Schuster (2000) found that a combination of community-based instruction and simulation training using a picture story board resulted in successful instruction and maintenance of grocery-shopping skills. Branham,

Simple Strategies for Teaching Students with Mental Retardation

- Teach students in small groups (three or four students).
- Teach one concept or skill at a time.
- Teach steps or strategies for learning (a plan for remembering or sequencing information).
- Provide ample opportunity for practice (practice often, but don't overload).
- Use prompts to promote correct responding (examples, modeling, physical guidance).

Collins, Schuster, and Kleinert (1999) found that a videotape of individuals modeling certain skills, such as mailing a letter and cashing a check, was an even more effective addition to community-based instruction than classroom simulation. As our knowledge of the most effective ways to combine alternative instructional strategies with community-based instruction grows, we increase opportunities for teaching a wide range of important life skills.

Instruction using real materials can help students generalize skills.

The use of real materials in natural environments is, however, a critical component of effective instruction for many students with mental retardation. Real materials can motivate as well as facilitate generalization. As we've mentioned, using an actual checkbook folder and checks can provide a good way to practice subtraction and addition skills that can easily be integrated into the regular curriculum. Many schools have had success at integrating the more functional objectives of a student's curriculum into their regular classroom curriculum.

Students who are in the regular classroom for the academic curriculum will probably use the same materials as everyone else. The resource or consulting teacher may work with the classroom teacher to develop strategies for helping the student interact with the text and other materials. Some materials are designed specifically for curriculum packages for students with learning difficulties. At the elementary level these materials are often found in programs for basic skills instruction (reading or math), such as the SRA Corrective Reading Series. At the secondary level, these materials might include low-vocabulary, high-interest reading materials such as teen magazines or plays. The regular education teacher can ask the resource teacher or consultant about available materials or catalogs.

Technology

Computer-based instruction has provided teachers of students with mild and moderate mental retardation with a number of instructional options. Computers can augment a curriculum, expand opportunities for practice, and facilitate new instruction. Hasselbring and Goin (1989) have identified the following most common and important uses for computer-based instruction:

Computer-based instruction provides teachers with additional resources for teaching students with mental retardation.

1. *Drill and practice* The computer is used to provide a range of practice activities, such as math problems to perform or words to read. Although this is the most common educational use of the computer, you should remember that drill and practice activities reinforce previous learning rather than teach new skills.
2. *Tutorial plus drill* In this type of lesson, some initial instruction takes place and then drill and practice activities follow. It is important for the teacher to evaluate the type of instructional strategies used in the lessons.
3. *Word processing* Using word-processing programs to produce written work may help develop students' skills in written language. The computer eliminates many of the problems students have with the actual production of letters, and the ease with which words can be moved or erased can also help to encourage more fluent writing.
4. *Thinking and problem solving* Some computer programs (such as Logo) can provide the student with exercise in developing higher-level thinking and problem-solving skills.

5. *Simulations* Computer simulations of real-life situations can provide students with practice making decisions without the risk of real consequences, dangers, or tight time constraints.

Technology also can be used to deliver instruction and instructional prompts to students in areas other than academic skills. For example, Mechling and Gast (1997) used a Digivox, an augmentative communication device, to teach skills such as using a dishwasher to students with moderate mental retardation. The Digivox contains pictures or symbols that the student presses to release a corresponding digitized speech recording. A series of photographs of the student or teacher performing each step of the task was placed over the computer symbols, and the verbal directions for each step were recorded, enabling the students to use the Digivox to learn the series of tasks.

It is important for you to evaluate software carefully and determine its appropriate instructional use. The types of available software are growing rapidly, and many companies are now producing exciting learning programs as well as the frequently used drill and practice activities. The computer can be a powerful teacher's aid in the classroom, as well as a motivating activity for many students. Computer programs can provide introductions and basic skill reviews of many areas that may not be a part of the regular classroom curriculum.

Transition to Adult Life

Many people with mild mental retardation integrate themselves successfully into the life of their community with little or no outside assistance. They find jobs and do them well; they marry and begin their own families. Others, though,

Technology often is used as a tool to learn new information—it also provides many children a way to share with the ones they love. (Photo courtesy of DynaVox Systems, LLC, Pittsburgh, PA)

continue to need the help and support of social agencies. In Robert Edgerton's study of the lives of adults with mental retardation, *The Cloak of Competence* (1967), adults had difficulties in three major areas: making a living, managing sexuality and marriage, and using leisure time. Although over thirty years have passed, these areas of concern remain (Edgerton, Bollinger, & Herr, 1984).

More and more, emphasis is being placed on the skills that young people need to make the transition from school to the working world. There is also a focus on the factors related to quality of life: social adjustment and integration into all aspects of the community. Research suggests the importance of community employment and living to the self-esteem of individuals with mental retardation (Griffin, Rosenberg, Cheyney, & Greenburg, 1996). The educational experiences that address the movement from school to work and from home or residential school to independent community living are referred to as **transitional programming**. All secondary students with mental retardation now have a separate component of their IEP that identifies and describes the transition training they will receive. The transition plan, now mandated by IDEA, has resulted in the identification and promotion of effective transition practices (Hasazi, Furney, & DeStefano, 1999). Figure 5.4 provides an example of a transition plan. The importance of transition in the curriculum of students with mental retardation is likely to continue to increase as specific needs of adults with mild mental retardation are identified. Greater cooperation between the educational system, the business world, and adult social agencies will help to improve transition services.

Transitional programming addresses the experiences students need to move on to life after school.

Many professionals assert the importance of the student's voice in effective transition programming. Self-determination, which describes the active role the student takes, includes decision-making and self-advocacy, which may need to be taught to students with mental retardation. Many educators feel that a deep level of participation by the student is critical to a successful transition plan (Devlieger & Trach, 1999; Hasazi, Furney, & DeStefano, 1999). Spencer and Sands (1999) found that student, school, and family factors, including extent of inclusion, possession of job-related skills, ability to self-regulate, and family environment, were related to the level of student participation in transition plans.

Transitional programming has become an integral part of the educational plans of most students with mental retardation. Recent research specific to the adjustment of students with mental retardation to the world of work suggests that more comprehensive and long-range transition support is necessary (Neubert, Tilson, & Ianacone, 1989).

Employment Opportunities

People with mild mental retardation continue to face serious problems finding meaningful work that uses their skills and that pays above the subsistence level. From the mid-1980s to the mid-1990s, hourly wages increased, as did the employment rate, but 65 percent of individuals with cognitive disabilities remained unemployed (Frank & Sitlington, 2000; Wehman, West, & Kregel, 1999). Because the needs of some students with mild mental retardation are not always obvious, many have not received the necessary preparation for transition.

People with moderate mental retardation are more likely to receive comprehensive preparation in the transition process related to employment. The fact that large numbers of adults with disabilities are unable to secure any employment continues to serve as an impetus for better transition programming during

Name DAVID RYAN		**Date** 7-1	
Transition Service Areas	**Person/Agency Responsible**	**Timeline**	**Comments**
A. Employment/ education goal: Seek and secure a job	Transition coordinator, student	January of school year	Prepare career planning packet. Identify job sites.
B. Home and family goal: Prepare for marriage and family	Teacher	October of school year	Identify community resources.
C. Leisure pursuits goal: Attend special neighborhood events	Teacher, student	September of school year	Link interests with local options.
D. Community involvement goal: Know about wide range of services available in the community.	Teacher	December of school year	Use community-based experiences.
E. Emotional/physical health goal: Seek personal counseling	Counselor, Teacher	October of school year	Locate and contact community services.
F. Personal responsibility and relationship goal: Get along with others	Teacher, Transition Coordinator	January of school year	Identify interpersonal job skills required in warehouse setting.

Source: M.E. Cronin & J.R. Patton, *Life Skills Instruction for All Students with Special Needs: A Practical Guide for Integrating Real Life Content into Curriculum* (Austin, TX: PRO-ED, 1993), p. 57. Copyright © 1993. Used by permission of PRO-ED.

Figure 5.4
Individualized Transition Plan
Scenario: David is a 16-year-old male who is tired of school and wants to get a job. He is interested in finding a job working in a warehouse. His reading skills are adequate, and his math skills are weak. He also has some problems relating appropriately to peers. His probable subsequent environment: working in a nearby community, living at home, and having a car.

the school years and for continuous opportunities for services throughout the adult years. The range of employment options for persons with disabilities includes (1) sheltered employment, (2) supported employment, (3) independent competitive employment in community settings. Although all these options are used as employment settings, employment in the community is a major vocational goal.

Sheltered Employment

Sheltered employment is the placement of individuals with mental retardation in work settings, usually set up as assembly-line workshops, in which individuals work on assigned contracts. Typically these contracts involve activities such as assembling items or putting packets together. The adults who work in sheltered workshops receive payment on a piecework basis; that is, they get paid for each task or product that is finished. This type of employment, which not so long ago was the primary work opportunity for individuals with moderate and severe disabilities, persists even in the face of the strong movement toward community-based employment and integration.

Supported Employment

Supported employment involves placing people in jobs that are located in community settings.

Supported employment is often used as a means of effecting the transition of individuals with disabilities into community employment settings. In supported work settings, people are placed in jobs that are either located in integrated settings or that facilitate social integration. The term *supported* refers to the training, supervision, and sometimes financial assistance that is provided to the individual and the employer in the work setting. Supported work is designed for individuals who traditionally have not found jobs in the community; therefore, comprehensive and long-term support may be necessary. Increasingly, supported work opportunities are initiated during high school so that students are placed in a job by the time they graduate or leave the secondary setting. The number of individuals involved in supported employment programs increased 34 percent between 1986 and 1995, although 30 percent of these people are not earning a minimum, competitive employment wage (Wehman, West, & Kregel, 1999). There are a number of different models for supported employment, including the mobile work crew, the enclave, and supported jobs (Kiernan & Stark, 1986).

The **mobile work crew** is a group of individuals with disabilities who have learned a specific trade or set of skills that can be applied in the community. Gardening and catering are two examples of the type of work mobile crews do. Often, the mobile work crew functions like any other business—advertising its services, traveling to jobs, and incorporating profits into salaries, equipment, and materials. Typically, the work crew is managed by a trainer or trainers who help the workers solicit jobs and manage finances and provide on-the-job assistance and instruction. Advantages of this model include the ability to select desired, competitive, and appropriate work; the potential for individuals to learn skills in management and independent contracting; and the ability to earn good wages. The mobile work crew also offers an avenue for supported employment in locations that have few businesses or work opportunities, such as in rural farming communities. A major disadvantage, however, is the fact that the crew continues to work as a segregated unit. All of the workers have disabilities, and although the work is done in the community, social integration may be limited to lunch and breaks during the workday. In addition, individuals in a mobile work crew receive continuous supervision and support, which does not facilitate eventual independent work.

A second supported employment option is the **enclave.** An enclave is a small group of individuals with disabilities who are placed in a work setting, usually within a large business or corporation. They receive on-the-job training and support from job coaches, schools, or social service agencies and from within the corporation itself. Training within an enclave may begin with an expected level of partial or limited skill performance; as individuals become more adept and receive more training, more work is required. The financial responsibility for paying individuals within an enclave will be gradually assumed by the employer as the employees become more competitive and independent. Although individuals working in an enclave are placed as a group, the workers do not necessarily work as a unit and may be scattered and integrated throughout the business. The enclave provides an opportunity for maximizing personnel resources, since one supervisor can provide support to a number of individuals, particularly when the employer also provides support personnel. In addition, the employee has the opportunity to earn a standard wage in a setting that facilitates physical and social integration.

The final supported employment model we will look at is the **individual supported job model.** This model involves one-to-one coaching and teaching of a single individual in a job setting. Supported jobs are likely to be used when the agency or school has a number of job coaches or support personnel, when only a few students or clients are placed at a given time, or when the individuals placed require limited or only occasional support. In an individual supported job model, the job coach provides on-site training and ongoing problem solving. Typically, the level of support will gradually diminish until only occasional visits are provided. Supported job models may lead to independent competitive employment as the need for support fades and the individual learns to perform effectively in the work setting. In addition to the obvious advantages of independent performance, regular wages, and constant opportunities for social integration and participation, this model also increases the probability that the individual may have some say in what type of job he or she gets. The role of choice in identifying an employment option cannot be underestimated in terms of maintaining motivation and performance; people who like their work are much more likely to do well.

Independent Competitive Employment

Given appropriate support, individuals with mild and moderate mental retardation can work successfully in the community.

Most students with mild mental retardation, and many with moderate mental retardation, will find independent competitive employment. Agencies such as vocational rehabilitation may be tapped, but often individuals seek and get jobs independently. Transitional programming can help students become equipped vocationally and socially to develop into productive and successful workers. In addition, factors such as gender, socioeconomic status, and general academic and living skills also seem to affect the probability of employment (Heal & Rusch, 1995). We do know, however, that many individuals with disabilities who find competitive employment independently work in low-paying jobs and are unsatisfied with their work (Edgar, 1988; Neel, Meadows, Levine, & Edgar, 1988). These people may be more likely to quit their jobs or to continue to depend on their families for housing or support. We hope that continued research on needed skills for adult employment, the requirements for transition planning at the secondary school level, and a wider recognition by persons with disabilities of the training and support services available to them will help to address these difficulties and result in more employment options and increased job satisfaction.

Residential Options

The movement from institutional to community living environments is called deinstitutionalization.

When today's adults with mental retardation were born, many of their parents were encouraged to place them in institutions as soon as their disabilities were diagnosed. These institutions seldom had educational programs and often simply provided custodial care for their residents. Over the last twenty years, however, three factors have contributed to the trend we now call **deinstitutionalization**—the movement from residential or institutional settings to community environments. First, the publication of books such as Blatt's *Christmas in Purgatory* (1966), which documented the abuses suffered by some residents of institutions, spotlighted those conditions for the general public. Second, a series of studies demonstrated the superior functional levels of persons with mental retardation who lived outside institutions (MacMillan, 1982). Third, the courts became involved in mandating alternatives to residential institutions. For example, in *Pennsylvania Association for Retarded Citizens v. Commonwealth of Pennsylvania* (1971), all children with mental retardation were determined to have the right to a free and appropriate public education.

As a result of these and other factors, a variety of community-based residential alternatives for people with mental retardation have been developed. Among them are **group homes,** in which several people with mental retardation live together, learning to care for themselves under the guidance of a trained supervisor. Another option is some form of apartment living involving small groups of people, again with support from trained supervisors. Sometimes people choosing to live in apartments may live alone or with a roommate with mental retardation. Supervisors might check to see that bills are being paid on time, that there is food in the refrigerator, or that the laundry is being done. Other times, the support person might just provide occasional transportation or help organize community-based activities.

Many adults with mild mental retardation support themselves and live in their own apartment or home. Preparation for community living, however, can be an important facet of the transition process. We have discussed the importance of teaching students the ways in which learned skills can be applied to real-life settings. Keeping a home, raising a family, and budgeting money are areas that can and should be addressed in school. An important part of the transition process is helping students with mild mental retardation achieve and maintain contacts with adult social service agencies that can provide assistance and information through adulthood. This can be particularly valuable in the areas of financial management, health care, employment counseling, and insurance.

Personal and Civil Rights

The battle for personal and civil rights for people with mental retardation is not yet over.

The history of educating individuals with mental retardation includes acts and philosophies that ignore personal and civil rights. Today, many legal and ethical dilemmas remain unresolved. The right to life and the right to education are issues still being addressed by advocates and the court system. (See Chapter 6 for further discussion.) Many adults with mental retardation also have to fight for access to fair housing, for the right to marry and have children, and for the opportunity to work in community settings.

It is difficult for most persons with mental retardation to wage an effective campaign for personal rights, since the mental competence of the individual is often determined to be unknown or insufficient and the parents or other legal surrogate must legally represent the individual. Often, the wishes of the parent and the individual may be different, resulting in decisions that are at odds with the individual's preferred outcomes. Another issue receiving a lot of attention today is the fact that the judicial system does not consider persons with mental retardation a protected class. This means that persons with mental retardation are eligible for, among other things, the death penalty. The apparent inequities in the legal system and the potential for abuse through representation suggest that advocacy is an important function for everyone interested in the fair treatment of *all* people.

Summary

- The AAMR definition of mental retardation includes three criteria: subaverage intellectual functioning, impairments in adaptive behavior, and manifestation during the developmental period.
- Mental retardation is usually classified as mild, moderate, severe, or profound. Approximately 1 percent of school-age students are identified as having mental retardation. Of these, 80 to 85 percent have mild mental retardation. The causes of retardation include both biological and environmental factors.
- Students with mental retardation may have trouble learning how to learn (metacognition), remembering, coming to and maintaining attention, and generalizing. Language development may be delayed, although most differences are quantitative rather than qualitative. Students may be smaller and more prone to health problems, although physical differences generally are not visible. Students may also exhibit inappropriate social behavior.
- Parents and siblings adjust their familial roles to accommodate a child with mental retardation. Siblings often spend more time on child care, though not at the expense of peer relationships.
- A functional curriculum emphasizes independent functioning, incorporating academic skills such as reading in a real-life context. Teaching strategies that can be used by regular or special educators include task analysis, the use of prompts, cooperative learning, and the use of concrete materials. Computers provide drill and practice, word processing, tutorials, and other instructional assistance.
- Transition programs are designed to help students achieve as much independence as possible through employment, living arrangements, and social relationships.

Key Terms

mental retardation
Stanford-Binet Intelligence Scale
Wechsler Intelligence Scale for Children, Third Edition (WISC-III)
adaptive behavior
AAMR Adaptive Behavior Scale
Vineland Adaptive Behavior Scales
skill transfer (generalization)
immature behavior

life-skills curriculum
functional academics
community-based instruction
task analysis
prompt
cooperative learning
transitional programming
self-determination
sheltered employment
supported employment
mobile work crew
enclave
individual supported job model
deinstitutionalization
group home

Multimedia Resources

ARC National Headquarters, 500 East Border, Suite 300, Arlington, TX 76010; (817) 261-6003. Information about programs and national policies affecting individuals with mental retardation and the ARC newsletter can be obtained from ARC Headquarters.

The Capitol Connection Policy Newsletter. Published by the Division on Career Development and Transition, The Council for Exceptional Children, 1920 Association Drive, Reston, VA 20191. This newsletter addresses interdisciplinary policy and practice in career preparation and transition to postsecondary education, employment, and responsible citizenship for special learners.

CAST (Center for Applied Special Technology), 39 Cross Street, Peabody, MA 01960, cast@cast.org. This center provides information on assistive technology resources and educational applications.

Cronin, M.G., and J.R. Patton, *Live Skills Instruction for All Students with Special Needs: A Practical Guide for Integrating Real-Life Content into Curriculum* (Austin, TX: Pro-Ed, 1993).

Down Syndrome News. Newsletter of the National Down Syndrome Congress; (800) 232-6372. This newsletter can serve as a source of information and support for professionals, parents, siblings, and individuals with Down syndrome.

Salvia, John, and James E. Ysseldyke. *Assessment*, 8th ed. (Boston, MA: Houghton Mifflin, 2001). An overview of a variety of assessment tools. Includes in-depth discussion of bias in assessment.

Siblings for Significant Change (support group), 105 East 22nd Street, Room 710, New York, NY 10010; (212) 420-0776. This organization presents strategies and support contacts for brothers and sisters of individuals with disabilities.

Sibling Information Network Newsletter. A. J. Pappenikou Center on Special Education and Rehabilitation, University of Connecticut, 249 Glenbrook Road, Box U-64, Storrs, CT 06269.

What You Can Do

1. Visit your local high school and make an appointment with a job coach for individuals with mental retardation. Try to arrange an observation of a community-based job training session. Observe the specific instructional strategies used by the job coach, the methods of job evaluation, and the social interaction between the trainee and his or her colleagues.

2. Send out a survey to local business people to find out their needs and attitudes regarding disabilities. Would they want to hire a person with a dis-

ability? For what type of job? What would be their expectations? Support? Pay? Security?

3. Visit a group home and talk with its residents and staff. Find out what type of contact residents have with the community (for example, shopping in local stores, riding public transportation). Discuss their views on the value of community living.

4. Observe either a secondary or elementary classroom in a local school. Note the teaching strategies and materials used in the classroom. What adaptations might the teacher have to make to accommodate and support a student with mild or moderate mental retardation? Talk with the teacher to see what types of instructional adjustments he or she may have made in the past.

Children with Severe Disabilities

6

STUDENTS WITH severe disabilities can benefit greatly from an educational program that prepares them for participation in the community. In this chapter, we introduce educational strategies designed to maximize these students' potential, and we raise questions about the protection of their rights. As you read, think about the following questions:

How has normalization affected the educational philosophies and options available to students with severe disabilities?

Why are physical and social integration both necessary for full inclusion, and how do they influence one another?

How does a teacher identify skills to be included in the life-skills curriculum?

Commonalities: What key ethical issues are faced by parents, teachers, and others who work with students with severe disabilities?

Collaboration: How can the educational team prepare a transition plan that will enable the student with severe disabilities to move to an integrated setting?

Can Do: What opportunities do technological aids provide to students with severe disabilities?

The outlook and opportunities for individuals with severe and profound disabilities are now greater than many parents and professionals ever anticipated. Someone with severe mental retardation may be living in a home down the street from you or working in your neighborhood grocery store. Unfortunately, however, many of us are not afforded, nor do we seek, the opportunity to interact in a meaningful way with people who have severe disabilities. Although

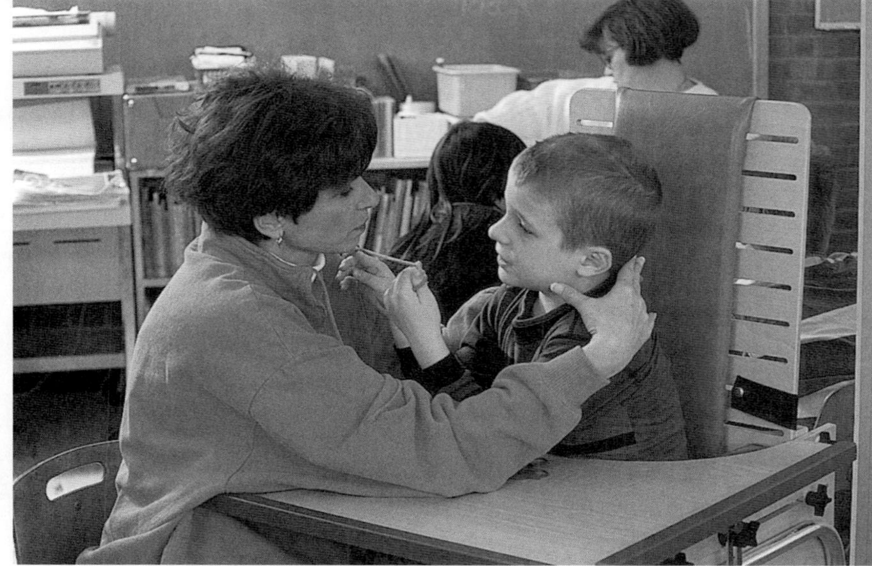

Communication, in all its forms, is the basis of all teaching and learning. (Ellen Senisi/The Image Works, Inc.)

programs that prepare persons with severe disabilities to work, live, or interact with other members of the community are steadily increasing in both quantity and quality, there are still not enough of them. Through our selection of programs, curricula, and activities, we can promote and develop attitudes and procedures for facilitating knowledge, acceptance, and interaction among all individuals, including those who have severe disabilities.

Definitions and Terms

Individuals who are identified as having severe disabilities may display a variety of primary disabilities. In this section, we will look briefly at the definition of severe disabilities as well as at definitions of some disability areas that are included in the broader term.

Severe Disabilities

Individuals with severe disabilities require extensive support in major life activities.

According to the Association for Persons with Severe Handicaps (TASH), individuals with **severe disabilities** "require extensive ongoing support in more than one major life activity in order to participate in integrated community settings and to enjoy a quality of life that is available to citizens with fewer or no disabilities. Support may be required for life activities such as mobility, communication, self-care, and learning as necessary for independent living, employment, and self-sufficiency" (1989, p. 30). Although any of the disabilities we discuss in this text can range in intensity from mild to severe (for example, learning disabilities, behavioral disorders), the term *severe disabilities* is used in this chapter to refer primarily to individuals who have severe or profound mental retardation. The life supports and educational programs required by these individuals are typically more extensive than those required by individuals with other types of disabilities.

Severe and Profound Mental Retardation

The federal definition of **severe mental retardation** includes an IQ of less than 40 and the manifestation of deficits in adaptive behavior, with both areas of deficit originating during the developmental period. **Profound mental retardation** varies only in the range of the IQ score, which is 20 and below. It is sometimes very difficult to determine the extent of mental retardation in an infant. This is particularly true when the child also has severe health or sensory impairments. Thus the extent of mental retardation often cannot be determined until the child is much older. Children thought to have severe or profound levels of mental retardation are often given the label developmentally disabled (Gentry & Olson, 1985).

Causes

There are numerous causes for severe and profound mental retardation, including genetic syndromes, physical trauma, and disease. Most disabilities considered to be severe or profound are the result of similar causes, including those presented in Chapter 5. Some children are born with a cluster of disabilities, one of which is severe mental retardation.

Genetic syndromes, which result in a number of common physical, behavioral, and intellectual characteristics, include Down syndrome, Klinefelter's syndrome, Turner's syndrome, fragile X syndrome, and Tay-Sachs disease. The probability of having a child with some of these conditions can be determined through genetic counseling. Some, such as Down syndrome, can be detected in utero.

Physical trauma to the head, caused by accidents or child abuse, can result in severe mental retardation. Medical abnormalities, such as brain tumors, and diseases, such as meningitis can also cause severe disabilities.

In most cases, the ways we teach students with severe disabilities will be the same regardless of the cause. However, knowing the cause of a disability can be important; for example, certain physical disabilities or health concerns are associated with specific syndromes, such as Down syndrome and cerebral palsy. As a teacher, you should become familiar with the characteristics of these conditions to avoid exposing your students to injury or health risks. Sometimes knowing the cause of severe disabilities can help teachers know what to expect and to be better prepared for instruction (Hodapp & Fidler, 1999). For example, if we know that children with some syndromes are likely to show extreme self-abusive behavior, we can be better prepared both emotionally and instructionally to deal with these difficult circumstances.

Neither social and economic status nor the general intellectual ability of the parents seem to be related to the incidence of severe or profound mental retardation, which is estimated to be .7 percent, or 7 per 1,000 births. Although medical technology has enabled many individuals with severe disabilities to live much longer than in previous years, infants born with severe and profound mental retardation have three times the mortality rate of nondisabled infants (Landesman-Dwyer & Butterfield, 1983).

Effects on the Developing Child

If you ask parents, siblings, and teachers of individuals with severe disabilities what the effects of those disabilities have been on the children themselves, you will get a wide range of answers. It is sometimes difficult to describe the effects

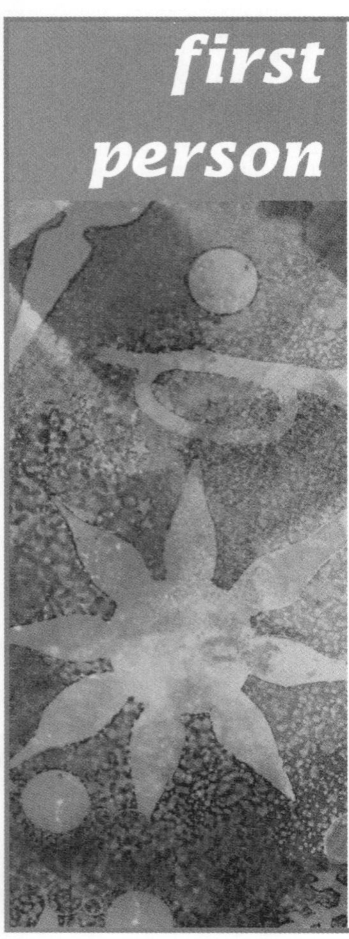

It is said that beauty is in the eye of the beholder. In Carolyn's eyes, everything is beautiful. She is always so happy that beauty seems to generate into the hearts of everyone around her.

Carolyn Dadd, 15, has moyamoya disease. She cannot walk, talk or feed herself, and she requires total care. She knows the people around her, though. I only wish more people could realize how capable she is.

I am 19 years old, and I have been Carolyn's sitter for the past seven years. I first met Carolyn when I was 12 and she was 9. I had never seen anyone quite like her. She was very small then, barely 60 pounds. Her smile was deep as if it sank back into her soul. When we met she raised her hand in a gentle motion to touch my face and laughed as if there was a joke beween us. Soon I found myself laughing, too. That day started our friendship—one that I will cherish the rest of my life. It was obvious that Carolyn was different from anyone I had ever met, and that is exactly what I liked about her.

Jessica Morgan

Moyamoya disease is a progressive disease that affects the blood vessels in the brain. It is characterized by narrowing and/or closing of the carotid artery. This lack of blood may cause paralysis of the feet, legs or upper extremities. Headaches, various vision problems, mental retardation, and psychiatric problems may also occur.

Source: "Good Things Come in Small Packages" by Jessica Morgan, *Exceptional Parent*, July, 2000.

of severe disabilities when you are personally involved. You keep thinking of the *person* with the disabilities—the person is wonderful and the interaction is rewarding even when the disabilities are very challenging and sometimes overwhelming.

Cognitive Development

The specific effects of mental retardation on cognitive development, which are discussed in detail in Chapter 5, include problems in such areas as selective attention, maintaining attention, short-term memory, metacognitive skills, and the maintenance, transfer, and generalization of skills. These problems may exist to an even greater degree in persons with severe and profound mental disabilities. Most people with severe or profound mental retardation experience disabilities across all cognitive skill areas.

The effects of severe disabilities on cognitive development are related partially to the learning experiences the person has throughout life, particularly in the early years. The frequent coexistence of physical or health impairments with severe cognitive disabilities often results in a reduction in the normal environmental interactions considered instrumental in the development of cognitive abilities. For example, an infant without severe disabilities, while lying in his crib, may accidentally hit the side of the crib with his hand and hear the noise it makes. After this happens a few times, the child will make the connection between his hand movement and the noise of it against the crib. This is called an understanding of cause and effect. The realization that something you do can have predictable consequences is an important tool for learning to control and interact with the environment. Another example, recognized immediately by parents and infants, is the connection between crying and parental attention. The child may begin to hit his hand against the crib for the purpose of making the noise or cry in order to be held. He intentionally does something to get a specific result—attention from a parent. This purposeful behavior is referred to as a *means-end relationship*. The development of an understanding of cause and effect and of means-end relationships is critical for children to begin to explore their environments actively and with purpose; these skills are also considered important in language development (Iacono & Miller, 1989).

Understanding cause and effect and means-ends relationships is critical for most cognitive skills.

The child with severe or profound disabilities may experience difficulty learning these early skills in the typical way. A child with severe physical disabilities or with very delayed motor development may not be aware that it is her hand that is hitting the side of the crib—or she may not have sufficient motor control to direct it to happen again. A child with severe mental retardation may be unable to understand that her mother appears two or three minutes after she has started crying. As a result, the child may have difficulty making a connection between the things she does and the results of these actions or behaviors. The infant, therefore, may not acquire these important behaviors unassisted and may not attempt to interact with the world around her. The child simply may not know that what she does makes any difference.

Physical Development and Health

Children with severe and profound mental retardation are usually much below average in physical size (Landesman-Dwyer & Butterfield, 1983) and experience a wide range of physical and health-related difficulties. As we have mentioned, mental retardation of this degree of severity is typically accompanied by other disabilities.

Infants born with severe and profound mental retardation often experience significant delays in physical development. Because of this delay, the infant may have very limited physical movement at the beginning of life.

Sometimes physical disabilities and health risks are associated with the specific syndrome or condition responsible for the retardation. Children with Down syndrome, for example, often require heart surgery at a very young age because of congenital heart defects, and they are at risk for respiratory problems. Children with severe mental retardation and cerebral palsy may have varying degrees of motor impairment; sometimes the physical disabilities may affect mobility, speech, and regulated motor activity. A number of children will be prone to a seizure disorder such as epilepsy, although most types of seizures can be controlled or reduced by appropriate medication. Other syndromes or conditions may be degenerative in nature: the conditions will worsen over time, and the child's health will become progressively worse, until death occurs. An example we have already mentioned is Tay-Sachs disease.

Children with severe and profound mental retardation often experience health-related difficulties and severe delays in physical development.

In some instances, the physical development of the child with severe or profound mental retardation is compromised as a side effect of extreme developmental delay. Intrusive procedures may be required on a regular basis to maintain comfort and sustain life. For example, a child who must be catheterized daily or fed through a stomach tube is exposed to more opportunities for infection.

A number of children with profound mental retardation may not be independently mobile and thus may not use their limbs with any regularity. This can result in atrophy of the muscles. Other individuals may have mobility, but also may require guidance and instruction to participate in physical activity of either a therapeutic or recreational nature. Therapeutic physical activity, including physical therapy, can increase strength and flexibility and prevent some health problems (Green & Reid, 1999). Physical activities not only have obvious health benefits but also can serve an important recreational function and contribute to independent movement and psychological well-being (Modell & Cox, 1999).

Language Development and Communication

Many people with severe or profound disabilities can use a verbal or nonverbal communication system.

Severe and profound disabilities can have extensive effects on an individual's language development and communicative abilities. Some people with severe or profound retardation will have limited spontaneous oral language, others will have nonfunctional oral language, and some, no oral language at all. The presence or lack of spontaneous oral language does not, however, imply that no communication system can be taught. Research suggests that by far the most common form of expressive communication used by children with severe disabilities is direct behavior, such as dragging adults to the desired place or object, getting the desired object, or throwing away an undesired object (Harvey & Sall, 1999). Once again we see the strong and obvious relationship between behavior and communication. New communication skills, whether they are verbal or nonverbal, must be as efficient and as easy to use as the behaviors students are currently using. In other words, the communication must be **functional communication**—easy to use and easily understandable (Ostrosky, Drasgow, & Halle, 1999). Table 6.1 presents a set of guidelines for developing functional communication skills for individuals with severe disabilities.

Nonverbal communication systems include sign language and language boards or communication boards. On communication boards, words or symbols that represent possible needs and requests are placed on a lap board, and the person communicates by indicating the appropriate word or picture. Many people with severe and profound mental retardation do find ways of communicating their wishes and controlling their environment by using nonverbal means. Regardless of the method of communication selected, critical factors for effective communication include the preparation and interest of communication partners and an environment that supports individual interaction and communication (Butterfield & Arthur, 1995).

Social Behaviors and Emotional Development

By definition, students with severe and profound mental retardation will have deficits in adaptive behavior. The extent to which appropriate adaptive behaviors, such as self-help skills and general social skills, are acquired will vary according to the severity of the disability, the type and breadth of educational programming, and the environment in which the person lives, works, or goes to school. For example, positive changes in different areas of adaptive behavior have been found when persons with mental retardation live in group homes

Table 6.1 Guidelines for Developing Functional Communication Systems

1. **Take advantage of the existing communication skills of students with severe disabilities.**
   - Observe the communication strategies students already use to communicate. Ask yourself: What forms of communication does this student consistently and intentionally use to communicate? Observe these forms across settings, routines, and activities.
   - Build on existing types of communicative behavior by teaching socially desirable and functionally equivalent forms of behavior that are more easily understood by others.
2. **Select functional communication targets and identify powerful teaching opportunities.**
   - When selecting communication targets, ask yourself: Will learning this behavior help the student become more independent?
   - Select potential teaching opportunities that will likely result in high levels of motivation by capitalizing on current student-initiated communicative occasions.
3. **Facilitate the widespread use of the new forms of behavior.**
   - Identify the situations in which students currently use their existing communication forms (e.g., generalized use of the existing form).
   - Determine the consequences that might be supporting this generalization.
   - Teach the new communication form in all situations where the student currently uses the existing form. Careful attention to, and reflection on, one's own behavior and prudent observation of student behavior are necessary.
4. **Ensure maintenance of the new behavior.**
   - When replacing existing forms of communicative behavior, take care to ensure that the new form requires less physical effort, and produces reinforcement more rapidly and more frequently than the old one.

Source: Ostrosky, M. M., Drasgow, E., & Halle, J. W. (1999). "How can I help you get what you want?", *Teaching Exceptional Children, 31* (4), 58.

rather than institutional settings and work in competitive employment versus sheltered workshops (Inge et al., 1988; Sullivan, Vitello, & Foster, 1988).

Because the labels *severe mental retardation* and *profound mental retardation* can encompass a wide range of ability and performance levels, it is difficult to characterize "typical" social behavior. For a few persons, social development may be very limited, and target skills may include establishing eye contact or acknowledging someone's presence. Some individuals will have inappropriate behaviors, and interventions may then focus on reducing acting-out or tantrum-like behaviors. For others, social development goals may include appropriate social interaction in a community work setting. Often, a drawback to successful social interaction is the lack of a common communication system. Storey and Provost (1996) found that the use of communication books (essentially picture books) increased the amount of social interaction as well as interpersonal communication between individuals with severe disabilities and their nondisabled coworkers in a community work setting. Problems in communicative ability are also related to the presence of inappropriate or aberrant behavior (Sigafoos, 2000). Children with severe levels of aberrant behavior, such as self-injury, displayed fewer communication skills.

Although there is very little descriptive research available on the emotional development of persons with severe or profound mental disabilities, we know that all people experience an array of emotions. In some instances, we must learn to recognize the indicators of basic human emotions such as love, trust, fear, and happiness. More likely, we can observe emotional development and expression easily. The management or appropriate demonstration of emotions is an important aspect of adaptive behavior. The development and nurturing of many emotions rests with the significant others in the person's life, including the family.

Effects on the Family

In this section, we will look at the joys and struggles of families of children with severe disabilities. We will also discuss the multiple roles that parents of children with severe disabilities must play.

Family Attitudes and Reactions

Most children with severe or profound mental retardation are diagnosed at birth.

Because most children with severe or profound mental retardation are diagnosed at birth, families must immediately confront the prospect of rearing a child with a severe disability (see the accompanying box, "A Family Perspective"). As you might expect, reactions to this diagnosis and the onslaught of ensuing emotions vary greatly. Parents have many questions about what the future holds for them and their other children: How can I care for this child? What will happen to her when I'm no longer around? How will my other children react to their brother? Some of these questions will be answered in time, some can be answered through education, and some can never be answered.

You may see many differences in the lives of families that include an individual with severe disabilities. It is interesting to note, however, that mothers of youngsters with severe disabilities, like all mothers, hope and expect that their children will be able to achieve independence (Lehmann & Baker, 1995). Although there are more services than ever before to assist families, many parents are concerned about the lack of community support and related services available to them—services that are necessary for community inclusion and maximum independence for their child (Turnbull & Ruef, 1997). Parents of children with severe disabilities, especially those who have complex medical needs, are particularly vulnerable to stress. Factors such as availability of services, financial issues, care of other children in the family, and continuing medical care are weighed by parents as they try to make appropriate and life-altering decisions about caring for their child (Bruns, 2000).

Parents, of course, are not the only family members affected by the presence of a child with severe disabilities. Brothers and sisters will have their own reactions and ways of dealing with them. Reactions can range from resentment to extreme protectiveness; probably the whole spectrum of emotions will be experienced at some point during the sibling's lifetime. Although it is not unusual for siblings of children with mental retardation to experience high levels of

~ A Family Perspective

In the following excerpt from her book *A Difference in the Family,* Helen Featherstone (1980) describes her reactions to the discovery that her child had severe disabilities:

> When Jody was fifteen days old we learned that he was blind. We wept for the experiences he would miss—the changing colors of a New England autumn, the splendor of a clear night sky, the faces of the people he would love. Yet we realized how much remained—if he were "only" blind. Most of the activities that gave our lives meaning and importance would still be within his reach. He could read, write, teach, play, and enjoy the fellowship of friends. He could talk and think, give comfort and, in time, go about his own life independently, perhaps with some special understanding born of his disability. Anyway, that is what we hoped. The idea of blindness made us sad. It led us to examine our values: it did not shatter them. However, as the months went by, we learned that Jody was not "only" blind. He had cerebral palsy; he was probably severely retarded. During the first eighteen months of his life he cried almost continually from the pain that no one could diagnose or relieve. His days and nights were passed in misery; his future looked bleak and limited. Hardly a day passed without our asking ourselves whether his life was worth living. Each of us, separately and together, wished for an end to his ordeal: a peaceful, painless death.
>
> He did not die. He was remarkably tough. Unexpectedly, after the doctor removed an infected shunt, his pain went. He cried less during the day and slept longer at night. He smiled more often, even laughed. Liberated from his inner torments, he responded to us. We began to like him. He gave more: his smiles, his laughter, his delighted shrieks. He asked less. He still needed a lot of special care, but we no longer performed our family routines with one hand while patting a wretched baby with the other. Each of us began to feel that Jody's life was worth living, and that he made his own special contribution to the family.

Source: Helen Featherstone, *A Difference in the Family: Life with a Disabled Child* (New York: Basic Books, 1980), pp. 222–223.

stress, many children develop very close relationships with each other (Lindsey & Stewart, 1989).

Family Roles in Education

The family of an individual with severe or profound disabilities can play an active role in educational programming from the very beginning. The passage of P.L. 99-457 in 1986 provided the legislative impetus needed for the establishment of federal programs for infants and young children with disabilities and their families (Campbell, Bellamy, & Bishop, 1988). The importance of early intervention and family responsiveness in the development of children with severe and profound mental retardation, as well as any type of disability, has been recognized. Parents who learn how to encourage language or communication or who are trained to provide at-home occupational therapy will not only feel more competent in dealing with their child, they will be helping that child to build an important and perhaps critical learning foundation. Educators must incorporate parents' goals and priorities, particularly in areas such as communication, into curriculum content and educational procedures (Stephenson & Dowrick, 2000).

Early intervention programs provide crucial services for children with severe disabilities and their families.

Not everyone agrees with the present focus on the provision of early service in the home environment. Krauss (1990), for example, suggests that some families may resent the fact that they must be evaluated before their child can receive services and may feel that their privacy is being threatened. Although you might think that most families would not feel this way, if you work with parents and families of infants or young children, it may be an important consideration to keep in mind.

In Classrooms and Other Educational Settings

A term like *profound mental retardation* provides little information on how to understand or educate persons with extensive mental disabilities (Bricker & Filler, 1985). Explaining the term to educators by saying it means an IQ of 20 or below simply is an inadequate description of a population and does not address the educational or health-related issues of individual children. It is important to visit a student's classroom or to meet with him or her to learn who the child is and what his or her educational needs are. When you meet a student or enter a class of individuals with severe disabilities, the first things that attract your attention are the differences. Puréed food, toilet training for people of all ages, unusual sounds, and strange equipment all stand out. When you meet a child, you may feel a sense of sadness because of his disabilities and what you may perceive as his limited possibilities for normal life experiences. All of the implications of severe or profound mental retardation seem to be foremost in your mind as you get to know the child. Then an amazing thing happens as you spend time with him. In a very short time, the things that come to mind are not the physical or cognitive limitations or the behavioral characteristics. Instead, you think of the skills the child has learned to perform, the look in his or her eyes when excited, the way the child responds to your voice, and the wealth of things the child will learn in the years to come. In short, you focus on *all* of the characteristics of the individual rather than only on the differences or the disabilities.

The future of children with severe disabilities will depend in part on the vision and commitment of their families, their teachers, and their peers—of people like you. The extent to which children with severe and profound levels of mental retardation will become adults who are accepted, valued, and integrated into the mainstream of society is your responsibility as well as theirs.

New educational philosophies and higher expectations have changed educational programming for people with severe and profound mental retardation.

The nature and content of educational programming for individuals with severe and profound levels of mental retardation have changed significantly in recent years. Most of the changes have come about because of new or different educational philosophies and greater expectations and goals for children, adolescents, and adults with severe disabilities. Strategies for teaching individuals with disabilities now reflect a clear behavioral philosophy and focus on the analysis of behavior. Specific interventions include the task analysis and prompt systems introduced in Chapter 5. Another important paradigm shift in recent years is toward empowerment (Polloway, Smith, Patton, & Smith, 1996). Person-centered planning, which allows individuals with severe disabilities to have an important role in decisions regarding their lives, is the underlying component of many educational programs (Reid, Everson, & Green, 1999).

Although there has been some disagreement among professionals about the rate or extent of some of the changes we will be discussing, we now recognize the importance and need for programs that emphasize normalization, social and physical inclusion, and life-skills curricula. Each of these areas will be discussed separately. As you will see, however, they are closely interrelated and together represent a continuing movement toward change for individuals with severe disabilities.

Normalization

One of the forces behind educational change for individuals with all levels of mental retardation is the movement toward normalization. The term **normalization,** or *social role valorization*, refers to an emphasis on conventional or normal behavior and attitudes in all aspects of education, socialization, and other life experiences (Wolfensberger, 1977, 1983). In other words, the focus of normalization is that all people should lead lives that are as normal as possible. For persons with mental retardation, this movement has great implications. Wolfensberger (1977) defines two dimensions of normalization: (a) direct contact or interaction with individuals and (b) the way an individual is described to others.

The focus of normalization is that all people should lead lives that are as normal as possible.

The first dimension involves the way we treat people with mental retardation and the things we decide to teach and encourage. It is important, for example, to consider a person's age and the usual criteria for normal behavior when we are interacting with someone or deciding what types of behaviors, skills, or recreational activities we will be teaching or doing. It may be easy and fast to feed a 10-year-old with severe disabilities, but it is not age-appropriate, and

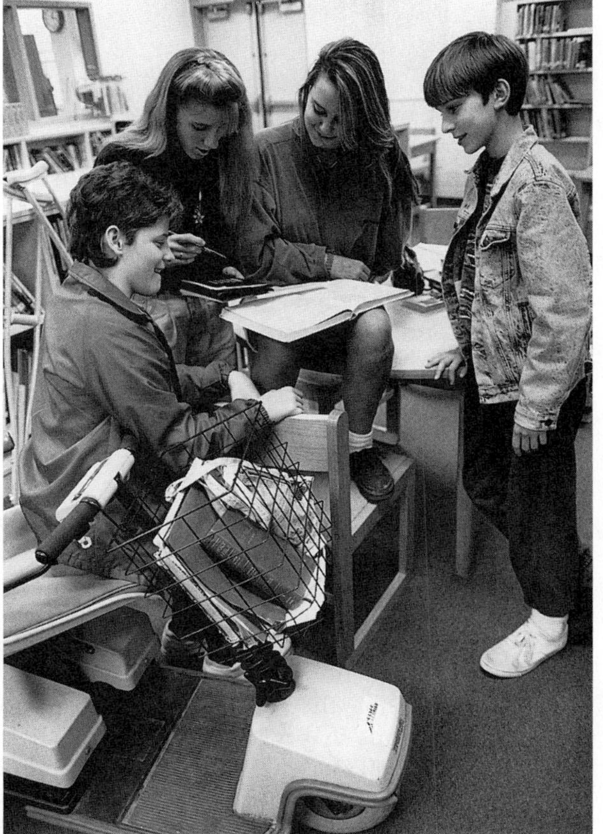

Environmental modifications can facilitate the physical and social integration of students with disabilities into community settings. (© Joel Gordon)

therefore, if it is at all possible, we should choose to implement a self-feeding program so that the child not only will become more independent but also will be expected to perform some of the skills of other children his or her age.

Sometimes it may be beyond a person's physical or cognitive abilities to perform some self-care skills (eating, toileting, dressing) or other types of tasks with complete independence. In these instances, we encourage **partial participation:** we enable the student to perform the parts of the skill or task that are within his or her ability range (Snell, 1988).

The second dimension of normalization refers to the way we portray or present persons with mental retardation to others. This dimension includes the way we may refer to a student in our class, the words or phrases we include in writing about or describing persons with mental retardation, and the way we select clothing or hairstyles for our children or clients. The types of housing or educational environments in which we place persons with disabilities and the extent to which legislation protects and enforces basic human rights reflect our society's perceptions of individuals with disabilities. Persons with mental retardation should live in environments and structures that approximate normal living arrangements and that include a small group of friends, family, or caretakers (Taylor, Racino, & Walker, 1992).

In general, the move toward a normalized existence for individuals with severe and profound mental retardation depends on the increased willingness of the public to recognize and accept the humanity, value, and contributions of persons with mental retardation. Normalization has served as a foundation for many of the major social as well as educational changes that we have observed in the area of mental retardation over the past few decades.

Inclusion

One term you will hear or see repeatedly in any educational program description or curriculum for students with severe mental retardation is *inclusion*, the incorporation of all individuals into the mainstream of society. There are several reasons why inclusion has become an important facet of instructional programming for individuals with mental retardation. First, it is proposed that individuals are more likely to develop functional patterns of behavior and higher levels of functioning if they have the opportunity to interact with people without disabilities. Second, it is considered to be every individual's right to access the opportunities and facilities that the community has to offer to the greatest extent possible. Third, an emphasis on inclusion will provide many individuals with the direct training and experiences they will need in order to achieve full or partial independence (Stainback, Stainback, & Ayres, 1996; Williams, Vogelsberg, & Schutz, 1985).

People with severe mental retardation may develop higher levels of functioning and independence when they interact with people without disabilities.

Inclusion also involves the acceptance of individuals with mental retardation by the community. Of course, acceptance and social interaction cannot be dictated, but they can be developed through encouragement, preparation, and the provision of opportunities for interaction (Shutz, Williams, Iverson, & Duncan, 1984). Obviously, it is easier to develop friendships and good working relationships with people who are living and working in the same environment as you are. It is also possible that early physical integration will encourage the development of friendships that may persist during the school years. Interestingly, research suggests that students with severe disabilities who are included in general education classrooms are more likely to be accepted by nondisabled peers than students with mild disabilities. Some research, however, suggests that these higher ratings of acceptance for students with severe disabilities are related to nurturing attitudes rather than true friendship behaviors (Cook & Semmel, 1999).

A key issue in inclusion is the extent to which people with severe mental retardation should be integrated into the school or community. Many professionals suggest that total inclusion should be the goal. An example of total inclusion in the public school setting would be the placement of students with severe disabilities in regular classes in order to promote socialization experiences. In many full inclusion programs, teachers attempt to adapt the general education content for the student with severe disabilities (Siegel-Causey, McMorris, McGowen, & Sands-Buss, 1998). Table 6.2 is an example of several eighth-grade science curriculum goals for a student with severe cognitive disabilities. Other professionals feel that inclusion to this extent may result in a reduced amount of needed educational programming for the students and that social integration can best be achieved in other settings. In addition, some parents are concerned about their child's safety and emotional well-being in integrated environments and prefer, at least initially, less risky program options (Stetson, 1984).

The attitudes of the nondisabled persons in the community, school, or work setting are critical to successful inclusion. Some educational programs have been developed to give nondisabled persons some knowledge about individuals with disabilities, and many teachers do take the time to discuss individual differences and specific disabilities with their classes.

Curriculum

■ ***The Functional Curriculum*** Most of the curricula currently used in instructional programs for individuals with severe and profound disabilities stress instruction in life skills and are designed to maximize independent functioning. A curriculum that emphasizes preparation for life and that includes skills that will be used by the student in home, school, or work environments is called a **functional curriculum.** A functional curriculum includes instruction in all of the important areas, or domains, of adult life: domestic, community, recreation and leisure, and vocational. All types of instruction, including training in self-help skills and communication skills, mobility training, physical therapy, and occupational therapy, are integrated so that they complement one another and focus on functional activities rather than isolated practice tasks (Snell & Drake, 1994). Each student must be taught the behaviors or tasks that are required in his or her home, work, or recreational setting (see the accompanying box, "Examples of Functional Curriculum Domains").

Instruction in language is an important part of the functional curriculum for most persons with severe or profound mental retardation. This is especially true for individuals who will be going out to work or who are living in community settings. Caro and Snell (1989) have identified the following three major goals of programs designed to teach language or communication to persons with severe disabilities: (1) to increase the frequency of communicative behavior, (2) to enlarge the student's repertoire of communicative functions, and (3) to promote the spontaneous and generalized use of communication skills in everyday life. Instructional programs in language and communication must focus on functional communication, as we have already mentioned. Communication interventions should occur in natural environments and focus on purposeful communication (Caro & Snell, 1989; Reichle & Keogh, 1986).

The technique that is frequently used to identify skills for instruction is called an **environmental inventory,** or **environmental analysis** (Nietupski &

Table 6.2 Inclusion Curriculum Goals for a Student with Severe Disabilities

Cory's Weather Station Activity

Curricular Goal: Increase understanding of weather instruments and meteorological concepts.

Assignments	Adaptations by Type and Description	Annual Goals	Monitoring	Outcomes
Check daily temperature readings, the type of cloud cover, precipitation, wind speed, humidity level, and barometric pressure.	*Teacher Support*—a behavior support plan used to increase participation was implemented by the teachers jointly. *Size*—reduced the number of steps required from 6 to 3 (check daily temperature readings, the type of cloud cover, precipitation).	Maintain socially acceptable behavior and read to get information.	Behavior rated on a monitoring card at the end of the class.	Participation increased to 100% and an unanticipated outcome that involved the improvement of his skills in dressing appropriately for the weather.
Record weather conditions on work sheets.	*Difficulty*—work sheets required approximated readings (e.g., estimate temperature to nearest 10-degree mark). *Input*—pictorial cues were provided on work sheets (e.g., picture of cloud conditions). *Output*—eliminated need to spell (e.g., color in thermometer to correct degree point).	Describe events and read to follow instructions.	Portfolio of work sheets and log of Cory's performance.	Increased ability to read and record thermometer numbers within 5 degrees and eliminated need for assistance to complete the work sheet.
Report readings to the class.	*Difficulty*—specific questions were asked that could be answered with short phrases. *Peer Supports*—modeling and input from peers were encouraged to promote greater participation.	Sustain communication and describe events.	Log of Cory's performance.	Increased answers from single words to short phrases, and increased use of adjectives, pronouns, and adverbs.
Record weather journal entries.	*Alternative Activity* (adapted content)—assigned to make a call to the national Weather Bureau to obtain their forecast and share this information verbally with the class.	Use telephone and describe events.	Log of Cory's performance and forecast report.	Became independent in dialing written phone numbers without assistance and improved speech.

Source: Siegel-Causey, E., McMorris, C., McGowen, S., & Sands-Buss, S. (1998). "In Junior High you take Earth Science: Including a student with severe disabilities into an academic class," *Teaching Exceptional Children, 31* (1), 71.

Examples of Functional Curriculum Domains

Domestic

Areas or subdomains: kitchen, bathroom, laundry room, bedroom

Community

Areas or subdomains: grocery store, bank, post office, restaurants, school

Recreation/Leisure

Areas or subdomains: park, YMCA, movie theater, bowling alley, fishing pond

Vocational

Areas or subdomains: specific job sites (hotel, restaurant, landscape)

Skill areas to be addressed across all domains: communication, transportation, social skills, attire, behavioral expectations, word/sign/symbol recognition, area-specific skills (for example, using the stove, depositing money, bowling, greeting customers), decision-making skills

Hamre-Nietupski, 1987). An environmental inventory involves a visit to the settings in which the student has to function. The environment might be a group home, the cafeteria in an elementary school, the local park, or the neighborhood bus station. A list is made of the specific skills needed by the average person to be successful in that environment. Then the skills of the individual student are compared to the needed skills, and specific behaviors or tasks are targeted for instruction. By using this procedure, the curriculum truly prepares the student to be successful in current or future life situations and channels valuable teaching time into meaningful instruction.

■ ***Community-Based Instruction*** One way that integration is incorporated into educational plans is through community-based instruction, which, as you learned in Chapter 5, involves actually conducting learning experiences in community settings. Students who are able to travel in the community will, for example, receive training on how to walk to their home or work site or how to take a bus. Instruction will take place on the very sidewalks or bus lines that the student will be using to travel. Community-based instruction provides students with direct training in skills they need to be integrated into society and also allows them to experience integration during the instructional process (Voeltz, 1984). The accompanying box, "A Closer Look: Can Do: Scope and Sequence Chart for General Community Functioning," reflects the integration of community-based instruction in curriculum planning.

Integration is a natural outcome of community-based instruction.

Technology

Technological advances in the areas of communication and cognitive development have contributed significantly to the quality of life of individuals with severe and profound levels of mental retardation. Technology has opened many avenues of communication not previously available to people with severe physical as well as cognitive disabilities. A description of these advances in communication is provided in Chapter 12. In this chapter, we will discuss the role of technology in the cognitive development of individuals, particularly infants. A few landmark studies have provided us with an increased awareness of the

A closer look

Can Do: Scope and Sequence Chart for General Community Functioning

Goal areas	Age and grade levels: Elementary school: Kindergarten (age 5)	Primary grades (ages 6–8)	Intermediate grades (ages 9–11)	Middle school (ages 12–14)	High school (ages 15–18)	Transition (ages 19–21)
Travel	Walk or ride bus to and from school Walk to and from school bus and to point in school (classroom, office) Cross street: stop at curb	Walk or ride bus to and from school Walk to and from school bus and to point in school (classroom, cafeteria, office, music room) Cross street: familiar, low-traffic intersections	Walk, ride bus, or ride bike to and from school Walk to various destinations in school and in the community (neighborhood grocery store, mailbox) Cross streets safely	Walk, ride bus, or ride bike to and from school Walk to various destinations in school and in the community (store, restaurant, job site) Cross streets safely Use public bus/subway for general transportation	Walk, ride bus, or ride bike to and from school Walk to various destinations in school and in the community (store, restaurant, job site) Cross streets safely Use public bus/subway for general transportation	Walk, ride bus, or ride bike to and from home and community sites Walk to various destinations Cross streets safely Use public bus/subway for general transportation
Community safety			Problem-solve if lost in new places Use caution with strangers	Problem-solve if lost in new places Use caution with strangers	Problem-solve if lost in new places Use caution with strangers	Problem-solve if lost in new places Use caution with strangers
Grocery shopping			Buy two to three items at neighborhood store for self (snack) or classroom snack activity	Buy items needed for specific planned menu	Buy items needed for specific meal or special event	Buy items needed for specific meal or special event
General shopping		Buy item at school store	Buy item at school store	Buy few items in store with limited money amount Purchase personal care items	Shop for desired items in shopping center Purchase personal care items	Shop for desired items in shopping center Purchase personal care items
Eating out	Carry milk/lunch money Follow school cafeteria routine	Carry milk/lunch money Follow school cafeteria routine	Carry milk/lunch money Follow school cafeteria routine Order and pay: familiar fast food restaurants, snack stand Buy snack/drinks from vending machine	Budget/carry money for lunch/snacks Eat in school cafeteria Order and eat in fast food restaurants Buy snack/drinks from vending machine	Budget/carry money for lunch/snacks Eat in school/public cafeteria Order and eat in fast food restaurants Buy snack/drinks from vending machines	Budget/carry money for meals and snacks Eat in public cafeteria Order and eat in fast food restaurants Buy snack/drinks from vending machines
Using services	Mail letter at corner mailbox	Mail letter at corner mailbox Use pay phone with help	Mail letters Use pay phone	Use post office Use pay phone Ask for assistance in stores	Use post office Use pay phone Ask for assistance in stores, information booths	Use post office Use pay phone Ask for assistance appropriately in stores, information booths

Source: From *The Syracuse Community-Referenced Curriculum Guide for Students with Moderate and Severe Disabilities,* edited by Alison Ford, Roberta Schnorr, Luanna Meyer, Linda Davern, Jim Black, and Patrick Dempsey, p. 78.

importance of early learning and the ways that modern technology can help to facilitate the educational process.

As we have mentioned already, the infant born with severe disabilities often experiences both cognitive and psychomotor developmental delays that can impede the acquisition of fundamental concepts such as personal control over the environment and the realization of cause-and-effect relationships. It is in the development of these initial and very important cognitive skills that technology can be instrumental.

One early example is the use of the microcomputer in the development of a contingency intervention curriculum (Brinker, 1984; Brinker & Lewis, 1982). Remember our discussion of the problems young infants might have in realizing that their hand hitting against the side of the crib made sounds or that their cries brought their mother to them? The results of their actions (the noise, the

~ Join the Circus

Join the circus [Don Johnston Developmental Equipment, Inc.] is a cause-effect program for Apple II series computers. It requires a color monitor, a switch, and the Echo speech synthesizer; a printer is optional. Join the Circus contains three activities: the Juggling J's (jugglers), Magnificent Maggy (a magician), and Katy the Lion Tamer. In the lion tamer's act, . . . the lion jumps on the stand and roars. For the finale, Katy places her head in the lion's mouth. . . .

All the activities in Join the Circus require switch responses. However, each activity can be used on four different levels. In level 1, one switch press shows the entire circus act. In level 2, the student must press the switch twice, once to start the act and once to see the finale. In level 3, five switch presses are required. In level 4, two students work cooperatively and take turns pressing their switches.

One advantage of this and many other programs from Don Johnston is the amount of control that teachers have over instructional variables. At the teacher's menu (called the Parameters Menu), teachers can make decisions related to the timing of the program and the cues and feedback provided to the learner. Among the choices in the Cues/Feedback menu are whether or not the program uses speech and sound effects, whether the screen should go blank when it's time to press the switch, and whether the synthesizer prompts the student if he or she has not responded after a set time limit. The Timing menu sets the level of the program (1, 2, 3, or 4), the amount of time the student has to respond, how long the switch must be held down, and the length of the action delay. The action delay is the amount of time between the switch press and the action on the screen; this is a useful feature for students who need time to shift their attention from the switch to the monitor. During the operation of the program, the teacher can press Control-W to change any of the Timing parameters. For example, the level of the program can be changed if it is too easy or too difficult for the student.

It is also possible to set the menu of Join the Circus to operate by switch or keyboard commands. With the menu in the switch mode, students can make their own decisions about which activity to work with. The program can be personalized to some extent by having the speech synthesizer address the student by name. To make this happen, the teacher chooses Names from the Parameters Menu and enters the phonetic spelling of the name of player 1 and, if level 4 of the program is being used, that of player 2.

Source: From Rena B. Lewis, *Special Education Technology: Classroom Applications*, p. 199. Copyright © 1993 by Brooks/Cole Publishing Company. Used by permission of Wadsworth Publishing Company.

appearance of the mother) can be described as *contingencies*. The **contingency intervention curriculum** involves the immediate and distinct presentation of contingencies, or consequences, to children to help them understand the relationship between what they do and what happens in the environment. In these studies, a microcomputer was used to help provide infants with contingencies, such as music or recordings of the mother's voice, for even minimal movement. Because the child participating in this type of programming receives evidence of the effects her movement has on the environment, she is given the opportunity to develop purposeful behavior and interact with the environment in a meaningful way.

Recent research in technology has also focused on developing cause-and-effect understanding for children with severe and profound cognitive disabilities. For example, cause-and-effect software has been developed that includes programs that use abstract design, sound, graphics, and games (Lewis, 1993). The accompanying box, "Join the Circus," describes a commercial program designed to teach cause-and-effect relationships.

Another new area of technology in this area is assistive robotics. Cook and Cavalier (1999) describe teaching young children with severe developmental disabilities to use robotic systems, such as robotic arms. These devices can help students become active participants in their environment and therefore increase their awareness of cause and effect. In the near future, it is likely that technology will play an even greater role in providing individuals with severe and profound levels of mental retardation with the experiences necessary for the development of critical cognitive and communication skills.

Technology also is playing an emerging role as a means of delivering and enhancing instruction for individuals with severe disabilities. Langone and Mechling (2000) used a computer-based program to teach students with severe disabilities to recognize photographic prompts for appropriate language use. In recent years, wearable computers have been developed: When attached to glasses or headphones, these may provide exciting options for community-based instruction and for performance feedback.

Transition Programming

As we've discussed throughout this text, *transition* refers to the process of preparing for and facilitating movement from one situation or place to another. In the area of severe and profound disabilities, the term usually refers to one of three types of movement: (1) movement from one level of school to another, (2) movement from a segregated school or home setting to an integrated or community-based school or residence, or (3) movement from school to a work setting, typically a work setting in the community. As we have seen, the educational and philosophical movements in the field today have been directed toward preparing individuals with severe disabilities for integration in local communities. The need for advance planning and continual instruction in the skills and behaviors needed to maximize the potential for successful experiences in future environments has resulted in the development of specific programs and extensive research focused on the transition process. The individualized transition plan prepares the child with disabilities for new environments. Figure 6.1 illustrates the six areas of adult life that should be addressed by transition programs. How do we know if our programs have been successful in these areas? How can we determine if someone is productive, happy, and healthy? A

The individualized transition plan prepares the child with disabilities for new environments.

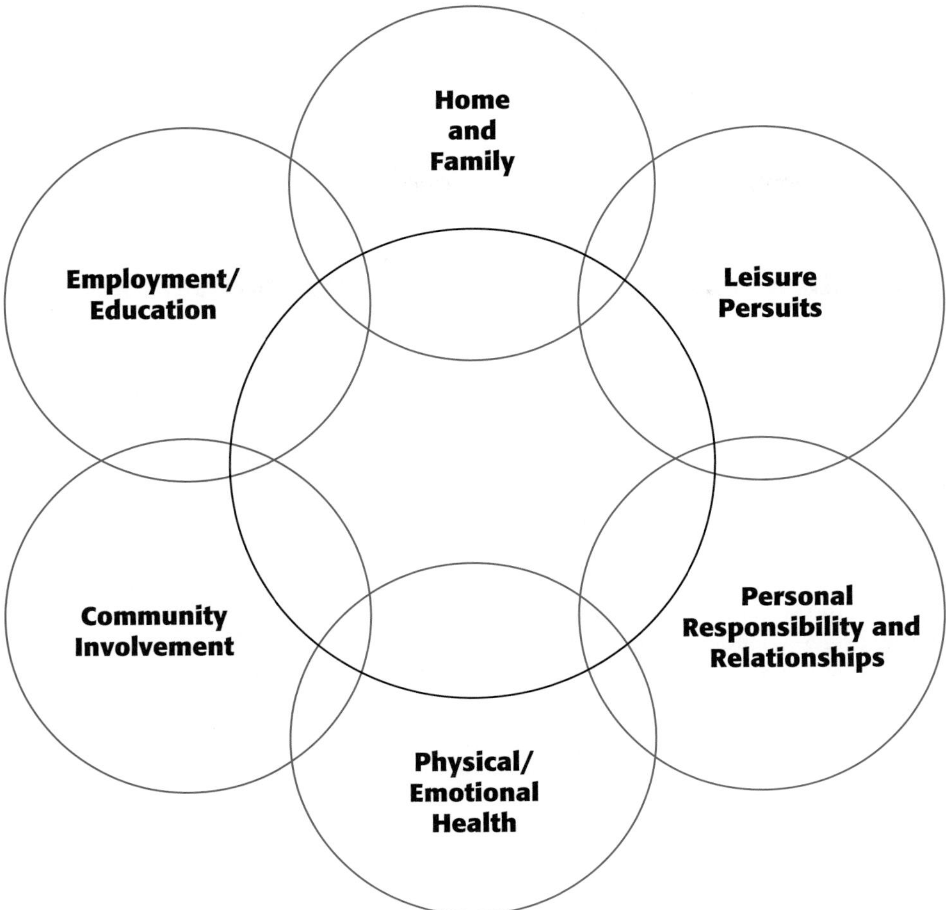

Figure 6.1
Domains of Adulthood

Source: M.E. Cronin & J.R. Patton, *Life Skills Instruction for All Students with Special Needs: A Practical Guide for Integrating Real Life Content into Curriculum* (Austin, TX: PRO-ED, 1993), p. 13. Copyright © 1993. Used by permission of PRO-ED.

number of research investigations are conducted to determine such things as employment rates, graduation rates, and living arrangements of individuals with disabilities.

Transition Between Levels of School

Transition programming in educational settings often begins immediately for the infant born with severe disabilities. As soon as the need for specialized services is recognized, interventions are put in place that are designed to prepare the child for success in future environments as well as the present one. Programs are available at day-care centers, through home-based instruction, and in preschools that are, in part, designed to help the infant or child move to an integrated setting or to prepare him or her for the next level of schooling.

The process of preparation for a new school situation will take place as long as the child is in the school system. If a child is already in an integrated setting, the change from elementary school to a middle school, or from junior high school to senior high school, will need to be addressed in the curriculum. All children must learn to cope with the new physical environment, the usually larger number of students, and the progressively greater freedoms that are present as they go from first through twelfth grade. The individual with severe mental retardation must be prepared to cope with these changes. For example, learning to use a locker may require a comprehensive instructional program (Felko, Schuster, Harley, & Collins, 1999).

Transition from Segregated to Integrated Settings

The education of students with severe or profound levels of disabilities has, on the whole, been segregated. The recent movement to end the practice of segregating students with severe disabilities is reflected in the transition plans of students of all ages. Many of these plans contain programming and educational goals intended to enable students to move to a partially or fully integrated school setting. In some instances, these goals may be to prepare students to move from a protective, residential school to a classroom in the local public school. For other students, the goals may be to move them from a separate lunch held in their classroom to a fully integrated lunch with all of the other students in the school, or for them to join the regular classroom for certain nonacademic or even academic subjects.

Transition plans that include a focus on inclusion will probably contain many skills and experiences that address different aspects of communication, socialization, and independent movement. A student who has little or no experience interacting with nondisabled peers will not have the skills needed to benefit from new school situations. The transition plans may thus include trial experiences in the new school to help the student gradually get accustomed to the change.

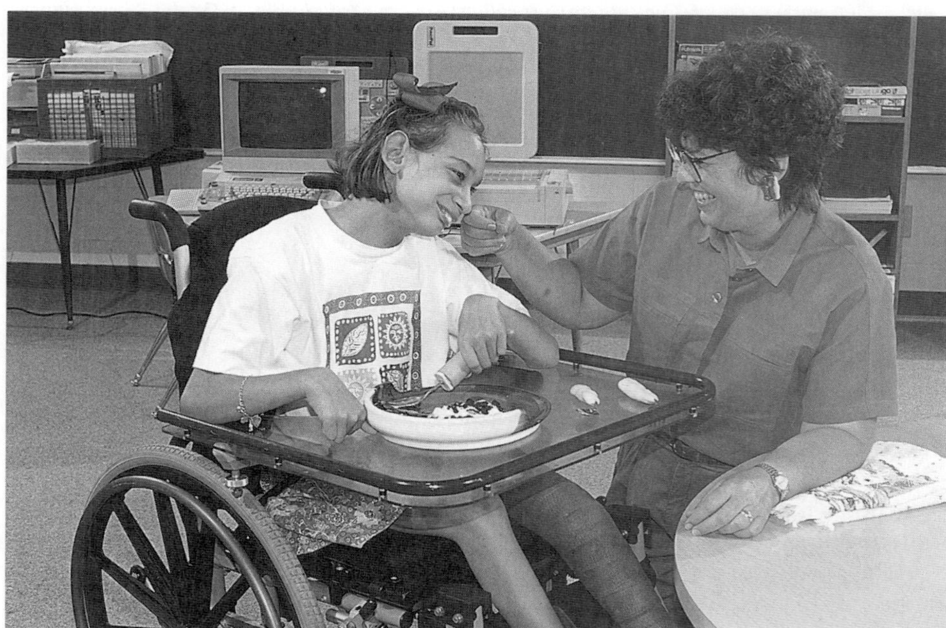

Instruction in life skills forms the core of the curriculum for many students. Adapted materials and equipment can facilitate the extent to which an individual can participate in important skills such as eating, dressing, and cooking. (Bob Daemmrich/The Image Works, Inc.)

Successful transition into an integrated environment depends on appropriate educational programs and support.

As you might expect, the success of a student's transition into an integrated environment will depend not only on the appropriateness of the educational program the student receives before the move but on the support the student receives once he or she is in the school as well. Cooperative planning between the student's present and future teachers will help to facilitate a smooth transition.

Although many school personnel are becoming more receptive to the integration process (Stainback, Stainback, & Stainback, 1988), those involved in transition plans should always anticipate possible resistance. Letting people know exactly what to expect and ways to deal with potential difficulties will help alleviate anxiety. Often, visits to schools with existing integrated programs for students with severe and profound disabilities, or films of such schools, can provide a demonstration of effective programming.

Another factor critical to the successful movement of students with severe disabilities from segregated to integrated facilities is the role of parents. This role may change over time. The accompanying box, "Roles of Family Members in Transition," outlines four roles of the family in the transition process. The strategies presented in the box can be used by service providers to ensure that parents are involved appropriately in all aspects of the transition process. Consideration of these roles and strategies also will help to facilitate a culturally sensitive transition program (Bruns & Fowler, 1999).

When it comes to decisions related to integrated placements, particularly if they involve changes in schools, parents may be concerned about the quality of programming in a new school or class situation and about the safety of their child, or they may be worried that their child will be rejected in the new situation. These feelings will be less pronounced if the parents have been planning for transitional placements during the course of the child's life. Parents may find support, encouragement, and strategies for helping to prepare themselves and their children through support groups composed of other parents of children with similar disabilities who have experienced the same concerns. Teachers and school administrators can help to get parents together if groups do not exist already in the community. Parents also might benefit from observing model programs that include integration and from communicating with personnel at the new school (Hanline & Halvorsen, 1989).

Transition from segregated to integrated settings can involve residential as well as school settings. Up until very recently, the vast majority of individuals of all ages who experienced severe or profound levels of mental retardation lived in segregated residential facilities. Most of these were institutional or private settings such as nursing homes. During the past two decades, however, many of these individuals have moved to smaller and more integrated residences, such as group homes, or to live with their families. According to Taylor, Lakin, and Hill (1989), the number of children and youth in long-term residential facilities decreased from 91,000 to 48,450 in the years from 1977 to 1986. Similarly, according to the U.S. Department of Education's *Eighteenth Annual Report to Congress on the Implementation of the Individuals with Disabilities Education Act* (1996), only 1.4 percent of students with disabilities ages 3 to 21 were served in residential or hospital environments during the 1993–1994 school year.

Transition to an integrated setting focuses on helping families keep and support their child in the home and on enabling adults to live as independently as possible and to maximize interaction within the local community. Both the child who has been living at home and the child who has lived in a segregated facility must receive transition training for adult living. In many cases, it will be possible for individuals with severe mental retardation to live in group homes or

~ Roles of Family Members in Transition: Strategies to Facilitate Culturally Appropriate Transition

Role: Family as . . .	**Strategies for Service Providers for Issues Related to:**
Guide	Continuity: Child's home culture and practices are respected in new placement. Family is involved in identifying and deciding how to manage conflicting practices and expectations. Sources of potential discontinuity between home and the new program are identified; steps are taken to minimize them.
Information specialist	Communication: Written material to families should be clear and concise. Written and oral information should be free of jargon and technical language. Written and oral information should be in the family's primary language. Information exchange should match family preferences (e.g., face-to-face meetings, involvement of community leader, community elder, or extended family member).
Decision maker	Collaboration: Child and family preparation and training for transition should be culturally appropriate (e.g., small-group instruction, oral transmission of information, multigenerational involvement). Families should be informed of their legal rights and responsibilities in a culturally sensitive manner. Include opportunities for feedback from families throughout the transition process.
Ally	Family concerns: Families are encouraged to share their concerns. Family concerns are addressed in a culturally sensitive manner. Families are consulted concerning culturally appropriate roles and level of involvement in transition; cultural brokers (e.g., a community leader) are involved as necessary.

Source: Bruns, D. A., & Fowler, S. A. (1999). "Culturally sensitive transition plans for young children and their families," *Teaching Exceptional Children, 31* (5), 26–30.

apartments in a community setting. People living in independent or semi-independent housing must be prepared emotionally and technically. Skills involved in cooking, cleaning, dressing recreational activities, and transportation must be taught and will usually require extensive planning and instruction. Preparation in these skills and in related ones must begin early and then be extended to enable the individual to function in the specific home or apartment setting. See the accompanying box, "Living Settings for Individuals with Severe Disabilities."

Transition from School to Work

Probably the most commonly perceived meaning of the term *transition* across the field of special education is the transition from school to work settings.

~ Living Settings for Individuals with Severe Disabilities

Individuals with disabilities often want to live in independent, community-based homes. For many people, these goals are realized through independent living arrangements. For others, the goals are adapted to include the most independent and normalized setting possible.

Institutions

Large, segregated residential buildings known as institutions were used for years to house thousands of individuals with mental retardation, mental illness, sensory impairments, or physical disabilities. After numerous allegations of neglect and abuse that often took place in institutions, a social and legal movement began in the 1960s and the 1970s to take people out of the institutional setting and relocate them in smaller, community-based settings. This movement, deinstitutionalization, led to the development of good community residential programs. However, the lack of existing support networks and adequate community-based housing also resulted in many displaced and homeless persons. Although institutions still exist, they are less frequently chosen as a residential placement of choice, and in some states are not considered at all.

Community-Based Residential Facilities

Some individuals who in times past lived in segregated settings have moved directly and successfully into the community. People with disabilities such as severe mental retardation, may live in settings that range from nursing homes to community-based homes or facilities. Opportunities for community-based residences are continuing to increase for all individuals, however, the more complex an individual's health-care and personal maintenance needs are, the more likely it is that the person continues to live in one of the more segregated settings. Often, these settings are able to employ support personnel, such as nurses and therapists, and have available more elaborate medical equipment than a group home or apartment.

Intermediate-Care Facilities

An intermediate-care facility (ICF) is composed of a number of individuals with disabilities living together in a supervised setting. Some large ICFs do not provide for community integration, however, and may serve as permanent, segregated living settings for individuals with disabilities. These facilities may include cottage living or other congregated living options.

Small group homes house several adults with disabilities who live with a nondisabled person responsible for general supervision and coordination of activities. Such living situations require not only financial resources and trained personnel but also a receptive community. The resistance of some communities to the placement of group homes adds one more obstacle to be overcome in the move toward normalized and independent living. The road to normalized socialization and integration within the community is an exciting option, but not an easy one.

A variety of living situations may also be found in apartment settings. For example, one or more individuals with disabilities may live independently in an apartment, with only periodic visits from a counselor or case manager. Another option may be a person with a disability living with a roommate without a disability. (The roommate may be a residential care provider—or just a friend.) Apartment living is one step closer to an independent, normal living arrangement for many young adults.

Living with Family

Another living option is the family home. Many individuals with disabilities continue to live in the family home during their adult years. Financial dependence, emotional dependence on the part of the family as well as the individual, and a lack of alternative living options may contribute to adults living in this setting.

Preparing students with severe disabilities to go into the work force, particularly the community work force, is a major educational goal.

Although it is suggested that transition programming from school to work begin at least five years before graduation from school, preparation is often a major component of the curriculum throughout the student's educational experience (Noonan & Kilgo, 1987; Wehman et al., 1987). The transition process will encompass not only skills directly related to a work situation but also the necessary skills involved in social interaction, self-help areas, and transportation.

Joining the community work force is a major educational goal for many students with severe disabilities.

An essential component of all school-to-work transition programs is community-based work experience. When possible, the student should try out several types of work experiences and have an important decision-making role in job selection (Brooke et al., 1995; Wehman et al., 1987). How receptive are business owners to training opportunities for students with severe disabilities? As you might expect, the receptivity will vary from person to person and from community to community. Aveno and Renzaglia (1988) approached sixty-one community businesses that could be potential job sites for persons with severe mental retardation (stores, restaurants, recreational facilities, etc.) and found that the business personnel had generally positive attitudes toward community integration of the students. Although the attitudes were generally supportive, Aveno and Renzaglia suggest that teachers recognize the need to develop strategies to help increase positive attitudes in the community. They suggested in-service training and opportunities for structured exposure to persons with severe disabilities.

Teaching in community-based settings involves some of the same processes and people discussed in Chapter 5. For example, job coaches go with students to the work site to provide on-the-job instruction. Supported employment is a desired goal for many young adults with severe disabilities. Continued business and community support is needed, however, to provide adequate opportunities for supported employment to interested individuals (Brooke et al., 1995). In fact, research suggests that individuals with severe disabilities remain underrepresented in supported employment positions, compared to individuals with other types of disabilities (Mank, Ciofi, & Yovanoff, 1998).

Self-management procedures facilitate independent performance.

Teachers also need to look at ways to teach students to work independently in the work situation. **Self-management procedures** have been taught to students with severe mental retardation to facilitate independent performance (Lagomarcino & Rusch, 1989). These procedures include self-monitoring or recording of completed tasks and giving praise or other reinforcement to yourself when a task or step of a task has been completed. For example, a student might have a series of five photographs that are used as prompts for the five steps needed to complete a task, such as setting a table in a restaurant. A self-recording procedure might involve putting a check or mark beside each picture as the task is completed. Students who can learn to monitor themselves accurately will require less direct supervision over time and therefore may be more likely candidates for permanent employment opportunities.

Permanent employment in community settings is the ultimate goal of transition programming from school to work; it requires not only effective instructional techniques but also extensive coordination among the school, family, employers, and adult service agencies. Remember that the primary service providers for people with severe and profound mental retardation will change from the school to adult agencies once the students reach the age of 22. Work-related goals that are intended to extend into the student's adult life must include the cooperation and participation of case managers from the community service agencies.

Ethical Issues

The ethical issues that have arisen in the area of severe and profound disabilities revolve around the basic rights of all individuals: the right to life and the right to education. Professionals in the areas of medicine, education, and law have become involved with children with severe disabilities and their parents in attempts to resolve some of these issues and to find answers to some very disturbing questions. The fact that questions are raised at all relative to the human and constitutional rights of individuals with severe or profound levels of disabilities is difficult for many of us to understand. As we present these issues, we will attempt to provide you with both sides of the controversies. It is inevitable, however, that our biases will be revealed through the discussion. We do not feel that it is appropriate for any professional in the field of special education to present noncommittal statements on issues that are so fundamental to the philosophy we espouse.

Ethical issues arising from severe disabilities concern the right to life, and the right to education.

The Right to Life

Do all newborn infants have the right to live? Should lifesaving surgery be performed on infants who have an assortment of potentially painful and disabling physical and mental disabilities? Should heroic measures be taken to save the life of an infant with suspected severe mental retardation? Do parents, doctors, lawyers, or the government have the right or responsibility to make life-and-death decisions for these children?

These questions are at the heart of the ethical issue of the right to life of children born with severe mental retardation and physical disabilities. In essence, the questions are asked because judgments are being made at the time of a child's birth about the prospective quality of life of that child. **Quality of life** refers to the extent to which an individual can participate in, enjoy, and be aware of the experience of living. When a child with severe mental and/or physical disabilities is born, assumptions are also made about his or her prospective quality of life. Sometimes these assumptions focus on whether or not the child's life is worth living, whether the mental or physical disabilities experienced by the child will enable him or her to have a meaningful life. Often these assumptions are accompanied by concern about the physical pain or discomfort the child is likely to experience, the prospect of a painful death later in life, or the likelihood of an existence filled with endless surgical procedures and medical treatment. In other instances, the presence of moderate, severe, or profound levels of mental retardation may lead to negative assumptions about the child's quality of life. All of these considerations have come into play when medical decisions have been made about whether or not to treat children with severe disabilities when life-threatening conditions occur. In some cases, the decision is made that, because of the prospect of a poor quality of life, the infant should be allowed to die.

Quality of life refers to the extent to which an individual is aware of, participates in, and enjoys life.

Although allowing any infant to die because of nontreatment is illegal (Orelove & Sobsey, 1987), such cases are rarely prosecuted, primarily because many individuals feel that these decisions can and should be made by the parents of the children and their physicians (Hentoff, 1985). When an investigation

A closer look

Can Do: Focus on the Future

All people bring important gifts to community life. Too often, however, the positive characteristics and qualities of many people with disabilities have been denied or ignored. Many human services focus on deficits and negative characteristics.

A positive alternative approach to planning for the future is called the "capacity search," which helps others see how competent people can be when they have the opportunity to express their gifts. The following profile contrasts the traditional "deficiency description" with a "capacity search description" for a woman named Alma.

Deficiency Description

- She is a physically large 18-year-old female.
- She is enrolled in an education program for children with moderate mental handicaps.
- She is physically handicapped.
- Her right side and arm seem partially paralyzed.
- Her speech is slow and considered related to brain dysfunction and injury.
- There are signs of scars on her right arm.
- She has speech deficits and lags in developmental speech
- She has epilepsy and delayed mobility.
- There is left hemiparesis associated with brain damage.
- She scores at first-grade level on information, spelling, and reading, and at second grade in math.
- She has a full-scale IQ of 58, a verbal quotient of 62, which indicates functioning within mild mental retardation, and an age equivalent of 10 years, 8 months.

Capacity Search Description

- Home: She could live independently if something were to happen to her grandmother. Alma wants to have her own apartment.

has occurred, it has usually resulted in extensive media coverage and publicity (Lyon, 1985), which has done little to encourage further prosecution. Certainly, any parent who chooses to withhold treatment, or, in some instances, nutrition from a child is making an incredibly difficult decision. Yet the fact remains that if this type of decision were made for an infant without a disability, the persons responsible for allowing the infant to die would unquestionably be punished.

Orelove and Sobsey (1987) present five basic alternatives for the right-to-life issue: (1) to treat all nondying newborns, (2) to terminate the lives of selected infants who are not determined to be viable individuals, (3) to withhold treatment according to parental discretion, (4) to withhold treatment according to a quality-of-life determination, and (5) to withhold treatment judged not to be in the child's best interest. All of these alternatives, with the exception of the first, involve subjective determinations that will result in the life or death of the child. Who, if anyone, has the right to determine if the child has the right to live? This, of course, is the root of the dilemma. Once this right has been placed in the hands of the parents or physicians, their personal criteria for the quality of life will serve as the basis for life-and-death decisions.

Smith (1989) points out that most of the individuals who make decisions about the potential quality of life for individuals with mental retardation, including parents, physicians, and lawyers, have had little, if any, experience liv-

- Health: She is generally healthy, although she has chronic allergies.
- People: She has fifteen significant people in her network. They include her teacher, friends from school, and family members. Her friendships with nonhandicapped peers have decreased over time.
- Places: Alma goes all over town on her own. She walks to the grocery store and other shops. She goes to the Freewill Baptist Church. She visits a lot of people. She would like to be able to get out of town more.
- Choices: Alma decorates her room. She chooses to visit her father. Her grandmother makes many choices for her and decides how her check is spent.
- Respect: Alma is congenial and helpful and has a pleasant personality. She is in the "trainable mentally retarded class" and likes to tell other people what to do.
- Personal preferences: Alma cooks simple meals. She gets up at 6 A.M. every day and cooks breakfast for everyone. She is a good babysitter for Maria, her little sister. She shows leadership ability. She likes to travel. She likes music and dancing. She likes "circle a word" and math exercises. She likes to help clean. She likes to watch TV. She doesn't like to wash dishes, tend to babies, or read.
- Personal images of the future: Alma wants to acquire a skill through the vocational technical school. She wants her own apartment and a job. She would like to be able to drive. She wants to have more friends.

Source: Beth Mount and Kay Zwernick, *It's Never Too Early, It's Never Too Late* (St. Paul, MN: Metropolitan Council, 1988), pp. 918–919.

ing, working, or spending time with persons with any degree of mental retardation. This lack of familiarity results not only in fear for the child's future but often in misconceptions about the potential quality of life of individuals with varying levels of mental retardation.

Quality of life is defined many different ways when used to measure adult outcomes. Halpern (1993) suggests that the major criteria for quality of life are (1) physical and material well-being, (2) performance of adult roles, and (3) personal fulfillment. Objective, quantitative evaluations, such as specific job requirements, are important tools for identifying target instructional skills in the environment that may lead to successful performance. Qualitative or descriptive analyses of an individual's performance and personal fulfillment also are considered necessary for an accurate picture of that person's quality of life. Dennis, Williams, Giangreco, and Cloninger (1993) suggest that there is no single definition of quality of life. They, too, recommend that an individual's performance be evaluated in the context of his or her environment, using indices that reflect that person's culture, family or support system, and personal preferences. These indices may be different for each person, reflecting those facets of life that are important to the individual and his or her significant others (see "A Closer Look: Can Do: Focus on the Future"). Storey (1997) asserts the need for broad, generally accepted operational definitions of quality of life, acknowledging that definitions might change according to the age and population.

The Right to Education

We may take it for granted that all children and adolescents have the right to receive an education. Legally, this was not the case for individuals with severe and profound levels of mental retardation until 1975, when P.L. 94-142, the Education for All Handicapped Children Act (now known as IDEA), was passed. Even now, although the law states specifically that all children have the right to a free and appropriate education, controversy persists. The source of the controversy lies in the extent to which education is actually possible for some individuals with profound mental retardation. If, as some contend, there arechildren or adolescents who cannot benefit from educational programs, there remains the question of whether these individuals would qualify for school-based programs.

Some people feel that not all children will profit meaningfully from educational programming.

There are a few students whose levels of disability are so severe that they severely limit the amount of instruction to which they can respond. These students will receive educational programming that may be limited to sensory stimulation and efforts to establish some type of communication skill or preskill, such as eye contact. Questions have been raised by some people about the need to continue educational programming for individuals with such profound levels of mental retardation. Their feeling is that it is misleading to describe every child as educable and that it must be recognized that some students will not profit meaningfully from educational programming and should not be subjected to such programs. This point of view, when expressed by special educators, is supposedly applicable only to a very small number of children, and proponents stress that documented educational efforts must precede the label of ineducability.

Other special educators, however, feel that no child should be identified as unable to benefit from educational programming. There are a number of reasons for this point of view. Some express a fear that because such judgments are subjective and cannot be monitored across educational settings, a large number of students with profound levels of mental retardation will be labeled ineducable without receiving adequate or appropriate programming. Others have suggested that such determinations will undermine the progress made in the area of education for students with severe and profound levels of mental retardation by placing a limit on instructional efforts and expectations. Certainly, few individuals who taught several decades ago would have anticipated the amount of learning and skill now routinely acquired by individuals with all levels of mental retardation.

Other professionals feel that no limits should be placed on instructional efforts and expectations.

Perhaps the most important concern, however, involves the philosophy of education revealed when instructional effort is evaluated in terms of the amount or quality of student response. Ferguson (1987) proposes that education should be presented because of our commitment to individuals and should not be measured in terms of a cost-benefit standard. She suggests that it is our criteria for "meaningful" responses or functional skill acquisition that contribute to the constant delineation of a portion of the population as ineducable, or not capable of meaningful learning. In other words, she suggests that as long as we feel the need to justify education in terms of the types or amount of skills students are able to learn, we will always find a group of students who will be considered ineducable. According to Ferguson, the right to education does not have to be earned by the student; we should simply espouse the philosophy that we are committed to educating everyone.

Summary

- Severe mental retardation is defined as an IQ score of 40 or below, and profound mental retardation as an IQ score of 20 or below accompanied by deficits in adaptive behavior. Severe and profound disabilities are caused by a variety of genetic and environmental factors and are usually identified at birth.
- The effects of a severe disability on the child include cognitive difficulty in making connections between the action and the environment, relatively small physical size and high risk of health problems, delays in or lack of oral communication, and limited social skills due to lack of interaction with others.
- Educational issues include normalization, integration, and an appropriate life-skills curriculum. Normalization involves age-appropriate treatment and providing environments and representations of individuals that are as close to normal as possible. Integration refers to both physical and social integration. The functional curriculum emphasizes preparation for life and instruction in integrated skills useful in school, work, or home.
- Transitional programming for children with severe and profound disabilities includes preparation for changes in schools, for movement from a segregated to an integrated setting, and for work after school.
- Basic rights, including the right to life and to education, have been questioned for people with severe disabilities. We have discussed both sides of the controversies.

Key Terms

severe disabilities
severe mental retardation
profound mental retardation
functional communication
normalization
partial participation
functional curriculum
environmental inventory (environmental analysis)
contingency intervention curriculum
self-management procedures
quality of life

Multimedia Resources

Adaptive Physical Education FAQ: http://www.cec.sped.org/faq/adaptpe.htm. This website is a resource page for articles or other printed information about adapting physical activities for individuals with disabilities.

The Association for Persons with Severe Handicaps (TASH), 26 West Susquehanna Avenue, Suite 210, Baltimore, MD 21204, (410) 828-8274. Website: http://www.tash.org.

Educational Electronic Robots, Elekit Company, 1160 Mahalo Place, Compton, CA 90220-5443. Phone (310) 638-7970. e-mail: http://www.owirobot.com/

menu.html. This company provides information about educational and assistive robotic programs.

Orelove, Fred P., and Dick Sobsey. *Educating Children with Multiple Disabilities: A Trandisciplinary Approach* (Baltimore: Brookes, 1987). This text gives a model for providing services that relies on cooperation among teachers, therapists, and parents and includes specific techniques and strategies for teaching children with severe mental retardation and motor or sensory impairments.

Wilcox, Barbara, and G. Thomas Bellamy. *The Activities Catalog: An Alternative Curriculum for Youth and Adults with Severe Disabilities* and *A Comprehensive Guide to the Activities Catalog* (Baltimore: Brookes, 1987). Both the catalog and the accompanying guide offer hundreds of innovative approaches for designing meaningful curriculum for persons with severe disabilities.

WHAT YOU CAN DO

1. Visit a teacher or transition coordinator in a local school who specializes in working with individuals with severe or profound mental retardation. Ask to observe the teacher working with students in community-based settings.
2. Identify a task you do frequently as part of your daily or weekly routine, such as doing laundry or preparing a meal. Carefully observe and write down all of the components of that task, including specific behaviors and any decisions that must be made to complete the task. Prepare some ideas for how you could teach all of these task components.
3. Locate several grocery stores or fast-food restaurants in your local community. Before visiting them, make a list of things you might need to know if you were teaching individuals with severe disabilities—for example, the location of specific food items, exits, and check-out lines in the grocery store; or methods of ordering, use of picture cues, and location of trays and condiments in the fast-food restaurants. Then visit each location. Identify the similarities and differences at each location. Which would be the easiest location at which to begin instruction?
4. Why is a functional or life-skills curriculum of primary importance for people with severe disabilities? Obtain several curricula from local public and/or residential schools. What characteristics do all the curricula have in common? Are there any significant differences? To what extent are individuals in community or home settings involved in the curricula?
5. What is your position on the issue of rights for people with severe disabilities? How did you develop your view?

Children with Behavioral and Emotional Disorders

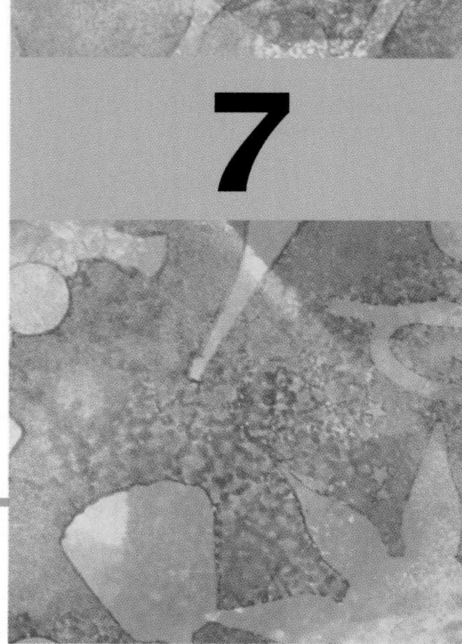

7

In This chapter, you will learn how behavioral disorders are identified and defined, the effects of these disorders on students and their families, and strategies that you can use to work with students who have them. We will also discuss some of the questions and problems surrounding the definition and identification of these disorders. As you read, think about how you would answer the following questions:

How are behavioral disorders defined and classified?

Why is the federal definition a source of controversy?

What techniques are used to identify and assess children with behavioral disorders?

Commonalities: **How can behavior-management strategies suggested for students with behavioral disorders be used to prevent or manage inappropriate behavior in other children?**

Collaboration: **Why is collaboration between teachers and parents so important for teaching children new behaviors?**

Can Do: **What strategies can you use to help students learn to manage their own behavior?**

There are many differences in the way people react to certain situations, act around other people, follow rules and regulations, and conform to society's expectations for behavior. A wide range of behavior patterns is considered "normal" and accepted as a reflection of individual differences. This is particularly true among adults, for we accept the fact that people choose their own lifestyles and behave in ways that are most comfortable to them. Concern is voiced only when there appears to be a chance that someone will harm others or himself or herself, or does not appear able to cope with the daily activities of life.

Our outlook on conformity and acceptable patterns of behavior is different when we look at children, particularly children in school settings. The range of behaviors considered acceptable in school settings is narrow. Our expectations, as adults, of how children should feel and act is also much more narrowly defined than are our expectations of acceptable adult behavior. In part, these expectations help ensure that children learn how to behave appropriately in a variety of situations and benefit from educational programming. Many children do, from time to time, behave in ways that appear to be out of bounds—beyond our typical standards of normal behavior. These children are not the focus of this chapter. As educators, we are concerned when inappropriate behavior persists, interferes with school performance, and appears harmful to the child or others.

Definitions and Terms

The children identified in this category of special education can be referred to in a number of ways. The terms used include *behavior disorders*, *severe emotional disturbance*, *emotional disturbance*, *emotionally handicapped*, and *behaviorally handicapped*. Professionals have many different opinions about which term is most appropriate (Forness, 1988). The differences result from whether educators focus on the causes of the behavior children exhibit or on the behavior alone.

The Federal Definition

At the present time, the federal definition in IDEA uses the term **emotional disturbance** and includes five major criteria for identification:

Federal law cites five major criteria for determining whether a child has an emotional disturbance.

i. The term means a condition exhibiting one or more of the following characteristics over a long period of time and to a marked degree, which adversely affects educational performance.
   a. An inability to learn which cannot be explained by intellectual, sensory, and health factors;
   b. An inability to build or maintain satisfactory interpersonal relationships with peers and teachers;
   c. Inappropriate types of behavior or feelings under normal circumstances;
   d. A general pervasive mood of unhappiness or depression; or
   e. A tendency to develop physical symptoms or fears associated with personal or school problems.

ii. The term includes children who are schizophrenic. The term does not include children who are socially maladjusted unless it is determined that they are emotionally disturbed. (*Federal Register* 42 [163], August 23, 1977, p. 42,478)

This definition, like most definitions in special education, is the source of much debate and discussion, and the term *emotional disturbance* is being challenged at the federal level. A number of professionals are urging that the term *emotional* or *behavior disorder* be used instead and are also proposing several changes in the existing definition (Forness & Knitzer, 1990). Some states have adopted the term **behavior disordered** because of its more direct relationship to assessment and identification procedures (Smith, 1985).

Much of the controversy revolves around the ambiguity of the terms used as diagnostic markers and concern that this ambiguity excludes children who require services. For example, phrases such as *inappropriate types of behavior* or *satisfactory interpersonal relationships* are difficult to translate into clear-cut measures of performance. It is not too difficult to imagine that different people would interpret these terms in different ways. There is also much concern over the exclusion of children identified as "socially maladjusted." The term is considered difficult to define, particularly in view of the possible overlap with behaviors (such as aggression, poor peer relationships) that *would* qualify a child for special education services.

The ambiguities of the federal definition subject it to much controversy.

It does seem likely that changes are imminent in the definition of emotional and behavioral disorders, because the definition is less effective than it could be in providing guidelines for identification, assessment, and treatment.

Rate, Intensity, Duration, Age Appropriateness

Behaviors can differ in frequency or rate, intensity, duration, and age appropriateness. Often these factors determine whether behavior is considered normal or abnormal. In other words, abnormal behavior can be normal behavior that is performed to such a degree that it becomes atypical.

■ ***Rate*** **Rate** refers to how often a behavior occurs in a given time period. Most children occasionally get out of their seats without asking permission or get into fights. A child who gets into a fight every day, however, or who gets out of his seat every two minutes would be demonstrating an unusually high rate of these behaviors.

■ ***Intensity*** **Intensity** refers to the strength or magnitude of the behavior. For example, if a child hit his fist against the desk because he became frustrated, he might just hit it loud enough to make a noise, or he could hit it so hard he breaks either his hand or the desk. One instance would be considered a normal response; the other, more intense behavior would be considered problematic.

■ ***Duration*** The length of time a behavior lasts is referred to as its **duration.** Any child might have an occasional temper tantrum or cry if his or her feelings are hurt. But a tantrum or crying spell that goes on for an hour or two will be considered differently than a ten-minute outburst.

■ ***Age Appropriateness*** **Age-appropriate behavior** refers to the fact that some behaviors are considered quite normal in children of a certain age but are considered problematic when they persist as the child ages or occur before they are expected. For example, clinging to a parent, throwing tantrums, or being afraid of monsters in the closet are behaviors we might expect from a 5- or 6-year-old but not from a preteen.

Some children with emotional or behavior disorders exhibit *unusual* behaviors—behaviors we do not typically see at any level in other children. Most of these children have a more severe level of behavior disorders. Examples of this type of behavior include unusual patterns of language, distinctive hand movements and walking patterns, and behaviors directed at harming the child or others. We will look at these behaviors more closely when we discuss severe emotional or behavioral disabilities later in the chapter.

A single episode of abnormal behavior does not mean that a child has a behavioral disorder.

An important point to keep in mind is that a single episode of what appears to be abnormal behavior does not mean that the child has a behavioral disorder. Events within the child's life, as well as the changes and pressures of growing up, can result in an incidence of problem behavior, or perhaps even a few weeks in which the child seems to be exhibiting new and difficult behaviors. Typically, look for behavior that persists over several months and does not seem to have a readily identifiable cause (such as parents going through a divorce, death in the family).

Classifying Behavioral Disorders

Behaviors are usually classified into groups or categories. Sometimes this is done for the purpose of diagnosis, sometimes for assessment, and other times for placement and educational treatment. For the most part, behaviors that seem related in some way are grouped together. Often children exhibiting one type of behavior in a group or cluster will exhibit others found in that same cluster. Those children may be identified as having a specific type of syndrome or disorder. Other children display behaviors from a number of different groups. A number of classification systems are used with children having behavioral or emotional disorders. In addition to the various behaviors described in this section, we have included a separate section on attention deficit/hyperactivity disorder (ADHD) later in this chapter. Although ADHD is not technically a behavioral disorder, it has been considered a disorder of behavior because of its historical relationship with hyperactive behavior. ADHD is not a separate category of special education under IDEA; however, it is a common diagnosis for students in general education classrooms and warrants a clear and thorough discussion (see pages 250–253).

The DSM-IV System

The DSM-IV classifies behavior by diagnostic categories.

One classification system is presented in *The Diagnostic and Statistical Manual of Mental Disorders of the American Psychiatric Association* (fourth edition, 1993), known as **DSM-IV.** This manual groups behaviors into diagnostic categories. In other words, the manual lists specific behaviors and other criteria that must be present before a disorder can be diagnosed. Because many behavioral and psychiatric disorders are diagnosed on the basis of behavior alone, rather than by a specific test or medical diagnosis, these behavioral descriptions can assist in the diagnosis of specific disabilities. Thus a psychologist may collect observations and reports of a child's behavior in a number of settings over time and compare those behaviors to the categories in DSM-IV to make a diagnosis.

In some schools, the school or clinical psychologist makes the diagnosis of behavior disorders. In other schools a psychiatrist or pediatrician may diagnose the disability. This is particularly important when severe problems are exhibited or when therapy or medication are part of the remediation process. An example of diagnostic criteria from DSM-IV is found in the section of this chapter on ADHD.

Educational Classification Systems

Other systems of classifying behavior are more informal and based on groupings of a more general nature. Rather than looking for specific disorders, we describe broad patterns of behavior or disorders. This type of classification system is used for educational placement, service delivery, and program development.

Kerr and Nelson (1989) grouped behaviors into the following categories based on the similarity of the instructional procedures or interventions that would be used to address them: disruptive behavior, socially inadequate and immature behaviors, social withdrawal, stereotypic behaviors, and aggressive behaviors.

Quay and Peterson (1983) devised a classification system based on extensive observations of children and the patterns of behavior that surfaced. They used six types of behavior as the basis for their classification scheme: conduct disorder, socialized aggression, attention problems–immaturity, anxiety–withdrawal, psychotic behavior, and motor excess.

Achenbach and Edelbrock (1979) classified behavior in even broader terms, as either externalizing or internalizing. **Externalizing behaviors,** also known as acting out or aggressive behaviors, encompass all of those behaviors that are expressed overtly and that appear, in some way, to be directed toward others or the environment. These outwardly directed behaviors may represent impulsivity or a lack of self-control and can often be confrontational, aggressive, or disruptive.

Children with externalizing behavior disorders typically stand out in a classroom because of the impact their behavior has on others. The child who throws tantrums or teases his or her neighbor will interfere with others' abilities to listen or participate in class; aggressive actions may result in more than one child on the floor or in tears.

Internalizing behaviors are self-directed behaviors, such as withdrawal, avoidance, or compulsiveness. A child with an internalizing behavior disorder may be sad or depressed, withdrawn or shy, or focused on disturbing fears or fantasies.

Because of the nature of internalizing behavior disorders, a child's problems may not be recognized immediately, if at all. This child, typically, will not be a disruptive influence in the class and will not exhibit behaviors that draw attention from peers or the teacher. The student's avoidance of social interaction and the presence of fears or interfering thoughts, however, can affect his or her ability to perform in school and to establish social relationships. Recently, in light of the publicity given to adolescent suicides, more attention has been directed to identifying children with this type of disorder. Interestingly, females who have been identified as learning disabled or seriously emotionally disturbed appear to be up to three times more at risk than males for developing symptoms of depression (Maag & Behrens, 1989).

Again, it is important to examine the extent and appearance of the behavior as well as the effects on the child when trying to identify internalizing behavior disorders. Many young children will exhibit excessively shy behavior when encountering new experiences or people (such as the first day of school). We might also expect a period of depressed or withdrawn behavior when a traumatic event such as death, divorce, or a move has occurred in a child's life. Table 7.1 depicts the relationships among the different systems of categorization.

Classification and the Teacher

In the rest of this chapter, we will be using the Achenbach and Edelbrock classification system of externalizing and internalizing behaviors to look at the effects of behavioral or emotional disorders on children and their educational needs.

Table 7.1 Systems of Categorization

Externalizing behaviors	Internalizing behaviors
Conduct disorder	Attention problems, immaturity
Socialized aggression	Anxiety-withdrawal
Motor excess	Psychotic behavior
Aggressive behavior	Socially inadequate and immature behavior
Disruptive behaviors	Social withdrawal
	Stereotypic behaviors

This system is the least complicated, encompasses all behaviors, and focuses on the fundamental difference in children's behavior patterns.

From the teacher's perspective, the system helps to emphasize the relevance of *both* types of behavior. Unfortunately, the behaviors found in the internalizing dimension are not recognized as easily or as often as problematic even though these behaviors can have a profound effect on a child. As you might expect, teachers are more motivated to identify problems that disrupt the classroom and cause daily conflict than to recognize problems like depressed or withdrawn behavior that affect only the child in question.

Prevalence

The prevalence rate of behavioral disorders is estimated to be about 8.6 percent of the school-aged population with disabilities, although estimates have reached as high as 20 to 30 percent. In the United States and territories, 455,194 students, ages 6–21, were served for emotional disturbance during the 1997–1998 school year (U.S. Department of Education, 1999).

Some feel that many children with emotional or behavioral disorders are not receiving needed attention.

Although these numbers may seem large, they actually represent a figure far lower than most estimates of the true number of students with behavioral disorders. The vague criteria in the definition and the subjective nature of assessment often make a definitive diagnosis difficult. For example, the percentage of students identified with emotional disturbance in one state could be very different from the percentage of children identified in another. Factors such as the state definition, school district identification practices, and the frequency or type of prereferral interventions could account for portions of the variance. Zanglis, Furlong, and Casas (2000) found that the number of children referred and identified for emotional and behavioral disorders doubled in one county after the establishment of a cross-agency service delivery system. Whatever the sources of variance, we know that there are important questions about the applicability of the definition. There are probably many students who are not receiving needed special education services.

Causes

It is difficult to pinpoint the causes of most behavioral and emotional disorders.

The causes of most behavioral and emotional disorders are difficult to pinpoint. We often see children with very similar behavior patterns yet very different learning and family histories. Sometimes it is easy to pinpoint factors or situations that possibly contribute to behavioral and emotional disorders; sometimes there are no readily identifiable causal factors. Let's look at the following two examples of students with externalizing behavior disorders.

> Sandy, age 10, was identified as behavior disordered at age 7. At that time, she began demonstrating a number of problematic behaviors: She used extremely violent and obscene language toward her teachers and classmates; threw loud and long temper tantrums; hit her teacher and threw things when she was denied a request; and said cruel things to the other children in the class. She was failing the second grade. About two years later, it was discovered that Sandy had been the victim of sexual abuse by her mother's boyfriend. Although the abusive situation had ended, Sandy's behavior persisted. The identification of the specific cause could not, by itself, heal Sandy's emotional distress or end the behaviors that she had acquired and practiced over time.

> Bill, age 13, has been identified as having emotional or behavioral disorders for five years. He is very active, always out of his seat and moving around. Although he can be compliant and cooperative, he flares up easily, becoming resistant and confrontational with teachers and principals. Bill constantly fights with other children. He seems to see every interaction as a challenge and responds with anger and aggression. He failed fourth grade and is barely passing his classes now. Most of the students in school dislike and avoid him. Bill lives with his mother and they apparently have a good relationship. Although Bill's behavior has improved some during the past few years, he is socially rejected and behind academically, and he still resorts to violent interactions when frustrated or when he feels challenged in any way.

Although Sandy's inappropriate behavior had a clear time of onset, Bill is an example of a child with a long history of problem behavior. He has trouble interacting with adults and peers and is not doing well in school. Bill seems to see things somewhat differently than other children; he feels others are out to get him, he can't control his temper, and he always uses aggression to respond. Why does Bill act this way? Does he live in a violent home or neighborhood? Does he have problems dealing with reality? Or is he just a bad kid? There are no simple answers to these questions for many students with behavior disorders. Sometimes we (as teachers) can speculate or make assumptions about the role of parents, peers, or temperament, but often this is all we can do. It is very difficult to determine why one child has a behavior disorder and another child in the same situation does not.

In spite of numerous theories and hypotheses about the causes of behavioral disorders, all we can do with certainty is identify factors that seem to coincide with the occurrence of behavioral differences. These factors can be grouped into two major categories: environmental and physiological. Environmental factors focus on the child's interactions with people and things external to him or her; physiological factors focus on the inner biology or psychology of the child. The accompanying box, "Factors Associated with Behavioral Disorders," summarizes these points.

~ Factors Associated with Behavioral Disorders

Environmental Factors

- Family factors
- Cultural factors
- School factors

Physiological Factors

- Organic factors
- Genetic factors
- Specific syndromes with behavioral correlates

Environmental Factors

Environmental factors that may contribute to behavioral disorders include family factors, cultural factors, and school factors. Family factors often revolve around the level and consistency of discipline; the history of violence and arrests in the family; and the way parents and siblings deal with feelings and each other. For example, Walker and Sylwester (1991) found that children who exhibit antisocial behaviors were more likely to live in homes with more negative and less competent family management styles. As you might expect, children who have experienced consistent behavior management practices, including positive as well as negative consequences for behavior, have a clearer idea of appropriate and inappropriate behavior. In other words, just as in the classroom, it is important for children at home to know the rules and be expected to follow them. Some other possible contributors to children's behavior can be the modeling of aggressive behavior by family members, neglect, or traumatic events such as death or divorce. Remember, however, that the way individual children respond to factors like these can vary considerably. Also, many children with behavioral disorders seem to have very supportive and loving family environments.

Cultural factors may include the cultural norms for accepted levels of deviant behavior and, some people suspect, the level of violence in the media. In the middle school years, students with antisocial behavior often develop peer groups that support and reinforce inappropriate behavior (Walker & Sylwester, 1991). Figure 7.1 presents a diagram of the interaction between environmental risk factors and the development of inappropriate behaviors.

Physiological Factors

Physiological factors that may influence the development of behavioral disorders include organic factors, such as dysfunctions of the central nervous system; genetic factors, such as a family history of schizophrenia; or specific syndromes, such as Tourette's syndrome, which are accompanied by unusual behavior patterns. A child's temperament has also been identified as a possible source of behavioral differences. Again, with the exception of some syndromes with distinct behavior correlates, we must rely primarily on assumptions when dealing with physiological causes of behavioral disorders.

It is interesting to note that a number of students receive drug treatment for behavioral disorders. Although the cause of the behaviors may be unknown, certain drugs ameliorate symptoms for some people. Because drug treatments work on the symptoms rather than on the causes, drug therapy must be con-

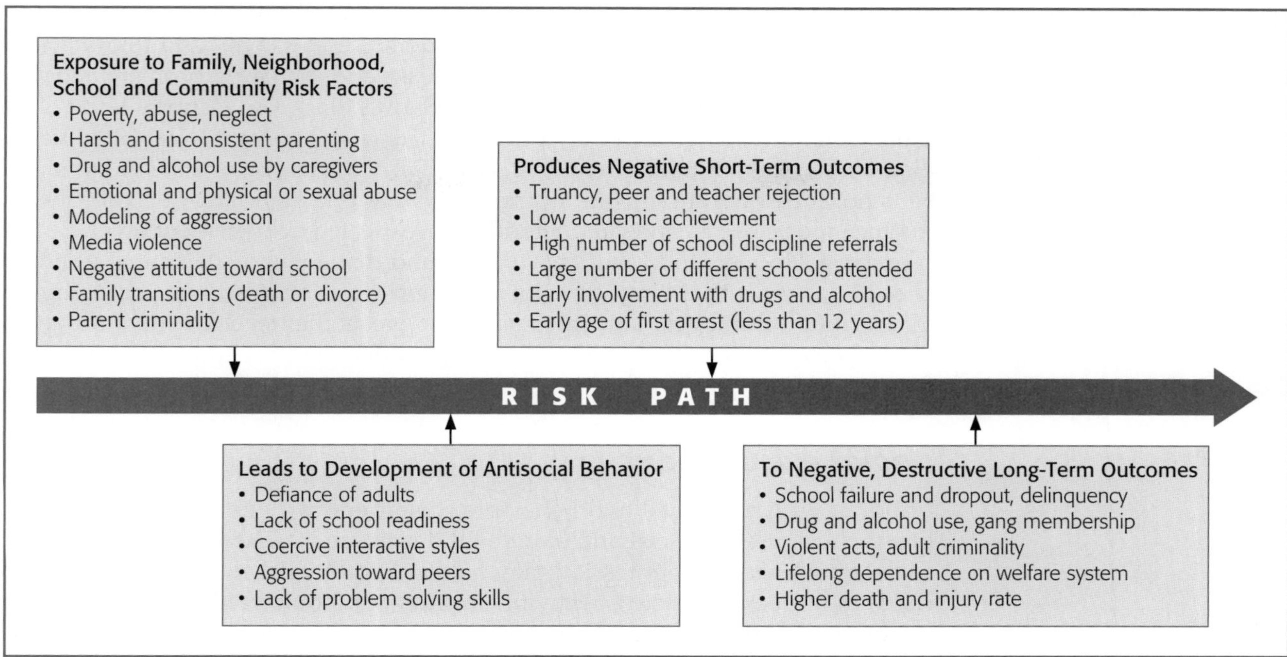

Figure 7.1
The Path to Negative Outcomes

Source: Sprague, J., & Walker, H. (2000). "Early identification and intervention for youth with antisocial and violent behavior," *Exceptional Children, 66,* 367–379.

stant in order for the symptoms to stay suppressed. A prominent example is the use of drug therapy for attention deficit/hyperactivity disorder. Although the exact cause of this disorder is not known, certain drugs have been found to suppress its symptoms in some students. Young people with depression or who demonstrate psychotic behaviors may also receive medication. A medical model for treatment may be used with increasing frequency as we learn more about the role of physiological contributions to behavioral disorders. Professionals stress, however, that effective programs include medication in conjunction with behavioral and educational interventions (Forness, Sweeney, & Toy, 1996).

Drug therapy can be an important component of a treatment plan for some students with behavioral disorders.

Effects on the Developing Child

Behavioral and emotional disorders, by definition, affect the way children interact with those around them as well as the performance abilities of the children themselves. In this section, we discuss some of the specific ways the child's life can be affected by behavioral disorders.

School Achievement

Most children with emotional or behavioral disorders are in the average range of intellectual functioning, yet do not do well in school. Although the extent to which behavior affects academic performance varies according to the individual

Most children with emotional or behavioral disorders are in the normal range of intelligence but tend to do poorly in school.

child, poor schoolwork and underachievement in class are often cited as characteristics of children with behavioral disorders. Researchers have found a relationship between more difficult academic tasks and increased problem behavior and lower attention to task (DePaepe, Shores, Jack, & Denny, 1996). Low achievement in school also may be associated with poor work habits, noncompliant behaviors, or poor attentional skills. Research suggests that students with behavioral disorders perform at approximately one standard deviation below the mean, or close to one year behind their expected achievement level. In fact, Glassberg, Hooper, and Mattison (1999) found that about 53 percent of a sample of students recently identified with behavior disorders also met the definition for learning disabilities. This information suggests that teachers must recognize the importance of academic assessment and effective educational interventions for these children.

Social Adjustment

Children with emotional and behavioral disorders by definition exhibit behaviors that affect their social and emotional development. Externalizing behaviors such as violence and aggression may be directed toward classmates, and many children with externalizing behavior disorders do not have the skills for reflecting on and restricting their behavior. As these children grow into adolescence, their lack of control can often lead to serious conflicts. The patterns of violent behaviors exhibited by students with behavior disorders change as students age. Violent behavior patterns may consist of bullying at the elementary level, fighting at the middle school level, and using weapons or drugs at the high school level (Furlong & Morrison, 2000).

Internalized behaviors such as withdrawal or depression may result in the children being teased or rejected by classmates, and may cause great difficulty interacting with others. Research shows that children with behavior disorders are not accepted well by their regular classmates, even in adolescence—a time when some noncompliant behavior is the norm (Sabornie et al., 1988).

Without education and intervention, the behaviors that characterize a behavioral disorder will continue to affect the student after he or she leaves the school environment. What will happen when an aggressive child grows into an adult? Will he punch his coworkers or have a tantrum while driving or arguing with his girlfriend? If a student doesn't learn new ways to control and respond to anger or frustration as he or she grows older, the probability of encounters with the law increases.

Many adolescents with behavioral disorders have been in trouble with the law.

High school classes for students with behavioral disorders often include students who have been in trouble with the law. The number of teens with behavioral disorders who have gone through the legal system at least once varies greatly from area to area; however, students with this diagnosis appear at higher risk for arrest both during and after the school years (Doren, Bullis, & Benz, 1996). Patterns of aggressive, rule-breaking, and risk-taking behavior are often found in students with behavioral disorders, and these behaviors set the stage for illegal activities.

Research has investigated patterns of drug use and dropout rates of junior and senior high school students with and without behavioral disorders. Devlin and Elliott (1992) found that 51 percent of students with behavior disorders were in the high-drug-use category, 20 percent were in the medium-drug-use category, and 28 percent were in the low- or negligible-drug-use category. Compare those figures with the ones for students without behavioral disorders:

Social acceptance by classmates is desired by every adolescent. The peer group can play an important role in identifying and supporting appropriate behaviors. (Brian Crites/ Kansas City Star/ CORBIS-SYGMA)

14 percent in the high-use group, 10 percent in the medium-use group, and 74 percent in the low- or negligible-use group. Walker, Colvin, and Ramsey (1995) found that boys identified with antisocial behavior disorders experienced seven times as many arrests during their school years as boys identified as at-risk for school failure. They also found the antisocial students were over five times as likely to drop out of school as the children at risk.

Language and Communication

As we look at the effects of emotional or behavioral disorders on communication, we must consider that in many ways behavior *is* communication. Some behaviors are learned as a way of responding to situations or events or of getting a response; some are developed because an individual has no other effective means of expression; and some are developed to enable an individual to control a situation. When we talk about teaching students appropriate behavior, or reducing inappropriate behavior, we are also teaching students alternative ways of communicating information, feelings, or needs.

Students with emotional or behavioral disorders may have great difficulty expressing themselves using verbal language, or they may experience much milder forms of language difficulty and delay. Some students with behavioral disorders are found to use fewer words per sentence, to have difficulty staying on a topic, and to have problems using language that is appropriate or meaningful in a given situation or conversation (McDonough, 1989). Students may also have difficulty organizing their thoughts to communicate effectively through oral or written language.

Language is crucial to academic performance, to interactions with peers and adults, and to the development of the sequential logical thought processes required in many self-management interventions, and it is an important component of the educational program. Communication, however, involves more than language. Teachers should always keep in mind the potential communicative intent of the *behaviors* students are exhibiting and be ready to provide appropriate alternatives—new ways of expressing how they feel or what they want—so they can successfully overcome their existing communication behaviors.

Severe Disorders

In the case studies presented earlier, we saw the great impact behavioral disorders can have on a child's life. Yet the continuum of emotional or behavioral disorders extends even further than what has been already described. Some individuals exhibit severe disorders of behavior—behaviors that require even more specialized attention and intervention, some of which are provided outside of the regular school setting. Others have unusual patterns of behavior, such as those found in autism (see Chapter 8), or a combination of disabilities that also require specialized interventions and that can have profound effects on the individual's behavior in all areas of life.

■ ***Severe Emotional or Behavior Disorders*** The children we refer to in this section may either have externalizing or internalizing behavioral disorders, but they exhibit behaviors that are markedly severe and intended to harm others or themselves. Other children in this category may be so withdrawn as to resist any semblance of normal social interaction. Their functioning may be severely inhibited because of withdrawal, disoriented thoughts, or depression. In general, these children require extensive and intensive educational assistance. Some children with severe disabilities receive educational services in public school settings, whereas others still are served, at least for a time, in segregated or residential facilities.

> John, who is barely 8 years old, lives in a residential facility for children with severe behavioral disorders. He is exceptionally bright yet works at a primer level. By the age of 7, John had stabbed his mother twice with a knife, pushed his younger brother down the stairs and off a high chair, and tried to set fire to his room on three separate occasions. Although most of the time John seemed to be a friendly, outgoing child, his behaviors were determined to be so potentially harmful that he was placed in the residential setting.

Behavior patterns similar to John's are among the most difficult for professionals and parents to handle. The child seems to be normal or above average in so many respects, yet exhibits incredibly hurtful behavior without any warning or apparent reason. Treatment for John will need to be very complex, and most likely it is outside of the realm of school personnel. Teaching him to recognize and control his impulses will be a key focus.

Other students with severe behavior disorders may be the target of their own destructive behavior.

> Rhonda is 17 years old. Although she has always been moody and aggressive, she was identified as having behavioral disorders only a few years ago. At that time, her behaviors became increasingly self-destructive and violent. She broke her hand by slamming it against her locker, gave herself cigarette burns on her arms, and, in the last year, made two suicide attempts. Although Rhonda was placed in a public school resource class ini-

tially, she was later placed in a residential setting for more intensive interventions and close supervision.

Such violent, self-destructive behavior is often interpreted as a plea for attention or a cry for help. Interventions for suicidal students include counseling, medication (when appropriate), helping them think more positively about themselves, teaching new and more positive ways to communicate anger, fear, or frustration, focusing on activities designed to demonstrate and accentuate their skills and abilities, and developing positive friendships.

The specific instructional strategies and therapies used for children with severe disabilities will vary widely and must be tailored to the specific needs of the individual. In a number of instances, drug therapy will be a component of the treatment plan. In part, drug treatment is a response to recent discoveries that some disorders, such as certain types of schizophrenia or depression, appear to have a strong physiological component.

Lewis (1988) suggests that the successful movement of children with severe emotional or behavioral disorders from residential treatment facilities to their home and school environments must be accompanied by extensive liaison work between the facility and the home and receiving school. In order for these children to continue to improve and function independently, they must be able to cope with life in their everyday environments, not just in the residential facility. The more teachers understand about the environments into which children will be returning, the more they can prepare the students to handle those emotional and behavioral requirements.

■ ***Childhood Schizophrenia*** Childhood schizophrenia is classified as a behavioral disorder. The primary characteristics of childhood schizophrenia are (1) disorders in speech and language—children's speech may take on peculiar pitch and intonation and language may be self-directed or meaningless; (2) disorders in the ability to relate to other people or the environment—children may be extremely clingy or virtually ignore other people; and (3) emotional disorders: Children may be extremely anxious and nervous and experience extreme mood swings that are often unpredictable and violent (Rosenberg, Wilson, Maheady, & Sindelar, 1992). Childhood schizophrenia is rare. In the classroom, the child with this disorder may experience great difficulty attending to work and interacting with others. The unusual and unpredictable behavior patterns may work against successful social integration or group activities.

Effects on the Family

Family Interaction

The effects on the family of a child with behavioral disorders can be significant. Some parents struggle with the feeling that they contributed to the problem; others find dealing with the child's behavior emotionally and physically exhausting. Some parents, and siblings as well, feel they have to focus all of their attention on a child with behavior disorders; others try to ignore the behaviors. Because a child's behavior is often taken to be a reflection of parenting skill, a child with behavioral disorders may cause a parent to feel embarrassed and guilty. Parents may try to "make it up" to the child or become angry with him or her—sometimes to the point of abuse. Try to remember this the next time you

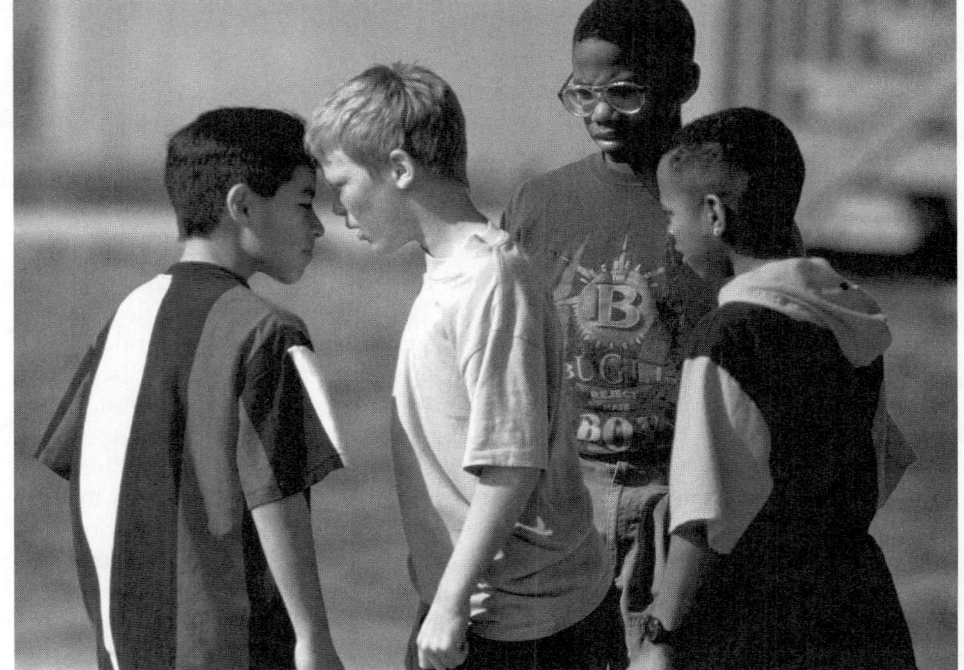

Some children experience difficulty adjusting to the behavioral requirements of social situations, which leads to inappropriate or aggressive behavior. (Bob Daemmrich/The Image Works, Inc.)

stare angrily at a parent whose child is crying in the grocery store. Parents may be faced continually with fear of what their child will do next or with feelings of helplessness.

A child with a behavioral or emotional disorder may become a victim of abuse. Zirpoli (1986) found that children with behavioral disorders are at increased risk for parental abuse. It is not clear whether abuse is more likely to cause behavioral disorders or whether behavioral disorders are more likely to cause abuse. Zirpoli, however, discusses the fact that the incidence of child abuse of children with all types of disabilities does not decrease after the age of 6, as it does with children without disabilities. One reason for this sad statistic may be that the presence of a lifelong disability is a continuing stressor to the family. (See the accompanying box, "A Closer Look: Commonalities: Schoolwide Behavior Management: Primary, Secondary, and Tertiary Prevention Programs.")

Teachers often involve parents in programs designed to teach behavior.

Because of specific stress factors and other individual needs of families, educational plans must take the family's needs into account. Some of the feelings of helplessness can be addressed when parents are given strategies to implement and carry over to the home, particularly in the area of dealing with crises—a need frequently expressed by parents of children with behavioral disorders (Simpson, 1988). For example, a family may be concerned about the tantrums their 10-year-old displays in public places when he is unable to get his way. Embarrassed by their child, the parents typically give in to him so that he will stop creating a public scene. The parents feel manipulated by their child and helpless. The teacher may come up with a set of techniques for the parents to try. These may include a checklist for the child to keep for himself while out in public. If all of the appropriate behaviors are checked off, the child could be eligible for some privilege or allowed to choose where to eat lunch. Other strate-

A closer look

Commonalities: Schoolwide Behavior Management: Primary, Secondary, and Tertiary Prevention Programs

Programs for All Students

Most schools are faced with the challenge of designing programs or plans for school discipline. Increasingly, these plans focus on the prevention of discipline problems as well as on teaching students and teachers new strategies for dealing with inappropriate behavior when it does occur. An example of a program that focuses on both prevention and remediation is the schoolwide discipline plan developed by Nelson, Crabtree, Marchand-Martella, and Martella (1998). These educators and researchers describe their discipline program as a multilevel plan for all students, with greater levels of services and more comprehensive services provided to students who exhibit more pervasive patterns of disruptive behavior. Some characteristics of their program are as follows:

1. *Prevention* The schoolwide intervention includes adjustments in ecological or environmental factors that could contribute to inappropriate behaviors (such as reducing congestion), the development of specific behavioral expectations for students in common areas (such as hallways), and the supervision of students in common areas.

2. *Prevention and remediation* The school establishes a schoolwide discipline plan and a schoolwide strategy for classroom management. The strategy for classroom management is called the Think Time Strategy. In the Think Time Strategy, students engaging in problem behavior move to a Think Time classroom and meet with a designated teacher. The student and teacher engage in a debriefing process that consists of several steps, including having the student identify his or her inappropriate behavior, the motivation and consequence of the behavior, and appropriate alternative behaviors before he or she returns to the classroom. Students who are at-risk for disruptive behavior also receive more intensive instruction in behavior management skills, as well as academic and/or behavioral interventions designed just for them.

3. *Remediation* The continuum of services includes "wraparound services" for children with consistent disruptive behavior patterns. Wraparound services include the involvement of social service agencies and parents or other caregivers, so that interventions are comprehensive and consistent across environments.

Source: J. R. Nelson, M. Crabtree, N. Marchand-Martella, and R. Martella, "Teaching Good Behavior in the Whole School," *Teaching Exceptional Children*, *30* (1998), 4–9.

gies include helping the parents develop consistent and firm consequences to implement if a tantrum should occur and taking the child on a number of short trips to places that usually do not result in problems (for example, the post office as opposed to the toy store) so that lots of praise and encouragement can be given when no tantrums occur.

Parents and the Schools

The family of the child with emotional or behavioral disorders plays a critical role in the development and implementation of effective educational programs. Educators suggest that, because of the need for mutual trust and recognition of behavioral goals, strong parent-teacher relationships may be particularly important when the teacher and student are from different cultural backgrounds (Cartledge,

Kea, & Ida, 2000). Many educators try to involve parents as much as possible when establishing consistent behavior-management strategies across settings. Programs with a home-based component that includes the delivery by parents of positive and negative consequences for behavior have resulted in decreases in noncompliant and antisocial behaviors as well as in symptoms of depression in children (Eddy, Reid, & Fetrow, 2000; Rosen, Gabardi, Miller, & Miller, 1990).

A key factor in consistent behavior management is communication between teacher and parent.

One major factor in consistent behavior management is the degree of communication between the teacher and the parent. Parents of a child with behavioral disorders should keep in close contact with their child's teachers so they can be aware of how he or she is progressing and how they can stress the same behavior patterns at home. Many teachers have devised daily or weekly forms that are sent home to let parents know how the child behaved that day and what the parents can do to help reinforce good behavior. Parents may provide consequences for good school behavior, such as taking the child to a movie on Saturday afternoon after a week of good reports. This type of teacher-parent alliance may be particularly helpful with older children who value their weekend and afterschool time.

Attention Deficit/Hyperactivity Disorder

As mentioned earlier, **attention deficit/hyperactivity disorder (ADHD)** refers to a disorder that affects an individual's ability to attend to or focus on tasks and that may involve high levels of motoric activity. As you can see in the accompanying diagnostic criteria from DSM-IV, the symptoms of ADHD are grouped into two major categories: (1) inattention and (2) hyperactivity-impulsivity. The number of symptoms a child displays in each category will determine if the child has primarily an attention disorder (ADHD, predominantly inattention type), a hyperactivity disorder (ADHD, predominantly hyperactive-impulsive type), or a combination (ADHD, combined type) (DSM-IV, 1994). You may hear the term *attention deficit disorder (ADD)* used by teachers or parents to refer to the inattention type of ADHD, or as a general description of attention problems.

Assessment and Diagnosis

Between 3 and 5 percent of children in the United States are identified as having ADHD (Lerner, Lowenthal, & Lerner, 1995). The methods used to determine if a student has ADHD include interviews of the child, parents, and teachers, and behavior checklists. If you look at the DSM-IV diagnostic criteria in the accompanying box, you will note that all children display some of these behaviors at one time or another. As with all behavior disorders, the clinicians look at the degree to which these behaviors are performed and how the behaviors affect academic and social performance before reaching a diagnosis. ADHD is diagnosed in individuals of all ages; however, the symptoms must have been present before 7 years of age (DSM-IV, 1994). Lerner, Lowenthal, and Lerner (1995) summarize research that indicates that approximately 25 percent of students with ADHD have an additional diagnosis—for example, learning disabilities or conduct-related behavior disorders. Although assessment and diagnosis can be done by psychologists in the school setting, many children are referred to pediatricians for evaluation. Some parents prefer a pediatrician's evaluation because the doctor can rule out other possible causes for the behavior and because drug therapy is often used, which must be prescribed by a physician.

~ Diagnostic Criteria for Attention Deficit/Hyperactivity Disorder

A. Either (1) or (2):

(1) six (or more) of the following symptoms of inattention have persisted for at least 6 months to a degree that is maladaptive and inconsistent with developmental level:

Inattention

(a) often fails to give close attention to details or makes careless mistakes in schoolwork, work, or other activities

(b) often has difficulty sustaining attention in tasks or play activities

(c) often does not seem to listen when spoken to directly

(d) often does not follow through on instructions and fails to finish schoolwork, chores, or duties in the workplace (not due to oppositional behavior or failure to understand instructions)

(e) often has difficulty organizing tasks and activities

(f) often avoids, dislikes, or is reluctant to engage in tasks that require sustained mental effort (such as schoolwork or homework)

(g) often loses things necessary for tasks or activities (e.g., toys, school assignments, pencils, books, or tools)

(h) is often easily distracted by extraneous stimuli

(i) is often forgetful in daily activities

(2) six (or more) of the following symptoms of hyperactivity-impulsivity have persisted for at least 6 months to a degree that is maladaptive and inconsistent with developmental level:

Hyperactivity

(a) often fidgets with hands or feet or squirms in seat

(b) often leaves seat in classroom or in other situations in which remaining seated is expected

(c) often runs about or climbs excessively in situations in which it is inappropriate (in adolescents or adults, may be limited to subjective feelings of restlessness)

(d) often has difficulty playing or engaging in leisure activities quietly

(e) is often "on the go" or often acts as if "driven by a motor"

(f) often talks excessively

Impulsivity

(g) often blurts out answers before questions have been completed

(h) often has difficulty awaiting turn

(i) often interrupts or intrudes on others (e.g., butts into conversations or games)

B. Some hyperactive-impulsive or inattentive symptoms that caused impairment were present before age 7 years.

C. Some impairment from the symptoms is present in two or more settings (e.g., at school [or work] and at home).

D. There must be clear evidence of clinically significant impairment in social, academic, or occupational functioning.

E. The symptoms do not occur exclusively during the course of a Pervasive Developmental Disorder, Schizophrenia, or other Psychotic Disorder and are not better accounted for by another mental disorder (e.g., Mood Disorder, Anxiety Disorder, Dissociative Disorder, or a Personality Disorder).

Characteristics

The characteristics of children with ADHD will vary both across and within types of the disorder. When a child has inattention symptoms, his work may be messy, incomplete, and disorganized; directions may be forgotten or only partially followed; and he may be easily distracted and forgetful. The student with

ADHD is likely to forget to bring pencils, paper, books, and lunch tickets to school—every day. Essentially, any activity that requires voluntary, sustained attention can be disrupted. For example, while you are giving directions for a test, the student may interrupt you to ask what is being served for lunch today. Long tasks or activities are particularly difficult, and the student may try to avoid them altogether. Your request for a student with ADHD to write a two-page essay in class could be met with (a) frequent trips to the bathroom or pencil sharpener; (b) a half-written sentence with the student gazing out the window; (c) a "completed" essay consisting of three sentences and written in less than five minutes; or (d) the student attempting the task, crumpling up the paper, and sulking with his head on his desk. A student's attention deficits can eventually result in learning deficits, because of difficulty attending to material long enough to learn and practice it.

The behavior of students who experience impulsivity/hyperactivity symptoms reflects high and constant levels of activity. The characteristics of impulsive cognitive style that we discussed in Chapter 4 apply to students with ADHD. They may react quickly to situations, without considering the consequences, or they may shout out answers to questions without waiting for recognition or reflecting on their responses. The activity level demonstrated by many students with ADHD is much higher than that of other children, and it is constant. The child with hyperactivity symptoms is always moving—running, twitching, tapping, shifting, and jumping. Parents of young children with hyperactivity report that their children have trouble sleeping or eating (Fowler, 1995). The constant motion, combined with impulsivity, obviously is at odds with the behavioral requirements of school settings and often puts kids with ADHD at risk for accidents and social altercations.

Educational Programs for Students with ADHD

Although ADHD is not a category of special education identified in IDEA, many students with the disorder do receive special education or other educational support services. Students with ADHD who do not have another identified disability may receive services under the IDEA category "Other Health Impaired" or, more typically, under Section 504 of the Rehabilitation Act of 1973. It is likely, therefore, that if you have a student with ADHD in your classroom, he or she will have an IEP that identifies specific accommodations and educational needs. Educational strategies for students with ADHD focus on attention, organization, behavior management, and self-management. The specific interventions used with students with ADHD overlap considerably with the strategies we discuss in each of these areas in both Chapter 4 and this chapter. Students with ADHD need structure, consistency, and clear consequences for behavior. It is important for teachers and parents to remember that students with ADHD need to learn specific skills for organizing, attending, and self-management.

Drug therapy is frequently a part of educational programs of students with ADHD. It is successfully used in many, but not all, cases to allow students time to think, reflect, and learn. Approximately 70 to 80 percent of students with ADHD respond to medication (DuPaul & Barkley, 1990). However, drug therapy does not *teach* students necessary skills, although it may give the students the time needed to learn them. If you have a student in your class who is receiving drug therapy for ADHD, it is important for you to provide feedback to the parents and the physician about the effects of the drug. Often, physicians must experiment with dosages before finding the correct one; your input will be important. The most common drugs used are psychostimulants, particularly Ritalin, Dexedrine, and Cylert (DuPaul & Barkley, 1990). Each child will react differently, and some side effects are indicated, so it is important to learn as much about each student's drug therapy regime as possible.

In Classrooms

Educational planning and programming for students with emotional or behavioral disorders involve several interrelated issues: early intervention, assessment, placing children with behavioral disorders within the school system, choosing a philosophical approach, designing curriculum and instructional strategies to enhance learning, and handling discipline in the school.

Early Intervention

There is so much variation in what behaviors and emotional reactions are considered developmentally appropriate among young children that it is difficult to identify emotional or behavior disorders in the early years. Many educators, however, believe that early intervention is critical, particularly for antisocial or noncompliant behaviors (Kamps & Tankersley, 1996). In fact, the current focus on prevention of behavior disorders has resulted in the screening procedures we will discuss in the next section being applied in preschool settings such as Head Start Programs (Feil, Walker, Severson, & Ball, 2000). Young children with behaviors that greatly concern parents may be eligible for services under Public Law 99-457, as we discussed earlier, without being labeled behavior disordered.

Identification and Assessment: The Classroom Teacher's Role

Identifying and assessing behavior disorders is not easy because of the ambiguity of the definition and the subjectivity involved in judging the appropriateness of behavior. For example, suppose I like my classroom busy and bustling, with chatter going on at all times, whereas you like your class perfectly still and quiet—no one moves without raising a hand. Further, suppose that little Bobby likes to roam around the class and talk. You and I will rate Bobby's behavior very differently. This point is important to keep in mind, because although there are many ways to assess behavior differences, including screening, rating scales, and psychological testing, the primary method of identifying students with emotional or behavior disorders is, increasingly, observations of the child's behavior.

■ ***Screening*** The purpose of screening is to identify children who exhibit behaviors that interfere with their classroom performance and academic achievement. Procedures designed to integrate screening and possible assessment for identification include the Standardized Screening for Behavior Disorders (SSBD), developed by Walker, Severson, and others (1988), and the Early Screening Project, an adaptation of the SSBD (Feil, Walker, Severson, & Ball, 2000).

Screening identifies children whose behavior interferes with academic achievement.

These procedures involve what the authors call a multiple-gating procedure. That is, there are three stages, or gates, of the screening and assessment process. In the first stage of the SSBD, teachers rank all of their students in two types of behavior patterns: externalizing behaviors (such as stealing, throwing tantrums, damaging property, using obscene language or physical aggression) or internalizing behaviors (such as shyness, sadness, thought disorders). This step requires teachers to look at all of their students, therefore increasing the teachers' awareness of and attention to specific behavior difficulties children might be experiencing. In the second stage the three children who rank highest in the class on each of the two behavioral dimensions are assessed using comprehensive behavior rating scales. If any of the children score beyond a certain point on the behavior-rating instruments, then the final stage, direct observation in various settings, occurs.

■ ***Testing*** In addition to the IQ and achievement tests that are a part of all special education evaluations, a few specific types of instruments are employed if emotional or behavioral disorders are suspected.

Behavior-Rating Scales After a child is referred, teachers, parents, and school psychologists observe him or her in school and home settings and complete **behavior-rating scales** designed to reflect patterns of behavior. Behavior-rating scales used frequently in the schools include the Conners' Behavior Ratings Scales and the Peterson-Quay Behavior Rating Scales. An example of the Abbreviated Conners' Rating Scale for Teachers is found in Figure 7.2.

It is important to understand that there is no standard or uniform battery of tests, checklists, or procedures to follow for the identification of children or adolescents with behavioral disorders. Each state education agency establishes its own guidelines and identifies the particular tests that can be used. Intelligence and achievement tests may be used to substantiate or rule out specific disability areas. Other assessment devices are largely subjective. All of the information is examined to determine if the child has a behavioral disorder. There is no specific test score, test average, or level of behavior agreed on by professionals as an appropriate criterion for identification.

■ ***Assessment Issues*** Because classroom teachers play an important role in the identification of students with behavioral or emotional disorders, it is important for them to understand the issues involved in defining and identifying children who fall into this category.

Teachers' personal biases can affect the referral and assessment process.

One issue that surfaces repeatedly when assessment is discussed is the problem of personal bias in the referral system. It is easy to see how the effects of personal bias and tolerance can influence behavior-rating scales. Each of the people involved in the rating process can have very different perceptions of what is normal or acceptable in terms of activity level or acting-out behavior; the raters may have different personal feelings toward the child, which could bias ratings; and the level of experience a rater has had with children can affect scoring—a parent with no other children might rate behavior differently than a parent with three or four other children. Currently, researchers are studying the effects of gender and cultural bias on behavioral ratings and student referrals (Reid et al., 2000). The box "Cultural Diversity and Serious Emotional Disturbance (SED)" describes some of the factors to keep in mind when identifying and instructing children from culturally diverse backgrounds.

Name of child ____________________ Grade ________
Sex of child ____________________ School ____________________
Age of child ____________________ Person filling out this scale ____________________

Please answer all questions. Beside each item below, indicate the degree of the problem by a check mark (√)	***Not at All Present***	***Just a Little Present***	***Pretty Much Present***	***Very Much Present***
1. Restless in the "squirming" sense				
2. Makes inappropriate noises when he shouldn't				
3. Demands must be met immediately				
4. Acts "smart" (impudent or sassy)				
5. Temper outbursts and unpredictable behavior				
6. Overly sensitive to criticism				
7. Distractibility or attention span a problem				
8. Disturbs other children				
9. Daydreams				
10. Pouts and sulks				
11. Mood changes quickly and drastically				
12. Quarrelsome				
13. Submissive attitude toward authority				
14. Restless, always up and on the go				
15. Excitable, impulsive				
16. Excessive demands for teacher's attention				
17. Appears to be unaccepted by group				
18. Appears to be easily led by other children				
19. Appears to lack leadership				
20. Fails to finish things he or she starts				
21. Childish and immature				
22. Denies mistakes or blames others				
23. Does not get along well with other children				
24. Uncooperative with classmates				
25. Easily frustrated in efforts				
26. Uncooperative with teacher				
27. Difficulty in learning				

Figure 7.2
Abbreviated Conners' Rating Scale for Teachers

Source: R. Sprague and E. Sleator, "Effects of Psychopharmacologic Agents on Learning Disorders." *Pediatric Clinics of North America, 20* (1973), p. 726. Copyright © 1973 by W. B. Saunders Co. Reprinted by permission.

~ Cultural Diversity and Serious Emotional Disturbance (SED)

Misperceptions Abound. Because many people lack understanding and cultural sensitivity toward cultures different from their own, teachers, administrators, ancillary personnel, and students may misinterpret culturally based behaviors and may view them as behavioral disorders. What teachers consider "discipline problems" are determined by their own culture, personal values, attitudes, and teaching style. More often than not, disciplinary problems seem centered around interpersonal discourse. Tension and negative consequences seem to intensify among the various communication styles of diverse ethnic groups when teachers and their students do not share the same cultural backgrounds, ethnic identities, values, social protocols, and relational styles.

Cultural Inversion and Other Behavior. Culturally different behaviors are not equivalent to social-skill deficits or behavior disorders. Standardized or European American-based social-skill assessments may not adequately reflect the social competence of culturally different students. The quick, high-intensity responses of African Americans, for example, may be seen as hostile, rude, or hyperactive. Acting-out, disruptive behaviors do not automatically signal conduct disorder and, in some cases, may be more a manifestation of "cultural inversion" where students are resisting the label of "acting white" by refusing to follow the established expectations of the classroom culture.

Cycles of Misinterpretation and Fear. Cultural misunderstandings can have negative effects for both students and teachers. Researchers noted the occurrence of vicious circles, explaining that when students find their playful acts are misinterpreted, they become angry and intensify the roughness of their activities; the result is greater fear on the part of whites. Students may feel empowered and rewarded by the effects of their actions on whites, particularly females. This false sense of power may lead them to escalate those behaviors, most likely at the expense of more productive behaviors that relate to school success.

Professionals urge that children be observed in a number of different settings, that ratings and observations be conducted by several different people, that observations be conducted over a period of time rather than during a single session, and that predisposing factors, including the influence of cultural differences and family expectations, be considered during assessment (Executive Committee of the Council for Children with Behavioral Disorders, 1989). Adherence to these suggestions will help reduce the influence of personal bias and episodic or situational behavior problems on the assessment and identification process. See the accompanying box, "Issues in the Assessment of Behavior Disorders," for a summary of related assessment issues.

■ ***Assessment for Instruction*** Although behavior checklists and screening procedures may help identify students with behavior disorders, they may not provide specific information about instructional objectives. Educators will conduct functional behavioral assessments to obtain information that can be translated into instructional goals when students with disabilities exhibit problem behaviors. The 1997 IDEA amendments require that a **functional behavioral assessment** (FBA) be administered to students with behavior problems in order to identify strategies that are positive and replacement behaviors that can serve the same function as the problem behaviors (IDEA Amendments, 1997). See the accompanying box, "What Is a Functional Behavioral Assessment?", for more information about this type of assessment.

The information from the FBA will serve as the basis for a **behavior intervention plan** (BIP). The BIP should contain positive, behavior support strategies

Excessive Compliance or Cultural Expectation? It also should be noted that exceptionally compliant behaviors are not necessarily indicative of the absence of some difficulty. For example, in one study Asian-American students received positive teacher and peer ratings but also indicated they were least likely to question unfair rules or do anything if treated unfairly. This emphasis on conformity and "saving face" may cause teachers to make erroneous assumptions about the child's well-being and lead to significant problems being overlooked.

Ecosystem Importance. The tendency for some children to need more "wait time" or to be verbally unassertive (e.g., Native and Hispanic American) may be interpreted as unmotivated or resistant to instruction. Researchers assert the need for an "ecosystemic" assessment, which takes an ecological approach to consider all aspects of the child's environment.

The issue of culturally relevant assessment for SED is probably most relevant for African- and Asian-American students who are proportionately overrepresented and underrepresented in SED diagnoses, respectively. Researchers recommend that one use norms based on members of the cultural group of the student being assessed and that evaluation materials be reviewed by people who know the child well and can provide culturally based interpretations of the child's behavior. Other suggestions for linguistically diverse students are to assess students in both languages, attend to verbal and nonverbal communication, and to focus on ways to support the student rather than on simply documenting student deficits.

Source: Cartledge, Kea, and Ida, "Anticipating Differences—Celebrating Strengths: Providing Culturally Competent Services for Students with Serious Emotional Disturbance," *Teaching Exceptional Children, 32* (2000), p. 32.

designed to teach and reinforce appropriate behavior (Kauffman, 2001). The BIP becomes a part of student's IEP and reflects both behavioral goals and interventions.

Instructional Setting

Children with behavioral disorders have the same placement options as other children with disabilities. These options range from the residential school to the regular classroom. Because of the nature of certain types of behavioral disorders, such as aggressive and threatening behavior, some segregated service-delivery models have persisted in many school systems. These placement options are usually reserved as a last resort for students, usually adolescents, who are deemed unable to cope with the regular school environment. Most students with behavioral disorders, however, are served through a resource setting. In the resource room, students with behavioral disorders may receive instruction in academic skills, as well as interventions or programs designed to increase appropriate behavior.

Recent research suggests that the number of adolescents with behavioral disorders mainstreamed into regular classes has grown in recent years. There has been very little research, however, on interventions that are successful for students with behavioral disorders in general education settings (Cullinan, Epstein, & Sabornie, 1992; Dunlap & Childs, 1996). The ability of the special education teacher and classroom teacher to work together is a critical factor in the successful adjustment of these students in general education classes. Specific

~ Issues in the Assessment of Behavior Disorders

All of the following factors may cause problems during the assessment process.

Problem

- Personal bias: For example, the referring teacher's bias in favor of talkative or quiet children.

Possible Solution

- A child should be observed by a variety of raters.

Problem

- Effect of the specific classroom environment

Solution

- Evaluate a child's behavior in the context of several classroom environments and other settings.

Problem

- Noticing students with withdrawn or depressed behavior

Solution

- Ask for information or training about all types of behavior that could indicate an emotional or behavior problem.

social skills or behaviors need to be targeted for instruction, and all individuals involved in educational planning need to agree on them.

Teaching Strategies

The curriculum for students with emotional and behavioral disorders must address both behavioral and academic needs.

■ ***Curriculum Focus*** The curriculum for students with behavioral and emotional disorders must address behavioral as well as academic needs. The teacher must include curriculum components that remediate behavioral excesses or deficiencies as well as those that teach the regular school curriculum. To address both of these major curriculum areas is quite a challenge for any teacher. Although the responsibilities of the classroom teacher and the special education teacher will vary depending on placement options and class size, the importance of collaboration in instruction and planning cannot be overemphasized. Students in self-contained or resource settings in the public schools typically receive programs that address their behavioral performance in current settings. This curriculum, however, does not adequately prepare them for the challenges they will face in future environments.

Academic Programming Although students with behavioral disorders usually have many learning difficulties, only recently have research efforts been devoted to identifying the most effective academic interventions for these students. Coleman and Vaughn (2000) found only eight publications in the past twenty-five years that addressed reading interventions for elementary students with emotional and behavioral disorders. Recent research and recommendations suggest that the teaching strategies and instructional programs used for students with learning disabilities are also effective for students with behavioral disorders (see Chapter 4). For example, the use of mnemonic interventions such as mnemonic strategy instruction and the use of memory aids such as keywords and pegwords (Scruggs & Mastropieri, 2000) improve memory performance as

What Is a Functional Behavioral Assessment?

According to the IDEA Amendments of 1997, all students with behavior problems served under IDEA must receive a functional behavioral assessment (Yell & Shriner, 1997). Brady and Halle (1997) describe a functional behavioral assessment as a way to determine the uses or functions of behavior. They identify the following components of a functional behavioral assessment:

1. Interviews: The student, parents, teachers, and other caregivers should be interviewed about the occurrence of the behavior and the surrounding circumstances.
2. Direct observation: The student should be observed in the setting or settings in which the behavior occurs. Observations should include what happens before, during, and after behavior occurrence.
3. Analog probes: The observer should manipulate specific variables, such as the setting or the number of opportunities for interaction (for example, between the student and teacher) to get a better understanding of when and why the behavior occurs.

What Can We Learn from a Functional Behavioral Assessment?

1. When a behavior is most likely to occur: after lunch, during unstructured time, when the student is fatigued.
2. If something specific prompts the behavior: difficult seatwork, teacher correction, teasing.
3. What the student is trying to tell you: I want to be left alone, I want to get out of work, I am embarrassed, I love all this attention.
4. What usually happens after the behavior occurs: The student is ignored, put into time-out, or receives a lot of negative comments; the class laughs or works quietly; different consequences occur at different times of the day.

What Do We Do After a Functional Behavioral Assessment?

In the IEP meeting, the teachers, parents, student (if appropriate), and other relevant personnel develop an appropriate behavior management plan based on the information from the functional behavioral assessment. Answers to the following questions will be used to develop the plan:

1. Can changes in the student's environment (seating, method of teacher questioning, shortening assignments) help to prevent the occurrence of behavior?
2. What new behaviors (requesting, self-removal from setting) can the student use to satisfy the same communicative intent of the problem behaviors?
3. How can we prompt use of the alternative behavior (signals, self-monitoring, modeling)?
4. What consequences shall we provide for (a) demonstration of new behavior and (b) demonstration of problem behavior?
5. How can we evaluate behavior change?

well as positive social behavior. In the area of reading comprehension, the use of story mapping instruction resulted in improved comprehension abilities for elementary-age students with behavior disorders (Babyak, Koorland, & Mathes, 2000).

Most of the instructional procedures recommended for students with behavior disorders include the direct instruction methods outlined in earlier chapters. Modeling, leading or guided practice, and then provision of independent practice or testing are the three teaching steps found in most effective instruction plans. Dawson, Venn, and Gunter (2000) compared teacher modeling of reading to computer modeling of reading using a voice synthesizer on the reading accuracy of students with behavior disorders. Although teacher modeling was more effective, the computer modeling also improved the students' reading rate and accuracy. This study reinforces the role of modeling in academic instruction for students with behavior disorders and identifies the computer as a viable option, particularly if a teacher does not use modeling in the classroom.

Direct instruction programs are recommended for students with emotional and behavioral disorders.

In the preceding paragraphs, we have looked at single components of instruction. Stein and Davis (2000) recommend the use of comprehensive direct instruction programs for students with behavior disorders—programs that include strategies for addressing both academic and social behavior. They base their recommendations on the philosophy of positive behavioral support. **Positive behavioral support** refers to an array of preventive and positive interventions designed to create and maintain a supportive and successful environment for individuals. Stein and Davis suggest that the specific, consistent, and structured interventions found in both the curriculum and methodology of direct instruction programs are crucial to providing effective instruction for students with behavior disorders. In Chapter 4, we provide an extensive description of direct instruction practices and corresponding programs. The accompanying box, "Direct Instruction Checklist," provides a set of questions that teachers of students with behavior disorders can ask to evaluate their use of direct instruction.

Behavioral goals for students with behavior and emotional disorders must be individualized to meet each student's needs; however, more general interventions designed to prevent behavior disorders may take place at the class or building level. These interventions can be described in terms of their intended effects. In the following sections, we examine three common curriculum goals and related instructional methodology: preventing inappropriate behaviors, developing appropriate cognitions, and teaching new behaviors.

Many interventions are targeted at preventing the occurence of behavioral disorders. Prevention includes primary, secondary, and tertiary levels.

Preventing Inappropriate Behaviors The current emphasis on prevention of behavioral disorders, as well as the general societal concern about violence in schools, has led to new programs designed to reduce the probability of inappropriate behavior through the implementation of school-based programs. These programs include three levels of prevention identified by the United States Public Health Service and match each level with a specific type of behavior inter-

~ Direct Instruction Checklist

1. Am I using flexible instructional grouping as a technique to increase academic engaged time?
2. Am I maintaining high levels of engagement at high levels of student success?
3. Am I monitoring student performance frequently, providing immediate feedback to students adjusting instruction according to student need?
4. Am I teaching all students to a high level of mastery?
5. Am I designing appropriate motivational strategies for my students?

Source: M. Stein, and C.S. Davis, "Direct Instruction as a Positive Behavioral Support," *Beyond Behavior, 10* (2000), p. 12.

vention. The three levels of prevention are primary, secondary, and tertiary. Primary prevention focuses on general, schoolwide programs—often called universal interventions—that are designed to prevent problems among all children. Secondary prevention targets specialized group interventions for students who are at risk for more severe problems or who already exhibit mild behavior problems. Tertiary programs include specialized individual interventions designed for students who are at great risk for serious problems or who are already demonstrating serious behavior problems (Sprague & Walker, 2000). For each level, the complexity of the intervention is matched to the severity of the target behaviors. See Figure 7.3 for an illustration of the multilevel system of school discipline programs.

Early research suggests that the tri-level approach is an effective way to prevent or delay the onset of behavior problems for at-risk children. Universal interventions appear to reduce inappropriate and aggressive behaviors (Serna, Nielson, Lambros, & Forness, 2000). Although the universal programs vary, most include both parent and school components. Most also include elements such as classroom management, peer tutoring, role playing, and problem-solving activities (Frey, Hirschstein, & Guzzo, 2000; Kamps et al., 2000).

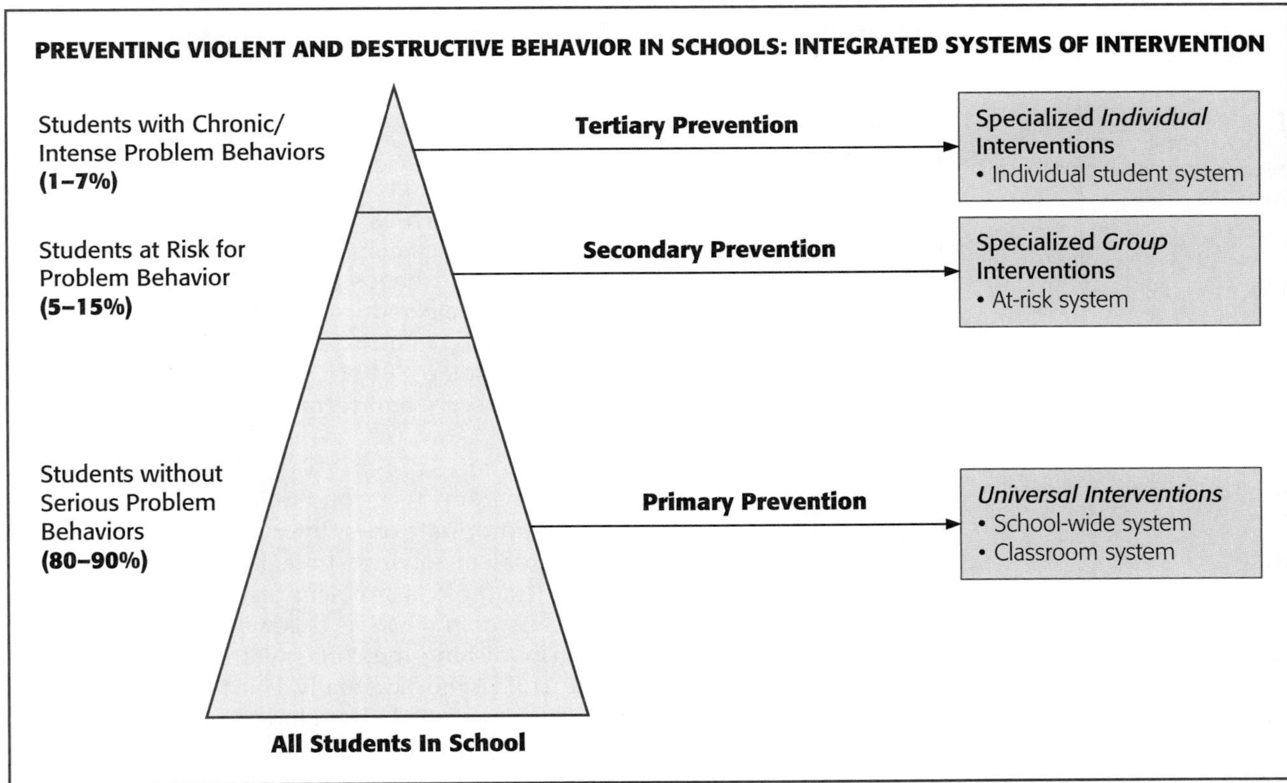

Figure 7.3
Multilevel system of schoolwide discipline strategies

Source: G. Sugai, J.R. Sprague, R.H. Horner, and H.M. Walker, "Preventing School Violence: The Use of Office Discipline Referrals to Assess and Monitor School-wide Discipline Interventions," *Journal of Emotional and Behavior Disorders, 8* (2000), p. 94.

Secondary programs may include structured group social skills and problem-solving activities, as well as group behavior management programs, such as the level system described below. Tertiary programs likely will focus on the BIP resulting from each student's functional behavioral assessment.

Developing Appropriate Cognitions One of the recurring problems experienced by children with behavioral disorders is difficulty interpreting events realistically and determining socially appropriate responses. For example, Hartman and Stage (2000) interviewed students with behavioral disorders who were assigned to in-school suspension. The interviews revealed that the students had reacted negatively to their perception that teachers deliberately provoked them. Studies like this one suggest the importance of interventions with a positive and reinforcing focus. They also suggest that students need instruction in skills to help them identify and cope with both real and exaggerated concerns and thoughts. Regardless of the cause, children who have retreated from social activities and relationships usually receive instruction that will enable them to make slow and nonthreatening steps toward appropriate social behavior.

Educational programs should include components designed to teach students how to monitor their own behavior (Maag, 1988). Because of the possible role of a child's thoughts in behavioral disorders, it is difficult for the teacher, who cannot observe these thoughts, to manage the behavior without student participation. One way to address this problem is to provide **self-management instruction.**

Instruction in self-management skills teaches students to attend to and record their own performance.

Instruction in self-management skills involves teaching children to pay attention to and record their own performance (Levendoski & Cartledge, 2000). For example, children record on a piece of paper every time they talk without raising their hand. Alternatively, children can record a mark for every five minutes they exhibit appropriate behavior such as time-on-task or time without fighting. With very young children, calling their attention to the "rules" with contingency statements ("If you keep your hands to yourself, then you can go outside at recess") has been found to help reduce aggressive or violent play (Sherburne, Utley, McConnel, & Gannon, 1988). Self-management programs can involve the use of videotapes (Falk, Dunlap, & Kern, 1996) and role play to assist in self-evaluation. Students can observe and record behaviors and practice giving alternative responses.

Teaching New Behaviors Some programs focus on the instruction of new behaviors to take the place of the inappropriate ones. Interventions of this nature may involve teaching students problem-solving strategies to use when they begin to feel angry or upset. For example, a problem teachers often face is a child throwing a tantrum in the classroom when he becomes frustrated. Simply telling the child to stop, or even punishing the child, will not necessarily address the problem, because the child who habitually has tantrums does not know what else to do when he gets frustrated. Therefore, the teacher can give him a signal when he starts to get angry. When he sees the signal, he has three choices: He can count to 10 and take a deep breath to calm down, he can raise his hand and ask the teacher for help, or he can get up and go sit in the reading corner for five minutes to relax. Now the child has options. Instead of throwing a book, he can choose an alternative behavior.

Viewing videotapes of appropriate behaviors, modeling by teachers and peers, and practicing appropriate responses are other activities that have been used effectively to teach new behaviors (Amish et al., 1988; Knapczyk, 1988). Recent research has examined the role of peers in helping students with behavior disorders to learn appropriate anger-management behavior. Presley and Hughes (2000) found that high school students with behavior disorders demonstrated appropriate anger-management behaviors in role play after receiving a combination of individual instruction from peers, self-management instruction, and a traditional anger-control program.

Some behaviors (such as stealing and using obscenities) may seem more deliberate and manipulative and less a result of lack of control. Usually, behavior-management techniques that involve the application of specific consequences for appropriate and inappropriate behavior are used to address these types of behaviors. Although the predominate philosophy in behavior management is to focus on using positive interventions to teach new behaviors, punishing and exclusionary strategies (loss of recess time, time out) are still used in many classrooms. All teachers must remember that negative approaches may produce negative reactions by students with behavior disorders; they should also realize that punishing a child does not tell him what he is supposed to do. Some research reveals that teachers tend to use these negative interventions most often with African American students (Ishii-Jordan, 2000; Townsend, 2000).

Some programs also include curriculum components devoted to moral development, such as decision-making and value judgment (Swarthout, 1988). A major goal of programs for children with behavioral or emotional disorders is to teach them a level of control that will enable them to perform appropriately in regular classes.

One example of this type of program is the **level system,** which involves a stepwise progression through a predetermined set of behavioral requirements, restrictions, and responsibilities. Through the demonstration of appropriate behavior over time, students can achieve higher levels of freedom and responsibility. Depending on the specific situation, the highest level reached could be eligibility for partial or full inclusion. This type of system has been shown to be effective even when the only consequence for appropriate behavior was increasing levels of independence and responsibility (Mastropieri, Jenne, & Scruggs, 1988). Some, however, have expressed concerns about the level system. For example, Scheuermann and Webber (1996) suggest that the least restrictive environment is an educational right, not something that can be earned only by students reaching a high level on the program. In addition, they report that a level system might emphasize a group, rather than an individualized curriculum, as mandated by law. See the accompanying box, "Level System Evaluation Checklist," for an example of an evaluation checklist for level systems.

Regardless of your ultimate behavioral goal for an individual student, several factors, such as consistency and clear consequences, are required for all behavior-management programs. It is also important for you, the parent, and the student to see the program as positive and practical. See the accompanying box, "Checklist for Positive Classroom Management," for a sample checklist. Although many behavior-management systems include tangible rewards for appropriate behavior, some students with behavioral disorders have actually rated good grades as their most desired reward (Maratens, Muir, & Meller, 1988). This type of reward structure (independence, responsibility, grades) is likely to appeal more to regular classroom teachers than one dependent on tangible rewards (stickers, toys, food). Consequently, they may be more inclined to continue implementing the system in the regular classroom setting.

~ Level System Evaluation Checklist

Below is a level system evaluation checklist. The person who is most familiar with the level system being evaluated should complete the form.

Answer each of the following questions regarding your level system.

I. Access to LRE [least restrictive environment]
   A. Are mainstreaming decisions made by each student's IEP committee, regardless of the student's status within the level system? YES NO
      If no, check below:
      ___ 1. Students are required to attain a predetermined level before they can attend a mainstream class.
      ___ 2. Mainstream classes are predetermined (e.g., P.E. for students on Level 2, P.E. and music for students on Level 3, etc.)

II. Placement in the level system
   A. Are students initially placed in the level system at the level that is commensurate with their needs and strengths? YES NO
   B. Is initial placement in the level system based on current, valid assessment? YES NO

III. Curriculum
   A. Does each student have individual target behaviors designated in addition to those designated for the whole group? YES NO
   B. Are group expectations considered by each student's IEP committee to determine if those expectations are appropriate for each individual student? YES NO
   C. Are criteria for mastery of target behaviors determined individually? YES NO
   D. Is the sequence of target behaviors developed individually for each student, based on that student's needs and areas of strength? YES NO
   E. Are target behaviors differentiated as skill deficits or performance deficits? YES NO
   F. Are reinforcers individualized? YES NO

Discipline in the Schools

According to federal law, children cannot be punished for behavior that is a result of their disability.

Most schools have established programs for the purpose of disciplining children who exhibit inappropriate behavior. These programs may include suspension, in-school suspension, time-out, corporal punishment, and expulsion. Children with externalizing behavioral disorders may seem to be prime candidates for experiencing some of these disciplinary actions, but federal law states that children cannot be punished for their disability. In other words, if a child's disability is considered responsible for the behavior, that child should not be punished for it. The IDEA amendments of 1997 present some guidelines for addressing the behavior problems of students with disabilities, including those with behavioral disorders. One requirement in the 1997 amendments is that a school review, called a **manifestation determination,** must be conducted after a school behavior problem has occurred to determine if the student's behavior is related to the disability. If the ruling is that the behavior is not related to the disability, the student may be disciplined like any other child (IDEA Amendments, 1997; Yell & Shriner, 1997). In addition, children with behavioral disorders must have a specific behavior management plan, including disciplinary procedures in their individual educational programs. Any disciplinary actions, such as suspension, that change the student's placement are limited to 10 days. Exceptions include

Schools must develop guidelines that enable them to implement discipline without violating students' rights.

G. Do you avoid using access to less restrictive environments/activities and nondisabled peers as reinforcers?
YES NO

IV. Procedures

A. Are advancement criteria (criteria for movement from one level to the next) individualized for each student?
YES NO

B. Are advancement criteria based on recent, relevant assessment data as well as expectations for age peers in general education environments?
YES NO

C. Does each student's IEP committee determine whether advancement criteria are developmentally appropriate for a particular student? YES NO

D. Are behavior reductive strategies used separately from the level system (i.e., downward movement is not used as a consequence for inappropriate behavior or for failure to meet minimum criteria for a given level)?
YES NO

If no, check below:

___ 1. Downward movement is used as a consequence for inappropriate behavior.

___ 2. Downward movement is used as a consequence for failure to earn minimum points for a certain number of days.

V. Efficacy

A. Is each student's progress through the level system monitored? YES NO

B. Is there a problem-solving procedure if data indicate a lack of progress through the level system? YES NO

C. Do students consistently "graduate" from the level system? YES NO

D. Do behaviors that are addressed in the level system maintain over time and generalize across environments?
YES NO

E. Do students who complete the level system maintain successfully in less restrictive environments? YES NO

F. Are self-management skills incorporated into the level system? YES NO

the possession of firearms or drugs in school or at school functions, which allows administrators to place the child in a temporary alternative educational setting for up to 45 days (IDEA Amendments, 1997; Yell & Shriner, 1997).

Transition

Few recent long-term outcome studies have been conducted on students with emotional and behavioral disorders. Because many such students do not voluntarily continue to receive state or federal services after graduation, they are probably difficult to track after they exit school. Data from the National Longitudinal Transition Study suggest that in addition to personal and family variables, school variables, such as high functional competency in basic skills and a high school diploma, were predictors of employment after high school (Rylance, 1998). Another area in which data exist is criminal activity. Research suggests that about half of all antisocial children become adjudicated as adolescents, and 50 to 75 percent of these adolescents go on to become adult criminals (Walker, Colvin, & Ramsey, 1995). This is dismal news, particularly when coupled with what we have already discussed about the high dropout rates and drug use by

~ Checklist for Positive Classroom Management

1. The teacher interacts positively with the student. Y N
2. The teacher communicates high expectations to the student. Y N
3. Opportunities are provided for students to become acquainted. Y N
4. Students are actively involved with peers through cooperative learning or peer tutoring. Y N
5. Classroom procedures are taught to students, who demonstrate understanding of the procedures. Y N
6. Students' instructional programs are appropriate to their needs, skill levels, and learning styles. Y N
7. The subject matter is relevant to the students' lives and they understand the connection. Y N
8. Students understand the teacher's instructional goals and why teaching strategies are being used to achieve these goals. Y N
9. Students have been involved in some form of academic goal setting and recording. Y N
10. The assessment system motivates the student to make good effort. Y N
11. Rules for managing student behavior are appropriate, succinct, stated positively, and applied to all. Y N
12. Consequences for inappropriate behavior are clear to all students. Y N
13. Consequences are educational, respectful, and implemented consistently. Y N
14. Students demonstrate understanding of rules and consequences. Y N
15. If a problem arises, the teacher meets privately with the student to discuss the problem and jointly develop a plan to help. Y N

Source: Vern Jones, "Responding to Student Behavior Problems," *Beyond Behavior* (Winter 1990), p. 20. Published by the Council for Children with Behavior Disorders, Council for Exceptional Children, 1920 Association Dr., Reston, VA 22091.

adolescents with behavior disorders. With such concern about the prognosis for students with emotional and behavior disorders, it is easy to understand why there currently is such an emphasis on prevention.

SUMMARY

- Federal law lists five criteria for identifying children who are emotionally disturbed: unexplained inability to learn, inability to relate satisfactorily to peers and teachers, inappropriate behavior under normal circumstances, pervasive unhappiness or depression, and a tendency to develop physical symptoms or fears associated with school or personal problems.
- Behavior can be evaluated in terms of rate, intensity, duration, and age appropriateness.
- It is difficult to determine the prevalence of behavioral disorders because of differences in instruments used to measure behavior, in terminology and interpretation of definitions, and in the subjectivity of behavior-rating systems.

- The causes of behavioral disorders are not known; however, certain environmental and physiological factors seem to relate to behavior differences.
- The effects of behavioral disorders on the child include underachievement in school, difficulties with social adjustment, and difficulties in self-expression or communication. Effects on the family include parental anger, stress, and guilt; helplessness; and an increased risk of child abuse.
- Assessment techniques include screening instruments, observation, and behavior-rating scales. States establish their own guidelines for selecting and administering tests, and professionals interpret the results based on the nature of the specific case and their own expertise. A teacher's conscious or unconscious bias can cause problems in assessment.
- Many educators recommend direct instruction programs and strategies for teaching students with emotional or behavior disorders.
- Regardless of a student's placement, regular and special education teachers should share the same expectations for appropriate behavior and use a consistent behavior-management system. The major strategies for working with students with behavior disorders involve developing appropriate cognitions, teaching new behavior, and eliminating inappropriate behavior.

Key Terms

emotional disturbance
behavior disordered
rate
intensity
duration
age-appropriate behavior
DSM-IV
externalizing behavior
internalizing behavior
attention deficit/hyperactivity disorder (ADHD)
behavior-rating scale
functional behavioral assessment
behavior intervention plan
positive behavioral support
level system
manifestation determination

Multimedia Resources

Barkley, Russel A. *ADHD: What Do We Know?* and *ADHD: What Can We Do?* (New York: Guilford Publications, Inc., 1992). Two comprehensive, informative, and practical videotapes on attention deficit/hyperactivity disorder; the tapes are appropriate for teachers and parents.

Fowler, Mary. *Maybe You Know My Kid* (New York: Carol Publishing Group, 1995). A parents' guide to identifying, understanding, and helping your child with attention deficit/hyperactivity disorder.

Gordon, Michael. *ADHD/Hyperactivity: A Consumer's Guide for Parents and Teachers* (DeWitt, NY: GSI Publications, 1991). A guide to essential concepts of ADHD and hyperactivity that covers obtaining a comprehensive and relevant evaluation, effective educational programs, and decisions about medication.

Kameenui, Edward J., and Craig B. Darch. *Instructional Classroom Management: A Proactive Approach to Classroom Management* (White Plains, NY: Longman,

1995). A text for classroom teachers about managing behavior in the context of instruction.

The Law and Special Education: http://www.ed.sc.edu/spedlaw/lawpage.htm. This site provides access to the latest updates in special education legislation and case law.

Resources in Emotional/Behavioral Disabilities: http://www.gwu.edu/~ebdweb/index.html. George Washington University's site for teachers and preservice teachers who relate experiences from a psychoeducational perspective.

Rockwell, Sylvia. *Tough to Reach, Tough to Teach: Students with Behavior Problems* (Reston, VA: CEC, 1993). This resource, written for both regular and special education teachers, contains many effective management strategies as well as anecdotal vignettes that every teacher will recognize.

Wilens, Timothy E. (1999). *Straight Talk About Psychiatric Medications for Kids*. New York: Guilford Press. This book provides parents with specific information about childhood psychiatric disorders and the use of medications to treat them.

What You Can Do

1. Speak to the school psychologist for a local school district. Discuss how the \school district defines and identifies children with behavioral disorders, and what terms are used in your state. Ask the psychologist what tests and assessment instruments are used to identify students with behavior disorders. Find out his or her perspective on the effectiveness of the assessment procedures.

2. Ask school guidance counselors or conflict-management specialists for suggestions of strategies and programs that teach students self-control and problem solving. Ask them for some examples of curricula related to self-management, social skills training, and affective development. Could you integrate these curricula into a general education classroom?

3. How do your expectations of classroom performance affect the ways you perceive students' behavior? Using a behavior checklist, visit several classrooms at various grade levels. Observe and record the behavior of a few children. Afterward, discuss your observations and ratings with the classroom teachers. Are your perceptions and observations similar to those of the classroom teacher? Evaluate your own biases and their effect on your ratings. Make a list of behaviors that you think will be important in your own classroom.

4. Interview a local pediatrician about the methods he or she uses to identify children with ADHD. Ask to see examples of behavioral checklists and forms for classroom observations and parent interviews. What criteria does the doctor use? If possible, interview several pediatricians and compare their diagnostic methods.

5. Observe a teacher conduct a functional behavior assessment for a student. Record the antecedents, behaviors, and consequences along with the teacher, and arrive at your own hypothesis about the function of the inappropriate behavior. Confer with the teacher and discuss his or her suggestions for appropriate replacement behaviors.

8

Autism and Related Syndromes

EDUCATIONAL PROGRAMS for children and adolescents with autism focus on instruction in functional communication, appropriate behavior, social interaction, and life skills. In this chapter, we discuss historical and current theories about autism and review effective interventions. Think about the following questions as you read this chapter:

Why is it sometimes difficult to get an early diagnosis of autism?

What is communicative intent, and why is it important when working with children with autism?

Commonalities: How do the goals of teaching students with autism compare to those of teaching other children?

Collaboration: What types of collaboration are necessary to provide effective early intervention programs for young children with autism?

Can Do: How can you determine the most effective interventions to use with individuals with autism?

Arguably, no other area of special education has been the subject of as much speculation and controversy as autism. In most areas of disability, we can easily see that individuals perform somewhere on an ability continuum in physical, cognitive, sensory, or emotional skills. We can observe our own or others' performances and logically understand deficits or exceptional abilities. Autism, however, sometimes seems to defy logic. The characteristic behaviors of autism, coupled with the apparently uneven distribution and range of deficits and abilities displayed by individuals with autism, seem to undermine a clear and rational explanation. Consequently, autism has been attributed to many different causes, and a wide variety of sometimes bizarre treatments has been explored through the years by confused parents and professionals. Although science is leading us ever closer to a good understanding of autism, many questions remain. We do, however, know that individuals with autism, like individuals with other pervasive disabilities, are in a better position than ever before to assume fulfilling and productive lives.

Definitions and Terms

Defining Autism

Autism was identified as a special education category in 1990.

Autism is a lifelong developmental disability that is best described as a collection of behavioral symptoms. Although autism has been recognized for many years, it was not identified as a separate category of special education until the IDEA reauthorization of 1990. The following is the federal definition of autism:

> Autism means a developmental disability significantly affecting verbal and nonverbal communication and social interaction, generally evident before age 3 that adversely affects a child's educational performance. Other characteristics often associated with autism are engagement in repetitive activities and stereotyped movements, resistance to environmental change or daily routines, and unusual responses to sensory experiences. The term does not apply if a child's educational performance is adversely affected primarily because the child has an emotional disturbance.
>
> A child who manifests the characteristics of "autism" after age 3 could be diagnosed as having "autism" if the criteria in the above paragraph are satisfied. (IDEA, Part B, p. 34.300-6A)

The federal definition provides us with a general definition. The accompanying box, "Autism: A Parent's Perspective," presents one mother's description of autism. Her words give us insight about the meaning of terms such as repetitive activity and resistance to change.

As with all disability categories that rely on observational measures, the diagnosis of autism may be subjective. The *Diagnostic and Statistical Manual of Mental Disorders,* Fourth Edition (DSM-IV), published by the American Psychiatric Association (1994), contains complex diagnostic criteria that parallel and attempt to quantify the behavioral characteristics present in the definition of autism. In addition, a simple five-step screening test called the *Checklist for Autism in Toddlers* (CHAT) is offered as a diagnostic tool for pediatricians (Foote & Tesoriero, 2000). See the accompanying box, "Two Sets of Diagnostic Criteria." Because the tools various professionals use to diagnose autism can range from incredibly simple to quite complex, and because many professionals also have their own criteria for what autism "looks like," it is no wonder that many parents have great difficulty obtaining a diagnosis for their child (Maurice, 1993).

The difficulty of arriving at a diagnosis of autism is compounded by the fact that there are a number of disorders related to autism, referred to as **pervasive developmental disorders (PDD)**, in which only a few of the characteristics are present, or the characteristics are present in a very mild form. Often physicians

~ Autism: A Parent's Perspective

Autism is when your two-year-old looks straight through you to the wall behind—through you, her father, her sister, her brother, or anybody else. You are a pane of glass. Or you are her own personal extension, your hand a tool she uses to get the cookie she will not reach for herself. Autism is when your eight-year-old fills a carton with three-quarter-inch squares of cut-up paper to sift between her fingers for twenty minutes, half an hour, longer, autism is when your eleven-year-old fills sheet after sheet with division, division by three, by seven, eleven, thirteen, seventeen, nineteen. . . . But that's enough, there are many books about autism now, anyone can read the symptoms. I need the image for what the symptoms can't convey: this child was *happy.* Is it not happiness to want nothing but what you have? Craving, the Buddha taught, was the source of all misery, detachment the road to the serene equilibrium of nirvana.

But nirvana at eighteen months? That's too soon.

Source: Claira Claiborne Park, "Exiting Nirvana," *The American Scholar, 67:*2(1998), 30.

or other diagnosticians want to delay the diagnosis of autism until these associated disorders can be eliminated. Because autism is the only category among the pervasive developmental disorders specifically identified in IDEA, however, it is important for parents to get a confirmed diagnosis as soon as possible so that they can obtain appropriate services. Professionals are evaluating the effectiveness of diagnostic criteria and instruments for PDD to distinguish between autism and other pervasive developmental disorders and to determine the reliability of these instruments when used by different evaluators (Klin, Lang, Cicchetti, & Volkmar, 2000; Stella, Mundy, & Tuchman, 1999).

Asperger's Syndrome

Pervasive developmental disorders include autism and Asperger's syndrome.

Although the term pervasive developmental disorders includes many specific disorders, we will address briefly the most common of these, **Asperger's syndrome.** Asperger's syndrome is increasingly being diagnosed in young children, and therefore there is a strong likelihood that you will have students with this diagnosis in your classrooms. Approximately 26 to 36 out of 10,000 school-age children are diagnosed with Asperger's syndrome (Ehlers & Gillberg, 1993).

Individuals with Asperger's syndrome may have many of the social and behavioral characteristics of autism but, importantly, *without* any marked delays in language and cognitive development. They experience difficulties in social functioning and relationships, but not in intelligence or language skills. Learning disabilities, motor clumsiness, and hypersensitivity to sensory stimuli are also common (Bock & Myles, 1999). The wide range of abilities can manifest in unique ways; a student may be as likely to become fixated on astronomy as on a piece of silverware.

Many of the educational approaches we present later in the chapter can be appropriate for children with Asperger's syndrome. A number of students with this syndrome are also treated with specific medications prescribed to address behavioral characteristics such as hyperactivity, aggression, and compulsive or ritualistic behaviors.

~ Two Sets of Diagnostic Criteria

How Psychologists Define Autism

Diagnostic criteria for 299.00 Autistic Disorder

A. A total of six (or more) items from (1), (2), and (3), with at least two from (1), and one each from (2) and (3):
  - (1) qualitative impairment in social interaction, as manifested by at least two of the following:
    - (a) marked impairment in the use of multiple nonverbal behaviors such as eye-to-eye gaze, facial expression, body postures, and gestures to regulate social interaction.
    - (b) failure to develop peer relationships appropriate to developmental level
    - (c) a lack of spontaneous seeking to share enjoyment, interests, or achievements with other people (e.g., by a lack of showing, bringing, or pointing out objects of interest)
    - (d) lack of social or emotional reciprocity
  - (2) qualitative impairments in communication as manifested by at least one of the following:
    - (a) delay in, or total lack of, the development of spoken language (not accompanied by an attempt to compensate through alternative modes of communication such as gesture or mime)
    - (b) in individuals with adequate speech, marked impairment in the ability to initiate or sustain a conversation with others
    - (c) stereotyped and repetitive use of language or idiosyncratic language
    - (d) lack of varied, spontaneous make-believe play or social imitative play appropriate to developmental level
  - (3) restricted repetitive and stereotyped patterns of behavior, interests, and activities, as manifested by at least one of the following:
    - (a) encompassing preoccupation with one or more stereotyped and restricted patterns of interest that is abnormal either in intensity or focus
    - (b) apparently inflexible adherence to specific, nonfunctional routines or rituals
    - (c) stereotyped and repetitive motor mannerisms (e.g., hand or finger flapping or twisting, or complex whole-body movements)
    - (d) persistent preoccupation with parts of objects

B. Delays or abnormal functioning in at least one of the following areas, with onset prior to age 3 years: (1) social interaction, (2) language as used in social communication, or (3) symbolic or imaginative play.

C. The disturbance is not better accounted for by Rett's Disorder or Childhood Disintegrative Disorder.

Source: *Diagnostic and Statistical Manual of Mental Disorders* (4th ed.) (Washington, DC: American Psychiatric Association, 1994), pp. 70–71.

The Problem of Dual Diagnosis

Another difficulty in attempting to diagnose autism is the fact that it coexists with a number of other conditions, such as **fragile X syndrome,** an inherited disorder caused by chromosomal abnormalities. Unlike autism, fragile X syndrome is diagnosed through genetic testing. Affected children exhibit many of the same behaviors as children with autism, such as communication delays, stereotypic movements, perseveration, and hyperarousal. Children with autism,

~ Two Sets of Diagnostic Criteria

How Pediatricians Diagnose Autism

A child who fails to accomplish each of the following five measures almost certainly has classic autism.

Questions for parents:

1. Does your child ever pretend, for example, to make a cup of tea using a toy cup and teapot, or pretend other things?
2. Does your child ever use his index finger to point, indicating interest in something?

Exercises for the child:

3. Get the child's attention, then point across the room at an interesting object and say, "Oh, look! There's a [name of object]!" Watch the child's face. Does the child look to see what you are pointing at?
4. Get the child's attention, then give the child a miniature toy cup and teapot and say, "Can you make a cup of tea?" Does your child pretend to pour out tea, drink it, etc.?
5. Say, "Where's the light?" Does the child point with his index finger at the light?

Source: D. Foote and H. W. Tesoriero, "Understanding Autism," *Newsweek*, July 31, 2000, p. 48.

however, tend to display greater variability in their developmental profile and greater deficits in social and communication skills than children with fragile X syndrome (Bailey et al., 2000). Nonetheless, there certainly is some overlap in diagnosis; 15 to 25 percent of children with fragile X syndrome also meet the criteria for autism, and 4 percent of children with autism are diagnosed with fragile X syndrome (Dykens & Volkmar, 1997).

The vast majority of individuals with autism (80 percent) also have mental retardation ranging from quite mild to profound. Although the level of mental retardation certainly affects the ultimate ability levels of individuals with autism, as well as the specific educational goals and expectations, it typically does not affect the general educational approaches used in the classroom or other educational settings.

Causes

Prevalence

About 16 of every 10,000 children are diagnosed with autism or as having autistic-like behaviors (Rodier, 2000). During the 1997–1998 school year, 0.07 percent of all students ages 6 through 21, or 42,511 students, were served as students with autism (U.S. Department of Education, 1999). This number does not include the many young children with autism who may be served under preschool programs for children with developmental disabilities. The number of children identified as having autism has increased dramatically in recent years. Of course, the relatively recent identification of autism as a separate category in special education is partially responsible for this increase: As school districts became more practiced and prepared in classification procedures, more children were identified. For example, during the six-year period following the special education categorization of autism, the number of children between the ages of 6 and 11 identified as having autism jumped 200 percent. Some professionals, however, suggest that the rise in the number of children identified as having autism represents a true increase in numbers, and they speculate about possible environmental and medical causes.

Historical Opinions About Causes

Autism has been attributed to a wide range of possible causes.

The true causes of autism are unknown; however, research is bringing us ever closer to answering the questions about the reasons for the disorder and the unusual cognitive, behavioral, and communicative patterns that occur with it. Because of the unusual nature of the behaviors associated with autism, the disorder has been attributed to a wide range of possible causes.

Although theories about the causes of autism now rest firmly in the physiological realm—the neurological, genetic, and metabolic—this certainly was not always the case. Autism was first defined in the mid-1940s by Leo Kanner (1943), who identified a cluster of behavioral characteristics that are essentially the same as those used today to diagnose children with autism. Kanner speculated about a range of possible causes, but it was Bettleheim (1967) who strongly felt that autism was a psychiatric response to an unsupportive and deprived environment. Naturally, the person responsible for the young child's environment was the mother, and it was she who was held responsible for the autistic state of her young child. How? It was assumed at the time that the child's withdrawal from social contact, abnormal focus on objects rather than people, and delayed language development reflected a lack of appropriate socialization and loving behaviors from the mother. In fact, the term *refrigerator mother* was used to describe the mothers of young children with autism—cold, unfeeling, icy. So, if you were a mother forty or fifty years ago and had a young child with autism, not only did you have the great challenge of trying to teach your toddler how to talk and play and smile, you also had to shoulder the burden of responsibility for *causing* these learning problems.

Fortunately, all we have learned about the nature of autism in the past decade or so has almost erased the stigma on parents, although we still see some interventions based on the concept of parents as the cause of autism.

Current Opinions About Causes

Today, hypotheses about the causes of autism focus on physiological factors.

Although there is still much speculation in the field, today our hypotheses about the causes of autism focus on physiological differences. The search for physiological causes for autism began in the 1960s (Rimland, 1964; Scott, Clark, & Brady, 2000) and has received increasing support in the past few decades. Most scientists agree that the collection of symptoms constituting autism, Asperger's syndrome, and pervasive developmental disorder arises from a set of inherited factors (Rodier, 2000). It also appears that most cases of autism begin very early in the embryonic development of the child. Children with autism have specific differences in brain development, specifically in the brain stem (see Figure 8.1). They also have specific genetic abnormalities. Although many genes appear to be associated with autism, no clear causal relationship between a specific genetic abnormality and the occurrence of autism has been established. Discovering the ultimate cause of autism will mean answering the following questions: What types of environmental or physiological insults trigger the brain differences? What factors influence the variety and intensity of charac-

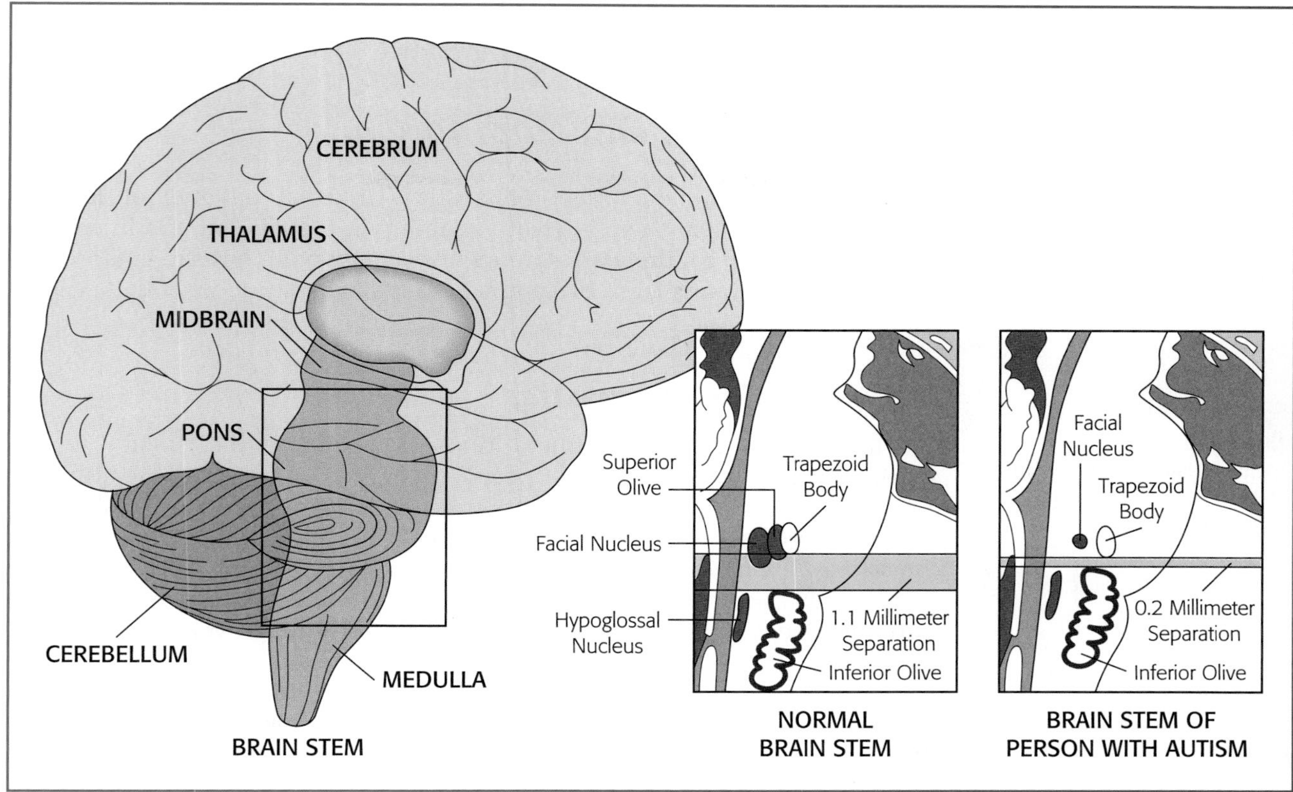

Figure 8.1
Autism's effects include changes to the brain stem, the region just above the spinal cord (*left*). The brain stem of a person with autism is shorter than a normal brain stem (*below*): the structures at the junction of the pons and the medulla (such as the facial nucleus and the trapezoid body) are closer to the structures of the lower medulla (the hypoglossal nucleus and the inferior olive). It is as though a band of tissue were missing. The brain stem of a person with autism also lacks the superior olive and has a smaller-than-normal facial nucleus. Such changes could occur only in early gestation

Source: Patricia M. Rodier, "The Early Origins of Autism," *Scientific American*, 282 (2), 56–63.

teristics related to autism? Is there a clear set of identifiable risk factors? The answers to these questions will depend on further knowledge about specific genetic and chromosomal factors, and they may lead to the discovery of the importance of environmental factors, such as drugs taken by the mother during pregnancy. Investigations designed to examine possible neurochemical factors common to children with autism have found only elevated levels of platelet serotonin, a finding that has led to highly speculative treatment protocols (Scott, Clark, & Brady, 2000).

Certainly one of the puzzling factors about the onset of autism is that in close to 50 percent of children diagnosed, the defining characteristics don't appear until the child is a toddler, at which point the child begins to regress markedly in communication and social abilities (Davidovitch et al., 2000). Although this characteristic may be attributed to genes which are active only during specific times of a child's development, it has fostered increased, yet sometimes unsubstantiated, speculation about direct environmental influences, such as childhood inoculations or prenatal exposure to diseases such as rubella.

Effects on the Developing Child

Individuals with autism often demonstrate unusual patterns of learning, speech, and behavior. There is great variability in the amount and intensity of symptoms among children who are identified as having autism. Children described as having autisticlike behaviors usually have only a few of these characteristics.

Cognitive Characteristics

Most individuals with autism have mental retardation and display unusual learning patterns.

Children with autism can be found in all ranges of intellectual ability. As we stated above, about 80 percent of people diagnosed with autism are also diagnosed with mental retardation. Individuals with autism, even those without significant mental retardation, display unusual, uneven learning patterns, often consisting of relative strength in one or two areas of learning. Although a very small number of children with autism are truly gifted in one area, many do have learning strengths that are surprising in light of the child's overall level of functioning.

A child with autism may demonstrate ability in auditory memory, organization, or telling time and yet have extreme difficulty in other learning skills, such as reading or writing. For example, Michael, a young man with autism and moderate mental retardation, has a sight word vocabulary of only twenty-five words, yet can remember all the words to songs and commercials he heard over fifteen years ago. Although he cannot do even simple addition or subtraction when it is presented in number problem format, he can instantly add or subtract

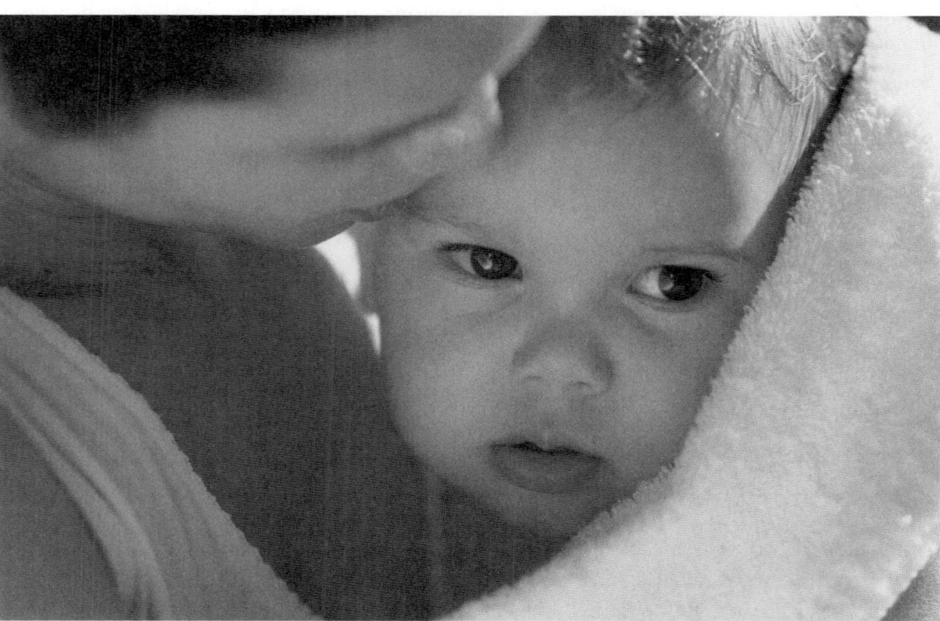

Parents may notice a lack of eye contact or social interaction in their young children with autism. (© Richard/CORBIS)

hours on his watch to accommodate changes due to Daylight Savings Time or Standard Time, before his watch is adjusted. He also can easily convert "military time" to standard time (e.g., 1400 hours to 2:00 P.M.). The skills alone are not exceptional (most of us can convert time), but they are surprising when compared to other skills with which Michael has difficulty.

We have seen that many children with cognitive or learning disabilities have difficulty with memory tasks. Children with autism may have variable memory skills, but we do see some similarities with other children who have disabilities in some aspects of remembering. For example, individuals with autism do not appear to use active memory strategies like organization and rehearsal of information (Renner, Klinger, & Klinger, 2000). On the other hand, children with autism recall events that happened to their peers better than they recall events that happened to themselves (Millward, Powell, Messer, & Jordan, 2000). This surprising learning characteristic seems incongruous with what we know about the social withdrawal of most children with autism.

Children with autism are often very rigid in their demands for environmental sameness.

Children with autism also may be very rigid in their demands for environmental sameness and dependent upon exact routines during the day (Koegel, Koegel, Frea, & Smith, 1995). For example, a student who catches the school bus at 7:15 in the morning will always leave the house at 7:10 A.M. and walk the exact same number of steps each time. If he leaves early, the student will walk very slowly so that he arrives and boards the bus at exactly 7:15. Some individuals will insist on sameness in their house or classroom, or in the sequence of events involved in going on a shopping trip or preparing lunch. The need for sameness may have significant implications when selecting instructional strategies and types of interventions.

Physical Characteristics

Children with autism are usually described as average in appearance, if not as unusually attractive children. There do appear, however, to be a few minor physical anomalies associated with autism. Most of these are related to the ear: The ears of children with autism may be placed a bit lower than those of children without autism, may tilt backward more that 15 degrees, and may have a slightly more square shape. The tops of the child's ears may also flop over, and the corners of the mouth may be low compared to the center of the upper lip (Rodier, 2000). These characteristics are truly minor and difficult to observe unless one knows to look for them.

There also appears to be an association between identified chromosomal abnormalities and minor physical anomalies. About 6.3 percent of children with autism have identified chromosomal abnormalities other than those associated with fragile X syndrome. Children with these chromosomal abnormalities are more likely to have minor physical anomalies and to be cognitively delayed (Konstantareas & Homatidis, 1999).

Social Interaction

Many children with autism withdraw from social interaction or display significant deficits in social skills.

Individuals with autism typically demonstrate patterns of social behavior that reflect social withdrawal and avoidance of others. These patterns can include failure to make eye contact and to attend to others in the room, even if the other individuals are attempting to play with or talk to the child. The individual with autism simply may not react or may actively avoid other people's efforts at social interaction or communication. In fact, a characteristic description given by parents is that the child with autism appears to look through or past them (Maurice, 1993; Park, 1998). Historically, young children with autism were often misdiagnosed as being deaf, because their inattention was so marked that parents assumed they couldn't hear the noises around them, including their own name.

Many children with autism focus their attentions on objects instead of other people. They seem to disregard the desire for **joint attention**—the mutual sharing of experiences, activities, or even objects with friends, teachers, or parents (Scott, Clark, & Brady, 2000). As you can imagine, these characteristics can be particularly difficult for parents as they attempt to interact with and come to know their young child.

> We start with an image—a tiny, golden child on hands and knees, circling round and round a spot on the floor in mysterious, self-absorbed delight. She does not look up, though she is smiling and laughing; she does not call our attention to the mysterious object of her pleasure. She does not see us at all. She and the spot are all there is, and though she is eighteen months old, an age for touching, tasting, pointing, pushing, exploring, she is doing none of these things. She does not walk, or crawl up stairs, or pull herself to her feet to reach for objects. She doesn't *want* any objects, Instead she circles her spot. Or she sits, a long chain in her hand, snaking it up and down, up and down, watching it coil and uncoil for twenty minutes, half an hour, longer. . . . (Park, 1998, p. 30)

Not all individuals with autism are so completely withdrawn from social interaction with others, but most experience significant delays or deficits in social skills. A dual diagnosis of autism and mental retardation suggests high rates of poor adaptive behavior (Kraijer, 2000). Even those with less severe social deficits may have difficulty seeing things from the perspective of others and engaging appropriately in reciprocal social exchanges.

The importance of these characteristic social behavior patterns cannot be overestimated, since they affect virtually all areas of functioning—school, work, home, and play. For just about all individuals with autism, therefore, acquiring appropriate social skills and adaptive behavior comprises a substantial portion of educational programs at any age. As we will see, appropriate social interaction is closely intertwined with language, communication, and behavior.

Language and Communication

Differences in language and communication are the hallmarks of children with autism.

Difficulties and delays with language and communication are the hallmarks of children with autism. Some have delayed speech; it is not unusual for a child with autism to just begin saying words at the age of 6 or 7. Sometimes, a toddler may begin talking at a normal developmental rate and then stop using previously acquired speech around age 2 (Davidovitch et al., 2000). Some children with autism may not acquire verbal language at all. A nonverbal child may use gestures, vocalizations, or facial expressions to communicate (Stephenson & Dowrick, 2000). Sign language or language boards are often used with nonverbal students to provide a means of communication.

If individuals with autism acquire oral speech, their speech patterns will take unusual forms. One common example is **echolalia,** the repetition of speech sounds. For example, if you asked a child, "What is your name?" the child would respond, "What is your name?" The child also may repeat certain words over and over—the jingle from a television advertisement or a sentence he or she has overheard. Although echolalic speech may seem to be nonfunctional—that is, not used for a specific purpose such as asking a question—it often does represent an attempt at direct communication. The student does not use typical forms of interpersonal communication, but the *intent* to communicate may be there. In fact, echolalic responses can indicate an attempt at the turn taking required in reciprocal speech (Scott, Clark, & Brady, 2000). In other words, the child may understand that a response is required but be unable to formulate an appropriate response, so he simply repeats what was just said. Research continues to increase our knowledge base in this area, and interventions now include teaching students to adapt echolalic speech into useful, or functional, language.

Individuals with autism may present other types of language differences. Some may speak telegraphically, omitting articles, conjunctions, and tense markers ("Dan eat apple"). People with autism also may refer to themselves in the third person and avoid using pronouns altogether. As an example of both characteristics, Jim might say, "Jim watch TV" instead of "I want to watch TV." The speech of individuals with autism also is characterized by a flat or monotone quality.

As you can probably see, many individuals with autism have a difficult time with reciprocal language—the use of language to give and receive information. **Reciprocal speech** combines the social or pragmatic aspects of communication, such as eye contact and turn taking, with the mechanical requirements of communication. It also involves skills in both **receptive language,** that is, understanding and interpreting information, and **expressive language.** Much research is devoted to the observation and development of reciprocal speech in young children with autism (Savelle & Fox, 1988; Simpson & Souris, 1988). Some investigators have found that structured interventions that emphasize social interactive skills can increase both social and communication skills (Hwang & Hughes, 2000). It makes sense that teaching language in the context of social interaction will facilitate the acquisition and generalization of both types of behaviors. See Figure 8.2 for a sample protocol for language instruction in pronoun use.

We still have much to learn about the receptive communication skills of individuals with autism. As we mentioned earlier, often individuals with autism do not respond to language directed toward them. Sigafoos (2000) conducted research that reinforced our knowledge base on the relationship of poor communication skills to inappropriate behavior. Interestingly, he found stronger correlations between inappropriate behavior and receptive communication than between inappropriate behavior and expressive language. These relationships indicate that children with autism may be even more frustrated by their inability to understand information than their difficulty in expressing themselves. This implies that teachers need to assess the clarity and efficiency of their own communication strategies during instruction. See Table 8.1 for "Considerations for Developing Communication Skills."

Behavior

Individuals with autism may display a unique range of characteristic, sometimes disturbing, behaviors. Some are typical of the types of behaviors you might see in any child, but they occur at greater rates and intensities and at unexpected times. Examples include throwing tantrums, crying, yelling or

PROGRAM: Pronouns (I and You)

Program Procedure

1. *I*—Prompt the child to perform an action (e.g., physically guide the child to clap his or her hands) and say "What are you doing?" Prompt the child to say what he or she is doing with the correct pronoun (e.g., "I am clapping my hands"). Reinforce the response. Fade prompts over subsequent trials. Differentially reinforce responses demonstrated with the lowest level of prompting. Eventually, only reinforce correct, unprompted responses.

2. *You*—Sit across from the child. Establish attending and demonstrate an action (e.g., clap your hands). Say "What am I doing?" Prompt child to say what you are doing with the correct pronoun (e.g., "You are clapping your hands"). Reinforce the response. Fade prompts over subsequent trials. Differentially reinforce responses demonstrated with the lowest level of prompting. Eventually, only reinforce correct, unprompted responses.

3. *Randomize I and You*—Prompt the child to perform an action (e.g., give the child some juice to drink) and demonstrate an action (e.g., eat a cookie). Say either "What are you doing?" or "What am I doing?" Prompt the child to say what are you doing (e.g., "You are eating a cookie") or to say what he or she is doing (e.g., "I am drinking juice"). Fade prompts over subsequent trials. Differentially reinforce responses demonstrated with the lowest level of prompting. Eventually, only reinforce correct, unprompted responses.

Suggested Prerequisites:

Labels actions, possession, and pronouns (***my*** and ***your***).

Prompting Suggestions:

Model the correct response and use a time-delay procedure.

Question 1. "What are you doing?" 2. "What am I doing?" 3. Either 1 or 2	**Response** 1. Describes what he or she is doing with correct pronoun "I am…" 2. Describes what you are doing with correct pronoun "You are…" 3. Either 1 or 2	**Date Introduced**	**Date Mastered**
1. I am			
2. You are			
3. Randomize I and You			
Helpful Hint: Be sure to ask your child to label pronouns in natural contexts.			

Figure 8.2
Pronouns: *I* and *You*

screaming, and hiding. You might expect an average two-year-old to throw a tantrum if you take a toy away, or a five-year-old to start crying if he is reprimanded for leaving his toys out over night. You would not, however, expect a ten-year-old to throw a tantrum because a certain spoon is in the dishwasher, a behavior you might see from a child with autism.

Other behaviors reflect the characteristics of rigidity, or need for structure, often present in children with autism. A common experience of parents of

Table 8.1 Considerations for Developing Communication Skills

- Make the communication an integral part of the child's life in and out of school.
- Communication, rather that rote responses, should be the goal.
- Emphasize spontaneous speech, whether pictorial, gestural, or verbal.
- Give the child many opportunities to communicate in all settings.
- Any socially acceptable attempt to communicate should be reinforced in all settings.
- Communication goals should be part of any plan to change maladaptive behavior.
- Initial communication goals should target obtaining items and activities that the student finds reinforcing.
- Communication goals should be developmentally and chronologically appropriate.
- Work together with all significant people in the student's environment to make the communication training as consistent as possible.

Source: J. Scott, C. Clark, and M. Brady, *Students with Autism: Characteristics and Instruction Programming* (San Diego: Singular, 2000), p. 225.

young children with autism is that the child will start crying or screaming because something is out of place. The parents and siblings then begin a long process of checking everything in the environment—every piece of furniture, book, lamp, rug—to identify and then fix the source of the child's dismay.

Individuals with autism often engage in repetitive behaviors referred to as stereotypic behaviors.

An unusual behavioral tendency demonstrated by some individuals with autism is the performance of repetitive patterns of behavior such as rocking, twirling objects, clapping hands, and flapping a hand in front of one's face. These repetitive, nonharmful behaviors are often referred to as **stereotypic behaviors.** Some people with autism display a number of stereotypic behaviors and perform them frequently, if not constantly. Others may engage in one or two behaviors, such as rocking during periods of inactivity.

Sometimes, the stereotypic nature of behavior is reflected in more disturbing actions. A few individuals with autism exhibit self-injurious or self-abusive behaviors, ranging from hand biting or head slapping to life-threatening behaviors such as head banging. The individuals seem oblivious to the pain and damage caused by these behaviors.

Inappropriate behavior may reflect attempts by individuals with autism to communicate or to manipulate the environment.

Why do individuals with autism display these behaviors, particularly harmful ones? Research suggests many possible reasons for self-injurious and other inappropriate behavior, including attempts at communication and efforts to manipulate the environment and avoid demanding or stressful situations (Chandler, Dahlquist, Repp, & Feltz, 1999; Durand & Carr, 1985; Sigafoos, 2000). In other words, most of these behaviors have a clear use or function for the child with autism. Often, they represent the individual's best effort to tell you how he or she is feeling and to achieve some control over his or her environment.

This knowledge is extremely important to those who make up the social support system of individuals with autism. As teachers, our first instinct is to try to eliminate inappropriate or harmful behavior. However, we must first assess the student's communicative intent and try to provide alternative behaviors

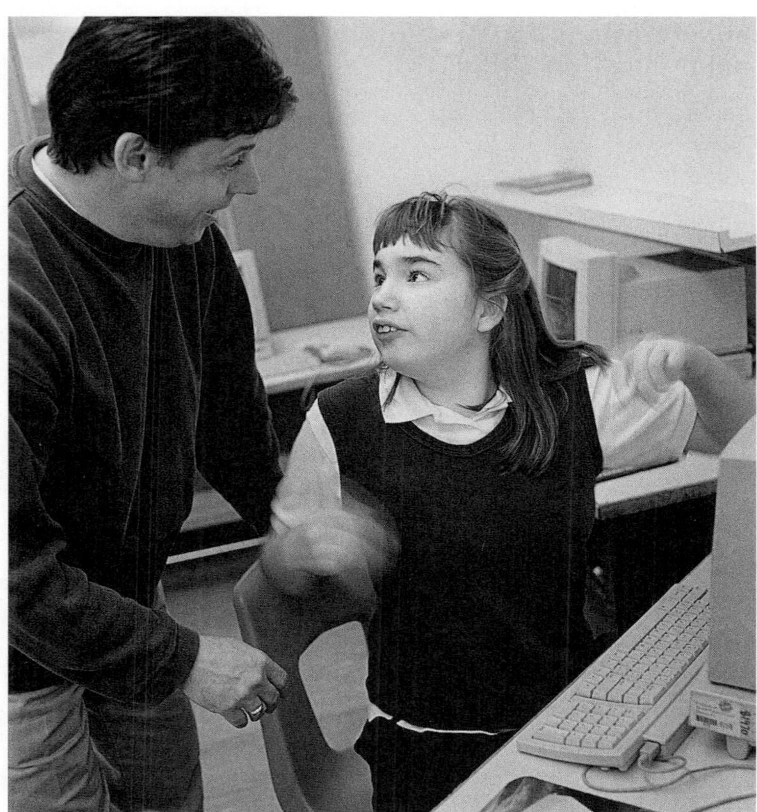

Individuals with autism often engage in repetitive, stereotypic behavior, such as hand-flapping. (© Susie Fitzhugh)

or skills in language and communication when attempting to reduce inappropriate behaviors. Our job, therefore, is twofold: (1) determine the purpose or function of the behavior, and (2) identify and teach an appropriate, alternative behavior that will serve the same function. To accomplish these goals, we conduct functional behavioral assessments (see Chapter 7). This procedure has been found to be effective in replacing inappropriate behavior with appropriate classroom behavior for students with autism (Chandler, Dahlquist, Repp, & Feltz, 1999).

Effects on the Family

Parents are major contributors to the knowledge base in the field of autism.

Several times throughout this chapter we have referred to issues and challenges faced by families of individuals with autism. It is difficult to talk about autism without including parents in the discussion. Parents have been substantial contributors to the knowledge base in the field, both as ethnographers and as sources of empirical data on the effectiveness of various interventions. Unfortunately, most parents are forced into the roles of treatment evaluator, teacher, and, in some cases, intervention designer. Because of the dearth of practical information about living with children with autism, difficulty getting an early diagnosis, inconsistency in treatment recommendations, and lack of early intervention programs, parents have taken the reins and brought the needs of children with autism into focus. This effort by parents is still under way, but now many parents and professionals are working together, and parent advocacy has resulted in a renewed demand for empirical proof of an intervention's effectiveness as well as increased intervention for very young children.

The literature written by parents is filled with concerns about the difficulties they have experienced as they have tried to get an accurate diagnosis for their child (Maurice, 1993). We have already pointed to some of the specific reasons for diagnostic delays, a situation we hope is becoming less and less common. It is important to recognize the importance of this issue, however, because parents may realize early on the level of effort they must put into getting appropriate services for their children.

Once a diagnosis is obtained, parents are faced with a growing body of literature and testimonials about literally dozens of interventions, all of which should begin when the child is about 2 years old. So, sifting through the research and trying to find the desired service provider in the community as soon as possible becomes the next priority. Of course, families with limited resources or those living in rural areas may experience even more difficulty finding appropriate services. It is no wonder that parent support groups and organizations such as the Autism Society provide valuable guidance and assistance as parents try to make their way through the intervention maze.

Once an intervention is chosen, the role of the parents and other family members will only increase. Almost all recommended interventions for young children with autism include intensive teaching, often within the child's home, and usually involving round-the-clock instruction, measuring, and evaluating by parents. So, by the time a child with autism is 3 or 4, his or her family will have devoted at least two to three years of nonstop searching, investigating, and teaching. Because of the intimate role parents play in service delivery, great care is taken to understand and incorporate their needs and educational concerns in areas such as communication priorities (Stephenson & Dowrick, 2000).

In Classrooms and Other Educational Settings

The recommended focus of curriculum and instruction for individuals with autism is essentially the same as it is for students with severe disabilties. Although some individuals with autism are able to progress through a general education academic curriculum, the majority of students require extensive support and benefit from a functional, community-based curriculum. The areas of communication, socialization, and generalization, or transfer of learning, are particularly important in programs for individuals with autism. Table 8.2 provides some guiding questions to help you match interventions to the specific needs of a child.

The majority of students with autism receive a functional, community-based curriculum.

Students with autism may receive special education services at all levels of the service delivery continuum. Many young children receive services at home, and some attend a preschool program. As with all children with disabilities, decisions about educational settings for children with autism will be based on short-term and long-range educational goals for the child and on his or her ability to perform in general education settings. You may find a child with autism and moderate mental retardation served in a self-contained class or in a high school vocational training program. Or, you may find a child with autism receiving academic instruction in the general education class, with accommodations for language and

Table 8.2 Criteria for Selecting Programs: Questions for Parents

1. Does your child have the necessary prerequisite skills for this program?

   When you choose a teaching program, ask yourself what skills your child may need to perform the response. For example, you may want your child to request in sentences, but she may not be able to repeat words. Breaking a skill down into its component parts can help you identify what other skills you may need to teach first.

2. Is this program developmentally age-appropriate for your child?

   Programs should loosely reflect a sequence of development that would be expected of a typical child. When identifying a skill to teach, ask yourself if another child of similar age could perform the same skill.

3. Will this skill help to reduce problem behaviors?

   Choose teaching programs that are likely to have a positive impact on your child's behavior. For example, teaching communicative responses such as pointing and gesturing yes and no may reduce problem behaviors that serve a communicative function.

4. Will this skill lead to the teaching of other skills?

   When choosing skills to teach, identify those that are likely to build on one another. For example, teaching your child to imitate sequenced gross motor actions (e.g., imitating two actions in the correct order) will probably lead you to teach your child to follow two-step verbal instructions.

5. Is this skill likely to generalize?

   Choose programs and target responses that your child will have ample opportunity to practice beyond the teaching sessions. For example, you are more likely to ask your child to "Shut the door," or "Turn on the light," throughout the day, as opposed to "Stomp your feet." Responses that are associated with naturally occurring positive consequences are more likely to generalize.

6. Will your child acquire this skill within a reasonable time frame?

   Priority should be given to teaching skills that your child is likely to acquire in a reasonable amount of time. For example, if your child does not speak, he will need to learn effective communicative responses. Your child can learn to point to desired items relatively quickly, in comparison to requesting in phrases. Skills that will be acquired in a reasonable time frame will be reinforcing for you, your child, and your teaching staff.

7. Is this an important skill for you and your family?

   Choose skills that will have positive implications for your child's participation in family activities. Although matching colors is an important readiness skill, teaching your child to identify family members will have a greater impact on your child's participation in the family.

8. Is this a skill that your child can use throughout the day?

   Choose to teach skills that are functional for your child. For example, learning to follow simple instructions, using yes and no, pointing to desired items, and completing play activities are useful for your child and can be incorporated into his day.

Adapted from B. A. Taylor and K. A. McDonough, Selecting teaching programs, in C. Maurice, G. Green, and S. C. Luce (Eds.), *Behavioral Intervention for Young Children with Autism: A Manual for Parents and Professionals* (Austin, TX: Pro-Ed, 1996), p. 64.

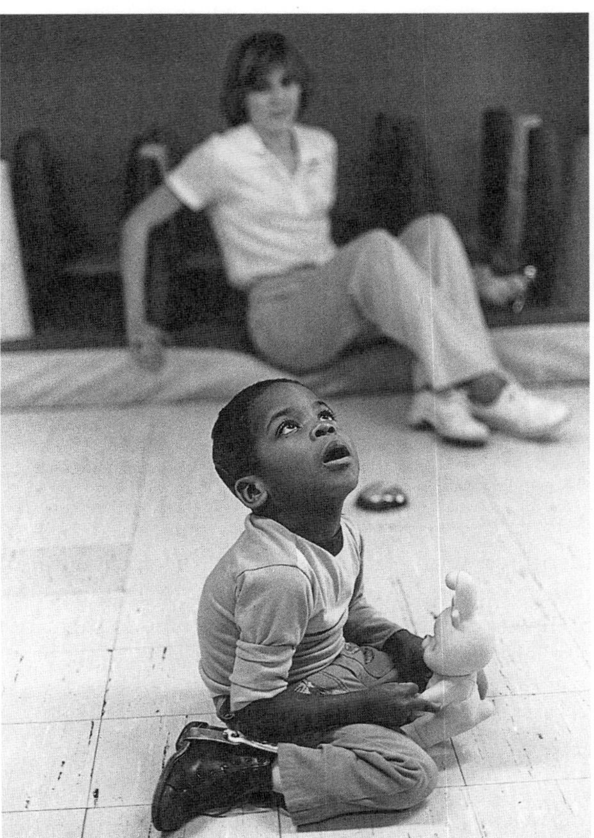

Even in classroom or play settings, a child with autism may be oblivious to those around him. (© David M. Grossman/Science Source—Photo Researchers, Inc.)

in-class instruction in social skills. It is important to ensure that students with autism, regardless of the classroom setting, receive the level of instruction they require, particularly in the areas of social behavior and communication. These areas are likely to continue to be crucial throughout the transition plan of adolescents as they relate to job training and other preparations for life after school.

The Importance of Early Intervention

Although there is great variety of available interventions for individuals with autism, the proponents of virtually all of them agree on one thing: the earlier the better. Harris and Handleman (2000) found that all children who received intensive applied behavior analysis programs beginning before the age of 4 showed both clear gains in IQ and an increased probability of placement in general education classes. Children who received early intervention and who had higher IQs had the best prognosis. Regardless of the type of early intervention program, those that were most effective included six common elements, as identified by Dawson and Osterling (1997) and as listed in the accompanying box, "Elements of Effective Early Intervention Programs."

Children with autism should receive intensive intervention at an early age.

These elements can serve as guidelines for both teachers and parents as they search for comprehensive preschool programs. Because of the requirements of PL 99-457, school districts must provide programs for individuals over age 3

~ Elements of Effective Early Intervention Programs

1. Curriculum content that emphasizes five basic skill areas
   - Attention to aspects of the environment
   - Motoric and visual imitation of others
   - Receptive and expressive language
   - Developmentally appropriate play with toys
   - Social interaction
2. Supportive teaching environments incorporating generalization strategies
3. Predictability and routine
4. Functional assessment of problem behaviors
5. Skills to transition students out of the preschool class
6. Involvement of parents and other family members

Source: G. Dawson and J. Osterling (1997), "Early Intervention in Autism," in M. J. Suralnick (ed.), *The Effectiveness of Early Intervention* (Baltimore: Brookes).

identified with autism or other developmental disabilities, and many districts offer programs for children between the ages of birth and 3 (see Chapter 2). State educational agencies will be able to identify the range and type of services available in specific communities.

Applied Behavior Analysis

Effective interventions for individuals with autism are based on applied behavior analysis.

The methods used most successfully for individuals with autism and other severe disabilities are based on the principles of applied behavior analysis. As we discussed in Chapter 6, applied behavior analysis focuses on clearly defining behavior in the context of the environment and then arranging the environment and providing consequences for increasing or decreasing specific behaviors. First one determines the role or function that the student's behavior plays in his or her environment, and then one identifies alternative behaviors that can serve the same function. New behaviors are taught through reinforcement-based opportunities for response. Complex or multistep behaviors, such as some vocational tasks, may be taught in segments and then linked together. Other skills, such as getting dressed, are presented as a whole, with the student gradually increasing participation. Students with autism may require many instructional trials (discrete trials) and explicit training across environments.

■ ***The Lovaas Method*** The UCLA Young Autism Project, an intensive, three-year program for young children with autism, recently received much attention by parents and some professionals. This project uses interventions based on strategies developed by Ivar Lovaas over thirty years ago. The project developers present data that support significant change in children's cognition, language, and behavior (Smith & Lovaas, 1997). The project is based on the principles of applied behavior analysis; however, some professionals question the curriculum context (what skills are taught and where they are taught) and criticize the quality and validity of the program's experimental research (Gresham & MacMillan, 1997).

The Lovaas Method, as this intervention is commonly called, requires intensive training of teachers or parents and begins when the child is 2 to 3 years of age. The trained interventionist provides intensive, discrete trial training with the child on a one-to-one basis in the child's home. Training is recommended for up to forty hours per week for a minimum of three years. Needless to say, this is an expensive and exhausting intervention approach, yet it is the treatment most commonly requested by parents of young children with autism. The existing empirical base of support has driven the widespread use of the program. In fact, the Lovaas program is one of the few specific educational approaches supported by the courts in litigation against school districts (Yell & Drasgow, 2000). Many school districts are attempting to create applied behavior analysis programs that provide substantial empirical support for learning, without requiring the expensive and limiting in-home training. The box titled "Recommendations for In-home Behavioral Programs" provides guidelines for parents or teachers to use when selecting a behavioral program for very young children.

Environmental Interventions: Project TEACCH

Other methods of teaching students with autism focus on arranging the environment to provide support and extensive opportunities for behavioral expression. The most prominent of these intervention approaches is Project TEACCH (Treatment and Education of Autistic and Related Communication Handi-

~ Recommendations for In-Home Behavioral Programs

Once when I sent a mother to one of the early-intervention programs in New York to try to recruit some therapists for her home program, she reported back to me that the director had informed her that it was "illegal and unethical" for "amateurs" to be attempting this kind of work

We parents *are* amateurs, in the true sense of the word: amateurs are lovers. We are lovers of our children, and until the professional community can offer us more effective programs, we will often have to take matters into our own hands.

A few parents are lucky enough to find an established behavioral program that has room for their child. From what a number of these parents have told me, however, I gather that some of these facilities are better than others. A good behavioral program, I believe, includes these basic qualities:

- A knowledgeable therapeutic team who know how to vary reinforcements and programs, how to keep accurate objective data, until they are *reasonably certain* that the child is doing as well as he can. In other words, they know how to push the child, and when to ease up on the pushing.
- Daily data collection, individualized programs for each child, one-on-one therapy, therapists trained in the principles and techniques of behavior analysis. One therapists to two students is probably not good enough, at least not at the beginning. Later, if the child reaches a higher level of functioning, he or she will probably benefit from small-group teaching. But in the beginning, your child most likely needs concentrated, intense, individual sessions, where the focus is on him or her alone.
- A director and staff who are willing to confer with you—not once a month, not once a week, but whenever you feel like getting or giving information.

In any case, however, these behaviorally oriented programs, whether excellent or mediocre, are few and far between at this time. At least half the families I have met have had to set up, at one time or other, their own home program, since there was literally nothing available to them.

Source: C. Maurice, *Let Me Hear Your Voice: A Family's Triumph over Autism* (New York: Fawcett Columbine, 1993), pp. 307–308.

capped Children program) (Mesibov, 1994). The TEACCH program began as a statewide service delivery system in North Carolina over thirty years ago and it has spread across the United States and Europe. The intervention emphasizes encouraging and maintaining existing behaviors and structured teaching of developmentally appropriate new skills, often using one-on-one instruction (Dawson & Osterling, 1997). Structured instruction takes place in context, to support performance within designated environments. Supports are gradually withdrawn as students become more independent.

A fundamental component of the TEACCH program is the close working relationship between the professionals in the program and parents and families (Scott, Clark, & Brady, 2000). The program focuses on early intervention but continues throughout adulthood, providing safe and interactive learning environments for individuals with autism. Intervention research supports the effectiveness of TEACCH programs in producing satisfaction in increasing independence, and in reducing problem behaviors among the families and children and adults with autism (Mesibov, 1997; Persson, 2000), although some professionals question the research outcomes (Smith, 1996).

Biochemical Interventions

Over the years, a number of interventions have focused on biochemistry, including diet-based interventions, vitamin-based therapies, and others. Most of these interventions lack supporting empirical data. The most recent of the proposed biochemical interventions involves the use of the gastrointestinal hormone secretin to reduce the symptoms of autism. In spite of personal testimony to the contrary, current research indicates that the administration of secretin produces no meaningful changes in the language or behavior of individuals with autism (Chez et al., 2000).

Pharmacological interventions are often a component of treatment protocols for individuals with autism.

Pharmacological interventions, on the other hand, are widely considered to be an important part of treatment protocols for many individuals with autism. Although not a primary educational intervention, drug treatment is often used to address some of the concomitant symptoms of autism, such as hyperactivity, depression, seizure disorders, agitation, aggression, and self-stimulatory behaviors (Heflin & Simpson, 1998).

Alternative Interventions

In addition to the interventions we have described above, many other treatments have been proposed. These treatments run the gamut from new, promising approaches, to historical, unsubstantiated interventions, and everything in between. Some of these interventions, including holding therapy, gentle teaching, and floor time, focus on the suspected psychopathology of autism, and address parental acceptance of children's behaviors and increasing the child's comfort as he or she attempts to communicate (Heflin & Simpson, 1998). Others focus on increasing communication skills (facilitated communication) or establishing neurological equilibrium (sensory integration).

Although many of these interventions may show up in any given community, they do not have empirical support. Some of the proposed interventions may appear idiosyncratic and quite far-fetched. Yet because parents are often desperate for answers, they may be drawn to unproven and often expensive treatments. The support of good, empirical research is the criterion that must be used to select an appropriate educational intervention for individuals

Table 8.3 Evaluating Evidence About Treatments for Autism

A great number of treatments for autism have surfaced over the years. Some professionals claim to have great success using these interventions to improve the performance of children, and some even suggest they can cure autism. All of the claims can be quite confusing to parents and teachers trying to find the most effective educational programs. Part of making treatment decisions is determining the extent to which the evidence presented for treatment efficacy can be trusted. Green (1996) identifies the following factors to look for when evaluating evidence for various treatments.

Speculation vs. Demonstration

Is there actual proof that a treatment produces definite results (demonstration), or is there a recommendation based on someone's theory or hypothesis (speculation)?

Subjective Evidence vs. Objective Evidence

Is the evidence provided by individuals who are biased about the treatment results without controls for such bias (subjective)? Or, is the evidence presented in a quantitative form—the data are clearly defined and carefully observed and assessed via multiple measures by individuals without a stake in the treatment outcomes (objective)?

Indirect Measures vs. Direct Measures

Is the evidence provided in the form of an individual's perceptions, feelings, anecdotes, or impressions that behavior has changed (indirect), or has the behavior been directly observed, counted, or measured (direct)?

Noncomparative Information vs. Comparative Information

Does the evidence result from looking only at the performance of children receiving that intervention (noncomparative), or does it document improved performance when evaluated with students receiving other interventions or no intervention at all (comparative)?

Descriptive Research vs. Experimental Research

Is the information acquired through general descriptions or observations of performance (descriptive), or are observations arranged so that they can be conducted systematically and controlled (experimental)?

Statistical Significance vs. Clinical Significance

Do the results presented indicate only significance based on statistical analysis (statistical), or do they represent real educational importance (clinical significance)?

Adapted from G. Green, "Evaluating Claims About Treatments for Autism," in C. Maurice, G. Green, & S. C. Luce. (Eds.), *Behavioral Intervention for Young Children with Autism: A Manual for Parents and Professionals* (Austin, Texas: Pro-Ed, 1996), pp. 15–28.

with autism. See Table 8.3 for criteria to use when evaluating programmatic research.

Transition to Adulthood

Adults with autism have the same range of opportunities for independence in work and residential settings as individuals with other disabilities.

Adults with autism have the same opportunities for independent performance at work and in residential settings as individuals with other disabilities. They may perform various types of work through competitive employment or sup-

Anecdotes must temper our yen for the miraculous, keep the account honest. Without them, Jessy's slow progress takes on too much of the aura of the success story everybody wants to hear. Suppose I say what is entirely true: that she has worked, rapidly and efficiently, for sixteen years in the Williams College mailroom; that she is hardly ever absent and never late; that she pays taxes; that she keeps her bank account accurately to the penny; that she has saved more money than any of her siblings; that increasingly she keeps house for her aging parents; that I haven't touched a vacuum cleaner in years; that she does the laundry, the ironing, some of the cooking, all of the baking; that she is a contributing member of her community and of her family. Who wouldn't hear, behind those words, others: miracle, recovery, cure? And I have as yet hardly mentioned the brilliant acrylics that seem to be, but are not, the crown of her achievements.

Indeed, they are remarkable. Black-and-white can convey the ordered exactitude of the outlines, the clarity and repetition of design elements, recalling the baby to whom shapes and colors were more significant than faces. There is no vagueness in her paintings, no dashing brush strokes, no atmospheric washes. It is hard-edge stuff, and always has been. Even in nursery school she never overlapped her colors, never scrubbed them together into lovely, messy mud. Her paintings then were as characteristic as these today, repetitive arrangements of shapes and patterns, always controlled, always in balance. What black-and-white can't convey is the incandescence of her colors, and even the finest reproduction could not convey their variety.

Jessy paints; paintings bring checks; the numbers in her bank account rise, as once the numbers rose (and occasionally fell) when she kept track of her behaviors on a golf counter. The checks are a significant motivator for her, as the growing recognition is for us, who must answer inquiries and learn to negotiate the world of galleries and shows—social complexities forever beyond Jessy's ken.

ported work programs. Of course, the particular social and behavioral characteristics of autism may present great challenges in postschool environments, even for individuals without cognitive disabilities. Skills such as language use and appropriate social interaction may be targets for instruction throughout the lifetime of an individual. Instructional approaches such as applied behavior analysis and TEACCH are used through adulthood. Most adults with autism

But for us, and for her, what's important about this demanding, absorbing activity, valued and rewarded by society, is not what it brings to her bank account or her reputation (a concept much harder to understand than stratification), but what it brings to her life. It interests people, predisposes them in her favor, encourages them to overlook behavior that needs overlooking. Autistic people need that. Yet its real meaning for her life is more ordinary: it gives her something to do.

Something to do when she's not working in the mailroom, or changing the cat's pan, or mending her clothes, or changing her sheets, or attending aerobics (a scheduled, predictable, repetitive, satisfying, autistic activity), or taking out the trash, or, as they say, whatever. But there isn't any whatever for Jessy. Her skills, however they have been expanded by years of teaching, do not and cannot embrace the huge range of normality; she doesn't know what to do with leisure. With nothing to do, she won't go for a walk or call a friend. She reverts to the old, stereotyped behaviors. She still likes to rock.

So it is that her real achievements are in the realm of the practical, the necessary, the unromanticizable. . . .

Claire Claiborne Park

Source: Claire Claiborne Park, "Exiting Nirvana," *The American Scholar, 67*:2(1998), 37–39.

live with the family; others live semi-independently in group homes or apartments; and some adults live in more restrictive settings. Often, individuals with autism who live independently benefit from support services, even if it is only an occasional visit from a relative or care provider. In the "First Person" box, a mother describes Jessy, her adult daughter with autism, and Figure 8.3 shows one of Jessy's many beautiful drawings.

Educational Issues

The Right to Nonaversive Interventions

One of the pressing issues both within and without the community of special educators is the use of **aversive interventions** for reducing or eliminating inappropriate, abusive, or self-abusive behaviors. Aversive interventions are typically defined as those that involve the presentation of unpleasant consequences or stimuli as a means of modifying behavior. This issue applies to the educational programming of all students with disabilities, but it is strongest in the area of autism and severe disabilities. Some students with autism, for example, exhibit some behaviors that may be self-destructive, injurious to others, or extremely inappropriate in any given setting or situation. Historically, a variety of interventions that could be considered aversive in nature have been used to reduce or eliminate these behaviors. These included the use of restraints, corporal punishment, and, in some cases, electric shock. Today, aversive treatments are used infrequently, and great care has been taken in special education planning procedures to avoid their use. A specific protocol and guidelines have been established for teachers to follow if they want aversive procedures to be considered for a specific student's educational program.

One area in which aversive procedures are still used to some extent, however, is the treatment of self-abusive behavior, particularly when that behavior could be considered life-threatening or could result in severe mutilation, such as head banging. Some teachers find aversive procedures to be an acceptable option because of their quick results. Other special educators feel strongly that no aversive consequences should be included in students' educational programs. The Association for Persons with Severe Handicapping Conditions (TASH) has issued several statements in support of a completely nonaversive philosophy of behavior management and education. This organization's statements reflect the feelings of many teachers and parents that aversive or painful techniques are unnecessary, obstruct the development of more efficient positive approaches to behavior management, and are contradictory to the individual's right to happiness and basic freedom from persecution.

SUMMARY

- Autism is a lifelong developmental disability that is best described as a collection of behavioral symptoms. Symptoms include deficits in verbal and nonverbal communication, social withdrawal, repetitive and stereotypical behaviors, resistance to change, and unusual responses to sensory experiences.
- It is often difficult to diagnose autism because of the similarity between autism and other disorders, all referred to as pervasive developmental disorders. Asperger's syndrome is one of the many disorders related to autism.
- The cause of autism is not known; however, current research suggests that the cause or causes of autism are physiological factors. At one time, autism was thought to be an emotional or psychological disorder.
- Autism greatly affects the areas of communication, cognition, and social behaviors. Individuals with autism may display unusual speech patterns, such

as echolalia, or may have no oral language. About 80 percent of people diagnosed with autism also have mental retardation. Most individuals with autism display stereotypic behaviors, such as rocking, twirling of objects, or hand clapping.

- Early intervention is a key factor for improving the prognosis of children with autism. Parents, therefore, play an important role in the education of their young children.
- The most effective interventions for individuals with autism are based on principles of applied behavior analysis; these programs involve the systematic instruction of discrete skills.

Key Terms

autism
pervasive developmental disorders
Asperger's syndrome
fragile X syndrome
joint attention
echolalia
reciprocal speech
receptive language
expressive language
stereotypic behaviors
aversive interventions

Multimedia Resources

Autism Society of America: autism-society.org. The Autism Society is a national organization for parents, professionals, and individuals with autism. Most states have their own branch.

Families for the Early Treatment of Autism: feat.org. This website provides information to families and advocates about early intervention options.

Maurice, C. *Let Me Hear Your Voice: A Family's Triumph Over Autism.* (New York: Fawcett Columbine, 1993). This book tells one family's story about the emotional and physical struggle for appropriate interventions for two young children with autism.

Maurice, C., G. Green, and S.C. Luce, Eds. *Behavioral Intervention for Young Children with Autism: A Manual for Parents and Professionals* (Austin, TX: Pro-Ed, 1996). This text is the standard in the field. It provides extensive and usable information about teaching programs and strategies for individuals with autism.

National Alliance for Autism Research: www.naar.org. This site provides information about the latest research in autism.

What You Can Do

1. Interview a pediatrician about the process he or she uses to diagnose a child with autism. Discuss the specific criteria he or she uses and the recommendations he or she gives to parents.
2. Attend a meeting of the Autism Society in your area. Talk with the members to identify the range and sources of services available in your area.

3. Observe or participate in an applied behavior analysis or Lovaas training session for individuals who work with young children with autism. Describe how the training program addresses the specific characteristics of children with autism.

4. Identify the services local school districts provide for preschool children with autism. Visit the classrooms or teaching sessions for each type of intervention and compare them. How do they differ?

5. Visit a secondary school program that includes adolescents with autism. Identify the range of skills being instructed in the areas of communication, social skills, work skills, and academic skills.

9

Children with Communication Disorders

CHILDREN WITH communication disorders may have subtle difficulties or obvious problems in speaking, understanding, or hearing. Because communication is central to the educational experience, teachers play a key role in recognizing students who are experiencing significant problems in communication, and in helping these students communicate effectively in the classroom. As you read this chapter, think about the following questions:

How do you envision your own role in helping your students communicate effectively?

Can you think of any area of schooling in which communication is not important?

Commonalities: How are language, speech, and communication crucial to classroom success for all children?

Collaboration: How can the classroom teacher and the speech-language pathologist work together to ensure the success of children with communication disorders—and those at risk for developing problems?

Can Do: What can the classroom teacher do to help children communicate more successfully?

Most of you reading this book are highly verbal individuals. You know how to change your communicative style to talk in different ways to different people in different situations. You know that talking to a toddler and talking to the school principal require distinct communicative styles. You can express a wide range of meanings, often in subtle ways, take your turn at speaking in all the many different situations you experience in a day, manage the flow and direction of

Communication in the classroom involves more than words.
(Ellen Senisil/The Image Works, Inc.)

conversations with both familiar and less familiar conversational partners, and fix breakdowns in understanding when they happen—for example, by asking for clarification. When it comes to reading and writing, you know how to read differently for different purposes—you can skim the newspaper versus reading a textbook—and you know what to do when you don't understand what you have read. You also know how to write for different purposes and audiences, how to adjust your style and form of writing for the occasion, and how to revise your meanings when you think they may not be clear for the reader. You are effective communicators. For you, communicating with others, either orally or through print, is relatively easy—at least in your native language.

Yet you have probably experienced difficulty in communication—the "fear and trembling" that can happen when a professor calls on you in class to answer a question, the frustration of having your speaking turn taken away when someone interrupts you, the inability to make sense of what you are reading, or the essay returned with a poor grade because the main ideas have not been communicated well.

Those who have experienced some disruption in the development and use of oral communication can experience similar difficulties every day, difficulties also reflected in their reading, writing, and spelling. Communication problems are common to many exceptional students studied in this book, such as those with mental retardation, learning disabilities, or behavioral and emotional disorders. For example, communication issues are at the core of autism, and students with a severe hearing loss or a physical disability may have difficulty acquiring effective oral communication skills.

The group of students emphasized in this chapter are different. Most of them have normal sensory and motor functioning and normal intellectual potential. Their primary disability involves the communication process; however, their problems with communication are often subtle. In the following sections we'll examine the components of communication, language, and speech, and their development, and then look at how teachers work with students with communication disorders.

Definitions and Terms

Communication, language, and *speech* are related terms. Since they constitute the foundation for teaching and learning in school, we will examine their meaning more closely.

Communication

Communication is the exchange of ideas, information, thoughts, and feelings (McCormick, Loeb, & Schiefelbusch, 1997). It involves two or more people interactively sending and receiving messages. Communication has many purposes, and its power cannot be overestimated: "No matter how one may try, one cannot *not* communicate. Activity or inactivity, words or silence all have message value: they influence others and these others, in turn, cannot *not* respond to these communications and are thus themselves communicating" (Watlawick, Beavin, & Jackson, 1967, p. 49).

We communicate—exchange ideas—through listening, speaking, reading, and writing.

We usually think of communication occurring through speaking, listening, reading, and writing. But it's important to think of communication as more than words. Don't people communicate with their clothing, their movement, and their facial expressions? Don't pets communicate to their owners when they are hungry or hurt? Even students with disabilities who lack the ability to speak express themselves in some way, as we will see in Chapter 12. Figure 9.1 displays some of the types of communication.

Language

Language is the verbal system by which human beings communicate. According to Bloom and Lahey (1978), it is "a code whereby ideas about the world are expressed through a conventional system of arbitrary signals for communication" (p. 2). Let's look at each component of this definition. A *code* is a symbolic means

We communicate verbally through language.

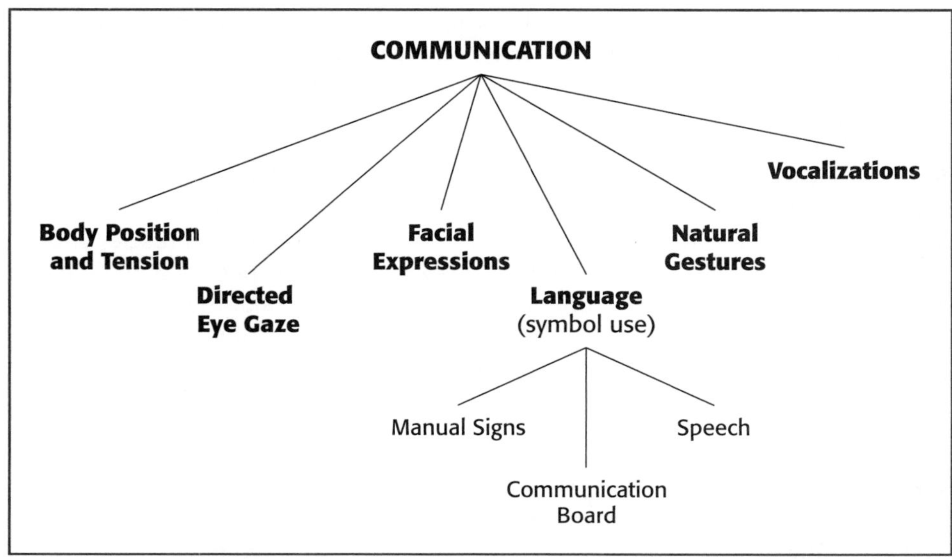

Source: M. Diane Klein, Division of Special Education, California State University, Los Angeles. Used with permission

Figure 9.1
Types of Communication

we use to represent one thing by another in order to think about it, store it, or share it with others (Bloom, 1988). For example, the word *cat* is a symbol we use to represent a small, furry animal. The linguistic code provides the form through which the speech sounds of spoken language (or the signs of a manual language) combine to represent objects and ideas. Each spoken language has its own sound code. For example, in English the sound combination /k/ /â/ /t/ means *cat*, but in Russian this meaning is expressed through the sound combination *koshka* and in French, *chat*. This linguistic code is designed to communicate meaning, which is expressed through the *content*, or semantic component, of language. When we speak of vocabulary, we are actually referring to the meaning of words, or their dictionary meaning. Of course, most words have many meanings, a fact which contributes significantly to the complexity of language learning.

Through the linguistic code, speech sounds combine to represent objects and ideas.

The linguistic code is rule-governed. This means that patterns of regularity exist in the form or structure of language, or what is often called its *grammar*. For example, if you were asked to complete the following sentence: "Here is a bik; here are two ______," you would most likely respond *biks*, demonstrating your knowledge of language as ordered by rules (Berko, 1958). Linguists describe five interrelated components of language, each having a rule system: (1) **phonology:** phonological rules govern how we combine **phonemes,** or sounds, in permissible ways to form words; (2) **morphology:** morphological rules tell us how word meaning may be changed by adding or deleting **morphemes**—prefixes, suffixes, and other forms that specifically indicate tense and number, such as *-ed* to mark the past tense (miss*ed*) and *-s* to mark the plural form (dog*s*); (3) **syntax:** syntactic rules govern how words may be combined to form sentences; (4) **semantics:** semantic rules specify how language users create and understand the meaning of words and word combinations (McCormick, Loeb, & Schiefelbusch, 1997); and (5) **pragmatics:** pragmatic rules indicate how to use language appropriately in a social context in order to achieve some goal. Pragmatic goals might include finding information, fulfilling a need, or sharing a thought. All speakers of a language share the knowledge of how to use language in accord with the social rules of their speech community. Shared communication, called conversation, or **discourse,** has specific rules for taking turns, responding appropriately, and managing topics. Figure 9.2 depicts the interrelationship of the primary components of language: they can be addressed separately but are interrelated.

The form or structure of language is its grammar.

Rules of grammar have phonological, morphological, and syntactic components.

Speech

Speech is the oral part of the language system.

Speech involves the physical action of orally producing words. It is a product of complex, well-coordinated muscular activity from respiration to phonation to articulation. Just to say "pop," for example, requires a hundred muscles coordinating their work at a speed of fifteen speech sounds per second (Haynes, Moran, & Pindzola, 1990). Figure 9.3 shows the structures of the speech mechanism. Every language uses a set of sounds, or phonemes, from a larger set of all possible sounds. Languages do not all have the same number of phonemes. English uses approximately forty to forty-five phonemes.

Language Development

The next few pages cover very briefly what other books spend hundreds of pages explaining and discussing—the process of normal language development. Obviously, there is much more to learn about this subject than we can

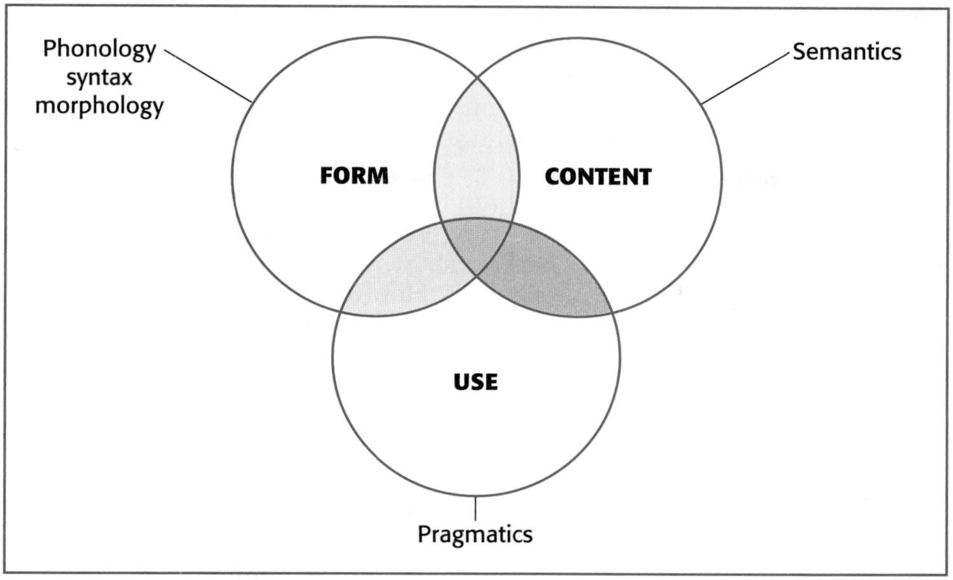

Phonology
syntax
morphology

Semantics

FORM

CONTENT

USE

Pragmatics

Figure 9.2
The Intersection of Content, Form, and Use in Language

Source: L. Bloom & M. Lahey, *Language Development and Language Disorders* (New York: Wiley, 1978), p. 22.

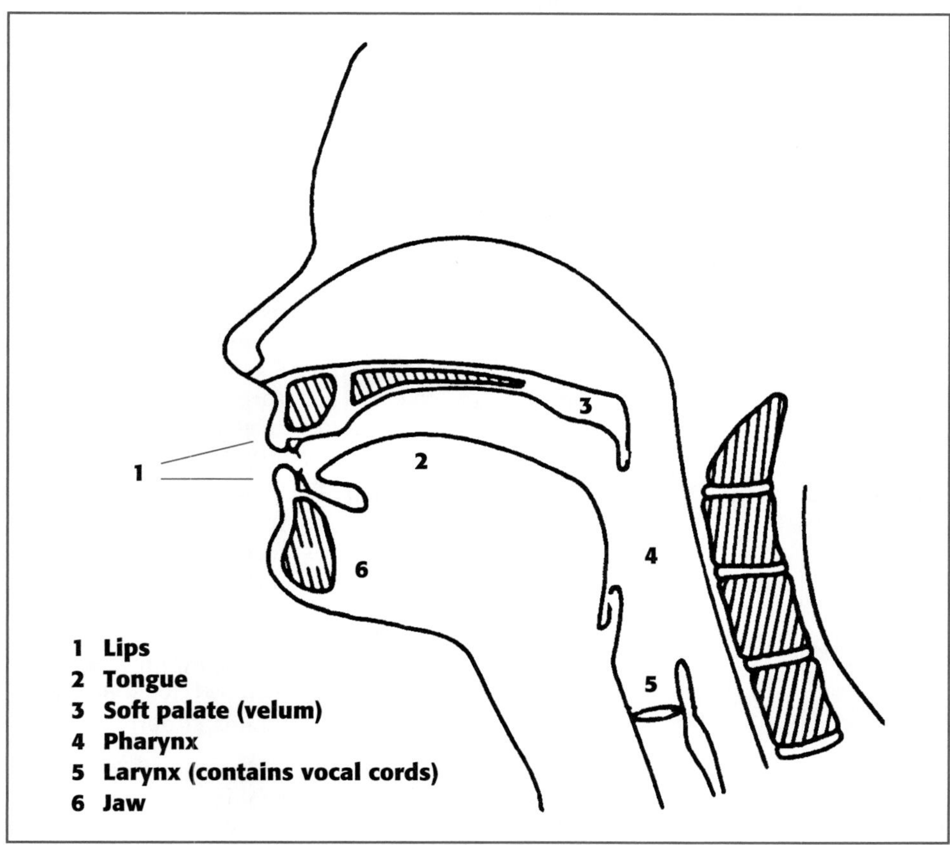

Figure 9.3
Structures of the Speech Mechanism

Source: M. L. Edwards, *Introduction to Applied Phonetics* (Austin, TX: Pro-Ed, 1986), p. 177.

present here. If you have not learned this material through another course or your own reading, we have provided additional resources on normal language and speech development at the end of this chapter. The following brief overview provides the foundation for our understanding of communication disorders, which occur when language and speech do *not* develop as expected.

In about a thousand days, from birth to age 3, most children develop initial competence as oral communicators. How do children acquire communication skills so rapidly? What do they have to know about the world and about language? How is this knowledge organized? How and why does this knowledge change during the school-age years? Theories of communication acquisition attempt to address these vital questions.

Language Acquisition

The oral communication process is complex, and there is no agreement on a single theory of communication development. Rather, competing perspectives attempt to explain how children learn to communicate. Two of these major perspectives on communication acquisition are outlined in Table 9.1.

Most major theories of language acquisition reflect a psycholinguistic and/or a social interaction perspective.

Most theories reflect a psycholinguistic or social interactional perspective, or a combination of both. Both perspectives stress the active, constructive nature of language learning and the interrelationships among biological, cognitive, social, and linguistic systems (Kamhi, 1992).

Psycholinguistic theories are primarily concerned with mental processes within the child—what goes on inside the child's head. Often, psycholinguists study the child alone. *Social interactional theories* assume that mental processes originate as social processes and are progressively internalized by the child

Table 9.1 Two Perspectives on Communication Acquisition

Perspective	Focus	Main Assumptions
Psycholinguistic	Child is an explorer	"You're basically taking this trip alone, but I'm here when you need me." Child is an active language processor whose task is to discover underlying rules based on the adult input.
Social interactional	Child is a collaborator	"I'm always with you for support, so don't worry about getting lost." Child and adult actively participate together to create communicative events; these events form communicative contexts through which the child progressively discovers and applies underlying rules.

Source: J. N. Bohannan & A. Warren-Lenbecker, "Theoretical Approach to Language Acquisition," in J. B. Gleason, ed., *The Development of Language*, 2d ed. (Columbus, OH: Merrill, 1989), pp. 167–223. Copyright © 1989 by Allyn & Bacon. Reprinted/ adapted by permission.

through interactions with a caregiver or teacher. This conceptual framework emphasizes the interpersonal context in which the child participates—how adults support the child as they collaborate to accomplish goals.

Although we do not know exactly how language is acquired, we do know when most children reach developmental milestones. There is variation in the age when individuals achieve these stages, but the process has a pattern and pace common among all languages and cultures. Table 9.2 summarizes five stages of language and communicative development from birth to age 12.

The age boundaries between phases, as well as the ages for the appearance of particular behaviors, represent data that have been compiled from many children and then averaged—so in working with individual children teachers should use this information only as a general guideline. It's also important to be cautious when applying milestones to children from cultural minority groups, because they have not typically been included in research studies.

You can see from the information in Table 9.2 how swiftly development proceeds during the first three to five years of life. For example, by approximately 12 months, the infant has become a highly social individual and has begun the transition to conventional first words. At 24 months, the child has begun to use two-word sentences, and at 48 months she is using complex utterances. Such rapid learning is possible, in part, because of the typical child's communicative environment. It is estimated that by age 4, in the course of everyday interaction, the average child has been exposed to 20 to 40 million words and has spoken 10 to 20 million words (Chapman et al., 1992). By age 5, the basic system of oral communication has been acquired. This system continues to grow in more sophisticated

We acquire the basic system of oral communication by age 5, and it forms the foundation for reading and writing.

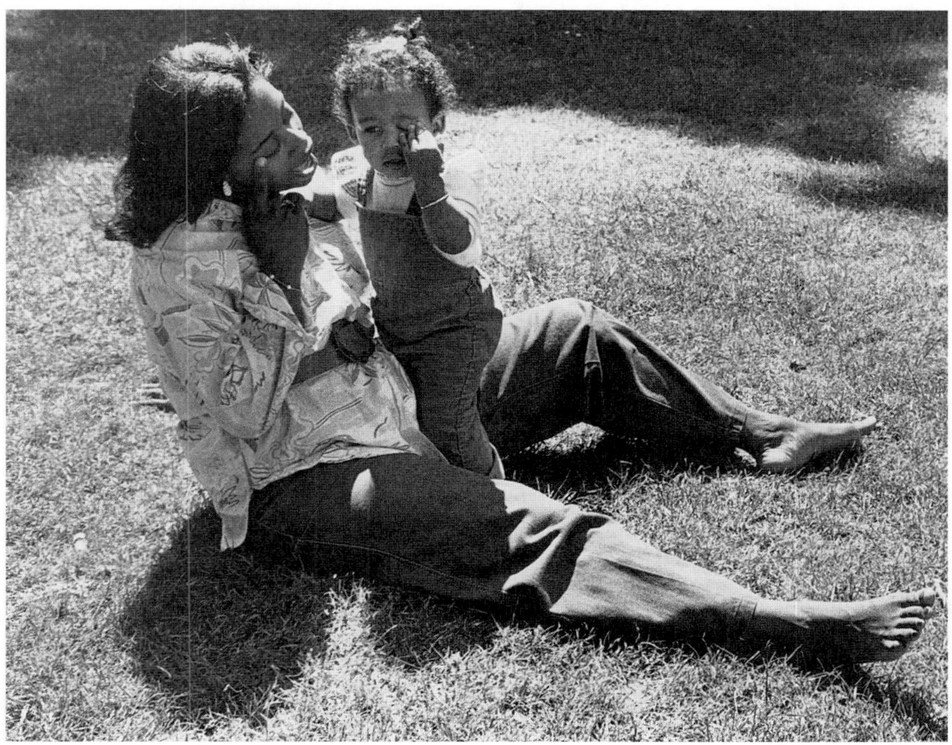

Children learn language through interaction with others during meaningful experiences. (Elizabeth Crews)

Table 9.2 Overview of Communicative Development: Birth to 12 Years

Age (Months)	Appearances
The examiner (1–6 mos.)	Responds to human voice; makes pleasure sounds (1 mo.)
	Produces strings of consonant-vowel or vowel-only syllables; vocally responds to speech of others (3 mo.)
	Smiles at person speaking to him/ her (4 mo.)
	Responds to name; smiles and vocalizes to image in mirror (5 mo.)
	Prefers people games, e.g., peek-a-boo, I'm going to get you; explores face of person holding him/her (6 mo.)
The experimenter (7–12 mos.)	Recognizes some words; repeats emphasized syllables (8 mo.)
	"Performs" for family; imitates coughs, hisses, raspberries, etc. (9 mo.)
	Obeys some directives (10 mo.)
	Anticipates caregiver's goal and attempts to change it via persuasion/protest (11 mo.)
	Recognizes own name; engages in familiar routines having visual cues (e.g., bye-bye); uses one or more words (12 mo.)
The explorer (12–24 mos.)	Points to toys, persons, animals named; pushes toys; plays alone; begins some make-believe; has 4- to 6-word vocabulary (15 mo.)
	Begins to use 2-word utterances (combines); refers to self by name; has about 20-word vocabulary; pretends to feed doll, etc. (18 mo.)
	Enjoys rhyming games; tries to "tell" experiences; understands some personal pronouns; engages in parallel play (21 mo.)
	Has 200- to 300-word vocabulary; names most common everyday objects; uses some prepositions (*in, on*) and pronouns (*I, me*) but not always accurately; engages in object-specific pretend play and parallel play; can role-play in limited way; orders other around; communicates feelings, desires, interests (24 mo.)
The exhibitor (3–5 yrs.)	Has 900- to 1,000-word vocabulary; creates 3- to 4-word utterances; talks about the "here and now"; talks while playing and takes turns in play; "swears" (3 yrs.)
	Has 1,500- to 1,600-word vocabulary; asks many questions; uses increasingly complex sentence constructions; still relies on word order for interpretation; plays cooperatively with others; role-plays; recounts stories about recent experiences (narrative recounts); has some difficulty answering *how* and *why* (4 yrs.)
	Has vocabulary of 2,100–2,200 words; discusses feelings; understands *before* and *after* regardless of word order; play is purposeful and constructive; shows interest in group activities (5 yrs.)
The expert (6–12 yrs.)	Has expressive vocabulary of 2600 words while understands 20,000–24,000 word meanings; defines by function; has many well-formed, complex sentences; enjoys active games and is competitive; identifies with same sex peers in groups (6 yrs.)
	Verbalizes ideas and problems readily; enjoys an audience; knows that others have different perspectives; has allegiance to group, but also needs adult support (8 yrs.)
	Talks a lot; has good comprehension; discovers he or she may be the object of someone else's perspective; plans future actions; enjoys games, sports, hobbies (10 yrs.)
	Understands about 50,000 word meanings; constructs adultlike definitions; engages in higher-order thinking and communicating (12 yrs.)

Source: R. E. Owens, *Language Development: An Introduction*, 5th ed. (New York: Merrill, 2001), pp. 76–111.

ways during the school years because it is influenced by two new tools the child learns for thinking and communicating: reading and writing.

Speech Production

During the first 6 months of life, infants primarily produce vowel-like sounds with some glottal and back consonant-like sounds. At about 6 months of age their vocalizations begin to include more consonant-like sounds ("ba-ba-ba"). This stage is called "babbling." These sounds tend to follow rather predictable patterns of development in all languages (Oller, Weiman, Doyle, & Ross, 1976; Oller & Eilers, 1982). Social interactions with caretakers involving imitative vocal play and turn taking, along with developing cognitive capabilities such as increased memory span, play a role in the transition from babbling to speech, along with the increasing fine motor control necessary for phoneme differentiation. Table 9.3 shows the path from vocalization to speech.

Table 9.3 The Path from Vocalization to Speech

Stage	Characteristic Behavior
Phonation (0–2 mos.)	Produces vowel-like sounds with vocal tract at rest.
	Produces reflexive sounds such as cries, grunts, hiccoughs, sneezes, which may sound consonantal.
Primitive articulation (1–4 mos.)	Produces coos and gurgles, which are primitive syllables using vowel sounds and some velar (back) sounds.
Expansion (3–8 mos.)	Produces more vowel sounds.
	Explores pitch through squeals, growls, yells, whispers, raspberries.
	Repeats particular sound types in vocal play.
Canonical syllable (5–10 mos.)	Produces babbling, which consists of well-formed syllables with combinations of consonants and vowels.
	Reduplicates sequences of these syllables, such as "ba-ba-ba."
Integrative (9–18 mos.)	Produces variegated sequences of babbling syllables.
	Mixes babbling and speech.
	Begins transition to meaningful speech (first words).

Note: These stages are based on age ranges. One infant may enter a new stage earlier or later than another infant.
Source: D. K. Oller and M. P. Lynch, "Infant Vocalizations and Innovations in Infraphonology," in C. A. Ferguson, L. Menn, and C. Stoel-Gammon, eds., *Phonological Development: Models, Research, Implications* (Timonium, MD: York Press, 1992), pp. 509–536. Used by permission.

Types of Communication Disorders

The IDEA definition of **communication disorder** is "a . . . disorder such as stuttering, impaired articulation, a language impairment, or a voice impairment that adversely affects a child's educational performance" (*Federal Register*, 1992). Disruptions to the communication process can affect language, speech, or hearing. Language disorders involve a delay in understanding others, participating in conversation, or using language appropriate to the listener or to the situation (ASHA, 1997). Speech disorders include phonological, fluency, and voice impairments. Figure 9.4 shows the relationship among communication disorders, language disorders, and speech disorders. Hearing loss, discussed in depth in the next chapter, also results in difficulties in acquiring and using language and speech.

Language Disorders

Although most children acquire language through natural interactions with the people around them, some do not: they experience either language delay (slower development) or language disorders (Fahey, 2000a). The American Speech-Language-Hearing Association (ASHA), the national professional organization for speech-language pathologists and audiologists, defines language disorder as

A language disorder is the impaired comprehension or use of spoken or written language.

> the abnormal acquisition, comprehension, or expression of spoken or written language. The disorder may involve all, one, or some of the phonologic, morphologic, semantic, syntactic, or pragmatic components of the linguistic system. Individuals with language disorders frequently have trouble in sentence processing or in abstracting information meaningfully for storage and retrieval from long-term memory. (ASHA, 1980, pp. 317–318)

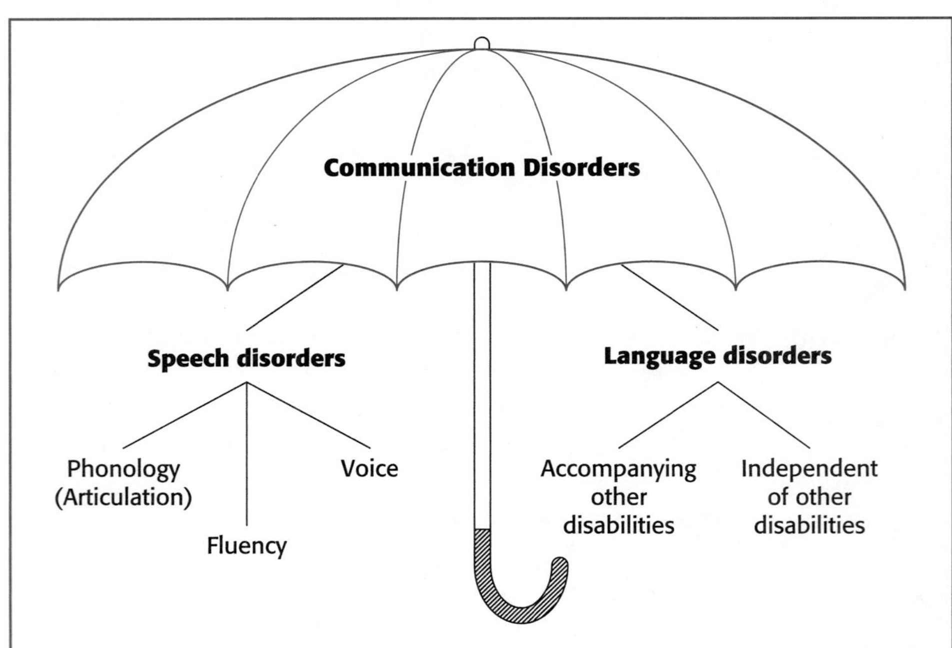

Figure 9.4
The Relationship of Communication, Language, and Speech Disorders

Communication: Strategies and Resources

We note in Chapter 9 that language-learning difficulties are at the core of many of the disabilities we cover in this book. These include communication disorders and deafness as well as learning disabilities, mental retardation, and autism. Language learning is also paramount for the millions of American schoolchildren who first learn English in school, whom we call English language learners. Even the most competent students, those often identified as gifted, can benefit from intensive focus on language learning—to further their vocabulary, perfect their spoken and written use of English, and help them develop fluency in other languages. Knowledge of language and language development strategies is the foundation for literacy instruction, as teachers need to possess this knowledge to help their students develop a sound command of spoken and written language.

It is helpful to think of three levels of language intervention strategies. Intervention becomes more focused and intensive at each level. Here are some examples of strategies that can be used by classroom teachers at each level.

Level One: Best practices for typical language learners; enrichment for students who are learning language successfully.

- Give your students plenty of opportunities to talk, and listen carefully to what they say. Students need to talk as much as or more than teachers.
- Tape record one of your lessons, then listen for who is doing the talking. Teachers should be providing every student with an opportunity to talk, and not monopolizing all the talking themselves.
- Provide a "wait time" when a student is called on, and try not to interrupt. Students from some cultures unfold their narratives more slowly than others (Reid, 2000).
- Respond to students' talk not with correction, but with an enriched, correct pattern.
- Provide plenty of contextual supports for new language learning as well as new concepts: pictures, graphic organizers, films, hands-on experiences, and so on.
- Have a place in your classroom where new vocabulary is recorded, and find opportunities to use new vocabulary in different contexts. Reward students for their use of new vocabulary as well.
- Through your dialogue with students, use scaffolding to move them to a higher level of speaking and understanding. Scaffolding is "a process of enabling students to solve a problem, achieve a goal, or carry out a task that would be beyond their ability if they were not given help" (Reid, 2000, p.28). Your goal is to improve students' levels of participation until they become independent.

Level Two: Procedures used with children who are not acquiring language at the same rate as their peers, or with those who are learning English.

- Find the time for work on English language development every day.
- Pre-teach critical vocabulary prior to student reading (Gersten & Baker, 2000).
- Provide the students with frequent opportunities to use oral language in the classroom. Don't let the more fluent students monopolize the discussion.
- Focus on vocabulary building, but do not overwhelm students with new vocabulary—lists of seven or fewer words should be worked on over relatively long periods. Vocabulary should convey key concepts and be useful, relevant to the concepts being taught, and meaningful to the students (Gersten & Baker, 2000).
- Use visuals as you teach. For students who are learning a new language, visuals such as semantic maps and story maps "help students visualize the abstractions of language" (Gersten & Baker, 2000, p. 463).
- Promote peer interactions, peer tutoring, and cooperative work groups. Students who are learning language, whether they be English language learners or students with disabilities, will benefit from peer models, prompts, and supports.

Level Three: Interventions that are disability-specific.

- Incorporate sign language and fingerspelling for students with hearing loss. It often helps other students, too. If you're not an expert, buy a book and learn with your students. Teach all of your students signs so they will use them with one another and develop new vocabulary.
- Build in concept development for students who are visually impaired. Concepts that sighted students learn through vision must be explicitly taught to students who are blind or have low vision.
- Through your school's speech-language pathologist, investigate augmentative communication systems for students who cannot or do not speak. Students with physical disabilities can use picture boards and computer systems with adaptations (see Chapter 12). Students with autism might use systems like the Picture Exchange Communication System (PECS; see Chapter 8).

Multimedia Resources

McCormick, L., Loeb, D.F., & Schiefelbusch, R.L. (1997). *Supporting Children with Communication Difficulties in Inclusive Settings: School-based Interventions.* Boston: Allyn & Bacon.

The American Speech-Language-Hearing Association (ASHA) has a consumer website with interesting information. Go to their site index from the home page for an overview. **http://www.asha.org**

You can find Internet Resources in Speech-Language-Hearing at

http://professional.asha.org/tech_resources/internet.htm

The ASHA journal *Language, Speech, and Hearing Services in Schools* frequently has articles dealing with classroom discourse. Find it in your university library, or see the index through the ASHA website, cited above.

Instructional Technology : Strategies and Resources

Although computers have become commonplace in classrooms, many of us still have questions about how to use instructional technology and how to identify the best programs for specific academic needs. These questions become even more numerous when we consider using instructional technology with and for students with disabilities. The actual practice of instructional technology in classrooms does not change because of the presence or absence of students with disabilities. You may, however, need to make more choices and survey a wider range of technological options. Because there are so many techniques for using instructional technology in the classroom, we will focus here on basic strategies for making decisions about using instructional technology.

Your decisions about how and why to use technology in your classrooms will depend on many things. We will look at two basic areas: establishing a purpose and meeting individual student needs.

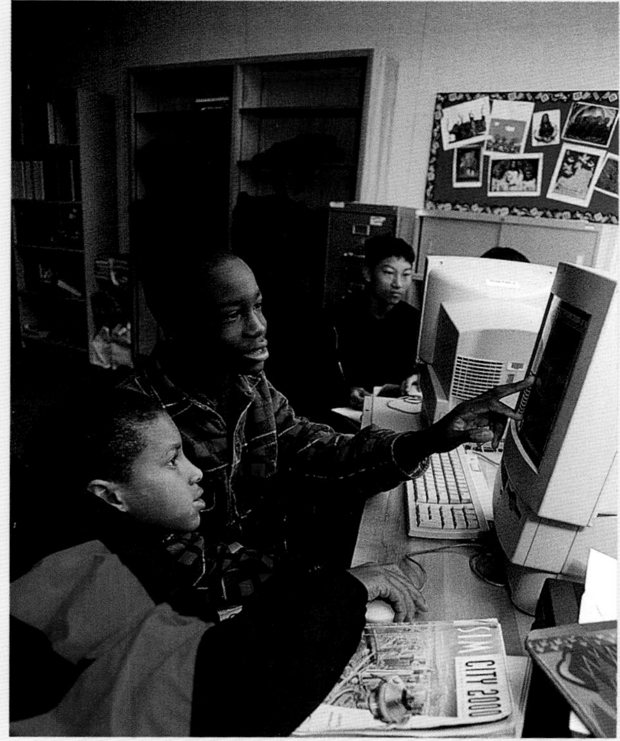

© Elizabeth Crews

Establish a Purpose for Instruction and Integrate Appropriate Instructional Technology

As we discussed in Chapter 4, research suggests that certain teaching strategies are effective for students with disabilities. Included in these strategies is direct instruction, which includes the elements of modeling (presenting information), leading (guided practice), and testing (independent performance). We also talk throughout the text about the importance of skill mastery and generalization. When you use technology for students with disabilities, it is important that you keep these basic principles of instruction in mind.

Alessi and Trollop (2001) identified and described eight specific types of technology. These are listed below, with a brief description of what they are and how they are used.

1. **Tutorials** Tutorials are used to give the student information—in other words, to teach something. They should include a modeling component and provide guided practice.
2. **Hypermedia** Hypermedia consists of providing access through a variety of navigational tools to a substantial data base related to a specific topic. Hypermedia often is used to provide students with opportunities for topical discovery and independent acquisition of information.
3. **Drills** Drills are repeated opportunities for practice. Like the worksheets of old, drills on a computer can be a boring series of problems. Technology does, however, offer options for more interesting drill or practice activities, including those which include providing corrective feedback to the student.
4. **Simulations** Simulations are models of an activity or experience that allow students to learn through participation. Simulations can be used to establish a purpose for learning, to acquire a new skill, or to practice or apply a skill that has already been learned.
5. **Games** Games in instructional technology have the same definition as games in a child's playroom. They are activities designed to be fun, to invoke a competitive spirit, and to establish a goal for the student to reach. Games can be used in all parts of the learning process, and are most often used to practice or apply skills or knowledge.

6. **Tools and open-ended learning environments** A number of programs teach students to use technological tools for such things as graphing, organizing, and drawing. Students can use this technology to apply, illustrate, and practice skills, or to develop aids to new learning by developing outlines, etc.

7. **Tests** The purpose of tests is to assess mastery. Tests given on the computer can be disguised in game formats or simulations, and can include learning tools such as providing corrective feedback. Many new programs can be very helpful to teachers by recording and graphing data on each student.

8. **Web-based learning** Web-based learning includes everything from sending e-mail, to participating in discussion groups, to hypermedia. The purposes also vary widely, focusing more on group or individual exploration of topics than on direct instruction of new skills (Alessi & Trollop, 2001).

Meeting Individual Students' Needs

When technology is integrated in the curriculum, it is important to address the individual needs of students with disabilities. To assess individual needs, you may refer to the student's IEP, as well as consider a task analysis of the content area skill and the software operation. Gardner and Edyburn (2000) suggest that two of the important questions teachers should ask are:

1. What prerequisite skills and knowledge are required for my students to use the program?
2. Will special instructional strategies be required for my students to successfully use the program? (p. 207)

Prerequisite skills and knowledge may pertain to the content presented in the program or to operating the program itself. For example, if a child is going to use a program designed to provide practice in two-operation word problems, he must be able to work two-operation word problems and to read the text in the program. Preskills for operating the program may be using a keyboard and reading the commands in the program menu. These skills must be taught before the student can use the program independently.

Special instructional strategies related to content may include teaching students specific steps to follow to evaluate their writing performance before presenting them with a program that prompts self-evaluation. Teachers must devote time to teaching students how to use a particular program. For students with disabilities, a series of commands, arrows, and several sets of directions can be overwhelming and confusing. Gardner and Edyburn (2000) suggest developing a strategy sheet or a written set of steps to follow so that students can have procedural prompts to guide them after instruction.

MULTIMEDIA RESOURCES

Websites with assistance, examples, and instructions for developing instructional technology:

TrackStar: **http://hprtec.org/track**

Web Toolboxes: **http://www.ed.sc.edu/caw/toolbox.html**

Federal search engine guide to a range of educational resources (including some free materials) **http://www.thegateway.org**

Software to Go—a collection of software evaluations for children who are deaf: **http://clerccenter2.gallaudet.edu/stg/index.html**

Journals that include instrumental technology reviews, guidelines for applications, and new websites for information on technology:

ConnSENSE Bulletin—an independent periodic publication focusing on software evaluation. Visit the website at **http://www.connsensebulletin.com**

Journal of Special Education Technology—the journal of the Technology and Media Division of the Council for Exceptional Children. Visit the website at **http://www.tamcec.org**

Special Education Technology Practice. Visit the website at **http://www.setp.net**

Think about the five components of language described earlier—**phonology, syntax, morphology, semantics, and pragmatics.** The ASHA definition tells us that a language disorder can occur as a result of a problem with one or more of those components. Since they are interrelated, difficulties often occur in combination.

There has been considerable debate among professionals about how to classify children with language disorders (Kamhi, 1998). Should it be by the primary label of disability, such as learning disability, autism, or motor disabilities? Certainly, many children who qualify for special education services in those specific disability areas have significant problems with language, spoken and written. Or should professionals describe children by the specific area of language that they have difficulty with—children with syntactical difficulties, for example? These descriptions would cut across traditional disability areas, but many children do have problems with language that involve more than one specific area.

Polloway and Smith (2000) use a model that describes language disabilities by degree of severity. Level I is severe language disabilities, and Level II, mild to moderate language disabilities. Table 9-4 fleshes out those categories.

One way to classify language disorders is by level of severity.

For this discussion, we refer to children whose *primary* difficulty is in learning and using language. (The language problems of children with other disabilities will be described in the chapters that focus on specific disabilities.) These children are sometimes referred to as those with **specific language impairment** (McCormick, Loeb, & Schiefelbusch, 1997). Their problems with learning and using language cannot be attributed to another disability—they have no other apparent problems. Later in their school careers, however, they are much more likely than children without language impairments to have difficulties with reading and writing and, therefore, with school achievement—so they may end up with the label of *learning disability***.** Table 9.5 describes some of the language problems associated with specific language impairment. Remember, in real life children do not appear in neat little chapters as they do in this book. Their

Most students with a specific language impediment do not have other major disabilities.

Table 9-4 A General Model for Classification of Language Disabilities

Level I: Severe Language Disabilities
- A. Absence of language
- B. Nonspontaneous acquisition of language
- C. Severe language delay or distortion

Level II: Mild-Moderate Language Disabilities
- A. Oral language delay
- B. Oral language disorders
- C. Written language disorders
  1. Reading disabilities
  2. Graphic disabilities
  3. Expressive disabilities

Source: E. A. Polloway & Tom E. C. Smith, *Language Instruction for Students with Disabilities (second ed.)*, p. 38. Denver: Love Publishing Company, 2000.

Table 9.5 Language Difficulties Associated with Specific Language Impairment

Language Dimension	Difficulties
Phonology	Failure to capitalize on regularities across words
	Slow development of phonological processes
	Unusual errors across sound categories
Morphology/syntax	Co-occurrence of more mature and less mature forms
	Fewer lexical categories per sentence than peers
	More grammatical errors than peers
	Slow development of grammatical morphemes
	Many pronoun errors
Semantics	Delayed acquisition of first words
	Slower rate of vocabulary acquisition
	Less diverse repertoire of verb types
Pragmatics	Intent not signaled through linguistic means
	Difficulty gaining access into conversations
	Less effective at negotiating disputes
	Less use of the naming function
	Difficulty tailoring the message to the listener
	Difficulty repairing communication breakdowns

Source: L. McCormick and D. F. Loeb, "Characteristics of Students with Language and Communication Difficulties," in L. McCormick, D. F. Loeb, and R. L. Schiefelbusch, *Supporting Children with Communication Difficulties in Inclusive Settings*, p. 85.

characteristics and needs are much more complex and challenging than the "categorical approach" we use here might suggest.

Most current evidence supports the concept that students with language disorders follow the normal pattern of development but more slowly and over a longer period of time (Bashir & Scavuzzo, 1992). Longitudinal studies of preschool children with language delay have found that 28 to 75 percent of these children continue to have speech and language problems during the school-age years (Scarborough & Dobrich, 1990). More than 50 percent of these children manifest significant problems with academic achievement over the course of their school careers (Nelson, 1993). This evidence suggests that, despite special education services, a substantial number of children will not catch up with their peers. In other words, a language disorder is usually a chronic condition that persists into adulthood (Bashir & Scavuzzo, 1992; Snyder & Downey, 1991).

Speech Disorders

■ ***Phonological Disorders*** Children with speech disorders may have difficulties performing the neuromuscular movements of speech as well as problems in the underlying conceptual knowledge of the sound system and the rules for its use. Speech problems can be described by their primary characteristics: articulation, fluency, or voice (Fahey, 2000b). *Articulation* is the accurate and clear production of sounds within words. Educators would probably identify **phonological disorders** (also referred to as **articulation disorders**), which are problems in understanding and using the sound system, as the most common communication problem seen during the elementary years. It is important to realize, though, that what appears to be a disorder may just be a normal difference in a child's rate of mastering certain phonological processes, particularly in young children (Haynes et al., 1990).

Types of Communication Disorders

The most common type of speech disorder is a phonological (articulation) disorder.

Normally developing children simplify adult speech so that they may acquire it. For example, they often simplify the production of a multisyllabic word (such as *nana* for *banana*). Another common process is simplifying two consonants produced together (such as *pin* for *spin*). Other pronunciation errors include addition, omission, substitution, and distortion of phonemes.

These processes are developmentally natural and are eventually discarded as the child becomes more skilled with the phonological system of the language. Whether a child has a phonological disorder is determined by two factors: (1) whether the phonological errors are being used far longer than normal, and (2) whether the errors themselves are unusual; that is, they are not seen in normally developing children at any age. If a child's speech characteristics are embarrassing or lead to teasing from classmates, or if you are uncertain about whether a child has a phonological disorder, consulting with your school speech-language pathologist will help you come to a decision about whether to take action.

■ ***Fluency Disorders*** **Fluency disorder** is a broad term that describes interruptions in the flow of speaking (American Speech-Language-Hearing Association, 1993). The most familiar fluency disorder is **stuttering.** The primary symptoms of stuttering are excessive sound, syllable, and word repetitions, and

Fluency disorders are interruptions in the flow of speaking, such as stuttering.

This student is working with a speech-language pathologist to improve his articulation. (Hattie Young/Science Photo Library—Photo Researchers, Inc.)

sound prolongations and pauses. A child who stutters may also display a visible or audible struggle when talking.

In the past, it was believed that stuttering was a learned behavior: Children were conditioned to stutter because of stress in their environment. Today that explanation has been largely abandoned, for two reasons. First, there is substantial evidence of genetic transmission (Pauls, 1990). Second, in many children who stutter, their fluent productions of speech, as well as their disfluent productions, are characterized by brief but subtle malfunctioning of the laryngeal muscles (Conture, 1990). Some children go on to develop more severe forms of stuttering and clearly need treatment, whereas the stuttering of others does not progress in severity and resolves with or without treatment.

Stuttering usually starts in the preschool or early elementary years.

Because the onset of stuttering most typically occurs in the preschool to early elementary years, teachers need to know that referral to a speech-language pathologist is essential for appropriate diagnosis and the development of an intervention plan. Conture (1990) recommends that therapy begin immediately when (1) two or more sound prolongations are produced per every ten instances of stuttering; (2) eye gaze is averted more than 50 percent of the time when the child is in the speaker role; and (3) delayed phonological development is also present (see the accompanying box, "Helpful Tips for the Child Who Stutters").

Voice disorders can affect the pitch, loudness, or quality of a voice.

■ ***Voice Disorders*** **Voice disorders** may result from difficulties in breathing, abnormalities in the structure or function of the larynx, and certain dysfunctions in the oral and nasal cavities. These disorders can affect the pitch, loudness, and quality of a voice, all of which can have important social and

~ Helpful Tips for the Child Who Stutters

Teachers should:

- Refer the child suspected of stuttering to the speech-language pathologist
- Create relaxed communication environments for the child who stutters
- Reduce the pressure to communicate
- Slow down their rate of speech
- Discuss teasing with the child and the class
- Be willing to talk to the child, the speech-language specialist, and family members about stuttering

Teachers should *not:*

- Assume that a child's stuttering will go away
- Directly address the behaviors that the child uses to attempt to hide his or her stuttering
- Interrupt or finish the child's sentences
- Instruct the child to slow down, think before speaking, or just spit it out
- Assume a child is stuttering to gain attention
- React with alarm to speech blocks or repetitions
- Assume that a child who stutters has additional speech, language, or learning problems

Sources: D. F. Williams, "The Child Who Stutters: Guidelines for the Educator," *Young Exceptional Children,* 2:3(1999), 9–14; and R. E. Cook, A. Tessier, and M. D. Klein, *Adapting Early Childhood Curricula for Children in Inclusive Settings* (5th ed.) (Englewood Cliffs, NJ: Merrill, 2000), p. 306.

emotional ramifications for a child. Whenever you become concerned that a child's voice is very unusual or abnormal, it's important to consult with the school nurse to rule out the possibility of a medical problem, then with the speech-language pathologist for suggestions about treatment.

Dialects and Language Differences

A dialect is a regional, social, or cultural variation of a symbol system; it is not a speech disorder.

Not all speech differences are disorders. Other kinds of pronunciation differences may be dialect-related. A **dialect** is "a variation of a symbol system used by a group of individuals that reflects and is determined by shared regional, social, or cultural/ethnic factors. A regional, social, or cultural/ethnic variation of a symbol system should not be considered a disorder of speech or language" (American Speech-Language-Hearing Association, 1993, p. 41). A dialect is *not* a communication disorder, but teachers need to be aware of how dialects are used in their students' communities to prevent misidentifying a language difference as a disorder. Teachers also need to be aware of dialects in order to recognize when a speech or language problem coexists with a dialect. Children's use of English will reflect the characteristics of their cultural and ethnic communities. Table 9.6 describes some of those differences in the use of English. We believe, along with many in the scholarly community (e.g., Gee, 1990; Reid, 2000), that schools must build understanding in their students about the relationships between the home dialect and Standard American English in a respectful context. Ideally, our students will become fluent "code-switchers" who are able to move back and forth between the dialect of their native community and Standard American English.

Hearing Loss

The normal processing of spoken language is through hearing. Children with hearing loss frequently have significant communication problems; we will discuss hearing loss in greater detail in Chapter 10 .

Causes of Communication Disorders

A number of communication disorders have known causes. In some cases, they are associated with genetic disorders such as congenital hearing impairment, fragile X syndrome, or cleft palate and other structural malformations.

Communication disorders may have a genetic, physical, or environmental cause.

Other communication disorders appear to be caused by biological and environmental factors. For example, maternal substance abuse affects fetal brain development and can result in delayed speech and language development. Head trauma and child abuse and neglect are also associated with communication disorders (Fahey, 2000). Multiple factors may play a role in conditions such as autism, stuttering, and language disabilities, which "run in families, affect more boys than girls, and are found in identical twins" (American Speech-Language-Hearing Association, 1991, p. 21). However, specific genes for language or speech have not been identified (Pembrey, 1992), and in many cases the causes of children's speech and language disorders are not clear or are unknown.

In general, it is difficult to pinpoint the cause of a communication disorder.

Table 9.6 Contrasting Cultural Conventions in the Use of English

	Black English	Asian Speakers of English	Standard American English	Hispanic English
	Morphological and Syntactical Components			
Plural *s* Marker	Nonobligatory use of marker *s* with numerical quantifier. *I see two dog playing. I need ten dollar. Look at the dogs.*	Omission of plural marker *s* or overregulation. *I see two dog. I need ten dollar. I have two sheeps.*	Obligatory use of marker *s* with a few exceptions. *I see two dogs. I need ten dollars. I have two sheep.*	Nonobligatory use of marker *s. I see two dog playing. I have two sheep.*
Past Tense	Nonobligatory use of *ed* marker. *Yesterday, I talk to her.*	Omission of *ed* marker or overregulation. *I talk to her yesterday. I sawed her yesterday.*	Obligatory use of *ed* marker. *I talked to her yesterday.*	Nonobligatory use of marker *ed. I talk to her yesterday.*
	Pragmatic Components			
Rules of Conversation	Interruption is tolerated. The most assertive person has the floor.	Children are expected to be passive; are discouraged from interrupting teachers; are considered impolite if they talk during dinner.	Appropriate to interrupt in certain circumstances. One person has the floor until point is made.	Official or business conversations may be preceded by lengthy introductions.
Eye Contact	Indirect eye contact during listening. Direct eye contact during speaking denotes attentiveness and respect.	May not maintain eye contact with authority figure but may make eye contact with strangers. May avert direct eye contact and giggle to express embarrassment.	Indirect eye contact during speaking. Direct eye contact during listening denotes attentiveness and respect.	Avoidance of direct eye contact is sometimes a sign of respect and attentiveness. Maintaining eye contact may be considered a challenge to authority.

Source: Adapted from Owens (1991) and Cheng (1987), in Ratner & Harris (1994).

Prevalence

The federal government uses the label "speech or language impairments" to describe the students we are discussing in this chapter. The *Twenty-second Annual Report to Congress on the Implementation of the Individuals with Disabilities Education Act* (2000) reported that 1,074,044 children were served by federally funded programs in this category during the 1998–1999 school year. Students with speech or language impairments constituted 19.3 percent of all students with disabilities between the ages of 6 and 11 in that school year, making this the second-largest group of students served in special education programs. Only the category of specific learning disabilities is larger.

Recognizing Risk for a Language Disorder

Teachers are often the first professionals to encounter children whose patterns of language development place them at risk for subsequent academic and social failure. Because you, as a future teacher, will have this unique "gatekeeping" role, it is important to know what patterns may indicate risk at different points in a child's school career. In the next sections, we discuss significant stages in language development and identifiable risk indicators.

Preschool Years

Under IDEA, many states now provide programs for infants and toddlers who are at risk developmentally. If you are an early childhood education teacher, you will encounter very young children who appear to have significant delays in the development of language and communication. Some of these children may be late talkers, and some may have a language delay. By definition, "late talker" refers to delayed onset of speech, and **language delay** refers to delayed development in all areas of language.

The age of 30 months appears to be a critical time for determining whether a real problem exists. We know now that there are links between preverbal and increasingly sophisticated verbal development (Stoel-Gammon, 1992). The "good babbler" tends to become a "good talker," even if an articulation problem is present. The "good talker" most likely becomes a good reader and writer. The opposite may also be true: The less adept babbler culminates in a less adept talker, reader, and writer unless appropriate early intervention is initiated. The child with language delay may have greater difficulties describing events, having conversations, and articulating sounds, and may be less likely to use meaningful gestures for communicating (Owens, 1999). As a teacher who may serve young children and their families, your understanding of risk for language delay becomes essential for effective early identification and intervention.

The age of 30 months appears to be critical for determining whether a language delay exists.

Kindergarten and the Early School Years

The profile of a language disorder changes over time. As children reach school age, patterns of difficulty can emerge that often involve learning to read and write. At this point, children with language disorders are often "relabeled" as learning disabled, or even as having emotional or behavioral disorders (Nelson, 1998). Again, teacher awareness of who may now be at risk is vital to assist children to remain in the regular education setting whenever possible.

■ ***Phonological Awareness as a Risk Indicator*** How does a teacher recognize risk in these early school years? One important indicator is **phonological awareness,** or the ability to recognize and analyze the sounds contained in words. This ability is critical to emerging literacy.

Phonological awareness is the ability to recognize that words consist of sounds.

Phonological awareness is the degree to which children's level of linguistic development has allowed them to develop the explicit awareness that words consist of sounds, or phonemes (Snow, Burns, & Griffin, 1998). Phonological

A closer look

Can Do: Language Delay in Young Children

Jesy Moreno started school last fall, a lucky recipient of one of the limited public preschool spots in Los Angeles. But one thing immediately set the small boy apart from most of his classmates: At age 4½, Jesy hardly spoke.

He could utter a few words—mostly names of family members—and he understood some of what was said to him. But carrying on a conversation was impossible, and he could not follow the simplest instructions.

There are thousands of youngsters like Jesy in Southern California—children who are not mentally retarded yet enter school lacking rudimentary communication skills in both their home language and English.

Expressed simply: The less children speak, the more limited their comprehension and vocabulary and the harder it is for them to learn to read and write, not to mention navigate the social complexities of school.

Even now, after a year of concentrated effort by his teachers, Jesy cannot count to 10 or name the colors in the classroom's crayon box. When another boy stole the wheels from a truck he had built, Jesy could not find the words to tell the teacher what had happened.

"Tell me, Jesy, what's wrong?" Maria Dolinsky asked in Spanish, crouching to his level and overenunciating her words, a practice everyone in the classroom follows with him.

"Ah, ah, *toda llanta,*" he answered haltingly. Um, um, all tire.

A classroom for children with language delays like Jesy's places new demands on a kindergarten teacher accustomed to teaching boisterous youngsters to raise their hands and wait their turn before speaking.

While the kindergartners next door were sitting in a neat circle and talking about their families and pets, Jesy's teacher, Toby Tilles, faced a clump of youngsters who ignored her and interacted with each other in grunts and baby talk and by hitting and "rolling around like puppies" on the classroom rug.

Slowly, she began coaxing words out of them, using techniques ranging from songs to sign language. When she talks, she pronounces each word carefully, repeats frequently, then urges the students to answer questions with more than a nod. Every lesson has a hands-on component, every response is recognized.

"I reward every approximation of a word. I started the year with very concrete rewards—stickers on hands—and now I can use mostly verbal rewards," Tilles said.

After they make Lego models during a free play period one morning, Tilles draws them together on the floor and has each describe what they have made.

"What is this?" she prompts one boy. *"Que es esto?"*

"Un ah-oh," he says, clutching an airplane-like structure.

"Un aeroplano? Say *'aeroplano.'"*

He tries.

"Good, good. *Muy bien!"*

Although nearly all the students are from Spanish-speaking families, Tilles teaches mostly in English—with translation support from an aide—so the children do not have the added burden of trying to learn two languages.

It is unclear whether children like Jesy can "catch up" to others their age through an intensive language-emphasis program. Most researchers agree that there are windows of language acquisition opportunity that, once missed, cannot be recreated.

Yet for Jesy's teachers, such deep concerns evaporated in one moment this spring:

He stood at the phonics board in front of his preschool classmates and, with help from the teacher's aide, he slowly pieced together two sound cards—*ta* and *sa.* He stepped back for a moment, considered his creation, then said in a clear voice: *"ta sa . . . tasa"*—cup in Spanish.

"Jesy!" the aide and his teacher shouted simultaneously.

Source: Adapted from Amy Pyle, "Teaching the Silent Student," *Los Angeles Times,* June 11, 1996, p. 1.

awareness is an aspect of metalinguistic awareness. When we consciously analyze and compare the sound structure of words or the meaning of words and sentences in either oral or written language, we are using metalinguistic strategies for thinking critically about language. A strong connection exists between aspects of oral language development and the word-recognition skills necessary for learning to read (decode) and spell. In fact, in kindergarten, the best predictor of learning to read in first grade is a child's level of phonological awareness (Catts, 1991a).

Metalinguistic awareness is the ability to think critically about language.

Children who are less sensitive to the sound structure of their language may also have a less-well-developed vocabulary, because words consist of phonemes. During the early school years, despite experience with reading, these same children may encounter persistent problems in learning new vocabulary words. Most likely, they will also have serious difficulties with phonics approaches that require breaking words into their phonemic parts (for example, "What sound does *dish* begin with?" or "How many sounds does *fish* have?") and blending the parts into a whole. Difficulty with phonemic segmentation and blending will also affect the ability to engage in more advanced manipulations of the phonological code, such as deleting, adding, or reversing phonemes, and in managing conventional spellings (Catts, 1991b; Ehri, 1989).

Reading is impaired by the lack of phonological awareness.

Research findings show that all students should have explicit instruction in phonological awareness to maximize success with word recognition in both reading and spelling (Blachman, 1991b; Snow, Burns, & Griffin, 1998). Some forms of reading failure may be avoided if students are given explicit instruction in phonological awareness, and the instruction follows a developmental sequence. See the accompanying box, "Developing Phonological Awareness," for some teaching tips.

Once the phonological awareness of sound-letter correspondences becomes automatic, children do not need to pay as much deliberate attention to phonemic segmentation and blending of words. At that point, phonological awareness probably begins to play a lesser role in reading and spelling (Kamhi, 1989). However, many students with language disorders have persistent problems with word recognition well into adolescence. They may learn to compensate by relying more on comprehension strategies, such as guessing meaning from the context (Snyder & Downey, 1991).

Phonological awareness helps all students maximize success with word recognition in reading and spelling.

~ Developing Phonological Awareness

- Beginning at the preschool level, teachers can integrate phonological awareness activities in meaningful ways by using good literature that plays with the sounds in language, for example, through nursery rhymes and word games, and only then moving to judgments about sound similarities and differences (Catts, 1991b; Blachman, 1991a, 1991b; Griffith & Olson, 1992).
- A variety of writing experiences offers children rich opportunities to pay attention in a deliberate way to each letter in a word as they or the teacher actually writes words (Treiman, 1993).
- All children need to show the developmental evidence that they can consistently engage in these earlier phonological awareness activities before explicit instruction in phoneme segmentation and blending is introduced.
- Finally, following mastery of segmentation and blending, children should be introduced to letter-sound correspondences.

In Classrooms

Identification

In most educational settings, the speech-language pathologist has primary responsibility for the identification, assessment, and treatment of students with communication disorders. When classroom teachers and speech-language pathologists work collaboratively, the best interests of children with speech and language problems can be met. (For more information about a career in speech-language pathology, see "A Closer Look: Collaboration: Who Is the Speech-Language Pathologist?")

The speech-language pathologist identifies, assesses, and treats students with communication disorders.

Speech-language pathologists do not engage in medical or psychological diagnoses. However, they do have the professional and ethical responsibility to (1) determine what may have caused the onset and development of the problem; (2) interpret whether other causal factors, such as the language demands of the classroom, may contribute to the maintenance of a speech or language problem; and (3) clarify the problem for a student and the family and counsel them appropriately (Lund & Duchan, 1993; Nation & Aram, 1991).

Identifying causes may not be possible given the many factors that can influence the changing profile of a language disorder. Moreover, knowing that an initial cause, such as a birth injury or fetal alcohol syndrome, is related to the communication problem is not always useful for planning meaningful intervention for individual students (Lahey, 1988).

Assessment is an ongoing, evolving process.

Regardless of the emphasis given to causal factors in assessment, there is common agreement that assessment is not a one-time snapshot of a student at a particular point in time. Rather, it is a portrait that continuously evolves because it incorporates diagnostic information with new information obtained from the ongoing monitoring of progress.

Assessment

Some states screen students for language disorders; in other states, the general education teacher refers students.

Identification of students who are at educational risk for a language disorder often begins with screening. Some states use standardized screening measures with large groups of students in order to determine whether students who do not meet the age-level criteria for language and speech should be formally referred to special education for a full assessment. In other states, mass screening of students is not used because it is not seen as cost effective. Instead, speech-language pathologists develop prereferral criteria for regular education teachers to document prior to the formal referral of a specific student for a suspected language disorder.

Referral criteria may lead to overreferral.

As a prospective teacher, it is important for you to be aware that referral criteria can sometimes result in overreferral. A major study on teacher decision-making about who should be referred to special education showed that the very existence of these referral criteria influenced teacher selection of students (Mehan, Hertweck, & Meihls, 1986). Teachers discovered in their students previously undetected symptoms of "disability," which then tended to be confirmed by the traditional assessment process. Although the primary purpose of referral criteria is to identify students for special education who might otherwise go unnoticed, the researchers found that in many cases students' behavior in the classroom was not the real rationale for referral. Videotapes of the classroom, for example, showed that the same behavior in two different students resulted in one student being referred for a learning disability or behavioral

A closer look

Collaboration: Who Is the Speech-Language Pathologist?

Speech-language pathologists in the schools are members of the educational team. Their traditional role has been to be the "expert" specialist who serves students in special education with speech, language, or hearing problems. This service has typically been provided outside of the classroom in a pullout model of service delivery. Today, the speech-language pathologist's role is changing from one of outside expert to a truer educational partnership with both regular and special education teachers. Because you are likely to work with these professionals, it's helpful to know about their background and training.

Speech-language pathologist is a professional title. Individuals holding this title must meet a number of academic and clinical requirements established by the American Speech-Language-Hearing Association (ASHA). This national organization is the professional, scientific, and credentialing body for more than 74,000 speech-language pathologists and audiologists. Approximately 45 percent of speech-language pathologists work in schools.

The professional credential is the Certificate of Clinical Competence (CCC). To be eligible for the CCC in either speech-language pathology (CCC-SLP) or audiology (CCC-A), individuals must have a master's or doctoral degree from an academic institution with an educational program accredited by ASHA.

In addition to these ASHA requirements for certification, forty-three states currently require licensing of speech-language pathologists and audiologists, similar to licensing for physicians and nurses. Licensure laws vary from state to state and are different from teacher certification. Many states have continuing education requirements as well to maintain the professional license.

The ASHA code of ethics states that only individuals who have the CCC, or are in the process of obtaining this certificate by working under an ASHA-certified supervisor, should practice speech-language pathology or audiology. However, to work in the public schools, a number of states require only a bachelor's degree in communication disorders, combined in some instances with teacher certification. Most states also require that, to continue working in the schools, a master's degree in communication disorders be obtained within a prescribed number of years. In all other settings, such as health-care facilities, the master's degree is the entry-level degree. Continuous efforts are being expended by ASHA and state professional organizations to have the master's degree also be the entry-level degree for school services.

Source: American Speech-Language-Hearing Association (1993). Implementation procedures for the standards for the certificates of clinical competence, *ASHA*, 35 (3), 76–83. Reprinted by permission of the American Speech-Language-Hearing Association.

disorder whereas the other student was not referred. The referred student may have been described as having "poor language skills and acting out," while the student not referred might be described as "less talkative and shy" (even though this student can be seen on a videotape to "act out" also).

This inconsistent pattern seemed to derive from expectations about communicative competence that teachers hold about different students. These expectations influence how teachers interpret certain behaviors and may often result in unnecessary referrals to special education, particularly for students from cultural minority groups. The referrals may lead to the confirmation of disability when none actually exists.

The example of Jesy in "A Closer Look" (see page 312) suggests how complicated the identification, assessment, and intervention of a language problem is when a child comes from a non–English-speaking background. A bilingual professional must conduct a careful assessment with such children in order to determine whether a language problem exists in the child's native language as well as in English. Only when the problem crosses both languages is it considered a language delay or disorder; otherwise, the child may simply be a nonfluent user of English. Professionals must take great care not to identify such children with a disability label. There is considerable evidence that this occurs with some frequency (Figueroa, Fradd, & Correa, 1989).

Grace Zamora-Duran and Elba Reyes (1997) urge school professionals to look for "communicative competence" in their English-language learning students. Communicative competence includes the ability to comprehend language as well as to use it in a variety of contexts, including conversation with different speakers and formal and informal speaking. The checklist in Figure 9.5 will help you assess communication competence.

Research makes the strongest possible case that a teacher must have good working knowledge of the language and communication system and its many normal developmental and cultural variations in order to know who should be referred. A delicate balance exists between failing to refer a child who needs assessment and referring a child who may be wrongly classified as disabled by the referral itself.

■ ***Approaches to Assessment*** The specific approaches used in traditional language assessment may be determined by special education policies at state or local levels. However, speech-language pathologists generally use a combination of four approaches, or tools, for information-gathering: the interview, or case history report; norm-referenced measures; criterion-referenced measures; and observation. These tools will be discussed next.

Direct interviews with the student can be a source for the case history report.

Case History Report Information for the case history report is obtained from direct interviews with parents, teachers, and, where appropriate, the student. Other sources of information may also be included, such as reports from the family physician, other medical specialists, teachers, or psychologists. The purpose of the case history report is to understand background information in order to be able to draw as complete a picture as possible of the student's current status and needs. The actual format and content of the case history will vary according to the requirements of individual school systems.

Standardized tests are norm-referenced measures of performance in which scores are compared to those of a norm group.

Norm-Referenced Measures Standardized tests are norm-referenced measures. Normal performance on a standardized test is defined according to a range of scores on the normal curve (Peterson & Marquardt, 1990), against which an individual student's score is compared. Norm-referenced tests are usually required to determine a student's eligibility for speech and language services. Many school systems also designate which tests should be used.

At the outset, three points should be made about language tests, which in reality are achievement tests: (1) "Normal" generally means proficient; however, there is a lack of agreement on what constitutes proficiency in a native or first language; (2) language tests tend to reduce the complexity of communication into isolated parts, such as syntax, semantics, or pragmatics; these isolated parts are unrepresentative of how language and communication work as a whole in and out of school; and (3) because language tests reduce complex be-

Figure 9.5
Checklist for Skills Illustrating Communicative Competency

✔	Grammatical	✔	Sociolinguistic	✔	Discourse	✔	Strategic
	Use noun/verb agreement		Demonstrates various styles of social register in speech, for example, when interacting with peers or adults		Retells an event with attention to sequence		Joins groups and acts as if understands language and activities
	Uses pronouns correctly		Uses diminutives		Explains activity in present or near future		Demonstrates expressive ability
	Uses proper syntax		Uses terms of endearment		Shares experiences spontaneously		Counts on friends for help
	Uses verb tenses appropriately		Uses courtesy, etiquette terms, and titles of respect		Tells stories with personal emphases		Switches language to resolve ambiguities
	Uses dialectical variations		Uses appropriate variations in intonation		Switches language for elaboration		Observes and imitates language patterns
	Uses complex sentence structure				Switches language to clarify statements		Asks for information
					Switches language to experiment with new language		Reads to gain information
							Uses a dictionary
							Asks for repetition
							Takes risks and guesses at language meaning
							Attempts difficult words and constructions

Grammatical: mastery of lexical items, rules of word and sentence formation, literal meaning, pronunciation, and spelling.
Sociolinguistic: Using language appropriately, in different social contexts, with emphasis on meanings and forms.
Discourse: Using language in an organized and effective manner.
Strategic: Using verbal and nonverbal strategies (such as paraphrasing, gesturing, or switching from Standard American English to a dialect) to enhance the effectiveness of communication and to compensate for breakdowns in communication.

Source: Adapted from G. Zamora-Duran and E. Reyes, (1997). From Tests to Talking in the Classroom: Assessing Communicative Competence, in A.J. Artiles and G. Zamora-Dunn (eds.), *Reducing Disproportionate Representation of Culturally Diverse Students in Special and Gifted Education* (Reston, VA: Council for Exceptional Children, 1997).

Jessie Alpaugh left school during her sophomore year, when she contracted a form of encephalitis which left her unable to speak and using a wheelchair. She returned to school at the beginning of her senior year. Here Jessie reminds us that we may take the ability to communicate freely for granted.

In the early stages of my illness, after I had started to recover from the initial shock of my new physical condition, I vowed that sometime in the future I would return to school and rejoin my class. It soon became evident, though, that if I did return, it would certainly not be under the same conditions as before my illness.

My first day back was tumultuous. After that, I calmed down a little. I came to realize that however uncomfortable and self-conscious I felt, this was the same school with the same friends and teachers I had known before I got sick. But overcoming my personal inhibition was problematic. While I recognized that this was the same school environment I had known two years ago, I did not feel at all like the same person inside. The way I interacted with the other students and my friends made me feel completely different. Just by the way countless strangers greeted me in the halls set me apart from everyone, and this was a daily reminder that I was different. It was a struggle to recon-

haviors that in real life cannot be reduced, tests create the illusion that they are objective (Oller & Damico, 1991; Stallman & Pearson, 1990; Weaver, 1991).

Because of these issues, it is critical to remember that "the blind use of a 'test battery' is not language assessment" (Damico & Simon, 1993, p. 279), even when testing is understood as one method of information collection. Teachers and speech-language pathologists have a professional obligation to be informed test consumers.

Criterion-referenced measures permit evaluation of the student's performance on specific tasks.

Criterion-Referenced Measures Criterion referencing is a third method of information gathering. Criterion-referenced measures judge the student's performance according to some predetermined standard. The standard of comparison is related to the student's own performance on specific tasks rather than the performance of a normative group. When a criterion-referenced approach is linked to language assessment, the focus shifts to whether the student is using specific kinds of language knowledge and strategies effectively to learn academic content (Nelson, 1998).

One advantage of the criterion-referenced approach over the norm-referenced approach is its clearer relationship to educational and intervention objectives. Also, the student's current level of performance is a primary emphasis, not what the student might be capable of with assistance.

Observation The fourth method for gathering information about students' performance is direct observation. In fact, all of the assessment methods mentioned so far involve various degrees of direct observation. All consist of look-

nect with my class members and other peers, and I often felt quite lonely or trapped because of my speech impairment. I desperately hoped that the enthusiastic support from everyone was not only out of pity, but I think for some people it was. In the classroom I had to adjust to being solely a listener and not being able to participate in the discussions. While I have never been an outgoing ringleader in class discussions, this was nevertheless hard for me.

I have made it through my first semester back at school. Really, not a day goes by that I don't stop to think about what my life was like here before my illness. Some days I feel more nostalgic than others. It is a constant struggle to let go of the past and not become imprisoned within myself. I realize that I have set strong goals for the future, and I can educate myself. I know it is going to take a lot of strength, courage, and determination to become the person who I want and need to become. This frightens me because I often question whether I hold enough of these qualities. Sometimes I know I don't, but I try to be optimistic and remind myself that only I have the power to control my own future.

Jessie Alpaugh

ing at and listening to what students and teachers actually do and say in order to interpret the meaning of their behaviors. There is a difference among them, however. The other methods focus on end results, which, sometimes, are far removed from the life of the classroom. Direct observation can provide information on teaching and learning as these actually happen in the classroom.

Direct, planned observation in the classroom can provide important information on teaching and learning.

For observation to be useful for teachers, it must be *planned*. This means that observation should be a systematic process with a clear purpose, one that involves a collaboration among teachers, speech-language pathologists, and other educational staff. Becoming a skilled observer also requires experience with this process in order for educators to have a shared frame of reference about classroom events.

The purpose of an observation must be clearly defined and understood by both teacher and speech-language pathologist.

The assessment process functions to determine whether a speech or language disorder exists, and, if present, its severity and variability. Eligibility for special education and service options depends on how this evaluation question is answered and whether a diagnostic category, or label, can be assigned, such as speech impairment or language disorder. Although these categories may be global and imprecise, they allow us to understand the commonalities that make up a particular disability and to design assessment and intervention approaches for students who share common symptoms (Nelson, 1998).

Placement and Service Options

The placement and service options for students with communication disorders are similar to those already discussed in previous chapters, with one exception: an emphasis on the pullout mode of service delivery. Students with speech impairments or language disorders are often removed from the regular or special education classroom for one-to-one or small-group treatment.

The thinking behind this service option for language intervention has had a practical basis. In a smaller group setting, the speech-language pathologist can control some of the many variables that affect a student's successful performance in the classroom. On another level, many children can be served, which gives the appearance of cost-effective services but in reality often results in caseloads exceeding seventy-five to one hundred students per week.

The "pullout" model used with students with communication disorders is coming under increasing criticism.

The pullout model may not be "best practice" and has been criticized for several reasons (Kamhi, 1993; McCormick, 1997). First, students' language learning may become increasingly isolated from the natural communication context of the classroom. Second, students tend to be stigmatized even further through their removal from the classroom and may suffer academically from missing important curricular content. Last, because speech-language pathologists were themselves isolated from the classroom and curriculum, teachers too often developed the unrealistic view that pulling students out was a way to "make them better and put them back" (Nelson, 1998).

In recent years, the trend has been toward integrated classroom-based services, in which language and communication instruction is provided in the context of daily activities *in the classroom*. When speech and language intervention is provided in the classroom, the general education or special education teacher can collaborate with the speech-language pathologist to provide the most effective intervention program for the child, in the natural setting in which the child will use the skills learned (see the accompanying box, "Advantages of Integrated Classroom-Based Speech and Language Intervention").

Although integrated intervention may be desirable, in many school districts across the country, students are still being "pulled out" of the classroom for speech and language services. There are many obstacles to changes in practice, such as (1) the evidence that accommodation to individual student needs within the regular classroom rarely occurs with ease; (2) the challenges presented by students with severe behavioral and emotional disorders; (3) the lack of adequate funding for an integrated system; and (4) the changes that must occur in teacher education as well as in the education of speech-language pathologists

~ Advantages of Integrated Classroom-Based Speech and Language Intervention

- The student gains and maintains access to "regular" educational opportunities and learning outcomes.
- Opportunities for team collaboration are maximized, and fragmentation (gaps, overlaps, and/or contradictions) in services are avoided.
- The input and methods of all team members are synthesized as they address a shared vision for the student's participation in social, educational, and vocational settings.
- Skills taught through integrated intervention are likely to generalize because they were learned and practiced in the integrated, natural environments where they need to be used.

Source: L. McCormick, "Policies and Practices," in L. McCormick, D. F. Loeb, and R. L. Schiefelbusch, *Supporting Children with Communication Difficulties in Inclusive Settings: School-Based Language Intervention.*

(Hoffman, 1993). Professionals in speech-language pathology are currently working to revamp their roles in inclusive school settings, with many suggesting that they become part of an in-classroom intervention team with shared responsibility for student success (Ehren, 2000; Prelock, 2000). Barbara Ehren (2000) describes two major functions for the speech-language pathologist providing in-classroom services:

1. Work with the classroom teacher to make modifications in curriculum, instruction, and assessment so that students with speech and language difficulties can be successful in the general education classroom.
2. Engage the teacher as a partner in the process by enlisting his or her help in practicing new skills, setting new objectives, and assessing progress. (p. 225)

Strategies for Working with Students with Communication Learning Needs

In Los Angeles, where I live and work, we have a large population of students who are English-language learners, so every teacher must focus on English-language acquisition with his or her students. This focus potentially benefits *all* students, from the fifth-grader identified with a learning disability to the newly immigrated seventh-grader from Central America to the academically gifted child of any age. Integrating the teaching of both social and academic language—through listening, speaking, writing, and reading—into daily routines and curriculum may strengthen school learning for every child.

■ ***Integrating Language and Literacy Learning*** Several principles of language and literacy learning are consistent with this approach:

1. All children naturally learn language through social interaction with adults and peers.
2. Children learn best when they are guided by a "big picture" or theme and when they understand the reasons for learning.
3. Real learning is functional; it is also "messy" because active choice and risk-taking are required.
4. Real learning is challenging and involves cooperating with others.
5. All children are capable of learning; the guiding premise is that the learner's ability to be successful is always the focus of assessment and instruction.

For students with language disorders, these principles mean that the goal for instruction remains one of enabling communicative competence. Guided by these principles, the focus of instruction is twofold: to support the student's abilities through the teaching of active learning-how-to-learn strategies and to help the student develop more effective communication.

Supportive Discourse Scaffolding The instructional strategies teachers use to help students achieve their goals are connected to the holistic view of language and learning. **Instructional discourse strategies** are the ways in which teachers communicate to students expectations for learning, how they are to learn, how they know they are learning, and, most importantly, the meaning of learning.

Teachers use discourse strategies to communicate expectations for learning to students.

Another way of thinking about these discourse strategies is to consider them as a scaffold, or support for learning. **Scaffolding** refers to supporting a child so that she can understand or use language that is more complex than she

Scaffolding is the guidance an adult or peer provides for students who cannot yet do a task alone.

could understand or use independently. Scaffolding occurs when a teacher asks questions about the elements of a story, or elaborates on the themes or vocabulary of a story, asks "thought" questions, or restates or summarizes concepts or themes. As the child is able to use the language independently, scaffolding is gradually withdrawn.

Supportive discourse scaffolding can provide a kind of "communication safety net" for students who need help in learning to communicate effectively (Silliman & Wilkinson, 1994). As the student becomes more capable, the discourse support is progressively removed. Thus, the transfer of responsibility for learning from the teacher to the student is built into the concept of supportive discourse scaffolding. Supportive discourse scaffolding provides opportunities for teachers and speech-language pathologists, as well as students, to act as working models in helping students to elaborate their own thinking (Shuy, 1988).

Members of the Collaborative Team

New roles for the speech-language pathologist are emerging.

A collaborative approach requires the willingness to cross disciplinary boundaries. Members of an educational team must be willing to maintain their existing roles, or expertise, and also to expand their roles, or even relinquish them, when appropriate, to meet students' needs. Classroom-based instruction and intervention mean that speech-language pathologists and general and special education teachers will work together in new ways to achieve the goals of an integrated curriculum.

There are at least seven new roles for the speech-language pathologist in language and literacy-based classrooms (Gerber, 1993; Miller, 1989; Nelson, 1993). None of these roles are exclusive—they can overlap in any combination—and all are compatible with inclusive schooling, an educational continuum, or other collaborative approaches. These new roles include:

- Teaching in a self-contained classroom for students with language disorders
- Teaching in a regularly scheduled class for these students, for example, at the secondary level
- Team teaching with the general education teacher
- Team teaching in the self-contained classroom with another specialist
- Team teaching in a combination of resource and general education modules
- Providing collaborative consultation to general and special education teachers
- Providing staff, curriculum, or program development

The first five roles have in common direct service to students, and the last two roles involve acting as a resource for classroom teachers, other specialists, administrators, and parents.

Teachers and speech-language pathologists can work together in collaborative teams.

Role expansion in a collaborative approach also means that general education teachers, with the support of speech-language pathologists, can learn to incorporate communication goals and strategies for individual students into everyday classroom activities. Most importantly, effective role expansion depends on continuous planning and communication among all team members, as well as on changes in attitudes and expectations. Ehren (2000) makes specific

Sharing Responsibility for Student Success

1. Promote the writing of individualized education program (IEP) goals that teachers and speech-language pathologists (SLPs) work collaboratively to achieve, as opposed to goals that are identified only with the teacher or the SLP.
2. SLPs should be prepared to make suggestions for modifications at IEP meetings. What can the teacher do to adjust assessment and instructional activities to accommodate a student's language disorder so that student can benefit from classroom instruction?
3. SLPs should make specific suggestions to teachers on how to modify lessons, tests, and assigned work, and consider demonstrating appropriate modifications for the teacher.
4. Teachers and SLPs should agree on progress assessment procedures and work together to assess progress based on specific progress criteria.
5. Broadcast successes to other faculty members and administration. Brag about each other's hard work and mutual accomplishments.

Source: B. J. Ehren, (2000) "Maintaining a therapeutic focus and sharing responsibility for student success: Keys to in-classroom speech-language services," *Language, Speech, and Hearing Services in Schools, 31* (3), 225–226.

suggestions for operationalizing shared responsibility in the classroom; see the accompanying box, "Sharing Responsibility for Student Success."

In shifting toward more collaborative and integrated models of education, including inclusive models, we need to start with the basics: challenging our existing beliefs about how we work together, and what students are capable of when given appropriate support.

Technology

Computer software in the area of literacy development can be effectively used to supplement classroom literacy experiences for students with language disorders, who need a great deal of practice and redundancy in the development of their reading, writing, and speaking. Students with severe communication disorders that limit their ability to speak may also benefit from assistive technology devices—"pieces of equipment used to increase, maintain, or improve the functional capabilities of students with disabilities" (Hourcade, Parette, & Huer, 1997, p. 40). Recommendations for assistive technology devices may be written into the student's IEP (Individualized Education Program). These students, who often have accompanying physical disabilities, can benefit from augmentative and alternative communication systems such as electronic communication boards and computerized speech synthesizers. These systems can provide a system of communication for students who cannot speak for themselves. They will be described in more detail in Chapter 12 .

Technological advances can provide a means of communication for students with the most severe communication disorders.

Developing useful communication skills can be challenging, but it is not impossible—even for students with the most significant communication disorders. You can be crucial to what may be the most important goal for your students—learning to communicate effectively, and therefore connect with others.

For twelve and a half years I couldn't talk. I used a speechboard, a typewriter, and my hands to communicate with my family, friends and teachers. Before I learned to spell, it was very hard for them to know what I wanted.

When I was twelve, I saw a machine called a Handi-Voice, which is a precision electronic speech synthesizer for people who can't talk. It has a voice kind of like a robot. It will speak, save, recall or repeat any message. Now I could talk with my family. I called my sister a turkey. She said that the Handi-Voice said that, not me.

A new world has opened up for me since I got the machine. I use it in school and at home. The one thing I really very much appreciate is if people give me time to talk. For example, when a teacher asks the class a question, and I know the answer. She or he will see that I'm pushing in the answer in the Handi-Voice. When I'm ready I push a button and it talks for me. Some people, like my family, friends and teachers can make out what the voice is saying. But others can't make out a darn word.

Jason J. Homyshin, 13

Source: Helen Exley, ed., *What It's Like to Be Me* (Watford, U.K.: Exley, 1981), p. 112. Reprinted with permission of Exley Publications, Ltd.

Summary

- Communication is the exchange of ideas. Language is one type of symbolic communication; its code expresses ideas or content. Language is functional, or pragmatic. A community of language users agrees on the appropriate ways to behave as speakers and listeners.
- Speech is one component of the total language system. It involves the physical actions needed to produce meaningful spoken words.
- Language develops very rapidly and in generally the same sequence in all children, although the ages at which children reach particular developmental milestones can vary significantly. Several theories have been proposed to explain the acquisition of language and communication. It is likely that social interaction with others in the language community plays a vital role in speech and language development. By 5 years of age, the basic system of oral communication has been acquired.
- Language disorders involve difficulties in the comprehension and expression of the meaning and content of language. Speech disorders include phonological, fluency, and voice impairments. *Communication disorders* is a more gen-

eral term used to include difficulties with speech and hearing, as well as language and speech disorders.

- Identification and assessment of students with communication disorders are typically the tasks of the speech-language pathologist. Approaches to assessment include case histories, norm-referenced tests, criterion-referenced tests, and observation.
- Placement options for students with communication disorders are increasingly focusing on inclusion in the integrated classroom. This has led to a shift in the philosophy, principles, and practices of educators. Instructional strategies focus on integrating language and literacy development and supporting the use of oral communication for a variety of functional purposes.

Key Terms

communication
language
phonology
phoneme
morphology
morphemes
syntax
semantics
pragmatics
discourse
speech
communication disorders
specific language impairment
phonological (articulation) disorders
fluency disorder
stuttering
voice disorder
dialect
language delay
phonological awareness
instructional discourse strategies
scaffolding

Multimedia Resources

American Speech-Language-Hearing Association website: http://www.ASHA.org. The ASHA website offers information and resources to professionals in the field and others interested in speech and language. The ASHA website also covers this topic at
http://www.asha.org/speech/development/index.cfm/.

Lue, Martha Scott, *A Survey of Communication Disorders for the Classroom Teacher* (Boston: Allyn & Bacon, 2001). This book provides ideas and strategies for teachers of students with communication problems.

National Institute on Deafness and Other Communication Disorders website: www.nih.gov/nidcd. This arm of the National Institutes of Health supports research on communication disorders and serves as a resource in the field. The area devoted to "Teachers and Kids" is particularly relevant for our readers.

Owens, Robert E. (2001). *Language development: An introduction* (Fifth Ed.). Boston: Allyn & Bacon.

Two journals will be particularly interesting for those of you writing papers or working on projects in this area. They are *Language, Speech, and Hearing Services in the Schools*, published by ASHA, and the *Journal of Communicative*

Disorders, published by the Division of Communication Disorders of the Council for Exceptional Children.

Earlier in the chapter we promised to provide you with further resources on normal language development. Here are two:

Owens, Robert E. (2001). *Language development*: An introduction (5th ed.). Boston: Allyn & Bacon.

The American Speech-Language-Hearing Association (ASHA) website (see above) also covers this topic at http://www.asha.org/speech/development/index.cfm/ or http://www.asha.org/speech/development/dev milestones.cfm/.

What You Can Do

1. Talk to a school speech-language pathologist.

- Ask her to describe the students she sees: How many are there on her caseload? What speech and language needs do the students have?
- Ask her about her training: Does she have both a graduate and undergraduate degree in communication disorders? How many hours did she work with children before obtaining certification?
- Ask her about collaboration: Does she see children in their classrooms or in a pullout program? How does she find time to confer with their classroom teachers?
- Write an article for your school newsletter or newspaper describing your interview.

2. Many well-known and successful adults have overcome childhood stuttering.

- Visit the Stuttering Homepage (**http://www.mankato.msus.edu/dept/comdis/kuster/stutter.html**) on the World Wide Web.
- Read about famous people who have stuttered, from Moses (yes, Moses—see the Book of Exodus) to Christopher Robin Milne to novelist John Updike and actor James Earl Jones.
- How could you sensitively structure an assignment for a student who stutters using these resources?

3. Classrooms that include students with communication disorders should encourage multiple modes of communication. Students can express their ideas and feelings through painting, drawing, singing or using a musical instrument, creative writing, drama, e-mail . . . the possibilities are vast. Can you design a classroom where multiple modes of communication will be encouraged? At the preschool level? At the secondary level?

Children Who Are Deaf and Hard of Hearing

10

STUDENTS WHO are deaf must be provided with a challenging academic curriculum. But first and foremost, schools must address their communication needs. Whatever the communication method used, the richness and complexity of Deaf culture provides a powerful context for learning and personal development for students with hearing loss and their families. As you read the chapter, think about the following questions:

What is the relationship between hearing and language development?

What is Deaf culture, and what role does it play in education?

Commonalities: What kinds of supports does a student with hearing loss need to be successfully included in the general education classroom?

Collaboration: What professional resources are available to help the classroom teacher of children who are deaf or hard of hearing?

Can Do: What communication options are available for students who are deaf?

I often tell my students how I got into the field of special education. I was in college, an English major, and a boy I had a crush on worked part-time at St. Mary's School for the Deaf. I decided to try to get a job there, too, so I could "run into him" accidentally. Well, I did get the job, and I never once saw him at work in the two years that I worked in the school. But serendipity was at work—I found out what I wanted to do professionally for the rest of my life.

Fingerspelling and signs make up the communication system of many students who are deaf. (Bob Daemmrich Photography, Inc.)

The little boys that I worked with were between 3 and 5 years old, and they lived at the school. (This was before the days of IDEA; parents who had no programs for their children in their communities were required to send their children to residential schools, often far from home.) Some spoke, some were silent, but they all used sign language as their preferred form of communication. The fascination I felt then with the possibility of teaching them more language has never left me. Do you remember the moment in the film *The Miracle Worker* when Annie Sullivan takes Helen Keller to the water pump, puts her hands under the water, and signs "water" into those hands? Helen's eyes light up. That is the moment that she finally understands that water has a name, and that all things have a name. I wanted to see the eyes of those little boys light up as they learned to communicate.

Many of you share my interest in teaching language. It is at the heart of our instruction of English-language learners, of instruction for children with many of the disabilities we discuss in this book, and of foreign language instruction. In fact, teaching the complexity and richness of language is important for every learner. Sign language, used by many deaf students, is a source of great fascination as well. Join me now in learning about the students who taught me to be a teacher—those who are deaf and hard of hearing.

Nancy Hunt

Definitions and Terms

Deafness is a hearing loss that precludes the learning of language through hearing.

Hard of hearing describes a loss that is less severe than deafness.

Deafness is defined as a hearing loss that precludes the learning of language through hearing (Northern & Downs, 1991). People who are deaf usually rely primarily on their vision both for their understanding of the world and for communication. **Hard of hearing** is a term used to describe a hearing loss that, although serious, is less severe than deafness and usually permits the understanding of spoken language with the use of hearing aids. **Hearing impairment** is an umbrella term that refers to all degrees of hearing loss, from slight to profound. Since many individuals in the **Deaf community**—those adults bound together by their deafness, the use of American Sign Language, and their culture, values, and attitudes—dislike the term *impairment*, we will avoid it in this chapter and instead use the term **hearing loss** when referring to individuals who are deaf and hard of hearing.

Very few people with hearing loss are totally deaf; most have some remaining hearing, however slight. It is this remaining hearing, called **residual hearing,** that, with the help of a hearing aid, detects sounds within the environment and can be used to learn speech. Sometimes a baby is born with a hearing loss; then it is called a **congenital hearing loss.** A hearing loss can also be acquired at any time, in which case it is referred to as an **acquired hearing loss.** Most educators of students with hearing loss, however, consider it most important to know whether the child has **prelingual** or **postlingual deafness**—that is, whether the hearing loss occurred before or after the child developed spoken language.

Residual hearing is the remaining hearing possessed by most people who are deaf.

Please note that in keeping with today's conventions, throughout this chapter, the word *Deaf* is capitalized when it refers to Deafness as a cultural entity.

Hearing and Hearing Loss

The human auditory system, as shown in Figure 10.1, is complicated and extremely delicate. Sound energy creates vibration, and the vibration travels in sound waves through a passageway called the ear canal to the eardrum, or tympanic membrane, a thin layer of tissue between the outer and middle ear. The vibration of the eardrum sets off a chain of vibrations in the three small bones of the middle ear: the malleus, incus, and stapes. The sound is transmitted through the cochlea, a tiny, spiral-shaped structure in the inner ear. Finally, it reaches the brain via the auditory nerve, where it is interpreted as meaningful.

Sound waves travel through the auditory canal to the eardrum, middle ear, cochlea, and (via the auditory nerve) to the brain.

Because hearing depends on the transmission of sound waves across numerous tiny structures throughout the auditory mechanism, malfunctions or

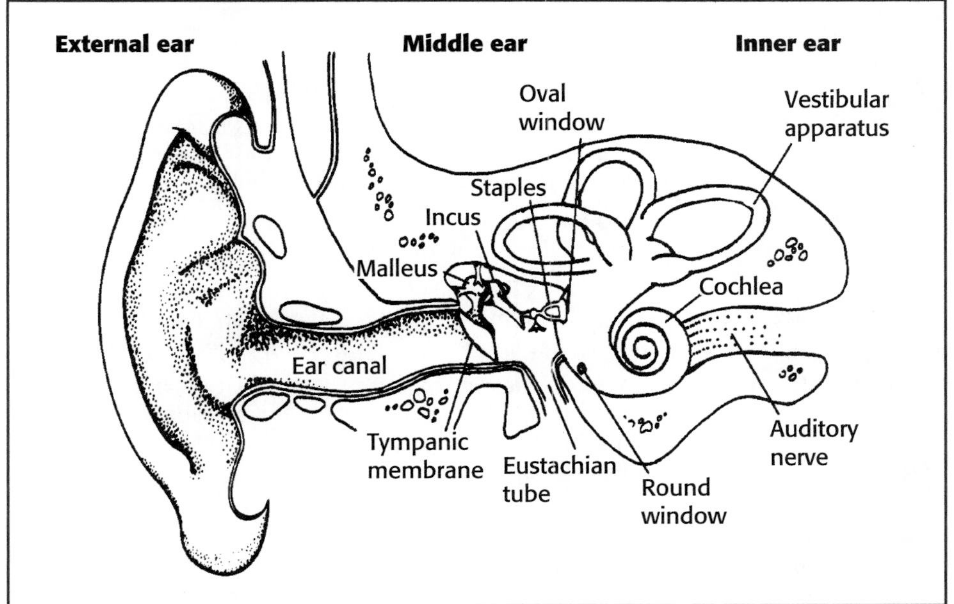

Figure 10.1
Structure of the Ear

Source: M.L. Batshaw and Y. M. Perret, *Children with Disabilities: A Medical Primer,* 3d ed. (Baltimore: Paul H. Brookes, 1992), p. 323. Used by permission of the authors.

Children Who Are Deaf and Hard of Hearing

damage to any part of the system can result in temporary or permanent hearing loss.

Damage or obstruction in the external or middle ear disrupts the passage of sound and causes conductive hearing loss.

Damage or obstruction in the external or middle ear that disrupts the efficient passage or conduction of sound through those chambers results in a **conductive hearing loss.** Most conductive losses can be successfully treated medically, but research has shown that recurrent conductive hearing loss in young children can have serious long-term effects on their language development and school learning (Roberts, Wallace, & Henderson, 1997).

Sensorineural hearing loss is usually caused by damage in the cochlea or auditory nerve.

Damage to the cochlea or the auditory nerve in the inner ear is called a **sensorineural hearing loss.** A sensorineural loss is permanent; at this time it cannot be medically treated (Northern & Downs, 1991). Most students with hearing loss in our schools have a sensorineural hearing loss, although some of them have a **mixed hearing loss,** with both conductive and sensorineural components.

Bilateral hearing loss is a loss in both ears; unilateral hearing loss is a loss in one.

Most school-age children who are deaf or hard of hearing have **bilateral hearing loss;** that is, they have a hearing loss in both ears (although one ear may have more hearing than the other). Some children, however, have normal hearing in one ear and a hearing loss in the other; they are said to have a **unilateral hearing loss.** Children with unilateral hearing losses may develop language normally, but some have problems in the classroom. They are at a disadvantage in noisy environments and may have difficulties picking out the most important source of sound, such as the teacher's voice. About half the children with unilateral hearing loss described in a recent study received special education services, and about one-quarter of them were functioning below grade level (English & Church, 1999). Table 10.1 is an overview of the two major kinds of hearing loss.

Table 10.1 Characteristics of the Two Major Kinds of Hearing Loss

	Conductive Hearing Loss	Sensorineural Hearing Loss
Duration	Usually temporary	Permanent
Location of the problem	Occurs as a result of a problem in the outer or middle ear	Occurs as a result of a problem in the inner ear or the auditory nerve
Treatment	Treatable by a physician with medication and/or surgery	Not routinely treatable*
Impact on hearing	Tends to be a mild or moderate hearing loss	Tends to be a severe or profound hearing loss
Impact on learning	Depends on the length of the problem; can vary from no impact at all to significantly affecting language learning	Usually affects oral language development
Educational services provided	Special education services not routinely provided for this short-term hearing loss	Special education provided when the hearing loss affects the student's educational performance

*Sometimes treated by a cochlear implant (see p. 365).

Classification Issues

Hearing loss can range in severity from slight to profound. Children with losses described as mild and moderate are usually called hard of hearing; those with severe and profound losses are considered deaf. Even most deaf people, though, have some residual hearing that can make a hearing aid helpful. See Table 10.2 for the effects of the varying degrees of hearing loss on children.

Table 10.2 Degrees of Hearing Loss

Average Hearing Level	Description	Possible Condition	What Can Be Heard Without Amplification	Handicapping Effects (If Not Treated in First Year of Life)	Probable Needs
0–15 dB*	Normal range		All speech sounds	None	None
15–25 dB	Slight hearing loss	Conductive hearing losses, some sensori-neural hearing losses	Vowel sounds heard clearly; may miss unvoiced consonants sounds	Mild auditory dysfunction in language learning	Consideration of need for hearing aid; speech read-ing, auditory training, speech therapy, prefer-ential seating
25–30 dB	Mild hearing loss	Conductive or sensorineural hearing loss	Only some speech sounds, the louder voiced sounds	Auditory learning dysfunction, mild language delay, mild speech problems	Hearing aid, speech reading, auditory training, speech therapy
30–50 dB	Moderate hearing loss	Conductive hearing loss from chronic middle ear disorders; sensorineural hearing losses	Almost no speech sounds at normal conversational level	Speech problems, language delay, learning difficulties	All of the above, plus consideration of other special education services
50–70 dB	Severe hearing loss	Sensorineural or mixed losses due to a combination of middle ear disease and sensorineural involvement	No speech sounds at normal conversational level	Severe speech problems, language delay, learning difficulties	All of the above; need for special education services
70+ dB	Profound hearing loss	Sensorineural or mixed losses due to a combination of middle ear disease and sensorineural involvement	No speech or other sounds	Severe speech problems, language delay, learning difficulties	All of the above; need for special education services

*dB stands for *decibels*, or units of loudness.
Source: Adapted from Jerry L. Northern and Marion P. Downs, *Hearing in Children*, 4th ed. (Baltimore: Williams & Wilkins, 1991). Copyright © 1991 by Williams & Wilkins. Used by permission of Waverly.

Causes of Hearing Loss

Knowledge of the cause of hearing loss in young children is important for several reasons. In the case of conductive losses, which are usually treatable, the cause dictates the treatment; in the case of sensorineural loss, which is permanent, knowledge will help families gather information about the probability of hearing loss in any subsequent children and may help them master the feelings of stress related to their child's disability.

Conductive Hearing Loss

Otitis media is the most common cause of conductive hearing loss in children.

The most common cause of conductive hearing loss in children is middle ear infection, or **otitis media.** When, because of a cold or for some other reason, fluid gathers in the middle ear, it dampens or restricts the movement of the eardrum, and hearing loss may result. Middle ear infection, or simply the presence of fluid in the middle ear, can have serious effects on hearing in children, and it should always be brought to the attention of the child's pediatrician. *Chronic* otitis media (ear infection that lasts for twelve weeks or longer), with long-term effects on hearing, can also delay the normal development of language and speech in young children (Schoem, 1999). This language delay may, in turn, have adverse effects over time on a child's achievement in school, long after the ear infection has disappeared.

Children should be treated by a physician when warning signs of middle ear infection appear, and especially when they persist over time. Some of those signs are fever, redness of the ear, rubbing of the ear, or, in a young infant, rubbing of the head against a mattress or blanket; reports of pain or itching; and, in extreme cases, dripping from the ear. Many middle ear infections can be effectively treated with antibiotics, and chronic cases are often treated with the insertion of small tubes into the ear, through which the liquid in the middle ear will drain out naturally (Schoem, 1999). Ear infections should always be treated promptly in babies and young children: their long-term effects can be very serious. You as a professional working with young children and families can play an important role in the prevention of conductive hearing loss by encouraging prompt medical treatment when an ear infection is suspected.

Sensorineural Hearing Loss

Children with sensorineural hearing loss usually require special education services.

Conductive hearing loss can often be successfully treated in young children, and it is not usually the major cause of hearing loss that places school-age children in special education services. Children with sensorineural hearing loss, though, usually have a permanent condition that cannot be medically treated and that makes special education services necessary.

Knowledge of the cause of a child's sensorineural hearing loss is often important for families. Parents may want to know if a child's hearing loss is hereditary. A genetic counselor can help a family know whether or not that determination can be made (Arnos, 1999). Also, many parents feel a strong desire to know the cause of their child's disability. In fact, Kathryn Meadow (1968) found that parents who knew the probable cause of their child's hearing loss were better able to cope with the complex feelings associated with the diagnosis. Summers, Behr, and Turnbull (1989) suggest that identifying the cause of disability may be a positive process of adaptation for families.

~ Causes of Sensorineural Hearing Loss

1. **Heredity.** We know that in a great number of cases hearing loss is caused by heredity, or genetic factors. It is believed that hereditary deafness accounts for about 60 percent of the cases of early childhood deafness in this country today (Moores, 2001).
2. **Meningitis.** Meningitis is a bacterial or viral infection that causes inflammation of the coverings of the brain and spinal cord. If the infection reaches the inner ear, it can destroy the delicate organs within, resulting in deafness. Meningitis is the major cause of acquired deafness in children. It may also be associated with other neurological disabilities.
3. **Prematurity.** Prematurity and the traumatic medical events frequently associated with premature birth and low birthweight are sometimes associated with hearing loss. When infants are born early, sick, and small, they are at considerably higher risk for hearing loss, but it is often difficult to isolate the factor that actually causes the deafness. With the increasing number of very low birthweight children who are surviving with the help of modern neonatal medicine, it is likely that the number of children with hearing loss in this category will increase.
4. **Cytomegalovirus (CMV).** CMV (see Chapter 2) accounts for a small but increasing number of cases of childhood hearing loss (Schildroth, 1994). CMV is common; 44 to100 percent of adult populations evaluated have been exposed to the virus (Strauss, 1999). When a pregnant woman contracts CMV, she can pass it to her fetus, which results in other disabilities as well as hearing loss.
5. **Other causes.** There are many other, less common causes of childhood hearing loss, including mother-child blood incompatibility, or RH incompatibility. This is decreasing as a cause of deafness because of rhogam treatments and improvements in blood transfusion techniques.

The major causes of sensorineural hearing loss in children change over time, depending on the occurrence of epidemics, the development of new drugs and medical treatments, and public health conditions. For example, most of the children who lost their hearing as a result of maternal exposure to rubella during the 1960s rubella epidemic have by now left special education services, and since the rubella vaccine was introduced in 1969, rubella has become a less prominent cause of hearing loss. See the accompanying box, "Causes of Sensorineural Hearing Loss," for a list of the current most common causes of sensorineural hearing loss in children.

Although there are benefits to knowing the cause of sensorineural hearing loss, that information is frequently unavailable. In at least 30 percent of the reported cases of hearing loss, despite the best efforts of parents and counselors to determine the cause, it remains unknown (Moores, 2001).

Students with Hearing Loss and Additional Disabilities

About 26 percent of the children who are deaf and hard of hearing and enrolled in special education programs have been identified with a disability in addition to their hearing loss (Gallaudet Research Institute, 1999). Table 10.3 shows the numbers of children with hearing loss and additional disabilities. The most common are the cognitive-behavioral disabilities: mental retardation and

About 26 percent of children with hearing loss have additional disabilities.

Table 10.3 Deaf and Hard-of-Hearing Students with Additional Disabilities, 1998–1999

Specific Classifications*	Percentage
Legal blindness	5.6
Learning disabled	33.9
Mentally retarded	30.8
Attention deficit disorder	17.0
Serious emotional disturbance	1.9
Cerebral palsy	10.8
Other	14.0
Totals:	
1 or more additional disabilities	25.7
No additional disabilities reported	74.3

Note: Figures do not add up to 100 percent because some students have more than one classification.
*Specific classifications refer to specific disabilities for which the student has officially been referred and diagnosed.
Source: Gallaudet Research Institute. (1999, December). *Regional and National Summary Report of Data from the 1998–99 Annual Survey of Deaf and Hard-of-Hearing Children & Youth.* Washington, DC: GRI, Gallaudet University.

specific learning disabilities. If 26 percent seems high to you, note that part of the explanation for this relationship comes from the linkage between the cause of hearing loss and the additional disability. Moores (2001) reminds us:

> All of the major contemporary known causes of early childhood deafness may be related to other conditions to some extent. These include maternal rubella, prematurity, cytomegalovirus, mother-child blood incompatibility, and meningitis. Even in the case of inherited deafness, whether dominant, recessive, or sex-linked, the hearing loss may be only one manifestation of a syndrome that includes a wide range of conditions. (p. 118)

There may also be social or environmental causes for an additional condition: An impoverished communication system, late entry to school, an inappropriate school program, and a lack of consistent behavioral limits, for example, could combine to allow the development of an additional disability.

Hearing loss is also frequently associated with other conditions that may be considered a student's primary disability, such as Down syndrome, cerebral palsy, and cleft palate (Chen, 1999). In addition, children who are both deaf and blind constitute a small but unique group of students who often have intensive communication and mobility needs and are best served by a multidisciplinary group of professionals (Chen & Dote-Kwan, 1995). Family members can learn to interpret communication cues in infants with multiple disabilities that include both hearing and vision; these cues can serve as the foundation for a system of communication (Klein, Chen, & Haney, 2001).

It is likely that the number of children who have hearing loss and multiple disabilities will increase over the coming years because of the improved survival rates of premature and medically at-risk infants and improved identification and diagnostic procedures. Effective strategies for teaching these children, always difficult to come by, must continue to be developed.

Prevalence

In comparison to other groups of children served in special education programs, the number of children who are deaf and hard of hearing is small. In fact, the number of children has declined slowly but steadily over the past three decades (Moores, 2001). Only 1.3 percent of the children served in special programs in the 1998–1999 school year were labeled hearing impaired (*Twenty-Second Annual Report to Congress on the Implementation of the Individuals with Disabilities Education Act,* 2000). As many as 18.7 million Americans have some kind of hearing loss (Meadow-Orlans & Orlans, 1990), but the great majority of these are adults. Counting the number of children with hearing loss is made difficult by the fact that many children have such a mild loss that they are not receiving any special education services at all; in addition, some students with hearing loss are in programs designed for other disabilities and are not included in most counts.

A small percentage of all the children served in special education programs are deaf or hard of hearing.

Measurement of Hearing Loss

If you work with students with hearing loss, you will most likely come into contact with a number of other professionals who interact with the child and family. As you review your students' records, you will see their reports.

The **otologist** is a physician whose specialization is diseases of the ear. He or she may participate in the diagnosis of hearing loss and treat the child later for related problems. The otologist is also the specialist many children see for chronic middle ear infections.

The **audiologist** has special training in testing and measuring hearing. Professionally trained audiologists have the skills and equipment needed to evaluate the hearing of any child at any age with a high degree of accuracy. Many audiologists also participate in the process of rehabilitation, or treatment of the effects of hearing loss, and prescribe and evaluate the effectiveness of hearing aids.

The audiologist is trained to test and measure hearing.

The traditional first hearing test given by an audiologist is called a pure-tone test. You have probably had a test like this yourself, since hearing screenings are common in schools. In a pure-tone test the individual, wearing headphones, is exposed to a series of tones or beeps measured in decibels (units of loudness). The tones vary in loudness, or intensity, from soft to loud, and in pitch, or frequency, from low to high. The **audiogram** is the chart on which the audiologist records the individual's responses to the tones. People with normal hearing generally respond to very soft sounds, whether they are high or low in frequency (pitch). Figure 10.2 explains an audiogram. Note that each ear is tested separately.

The audiogram is the chart on which the audiologist records the individual's responses to sounds presented.

There are a couple of simple principles that make interpreting an audiogram easier. First, the farther down on the audiogram the responses are recorded, the less residual hearing a person has, or the louder the tones have to be before the person responds to them. Second, the most crucial sounds for a

An audiogram is a picture of your hearing. The results of your hearing test are recorded on an audiogram. The audiogram to the right demonstrates different sounds and where they would be represented on an audiogram. The blue, banana-shaped figure represents all the sounds that make up the human voice when speaking at normal conversational levels.

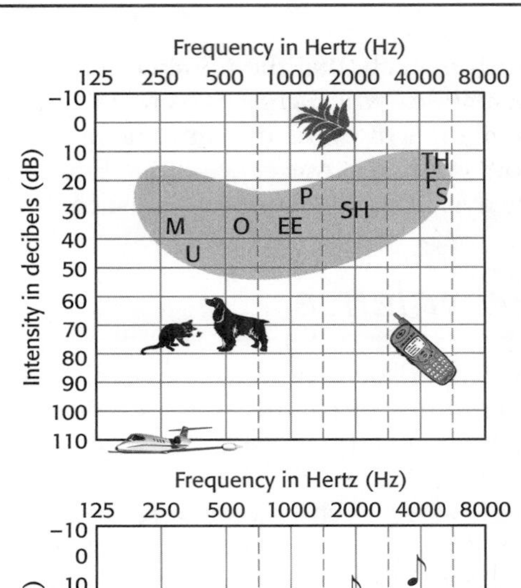

The vertical lines on an audiogram represent pitch or frequency. The 125 Hertz (Hz) vertical line on the left side of the audiogram represents a very low pitch sound and each vertical line to the right represents a higher pitch sound. Moving from left to right on the audiogram would be consistent with moving from left to right on a piano keyboard. The most important pitches for speech are 500–3,000 Hz.

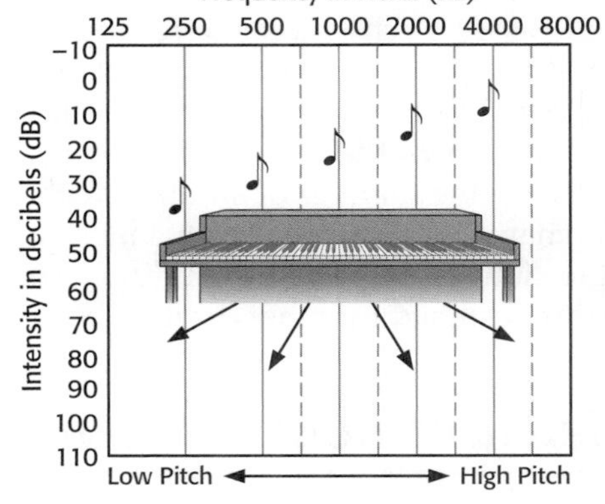

The horizontal lines represent loudness or intensity. The 0 decibel (dB) line near the top of the audiogram represents an extremely soft sound. Each horizontal line below represents a louder sound. Moving from the top to the bottom would be consistent with hitting the piano key harder or turning up the volume control on your stereo.

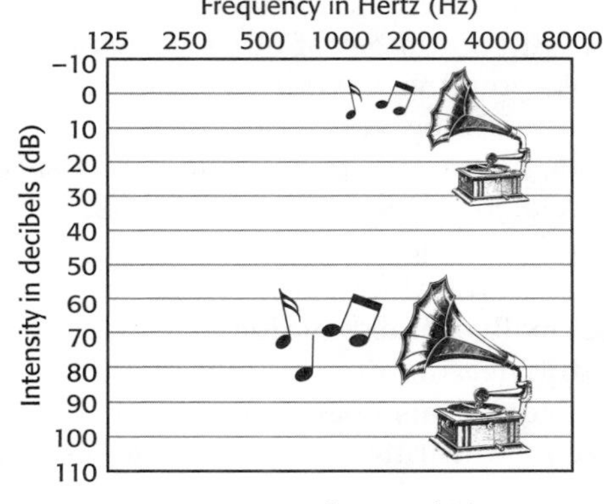

Therefore, every point on an audiogram represents a different sound. For example, point A on the audiogram to the right represents a soft low-pitch sound and point B represents a soft-high pitch sound. Point C represents a loud mid-pitch sound.

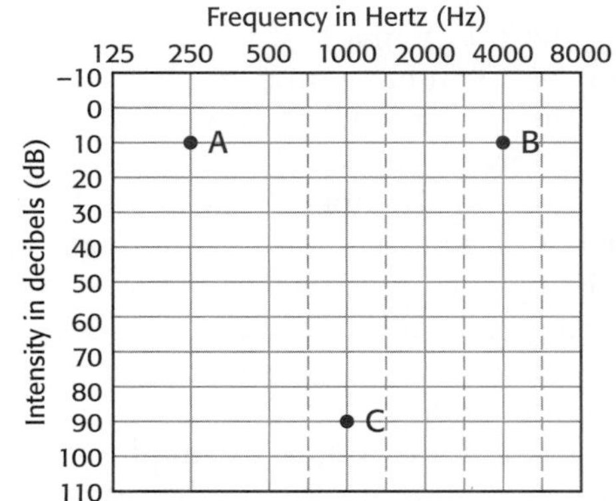

Figure 10.2
Understanding Your Audiogram

The softest sound you are able to hear at each pitch is recorded on the audiogram. The softest sound you are able to hear is called your threshold. Thresholds of 0-25 dB are considered normal (for adults). The audiogram on the right demonstrates the different degrees of hearing loss.

Frequency in Hertz (Hz)
125 250 500 1000 2000 4000 8000
Intensity in decibels (dB)
-10 0 10 20 30 40 50 60 70 80 90 100 110
NORMAL HEARING
MILD HEARING LOSS
MODERATE HEARING LOSS
SEVERE HEARING LOSS
PROFOUND HEARING LOSS

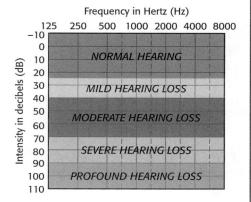

The audiogram on the right represents the hearing of an individual with normal hearing in the low frequencies (pitch) sloping to a severe high frequency hearing loss in the left ear and a moderate to severe hearing loss in the right ear. The blue Xs indicate the thresholds for the left ear and the black Os indicate the thresholds for the right ear.

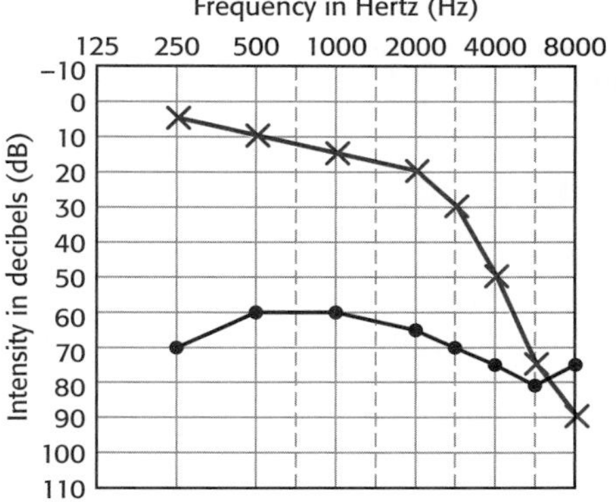

If we now superimpose the normal speech area on the audiogram, we can obtain some information regarding this individual's ability to hear speech. The listener is able to hear all the low and mid speech sounds but is not able to hear the high pitch speech sounds (F, S, TH) in the left ear (blue Xs). The listener is not able to hear any of the normal speech sounds in the right ear. This person would rely on the left ear for speech understanding and would probably experience difficulty hearing in noisy environments.

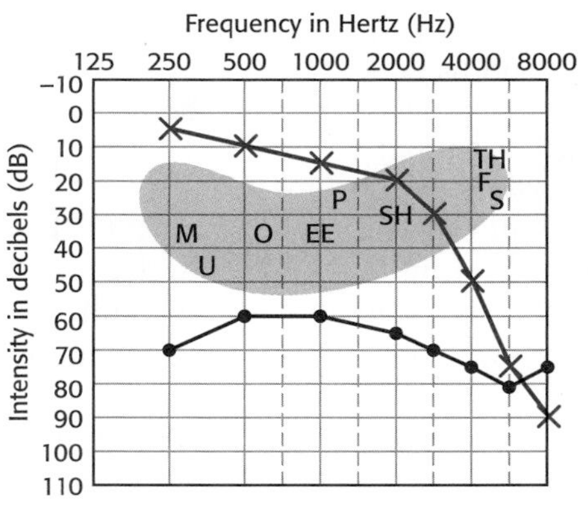

Figure 10.2 (continued)

Source: Allan S. Mehr, "Understanding Your Audiogram," *Consumer Guides*, Feb. 2001. http://www.audiology.org/consumer/guides/uya.php

person to hear are those that fall primarily between 500 and 3,000 Hertz, or cycles per second. Those are the "speech frequencies," the pitch range within which most speech sounds fall. Many professionals believe that children with hearing loss should hear speech sounds more than any other sounds. It is through amplification with hearing aids and the training of their residual hearing to respond to speech sounds that children can most efficiently learn to understand and express spoken language.

Effects on the Developing Person

The impact of hearing loss on a person's ability to naturally acquire the spoken language of his or her community is often substantial. Those communication difficulties may then adversely influence school achievement, social and emotional development, and interaction with others. Relationships within families can be touched by these issues, too, as we will see.

Language Development

Hearing loss has its most pervasive effect on the development of spoken language. It does not appear to affect cognitive or intellectual development, but it can have a significant impact on school achievement.

If you were to become deaf right now, your primary disability would be your inability to hear. Your relations with your family and friends might be strained by your inability to understand everything they say through lip reading. You would be particularly uncomfortable at parties and restaurants, where the noisy background would make it difficult for you to use your residual hearing to follow the conversation. Television and movies would be harder to follow, and listening to music would bring you less pleasure. Well, you might say, that's what deafness is all about, isn't it? Well, yes—for those of us who have already acquired language. For the prelingually deaf child, deafness is much more than that.

Kathryn Meadow-Orlans (1980) has said that for a child the primary disability of hearing loss is not the deprivation of sound, but the deprivation of *language*. Think about it. Young children with normal hearing learn how to talk by listening to the people around them use language meaningfully. They begin to understand and to say words. As they have more experiences listening and using language for different communicative purposes, and mature cognitively, their ability to communicate becomes much more sophisticated. But for the child who does not hear, or does not hear well, that listening experience does not occur, or occurs much less consistently. Unless sign language is used in the home, there are fewer occasions for practice in using language to communicate. Many children who are deaf, particularly those who have not been involved in early intervention programs, come to school at age 3 (and sometimes much later) without any speech or signing skills at all. So, although there are exceptions, most children who are deaf or hard of hearing start school with a language delay, and many of them never catch up to their hearing peers linguistically or academically while they are in school.

Carlos, for example, was a 15-year-old boy who was profoundly deaf. His family had recently moved from El Salvador to Los Angeles, and he had never been in school or had any communication development services. The language of his home was Spanish, but his family reported that he used no recognizable

Spanish words. The language of the school was English (presented orally and accompanied by an English-order sign language system), but on entering school Carlos used no recognizable English vocabulary, either signed or spoken. This boy was very bright and sociable; he had developed his own gesture language, and through this pantomime could communicate simple needs and actions. But catching up to the other students who were deaf in his class presented a formidable challenge to Carlos and his teachers.

The more residual hearing children have, the more likely they will speak the language of their home.

The first language of children who are deaf and hard of hearing depends to some extent on the language they are exposed to in the home. The more residual hearing a child has, the more likely it is that the child will learn to speak the language of the home. Children who have little usable residual hearing, however, may develop a relatively unique "first language" based on what they are exposed to—spoken words and formal signs, for example—and what they invent themselves—gestures and "home signs" that may be understood only by the child and family members (Luetke-Stahlman & Luckner, 1991). On the other hand, deaf children of deaf parents who use American Sign Language may begin school with communication abilities that are developmentally appropriate for their age—and continue to excel throughout their school careers.

Many children with hearing loss do not learn English until they begin school.

Many children with hearing loss begin learning *English* when they enter school. Research that has examined the acquisition of English literacy skills—speaking, reading, and writing—of children with hearing loss tells us that the English language of children who are deaf typically develops in the same order as that of hearing children, but at a considerably slower rate (Paul, 1998).

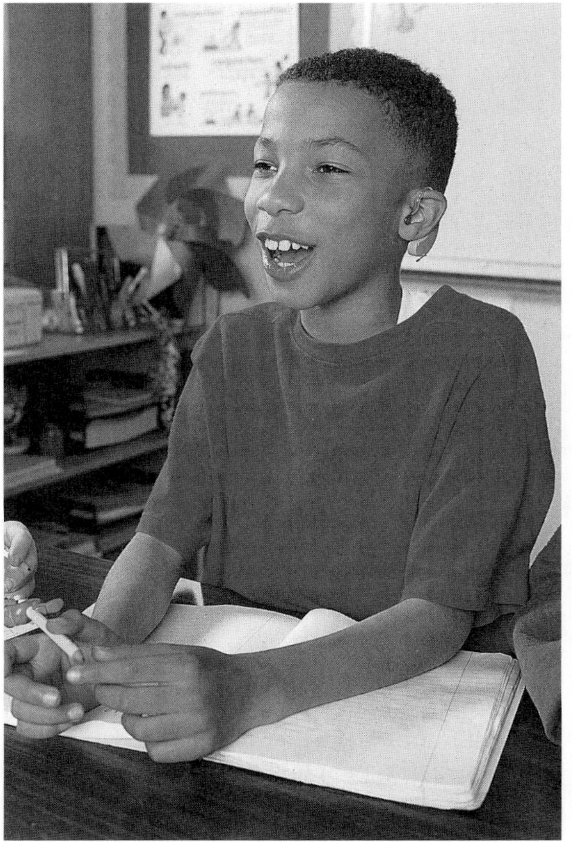

Children with hearing loss can feel sound vibrations and watch lip movements, giving them an understanding of spoken language that can be supplemented by a hearing aid. (© Michael Newman/PHOTO EDIT)

Bridget and Books

When our daughter, Bridget, came into this world, we greeted her with awe—and language. Bridget, like us, is Deaf. From those first wonderful moments in the hospital, we signed and fingerspelled to her. Perhaps because of all this language, she was an alert baby and we introduced her to books quickly. At 34 months old, she has been entertained by over 200 books, an average of four books a day.

We point to the pictures, tell stories, and translate printed English (text and phrases) into signs and fingerspelling. We talk about the letters, too, and how they can be printed or fingerspelled.

Fingerspelling is critical because we know it helps with reading skills. While Bridget was still a baby, we introduced her to the sequence of letters that make up the alphabet. As she watched, we would fingerspell all 26 letters, A to Z, in rhythmic motions. We did this on a regular basis, if not every day. In addition, we signed numbers, one through 10, then one through 20, with a similar rhythmic flow. We also included fingerspelling when we communicated with her.

Bridget was fascinated by this. She loved watching. She asked us to do it again and again. During the same time, we exposed her to printed letters, both capital and lower case. We enjoyed print in other ways too—books, posters, object manipulation boards, puzzles, magnets, and erasers. We called her attention to posters that listed the ABCs with their accompanying handshapes that corresponded with the letters. We brought writing and print constantly into her environment, and made English as visible as possible. By two years old, Bridget started to recognize numbers and letters on shirts, license plates, and store names, and would initiate conversations about them.

Bridget and Fingerspelling

Bridget has witnessed countless examples of fingerspelling in countless situations. As we read to her before she goes to sleep, she sees fingerspelling. Of course, she was exposed to numerous fingerspelled words. By the time she was one year old, we realized that she attended to our fingerspelling as she did to the rest of our conversation. She may

Cognitive and Intellectual Development

Most people with hearing loss have normal cognitive and intellectual abilities.

The best information that we have today, based on the most recently conducted research, is that people who are deaf and hard of hearing as a group have normal cognitive and intellectual abilities (Paul & Jackson, 1993). However, that conclusion is a fairly recent one; for many years psychologists believed that the

not have been able to understand all fingerspelled words, but she knew that use of fingerspelling identified real things in conversation. At 19 months, Bridget began fingerspelling clearly back to us. Her first letters were generated on her fingers before she was able to recognize them in print. These were *A, B, C, Z,* and *OK* (in a sign play form).

Bridget made the transition to reading quickly after that. When she first noticed the word *moon* from her storybook, *Goodnight Moon,* she pointed to it and signed *mom.* We praised her for noticing that both words have the same first letter *m,* and noted that different letters follow. *MOON, MOM.* We fingerspelled, signed, and pointed to the print with each word. Bridget looked at the title of the book on the cover and visibly pondered. Then she pointed to the print *M-O-O-N* and signed *MOON.*

From Fingers to Print

She was quick in her associations—*M* indicated *MOM, W* indicated her friend, *WOLFGANG,* and *I* was for *ICE CREAM.* She also picked up *I* for her name, catching the last letter as we fingerspelled *BRI,* which we use as her nickname. She knew *B* led the three letter progression that was her name though, and one meal time when we fingerspelled *BIB,* she pointed directly to herself. Then we fingerspelled each word slowly so she could see how *BIB* and *BRI* differ. She learned fingerspellings. Then she matched the fingerspelling to the print. Thereafter, she knew the words were separate and identified them correctly.

At 30 months old, Bridget began to try to fingerspell the entire alphabet. She started with *A* and fingerspelled each letter in its place to *G.* Then she returned to *E* and *T.* Her fingerspelled alphabet looked like this, *A-B-C-D-E-F-G-E-T.* Why this order? We wondered if she confounded the order of the letters in the alphabet with those of her first name. Shortly afterward, with the stumbling block behind her, she successfully generated all 26 handshapes of the manual alphabet.

Letters + Play = Literacy

Every day we take turns playing with Bridget using a variety of literacy-related activities. Each session is about 20 minutes and each of

thinking and reasoning capacities of deaf people were "inferior" (Pintner & Patterson, 1917) or qualitatively different (Myklebust, 1964).

These earlier conclusions stemmed from the assessment process. People who are deaf or hard of hearing have, at times, been administered IQ tests that weigh verbal skills heavily; when they did not do well because of their limited

us may do a session two or three times a day. As a result, Bridget has come to enjoy reading books with us. She has her favorite books that she wants us to read to her again and again, often over several days and weeks.

At 30 months old, two of Bridget's favorite books were *Franklin Is Lost* and *Franklin in the Dark* by Paulette Bourgeois. We fingerspelled many words as we read this book to Bridget, including *SHELL, GOOSE, PARACHUTE, SUPPER, BED,* and *FRANKLIN.* We fingerspelled the name of Franklin, the turtle star of both books, and Bridget recognized both the fingerspelled and printed name and frequently fingerspelled the word to us. Here's our record of how her fingerspelling evolved over a two-week span.

F-L-N
F-R-L-N-I
F-R-K-L-N-I
F-R-A-N-K-L-N-I
F-R-A-N-K-L-I-N-I
F-R-A-N-K-L-I-N

Just before Bridget's final mastery of Franklin's name, she spelled it with an extraneous *I,* i.e., *F-R-A-N-K-L-I-N-I.* We never corrected Bridget's fingerspelling, teaching her instead through modeling. But on one occasion, when she attempted to correct Dennis as he spelled the turtle's name without its phantom *I,* he offered an explanation. "There's no *I* at the end of Franklin," he told her. He pointed to the word in the book, and then he fingerspelled it again. Bridget watched intently. The next time she fingerspelled Franklin, the extraneous *I* was gone. It never resurfaced on her fingers again.

Since that time, Bridget has recognized the printed word Franklin in many different contexts throughout her environment. She has pointed out the familiar spelling in Franklin Mint, Franklin Street, and on a basketball that carries the Franklin brand name. One day as we were reading, Bridget bestowed a last name on Franklin the Turtle. It was Berrigan. She fingerspelled the entire production clearly, F-R-A-N-K-L-I-N B-E-R-R-I-G-A-N.

The process through which Bridget's language and reading skills emerge continues to amaze us. She is acquiring American Sign Lan-

understanding and use of English, they were judged to be cognitively below normal—sometimes even mentally retarded (Moores, 2001). Even when a relatively "fair" test is used, the person with hearing loss may not understand the test directions given by a psychologist who does not have the skills necessary for communicating with him or her. Although psychologists and other test ad-

guage and learning printed English quickly and naturally—and at a very young age. At 34 months old, she recognizes approximately 150 fingerspelled words. She is able to generate about 50 of the fingerspelled words intelligibly herself.

She enjoys many theme-based books, such as the Franklin books and stories about the Berenstein Bears. Every three weeks we go to the library, and recently Bridget chooses books that focus on words and word lists. These books are not exciting to us, but Bridget loves them. She has us read them again and again. This week's book focuses on words for body parts. We sign and fingerspell each word, pointing to the body part that it signifies and then pointing to the printed word in the book to refer to what was signed. We made some flash cards and were pleased to see how many body parts Bridget recognizes in print.

For example, when Bridget saw *KNEE* on a card, she pointed to her knee. "I remember when I fell and hurt my knee," she said. The flashcard that said *ears* stumped her briefly. She didn't recognize the word until we fingerspelled, *E-A-R-S.* Then she pointed to her own ears and explained about Dumbo, the flying elephant whose tales appear in books and on television. We find it interesting that, at this stage in her literacy development, Bridget uses fingerspelling to recognize printed words. She recognizes the print and fingerspelling for *hair, eyes, nose, mouth, arms, belly button, legs, toes, feet,* and *hands.*

Bridget's recent selection, Dr. Seuss's *Hop on Pop,* has us marveling at her joy in reading and exploring English words. As she makes her way through sequences of words like *hop* and *pop,* and *three, tree,* and *bee,* Bridget discovers, recognizes, and delights in rhyme.

With fingerspelling, story reading, lots of print, and natural communication, Bridget has learned to love books. At night when she falls asleep, there are often books tucked under her pillow. She is becoming richly bilingual—and she is loving it.

Source: Dennis Berrigan and Sharon Berrigan, "Bridget & Books," *Odyssey,* Summer 2000, pp. 6–9.

ministrators have become more knowledgeable about testing people who are deaf and thus fewer abuses seem to occur today, great care should always be taken in interpreting test scores (Eccarius, 1997). As always, they are just one piece of the puzzle.

School Achievement

Despite normal abilities, most children with hearing loss do not achieve at grade level.

Despite the normal cognitive and intellectual abilities of most children with hearing loss, their average school achievement has been significantly below that of their hearing peers. Paul and Jackson (1993) report that "one of the most robust findings is that there is an inverse relationship between hearing impairment and achievement: the more severe the impairment, the lower the achievement" (p. 34). Donald Moores (2001) documents a slow but steady rise in achievement among the students whose schools participate in the Annual Survey of Children and Youth conducted by the Gallaudet Research Institute, but still, "achievement on the average seems to peak around the fourth-grade level in reading comprehension and the seventh-grade level in math computation" (p. 322).

Why this discrepancy between ability and achievement? It hinges on the lack of mastery of the English language among students who are deaf. If a person can't comprehend and use the language fluently, then he or she can't read it, since even basal reading materials incorporate sophisticated grammatical structures at preprimer and first-grade levels (King & Quigley, 1985). Reading ability is crucial for success in nearly all academic areas.

Social and Emotional Development

Inadequate psychological assessment labeled individuals with hearing loss as socially and emotionally deficient.

Traditionally, psychologists and other professionals concerned with the social and emotional development of individuals who are deaf have concentrated on the differences in this group from the "norms" set by hearing subjects. From this approach has arisen what Donald Moores (2001) calls a "deviance model," which implies that there is something deficient in the psychological makeup of people who are deaf. Many of these conclusions have arisen because of the psychological assessment of students with hearing loss by examiners who are not trained in using sign language and who administer tests that are not appropriate.

Moores (2001) describes another view of the social and emotional development of individuals with hearing loss. This perspective focuses on the development of a healthy, whole, well-integrated person rather than concentrating on what is different or deficient. It assumes that all humans have similar basic needs, which must be met satisfactorily for healthy personal development—among them, the need to communicate with others. For people who are deaf, this need for basic human communication is not always met. Think about this example: Parents of young children who are deaf often feel they do not have the command of communication necessary to explain complicated events, such as a relative's death, a separation, a forthcoming move, or marital problems, and so do not fully communicate the meaning of these experiences to their child. As a result, the child's world may change drastically from one day to the next with no explanation, leaving him or her anxious, frightened, resentful, or confused (Meadow-Orlans, 1980). The frustration that can arise from poor communication can spill over into the child's behavior, relationships, and motivation.

Frustration over inadequate communication may result in behavior or emotional problems for children who are deaf.

This is not to say that people who are deaf and hard of hearing, young and old, do not have problems like everyone else, only that those problems are not particular to hearing loss. Rather, they may arise from experiences within the family, school, and community where poor communication or no communication is the rule.

In summary, the primary effect of deafness on the developing child is to place the development of communication at risk. Because communication skills are so essential for school learning, when these skills are affected, school achievement is, too. But cognitive and social development need not be delayed in children with hearing loss when they are provided with a means and reason to communicate from an early age.

Effects on the Family

Many parents do not begin to suspect a hearing loss until their child's second year.

In most states, hearing loss is not routinely screened for at birth, and many families do not begin to suspect that their child's hearing is impaired until the child's second year, when he or she does not begin to talk (see the accompanying box, "Speech and Hearing Checklist"). Even when parents have doubts about their child's hearing during the first year, they are frequently reassured by their pediatricians that the child is normal and that they are "overanxious." One mother, Elsa, told her story this way:

> I felt Pablo couldn't hear from the time he was about 6 months old. But my pediatrician clapped his hands behind Pablo's head and when he turned, the doctor told me he was fine, and I was worrying too much. I believed him for a while, but eventually I went to two more doctors before I found one who would listen to me and recommend a hearing test. Pablo wasn't diagnosed as deaf until he was 18 months old—one year after I first suggested there was a problem . . . and he is profoundly deaf!

Once a family has had its child's hearing tested by an audiologist and a diagnosis of deafness has been given, reactions may range from shock to anger to depression. Most parents feel overwhelmed by helplessness and their own emotions and have a difficult time taking in the information that professionals—in this case usually the audiologist or teacher of the deaf—are eager to present to them. Involvement in an early intervention program is very important for the young child and the family, but it takes some time for the implications of hearing loss for language learning to become clear.

However, most parents can and do learn to cope with their child's hearing loss. Here is Elsa again:

> I had to be able to cope with Pablo's deafness—at such a young age he had to get hearing aids and start school, and I had to be there to help him. I participated in the program with him, and began to learn sign language. Being with other parents in the same situation and having something to do really helped me, although sometimes at night I would get into bed by myself and cry. But for my husband it was much harder. He couldn't be as involved as I was, and for a long time he couldn't understand the deafness or accept it.

Koester and Meadow-Orlans (1990) describe the need of parents of young children who are deaf for social support from a network of family, friends, and professionals. But some reports indicate that families with young children who are deaf are less likely than others to have that social network; families report that unwanted advice-giving, misconceptions about the child, and underestimates of the child's ability often cause problems between parents and their family and friends.

Parents with children who are deaf and have additional disabilities may experience heightened levels of stress, and they may need greater support from

~ Speech and Hearing Checklist

This checklist will help you to detect any hearing or speech problems in your child at a very young age. *Even if a hearing loss was not detected during your child's infant screening,* it is important to continually monitor speech and language development in order to identify a potential later loss as soon as possible.

Early detection is crucial because undetected hearing loss has a direct effect on the development of speech and language in young children. It is through the sense of hearing that infants begin to naturally learn their native language. If your child can't hear sounds or differences in sounds, then understanding words and speaking will be difficult. No child is too young to be tested or to be helped if a hearing loss is suspected. The earlier a child with hearing loss is identified, the less effect the loss will have on his/her speech development, social growth, learning ability, and classroom performance.

If your child fails to respond as the checklist for the appropriate age level suggests, have your child's hearing tested immediately. Don't delay! If your child does have a hearing loss, early detection means early solutions to hearing and speech problems through the help of medical intervention, education, and amplification. The earlier a hearing loss is identified, the less effect the loss will have on your child's future.

Average Speech and Hearing Behavior for Your Child's Age Level

Birth–3 Months

Startled by loud sounds
Soothed by caretakers' voices

3–6 Months

Reacts to the sound of your voice
Turns eyes and head in the direction of the source of sounds
Enjoys rattles and noisy toys

7–10 Months

Responds to his/her own name
Understands *mama, dada, no, bye bye,* and other common words
Turns head toward familiar sounds, even when he/she cannot see what is happening:

- Dog barking or paper rustling
- Familiar footsteps
- Telephone
- Person's voice

11–15 Months

Imitates and matches sounds with own speech production (though frequently unintelligible), especially in response to human voices or loud noises
Locates or points to familiar objects when asked
Understands words by making appropriate responses or behavior:

- "Where's the dog?"
- "Find the truck."

15–18 Months

Identifies things in response to questions, such as parts of the body
Uses a few single words; while not complete or perfectly pronounced, the words should be clearly meaningful
Follows simple spoken directions

2 Years

Understands yes/no questions
Uses everyday words heard at home or at day care/school
Enjoys being read to and shown pictures in books; points out pictures upon request
Interested in radio/television as shown by word or action
Puts words together to make simple sentences, although they are not complete or grammatically correct:

- "Juice all gone"
- "Go bye-bye car"

Follows simple commands without visual clues from the speaker:

- "Bring me that ball."
- "Get your book and give it to Daddy."

2½ Years

Says or sings short rhymes and songs; enjoys music
Vocabulary approximately 270 words
Investigates noises or tells others when interesting sounds are heard:

- Car door slamming
- Telephone ringing

3 Years

Understands and uses simple verbs, pronouns, and adjectives:

- Go, come, run, sing
- Me, you, him, her
- Big, green, sweet

Locates the source of a sound automatically
Often uses complete sentences
Vocabulary approximately 1,000 words

4 Years

Gives connected account of some recent experiences
Can carry out a sequence of two simple directions:

- "Find your shoe and bring it here."
- "Get the ball and throw it to the dog."

5 years

Speech should be intelligible, although some sounds may still be mispronounced—such as the /s/ sound, particularly in blends with other consonants (e.g., *street, sleep, ask*). Neighbors and people outside the family can understand most of what your child says and her grammatical patterns should match theirs most of the time.
Child carries on conversations, although vocabulary may be limited
Pronouns should be used correctly:

- *I* instead of *me*
- *He* instead of *him*

Does Your Child Have Any of the Indicators for Hearing Loss?

If your child has one or more of these indicators, he or she may have a better than average chance of having a hearing loss. Consult your pediatrician, family doctor, ear, nose, and throat doctor, or an audiologist who has experience with pediatric hearing loss. Request a complete medical and hearing evaluation. Parents, not medical professionals, are often the first to suspect their child has a hearing loss! Do not hesitate to have your child's hearing tested. Prompt and accurate screening will help you to detect any hearing or speech problems in your child at a very young age.

Prenatal and Early Infancy Indicators

- Infection or illness during pregnancy (especially cytomegalovirus, rubella, herpes, syphilis, flu)
- Drug or alcohol consumption during pregnancy
- APGAR scores lower than 4 at one minute and below 6 at five minutes (APGAR scores measure newborn vital signs at birth)
- Low birthweight (below 3.5 pounds)
- Admission to Newborn Intensive Care for more than 5 days
- Neonatal jaundice at birth requiring transfusion
- Craniofacial anomalies

- Use of ototoxic medications given in multiple courses or in combination with loop diuretics (Lasix)

Genetic and Environmental Indicators

- Suspicion that your child may not be hearing well
- Visible malformations of the head, neck, or ears
- Family history of permanent or progressive hearing loss in childhood
- Malformations of the middle and/or inner ear structures
- Childhood diseases (especially meningitis, scarlet fever, mumps)
- Chronic middle ear infections with persistent fluid in the ears for more than 3 months
- Childhood injuries (especially skull fracture, sharp blow to the head or ears, loud noise exposure, and items accidentally inserted into ears resulting in damage)

Don't Delay!

If your child does not exhibit the average behavior for his/her age, get professional advice from your doctor, your hospital, or a local speech and hearing clinic. No child is too young to be tested or to be helped if a hearing loss is suspected. Keep in mind that clapping hands or making loud noises behind a child's back are never accurate tests for hearing loss!

Source: http://www.agbell.org/information/checklst.html

professionals and other parents than those with children whose only disability is deafness (Hintermair, 2000).

The feelings that often accompany the diagnosis of hearing loss do not go away quickly. But sensitive professionals can do much to assist families through this period by listening to them, by accepting the inevitability of their reactions, and by pointing out to them the strengths and beauties of their child. In addition, other parents with children who are deaf will provide significant support and models for successful coping for young families; meetings with groups that can enable experienced families and young families to share their feelings and experiences should be built into early intervention programs (Koester & Meadow-Orlans, 1990).

Other parents with children who are deaf can provide significant support and models for successful coping.

Some of the reactions that families experience may come as a result of not being familiar with positive images of adults who are deaf. The work that is being done to identify the cultural components of deafness may someday change our society's perception of hearing loss.

Deafness and Culture

Our discussions so far in this chapter have centered around definitions and descriptions that place deafness in the context of *disability*—and that tend to measure people who are deaf by the yardstick of people who are hearing. We speak of deafness as hearing *loss* or hearing *impairment*—yet, as one deaf professional put it: "How would women like to be referred to as male-impaired, or whites like to be called black-impaired? I'm not impaired; I'm deaf!" Many professionals in the field of deafness, particularly those who are deaf themselves, have

The clinical perspective of deafness views it as a disability; many prefer that a cultural perspective be adopted.

been urging teachers of deaf children to drop the clinical perspective, in which deafness is seen as a pathology, a deviance from the "normal" condition of hearing, a condition that must be "cured" or "fixed." These deaf professionals are exhorting the field to adopt the *cultural* perspective, which describes people who are deaf as members of a different culture—a culture with its own language, social institutions, class structure, history, attitudes, values, and literature—that must be studied, understood, and respected (Crittenden, 1993).

Deaf culture unites those in the Deaf community who share common goals.

Adoption of a cultural perspective on deafness demands a knowledge of **Deaf culture,** which Crittenden (1993) defines as "the view of life manifested by the mores, beliefs, artistic expression, understandings, and language particular to Deaf people" (p. 218). Deaf culture is the mainstay of the Deaf community, that group of people who share common goals deriving from Deaf cultural influences and work together toward achieving these goals. Crittenden (1993) describes the characteristics that members of the Deaf community share as follows:

- "Attitudinal deafness," the desire to associate with other deaf people with whom values and experiences are shared
- The use of American Sign Language (ASL), considered by members of the Deaf community to be their native language
- The similar life experiences of many people who are deaf in relation to family, schooling, and interaction with "the hearing world"
- The bond between deaf people, the friendships and relationships that grow out of those shared experiences

Members of the Deaf community may not be physically deaf (that is, they may be hearing people), but they must actively support the goals of the Deaf community and work together with people who are deaf to achieve them (Padden, 1980). Padden and Humphries's book *Deaf in America: Voices from a Culture* (1988) portrays members of the Deaf community. These authors, deaf themselves, write:

> In contrast to the long history of writings that treat [deaf people] as medical cases, or people with "disabilities," who "compensate" for their deafness by using sign language, we want to portray the lives they live, their art and performances, their everyday talk, their shared myths, and the lessons they teach one another. We have always felt that the attention given to the physical condition of not hearing has obscured far more interesting facets of Deaf people's lives. (p. 1)

Thomas Holcomb (1997) argues that it is important to offer deaf children opportunities to develop a deaf identity from a young age, so that they see themselves as bicultural in a diverse world (see the accompanying box, "Deaf Culture and History"). David Stewart and Thomas Kluwin (2001) describe how a teacher can integrate Deaf Studies into the curriculum, and describe the basic premises of the study of deaf people:

- Deaf people are individuals first.
- The thoughts of a deaf person are shaped by a unique set of experiences that occur inside and outside of the classroom.
- A variety of information about deaf people is available from a variety of resources.

~ Deaf Culture and History

In March 1998 the Deaf community celebrated the tenth anniversary of the 1988 watershed political event at Gallaudet University, "Deaf President Now." Gallaudet students, faculty, and sympathetic deaf people from all over the country gathered to close down the university in protest because a hearing woman with little knowledge of deafness was named president. After a week of protests, the new president resigned and the university board of trustees named I. King Jordan, a man who became deaf early in life, president. In Jordan's first statement after he was named president, he stated, "We know that deaf people can do anything hearing people can do except hear" (Sacks, 1989). Many people who are deaf view that week at Gallaudet as a milestone in their history, and a powerful expression of the values of the Deaf community.

The Deaf President Now movement became a catalyst for a new study of the culture and history of deafness (Parasnis, 1996). If the values and culture of the Deaf community are to be integrated into the education of students who are deaf, then it is important to bring more teachers who are deaf into school programs. Deaf teachers can bring their own knowledge of Deaf culture and their own experiences to their students, as well as provide examples of successful adult life. In addition, many adults who are deaf are fluent ASL users but can also use manually coded English systems—they are bilingual.

Many professionals now believe that a knowledge and understanding of Deaf culture should be part of the school curriculum for students who are deaf, so that they are provided with opportunities to learn about other individuals with deafness and their achievements (Christensen, 1993; Schirmer, 1994).

- There are diverse perspectives about deaf people that are related to their use of communication, interactions with deaf and hearing people, cultural affiliation with different ethnic groups, social patterns, use of technology, educational experiences, participation in the workforce, and more.
- Studying about deaf people is an opportunity for gaining knowledge about and appreciation for these perspectives.
- Deaf studies is a means for helping deaf students discover their own identity. (p. 119)

Deaf Studies can help deaf students discover their own identity.

Table 10.4 shows how topics within Deaf Studies can be integrated into the elementary curriculum.

In Classrooms

Students with hearing loss need the benefit of an interdisciplinary team of professionals who will cooperatively plan and implement their educational program, whether it is an individualized family service plan (IFSP) for the child from birth to age 3, an individualized education program (IEP) for the school-aged child, or an individualized transition plan (ITP) for the high school student. First we will discuss the implementation of programming for the youngest children.

Table 10.4 Integrating Deaf Studies into the Curriculum

Grade Level	Content Area Topics	Deaf Culture Components
Kindergarten	Science/Social Studies: sound awareness and Deaf awareness	Basics for interacting with Deaf people
First grade	Social Studies: family life of the Deaf	Deafness and communication
Second grade	Social Studies: Deaf people in the community	Sensitivity activities, ASL as a language
Third grade	Sound, hearing measurement, and amplification	Deaf vs. hard of hearing, social interaction norms
Fourth grade	Reading: biography and history of Deaf people	Deaf history, Deaf identity, interview Deaf adult
Fifth grade	Health: hearing and deafness	Deaf community, organizations, and recreation
Sixth grade	Science: communication and assistive devices for the Deaf	Deafness and literature, Deaf values

Source: David A. Stewart and Thomas Kluwin (2001). *Teaching Deaf and Hard of Hearing Students: Content, Strategies, and Curriculum* (p. 118). Boston: Allyn & Bacon.

Early Identification and Intervention

Because hearing loss affects language development so directly, and the years from birth to age 3 are so critical for language, the early diagnosis of hearing loss is essential so that work with the family and language intervention with the child with hearing loss can begin. LaVonne Bergstrom (1984) described the ideal: that all major losses be detected and rehabilitation begun by age 3 months so that the child has the opportunity to hear language and other sounds.

The early diagnosis of hearing loss is essential so that intervention can begin.

The ideal, however, is far from being realized in everyday practice; in Dr. Bergstrom's large urban clinic, the average hearing loss was first suspected by the family at 10 months and detected by a professional at 21 months. Amplification and training did not typically begin until 27 months (Bergstrom, 1984). Many normally hearing children are speaking in sentences by that age, so the child who is deaf is at a disadvantage immediately; some feel that it is one from which the child never fully recovers.

The national trend to provide newborn hearing screenings may lower the age at which children with hearing loss are identified and begin intervention. There is hope that, ultimately, earlier intervention will improve the long-term outcomes for children who are deaf or hard of hearing (Joint Committee on Infant Hearing, 2000).

Newborn hearing screenings may lower the age of identification of hearing loss.

An early intervention program can serve many purposes for the family of a newly diagnosed child with hearing loss. Parents often need support from professionals in dealing with their reactions to the diagnosis of hearing loss; they also need information about the effects of hearing loss on language development. Families must make the important decision about how they will teach their child to communicate—will it be signs or speech? If signs are chosen, will it be American Sign Language (ASL) or manually coded English?

The early intervention teacher will help the family continue to communicate naturally to the child about everyday experiences, sometimes with the addition of sign language. She will help the family and the child understand how hearing aids are used and what they can and cannot do. Children with hearing loss do not automatically know where a sound comes from the first time they hear it with their hearing aids; they must be taught the association, for example, between the noise they hear and the airplane flying overhead. The child, the family, and the teacher must collaborate to maximize every communication opportunity during the child's waking hours.

Developing Communication Skills

Most educators of children who are deaf or hard of hearing agree that early diagnosis, amplification, and intervention are of paramount importance for their students, but there is no such unanimity on the topic of how these children should be taught to communicate. Should speech alone be emphasized, or signs be added? How much emphasis should there be on the use of residual hearing? Which sign language system should be used? What should be the role of the native language of the student, be it Spanish, Russian, or ASL, in school learning? Before we attempt to grapple with these thorny issues, let us discuss the communication methods or modalities that are currently used in classrooms with students who are deaf or hard of hearing.

Most teachers of students who are deaf or hard of hearing have as their ultimate goal that their students become fluent, competent users of English. There is also increasing emphasis placed on the acquisition of fluency in American Sign Language. Although the most intensive language teaching will take place in early intervention programs and in special schools and classes, the regular class teacher who works with the deaf or hard-of-hearing student will also play a role in introducing and expanding English vocabulary, structures, and use. Because of this emphasis, much of the training of teachers of students with hearing loss is on the development of skills related to language development, assessment, and teaching.

Traditionally, programs for students who are deaf and hard of hearing have differed in their approach to teaching communication skills. Some have emphasized the development of speech and auditory skills, while others have encouraged the growth of signs along with those skills. Let us take a closer look at these philosophies, the oral approach and the manual approach.

The oral communication approach is based on the belief that children with hearing loss can learn to speak.

■ ***The Oral Approach*** The **oral communication approach** is built on the belief that children who are deaf and hard of hearing can learn to talk and that speech should be their primary method of expression. Also, they should understand the speech of others through a combination of speech reading (lip reading) and residual hearing. The overall goal of oralism is that children with hearing loss learn intelligible speech and age-appropriate language (Connor, 1986). There are several different oral methods, but all high-quality oral programs share common goals:

- The earliest possible detection of hearing loss
- Amplification and intervention
- Intensive parent involvement in the child's education

- The use of residual hearing
- The exclusive use of speech, without sign language, for communication

Teaching speech takes considerable training and skill.

Teaching speech and auditory skills is theoretically part of the educational program for the majority of children with hearing loss. Teaching speech is one of the teacher's most complicated and challenging responsibilities (Calvert, 1986; Wolk & Schildroth, 1986), and doing it well takes considerable training and skill.

In many programs for students who are deaf and hard of hearing throughout the country, responsibility for teaching speech has been shifted to the school speech-language pathologist. This situation works best for students when the classroom teacher, whether a regular education teacher or a teacher of students with hearing loss, works collaboratively with the speech-language pathologist to help the students reach their speech goals and incorporate them into ongoing activities.

The teaching of listening skills, sometimes called **auditory training,** requires that the child be fitted with effective, appropriate hearing aids—preferably one in each ear (Ross, 1986). It begins with developing the child's awareness of all the sounds in the environment—doorbells ringing, dogs barking, people calling the child's name. The most important goal of training residual hearing, however, is to assist the child in understanding spoken language, and thereby support the development of oral language and speech (Flexer, 1994).

Auditory training itself does not enable the child to hear new sounds or words; it simply helps the child make sense of what is heard and use his or her residual hearing as well as possible. Attention to listening skills is important for the regular class teacher as well as the specialist, since there are safety issues involved for the student as well as language-learning issues. For example, attention to environmental sounds will help the student stay safe while riding a bike or crossing the street. Oral programs vary in the emphasis they give to speech reading and residual hearing. Those that emphasize speech reading are sometimes called *multisensory* or *visual-oral*, and those that emphasize residual hearing, *auditory-oral* or *aural-oral*. Some professionals advocate a *unisensory* approach, which calls for total reliance on residual hearing to the exclusion of speech reading, and early mainstreaming of children with hearing loss into preschool programs.

■ ***The Manual Approach*** The use of the **manual communication approach** by and with people who are deaf has a long history. According to Baker and Cokely (1980), "Wherever there were deaf people who needed to communicate there have been signed languages that they and their ancestors have developed" (p. 48). The first to systematize a sign language for teaching purposes was the Abbé de l'Epée, a French monk who started the first school for deaf children in Paris in 1755 (Quigley & Paul, 1984).

The manual communication approach has two components—fingerspelling and signs.

Manual communication has two components: **fingerspelling,** in which words are spelled out letter by letter using a manual alphabet (see Figure 10.3), and **signs,** which are symbolic representations of words made with the hands. The box on fingerspelling describes its importance in literacy development.

American Sign Language uses the same vocabulary as English but has a different grammatical structure.

The sign language considered by many deaf adults to be their "native language" is **American Sign Language (ASL).** ASL uses the same lexicon, or vocabulary, as English, but a different grammatical structure. Today, linguists consider ASL a legitimate language of its own, not simply a form of English (Hoffmeister, 1990; Stokoe, 1960). Because it does not correspond directly to

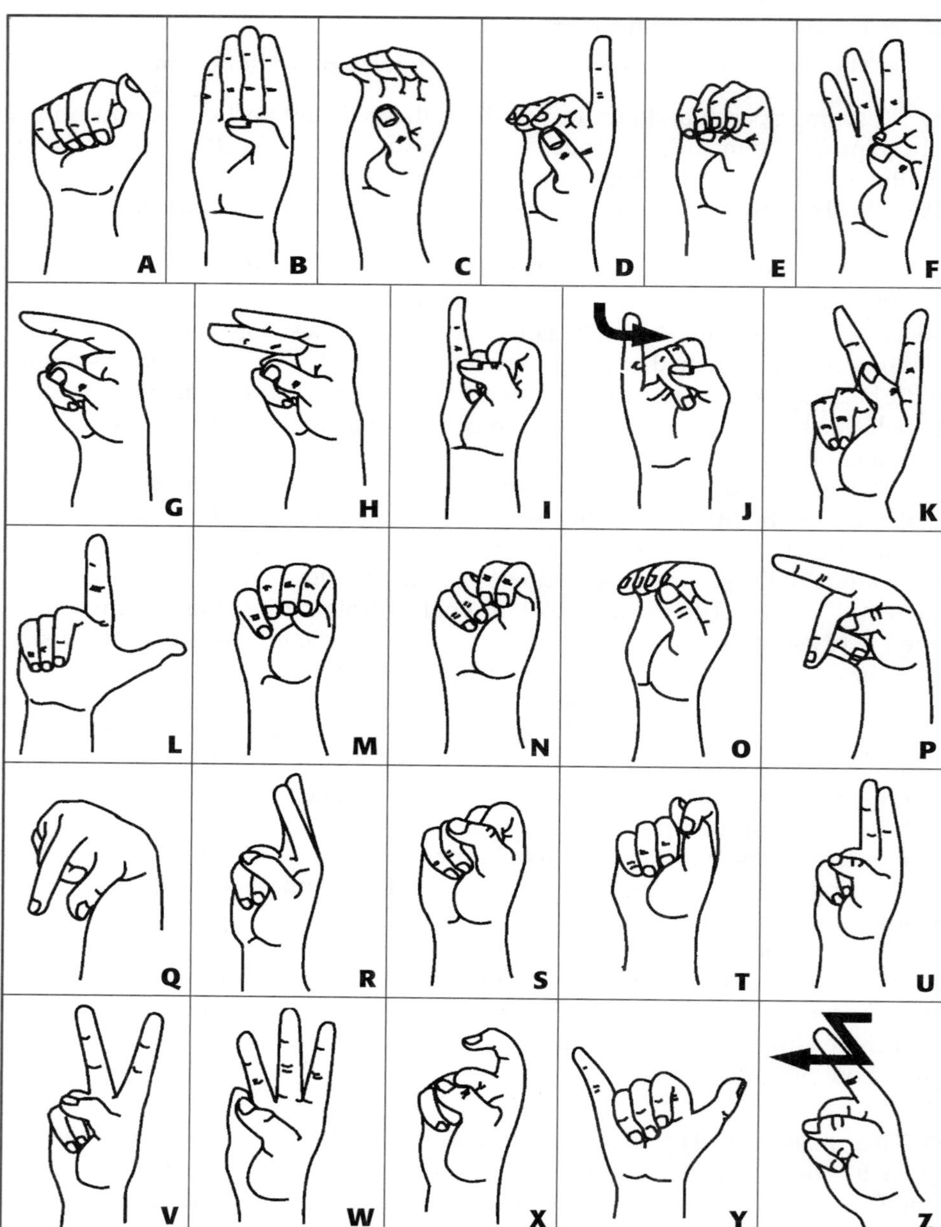

Figure 10.3
The Manual Alphabet

Source: T. Humphries, C. Padden, T. J. O'Rourke, *A Basic Course in American Sign Language* (Silver Spring, MD: T.J. Publishers, 1980). Reprinted by permission.

English, and because there is no widely practiced method of writing in ASL, it has not traditionally been used as the primary language of instruction for children who are deaf. Instead, sign language systems that have been designed to represent English manually are usually used for educational purposes, since it is thought that their correspondence to reading and writing in English is closer. In these English-order systems, the intent is that every word and every inflection (for example, verb tense markers like *-ed* and *-ing*) of English are signed. The

~ Fingerspelling: Critical for Literacy Development

Fingerspelling—representing the letters of the alphabet on the fingers—may be a critical bridge for deaf and hard-of-hearing children in learning English. Children should be exposed to fingerspelling on a regular basis. This exposure begins with the child's identification as deaf or hard of hearing. Infants and toddlers should be immersed in fingerspelling. They may not immediately understand the letters, but the exposure will prepare them for acquisition of reading and literacy.

Experts emphasize the importance of practice. It is important to make transitions between the letters of words as smoothly as possible. For example, do not fingerspell *CAT* as *C* pause *A* pause *T* pause. Instead, hold the wrist steady and practice until able to move easily between the letters *C-A-T.*

Two techniques—the Sandwich Technique and the Chaining Technique—are useful in reading to deaf children. In the Sandwich Technique, signs are "sandwiched" between fingerspellings. Individuals fingerspell the word or the phrase that appears in the book, then sign the word or phrase, then fingerspell it again (Blumenthal-Kelly, 1995; Humphries and MacDougall, 1997).

In the Chaining Technique, the process is elongated. Individuals point to the word in the book, fingerspell it, sign it, then point to the printed word again.

REFERENCES: Blumenthal-Kelly, A. (1995). Fingerspelling interaction: A set of deaf parents and their deaf daughter. In C. Lucas (Ed.), *Sociolinguistics in Deaf Communities* (pp. 62–73). Washington, DC: Gallaudet University. Humphries, T., & MacDougall, F. (1997). *Adding Links to the Chain: Discourse Strategies in American Sign Language Teaching.* Unpublished manuscript. Teacher Education Program, University of California, San Diego.

SOURCE: David R. Schleper, "Fingerspelling: Critical for Literacy Development," *Odyssey* (Summer 2000), p. 10. Washington, DC: Laurent Clerc National Deaf Education Center, Gallaudet University.

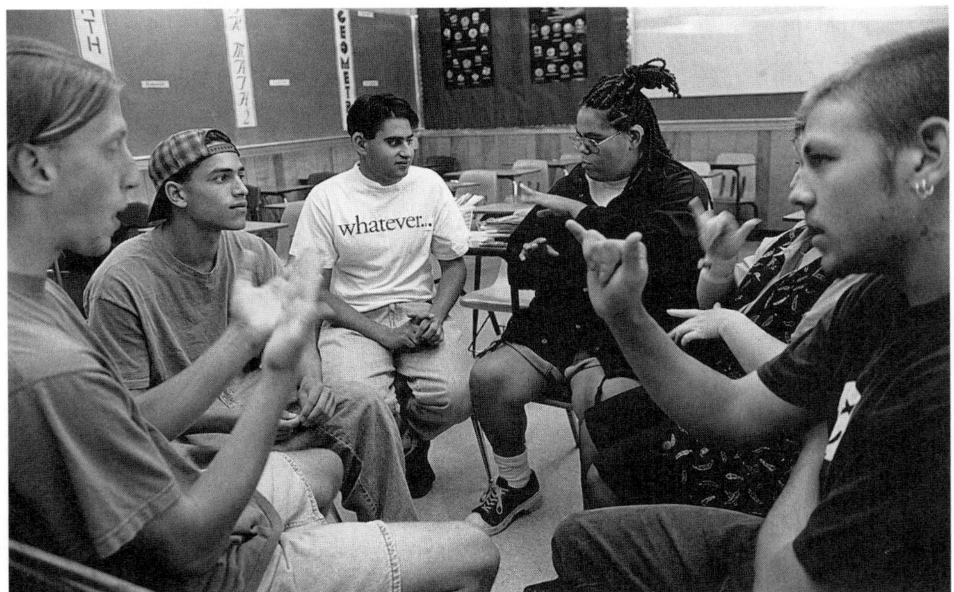

High school students who are deaf need the experience of communicating effectively with their peers. (© 2001 David Bacon/Impact Visuals)

most commonly used of these systems are Signed English (Bornstein, 1990b) and Signing Exact English (SEE II) (Gustason, 1990).

Other terms are used to describe communication systems that incorporate elements of manual communication. The use of fingerspelling along with speech is called the *Rochester method*. Using an English-order sign system along with speech is *simultaneous communication*. *Cued speech* is a system that uses hand signals near the face (not signs or fingerspelling) to differentiate speech sounds that look alike in speech reading (Kipila & Williams-Scott, 1990). The philosophy that advocates the use of whatever communication system (ASL, English-order signs, speech, speech reading, fingerspelling, gestures, etc.) is appropriate for a given child at a given time is called **total communication.**

Total communication advocates the use of the communication system appropriate for a child at a given time.

■ ***Communication Controversies*** Since education of deaf children began in the sixteenth century, teachers have argued passionately about the best method of instruction. Advocates of the oral approach have maintained that teaching the child who is deaf to speak and to use residual hearing and speech reading to comprehend language provides the skills the individual needs to function both in the hearing world and in the community of deaf people. But teaching oral language and speech to a child who is profoundly deaf is an extremely difficult and laborious process.

Children taught with the oral method do best when early diagnosis is combined with early amplification and family involvement.

The best results seem to occur when early diagnosis is combined with early amplification and early and consistent family involvement. Family involvement is the key. Typically, a preschool-aged child who is deaf speaks only a handful of words. Therefore, the family's commitment to teaching the child to talk is crucial in an oral program, and parents must be willing to experience the slow growth of communication skills in their child. For children who are hard of hearing, the growth of oral skills proceeds significantly faster; they frequently can learn oral language in the regular classroom, with support from a resource teacher or a speech-language specialist.

However, for many children who are deaf—those whose hearing loss is diagnosed after age 2, those with additional handicapping conditions, or those whose families are unable to supply them with the complete support that they need—the oral approach is frequently not satisfactory. During the 1960s and 1970s, dissatisfaction with the oral approach grew, and school programs using total communication proliferated. By 1999, about 55 percent of the students included in the Annual Survey of Hearing-impaired Children and Youth attended schools in which some form of sign was used (Gallaudet Research Institute, 1999).

Total communication was designed to use any and all methods of communicating with students who are deaf—speech, fingerspelling, English-order sign language, American Sign Language—depending on the learning needs of the student at the moment (Garretson, 1976). In practice, however, most professionals equate total communication with the simultaneous method—using speech and manually coded English together.

Many in the Deaf community believe that ASL should be the first language of all children who are deaf.

Today the controversies in the field revolve not so much around whether speech or sign should be used but on which form of sign should be used in the classroom. Some professionals believe that advocates of the oral approach are operating under the clinical model of understanding deafness, where it is still seen as deviant; they believe that oralists want to turn children who are deaf into children who are hearing (Paul & Quigley, 1990). Proponents of viewing Deafness as a cultural difference rather than as a disability believe that American Sign Language should be the first language of all children who are deaf and that therefore it should be the first language taught in schools (Drasgow, 1998). These professionals, both deaf and hearing, use theories of first- and second-language acquisition of spoken language to support their argument that once fluency in the first language is acquired, second-language learning can and will follow (Drasgow, 1998). They propose teaching ASL first and then, when children have a solid ASL base, introducing English as a second language (Newell, 1991). Other professionals object to this model, suggesting that since there is no widely accepted written form of ASL, reading and writing skills in English will be introduced too late. Also, since ASL is used without speech, young children may not be given the opportunity to develop speech skills through listening and observation.

Only research, study, and the introduction of model programs will demonstrate whether teaching ASL as a first language in a bilingual program will ultimately succeed in improving the English literacy of children who are deaf, and in the process make them fluent ASL users who are comfortable in their own culture as well as in the "hearing world." We must continue to try to improve services, and therefore opportunities, to children who are deaf, and new ideas and efforts to this end deserve our support.

Curriculum

Students who are deaf or hard of hearing should learn the same subject matter in school as their hearing peers, but there is some evidence that they do not. Donald Moores (2001) believes that the emphasis on teaching communication skills in most programs for students who are deaf or hard of hearing has resulted in neglect of the traditional academic areas such as math, science, and social studies. Moores's own research (Kluwin & Moores, 1985) concludes that students with hearing loss who are mainstreamed for math at the secondary level have higher levels of math achievement than those who are in special classes. These researchers suggest that the more rigorous subject-area training of the secondary math teachers may be responsible for the superior achievement of their students with hearing loss. As Moores (2001) suggests, educators must pay more attention to the teaching of traditional content areas in order to prevent their students with hearing loss from experiencing a major "knowledge gap."

There is evidence that students with hearing loss do not learn the same subject matter as their hearing peers.

David Stewart and Thomas Kluwin (2001) believe that, because of lack of experiences and adequate opportunities for communication in their home environments, the curriculum for deaf students must reflect these themes:

Curriculum should incorporate authentic experiences.

- *Creating authentic experiences.* Teachers must engineer experiences for students that are directly tied to the teaching content.
- *Integrating vocabulary development.* Teachers must make words visible and teach them as part of broader concepts and in meaningful contexts.
- *Creating opportunities for self-expression.* Deaf students need opportunities to practice elaborate verbal skills, as well as opportunities for defining and refining ideas.
- *Providing deaf role models.* Deaf role models let deaf students know "This is what you need to do to succeed."

As we mentioned earlier in the chapter, in addition to the study of communication and the content areas, many professionals advocate for the study of Deaf culture in the school curriculum. There is hope that an understanding of the history and heritage of people who are deaf will help students "develop an appreciation for both their hearing and Deaf cultural and linguistic linkages with people throughout the world and . . . appreciate more fully the value and relevance of their educational experience" (Luetke-Stahlman & Luckner, 1991, p. 347).

Teachers and researchers alike are focusing on improving the literacy of deaf children.

Today the focus of the curriculum for most deaf students is in the area of literacy. The skills involved in learning to read and write and the application of those skills in life have not traditionally come easily to deaf students, and teachers and researchers are working to address the best ways for deaf students to acquire literacy skills (Luetke-Stahlman, 1999; Paul, 1998; Schirmer, 1994; Stewart & Kluwin, 2001). The Shared Reading Project has provided models of deaf adults reading books to deaf children that have demonstrated the importance of reading "aloud" (Schleper, 1997), and teachers of deaf children are taking the "best practices" for teaching reading from general education and applying them in their work with deaf children. Stewart and Kluwin apply their "themes" to the teaching of literacy:

> The strategies that we described for teaching literacy are similar to those for teaching other subject matter to deaf students. Authentic activities must be incorporated into the learning experience, the students must be provided with opportunities to talk about what they are reading and writing, and modeling and guidance must be provided to help them overcome their lack of proficiency in the English language. (p. 109)

Assessment

Many tests are not reliable or valid for use with test takers who are deaf.

Undertaking an educational assessment with a student who is deaf or hard of hearing is a difficult endeavor, because the typical student's English-language competency is often significantly delayed for his or her age (Paul & Quigley, 1990). As a result, each test, with directions and questions written (or spoken) in English, becomes a test not of its content but of the student's mastery of English. When a student does not do well on a test, it is often because he or she does not understand the language of the directions or the test items. Rephrasing or paraphrasing the language makes the test standardization invalid, so the results cannot be used comparatively (Salvia & Ysseldyke, 1998). Although it is possible to work around these complicating factors, it takes skill and considerable experience in communication to obtain valid assessment results with students with hearing loss, particularly those who are deaf (Eccarius, 1997).

School Placement

Deaf and hard-of-hearing students can be found in every educational setting.

Students who are deaf and hard of hearing can be found in a wide variety of educational settings, from the regular classroom to the residential school. According to the Gallaudet Research Institute (1999), about 57 percent of the children with hearing loss were placed in the regular class or regular class with resource room, 30 percent were in separate classes on regular campuses, and 29 percent were in special schools or residential schools (the numbers don't add up to 100 percent because some children were enrolled in more than one of these options). Let us discuss the variations on those three placement options.

■ ***The General Education Classroom*** More and more deaf or hard-of-hearing students are included in the general education classroom. From that classroom base they may receive a variety of specialized services. Their classroom amplification devices, whether they be personal hearing aids, cochlear implants, or classroom hearing aids connected to a teacher microphone, may be evaluated regularly by the school audiologist; they may receive direct services in speech, signs, or the development of auditory skills from the itinerant teacher with a specialization in hearing loss or from the speech-language therapist; perhaps they receive extra help with communication skills or academic subjects from the resource teacher, who is also a specialist in hearing loss. Students who participate in school programs with their hearing peers are likely to have more residual hearing than those who do not (*Annual Survey of Deaf and Hard-of-Hearing Children and Youth, 1996–1997*); they are also likely to have better communication skills.

Moores and Kluwin (1986) found that three factors—academic achievement or ability, communication skill, and personal or social adjustment—should be considered when deciding whether to mainstream a student with hearing loss. According to these authors, most mainstreaming is for nonacademic activities, followed by vocational education. Academic integration of students who are deaf and hard of hearing is less frequent and more selective. Integration occurs most frequently in mathematics classes and least often in English classes. It appears that in many school programs, although students with hearing loss enjoy proximity to their hearing peers, the amount of *meaningful* academic integration between the two groups is surprisingly low. Inclusion has sparked much debate among professionals, with many arguing that the general education classroom does not provide an optimal communication environment for students who are deaf (Stinson & Lang, 1995).

Teachers should consider a student's academic achievement, communication skill, and social adjustment when contemplating inclusion for a student with hearing loss.

Some students with hearing loss will be integrated in the regular classroom with a sign language interpreter (see the accompanying box, "A Closer Look: Collaboration: Get to Know Your Student's Interpreter"); others will rely on their speech-reading skills and residual hearing to gain information in the classroom. Most integrated students, whether they are in the regular classroom full time or part time, will need preferential seating so they are close enough to the teacher or other speaker to speech-read. Remember that in a noisy setting students with hearing loss must rely heavily on vision to obtain information; often if they are not looking at the source of the sound, they are not "hearing" it or getting the information. The accompanying box, "Communication Tips for Deaf and Hard-of Hearing Children in the Classroom," outlines some strategies designed to eliminate classroom problems.

■ ***Special Classes*** A special class is composed of a group of students who are deaf and hard of hearing of similar age and who are taught on an elementary, middle school, or high school campus by a specialist teacher of deaf and hard-of-hearing students. More and more children with hearing loss are attending special classes on public school campuses, because this placement provides a home base for integrating these students with their hearing peers.

Some students in the special class are integrated with their hearing peers for academic subjects, and others for subjects like art, music, or physical education; still others may have contact with their hearing peers only at recess and lunch. The amount of time each student spends with hearing peers is specified on his or her individualized education program (IEP). Although characteristics of the student are obviously of prime importance in the decision whether or not to integrate, the availability of willing and competent regular education teachers to work with the students with hearing loss is often what makes or breaks the opportunity for the student.

A closer look

Collaboration: Get to Know Your Student's Interpreter

Interpreters provide an essential service to both students and teachers in classrooms. Whether you are working with an oral interpreter or a sign language interpreter, it will be important to work collaboratively with that person to ensure that your student is receiving the kind of assistance you intend (Seal, 2000).

Oral interpreters silently repeat, with clear but unexaggerated lip movements, the message of another speaker. Why are they necessary? Try putting earplugs into your own ears. You will find that lipreading (also called speech reading) is extremely difficult, and some people are much easier to lipread than others. People who have mustaches and beards, who speak very quickly, or who move as they speak and turn their backs on the student (such as an instructor at a blackboard) are among those difficult to lipread. Many adults and students with hearing loss who use the oral method to communicate prefer to have the help of an oral interpreter in difficult communication circumstances (Northcott, 1984).

Sign language interpreters translate the spoken message into signs. Sometimes they provide a word-for-word translation, but if you have ever watched a fluent sign interpreter interpret a song, you will know that sometimes whole concepts can be communicated in a sign or two, and sometimes very beautifully. Since most sign interpreters in American classrooms are interpreting English, they usually sign in an English-order system. Often sign interpreters use Pidgin Sign English—ASL signs in English order—and sometimes they silently articulate the words they are signing. Teachers should know what form of sign system the interpreter is using and whether that conforms to the expectations of the school district, the student, and the student's family. The most competent sign interpreters are certified by the National Registry of Interpreters for the Deaf; they have often undergone extensive and rigorous training in sign language and interpreting to prepare for their work (Frishberg, 1986).

Often educational interpreters are asked to perform additional duties within the school or classroom, such as tutoring, general classroom assistance, educational planning, and sign language instruction (Stuckless, Avery, & Hurwitz, 1989). Teachers should consider two factors when asking the interpreter for this kind of assistance. First and foremost, will the additional responsibility interfere with interpreting for the student? This should be the absolute priority responsibility for the interpreter. Second, is the interpreter qualified to perform the additional responsibility? Most educational interpreters are not trained as teachers or teacher's aides; they should provide tutoring and educational planning only under the close supervision of the classroom teacher.

Leah Ilan is an interpreter in Los Angeles who has a busy career as both an oral and sign language interpreter. Leah believes that the most important factors in the relationship between the classroom teacher and the interpreter are communication and trust, and that the better the interpreter knows the teacher, the better work she does. Leah finds oral interpreting somewhat more difficult than sign interpreting. She describes the job as "sounding out every single sound and making it visible—with the mouth, jaw, eyes, and facial expression. I use it all." Leah finds the need for concentration greater with oral interpreting, since the oral "consumer"—the person with hearing loss—relies on small parts of speech and word endings for comprehension. She hastens to add that sign interpreting is not easy; in fact, the preference now is that sign interpreters work in teams of two on long assignments. This allows sign interpreters periods of rest and avoids the appearance of hand and arm injuries such as carpal-tunnel syndrome, which can limit or end their careers.

■ ***Residential Schools*** The deinstitutionalization movement (see Chapter 1) has had an important influence on the education of children who are deaf. Twenty years ago, most children with hearing loss attended large residential schools, either as day students or as residents. These schools hold a special place in the heart of the Deaf community. Many people who were deaf had left their homes to live at residential schools when they were very young; they learned to communicate there, made their lifelong friends there, met their spouses there, and settled in the surrounding area. They were anxious that their own deaf children attend these schools, too.

The concept of the "least restrictive environment" in IDEA has mandated a less segregated school setting for most children who are deaf, and the nature of residential schools has changed dramatically since the law was signed by President Ford in 1975, much to the dismay of many members of the Deaf community. Student enrollment has declined notably (Moores, 2001). Some of the schools have closed; many of them have become centers for students who are deaf with multiple disabilities; most have become day schools.

The nature of residential schools has changed dramatically since 1975, when IDEA mandated less segregated school settings.

With a wider range of program options available in public schools, some professionals, often from outside the field of deafness, have seen very little justification for the removal of a child from his or her family in order to attend school. Nonetheless, many members of the Deaf community and professionals in the field of deafness continue to fight for the right to choose a residential school for a child who is deaf. The schools are sometimes seen as the birthplace of Deaf culture in this country, places where students who are deaf can develop their own positive identity rather than being forced to accept the values and norms of the hearing world.

Residential schools are often places where students can develop positive identities.

Educational Quality for Deaf Students

In 1986, Congress established the Commission on the Education of the Deaf to assess the quality of all educational services provided to students who are deaf, from infancy and early childhood through postsecondary and adult education. Eight of the twelve commissioners were deaf or hard of hearing. The commission's 1988 report, *Toward Equality*, came to a strong and serious conclusion: The present status of education for persons who are deaf in the United States is unsatisfactory.

The Commission on the Education of the Deaf assessed the quality of educational services for students who are deaf.

The commission made fifty-two recommendations for the improvement of educational services to students who are deaf. The report, calling for significant changes in the focus of educational services, was supported nearly unanimously by adults who were deaf as well as by other professionals in the field.

One of the commission's major recommendations was that the federal government emphasize English language development among students who are deaf—including vocal, visual, and written language. It also called for recognition of the "unique needs" of students who are deaf when developing their IEPs, including severity of hearing loss and the potential for using residual hearing; academic level and learning style; communicative needs and the preferred mode of communication; linguistic, cultural, social, and emotional needs; placement preference; individual motivation; and family support.

Another important recommendation urged that the federal Department of Education reconsider the emphasis of IDEA on the least restrictive environment and instead focus on the *appropriateness* of the placement of each student who is deaf. In appropriate placements for students who are deaf, the commissioners believed, educators and other staff members must have the skills needed to

The commission focused on appropriate placement of students who are deaf rather than on the least restrictive environment.

~ Communication Tips for Deaf and Hard-of-Hearing Children in the Classroom

Classrooms often move at a fast pace. Making sure that the deaf or hard-of-hearing child has access to everything that is going on will be of the utmost importance. Here are some considerations that may help facilitate communication in the classroom. Many of these strategies, which make the classroom a more visual environment, will be helpful for all of the children in the classroom.

For All Deaf or Hard-Of-Hearing Students

- The student should have a clear view of the faces of the teacher and the other students.
- Do not seat the student facing bright lights or windows where a glare or strong backlighting will make it difficult to see the faces of others.
- Remember that the best place for a deaf or hard-of-hearing student may change with the teaching situation. Make sure the student feels free to move about the room for ease of communication.

For Students Depending on Spoken Language Communication

- When possible, seat the student close to the teacher's desk for the best listening and viewing advantage.
- Familiarize yourself with how to check a child's hearing aid.
- Do not exaggerate mouth movements or shout; this may cause distortion of the message through the hearing aid and cause greater difficulty for the student.
- If communication breakdowns occur, try repair strategies such as rephrasing the message, saying it at a slower pace, or writing the message when appropriate.

For Students Depending on Visual Communication

- Try to remove "visual noise" (visual interference) from communication situations (e.g., bottle on table, door open, paper in hand while signing, jewelry of signer, overhead projector in the way).

communicate with the student. Bowe (1991) explained that these skills might include ASL fluency, Signed English ability, or clear enunciation. The Department of Education could look to the communication capabilities of the staff rather than the "least restrictive" nature of the setting.

In 1992 the federal government issued new policy guidelines relative to the education of students who are deaf in response to the commission report (Department of Education, 1992). The guidelines describe the current status of students who are deaf and identify the primacy of their needs for direct and meaningful communication with teachers and peers, which may be a primary consideration in making educational placement decisions. The box, "Improving Educational Quality," summarizes the priorities for developing an IEP for the student who is deaf.

Consideration of appropriate placement must recognize the communication needs of the child.

The guidelines make a crucial point: "Any setting, *including a regular classroom* [italics added], that prevents a child who is deaf from receiving an appropriate education that meets his or her needs, including communication needs, is not the LRE [least restrictive environment] for that child" (Department of Education, 1992, p. 49275). So the regular classroom may not always be the least re-

- When a sign language interpreter is being used in the classroom, make sure the interpreter has an opportunity to complete the message before moving on to the next point.

Facilitating Classroom Discussions

- When possible, have students sit in a circle.
- Remind students to speak one at a time.
- Point to the student who will speak next. Wait for the deaf or hard-of-hearing student to locate the speaker.

DO's That Will Help Deaf or Hard-of-Hearing Students

- DO use as many visual aids as possible. Use written instructions and summaries, and write key words and concepts on the blackboard. Utilize captioned films when possible.
- DO use attention-getting techniques when they are needed: touch the student lightly on the shoulder, wave your hands, or flash the lights in the classroom.
- DO set up a buddy system to help deaf or hard-of-hearing students with taking notes, clarifying assignments, etc.
- DO ask questions and spend individual time with deaf or hard-of-hearing students periodically to make sure they are following the instructions.

DON'T's to Keep in Mind

- DON'T change the topic of conversation quickly without letting the deaf or hard-of-hearing students know that the topic has changed.
- DON'T talk with your back to the class, your face obstructed by a book, or with a pencil in your mouth.
- DON'T call attention to misunderstandings or speech errors in front of the class. If this becomes a problem, discuss it with the child's family or other support personnel who may be working with the child.

Source: Developed by: Debra Nussbaum, Audiologist, Kendall Demonstration Elementary School Laurent Clerc National Deaf Education Center, Gallaudet University, Series Number 4009.

strictive environment for the child who is deaf; consideration of appropriate placement must include a priority placed on the communication needs of the child. The guidelines go further to conclude that, for some children, a special school may be the least restrictive environment in which their needs can be met.

Although it is too soon to measure the effect of these guidelines on educational decision-making for students who are deaf, there is little doubt that they will have a significant effect on placement decisions, as well as provide ammunition for the fight of the Deaf community against full inclusion.

Technological Advances

Many of the advances in services and opportunities for people who are deaf have occurred in the area of technology. Improved hearing aids, telecommunication devices and relay systems, and television captioning have made life more convenient and everyday experiences more accessible for many people with hearing loss.

~ Improving Educational Quality

Considerations for the IEP. When writing an IEP for a child with hearing loss, the team should consider the following:

- The child's communication needs and the family's preferred mode of communication
- Severity of hearing loss and potential for using residual hearing
- Academic level
- Social, emotional, and cultural needs, including opportunities for peer interactions and communication

Least Restrictive Environment. The least restrictive environment for the child who is deaf is the setting that best meets the child's needs, including communication needs. In some cases, the general education classroom may not be the least restrictive environment.

Source: U.S. Department of Education, "Guidelines for Educational Programs for Deaf Students," *Federal Register* (1992), pp. 49275–49276.

Hearing Aids

Twenty-five years ago amplification was just emerging from the period in which it was viewed as an imposition by audiologists and other technocrats on helpless children (Ross, 1986). According to Mark Ross, at that time hearing aids were worn primarily by young children. Older children refused to wear the relatively cumbersome "body aids" that were widely used then, and most students did not wear their hearing aids outside the classroom.

Modern hearing aids are much more efficient and compact than their predecessors.

Hearing aids today are considerably more efficient. They have been reduced in size, so they are more appealing cosmetically, and the majority of children are now fitted with behind-the-ear aids. More important, their capabilities have improved, and they can be designed to match each individual's hearing loss. Most children can benefit from wearing two hearing aids. New designs in hearing aids include those that have been miniaturized to the point that they fit completely in the ear. Although these tiny and lightweight in-the-ear hearing aids are just beginning to be recommended for young children or profoundly deaf users, they are prescribed more frequently for adolescents and adults, who often have great concerns about the visibility of their hearing aids.

Digital hearing aids can be customized for each person's hearing loss.

In the last few years hearing aid technology has changed and improved dramatically (Sweetow & Tate, 1999). Today's newest hearing aids are digital—they can be programmed by computer and customized to match an individual's hearing loss and characteristics of the environment. The traditional analog hearing aid amplified all sounds to the same volume. That means that in the classroom, for example, the teacher's voice, children talking, and the sounds of the hallway outside would be heard at a similar volume. Digitally programmed hearing aids can improve the wearer's ability to hear in the presence of background noise, and can be set to work differently in different listening environments.

Not all children need digital hearing aids, and they are considerably more expensive than analog aids. Families must discuss the pros and cons of this expense with their audiologist before committing to digital hearing aids (Sweetow

& Tate, 1999). It is likely that the appearance and the functioning of hearing aids will continue to improve through the refinement of digital-based technology.

Cochlear Implants

Researchers around the country have been surgically inserting **cochlear implants** in a relatively small number of profoundly deaf children with sensorineural hearing loss. Although the cochlear implant is not a cure for deafness, implants do appear to improve the perception of sound. The implants have become a source of controversy, however, as the accompanying box, "Cochlear Implants," explains.

Assistive Listening Devices

Although a hearing aid makes all sounds in the environment louder, assistive listening devices increase the loudness of a desired sound—the teacher's voice, the actors on a stage, or the voice on the telephone. There are different types of assistive listening devices for different settings: Some are used with hearing aids, and some without. An audiologist can help a teacher or an individual determine which assistive listening device will be most helpful (American Speech-Language-Hearing Association, 1997).

Telecommunication Devices

Until fairly recently, most people who were deaf did not have access to telephone services; when they wanted to send a message, they wrote a letter and waited for a response, or drove across town. This began to change in 1964 when Robert Weitbrecht, an American physicist who was profoundly deaf, discovered a way for two teletype machines to communicate with each other over a standard telephone line (Bellefleur, 1976). This device became the teletypewriter (TTY). Since then, the use of **telecommunication devices for the deaf (TDDs)** has slowly grown to the point where most adolescents and adults with hearing loss have access to this means of communication. TDDs are telephones with small screens that display the message of the sender. The system works like this: One person dials the number of a friend. The phone rings, and a light flashes in the home of the person receiving the call. When the receiver is picked up and placed in the cradle of the TDD, the two people can begin to type their communication into the TDD. The messages appear on paper, or, in the newest models, on a tiny screen on the TDD. Many agencies and businesses now routinely train their employees to use the TDD; they are used for business as well as social calls.

Today most people with hearing loss can use TDDs.

Since the passage of the Americans with Disabilities Act (1990), most states have developed telephone relay systems that allow a TDD user to communicate directly with a hearing person who does not have a TDD. The TDD user dials a relay operator, who also has a TDD. The relay operator then dials the number of the person with whom the TDD user wishes to communicate and reads the messages from the TDD user to the other person. That person responds orally, and the operator then types the oral message into the TDD for the TDD user. This goes on until the two people have finished their conversation, when they sign off. The ADA requires that all telephone companies offer relay systems to TDD users twenty-four hours a day, seven days a week. This national relay system allows TDD users access to every telephone in the United States.

TDD users now can access any telephone in the United States.

A closer look

Cochlear Implants

A cochlear implant—"one of the twentieth century's most consequential developments in communication" (Niparko, 2000, p. 1)—is an electronic device designed to provide sound information for adults and children who have sensorineural hearing loss in both ears and obtain limited benefit from appropriate hearing aids. In the last thirty years, the technology has evolved from a device with a single electrode (or channel) to systems that transmit more sound information through multiple electrodes (or channels). The cochlear implant has been approved for use with children since 1990. A small but growing number of children with deafness are currently using cochlear implants; the *Annual Survey* done by the Gallaudet Research Institute reported that 4.4 percent of students in surveyed programs had cochlear implants (Gallaudet Research Institute, 1999). Since the implant is expensive and not routinely covered by medical insurance, some are concerned that it is only available to relatively affluent families.

Advocates such as Dr. Mary Jo Osberger, a researcher who has studied children with cochlear implants, assert that they can help children who do not benefit from hearing aids develop speech and language understanding and skills. She says that "no other sensory aid has had such a dramatic impact on improving the acquisition and use of spoken language by children with profound hearing impairments." The earlier the children receive implants, the greater their chances of improvement.

Recent research suggests that the benefits of the cochlear implant vary greatly among individuals, but in general, children with cochlear implants surpass children who wear conventional hearing aids in speech perception, speech production, and speech intelligibility (Cheng & Niparko, 2000; Kirk, 2000). The best outcomes appear in children who receive their implants early in life, who undergo a period of intensive training after the implant, and who have had the implant for at least two years.

However, the implant has been called "cultural genocide" by many in the Deaf community who believe American Sign Language is the linguistic base for a separate culture. Their response is built on a legacy of failed attempts to teach deaf children oral communication—in their view, to be more like hearing children. In the view of Harlan Lane, a psychology professor at Northeastern University, "It's simply unethical to use force, surgery, or education to take children who would normally be members of a linguistic minority and try to make them into members of another linguistic group."

To many, the argument implies that deaf children belong to the Deaf community and not to their hearing parents, a view to which people like Donna Morere take exception. "There is a large segment within the community that identifies with Deaf culture and feels like hearing parents are not competent to make a decision like choosing a cochlear implant for their children," she says.

Captioning

Closed captioning allows viewers with hearing loss to receive captions that parallel the verbal content of many TV programs.

Television captioning for viewers with hearing loss began as a system of open captioning in which captions that paralleled the verbal content of the television program appeared on the bottom of every viewer's screen. Today, though, a system called **closed captioning** exists. Viewers with hearing loss can buy a decoder that, when connected to their television set, allows them to receive broadcasts carrying a coded signal that the decoder makes visible (Withrow, 1976). Since July 1, 1993, all TV sets thirteen inches or larger that are sold or built in the United States have been caption-chip-equipped (Bowe, 1991), allowing viewers to select.captioning of all available programs.

A closer look

Morere is in a unique position to see both sides of the debate. As a psychology professor at Gallaudet University—the only liberal arts college for the deaf in the United States—she has taught at the heart of the Deaf culture movement. Morere has normal hearing, but when her son, Thomas, was diagnosed as profoundly deaf, she was suddenly faced not with the abstract arguments of ethicists and anthropologists, but with the hard reality that her child could not hear.

Initially, Morere says, she was persuaded by some of her colleagues at Gallaudet who cautioned her against opting for a cochlear implant. Her eventual decision to go ahead with the procedure is one she now says she wished she'd made earlier. "When I saw what the CI could do, I really regretted the little over a year that he didn't have it," she says. "I'm so relieved when Thomas can ride his bicycle in the street with other kids and instead of having to run after him and drag him off the street when a car comes, I can yell 'Car!' and he will ride his bike off the street," Morere says. "If that was all the cochlear implant accomplished, that would have satisfied me, but it's gone way beyond that."

The National Organization of the Deaf (NAD) is an education and advocacy group that has long worked on behalf of deaf individuals. In its recent position statement on cochlear implants, the NAD has provided a measured (but still passionate) view of the potential drawbacks and benefits of the implant. The paper's authors describe the importance of viewing people who are deaf according to a "wellness model," emphasizing the large number of deaf adults who live productive lives; they believe that "cochlear implants are not appropriate for all deaf and hard-of-hearing children and adults" (p. 2) and that they do not eliminate or "cure" deafness. The recommendations to parents are sound:

> Despite the pathological view of deafness held by many within the medical profession, parents would benefit by seeking out opportunities to meet and get to know successful deaf and hard of hearing children and adults who are fluent in sign language and English, both with and without implants. The NAD encourages parents and deaf adults to research other options besides implantation. If implantation is the object of choice, parents should obtain all information about the surgical procedure, surgical risks, post-surgical auditory and speech training requirements, and potential benefits and limitations so as to make informed decisions. (pp. 3-4)

Local branches of the NAD would be a good place for families to start looking for such models.

Sources: Adapted from Mary Jo Osberger and Harlan Lane, "The Debate: Cochlear Implants in Children," *Hearing Health, 9* (2) (February–March 1993), pp. 19–22. NAD Position Statement on Cochlear Implants: www.nad.org/infocenter/newsroom/papers/CochlearImplants.html.

The Commission on Education of the Deaf described the potential benefits of captioning for older Americans with hearing loss, as well as for people who are learning English, preschool children, and illiterate adults (Bowe, 1991). Captioning can thus potentially assist many more people than the relatively small number who were born deaf or acquired deafness early in life.

Not all television programs are closed captioned, but because of the rapidly expanding market for such services, television networks are making an increasing number of programs available to viewers with hearing loss. The Americans with Disabilities Act of 1990 requires that any television public service announcement that is produced with federal funds be captioned. Viewers with hearing loss and the National Captioning Institute are also working with television networks to increase the amount of real-time captioning on the screen (the immediate captioning of live television programs such as news broadcasts). The National Center to Improve Practice in Special Education Through Technology, Media, and Materials is a good place to start looking for captioned materials (http://www2.edc.org/NCIP/library/v&c/toc.htm).

Technology for Instruction

Since many students who are deaf are dependent on their sight for processing information, visual representation of course content is highly important. Classroom computers can provide a crucial supplement to the school curriculum. Use of the classroom computer for instruction and curricular support, practicing literacy skills, access to content, research resources, and communication with others will enrich learning opportunities for students who are deaf or hard of hearing. These and other new forms of technology have shown promise of becoming an integral part of classroom instruction (Lang, 1996). Internet sites for users who are deaf are proliferating (see Multimedia Resources at the end of this chapter).

The Center for Applied Special Technology (CAST) has developed *Bobby*, a system that can evaluate whether websites are accessible to users with hearing loss (and others with disabilities as well). Look for the Bobby icon (a picture of a British policeman, or Bobby, in his tall blue hat) to determine whether a website is accessible for students with disabilities, or **Bobby-approved** (http://www.cast.org/Bobby/AboutBobby313.cfm).

Websites that are accessible to people with disabilities are said to be Bobby-approved.

Summary

- Deafness is hearing loss that prevents the learning of language through hearing. Conductive hearing loss results from damage to the outer or middle ear and can usually be corrected. Sensorineural loss involves damage to the cochlea or auditory nerve and as of now cannot be corrected.
- The most common causes of hearing loss are otitis media, inherited genetic factors, rubella, meningitis, and premature birth. Approximately 26 percent of children with hearing loss have additional disabilities.
- Hearing loss is measured by an audiologist using a series of tests, including pure-tone tests. The results of these tests are illustrated by an audiogram.
- Language is the most critical area affected by hearing loss, especially because hearing loss is usually not identified until after language normally appears.
- The cognitive abilities of students who are deaf and hard of hearing as a group are the same as those of hearing individuals. Despite this, students with hearing loss frequently underachieve in school because of the heavy emphasis on English-language skills.
- The Deaf community views deafness as a culture rather than a deficit and urges that understanding of Deaf culture be integrated into the curriculum for students.
- Manual communication includes fingerspelling and signs. American Sign Language (ASL) is considered a language of its own and does not correspond

directly to English. Total communication uses oral, aural, and manual modes of communication and advocates adopting whatever system seems most appropriate for a child at a given time.

- Many students with hearing loss attend general education classes and use amplification devices, special services provided by an audiologist or itinerant teacher, or an oral or sign language interpreter.
- Hearing aids and telecommunication devices have greatly improved in recent years, and technological advances continue to provide opportunities for people with hearing loss to communicate freely across long distances.

Key Terms

deafness
hard of hearing
hearing impairment
Deaf community
hearing loss
residual hearing
congenital hearing loss
acquired hearing loss
prelingual deafness
postlingual deafness
conductive hearing loss
sensorineural hearing loss
mixed hearing loss
bilateral hearing loss
unilateral hearing loss
otitis media
otologist
audiologist
audiogram
Deaf culture
oral communication approach
auditory training
manual communication approach
fingerspelling
signs
American Sign Language (ASL)
total communication
cochlear implants
telecommunication devices for the deaf (TDDs)
closed captioning
Bobby-approved

Multimedia Resources

The Alexander Graham Bell Association for the Deaf (www.agbell.org) has published an excellent booklet for parents whose young child has been diagnosed with hearing loss. Called *So Your Child Has a Hearing Loss: Next Steps for Parents*, it is available free of charge from A.G. Bell. It's an excellent introduction to hearing loss for teachers as well.

Gallaudet University Press (http://gupress.gallaudet.edu) publishes a range of books of interest to deaf and hearing readers; many are about sign language. For teachers, there is *Come Sign with Us* by Jan C. Hafer and Robert M. Wilson, which describes activities for teaching children sign language. For parents, there is *You and Your Deaf Child,* by John W. Adams. There is also an extensive collection of books for children that incorporate sign language.

Handspeak is a sign language dictionary online that contains video illustrations of over 3,000 signs (www.handspeak.com). Another excellent source is the *American Sign Language Dictionary* at www.commtechlab.msu.edu/sites/aslweb/browser.htm.

HiP Magazine Online website: http://www.hipmag.org. This is a website tied to a paper magazine designed for "deaf and hard-of-hearing kids and their pals." Each issue contains *HiP Tips–A Teaching Guide for Professionals and Parents.*

The National Deaf Education Network and Clearinghouse (http://clerccenter.gallaudet.edu/clearinghouse/index.html) has a service called *Info to Go* that is an excellent source of additional information on deafness. *Info to Go*, formerly the National Information Center on Deafness, is a centralized source of accurate, up-to-date, objective information on topics dealing with deafness and hearing loss in the age group of 0–21. *Info to Go* responds to a wide range of questions received from the general public, deaf and hard-of-hearing people, their families, and professionals who work with them. It collects, develops, and disseminates information on deafness, hearing loss, and services and programs related to children with hearing loss from birth to age 21. Phone: (202) 651-5051, (202) 651-5052 TTY, (202) 651-5054 FAX. E-mail: Clearinghouse.Infotogo@gallaudet.edu.

Padden, Carol, and Tom Humphries. *Deaf in America: Voices from a Culture* (Cambridge, MA: Harvard University Press, 1988). This book, now a classic, focuses on the stories of people who are deaf and offers intriguing insights into those who share the culture of American Sign Language.

Schleper, David R. *Reading to Deaf Children: Lessons from Deaf Adults* (Washington, DC: Pre-College National Mission Programs, Gallaudet University, 1997). This book and the accompanying videotapes present strategies for reading to children with hearing loss culled from observations of deaf adults.

WHAT YOU CAN DO

1. Explore Deaf culture and interact with deaf individuals:
   - Contact an adult service agency to find out how services are provided to deaf people.
   - Volunteer to be a note-taker for a deaf student.
   - Volunteer at a nursing home for elderly people who are deaf.

2. How does your college or university provide support services to students with hearing loss? In particular, find out what types of career counseling are offered. How might these services be improved? With others in your class, create a list of career services that could be used by students who are deaf.

3. Devise a unit on deafness and Deaf culture to include in your curriculum. Its components might include the following:
   - What is sound? How is it made?
   - What are the parts of the ear? What causes deafness?
   - How does a cochlear implant work?
   - What is Deaf culture and the Deaf community?
   - Invite a mime group, signing song group, or Deaf theater group to visit your classroom.
   - Describe the types of manual languages and systems to transcribe them.
   - What are the abilities, attitudes, and accomplishments of deaf artists?
   - Who are some famous deaf people?
   - Making communication work: What can deaf students tell their hearing friends so that they can improve their communication?
   - Organize a Deaf Awareness Week at school.
   - Explore jobs and higher education opportunities for deaf students.

- Offer sign classes by students with hearing loss for hearing students.
- Visit or host pen pal programs with students who are deaf in other programs, states, or countries.

Source: Adapted from Barbara Luetke-Stahlman and John Luckner, *Effectively Educating Students with Hearing Impairments* (New York: Longman, 1991), p. 352. Copyright © 1991. Used by permission of the authors.

4. Visit some websites on the Internet to learn more about deafness and Deaf culture. For example:

- Deaf World Web: http://deafworldweb.org
- Gallaudet University: http://www.gallaudet.edu
- National Association for the Deaf: http://www.nad.org
- National Technical Institute for the Deaf: http://www.isc.rit.edu/~418www/

Children Who Are Blind and Have Low Vision

11

IN THIS chapter we discuss how a visual impairment can affect a child's learning and development. Students with visual impairments experience difficulty seeing even with corrective measures such as glasses. Thus educational goals related to learning to read, developing mobility, and planning for life after school are vital. As you read, think about the following questions:

Commonalities: **How should education for children with visual impairments be different from that of sighted students, and how should it be the same?**

Collaboration: **Who are the school professionals who must work together to plan a high-quality educational program for students with visual impairments?**

Can Do: **What can we do to promote the social acceptance of students with visual impairment?**

People who are sighted develop a concept of what it is like to be blind from maneuvering in the dark or wearing a blindfold during childhood games. As a result of these experiences, most of us believe that we understand what it is like to be blind. We are probably wrong. In the first place, our experiences are based on the condition of total blindness. Most people who are visually impaired respond to some visual stimuli, such as shadows, light and darkness, or moving objects. The majority of people with visual impairments can read print, either regular print or print that is magnified or enlarged; only 10 percent of students meeting the requirements of legal blindness use Braille as their primary learning medium (American Printing House for the Blind, 2001).

Second, some of our early experiences of "blindness" may have been negative or frightening because we lacked certain skills. Most people rely on vision for protection and information. So, during the course of our childhood games we were usually tempted to peek or turn on the light for reassurance and confirmation. In contrast, people who are blind receive instruction in daily living skills and rely on their other senses to gain information about their world. Most people who are blind can move independently around their homes and travel in the community; they are productively employed and active in their communities. Our negative or fearful concepts of blindness, therefore, do not reflect the real life of a person who is blind.

These common misconceptions about the ability of people who are visually impaired are important to remember when preparing to teach a child who is blind or visually impaired. We must look beyond our traditional view of blindness and our misconceptions to realize that, with specialized instruction, children with visual impairments are capable of succeeding in our classrooms.

Definitions and Terms

The term *visual impairment* covers all degrees of vision loss.

Like *hearing impairment*, **visual impairment** is an umbrella term that includes all levels of vision loss, from total blindness to uncorrectable visual limitations. A number of terms are used interchangeably to describe children whose vision is impaired, including *visually impaired, visually handicapped, visually disabled, blind, partially sighted*, and *low vision*.

The IDEA definition states that visual impairment, including blindness, is "an impairment in vision that, even with correction, adversely affects a child's educational performance. The term includes both partial sight (low vision) and blindness" (Knoblauch & Sorenson, 1998). It is helpful to think about the phrase *with correction* in this definition. Even with the best possible corrective lenses, these children have a vision problem that interferes with their learning at

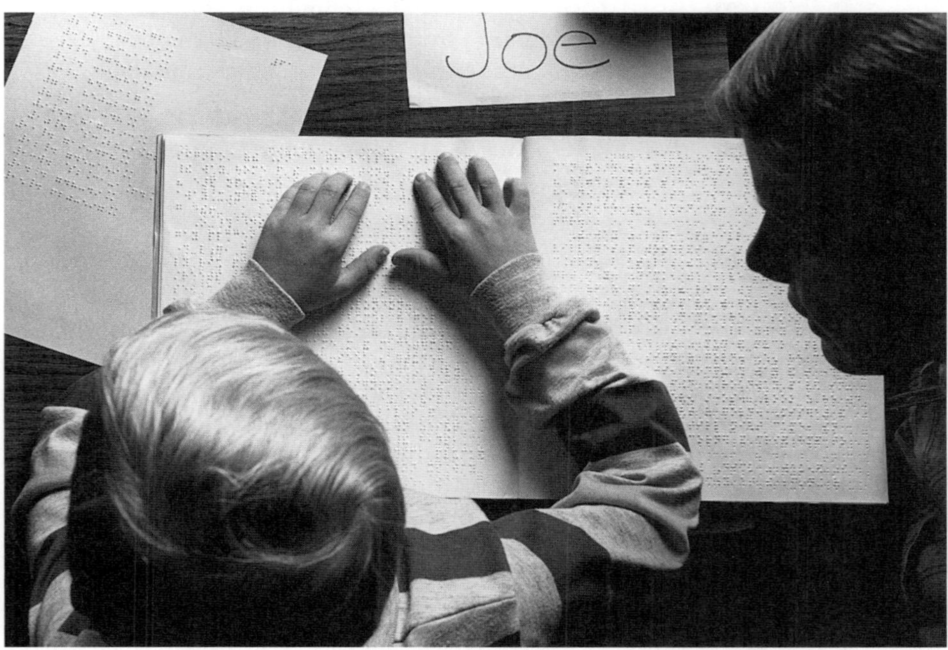

Reading Braille requires tactile recognition, decoding, and memory skills. (Will and Deni McIntyre/Photo Researchers, Inc.)

school. Many of us wear glasses or contact lenses that correct our vision. But we are not considered visually impaired, since our learning is not adversely affected.

It is important to distinguish between legal definitions and educational definitions. A person is considered **legally blind** when his or her **visual acuity,** or sharpness of vision, is 20/200 or worse in the better eye *with* correction, or when he or she has a visual field no greater than 20 degrees. If vision can be corrected through glasses or contact lenses to 20/200 or better, the person is not considered legally blind. The term *legal blindness* describes visual impairments that qualify a person for a variety of legal and social services. This definition is used to determine eligibility for governmental funding, tax deductions, rehabilitation, and other services. Although the legal definition is widely used, it is somewhat misleading, since many legally blind people have a good deal of useful vision.

Legal blindness refers to visual acuity of 20/200 or less in the better eye after correction or a visual field of less than 20 degrees.

For educators, actual measurements of visual acuity are less important than a description of how the student functions in school. **Educational definitions** are generally based on the way a student uses his or her vision in an educational setting. For educational purposes, children who use Braille may be considered blind, and those who read large print may be designated as having **"low vision."** Students with low vision are those whose primary source of information is visual (Hatlen, 2000a). Table 11.1 lists the levels of visual impairment and their educational implications. These definitions rely less on visual acuity measurements and more on **functional vision**—"what a person can do with his or her available vision" (Corn, DePreist, & Erin, 2000, p. 470). At times, students with exactly the same acuity will function very differently. In fact, professionals in the field of blindness and visual impairment often say that no two people see exactly alike (Augusto, 1996). Whereas one student might respond visually to educational tasks, the other might rely more on hearing or sense of touch, depending on his or her background, experience, type of visual impairment, and learning style. The real test of how well a student sees is how she accomplishes daily activities while using her sight as well as her other senses. An assessment

Educational definitions of visual impairment are based on whether the student reads print or Braille.

Functional vision refers to how well a person uses remaining vision.

Table 11.1 Educational Implications of Visual Impairments

Levels of Visual Impairment	Educational Implications
Total blindness	Students are totally blind or are able only to distinguish the presence or absence of light; they may learn best through tactile or auditory senses, although, if they do have some vision, they may use it effectively for orientation and mobility and other tasks.
Low vision	Students are severely visually impaired but may be able to see objects at near distances, sometimes under modified conditions, or may have limited use of vision under average circumstances.
Blindness in one eye	Students with vision in only one eye may or may not be considered visually impaired, depending on the vision in the sighted eye; they may have difficulty with depth perception and may need special consideration in physical education or other classroom activities.

of functional vision will provide the most useful information on how much the student will use her vision in your classroom. You may be asked to participate on a functional vision assessment team, which will be spearheaded by a vision specialist or orientation and mobility specialist with unique training in this area.

Prevalence

The American Printing House for the Blind (APH) annually compiles data regarding the number of children, birth through age 21, who receive federal support for educational materials (American Printing House for the Blind, 2001; see Table 11 .2). The APH reported that in 1998, 57,425 students enrolled in residential schools, public schools, programs for students who are multihandicapped, and rehabilitation programs were registered to receive such assistance. The APH register includes only those students who are, by legal definition, blind; other students with less severe visual impairments are not included. The *Twenty-second Annual Report to Congress* (2000) reported that students with visual impairments still account for just 0.5 percent of the total number of students aged 6–21 served under IDEA. As with many other handicapping conditions, accurate counts are difficult because of differences in definition and classification (Huebner, 2000). However, even when the highest estimates are used, visual impairments are still among the low-incidence (or least frequently occurring) disabling conditions in children. Visual impairment is much more common among adults, especially those aged 65 and older.

As many as 75 percent of students who are blind have additional disabilities as well.

A relatively large number of children who are visually impaired have additional disabilities as well. Although the exact number is hard to come by, it may be as high as 75 percent of children with visual impairments (Silberman, 2000).

How We See

The eye is a small but extremely complex structure that contains an immense network of nerves, blood vessels, cells, and specialized tissues (Ward, 2000). For most people, this complicated structure works quite efficiently; even if we need

Table 11.2 Prevalence of Visual Impairments, Birth through Age 21

Reading Medium	Number of Children Reported	Percentage
Visual readers (print readers)	14,461	25
Braille readers	5,461	10
Auditory readers	4,051	7
Prereaders	14,924	26
Nonreaders	18,528	32
Total	57,425	100

Source: American Printing House for the Blind (2001). *Distribution of Federal Quota*. Louisville, KY: American Printing House for the Blind, Inc. (http://www.aph.org/)

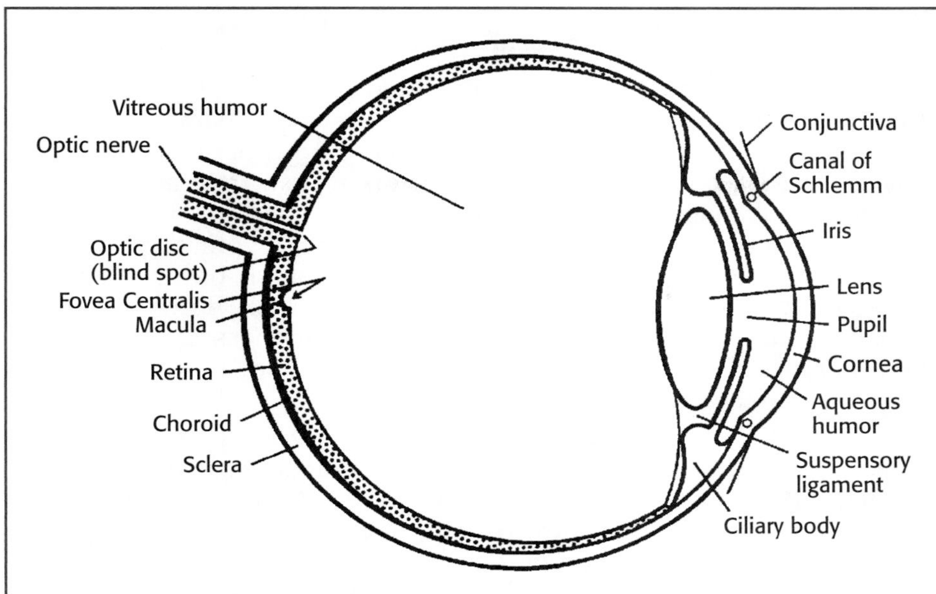

Figure 11.1
Structures of the Eye

Source: Used by permission of National Society to Prevent Blindness.

corrective lenses, most of us can see well. (Figure 11.1 shows the eye and its structures.) But impairments of vision can result from any interference with the passage of light as it travels from the outer surface of the eye, through the inner structures of the eye, and back through the visual pathways in the brain to the cortical brain centers.

Light rays pass through the cornea, pupil, and lens and are then projected onto the retina, which sends signals of the image by the optic nerve to the brain.

When we look at an object, the light rays reflecting off it first pass through the outer membrane of the eye, the transparent, smooth **cornea,** through the **pupil** (the opening in the center of the eye), and through the **lens,** a transparent structure that lies between the iris and the tissue inside the eyeball, called the **vitreous humor.** The muscles in the **iris,** or colored part of the eye, expand or contract according to the amount of light available. The lens focuses the light rays so that they form clear images where they strike the **retina,** a layer of specialized cells at the back of the eye. The light rays activate the special cells on the the retina, which then transmit signals of the images through the fibers of the **optic nerve,** which connects the eye to the brain, where they are interpreted. Damage to any of these structures, or a breakdown in the processing of visual information, can result in visual impairment. In the next section, we discuss some of the more common causes of visual impairment and their implications for learning.

Causes of Visual Impairment

Most visual impairments in children are congenital.

Most cases of visual impairment in school-age children are congenital in origin. Congenital conditions may be caused by heredity, maternal or fetal infection, or damage during fetal development or shortly after birth. Hereditary conditions include albinism, some forms of glaucoma, and retinitis pigmentosa. Other conditions, such as cataracts and underdevelopment or absence of parts of the eye structure, may be caused by damage during fetal development. It is important

~ Causes of Visual Impairment in Children

- ***Cortical visual impairment*** results from damage to the brain rather than to the eye. The occipital lobes in the brain contain the visual cortex, which may be thought of as the screen on which the visual fields are projected (Bishop, 1996). If they are damaged, the brain cannot receive the images from the eye. Causes of cortical visual impairment in infants and children are numerous; they include trauma and hydrocephaly. Children with this condition often have other disabilities as well (Ward, 2000).
- ***Retinopathy of prematurity* (ROP)** occurs most commonly in premature babies or even full-term babies suffering from respiratory distress syndrome (see Chapter 2) who require high levels of oxygen over an extended period of time for survival. With the advent of technology that allows very-low-birthweight babies to survive, new cases of ROP are becoming more frequent (Wright, 1997).
- In ***optic nerve hypoplasia*** and *optic nerve atrophy*, the optic nerve does not develop normally or degenerates, causing vision loss (Ward, 2000).
- ***Albinism*** is the congenital absence of pigmentation (including that of the eye), which can result in vision loss.
- ***Glaucoma*** is a leading cause of blindness across all age groups (Ward, 2000). It occurs when fluid within the eye cannot drain properly, resulting in a gradual increase of pressure within the eye and damage to the optic nerve. Warning signs of glaucoma are often overlooked because they are subtle and develop slowly. In advanced stages, symptoms include painful pressure, hazy vision, discomfort around bright lights, and excessive tearing. When left untreated, glaucoma can cause blindness; if it is diagnosed and treated in time, vision can be saved.
- A ***cataract*** is a clouding of the lens of the eye. Congenital cataracts occur in about 1 in 250 births (Ward, 2000). Children with cataracts will have difficulty seeing the board clearly and may need increased lighting or high-contrast educational materials.
- Diabetes can result in a condition known as ***diabetic retinopathy,*** another major cause of blindness in this country. The circulation problems associated with diabetes can result in damage to the retinal blood vessels, resulting in loss of vision. Although diabetic retinopathy can occur in children, it is most common in older persons who have had diabetes for a long period of time.

There are many other less frequently occurring causes of visual impairment on children and adults. For more information, consult an ophthalmology textbook, such as the Wright text cited above.

for classroom teachers to understand the eye conditions of their students, since the specific condition may affect what we expect for the child's visual functioning in the classroom. See the accompanying box, "Causes of Visual Impairment in Children," for additional details.

Effects of Visual Impairment

Effects on the Developing Person

Tasha is 9 years old and is in the fourth grade. She was born prematurely and is blind because of retinopathy of prematurity. Tasha has above-average intelligence and is on grade level in every academic subject. In some subjects, she requires more time than the rest of the class to complete daily assignments. During the first and second grades, Tasha's general education teachers decided that she should not be required to do all of the work that the rest of the class was required to do. When the rest of the class was assigned twenty addition problems, Tasha was told to complete only ten. By the time Tasha was in the third grade, she would complain that the assignments she was given were too hard, or that she couldn't complete them because she was blind. Tasha's third-grade teacher, Ms. Garcia, was concerned and contacted a vision specialist teacher and Tasha's parents. They all agreed that this attitude could lead to a decline in Tasha's self-esteem and confidence. At their meeting it was decided that Tasha would benefit from completing all class assignments.

Ms. Garcia re-examined the assignments she gave to her entire class realizing that if ten addition problems were enough for her to determine mastery for Tasha, they were enough for the other members of her class, as well. However, at this point in her education, it takes Tasha longer to complete the assignment than her classmates, regardless of the amount of material. Ms. Garcia, therefore, arranged her class schedule so that all students would have some time to complete assignments during school hours and could also take work home to complete.

It still takes Tasha more time to accomplish these assignments, but when she is finished she is confident that she can compete with the other students in her class. At the same time, she is learning strategies to help her complete her work more efficiently.

There is great variability in the ages at which children with visual impairments acquire developmental milestones.

Until recently, it has been believed that the development of children with visual impairments is similar to that of their nondisabled peers (Scholl, 1986), with any differences a direct or indirect result of the visual impairment. The recent work of Kay Ferrell and her colleagues in Project PRISM (Ferrell, Shaw, & Dietz, 1998) has suggested that we should re-examine that premise. There is tremendous variability among young children with visual impairments, including the ages at which they acquire important milestones in development. The factor that has the greatest impact on development is not degree of vision loss, but the presence or absence of additional disabilities. These findings led Ferrell to support an "individual differences approach" to intervention with children with visual impairments that seeks to support the development of each child within the context of individual experiences (Ferrell, 2000; Warren, 1984). Ferrell writes:

> Children with blindness and visual impairment learn differently, if for no other reason than the fact that in most cases they cannot rely on their vision to provide information. The information they obtain through their other senses is *inconsistent* (things do not always make noise or produce an odor), *fragmented* (comes in bits and pieces), and *passive* (not under the child's control). It takes practice, training, and time to sort all this out. (1997, p. v)

Negative attitudes and expectations can deprive the student with visual impairment of important experiences and opportunities.

Society's lack of knowledge or negative attitudes may indirectly affect the child with a visual impairment by depriving her of opportunities or experiences important for development. As we saw with the example of Tasha, it is a fairly common belief that people who are blind cannot accomplish certain tasks; unfortunately, this attitude may deprive them of the opportunity to compete with people who are sighted.

Even when differences are caused directly by the visual impairment, the degree to which the person's development is affected depends on the severity and cause of the visual impairment and on whether the child has additional disabilities. Environmental factors, such as family background and the child's daily experience, are also significant. Ferrell states that what makes a difference in how a child with visual impairments develops is the opportunities to learn and the presence or absence of additional disabilities (2000). As you read the following sections, think about the ways in which the areas of development are related to one another.

Children with visual impairments may be prone to verbalisms; they may use words without firsthand knowledge of their meanings.

■ ***Language and Concept Development*** Although communication through babbling and early sound production is generally the same for children who are blind and children who are sighted (Warren, 1984), developmental differences arise when children begin to associate meaning with words. In a classic study, Thomas Cutsforth (1932) researched the use of words and the understanding of their meaning by children who were totally blind from birth. He discovered that children who are blind often use words for which they could not have firsthand knowledge through other senses, such as when describing a blue sky. Cutsforth (1951) called this use of words without concrete knowledge of their meanings **verbalisms.**

Children who are blind may have other unusual language characteristics. For instance, they may ask frequent inappropriate or off-the-topic questions in order to maintain contact with partners or to respond to frightening or confusing situations (Fazzi & Klein, in press). They may also engage in **echolalia,** the repetition of statements used by other people. Interventions should be responsive to the content of the child's utterance, but teachers should not reinforce language behaviors that would not be acceptable in a sighted child.

Children with visual impairments should have direct experience with complex concepts.

Those of us who are sighted may take for granted the role that vision plays in learning and development, but Kay Ferrell (2000) reminds us that vision provides an incentive for communication and helps children develop concepts. Teachers and families of children with visual impairments must make all the features of concepts explicit. For example, an apple is not just red (or green or yellow); it is white on the inside, and the seeds are brown. Teachers working with children who are blind should be aware that even though a child may use verbal expressions that indicate an understanding of a concept, she may not really have the deeper understanding that comes with actual personal experience. If a child writes or reads a story about a big gray elephant and has had no firsthand experience with an elephant or the color gray, she is writing and/or reading about something that she does not truly understand. The teacher may want to work more closely with the child on these concepts, providing rich and meaningful experiences (see the accompanying box, "Promoting Language Development: Intervention Strategies"). By the way, this may also be true of children who are sighted; teachers can never assume that children's use of concepts in verbal or written communications indicates a clear understanding of those concepts. The challenge to educators, therefore, is to provide *all* children with a wealth of opportunities that increase their experiences through all senses, thus increasing their understanding of the language they use.

The acquisition of motor development skills may be delayed by lack of vision.

■ ***Motor Development*** From infancy, motor development is stimulated by vision. An infant who sees a brightly colored object or her mother's face reaches out for it and thus begins the development of gross motor skills. Children who are blind have difficulty in this area. Children who are sighted learn how to

~ Promoting Language Development: Intervention Strategies

The following strategies will help promote language development in young children with visual impairments.

- Maintain high expectations for the child's language. Do not always guess the child's needs or wants; instead encourage the child to make her needs known.
- Acknowledge the child's efforts to communicate. A child's early attempts to communicate should be encouraged. When parents and professionals imitate and expand on children's language, children are encouraged to continue talking.
- Provide opportunities for exploration and listening. Children who are visually impaired learn by listening and by exploring the environment. However, too much input can be overwhelming and can cause a child to tune out sounds in his surroundings.
- Try to provide extra information about things that are discussed. Instead of merely labeling, describe the persons and objects that are of interest to the child.
- Provide hands-on experiences. The language spoken to a child who is visually impaired should be reinforced with firsthand experiences. When children with visual impairments understand language, they are less likely to be echolalic.
- Respond to the ideas and feelings in the child's speech. If careful attention is paid to the child's actions and the events taking place around him, others will be able to respond to the child's underlying intentions.
- Express your feelings and put the child's feelings into words. Children with visual impairments cannot read feelings from the frowns, smiles, and expressions of others. Other persons' feelings should be explained, and the child should be taught to express feelings appropriately.
- Assist the child in developing socially appropriate responses. Attention should be paid to social skills. For instance, the child may be taught to listen to what other children are doing and to imitate their behavior when she wants to join in friends' play.
- Be supportive and encouraging. It is important that interactions be fun and that children talk about shared interests and enjoy interacting with one another. Respect the child's attempts to communicate.

Source: Adapted from K. M. Finello, N. H. Hanson, and L. S. Kekelis, "Cognitive Focus: Developing Cognition, Concepts, and Language in Young Blind and Visually Impaired Children," in R. L. Pogrund, D. L. Fazzi, and J. S. Lampert (eds.), *Early Focus: Working with Young Blind and Visually Impaired Children and Their Families* (New York: American Foundation for the Blind, 1992).

move by watching the movement of others and imitating it. Then, they practice variations of this movement and observe their own movement, which gives them the feedback they need to change and modify their movements. Children who are blind, however, cannot observe others and imitate their movements; they are slow to begin to move in response to the sounds around them (Orel-Bixler, 1999).

IDEA, as you have learned, provides that children with disabilities receive "related services" in order to fully benefit from schooling. Under this law, children who are blind may receive instruction in **orientation and mobility,** a set of skills involved in establishing one's location in the environment and moving safely through it (Anthony et al., in press). When children who have visual impairments enter school, they should be able to move efficiently and safely through their environment.

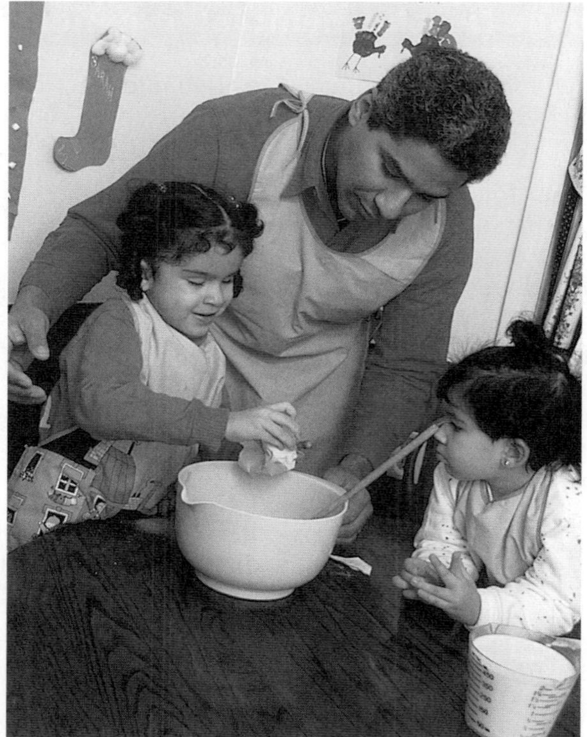

Daily living skills are everyday activities, like making pudding, which need to be taught specifically to people with visual impairments. Mastering daily living skills will eventually lead to independent living. (Laura Dwight)

Blindness affects cognitive development by restricting the range and variety of a child's experiences.

■ ***Cognitive and Intellectual Development*** Blindness affects cognitive development in young children in much the same way as it affects motor development, by restricting the range and variety of their experiences, by limiting their ability to move around, and by diminishing their control of the environment and their relationship to it (Lowenfeld, 1981).

With emerging research on newborns and infants, we are discovering more and more about the importance of vision in early learning. In early infancy the eyes are the child's primary avenue for exploring the world. The newborn uses vision to follow objects with her eyes, for example, and can stick out her tongue after watching someone else do it (Freidrich, 1983). The visual sense motivates the infant to interact with people and objects, guides that interaction, and verifies the success of the interaction. Vision thus stimulates motor activity and exploration, forming the basis for cognitive growth.

Some research has suggested that there are critical periods for certain kinds of learning (Langley, 1980). If infants who are visually impaired miss out on those critical periods for reaching, crawling, or walking, for example, it may be difficult or impossible for them to "catch up" and develop at a normal rate later in life. School-age children may continue to experience difficulties in their developmental progress. Thus early intervention for infants with visual impairments is designed to use the child's intact senses to provide the kind of experiences that will promote cognitive growth (Fazzi & Klein, in press).

■ ***Social and Emotional Development*** There is no unique psychology of blindness. The principles and issues related to the social and emotional development of people who are sighted are the same as those related to the social and emotional development of people who are blind (Tuttle & Tuttle, 2000). However, children who are blind do encounter unique difficulties in social situations. Primarily, the difficulties arise because of the way that the child is perceived by society and the way that the child perceives himself (Sacks, 1996).

Children who are blind often encounter social difficulties because of how society perceives them and how they perceive themselves.

For example, the child who completes class assignments develops a clear sense of accomplishment. Children who are visually impaired, however, are often allowed to turn in incomplete work or partial assignments, as in the case of Tasha. As a result, such children may believe that they are not "smart enough" to do the same work that other children in the class do. The perception of other children in the class may also be that the child with a visual impairment cannot accomplish as much as the rest of the class.

■ ***School Achievement*** With appropriate assistance and placement, a student who is visually impaired and has no additional disabilities should be able to participate actively in all aspects of school and compete with sighted peers in academic areas. If a student with visual impairment is having trouble achieving academic goals, the teacher and the vision specialist should work together to determine if he is receiving proper instruction and has the needed adapted materials. The sections later in this chapter on teaching strategies and technological aids will provide more information for this purpose.

Effects on the Family

The reaction of families to the fact that their infant or child is blind or has low vision depends on many factors. Most important, as we saw in Chapter 3, may be the degree of support available to the family through its informal network of relatives and friends and its formal network of helping agencies and professionals.

Several other characteristics of the family and the child may affect the parents' attitude toward their child's visual impairment (Ferrell, 1986):

1. *The severity of the handicap* may be an important issue, because many children with visual impairments also have additional disabilities. Parents of children whose visual impairment is severe or is complicated by other disabilities must respond to a variety of physical and developmental issues; in some cases they must also cope with anxiety about life-threatening medical procedures.
2. *The age of onset of the visual impairment.* The later the diagnosis of disability, the more difficult the news is for the parents; they have had more time for their hopes and expectations for their child to develop. On the other hand, the development of bonding, that crucial early parent–child tie that is so important to social and emotional development, may be affected when the infant is congenitally blind. Babies who have visual impairments are less likely to make eye contact with their mothers, which can reduce the amount of the "mutual gazing" that occurs between infants and mothers. In addition, these babies may smile less regularly and consistently at their parents. Smiling in infants is important to elicit social interactions with other people and serves as a means to include the infant in the social relationship (Warren, 1984).
3. *How the information or diagnosis concerning visual impairment was initially received.* Stotland (1984), the parent of a child who is blind, says, "Ask any five

parents of visually impaired children how they first learned their child had vision problems and you will get five different horror stories. These stories will range from blatant misdiagnoses to inaccurate predictions of total blindness, to expressions of pity" (p. 69).

Parents' attitudes toward their child's visual impairment are affected by its severity, age of onset, delivery of diagnosis, and medical and educational support.

4. *Support from medical professionals and educators* is critical in the initial discovery of a child's visual impairment. Parents must feel comfortable asking questions and expressing concerns if they are to accept their child's visual impairment.

A child with visual impairment creates a dynamic within the family that can affect it in many ways long after the initial diagnosis. These effects might include changes in daily routines, social interactions, and parent involvement at school (J.B. Chase, in Wolffe, 2000).

Families of children with visual impairments are often able to incorporate their child into the family routine, ensuring that the child feels she is a vital member of the family. In some cases, caregivers allow more time for the child to complete a particular task, such as clearing the dishes from the table. Caregivers can also use special adapted materials for more complicated tasks—for example, Braille labels on the washing machine and dryer. Participation in family routines helps children learn to complete tasks that they have started, to perform as independently as possible, and to take responsibility for their actions.

Parents may have difficulty dealing with the attitudes and misconceptions of others.

Outside their daily routines, families often must deal with changes in their social relationships as an indirect result of their child's visual impairment. Parents, for example, may have difficulty coping with the attitudes and misconceptions of their friends. Deborah Barton (1984), the parent of a child who is blind, recalls, "When my child started walking and talking, my friends considered him a genius and thought of me as a saint. They misinterpreted what they saw, and I let them. They praised Jed for ordinary behavior ('he's walking,' 'he likes peanut butter,' 'he doesn't whine') and talked about me as if I was a cross between Madame Curie and the Flying Nun" (p. 67). Although at first this kind of acknowledgment might seem welcome, it is difficult for parents to endure misconceptions such as these over time because they indicate a lack of understanding of their child's needs and abilities.

Social interactions between the child who is visually impaired and children who are sighted may also require special attention and effort. Families of children with a visual impairment must be even more careful to provide social activities for that child outside of the family so that good social skills are established throughout the early years of a child's development. Unfortunately, some parents of sighted children may be reluctant to invite the child who is blind to participate in activities such as birthday parties or slumber parties because of their lack of understanding about blindness. Parents of children with visual impairments may need to initiate some of this social interaction and to educate the parents of their child's sighted peers. When inexperienced adults begin to learn about the abilities and needs of a child with visual impairment, they can model acceptance and understanding for their own children. See the box titled "Strategies for Promoting Social Inclusion at Home and at School" for ideas that family members can use to promote social relationships.

Family participation in the child's education, especially on the IEP team, is crucial.

School is another area in which family participation and adaptation are important. Parents or caregivers should participate in the interdisciplinary team, which gathers as much information as possible concerning the child's abilities and needs, including the degree to which the child uses remaining vision. The family has a crucial role in providing the professionals with information on how

~ Strategies for Promoting Social Inclusion at Home and at School

- Encourage the child to explore the environment by providing many hands-on experiences. Take him or her on outings to various community sites (such as parks, playgrounds, and restaurants) and on shopping trips (to the grocery store, shopping mall, or video store), for example.
- Allow the child to be an active participant in each hands-on experience. For example, when grocery shopping, have the child choose a favorite snack or select a favorite fruit from the produce section.
- Provide opportunities for the child to participate in structured group activities that facilitate socialization, such as swimming lessons, gymnastics, story hour at the public library, and rhythm and music groups. Many of these activities can be done with a parent or other family member.
- Encourage the child to take risks and try new activities. Provide opportunities for the child to experience a variety of multisensory activities (such as tasting new foods and feeling a variety of textures; playing rough-and-tumble games; engaging in climbing activities; and playing in water, sand, and snow).
- Provide opportunities for the child to assume responsibility for classroom jobs or home chores on a consistent basis. Young children can be responsible for putting away their toys, putting their dirty clothes in a clothes hamper, helping to set the table for a family meal, clearing the table after eating a meal, or helping to take out the trash or recycle bins.
- Form partnerships with other parents and teachers and become involved in play groups and community groups (such as a church, Tiny Tots, dance classes, music lessons, ice skating, and skiing).

Source: Sacks, S. Z., & Silberman, S. K. (2000). Social skills. In A. J. Koenig & M. C. Holbrook (Eds.), *Foundations of Education* (2nd ed.), Vol. II, pp. 633–634. New York: American Foundation for the Blind.

the child uses his vision. Once decisions have been made regarding adaptive materials and curricular activities, parents become vital participants in their child's education. If, for example, a child is learning to travel independently with a cane, the parents can reinforce this skill by communicating closely with their child's teachers to monitor progress and to learn about the skill from them. In doing so, they encourage independence for their child. If a child is learning Braille, parents can learn it too. Close communication between parents and teachers and direct involvement of parents in the education of the child are critical to educational success.

In Classrooms

Understanding the following issues will help teachers and parents provide an appropriate education for children with vision loss, including necessary adaptations.

Early Intervention

Professionals have long recognized the need for intervention programs for infants and their parents as soon as a visual impairment is diagnosed. For babies with congenital blindness, this diagnosis comes at birth or soon after; for babies

Teachers must expect children with visual impairments to follow the same routines as other students. There are benefits when friends stand in line together! (Ellen Senisi/The Image Works, Inc.)

with lesser degrees of visual impairment, the diagnosis may occur later in infancy. Children with a moderate degree of impairment may receive a diagnosis only after they encounter difficulty in completing school tasks.

Early intervention with infants with visual impairments may prevent the development of secondary handicaps.

Kay Ferrell (1986) has described several reasons for early intervention with infants who are visually impaired. First, as discussed earlier, vision is an important component of early cognitive development, and there may be particular periods of early development when optimal learning occurs. Early intervention may also prevent the development of secondary disabilities. Failure to develop language, ear–hand coordination, or attachment to a significant adult may form the foundation for disabilities in addition to visual impairment that will emerge later in the child's life.

Early intervention can take numerous forms. Teachers of young children with visual impairments will encourage parents to continue to talk to their baby, to "show" things to the baby by allowing her to touch and explore them, to teach the baby to listen for clues to what is happening around her, to play games that involve moving and identifying parts of the body, using the baby's hands to find her head, nose, ears, tummy, knees, and so on. Teachers can also help parents make the most of the learning opportunities that arise in daily life with their baby, so that he or she will grow into a healthy and well-adjusted child. This role is important, since parents sometimes alter their interactions with a child who is visually impaired. They may assume that a child who cannot see is less interested in his or her environment or does not need the stimulation of playing with household objects and toys or of playing baby games with parents.

Infants with visual impairment and additional disabilities need intensive intervention.

Infants who are visually impaired and have additional disabilities as well have especially intensive intervention needs, and their parents need a great deal of support (Chen, 1999). Reading the cues of a baby who is blind and may be deaf, mentally retarded, or physically disabled can be complex. How can a mother tell when the baby is pleased or sad? What are the baby's preferences? How do the family members and the baby build relationships? Effective intervention for these families requires an early intervention specialist who knows each disability area well and can build on the family strengths to foster communication and loving relationships (Klein, Chen, & Haney, 2000).

Early Intervention

Identification and Assessment

Assessment for students who are visually impaired is especially difficult for three reasons: the lack of standardized assessment instruments, the need for adaptations of existing assessment instruments to meet the needs of students with visual impairments, and the need for a fair interpretation of test results. The lack of standardized assessment instruments is a direct result of the small number of students with visual impairments. It has been impossible to standardize tests on this population because of the lack of homogeneity caused by differences in age of onset of visual impairment, degree of visual impairment, and differences in educational experiences.

Assessment of students who are visually impaired is difficult, mostly because of lack of standardized tests for this population.

■ ***Identification in School*** Every state mandates vision screening in the schools to determine which students have visual problems that warrant further assessment. At least 25 percent of school-age children have eye problems that need professional attention (Harley & Lawrence, 1984), and that percentage is considerably higher among children with other disabilities.

The most common visual screening test is one you have probably taken yourself, although you may not know the name of it—the **Snellen Chart.** The person being examined is positioned twenty feet from the chart, on which eight rows of letters ranging from large to small are printed, and is asked to read the letters with each eye (while the other eye is covered). If there is difficulty reading any of the letters on the chart, the school nurse or other person conducting the screening usually makes a referral for a more comprehensive evaluation of vision.

The Snellen Chart is the most common visual screening test.

The Snellen Chart is used to screen for distance vision problems only. If you suspect that one of your students has a near vision problem (which would affect reading) or another kind of vision problem, then urge your school nurse to conduct or recommend a more complete visual evaluation for that student. (See the accompanying box, "Detection of Vision Problems.")

There are a number of ways to screen for visual impairments in very young children or those who do not know the letter names. The most common are the Snellen E Chart and the Apple/House/Umbrella Screening. There are also a variety of means for evaluating the vision of students with severe handicaps that the experienced examiner will be able to use (Harley & Lawrence, 1984). No student should be excluded from vision screening because he or she cannot provide traditional responses.

Ideally, vision screening should be the product of a team approach, with educational and medical staff working together (Harley & Lawrence, 1984). Continuous observation of the student in the classroom and in other natural settings should accompany the screening, plus referral of identified students for further visual evaluation and follow-up to ensure that the recommendations have been carried out.

In addition to medical evaluations of vision, it is critical to test a student's functional vision.

■ ***Functional Vision Assessment*** In addition to the medical evaluations just discussed, it is critical to test students' functional vision—in other words,

~ Detection of Vision Problems

Teachers are often the first to detect visual problems in their students. Symptoms of visual impairment may include:

- Physical changes in or about the eyes and face. Physical changes may include an eye that tends to wander or eyes that are bloodshot or show recurrent redness or watering. Children may complain that their eyes hurt or feel "dusty." Frequent rubbing of the eyes, facial distortions, frowning, and an abnormal amount of squinting or blinking may be other symptoms of trouble. Children may show a preference for using only one eye or for viewing only at a distance or only at close range, or they may tilt their heads or bring objects unusually close to their eyes.
- Changes in vision. Children may complain that objects look blurry or that they are unable to see something at a distance. Note also an inability to use vision in different situations or with different illumination.
- Changes in behavior. Children may become irritable when doing desk work or have a short attention span when watching an activity that takes place across the room. They may report headache or nausea after close work, hold books close to the eyes, or lean down close to the book.

If the teacher suspects a visual impairment, he or she should immediately notify the parents and refer the student to the school nurse or physician for evaluation.

Source: Adapted from I. Torres and A. L. Corn, *When You Have a Visually Handicapped Child in Your Classroom: Suggestions for Teachers* (2d ed.) (New York: American Foundation for the Blind, 1990), pp. 32–33.

how well they use the vision that they do possess. If, for example, it is noted during a functional vision assessment that a student has difficulty moving and performing tasks in limited lighting, teachers will be more prepared to accommodate him in low-lighting situations.

Functional vision assessments vary according to the type of information needed. Commercially produced functional vision assessments are available, such as the Program to Develop Efficiency in Visual Functioning (American Printing House for the Blind) and Project IVEY: Increasing Visual Efficiency in Young Children (Florida Department of Education), but most functional vision assessments are informal and may be a compilation of other assessments. Functional vision assessments are usually conducted by a vision specialist and an orientation and mobility specialist and may include the following (Erin & Paul, 1996; Roessing, 1982):

- Information on the student's visual disability and prognosis
- Classroom modifications for distance vision tasks
- Classroom modifications for near vision tasks
- Informal assessments of visual field and color vision
- Equipment adaptations for classes
- Travel skills

Functional vision assessments are individualized. By carefully considering the information provided by the assessment, teachers can make more informed decisions about educational programming.

■ ***Assessment for Teaching*** Students who are visually impaired must demonstrate knowledge through both informal classroom evaluations and formal standardized tests, just as their sighted peers do. They should be required to participate in evaluation activities along with their mainstreamed class; however, these students must be given every opportunity to take the test in such a way that their performance gives an accurate picture of their true abilities. In most cases students with visual impairments need modifications in the presentation of testing materials and in time requirements. Most commercially produced achievement tests are available in Braille and large-print versions. A vision specialist will be able to obtain copies of these tests.

Most commercially produced achievement tests are available in Braille and large print.

Students who are visually impaired have difficulty completing tests with time limits since it generally takes longer to read material in Braille or in large print. Decisions regarding the testing time limit for a student who is visually impaired should be made by evaluating the student's needs and abilities.

Finally, interpretation of test results should take into consideration the modification of test items and the testing situation as well as whether any test items rely heavily on visual experiences for correct answers. The scores of students who are visually impaired should not be compared with standardized scores since standardized scores do not reflect modifications for these students. Vision specialists can assist in the interpretation of test results for individual students.

Curriculum

Students who are visually impaired require instruction not only in academic areas but also in skills needed to compensate for their loss of vision. These skills are critical to students' success in life after school and so are an important part of the curriculum. Phillip Hatlen (2000b) has described the necessary school program for students with visual impairments as the **expanded core curriculum**—the existing core curriculum plus the additional areas of learning needed by students who are visually impaired, including those with additional disabilities (see Table 11.3).

The extended core curriculum includes the specialized skill areas that students with visual impairments need.

Not every student who is blind or has low vision will need instruction in every component of the expanded core curriculum. Each student's needs must be determined individually through careful, comprehensive assessment.

For Hatlen, compensatory academic skills are the skills that students with visual impairments need to access all areas of the core curriculum. They include concept development, spatial understanding, study and organizational skills, speaking and listening skills, and the adaptations necessary for accessing all areas of the core curriculum. Communication modes might include Braille, large print, print with the use of optical devices, regular print, tactile symbols, a calendar system, sign language, recorded materials, or combinations of these means. Let's take a closer look at the most common of these methods.

■ ***Braille*** Learning Braille is essential for students who are so severely visually impaired that they cannot read print. It is also recommended for students who are legally blind and those with visual impairments that are progressive (will worsen over time). **Braille** was devised by Louis Braille, a French musician and educator, in 1829. It is a code that uses raised dots instead of printed characters (letters). A unit in Braille is called a *cell*. Each cell consists of six dots, three dots high and two dots wide. The dots are numbered from 1 through 6, and the

Students who are blind read by using Braille, a tactile code of raised dots.

Table 11.3 Curriculum for Students with Visual Impairments

Existing Core Curriculum	Expanded Core Curriculum
English language arts	All of the existing core curriculum, PLUS
Other languages, to the extent possible	Compensatory academic skills, including communication modes
Mathematics	Orientation and mobility
Science	Social interaction skills
Health	Independent living skills
Physical education	Recreation and leisure skills
Social studies	Career education
History	Use of assistive technology
Economics	Visual efficiency skills
Business education	
Fine arts	
Vocational education	

Braille alphabet is made of combinations of these six dots (Figure 11.2). The Braille alphabet is only a small part of the literary Braille code, which also consists of contractions (or combinations of letters). Braille is produced on a Braillewriter or on a hand-held slate and stylus. It can also be produced by a computer with a Braille printer.

Learning to read Braille should begin long before a student enters school, just as learning to read print should (McComiskey, 1996). Sighted children begin the reading process by recognizing symbols in the environment. For example, children at an early age might learn to associate a hamburger and french fries with the golden arches of McDonald's. Children who are sighted have experience watching adults read books, looking at picture books, and having books read to them long before they know how to read. They also build background experiences through observation and participation.

In contrast, children who are severely visually impaired will not have experiences equating symbols with their meanings unless they are given tactile symbols. Children who are blind cannot watch adults read books, so they gain knowledge about books only if they have the opportunity to explore Braille books prior to school. Parents who give children opportunities to become familiar with Braille and tactile symbols help them achieve readiness for Braille reading. Without these experiences, it becomes necessary for the teacher to begin the process of developing an understanding of symbols. Children with visual impairments also need to be provided with the experiences that are described in basal reading series—usually the games and routines of sighted children (Koenig & Farrenkopf, 1997). All children need experiential background to understand fully what they read, but it is especially important to provide background experiences for children who are blind, for they may not have developed symbolic meanings for themselves (Koenig & Holbrook, 2000). Classroom teachers should request Braille copies of all classroom materials so that the student who is blind can be included in all activities.

Classroom teachers should request Braille copies of all classroom materials for students who need them.

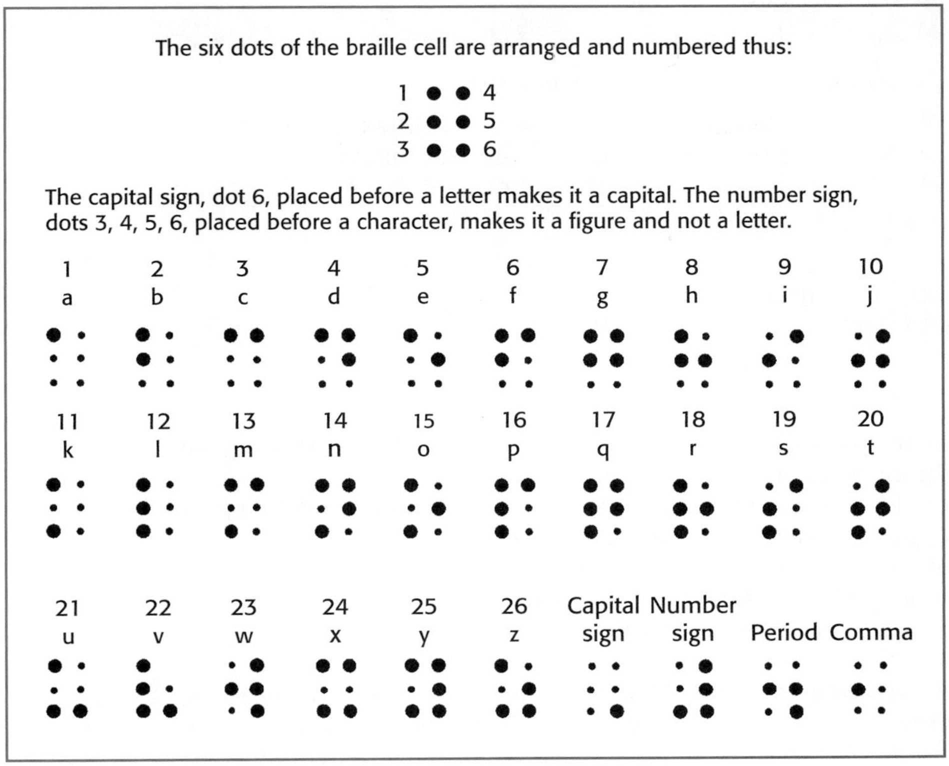

The six dots of the braille cell are arranged and numbered thus:

1 ● ● 4
2 ● ● 5
3 ● ● 6

The capital sign, dot 6, placed before a letter makes it a capital. The number sign, dots 3, 4, 5, 6, placed before a character, makes it a figure and not a letter.

1	2	3	4	5	6	7	8	9	10
a	b	c	d	e	f	g	h	i	j
11	12	13	14	15	16	17	18	19	20
k	l	m	n	o	p	q	r	s	t
21	22	23	24	25	26	Capital	Number		
u	v	w	x	y	z	sign	sign	Period	Comma

Figure 11.2
Braille Alphabet and Numerals

Source: Division for the Blind and Physically Handicapped, Library of Congress, Washington, DC 20542.

■ ***Low-Vision Aids and Training*** Many students who are visually impaired do not use Braille as their primary literacy medium; instead, they can learn to use large print or even regular print with magnification or low-vision aids. In other words, their primary source of information is still visual (Hatlen, 2000a, see the accompanying box, "Aids for Students with Low Vision").

Students with low vision get most of their information through their vision.

Professionals in visual impairment no longer believe that using vision can damage it. In fact, professionals who work with students who are visually impaired now realize that instruction can actually help children develop better use of their vision.

Instruction in the use of low vision touches on three areas: environmental adaptations, which may involve making changes in distance, size, contrast, illumination, or time; enhancement of visual skills, such as attention, scanning, tracking, and reaching for objects, through integration of these skills into functional activities; and integration of vision into activities, or teaching skills within the actual activities where they are needed (Erin & Paul, 1996). Low-vision instruction is designed to help the student make the best possible use of the vision that she has.

■ ***Developing Listening Skills*** Since students who are visually impaired receive a large percentage of information through their auditory sense, it is important to give them instruction and experience in using this sense to the fullest.

Aids for Students with Low Vision

- Optical aids, such as a hand-held magnifying glass
- Closed-circuit television (CCTV) sets that enlarge printed material onto a screen
- Computer software that varies type size and typeface
- Computer hardware such as large monitor screens and screen magnifiers
- Large-print textbooks
- Materials used to provide greater contrast in written and printed matter: yellow acetate, bold-line paper, felt-tip markers

Source: Adapted from G. J. Zimmerman, "Optics and Low Vision Devices," in A. L. Corn and A. J. Koenig (eds.), *Foundations of Low Vision: Clinical and Functional Perspectives* (New York: AFB Press, 1996).

Many people believe that people who are blind automatically have superior auditory skills, but this is not true.

Students with visual impairments benefit from instruction in listening skills.

Listening to recorded materials does not replace reading print or Braille as a means for developing literacy; however, it is important for students who are blind since it allows for efficient gathering of large amounts of materials over a short period of time. With instruction, a student can become more efficient in the use of listening for learning.

■ ***Orientation and Mobility*** In addition to academic skills, students with visual impairment must develop skills to ensure that they can be independent adults, able to work and to move around in their environment with as little assistance as possible. For this reason, instruction in orientation and mobility is a critical component of the curriculum for students who are blind (see the accompanying box, "A Closer Look: Collaboration: Who Are the Professionals Interacting with the Student Who Is Visually Impaired?"). **Orientation and mobility training** is "teaching the concepts and skills necessary for students to travel safely and efficiently in their environmental settings" (Griffin-Shirley, Trusty, & Rickard, 2000, p. 530).

Orientation is the ability to use one's senses to establish one's relationship to objects and people; mobility is the ability to move about the environment.

Orientation and mobility consists of two equally important subparts: *orientation,* the ability to use one's senses to establish where one is in space and in relation to other objects and people, and *mobility,* the ability to move about in one's environment. Skill in orientation and mobility is crucial for several reasons:

- Psychological reasons, including the development of a positive self-concept
- Physical reasons, including the development of fitness
- Social reasons, including the increase of opportunities for social interactions through independent travel
- Economic reasons, including the increase of employment opportunities and options

There are four generally accepted orientation and mobility systems: **human guide, cane travel, dog guide,** and **electronic travel aids.** The first three systems will be discussed in this section, and electronic travel aids will be discussed in the section on technological advances. People who are blind often use a combination of these systems, depending on the nature of the task they wish to accomplish.

A closer look

Collaboration: Who Are the Professionals Interacting with the Student Who Is Visually Impaired?

A number of professionals with different educational backgrounds and specialized skills will likely work with the student who is visually impaired, and you as the teacher will have the opportunity to collaborate with some of them to provide services to the student. First, there are three groups of professionals involved with different aspects of evaluating vision and prescribing and fitting corrective lenses. An **ophthalmologist** is a physician who specializes in the treatment of eye diseases. This medical doctor can perform a complete eye examination, prescribe medicine, and perform surgery; the ophthalmologist should be consulted if there is any suspicion of eye disease. An **optometrist,** or doctor of optometry, although not a physician, undergoes postgraduate training enabling him or her to examine the eyes, evaluate visual problems, and prescribe corrective lenses. An **optician** grinds and fits corrective lenses that have been prescribed by an ophthalmologist or optometrist.

Next are the specialists working in school settings. The teacher of students with visual impairments has advanced training in providing specialized skills—reading skills, including Braille and large print; concept development; daily living skills; and so on. The teacher may provide direct services to students on an itinerant basis or in a special day class, resource room, or residential school; or may consult with the general education teacher. The teacher may work with students from infancy through transition to the workplace.

The **orientation and mobility specialist** teaches the skills for safe and independent travel, from toddlerhood through adulthood, as well as the use of specialized travel devices. Orientation and mobility instructors help students learn to detect obstacles and eventually to cross streets alone; they will be needed whenever a student needs to become familiar with a new setting, such as a new school. The **vocational rehabilitation counselor,** usually associated with a state or private agency, assists adolescents with visual impairments making the transition from school to work by helping them and their families plan for post–high school education and training, as well as job placement.

Lisa Pruner, a teacher-consultant with students with visual impairments, developed these tips for working with a consultant:

1. Use the telephone! Your consultant won't know that you have questions or concerns unless you let her know. Don't try to "make do" until the next scheduled visit. That can be frustrating for everyone. When in doubt, call your consultant.
2. Set aside a block of time to talk to your consultant during her visit. It's important to be able to share observations and concerns immediately in a relatively distraction-free environment.
3. Let your consultant know what you need. If you need an observation, some suggestions for adaptations, or if you want to observe the consultant interacting directly with a student, tell your consultant. Every classroom has different needs, and every teacher has a different level of comfort with vision issues. Let your consultant know what she can do for you.
4. Make a list of questions to ask before each visit.
5. Contact therapists, specialists, administrators, and parents regarding the consultant's visit. Invite them to join you or submit questions through you if they can't attend.
6. Remember, the consultant's job is to provide technical assistance in an area in which classroom teachers aren't usually trained. Make good use of your consultant.

Sources: Adapted from Appendix A: "Who Are the Professionals Who Work with Visually Impaired People?" in I. Torres and A. L. Corn, *When You Have a Visually Impaired Child in Your Classroom: Suggestions for Teachers* (New York: American Foundation for the Blind, 1990); and Lisa W. Pruner, "Tips for Working with a Consultant," *RE:view, 25*(4) (1994), 174.

A *human guide* can help a person who is blind travel safely but may also lead to a high level of dependence.

Human Guide In this system the person who is blind can travel safely through the environment, including maneuvering around stairs and obstacles, by holding lightly onto the elbow of a sighted person and following the movement of that person as he or she walks. Even though these techniques are relatively safe and efficient and human guides are often able to assist the person who is blind in the development of kinesthetic awareness (awareness of movement), the continuous use of a human guide may also lead to a level of dependence instead of the independence that is the goal of instruction in orientation and mobility (Griffin-Shirley, Trusty, & Rickard, 2000). It is also difficult to use human guide techniques properly, since few members of the general public are aware of them.

With proper training, students who are visually impaired can use a cane to travel independently.

Cane Travel One of the most common systems of orientation and mobility is the use of the long cane for independent travel. Students who are visually impaired and use a cane must learn a variety of techniques in order to travel efficiently and safely. The canes used today are generally made from aluminum and vary in length according to a person's height, stride, and the time it takes him or her to respond to information gathered by moving the cane (Hill, 1986). Instruction in the use of the cane is very specialized and should be provided individually. This instruction is very important, since in many cases the safety of the student depends on the use of proper techniques. Instruction is most commonly given by an orientation and mobility specialist. Orientation and mobility specialists must undergo hundreds of hours of training while blindfolded themselves in order to learn to teach independent travel skills to people who are visually impaired.

Dog guides are used only by a small percentage of people with visual impairments.

Dog Guides The use of dog guides, though well publicized, is very limited. Only about two percent of people with visual impairments use a dog guide for travel (Hill, 1986). Dog guides are trained to assist people who are blind in safe travel; however, it is the person who is blind who makes decisions regarding travel route and destination. The use of a dog guide does not negate the need for a person who is blind to have good independent orientation and mobility skills.

One of the responsibilities of the vision specialist is to teach independent living skills.

■ ***Development of Independent Living Skills*** An important element in the expanded core curriculum is the development of **independent living skills** for students with visual impairments, which increases their ability to accomplish daily routines, such as selecting and caring for clothes, managing (including identifying) money, preparing food, shopping, and so on (Hill, 1986).

Children who are sighted learn most daily living skills through observation and imitation or instruction from parents or family members. Children who are blind may not be able to observe daily living activities with enough detail to imitate, and their parents may be unaware of adapted techniques for instruction. It is usually the responsibility of the vision specialist to provide this instruction. Consider, for example, Roberto's predicament:

> The vision specialist was unaware until Roberto was in the eighth grade that he was unable to tie his shoes. After investigating, the teacher found out that Roberto's parents had attempted several times to teach him, but he had difficulty accomplishing the task as it was described to him and consequently took a very long time to tie his shoes. As in most families, the

> mornings were hectic, so, two minutes before Roberto's bus arrived each morning, his mother gave in and tied his shoes. The problem came in junior high school, when Roberto had to get dressed and undressed for gym class, and no one was there to tie his shoes. Had instruction in independent living skills been a priority in earlier grades, this difficulty (and embarrassment for Roberto) might have been avoided. The vision specialist immediately began intensive instruction in independent living skills with Roberto. She taught him not only how to tie his shoes but also how to fold the bills in his wallet so that he could tell the difference between a $5 bill and a $10 bill and how to make healthy after-school snacks. As a result, Roberto is more confident and more independent.

See Table 11.4 for examples of daily living skills that can be taught to children who are visually impaired.

Social Interaction Skills Think about how much of what we have learned about interacting with others came through watching others—through vision. Posture, eye contact, facial expression, when to shake hands, when to touch and not to touch—all of these skills and more we unconsciously imitate what we see. Without vision, these skills must be taught explicitly, so that people with visual impairments can be accepted by others and form friendships (Sacks & Silberman, 2000).

Recreation and Leisure Skills Many students with visual impairments may not know how many options there are for the use of leisure time (McGregor & Farrenkopf, 2000). Learning about these options and acquiring the skills needed

Table 11.4 Typical Independent Living Activities for Children with Visual Impairments

Preschool	Dressing
	Mealtime routines
	Toileting
	Use of eating utensils
Elementary years	Selection of clothes according to preference and weather
	Washing and caring for hair
	Household chores
	Handling small amounts of personal money
High school years	Grooming
	Self-care
	Organization of personal possessions
	Ordering and maintaining special devices and equipment
	Application of appropriate social skills

Source: N. C. Barraga and J. N. Erin, *Visual Handicaps and Learning* (Austin, TX: Pro Ed, 1992), pp. 152–153. Used by permission of Pro-Ed, Inc.

to perform them are part of the responsibility of the specialized teacher. Among the options that can be learned by people with visual impairments are cross-country and downhill skiing, bicycling, sailing and canoeing, running, skating, bowling, swimming, waterskiing, scuba diving, snorkeling, and martial arts—you name it, and it can be adapted.

Use of Assistive Technology The technology adaptations for people with visual impairments are impressive, although not all students have access to them. We will discuss technology separately later in the chapter.

Career Education Career education must start early for the child with visual impairment and must focus on developing knowledge of the range of possible careers and interest and skills in particular areas (Hatlen, 2000b). Since underemployment is a serious issue for adults with visual impairment, this is an essential part of the core curriculum (Wolffe, 2000).

Visual Efficiency The term *visual efficiency* refers to the best possible use of the remaining vision in the person who is blind or has low vision. The specialized teacher must assess functional vision, plan learning activities, and teach students to use their functional vision effectively (Hatlen, 2000b).

Allen Koenig and Cay Holbrook (2000) describe Lowenfeld's (1973) three principles of special methods for teaching students with visual impairments: the need for concrete experiences, the need for learning by doing, and the need for unifying experiences. Table 11.5 gives examples of how to use those special methods.

Table 11.5 Applications of the Principles of Special Methods

	Principles of Special Methods		
Unique Skill	**Concrete Experiences**	**Learning by Doing**	**Unifying Experiences**
Making lemonade	Use real ingredients, real utensils, and real dinnerware.	Make the lemonade, completing each step in the process with or without guidance or prompting from the teacher.	Purchase ingredients from a grocery store. Integrate measurement concepts learned in math class. Drink lemonade as part of an after-school party for peers and parents.
Writing with slate and stylus	Use the actual slate and stylus. Use slate instructional tool from the American Printing House for the Blind to introduce cell configurations.	Use the slate and stylus with guidance from the teacher, as needed. Explore other specialty slates, such as one-liner notecard slate, full-page slate, and cassette-labeling slate.	Use the slate and stylus to jot assignments. Use the slate and stylus to take notes in a classroom. Use a slate and stylus at home to label CDs.

Source: Holbrook, M. C., & Koenig, A. J. (2000). Basic techniques for modifying instruction. In A. J. Koenig & M. C. Holbrook (Eds.), *Foundations of education* (Vol. II), (2nd ed.), p. 200. New York: American Foundation for the Blind.

Placement for Students Who Are Visually Impaired

Students with visual impairments can be found in every kind of educational setting. In general, the greater the student's need for specialized services, the more restrictive the setting. Remember, though, that each decision about *where* the child learns is made on the basis of the individual student's needs, by the IEP team. Here we will discuss options ranging from the least restrictive to residential schools.

Most children with visual impairments are now educated in public schools.

■ ***Public School Programs*** Public school programs for students who are blind began as early as 1900. They are today the most frequently used service delivery model for students who are visually impaired. The major educational models used within public schools are consultative services, itinerant services, resource rooms, and self-contained classrooms.

In the consultant model, the student with visual impairment does not receive direct services from the specialized teacher of students with visual impairments. Instead, the general education teacher and the specialized teacher set up the needed classroom adaptations together, and the specialized teacher is available to the general education teacher for help as needed. This model might be appropriate for the blind student functioning at grade level or for the student with multiple disabilities which include visual impairment (Lewis & Allman, 2000).

Itinerant teachers travel from school to school to provide services to students with visual impairments.

Itinerant services, in which a trained teacher travels from school to school within a specific area, providing direct or indirect services to students with visual impairments, are available for students enrolled in public schools who need additional assistance. Itinerant teachers provide a variety of services to these students, depending on their individual needs; for example, they may see one child every day of the week, and another one day each week or less. See the accompanying box, "What Specialized Instruction Do Students with Visual Impairments Need?" for further details on these service-delivery models.

~ What Specialized Instruction Do Students with Visual Impairments Need?

Specialized instruction from the resource teacher includes compensatory skills needed to allow full participation in a regular classroom, such as Braille, use of technology, keyboarding, and listening skills. Although instructing the student in academic skills is primarily the responsibility of the general education teacher, resource teachers who are fully qualified to teach students with visual impairments serve as a resource to both the classroom teacher and the student.

The resource teacher can help students develop special skills and assist in teaching academic skills that may rely somewhat on vision for understanding (such as fractions, biology, and geography). The resource teacher will work with the classroom teacher to develop materials so that instruction in academic skill areas can occur within the regular classroom.

Itinerant teachers also provide instruction in special skills (such as use of technology, listening skills, daily living skills) to students who are visually impaired as well as consultation services to regular classroom teachers. In some cases the itinerant teacher will not provide the student with direct service but may assist the classroom teacher by giving adaptive materials or strategies for the presentation of academic material to a child who is visually impaired.

Some children are instructed in the regular education classroom but get specialized instruction from the resource room teacher.

In resource room programs, the student who is visually impaired is enrolled in the general education classroom, where he receives most instruction. A resource teacher with special training then provides special assistance through direct instruction and consultation to the student and classroom teacher.

Some children are taught in self-contained classrooms for students who are visually impaired.

Self-contained classrooms are classrooms within a public school in which only children with visual impairments are enrolled. The teacher of the class is certified in special education that focuses on the needs of students with visual impairments. Self-contained classrooms are not necessarily uninvolved with the general education class: Sometimes both groups of students participate in the same activities. But the majority of instruction for students enrolled in a self-contained classroom is provided in that classroom by the certified teacher. Some students need additional instruction in adaptive learning techniques (such as Braille, listening skills, or use of adaptive technology) and, after such instruction, will be capable of entering the regular classroom and succeeding. Self-contained classrooms may be very useful in the education of very young children who are blind in order to prepare them for full, successful inclusion in general education classrooms.

One of the most critical decisions to be made for children with visual impairments and their families is placement. It is difficult to obtain the "ideal" placement for the student who is blind or has low vision, since each student has such a complex set of needs (Lewis & Allman, 2000). Following the initial placement decision, it is important that the appropriateness of the decision be re-evaluated frequently so that the child will receive not only the best possible instruction, taking into account the need for adaptive skills, but also the social interactions and experiences that will prepare the child for adult life in a competitive world.

Residential schools have played a major role in the education of children with visual impairments and today offer support for regular public schools.

■ ***Residential School Programs*** The first opportunity for students with visual impairments in the United States to receive an education was provided by residential schools, which were modeled after European residential schools for the blind. The first American residential schools were opened in New York and Massachusetts in 1832. By the end of the nineteenth century, thirty-six schools for the blind had been established throughout the United States, and today there are fifty-two schools in forty-two states that serve about 9 percent of students with visual impairments (Lewis & Allman, 2000). Residential schools, in which students go to classes and live on campus, have traditionally offered comprehensive services, providing instruction in academic skills, daily living skills, and vocational skills.

Lewis and Allman (2000) see the following advantages for residential schools:

- All the adults are trained and knowledgeable about the complex educational needs of students with visual impairments;
- The students spend all their day learning, rather than spending time waiting while sighted students are instructed visually;
- Students continue learning beyond the six-hour school day, since instruction occurs in dormitories and in community-based settings on weekends and after school;
- Goals related to the expanded core curriculum are infused into all activities by knowledgeable specialists;
- Students have the opportunity to interact with other students with visual impairments.

These advantages must be weighed against the drawbacks of being separated for long periods from family and community.

Education for Students with Additional Disabilities

Many students with visual impairment have additional disabilities such as deafness, emotional disturbance, mental retardation, learning disabilities, and physical impairment. Regardless of additional handicapping conditions, students with visual impairments should be encouraged to make use of their functional vision and also be taught adaptive techniques for independent living and vocational skills. In most cases, special education teachers who have students with multiple disabilities in their classroom will receive consultation services from the vision teacher in order to provide them with adaptive instruction (Erin, 1996).

Students with visual impairment and other disabilities will also need specialized instruction.

Technological Advances

Technological changes have had a significant effect on the educational and vocational outlook for students with visual impairments. Under IDEA, the specialized equipment available to students with disabilities is referred to as **assistive technology.** (See the box, "Assistive Technology Mandates in IDEA.") Many assistive technology devices are now available to increase a student's ability to

Assistive technology allows people who are blind or have low vision to function independently.

~ Assistive Technology Mandates in IDEA

According to IDEA, mandated assistive technology services include the following:

1. The evaluation of the needs of a child with a disability, including a functional evaluation of the child in the child's customary environment;
2. Purchasing, leasing, or otherwise providing for the acquisition of assistive technology devices for a child with a disability;
3. Selecting, designing, fitting, customizing, adapting, applying, retaining, repairing or replacing assistive technology devices;
4. Coordinating and using other therapies, interventions, or services with assistive technology devices, such as those associated with existing educational rehabilitation plans and programs;
5. Training or technical assistance for a child with a disability or, if appropriate, the child's family; and
6. Training or technical assistance for professionals, including individuals providing educational or rehabilitation services, employers, or other individuals who provide services to, employ, or are otherwise substantially involved in the major life functions of children with disabilities.

Assistive technology can also be part of a Section 504 plan (see Chapter 1). According to Section 504 of the Rehabilitation Act of 1973, schools are required to ensure that students with disabilities are not discriminated against in gaining access to the full range of programs and activities offered by the schools. If, for example, computers are used in the general education curriculum, a school must take all reasonable steps to make those computers usable by students with disabilities.

Source: *Individuals with Disabilities Education Act Amendments of 1997,* Sec. 602, 20 USC 1401, CFR Sec. 300.6.
From G. Kapperman & J. Stricken (2000), Assistive technology (p. 502). In A. J. Koenig & M. C. Holbrook (eds.) *Foundations of education* (Vol. II) (Second ed.). New York: American Foundation for the Blind.

Can Girls with Impaired Vision Be Mommies?

I was 26 the first time someone raised the question of whether I, who had been blind since age 5, could have and raise children. I had three advanced degrees and three years of teaching to my credit and had lived on my own (first single, then married) since age 21. Now, here I sat in the hospital with a pink-blanketed bundle in my arms, awestruck, wondering what I would do next.

I wanted some hands-on experience in diapering. I told a nurse who was going off duty, and when her replacement came in, the experience was brutal. She pushed my hands away gruffly and impatiently, saying she could do it better. I felt inadequate and embarrassed. This episode shook my confidence in my ability to cope with this incredible responsibility of being a mother.

Of course, within hours, I learned that the problem was the nurse's ignorance about blindness—not my ability to fasten a baby's diaper! I would also learn that the attitudes of others would continue to be the most significant problem unique to parents with impaired vision.

Sure, I had to make adaptations along the way—just as I had to make certain adaptations in riding a bike, climbing a tree, or going to college as a kid who couldn't see. I read books, I talked to other mothers. I invented solutions as I went along.

Organizing objects and clearly defining spaces were two keys in the first three years. Toys, books, food—everything that needed a Braille label got one. I pinned outfits together before laundering, so that my babies were color-coordinated, and I always put toys away in the same place. I carried my babies first in front carriers and later in backpacks, and when they became toddlers, I used child safety harnesses to keep them close to me in public places.

My children have all been extremely verbal, as I've noticed many children of parents with impaired vision to be. They have also been

function independently in educational and employment settings, and, most importantly, to increase access to print. Teachers have a role to play, though, in making this technology accessible and understandable to their students (Mack, Koenig, & Ashcroft, 1990). Teachers need to provide effective instruction, to maximize time management, and to advocate for purchase of equipment. There are four major categories of available technology:

1. *Devices to increase visual access to print,* including closed-circuit televisions (CCTV) that enlarge print size on a television screen. A student may use

early avid readers, probably a consequence of all my talking out of necessity and my obsession with being sure there were plenty of opportunities for learning.

It always amuses me that sighted people are so particularly focused on the fact that I cared for my children as babies. That was, without doubt, the easy part. A baby stays where you put her. Even when crawling or early walking, a baby is easy to keep within a defined area. It's when they become truly mobile—and later, truly individualized with their own opinions—that parenting, with or without sight, gets most challenging.

Sure, there have been some things we couldn't do. Someone else has to kick a soccer ball around with my eight-year-old, and someone else had to teach my older kids to drive. But no parent can do it all. On the other hand, I have taught other kids to bake cookies, write stories, sing songs.

Over the years I have known many other parents who are blind and seen many styles of parenting. Why should we expect anything less? Vision impairment is an equal opportunity disability and affects people of all temperaments and leadership capabilities.

What I know for sure is that when it comes to parenting, the same rules apply for people with impaired vision as for all others. Anyone who wants to have children should do so and will figure out the logistics as they go along. We have loved, laughed, and lived family life to the fullest in my household, and there is no person, no professional accomplishment, no privilege I could ever cherish more than my three children.

Deborah Kendrick

Source: "Can Girls with Impaired Vision Be Mommies?" by Deborah Kendrick, *Envision,* August 1997, pp. 5–7.

such devices to magnify all or some of her classwork. The CCTV should be available in a place where the student has easy access and is also still a part of the class. As soon as the student is introduced to the CCTV, she will receive instruction from the vision specialist on its use and should, within a short time, be able to use it independently. The student should then be allowed to use the CCTV whenever she believes it will help accomplish the classwork. Some students use the CCTV only for reading, preferring to complete written assignments without it, while other students use it for both reading and writing. If the student is just beginning to use the CCTV, a

~ Scope and Sequence of Technology Skills and Applications

Primary Grades (K–3)

In these grades, the teacher of students with visual impairments needs to teach or foster the following:

- An awareness of technology, by having students explore the layout of equipment and how components are connected.
- The basic rules of computer uses, such as shutting the computer down properly.
- How to navigate the screen using screen readers with synthesized speech or a refreshable Braille display.
- Prekeyboarding activities using touch tables and tactile overlays.
- Keyboarding skills when a student has the necessary motor and academic skills for the task using "touch-typing" techniques.
- Early word-processing skills, such as naming, saving, and printing files: inserting and deleting text; and completing written assignments.
- The use of screen-enlargement features, including built-in features of word-processing programs and specialized software.
- The use of screen-reading programs to read sentences, then words and characters; spell out individual words; adjust voice and punctuation settings; and so forth.
- The use of refreshable Braille displays, either alone or in conjunction with speech synthesis when a student is proficient in uncontracted Braille.

Middle School (Grades 4–8)

In these grades, the specialist instructs students in these skills:

- More advanced word-processing skills, such as cutting and pasting text, using a spell checker, using formatting features (including centering and underlining), and using the dictionary feature.
- More advanced screen-reading skills, such as using customized screen-reading settings and skimming long documents with search-and-find features.
- The use of portable note takers, beginning with simple applications (such as word-processing file management, and using the calendar and calculator functions).
- Internet applications, such as using e-mail, a Web browser, off-line browsing and search engines.
- The use of Braille-translation software and Braille embossing.

High School (Grades 9–12)

In high school, the specialist helps students master advanced skills:

- Advanced functions of applications.
- More detailed use of the Internet and World Wide Web, such as using advanced e-mail features and creating web pages.
- The use of scanners and optical character recognition (OCR) software to create Braille documents from print materials.
- Higher-level functions, including advanced mathematics and computer programming.
- The use of an electronic Brailler and other types of specialized equipment.

Source: Adapted from F.M. D'Andrea and K Barnicle, "Access to information: Technology and Braille," in D.P. Wormsley and F.M. D'Andrea, Eds., *Instructional Strategies for Braille Literacy* (New York: AFB Press, 1997), pp. 269–307.

gentle reminder may be helpful when the student has an academic task that may be more efficiently completed with the device.

2. *Devices to increase auditory access to print,* including voice output for personal computers and devices that convert print to auditory output, such as the Kurzwiel Reading Machine. A Kurzwiel Reading Machine is quite expensive and will probably not be available in the classroom; however, this device may be available through the library or vision resource center in your school or region. In addition, voice output devices are becoming more widely available. For students who are unable to read the print on a computer screen, a voice output device may allow them to use the computer to complete assignments. Headphones are available so that the student can use the device without disturbing other students.

Technology can improve access to print through visual, auditory, or tactile modalities.

3. *Devices to increase tactile access to print,* including Braille printers that can be attached to word processors for immediate access to print work and devices that convert print to a tactile output, such as the Optacon. In the past, students who were blind would complete assignments in Braille, but the classroom teacher who was unable to read Braille would have to wait for the vision specialist to transcribe the Braille into print before grading the assignment. With the introduction of devices that can convert print into Braille and Braille into print, students can print their assignments in both Braille and English.
4. *Devices to increase independent travel,* including electronic travel aids that are independent or that attach to a long cane and provide supplementary information about the environment. Although these devices are not directly relevant to academic work, the classroom teacher should know as much as possible about any device the student is using, including how it works, when the student should use it, and how to reinforce the student's proper use of the device. An orientation and mobility specialist will be able to answer all of these questions.

Using some of these adaptive devices, people with visual impairments can also use the Internet. Websites that are "Bobby approved" (see Chapter 10) are accessible for users who are blind or have low vision. See the accompanying box, "Scope and Sequence of Technology Skills and Applications," for information on grade-appropriate technology skills.

As you know, change in technology occurs so quickly that it can be difficult to keep up to date. Consult the "Multimedia Resources" section at the end of this chapter for some websites that can provide you with the most current information about assistive technology.

Summary

- Students with visual impairments make up a relatively small percentage of school-age children. This low-incidence population includes children who are blind, who have low vision, and who are visually impaired and have additional disabilities. Although legal blindness is required for some services, educational services are also offered to students with less severe visual impairments.
- The process of seeing involves the passage of light through the eye and interpretation of the image by the brain. Damage to any of the eye structures, the

nerves connecting them to the brain, or the brain itself can result in visual impairment.

- Visual impairments may affect a child's development by limiting one source of sensory feedback from the environment. In language, children may use verbal expressions without understanding what they mean; in physical development, children may be less motivated to move and explore; in cognitive development, children may interact less with the environment, which may result in poorer concept development.
- Early intervention involves allowing the child to explore and touch and helping parents make the most of learning opportunities in daily life.
- Teachers are often the first to recognize milder visual impairments. The most common screening test is the Snellen Chart. Ideally, vision screening is the product of a team approach, with continuous observation in the classroom, referral for evaluation, and follow-up provided by appropriate professionals.
- A functional vision assessment is used to make decisions about the student's educational program. Interpretation of test results should take into account modifications to the test and items that rely heavily on visual experience.
- The expanded core curriculum for students who are blind or have low vision includes instruction in the core academic areas and in specialized skill areas such as: instruction in Braille, instruction in low-vision aids, development of listening skills, and orientation and mobility.
- Placement options for students who have visual impairments were initially limited to residential schools; however, public schools now provide self-contained classrooms, as well as resource programs, itinerant services, and consultation services for students included in the general education classroom.
- Advances in assistive technology have resulted in increasing visual, auditory, and tactile access to print; new technology for mobility has also been developed.

Key Terms

visual impairment
legal blindness
visual acuity
educational definitions
low vision
functional vision
cornea
pupil
lens
vitreous humor
iris
retina
optic nerve
cortical visual impairment
retinopathy of prematurity (ROP)
optic nerve hypoplasia
albinism
glaucoma
cataract
diabetic retinopathy
verbalisms
echolalia
orientation and mobility
Snellen Chart
expanded core curriculum
orientation and mobility training
ophthalmologist
optometrist
optician

orientation and mobility specialist
vocational rehabilitation counselor
human guide
cane travel
dog guide
electronic travel aids
independent living skills
assistive technology

Multimedia Resources

American Foundation for the Blind. *AFB Directory of Services for Blind and Visually Impaired Persons in the United States and Canada* (with accompanying CD-ROM) (New York: AFB Press). This directory, updated yearly, is a compilation of schools, agencies, organizations, and programs that serve individuals who are blind or have low vision and their families. The CD-ROM contains the same information, making it accessible to users with vision loss with adaptive equipment.

American Foundation for the Blind website: http://www.afb.org/afb/; AFB InfoLine: (800) 232-5463. The AFB InfoLine provides information about Talking Books, as well as other AFB services.

American Printing House for the Blind website: http://www.aph.org/. APH provides special media, tools, and material needed for education and daily life by people with visual impairments.

Blind Children's Center. This group publishes a series of booklets that are useful, inexpensive, and reader-friendly on topics such as communicating and encouraging movement with the young child with visual impairments. They are written with parents in mind but are helpful for early intervention specialists and teachers, too. Contact them at 4120 Marathon Street, Los Angeles, CA 90020, (800) 222-3566, http://www.blindcenter.org/.

Keller, Helen. *The Story of My Life* (Garden City, NY: Doubleday, 1954). This autobiography has inspired many a reader; for even more detail, read *Helen and Teacher* by Joseph Lash (republished in 1997 by the American Foundation for the Blind), or rent the movie version of *The Miracle Worker*, which tells the story of Helen's discovery of the meaning of language with Annie Sullivan.

Lewis, Sandra, and Carol B. Allman *Seeing Eye to Eye: An Administrator's Guide to Students with Low Vision* (New York: American Foundation for the Blind 2000). This booklet explains the needs of students with low vision and the practical services essential for helping them become literate and successful. An ideal resource for administrators and educators.

Library of Congress National Library Service for the Blind and Physically Handicapped. A free library program of Braille and recorded materials circulated to eligible borrowers through a network of cooperating libraries. Telephone: (202) 707-9275; website: http://lcweb.loc.gov/nls.html/.

D'Andrea, Frances Mary, & Carol Farrenkopf. *Looking to Learn: Promoting Literacy for Students with Low Vision* (New York: American Foundation for the Blind 2000). This handbook provides teachers with practical tips and advice on improving literacy skills for students with low vision.

About *Louis http://www.aph.org/louis.htm*. The American Printing House for the Blind (APH) currently houses a database called the *Louis* Database of Accessible Materials for People who are Blind or Visually Impaired. *Louis* contains information about more than 152,000 titles of accessible materials, including Braille, large print, sound recordings, and computer files from over 200 agencies throughout the United States. You can access *Louis* two ways.

1. Through the Internet. Go to the APH website at www.aph.org/ and follow the links for *Louis*. There is a nifty help page available from the Help button on the first search page.
2. Call, e-mail, or fax the information to be searched.

   Phone: 800-223-1839

   E-mail: resource@aph.org

   Fax: 502-899-2363

The National Agenda for Children and Youths with Visual Impairments, Including Those with Multiple Disabilities (New York: American Foundation for the Blind, 1995). This resource lists the national priorities for children with visual impairments as identified by noted professionals in the field.

Torres, Iris, and Anne L. Corn. *When You Have a Visually Impaired Child in Your Classroom: Suggestions for Teachers* (New York: American Foundation for the Blind, 1990). This small book is available free from the American Foundation for the Blind. It is a very straightforward and useful resource for teachers who are including students with vision loss.

AccessWorld: Technology for Consumers with Visual Impairments is a new bimonthly journal from the American Foundation for the Blind that plans to cover assistive technology and visual impairment. It is available online, in large print and Braille, or on tape or disk. Go to www.afb.org for more information.

What You Can Do

1. Now that you've read the chapter, have your assumptions about what it is like to have a visual impairment changed? Try a simulation exercise: Wear a blindfold during the first half of class. Concentrate on orientation and mobility, using listening skills, and memorizing spatial relationships. What were your impressions?
2. What are the limitations of the simulation exercise you just experienced? Now that you've experienced the simulation, what are you going to do to improve the quality of life for people with visual impairments?
3. Find out what's involved in raising a dog guide puppy. Contact 4-H Clubs of America, Room 50355, U.S. Department of Agriculture, Washington, DC 20250.
4. Contact the Office for Students with Disabilities on your campus and ask if there is a need for readers for students who are blind. Some textbooks are not immediately available in Braille or large print, so listening to a book on audiotape is the only way students have access to text material.
5. Learn human guide techniques so that you can accompany and assist a person with vision loss.
   - Let the person take your elbow, and walk half a step in front of her.
   - Describe objects or obstacles.
   - If approaching a stairway, say whether the stairs are going up or down.

- Describe a chair before placing a person's hand on the back of it; he can seat himself.
- Make sure doors are fully closed or open.
- Describe any changes in a familiar furniture arrangement.
- Converse naturally; provide detailed descriptions; don't worry about using words like *see* or *look;* don't hesitate to ask if it's not apparent what kind of help to provide.

6. Plan a social studies or science lesson and modify it to meet the needs of students who are blind.

Children with Physical Disabilities and Health Impairments

12

CHILDREN WITH physical disabilities and health impairments are a diverse group. This category includes a wide range of individual differences. Because many students with physical disabilities and health impairments have acquired their disabilities after infancy or have short life expectancies, they face emotional stress that teachers and parents must address. As you read, think about these questions:

What are the differences between physical disabilities and health impairments?

How can knowing the cause and treatment of a student's condition help you work with the student most effectively?

How can age of onset and severity of a condition affect a child's social and emotional development?

Commonalities: How can technology facilitate communication and social interaction among all students in a classroom, including those with significant physical disabilities?

Collaboration: What is the transdisciplinary approach? How is it implemented in the classroom?

Can Do: How has legislation affected the accessibility of schools and other public buildings to individuals with physical disabilities?

Many individuals with physical disabilities or health impairments play a pivotal role in the ongoing fight for civil and human rights due all people with disabilities. Their participation in this struggle resulted not only in many legal and physical changes in the environment, but also in a long tradition of self-advocacy. The visibility of physical disabilities creates a common bond and allows advocates to make powerful statements. That visibility, however, can set up nonphysical barriers and other difficulties in interpersonal situations, particularly for young children. For example, imagine having to explain many times a day why you have no hair, why your hands are in splints, or why you have to rest a few seconds between words. In this chapter, we will rely frequently on the voices of persons with physical disabilities and health impairments as they answer these types of questions to help you learn more about them as people—friends, relatives, students.

Definitions and Terms

Probably more than any other disability, the presence of a physical disability makes us explore the meaning of such words as *disability*, *handicap*, and *severity*. This is because the degree of physical involvement and the degree to which the disability affects an individual's life are not necessarily correlated. You might consider paralysis from the neck down to be an extremely severe disability. Yet many persons with this condition lead fulfilling lives. They may not view them-

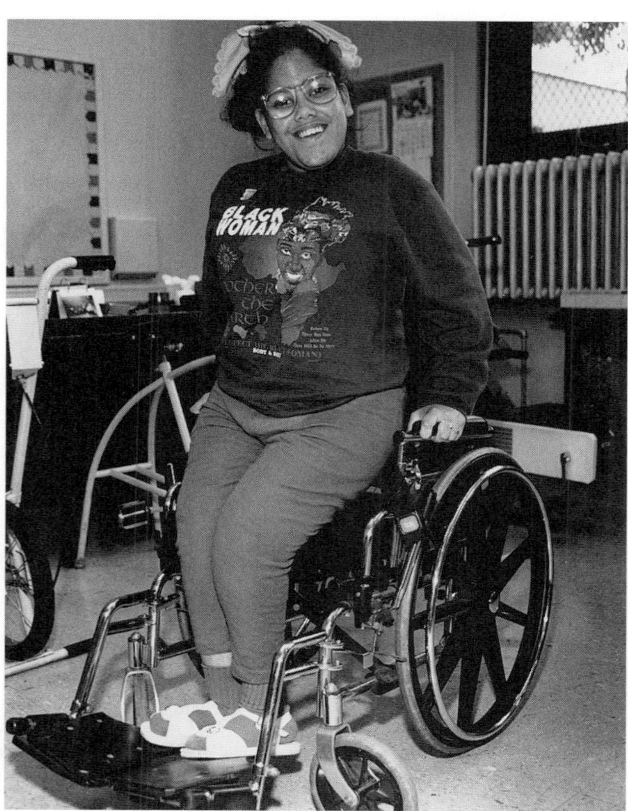

This teenager's face reflects independence, strength, and joy. (Pam Hasegawa/Impact Visuals)

selves as "handicapped" at all. The individual adjusts, adapts, and contributes to the community. Disabilities become handicaps only when society uses them as a reason to discriminate against and segregate people.

Many people with physical disabilities prefer to use the term **physically challenged.** They view their physical conditions as a challenge to be faced rather than as a situation that disables or handicaps their existence. "Living as a spinal cord injured individual is really no different than living as an able bodied individual, except that you're doing it on wheels. Some of the technical aspects of living on wheels are different" (Corbet, 1980, p. 54).

Many people with physical disabilities view their physical condition as a challenge rather than a handicapping condition.

Physical disability refers to a condition that incapacitates the skeletal, muscular, and/or neurological systems of the body to some degree. Many individuals with physical disabilities have no concurrent mental disability. This is an important point for us to keep in mind. Later in the chapter we will discuss conditions of coexisting mental and physical disabilities.

The Individuals with Disabilities Education Act (IDEA) identifies students who experience physical disabilities as "orthopedically impaired":

> "Orthopedically impaired" means having a severe orthopedic impairment. The term includes an impairment caused by a congenital anomaly (e.g., clubfoot, absence of some member, etc.), an impairment caused by disease (e.g., poliomyelitis, bone tuberculosis, etc.), and an impairment from any other cause (e.g., cerebral palsy, amputations, and fractures or burns which cause contractures). (Individuals with Disabilities Education Act, 1990, sec. 300.6[6])

The term **health impairment** also focuses on the physical condition of individuals. It includes conditions in which one or more of the body's systems are affected by diseases or conditions that are debilitating or life-threatening or that interfere with the student's ability to perform in a regular classroom setting. The definition of health impairment found in IDEA is as follows:

> "Other health impaired" means having limited strength, vitality, or alertness, due to chronic or acute health problems such as heart condition, tuberculosis, rheumatic fever, nephritis, asthma, sickle cell anemia, hemophilia, epilepsy, lead poisoning, leukemia, or diabetes. (Amendments to the Individuals with Disabilities Education Act, 1990, sec. 300.5[7])

Prevalence

Children with physical disabilities and other health impairments are among the smallest groups served under the federal laws known as IDEA. The *Twenty-Second Annual Report to Congress on the Implementation of the Individuals with Disabilities Act* (USDOE, 2000) reported 69,492 children from the ages of 6 to 21 with orthopedic impairments and 106,000 with other health impairments in the 1998–1999 school year.

Types of Physical Disabilities

In this section, we will look at the most prevalent types, causes, and treatments of physical disabilities in children. There are several reasons why you, as a prospective teacher, should know about particular disabilities. Understanding

Children with Physical Disabilities and Health Impairments

the cause may help you to know what to expect from a student, since certain causes lead to characteristic behavior. Understanding treatment requirements can also help you plan classroom time (for example, a student may need to miss class for dialysis) and become comfortable with helping the student with in-school treatment such as tube feeding. Once you know what to expect, you will be better able to plan instruction and to prepare the classroom from a physical perspective.

Within each disability category, the individual range of ability is very large.

The abilities of students within each type of physical disability can vary widely. Resist stereotyping and base your expectations on the abilities and efforts of each individual student.

Neurological Conditions

A neurological condition affects the nervous system—the brain, nerves, and spinal cord (Fraser, Hensinger, & Phelps, 1990). The muscles and bones are healthy but the neurological messages sent to them are faulty or interrupted. Three of the neurological conditions are cerebral palsy, spina bifida, and seizure disorders.

Cerebral palsy—caused by damage to the brain before birth or infancy—results in disabilities in movement and posture.

■ ***Cerebral Palsy*** **Cerebral palsy** is a condition involving disabilities in movement and posture that results from damage to the brain before or during birth or in infancy (Fraser, Hensinger, & Phelps, 1990). The muscles and the nerves connecting the muscles to the brain are normal; the problem lies in the "communication" process between the brain and the muscles. Events like cerebral hemorrhages (bleeding in the brain), anoxia (lack of oxygen at birth), and fetal strokes can cause neurological damage that results in some type of cerebral palsy. However, in almost half of the instances of cerebral palsy, no specific cause can be identified (Healy, 1983).

The area and severity of brain injury, the cause of the injury, and when it occurs determine the type of cerebral palsy that appears and the extent of its effect on the body. Although incidence figures vary, it is estimated that 1.5 to 2 instances of cerebral palsy occur for every 1,000 live births (Batshaw & Perret, 1992).

Some children are identified as having cerebral palsy at birth, whereas others are not definitively diagnosed until they are a year old or even older. Young children are often identified as having cerebral palsy because of delay in meeting developmental milestones of motor development and the persistence of certain infant reflexes. Cerebral palsy also can be diagnosed in children up to age 6 who have brain damage due to external causes such as suffocation, near drowning, or encephalitis.

Cerebral palsy is often classified by type of motor dysfunction (see Figure 12.1). The most common type of dysfunction is *spasticity*, or hypertonia. Spasticity involves a mild to severe exaggerated contraction of muscles when the muscle is stretched (Denhoff, 1975). Spasticity is present in about 60 percent of all cases of cerebral palsy and occurs when the area injured is on the surface of the brain or on the nerves leading from the surface to the interior of the brain (Grove, Cusick, & Bigge, 1991). Spasticity can involve the entire body or only some parts of the body.

Dyskenesia is a type of cerebral palsy characterized by involuntary extraneous motor activity, especially under stress (Blackburn, 1987). This type of cerebral palsy occurs in about 20 percent of all cases and is caused by injury to the basal ganglia, the brain's motor switchboard (Healy, 1983). The involuntary

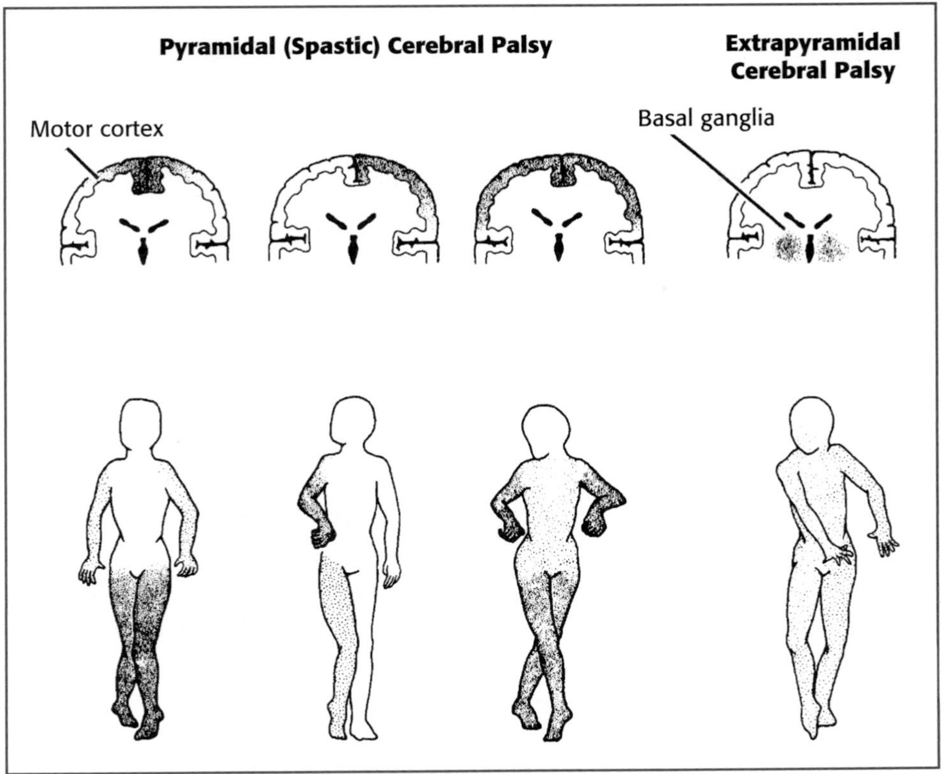

Figure 12.1
Regions of the Brain Affected in Various Forms of Cerebral Palsy

Source: M. L. Batshaw and Y. M. Perret, *Children with Handicaps: A Medical Primer,* 3d ed. (Baltimore: Paul H. Brookes, 1992), p. 444. Copyright © 1992. Used by permission of the author. Note: The darker the shading, the more severe the involvement.

movements sometimes accompany the individual's attempts at voluntary movement. One type of movement (*athetosis*) involves a slow, writhing type of movement. The person may appear to be repeatedly and slowly stretching his or her arms or legs when simply trying to reach for a book. *Choreoathetosis* refers to quick, jerky movements that may accompany the athetoid movements. Movements also may be slow and rhythmic and involve the entire limb or trunk (*distonia*).

Ataxia, a third type of cerebral palsy, is much less common. It occurs in about 1 percent of all cases, when the injury has occurred in the cerebellum. Ataxia refers to a lurching walking gait. People with ataxia also experience difficulty maintaining their balance.

About 30 percent of the individuals with cerebral palsy have a mixture of types (Healy, 1983). For example, a student might have spastic quadriplegia and ataxia. As we have already mentioned, the range of severity and involvement can be great. Some individuals may experience slight difficulty in muscle control—difficulty that may be undetectable by an observer. Others have almost no voluntary movement.

Some children with cerebral palsy also experience mental retardation, hyperactivity, or other disabilities such as visual impairment and hearing loss. The coexistence of other types of disabilities depends on the extent and location of brain injury as well as on early interventions. Some recent statistics suggest that around 30 percent of individuals with cerebral palsy have no coexisting mental

My Life

Hi! My name is Jessica Smallman. I am 14 years of age; I was born May 3, 1982, in Halifax, Nova Scotia. Before I was born my parents, Faye Smallman and John Smallman, Jr., were told that I had a birth defect called spina bifida. I also had something called hydrocephalus, which means I had water on and near the brain. After I was born the doctors did an operation on me to insert a shunt (a tube from my head to my stomach to drain the water from my head to my stomach). I was hospitalized for a little while after birth.

As I got older I needed special equipment to help me go to the washroom, stand, walk, and just for mobility reasons. Since my dad is in the navy, we move a lot and I went to several elementary schools and a new hospital in Montreal. When I went to new schools it was very hard because of the students at these schools. The kids didn't know what was wrong with me and they didn't know how to react around me. In class they would call me stupid. One day, I just could not take it anymore and I did a presentation in front of my grade five classmates on spina bifida. After the presentation they stopped bugging and teasing me. My parents pushed me to be more active and independent even though they saw how much I was hurting. In the summer I went to the rehabilitation centre for four weeks. They taught me how to live on my own, how to keep fit, and how to protect myself. They also taught me not to be so upset about the way people treat me since the reason they act this way is because they don't understand me. They think they have to do everything for me, and if they move me a certain way I will break. This is not true because I'm very, very strong, and I'm not glass or something fragile or delicate.

I also have to say that I am not lazy and I don't like people saying that. People used to laugh because I couldn't do some of the things they could, but I try my best to do many things. I think I am almost the same as any kid I know. I think like everyone else and I talk like

retardation, and only 10 percent have moderate to severe mental retardation; others suggest that approximately 41 percent of individuals with cerebral palsy have IQs below 70 (Nelson & Ellenberg, 1986).

The variability in the estimates of IQ ranges for children with cerebral palsy is largely due to difficulties in administering intelligence tests to individuals with severe physical disabilities. Because many children with severe cerebral palsy have significant differences in both speech and motor abilities, even non-

everyone else. The only things I don't do like everyone else is walk and go to the bathroom by myself. That is why I have to wear diapers and I do self-catheterizations every four hours, and I can't drink much after I do my catheters. If I do I will leak a lot more than I usually do. I also get infections a lot easier than other people. If I could tell people one thing, it is "please don't treat me like I'm fragile."

Life.....................

Life is like an elevator, some days are good some days are bad.
Life is like a book, some parts are boring and some are lots of fun.
Life is a bunch of songs, some are happy ones and some are sad ones.
Life is about heartaches and headaches and other different feelings.
Life is like school, you're always being educated.
And some things you may not like, but you've got to continue.
Life is full of surprises that are waiting for us to discover them.
Some may cause pain and some may cause happiness.
And life is having friends around you that care about you no matter what.
They won't do stuff behind your back or not believe you
or the things you say,
And that's what life is all about (at least that's what my life is all about).

by Jessie Smallman

Jessie Smallman is a grade nine student at Gaetz Brook Junior High, Nova Scotia.

Source: "My Life" by Jessica Smallman, *Ability Network Magazine,* Vol. 5, Number 2. Winter 1996/97. Reprinted by permission of Ability Network Publishing, Inc.

verbal IQ tests are difficult to administer. Parents, teachers, and psychologists must therefore attend closely to academic, task-oriented, and behavioral characteristics of students with cerebral palsy to get a clearer idea of each student's abilities. Characteristics such as maturity, determination and persistence, goal orientation, insight, and the use of one's intellect to cope with disability have been coupled with early academic success in students with severe cerebral palsy (Willard-Holt, 1998). Although typical standardized tests may be difficult to administer, students will find other ways of revealing their potential. Clearly, identifying a truly efficient method of communication is the critical factor in both assessment and instruction.

Medical interventions such as braces, surgery, and prescribed therapies can help a student with cerebral palsy. For example, physical and occupational therapies exercise, strengthen, and position muscles, bones, and joints. Prevention of serious and painful contractures, dislocations, and rigidity is critical for individuals with cerebral palsy. Physical and occupational therapies facilitate the development of normal reflexes and maximize the control a person can have over the environment.

Positioning is a critical intervention for persons with limited mobility, especially in helping them meet the demands of the classroom. For example, although a physically capable individual can change positions when uncomfortable or fatigued, a student in a wheelchair or one who wears braces may need assistance for minor repositioning. A student with cerebral palsy may need an adult, such as the teacher, to provide physical assistance related to positioning, feeding, and other everyday needs. In the classroom, use of a tape recorder or a "note buddy" for writing notes are simple accommodations that teachers commonly arrange. Assistive technology, another significant intervention for students with cerebral palsy, will be discussed later in the chapter.

In spina bifida, the spine does not close properly during fetal development, resulting in varying degrees of paralysis.

■ ***Spina Bifida*** **Spina bifida,** or open spine, and *neural tube defects (NTDs)* are general terms used to describe a midline defect of the skin, spinal column, and spinal cord that occurs during fetal development (Caldwell, Todaro, & Gates, 1988). An estimated 1 out of every 2,000 births is affected (Grove, Cusick, & Bigge, 1991). Spina bifida is most common in persons of Irish, Scotch, and English ancestry, and high-incidence regions in the United States, such as southern Appalachia, North and South Carolina, and Tennessee, reflect this heritage (Greenberg, James, & Oakley, 1983). Spina bifida and other NTDs have been correlated with a lack of folic acid, a vitamin found in green vegetables and fresh fruit, in the diet early in the pregnancy. Studies have found that minimal intakes of folic acid before and during pregnancy significantly decrease the incidence of spina bifida and other NTDs even in women who have had children with NTDs. Women of childbearing age should carefully evaluate their diets for proper amounts of folic acid or consult with a doctor about appropriate vitamin supplements.

Children with spina bifida have spines that did not properly close during development, so the spinal cord protrudes from the weak point. As a result, nerves that control the lower parts of the body are not properly connected to the brain. Spina bifida usually results in limited or even no muscle control of the affected area. The extent of the defect depends on the location of the spinal cord damage (Grove, Cusick, & Bigge, 1991). If the damage is at the base of the spine, the weakness may be limited to the muscles of the ankles and feet and the child may require only short leg braces for walking. A defect in the middle of the spine may result in paralysis below the waist, necessitating the use of a wheelchair. Bladder control problems and recurring kidney infections are also present (Caldwell, Todaro, & Gates, 1988).

In hydrocephalus, cerebrospinal fluid builds in the skull, sometimes causing brain damage and mental retardation.

Hydrocephalus, a condition in which cerebrospinal fluid builds up in the skull and puts pressure on the brain, occurs in about 80 percent of cases of spina bifida. Untreated hydrocephalus may cause brain damage and mental retardation. Since spina bifida and other NTDs can now be detected early in pregnancy, children with this disability are likely candidates for prenatal surgery. Shunts (artificial openings) can be inserted while the fetus is still in the uterus to minimize damage to the brain from excess spinal fluid. Although the paralysis itself cannot be corrected, shunt implants, physical therapy, and surgery can help minimize the effects of the disability (Korabek & Cuvo, 1986).

■ ***Seizure Disorders*** Seizures occur when the normally ordered pattern of movement of electricity along the nerve pathways of the brain is disrupted by an unorganized burst of electric impulses. These bursts periodically disrupt the normal functioning of the brain. Seizure disorders occur in about 6 percent of the population (Batshaw & Perret, 1992). A condition of the nervous system that results in the recurrence of seizures is known as **epilepsy** (Wolraich, 1983b). There are a number of possible causes, including any direct injury to the brain, conditions such as cerebral palsy, or scarring of the brain as a result of infections or illness such as meningitis or rubella. In some instances, there appears to be a genetic component or predisposition. In many instances of epilepsy, however, there is no identifiable cause. It is important to know that not all seizures are epileptic in nature. For example, sometimes a young child with a high fever has an isolated seizure.

Epilepsy is a neurological condition characterized by recurrent seizures.

Two types of seizures found frequently in school-age children are grand mal seizures and petit mal seizures. **Grand mal seizures,** also called generalized tonic-clonic seizures, are experienced by about 60 percent of all individuals with seizure disorders (Wolraich, 1983b). The seizures, which involve the whole body, usually last a few minutes and often result in a loss of consciousness. Most people experience a warning (called an *aura*) before the occurrence of a grand mal seizure. The aura may be characterized by unusual feelings or numbness. The seizure itself begins with a *tonic phase,* in which there is a stiffening of the body, often a loss of consciousness, heavy and irregular breathing, and drooling. In a few seconds, the seizure goes into the second, or *clonic phase.* At this time, the muscles alternately clench and relax. Finally, the seizure is followed by a period of fatigue or disorientation. (See the accompanying box, "What to Do If Someone Has a Tonic-Clonic Seizure.")

Petit mal seizures, also called absence seizures, occur most frequently in children between the ages of 4 and 12 (Wolraich, 1983b). Petit mal seizures often disappear as the child grows older; however, one-third to one-half of children with a history of petit mal seizures are likely also to have or eventually develop grand mal seizures. Petit mal seizures are very brief—usually lasting between 15 and 30 seconds. The episodes are sometimes difficult to recognize. The child will lose consciousness, but this is not accompanied by any observable physical changes. In other words, the child may appear to be just blinking his eyes or staring into space for a few seconds.

Medications are used extensively in the treatment of seizure disorders. In most cases, appropriate medication can prevent seizures; some adjustment in prescription may be necessary as the child gets older or if different types of seizures begin to occur. It is important for teachers to know when students are receiving medication for seizures because medication can affect school performance by causing changes in alertness and other school-related behaviors. A few children who experience a number of different kinds of seizures or who have extensive brain damage may have seizures that are difficult to keep under control. A recently approved treatment for epilepsy, especially for people who do not benefit from medications, is electrical stimulation of the vagus nerve. An electrode implanted in the chest sends signals to the vagus nerve, which is located in the neck. Research indicates that this procedure significantly reduces the occurrence of seizures (Finesmith, Zampella, & Devinsky, 1999).

What to Do If Someone Has a Tonic-Clonic Seizure

- Keep calm. Reassure the other children that the child will be fine in a minute.
- Ease the child gently to the floor and clear the area of anything that could hurt him.
- Put something flat and soft (like a folded jacket) under his head so it will not bang against the floor as his body jerks.
- Turn him gently onto his side. This keeps his airway clear and allows any fluid in his mouth to drain harmlessly away.

  Don't try to force his mouth open.

  Don't try to hold on to his tongue.

  Don't put anything in his mouth.

  Don't restrain his movements.
- When the jerking movements stop, let the child rest until full consciousness returns.
- Breathing may have been shallow during the seizure and may even have stopped briefly. This can give the child's lips or skin a bluish tinge, which corrects naturally as the seizure ends. In the unlikely event that breathing does not begin again, check the child's airway for any obstruction. It is rarely necessary to give artificial respiration.

Some children recover quickly after this type of seizure; others need more time. A short period of rest, depending on the child's alertness following the seizure, is usually advised. However, if the child is able to remain in the classroom afterward, he or she should be encouraged to do so.

Source: From *Children and Epilepsy: The Teacher's Role* (Landover, MD: Epilepsy Foundation of America, 1992), pp. 3–4.

Musculoskeletal Conditions

In addition to physical disabilities caused by damage to the brain are conditions that directly affect muscles and bones. These musculoskeletal and neuromuscular conditions debilitate the muscles, bones, or joints to such a degree that they cause limitations in their functional use.

In muscular dystrophy, the voluntary muscles of the body progressively weaken.

■ ***Muscular Dystrophy*** **Muscular dystrophy** is a neuromuscular condition in which the voluntary muscles of the body are affected by progressive weakness. Although there are several types of muscular dystrophy, the most common in school-age children is Duchenne's muscular dystrophy. This often hereditary condition, which affects boys, is usually diagnosed between the ages of 2 and 6. Neither the cause of Duchenne's muscular dystrophy nor a specific treatment has yet been discovered. The incidence is usually cited as 1 per 3,500 live male births (Grove, Cusick, & Bigge, 1991).

Because muscular dystrophy is a progressive condition, the child becomes increasingly weak and less mobile with age. A young child with muscular dystrophy may have barely noticeable weakness; by the time the child reaches his teens, however, walking may no longer be possible. The muscle weakness usually begins in the shoulders and hips and then spreads to other areas. Secondary effects of muscular dystrophy include scoliosis (curvature of the spine) and a gradual loss of respiratory function. Respiratory disease is often a cause of death of individuals with muscular dystrophy, who frequently live only until adolescence or early adulthood (Grove, Cusick, & Bigge, 1991).

Teachers must develop individualized modifications in the curriculum, depending on the child's age and the condition's progress. It is important to be

Musculoskeletal conditions vary widely; they may affect a child's ability to use his or her arms or legs or result in no visible limitations at all. (Bob Daemmrich/Stock, Boston, Inc.)

aware of the social and emotional effects that muscular dystrophy may have on the child's understanding of his or her own mortality. See Figure 12.2 for an illustration of related concerns.

■ ***Juvenile Rheumatoid Arthritis*** **Juvenile rheumatoid arthritis (JRA)** is a condition that affects the tissue lining of the joints, primarily the joints of the knees, ankles, elbows, hips, wrists, and feet, causing them to become painful and stiff. JRA is found in children between the ages of 3 and adolescence and affects twice as many girls as boys. It is estimated that only 3 new cases per 100,000 children occur each year (Grove, Cusick, & Bigge, 1991). Although the cause of JRA is unknown, it is suspected that infection or a defect in the body's immune system may be responsible (Caldwell, Todaro, & Gates, 1988).

Juvenile rheumatoid arthritis affects the tissue lining of the joints, making them painful and stiff.

One complication of JRA is *iridocyclitis*, an inflammation of the eye that occurs without warning. If a student with JRA complains about bright lights or painful eyes, a teacher should help the student seek immediate medical attention.

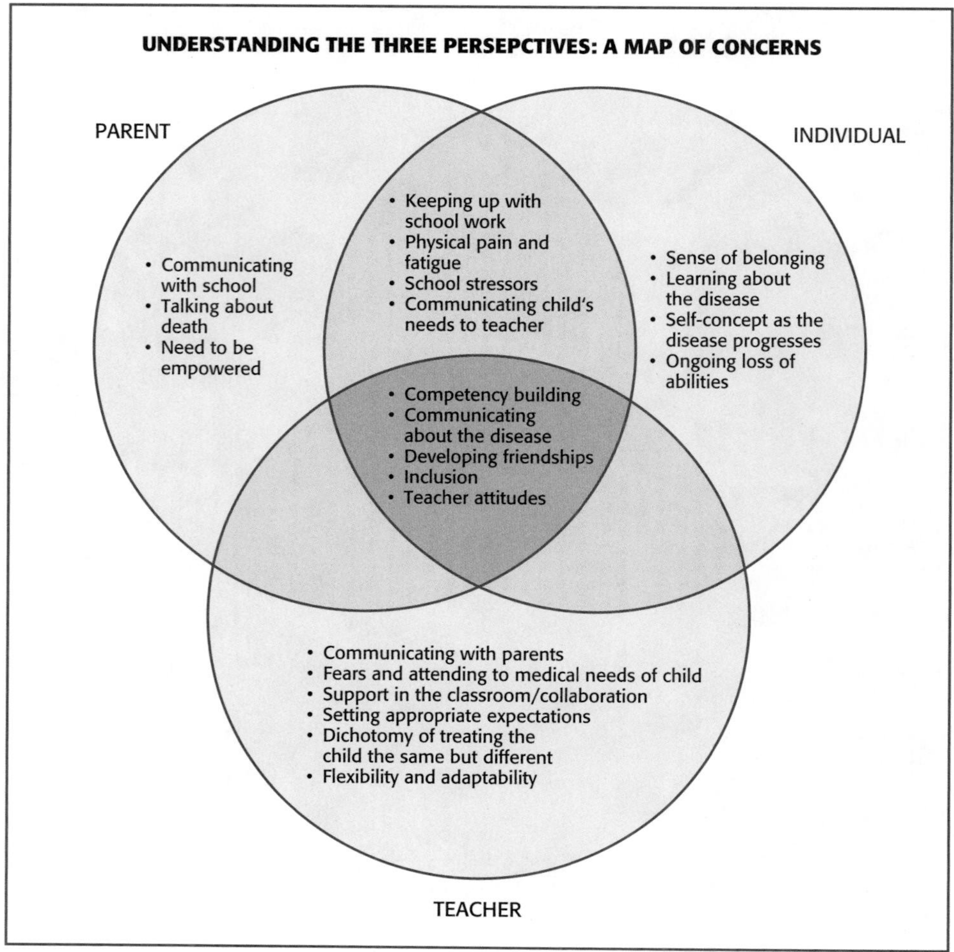

Figure 12.2
Common and Unique Concerns for Students with Neuromuscular Disabilities

Source: K. Strong and J. Sandoval, "Mainstreaming Children with a Neuromuscular Disease: A Map of Concerns," *Exceptional Children, 65* (1999), 358.

■ ***Congenital Malformations*** A **congenital malformation** is an incomplete or improperly formed part of the skeletal or muscular system that is present at birth. Congenital malformations occur in approximately 3 percent of all live births (Batshaw & Perret, 1992). Often, there is no known cause for these malformations, although many of the risk factors discussed in Chapter 2 have been partially implicated. In some instances, there may be a genetic component. In other cases, birth defects have been associated with medications or drugs taken during pregnancy, with illness, such as rubella, and with infections experienced by the mother during pregnancy. As discussed in Chapter 2, the use of the drug thalidomide by pregnant mothers during the 1950s resulted in a number of infants born with absent or shortened limbs (Batshaw & Perret, 1992).

Congenital malformations can take many forms; a few of them have particular implications for physical movement. One example is a clubfoot, in which the foot is structured so that the forefoot and heel are turned in and down toward the body and the toes are turned down and away from the body. A clubfoot is sometimes hereditary, with an incidence of 2 per every 1,000 live births. Surgery, physical therapy, and the use of casts are treatment options for children with this condition. Other malformations that can affect mobility are congenital hip dislocations, discrepancies of leg length, shortened or missing limbs, and scoliosis, or curvature of the spine. In some instances, treatment options include surgery, braces, special shoes, physical therapy, and the use of artificial limbs, or prostheses.

Many students with congenital physical malformations have no other accompanying disabilities. When the condition interferes with the student's regular education—because of surgery-related absences, for example—the student may qualify for special education and related services, such as physical or occupational therapy and transportation.

Traumatic Injury

Traumatic injury refers to damage inflicted to the brain or body after birth. There are many possible causes of traumatic injury, including child abuse and accidents, spinal cord injury, and closed-head injury.

Traumatic injury is damage to the brain or body that occurs after birth.

■ ***Spinal Cord Injuries*** Spinal cord injuries, in which the spinal cord is damaged or severed, occur most frequently in adolescents and young adults. Diving, automobile, and motorcycle accidents are frequent causes of this injury in young people. As in spina bifida, the location of the injury determines its effects. A lower-spine injury may result in limited use or paralysis of the legs. An injury higher up the spine or to the neck may result in more extensive involvement, including the arms, trunk, and neck. In some cases, respiration is greatly affected and only facial muscles can be moved voluntarily.

Consider a student who falls from a tree or is involved in a car accident. The student recovers but must now use a wheelchair. The student has missed several months of school, his friends have moved on to the next grade, and he must adjust to a new perception of himself. A severe spinal cord injury may change how the student approaches all aspects of education. One very promising area for assisting students is technology. Technological advances have provided new opportunities for mobility of individuals with spinal cord injury. We will discuss these advances in more detail later on in this chapter.

■ ***Traumatic Brain Injuries*** **Traumatic brain injury (TBI),** or acquired brain injury, is a "traumatic insult to the brain capable of producing physical, intellectual, emotional, social, and vocational changes" (National Head Injury Task Force, 1985). TBI is a separate diagnostic category in the Individuals with Disabilities Education Act (IDEA, 1990).

Traumatic brain injuries are caused by an external physical force and may result in functional disability or psychosocial impairment.

Since the brain controls and processes how one acts, damage to the brain can cause serious disabilities. The student who survives an automobile accident but who suffers a moderate or severe brain injury may physically recover well, but changes in memory, problem solving, attention span, impulse control, and overall cognition are likely to persist. The student may look the same, but these behavior changes have a significant impact on school, home, and friends.

About 23 in 10,000 children sustain TBI each year (Grove, Cusick, & Bigge, 1991). It is suspected that the actual incidence is much higher but that less severe cases are not reported. Most cases involve individuals between the ages of 15 and 24, but the number of younger children affected is almost as high (Kraus, 1987). A small school district can anticipate having several children with traumatic brain injury; a large district can anticipate having over a hundred such students (Mira, Tucker, & Tyler, 1992). Although the use of seat belts and bike and motorcycle helmets has reduced the rate of death and of severe brain injury, improvements in emergency medical services and technology have increased the number of students who become TBI survivors (Mira, Tucker, & Tyler, 1992; Witte, 1998).

An individual who survives TBI will usually be in a coma for a period of time. The length of the coma is one of the predictors of how severe the injury is. A mild brain injury usually results in loss of consciousness for less than an hour without skull fracture. A moderate injury results in one to twenty-four hours of unconsciousness and may be complicated by swelling of the brain and skull fractures. These symptoms persist for some time. A severe injury results in loss of consciousness for more than twenty-four hours. Bruising of the brain tissue (*contusion*) or bleeding in the brain (*intracranial hematoma*) is usually present. These serious conditions can result in lifelong cognitive deficits and difficulty with learning new information. Some deficits will be apparent immediately, and some will appear only after a period of time (Mira, Tucker, & Tyler, 1992; Witte, 1998).

Brain injuries affect each individual differently.

Teachers should be aware that the student returning to school with a traumatic brain injury will fatigue quickly for the first few months. Adjustment to schedules, reduction in the amount of reading and writing, memory helpers, and organizers are strategies that will help the student who survives brain injury become adjusted to school. Generally, the establishment of specific routines and highly structured learning environments is recommended for students returning to the classroom. Teachers must be flexible and must remember that each student with a traumatic brain injury will have different symptoms and may respond to different interventions (Witte, 1998).

■ ***Child Abuse*** According to Solomons (1983), a child who is battered may suffer burns, bruises, abrasions, and broken limbs—all injuries that could result from ordinary accidents. How, then, can abuse be detected? One key sign is the *number* of injuries a child exhibits. A discrepancy between the type of injury and how the injury occurred is also cause for concern.

The incidence of child abuse and neglect is not known, but a commonly accepted figure is one million cases per year. Each state has its own legal definition of child abuse. If all kinds of abuse and neglect are included, the figure would quadruple (Solomons, 1983). One-third of physical abuse cases involve children under 5. Sexual abuse of children is four to six times more common than physical abuse. Neglect is five to eight times more common (Solomons, 1983). It is estimated that 60 to 90 percent of abusers were abused themselves. Child abuse occurs in all socioeconomic levels and cultural backgrounds, and parents are not the only abusers. Friends, close family, neighbors, religious leaders, and trusted community members can also be abusers.

Child abuse is most likely to occur when there are high levels of stress in a family, when the parents' expectations for the child are too high, and when parents are emotionally and socially isolated. Children at high risk for abuse include low-birthweight infants and children with disabilities (Beckwith, 1990).

Teachers must report suspected child abuse.

Every state has laws that require teachers and health professionals to report child abuse when it is suspected. Penalties for not reporting suspected child abuse include loss of jobs and jail terms. An abused student may look to the teacher as a trusted individual. Remember that a student who tells you about abuse is seeking help. You must report these incidents to the proper authorities

~ Physical and Behavioral Indicators of Possible Neglect and Abuse

Emotional abuse and neglect

Physical indicators

- Height and weight significantly below age level
- Inappropriate clothing for weather
- Scaly skin
- Poor hygiene, lice, body odor
- Child left unsupervised or abandoned
- Lack of a safe and sanitary shelter
- Unattended medical or dental needs
- Developmental lags
- Habit disorders

Behavioral indicators

- Begging or stealing food
- Constant fatigue
- Poor school attendance
- Chronic hunger
- Dull, apathetic appearance
- Running away from home
- Child reports that no one cares/looks after him/her
- Sudden onset of behavioral extremes (conduct problems, depression)

Physical abuse

Physical indicators

- Frequent injuries such as cuts, bruises, or burns
- Wearing long sleeves in warm weather
- Pain despite lack of evident injury
- Inability to perform fine motor skills because of injured hands
- Difficulty walking or sitting

Behavioral indicators

- Poor school attendance
- Refusing to change clothes for physical education
- Finding reasons to stay at school and not go home
- Frequent complaints of harsh treatment by parents
- Fear of adults

Sexual abuse

Physical indicators

- Bedwetting or soiling
- Stained or bloody underclothing
- Venereal disease
- Blood or purulent discharge from genital or anal area
- Difficulty walking or sitting

Behavioral indicators

- Excessive fears, clinging
- Unusual, sophisticated sexual behavior/knowledge
- Sudden onset of behavioral extremes
- Poor school attendance
- Finding reasons to stay at school and not go home

Source: D. L. Cates, M. A. Markell, and S. Bettenhausen, "At Risk for Abuse: A Teacher's Guide to Recognizing and Reporting Child Neglect and Abuse," *Preventing School Failure, 39* (2) (1995), 6–9, p. 7, Winter 1995, pp. 6–9. Copyright © 1995. Reprinted by permission of the author.

so that the student can be protected from the abuser. Perhaps a student will not tell you of abuse, but certain indicators may be present. See the accompanying box, "Physical and Behavioral Indicators of Possible Neglect and Abuse," for some of the signs that might suggest concern is warranted. It is important to look at the student's age and other historical information when evaluating these indicators (Sobsey, 1994). If you or one of your students seeks help for overcoming an abusive situation, confidentiality is guaranteed in counseling centers.

Types of Health Impairments

Many conditions and diseases can significantly affect a child's health and ability to function successfully in school. Most health impairments are chronic conditions; that is, they are always present, or they recur. Many of these conditions result in gradual deterioration of health and eventual death.

Students with health impairments typically stay in the regular classroom for as long as possible.

Students with health impairments typically receive their education in the regular classroom as long as their health allows. Some require home-based instruction for periods of time or support services when they must miss school for an extended time. Teachers will need to be sensitive to the obstacles to learning that can arise from the condition itself, the side effects of prescribed treatments, and the emotional challenges the student faces. Knowledge of the condition and the individual student's treatment regimen will help you plan and prepare appropriate educational programs.

Let's look at some conditions that can fall into the category of health impairment. In some cases, only some forms of the condition are severe enough to warrant special education or support services.

Asthma

Asthma is a chronic obstructive lung condition characterized by an unusual reaction to a variety of stimuli that cause difficulty in breathing and coughing, wheezing, and shortness of breath (Caldwell, Todaro, & Gates, 1988). As many as five million children in the United States have some level of asthma, making it the most common chronic health impairment of young children (Feldman, 1996; Getch & Neuharth-Pritchett, 1999). Many things can trigger an asthma attack. Some of the more common irritants are smoke, a cold or other infection, chalk dust, exercise, cold air, pollen, animal hair, emotional stress, and classroom pets.

Asthma can be managed. Special attention should be paid to the child's overall fitness (Mitchell, 1985). Allergens that cause the reactions can be removed or minimized wherever possible. Children can also receive *bronchodilators,* which are drugs that reverse the narrowing of the airways (Mitchell, 1985). Because there may be side effects to any drug treatment, parents and teachers should learn the possible side effects of the particular medications a child is receiving.

Some forms of exercise are better tolerated than others by children with asthma. Running may result in narrowing of the airways and severe wheezing. Swimming is less likely to cause wheezing, but the child should be carefully watched, for obvious reasons. Overall participation in regular games and activities is encouraged, and many students have little or no difficulty participating in active sports.

Much attention has been given to the psychosocial effects of asthma. Loss of sleep is a frequent problem when attacks flare up at night (Caldwell, Todaro, & Gates, 1988), and it can be terrifying for a parent to watch a child fighting to breathe. Sometimes parents hesitate to discipline their child or to set limits for fear of triggering an asthmatic reaction. The child may also experience low self-esteem from a deformity in the chest cavity caused by the condition. Locker-room shyness may cause distress and anxiety (Mitchell, 1985). In general, however, the prognosis for future health is good for these children.

As a teacher you need to know the recommended physical activity levels for the student with asthma. Also, you should know the early warning signs of asthmatic episodes and what emergency procedures to take if a student has an asthma attack. Figure 12.3 illustrates a detailed asthma care plan for teachers or caregivers of a child with asthma. This figure also can serve as a model care plan for children with other health impairments or physical disabilities that require emergency action and special procedures.

Juvenile Diabetes

Juvenile diabetes is a disorder of the metabolism caused by little or no insulin being produced by the body, which results in difficulties in digesting and obtaining energy from food. It is estimated that **juvenile onset diabetes** affects over 1.5 million children, and the overall prevalence appears to be increasing at the rate of 6 percent a year.

Juvenile onset diabetes can appear at any point between birth and the age of 30; it cannot be cured, but it can be controlled by daily intake of insulin, by exercise, and by a special diet (Rosenthal-Malek & Greenspan, 1999). Sometimes diabetes can also affect the eyes and the kidneys; unmanaged or severe diabetes may result in early blindness.

Even when children are receiving treatment for diabetes, teachers should be aware of two possible emergency conditions caused by insulin reactions. One condition, which results from low blood sugar and can cause unconsciousness and seizures, is called **hypoglycemia.** Symptoms include confusion, drowsiness, perspiration, a pale complexion, sudden hunger, lack of coordination, trembling, or the appearance of intoxication. Hypoglycemia is most likely to occur if the child has gone without eating for a while or has been exerting himself or herself physically. Although parents should be informed of the reaction, certain foods, such as sugar, can be given to the child immediately to mitigate the condition. A tin of cake frosting is a good thing to keep on hand, since it not only contains sugar but is also easy to administer.

Another condition, **hyperglycemia,** results from high blood sugar. Its symptoms include extreme thirst, lethargy, dry hot skin, heavy labored breathing, and eventual unconsciousness. Severe hyperglycemia can result in ketoacidosis, which may result in unconsciousness, coma, and death (Rosenthal-Malek & Greenspan, 1999). Students experiencing hyperglycemia will need to drink water, diet soda, or other sugarless fluids.

If you have a child with juvenile diabetes in your class, it is a good idea to have a complete list of symptoms and emergency actions ready. You will need to be flexible regarding certain aspects of your classroom management. For example, students with juvenile diabetes must have immediate bathroom privileges, immediate access to a nurse, and may need to eat at specific times during the day. Communicate regularly with parents regarding classroom activities, patterns of high and low blood sugar episodes, and any deviations from those patterns (Rosenthal-Malek & Greenspan, 1999).

Cystic Fibrosis

Cystic fibrosis is a progressive and usually fatal disorder characterized by lung damage, abnormal mucus production, and difficulties in the absorption of protein and fat. Damage to the lungs results in inadequate amounts of oxygen being delivered to the body, which stresses the heart. Children with cystic fibrosis are susceptible to lung infections, pneumonia, and collapsed lungs.

Note to Teachers or Caregivers: The Asthma Care Plan is a useful tool for parents, day-care centers, babysitters, and schools. Included in the plan are specific instructions on what to do in the event of an asthma episode. Parents should fill out the form completely; and the form should be signed by the parent(s) and the child's physician. If parents are unable to fill out the form, they may need to obtain more information from their child's doctor.

Parents should describe to caregivers what asthma symptoms look like. Although the symptoms are listed on this form, a caregiver might not know what "nasal flaring" or "retractions" look like. It is also important for the parents and teacher to discuss the information contained on this form. The sample form included here has been filled out for a child with asthma. (Pseudonyms are used.)

Instructions for Parents:

- List *all medicines* that your child is currently taking (including over-the-counter drugs). This is very important in a medical emergency. Emergency personnel treating a child need to know what medicine(s) he or she is currently taking.
- The *allergies section* is also important. Caretakers must know what *not* to expose your child to. If the child is accidentally exposed, the caretaker or teacher must know what the child's typical reaction is.
- List *other symptoms* that may indicate your child is not breathing well. You know your child better than anyone else. Are there specific kinds of behaviors your child shows when he or she is not breathing well? List these, even if they sound silly.
- What is the child's *typical* behavior? Caregivers, especially new ones, need to know what is normal for your child. This will help them detect if the child is not behaving as he or she normally does.
- The information on this sheet will help caregivers or teachers monitor your child's asthma and obtain appropriate medical care, if needed. This sheet can also help caregivers recognize the early signs of an asthma episode. Both a parent and the child's doctor must sign the form.

Asthma Care Plan

Child's Name: Ronnie Childress
Date of Birth: 9-17-92
Parent(s) Name: Anna Childress 555-0000 (work) 555-0000 (home)
Chad Childress 555-0000 (work) 555-0000 (home) 555-0000 (cellular phone)
Other Emergency Contact: Bonnie Childress 555-0000 Grandmother
Physician: Dr. Robert Smith 555-0000
Ambulance: 911

What to Do If Asthmatic Symptoms Occur

Step 1: Shake the inhaler and place the inhaler into aerochamber.

Step 2: Place mask over Ronnie's nose and mouth.

Step 3: Depress the inhaler to release the medicine (it sounds like a *puff*) and allow Ronnie to breath in. Allow Ronnie to breathe into the mask 6 times.

Step 4: Repeat Step 3 until 8 puffs have been given and check Ronnie's peak flow reading on the peak flow meter.

Step 5: If his peak flow reading is 200 ml (Green Zone) or above, just relax.
- Check his peak flow again if you detect problems.
- If you don't detect problems, check his peak flow every hour.
- Plan to give 4 puffs of Albuterol inhaler ever 4 hours unless he seems worse or peak flow meter reading drops.

Step 6: If peak flow reading is 170-200 ml (Yellow Zone), give 6 puffs of Albuterol inhaler.
- Check his peak flow again if you detect problems.
- If you don't detect problems, check his peak flow every hour.
- Plan to give 6 puffs of Albuterol inhaler every 4 hours unless he seems worse or peak flow meter drops.

Step 7: If peak flow reading is 130-170 ml (Yellow Zone), give 8 puffs of Albuterol inhaler.
- Check his peak flow again if you detect problems.
- If you don't detect problems, check his peak flow every hour.
- Plan to give 8 puffs of Albuterol inhaler every 2 hours unless he seems worse or peak flow meter reading drops.
- Call parents.

Step 8: If peak flow reading is 100–130 ml (Yellow Zone), give 8 puffs of Albuterol inhaler and call parents.

Figure 12.3
Asthma Care Plan

Source: Y. Q. Getch and S. Neuharth-Pritchett, "Children with Asthma: Strategies for Educators," *Teaching Exceptional Children, 31*(3)(1999), 34–35.

- If you can't get parents immediately, call Ronnie's doctor and follow the doctor's instructions.
- If the Albuterol doesn't help and Ronnie appears in any distress or is lethargic, call 911.

Step 9: If peak flow reading is below 100 ml (Red Zone), give 8 puffs of Albuterol inhaler and call 911. This is an emergency!!

- Follow instructions given by emergency personnel.
- Call parents as soon as you can.

Medicines

(Include medications currently taken, medications used for asthma control, medications used in an emergency, and over-the-counter medications.)

- Name: Flovent
  Dose: 2 puffs via aerochamber
- Name: Albuterol
  Dose: 2 to 8 puffs via aerochamber (according to peak flow reading
- Name: Albuterol
  Dose: .25 ml mixed with 3 ml saline in nebulizer
- Name: Prelone
  Dose: 1 teaspoon

Obtain Immediate Medical attention If

- Lips or fingernails are blue
- Has difficulty talking or crying
- Is unresponsive to stimuli
- Chest sinks in deeply when breathing
- Cannot drink liquids
- Is just lying around and looks limp or extremely lethargic

Allergies

- Trigger: Dogs
  Typical Reaction: Coughing, drop in peak flow reading
- Trigger: Cigarette Smoke
  Typical Reaction: Coughing, labored breathing, wheezing, drop in peak flow reading
- Trigger: Milk/milk products
  Typical Reaction: Delayed reaction (4-12 hours after ingestion): wheezing, dark circles under eyes, runny nose, drop in peak flow reading
- Trigger : Strong Chemicals (Bleach)
  Typical Reaction: Wheezing, coughing

Asthmatic Symptoms

- Wheezing
- Nasal flaring
- Coughing
- Rapid shallow breathing
- Difficulty catching breath
- Appears lethargic or unduly tired
- Chest sinks in deeply when breathing

Other Symptoms That May Indicate Breathing Difficulty

- Very cranky or irritable
- Does not want to join in activities

Child's Typical Behavior

Ronnie is typically happy, social, energetic, and outgoing. He is not a cranky kid and tends to be lively and friendly. If Ronnie is ever lethargic, he is probably not breathing well.
Important: If his wheezing or difficulty breathing scares you, it is probably severe enough to require immediate medical attention. Please feel free to call 911.

Reactions or Side Effects Associated with Medications

Albuterol: Jittery, hyper, irritable (bouncing off the walls). Prelone: Same as Albuterol except more pronounced, increased heart rate, may be very distracted, doesn't listen or pay attention well.

Other Special Instructions

If you are unsure about Ronnie's condition, call his parents or the doctor. Ronnie's activities are not restricted. He can participate in all outdoor activities. Restrictions are only necessary if he is having problems with his asthma or the activity involves exposure to lots of dust (e.g., rolling in autumn leaves) or involves exposure to smoke (e.g., no roasting marshmallows over the campfire).

Food Allergies

(If child has food allergies, provide a list of food the child can or cannot have.)
Milk and milk products (e.g., pudding, cheese, yogurt, ice cream, chocolate candy bars, sour cream, cream soups, cheese crackers).

Medication Sheet

If Ronnie is having trouble with his asthma before school, the medications he has taken that morning will be documented and given to the teacher in case of increased breathing difficulty. This information must be given to emergency medical personnel if Ronnie's condition escalates and emergency personnel are contacted.

Signature of Parent/ Guardian:____________________ **Date:**________
Signature of Physician: ____________________ **Date:**________

Figure 12.3 (continued)

The disorder is an inherited recessive gene disorder; that is, both parents must be carriers in order for the child to have the condition. Parents who are carriers have a 25 percent chance per pregnancy of having a child with cystic fibrosis. The condition is most common in Caucasian populations and occurs in approximately 1 of every 2,000 births (Mitchell, 1985)—about 30,000 Americans each year (Angeter, 1992). Children with cystic fibrosis often die at a young age; the average lifespan is about 20 years. With early and continuous treatment, however, individuals with cystic fibrosis continue to live longer. In 1990, the gene carrying cystic fibrosis was identified; this is the crucial first step in finding a cure or treatment for this condition. This discovery led to the establishment of the first gene therapy centers. Although treatment is still in the earliest stages, it is apparent that a major breakthrough is at hand (Welsh & Smith, 1995).

Treatment for cystic fibrosis is extremely vigorous and often painful, including physical therapy (in some cases daily) to loosen the mucus secretions in the lungs. Because of problems in digestion, children must have dietary supplements of vitamins and enzymes, as well as antibiotics to fight off frequent infections. Hospitalization may be required because of bouts with pneumonia, other serious lung conditions, or lung collapse.

Teachers must be aware of the reduced energy level characteristic of children with cystic fibrosis and must understand that they may miss school because of therapy or hospitalization. Particularly difficult aspects, of course, are the child's awareness of the course of the disease, the fact that it is often a very painful condition, and the prospect of early death.

Acquired Immune Deficiency Syndrome (AIDS)

Acquired immune deficiency syndrome (AIDS) is a condition that has had a great impact on health concerns in recent years, and its effect on children has been recognized for some time (see the HIV/AIDS Fact Sheet in Chapter 2). AIDS is a viral disease that breaks down the body's immune system, destroying its ability to fight infections (Caldwell, Todaro, & Gates, 1988). When a child gets even the slightest cold or infection, the symptoms linger as the child weakens. AIDS is progressive, resulting in increasingly greater weakness and illness, particularly lung disease and pneumonia, which are frequently the immediate cause of death. AIDS also can affect many areas of child development, including cognitive development as the infection attacks the central nervous system (Belman et al., 1988; Lesar, Gerber, & Semmel, 1995).

AIDS is transmitted by the exchange of body fluids from an infected individual engaged in unprotected, high-risk behavior, such as unprotected sexual contact or sharing needles. AIDS has also been transmitted through blood transfusions and at birth from an infected mother to a newborn. Tragically, the number of children born with AIDS is increasing each year. Although much money and effort have been devoted to research on the virus that causes AIDS, no cure or vaccine is available yet.

Children with AIDS often face social isolation.

AIDS is the only condition we have discussed that can be transmitted to others. So, in addition to the health maintenance procedures, hospitalization, and medication required for children with this condition, children often face the unwarranted prospect of social isolation. There have been many instances in which children with AIDS have been avoided or ostracized because of fear.

Although transmission of AIDS in the normal course of school activities has never been documented, many parents—and therefore their children—have an extreme fear of this condition and sometimes fight the presence of the child with

AIDS in the regular classroom. When a teacher is aware of a student with AIDS, he or she must work to facilitate appropriate and normal social interaction and to educate other children in the classroom. Children with AIDS and their families have the most difficult task of not only dealing with a painful and probably fatal illness but also of fighting for love and acceptance from the people around them.

Childhood Cancer

Although the prognosis for children with cancer is steadily improving, cancer continues to result in more fatalities among school-age children than any other disease (Verhaaren & Connor, 1981). The extent to which childhood cancer will affect a child in school depends on whether the child is undergoing active treatment such as chemotherapy, the immediate state of the disease, and the general prognosis for the child.

Attention Deficit Hyperactivity Disorder (ADHD)

Although we have already discussed ADHD in some detail in Chapter 7, educational practice also places it in the category of Other Health Impaired. Because ADHD is a specific diagnosis but is not a separate category of special education, teachers and particularly parents seeking comprehensive services must find a category that will include their children. Children may not meet the specific identification criteria of categories that commonly co-occur with ADHD, such as learning disabilities or behavior disorders. The category of health impairments is defined in fairly general terms, and many school districts include some children with ADHD in this category. The use of this category to serve children with ADHD, not surprisingly, has resulted in great increases in the number of children served who are identified as Other Health Impaired. Remember, however, that despite the name of the category, the interventions used with students with ADHD will parallel those presented in Chapters 4 and 5.

Multiple Disabilities

This chapter focuses on individuals whose primary disability is a physical disability or health impairment. Some children born with other disabilities, including mental retardation, hearing or visual impairments, and communication disorders also experience physical disabilities or health impairments. For example, some children with Down syndrome experience congenital heart problems, and some children born with cerebral palsy have mental retardation. The Education of the Handicapped Act Amendments of 1990 (sec. 300.6[5]) define multiple disabilities as "concomitant impairments (such as mental retardation—blindness, mental retardation—orthopedic impairments, etc.) the combination of which causes such severe educational problems that they cannot be accommodated in special education programs solely for one of the impairments. The term does not include deaf-blindness."

Children whose multiple disabilities include physical or health disabilities may need comprehensive treatment and educational programming. A child with both severe cerebral palsy and mental retardation, for example, requires an effective avenue for communication, mobility instruction, physical and occupational therapy, and a program that facilitates maximum physical, social, and intellectual development.

Effects on the Developing Child

The severity and comprehensiveness of a physical disability or health impairment are gauges of how it will affect the child. In some instances, mobility or communication may be the areas in which a child feels the greatest effect; in others, the child's overall energy and motivation for making it through a day may be his or her most difficult task. The visibility of the disability may also play a major role, but not always in the way you might think. A mild disability or condition such as infrequent asthma attacks may affect the child a great deal if unwanted attention during an attack makes the child feel embarrassed. A child with a visible orthopedic disability may adjust well to challenges. It's important for you as a teacher to understand that each child is an individual with unique needs and abilities, rather than a collection of characteristics of a particular condition.

Cognitive and Intellectual Development

In most cases, a physical disability has no direct effect on intellectual disability.

In most instances, a physical disability or illness has no direct effect on intellectual growth or development. The presence of a physical disability, even a severe physical disability, does not mean that the individual's intellectual ability has been affected. Sometimes, however, both physical and cognitive disabilities occur. Cerebral palsy, for example, may include mental retardation, and some children who experience extensive brain damage are affected in many areas of functioning, including intellectual ability.

A health impairment can interfere directly with learning by affecting the speed of mental processing or the ability to focus for long periods of time. Children with asthma, muscular dystrophy, or other chronic or progressive conditions may require extensive therapy or stays in the hospital, which may interrupt their academic progress. A serious illness or condition also might greatly affect the child's stamina. As children tire more and more easily and lose energy, they may require school accommodations so that they can more readily handle academic work and attend to tasks.

Finally, cognitive development is closely dependent on communication abilities. This is particularly obvious in educational settings. Students with severe physical disabilities are most likely to succeed in academic subjects, particularly in regular classroom settings, if they are able to communicate visually, orally, or in writing. Students with physical disabilities who are able to speak and write may experience no exceptional difficulty with their academic tasks. We discuss communication further in the next section.

Communication and Language Development

Communication can be affected by many types of physical disability. The effects of a congenital disability, however, may be quite different from those of a condition with a gradual or sudden onset. Most persons with progressive conditions, or those who experienced a sudden onset of a disability, have had a number of years during which they could communicate using more conventional means. Their intellectual abilities were probably tested using standard assessment instruments, and there was time to plan for the future and teach alternative communication systems to the student and to others in his or her home, school, and social environments.

Children born with severe physical disabilities face a different challenge, because they may not be able to communicate through conventional means. Their cognitive capabilities may remain hidden until they are old enough to use an alternative system, several of which we will describe later in the chapter. People born with severe physical disabilities have faced extreme bias concerning their intellectual abilities, largely because of their inability to communicate with those around them. The assumption that severe physical disabilities were automatically associated with severe mental retardation resulted in the placement of many individuals in institutional settings with very little, if any, attempt to engage in reciprocal social interaction or communication. As you might imagine, this was not only a deplorable condition in its own right but extremely frustrating and painful for the people involved. One eloquent spokesperson, Ruth Sienkiewicz-Mercer, who lost bodily control and speech at age 5 due to encephalitis, describes her first communication breakthrough with her caretakers in a residential placement. At this point she had lived in the institution for three years without communicating with any of the adults present.

People with severe physical disabilities find their intellectual abilities underestimated because they communicate differently.

> As she brought the next spoonful of food to my mouth, she noticed that I was doing something funny with my eyes, obviously in reaction to what she had just said. I kept looking up at the ceiling, but Wessie couldn't figure out why I was doing that. She put the spoon down and thought for a few seconds, then asked, "Ruthie, are you trying to tell me something?"
>
> With a broad grin on my face, I looked at her squarely. Then I raised my eyes up to the ceiling again with such exaggeration that I thought my eyes would pop up through the top of my head.
>
> Wessie knew she was on to something, but she wasn't sure just what. She pondered for a few more seconds . . . then it clicked! A silent conversation flashed between us as loud and clear as any spoken words. Even before she asked me a dozen times over, and before I exuberantly answered a dozen times with my eyes raised skyward, Wessie knew. And I knew that she knew.
>
> I was raising my eyes to say yes.
>
> We both started laughing. Then I started laughing really hard, and before I knew it I was crying so uncontrollably that I couldn't see because of the tears. They were tears of pure joy, the kind of tears a person sheds on being released from prison after serving three years of what she had feared would be a life sentence. (Sienkiewicz-Mercer & Kaplan, 1989, p. 110)

Social and Emotional Development

Children with physical disabilities and health impairments are faced with an incredible array of stressful emotions—both their own and the emotions of others. They must struggle with perceptions of themselves, the reactions of others, and the impact on their families.

Young people with physical disabilities or health impairments may experience difficulty making friends, or just meeting new children. Sometimes, we

Don't Patronize Me—Communicate with Me

Jim Viggiano is a 37-year-old man who has cerebral palsy and spent twenty years in a state hospital in Massachusetts. Mr. Viggiano formerly used a word-board to communicate, but now uses an Autocom which will soon be configured with speech. He is an active advocate for nonverbal individuals and currently consults and lectures. The following is excerpted from a speech Mr. Viggiano gave at the Symposium on Nonverbal Communication in Boston, Massachusetts.

When I was young, I asked my mother, "Why did God make me like this?" She said to me, "God has His reasons." As time went on, I began to understand more and more of what she meant, especially in the past five years. In this time I have been able to help change things for other people and for myself. "We all get by with a little help from our friends" is my theme song. My goals are to work with people as a counselor and advocate and to help galvanize ideas as I was able to do for my friend Bob and his communication system.

Bob can only lie in bed and communicate by eye movements, since he cannot move his arms to spell. Some people talk to him like he is a 3-year-old, even though he is 40 and very much "with it." I shudder when hearing some people say to him such patronizing things like, "Hi Babykins, here's your bunny!" Granted, to look at Bob you wouldn't think he is "with it," but he understands French just as well as English.

As I got to know Bob better, I got to know what he wanted just by his facial expressions and his eyes. I would tell a nurse what he wanted, that is, if they would listen to me. Often they wouldn't listen to me and would try to figure it out themselves. Five minutes later I would hear, "O.K. Viggiano, what does he want?" and Bob would be laughing his head off when I was right to start with.

When I first met Bob, I promised myself somehow he would get some way to communicate. I asked his brother many questions about

avoid interacting with persons with physical disabilities not because we are insensitive or uncaring, but because we are confused about how to act. Sometimes it's difficult to judge whether or not you should provide assistance to someone, and often we become aware that we are noticing the disability—and this makes us uncomfortable with ourselves. Unfortunately, these concerns may result in the appearance of indifference or actual avoidance of persons with physical disabilities. Regardless of our reasons, the result is the same—a lack of communication and interaction with someone simply because of his or her physical appearance.

As you consider your reactions to persons with physical disabilities, past and future, remember our axiom of looking at the *person* first. We've alluded to the fact that sometimes our fear of acting patronizing or too helpful will insult

Bob's education, because obviously he understands everything. I went to Tufts–New England Medical Center for a project they were working on. While there, I saw clear plastic sheets that had pictures on them (Etrans) and that is when it hit me that this was one way for Bob to communicate. I told one of the people there, Cheryl Goodenough-Trepagnier, about how I really wanted to help Bob and she agreed to see him. Meanwhile I wrote to Bob's brother to tell him about what we planned to do and he was so enthusiastic about it that he gave his full cooperation. But the staff at the state hospital gave me so much negativism and said things like, "Why don't you mind your business!" and "Bob isn't smart enough to do that." I asked, "How would you know by how you just baby him like he was 3-years-old?"

Cheryl adapted the Etran, configuring it with one side in French for communication with his family. At first it just had pictures that Bob would fix his eyes on to tell what he wanted, like TV and drink. Now it has phonics on it with parts of words standing for sounds. He is doing great with it. But they said it couldn't be done.

However, only a handful of people use Bob's Etran. Most of the time it just sits there since most people aren't willing to take time to use it. They "cop out" by saying that it's too complex for them. It's so paradoxical, because the same people who said that Bob was too retarded to learn are so befuddled, while Bob is doing so well! It's their loss, because he has so much to give if people take the time. It goes to show that all mountains aren't formed from stone, and all handicaps aren't physical.

I have problems with people accepting my communication system as well. Perfect strangers look at my spelling board and the first words out of their mouths are, "How do you play that game?!" or they say, "Can you spell cat?" or, "Where's the letter A?" Some people act like I am deaf, and some people just pat me on the head and say, "You are a good little boy!" I point to the sign on my board that says "I talk by spelling words," then I point to the sign on my board

or embarrass the individual with whom we are interacting. People with physical disabilities realize your apprehension (many may have experienced these feelings themselves if their disability is injury-related) and appreciate the fact that any meaningful social interaction must be reciprocal in nature.

Most of us are only too aware of the importance society places on appearance. As children get older, teasing of someone who looks different is, unfortunately, fairly common. Unkind and humiliating situations are encountered. The child with a disability must have the opportunity to cry, vent anger, and talk in order to learn to deal with these situations. A key factor in a child's ability to develop a positive self-image is the extent to which he or she can accept his or her physical differences.

A key factor in a child's development of a positive self-image is accepting his or her physical disability.

that says, "Don't Patronize Me!" That sign was inspired by one of my idols, Jill Kinmont, of *The Other Side of the Mountain* fame. The part of that movie that was especially good was when she applied for a teacher's job and the interviewer said to Jill, "You people really inspire me, Jill, but you are too handicapped to teach from a wheelchair." Jill replied, "Don't patronize me! Right now my handicap is your negativism that won't give me a chance!" Everybody at the movie heard a titillated yell from me as if to say, "Give 'em hell, Jill!" since so many people have said that I'm too handicapped to do things that I really wanted to do. One of my goals is to meet Jill, since she inspires me.

Even my own family had said things like I could not use an electric typewriter, and I would kill myself in a motorized wheelchair. They also said that I couldn't push *play* and *record* on my cassette recorder. Those things and more were mastered because nobody was about to tell me that I couldn't do it before having a fair chance to decide the facts for myself.

It seems that so-called free speech isn't for all Americans. Especially for people who can't verbalize their frustrations. Obviously the total answer to this acute communication problem isn't with building more complex equipment so nonverbal people can communicate with "normal" people who are so ill-bred and patronizing to start with. Maybe the answer to the problem is to teach people what it means to be handicapped and nonverbal. The most complex communication equipment is worthless if "normal people are not willing to let nonspeaking persons say their thoughts"! As the saying goes, "It takes two people to start a fight," and it also takes two people to communicate rationally.

By Jim Viggiano

Source: J. Viggiano (1982), "Don't patronize me—communicate with me," *Communication Outlook, 3*(4), 13.

Another significant source of stress is the struggle for independence. For people with certain types of disabilities, such as seizure disorders or diabetes, it is very difficult to accept the fact that a certain level of dependence on others or on medications will be a continuing part of their lives (Bigge, 1982). The protectiveness of parents and other family members, and the possible adjusted expectations of others, may make the process of growing up very difficult.

Some children with progressive illness or deteriorating conditions must face the inevitable fact of an early death. Clearly, family, friends, and other support services and people can help children as they try to face this possibility. Experts advise teachers and other adults to be gentle, yet direct, with children who want to discuss death. Often, because children find it difficult to discuss this emotional topic with their parents, they may need to confide in another trusted adult. Although many children display incredible courage and consideration of others in the face of their disabilities, it is only natural for a part of this process to include the inevitable questions of "why me?" and "what if. . . ?" Sometimes these questions are directed at the condition itself, and sometimes at the pain or discomfort involved.

Effects on the Family

The impact of a child's physical disability or health impairment on a family can vary as greatly as the types of disabilities. The effects on the family of a child with cerebral palsy will be very different from the effects on the family of a child with muscular dystrophy, cancer, an amputated leg, or epilepsy. Yet parents of children with special needs do share many common experiences, such as dealing with medical professionals, educators, community prejudices, and the joys of loving a child.

Some families will be able to accept the child for who he is and become strong while dealing with challenges and decisions that may overwhelm most of us. Other families will become frayed as the child with the disability siphons all their emotional and physical energies. Some families face a potentially lifelong commitment to the education of their child; others must face daily the agony of watching their child's physical abilities and health deteriorate.

Children are often well aware of the impact of their disability on their families and may themselves feel a sense of guilt or responsibility for the ensuing emotional or financial strain. Sometimes, children will respond to this by avoiding discussion of their condition with their parents (Bigge, 1982) or by being careful of what they say or do. The child may focus on "taking care" of his or her parents. This unexpected interaction is illustrated in a touching passage from Frank Deford's book *Alex: The Life of a Child*, the story of his young daughter, who died of complications from cystic fibrosis.

> And so then Alex and I laughed. Unfortunately, at that point, late in her life, it was difficult for her to laugh without coughing and starting to choke. So she made sure she laughed gently, and I laughed extra hard, for both of us. Then she came over, sat in my lap, and this is what she said: "Oh, Daddy, wouldn't this have been great?"
>
> That is what she said, exactly. She didn't say, "Hasn't this been great?" She said, "Oh, Daddy, wouldn't this have been great?" Alex meant her whole life, if only she hadn't been sick.
>
> I just said, "Yes," and after we hugged each other, she left the room, because, I knew, she wanted to let me cry alone. Alex knew by then that, if I cried in front of her, I would worry about upsetting her, and she didn't want to burden me that way. She was the only one dying. (Deford, 1983, p. 9)

Because physical disabilities and deteriorating health are usually apparent to others, families also try to cope with the emotional pain faced by their children as they integrate into educational and social settings and deal with the countless questions about "what happened to you?" or "what's wrong with you?" Although it is important for families to encourage independence for their children, it is often difficult for them to let go of their desire to protect the child from more potentially painful situations (Haring, Lovett, & Saren, 1991). One of

Practical issues faced by the family include decisions about treatment and placement.

the greatest tasks faced by families of children with physical or health disabilities is to encourage their children to experience life and take risks, just as they would with children without disabilities.

Practical issues faced by the family include treatment decisions. Families must make constant decisions about the type or extent of therapy they will select for the child involved. In some instances, these decisions may be relatively simple (selecting a type of medication, choosing a particular kind of prosthesis). When the child has a severe illness or disability, however, these decisions can be very complex and include considerations of time allocated to the child and other family members; finances; emotional stress on the part of the parents, siblings, and involved child; and sometimes the actual physical abilities of the family caretakers. Certainly one of the biggest decisions related to treatment is whether the child with severe physical involvement, particularly a child with multiple disabilities, should be at home or in a residential placement. Let's listen to the experiences of one parent, Helen Featherstone, the mother of a child with severe cerebral palsy, blindness, and mental retardation:

> Sometimes mothers and fathers of exceptional children face peculiar difficulties because they are divided internally as well as between themselves. Each partner feels deeply ambivalent—about the child, the future, the advice of experts, and many other problems. Ambivalence is, however, confusing and upsetting. Sometimes mixed feelings get swept under the rug, to be expressed in a conflict between husband and wife. This occurred with us. When Jody was around eighteen months old, Jay (and several other people) felt strongly that we should begin to make inquiries about residential placement. I felt equally strongly that we should wait. Although I expected that Jody might eventually live elsewhere, I wanted to care for him at home while he was still small. Without being unpleasant, I refused to budge from my position. Yet my feelings were, of course, profoundly divided. Jody exhausted both of us; his care consumed all my energy and most of my time. Residential placement would have offered unimaginable freedom. I am sure that a part of me yearned for a simple long-term solution to the problem. But another part—a part that I liked better, and therefore gave license to speak—wanted to give Jody everything I could. Jay's feelings were probably equally mixed, but after weighing the issues, he came down on the other side for a while. We survived what amounted to an undeclared war. (Featherstone, 1980, p. 119)

Although there may be some similarities in the ways families deal with the impact of a physical disability or health impairment, families are composed of individuals. The child with the disability and the other family members develop the pattern of interaction that works for them. Educators must be aware of the needs of individual families and the type of support services that might help them make informed decisions about the education and placement of their children.

Fortunately, the emphasis on parent services and training available through P.L. 99-457 enables greater education and support for parents of young children with physical disabilities and health impairments. Parents and families of older children who incur physical or health disabilities need immediate and continued information and assistance. Social, spiritual, and physical support are all important predictors of more successful family adaptations (Lin, 2000). Often, local, state, or national groups related to a specific disability area can be a great source of available services, information, and emotional support.

In Classrooms

In the past, the diverse educational needs of children with physical disabilities and health impairments often kept them away from public education. Today's teacher needs to know, however, that in most cases these children can be part of the regular class with accommodations and support.

Early Intervention

For many children with physical disabilities or health impairments, the first educational issue to arise is the appropriate and early diagnosis of the condition and assessment of physical, cognitive, and language abilities. These diagnoses tend to be made by physicians rather than school personnel, and many diagnoses are made long before the child reaches school age.

As with other disabilities, early intervention services significantly affect the well-being of these children. For some of them, early intervention can mean the difference between life and death. For others, early intervention can mean the difference between a mild disability and a severe and long-term disability. Early and consistent therapy can help children to maximize their physical skills and sometimes prevent the occurrence of muscular atrophy and skeletal deformities.

Early intervention services that focus on family-centered service delivery models may have positive effects on the family as well as the child. Family-centered services can help parents establish a support network, as well as provide them with knowledge about their child's disability and a sense of empowerment (Thompson et al., 1997).

Identification and Assessment: The Classroom Teacher's Role

Most physical disabilities and health impairments are diagnosed before schooling begins, but some conditions will not be identified until later in the child's life. As a teacher you should be alert to gradual or sudden changes in children's physical abilities, energy level, and general behavior.

Regardless of the severity of any condition, it is your responsibility continually to assess and address the educational needs of the individual child. If you notice motor difficulties, a physical or occupational therapist may be called in to consult on the case or to provide assistance. See the accompanying box, "Some Considerations for Students with Mobility Impairments," for some general recommendations for interacting with students with physical disabilities or health impairments.

The Transdisciplinary Approach

In the transdisciplinary model, all interventions are delivered by one or two professionals to ensure continuity for the child.

Integrated, multidisciplinary planning is a requirement for appropriate education (York & Vandercook, 1991). IDEA requires that a multidisciplinary team evaluate each student in special education programs. However, on a

~ Some Considerations for Students with Mobility Impairments

- Many students with mobility impairments lead lives similar to those without impairments. Dependency and helplessness are not characteristics of physical disability.
- A physical disability is often separate from matters of cognition and general health; it does not imply that a student has other health problems or difficulty with intellectual functioning.
- People adjust to disabilities in myriad ways; students should not be assumed to be brave and courageous on the basis of disability.
- When talking with a wheelchair user, attempt to converse at eye level as opposed to standing and looking down. If a student has a communication impairment as well as a mobility impairment, take time to understand the person. Repeat what you understand, and when you don't understand, say so.
- A student with a physical disability may or may not want assistance in a particular situation. Ask before giving assistance, and wait for a response. Listen to any instructions the student may give; by virtue of experience, the student likely knows the safest and most efficient way to accomplish the task at hand.
- Be considerate of the extra time it might take a student with a disability to speak or act. Allow the student to set the pace walking or talking.
- A wheelchair should be viewed as a personal assistance device rather than something one is "confined to." It is also part of a student's personal space; do not lean on or touch the chair, and do not push the chair, unless asked.
- Mobility impairments vary over a wide range, from temporary to permanent. Other conditions, such as respiratory conditions, affect coordination and endurance; these can also affect a student's ability to perform in class.
- Physical access to a class is the first barrier a student with a mobility impairment may face, and this is not related only to the accessibility of a specific building or classroom. An unshoveled sidewalk, lack of reliable transportation, or mechanical problems with a wheelchair can easily cause a student to be late.
- Common accommodations for students with mobility impairments include priority registration, notetakers, accessible classroom/location/furniture, alternative ways of completing assignments, lab or library assistants, assistive computer technology, exam modifications, and conveniently located parking.

Source: Used by permission of Disability Services.

multidisciplinary team, professionals work independently, or directly, with the child. According to Orelove and Sobsey (1991), this model lacks methods for coordinating assessment and prioritizing the student's educational needs. Instead of the multidisciplinary approach, then, Orelove and Sobsey recommend the **transdisciplinary model.**

The transdisciplinary, or indirect service, model differs from the multidisciplinary approach because all interventions are delivered by one or two professionals. For example, a student who needs physical therapy to learn to walk is helped by his or her regular teacher to complete mobility exercises several times a day. This does not mean that the physical therapist never sees the student. It does mean that the physical therapist works closely with the teacher to carry out therapeutic activities properly and sees the student directly as needed. In a mul-

~ Continuum of Service Models

Direct Service Model

- One-on-one therapy* The therapist treats the student in a separate therapy room or a segregated portion of the classroom.
- Small group therapy* The therapist treats several students with similar needs at one time.
- One-on-one therapy (inclusive) The therapist works with the student during a classroom activity to facilitate his or her participation. Therapy can also occur during activities in the gymnasium, on the playground, or at a community site.
- Small-group therapy (inclusive) The therapist works with the student with special needs and a group of his or her classmates on an educationally appropriate activity. The activity also promotes the therapeutic goal for the student with special needs. For example, the therapist leads a craft project that facilitates the fine motor manipulation for all students, yet the project is modified to include and instruct the student with special needs.

Transdisciplinary Indirect Service Model

- Consultation The therapist recommends and instructs educators, paraprofessionals, or caregivers to carry out therapeutic programs. This may include instruction modification, activity enhancement, environmental modification, adaptation of materials, routine or schedule alterations, or team member training.
- Monitoring The therapist maintains contact with the student to monitor his or her status. Effective monitoring consists of checkups scheduled on a regular basis in the student's educational environment.

Note: *Restrictive model of treatment used only as a last resort. Therapy should be provided in a manner that facilitates integration with peers. Source: J. L. Szabo, "Maddie's Story," *Teaching Exceptional Children, 33*(2), 2000, p. 15.

tidisciplinary or interdisciplinary team, the student would be pulled out of the class and given physical therapy once a week for thirty minutes. The teacher and parents would have little idea of how to help the student learn and practice mobility the rest of the week. The accompanying box, "Continuum of Service Models," illustrates the traditional Direct Service Model and the transdisciplinary Indirect Service Model.

A transdisciplinary team of professionals, in conjunction with the family and, when appropriate, the child, works together to assess educational needs in a variety of areas and to determine appropriate program goals. For example, this group would work together to determine what type of computer keyboard is most appropriate for a student with cerebral palsy who cannot use a regular keyboard.

The family's role on the transdisciplinary team is critical because family members are able to give insight into the child's demonstrated abilities, motivation, emotional adjustment, and goals. Whenever special therapy, communication systems, or adaptive equipment is suggested, the willingness and ability of the family members to accept and use them or to participate must be assessed and evaluated.

When interventions are integrated into the classroom, teachers better understand how to help students learn useful skills.

When interventions are integrated into the home and classroom setting, not only does the student learn meaningful and useful skills, but the teacher and parents get a better understanding of how to facilitate the development of those skills on a day-to-day basis.

Educational Setting

In the past, children whose only disabilities were physical or health-related were placed in a variety of educational settings, ranging from a state hospital or institution to the regular classroom. Although there are still separate classes for children with "orthopedic handicaps," these classes are moving away from serving as the primary educational placement for children with physical disabilities and toward the role of a transition or support service (McLesky, Henry, & Hodges, 1999). They provide a setting for initial instruction in skills such as mobility and language, which can then be used in regular class settings. Support or special education services are often provided in physical therapy, occupational therapy, speech or language therapy, counseling, and, in some instances, homebound instruction for periods of time.

Special education services should be structured to support placement in the regular classroom.

Most placement options now focus on the regular classroom, and many general education teachers are responsible for educating students with physical or health impairments in their classrooms. In some instances, it is not necessary to make any specific instructional modifications for the student; in other cases, you will need assistance from special education teachers or other members of the student's education team to learn the best ways to encourage and facilitate communication, class participation, class interaction, and physical movement or activity. In fact, some of the responsibilities of teachers who work with children with physical disabilities and other health impairments can be quite different from those who work with other students in the general education setting. Even special education teachers often feel unprepared to deal with situations such as working with terminally ill students and their families, or identifying appropriate forms of augmentative communication and assistive technology (Heller et al., 1999). Salisbury, Evans, and Palombaro (1997) found that teachers in the primary grades used collaborative problem solving with all of their students to identify solutions to help students with significant disabilities participate more actively in the classroom. Sometimes, individuals with severe physical disabilities may have an aide who travels with them to assist in educational and health-care activities. It is important for the aide to step back whenever possible to allow full integration of the student and to encourage communication and other interactions with peers (Giangreco, Edelman, Luiselli, & MacFarland, 1997). See the accompanying box, "Specific Strategies for Integrating Students with Physical Disabilities or Health Impairments in the Classroom."

When a student is too sick to attend school, he or she may receive a homebound program, either in the student's home or at a hospital. This homebound program should always include plans for the student to re-enter school as soon as possible. The teacher who visits the student at home or in the hospital coordinates with the student's regular teachers so that proper assignments, homework, tests, and other activities are completed.

Technology is quickly improving the quality of homebound programs. In some school districts, distance learning is now available, which permits the student to watch educational television programs along with classroom peers. For students with long-term homebound needs, telephones can be set up in the classroom that allow the student to listen to the teacher and respond to questions just like the other students. The homebound teacher makes sure the student has the necessary materials each week to follow along with the class. Fax

~ Specific Strategies for Integrating Students with Physical Disabilities or Health Impairments in the Classroom

- Place students with limited physical movement front and center in a traditional classroom setting, to facilitate access to the teacher's presentation and material on the board. There are exceptions to this guideline; for example, a student with a traumatic brain injury might have a limited field of vision on one side and might follow the visual presentation of material more easily if seated at an angle.
- If students gather around small tables or learning centers, make sure the tables are at an appropriate height for the student who is in a wheelchair. If the students gather in groups on the floor, try to use chairs instead, so the child in a wheelchair is not sitting above and apart from the group. This is important for social integration as well as physical accessibility.
- Use bookshelves, material drawers, pencil sharpeners, and cubbies that are the appropriate height and can be reached by a student in a wheelchair. If a student cannot physically reach and grasp, make sure he or she has a trustworthy assistant for retrieving and putting away materials.
- Avoid the use of carpet squares or other floor materials, such as number lines, with raised sides or edges.
- Classrooms with fixed furnishings, such as science labs, can be particularly problematic for the student in a wheelchair. Creating an accessible work area may require significant changes in the classroom construction, so that the student will be truly integrated into the classroom setting.
- If a student requires assistive technology for communication, establish clear signals for typical classroom activities such as hand raising and asking a question. These signals should be clearly recognized by all students in the classroom, as well as the teacher. Provide training to all of the students in the classroom on how to communicate with the student using his specific assistive device. Always be careful to allow the student time to respond.
- Become an expert at identifying and creating learning experiences that allow all students in the classroom to participate fully.

machines are also used to connect the homebound student to the regular classroom.

Students Who Are Technologically Dependent

As a teacher, you may be required to assist students with physical disabilities in the use of equipment for moving, eating, breathing, and other bodily functions. These aspects of care are called physical handling and health maintenance.

Physical handling involves moving the student from one place to another or adjusting his or her placement in a fixed setting. For example, you might need to move a student from a wheelchair to another setting such as a group activity on the floor. There are very specific guidelines for picking up and carrying students with physical disabilities. It is important that you not try to lift or move students until you have received the information necessary to do it appropriately. In some instances, more than one person is needed to move a child, and in others, a specially trained aide or nurse will assist or do the lifting.

Other aspects of physical handling include adjusting physical placement or using physical props to allow greater range of motion. If students have a tendency to lean to one side or have difficulty reaching needed materials, you can make simple adjustments such as by using pillows to prevent leaning, having armrests or trays attached to wheelchairs to allow the closer placement of manipulative materials, or providing wedge-shaped props that children can lie on to allow greater range of arm movement (Kraemer, Cusick, & Bigge, 1982; Lough, 1983). Again, the physical and occupational therapist can provide needed information and equipment.

Health maintenance involves assisting students in eating, drinking, and using the bathroom. A student with severe cerebral palsy, for example, might be unable to feed herself. Some students run the risk of choking when they eat or drink, so it is important that the person feeding the student be skilled in CPR. Often a nurse or trained aide will assist in this process, as they will when medically oriented processes such as catheterization are required. Because the courts consistently rule that the school is responsible for providing any and all medical care to students in school as long as it does not require a physician, children with very severe medical needs may be in your classroom (Katsiyannis & Yell, 2000). Students requiring medical technology for support, such a ventilators for breathing, and students with other conditions requiring constant health maintenance, such as gastrostomies and tracheostomies, may be placed in the general education class for instruction and require monitoring and maintenance procedures by nurses or other health-care professionals (Levine, 1996; Thomas & Hawke, 1999).

Other health maintenance activities may include administration of medication, injections, and monitoring students for signs of distress such as diabetic shock. School nurses typically are responsible for the administration of any medical procedures, but as we mentioned previously, it is important for you to be aware of any particular signs or symptoms that signal a specific health problem. If you assist students with these activities, you must be taught correct procedures and be aware of potential risks. Federal guidelines and school district interpretations regulate who may or may not perform health-care services (Rapport, 1996). These guidelines should be reviewed by the evaluation team when decisions are being made about the delivery of these services in school.

Classroom Accessibility

With the passage of the Americans with Disabilities Act in 1990, all public facilities and buildings were required to be barrier-free by 1994. Your classroom, therefore, will probably be adapted to the needs of students with physical disabilities.

Sometimes, however, schools may not take into account accessibility to such things as play equipment, furniture, or educational equipment. One potential problem area is the surface of floors and walls (Lewis & Doorlag, 1987). For example, carpeting, rugs, or uneven floor surfaces can cause difficulties for students using wheelchairs or other types of assistance for walking.

Teachers should be sure that equipment and furniture are arranged for maximum accessibility.

Although some of these areas should be addressed by working in conjunction with the student's therapists, you can take some simple precautions yourself to ensure optimum accessibility. Widening aisles between desks and placing equipment such as computers, tape recorders, and bookshelves appropriately are some tasks that teachers can attend to in their classes. When planning field trips, it is always a good idea to call ahead and check to ensure that the visiting site has been adapted to accommodate students with disabilities. Although adapted school buses are quite common, some public buses still cannot be used by persons in wheelchairs. The student then needs to be lifted onto the bus and the wheelchair folded up and carried along. This may present difficulties, particularly with an older student, so advance planning will be necessary.

Technology

We have alluded throughout this chapter to the importance of technology to many individuals with physical disabilities and health impairments. For individuals with physical disabilities, most of the technological assistance is either medical technology or assistive technology that is designed to help the individual perform life tasks. For school-age students with disabilities, assistive technology may be considered special education or a related service. Teachers, parents, students, and other members of the evaluation team must evaluate the student's needs and indicate the need for appropriate assistive technology on the student's IEP (Menlove, 1996). When selecting appropriate technology for a student, it is most important to look at the way the individual functions in his or her environment and to determine what specific pieces of equipment or training may help to support the student in various settings (Blackhurst, 1997). The accompanying box, "Assistive Technology Assessments: Determining a Student's Needs," gives guidelines for determining technology needs.

Lau (2000) suggests that technology also can serve an important role as a focal activity for prompting social interaction among young children with physical disabilities and their peers. She suggests that when an appropriate software program is used in a well-structured cooperative learning group, young children can learn social interaction skills. This type of instructional activity can be used to teach the young children with or without physical disabilities skills such as turn taking, group decision-making, and helping. Table 12.1 provides a checklist for teachers to use to determine proper positioning at the computer for children with physical disabilities.

~ Assistive Technology Assessments: Determining a Student's Needs

Conduct an Assistive Technology Environmental Use Assessment

- List times and subjects in which student needs assistance to satisfactorily complete assignments.
- List times student needs assistance to satisfactorily function in his or her school environment.
- List adaptations currently in use (shortened assignment, note takers, etc.).
- List an assistive technology device currently used by student, what setting, and time used.

Conduct an Assistive Technology Functional Use Assessment

- Describe student's present level of functioning.
- List characteristics of student.
- What are the student's academic skills?
- Does student have keyboarding skills and at what level?
- What are the student's preferences for types of assistive technology?
- What technology courses are available in the current curriculum?
- What technology instructional services are available at the school site?

Match Environmental Use Assessment with Functional Use Assessment to Identify Appropriate Assistive Technology Services

Webb. B. J. (2000). Planning and organizing assistive technology resources in your school. *Teaching Exceptional Children, 32*(4), p. 51.

Table 12.1 Classroom Checklist for Proper Positioning at the Computer for Social Interaction

Criterion	Met	Not Met
1. Is the child's head at midline? (e.g., ears are directly over shoulders and face is facing forward)		
2. Is the child's pelvis at midline? (e.g., hips are in the back of the seat and are not tilted to one side)		
3. Is the child's trunk at midline? (e.g., trunk is not tilted to one side)		
4. Are the child's shoulders at midline? (e.g., shoulders are not hunched forward)		
5. Are the child's forearms supported? (e.g., elbows are flexed at 90 degrees and supported by the table, arm rest, or tray)		
6. Are the child's legs in a neutral position? (e.g., thighs are slightly apart; knees and ankles are bent at 90 degrees)		
7. Are the child's feet in a neutral position and supported? (e.g., feet are directly under the knees and facing forward; feet are supported by the floor or foot rest)		
8. Is the child seated at the same height as other children at the computer? (e.g., eye contact and verbal exchange can easily be achieved among children in the group)		
9. Is the computer monitor at the child's eye level? (e.g., the child can easily see the monitor without tilting his or her head)		
10. Is the computer table accessible to the child? (e.g., the child can easily reach the computer peripherals)		

Source: C. Lau, "I Learned How to Take Turns," *Teaching Exceptional Children, 32*(4)(2000), 8.

Although social interaction is a new and exciting application of technology, technology use by students with physical disabilities and health impairments typically focuses on mobility and communication skills.

Mobility

New designs in wheelchairs and controls for wheelchair movement have resulted in opportunities for independence for people who previously were dependent on others for even limited transportation. For example, individuals with very severe disabilities were unable to use conventionally designed wheelchairs to move because they had limited or no arm movement. A now-common mouth apparatus allows them to control wheelchair movement by blowing puffs of air through a tube.

Muscles that are not used because of injury (typically a spinal cord injury) can be given electronically stimulated "exercise" to prevent atrophy, contractions, and skeletal deformities. Some experiments using electrical stimulation and feedback have taken place that have allowed paralyzed individuals to walk a few steps (Dickey & Shealy, 1987).

Technology has also made it possible for people with physical disabilities to control some aspects of their home environment. Through the use of switches from a wheelchair panel or a voice-activated control device, it is possible to open doors or turn on lights from across the room (Bigge, 1991a). These devices provide an option for independent living that might not otherwise be available. Home accounting and banking software are examples of how technology has facilitated personal life-skills management for individuals with severe physical disabilities (Bigge, 1991b).

Communication

The most critical factor in using technology to meet communication needs is to identify processes that meet the individual's needs, allow and encourage intellectual and physical growth and development, and can be used by others in the environment. This last point is of the greatest importance. The latest high-tech system is useless if no one else takes the time to understand how it is used and to participate in the communication process. In this section we discuss some of the major developments in communication technology for people with physical disabilities.

Most advances in communication technology provide access to the symbols of written or oral language. The majority of these advances are associated with computer use. **Eye-gazing scanning systems** are a good example. As the individual scans a keyboard and focuses, a small and very sensitive camera detects the direction of the person's eyes and registers the letters, words, or phrases. A typed message can then be produced.

Augmentative communication aids are designed to be used in addition to the individual's existing speech or vocalizations (Bigge, 1991c). A person using an augmentative communication aid can directly select the desired message elements (such as words or pictures) from the display or can scan and then identify one of a series of potential message elements. In direct selection, the individual points to the desired message or message component using a finger, an adapted handpiece with a pointer attached, or a light beam attached to the head. In school settings, direct selection aids often take the form of alternative computer keyboards and overlays. These keyboards can look like an enlarged version of the typical keyboard, may contain numbers, pictures, or other symbols, and are designed to accommodate specific difficulties a person with limited motor control might encounter (such as difficulty pressing two keys at one time) (Intellitools, 1996).

In scanning, message elements are presented one at a time on flashcards, transparent charts, or a computer screen. As the potential messages are presented, the individual indicates which message(s) he or she wants to choose by making a sound, flexing a muscle, or fixing a visual gaze for a few seconds. This process eliminates the need for great mobility.

An adapted form of scanning is a multisignal process, in which the individual (a) scans groups (for example, fifteen groups of four messages), (b) selects a group (for example, group 9: I want to go see a movie. I want to see a television show. I want to turn the television off. Let's go to the video store.), and then

(c) scans the message elements in that group to select the appropriate message (I want to see a television show.). This type of encoding allows the individual with limited movement and a large message vocabulary to cover a wide range of potential messages. Computers facilitate scanning because they can store and present many groups of messages quickly.

Another communication option available through advanced technology is synthesized and digitized speech. **Digitized speech** is the storage of words or phrases that can be recalled as needed; **synthesized speech** is the storage of speech sounds—a phonetic alphabet that can be put together to form any word using a sound-by-sound process similar to the spelling process (Bigge, 1991c). Synthesized speech allows greater variety of words and phrases but can be a much slower process. These devices can be designed in various sizes and can be portable or connected to a large computer screen. Digitized speech devices can be designed with customized keyboard overlays and can present language at various speeds (Breakthroughs, 1997). Recent research suggests that synthetic speech can do more than serve as augmentative communication. Blischak (1999) found that young children with severe speech difficulties who used synthetic speech during language training sessions significantly increased their production of natural speech, when compared to students who used graphic or pictoral representations of speech. This research suggests that children can actually improve their speech while using synthesized speech technology.

Technological advances clearly have opened many new avenues for individuals with severe difficulties in communication. Not all procedures need to have a high-tech component; many augmentative communication processes can be integrated in very simple ways. The role of technology is to expand these options, particularly for individuals with limited movement or advanced cognitive capabilities.

Adult Life

Recent legislation has helped to refine the legal requirements for public services and places of employment as well as to put in place a system of preparation for work while individuals are still in the school system. For example, the **Education for Handicapped Children Amendments of 1984 (P.L. 98-199)** allocated educational funds for the purpose of facilitating the transition of adolescents to adult life. The **Education of the Handicapped Act Amendments of 1990 (P.L. 101-476)** required that a formal transition plan be developed for all secondary students identified as disabled. The **IDEA Amendments of 1997** required that transition services be included in a student's IEP when the student is 14 years old and that the transition services focus on the student's educational plan (Yell & Shriner, 1997).

The **Americans with Disabilities Act (ADA) of 1990 (P.L. 101-336)** extends civil rights protection to individuals with disabilities in private-sector employment. In addition, the law requires that public services such as transportation make accommodations for individuals with disabilities. For example, transportation systems such as buses and railroads must include access for individuals with physical disabilities. Other public accommodations and facilities (stores, hotels, schools) must be accessible and must provide any supporting material necessary to allow individuals to use their services (Council for Exceptional Children, 1990).

Supportive legislation helps to ensure that integration will take place and normalized interpersonal relationships will develop. A less obvious benefit of this legislation is the implicit acceptance and recognized importance of all persons in our society. Legislation is one of the ways our nation has of conveying information important to our culture. The message sent by these laws is that our society should and will encourage participation by all people in the socially important roles of adulthood. Legislation does not, however, assure that all individuals with disabilities will be successful in the workplace.

Social acceptance continues to be an obstacle for some individuals with disabilities.

Data from a national longitudinal transition study (Blackorby & Wagner, 1996) reveal that approximately 56.8 percent of individuals with disabilities were competitively employed three to five years after leaving secondary school. Other studies, however, suggest that between 66 and 90 percent of individuals with disabilities who graduate from public schools fail to find competitive employment (Harris & Associates, 1989; Stark, Kiernan, Goldsburg, & McGee, 1986). Although there is some variability in the results of these studies, it is clear that many persons with disabilities encounter greater difficulty finding and keeping jobs than do individuals without disabilities.

One avenue to successful employment is through college or other postsecondary training programs. Many high schools now offer programs that help students prepare for college or university: courses or curriculum components in study skills, notetaking, time management, and organization. Although individuals with other health impairments or physical disabilities attend postsecondary institutions at about twice the rate of many other students with disabilities (Blackorby and Wagner, 1996), the process often is difficult and frustrating. Lehmann, Davies, and Laurin (2000) organized a summit of a number of college students with disabilities, including a number with physical disabilities and other health impairments. These students identified barriers to their successful transition to postsecondary programs. The students then listed specific suggestions for students and teachers at both the secondary and postsecondary levels. These suggestions are found in the accompanying box, "Tips for Eliminating Barriers to Postsecondary Education."

The issues of transition, particularly for individuals who are dependent on technology, can be further complicated by cultural issues related to the use of assistive technology. Parette (1999) suggests that areas of cultural sensitivity include (1) the family's desire for the degree of independence technology can provide, (2) the balance between providing technological assistance and what may be perceived as the stigma of drawing attention to an individual because of technology use, (3) the range of information needs by a given family about the choices, costs, and goals of assistive technology, (4) the impact of assistive technology on family routines and demands, and (5) the experiences with assistive technology of the child and the family. Teachers and transition coordinators must be sensitive to these issues as they work with families and students to identify appropriate assistive technology for adult life.

Transition programs help students establish initial contacts with the **adult service agencies** that can provide guidance and assistance once the students have graduated from high school or college. Adult service agencies can provide medical and psychological examinations and counseling, training and job placement, and financial assistance for adaptive equipment, prostheses, and basic living costs during training (Smith, Price, & Marsh, 1986). The accompanying box, "Adult Services: Vocational Rehabilitation Department," illustrates one state department of vocational rehabilitation's eligibility requirements, financial considerations, and list of services. Once a person is determined to be eligible for vocational rehabilitation services, a vocational rehabilitation counselor will serve as case manager and outline specific employment goals and needed services in an Individual Plan

~ Tips for Eliminating Barriers to Postsecondary Education

- Ask students to conduct workshops that describe the nature of various disabilities to faculty and staff.
- Provide staff development to postsecondary faculty regarding adaptations and accommodations they can implement.
- Reward faculty who are willing to adapt instruction to address the learning needs of students.
- Evaluate transportation availability to campus and on campus.
- Inform students about the documentation requirements of local postsecondary institution before their senior year at high school.
- Identify potential financial resources for students entering into postsecondary settings.
- Teach high school students time and money management skills.
- Tour the college campus with interested students during transition planning.
- Provide summer classes addressing compensatory strategies on college campuses for high school students interested in obtaining a postsecondary education.
- Role-play with students ways of communicating to college faculty about students' disability and learning needs.
- Encourage networking between college students via focus groups, student meetings, and informational workshops.

Source: J. P. Lehmann, T. G. Davies, and K. M. Laurin (2000), "Listening to Student Voices About Postsecondary Education," *Teaching Exceptional Children, 32*(5), p. 63.

of Employment (IPE) (Neubert & Moon, 2000). Although such services may be provided automatically for persons under the care of state-run facilities, individuals with disabilities who are living on their own will need to seek and secure available services. Knowing what services are available and how to go about finding assistance may be important elements in the search for employment.

In addition to postsecondary education and employment opportunities, residential options are important considerations for individuals with physical disabilities and health impairments. Historically, many individuals with extensive physical disabilities, such as severe cerebral palsy, lived in institutional settings. Today, most of the individuals who in times past lived in segregated settings have moved directly and successfully into the community; some, however, continue to live in smaller segregated settings such as nursing homes. Many individuals with physical disabilities or health impairments live independently in homes within the community. Sometimes adaptive equipment is necessary or a personal attendant is required, so financial resources may be the factor that determines independent living for some people.

The more complex an individual's health-care and personal maintenance needs, the more likely it is that the person continues to live in one of the more segregated settings. Often, these settings are able to employ support personnel, such as nurses and therapists, and have available more elaborate medical equipment than a group home or apartment. As federal and state agencies become more experienced in integrated service delivery, however, it is likely that soon all individuals with disabilities will have service options that include integrated community placement.

Another important aspect of adult living is the ability to choose recreational activities that interest you. Many individuals with disabilities enjoy diverse recreational and leisure activities, which they choose, as we all do, on the basis

~ Adult Services: Vocational Rehabilitation Department

Eligibility

A. The individual must have an impediment to employment caused by a physical or mental impairment that substantially limits the ability to work.

B. The impaired individual must require vocational rehabilitation services to prepare for, enter, engage in, or retain gainful employment; and must benefit from these services in terms of an employment outcome.

Financial Considerations

In some states, clients are responsible for helping to pay for rehabilitation training and other services. A vocational rehabilitation counselor will help the client apply to funding sources such as educational grants, federal tuition grants, social services, and social security.

Services

Step 1. Referral and intake: Individuals must apply for services in person, in writing, or by phone.

Step 2. Evaluation: A medical examination, vocational evaluation, and, sometimes, a psychological evaluation may be required to determine eligibility for services and rehabilitation needs.

Step 3. Rehabilitation planning: An Individualized Written Rehabilitation Program is developed by the individual and his or her assigned counselor. Long-term and short-term employment goals are identified.

Step 4. Treatment: Medical or psychiatric care may be provided on a short-term basis along with specific therapies such as speech therapy or physical therapy. When necessary for job performance, equipment such as artificial limbs, hearing aids, and wheelchairs, and materials such as books, supplies, and licenses may be provided.

Step 5. Training: If needed, training in personal and social skills, work performance, and work adjustment is available. Vocational training may include education in technical schools or colleges.

Step 6. Placement: The counselor will assist in identifying job opportunities and helping to match the individual with the position of his or her choice.

Step 7. Closure: After an individual has been employed for a length of time, vocational rehabilitation services may be discontinued. Individuals may return for services if needed again; however, if more than a year has passed, reapplication may be necessary to reassess eligibility.

Source: Your Handbook of Vocational Rehabilitation Services, South Carolina Vocational Rehabilitation Department, 1991, pp. 1–11.

of what relaxes and challenges them. A number of community recreational centers and athletic competitions include specific programs for individuals with disabilities, while others simply integrate individuals with disabilities into their existing programs. Programs that require specialized supervision and training, such as horseback riding for individuals with physical disabilities, can also be found across the country.

Still, there are a number of individuals with disabilities who do not have access to desired recreational activities because of physical barriers or who have difficulty identifying and finding a way to participate in recreational opportunities. Helping individuals experience and identify a range of leisure options, providing necessary training or adaptations to facilitate independent participation

Many individuals with disabilities enjoy diverse recreational and leisure activities, but others have difficulty participating.

in the activities, and providing support services such as transportation and social interaction skills are important transition goals.

Individuals with physical disabilities and health impairments are increasingly participating fully and successfully in all aspects of adult life. Because many of us view a disability as an adverse condition, we may ascribe certain characteristics to the person with a disability who has been able to get a successful job and conduct a relatively normal existence. We speak frequently of the bravery of people who must deal with sensory impairments, debilitating illnesses, or physical conditions. Sometimes we wonder if we would be able to exhibit the same strength if we were in similar situations. There is no doubt that many people with disabilities are engaged in mighty struggles and exhibit courage and tenacity.

People with disabilities may struggle more with physical and social barriers imposed by others than with their own disabilities.

It is important for us to realize, however, that these struggles are often due to the physical and social barriers imposed by others—they are not a necessary consequence of disability. As in all historical battles for human and civil rights, ordinary people must become heroes in order to gain their rightful place in society. Although we admire the risks heroes take and the strength they show, it is unfortunate that we still live in a society in which heroic acts are necessary before basic rights and acceptance can be obtained.

Advocacy

For the person with a physical disability or health impairment, life may sometimes seem an unending series of barriers that need to be overcome. Although we all face challenges in our lives, many individuals with physical disabilities are challenged every step of the way—telephones that can't be reached, doors that can't be opened, buildings that can't be entered, eye contact that doesn't take place, communication that isn't attempted, and assumptions that are made.

Educating people about the challenges faced by individuals with physical disabilities has an important purpose, far removed from emotional responses such as sympathy, pity, or even empathy. Rather, the purpose of awareness is to facilitate change. Although it's been a long time coming, public awareness and technology are combining to create a much more accessible environment for persons facing physical challenges. Change in interpersonal areas—efforts at communication, comfortable social exchanges, and acceptance—cannot be legislated and must be instigated at an individual level.

We hope that by listening to our words as well as to the words of children and adults who have experienced disabilities, you have gained some insight into their strength, optimism, struggles, and educational needs. The past decade has resulted in great strides in medical management and technology, which have dramatically increased the options for individuals with physical disabilities and health impairments. We look forward to the doors that will be opened in the future through continued advances in science, social awareness, and knowledge.

Summary

- Physical disabilities and health impairments as currently defined by IDEA include a wide range of conditions. Physical disabilities can be grouped into neurological conditions, musculoskeletal conditions, and traumatic injuries. Health impairments include debilitating or life-threatening diseases or conditions like cystic fibrosis and AIDS. Being familiar with what is known about the causes, prevalence, and treatment of these various conditions may help you to know what to expect from the student, plan time for the student's treatment, and become comfortable with helping the student with in-school treatment.

- One of the most difficult aspects of physical disabilities and health impairments is the issue of mortality, since many conditions involve shortened life expectancy. Another issue is the continual need to educate others.
- Educational issues to be aware of include transdisciplinary planning, the importance of early intervention, and the use of technology to increase access for students in the regular class as well as to provide opportunities to students at home.
- New technologies for environmental control and communication have allowed people with physical disabilities and health impairments to participate more fully in many aspects of life. Legislation provides safeguards and regulations that facilitate the integration of individuals with physical disabilities and health impairments into the work force and the community.

Key Terms

physically challenged
physical disability
health impairment
cerebral palsy
spina bifida
hydrocephalus
epilepsy
grand mal seizure
petit mal seizure
muscular dystrophy
juvenile rheumatoid arthritis (JRA)
congenital malformation
traumatic brain injury (TBI)
asthma
juvenile onset diabetes
hypoglycemia
hyperglycemia
cystic fibrosis
acquired immune deficiency syndrome (AIDS)
transdisciplinary model
physical handling
health maintenance
eye-gazing scanning systems
augmentative communication aid
digitized speech
synthesized speech
Education for Handicapped Children Amendments of 1984 (P.L. 98-199)
Education of the Handicapped Act Amendments of 1990 (P.L. 101-476)
IDEA Amendments of 1997
Americans with Disabilities Act of 1990 (P.L. 101-336)
adult service agency

Multimedia Resources

Adaptive Environments Center, Inc., 347 Congress Street, Suite 301, Boston, MA 02210; website: adaptive@adaptenv.org. This site provides sources and general information about adapting home and work environments.

Children's Software Review. This is a newsletter that focuses on reviews of contemporary software, including software that can be used with assistive technology. Website: http://www2.childrenssoftware.com.

The Disability Rights Activist. Website: http://www.disrights.org. This site provides information to individuals with disabilities and their parents and advocates about legal rights and courses of political action.

Freedom Writer Software, Academics with Scanning: Language Arts and Math (World Communications, ACS Software). A source for software designed for students who use scanning techniques for communication.

Muscular Dystrophy Association, National Headquarters, 3300 East Sunrise Drive, Tucson, AZ 85738, (800) 572-1717. Information sources and resources for parents, professionals, and students interested in muscular dystrophy.

The National Organization for Rare Disorders (NORD). Website: http://www.pcnet.com/~orphan/. NORD is a unique federation of voluntary health organizations dedicated to helping people with rare "orphan" diseases and assisting the organizations that serve them. NORD is committed to the identification, treatment, and cure of rare disorders through programs of education, advocacy, research, and service. Since its inception in 1983, NORD has served as the primary nongovernmental clearinghouse for information on over 5,000 rare disorders. NORD also provides referrals to additional sources of assistance and ongoing support.

National Sports Center for the Disabled, P.O. Box 36, Winter Park, CO 80482, (303) 726-5514. Information and contacts for individuals with disabilities who wish to engage in a variety of sports.

President's Committee on Employment of People with Disabilities. Website: http://www.pcepd.gov/. Provides information in many areas related to the employment of individuals with disabilities, including laws, benefits, publications, federal programs, and special projects.

Rehabilitation Robotics Research Program, Applied Science and Engineering Laboratories, DuPont Hospital for Children and the University of Delaware. Website: http://www.asel.udel.edu/robotics/. Updates and summaries of research involving robotics for individuals with physical disabilities.

Sienkiewicz-Mercer, Ruth, and Steven B. Kaplan. *I Raise My Eyes to Say Yes: A Memoir* (Boston: Houghton Mifflin, 1989). Now an advocate for all people with disabilities, Ruth Sienkiewicz tells the story of her loss of bodily control and speech due to encephalitis at the age of 5.

What You Can Do

1. Make an appointment with a physical therapist or occupational therapist who serves your school district. Discuss with him or her the types of activities typically provided to the students he or she serves. If possible, accompany the therapist on a visit to a local school to observe individual service delivery.

2. Visit the center for disability services at your college or university. Review the services and materials that are available for college students with physical disabilities. Talk to some of the students who provide services, or, if possible, with some of the college students who receive services.

3. What are the important components of communication? Think about the messages you would select if you were creating your own communication board or scanning system. What messages would be most meaningful for you? For your friends? Have each student in your class make a communication board; compare similarities and differences in pictures, symbols, or

messages. Have the students try to communicate with one another using the communication boards.

4. Identify a job in your community often held by high school students (working in a fast-food restaurant or grocery store). Observe and identify the specific skills that are required. What adaptations would be needed for a student who is in a wheelchair to do that job?

5. Invite an adult with a physical disability to visit your class and talk about work, living, social opportunities, challenges to acceptance, and achievement. Perhaps an adult with a disability is in your class and would also be interested in sharing his or her experiences.

Children Who Are Gifted and Talented

13

THIS CHAPTER examines the highly capable students who are identified in our schools as gifted and talented. We discuss changes in the definition of giftedness over time, the effects of high ability on a student and his or her family, the teacher's role in identifying students who are gifted, and the influence of programs designed for gifted students on the education of *all* students. As you read, think about these questions:

What does it mean to be gifted? Is being talented something different?

What is the teacher's responsibility toward students with high ability?

What can a teacher do to modify the curriculum for the needs of a student who is gifted?

Commonalities: **What teaching strategies and enrichment activities can you use to improve the critical thinking and problem-solving skills of *all* children in your classroom?**

Collaboration: **How can you include other teachers and members of the community in providing a challenging education for students who are gifted and talented?**

✔ Can Do: **What specific strategies and techniques will be most helpful for students who are especially capable?**

Each of us has something that we are very good at, and each of our students has an ability or potential that deserves nurturing. But who is *gifted?* Who is *talented?* And once we've decided, what should be done about it? What kinds of school programs, curriculum, and teaching strategies are the ones that will nurture and develop our students' gifts and talents and keep them from becoming underachievers or dropouts?

In order to develop gifts and talents, children need *opportunities.* Would you have learned to be good at what you're good at without the opportunity to be exposed and to practice? Would Yo-Yo Ma have become a cellist if his parents hadn't been musicians? Would Colin Powell have become a leader without the hierarchy of the military? Would J.K. Rowling have become a writer without the encouragement of family and teachers? Some families can provide many opportunities to their children—lessons, summer camp, traveling, meeting accomplished people. And some cannot. In either case, the school is the place where opportunities for all students should be found—opportunities to find their strengths and develop their talents. It's a tall order. But (to steal from the United Negro College Fund) a mind is a terrible thing to waste.

Definitions and Terms

Generally, it would be appropriate to begin a chapter on giftedness with a definition of that term. However, that is easier said than done. Instead, in this section you will read about the various conceptions of giftedness that have evolved over the past hundred years or so. You will also read about some individuals who have devoted their lives to studying students with gifts and talents, as well as current ideas about intelligence and giftedness. As you read, think about someone you know (or know of) whom *you* consider gifted or talented. What are the characteristics of that individual that distinguish him or her? In short, how would *you* define giftedness?

It's hard to find two "experts" who agree on a single definition of giftedness. For that matter, it is difficult to find two experts who agree on whether *giftedness* and *talent* are synonyms or merely related terms. **Giftedness** often refers to exceptional intelligence or academic ability, whereas **talent** is often used to indicate exceptional artistic or athletic ability. Jane Piirto (1999) says that "to be talented is to possess the skills to do something well" (p. 16). These distinctions are too simplistic, however, in a time when, as we shall see, new theories and research are challenging our traditional ideas about intelligence, giftedness, and talents.

Giftedness is a complex and controversial subject.

Although the problem of defining giftedness has perplexed educators and psychologists for generations, everyone seems to agree on at least one thing: There is a universal fascination with people—especially children—who are intellectually very capable.

Early Scholars and Their Thoughts on Giftedness

According to early views of giftedness, it is a step away from insanity, and environment plays no role in developing talent.

From the time of the earliest scholars to today's most influential theorists, debate has centered on whether abilities and talents are born or made. This question continues to be of interest to teachers, who have a considerable stake in the belief that experiences can make a difference. In the 1800s, giftedness was often considered a personality flaw. Lombroso, a nineteenth-century physician, proffered a popularly held view that genius was just a short step from insanity. Other nineteenth-century theorists believed that each individual had only so much brain power to expend and that if a person used up this intellect early in life, she or he could expect an adulthood filled with madness or imbecility. This "early ripe, early rot" theory, though scientifically groundless, was believed by many nineteenth-century scholars.

■ ***Galton*** When Sir Francis Galton began his study of eminent scientists (*English Men of Science*, 1890), he concluded that "genius" (the nineteenth-century term for *giftedness*) was a natural talent composed of three traits: intellectual capacity, zeal, and the power of working. However, Galton believed fully in the idea that geniuses were born, not made. He dismissed the role of environment in the development of talent, even going so far as to suggest that "inferior specimens—for example, the mentally handicapped" (Kitano & Kirby, 1986, p. 36)—be sterilized to safeguard society from the further production of mental defectives.

■ ***Terman*** Using Galton's work as a cornerstone of his own, Lewis M. Terman became credited as being the "grandfather" of gifted education in the United States. Beginning with the publication of his article "Genius and Stupidity" (1906) and continuing until his death in the 1960s, Terman left his mark on all psychological research with his longitudinal study of over 1,500 children determined to be gifted because of an IQ score of 140+ on the Stanford-Binet Intelligence Test. Today, this original group of 1,500 "Termites" is still being studied (Friedman et al., 1995). The Terman legacy can be found in his five-volume series, *Genetic Studies of Genius* (Terman et al., 1925, 1926, 1930, 1947, 1959).

Terman's longitudinal study of 1500 gifted children dispelled many misconceptions about giftedness.

Terman's work did much to dispel the myths of the eventual mental breakdown of individuals with gifts or talents, for his picture of highly able children was one of absolute mental health—of children who were immune from social and emotional crises. As his career progressed and his knowledge of gifted persons deepened, Terman realized how complex the phenomenon of giftedness was. Near the end of his career, Terman acknowledged the powerful influence of family, marriage, self-confidence, work habits, and mental health on the development of talent, for even among his 1,500 high-IQ subjects, vast discrepancies existed in their contributions to society (Delisle, 2000).

■ ***Hollingworth*** Leta S. Hollingworth, a contemporary of Terman at Columbia University, added another dimension to the understanding of people with gifts and talents. A psychologist by training, she had tested thousands of children with mental disabilities before becoming interested in extreme intelligence. Hollingworth, who began a public school program for gifted elementary students in New York City, is best remembered for her recognition of the element of vulnerability that she knew to be a part of these very bright children.

Hollingworth identified social and emotional concerns that might affect students who are gifted and talented.

Hollingworth's research and writing concentrated on the humanity of children with gifts and talents and on the idea that individual students had unique personalities in addition to their IQs. In effect, Hollingworth presented a middle ground: She identified specific social and emotional concerns that might affect the behavior of students with gifts and talents. A tribute to Hollingworth's continuing impact on the field is shown by renewed interest in her work (Delisle, 2000).

Current Definitions of Giftedness

A complete history of ideas about giftedness, talent, or intelligence cannot be written in these few pages. More thorough analysis of these topics is available elsewhere (Thurstone, 1924; Gould, 1981), and you may wish to consult them once you have completed this book and this course. Now let us turn to the theorists who are influential today in the education of gifted children.

Contemporary views on the nature and scope of giftedness are still tied to concepts of that nebulous construct, **intelligence.** As you recall from Chapter 4, intelligence is the capacity to acquire, process, and use information. Terman's early work suggested that giftedness was limited to a select few who scored 140+ on an IQ test. One important contributor to contemporary understanding, Paul Witty, moved the thinking in a different direction. Witty suggested that anyone "whose performance is consistently remarkable in any potentially valuable area" (Witty, 1940, p. 516) should be considered gifted. He based this assertion less on statistical evidence and more on observation of the world around him. Thus, the poet whose words make you weep, the teacher who inspires you to learn, and the architect who causes you to look skyward in awe would be considered gifted, regardless of their IQ scores. Today, Nancy Ewald Jackson echoes Witty; she defines giftedness "simply as exceptional performance or exceptionally rapid learning" (2000, p. 38).

According to Renzulli, giftedness includes creativity and task commitment as well as above-average intellectual ability.

Taking this thought a few steps further, Joseph Renzulli (1978) elaborated on the idea that giftedness lies not so much in the traits you have as in the deeds you do. His conception of giftedness highlights the importance of **creativity** (the ability to generate original or imaginative ideas) and **task commitment** (the ability to stay focused on a task to its completion), in addition to above-average intellectual abilities, in the development of gifted behaviors (see Figure 13.1). Like Witty, Renzulli believed that IQ alone provides insufficient evidence of giftedness, and only after a student, an architect, or a poet creates a visible product can an analysis be made of that person's intellect. This product-based formula for giftedness fits right in with our own culture's current emphasis on performance and educational accountability. For these reasons, Renzulli's conception of giftedness has enjoyed wide popularity among educators.

Gardner postulates at least eight kinds of intelligence.

Robert Sternberg and Howard Gardner, two psychologists whose work has revitalized the debate on intelligence, propose broader views of human capabilities. Gardner defines intelligence as "a biophysical potential" and giftedness as "a sign of early or precocious biophysical potential in the domains of a culture" (2000, pp. 78–79). Gardner is best known in education for his **theory of multiple intelligences** (1983), which postulates that there are at least eight distinct intelligences (see the accompanying box, "Gardner's Intelligences"). An abundance of talent in any of these areas constitutes giftedness, according to Gardner, and although people can be capable in several different intelligences, one does not have to excel in every area to be considered gifted. Gardner points out that the manifestation of intelligence depends on what is valued in a culture; if a person is good at something that is not valued in a culture, then that capacity would not be considered an intelligence (Gardner, 2000).

Sternberg proposes knowledge-based skills, social/practical intelligence, and fluid abilities.

Robert J. Sternberg adds yet another tile to this ever-expanding mosaic with his **triarchic theory,** which includes three kinds of intellectual giftedness: analytic, creative, and practical (Sternberg, 1997; Sternberg & Clinkenbeard, 1995). Students who are analytically gifted are effective at analyzing, evaluating, and critiquing; those who are creatively gifted are skillful at discovering, creating, and inventing; and those who are practically gifted are good at implementing,

General Performance Areas

Mathematics	Visual arts	Physical sciences
Philosophy	Social sciences	Law
Religion	Language arts	Music
Life science		Movement arts

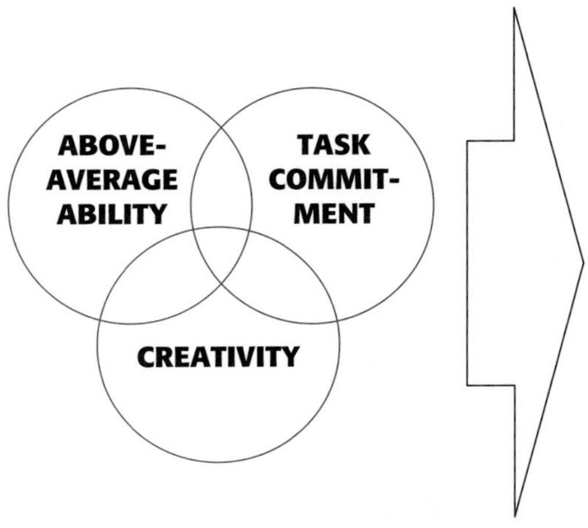

Specific Performance Areas

Cartooning	Demography	Electronic music
Astronomy	Microphotography	Child care
Public opinion polling	City planning	Consumer protection
Jewelry design	Pollution control	Cooking
Choreography	Fashion design	Furniture design
Biography	Weaving	Navigation
Film making	Play writing	Genealogy
Statistics	Advertising	Sculpture
Local history	Costume design	Wildlife management
Electronics	Meteorology	Set design
Musical composition	Puppetry	Agriculture research
Landscape architecture	Marketing	Animal learning
Chemistry	Game design	Film criticism
Etc.	Journalism	Etc.
	Etc.	

Figure 13.1
A Graphic Representation of Renzulli's Definition of Giftedness

Source: Joseph S. Renzulli, "What Makes Giftedness?" *Phi Delta Kappan 60* (1978): 180–184. Used by permission of the author.

~ Gardner's Intelligences

Gardner calls these *human competences, talents*, or "intelligences":

- Linguistic intelligence (verbal facility)
- Logical-mathematical intelligence (symbolic reasoning)
- Musical intelligence (performance-based or the ability to perceive great music)
- Spatial intelligence (heightened awareness of structural components of ideas and objects)
- Bodily-kinesthetic intelligence (lithe movement and expression)
- Interpersonal intelligence (ability to lead or inspire others)
- Intrapersonal intelligence (deep self-knowledge and actualization)
- Natural intelligence (knowledge of nature and the environment)

Source: Howard Gardner (1999). *Intelligence reframed: Multiple intelligences for the 21st century.* New York: Basic Books; and The giftedness matrix: A developmental perspective, in R. C. Friedman & B. M. Shore (eds.), *Talents unfolding: Cognition and development,* pp. 77–88. Washington, DC: American Psychological Association.

Gardner's multiple intelligences theory identifies musical intelligence as an important characteristic in young people. (*Newsweek*—Cynthia Harris/© 1991 Newsweek, Inc. All rights reserved. Reprinted by permission)

utilizing, and applying (see Figure 13.2). In Sternberg's view, "the big question is not how many things a person is good at, but how well a person can exploit whatever he or she is good at and find ways around the things that he or she is not good at" (1991, p. 51). That is a thoughtful proposition to examine for each one of us.

Sternberg identifies wisdom as a form of intelligence, and believes that schools should try to teach wisdom.

Sternberg's current interest lies in the nature of *wisdom* as a form of giftedness (2000). He asks that we think, for example, of four extremely gifted individuals of the twentieth century—Mahatma Gandhi, Mother Theresa, Martin Luther King, Jr., and Nelson Mandela. Would their gifts have been identified through any kind of test, or with the definitions we identify in this chapter? Perhaps not. But they instigated change that led to the common good in the world, the scope of which few others can claim. Sternberg argues that we need to start developing wisdom in children:

> For example, students need to learn how to think dialogically, understanding points of view other than their own, and to think not only in terms of their own interests, but in terms of the interests of others and of the society, as well. . . . Unless students are specifically taught to focus upon the common good, rather than only upon the good of themselves and those close to them, they may simply never learn to think in such a fashion. (Sternberg, 2000, p. 252).

The accompanying box provides Sternberg's suggestions for developing wisdom in children. These strategies would be particularly successful with teenagers.

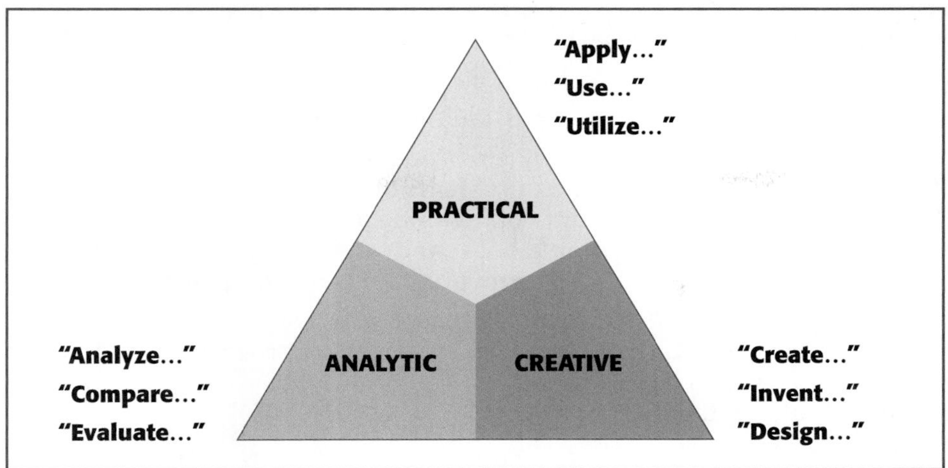

Figure 13.2
Sternberg's Triarchic Theory of Intelligence
According to Robert Sternberg, intelligence comprises analytic, creative, and practical abilities. In *analytical thinking,* we try to solve familiar problems by using strategies that manipulate the elements of a problem or the relationships among the elements (e.g., comparing, analyzing). In *creative thinking,* we try to solve new kinds of problems that require us to think about the problem and its elements in a new way (e.g., inventing, designing). In *practical thinking,* we try to solve problems that apply what we know to everyday contexts (e.g., applying, using).

Source: Figure from *In Search of the Human Mind* by Robert J. Sternberg, p. 395. Copyright © 1995 by Harcourt Brace & Company, reproduced by permission of publisher.

P.L. 97-35 defines giftedness as high erformance in intellectual, creative, artistic, leardership, and academic areas.

Finally, the "official" definition of giftedness is the one in federal law, which states that gifted children are those

> who give evidence of high performance capability in areas such as intellectual, creative, artistic, leadership capacity, or specific academic fields, and who require services or activities not ordinarily provided by the school in order to fully develop such capabilities. (P.L. 97-35, Education Consolidation and Improvement Act, sec. 582, 1981)

The federal definition specifies areas of giftedness; it allows for gifted traits and gifted behaviors; and it ties in the definition of giftedness with the need to provide special educational programs for children identified as gifted. Overall, it is a comprehensive definition that has been adopted enthusiastically by many states.

Federal law does not require educational services for gifted students but encourages state initiatives for serving these students.

Unlike IDEA, P.L. 97-35 does not *require* educational services for students identified as gifted, nor does it provide any funds for implementation of gifted programs. Since its enactment, however, many individual states have incorporated the federal definition into state legislation; and, since more than half the states now require special educational provisions for students identified as gifted or talented, this federal definition has encouraged a substantial increase in state-based initiatives for serving students with gifts or talents.

It is doubtful that one definition of giftedness will ever be written that satisfies every theorist, educator, and parent. Nor is it likely that all gifted children

~ Developing Wisdom in Children: The Work of Robert Sternberg

What we consider wisdom, argues Sternberg, is inextricably tied to our values, and we must begin by valuing wisdom itself and what it can contribute to society. Do we? Think of how older people are perceived in our culture to answer that question.

Here are Sternberg's words:

Wisdom is a form of giftedness that can be developed in a number of ways. Seven of these are particularly important:

- *First*, provide students with problems that require wise thinking.
- *Second*, help students think in terms of a common good in the solution of these problems.
- *Third*, help students learn how to balance their own interests, the interests of others, and the interests of institutions in the solution of these problems.
- *Fourth*, provide examples of wise thinking from the past and analyze them.
- *Fifth*, model wisdom for the students. Show them examples of wise thinking you have done and perhaps not-so-wise thinking that has taught you lessons.
- *Sixth*, help students to think dialectically... most problems in the world do not have right or wrong answers, but better or worse ones, and what is seen as a good answer can vary with time and place.
- *Seventh*, show your students that you value wise information processing and solutions.

Finally, carry what you learn and encourage students to carry what they learn outside the classroom. The goal is not to teach another "subject" that will serve as the basis for an additional grade to appear on a report card. The goal is to change the way people think about and act in their own lives. (Sternberg, 2000, pp. 257–258)

For more information on teaching wisdom, read the source: Sternberg, R. J. (2000). Wisdom as a form of giftedness. *Gifted Child Quarterly, 44* (4), 252–260.

will ever be identified for the special education they require. Still, it is important for you to realize that if you are unsure about "exactly" who is gifted, you are joined in your lack of certainty by some of the world's experts on the theory and measurement of intelligence.

Criteria for Identification

If a child begins to read independently at the age of 3 or a 15-year-old graduates as high school valedictorian, it is quite apparent that you are observing atypical behavior—not "abnormal" behavior, but behavior that appears in advance of its usual developmental onset.

Advanced development is one of the most commonly applied criteria in the identification of students with gifts and talents. Measurement of this advanced development historically has been through standardized tests commonly given by school psychologists or teachers.

Students scoring two or more standard deviations above the mean on IQ tests are usually classified as gifted.

Individual IQ tests, like the WISC-III or the Stanford-Binet (see Chapter 4), can be used to assess intellectual capacity. However, the extensive costs in terms of time and money needed to administer and score the tests have caused most school districts to forgo their use. Instead, standardized group intelligence tests are often used. When given as part of the annual battery of achievement tests administered to all students, these group tests provide a general assessment of how students compare intellectually with their classmates. Those students who score two or more standard deviations above the mean of the test (which generally results in an IQ of 130–135) are often classified as gifted. Similarly, students who score at the 95th percentile or above on standardized achievement tests of reading, math, and other content areas are often identified as academically gifted.

Achievement and IQ tests, though, have been criticized as being too narrow in focus. Barbara Clark (1997) points out that tests do not give an accurate description of a person's capacity or potential, and Frasier (1987) cautions that standardized tests often ignore the special background and characteristics of culturally diverse populations. Many scholars have noted that using IQ tests as the primary means of identifying candidates for gifted programs inevitably leads to underrepresentation of children with disabilities as well as those from culturally and linguistically diverse backgrounds (Salvia & Ysseldyke, 1998).

Standardized tests that determine giftedness are criticized because they may lead to underrepresentation of children from minority groups.

Informal assessment by parents, teachers, peers, and community members who know the student can provide school personnel with non–test-based information about the range of a student's specific skills or talents. The yardsticks for measuring giftedness are many and varied. The teacher's role in identifying and assessing giftedness and talent is discussed later in the chapter.

Factors Contributing to Giftedness

For as long as gifts and talents have been recognized and studied, the question of nature versus nurture has been pondered. Are individuals with gifts and talents endowed with a pool of superior genes, or is their environment responsible for the emergence of superior performance? The best answer seems to be "It depends."

Hereditary and Biological Factors

Scientists and educators agree that genes are but one element in the complex development of human intelligence. Even geneticists disagree about the relative contributions of our genes to our abilities—estimates range from about 40–80 percent. Gage and Berliner (1998) see the influences of heredity and environment on intelligence as about equal. Vernon (1989), in arguing against overemphasizing any one element—genes, environment, or opportunity—in the development of intelligence, reminds us that since none of these factors occurs in total isolation from the others, it is impossible to tell where the effects of heredity end and the impact of environment takes over.

Both genetics and environment play crucial roles in determining giftedness.

Environmental Factors

The role played by the family in the development of gifts and talents has been studied extensively, and virtually every study has shown the importance of nurturance. Benjamin Bloom (1985), in his study of Olympic athletes, musical prodigies, and others of exceptional achievement, points to the vital role played by the family (not just the parents) in channeling these remarkable talents and downplays the role of the school in the realization of noteworthy accomplishments.

Family encouragement of the child's talents is of critical importance.

The role played by peers, especially among economically disadvantaged children, has also been shown to have a significant impact on the desire to

A closer look

Where Budding Geniuses Can Blossom

A private school for children with exceptionally high IQs nurtures an unfettered, unapologetic appetite for knowledge. Experiments in terminal velocity, anyone?

At 10 a.m. on a recent Wednesday morning, the 5-year-olds were writing. Not, mind you, their ABCs, as most kindergartners would be doing. No, these tots were composing sentences, an entire paragraph—and with few errant periods or funny spellings. Their topic: "What I Would Do if I Were President."

In another room, the 11-year-olds were doing math. Not long division, not multiplication of fractions, but algebraic equations. X intercept, Y axis, eyes gleaming at the very mention. Manipulating fancy graphing calculators, these kids were not merely paying attention to the lesson, they were absorbed in it.

In the science lab, the 13-year-olds were furiously swaddling eggs in typing paper, masking tape and paper clips, which they soon would launch from the roof of a nearby building. They were conducting a physics experiment in terminal velocity—splat rate, for you dimwits out there. By the time these teens enter high school, they'll be years ahead of the crowd in physics and chemistry.

Extracurricular reading? Of course, plenty of it. But forget Harry Potter. Try "The Nothing That Is: A Natural History of Zero."

"It was brilliant," said Nicholas Sofroniew, the 13-year-old who gobbled up math teacher Robert Kaplan's weighty work of nonfiction in his free time.

If you've guessed that we're inside a school for geniuses, you are partially correct. To be labeled gifted, an IQ of 132 will do, but that still isn't enough to win passage through the black iron gate of the Mirman School in Bel-Air.

Mirman, a private school founded in 1962, is one of a handful in the country to cater to the tiptop of the intelligence scale: Only the highly gifted—children with an IQ of 145 and above—may apply.

Such exclusivity comes at a price. First of all, there's tuition—more than $12,000 a year for most of the 355 students (about 10 percent are on scholarship). The school, which serves youngsters ages 5 to 14, admits only about 40 new students a year, most of them at the earliest level.

Then there is the social fallout. Some parents feel that Mirman admission gives them bragging rights, a colossal turnoff for other parents who may already feel that schools for geniuses are undemocratic.

Mirman may be Egghead Central, but not in any stereotypical way. The students don't wear ink-smeared pocket protectors and they "don't all have big round glasses or oversized heads," says Norman Mirman, the octogenarian former Los Angeles city schoolteacher who founded the school with his wife, Beverly.

Socially and emotionally, the students, most of them Anglo, generally act their ages. Eight-year-olds still get in trouble for throwing sand—even the one who left at age 9 to attend Loyola University in Chicago. Eleven-year-olds study high school Spanish, but sometimes they forget their homework and cry.

In other ways, though, Mirman clearly is beyond the norm. It has no grades per se, just flexible age groups that allow students to learn at their own accelerated pace, studying material typically tackled by youngsters three to five years older. Here, if a 6-year-old, for instance, is especially talented in math, she's not stuck with others of her age; she can move up to an older class for part of the school day. By the time students finish Mirman, they have covered at least a ninth-grade curriculum and some far more. Over the years, about half a dozen prodigies have gone straight to college—a leap frowned on by Mirman but often pushed by parents.

Another difference: When a Mirman teacher asks a question, almost every hand waves for attention. Enthusiasm for learning is unbridled. Precocity is a given. Eyes don't roll—much—when a boy in a cast announces not that he busted his hand but that "I broke my third metacarpal."

Eight decades after influential psychologist Lewis Terman warned against indifference to the

A closer look

special needs of budding geniuses, the general attitude hasn't changed: Why invest in the high-IQ child who'll learn fine wherever he is? It's the struggling masses who need the help.

"The argument is, if we just have limited resources, why do we help the kids who don't need help? But that assumes they don't need help," said Ellen Winner, a Boston College psychology professor and author of the 1996 book *Gifted Children: Myths and Realities.*

"They need education that is challenging" but don't often get it, Winner noted. "These children are miserable in school when they are forced to work way below their level."

Winner goes so far as to argue that the highly gifted are more in need of specialized education than the moderately gifted—a distinction that makes her about as popular as a fox in a chicken coop among colleagues in the gifted world.

Most gifted students are educated in public schools. Los Angeles Unified, for instance, offers five full-time highly gifted magnet schools. However, in most districts the majority of students identified as having above-average intelligence are not in full-day gifted programs but may receive special instruction for an hour or two a day. The latter approach is, in Winner's view, woefully inadequate for the ablest minds.

An estimated 20 percent of high school dropouts are gifted students who got bored in school and 85 percent are underachievers, according to Barbara Clark, president of the World Council for Gifted and Talented Children and professor emeritus in the School of Education at Cal State Los Angeles. Yet such figures set off few alarms.

The "severely gifted," as students like those at Mirman are sometimes called, constitute about 1 percent of the 2 to 3 percent of the population who have above-average intelligence. That is, the gifted represent about 3 out of 100 people, the highly gifted 1 out of 10,000.

The ultra-intelligent largely remain victims of benign neglect in public schools. A 1993 report by the U.S. Department of Education found that only 2 cents out of every $100 spent on precollegiate education in 1990 went to gifted programs. Education Secretary Richard W. Riley described the situation as a "quiet crisis" in which the needs of the nation's ablest students are seldom met.

"There are students out there right now who are staring out the window. Their talents will atrophy," said Richard S. Maddox, director of the Early Entrance Program at Cal State L.A., which admits gifted students as young as 11.

As in many private schools, most of Mirman's students enroll at age 5. Those who come in later, especially from schools where few accommodations were made for the supremely gifted, say Mirman was liberating for them.

Take 10-year-old Sydney Ember. At the private San Fernando Valley school she attended until this year, she was the know-it-all who stuck her hand in the air every time the teacher asked a question. It got to the point that teachers told her, "Stop raising your hand, we know you know the answer." One teacher didn't understand why she begged for more homework, suggesting she should be happy that she had more time for TV.

Now, Sydney "comes home every day happy," said her mother, Laurie Ember. Sydney, whose 5-year-old sister, Jamie, also attends Mirman, has only one complaint: "Why didn't I come here sooner?"

Elaine Woo, *Los Angeles Times,* 11/22/00, Living Section, pp. 1,3.

achieve academically (Reis & McCoach, 2000). In short, the debate over the development of gifts and talents has grown far beyond the nature-nurture arguments of past generations. Today, the emphasis is on the practical: designing structure and strategies at home and at school that encourage these talents to bloom and blossom.

Prevalence

In most states, the prevalence of giftedness among the population is placed at 5 percent.

Considering the variety of definitions of giftedness, it is not surprising that the prevalence of gifts and talents in the population is also open to debate. For example, if you were to use the criterion of an IQ of 140 as the baseline for intellectual giftedness, you would exclude 99 percent of the population. If, however, you were to use the federal definition of giftedness written in P.L. 97-35, 3 to 5 percent of the school-age population would qualify as having gifts or talents. Renzulli's conception of giftedness (1986) identifies a set of behaviors that can emerge in students who are above average (though not necessarily superior) in ability. Thus, he suggests a figure of 15 to 20 percent of the population as capable of performing gifted behaviors. And Henry Levin (1996) believes that if we take time to look, we will find that almost every student in a class is above average in some skill, ability, or knowledge area—everyone is gifted in some way.

Many theorists and researchers, although arguing about the exact prevalence of gifts and talents, do agree that for funding purposes the figure of 5 percent is useful. Thus, although experts may disagree philosophically on where giftedness begins and ends, the prevalence figure of 5 percent is common in most states.

Special Populations of Gifted Students

The following sections address some special populations of gifted children and the special needs these young people have.

Gifted Girls

Gifted girls must be identified, supported, and challenged, particularly in the middle school years.

Until the impact of the women's movement began to be felt in American education in the 1970s and 1980s, little was done to identify and develop giftedness and talents in girls. Although it is now generally understood that it is illegal to discriminate on the basis of gender in any arena, unconscious biases may still prevent girls who are gifted and talented from being identified and from persevering through rigorous educational programs, particularly in middle and secondary school. It should be recognized that gifted girls often have a broader conception of what constitutes *achievement* than boys; it is not limited to degrees and career status, but is the successful balance of professional, personal, and relationship achievements in their lives (Hollinger & Fleming, 1992). Gifted girls should be encouraged to take the most challenging coursework available, to engage in play activities that are physically challenging and occasionally competitive, and to speak out and defend their opinions in groups (Kerr, 1997). See the accompanying box, "Profile of Gifted Females," which lists some distinguishing characteristics of girls who are gifted.

~ Profile of Gifted Females

Regarding younger gifted girls:

- Many gifted girls are superior physically, have more social knowledge, and are better adjusted than are average girls, although highly gifted girls may not seem as well adjusted.
- Highly gifted girls are often second-born females.
- Highly gifted girls have high academic achievement.
- In their interests, gifted girls may be more like gifted boys than they are like average girls.
- Gifted girls are often confident in their opinions and willing to argue for their point of view.
- By age 10, gifted girls express wishes and needs for self-esteem and are interested in fulfilling those needs through school and club achievements; highly gifted girls, though, may be loners without much need for recognition.
- Actual occupations of parents do not affect gifted girls' eventual career choices.
- Gifted girls have high career goals, although highly gifted girls aspire to careers having moderate rather than high status.

Regarding adolescent females:

- Gifted girls' IQ scores drop in adolescence, perhaps as they begin to perceive their own giftedness as undesirable.
- Gifted girls are likely to continue to have high academic achievement as measured by grade point average.
- Gifted girls take less rigorous courses than gifted boys in high school.
- Gifted girls maintain a high involvement in extracurricular and social activities during adolescence.
- Highly gifted girls do very well academically in high school; however, they often do not receive recognition for their achievements.
- Highly gifted girls attend less prestigious colleges than do highly gifted boys, which may lead to lower-status careers.

Remember that, like any list of group characteristics, these are not hard-and-fast rules; there will be exceptions to all of them in gifted females.

Source: Adapted from *Smart Girls* (Revised Edition) by Barbara Kerr. Copyright © 1998. Used by permission of Gifted Psychology Press.

Gifted Students with Disabilities

As early as 1942, Hollingworth saw the possibility that disabilities could coexist with giftedness. But only recently have the needs of these "twice exceptional" students been addressed.

Some gifted students have learning disabilities, sensory impairments, or motor limitations.

June Maker (1977) was among the first to suggest that options should be provided in schools for highly able students who also had learning disabilities, sensory impairments, or physical disabilities. But she warned that her work was merely a beginning, serving to "identify issues and raise questions to a greater degree than it solves or answers them" (p. xi). Later, Whitmore and Maker (1985) combined their efforts and experiences to produce more specific suggestions for working with students who are gifted and disabled in school and community settings. Their suggestions appear in the accompanying box, "Strategies for Working with Students Who Are Gifted and Disabled."

Students with learning disabilities are a unique group. Sally Reis and her colleagues (Reis, Neu, & McGuire, 1997; Reis, McGuire, & Neu, 2000) conducted in-

~ Strategies for Working with Students Who Are Gifted and Disabled

- Find alternate ways to help these students attain their goals rather than change (that is, lower) their aspirations.
- Locate specialized equipment and technology that can help students attain their objectives and share their talents with others.
- Allow students to explore their environments fully, rather than isolating them from others or making every activity a "safe" one.
- Plan activities and interventions that take advantage of the students' individual strengths.

depth interviews with twelve young adults who were successful in college while receiving support services for their identified learning disabilities. All had been tested earlier in their schooling and were found to have high IQs. The researchers found that these students uniformly reported negative experiences in elementary and secondary school. Their learning disabilities tended to be identified relatively late in their schooling, despite problems that had appeared early; they reported negative interactions with teachers, some of whom told the students they were lazy and could achieve if they worked harder; and they felt isolated from peers and unaccepted by them. But because these students developed compensation strategies, had parental support, and participated in a university learning disability program, they succeeded despite their early negative experiences (see the accompanying box, "Compensation Strategies Used by Gifted Students with Learning Disabilities"). Reis and her colleagues suggest that it was the combination of their high abilities and disabilities that set them up for problems in school, such as the late referrals to special education and poor relationships with teachers.

High-ability students with learning disabilities can succeed in college with the right supports.

These students had other advantages and a secret weapon: "Each person in this study had a mother who devoted herself to using different strategies to help her child succeed. This assistance was given regardless of whether the mother worked outside of the home and regardless of how many other children were in the family. One may ask, therefore, what happens to children who do not have a similar source of support?" (Reis, Neu, & McGuire, 1997, p. 477).

There is some concern that students who are gifted might inadvertently be identified as attention-deficit disordered because of the behaviors they display when they are bored (Willard-Holt, 1999). Children with attention-deficit disorder demonstrate the same inattentive behaviors consistently across situations; the behavior of students who are gifted and bored would vary, depending on how engaged in the material the student found himself.

Students with disabilities who are gifted may show their abilities in unusual ways and may need unconventional assessment techniques because traditional assessments are not appropriate. In the end, underlying all approaches to locating and serving gifted children with disabilities is a need to change society's attitudes and perceptions. There remains a need for each of us to see that *cap*ability is more important than *dis*ability.

Underachieving Gifted Students

Some gifted students do not achieve at the level of their potential.

Think of someone you knew in school who was always told by teachers, "You're a smart kid; I know you could do better if you wanted to." Usually, this type of student frustrates teachers and parents, for they see a lot of talent going to waste. The technical term applied to students whose aptitude is high but

~ Compensation Strategies Used by Gifted Students with Learning Disabilities

Students who had high ability levels and also had learning disabilities found that the following strategies and supports helped them succeed in college work.

Strategy	Components
Study and Performance Strategies	Notetaking Test-taking preparation Time management Monitoring daily, weekly, and monthly assignments and activities Using weekly and monthly organizers to maximize use of time; chunking assignments into workable parts Library skills Written expression Reading Mathematical processing
Cognitive/Learning Strategies	Memory strategies such as mnemonics and rehearsal using flash cards Chunking information into smaller units for mastery
Compensation Supports	Word processing Use of computers Books on tape

These students also had other supports and strengths:

Parental support

- Parents, particularly mothers, were energetic advocates for their children.
- The students in the university learning disabilities program cited help with study skills, a network of support, and a consistent program director as important components of the program.

Self-perceived strength and future aspirations

- Students had a strong work ethic and the conviction that they could succeed.

Sources: S. M. Reis, T. W. Neu, and J. M. McGuire, "Case Studies of High-Ability Students with Learning Disabilities Who Have Achieved," *Exceptional Children 63*:4 (1997), 463–479; S. M. Reis, J. M. McGuire, and T. W. Neu, "Compensation Strategies Used by High-Ability Students with Learning Disabilities Who Succeed in College," *Gifted Child Quarterly 44*:2 (2000), 123–134.

whose performance is low (or mediocre) is **gifted underachiever,** but the less technical terms are the ones that sting—terms like *lazy*, *unmotivated*, or *disorganized*. Whatever you call these students, one thing is certain: When *you* get one in *your* classroom, you'll wish there was some magic elixir available that would cause this "underachievement" to disappear.

What causes this disheartening underachievement? Hollingworth (1942) believed that students with an IQ of 140 spend half of each school day in activities that are unchallenging and monotonous, and the result is often a poor attitude

Intellectually gifted students who dislike school may not develop their talents.

toward school ("school is boring") or even misbehavior, as shown by the comment of this 12-year-old girl: "I learned I was gifted in third grade. I would finish my work early and disturb others because I had nothing to do" (Delisle, 1984, p. 11). Family, cultural, and peer issues contribute to underachievement as well (Reis & McCoach, 2000).

Methods of modifying school curriculum and structure for students with gifts and talents are discussed later in this chapter. What is important to note here is the intimate link between school achievement and school attitude; for if intellectually able students perceive school as drudgery, or irrelevant, it is unlikely that they will develop their talents fully (Whitmore, 1980).

Joanne Whitmore (1980) has produced the definitive work on gifted underachievers, and her approach combines curricular changes (focusing on a child's strengths and interests), family involvement (parent conferences and "partnership" in rewarding even small improvements in performance), and self-concept education (based on the premise that students who feel good about themselves will choose to achieve).

Later efforts have suggested more mechanistic solutions—like behavioral contracts—and more coercive measures—like punishment (Rimm, 1986). These efforts, though possibly successful in the short term, tend to be less effective than the approaches described by Whitmore. Reis and McCoach (2000) point out that none of the suggested interventions has been well researched, but it is likely that a combination of curricular modifications, counseling, and self-regulation training will be most effective.

When underachievement is detected early, the prognosis for positive change is good.

However, there is one point on which all researchers agree: The earlier the problem of underachievement is detected and addressed, the more hopeful is the prognosis for positive change. The problem of underachieving behaviors will not be easy to solve, but if you look toward making the gifted child's school time relevant, interesting, and intellectually stimulating, chances are good that the student's response will be positive.

Culturally Diverse Gifted Students

Using non-test-based indicators, children with gifts and talents can be found in every race, culture, and socioeconomic group.

Gifts and talents exist in children of every race, culture, and socioeconomic group. However, gifted program planners have often been criticized for not looking hard enough to find talents in children who may not represent the majority culture or its values. Indeed, blacks are overrepresented in all categories of special education except for one, gifted education, where they are significantly underrepresented (Baldwin & Vialle, 1999). So, although every thinking person agrees that one's skin color and primary language are not intrinsic limitations to the expression of one's talents, many gifted programs are filled with students from the white, middle-class culture of our population.

Cohen (1990) saw this as a problem related to *misuse* and *nonuse:* misuse of assessment instruments (like IQ tests) that were normed on middle-class students with middle-class experiences and nonuse of alternative methods of non-test-based indicators of giftedness—like nominations from parents or community leaders or a portfolio of a student's work samples that indicate superior performance. Paul Torrance (1969), ever conscious of the fact that different cultures have different standards of appropriate behavior, reminded us to look for qualities like *expressive speech, enjoyment and leadership in group-based activities,* and *the ability to improvise with commonplace materials and objects* as indicators of giftedness in culturally diverse groups.

Identifying gifted children from diverse cultural backgrounds has become a major goal of professionals involved in gifted child education (Clark, 1997). Once the students are identified, the program itself must be tailored to suit the needs, interests, learning styles, and cultural values of its participants. Ford and Harris (1999) encourage approaches that promote multiculturalism so that all students come to appreciate each other's cultures and backgrounds, and they believe in the importance of establishing links with the child's family, especially with someone who is familiar with the cultural heritage of the program's students.

As the twenty-first century develops and our world becomes even smaller through the wonders of travel and technology, program planners for gifted students, and *all* educators, must look for new ways to identify and foster the talents of each child. The challenge is great, but the individual and societal benefits, should we succeed, are even greater.

Highly Gifted Students

Just as educators who work with students with developmental disabilities classify disabilities by level of severity—mild, severe, or profound, for example—gifted child educators sometimes do the same thing regarding the label of gifted. Often, an IQ score is used to define a population that has come to be called the **highly gifted.** Terman and Merrill (1973) and Whitmore (1980) use an IQ score of 140 to classify a child as highly gifted, while McGuffog, Feiring, and Lewis (1987) call an IQ of 164 "extremely gifted." And Hollingworth (1942), in an early and classic study, used an IQ of 180 as the point at which giftedness is manifest in an extreme form.

Most highly gifted children are placed in regular classrooms, which often don't meet their needs.

A regular classroom placement for a child whose intellect surpasses that of 99.99 percent of his or her classmates can pose problems. Yet Gaunt (1989) found that most highly gifted children are placed in regular school classes, and even though many of these students are involved in part-time enrichment programs, the majority of their time is spent in classes that take their extreme intelligence into account only minimally (Kearney, 1988).

Gallagher (2000) believes that highly gifted students (who may constitute less than 1 percent of the total student population) need something different from other very capable students, and suggests the following:

Highly gifted students make up less than one percent of the school-aged population.

- These students should be the instructional responsibility of the specialist in gifted education rather than the general education teacher.
- Highly gifted students need more individual attention, perhaps through tutoring, acceleration, or individualized studies and projects.

The problems and solutions involving highly gifted students are complex and varied, but the highly gifted child has been receiving increasing attention over the past years. Advocates for this population of students point out that even the best school program that includes opportunities for **academic enrichment** (broadening the experience base of the students without changing the instructional objectives) and acceleration may fall far short of meeting the needs of highly gifted children. **Radical acceleration** (for example, skipping several grades), early entrance to college (some preteen students have attended university full time), and home schooling are some options that have been used effectively to meet the needs of this population.

Effects on the Developing Person

Students who are gifted and talented represent a cross-section of humanity: All races, cultures, sizes, and shapes are apparent. Yet as different as these individual students seem at first glance, their intelligence has affected their cognitive and social-emotional development in similar ways. The following sections highlight some of these effects, as well as the impact of the gifted or talented student on the family. We will first look at how giftedness affects individuals in the areas of cognitive, social and emotional, and physical development.

Cognitive Development

As discussed in the first part of the chapter, there are many perspectives on the nature of giftedness and cognitive development. In general, cognitive development is frequently accelerated, which can cause problems in the classroom. For example, a child who learned to read independently at the age of 3 may have difficulty in a kindergarten class where he or she is expected to learn the alphabet. A junior high student well versed in algebra may question the point of completing pages of long-division problems. A 10-year-old who perceives subtle distinctions in moral reasoning may be frustrated by agemates who see only cut-and-dried, right-and-wrong solutions.

Social and Emotional Development

Some gifted students experience social isolation.

Very closely tied to the cognitive effects of giftedness and talents is the social and emotional impact of these talents on students' performance. Students may feel "different," misunderstood, and socially isolated. To address these issues, several authors (Adderholt-Elliot, 1987; Buescher, 1984; Colangelo, 1989) have recommended particular strategies:

- Explaining their abilities to students so they can understand their specific areas of talent
- Reviewing expectations and setting them realistically, so that gifted students do not interpret any level other than perfection to be failure
- Establishing short-term, reachable goals and various ways of reaching these goals
- Concentrating on the idea that although they may be better at some activities and academic areas than other students, they are intrinsically no better than these students

The interplay between intellect and emotion is clear to people who work with students with talents and gifts. An intellectually able 6-year-old may cry uncontrollably when confronted with inequity or injustice, either on the schoolyard or while watching the evening news. A fastidious high school junior may consider herself a failure if she receives a grade of B+ in advanced physics. It is your job, as a teacher, to understand that intellectually capable students, whatever their ages, be appreciated for their strengths and their vulnerabilities; for even though these young people are smart, they are not small adults.

Physical Development

Effects on the Developing Person

Early research by Terman (1954) showed students with gifts to be stronger, bigger, and healthier than their agemates. In fact, Terman's findings did much to dissolve the stereotype of the gifted student as a bespectacled weakling who carries a briefcase to school instead of a backpack. However, Terman's research included primarily children from advantaged backgrounds whose physical prowess was bolstered by nurturing and plentiful home environments. Today, as gifted programs expand to students from all cultures and socioeconomic backgrounds, we see an array of physical characteristics that defies any simple categorization. In effect, a gifted student has no certain look or appearance. Indeed, students with physical disabilities must not be overlooked in the identification of giftedness; they may have an impressive store of knowledge despite limited experiences, and they use exceptional creativity in finding ways of communicating and accomplishing tasks (Willard-Holt, 1999).

The gifted student cannot be identified by appearance.

School-age students who are gifted may face a physical challenge if they are accelerated. **Acceleration** involves skipping several grades to provide a more appropriate curriculum; as a result, accelerated students are two or more years younger than classmates. Especially in junior high and high school, this becomes an important consideration, since few adolescents want to be left behind when growth spurts occur for everyone but them. This possibility, which can also have social side effects, should be reviewed before acceleration is undertaken.

Acceleration may have social implications for students, particularly in adolescence.

Gifted Adolescents

Struggling for social acceptance, experiencing physical changes, and conducting inner searches for meaning in one's life are some of the benchmarks of adolescence. Gifted adolescents are as concerned about these issues as are their agemates, but there may be unique implications for them (See the accompanying "First Person" for an example).

Birely and Genshaft (1991) point out that adolescence for gifted students involves special concerns in the social and emotional, educational, ethical and spiritual, and career and lifestyle domains. In the area of social and emotional issues, gifted females may struggle with decisions related to the often conflicting needs for social acceptance and the full expression of their talents (Kerr, 1985). In effect, gifted girls often feel they must suppress or disguise their abilities to be accepted by boys. Conversely, Alvino (1989) contended that most gifted males feel obligated to use their academic talents, often at the cost of the emotional aspects of their lives; the result may be increased stoicism and tendency to overwork. Teachers should be aware of these potential issues and be prepared to provide appropriate support.

Gifted adolescent girls often feel they must suppress or disguise their abilities to be accepted.

Educationally, adolescents with gifts and talents tend to question how best to further their intellectual development. For example, if they are admitted to college after their junior year in high school, do they stay in high school and not miss the senior prom and varsity football, or do they go on to college and seek social outlets there? Or, given the opportunity to pursue intellectual challenges independently, do they choose this route and forgo other options? Chad Gervich, a 15-year-old gifted student, summarizes these issues when describing his difficult decision whether to attend a summer residential program for gifted students:

first person

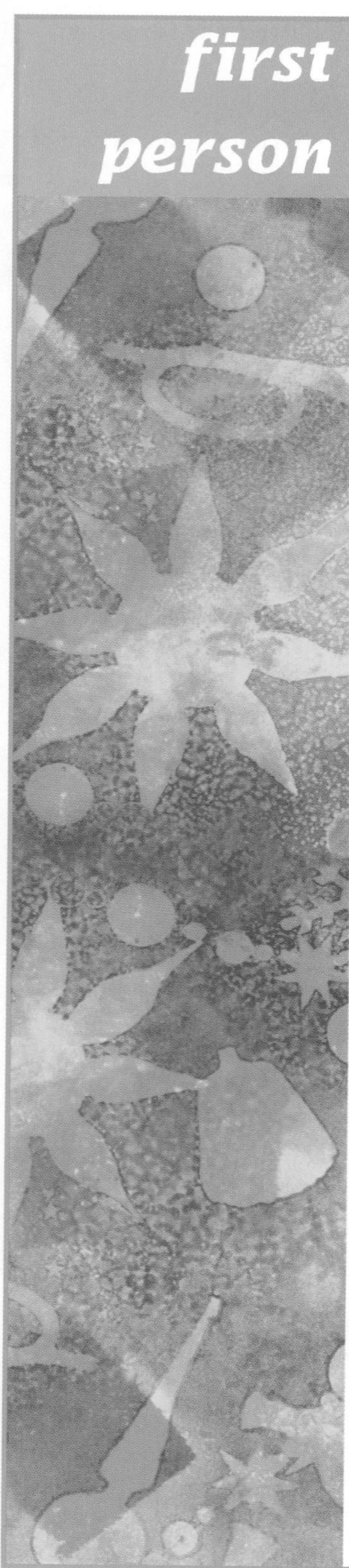

Janet McDonald grew up in a public housing project in New York, the middle child of seven children, and attended Erasmus Hall High School in Brooklyn and Harlem Prep. This vignette from her memoir Project Girl *follows the death of a classmate, Carleton, from an overdose of heroin.*

Carleton's death shook me—life wasn't guaranteed, not even for the young, gifted, and black. I decided to stop procrastinating and go to college. . . . I showed the college counselor a list of colleges that interested me. Lone Mountain College had a poetic name; the University of Hawaii sounded like paradise; and City College was a sure admit. "Why don't you apply to Vassar? They've already taken one of our students and say they'd be willing to take others." I flinched. "Isn't that the school for rich white girls like Jackie Kennedy?" "Now don't start your rich white girl thing again. Vassar is a top school, one of the seven sisters, and we need as many of us in schools like that as we can get." I wanted to say, *Then send your mama.* Why did *I* always have to be the one to carry the flag and plant it in foreign soil? He answered my unspoken question. "You're a straight-A student and you did extremely well on the SATs. You're the perfect candidate." Wondering who the "seven sisters" were, I wrote Vassar for an application and a fee-waiver form.

It was spring and I was on my way to Vassar College for an interview. . . .The taxicab driver pulled through the Gothic Vassar arch, slowed down for an approving nod from the security guard, and left me standing in the middle of acres of verdure and evergreen trees. Ivy crawled up the front of Main Building, my destination. I exhaled stress. Then inhaled the smell of Christmas and clean air. The inscription above the doorway read: "Vassar College, Founded 1861." My ancestors were still slaves while Matthew Vassar was worrying about the education of white women. . . . this school wasn't intended for me. . . . I had nothing in common with Jacqueline Bouvier Kennedy Onassis. What was I doing standing at the front door of her college?

"You must be Janet!" The voice of a WASP. The youthful director of admissions had dark brown hair and a big smile. "Welcome!" . . . "Yes," I answered, not knowing what else to say. He led me to his office, chatting about dormitories, language labs, and tennis courts. A student-guided tour had been arranged for me and other prospective students, he said, and some of the black students were very eager to meet me. "Okay," I said, once again waxing articulate. The interview was one of those "So, tell me about yourself" ordeals that leave perspiration stains on your best blouse. There's no telling what a teenager might babble under such stress. Nevertheless, by the end of the interview, I had the impression he liked me, and that made me like him back.

The campus tour was spectacular. I wanted what Vassar had to offer: not the education, but the *life*. Sunlight reflected off the long windowpanes of the Central Dining Hall, the well-groomed golf course stretched beyond the eye's reach, the castle-like library flashed color from its stained-glass windows, and barefoot white kids in cut-off jeans chased Frisbees. Vassar was a place where you strolled in soft grass, ate as much as your stomach could hold, and lived without fear of muggings, robberies, or assault. And all I had to do was sit in a classroom a few hours a day and write some research papers. What a deal! No wonder white people were so happy.

Meeting the black students dispelled the one lingering concern I had about the college. The students I met had not become white at all. They were unlike my own project tribe and my Prep peers—but definitely black. Shenim, a senior, greeted me wearing African dress. Laura, a witty Londoner, cursed as fluently as Joy from the Prep, only with an English accent. The idea of black people in Europe was so incongruous to me that I found myself staring at her. She was cocky and irreverent, or maybe the accent made it seem so. She instantly became the model of how I wanted to turn out if I did go to Vassar: smart, bold, and still black. I had outgrown my prejudice against non-American blacks and identified with Laura because of what distinguished us, albeit in different ways—we were both foreigners. I decided I would attend Vassar if they accepted me.

A few weeks later, Mother made her usual morning stop at the mailbox. She returned carrying a thin letter. "Here, you got mail from that college." She was still holding the six-inch nail she carried for protection against muggers. She'd explained that it offered her the best of both worlds—a weapon that wasn't illegal. I scrutinized the envelope. It was too soon for a decision. Unless, of course, it was negative. I braced myself. Who wanted to be a white girl, anyway? "We are pleased to inform you . . ." I read no further. "Yes!" Mother raised her hands to the heavens. "Well, knock me down and fan me with a brick! My baby's going to college. You know you got your brains from me." "I'm going to be a rich white girl like Jackie Kennedy!" I squealed, happier than I'd been in a long time.

Excerpted (and edited slightly) from *Project Girl* by Janet McDonald, pp. 53–55. New York: Farrar, Strauss, & Giroux, 1999.

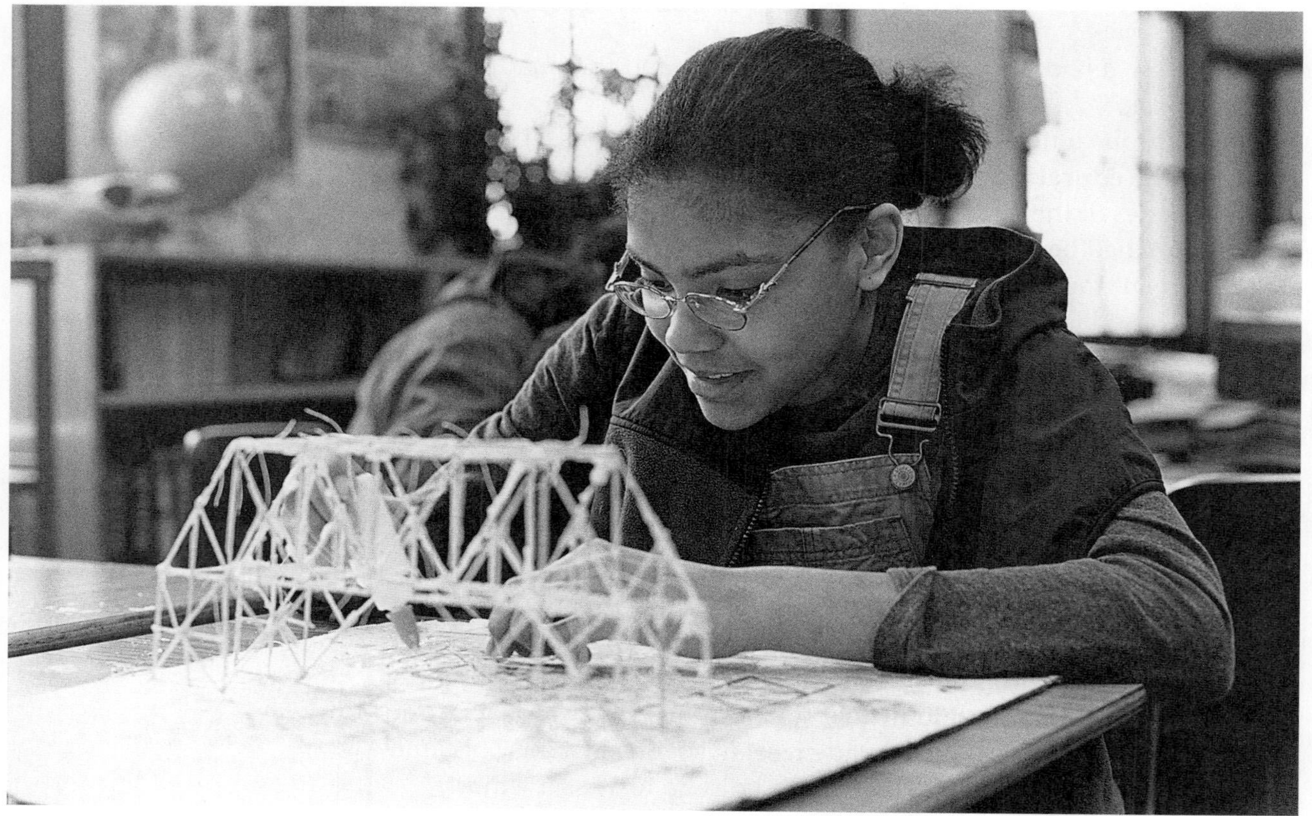

Adolescent girls need to know that their academic gifts are valued. (© Susie Fitzhugh)

> The biggest problem I encountered was my friends. They never let me forget I was applying to "Nerd Camp," "Geek City," and "Dweebville." "It's summer; school's out," they'd say. "Why do you want to go back?" That was a question I couldn't easily answer. Even I didn't know. (Delisle, 1992)

Ethical and spiritual issues may be especially important to gifted students during adolescence.

Ethical and spiritual issues may become important to gifted students at an earlier age than is typically expected. Clark and Hankins (1985) posed twenty-five philosophical questions to children ages 6 to 10 who were matched on all variables except intellectual ability. They found that in response to such questions as "What is the worst thing that could happen in the world?" and "Who is the best person in the world, living or dead?" the gifted children were found to be more knowledgeable about their world and more pessimistic about their future.

Career and lifestyle issues include a problem that many people see as a benefit: the ability to be successful in so many fields that selecting a career becomes problematic (Birely & Genshaft, 1991). The societal expectation that gifted students should become highly valued professionals (doctors, lawyers, professors) may intrude on an adolescent's personal choice if he or she wishes to enter a career such as artisan, laborer, or homemaker (Hollinger, 1991).

Through discussion with other adolescents with similar talents, or through academic and curricular programs that address intellectual and emotional growth, many of these issues can be addressed before they become problems (Silverman, 1990).

Gifted adolescents who may need special understanding and support are those who are gay, lesbian, or bisexual. Peterson and Rischar (2000) note that exceptional ability may contribute to a sense of "differentness" and may affect social relationships. When a gifted child is also gay, lesbian, or bisexual (GLB), that sense of differentness may intensify. A quest for perfection and a sexual identity that may not be approved of by the student's family and community can combine to form serious feelings of inadequacy in the adolescent who is gifted. Students who fall into these categories may be at particular risk of depression and thoughts of suicide. Peterson and Rischar write:

Students who are gifted can become depressed and suicidal if their emerging sexual identity does not conform with societal expectations.

> All educators, particularly those involved in education for the gifted, need to be courageous in their support for GLB students, ensuring that their classrooms are physically and psychologically safe and intervening on behalf of students who are "out" or are bullied or teased when their behaviors fit popular GLB stereotypes. Even quiet acknowledgement that gayness is worthy of discussion, that some respected individuals in textbooks are/were GLB, that concerns about sexual orientation are common during childhood and adolescence, and that GLB individuals are probably present in all schools and classrooms may help to lessen the distress of those who believe that no one has ever felt as they do. (2000, p. 231)

Effects on the Family

The effects of a student's giftedness or talents on the family have received considerable attention, and much research has been conducted to determine the effect of labeling a gifted child and on the transfer of values between parents and a gifted child.

Joyce van Tassel-Baska (1989) investigated the variables attributed to the success of gifted students from economically disadvantaged families and found that genuine support and encouragement of talents predicted high achievement—a reaffirmation of the important role of parents in the full development of their children.

There are, unfortunately, cases where a gifted student is exploited by the family or put on public display for all to see. There is also the possibility that a gifted child's talents may be ridiculed by parents, although the parents in Roald Dahl's *Matilda* are not representative. In those instances, the underlying problem may be related to dysfunctional family dynamics rather than the direct result of the child's giftedness.

Families from culturally and linguistically diverse backgrounds may have other beliefs about their child's abilities than those that are held by the dominant culture. Ford and Harris (1999) give us an example:

> For instance, the Navajo conception of giftedness includes talent for working in the crafts or performing in cultural rituals. Further, being gifted means doing things considered constructive, taking on leadership roles when necessary, and helping one's family. These values are not to be measured by traditional standardized tests of achievement and intelligence. (p. 4)

Conflicting beliefs about what constitutes giftedness and what constitutes acceptable behavior in the child may lead to confusion, stress, and conflict for the child, the parents, or within the home-school relationship (Silverstein, 2000). Including family members in the process of identifying and planning for the child's program is crucial to avoiding such conflicts and stresses.

Early Intervention

Children are often not formally identified as gifted or talented until sometime during their school career, usually in third or fourth grade. Because of particular advanced behaviors, though, many gifted young children show signs of high potential before they enter the classroom, and the people who identify these talents are often the child's parents.

Disagreement exists regarding the appropriateness of early identification of gifts and talents. On the one hand, some educators believe that it is imperative to identify and challenge talents at the youngest age possible. Eby and Smutny (1990) argue that such identification helps not only the child but also the child's caregivers; for if teachers, child-care workers, and parents are informed of a young child's strengths, they will be better able to provide academic and creative options that match those strengths. Joanne Whitmore (1980), in her classic study of underachieving gifted students, found that patterns of underachievement were developed during the primary school years, yet intervention seldom occurred until the intermediate grades. This unwillingness to address problems as they emerge means that much remediation will have to be done later, whereas preventive measures could have been less extreme yet equally effective.

Some professionals are concerned that early identification of gifts and talents creates the "superbaby syndrome."

On the other hand, critics of early identification of gifts and talents point to the "superbaby syndrome" as a problem that cannot be ignored. Parents who replace their gifted children's toys and free play with flash cards and classical concerts are, to the critics, misguided in their attempts to challenge their children. Eby and Smutny (1990), in critiquing these efforts, state that such "programs impose adult agendas on their young participants and forget that children learn best through experience" (p. 158).

The label of "gifted" tells us little about a child's specific unique talents. As parents and teachers work together to match a child's needs with appropriate services, they must keep in mind that the child's individual physical, emotional, and intellectual needs must be considered in order to provide a healthy balance of rigor and fun.

Identification and Assessment: The Teacher's Role

It was once considered easy to identify gifted students. An individual intelligence test on which a student scored 130 or higher qualified him or her as intellectually gifted. A student who scored 126 was summarily excluded.

Today there is a greater likelihood that multiple measures will be used to identify giftedness.

Today, as the validity of standardized intelligence test scores has become more suspect, especially for students from minority cultures (Baldwin, 1991), and as educators and parents have become more involved in the assessment of exceptional children, best practices call for multiple measures to be used to identify giftedness in students (Delisle, 2000). Most often, classroom teachers will be asked to supplement information about a child through the use of behavioral checklists. These checklists come in many varieties, but they generally require the teacher to rate a child on a scale of 1 to 4 (1 = seldom; 4 = always) on how often he or she observes behaviors like these:

- Learns rapidly, easily, efficiently
- Prefers to work alone
- Has a vocabulary above that of classmates
- Displays curiosity and imagination
- Goes beyond the minimum required with assignments
- Follows through on tasks
- Is original in oral and written expression

Essentially, teachers are being asked to select children who "go to school well" and whom teachers love to have in their classes. Yet if teachers are asked to consider only positive student traits and behaviors, they may not identify some gifted children who could surely benefit from advanced instruction. (See Table 13.1.)

Consider your own education. Were you ever in a class where you felt that your time was being wasted or your talents ignored? Perhaps it was a class that was repetitive to you, or one that provided few challenges or little outlet for creative expression. Whatever the reason for your dissatisfaction, do you recall how you acted in that class? It's unlikely that you led an animated discussion or that you were overly eager to answer the teacher's easy questions. In fact, if someone were to observe you in that class, he or she might find that you appeared bored, off-task, or looking for excitement in all the wrong places (like talking to your friends or passing notes). These would hardly seem to be behavioral indicators of giftedness but, in fact, they might be exactly that.

Some indicators of giftedness are behaviors that teachers find irritating.

The point is this: When you, as a teacher, are asked to select children for gifted program services, remember that some indicators of giftedness in children are those very behaviors that teachers usually find distasteful—boredom, misbehavior, even incomplete assignments on easy tasks or worksheets. This is not to say that all gifted children display negative behaviors in class, but it is a reminder to you that some gifts are wrapped in packages (that is, "behaviors") that are not so pretty. Be aware of this possibility when you question why a seemingly bright child is responding negatively to a class assignment or lecture.

The identification of gifted children is a complex, ongoing process (Davis & Rimm, 1989), and it sometimes appears that the main goal is not to locate talents in children but to find ways to exclude them from gifted program services. However, with the insights that can be provided by using a variety of standardized test scores (achievement and intelligence tests), parent, teacher, and peer nominations, and students' prior projects or portfolios as evidence of talent, we will do a better job of locating the variety of abilities that students display both inside and outside of school.

Curriculum Modifications in the General Education Classroom

Many gifted educators believe that the curriculum should be differentiated for the gifted student.

Much of what is written about curriculum and instruction for highly able students is based on the belief that programming should be differentiated for gifted learners. Jim Delisle describes **differentiation** as a "commitment to matching an individual student with educational options that make sense for her throughout the elementary and secondary years" (2001, p. 37). Differentia-

Table 13.1 Gifted Education Programming Criterion: Student Identification

Description: Gifted learners must be assessed to determine appropriate educational services.

Guiding Principles	Minimum Standards	Exemplary Standards
1. A comprehensive and cohesive process for student nomination must be coordinated in order to determine eligibility for gifted education services.	1.0 Information regarding the characteristics of gifted students in areas served by the district must be annually disseminated to all appropriate staff members. 1.1 All students must comprise the initial screening pool of potential recipients of gifted education services. 1.2 Nominations for services must be accepted from any source (e.g., teachers, parents, community members, peers, etc.). 1.3 Parents must be provided information regarding an understanding of giftedness and student characteristics.	1.0 The school district should provide information annually, in a variety of languages, regarding the process for nominating students for gifted education programming services. 1.1 The nomination process should be ongoing and screening of any student should occur at anytime. 1.2 Nomination procedures and forms should be available in a variety of languages. 1.3 Parents should be provided with special workshops or seminars to get a full meaning of giftedness.
2. Instruments used for student assessment to determine eligibility for gifted education services must measure diverse abilities, talents, strengths, and needs in order to provide students an opportunity to demonstrate any strengths.	2.0 Assessment instruments must measure the capabilities of students with provisions for the language in which the student is most fluent, when available. 2.1 Assessments must be culturally fair. 2.2 The purpose(s) of student assessments must be consistently articulated across all grade levels. 2.3 Student assessments must be sensitive to the current stage of talent development.	2.0 Assessments should be provided in a language in which the student is most fluent, if available. 2.1 Assessment should be responsive to students' economic conditions, gender, developmental differences, handicapping conditions, and other factors that mitigate against fair assessment practices. 2.2 Students identified in all designated areas of giftedness within a school district should be assessed consistently across grade levels. 2.3 Student assessments should be sensitive to all stages of talent development.
3. A student assessment profile of individual strengths and needs must be developed to plan appropriate intervention.	3.0 An assessment profile must be developed for each child to evaluate eligibility for gifted education programming services. 3.1 An assessment profile must reflect the unique learning characteristics and potential and performance levels.	3.0 Individual assessment plans should be developed for all gifted learners who need gifted education. 3.1 An assessment profile should reflect the gifted learner's interests, learning style, and educational needs.

(continued)

Table 13.1 Gifted Education Programming Criterion: Student Identification (cont.)

Guiding Principles	Minimum Standards	Exemplary Standards
4. All student identification procedures and instruments must be based on current theory and research.	4.0 No single assessment instrument or its results must deny student eligibility for gifted programming services.	4.0 Student assessment data should come from multiple sources and include multiple assessment methods.
	4.1 All assessment instruments must provide evidence of reliability and validity for the intended purposes and target students.	4.1 Student assessment data should represent an appropriate balance of reliable and valid quantitative and qualitative measures.
5. Written procedures for student identification must include at the very least provisions for informed consent, student retention, student reassessment, student exiting, and appeals procedures.	5.0 District gifted programming guidelines must contain specific procedures for student assessment at least once during the elementary, middle, and secondary levels.	5.0 Student placement data should be collected using an appropriate balance of quantitative and qualitative measures with adequate evidence of reliability and validity for the purposes of identification.
	5.1 District guidelines must provide specific procedures for student retention and exiting, as well as guidelines for parent appeals.	5.1 District guidelines and procedures should be reviewed and revised when necessary.

Source: http://www.nagc.org/table7.htm.

tion can involve modifications in *conent,* by putting more depth in the curriculum; *process,* by using a variety of methods and materials; *products, classroom environment,* and *teacher behavior* (Renzulli, 1997, in Dinnocenti, 1998). For teachers to individualize their teaching for gifted students, they must have models of differentiation, such as those prepared by van Tassel-Baska (1997) in science or Gallagher and Stempiak (1998) in social studies. A commitment to differentiating learning for students who are gifted and talented takes time, energy, and some inspiration, especially for those middle- and high school teachers who see large numbers of students at all ability levels throughout the day.

Differentiated instruction can involve modifications in content, process, products, classroom environment, and teacher behavior.

Every classroom teacher has (or can develop) the skills to work with gifted students within a regular classroom structure. By adapting, modifying, and differentiating the basic curriculum through techniques such as curriculum telescoping and content acceleration, teachers can determine when students have mastered particular skills, allowing them to move on to explore new ideas. Effective use of options such as independent study, cluster grouping, and cooperative learning can help satisfy students' individual learning interests. Finally, the appropriate use of higher-level thinking strategies and creative thinking skills can benefit *all* students, including those who are highly able. We'll discuss each of these methods of modifying the regular classroom in further detail.

■ ***Curriculum Telescoping*** **Curriculum telescoping,** or compacting, involves an analysis of the specific subject matter (for example, spelling, math, language arts) to determine which parts of those subjects are inappropriate for gifted students because they have already mastered them. Return for a minute to your fourth-grade class. It's math time, and let's assume you are a strong

Curriculum telescoping allows students to explore new concepts or subjects.

math student. As the teacher hands out worksheets, you have a sinking sense of *dèja vu*, for you are confronted with fifty problems like these: 26 × 247; 69 × 189; 24 × 790; 126 ÷ 4; 4216 ÷ 57. You think to yourself, "Didn't I see these yesterday? And the day before, too?" A conscientious math teacher would know that not all students in the class need extensive instruction in the basic math operations involved in these problems. In fact, a teacher who knew something about curriculum telescoping would probably not even require good math students like you to complete basic skill worksheets once you had mastered the concepts involved. What would be the point? If you already know how to multiply and divide large numbers, what possible benefit could there be to your completing more of these problems? There are dozens of more difficult concepts in math that you could probably work on instead of these basic skills.

That is the core of curriculum telescoping: determining what individual students already know and giving them the chance to explore concepts, subjects, or topics that better tap into their talents (Renzulli & Reis, 1985, 1991). Several authors have addressed the logistical problems of curriculum telescoping. Starko (1986) recommends several management techniques, including **group telescoping,** in which the teacher uses preexisting "top groups" in reading or math as the core group to telescope a particular concept or content area (see the accompanying box, "Steps in Curriculum Telescoping"). Figure 13.3 shows documentation for curriculum telescoping, or "compacting."

■ ***Content Area Acceleration*** Content area acceleration is another modification available to regular classroom teachers. Most often, educators equate *acceleration* with grade skipping, a practice that is not endorsed as enthusiastically today as in past generations (Pendarvis, Howley, & Howley, 1990). However, **content area acceleration** can occur within regular classes at virtually every grade level and within virtually every subject area. It happens every time a teacher allows students to "jump ahead" at a faster pace than most of their classmates. Thus, the first-grade teacher who provides literature to a child who has outgrown a basal reader is accelerating curriculum content for that child; so is the high school science teacher who works with a tenth-grader on physics experiments, even though physics is generally taken by twelfth-graders.

With content acceleration, students proceed at a faster pace than most of their classmates.

When you accelerate a student's curriculum in a basic skill area, there is always the possibility that other teachers (especially those in subsequent grades) will disapprove of this strategy. Some may prefer that students pursue areas of study that do not infringe on the content they will teach. Others may believe that content acceleration complicates their role as teachers since not all students are taught the same thing at the same time.

The most important consideration, however, remains the student's learning needs, even if fulfilling those needs complicates scheduling or planning. If

~ Steps in Curriculum Telescoping

1. Provide evidence of students' mastery (left column of Figure 13.3).
2. Describe how students may have their basic curriculum modified (center column of Figure 13.3).
3. List options for enrichment activities that take advantage of students' talents (right column of Figure 13.3).

Source: A. J. Starko, "Meeting the Needs of the Gifted Throughout the School Day: Techniques for Curriculum Compacting," *Roeper Review* 9:11 (1986), 27–33.

IEP COMPACTOR

Name Wendy, Mike, Carol, Paul, Chris, Kurt **Age** ______ **Teacher(s)** ______

School Smith **Grade** ______ **Parent(s)** ______

Individual conference dates and persons participating in planning of IEP ______

CURRICULUM AREAS TO BE CONSIDERED FOR COMPACTING: Describe basic material to be covered during this marking period and the assessment information or evidence that suggests the need for compacting.	PROCEDURES FOR COMPACTING BASIC MATERIAL: Describe activities that will be used to guarantee proficiency in basic curricular areas.	ACCELERATION AND/OR ENRICHMENT ACTIVITIES: Describe activities that will be used to provide advanced levels of learning experiences in each area of the regular curriculum.
Math: Houghton Mifflin Mathematics Level 6	Pre- and posttests will be used to check skill proficiency.	Selected enrichment masters
This group scored above 90% ile on CTBS math.	No assignment of math text examples or basic masters for skills already mastered.	Pre-algebra with Pizzaz and After-Math materials
	Students will be individually assigned student text pages and skill sheets as indicated by pretests.	Logic puzzles: mind benders, logic box
		Individual or small-group advanced-level independent study.

Figure 13.3
Individual Educational Programming Guide: The Compactor

Source: Alane J. Starko, "Meeting the Needs of the Gifted Throughout the School Day: Techniques for Curriculum Compacting," *Roeper Review 9:* 1 (1986): 27–33. Copyright © 1986. Reprinted by permission of *Roeper Review,* P.O. Box 329, Bloomfield, MI 48303, and the author.

teachers lose sight of this basic principle, students may be deprived of instruction or content that matches their level of ability. In extreme cases, students may adopt a negative attitude toward school.

Content area acceleration can be a nonobtrusive way to modify the curriculum for gifted students, but like any other activity, it will take practice for you to perfect. See the accompanying box, "Guidelines for Modifying Curriculum," for some tips.

■ ***Independent Study and Self-Directed Learning*** Independent study is one of the more popular forms of classroom modification for gifted students. **Independent study** provides "a chance for students to inquire about topics of interest to them in a manner that allows extensive exploration" (Parke,

In independent study, students pursue topics on their own, under teacher supervision.

~ Guidelines for Modifying Curriculum

1. Assess the student's skill level accurately, making sure he or she understands each of the concepts involved in any material that might be replaced or skipped over.
2. Talk with the student's teachers from the previous year and the teacher(s) who may be receiving this student the following year. Team planning can avoid many problems of miscommunication.
3. Remember that an option other than accelerating content is enriching it. So, if a student skilled in reading and language arts wants something more complex to do, consider activities such as play writing, cartooning, interviewing, or designing posters for a schoolwide project. These projects increase the student's breadth and depth of understanding of a subject.
4. Speak with your school district's director of curriculum or assistant superintendent about materials, resources, and options about which you might be unaware.

1989, pp. 99–100). Teachers have come to realize, however, that even highly able students need differentiated levels of support for directing their own learning.

Webbing focuses a child's specific interests within a broad topic by subdividing it into many smaller topics.

Kaplan et al. (1980) suggest using a process called webbing to help focus a child's specific interests within a broad topic, and Delisle (2000) notes that the independent study topic should be student-initiated, rather than dictated by the teacher. **Webbing** is a graphic representation of ideas and the relationships among them. In Figure 13.4, the topic of magnets is subdivided into many smaller, manageable subtopics. Students should not be required to complete all of these subtopics, but rather only those aspects of magnets that interest them. A secondary benefit to webbing is that it allows students to see how various content areas relate. For example, students may explore geography ("magnetic poles of the Earth"), English ("famous attractions and repulsions in literature"), and social studies ("history of man's use of magnets"), in addition to the expected scientific aspects of magnets.

Once webbing has been done, students can decide what resources they will need to research their topic and how they will display the knowledge they have gained. By following these steps and by putting a specific timeline on the student's efforts, you can use an independent study project to fill the time you have "bought" by telescoping the regular curriculum.

Like any strategy, independent study can be done improperly. Perhaps the most common mistake teachers make is to assume that since they're so smart, gifted students can succeed without any help. Teachers should introduce research skills such as library and computer information searching, hypothesis generation, and basic statistical analysis, which will give students tools for higher-level independent study. Unless a student selects a topic that is specific enough to be manageable, even a gifted student may wallow in a sea of confusion. As a teacher, you will need to provide appropriate direction through a technique such as webbing, as well as support for the independent work.

Cluster grouping allows gifted learners to be grouped for some activities and not others.

■ ***Cluster Grouping*** In **cluster grouping,** students who are identified as gifted at a given grade level are grouped together in the same classroom with a teacher who has training in educating students who are gifted. The rest of the class is a diverse group of learners. The cluster arrangement allows the gifted

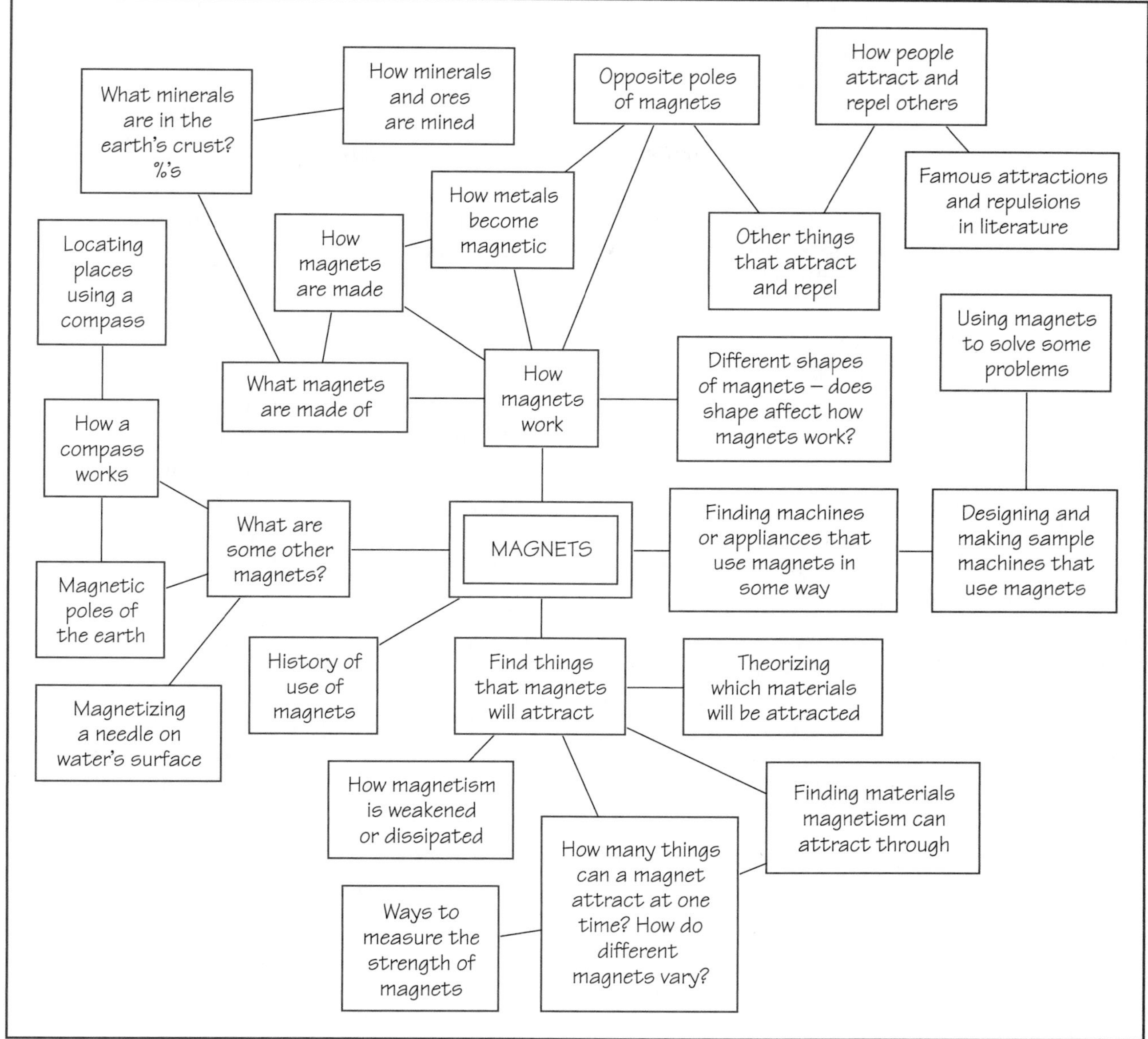

Figure 13.4
A Learning Web

Source: Sandra Kaplan, JoAnn Kaplan, Sheila Madsen, and Bette Gould, *Change for Children: Ideas and Activities for Individualizing Learning* (Santa Monica, CA: Goodyear, 1980), p. 179. Copyright © 1980 by Scott, Foresman and Company. Reprinted by permission.

learners to be grouped together for some activities and to be mixed with their age peers for others. Cluster grouping appears to be an increasingly popular option (Schuler, 1997).

■ ***Cooperative Learning*** **Cooperative learning** operates under the assumption that "all students are learners and teachers; all have an equal responsibility to explain to others and discuss with others. The pace of instruction is similar to what it would be in a traditional class, so high achievers are exposed to the same material they would have otherwise been taught" (Slavin, 1990, pp. 6–7). Thus, under cooperative learning strategies, students are grouped heterogeneously in clusters of five or six, and they learn a body of material by capitalizing on the strengths each member brings to the "team." Often, the same grades are awarded to all group members, which is meant to engender a team spirit in which everyone pulls his or her own weight.

Johnson and Johnson (1989) report that "performance on daily assignments and . . . retention tests [shows that] high achievers working in heterogeneous cooperative groups have never done worse than their counterparts working competitively and individualistically" (p. 318). However, critics of cooperative learning contend that "not doing worse than their counterparts" is not a reason to adopt cooperative learning for gifted students. One opponent enumerates the objections:

> The disadvantages of cooperative learning for academically talented students are primarily those of limiting instruction to grade level materials, presented at the pace of a grade level group and evaluated primarily on basic skill measures. The corollary is that opportunities which can meet intellectual needs may be made unavailable to talented students because cooperative learning is assumed to be a substitute. (Robinson, 1990, p. 22)

Teachers should be cautious in using cooperative learning with highly able students.

Since there is no clear-cut agreement as to whether cooperative learning should be used with gifted students, and if so, how frequently, the new teacher should approach this technique cautiously.

■ ***Creative and Higher-Level Thinking*** Creative and higher-level thinking processes are another area in which the curriculum can be modified. Consider the following two questions, either of which could appear on an elementary-level geography test:

1. What is the capital of Massachusetts?
2. Considering the geography of the state of Massachusetts, why might Boston have been chosen to be the state's capital?

Higher-level thinking skills should be incorporated into the curriculum for gifted students.

The first question requires little thought, merely a good memory. Students need to know nothing about Boston other than that it is the state capital. The second question, though, requires analytical thought and some comprehension of the role that geography, location, and politics may have played in choosing the site for a state's capital.

Gifted students often think naturally—with little direction from parents or teachers—about these "bigger questions," the ones that require the use of more complex levels of thinking. When they are in a classroom setting where the majority of time is spent on activities or questions that have one right answer requiring only rote memorization to deliver, they often feel stifled intellectually. To compound this problem, classroom materials and texts usually emphasize the acquisition of low-level thinking skills (like memorization) rather than the more sophisticated thinking patterns required to answer questions like the second one (Raths, Wassermann, Jones, & Rothstein, 1986).

There are, however, methods and systems for incorporating higher-level thinking skills into your curriculum. Benjamin Bloom (1956) developed a taxonomy of educational objectives to distinguish among the various ways that questions and teaching strategies can be designed to promote varied levels of thinking (see Table 13.2). Another scholar proposed that teachers should train their students to use three distinct types of critical thinking strategies, which are outlined in the accompanying box, "Critical Thinking Strategies" (Ennis, 1985).

Effects on the Developing Person

Some problems, however, do not require analytical thinking as much as they require creative thinking. That is, rather than trying to find a *solution* to a problem, it is more important to first determine what the problem itself really is. **Brainstorming** (Osborn, 1963) is a basic creative problem-solving technique. In brainstorming, there are no right or wrong answers, students cannot criticize each others' responses, and "piggybacking" an idea on someone else's is encouraged. Group brainstorming can be the beginning step to positive problem solving.

In brainstorming, participants come up with many ideas on a specific subject.

■ ***Problem-Based Learning*** **Problem-based learning** describes a method used in medical schools to focus on an "ill-structured problem" as a way for students to begin to ask questions and begin to hypothesize about how to clarify and solve the problem (Delisle, 2000). See the accompanying box for examples of problem-based learning at work.

The National Association for Gifted Children has developed program standards for gifted education. Table 13.3 describes the programming criteria for curriculum and instruction.

Placement Alternatives

The majority of students who are gifted and talented are served in the general education classroom—both those who have been identified and those who have not. Even though elementary and secondary classroom teachers can provide rich intellectual stimulation for gifted students, many school districts offer other options that take place outside of a regular classroom setting. Probably the most common service delivery model is **enrichment.** According to Barbara Clark (1997), "Enrichment can refer to adding disciplines or areas of learning not normally found in the regular curriculum, using more difficult or in-depth material to enhance the core curriculum, or enhancing the teaching strategies used to present instruction" (p. 204). Typically, students identified as gifted participate

Enrichment activities supplement the core curriculum for students identified as gifted.

~ Critical Thinking Strategies

- Defining and clarifying problems, including the ability to identify a problem's central issue, identify assumptions underlying a problem, and identify appropriate questions to ask to better understand a situation.
- Judging information, including the ability to determine the relevance of information and the credibility of sources and observations.
- Inferring solutions, including the ability to make deductive and inductive conclusions and to predict probable consequences of particular actions.

Classroom strategies based on Ennis's theory will prompt independent and logical thinking in children, especially in problem-solving situations encountered in math, science, social studies, and interpersonal relationships.

Source: R. H. Ennis, "A Logical Basis for Measuring Thinking Skills," *Educational Leadership 43*:2 (1985), 44–48.

Table 13.2 Bloom's Taxonomy: Cognitive Domain

Area of Taxonomy	Definition	What Teacher Does	What Student Does	Process Verbs	
Knowledge	Recall or recognition of specific information	Directs, tells, shows, examines	Responds, absorbs, remembers, recognizes	define repeat list name label	memorize record recall relate
Comprehension	Understanding of information given	Demonstrates, listens, questions, compares, contrasts, examines	Explains, translates, demonstrates, interprets	restate describe explain identify report tell	discuss recognize express locate review
Application	Using methods, concepts, principles, and theories in new situations	Shows, facilitates, observes, criticizes	Solves problems, demonstrates use of knowledge, constructs	translate apply employ use practice shop	interpret demonstrate dramatize illustrate operate schedule
Analysis	Breaking information down into its constituent elements	Probes, guides, observes, acts as a resource	Discusses, uncovers, lists, dissects	distinguish calculate test contract criticize debate question solve analyze	appraise differentiate experience compare diagram inspect inventory relate examine
Synthesis	Putting together constituent elements or parts to form a whole requiring original, creative thinking	Reflects, extends, analyzes, evaluates	Discusses, generalizes, relates, compares, contrasts, abstracts	compose propose formulate assemble construct set up manage	plan design arrange collect create organize prepare
Evaluation	Judging the values of ideas, materials, and methods by developing and applying standards and criteria	Clarifies, accepts, harmonizes, guides	Judges, disputes, develops criteria	judge evaluate compare score choose estimate predict	appraise rate value select assess measure

Source: Bloom, Englehart, Furst, Hill, and Krathwohl (1956).

in pullout or afterschool enrichment activities. Clark believes that enrichment is the least desirable option for the gifted student, since it involves the least change in learning opportunities.

Some school districts have special schools or self-contained classes for students who are gifted and talented. In other locales, a resource room model is

Table 13.3 Gifted Education Programming Criterion: Curriculum and Instruction

Description: Gifted education services must include curricular and instructional opportunities directed to the unique needs of the gifted child.

Guiding Principles	Minimum Standards	Exemplary Standards
1. Differentiated curriculum for the gifted learner must span grades pre-K–12.	1.0 Differentiated curriculum (curricular and instructional adaptations that address the unique learning needs of gifted learners) for gifted learners must be integrated and articulated throughout the district.	1.0 A well-defined and implemented curriculum scope and sequence should be articulated for all grade levels and all subject areas.
2. Regular classroom curricula and instruction must be adapted, modified, or replaced to meet the unique needs of gifted learners.	2.0 Instruction, objectives, and strategies provided to gifted learners must be systematically differentiated from those in the regular classroom.	2.0 District curriculum plans should include objectives, content, and resources that challenge gifted learners in the regular classroom.
	2.1 Teachers must differentiate, replace, supplement, or modify curricula to facilitate higher level learning goals.	2.1 Teachers should be responsible for developing plans to differentiate the curriculum in every discipline for gifted learners.
	2.2 Means for demonstrating proficiency in essential regular curriculum concepts and processes must be established to facilitate appropriate academic acceleration.	2.2 Documentation of instruction for assessing level(s) of learning and accelerated rates of learning should demonstrate plans for gifted learners based on specific needs of individual learners.
	2.3 Gifted learners must be assessed for proficiency in basic skills and knowledge and provided with alternative challenging educational opportunities when proficiency is demonstrated	2.3 Gifted learners should be assessed for proficiency in all standard courses of study and subsequently provided with more challenging educational opportunities.
3. Instructional pace must be flexible to allow for the accelerated learning of gifted learners as appropriate.	3.0 A program of instruction must consist of advanced content and appropriately differentiated teaching strategies to reflect the accelerative learning pace and advanced intellectual processes of gifted learners.	3.0 When warranted, continual opportunities for curricular acceleration should be provided in gifted learners' areas of strength and interest while allowing sufficient ceiling for optimal learning.
4. Educational opportunities for subject and grade skipping must be provided to gifted learners.	4.0 Decisions to proceed or limit the acceleration of content and grade acceleration must only be considered after a thorough assessment.	4.0 Possibilities for partial or full acceleration of content and grade levels should be available to any student presenting such needs.
5. Learning opportunities for gifted learners must consist of continuum of differentiated curricular options, instructional approaches, and resource materials.	5.0 Diverse and appropriate learning experiences must consist of a variety of curricular options, instructional strategies, and materials.	5.0 Appropriate service options for each student to work at assessed level(s) and advanced rates of learning should be available.
	5.1 Flexible instructional arrangements (e.g., special classes, seminars, resource rooms, mentorships, independent study, and research projects) must be available.	5.1 Differentiated educational program curricula for students pre-K–12 should be modified to provide learning experiences matched to students' interest[illegible] readiness, and learning sty[illegible]

Source: http://www.nagc.org/table1.html. ©1998 National Association for Gifted Children

~ Problem-Based Learning (PBL)

What is Problem-Based Learning?

Problem-based learning instruction is built upon "ill-structured and complex problems" just like those encountered in real life. The problems require that students "search beyond the readily available information to solve the problem" that is posed to them (Torp & Sage, 1998). Students become inquirers and active learners, collaborating, creating, and using knowledge to construct solutions. Teachers facilitate, model, and coach students as they work together in small groups.

Why is this Model Used?

Students learn best when they must "do" and when they are asked to think in authentic ways rather than abstractly. Use this model when you want students to apply, analyze, synthesize, and extend knowledge, and when you want students to apply research skills.

What are "Ill-Structured and Complex Problems" for PBL and What are Some Examples?

Delisle (2000) explains:

> Unlike a thinking exercise that includes all necessary information or a traditional project that requires students to use information they already know, PBL problems should be designed so that students must perform research to gather the information needed for possible solutions. It should require students to think through information they already know and find additional information, interpreting preexisting knowledge in light of new data they discover. In addition, the problem should lead students to discover that there may be a number of solutions.

Here are three examples of problems used from elementary through high school:

- Some students and our cafeteria staff have been complaining that the cafeteria is becoming so loud that it is hard to hear. We have been asked by our School Council to investigate this challenge and make a recommendation back to them by next week. You will need to create a presentation to the Council that includes the facts and conclusions we have reached.
- You are part of the Natural Science Museum Display team. You design all the display areas in the museum so that the people who come to the museum can easily see and learn from the museum display. This week, the museum was given $50,000 to create an area of the museum

preferred. Just as there are a variety of ways to serve students with gifts and talents within a classroom setting, there are multiple options for meeting the needs of these students in other settings. Some of the more popular out-of-class methods are reviewed here.

■ ***Resource Rooms*** The most popular option at the elementary school level may be the resource room approach. Similar in design and structure to such programs for children with disabilities, the gifted education resource room allows gifted students to work together. Often, cross-age grouping is used, and it is not unusual to see third-grade students working alongside fifth-grade students. However, some consequences of resource rooms are undesirable, as this 10-year old girl expresses:

> Last year I wasn't at school one day a week (my gifted program was in another school), so I didn't finish all my classwork. I would have finished, but my teacher wouldn't let me bring anything home as homework. When my

for four wolves who cannot be released into the wild because they have lived all their lives in a zoo. The museum staff wants an area that is as close as possible to the natural habitat of the wolf, and with a safe (for both wolves and public) viewing area. The museum curator wants your team plans within two weeks so that plans for construction can be made. The curator would like you to present the background information your teams used to develop its plans, as well as sketches or a model of what your team suggests.

- You are a new staff member of your local newspaper. Your Series Editor (your teacher) has called together a team of writers and researchers for an important series of stories that are developing. You are a member of that team. The task is described in a memo from the Managing Editor: Recently our newspaper has received many calls from extremists related to an article we ran about events in the Middle East and Israel. These calls and letters include derogatory references to various minority groups and religions, and deny that the Nazi Holocaust—the extermination of Jews, Catholics, Gypsies, and other minorities—had occurred. . . Due to these events, we have decided to produce a special series of stories on The Holocaust, with reference to the "denialists" and their arguments that the Holocaust did not occur. The series will include photos, interviews, and extensive documentation. The series will address major issues in this controversy, and provide an objective analysis—not only of the history of the Holocaust, but with references to how it relates to our current situation. Your task is to produce a newspaper layout and report to address this need.

Source: National Center for the Accelerated Schools Project, University of Connecticut Neag School of Education, 2131 Hillside Road, Unit 3224, Storrs, CT 06269-3224.

> mother asked her about my grade, the teacher said that "if I was smart enough to go to another school I should be smart enough to keep up with my own classwork." (Delisle, 1984, p. 75)

The resource room is a part-time solution to the full-time challenge of educating gifted students.

"Makeup work"—needing to complete worksheets and text assignments in addition to the work in the gifted program—can cause students to question the benefits of their resource room participation. The conscientious classroom teacher, by using pretesting and curriculum telescoping, can relieve many of these problems.

Another problem occurs when the classroom teacher relinquishes responsibility for educating gifted students by assuming that "they're getting all they need in the resource room." Teachers must remember that the resource room presents only a part-time solution to the full-time problem of educating gifted students (Cox, Daniel, & Boston, 1985). The resource room works best when its teachers communicate frequently with regular classroom teachers and both work together to benefit gifted students.

Children Who Are Gifted and Talented

The self-contained gifted education classroom denies program services to students who may have talents only in one area.

■ ***Self-Contained and Homogeneously Grouped Classes*** Often the option of choice a generation ago, the self-contained gifted classroom is still used today, but less frequently. In this type of class, gifted students are identified and placed together for instruction. This placement limits participation to a select group of gifted children—enough to fill one classroom—while denying gifted program services to those students who may have talents only in particular areas. An additional concern is more sociological in nature, "based upon the apprehension that such a grouping of the bright children will cause the nongifted to regard the gifted negatively, resentfully or hypercritically, and that the gifted, by virtue of being in separate groups, will come to look disdainfully or contemptuously upon the nongifted" (Newland, 1976, p. 271). Whether real or imagined, this fear goes back to our ambivalence about labeling children, especially when one group of students is selected because they have "more" of something than their classmates.

Homogeneously grouped classes are similar to those that are self-contained, with this one exception: Students are grouped according to content area or specialty, based on similar levels of aptitude or achievement. Thus, a student may be in a homogeneously grouped accelerated math class one hour and in a reading class for children of average reading ability the next. Most often used in middle and high schools, academic ability grouping, or tracking, has been criticized for its negative impact on children not in the highest tracks (Oakes, 1985), since it is believed that these children begin to see themselves as less capable, less smart. Others believe that the practice of academic tracking is still open to debate (George, 1988; Slavin, 1988), and in fact, "at the middle [grades] level, [tracking] may be the single most important unresolved issue in education" (George, 1988, p. 22).

Tracking, or academic ability grouping, has been criticized for its negative impact on children not in the highest tracks.

■ ***Magnet Schools and State-Sponsored Residential Schools*** Magnet schools are designed to place special emphasis on science, the arts, or some other content area and to attract students with interests or talents in that area. These students work with teachers who are specialists in the particular content area.

Often used in large school districts or urban settings, magnet schools can exist at both the elementary and secondary levels. In recent years, they have been heavily subsidized by federal government funds targeted toward racial desegregation. It was believed that if all students had the chance to attend the school of their choice because of the specialized focus of that school's curriculum, then each school would attract a mixture of racial, ethnic, and economic groups. This goal, as well as the goal of meeting the specific intellectual needs of students with specialized talents, has met with varying degrees of success.

Magnet schools attract a racial, ethnic, and economic mixture while meeting the needs of students with specialized talents.

In a magnet school, students receive accelerated and enriched instruction in their areas of greatest strength and interest. For example, if students attend a science magnet, they may spend a lot of time in laboratories conducting experiments. In a creative arts magnet, a portion of each school day will emphasize art, dance, or other creative endeavors. In magnet schools, other basic content areas (reading, language arts, math) are taught, but it is not assumed that students are highly capable in all areas. Thus, a student attending the science magnet may be enrolled in a basic English class as well as an advanced chemistry or biology class.

State-sponsored residential schools, often called "governor's schools," because they are established by an individual state's legislature and governor, have continued to increase in popularity in recent years. Highly competitive, these schools seek nominations from across the state's high schools for unusually talented juniors and seniors who will spend up to two years at the residential setting. The first governor's schools focused almost exclusively on math and science, but now many states have incorporated the arts and humanities into their stringent curricula. Among the states with well-established governor's schools are North Carolina, Louisiana, Indiana, and Illinois. Criticized by some as "hothousing" gifted students by surrounding them only with classmates who are similarly gifted, these residential schools still continue to flourish—as do their students.

State-sponsored residential schools for the gifted and talented have increased in popularity.

■ ***Other Options*** Not all educational options for gifted students take place within the school building or, for that matter, within the school year. **Mentorships,** during which time secondary students work with a community member to learn, firsthand, a specific skill, trade, or craft, are common. Research on the effectiveness of mentorships shows the very positive results of these community-school interactions, since participating students learn from the mentor's skill and expertise, receive valued and substantive praise and encouragement, and have as a role model a person who loves his or her field of study as much as does the student (Torrance, 1984).

In mentorships, secondary students learn specific skills, trades, or crafts from community members.

Summer and weekend programs are also offered for gifted students at many colleges and universities. Purdue University's Super Saturday Program, for example, serves children from preschool through high school with a variety of accelerated and enrichment classes each semester (Feldhusen, 1991). The Purdue model has been replicated across the country.

Summer programs can be either day programs or residential in nature, depending on the student's age. In Ohio, each of the thirteen state universities and several private colleges offer one- to three-week "summer institutes" that are financially supported by the state. Michigan and Iowa also offer extensive summer programs for gifted students.

With summer and weekend programs gifted children remain with their peers; in other programs they progress rapidly through high school and college.

In addition, early entrance to college or dual enrollment programs allow gifted secondary school students to progress through high school and college at a more rapid pace. In high schools, students enrolled in advanced placement courses may earn up to a year's worth of transferable college credit by taking rigorous courses and advanced placement tests, generally in their junior and senior years. Also, many colleges have an "honors college" component, which offers rigorous, and often accelerated, courses to highly able students. Some colleges encourage full-time enrollment by students as young as 15. Simon's Rock of Bard College in Great Barrington, Massachusetts, has been doing this for over twenty-five years, and Mary Baldwin College in Staunton, Virginia, has a similar program, called PEG (Program for the Exceptionally Gifted), which is open only to young women; these students generally attain both a high school diploma and a college degree within five years.

Program Models

Acceleration and enrichment options for gifted students, as we have seen, have existed for generations. But only within the past fifteen years have organizational models been developed. These models structure the activities in which gifted children participate to provide a "skeleton" format for teachers and gifted program planners.

■ ***The Enrichment Triad Model (Grades 4–6)*** The **enrichment triad model** (ETM) (Renzulli, 1977) is based on the following premises:

- Some types of academic and creative enrichment are good for all children.
- Students must master certain "process skills" (such as research skills and creative problem-solving) if they are to master curriculum content.
- Students should investigate problems of their own interest, rather than topics chosen by teachers, and they should share the results of their work with audiences outside of their school.

The ETM model builds in the teaching strategies from gifted education for a wider group of students, and allows children to express their talents to others in visible ways.

■ ***Schoolwide Models*** With so many interesting and innovative teaching strategies and models designed for students identified as gifted and talented, why not use them to benefit all children? Two school reform efforts attempt to do just that. The **Accelerated Schools Project** (Levin, 1996) operates on the principle that every child is a gifted child (Hopfenberg, Levin, and Associates, 1993). According to Levin,

> all students are treated as gifted and talented students, because the gifts and talents of each child are sought out and recognized. Such strengths are used as a basis for providing enrichment and acceleration. As soon as one recognizes that all students have strengths and weaknesses, a simple stratification of students no longer makes sense. Strengths include not only the various areas of intelligence identified by Gardner (1983), but also areas of interest, curiosity, motivation, and knowledge that grow out of the culture, experiences, and personalities of all children. (1996, p. 17)

Accelerated schools operate with the philosophy that building on the strengths of each student is more successful than identifying and remediating weaknesses. (For more information, visit the Accelerated Schools website at http://www.acceleratedschools.net/.)

Enrichment models help teachers differentiate the curriculum.

Renzulli's **Schoolwide Enrichment Model** was originally developed for gifted education programs as the enrichment triad model (1977; see above). It is now being used on a schoolwide basis to improve the creative productivity and academic achievement of *all* students (Renzulli, 1996). The model serves as a framework for organizational and curricular changes and rests on specific curriculum modification techniques, enrichment learning and teaching, and the recognition and development of student talents. (For more information, visit the National Research Center for the Gifted and Talented website at http://www.ucc.uconn.edu/~wwwgt/nrcgt.html.)

Technology

It is difficult to overestimate the importance of technology as a tool for research and creative efforts for students who are gifted and talented. Access to various kinds of software and to the Internet is essential for students who can learn independently, and the computer skills of these students grow quickly—often they teach *us* in this arena. Vahidi (1998) notes that the Internet can be used for research, for expressing views, for teleconferencing and telementoring, and for plugging into advanced online curricula. Students may develop their future careers by pursuing a hobby or interest on the Internet.

Johnson (2000) describes how technology can support the needs of the gifted, using mathematics as an example:

> Technology can provide a tool, an inspiration, or an independent learning environment for any student, but for the gifted it is often a means to reach the appropriate depth and breadth of curriculum and advanced product opportunities. Calculators can be used as an exploration tool to solve complex and interesting problems. Computer programming is a higher-level skill that enhances problem-solving abilities and promotes careful reasoning and creativity. The use of a database, spreadsheet, graphic calculator, or scientific calculator can facilitate powerful data analysis. The World Wide Web is a vast and exciting source of problems, contests, enrichment, teacher resources, and information about mathematical ideas that are not addressed in textbooks. Technology is an area in which disadvantaged gifted students may be left out because of lack of access or confidence. It is essential that students who do not have access at home get the exposure at school so that they will not fall behind the experiences of other students.

In this age of technology, the proliferation of information, and access to information in our "global village," the sky's the limit for our very capable students.

Summary

- The concept of giftedness has changed greatly over time, as has our view of students who are gifted. Giftedness has been described in terms of creativity and task commitment, multiple intelligences, successful manipulation of the environment, and heightened sensitivity and understanding.
- Standardized test scores are one criterion for identifying giftedness, but they should be supplemented by other measures, as well as by informal observations by teachers and parents.
- Although biological factors may play a role in giftedness, educators focus on environmental factors, especially family support, guidance, and encouragement, that can contribute to the full expression of a student's gifts.
- The prevalence of giftedness varies because of differing definitions and criteria; for funding purposes many states use a figure of 5 percent. Gifted females, students who are gifted and disabled, gifted underachievers, culturally diverse students, and the highly gifted are often underrepresented.
- Teachers usually play a central role in identifying gifted students through multiple measures, including observations of behavior (which might include boredom with regular classwork) as well as test scores and grades.
- The curriculum can be modified through telescoping, content area acceleration, independent study, cluster grouping, and cooperative learning. Modifications should be based on the student's needs and interests. Gifted students

are usually served in the regular classroom and pulled out for resource-room time. If self-contained classes are used, the students may be grouped according to their level or type of ability. Magnet schools are another setting in which students can receive a special emphasis on a specific type of ability.

- Many models for organizing gifted education have been proposed. These models help teachers plan curriculum modifications and activities to fulfill the social and emotional needs of gifted students.

Key Terms

giftedness
talent
intelligence
creativity
task commitment
theory of multiple intelligences
triarchic theory
gifted underachiever
highly gifted
academic enrichment
radical acceleration
acceleration
differentiation
curriculum telescoping
group telescoping
content area acceleration
independent study
webbing
cluster grouping
cooperative learning
brainstorming
problem-based learning
enrichment
mentorships
enrichment triad model
Accelerated Schools Project
Schoolwide Enrichment Model

Multimedia Resources

Bireley, Marlene. *Crossover Children: A Sourcebook for Helping Children Who Are Gifted and Learning Disabled,* 2d ed. (Reston, VA: Council for Exceptional Children, 1995). This book provides specific strategies to help students who are gifted and learning disabled increase attention, enhance memory, and improve social skills, as well as recommendations for academic interventions and enrichment activities.

Delisle, James R. *Once Upon a Mind: The Stories and Scholars of Gifted Child Education.* (Fort Worth: Harcourt Brace College Publishers, 2000). Jim Delisle has written a textbook for readers interested in gifted child education that is unconventional, creative, informative, and entertaining.

The ERIC Clearinghouse on Disabilities and Gifted Education has assembled the Gifted Education Searchable Online Database of selected gifted and talented programs in the United States. Using the database, educators may gather information on a wide variety of service options that match the needs of their student populations. The database enables professionals working in both general education and gifted education to find current programs and take advantage of research findings and work that was accomplished by those programs. The database is available on the ERIC EC website GIFTED menu at http://ericec.org/gifted/gt-menu.htm.

National Association for Gifted Children (NAGC) 1701 L Street, NW, Suite 550, Washington, DC 20036 (202) 785-4268 Fax: (202) 785-4248.

Parenting for High Potential. A publication of the National Association for Gifted Children, 1707 L Street, NW, Suite 550, Washington, DC 20036. Telephone: (202) 785-4268. Website: http://www.nagc.org. This quarterly magazine is designed for parents who want to make a difference in their children's lives, who want to develop their children's gifts and talents, and who want to help them develop their potential to the fullest. Each issue includes special features, expert advice columns, software and book reviews, ideas from parents, and a pullout children's section.

Selected Internet Resources for Gifted Education, ERIC Clearinghouse on Disabilities and Gifted Education. Website: http://www.cec.sped.org/faq/gt-urls.htm. The ERIC Clearinghouse has created and updates a list of links to research centers and organizations centered on gifted children.

van Tassel-Baska, Joyce. *Planning Effective Curriculum for Gifted Learners* (Reston, VA: Council for Exceptional Children, 1992). This book provides specific ideas for designing and implementing a curriculum that works, including practical ideas and sample units for teaching gifted students.

Winebrenner, Susan. *Teaching Gifted Kids in the Regular Classroom* (Minneapolis: Free Spirit Publishing, 1992). An excellent source for teaching ideas.

What You Can Do

1. Commonalities: Explore the diversity of gifted students.

- Visit local schools and talk to teachers who work with students identified as gifted and talented.
- Talk with gifted students about their diverse backgrounds and their attitudes and aspirations.
- Select one or two books or articles about gifted students from the list in the Multimedia Resources section or the references used in this chapter. Compare the authors' perspectives with your own knowledge and experiences.

2. Investigate popular culture and media images.

- How do films and television shows portray gifted children? How have those images changed?
- Interview a gifted student, classmate, or other person and note how that person differs from media stereotypes. Why might these stereotypes exist?
- Rent the video of the film *Little Man Tate*. Do you consider that portrait of a gifted child and his mother realistic? Write a review of the movie based on your analysis.
- Identify a public figure whom you consider gifted or talented. Using the characteristics described in this chapter, explain how this person fits the criteria for giftedness.

3. Can Do: Survey attitudes in your class.

- Find out what stereotypes or preconceptions students hold about gifted children.
- Have students write about one area in which they feel they are gifted. Does this ability shape their view of themselves, or is it just one characteristic?
- Compile the responses about individual areas of giftedness into a poster to show the range of gifts in the class.

4. Can Do: Using the information on curriculum modifications provided in this chapter and the recommended readings, develop some activities that would allow gifted students to enrich their learning in the regular class.

5. Collaboration: Where are gifted students in your school district served? Arrange to visit a local public school and see what combination of regular class, resource room, and self-contained class instruction gifted students receive. If possible, observe students in each of these environments. How do the settings vary?

Looking at Special Education Programs

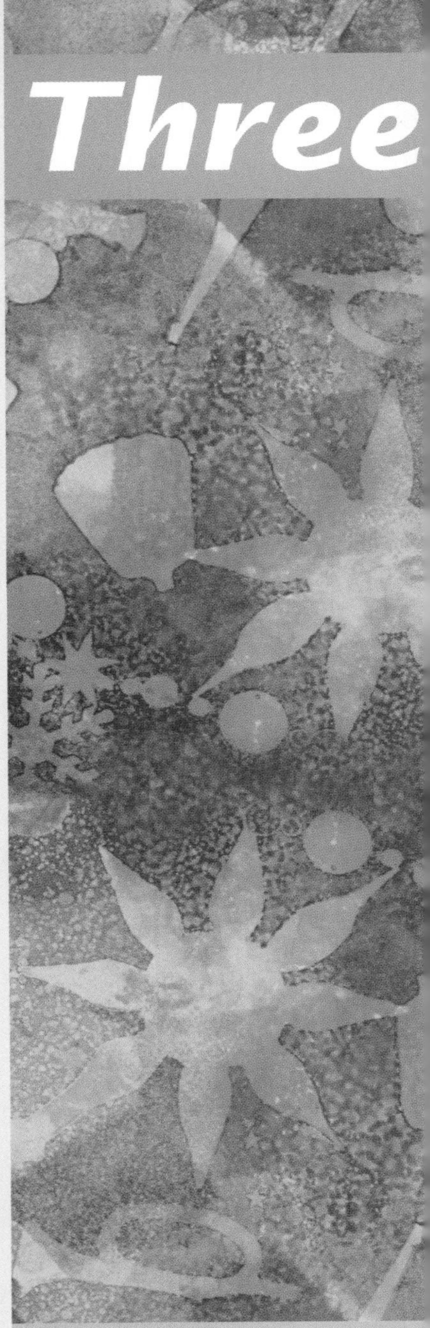

IN THIS final section, we will give you a brief glimpse of how special education should look in classrooms. We will examine some of the key decision-making factors that should be a part of every educator's plan for providing appropriate services to students with disabilities. Finally, we will show you how classrooms that serve students with disabilities might look.

Inside Special Education Classes

14

TODAY, VIRTUALLY all classrooms can be described as special education classes, because children with disabilities can be found in almost all of them. These classes may have a variety of purposes and reveal a wide range of teaching approaches and educational programs. In this chapter, we will reflect on the content of past chapters and illustrations of instructional options to provide insight into the many ways effective special education can be defined. As you read, answer the following questions:

Commonalities: What is the common thread in all special education services?

Collaboration: What specific collaborative models can general education and special education teachers use?

Can Do: What can a special education teacher do to facilitate effective inclusion of a student in a new general education class?

What is the probability that you will be teaching students with disabilities? How will you know if you are an effective teacher?

Inside Special Education Classes

As we begin our look inside special education classes, let's again ask ourselves the question we reviewed in Chapter 1: What is special education? Although it may seem unnecessary to revisit this question near the end of your course, it is only after you have learned about the many interventions, materials, and curricula used to teach students with disabilities that you can attempt to answer it. Answering this question may be further complicated by what you have learned about where special education services occur—in the home, at work, and in the community, as well as in classrooms. It is the great variety found in special education, however, that gives us our answer—special education is not a single method, a certain curriculum, or a specific place. To expand on our original definition: Special education is a planned and purposeful instructional program designed so that each individual with a disability can acquire necessary, appropriate, and meaningful skills. Each special education program can be and should be as unique as the individual for whom it is designed. Each program is guided by the individual needs and goals of each person (Zigmond & Baker, 1995).

If we examine our description of special education, we can see the common threads connecting all special education interventions. First, special education is planned in advance by professionals, family, and often the student with a disability, using tools such as the Individualized Family Service Plan, Individualized Education Program, Transition Plan, and Behavior Intervention Plan. Special education plans tell us exactly what will be done in the classroom or other environments and who is going to do it. Second, special education is purposeful. The purpose of the plan is to allow the student to reach his or her short-term instructional objectives and long-range life goals. Finally, individuals with disabilities will acquire the skills they need to achieve their goals. The importance and relevance of the skills to the individual must be evident.

Special education must address the individual needs of each student.

The bottom line in evaluating special education services is the extent to which they address the individual needs of each student. Although this factor is critical to the definition of special education, it is the factor most frequently lost in the face of realities such as overcrowded classes, limited curriculum options, and the limited time allotted for specialized instruction. Educators recognize that the goals and purposes of special education may sometimes be at odds with the practice of general education. The question that is often debated is "How can special education be delivered effectively within general education classes?" One of the shared responsibilities of both special education teachers and general education teachers is to answer that question by creating an environment in which the student with an individualized educational plan can have access to a general education curriculum, yet still receive the specialized support he or she needs. In the rest of this chapter we will examine the relationship between general education and special education, identify factors that appear common to successful programs, present some strategies for promoting effective programs in your own school, and look at how these factors and strategies appear in some innovative school programs.

Special Education and General Education: Commonalities, Collaboration, and Conflict

As you have learned in earlier chapters, special education gradually has become an accepted and integrated part of public education. We discussed the principles of inclusion, mainstreaming, and normalization and the effects they have had and continue to have on our conceptualization and practice of special education. As more and more students with disabilities spend increasing amounts of time in general education classrooms, we recognize that all teachers are or will be teaching students with disabilities. In fact, 82 percent of all children with disabilities between 1996 and 1997 were served in general education classes for all or part of the school day (*Twenty-Second Annual Report to Congress on the Implementation of the IDEA* 2000.) This information suggests that for many students the effectiveness of their program will be at least partially determined by how successful they are in general education.

All teachers will teach students with disabilities.

Are special education and general education more alike than different? One could argue that education is education. All schools have the common goals of providing curricula, instruction, and materials that provide students with basic skills and prepare them to achieve their professional goals (Kauffman & Hallahan, 1993). Schools often have a variety of general education curricula or tracks that lead to different types of preparation—for example, college preparatory curricula and vocational preparatory curricula. The idea of preparing some children differently to meet their individual needs and educational goals can be seen as compatible with the fundamental purposes of special education.

On the other hand, general education is designed to prepare large numbers of students to achieve a common outcome, such as a high school diploma. The curriculum is based on society's determination of what the majority of individuals need in order to be successful in life. Teaching materials and methods are determined on the basis of what is most effective for all typically achieving students. In general education, therefore, what students will learn and how they will be taught is determined before they walk in the door of their first grade class.

In special education, however, we have learned that the direction of educational programming is different from that of general education. Once a child is identified with a disability, it becomes the immediate responsibility of the parents, the teachers, the support personnel, and the individual to determine what *this child* needs to learn to maximize his potential for success, and how he or she will be taught.

It often is difficult to determine how to meet the needs of students with disabilities in the general education classroom.

Although students' goals often include successful academic or behavioral performance in the general education classroom, it can be difficult to determine how best to meet the needs of students with disabilities in the context of general education. The overriding and much debated concern is how to provide necessary special education support services while giving students as much experience possible in inclusive environments with their typical peers (Vaughn, Bos, & Schumm, 1997). Although this has been a long-standing concern, recent reform movements in general education, coupled with changes to special education law, have increased educators' concerns (Mamlin, 1999).

General education has moved to standards-based performance measures that are assessed with statewide assessment instruments. This means that all students in one grade are expected to be working on the same skills, and the outcome of their instruction should be the same. The standards-based assessment practice is called "high-stakes testing" because of the great importance state educational agencies, as well as local schools, give to these scores. An individual's performance may determine whether he or she passes a grade or graduates from high school. A school's overall performance can have consequences for individual teachers, administrators, and school funding.

Because the 1997 amendments to IDEA align special education with standards-based instruction and testing, many educators feel it is now even more difficult to integrate a student's special education objectives into general education classrooms (McLaughlin, Nolet, Rhim, & Henderson, 1999). General education teachers have less time for remedial or alternative instruction and are reluctant to have low-achieving students, who may not score well on high-stakes tests, in their classrooms. Special education teachers struggle to justify aligning a student's IEP objectives with grade-level performance standards. They fear that the result will be less meaningful IEP objectives and less time spent on meaningful instruction, because they are being asked to impose the predetermined, general education curriculum on the specific needs of individual students (McLaughlin et al., 1999). Nevertheless, the majority of students with disabilities are served primarily in general education classrooms. Let's take a look at some of the other issues in inclusive special education programs.

Are Inclusive Special Education Programs Effective?

If asked the question "Are inclusive special education programs effective?" most teachers, regardless of their personal feelings about inclusion, probably would reply, "Well, they can be if there is administrative support, interest, planning time, instructional time, and capable and cooperative teachers." Good inclusive programs require immense commitment of time, energy, and resources by general and special educators. Research suggests that when different service delivery options are compared (inclusion and resource, inclusion and self-contained classrooms, resource and self-contained classrooms), the critical variable is always instruction (Moody, Vaughn, Hughes, & Fisher, 2000). Factors such as how students are taught, the amount of instructional time, and the extent of individualized instruction are important—*where* the service is provided is not. The question, therefore, becomes not whether inclusive programs are effective, but whether effective instructional practices are provided in inclusive settings for students with disabilities.

The most critical variable when comparing programs is instruction, not location.

The research comparing the use of best instructional practice in general education classrooms with practice in other educational settings provides us with

Many students with disabilities require only a few accommodations to work successfully in general education classes. (© Paul Conklin/ PHOTO EDIT)

Procrastination of vital tasks is a close relative of incompetence and a handmaiden of inefficiency.
— R. Alec MacKenzie

Monthly Focus:
Productivity—*You reap what you sow. Are your efforts bringing forth the desired results?*

20
Thursday
September 2001

Daily Record of Events

263rd Day 102 Left Week 38

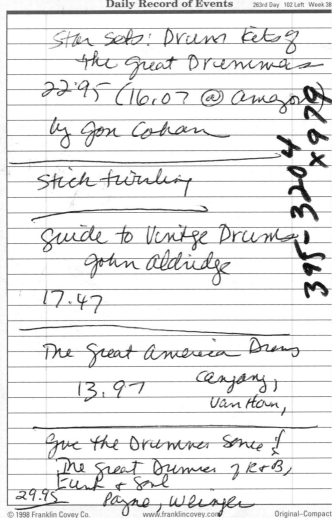

Star sets: Drum Kits of the Great Drummers
22.95 (16.07 @ amazon)
by Jon Cohan

Stick twirling

Guide to Vintage Drums
John Aldridge
17.47

The Great America Drum
13.97 Carjany,
Van Horn,

Give the Drummer Some!
The Great Drummers of R+B,
Funk + Soul
29.95 Payne, Weinger

395-3204 x 997

21

Friday
September 2001

S	M	T	W	T	F	S
30						1
2	3	4	5	6	7	8
9	10	11	12	13	14	15
16	17	18	19	20	**21**	22
23	24	25	26	27	28	29

✓ Task Completed
→ Planned Forward
× Task Deleted
G✓ Delegated Task
● In Process

↓ **ABC Prioritized Daily Task List**

~~Conversation~~
The Drummers' Time: Conversations w/ the great Drummers of Jazz

10.36 (Canyon)

562 799-5143 Deb.

Daily Expenses

Appointment Schedule

6
7
8
9
10
12
1
34. mi
2
3
4
30 hr
5
6
50 hr.
7
8
9

some interesting and useful information. When students with similar profiles were served in inclusive rather than separate resource settings, they had fewer long-range goals identified on their IEPs, they received programs that were less individually designed and less related to their assessed performance ability, and they received far fewer service minutes during the school day (Espin, Deno, & Albayrak-Kaymak, 1998). This research contributes to the perception that special education is watered down and less effective when delivered in general education classrooms and that teachers are less able to provide appropriate special education services in inclusive settings.

On the other hand, Logan and Malone (1998) found that similar amounts of time devoted to individualized instruction were provided to children with severe disabilities in both inclusive and self-contained settings. They also found that the individualized instruction in the general education classroom was always provided by either a special education teacher or paraprofessional. In other words, appropriate personnel is a key factor when addressing the issue of how to provide appropriate individualized services to students with disabilities in general education classrooms.

The presence of more than one teacher allows for more careful attention to student performance.

It may be extremely difficult for one teacher to address the overall academic and social needs of twenty-eight students and to provide even five minutes of individualized instruction for one child with a severe learning disability. Once the teacher-to-student ratio changes, individualization is increased. Two teachers in a classroom also introduces the option of co-teaching, which includes the ability to use small groups for instruction. Individualization occurs more frequently in smaller groups, and student attending behaviors and academic achievement increase when group size decreases (Russ, Chiang, Rylance, & Bongers, 2001).

The presence of more than one teacher also allows for more careful attention to and monitoring of student performance. If a teacher is aware of how the student with disabilities is progressing, she is then able to adapt her methods of instruction (Vaughn, Bos, & Schumm, 1997). When a special education teacher is in the general education class, she can also suggest materials or teaching methods to the general education teacher, or make the changes herself.

From the research mentioned above, it is clear that two sets of hands not only are better than one, but may be necessary in some classes so that effective and individualized instruction can be provided in general education settings. We are not recommending that all inclusion classes have both general and special education teachers. We are only pointing out that the best way to ensure many best practices in some inclusive settings is through teacher partnership and collaboration. Research in preschool settings, which typically include several teachers and teaching assistants, suggests that inclusive preschool programs tend to be of higher quality on traditional measures than preschools that are not inclusive (Buysse, Wesley, Bryant, & Gardner, 1999).

We look for guidelines for serving students with disabilities in general education programs by examining what works for others. We know that specific instructional skills and strategies are necessary for creating effective programs, and we've looked at those in earlier chapters. We've just looked at the importance of providing appropriate individualized instruction in all educational environments in which students with disabilities are served. Next, we will discuss some fundamental recommendations that will lead to better programs across the board—whether you are teaching a teenager with severe mental retardation or a young child with a behavior problem. In the next section, we will look at what you can do to promote collaboration and good instruction in inclusive settings.

Inside Special Education Classes

Strategies for Promoting Effective Programs

When special education teachers and general education teachers work together to deliver services in the general education classroom, many factors may contribute to the success of their partnership and the effectiveness of any individual student's educational program. Teamwork among educators is necessary for inclusion to have the greatest chance at success (Mamlin, 1999).

As you enter a partnership with another teacher, or are assessing teachers' interest at a schoolwide level, it is important to have a good understanding of the other teacher's knowledge base and personal perceptions of needs, strengths, and weaknesses, and interest. Daniels and Vaughn (1999) adapted core knowledge and skills teaching standards from the National Council for Exceptional Children and created a very helpful evaluation tool. This evaluation instrument (see Figure 14.1) is designed to look at general education teachers' knowledge of the skills important for teaching students with disabilities. With this information, special education teachers can identify teachers in general education who are prepared to work effectively with students with disabilities. The instrument also can be used to identify important sources of teacher support—for example, ensuring that a teacher has access to consultation from a behavior-management specialist, or the development of schoolwide inservice programs on critical skills, such as teaching communication skills, or broad areas of knowledge, such as visual impairments.

Not all teachers will want to become involved in inclusion programs.

Not all teachers with the necessary knowledge will want to become involved in inclusion programs. Although administrative support for collaboration is essential, administrative mandates can undermine the potential for success. The source of the change—principal, single teacher, special education administrator—can influence the way inclusion programs develop and succeed (Lieber et al., 2000).

Once willing and knowledgeable teachers are identified, it is important to place students carefully by matching individualized need with instructional options. Figure 14.2 is a sample chart that can be used to match aspects of the classroom environment to students' specific needs (Friend & Bursuck, 1996).

It is important not to overload teachers with included children with disabilities.

As collaborative teams are formed, it is important not to overload experienced or willing teachers with included students with disabilities. Overloading may result in even experienced teachers feeling that they cannot be effective with or concerned about these challenging students (Cook, Tankersley, Cook, & Landrum, 2000). Larger caseloads also negatively affect student achievement (Russ et al., 2001). A general education class that includes fifteen students with disabilities is really a special education class. Although this may be an appropriate service delivery option for these students, it is not an inclusion program.

Teachers must ensure that the content their students need can be provided in general education classes.

Finally, it is important to ensure that the content the students need can, in fact, be provided without compromise in the general education classroom. If the structure of any setting does not allow for appropriate content or identified best practices, then perhaps it is not the best choice for the given students (Moody et al., 2000). Appropriate content may extend beyond academic coursework to functional skills, community skills, social skills, and direct work experience (Benz, Lindstrom, & Yovanoff, 2000).

Although it is a challenge, effective instruction can be provided in general education settings when teachers take the initiative. You may have your own ideas of how to collaborate with other teachers or service providers to create a supportive and effective educational program. In the following section, we share some current teachers' educational practice.

Part I: Demographic Information

Directions: Please answer the following questions about yourself and your school by placing a check (✓) in the appropriate blank, or by providing appropriate information in the blank.

1. Professional Training (Highest Degree)
   ___ Bachelor's Degree
   ___ Master's Degree
   ___ Specialist Degree
   ___ Doctorate
2. Area(s) of Certification
   ___ Elementary Education
   ___ Secondary Education
   ___ Special Education
      ___ Mild/Moderate Disabilities
      ___ Severe/Profound Disabilities
   ___ Other (specify) ________
3. Present Teaching Level
   ___ Elementary School, Grade Level ______
   ___ Middle School, Grade Level ______
   ___ Other (Specify) ________
4. Total Years of Teaching Experience (for each setting)
   ___ General (Regular) Education
   ___ Special Education
   ___ Full Inclusion
   ___ Inclusion
5. Are you currently teaching in an inclusion setting?
   ___ yes
   ___ no

If no, please go to item 13.

6. Approximately how many students do you teach who are identified as having disabilities?
   ___ 1–2
   ___ 3–5
   ___ 6–8
   ___ 9–11
   ___ 12–14
   ___ more than 14
7. Most of the students that you teach with disabilities are
   ___ minority students
   ___ non-minority students
8. What is the average class size of the classes you teach that include students with disabilities?
   ___ 1–5
   ___ 6–10
   ___ 11–15
   ___ 16–20
   ___ 21–25
   ___ more than 25
9. What are the disabilities of the students you currently teach? Check all that apply.
   ___ emotional/behavioral disordered
   ___ hearing impaired
   ___ learning disabled
   ___ mildly mentally disabled
   ___ moderately mentally disabled
   ___ multidisabled
   ___ orthopedically impaired
   ___ severely/profoundly mentally disabled
   ___ speech/language disordered
   ___ other (specify) ________
10. The students with disabilities that you teach receive instruction in
   ___ your class only
   ___ special education and your class
   ___ other (specify) ________
11. Your primary teaching responsibility is
   ___ academic subjects
   ___ art/music
   ___ physical education
   ___ band
   ___ other, (specify) ________
12. Indicate the source(s) from which you have received training on inclusion.
   ___ college course work
   ___ professional conferences/meetings
   ___ inservice workshop(s) at local school
   ___other, (specify) ________
13. Indicate the source(s) from which you have received content knowledge of cultural diversity.
   ___ college course work
   ___ professional conferences/meetings
   ___ inservice workshop(s) at local school
   ___ other, (specify) ________
14. Did your college training prepare you for the reality of teaching in an inclusion setting?
   ___ yes
   ___ no
15. Would you advocate that the primary placement for "all" students with disabilities be the general education classroom?
   ___yes
   ___no

Figure 14.1
Scale of Knowledge and Skills for Instruction and Management of Students with Disabilities

Part II: Instructional Content and Practice

Directions: Please indicate your perceived level of "knowledge" and "skills" in the area of "Instructional Content and Practice" as related to students with disabilities. Rate each item based on the scale below. Circle only one response per item.

Knowledge	Skills
1 = No Knowledge	1 = No Skills
2 = Limited Knowledge	2 = Limited Skills
3 = Undecided	3 = Undecided
4 = Moderate Knowledge	4 = Moderate Skills
5 = Adequate Knowledge	5 = Adequate Skills

Knowledge:	Response				
1. Learning styles					
a. differing learning styles of students	1	2	3	4	5
b. how to adapt teaching to these styles	1	2	3	4	5
2. Demands of various learning environments (e.g., individualized instruction in general education classes).	1	2	3	4	5
3. Curricula for the development of:					
a. cognitive skills	1	2	3	4	5
b. academic skills	1	2	3	4	5
c. social skills	1	2	3	4	5
4. Instructional and remedial:					
a. methods	1	2	3	4	5
b. techniques	1	2	3	4	5
c. curriculum materials	1	2	3	4	5
5. Techniques for modifying:					
a. instructional methods	1	2	3	4	5
b. instructional materials	1	2	3	4	5
Skills:	**Response**				
6. Interpreting and using assessment data for instructional planning.	1	2	3	4	5
7. Developing and/or selecting assessment measures and instructional programs and practices which respond to:					
a. cultural differences	1	2	3	4	5
b. linguistic differences	1	2	3	4	5
c. gender differences	1	2	3	4	5
8. Choosing and using appropriate technologies to accomplish instructional objectives and to integrate them appropriately into the instructional process.	1	2	3	4	5
9. Preparing appropriate lesson plans.	1	2	3	4	5
10. Involving the student in setting instructional goals and charting progress.	1	2	3	4	5
11. Conducting and using task analysis.	1	2	3	4	5
12. Instructional strategies and materials:					
a. selecting instructional strategies and materials according to characteristics of the learner	1	2	3	4	5
b. adapting instructional strategies and materials according to characteristics of the learner	1	2	3	4	5
c. using instructional strategies and materials according to characteristics of the learner	1	2	3	4	5

Figure 14.1 (continued)

13. Student learning objectives					
a. sequencing individualized student learning objectives	1	2	3	4	5
b. implementing individualized student learning objectives	1	2	3	4	5
c. evaluating individualized student learning objectives	1	2	3	4	5
14. Integrating the following skills with academic curricula:	1	2	3	4	5
a. affective	1	2	3	4	5
b. social	1	2	3	4	5
15. Using strategies for facilitating maintenance and generalization of skills across learning environments.	1	2	3	4	5
16. Using instructional time properly (adequately).	1	2	3	4	5
17. Teaching students to use thinking, problem-solving, and other cognitive strategies to meet their individual needs.	1	2	3	4	5
18. Establishing and maintaining rapport with learner.	1	2	3	4	5
19. Using verbal and nonverbal communication techniques.	1	2	3	4	5
20. Conducting self-evaluation of instruction.	1	2	3	4	5

Part III: Planning and Managing the Teaching and Learning Environment

Directions: Please indicate your perceived level of "knowledge" and "skills" in the area of "Planning and Management of the Teaching and Learning Environment" as related to students with disabilities. Rate each item based on the scale below. Circle only one response per item.

Knowledge	Skills
1 = No Knowledge	1 = No Skills
2 = Limited Knowledge	2 = Limited Skills
3 = Undecided	3 = Undecided
4 = Moderate Knowledge	4 = Moderate Skills
5 = Adequate Knowledge	5 = Adequate Skills

Knowledge:	Response				
21. Basic classroom management for students with exceptional learning needs in terms of:					
a. theories	1	2	3	4	5
b. methods	1	2	3	4	5
c. techniques	1	2	3	4	5
22. Research based best practices for effective management of teaching and learning.	1	2	3	4	5
23. Ways in which technology can assist with planning and managing the teaching and learning environment.	1	2	3	4	5
Skills:	**Response**				
24. Creating a safe, positive, and supporting learning environment in which diversities are valued.	1	2	3	4	5
25. Using strategies and techniques for facilitating the functional integration of exceptional individuals in various settings.	1	2	3	4	5
26. Preparing and organizing materials in order to implement daily lesson plans.	1	2	3	4	5
27. Incorporating evaluation, planning, and management procedures which match learner needs with the instructional environment.	1	2	3	4	5

Figure 14.1 (continued)

Skills:	Response
28. Designing a learning environment that encourages active participation by learners in a variety of individual and group learning activities.	1 2 3 4 5
29. Designing, structuring, and managing daily classroom routines, including transition time, effectively for:	
a. students	1 2 3 4 5
b. other staff	1 2 3 4 5
c. the general classroom	1 2 3 4 5
30. Directing the activities of a classroom:	
a. paraprofessional	1 2 3 4 5
b. aide	1 2 3 4 5
c. peer tutor	1 2 3 4 5

Part IV: Managing Student Behavior and Social Interaction Skills

Directions: Please indicate your perceived level of "knowledge" and "skills" in the area of "Managing Student Behavior and Social Interaction Skills" as related to students with disabilities. Rate each item based on the scale below. Circle only one response per item.

Knowledge	Skills
1 = No Knowledge	1 = No Skills
2 = Limited Knowledge	2 = Limited Skills
3 = Undecided	3 = Undecided
4 = Moderate Knowledge	4 = Moderate Skills
5 = Adequate Knowledge	5 = Adequate Skills

Knowledge:	Response
31. Applicable laws, rules and regulations, and procedural safeguards regarding the planning and implementation of management of student behaviors.	1 2 3 4 5
32. Ethical considerations inherent in classroom behavior management.	1 2 3 4 5
33. Teacher attitudes and behaviors that:	
a. positively influence student behavior	1 2 3 4 5
b. negatively influence student behavior	1 2 3 4 5
34. Social skills needed for:	
a. educational environments	1 2 3 4 5
b. functional living environments	1 2 3 4 5
35. Effective instruction in the development of social skills.	1 2 3 4 5

Skills:	Response
36. Demonstrating a variety of effective behavior management techniques appropriate for the needs of exceptional individuals.	1 2 3 4 5
37. Implementing the least intensive intervention consistent with the needs of the exceptional individual.	1 2 3 4 5
38. Modifying the learning environment (schedule and physical arrangement) to manage inappropriate behaviors.	1 2 3 4 5
39. Identifying realistic expectations for:	
a. personal behavior in various settings	1 2 3 4 5
b. social behavior in various settings	1 2 3 4 5

Figure 14.1 (continued)

		1	2	3	4	5
40.	Integrating social skills into the curriculum.	1	2	3	4	5
41.	Using effective teaching procedures in social skills instruction.	1	2	3	4	5
42.	Demonstrating procedures to increase:					
	a. student self-awareness	1	2	3	4	5
	b. student self-control	1	2	3	4	5
	c. student self-reliance	1	2	3	4	5
	d. student self-esteem	1	2	3	4	5

43. What kind of teacher do you perceive yourself to be?
___ General Education Inclusion Teacher ___ General Education Noninclusion Teacher

44. How would you describe your classroom setting?
___ General Education Setting ___ Full Inclusion Setting ___ Inclusion Setting

45. Overall, how would you rate your knowledge and skills for teaching students with disabilities?
____ Excellent ____ Good ____ Fair ____ Insufficient

Comments: ____________________

Source: Vera I. Daniels and Sharon Vaughn, "A Tool to Encourage 'Best Practice' in Full Inclusion," *Teaching Exceptional Children*, May/June 1999, pp. 49–53.

Figure 14.1 (continued)

Featured Programs

Sometimes it is difficult to imagine what a special education program might look like, especially one that involves innovative approaches to education. In this section, you will get an idea of how special education can work. We identified two unique programs that reflect very different types of special education instruction and asked teachers in the programs to describe them. The first description you will read focuses on a program in which elementary students with moderate to severe disabilities receive services in an inclusive, general education setting. The second program addresses the transition of students with mild to moderate disabilities from middle school to high school and gives insight into the preparation and options available to the students in one school district. As you read about these programs, consider the issues and guidelines we just discussed. How do these programs provide appropriate services and stay true to the individualized nature of special education, while still operating within general education classrooms?

Inclusive Program for Elementary Students with Moderate to Severe Disabilities

School: Westside Elementary School, Douglas, Georgia
Special Education Teacher: Windy Schweder

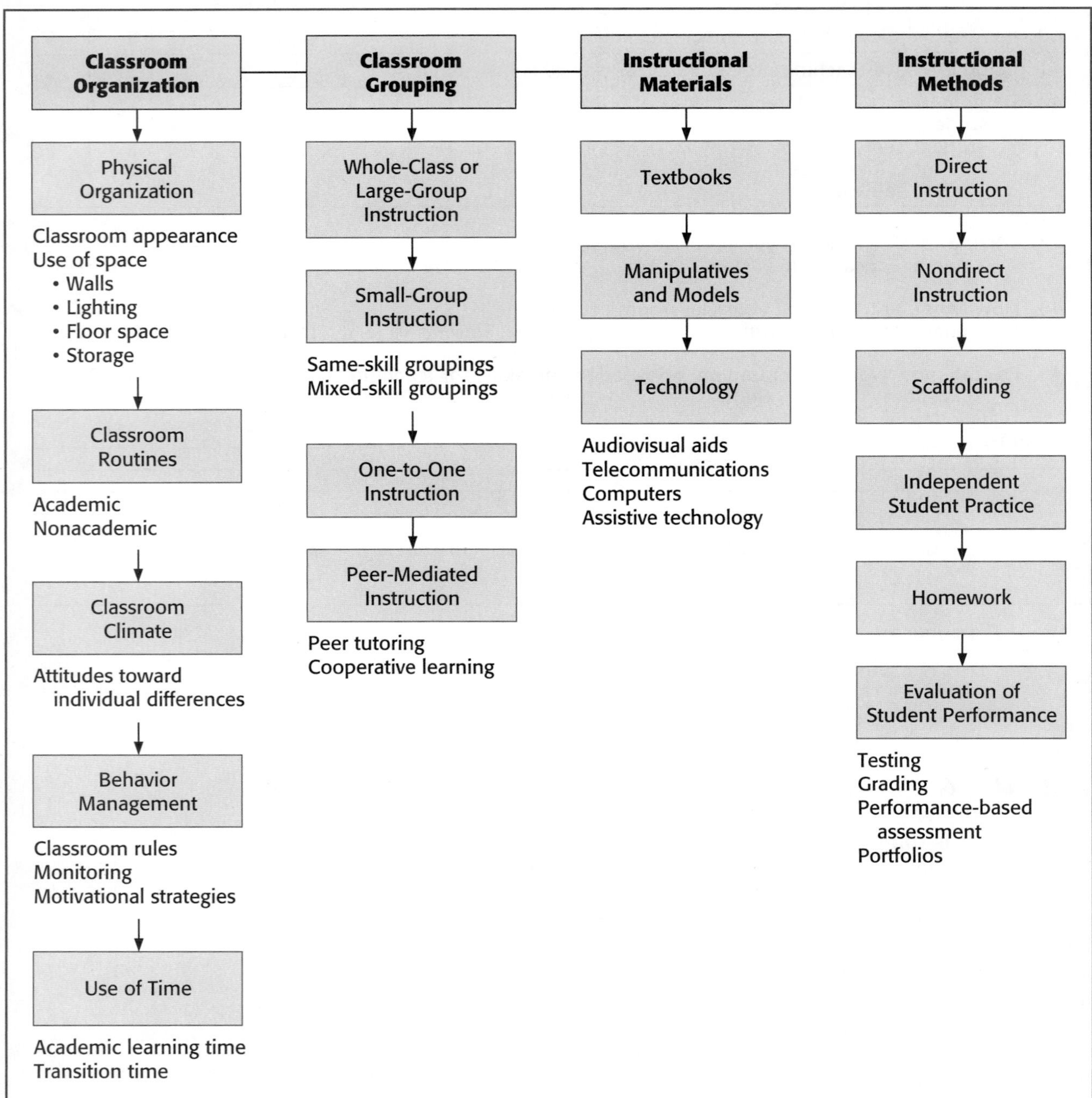

Figure 14.2
Overview of Classroom Environments

Source: Marilyn Friend and William D. Bursuck, *Including Students with Special Needs* (Boston: Allyn and Bacon, 1996), p. 221.

■ *Purpose of Program*

I was fortunate to have the opportunity to teach in an elementary school that was included in a program funded by a federal grant to Georgia State University (Gallagher et al., 2000). The program was part of a study designed to evaluate the progress students with moderate to severe disabilities make on their IEP objectives while being educated in inclusive settings.

■ *Description of Program*

Population The students who participated in the program were identified with mental retardation and had full-scale IQs ranging from 35 to 55, with a vast range of abilities. Although the study looked at many students, the students with whom I worked ranged in age from 5 to 21.

Setting During the first two years of the program, we mainstreamed the students with moderate to severe disabilities into nonacademic settings, such as P.E., recess, and lunch. Because these were nonacademic settings, I did not focus adequately on preparing the personnel in these settings. This was the wrong thing to do, and I later paid for sending my students into these settings without adequate support, because it turned more than one general education teacher against "inclusion." The third year, our principal and special education director merged two of our classrooms for students with moderate, severe, and pro-

Co-teaching can provide rich opportunities for student-teacher interaction and improved learning. (© Will Hart/PHOTO EDIT)

found disabilities because of a lack of physical space to house the separate classes. We went from two classrooms, each with six students, an instructional assistant, and a teacher, to one large room with two certified teachers, twelve students, and three instructional assistants. This turned out to be the best thing that could have happened to us, because it freed me to go out into the general education setting. During the four years I taught in this program, we managed to include ten of our students with disabilities into P.E., recess, lunch, reading, language arts, social studies, science, and math. Two of our included students had Down syndrome, and one had autism; five students were identified with moderate intellectual disabilities and five were identified with severe intellectual disabilities; two students were in wheelchairs. Yet these ten students participated in all field trips, PTA programs, and school activities with their typical peers, even if it meant the general education teacher or I would be sitting on the stage during the Christmas program to keep a student with autism from running off the set.

Inclusion takes lots of time and planning. We usually started around April of one year planning for the next year. In April, I would ask the teachers I was working with if they wanted to be involved again the next year. I also approached new teachers we thought would be receptive to the program. We tended to approach teachers who showed an interest in our students in the hall or at lunch, those who were our friends, or those who we considered to be good teachers who were accepting of all students. A few teachers we worked with offered to do it every other year, because the program was time-consuming and draining. Many teachers did volunteer to participate again. We also decided which students we thought would fit best with certain general education teachers and which subjects were most closely related to IEP objectives.

When I first approached a teacher about inclusion, I usually had a student or two in mind to include in the classroom, and would suggest that the teacher come to the special education classroom or general education classroom to observe the student before he or she committed. I encouraged the teacher to come to one of the general education classes where I was co-teaching to get an idea of what we would be doing if we worked together. I showed the teachers the IEP objectives and asked for suggestions about which of their classes would be the best choices for teaching the objectives.

By June, we usually knew who was going to be placed in whose general education classroom and for what period of time. Once we got students into a general education setting, we tried to increase gradually the amount of time they spent with their peers without disabilities. We started in nonacademic settings and moved to less structured academic classes, such as science and social studies. Last, we included students in academic subjects such as math, reading, and language arts.

Some students were mainstreamed for P.E., recess, and lunch and received support in academic settings such as reading and math. Those who needed support for nonacademic settings received it from an instructional assistant or special education teacher. One of my little boys in a wheelchair and both my students with Down syndrome needed support in all settings. We made sure that we didn't overload the general education classes with students who had disabilities. I never included more than two or three students with moderate or severe disabilities in one general education classroom. I didn't want to end up with a general education classroom that was really one big special education classroom.

Service Providers and Responsibilities Our philosophy of inclusion was that students should be included in general education settings only when they could achieve success on IEP objectives. Therefore, we did not advocate full inclusion for all. We looked at children on an individual basis when including them. We all shared the load. I co-taught in academic settings. We used many different models of co-teaching, depending on what was needed. For example, we might have one person teach and one float and assist, each teacher working with a separate group, or both of us teaching at the same time. On a few occasions, one of my instructional assistants did a little co-teaching. The general education teachers and I shared responsibilities for the classes we co-taught. I helped the teacher research activities to teach certain objectives, and I also helped to grade papers. Either an instructional assistant or myself was responsible for collecting the data on student progress on IEP objectives.

Degree of Individualized Programming and Instruction We gave individualized instruction to all students who needed it. That was the beauty of having more than one teacher in the general education classroom. For example, when we were using the one teach, one assist model of co-teaching, the floating teacher could stop to help those who needed it. In one second-grade class, we read to the students for 30 minutes each day after lunch. The general education teacher and I took turns reading and giving individualized instruction. Center time was also a good time to give students individual attention. Since our students with disabilities were not included all day, they could receive any individualized instruction that they didn't get in the general education class in the special education class.

■ ***Description of a Typical Day*** We had many different schedules. As an example, one year I took two of my students to a third-grade classroom at 8:00 for reading, language arts, math, and recess. One girl who had a severe intellectual disability and a severe seizure disorder (she had at least fifteen seizures a day) joined us for recess and also attended P.E. and lunch with the third-grade class, with the support of an instructional assistant. Some days I taught social and recreation/leisure skills during recess, and some days the general education teacher and I used the time to plan while sitting on a bench watching the children. At 11:30, I dropped these students off in the special education classroom and ate lunch. At 12:00, I met two students and an instructional assistant in a kindergarten room where we were included for centers and recess. This instructional assistant had been with the students in the kindergarten class since 11:00. When I arrived, she left to pick up the third-grade students and take them to lunch and P.E. At 1:30, I dropped the two kindergarten students off and picked up a fifth-grade student to attend a social studies class. I would take him back to the special education class at 2:30.

A second instructional assistant began her day in a fourth-grade classroom for reading, language arts, and math with three students—two with moderate disabilities and one with severe disabilities. She left them at 11:00 while the general education class had recess and P.E. to take our fifth-grade student to science. The three fourth-grade students were included for recess, lunch, and P.E. During that time they didn't have direct support from a special education teacher or instructional assistant.

I spent my afternoons planning with the kindergarten and third-grade teacher and trying to catch up with the fifth-grade science teacher and any other

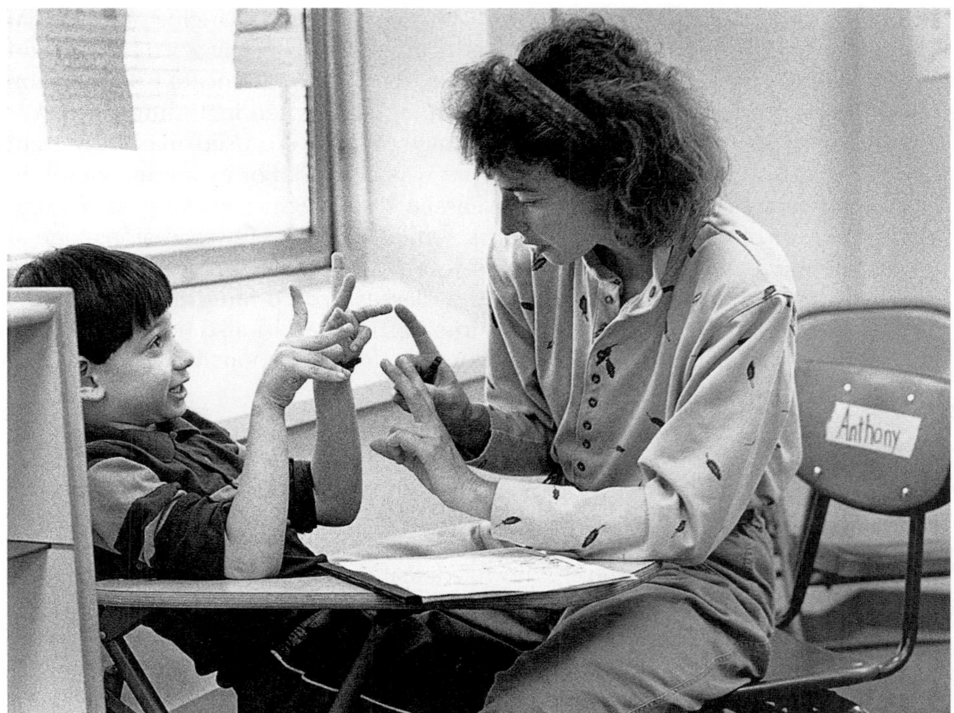

Specialized instruction, such as sign language or braille, is often taught in tutorial settings. (© Suzie Fitzhugh)

teacher I didn't see during the day. The other special education teacher and instructional assistant remained in the special education classroom, delivering instruction to the students who were not included.

■ ***Did the Program Accomplish Its Goals?*** According to the data that were gathered twice a week on all IEP objectives, all students made progress on IEP objectives each year they were in the study. Two of our students who were included changed labels during re-evaluations while being taught in inclusive settings: one from moderate disabilities to mild disabilities and the other from severe disabilities to moderate disabilities.

What Factors Were Critical to the Success of the Program?

Administrative Support Our school also worked to include children with mild disabilities and hearing loss. Our administrators made sure that our students with moderate and severe disabilities received the services we needed, and they hired the necessary personnel. They provided us with three special education instructional assistants and two certified special education teachers for twelve students to make sure we had the staff to make the inclusion model work. The general education teachers were given release time to visit other classrooms to observe students with disabilities. The kindergarten teacher and I were given release time to visit the prekindergarten special education classrooms located at another school, to observe the students who would be moving to our school the next year. This was great for me, because I could start matching children with teachers and classes.

Flexibility, a Sense of Humor, and the Ability to Get Along with Others These traits are important because you never know what will happen next. As you can see from the schedule, there is a lot of coming and going of adults to get everyone in the right place at the right time. Special education teachers are accustomed to the revolving door of physical therapy, occupational therapy and speech therapy; general education teachers are not.

Knowledge and Creativity It took us a while to get accustomed to coming up with modifications and accommodations for students. We didn't want to end up with two separate classes in one room. For example, in a fourth-grade science class, I taught one of my students the parts of a flower (leaf, petal, stem) using real flowers, while the other fourth-graders were learning terms such as *pistil* and *stamen.*

Good Teachers Who Care About Teaching All Children This is important because teaching in an inclusive environment means sharing control of your materials, space, and students. This is hard for some teachers. Inclusion also requires planning time before and after school. Teachers must be motivated by the program to invest their time, energy, and materials.

Support from the Experts at Georgia State Having direct access to experts helped me to troubleshoot and problem-solve. The faculty held summer inservice programs for general and special education teachers. They also conducted meetings after school every month or two to provide assistance on more immediate problems.

Transition from Middle School to High School

Richland Northeast High School, Columbia, South Carolina; Blythewood Middle School, Columbia, South Carolina

Teachers: Linda Rayl, Transition Coordinator, Richland Northeast High School; Angie Bankhead, Resource Teacher, Blythewood Middle School

■ ***Purpose of Program*** The purpose of this program is to ease the transition of eighth-grade students as they move from the middle school to the high school setting. The transition program begins in the eighth grade at the middle school and goes through the ninth grade at the high school. The ninth-grade program is designed not only to help students with the transition to high school but also to prepare them for the high school curriculum and life after high school. The ultimate goal is to keep the students in school and to make sure they are prepared for graduation.

■ ***Who Participates in This Program?*** The program was created for students with learning disabilities, emotional and behavioral disabilities, and mild mental retardation. The transition program is designed to serve both students who have been in self-contained classes and those who have been in less restrictive service-delivery models.

This group of rising ninth-graders needs our attention because there is a high failure rate among ninth-graders, especially in math. These students also have a difficult time adjusting to the academic and social rigors of high school. As they enter the ninth grade, they need to develop the personal responsibility that is necessary for a successful high school career.

The teachers who participate include at least one special education teacher from all of the middle schools, plus the high school transition coordinator. Other general education teachers at the high school level are invited to participate in some activities and do participate as teachers in the included classes.

■ ***The Eighth-Grade Transition Program*** In the eighth grade, the scheduling and content of students' academic courses are adjusted to align with high school curriculum and service delivery. Students are included in co-taught arts and math general curriculum courses, and may receive academic support for content area courses in an enrichment course titled Support Lab. Preparation also includes instruction in notetaking, study skills, and test-taking skills. In addition to academic preparation, students take an occupational inventory test to help identify their course and career interests, and, of course, schedule planning time with the guidance counselor.

The teachers also have some responsibilities at this time. In addition to preparing students, we also have to prepare ourselves. The high school teachers visit the feeder middle schools. The middle school and high school teachers share information about ideas and methods that may pertain to a particular student or group. Students, along with their parents and teachers, are invited to tour the high school and visit the various programs. A high school representative also attends the IEP meetings of each eighth-grade student.

Before the last two steps occur, the high school sends each eighth-grader a letter that outlines the different program options at the high school. This is an important time, because students and their parents are deciding which academic or nonacademic track they will pursue. They need to have a clear idea of what the options are and where each one leads. After the parents and student receive the necessary information, they can visit the school to see if they have any questions before identifying IEP goals.

■ ***The Ninth-Grade Transition Program*** As students make the move to high school, there is one additional attempt to ease transition: The middle school special education teachers attend the high school orientation held at the beginning of the school year. Once school begins, the ninth-grade transition program focuses on movement to an appropriate high school curriculum, and the general education and special education faculty at the high school work together to accomplish this goal. Ninth-grade students with disabilities will participate in the Freshman Focus Program and in one of three transition curriculum options: resource programs, HIRE-Career Preparation, and self-contained programs.

Freshman Focus All ninth-grade students take a freshman seminar class called the Freshman Focus. This helps to promote social and academic transition from middle to high school. Students learn general educational strategies that can be used across the curriculum (for example, technology and media research skills, and test-taking and learning strategies). The students also participate in group problem-solving activities that allow them to develop leadership abilities and working relationships with teachers and other students.

Resource Programs If a student selects the resource program, he or she has decided to earn a South Carolina high school diploma—a typical academic diploma. In order to do this, the student with a disability, just like all other diploma-track students, must earn 24 credits and pass the Exit Exams in reading, math, and writing. The academic diploma has two tracks—college preparatory and technical preparatory. In the ninth grade the student will participate in academic classes that are co-taught by general and special educators and participate in the academic support lab. The academic support lab is designed to give academic support for content area classes, provide practice on basic academic skills, and include instruction in test and study skills.

HIRE—Helping Individuals Reach Excellence If a student selects the HIRE program, he or she is pursuing a District 2 Career Preparatory diploma. This is a diploma created by the school district, not the state, so that students who cannot complete an academic diploma can graduate with a certificate that ensures that a meaningful curriculum has been successfully completed. The district's Career Prep diploma is recognized by local community colleges, area businesses, and the military. The HIRE program for ninth-grade students provides instruction in academic skills related to success in work and community environments. The ninth-grade HIRE class is a foundation for the Career Prep curriculum, in which the student must meet 115 basic skills and real-world competencies.

Self-Contained Programs The self-contained programs at the high school focus on different things for students with different disabilities. Students with learning disabilities may become eligible for the HIRE program or for later participation in the Career Prep curriculum. Students with emotional or behavior disabilities are mainstreamed into general education curriculum courses and receive a Support Lab course to address academic and behavioral concerns. The goal for many of these students is an academic diploma. Finally, the goal for students with mild mental disabilities is direct community skills and job training. In grades 10–12, the goal is for the students to spend half of the school day on a job site and the other half of the day receiving instruction in social skills or independent living skills.

Although the transition program and career preparatory curriculum have only been in place for a few years, the teachers, students, and parents are all excited about the new programs. In a few years, graduation, employment, and school completion rates will help to evaluate the success of the complete transition package.

After reading about these two featured programs, we hope you were able to get a better sense of how special education professionals and general education professionals can work together to present appropriate curriculum and effective instruction to students with disabilities. In the first program, the instructional coordination and teacher planning focused on serving students in the general education class whenever possible. The *process* of merging general and special education to achieve appropriate inclusion in elementary school was the goal of the program. Because the students had moderate to severe disabilities, the process was quite challenging. In the second description, the transition program had multiple goals and involved a multitude of general and special education faculty. In this program, the emphasis appeared to be on student *outcome,* as defined by the high school curriculum and diploma options. Perhaps the urgency of approaching graduation helped to shape the appropriate focus on long-range outcomes. Certainly both program descriptions revealed that complex scheduling and planning and continued teacher-to-teacher collaboration are essential when special educator and general educators work together to deliver services to students with disabilities.

Inside Special Education Classes

Summary

- The majority of students with disabilities receive special education services in general education settings, and, therefore, virtually all teachers will have students with disabilities in their classrooms.
- One of the most challenging aspects of teaching students with disabilities in general education classes is providing the students with the individualized instruction they may need.
- Factors that appear to have a strong influence on the effectiveness of providing special education services in general education settings include the number of qualified special education personnel, the use of small-group instruction, and the monitoring of student performance.
- Collaboration and teacher partnerships are critical to the effective delivery of special services in all environments, including the general education classroom.

What You Can Do

1. Visit an inclusive preschool setting in a local elementary school. Observe the teacher and instructional assistants and record the different types of teaching strategies you see used. Are the strategies the same for all of the students? Do the students with disabilities receive individual instruction?
2. Create a notebook of articles and first-hand descriptions of special education programs delivered in general education or community settings. Record or note the strategies or materials that you find particularly interesting and potentially useful in your own classroom.
3. Visit all of the high schools in a local school district. Look at the range of programs that are available to adolescents with disabilities. What options for graduation, curriculum, study skills, academic support, and vocational preparation are available to students with disabilities in that school district?
4. Scan school and university websites for descriptions, pictures, and videos of new and innovative special education programs. Keep a record of these websites to share with other teachers, administrators, and parents.

Multimedia Resources

Marquita Grenot-Scheyer, Mary Fisher, and Debbie Staub (Eds.), (2001). *At the end of the day: Lessons learned in inclusive education.* Baltimore: Brookes. This book includes discussion about the inclusive programs for eight students with disabilities. It presents descriptions of the successes and barriers to inclusive education.

Mary Susan E. Fishbaugh (2000). *The collaboration guide for early career educators.* Baltimore: Brookes. This text focuses on presenting specific teacher collaboration strategies to new teachers.

http://www.richland2org/svh/CareerPrep/Career Prep.htm: This website will provide you with more specific information about the secondary transition career diploma curriculum at Richland Northeast and other high schools in the Richland 2 School District.

http://www.dssc.org/nta/html/indes 2.htm: This is the address for the homepage for the National Transition Alliance for Youth with Disabilities. Links are provided to many related resources, databases, and model programs.

http://www.ssstw.ed.gov: The National School-to-Work website contains information about current activities and available information at both state and national levels.

http://www.uni.edu/coe/inclusion/index/html: This website provides philosophy, strategies, legal requirements, and resources for inclusion programs.

Exceptional Parent Magazine (September, 2000): This magazine issue includes short descriptions of inclusion programs that received Models of Excellence in Education awards.

Glossary

AAMR Adaptive Behavior Scale one of the most widely used instruments for measuring adaptive behavior.

academic enrichment broadening the experience base of the students in an academic content area without changing the instructional objectives.

Accelerated Schools Project school reform model that extends the expectations and strategies used in gifted education to all students in the school.

acceleration providing a more appropriate program for a gifted student by moving the student ahead in the curriculum; the most common example is grade-skipping.

acquired hearing loss a hearing loss acquired at any time after birth.

acquired immune deficiency syndrome (AIDS) a viral disease that breaks down the body's immune system, destroying its ability to fight infections; AIDS is transmitted by the exchange of body fluids which can occur through sexual contact or sharing contaminated needles to inject intravenous drugs.

adaptive behaviors the age- and situation-specific social, maturational, self-help, and communicative acts that assist each individual in adapting to the demands of his or her environment.

adult service agencies agencies that provide medical and psychological examinations and counseling, training and job placement, and financial assistance for adaptive equipment, prostheses, and basic living costs during training to adults with disabilities.

age-appropriate behavior behavior considered normal for a particular age.

American Sign Language (ASL) the sign language considered by many deaf adults to be their "native language"; it has the same vocabulary as English but a different grammatical structure.

Americans with Disabilities Act of 1990 (P.L. 101-336) a law that extends civil rights protection to individuals with disabilities in private-sector employment and requires that public services like telecommunications and transportation make accommodations for individuals with disabilities.

amniocentesis a prenatal testing technique that analyzes amniotic fluid to identify certain chromosomal and neural tube abnormalities.

anxiety-withdrawal behaviors, such as extreme sensitivity or depression, that reflect fear of performance and avoidance.

Asperger's syndrome A syndrome in which individuals have social and behavioral deficits similar to those experienced by children with autism, but do not experience delays in language and cognition.

assimilation the process of subordinating old cultural patterns to the patterns of the dominant culture.

asthma a chronic obstructive lung condition characterized by an unusual reaction to a variety of stimuli that causes difficulty in breathing, coughing, wheezing, and shortness of breath.

at-risk infants and young children who have a higher likelihood of developing a disability because of factors like extreme prematurity, chronic poverty, or medical problems.

attention the ability to focus on information.

attentional deficits the inability to come to attention, to maintain attention, or to pay attention selectively.

attention deficit disorder (ADD) a condition determined by difficulty in focusing on information and in sustaining attention.

attention deficit with hyperactivity disorder (ADHD) a condition determined by difficulty in focusing on information, sustaining attention, and hyperactive behavior.

audiogram the chart on which the audiologist records an individual's responses to a hearing test.

audiologist the professional who tests and measures hearing.

auditory training enhancing the residual hearing of a student with hearing loss by teaching listening skills.

augmentative communication aid a system designed to give individuals assistance in communication, such as a scanning system or communication board.

autism a severely incapacitating lifelong developmental disability characterized by certain types of behaviors and patterns of interaction and communication. Symptoms include disturbance in the rate of appearance of physical, social, and language skills; abnormal response to sensation; delayed or absent speech and language; and abnormal ways of relating to people, objects, and events. It usually appears during the first three years of life.

behavior disordered a term used by some states instead of "serious emotional disturbance" to classify children with behavior and emotional disorders.

behavior intervention plan (BIP) An empirically-based individual program to address problem behavior, that contains positive behavior support strategies designed to teach appropriate behavior.

behavior-rating scale an observation form that allows teachers, parents, and psychologists to rate patterns of behavior.

Bell, Alexander Graham 19th-century teacher of speech to deaf children; inventor of the telephone.

bilateral hearing loss hearing loss in both ears.

biological aging the physiological changes that occur over the lifespan.

biological risk the risk associated with damage to a child's developing systems before, during, or after birth.

Board of Education of Hendrick Hudson School District* v. *Rowley a 1982 Supreme Court decision that an "appropriate" education does not mean that a student must reach his or her maximum potential, only that the student have access to educational opportunity.

Bobby-approved symbol indicating that website content is accessible to people with disabilities.

Braille a system of reading that uses raised dots to signify numbers and letters.

brainstorming a basic creative thinking technique used in problem solving; participants are asked to come up with as many ideas as possible relative to a certain topic—there are no right or wrong answers; responses cannot be criticized; and piggybacking an idea onto someone else's is encouraged.

Brown* v. *Board of Education of Topeka, Kansas a 1954 Supreme Court ruling prohibiting the use of "separate but equal" schools for African American and white students.

cane travel using a long white cane to scan the environment while walking.

caregiver any person who takes care of or raises a child.

cataract a clouding of the lens of the eye.

cerebral palsy a neurological condition resulting from damage to the brain before or during birth or in infancy; it is characterized by disabilities in movement and posture.

chorionic villous sampling (CVS) a prenatal testing technique that analyzes cells from the chorion to determine if certain genetic abnormalities are present.

civil rights movement the 1960s movement for social and political equality for African Americans; it provided a model for activists seeking similar rights for people with disabilities.

classroom discourse strategies ways in which teachers communicate their expectations for learning to students.

Clerc, Laurent 19th-century French man who became the first teacher at the school for deaf children founded by T.H. Gallaudet. Clerc was deaf himself.

closed captioning captions that parallel the verbal content of a television show; they are made visible through decoders built into all television sets manufactured after July 1, 1993, which allow viewers to select captioning of all available programs.

cluster grouping students who are identified as gifted at a given grade level are grouped together in the same classroom with a teacher who has training in educating students who are gifted. The rest of the class is a diverse group of learners.

cochlear implants tiny processors that are surgically implanted in the cochlea and serve to electrically stimulate the auditory nerve fibers and improve perception of sound.

cognitive style the cognitive activity that takes place between the time a student recognizes the need to respond to something and actually does respond; cognitive styles are categorized along a continuum ranging from impulsive to reflective.

collaboration professionals working together with a shared purpose in a supportive, mutually beneficial relationship.

collaborative consultation teachers and other school professionals working together on an equal footing to solve students' problems.

communication the exchange of ideas.

communication disorders a language or speech disorder that adversely affects a child's educational performance.

community-based instruction working on a student's instructional goals in the community setting in which they would naturally be used.

conduct disorder individual disruptive, aggressive, noncompliant behaviors.

conductive hearing loss hearing loss resulting from damage or blockage to the outer or middle ear that disrupts the efficient passage or conduction of sound; most conductive losses can be treated medically.

congenital a condition present at birth.

congenital hearing loss a hearing loss present at birth.

congenital malformation an incomplete or improperly formed part of the skeletal or muscular system that is present at birth.

consultation a means of providing specialized services in the general education classroom whereby the special education teacher observes students with disabilities and provides suggestions to the teacher about adapting instruction or materials to meet students' needs.

consultation model special education resource teacher meets with classroom teachers to plan instructional adaptations for students and provides direct services in the classroom.

content area acceleration a curriculum modification for gifted students that allows students to proceed at a faster pace than their classmates.

contingency intervention curriculum the immediate and distinct presentation of consequences in order to facilitate an understanding of the relationship between actions and their results; this curriculum is used to give infants with severe disabilities the opportunity to develop purposeful behavior and interact with the environment in a meaningful way.

cooperative learning a learning strategy that involves providing small groups of students of various skill levels with a task to complete so that each student makes a significant contribution.

coping strategies things people do to enhance a sense of well-being and avoid being upset by stressful demands.

cornea the transparent outer membrane of the eye.

cortical vision loss vision loss resulting from damage to the brain rather than the eye.

cultural competence a respect for and knowledge of cultural differences and a willingness to accept that there are many ways of viewing the world.

cultural diversity the wide range of cultural characteristics and norms that exist within our society.

cultural reciprocity a two-way process of information sharing and understanding between school professionals and families which can be truly reciprocal and lead to genuine mutual understanding and cooperation.

culture a way of perceiving, believing, evaluating, and behaving shared by a group of people.

curriculum-based assessment (CBA) a method of assessment based on materials in the child's curriculum rather than on a general achievement test.

curriculum telescoping a curriculum modification for gifted students that involves determining what the students already know and allowing them the chance to explore concepts, subjects, or topics that they have yet to learn.

cystic fibrosis a progressive and usually fatal disorder characterized by lung damage, abnormal mucus production, and difficulties in the absorption of protein and fat.

cytomegalovirus (CMV) a relatively common infection that if contracted by a pregnant woman can cause microcephaly, mental retardation, neurological impairments, and hearing loss in the surviving infant.

Deaf community those adults bound together by their deafness, the use of American Sign Language, and their culture, values, and attitudes.

Deaf culture the view of life manifested by the mores, beliefs, artistic expression, and language particular to Deaf people.

deafness a hearing loss that precludes the learning of language through hearing.

deinstitutionalization the movement away from housing people with mental retardation in residential institutions and toward integrating them more fully into the community.

diabetic retinopathy a condition of the eye that can cause blindness; it occurs when the circulation problems associated with diabetes result in damage to the blood vessels of the retina.

diagnostic assessment the gathering of information about a child's developmental levels, usually through observation, interview, and formal testing, to determine whether the child has a disability.

dialect a variation of a spoken language used by a group of individuals that reflects and is determined by shared regional, social, or cultural/ethnic factors.

Diana* v. *Board of Education a 1970 California decision that children must be tested in their primary language when special education placement is being considered.

direct instruction the identification and instruction of specific academic skills and the use of teaching techniques that have been empirically demonstrated to be effective with students with learning difficulties.

disability a limitation, such as difficulty learning to read or inability to see.

discourse shared communication or conversation.

discrepancy the gap between a student's performance in school and his or her intellectual potential.

dog guide a trained dog used to identify obstacles to safe travel.

Down syndrome a condition caused by an extra twenty-first chromosome that results in mental retardation and physical anomalies.

DSM-IV *The Diagnostic and Statistical Manual of Mental Disorders of the American Psychiatric Association*, fourth edition. A classification system for behavior and emotional disorders.

dual diagnosis the coexisting conditions of mental retardation and behavioral disorders.

duration the length of time a behavior lasts.

early intervention a comprehensive set of services provided to children from birth to 3 years and their families designed to minimize the effects of risk status or disability.

echolalia the immediate or delayed repetition of someone else's utterance.

ecocultural theory seeks to explain family adaptations and activities through an understanding of the family's goals, dreams, and beliefs and the reality of the physical, material, and socio-cultural environment in which they live.

Education of the Handicapped Act Amendments of 1990 (P.L. 101-476) amendments to IDEA that require that a formal transition plan be developed for all secondary students identified as having a disability.

educational definitions those definitions of degrees of vision loss focusing on academic functioning and reading medium.

electronic travel devices devices that use sonic waves to detect obstacles in the environment.

enclave a small group of individuals with disabilities who are placed in a work setting, usually within a large business or corporation, and receive on-the-job training from job coaches or social service agencies and from the business itself.

encoding processes processes used to organize information so it can be learned.

enrichment adding disciplines or areas of learning not normally found in the regular curriculum, using more difficult or in-depth material to enhance the core curriculum, or enhancing the teaching strategies used to present instruction.

enrichment triad model (ETM) a program option for upper-elementary gifted children that exposes students to new curricular areas they might wish to explore in greater depth.

environmental analysis *see* environmental inventory.

environmental inventory (environmental analysis) a technique used to identify skills for instruction; it involves a visit to the settings in which the student lives or works so a list can be made of the specific skills needed to be successful in that environment.

environmental risk risk factors related to the environment in which a child develops.

epilepsy a condition of the nervous system that results in seizures that disrupt the normal functioning of the brain.

ethnic minority group an ethnic group that holds a subordinate power position to the majority group.

ethnicity the common history, values, attitudes, and behaviors that bind a group of people.

exceptional the label used to describe the range of students who receive special education services in the school.

exclusion clause the sentence in the federal definition of learning disabilities that excludes from the definition learning problems that are primarily the result of visual, hearing, or motor handicaps, mental retardation, emotional disturbance, or environmental, cultural, or economic disadvantage.

expert consultation the special educator advises the regular educator about the management and instruction of students with special needs.

expressive language The language abilities involved in generating and presenting information.

extended family grandparents, aunts, uncles, cousins, and other relations who may or may not live with a child and parent(s).

externalizing behavior overtly expressed behavior directed toward others or the environment.

eye-gazing scanning system a system that allows an individual to select letters, words, and phrases from a display by simply focusing his or her eyes on the display; a small, sensitive camera detects the direction of the person's eyes and registers the selected elements so a typed message can be produced.

families with multiple risks those families which experience a number of social stressors which place the development of their children in jeopardy.

family two or more people who live together and are related by blood or marriage.

family characteristics the traits, such as size, socioeconomic status, cultural background, and geographic location, that give each family its unique identity.

family configuration the people present in a family.

family functions all the life tasks of the family necessary for meeting family needs, including economic, daily care, recreation, socialization, self-identity, affection, and educational/vocational functions.

family interaction the relationships among family members.

family life cycle the lifespan of a family, starting with the marriage of a man and a woman and evolving through the birth and growth of their children.

family size the number of children in a family.

family systems approach a framework for understanding the family as an interrelated social system with unique characteristics and needs.

fetal alcohol effects the cognitive and behavioral characteristics associated with fetal alcohol syndrome (FAS) without the characteristic physical abnormalities.

fetal alcohol syndrome (FAS) a syndrome resulting from maternal alcohol intake during pregnancy; it is characterized by altered facial features, developmental delays in language and cognition, and behavior problems.

field independent student a student who does well on independent projects and on analytical tests.

field independent teacher a teacher who prefers to use the lecture approach, with limited interactions with students, and who encourages student achievement and competition among students.

field sensitive student a student who performs well in group work and cooperative learning situations.

field sensitive teacher a teacher who prefers to use interpersonal teaching methods, such as personal conversations.

fingerspelling spelling the manual alphabet with the fingers.

first trimester the first three months of pregnancy.

fluency disorder an interruption in the flow of speaking which significantly interferes with communication.

formal assessment using standardized tests to compare a student's performance with that of his or her peers.

fragile X syndrome An inherited disorder, caused by chromosomal abnormalities, that may result in mental retardation, social and communication defictis.

functional academics basic academic skills taught in the context of real-life activities; a curricular emphasis on academic skills that are meaningful and useful for daily living.

functional communication Verbal or nonverbal communication that is efficient, useful, understandable, and easy to use.

functional curriculum a curriculum that emphasizes preparation for life and includes only skills that will be useful to the student in home, community, school, or work environments.

functional vision how well a student uses whatever vision he or she may possess.

Gallaudet, Thomas Hopkins 19th-century minister and educator who was instrumental in starting the first school for deaf children in the United States.

generalization *see* skill transfer.

genetic counseling the process of discussing with a trained counselor the likelihood that a child will inherit a genetic condition.

giftedness high performance capability in intellectual, creative, artistic, leadership, or academic areas.

gifted underachiever the term applied to students whose aptitude is high but whose performance is low.

glaucoma a disease of the eye that can lead to blindness if untreated; it occurs when fluid within the eye cannot drain properly, resulting in a gradual increase of pressure within the eye.

grand mal seizure an epileptic seizure that involves the whole body, usually lasts a few minutes, and often results in a loss of consciousness.

group home a community residence shared by people with disabilities under the guidance of a trained supervisor.

handicap the limitations imposed by the environment of a person with a disability or by people's attitudes toward disability.

hard of hearing a term that describes a hearing loss less severe than deafness that usually permits the understanding of oral speech through the use of hearing aids.

health impairment a term used to describe a condition in which one or more of the body's systems are affected by debilitating or life-threatening conditions or diseases.

health maintenance the assisting of or instruction of a student with a physical disability or health impairment in eating, drinking, or using the bathroom.

hearing impairment a term that refers to all degrees of hearing loss from slight to profound.

hearing loss a term used to describe hearing problems.

highly gifted a term used to designate someone whose IQ score is in the 140+ range.

home- or hospital-based instruction instruction provided by a special education teacher to students with chronic illness or other medical needs; it is usually temporary.

household one or more people, members of a family and others, who live under the same roof.

Howe, Samuel Gridley 19th-century educator and advocate for people with disabilities.

human guide a person, usually sighted, accompanying someone with vision loss while walking.

hydrocephalus a condition in which cerebrospinal fluid builds up in the skull and puts pressure on the brain; if untreated, it can cause brain damage and mental retardation.

hyperglycemia A condition in which individuals with juvenile onset diabetes have high blood sugar, with potentially serious side effects, including unconsciousness and coma.

hypoglycemia A condition in which individuals with juvenile onset diabetes have low blood sugar, with potentially serious side effects including unconsciousness and seizures.

hypoxia decreased availability of oxygen during pregnancy, labor, delivery, or newborn life; it can result in death or brain damage.

immature behavior behavior that exhibits a low level of frustration tolerance and the inability to say and do socially appropriate things.

inclusion the provision of services to students with disabilities in the general education classroom.

independent study a curriculum modification for gifted students that allows them to explore topics of interest to them; the student does require teacher guidance to be sure a manageable topic is selected.

individual supported job model a form of supported employment in which a job coach provides on-site training and problem solving for a single individual; the goal is to gradually decrease the level of support until the individual is ready for independent competitive employment.

individualized education the concept that each student should have a program tailored to his or her unique learning needs.

individualized education program (IEP) the written plan for each student's individual education program.

individualized family service plan (IFSP) a written account of the personal and social services needed to promote and support the child and family for the first three years of an exceptional child's life.

Individuals with Disabilities Education Act (IDEA) the name given in 1990 to what was formerly known as the Education for All Handicapped Children Act, P.L. 94-142 and its amendments.

informal assessment measures of student performance and progress in academic or behavioral tasks; focuses on individual growth and skill acquisition rather than on a comparison of one child's performance with that of others.

informal inventories a series of sequential passages or tasks, on different grade levels, used to assess the specific difficulties a student is having with reading, writing, or math skills.

inoculation vaccination against such infectious diseases as rubella, pertussis, measles, mumps, and polio.

institution a large, segregated, residential building used to house individuals with mental retardation, mental illness, or physical disabilities.

intensity the strength or magnitude of a behavior.

interdisciplinary team a group of professionals from a variety of disciplines who work with a family to plan, coordinate, and deliver services.

intermediate-care facility (ICF) a community-based residential placement comprised of a number of individuals with disabilities living together in a supervised setting.

internalizing behavior self-directed behavior, such as withdrawal, avoidance, or compulsiveness.

iris the colored part of the eye.

Irving Independent School District* v. *Tatro a 1984 U.S. Supreme Court decision that schools must provide medical services that a nonphysician can perform if a child needs them to remain in school.

Itard, Jean-Marc-Gaspard early 19th-century French physician who attempted to teach the "wild boy of Aveyron" to talk.

job coach a person trained in special education who trains people on the job and works with on-site supervisors to help integrate the person with disabilities into the employment setting.

joint attention two or more individuals sharing experiences, activities, or objects.

juvenile onset diabetes a metabolic disorder caused by an insufficient amount of insulin produced by the body, which results in difficulties in digesting and obtaining energy from food; it can appear at any point between birth and age 30.

juvenile rheumatoid arthritis a condition that affects the tissue lining of the joints.

Kennedy, John F. a president with a strong personal interest in improving the quality of life for people with mental retardation.

language the verbal means by which humans communicate.

language delay a delay in the acquisition of normal language milestones.

language disorders the impaired comprehension and/or use of spoken, written, and/or other symbol systems that may involve the form, content, or function of language.

Larry P.* v. *Riles a 1979 California state court decision that IQ tests not be used in placing African American students in classes for students with mental retardation.

learning disability a disorder in one or more of the basic psychological processes involved in understanding or using language. A student who has a learning disability does not achieve at the expected age and ability level in one or more academic areas and shows a severe discrepancy between achievement and intellectual ability.

learning style the way a student approaches learning.

Learning Strategies Curriculum a well-known curriculum developed at the University of Kansas Institute for Research in Learning Disabilities that focuses on strategy instruction.

least restrictive environment the setting that allows each child to be educated with his or her nondisabled peers to the maximum extent appropriate.

legal blindness a visual acuity of 20/200 or worse in the better eye after correction or a visual field of no greater than 20 degrees; this level of visual impairment qualifies a person for a variety of legal and social services.

lens the clear structure between the iris and the tissue inside the eyeball, which focuses light on the retina.

level system an educational program that involves a stepwise progression through a predetermined set of behavioral requirements, restrictions, and responsibilities that allow students to achieve higher levels of freedom and responsibility once they demonstrate appropriate behavior.

life-skills curriculum a course of study intended to provide the skills necessary to enable a student to live and work independently.

low birthweight a weight less than five and a half pounds at birth.

low vision a visual impairment in which there is enough remaining vision to use as the primary source of information.

macroculture the core, or universal, culture of a country; in the United States it is characterized by traits such as individualism, industriousness, ambition, competitiveness, self-reliance, and independence.

Macy, Anne Sullivan teacher and companion of Helen Keller.

mainstreaming the practice of providing children with disabilities an education with their nondisabled peers.

manual communication approach an approach to the teaching of students who are deaf or hard-of-hearing that emphasizes the use of signs and sign language; its basic components are finger spelling and signs.

mediation discussion between families and school districts over a point of disagreement, for the purpose of resolving the disagreement before a due process hearing must be held.

meningitis a serious illness that can cause brain damage and result in a range of disabling conditions such as hearing and vision loss and mental retardation.

mental retardation a mild, moderate, or severe condition that is manifested in childhood and characterized by subaverage intellectual functioning and impairments in adaptive behavior.

mentorship an arrangement whereby a secondary-level student works with a community member to learn a specific skill, trade, or craft.

metacognition "thinking about thinking"; the ability to identify how one learns and to evaluate, monitor, and adapt the learning process.

microculture a subsociety, or subculture, that has its own distinctive cultural patterns while at the same time shares core values with the macroculture.

Mills* v. *Washington, D.C. Board of Education a 1972 decision that required the District of Columbia to provide a free, appropriate public education for students with disabilities.

minority a numerical minority; it also suggests a subordinate position in society.

minority group a group that can be categorized by ethnicity, gender, language, religion, handicap, or socioeconomic status.

mixed hearing loss a hearing loss with both conductive and sensorineural components.

mobile work crew a group of individuals with disabilities who have learned a specific trade or set of skills that can be applied in the community.

mobility the ability to move about in one's environment.

Montessori, Maria early 20th-century Italian physician, teacher, and advocate of children with developmental disabilities; developed method of teaching which is used with typically developing children today.

morphemes the smallest units of meaning in a language.

morphology the rules that govern how word meanings may be changed by adding prefixes, suffixes, and other forms that specifically indicate tense and number.

multiple intelligences Howard Gardner's theory that there are at least eight distinct intelligences. An abundance of talent in any of these areas constitutes giftedness, according to Gardner.

muscular dystrophy a condition in which the voluntary muscles of the body are affected by progressive weakness.

neonatal intensive care unit a specialized unit of the hospital for the care of high-risk newborns.

neonatology the study of high-risk newborns.

nondiscriminatory evaluation evaluation procedures must be conducted with fairness in the child's native language.

normalization an emphasis on conventional or normal behavior and attitudes in all aspects of education, socialization, and other life experiences for people with disabilities.

nystagmus a repetitive, involuntary, rhythmic movement of the eyes common among children with visual impairments.

ophthalmologist a physician who specializes in the treatment of eye diseases.

optic nerve the nerve that connects the eye to the brain.

optician someone who grinds and fits corrective lenses.

optometrist a professional trained to examine eyes, evaluate visual problems, and prescribe corrective lenses.

oral communication approach an approach to the teaching of students who are deaf and hard-of-hearing that emphasizes the development of speech and auditory skills through a combination of speech reading and residual hearing.

organization a cognitive skill that involves the ability to see and use similarities and differences and to categorize, arrange, and plan.

orientation the ability to use one's senses to establish where one is in space and in relation to other objects and people.

otitis media middle ear infection; the most common cause of conductive hearing loss in children.

otologist a physician who specializes in diseases of the ear.

overrepresentation a representation in a specific group or class that is greater than would be expected based on actual population numbers.

parent-to-parent model a model for parent support that links experienced parents of children with disabilities to parents who are new to the programs and processes.

partial participation performing parts of a skill or activity that are in an individual's ability range.

pegwords a word that rhymes with a piece of information to be learned, that is then associated with a picture to assist in remembering.

Pennsylvania Association for Retarded Citizens (PARC)* v. *Commonwealth of Pennsylvania a 1972 state decision that required Pennsylvania to provide a free, appropriate public education for students with mental retardation.

people-first language language that concentrates on describing the person first, then the disability.

perception ability to organize and interpret what one experiences through the senses.

perinatal period the period from the twelfth week of pregnancy to the twenty-eighth day of life.

perinatal stress traumatic events such as difficult or prolonged labor and delivery, hypoxia, low birthweight, or illness that occur during birth or the first twenty-eight days after birth.

pervasive developmental disorders a term given to a collection of developmental disabilities including autism, Asperger's syndrome, and other disorders including autistic-like behavior.

petit mal seizure an epileptic seizure that occurs most frequently in children between the ages of 4 and 12; these seizures are very brief—usually only a few seconds—and although the child may lose consciousness, there may be no observable physical changes.

phoneme the smallest unit of speech.

phonological awareness the ability to recognize the sounds contained in words.

phonological disorders problems with the consistent articulation of phonemes, the individual sounds of speech.

phonology the rules for combining sounds in permissible ways to form words.

physical disability a condition that incapacitates to some degree the skeletal, muscular, and/or neurological systems of the body.

physical handling the moving of a student with a physical disability from place to place.

physically challenged the descriptive term preferred by many people with a physical disability; it describes their physical condition as a challenge to be faced rather than as a handicap.

polysubstance abuser someone who uses a combination of illegal drugs, plus alcohol.

positive behavior support preventive and positive interventions designed to create and maintain a supportive and successful environment.

postlingual deafness deafness that occurs after language is acquired.

postnatal period the period from the twenty-eighth day of life through early childhood.

pragmatic language the ability to use language effectively in different settings and for different purposes.

pragmatics the rules governing language use in differing situations.

predictive validity how accurately a test can predict academic performance.

prelingual deafness deafness that occurs before language is acquired.

premature a baby born before thirty-seven weeks' gestation.

prenatal care the care provided to an expectant mother during pregnancy by her physician, usually an obstetrician.

prenatal period the period from conception to birth.

prereferral intervention team a team of teachers and other professionals that works to keep children in the general education classroom instead of referring them to special education.

preterm *see* premature.

prevalence the number of students within a given special education category.

profound mental retardation a level of retardation characterized by an IQ of less than 20 and deficits in adaptive behavior.

projective test an open-ended test that provides an opportunity for a child to express himself or herself and perhaps reveal evidence of behavioral or emotional trauma.

prompt a cue or guide that helps a student attend to or learn the appropriate material.

Public Law 94-142 a 1975 federal law (known now as the Individuals with Disabilities Education Act, or IDEA) that requires that every child between the ages of 3 and 21 with a disability be provided a free, appropriate public education in the least restrictive environment.

pullout program a service that involves the student leaving the classroom to receive specialized instruction.

pupil the opening in the center of the eye.

quality of life an index of adult performance, adjustment, and happiness.

rate how often a behavior occurs in a given time period.

reading comprehension the ability to understand the meaning of sentences and passages.

receptive language the language abilities involved in understanding and interpreting information.

reciprocal speech using language to give and receive information appropriately.

related services those services, such as speech, adaptive physical education, and others, which the student with disabilities requires in order to benefit from schooling. Related services must be specified on the IEP.

refractive errors myopia, hyperopia, and astigmatism resulting from differences in the shape of the eye.

relational meaning the meaning that goes beyond the individual meanings of words and links word meanings together into topics.

remedial instruction teaching the basic skill or content subject in which a student is having difficulty.

residential school a special school where students live during the school year.

residual hearing the remaining hearing most people with hearing loss possess.

resiliency the ability to resist stress, overcome risk factors, and develop well.

resource room a service that involves students leaving the regular classroom for specialized instruction in academic areas of need.

respite care care given to a family member with a disability by a trained substitute caregiver.

retina a layer of specialized cells at the back of the eye that are highly sensitive to light.

retinitis pigmentosa a hereditary condition of the eye characterized by degeneration of the retina caused by a deposit of pigment in the back of the eye; it is a progressive disease that results in tunnel vision.

retinopathy of prematurity damage to the eye that can cause vision loss in premature infants.

right to due process hearing a procedure to resolve a conflict between a school and family over the evaluation, placement, or program of a child with a disability.

risk factors biological and environmental conditions associated with the increased probability of developmental problems.

rubella also known as German measles; a highly contagious virus that can cause severe damage to the fetus if contracted by a mother in the first sixteen weeks of pregnancy.

scaffolding the guidance an adult or peer provides through verbal communication as a way of doing for the student what the student cannot yet do alone.

screening quick evaluation of large numbers of children for developmental and health problems.

Schoolwide Enrichment Model Joseph Renzulli's model for school change that is based on curriculum modifications and enrichment strategies used with gifted students.

Section 504 of the Rehabilitation Act of 1973 a law requiring that all facilities that receive federal funds be accessible to people with disabilities and prohibiting discrimination against people who are disabled.

Seguin, Edouard 19th-century teacher and advocate for children with mental retardation.

semantics the rules used to create and understand meaning in words and word combinations.

sensorineural hearing loss permanent hearing loss that usually results from damage to the cochlea or auditory nerve.

serious emotional disturbance a condition including one or more of the following characteristics over a long period of time and to a marked degree, which adversely affects educational performance: an inability to learn, an inability to build satisfactory interpersonal relationships, inappropriate types of behavior, a general mood of unhappiness or depression, and a tendency to develop fears associated with personal or school problems.

severe disabilities disabilities that require ongoing support in one or more major life activity, such as mobility, communication, self-care, and learning, in order to participate in integrated community settings and enjoy a quality of life available to people with fewer or no disabilities.

severe mental retardation a level of retardation characterized by an IQ of less than 40 and deficits in adaptive behavior.

sexually transmitted diseases (STDs) diseases spread by sexual intercourse.

sheltered employment contract work conducted in settings designed for individuals with disabilities—usually assembly-line workshops.

sheltered workshops large facilities for people with disabilities that provide simple contract work.

signs manual symbols for a word or concept.

skill transfer (generalization) the ability to apply a specific skill learned in one context to a different context.

Snellen Chart the most common visual screening test; it consists of eight rows of letters, each row smaller in size than the previous one; the person being tested is asked to read the letters with each eye while the other eye is covered. Each row represents the distance at which a person with normal vision can see the letters.

social aging the different roles a person acquires and abandons over the course of the lifespan.

socialized aggression aggressive and disruptive behaviors on the part of a group.

socioeconomic status a measure of a family's social and economic standing based on family income and education and employment of the parents.

special class a class within a regular elementary or high school that groups children by exceptionality; a specialist teacher instructs these students together.

special education the educational program designed to meet the unique learning and developmental needs of exceptional students.

special school a school designed exclusively for students with exceptionalities.

specific language impairment primary difficulty in learning and using language which cannot be attributed to another disability.

speech the spoken part of the language system; it is produced by complex, well-coordinated activity from respiration to phonation to articulation.

speech disorders impairments of articulation, fluency, or voice.

speech-language pathologist the specialist concerned with the identification, assessment, and treatment of students with communication disorders.

spina bifida a midline defect of the skin, spinal column, and spinal cord that occurs during fetal development; it is characterized by varying degrees of paralysis.

stage theory an assumption that changes occur in a predictable order and that movement to the next stage depends on successful resolution of the prior stage.

Stanford-Binet a widely used standardized test of intelligence that places great emphasis on verbal judgments and reasoning.

stereotypic behaviors repetitive, nonharmful behaviors sometimes exhibited by people with severe mental retardation and autism; examples include rocking, twirling of objects, clapping of hands.

strabismus a structural defect associated with the muscles of the eye resulting in the appearance of crossed eyes or wall eyes; the result of this deviation is that the eyes focus on two different things at the same time, leading the brain to suppress one of the images.

strategy instruction an approach to teaching students with learning disabilities that involves first breaking down the skills involved in a task or problem into a set of sequential steps and then preparing the steps so that students may read and later memorize them in order to perform the task correctly.

stuttering the habit of repeating a sound, syllable, or word while speaking, which significantly interferes with communication.

supported employment an employment setting in which a job coach trains a student at the job site, and a support system is established to help the student maintain the job and adjust to new job requirements over time.

syntax rules governing how words may be combined to form sentences.

synthesized speech the storage of words or phrases that can be recalled as needed, or the storage of speech sounds that can be put together to form words using a sound-by-sound process.

talent a mental or physical aptitude or ability.

task analysis the process of breaking down a task or skill into its component parts.

teacher assistance team (intervention assistance team) a group of teachers and other professionals who work together to assist the general education teacher.

team teaching shared instruction of a lesson, a subject area, or an entire instructional program.

telecommunication devices for the deaf (TDDs) telephones with screens and keyboards that allow people who are deaf to communicate with others.

teratogen a substance that can cause birth defects.

Thalidomide a drug prescribed to pregnant women in the 1950s that caused severe birth defects.

total communication the philosophy that advocates the use of whatever communication system is appropriate for a given child with a hearing loss at a given time.

transdisciplinary model an approach to assessment and planning in which professionals with differing specializations work together on an equal footing.

transition movement from one life period or event to another. In special education, the transition most frequently prepared for is that from school to work and adult life.

transition coordinator a person designated by the state, school district, or school to plan, coordinate, and supervise transition services.

transition programs programs designed to facilitate movement from school to work, from segregated to integrated settings, and from isolated living to community living and employment.

traumatic brain injury an acquired injury to the brain caused by an external physical force resulting in total or partial functional disability or psychosocial impairment.

triarchic theory Robert Sternberg's theory which describes three kinds of intelligence: analytic, creative, and practical.

tutorial instruction helping the student in the specific subject in which he or she is having difficulty.

underrepresentation a representation in a specific group or class that is less than would be expected based on actual numbers in the population.

unilateral hearing loss normal hearing in one ear and hearing loss in the other.

verbalism the use of words without concrete knowledge of their meanings.

Vineland Adaptive Behavior Scale one of the most widely used instruments for measuring adaptive behavior.

visual acuity sharpness of vision.

visual impairment a term that describes all levels of vision loss, from total blindness to uncorrectable visual limitations.

vitreous humor liquid-filled "eyeball."

vocational rehabilitation counselor person who assists adolescents and adults with disabilities in making the transition from school to work by helping them plan for post high school education and training, and job placement.

voice disorder any disorder resulting from difficulties in breathing, abnormalities of the larynx, or dysfunctions in the oral and nasal cavities that can affect the pitch, loudness, and/or quality of a voice.

webbing a process that can help focus a child's specific interests within a broad topic by subdividing it into many smaller, manageable subtopics.

Wechsler Intelligence Scale for Children, Third Edition (WISC-III) a test frequently used to predict academic achievement in school-age children.

word analysis the process of identifying written words; it involves the use of phonics, sight words, and context clues.

zero reject the principle that no child with a disability shall be refused an appropriate education by the schools.

References

Abelson, A.G. (1999). Respite care needs of parents of children with developmental disabilities. *Focus on autism and other developmental disabilities, 14* (2), 96–100.

Abuzaitoun, O.R., & Hanson, I.C. (2000). Organ-specific manifestations of HIV disease in children. In Martha F. Rogers (Ed.), *The pediatric clinics of North America, 47*(1), 109–126.

Achenbach, T., & Edelbrock, C. (1979). The child behavior profile II: Boys aged 12–16 and girls aged 6–11 and 12–16. *Journal of Consulting and Clinical Psychology, 47,* 223–233.

Adderhold-Elliott, M. (1987). *Perfectionism: What's bad about being too good?* Minneapolis: Free Spirit.

Adelman, H.S. (1996). Appreciating the classification dilemma. In W. Stainback & S. Stainback (Eds.), *Controversial issues confronting special education: Divergent perspectives* (2d ed.) (pp. 96–111). Boston: Allyn & Bacon.

Agency for Toxic Substances and Disease Registry (1988). *The nature and extent of lead poisoning in children in the United States: A report to Congress.* Washington, DC: U.S. Department of Health and Human Services.

Albert, R.S. (1978). Observations and suggestions regarding giftedness: Familial influences and the achievement of eminence. *Gifted Child Quarterly, 28*(3), 201–211.

Alberto, P.A., & Troutman, A.C. (1990). *Applied behavior analysis for teachers* (3d ed.). Columbus, OH: Merrill.

———. (1999). *Applied Behavior Analysis for teachers* (5th ed.). Columbus, OH: Merrill.

Alessi, S.M., & Trollop, S.R. (2001). *Multimedia for learning: Methods and development* (3rd ed.). Boston: Allyn and Bacon.

Allen, R., & Petr, C.G. (1996). Toward developing standards and measurements for family-centered practice in family support programs. In G.H.S. Singer, L.E. Powers & A.L. Olson (Eds.), *Redefining family support: Innovations in public-private partnerships* (pp. 57–86). Baltimore: Brookes.

Alvino, J. (1989). From the editor. *Gifted Children Monthly, 10*(2), 23.

American College of Medical Genetics. (2001). Statement on guidance for genetic counseling in advanced paternal age. http://www.faseb.org/genetics/acmg/pol-20.htm.

American Printing House for the Blind (2001). *Annual Report.* Louisville, KY: American Printing House for the Blind.

———. (2001, updated). *Distribution of Eligible Students Based on the Federal Quota Census of January 5, 1998. www.aph.org/.*

American Speech-Language-Hearing Association. (1991). The prevention of communication disorders tutorial. *ASHA, 33* (Suppl. 6), 15–41.

———. (1993). Definitions of communication disorders and variations. *ASHA, 35* (Suppl. 10), 40–41.

———. (1997). *Assistive listening devices.* Rockville, MD: American Speech-Language-Hearing Association.

Amish, P.L., Gesten, E.L., Smith, J.K., Clark, H.B., & Stark, C. (1988). Social problem-solving training for severely emotionally and behaviorally disturbed children. *Behavioral Disorders, 13,* 175–186.

Anastasiow, N.J. (1986). The research base for early intervention. *Journal of the Division for Early Childhood, 10,* 99–105.

Anderson, H.R., Bailey, P.A., Cooper, J.S., Palmer, J.C., & West, S. (1983). Morbidity and school absence caused by asthma and wheezing illness. *Archives of Disabled Children, 58,* 777–784.

Angier, N. (1992). *New York Times,* Friday, Dec. 4.

Anthony, T., Bleier, H., Fazzi, D.L., Kish, & Pogrund, R.L. (in press). Movement focus: Orientation and mobility for young children who are blind and visually impaired. In R.L Pogrund, D.L. Fazzi, & Jessica S. Lampert (Eds.), *Early focus: Working with young children who are blind and visually impaired and their families* (2d ed.). New York: American Foundation for the Blind.

Arnold, L., Christopher, J., & Huestis, R. (1978). Megavitamins for minimal brain dysfunction: A placebo-controlled study. *Journal of the American Medical Association, 240,* 2642.

Artiles, A.J., & Trent, S.C. (1994). Overrepresentation of minority students in special education: A continuing debate. *Journal of Special Education, 27,* 410–437.

ASHA (American Speech, Language, and Hearing Association) (1997). *Preventing speech and language disorders.* Rockville, MD: American Speech, Language, and Hearing Association.

ASHA Committee on Language Speech and Hearing Services in the Schools. (1980, April). Definitions for communicative disorders and differences. *ASHA, 22,* 317–318.

Association for Persons with Severe Handicaps. (1989). *TASH resolutions and policy statements.* Seattle, WA: TASH.

Augusto, C. (1996). Foreword. In A.L. Corn & A.J. Koenig (Eds.), *Foundations of low vision: Clinical and functional perspectives* (p. v). New York: AFB Press.

Aune, E. (1991). A transition model for postsecondary-bound students with learning disabilities. *Learning Disabilities Research and Practice, 6,* 177–187.

Aveno, A., & Renzaglia, A. (1988). A survey of attitudes of potential community training site staff toward persons with severe handicaps. *Education and Training in Mental Retardation, 23,* 213–223.

Babyak, A.E., Koorland, M., & Mathes, P.G. (2000). The effects of story mapping instruction on the reading comprehension of students with behavioral disorders. *Behavioral Disorders, 25,* 239–258.

Baer, D. M., Wolf, M.M., & Risley, T. (1968). Current dimensions of applied behavior analysis. *Journal of Applied Behavior Analysis, 1,* 91–97.

Bailey, D.B., Hatton, D.D., Mesibov, G., Ament, N., & Skinner, M. (2000). Early development, temperament, and functional impairment in Autism and Fragile X Syndrome. *Journal of Autism and Developmental Disorders, 30,* 49–59.

Bailey, D.B., Skinner, D., Rodriguez, P., Gut, D., & Correa, V. (1999). Awareness, use, and satisfaction with services for Latino parents of young children with disabilities. *Exceptional Children, 65* (3), 367–381.

Baker, C., & Cokely, D. (1980). *American Sign Language: A teacher's resource on grammar and culture.* Silver Spring, MD: T.J. Publishers.

Baker, R.L., Mednick, B.R., & Hunt, N.A. (1987). Academic and social characteristics of low-birth-weight adolescents. *Social Biology, 34*(1–2), 94–109.

———. (1991). Ethnic and cultural issues. In N. Colangelo & G.A. Davis, *Handbook of gifted education.* Boston: Allyn & Bacon.

Barnard, K.E., & Kelly, J.F. (1990). Assessment of parent-child interaction. In S.J. Meisels & J.P. Shonkoff (Eds.), *Handbook of early childhood intervention* (pp. 278–302). New York: Cambridge University Press.

Barton, D.D. (1984). Uncharted course: Mothering the blind child. *Journal of Visual Impairment and Blindness, 78*(2), 66–69.

Bashir, A.S., & Scavuzzo, A. (1992). Children with language disorders: Natural history and academic success. *Journal of Learning Disabilities, 25,* 53–64.

Batshaw, M.L., & Conlin, C.J. (1997). Substance abuse: A preventable threat to development. In M.L. Batshaw (Ed.), *Children with disabilities* (pp. 143–162). Baltimore: Brookes.

Batshaw, M.L., & Rose, N.C. (1997). Birth defects, prenatal diagnosis, and prenatal therapy. In M.L. Batshaw (Ed.), *Children with disabilities* (pp. 35–52). Baltimore: Brookes.

Beckman, P.J., Frank, N., & Newcomb, S. (1996). Qualities and skills for communicating with families. In P.J. Beckman (Ed.), *Strategies for working with young children with disabilities,* pp.31–46. Baltimore: Paul H. Brookes.

Beckwith, L. (1990). Adaptive and maladaptive parenting: Implications for intervention. In S.J. Meisels & J.P. Shonkoff (Eds.), *Handbook of early childhood intervention.* New York: Cambridge University Press.

Bellefleur, P.A. (1976). TTY communication: Its history and future. *Volta Review, 78*(4), 107–112.

Belman, A.L., Diamond, G., Dickson, D., Horoupian, D., Llena, J., Lantos, G., & Rubenstein, S. (1988). Pediatric acquired immunodeficiency syndrome. *American Journal of Diseases in Children, 142,* 29–35.

Belsky, J., Lang, M.E., & Rovine, M. (1985). Stability and change in marriage across the transition to parenthood: A second study. *Journal of Marriage and the Family, 47,* 855–865.

Benson, H.A. (1989). An investigation of respite care as a mediator of stress in families with members with developmental disabilities. Doctoral dissertation, University of Kansas.

Benz, M.R., Lindstrom, L., & Yovanoff, P. (2000). Improving graduation and employment outcomes of students with disabilities: Predictive factors and student perspectives. *Exceptional Children, 66,* 509–529.

Benz, M.R., Yovanoff, P., & Doren, B. (1997). School-to-work components that predict postschool success for students with and without disabilities. *Exceptional Children, 63,* 151–165.

Bergstrom, L. (1984). Congenital hearing loss. In J.L. Northern (Ed.), *Hearing disorders* (2d ed.). Boston: Little, Brown.

Berko, J. (1958). The child's learning of English morphology. *Word, 14,* 150–177.

Bernbaum, J.C., & Batshaw, M.L. (1997). Born too soon, born too small. In M.L. Batshaw (Ed.), *Children with disabilities* (pp. 115–139). Baltimore: Brookes.

Bernheimer, L.P., & Keogh, B.K.(1995). Weaving assessment into the fabric of everyday life: An approach to family assessment. *Topics in early childhood special education, 15* (4), 415–433.

Bernheimer, L.P., Gallimore, R., & Weisner, T.S. (1990). Ecocultural theory as a context for the Individualized Family Service Plan. *Journal of Early Intervention, 14* (3), 219–233.

Berry, J.O., & Hardman, M.L. (1998). *Lifespan perspectives on the family and disability.* Boston: Allyn & Bacon.

Berry, M.R., Lindstrom, L., & Vovanoff, P. (2000). Improving graduation outcomes of students with disabilities: Predictive factors and student perspectives. *Exceptional Children, 66,* 509–529.

Bettleheim, B. (1967). *The empty fortress: Infantile autism and the birth of the self.* New York: Free Press.

Biederman, G.B., Fairhall, J.L., Raven, K.A., & Davey, V.A. (1998). Verbal prompting, hand-over-hand instruction, and passive observation with developmental disabilities, *Exceptional Children, 64,* 503–511.

Bigge, J. (1991a). Self care. In J. Bigge, *Teaching individuals with physical and multiple disabilities* (3d ed.) (pp. 379–398). New York: Merrill.

———. (1991b). Life management. In J. Bigge, *Teaching individuals with physical and multiple disabilities* (3d ed.) (pp. 399–427). New York: Merrill.

———. (1991c). Augmentative communication. In J. Bigge, *Teaching individuals with physical and multiple disabilities* (3d ed.) (pp. 199–246). New York: Merrill.

———. (1982). *Teaching individuals with physical and multiple disabilities* (2d ed.). Columbus, OH: Merrill.

Bigler, E.D. (1992). The neurobiology and neuropsychology of adult learning disorders. *Journal of Learning Disabilities, 25,* 488–506.

Bireley, M., & Genshaft, J. (1991). *Understanding the gifted adolescent.* New York: Teachers College Press.

Bishop, V.E. (1996). Causes and functional implications of visual impairment. In A.L. Corn & A.J. Koenig (Eds.), *Foundations of low vision: Clinical and functional perspectives* (pp. 86–114). New York: AFB Press.

Blacher, J. (Ed.). (1984). *Severely handicapped young children and their families: Research in review.* Orlando, FL: Academic Press.

Blachman, B.A. (1991a). Getting ready to read: Learning how to print maps of speech. In J.F. Kavanagh (Ed.), *The language continuum: From infancy to literacy* (pp. 41–62). Parkton, MD: York Press.

———. (1991b). Early intervention for children's reading problems: Clinical applications of the research in phonological awareness. *Topics in Language Disorders, 12*(1), 51–65.

Blackburn, J.A. (1987). In M.L. Wolraich (Ed.), *The practical assessment and management of children with disorders of development and learning* (pp. 164–193). Chicago: Yearbook.

Blackhurst, A.E. (1997). Perspectives on technology in special education (1997). *Teaching Exceptional Children, 29*(5), 41–48.

Blatt, B. (1966). *Christmas in purgatory.* Boston: Allyn and Bacon.

Blischak, D.M. (1999). Increases in natural speech production following experience with synthetic speech. *Journal of Special Education Technology, 7*(2), 44–53.

Bloom, B. (Ed.). (1956). *Taxonomy of educational objectives, Handbook I: Cognitive domain.* New York: David McKay.

———. (1985). *Developing talent in young people.* New York: Ballantine.

Bloom, B., Englehart, M., Furst, E., Hill, W., & Krathwohl, D., (1956). *Taxonomy of educational objectives, Handbook 1: Cognitive domain.* New York: McKay.

Bloom, L. (1988). What is language? In M. Lahey (Ed.), *Language disorders and language development* (pp. 1–19). New York: Macmillan.

Bloom, L., & Lahey, M. (1978). *Language development and language disorders.* New York: John Wiley.

Bock, S.J., & Myles, B.S. (1999). An overview of characteristics of Asperger Syndrome. *Education and Training in Mental Retardation and Developmental Disabilties, 34,* 511–520.

Boland, M.G. (2000). Caring for the child and family with HIV disease. In Martha F. Rogers (Ed.), *The pediatric clinics of North America, 47*(1), 189–202.

Bornstein, H. (1990a). A manual communication overview. In H. Bornstein (Ed.), *Manual communication: Implications for education.* Washington, DC: Gallaudet University Press.

———. (1990b). Signed English. In H. Bornstein (Ed.), *Manual communication: Implications for education.* Washington, DC: Gallaudet University Press.

Bowe, F. (1991). *Approaching equality: Education of the deaf.* Silver Springs, MD: TJ Publications.

Brady, N.C., & Halle, J.W. (1997). Functional analysis of communicative behaviors. *Focus on Autism and Other Developmental Disabilities, 12,* 95–104.

Branham, R.S., Collins, B.C., Schuster, J.W., & Kleinert, H. (1999). Teaching community skills to students with moderate disabilties: Comparing combined techniques of classroom simulation, videotape modeling, and community-based instruction. *Education and Training in Mental Retardation and Developmental Disabilities, 34,* 170–181.

Breakthroughs. (1997). Augmentative communication product catalog. Pittsburgh, PA: Sentient Systems Technology, Inc.

Bredekamp, S. (Ed.) (1987). *Developmentally appropriate practice in early childhood programs serving children from birth through age 8.* Washington, DC : National Association for the Education of Young Children.

Bredekamp, S., & Copple, C. (Eds.) (1997). *Developmentally appropriate practice in early childhood programs, revised edition.* Washington, DC : National Association for the Education of Young Children.

Breslau, N., Staruch, K.S., & Mortimer, E.A. (1982). Psychological distress in mothers of disabled children *American Journal of the Disabled Child, 136,* 682–686.

Bricker, D., & Filler, J. (1985). The severely mentally retarded individual: Philosophical and implementation dilemmas. In D. Bricker & J. Filler (Eds.), *Severe mental retardation: From theory to practice* (pp. 2–10). Reston, VA: Division for Mental Retardation of the Council for Exceptional Children.

Brinckerhoff, J.L., & Vincent, L.J. (1986). Increasing parental decision-making at their child's individualized education program meeting. *Journal of the Division for Early Childhood, 11*(1), 46–58.

Brinker, R.P. (1984). The microcomputer as a perceptual tool: Searching for systematic learning strategies with handicapped infants. In R.E. Bennet & C.A. Maher (Eds.), *Microcomputers and exceptional children* (pp. 21–36). New York: Haworth Press.

Brinker, R.P., & Lewis, M. (1982). Making the world work with microcomputers: A learning prosthesis for handicapped infants. *Exceptional Children, 49,* 163–170.

Bronfenbrenner, U. (1979). *The ecology of human development.* Cambridge, MA: Harvard University Press.

———. (1993). Forward. In T. Luster and L. Okagaki (Eds.): *Parenting: An Ecological Perspective.* Hillsdale, NJ: Lawrence Erlbaum.

Brooke, V., Wehman, P., Inge, K., & Parent, W. (1995). Toward a customer-driven approach of supported employment. *Education and Training in Mental Retardation and Developmental Disabilities, 30,* 308–320.

Brooks, P.H., & McCauley, C. (1984). Cognitive research in mental retardation. *American Journal of Mental Deficiency,* 88, 479–486.

Browder, D.M., & Minarovic, T.J. (2000). Utilizing sight words in self-instruction training for employees with moderate mental retardation in competitive jobs. *Education and Training in Mental Retardation and Developmental Disabilities, 35,* 78–89.

Browder, D.M., & Snell, M.E. (1987). Functional academics. In M.E. Snell (Ed.), *Systematic instruction of persons with severe handicaps* (3d ed.) (pp. 436–468). Columbus, OH: Merrill.

Bruns, D.A. (2000). Leaving home at an early age: Parents' decisions about out-of-home placement for young children with complex medical needs. *Mental Retardation, 38,* 50–60.

Bruns, D.A., & Fowler, S.A. (1999). Culturally sensitive transition plans for young children and their families. *Teaching Exceptional Children, 31*(5), 26–30.

Bryan, T. (1991). Social problems and learning disabilities. In B. Wong (Ed.), *Learning about learning disabilities* (pp. 196–231). San Diego: Academic Press.

Bryson, S. (1996). Brief report: Epidemiology of autism. *Journal of Autism and Developmental Disorders, 26,* 165–167.

Buescher, T.M. (1984). Gifted and talented adolescents: Challenging perspectives. *Journal for the Education of the Gifted, 8*(1), 1–8.

Burns, S.M., Griffin, P., Snow, C.E. (1999), (Eds.). *Starting out right: A guide to promoting children's reading success.* Washington, DC: Committee on the Prevention of Reading Difficulties in Young Children, National Research Council.

Buysse, V., Wesley, P.W., Bryant, D., & Gardner, D. (1999). Quality of early childhood programs in inclusive and noninclusive settings. *Exceptional Children, 65,* 301–314.

Bufkin, L.J., & Altman, R. (1995). A developmental study of nonverbal pragmatic communication in students with and without mild mental retardation. *Education and Training in Mental Retardation and Developmental Disabilities, 30,* 199–207.

Burton, B.K., Schulz, C.J., & Burd, L.I. (1992). Limb anomalies associated with chorionic villus sampling. *Obstetrics and Gynecology, 79,* 726–730.

Butterfield, N., & Arthur, M. (1995). Shifting the focus: Emerging priorities in communication programming for students with a severe intellectual disability. *Education and Training in Mental Retardation and Developmental Disabilities, 31,* 41–50.

Caldwell, T., Todaro, A.W., & Gates, A.J. (Eds.). (1988). *Community provider's guide: An information outline for working with children with special needs.* Children's Hospital, New Orleans, LA.

Calvert, D.R. (1986). *Physician's guide to the education of hearing-impaired children.* Washington, DC: Alexander Graham Bell Association for the Deaf.

Campbell, P.H., Bellamy, G.T., & Bishop, K.K. (1988). Statewide intervention systems: An overview of the new federal program for infants and toddlers with handicaps. *Journal of Special Education, 22,* 25–40.

Carlson, C.I. (1987). Social interaction goals and strategies of children with learning disabilities. *Journal of Learning Disabilities, 20,* 306–311.

Carnine, D. (1991). Curricular interventions for teaching higher order thinking to all students: Introduction to the special series. *Journal of Learning Disabilities, 24,* 261–269.

Caro P., & Snell, M.E. (1989). Characteristics of teaching communication to people with moderate and severe disabilities. *Education and Training in Mental Retardation, 24,* 63–77.

Carr, E.G., Levin, L., McConnachie, G., Carlson, J.I., Kemp, D.C., & Smith, C.E. (1998). *Communication-based intervention for problem behavior: A user's guide for producing positive behavior change.* Baltimore: Paul H. Brookes.

Cartledge, G., Kea, C.D., & Ida, D.J. (2000). Anticipating differences–celebrating strengths: Providing culturally competent services for students with serious emotional disturbance. *Teaching Exceptional Children, 32*(3), 30–37.

Cates, D.L., Markell, M.A., & Bettenhausen, S. (1995). At risk for abuse: A teacher's guide for recognizing and reporting child neglect and abuse. *Preventing School Failure, 39*(2), 6–9.

Catts, H.W. (1991a). Early identification of reading disabilities. *Topics in Language Disorders, 12*(1), 1–16.

———. (1991b). Facilitating phonological awareness: Role of speech-language pathologists. *Language, Speech, and Hearing Services in Schools, 22,* 196–203.

Cawley, J.F., Parmar, R.S., Yan, W.F., & Miller, J.H. (1996). Arithmetic computation abilities of students with learning disabilities: Implications for instruction. *Learning Disabilities Research and Practice, 1,* 230–237.

Cazden, C.B. (1988). *Classroom discourse: The language of teaching and learning.* Portsmouth, NH: Heinemann.

Chan, S. (1986). Parents of exceptional Asian children. In M.K. Kitano & P.C. Chinn (Eds.), *Exceptional Asian children and youth* (pp. 36–53). Reston, VA: The Council for Exceptional Children.

Chandler, L.K., Dahlquist, C.M., Repp, A.C., & Feltz, C. (1999). The effects of team-based functional assessment on the behavior of students in classroom settings. *Exceptional Children, 66,* 101–122.

Chapman, R.S., Streim, N.W., Crais, E.R., Salmon, D., Strand, C.A., & Negri, N.A. (1992). Child talk: Assumptions of a developmental process model for early language learning. In R.S. Chapman (Ed.), *Processes in language acquisition and disorders* (pp. 3–19). St. Louis: Mosby Year-Book.

Chedd, N.A. (1995). Genetic counseling. *Exceptional Parent, 25*(8), 26–27.

Chen, D.(Ed.)(1999). *Essential elements in early intervention: Visual impairment and multiple disabilities.* New York: American Foundation for the Blind.

Chen, D., & Dote-Kwan, J. (1995). *Starting points: Instructional practices for young children whose multiple disabilities include visual impairment.* Los Angeles: Blind Children's Center.

Cheng, A.K., & Niparko, J.K.(2000). Analyzing the effects of early implantation and results with different causes of deafness: Meta-analysis of the pediatric cochlear implant literature. In J.K., Niparko, K.I., Kirk, N.K., Mellon, A.M., Robbins, D.L., Tucci, & B.S. Wilson (Eds.), *Cochlear implants: Principles and practices* (pp.259–265). Philadelphia: Lippincott Williams & Wilkins.

Cheng, I. (1987). Cross-cultural and linguistic considerations in working with Asian populations, *ASHA 29*(6), 33–38.

Chez, M.G., Buchanan, C.P., Bagan, B.T., Hammer, M.S., McCarthy, K.S., Ovrutskaya, I., Nowinski, C.V., & Cohen, Z.S. (2000). Secretin and Autism: A two-part clinical investigation. *Journal of Autism and Developmental Disorders, 30,* 87–94.

Children's Defense Fund. (2000). *The state of America's children yearbook.* Washington, DC: Children's Defense Fund.

Christensen, K.M. (1993). A multicultural approach to education of children who are deaf. In K.M. Christensen & G.L. Delgado (Eds.), *Multicultural issues in deafness.* White Plains, NY: Longman.

Clark, B. (1997). *Growing up gifted* (5th ed.). Upper Saddle River, NJ: Merrill.

Clark, W., & Hankins, N. (1985). Giftedness and conflict. *Roeper Review, 8,* 50–53.

Clement-Heist, K., Siegel, S., & Gaylord-Ross, R. (1992). Simulated and in-situ vocational social skills training for youths with learning disabilities. *Exceptional Children, 58,* 336–345.

Cline, B.V., & Billingsley, B.S. (1991). Teachers' and supervisors' perceptions of secondary learning disabilities programs: A multi-state survey. *Learning Disabilities Research and Practice, 6,* 158–165.

Cohen, O. (1994). Replacing myths about deafness. In R.C. Johnson & O.P. Cohen (Eds.), *Implications and complications for deaf students of the full inclusion movement* (Gallaudet Research Institute Occasional Paper 94-2). Washington, DC: Gallaudet University.

Cohen, S.E., & Parmalee, A.H. (1983). Prediction of five-year Stanford-Binet scores in preterm infants. *Child Development, 54,* 1242–1253.

Colangelo, N. (1989). Moral dilemmas as formulated by gifted students. *Understanding Our Gifted, 1*(6), 10–12.

Coleman, M., & Vaughn, S. (2000). Reading interventions for students with emotional/behavioral disorders. *Behavioral Disorders, 25,* 93–104.

Coles, R. (1977). *Children of crisis: Vol. IV. Eskimos, Chicanos, Indians.* Boston: Little, Brown.

Connor, L.E. (1986). Oralism in perspective. In D.M. Luterman (Ed.), *Deafness in perspective* (pp. 117–129). San Diego: College-Hill.

Conture, E.G. (1990). *Stuttering* (2d ed.). Englewood Cliffs, NJ: Prentice-Hall.

Cook, A.M., & Cavalier, A.R. (1999). Young children using assistive robotics for discovery and control. *Teaching Exceptional Children, 31*(5), 72–78.

Cook, B.G., & Semmel, M.I. (1999). Peer acceptance of included students with disabilities as a function of severity of disability and classroom composition. *Journal of Special Education, 33,* 50–61.

Cook, B.G., Tankersley, M., Cook, L., & Landrum, T.J. (2000). Teachers' attitudes toward their included students with disabilities. *Exceptional Children, 67,* 115–135.

Cook, P.S., Petersen, R.C., & Moore, D.T. (1990). *Alcohol, tobacco, and other drugs may harm the unborn.* Rockville, MD: Office for Substance Abuse Prevention, U.S. Department of Health and Human Services.

Cook, R.E., Tessier, A., & Klein, M.D. (2000). *Adapting early childhood curricula for children in inclusive settings* (5th ed.). Englewood Cliffs, NJ: Merrill.

Cooper, J.O., Heron, T.E., & Heward, W.L. (1987). *Applied Behavior Analysis.* UpperSaddle River, NJ: Merril.

Corbet, E.B. (1980). Elmer Bartels. *Options: Spinal cord injury and the future* (pp. 145–147). Denver: Hirschfield Press.

Corn, A.L, DePriest, L.B., & Erin, J.N. (2000). Visual efficiency. In A.J. Koenig and M.C. Holbrook (Eds.), *Foundations of Education: Vol. II* (2d ed., pp.464–499). New York: American Foundation for the Blind.

Cott, A. (1972). Megavitamins: The orthomolecular approach to behavioral disorders and learning disabilities. *Academic Therapy, 7,* 245–257.

Council for Exceptional Children. (1990). Americans with Disabilities Act of 1990: What should you know? *Exceptional Children, 57,* Supplement.

———. (1997). *CEC policy manual: Basic commitments and responsibilities to exceptional children.* http://www.cec.specl.org/pp/policies/ch3. htm#35.

Cox, J., Daniel, N., & Boston, B. (1985). *Educating able learners: Programs and promising practices.* Austin: University of Texas Press.

Craig, S., Hull, K., Haggart, A.G., & Perez-Selles, M. (2000). Promoting cultural competence through teacher assistance teams. *Teaching Exceptional Children, 32*(7), 6–12.

Crittenden, J.B. (1993). The culture and identity of deafness. In P.V. Paul & D.W. Jackson, *Toward a psychology of deafness.* Boston: Allyn & Bacon.

Cronin, M.G., & Patton, J.R. (1993). *Life skills instruction for all students with special needs: A practical guide for integrating real-life content into curriculum* (pp. 5–6, 57, 63–65). Austin, TX: Pro-Ed.

Cullinan, D., Epstein, M.H. & Sabornie, E.J. (1992). Selected characteristics of a national sample of seriously emotionally disturbed adolescents. *Behavioral Disorders, 17,* 273–280.

Cutsforth, T.D. (1932). The unreality of words to the blind. *Teachers Forum, 4,* 86–89.

———. (1951). *The blind in school and society.* New York: American Foundation for the Blind.

Damico, J.S., & Simon, C.S. (1993). Assessing language abilities in school-age children. In A. Gerber (Ed.), *Language-related learning disabilities: Their nature and treatment* (pp. 279–299). Baltimore: Brookes.

Daniels, V.I., & Vaughn, S. (1999). A tool to encourage "Best Practice" in full inclusion. *Teaching Exceptional Children, 31(5),* 48–55.

Davidovitch, M., Glick, L., Holtzman, G., Tirosh, E., & Safir, M.P. (2000). Developmental regression in Autism: Maternal perception. *Journal of Autism and Developmental Disorders, 30,* 113–119.

Dawson, G., & Osterling, J. (1997). Early intervention in autism. In M.J.Guralnick (Ed.), *The effectivenesss of early intervention.* Baltimore: Brookes.

Dawson, L., Venn, M.L., & Gunter, P.L. (2000). The effects of teacher versus computer reading models. *Behavioral Disorders, 25,* 105–113.

Deford, F. (1983). *Alex: The life of a child.* New York: Viking Press.

De La Paz, S., & Graham, S. (1997). Strategy instruction in planning: Effects on the writing performance and behavior of students with learning difficulties. *Exceptional Children, 63,* 167–181.

De La Paz, S., Owen, B., Harris, K.R., & Graham, S. (2000). Riding Elvis' motorcycle: Using self-regulated strategy development to PLAN and WRITE for a state writing exam. *Learning Disabilities Research and Practice, 15,* 101–109.

DeFries, J.C., Gillis, J.J., & Wadsworth, S.J. (1993). Genes and genders: A twin study of reading disability. In A.M. Galaburda (Ed.), *Dyslexia and development: Neurological aspects of extra-ordinary brains* (pp.187–204). Cambridge, MA: Harvard University Press.

Delisle, J.R. (1984). *Gifted children speak out.* New York: Walker.

———. (1992). *Kidstories: Biographies of twenty young people you'd like to know.* Minneapolis: Free Spirit.

———. (2000). *Once upon a mind: The stories and scholars of gifted child education.* Fort Worth: Harcourt Brace College Publishers.

Denhoff, E. (1976). Medical aspects. In W.M. Cruickshank (Ed.), *Cerebral palsy, a developmental disability* (3d ed.) (pp. 29–72). Syracuse: Syracuse University Press.

Denning, C.B., Chamberlain, J.A., & Polloway, E.A. (2000). Guidelines for Mental Retardation: Focus on definition and classification practices. *Education and Training in Mental Retardation and Developmental Disabilities, 35,* 226–232.

Dennis, R.E., Williams, W., Giangreco, M.F., & Cloninger, C.J. (1993). Quality of life as context for planning and evaluation of services for people with disabilities. *Exceptional Children, 59,* 499–512.

DePaepe, P.A., Shores, R.E., Jack, S.L., & Denny, R.K. (1996). Effects of task difficulty on the disruptive and on-task behavior of students with severe behavior disorders. *Behavioral Disorders, 21,* 216–225.

Department of Education. (1992). Deaf students education services: Policy guidance. *Federal Register, 57*(211). (Friday, October 30, 1992): 49274–49276.

Deshler, D.D., Warner, M.M., Schumaker, J.B., & Alley, G.R. (1983). Learning strategies intervention model: Key components and current status. In J.D. McKinney & L. Feagans (Eds.), *Current topics in learning disabilities.* Norwood, NJ: Ablex.

Dettmer, P., Thurston, L.P., & Dyck, N. (1993). *Consultation, collaboration, and teamwork for students with special needs* (pp. 1–35). Boston: Allyn & Bacon.

Devlieger, P.J., & Trach, J.S. (1999). Mediation as a transition process: The impact on postschool employment outcomes. *Exceptional Children, 65,* 507–523.

Devlin, S.D., & Elliott, R.N. (1992). Drug use patterns of adolescents with behavioral disorders. *Behavioral Disorders, 17,* 264–272.

Dew, N. (1984). The exceptional bilingual child: Demography. In P. Chinn (Ed.), *Education of culturally and linguistically different exceptional children* (pp. 1–41). Reston, VA: The Council for Exceptional Children.

Diagnostic and Statistical Manual of Mental Disorders (4th ed.) (1994). Washington, DC: American Psychiatric Association.

Dickey, R., & Shealy, S.H. (1987). Using technology to control the environment. *American Journal of Occupational Therapy, 41*(11), 717–721.

Dingle, M., & Hunt, N. (2001). Home Literacy Practices of Latino Parents of First Graders. Paper presented at the American Educational Research Association Annual Meeting, Seattle.

Disability Services: webmaster@disserv.stu.umn.edu.

Dixson, B. (1989). *Environmental effects on fetal development.* Sacramento: California State Department of Education.

Doren, B., Bullis, M., & Benz, M.R. (1996). Predicting the arrest status of adolescents with disabilities in transition. *Journal of Special Education, 29,* 363–380.

Dorris, M. (1989). *The broken cord.* New York: Harper Perennial.

Drasgow, E. (1998). American sign language as a pathway to linguistic competence. *Exceptional Children, 64*(3).

Dunlap, G., & Childs, K.E. (1996). Intervention research in emotional and behavioral disorders: An analysis of studies from 1980–1993. *Behavioral Disorders, 21,* 125–136.

Dunn, L.M. (1968). Special education for the mildly retarded: Is much of it justifiable? *Exceptional Children, 35,* 5–22.

Dunst, C.J. (1993). Implication of risk and opportunity factors for assessment and intervention practices. *Topics in Early Childhood Education, 13*(2), 143–153.

DuPaul, G.J., & Barkley, R.A. (1990). Medication therapy. In R.A. Barkley, *Attention deficit hyperactivity disorder: A handbook for diagnosis and treatment* (pp. 573–612). New York: Guilford Press.

Durand, V.M., & Carr, E.G. (1985). Self-injurious behavior: Motivating conditions and guidelines for treatment. *School Psychology Review, 14,* 171–176.

Dykens, E., & Volkmar, F.R. (1997). Medical conditions associated with autism. In D.J. Cohen & F.R. Volkmar (Eds.), *Handbook of autism and pervasive developmental disorders* (2nd. ed., pp. 388–410). New York: Wiley.

Eby, J.W., & Smutny, J.F. (1990). *A thoughtful overview of gifted education.* New York: Longman.

Eccarius, M. (1997). *Educating children who are deaf or hard of hearing: Assessment.* ERIC Digest (EDO-EC-96-5). Reston, VA: ERIC Clearinghouse on Disabilities and Gifted Education.

Eddy, J.M., Reid, J.B., & Fetrow, R.A. (2000). An elementary school-based prevention program targeting modifiable antecedents of youth delinquency and violence: Linking the Interests of Families and Teachers (LIFT). *Journal of Emotional and Behavioral Disorders, 8,* 165–176.

Edgar, E. (1988). Employment as an outcome for mildly handicapped students: Current status and future directions. *Focus on Exceptional Children, 2*(1), 1–8.

Edgerton, R.B. (1967). *The cloak of competence: Stigma in the lives of mentally retarded.* Berkeley: University of California Press.

Edgerton, R.B., Bollinger, M., & Herr, B. (1984). The cloak of competence: After two decades. *American Journal of Mental Deficiency, 88,* 345–351.

Ehlers, S., & Gillberg, C. (1993). The epidemiology of Asperger Syndrome: A total population study. *Journal of Child Psychology and Psychiatry, 34,* 1327–1350.

Ehren, B. J.(2000). Maintaining a therapeutic focus and sharing responsibility for student success: Keys to in-classroom speech-language services. *Language, Speech, and Hearing Services in Schools, 31* (3), 219–229.

Ehri, L.C. (1989). Movement into word reading and spelling. In J.M. Mason (Ed.), *Reading and writing connections* (pp. 65–81). Boston: Allyn & Bacon.

Ehrlich, M.I. (1983). Psychofamilial correlates of school disorders. *Journal of School Psychology, 21,* 191–199.

Ellis, E.S., Sabornie, E.J., & Marshall, K.J. (1989). Teaching learning strategies to learning disabled students in postsecondary settings. *Academic Therapy, 24,* 491–501.

Eng, T.R., & Butler, W.T. (Eds.).(1997). *The hidden epidemic: Confronting sexually transmitted diseases.* Committee on Prevention and Control of Sexually Transmitted Diseases, Institute of Medicine, Division of Health Promotion and Disease Prevention. Washington, DC: National Academy Press.

Engelmann, S., & Bruner, E. (1988). *Reading Mastery Fast Cycle.* Chicago: Science Research Associates.

Engelmann, S., & Carnine, D. (1982). *Corrective mathematics program.* Chicago: Science Research Associates.

Engelmann, S., Carnine, L., & Johnson, G. (1988). *Word-Attack Basics: Decoding A.* Chicago: Science Research Associates.

Engelmann, S., Carnine, D., & Steely, D.G. (1991). Making connections in mathematics. *Journal of Learning Disabilities, 24,* 292–303.

Engelmann, S., & Hanner, S. (1982). *Reading mastery, level III: A direct instruction program.* Chicago: Science Research Associates.

Engelmann, S., Johnson, G., Hanner, S., Carnine, L., Meyers, S., Becker, W., & Eisele, J. (1988). *Corrective reading: Decoding strategies.* Chicago: Science Research Associates.

English, K., & Church, G. (1999). Unilateral hearing loss in children: An update for the 1990s. *Language, Speech, and Hearing Services in Schools, 30,* (1), 26–31.

Ennis, R.H. (1985). A logical basis for measuring critical thinking skills. *Educational Leadership, 43*(2), 44–48.

Epstein, M.H., Kinder, D., & Bursuck, B. (1989). The academic status of adolescents with behavioral disorders. *Behavioral Disorders, 14,* 157–165.

Epstein, M.H., Polloway, E.A., Patton, J.R., & Foley, R. (1989). Mild retardation: Student characteristics and services. *Education and Training in Mental Retardation, 24,* 7–16.

Erikson, E.H. (1968). *Identity: Youth and crisis.* New York: Norton.

Erin, J.N. (1996). Functional vision assessment and instruction of children and youths with multiple disabilities. In A.L. Corn & A.J. Koenig (Eds.), *Foundations of low vision: Clinical and functional perspectives* (pp. 221–245). New York: AFB Press.

Erin, J.N., & Paul, B. (1996). Functional vision assessment and instruction of children and youths in academic programs. In A.L. Corn & A.J. Koenig (Eds.), *Foundations of low vision: Clinical and functional perspectives* (pp. 185–220). New York: AFB Press.

Espin, C.A., Deno, S.L., & Albayrak-Kaymak, D. (1998). Individualized Education Programs in resource and inclusive settings: How "individualized" are they? *Journal of Special Education, 32,* 164–174.

Executive Committee of the Council for Children with Behavioral Disorders. (1989). White paper on best assessment practices for students with behavioral disorders: Accommodation to cultural diversity and individual differences. *Behavioral Disorders, 14,* 263–278.

Fahey & D.K. Reid (Eds.) *Language development, differences, and disorders,* pp.219-244. Austin, TX: Pro-Ed.

Falk, G.D., Dunlap, G., & Kern, L. (1996). An analysis of self-evaluation and videotape feedback for improving the peer interactions of students with externalizing and internalizing behavior problems. *Behavioral Disorders, 21,* 261–276.

Falvey, M. (1995). *Inclusive and heterogeneous schooling.* Baltimore: Brookes.

Featherstone, H. (1980). *A difference in the family: Life with a disabled child.* New York: Basic Books.

Federal Register. (1992). Washington, DC: U.S. Government Printing Office, September 29.

Feil, E.G., Walker, H., Severson, H., & Ball, A. (2000). Proactive screening for emotional/behavioral concerns in Head Start preschools: Promising practices and challenges in applied research. *Behavioral Disorders, 26,* 13–25.

Feingold, B.F. (1975). Hyperkinesis and learning disabilities linked to artificial food flavors and colors. *American Journal of Nursing, 75,* 797–803.

Feldhusen, J.F. (1991). Saturday and summer programs. In N. Colangelo & G.A. Davis (Eds.), *Handbook of gifted education* (pp. 197–208). Boston: Allyn & Bacon.

Feldman, W. (1996). Chronic illness in children. In R.H.A. Haslam & P.J. Valletutti (Eds.), *Medical problems in the classroom: The teacher's role in diagnosis and management* (3rd ed., pp. 115–123). Austin, TX: Pro-Ed.

Felko, K.S., Schuster, J.W., Harley, D.A., & Collins, B.C. (1999). Using simultaneous prompting to teach a chained vocational task to young adults with severe intellectual disabilities. *Education and Training in Mental Retardation and Developmental Disabilities, 34,* 318–329.

Ferguson, D.L. (1987). *Curriculum decision making for students with severe handicaps: Policy and practice.* New York: Teachers College Press.

Ferrell, K.A. (1985). *Reach out and teach.* New York: American Foundation for the Blind.

———. (1986). Infancy and early childhood. In G.T. Scholl (Ed.), *Foundations of education for blind and visually handicapped children and youth: Theory and practice.* New York: American Foundation for the Blind.

———. (2000). Growth and development of young children. In M.C. Holbrook and A.J. Koenig (Eds.), *Foundations of Education: Vol.1* (2d ed., pp.111–134). New York: American Foundation for the Blind.

Ferrell, K.A., Shaw, A.R., & Dietz, S.J.(1998). *Project PRISM: A longitudinal study of developmental patterns of children who are visually impaired.* (Final Report, CFDA 84.023C, Grant HO23C10188). Greeley: University of Northern Colorado, Division of Special Education.

Figueroa, R.A., Fradd, S.H., & Correa, V.I. (1989). Bilingual special education and this special issue. *Exceptional Children, 56*(2), 174–178.

Finesmith, R.B., Zampella, E., & Devinsky, O. (1999). Vagal nerve stimulator: A new approach to medically refractory epilepsy. *National Journal of Medicine, 96*(6), 37–40.

Fitzsimmons, M. K. & Hunt, N. (1998). *Beginning Reading.* ERIC/OSEP Digest No. #565.

Flexer, C. (1994). *Facilitating hearing and listening in young children.* San Diego: Singular.

Foorman, B.R., Francis, D.J., Fletcher, J.M., Schatschneider, C., & Mehta, P. (1998). The role of instruction in learning to read: Preventing reading failure in at-risk children. *Journal of Educational Psychology, 90,* 37–55.

Ford, A., Schnorr, R., Meyer, L., Davern, L., Black, J., & Dempsey, P. (1989). General community functioning. In A. Ford, R. Schnorr, L. Meyer, L. Davern, J. Black, & P. Dempsey (Eds.), *The Syracuse community-referenced curriculum guide for students with moderate and severe disabilities* (pp. 77–88). Baltimore: Brookes.

Forness, S.R. (1988). Planning for the needs of children with serious emotional disturbance: The national special education and mental health coalition. *Behavioral Disorders, 13,* 127–139.

Forness, S.R., & Knitzer, J. (1990). A new proposed definition and terminology to replace 'Serious Emotional Disturbance' in Education of the Handicapped Act. Workgroup on Definition, the National Mental Health and Special Education Coalition, National Mental Health Association.

Forness, S.R., Sweeney, D.P., & Toy, K. (1996). Psychopharmacologic medication: What teachers need to know. *Beyond Behavior, 7*(2), 4–11.

Fowler, M. (1995). *Maybe you know my kid.* New York: Carol Publishing Group.

Frank, A.R., & Sitlington, P.L. (2000). Young adults with mental disabilities: Does transition planning make a difference? *Education and Training in Mental Retardation and Developmental Disabilities, 35,* 119–134.

Frankenberger, W., & Fronzaglio, K. (1991). A review of states' criteria and procedures for identifying children with learning disabilities. *Journal of Learning Disabilities, 24,* 495–500.

Fraser, B., Hensinger, R.N., & Phelps, J. (1990). *Physical management of multiple handicaps.* Baltimore: Brookes.

———. (1987). The identification of gifted black students: Developing new perspectives. *Journal for the Education of the Gifted, 10*(3), 155–180.

Frey, K.S., Hirschstein, M.K., & Guzzo, B.A. (2000). Second step: Preventing aggression by promoting social competence. *Journal of Emotional and Behavioral Disorders, 8,* 102–112.

Friedman, H.S., Tucker, J.S., Schwartz, J.E., Tomlinson-Keasey, C., Martin, L.R., Wingard, D.L., & Criqui, M.H. (1995). Psychosocial and behavioral predictors of longevity: The aging and death of the "Termites." *American Psychologist, 50*(2), 69–78.

Friedrich, O. (1983, August). What do babies know? *Time,* pp. 70–76.

Friend, M. (1996). *The Power of 2: Making a difference through co-teaching.* Bloomington, IN: Indiana University Press.

Friend, M., & Bursuck, W. (1996). *Including students with special needs.* Boston: Allyn & Bacon.

Friend, M., & Cook, L. (1996). Collaboration as a predictor for success in school reform. *Journal of Educational and Psychological Consultation, 1*(1), 69–86.

———. (1996). *Interactions: Collaboration skills for school professionals.* White Plains, NY: Longman.

———. (2000). *Interactions: Collaboration skills for school professionals* (third ed.). New York: Longman.

Frishberg, N. (1986). *Interpreting: An introduction.* Silver Spring, MD: RID Publications.

Fuchs, D., Fuchs, L., & Burish, P. (2000). Peer-Assisted Learning Strategies: An evidence-based practice to promote reading achievement. *Learning Disabilities Research and Practice, 15,* 85–91.

Fuchs, D., Fuchs, L.S., Mathes, P.G., & Simmons, D. C. (1997). Peer-assisted learning strategies: Making classrooms more responsive to diversity. *American Educational Research Journal, 34,* 174–206.

Furlong, M., & Morrison, G. (2000). The school in school violence: Definitions and facts. *Journal of Emotional and Behavioral Disorders, 8,* 71–82.

Gable, R.A., Hendrickson, J.M., Warren, S.F., Evans, W.H., & Evans, S.S. (1988). The promise and pitfalls of an ecological perspective on children's behavioral disorders. In R.B. Rutherford, Jr. & J.W. Maag (Eds.), *Monograph in Behavioral Disorders: Severe Behavioral Disorders of Children and Youth, 11,* 156–166.

Gajar, A. (1992). Adults with learning disabilities: Current and future research priorities. *Journal of Learning Disabilities, 25,* 507–519.

Gajira, M., & Salvia, J. (1992). The effects of summarization instruction on text comprehension of students with learning disabilities. *Exceptional Children, 58,* 508–516.

Garbarino, J. (1990). The human ecology of early risk. In S.J. Meisels & J.P. Shonkoff (Eds.), *Handbook of early childhood intervention.* Cambridge: Cambridge University Press.

Garbarino, James. (1997). Educating children in a socially toxic environment. *Educational Leadership, 54*(7), 12–16.

Gardill, M.C., & Jitendra, A.K. (1999). Advanced story map instruction: Effects on the reading comprehension of students with learning disabilities. *Journal of Special Education, 33,* 2–17, 28.

Gardner, H. (1983). *Frames of mind.* New York: Basic Books.

———. (2000). The giftedness matrix: A developmental perspective. In R.C. Friedman & B.M. Shore (Eds.), *Talents unfolding: Cognition and development*, pp.77–88. Washington DC: American Psychological Association.

Gardner, J.E., & Edyburn, D.L. (2000). Integrating technology to support effective instruction. In J.D. Linsey (Ed.). *Technology and exceptional individuals* (3rd ed.). Austin, TX: Pro-Ed.

Garretson, M.D. (1976). Total communication. *Volta Review, 78*(4), 107–112.

Gartin, B.C., Rumrill, P., & Serebreni, R. (1996). The higher education transition model: Guidelines for facilitating college transition among college-bound students with disabilities. *Teaching Exceptional Children, 29*(1), 30–33.

Gaunt, R.I. (1989). A comparison of the perceptions of parents of highly and moderately gifted children. Doctoral dissertation, Kent State University. *Dissertation Abstracts International, 50,* A.

Gee, J.P.(1990). *Social linguistics and literacies: Ideology in discourse.* Bristol, PA: Falmer Press.

Gelfand, D.M., Jenson, W.R., & Drew, C.J. (1988). *Understanding child behavior disorders* (2d ed.). New York: Holt, Rinehart & Winston.

Gentry, D., & Olson, J. (1985). Severely mentally retarded young children. In D. Bricker & J. Fuller (Eds.), *Severe mental retardation: From theory to practice* (pp. 50–75). Reston, VA: Division on Mental Retardation of the Council for Exceptional Children.

George, P.S. (1988). Tracking and ability grouping—which way for the middle school? *Middle School Journal* (Sept.), 21–28.

Gerber, A. (1993). Interdisciplinary language intervention in education. In A. Gerber (Ed.), *Language-related learning disabilities: Their nature and treatment* (pp. 301–322). Baltimore: Brookes.

Gerber, P.J., Ginsberg, R., & Reiff, H.B. (1992). Identifying alterable patterns in employment success for highly successful adults with learning disabilities. *Journal of Learning Disabilities, 25,* 475–487.

Gersten, R., & Baker, S. (2000).What we know about effective instructional practices for English-language learners. *Exceptional children, 66* (4), 454–470.

Getch, Y.Q., & Neuharth-Pritchett, S. (1999). Children with asthma: Strategies for educators. *Teaching Exceptional Children, 31*(3), 30–36.

Giangreco, M.F., Edelman, S.W., Luiselli, T.E., & MacFarland, S.Z.C. (1997). Helping or hovering? Effects of instructional assistant proximity on students with disabilities. *Exceptional Children, 64,* 7–18.

Gibbs, D.P., & Cooper, E.B. (1989). Prevalence of communication disorders in students with learning disabilities. *Journal of Learning Disabilities, 22,* 60–63.

Glassberg, L.A., Hooper, S.R., & Mattison, R.E. (1999). Prevalence of learning disabilities at enrollment in special education students with behavioral disorders. *Behavioral Disorders, 25,* 9–21.

Goldberg, S. (1987). *Ophthalmology made ridiculously simple.* Miami, FL: MedMaster.

Gollnick, D.M., & Chinn, P.C. (1998). *Multicultural education in a pluralistic society* (5th ed.). Columbus, OH: Macmillan.

Goodenough, N. (1987). Multi-culturalism as the normal human experience. In E.M. Eddy & W.L. Partridge (Eds.), *Applied anthropology in America* (2d ed.). New York: Columbia University Press.

Gorski, P.A., & VandenBerg, K.A. (1996). Infants born at risk. In M.J. Hanson (Ed.), *Atypical infant development* (2d ed.) (pp. 85–114). Austin, TX: Pro-Ed.

Gould, S.J. (1981). *The mismeasure of man.* New York: Norton.

Graden, J.L. (1989). Redefining "prereferral" intervention as intervention assistance: Collaboration between general and special education. *Exceptional Children, 56*(3), 227–231.

Graham, E.M., & Morgan, M.A. (1997). Growth before birth. In M.L. Batshaw (Ed.), *Children with disabilities* (pp. 53–69). Baltimore: Brookes.

Graves, D.H. (1983). *Writing: Teachers and children at work.* Exeter, NH: Heinemann.

Green, C.W., & Reid, D.H. (1999). Reducing indices of unhappiness among individuals with profound multiple disabilities during therapeutic exercise routines. *Journal of Applied Behavior Analysis, 32,* 137–147.

Green, G. (1996). Evaluating claims about treatments for Autism. In C. Maurice, G. Green, & S.C. Luce, S. (Eds.), *Behavioral intervention for young children with autism: A manual for parents and professionals* (pp. 15–28). Austin, TX: Pro-Ed.

Greenbaum, B., Graham, S., & Scales, W. (1995). Adults with learning disabilities: Educational and social experiences during college. *Exceptional Children, 61,* 460–471.

Greenberg, F., James, L.M., & Oakley, Jr., G.P. (1983). Estimates of birth prevalence rates of spina bifida in the United States from computer generated maps. *American Journal of Obstetrics and Gynecology, 145,* 570–573.

Greene, G. (1999). Mnemonic multiplication fact instruction for students with learning disabilities. *Learning Disabilities Research and Practice, 14,* 141–148.

Greenwood, C.R., Delquadri, J.C., & Hall, R.V. (1989). Longitudinal effects of classwide peer tutoring. Journal of Educational Psychology, *81,* 371–383.

Gresham, F.M., & MacMillan, D.L. (1997). Autistic recovery? An analysis and critique of the empirical evidence on the Early Intervention Project. *Behavioral Disorders, 22,* 185–201.

Griffin, D.K., Rosenberg, H., Cheyney, W., & Greenburg, B. (1996). A comparison of self-esteem and job satisfaction of adults with mild mental retardation in sheltered workshops and supported employment. *Education and Training in Mental Retardation and Developmental Disabilities, 31,* 142–150.

Griffin-Shirley, N., Trusty, S., & Rickard, R.(2000). Orientation and mobility. In A.J. Koenig and M.C. Holbrook (Eds.), *Foundations of Education: Vol. II* (2d ed., pp.529-568). New York: American Foundation for the Blind.

Griffith, D.R. (1992). Prenatal exposure to cocaine and other drugs: Developmental and educational prognoses. *Phi Delta Kappan, 74*(1), 30–34.

Griffith, P.L., & Olson, M.W. (1992). Phonemic awareness helps beginning readers to break the code. *The Reading Teacher, 45,* 516–523.

Grigorenko, E.L., & Sternberg, R.J. (1997). Styles of thinking, abilities, and academic performance. *Exceptional Children, 63*(3), 295–312.

Grove, N., Cusick, B., & Bigge, J. (1991). Conditions resulting in physical disabilities. In J. Bigge, *Teaching individuals with physical and multiple disabilities* (3d ed.) (pp. 1–15). New York: Merrill.

Gunn, B., Biglan, A., Smolkowski, K., & Ary, D. (2000). The efficacy of supplemental instruction in decoding skills for Hispanic and non-Hispanic students in early elementary school. *Journal of Special Education, 34,* 90–103.

Guralnick, M.J. (1997). *The effectiveness of early intervention.* Baltimore: Brookes.

Gustason, G. (1990). Signing exact English. In H. Bornstein (Ed.), *Manual communication: Implications for education.* Washington, DC: Gallaudet University Press.

Hack, M., & Fanaroff, A.A. (2000). Outcomes of children of extremely low birthweight and gestational age in the 1990s. *Seminars in Neonatology,* 5 (2), 89-106.

Hallahan, D.P. (1992). Some thoughts on why the prevalence of learning disabilities has increased. *Journal of Learning Disabilities, 25,* 523–528.

Hallahan, D.P., Kauffman, J.M., & Lloyd, J.W. (1999). *Introduction to learning disabilities* (2nd ed.). Boston: Allyn and Bacon.

Halpern, A.S. (1993). Quality of life as a conceptual framework for evaluating transition outcomes. *Exceptional Children, 59,* 486–498.

Halvorsen, A.T., Doering, K., Farron-Davis, P., Usilton, R., & Sailor, W. (1989). The role of parents and family members in planning severely disabled students' transitions from school. In G.H.S. Singer and L.K. Irwin (Eds.), *Support for caregiving families* (pp. 253–268). Baltimore: Brookes.

Hanline, M.F., & Halvorsen, A. (1989). Parent perceptions of the integration transition process: Overcoming artificial barriers. *Exceptional Children, 55,* 487–492.

Hanson, M.J. (1996). Early intervention goals and outcomes. In M.J. Hanson (Ed.), *Atypical infant development* (2d ed.) (pp. 477–513). Austin, TX: Pro-Ed.

———. (1998). Ethnic, cultural, and language diversity in intervention settings. In E.W. Lynch & M.J. Hanson (Eds.), *Developing cross-cultural competence* (2d ed.) (pp. 3–22). Baltimore: Brookes.

Hanson, M.J, & Carta, J.J. (1996). Addressing the challenges of families with multiple risks. *Exceptional Children, 62*(3), 201–212.

Hanson, M.J., Ellis, L., & Deppe, J. (1989). Support for families during infancy. In G.H.S. Singer & L.K. Irvin (Eds.), *Support for caregiving families* (pp. 207–219). Baltimore: Brookes.

Haring, K.A., Lovett, D.L., & Saren, D. (1991). Parent perceptions of their adult offspring with disabilities. *Teaching Exceptional Children, 23*(2), 6–11.

Harkness, S., Super, C., & Keefer, C. (1994). Learning to be an American parent. In R. D'Andrade & C. Strauss (Eds.), *Human motives and cultural models.* Cambridge, UK: Cambridge University Press.

Harley, R.K., & Lawrence, G.A. (1984). *Visual impairment in the schools.* Springfield, IL: Thomas.

Harris, C.A., Miller, S.P., & Mercer, C.D. (1995). Teaching initial multiplication skills to students with disabilities in general education classrooms. *Learning Disabilities Research and Practice, 10,* 180–195.

Harris, S.L., & Handleman, J.S. (2000). Age and IQ at intake as predictors of placement for young children with autism: A four- to six-year follow-up. *Journal of Autism and Developmental Disorders, 30,* 137–142.

Harry, B. (1992a). Making sense of disability: Low-income, Puerto Rican parents' theories of the problem. *Exceptional Children, 59*(1), 27–40.

———. (1992b). Restructuring the participation of African-American parents in special education. *Exceptional Children, 59*(2), 123–131.

Harry, B., Allen, A., & McLaughlin, M. (1995). Communication versus compliance: African-American parents' involvement in special education. *Exceptional Children, 64*(4), 364–377.

Harry, B., Rueda, R., & Kalyanpour, M. (1999). Cultural reciprocity in sociocultural perspective: Adapting the normalization principle for family collaboration. *Exceptional Children, 66* (1), 123–136.

Harry, Beth , Kalyanpur, Maya, and Day, Monimalika (1999). *Building cultural reciprocity with families: Case studies in special education.* Baltimore: Paul H. Brookes.

Hartman, R., & Stage, S.A. (2000). The relationship between social information processing and in-school suspension for students with behavioral disorders. *Behavioral Disorders, 25,* 183–195.

Harvey, H.M., & Sall, N. (1999). Profiles of the expressive communication skills of children and adolescents with severe cognitive disabilities. *Education and Training in Mental Retardation and Developmental Disabilities, 34,* 77–89.

Hasazi, S.B., Furney, K.S., & DeStefano, L. (1999). Implementing the IDEA transition mandates. *Exceptional Children, 65,* 555–566.

Hasselbring, T.S., & Goin, L.I. (1989). Use of computers. In G.A. Robinson, J.R. Patton, E.A. Polloway & L.R. Sargent (Eds.), *Best practices in mild mental disabilities* (pp. 395–412). Reston, VA: The Division on Mental Retardation of the Council for Exceptional Children.

Hatlen, P.(2000a). Historical perspectives. In M.C. Holbrook and A.J. Koenig (Eds.), *Foundations of Education: Vol.1* (2d ed., pp.1–54). New York: American Foundation for the Blind.

———. (2000b). The core curriculum for blind and visually impaired students, including those with additional disabilities. In A.J. Koenig and M.C. Holbrook (Eds.), *Foundations of Education: Volume II* (2d ed., pp.779–784). New York: American Foundation for the Blind.

Hayden, M., Gersten, R., & Carnine, D. (1992). Using computer networking to increase active teaching in general education math classes containing students with mild disabilities. *Journal of Special Education Technology, 11,* 167–177.

Haynes, W.O., Moran, M.J., & Pindzola, R.H. (1990). *Communication disorders in the classroom.* Dubuque, IA: Kendall/Hunt Publishing.

Heal, L.W., & Rusch, F.R. (1995). Predicting employment for students who leave special education high school programs. *Exceptional Children, 61,* 472–487.

Health Indicators (2000). National Health Interview Survey, National Center for Health Statistics. Atlanta: Centers for Disease Control and Prevention.

Healy, A. (1983). Cerebral palsy. In J.A. Blackman (Ed.), *Medical aspects of developmental disabilities in children birth to three* (pp. 31–37). Iowa City: University of Iowa.

Heflin, L.J., & Simpson, R.L. (1998). Interventions for children and youth with autism: Prudent choices in a world of exaggerated claims and empty promises. Part I: Intervention and treatment option review. *Focus on Autism and Other Developmental Disabilities, 13,* 194–211.

Heller, K.W., Fredrick, L.D., Dykes, M.K., Best, S., & Cohen, E.T. (1999). A national perspective of competencies for teachers of individuals with physical and health disabilities. *Exceptional Children, 65,* 219–234.

Henley, M., Ramsey, R.S., & Algozziue, R. (1984). *Education of exceptional learners.* (3d ed.). Boston: Allyn & Bacon.

Hill, E.W. (1986). Orientation and mobility. In G.T. Scholl (Ed.), *Foundations of education for blind and visually handicapped children and youth: Theory and practice.* New York: American Foundation for the Blind.

Hobbs, N. (1975). *The futures of children: Categories, labels, and their consequences.* Nashville: Vanderbilt Institute for Policy Studies.

Hodapp, R.M., & Fidler, D.J. (1999). Special education and genetics: Connections for the 21st century. *Journal of Special Education, 33,* 130–137.

Hoffman, L.P. (1993). Language in the school context: What is least restrictive? *Proceedings of contemporary issues in language and learning: Toward the year 2000, point and counterpoint* (pp. 16–18). Rockville, MD: American Speech-Language-Hearing Association, Division 10, Language Learning and Education.

Hoffmeister, R.J. (1990). ASL and its implications for education. In H. Bornstein (Ed.), *Manual communication: Implications for education.* Washington, DC: Gallaudet University Press.

Hollinger, C.L. (1991). Career choices for gifted adolescents: Overcoming stereotypes. In M. Bireley & J. Genshaft (Eds.), *Understanding the gifted adolescent* (pp. 201–214). New York: Teachers College Press.

Hollinger, C., & Fleming, E.S. (1992). A longitudinal examination of life choices of gifted and talented young women. *Gifted Child Quarterly, 36*(4), pp. 207–212.

Hollingworth, L.A. (1942). *Children above 180 I.Q. Stanford-Binet: Origin and development.* Yonkers-on-Hudson, NY: World Book Company.

Hollingsworth, M., & Woodward, J. (1993). Integrated learning: Explicit strategies and their role in problem-solving instruction for students with learning disabilities. *Exceptional Children, 59,* 444–455.

Hom, J.L., O'Donnell, J.P., & Leicht, D.J. (1988). Phonetically inaccurate spelling among learning-disabled, head-injured, and nondisabled young adults. *Brain and Language 33,* 55–64.

Hopfenberg, W.S., Levin, H.M., Chase, C., Christensen, S.G., Moore, M., Soler, P., Brunner, I., Keller, B., & Rodriguez, G. (1993).

The Accelerated Schools resource guide. San Francisco: Jossey-Bass.

Houston, W.R. (Ed.). *Handbook of research on teacher education* (pp. 826–857).

Huebner, K.M.(2000). Visual impairment. In M.C. Holbrook and A.J. Koenig (Eds.), *Foundations of Education: Vol.1*(2d ed., pp. 55–76). New York: American Foundation for the Blind.

Hughes, C., Kim, J., Hwang, B., Killian, D.J., Fischer, G.M., Brock, M.L., Godshall, J.C., & Houser, B. (1997). Practitioner-validated secondary transition support strategies. *Education and Training in Mental Retardation and Developmental Disabilities, 32,* 201–212.

Hunt, N.A. (1982). The relationship of medical, social, and familial variables with school-related performance of adolescents born at low weight. Doctoral dissertation, University of Southern California.

Hutchinson, M.K., & Sandall, S.R. (1995). Congenital TORCH infections in infants and young children: Neurodevelopmental sequelae and implications for intervention. *Topics in Early Childhood Special Education, 15*(1), 65–82.

Hwang, B., & Hughes, C. (2000). The effects of social interactive training on early social communicative skills of children with autism. *Journal of Autism and Developmental Disorders, 30,* 331–343.

Iacono, T.A., & Miller, J.F. (1989). Can microcomputers be used to teach communication skills to students with mental retardation? *Education and Training in Mental Retardation, 24,* 32–44.

Individuals with Disabilities Education Act Amendments of 1997. (1997). P.L. 105-17, 105th Cong., 1st sess.

Individuals with Disabilities Education Act of 1990, 20 U.S.C. § 1400 et seq.

Inge, K.J., Banks, P.D., Wehman, P., Hill, J.W., & Shafer, M.S. (1988). Quality of life for individuals who are labeled mentally retarded: Evaluating competitive employment versus sheltered workshop employment. *Education and Training in Mental Retardation, 23,* 97–104.

Intellitools. (1996). Spring Catalog. Novato, CA: Intellitools.

Ishii-Jordan, S.R. (2000). Behavioral interventions used with diverse students. *Behavioral Disorders, 25,* 299–309.

Jackson, N.E.(2000). Strategies for modeling the development of giftedness in children. In R.C. Friedman & B.M. Shore (Eds.), *Talents unfolding: Cognition and development*, pp.27–54. Washington DC: American Psychological Association.

Jansson, L.M., & Velez, M. (1999). Understanding and treating substance abusers and their infants. *Infants and Young Children, 11(4),* 79–89.

Joe, J.R., & Malach, R.S. (1998). Families with Native-American roots. In E.W. Lynch & M.J. Hanson (Eds.), *Developing cross-cultural competence* (2d ed.). Baltimore: Brookes.

Johnson, D.W., & Johnson, R.T. (1989). The high achieving student in cooperative learning groups. *Cooperative Link, 5*(2), 317–321.

Joint Committee on Infant Hearing (2000). Year 2000 Position Statement: Principles and Guidelines for Early Hearing Detection and Intervention Programs. http://www.asha.org/infant_hearing/y2kpstn_stmnt.htm

Kalyanpur, Maya, and Harry, Beth. (1999). *Culture in special education: Building reciprocal family-professional relationships*. Baltimore: Paul H. Brookes.

Kamhi, A.G. (1989). Causes and consequences of reading disabilities. In A.G. Kamhi & H.W. Catts (Eds.), *Reading disabilities: A developmental language perspective* (pp. 67–99). Boston: College-Hill.

———. (1992). Three perspectives on language processing: Interactionism, modularity, and holism. In R.S. Chapman (Ed.), *Processes in language acquisition and disorders* (pp. 45–64). St. Louis: Mosby Year-Book.

———. (1993). Some problems with the marriage between theory and clinical practice. *Language, Speech, and Hearing Services in the Schools, 24,* 57–60.

———. (1998). Trying to make sense of developmental language disorders. *Language, Speech, and Hearing in the Schools,* January, 35–44.

Kamps, D., Kravits, T., Rauch, J., Kamps, J.L., & Chung, N. (2000). A prevention program for students with or at risk for ED: Moderating effects of variation in treatment and classroom structure. *Journal of Emotional and Behavioral Disorders, 8,* 141–154.

Kamps, D.M., & Tankersley, M. (1996). Prevention of behavioral and conduct disorders: Trends and research issues. *Behavioral Disorders, 22,* 41–48.

Kanner, L. (1943). Inborn disturbances of affective contact. *Nervous Child, 2,* 217–250.

Katsiyannis, A., & Yell, M.L. (2000). The Supreme Court and school health services: Cedar Rapids v. Garret F. *Exceptional Children, 66,* 317–326.

Kauffman, J.M. (1989). The regular education initiative as Reagan-Bush education policy: A trickle-down theory of education of the hard-to-teach. *Journal of Special Education, 23,* 256–278.

———. (2001). *Characteristics of Emotional and Behavioral Disorders of Children (7th ed.).* Upper Saddle River, NJ: Prentice-Hall.

Kauffman, J.M., & Hallahan, D.P. (1993). Toward a comprehensive service delivery system for special education. In J.I.Goodlad and T.C. Lovitt (Eds.), *Integrating general and special education* (pp.73–102). New York: Merrill.

Kavale, K.A., & Forness, S.R. (1983). Hyperactivity and diet treatment: A meta-analysis of the Feingold hypothesis. *Journal of Learning Disabilities, 16,* 324–330.

Kazdin, A.E. (2001). *Behavior Modification* (6th ed.). Belmont, CA: Wadsworth/Thomson Learning.

Kearney, K. (1988). The highly gifted. *Understanding Our Gifted, 1*(1), 13.

Keogh, B.K., Gallimore, R., & Weisner, T. (1997). A sociocultural perspective on learning and learning disabilities. *Learning Disabilities Research and Practice, 12,* 107–113.

Keogh, B.K., Wilcoxen, A.G., & Bernheimer, L. (1986). Prevention services for high risk children: Evidence for policy and practice. In D.C. Farran & J.D. McKinney (Eds.), *Risk in intellectual and psychosocial development* (pp. 287–315). New York: Academic Press.

Kerr, B.A. (1985). *Smart girls, gifted women.* Columbus: Ohio Psychology Publishing.

———. (1997). Smart girls two: A new psychology of girls, women, and giftedness. In B. Clark, *Growing up gifted* (5th ed.). Upper Saddle River, NJ: Merrill.

Kerr, M.M., & Nelson, C.M. (1989). *Strategies for managing behavior problems in the classroom* (2d ed.). New York: Merrill/Macmillan.

Kiernan, W.E., & Stark, J.A. (1986). *Pathways to employment for adults with developmental disabilities.* Baltimore: Brookes.

Kinder, D., & Bursuch, W. (1991). The search for a unified social studies curriculum: Does history really repeat itself? *Journal of Learning Disabilities, 24,* 270–275.

King, C., & Quigley, S. (1985). *Reading and deafness.* San Diego: College-Hill.

Kipila, E.L., & Williams-Scott, B. (1990). Cued speech. In H. Bornstein (Ed.), *Manual communication: Implications for education.* Washington, DC: Gallaudet University Press.

Kirk, K.I.(2000). Challenges in clinical investigations of cochlear implant outcomes. In J.K., Niparko, K.I., Kirk, N.K., Mellon, A.M., Robbins, D.L., Tucci, & B.S. Wilson, (Eds.), *Cochlear implants: Principles and practices* (pp. 225–255). Philadelphia: Lippincott Williams & Wilkins.

Klein, M.D., & Briggs, M.H. (1987). Facilitating mother-infant communicative interaction in mothers of high-risk infants. *Journal of Childhood Communication Disorders, X,* 91–106.

Klein, M.D., & Chen, D. (2001). *Working with children from culturally diverse backgrounds.* Albany, NY: Delmar.

Klein, M.D., Chen, D., & Haney, M.(2000). *Project PLAI.* Baltimore: Paul H. Brookes.

Klein, M.D., Fazzi, D.L., & Kekelis, L. (in press).Cognitive focus: Developing cognition, concepts, and language in young children who are blind and visually impaired. In R.L Pogrund, D.L. Fazzi, & Jessica S. Lampert (Eds.), *Early focus: Working with young children who are blind and visually impaired and their families* (2d ed.). New York: American Foundation for the Blind.

Klin, A., Lang, J., Cicchetti, D.V., & Volkmar, F.R. (2000). Brief report: Interrater reliability of clinical diagnosis and DSM-IV Criteria for Autistic Disorder: Results of the DSM-IV Autism field trial. *Journal of Autism and Developmental Disorders, 30,* 163–167.

Kluwe, R. (1987). Executive decisions and regulation of problem-solving behavior. In F. Weinert & R. Kluwe (Eds.), *Metacognition, motivation and understanding* (pp. 31–64). Hillsdale, NJ: Erlbaum.

Kluwin, T., & Moores, D.F. (1985). The effects of integration on the mathematics achievement of hearing-impaired adolescents. *Exceptional Children, 52,* 153–160.

Knapczyk, D.R. (1988). Reducing aggressive behaviors in special and regular class settings by training alternative social responses. *Behavioral Disorders, 14,* 27–39.

Knoblauch, B., & Sorenson, B.(1998). IDEA's definition of disabilities. *ERIC Digest*, April, EDO-EC-97-7. Reston, VA: ERIC Clearinghouse on Disabilities and Gifted Education.

Knoblock, P. (1982). *Teaching and mainstreaming autistic children.* Denver: Love.

Koegel, R.L., Koegel, L.K., Frea, W.D., & Smith, A.E. (1995). Emerging interventions for children with autism: Longitudinal and lifestyle implications. In R.L. Koegel & L.K. Koegel (Eds.), *Teaching children with autism: Strategies for initiating positive interactions and improving learning opportunities* (pp. 1–16). Baltimore: Brookes.

Koenig, A.J., & Farrenkopf, C. (1997). Essential experiences to undergird the early development of literacy. *Journal of Visual Impairment and Blindness, 91*(1), 14–24.

Koenig, A.J., & Holbrook, M.C.(2000). Planning instruction in unique skills. In A.J. Koenig and M.C. Holbrook (Eds.), *Foundations of Education: Vol. II* (2d ed., pp. 196–224). New York: American Foundation for the Blind.

Koester, L.S., & Meadow-Orlans, K.P. (1990). Parenting a deaf child: Stress, strength, and support. In D.F. Moores & K.P. Meadow-Orlans (Eds.), *Educational and developmental aspects of deafness* (pp. 299–320). Washington, DC: Gallaudet University Press.

Konstantareas, M.M., & Homatidis, S. (1999). Chromosomal abnormalities in a series of children with autistic disorder. *Journal of Autism and Developmental Disorders, 29,* 275–285.

Kopp, C.B. (1983). Risk factors in development. In M. Haith & J. Campos (Eds.), *Infancy and the biology of development* (Vol. II). In P. Mussen (Ed.), *Manual of child psychology.* New York: Wiley.

Korabek, C.A., & Cuvo, A.J. (1986). Children with spina bifida: Educational implications of their medical characteristics. *Education and Treatment of Children, 9,* 142–152.

Kraemer, K., Cusick, B., & Bigge, J. (1982). Motor development, deviations, and physical rehabilitation. In J. Bigge, *Teaching individuals with physical and multiple disabilities* (2d ed.) (pp. 12–14). Columbus, OH: Merrill.

Kraijer, D. (2000). Review of adaptive behavior studies in mentally retarded persons with Autism/Pervasive Developmental Disorder. *Journal of Autism and Developmental Disorders, 30,* 39–47.

Krauss, M.W. (1990). New precedent in family policy: Individualized family service plan. *Exceptional Children, 56*(5), 388–395.

Lagomarcino, T.R., & Rusch, F.R. (1989). Utilizing self-management procedures to teach independent performance. *Education and Training in Mental Retardation, 24,* 297–323.

Lahey, M. (1988). *Language disorders and language development.* New York: Macmillan.

Landesman-Dwyer, S., & Butterfield, E.C. (1983). Mental retardation: Developmental issues in cognitive and social adaptation. In M. Lewis (Ed.), *Origins of intelligence: Infancy and early childhood* (2d ed.) (pp. 479–519). New York: Plenum Press.

Lane, H. (1976). *The wild boy of Aveyron.* Cambridge: Harvard University Press.

Lang, H.G. (1996). Teaching science, engineering, and mathematics to deaf students: The role of technology in instruction and teacher preparation. *Proceedings of the Symposium on Technology for Persons with Disabilities.* Northridge: California State University.

Langley, M.B. (1980). *Assessment of multihandicapped visually impaired children.* Chicago, IL: Stoelting.

Langone, J., & Mechling, L. (2000). The effects of a computer-based instructional program with video anchors on the use of photographs for prompting augmentative communication. *Education and Training in Mental Retardation and Developmental Disabilities, 35,* 90–105.

Larson, K.A., & Gerber, M.M. (1987). Effects of social metacognitive training for enhancing overt behavior in learning disabled and low achieving delinquents. *Exceptional Children, 54,* 201–211.

Lau, C. (2000). I learned how to take turns. *Teaching Exceptional Children, 32*(4), 8–13.

Leffert, J.S., Siperstein, G.N., & Millikan, E. (2000). Understanding social adaption in children with mental retardation: A social-cognitive perspective. *Exceptional Children, 66,* 530–545.

Le Grice, B., & Blampied, N.M. (1994). Training pupils with intellectual disability to operate educational technology using video prompting. *Education and Training in Mental Retardation and Developmental Disabilities, 29,* 321–330.

Lehmann, J.P., & Baker, C. (1995). Mothers' expectations for their adolescent children: A comparison between families with disabled adolescents and those with non-labeled adolescents. *Education and Training in Mental Retardation and Developmental Disabilities, 31,* 27–40.

Lehmann, J.P., Davies, T.G., & Laurin, K.M. (2000). Listening to student voices about postsecondary education, *Teaching Exceptional Children , 32*(5), 60–65.

Leiberman, L.M. (1996). Preserving special education... for those who need it. In W. Stainback & S. Stainback (Eds.), *Controversial issues confronting special education: Divergent perspectives* (2d ed.) (pp. 16–27). Boston: Allyn and Bacon.

Lerner, J. (1993). Young children with disabilities. *Learning disabilities: Theories, diagnosis, and teaching strategies* (6th ed.) (pp. 245–271). Boston: Houghton Mifflin.

Lerner, J.W., Lowenthal, B., & Lerner, S. (1995). *Attention deficit disorders: Assessment and teaching.* Pacific Grove, CA: Brooks/Cole.

Lesar, S., Gerber, M.M., & Semmel, M.I. (1995). HIV infection in children: Family stress, social support, and adaptation. *Exceptional Children, 62,* 224–236.

Levendoski, L.S., & Cartledge, G. (2000). Self-monitoring for elementary school children with serious emotional disturbances: Classroom applications for increased academic responding. *Behavioral Disorders, 25,* 211–224.

Levin, H.M. (1996). Accelerated schools: The background. In C. Finnan, E.P. St. John, J. McCarthy & S.P. Slovacek (Eds.), *Accelerated schools in action: Lessons from the field* (pp. 3–23). Thousand Oaks, CA: Corwin Press.

Levine, J.M. (1996). Including children dependent on ventilators in school. *Teaching Exceptional Children, 28*(3), 24–29.

Lewis, B.A. (1992). Pedigree analysis of children with phonology disorders. *Journal of Learning Disabilities, 25,* 586–597.

Lewis, R.B. (1993). *Special education technology: Classroom applications* (pp. 176–219). Pacific Grove, CA: Brooks/ Cole.

Lewis, R.B., & Doorlag, D.H. (1987). *Teaching special students in the mainstream* (2d ed.). Columbus, OH: Merrill.

Lewis, S., & Allman, C.B.(2000). Educational programming. In M.C. Holbrook and A.J. Koenig (Eds.), *Foundations of Education: Vol.1*(2d ed., pp. 218–259). New York: American Foundation for the Blind.

Lewis, W.W. (1988). The role of ecological variables in residential treatment. *Behavioral Disorders, 13,* 98–107.

Lieber, J., Hanson, M.J., Beckman, P.J., Odom, S.L., Sandall, S.R., Schwartz, I.S., Horn, E., & Wolery, R. (2000). Key influences on the initiation and implementation of inclusive preschool programs. *Exceptional Children, 67,* 83–98.

Lin, S.L. (2000). Coping and adaptation in families of children with cerebral palsy. *Exceptional Children, 66,* 201–218.

Lindegren, M.L., Steinberg, S., & Byers, R.H. (2000). Epidemiology of HIV/AIDS in children. In Martha F. Rogers (Ed.), *The pediatric clinics of North America, 47*(1), 1-20.

Lindsey, J.D., & Stewart, D.A. (1989). The guardian minority: Siblings of children with mental retardation. *Education and Training in Mental Retardation, 24,* 291–296.

———. (Ed.). (1984). *Early intervention for hearing-impaired children: Oral options.* San Diego: College-Hill.

Locke, J.L. (1986). The linguistic significance of babbling. In B. Lindblom & R. Zetterstrom (Eds.), *Precursors of early speech* (pp. 143–157). New York: Stockton Press.

Logan, K.R., & Malone, D.M. (1998). Comparing instructional contexts of students with and without severe disabilities in general education classrooms, *Exceptional Children, 64,* 343–358.

Lopez-Reyna, N.A. (1996). The importance of meaningful contexts in bilingual special education: Moving to whole language. *Learning Disabilities Research and Practice, 11,* 120–131.

Lough, L.K. (1983). Positioning and handling. In J.A. Blackman (Ed.), *Medical aspects of developmental disabilities in children birth to three* (pp. 203–206). Iowa City: University of Iowa.

Loveday, E.B. (1993). Postsecondary transition services for students with learning disabilities within South Carolina. Doctoral dissertation. Columbia, SC: University of South Carolina.

Lowenfeld, B. (1981). *On blindness and blind people.* New York: American Foundation for the Blind.

Luetke-Stahlman, B.(1999). *Language across the curriculum: When students are deaf or hard of hearing.* Hillsboro, OR: Butte Publications.

Lund, N.J., & Duchan, J.F. (1993). *Assessing children's language in naturalistic contexts* (3d ed.). Englewood Cliffs, NJ: Prentice-Hall.

Lyon, J.S. (1985). *Playing God in the nursery.* New York: Norton.

Maag, J.W. (1988). Treatment of childhood and adolescent depression: Review and recommendations. In R.B. Rutherford, Jr. & J.W. Maag (Eds.), *Monograph in Behavioral Disorders: Severe Behavior Disorders of Children and Youth, 11,* 11–21.

Maag, J.W., & Behrens, J.T. (1989). Epidemiologic data on seriously emotionally disturbed and learning disabled adolescents: Reporting extreme depressive symptomatology. *Behavioral Disorders, 15,* 21–27.

Maag, J.W., & Katsiyannis, A. (2000).Recent legal and policy developments in special education. NASSP Bulletin, February, 1-8.

Maccini, P., & Hughes, C.A. (2000). Effects of a problem-solving strategy on the introductory algebra performance of secondary students with learning disabilities. *Learning Disabilities Research and Practice, 15,* 10–21.

Mack, C.G., Koenig, A.J., & Ashcroft, S.C. (1990). Microcomputers and access technology in programs for teachers of visually impaired students. *Journal of Visual Impairment and Blindness, 84*(10), 526–530.

MacMillan, D. (1989). Mild mental retardation: Emerging issues. In G.A. Robinson, J.R. Patton, E.A. Polloway & L.R. Sargent (Eds.), *Best practices in mild mental disabilities* (pp. 1–20). Reston, VA: Division on Mental Retardation of the Council for Exceptional Children.

MacMillan, D.L. (1982). *Mental retardation in school and society* (2d ed.). Boston: Little, Brown.

MacMillan, D.L., & Hendrick, I.G. (1993). Evolution and legacies. In J.I. Goodlad & T.C. Lovitt (Eds.), *Integrating general and special education.* New York: Macmillan.

MacMillan, D.L., Semmel, M.I., & Gerber, M.M. (1994). The social context of Dunn: Then and now. *Journal of Special Education, 27,* 466–480.

MacMillan, D.L., & Turnbull, A.P. (1983). Parent involvement with special education: Respecting individual differences. *Education and Training of the Mentally Retarded, 18,* 4–9.

Magnusson, D. (1994). Human ontogeny: Longitudinal perspectives. In D. Magnusson & P. Casaer (Eds.), *Longitudinal research on individual development: Present status and future perspectives.* Cambridge, UK: Cambridge University Press.

Maker, C.J. (1977). *Providing programs for the gifted handicapped.* Reston, VA: Council for Exceptional Children.

Male, M. (1997). *Technology for inclusion: Meeting the special needs of all students* (3rd ed). Boston: Allyn and Bacon.

Malone, L.D., & Mastropieri, M.A. (1992). Reading comprehension instruction: Summarization and self-monitoring training for students with learning disabilities. *Exceptional Children, 58,* 270–279.

Mamlin, N. (1999). Despite best intentions: When inclusion fails. *The Journal of Special Education, 33,* 36–49.

Mangrum, C., & Strichart, S. (Eds.). (1988). *Colleges with programs for learning disabled students.* New Jersey: Peterson's Guides, Inc.

Mank, D., Cioffi, A., & Yovanoff, P. (1998). Employment outcomes for people with severe disabilities: Opportunities for improvement. *Mental Retardation, 36,* 205–216.

Maratens, B.K., Muir, K.A., & Meller, P.J. (1988). Rewards common to the classroom setting: A comparison of regular and self-contained room student ratings. *Behavioral Disorders, 13,* 169–174.

Masten, A.S., & Coatsworth, J.D. (1998). The development of competence in favorable and unfavorable environments: Lessons from research on successful children. *American Psychologist, 53,* p.212.

Mastropieri, M.A., Jenne, T., & Scruggs, T.E. (1988). A level system for managing problem behaviors in a high school resource program. *Behavioral Disorders, 13,* 202–208.

Mastropieri, M.A., & Scruggs, T.E. (1991). *Teaching students ways to remember: Strategies for learning mnemonically.* Cambridge, MA: Brookline Books.

———. (2000). The inclusive classroom: Strategies for effective instruction. Columbus, OH: Merrill.

Mathes, P.G., Grek, M.L., Howard, J.K., Babyak, A.E., & Allen, S.H. (1999). Peer-Assisted Learning Strategies for first-grade readers: A tool for preventing early reading failure. *Learning Disabilities Research and Practice, 14,* 50–60.

Maurice, C. (1993). *Let me hear your voice: A family's triumph over autism.* New York: Fawcett Columbine.

McClesky, J., Henry, D., & Axelrod, M.I. (1999). Inclusion of students with learning disabilities: An examination of data from reports to Congress. *Exceptional Children, 66,* 55–66.

McCollum, K. (1998). Web-standards group releases draft rules to help the disabled explore cyberspace. *Chronicle of Higher Education,* February 4, p. 1.

McComiskey, A.V. (1996). The Braille readiness skills grid: A guide to building a foundation for literacy. *Journal of Visual Impairment and Blindness, 90*(3), 190–193.

McCormick, L. (1997). Policies and practices. In L. McCormick, D.F. Loeb & R.L. Schiefelbusch, *Supporting children with communication difficulties in inclusive settings: School-based language intervention* (pp. 149–178). Boston: Allyn & Bacon.

McDonnell, A., & Hardman, M. (1988). A synthesis of "best practice" for early childhood services. *Journal of the Division for Early Childhood, 12,* 32–341.

McDonough, K.M. (1989). Analysis of the expressive language characteristics of emotionally handicapped students in social interactions. *Behavioral Disorders, 14,* 127–139.

McGregor, D., & Farrenkopf, C.(2000). Recreation and leisure skills. In A.J. Koenig and M.C. Holbrook (Eds.), *Foundations of Education: Vol. II* (2d ed., pp. 653–678). New York: American Foundation for the Blind.

McGuffog, C., Feiring, C., & Lewis, M. (1987). The diverse profile of the extremely gifted child. *Roeper Review, 10*(2), 82–89.

McIntosh, R., Vaughn, S., & Zaragoza, N. (1991). A review of social interventions for students with learning disabilities. *Journal of Learning Disabilities, 24,* 451–458.

McKinney, J.D., Hocutt, A.M., Giambo, D.A., & Schumm, J.S. (2000). Research on a teacher-implemented phonological awareness intervention for Hispanic kindergarten children. Paper presented at the Council for Exceptional Children Convention, Vancouver, BC.

McLaren, J., & Bryson, S.E. (1987). Review of recent epidemiological studies of mental retardation: Prevalence, associated disorders, and etiology. *American Journal of Mental Retardation, 92,* 243–254.

McLaughlin, M.J., Nolet, V., Rhim, L.M., & Henderson, K. (1999). Integrating standards: Including all students. *Teaching Exceptional Children, 31*(3), 66–71.

McLaughlin, T.F., Krappman, V.F., & Welsh, J.M. (1985). The effects of self-recording for on-task behavior of behaviorally disordered special education students. *Remedial and Special Education, 6*(4), 42–45.

McLesky, J., Henry, D., & Hodges, D. (1999). Inclusion: What progress is being made across disability categories? *Teaching Exceptional Children, 31*(3), 60–64.

McLloyd, V.C. (1998). Socioeconomic disadvantage and child development. *American Psychologist, 53* (2), 185-204.

McLoughlin, J.A., & Lewis, R.B. (1986). *Assessing special students* (2d ed.). Columbus, OH: Merrill.

Meadow, K. (1968). Parental responses to the medical ambiguities of deafness. *Journal of Health and Social Behavior, 9,* 299–309.

Meadow-Orlans, K.P. (1980). *Deafness and child development.* Berkeley: University of California Press.

Meadow-Orlans, K.P., & Orlans, H. (1990). Responses to loss of hearing in later life. In D.F. Moores & K.P. Meadow-Orlans (Eds.), *Educational and developmental aspects of deafness* (pp. 417–429). Washington, DC: Gallaudet University Press.

Mechaty, I.R., & Thompson, J.E. (Eds.). (1990). *New perspectives on prenatal care.* New York: Elsevier.

Mechling, L.C., & Gast, D.L. (1997). Combination audio/visual self-prompting system for teaching chained tasks to students with intellectual disabilities. *Education and Training in Mental Retardation and Developmental Disabilities, 32,* 138–153.

Medley, L.P., Roberts, J.E., & Zeisel, S.A. (1995). At-risk children and otitis media with effusion: Management issues for the early childhood special educator. *Topics in Early Childhood Special Education, 15*(1), 44–64.

Mehan, H., Hertweck, A., & Meihls, J.L. (1986). *Handicapping the handicapped: Decision making in students' educational careers.* Stanford, CA: Stanford University Press.

Meisels, S.J., & Provence, S. (1989). *Screening and assessment: Guidelines for identifying young disabled and developmentally vulnerable children and their families.* Washington, DC: National Center for Clinical Infant Programs.

Meisels, S.J., & Wasik, B.A. (1990). Who should be served? Identifying children in need of early intervention. In S.J. Meisels & J.P. Shonkoff (Eds.), *Handbook of early childhood intervention.* Cambridge: Cambridge University Press.

Menlove, M. (1996). A checklist for identifying funding sources for assistive technology. *Teaching Exceptional Children, 28*(3), 20–24.

Mercer, C.D. (1987). Definitions and characteristics. *Students with learning disabilities* (3d ed.) (pp. 28–51). Columbus, OH: Merrill.

Mercer, C.D., & Mercer, A.R. (1993a). Assessing and teaching handwriting and written expression skills. *Teaching students with learning problems* (4th ed.) (pp. 533–581). New York: Merrill.

———. (1993b). Teaching math skills. In *Teaching students with learning problems* (4th ed.) (pp. 273–342). New York: Merrill.

Mercer, C.D., & Miller, S.P. (1992). *Multiplication facts 0 to 81.* Lawrence, KS: Edge Enterprises.

Mercer, J. (1973). *Labeling the mentally retarded.* Berkeley: University of California Press.

Mesibov, G.B. (1994). A comprehensive program for serving people with autism and the families: The TEACCH model. In J.L. Matson (Ed.), *Autism in children and adults: Etiology, assessment, and intervention* (pp. 85–97). Belmont, CA: Brooks/Cole.

———. (1997). Formal and informal measures on the effectiveness of the TEACCH programmme. *Autism: The International Journal of Research and Practice, 1,* 25–35.

Miller, L. (1989). Classroom-based language intervention. *Language, Speech, and Hearing Services in Schools, 20,* 153–169.

Millward, C., Powell, S., Messer, D., & Jordan, R. (2000). Recall for self and other in Autism: Children's memory for events experienced by themselves and their peers. *Journal of Autism and Developmental Disorders, 30,* 15–28.

Milstead, S. (1988). Siblings are people, too! *Academic Therapy, 23,* 537–540.

Mira, M., Tucker, B.F., & Tyler, J.S. (1992). *Traumatic brain injury in children and adolescents: A source book for teachers and other school personnel.* Austin, TX: Pro-Ed.

Mitchell, I. (1985). The child with chronic illness. In H.A. Haslam & P. Balletutti (Eds.), *Medical problems in the classroom.* Austin, TX: Pro-Ed.

Moats, L.C., & Lyon, G. R. (1996). Wanted: Teachers with knowledge of language. *Topics in Language Disorders, 16* (2), 23–86.

Modell, S.J., & Cox, T.A. (1999). Lets get fit! Fitness activities for children with severe/profound disabilities. *Teaching Exceptional Children, 31*(3), 24–29.

Montague, M., Warger, C., & Morgan, T.H. (2000). Solve it! Strategy instruction to improve mathematical problem-solving. *Learning Disabilities Research and Practice, 15,* 110–116.

Moody, S.W., Vaughn, S., Hughes, M.T., & Fischer, M. (2000). Reading instruction in the resource room: Setup for failure. *Exceptional Children, 66,* 305–316.

Moores, D.F. (1969). The vocational status of young deaf adults in New England. *Journal of Rehabilitation of the Deaf, 2*(1), 29–41.

———. (1987). *Educating the deaf: Psychology, principles, and practices* (3d ed.). Boston: Houghton Mifflin.

———. (2001). *Educating the deaf: Psychology, principles, and practices* (5th ed.). Boston: Houghton Mifflin.

Moores, D.F., & Kluwin, T.N. (1986). Issues in school placement. In A.N. Schildroth & M.A. Karchmer (Eds.), *Deaf children in America* (pp. 105–123). San Diego: College-Hill.

Morgan, R.L., Moore, S.C., McSweyn, C., & Salzberg, C.L. (1992). Transition from school to work: Views of secondary special educators. *Education and Training in Mental Retardation, 27,* 315–323.

Morse, T.E., & Schuster, J.W. (2000). Teaching elementary students with moderate intellectual disabilities how to shop for groceries. *Exceptional Children, 66,* 273–288.

Morsink, C.A. (1984). *Teaching special needs students in regular classrooms.* Boston: Little, Brown.

Morton, K. (1985). Identifying the enemy: A parent's complaint. In H.R. Turnbull & A.P. Turnbull. *Parents speak out: Then and now* (pp. 143–147). Columbus, OH: Merrill.

Mortweet, S.L. (1999). Classwide peer tutoring: Teaching students with mild mental retardation in inclusive classrooms. *Exceptional Children, 65,* 524–536.

Murray, C., Goldstein, D.E., Nourse, S., & Edgar, E. (2000). The postsecondary school attendance and completion rates of high school graduates with learning disabilities. *Learning Disabilities Research and Practice, 15,* 119–127.

Myers, B.J., Olson, H.C., & Kaltenbach, K. (1992). Cocaine-exposed infants: Myths and misunderstandings. *Zero to Three, 13*(1), 1–5.

Myklebust, H. (1964). *The psychology of deafness* (2d ed.). New York: Grune & Stratton.

Nation, J.E., & Aram, D.M. (1991). *Diagnosis of speech and language disor-*

ders (2d ed.). San Diego: Singular Publishing.

National Center for Education Statistics (1999). Inclusion of students with disabilities in the least restrictive environment - Section 2 - Condition of Education

National Head Injury Task Force. (1985). *An educator's manual.* Framingham, MA: National Head Injury Foundation.

Needleman, H.L. (1992). Childhood exposure to lead: A common cause of school failure. *Phi Delta Kappan, 74*(1), 35–37.

Needleman, H.L., et al. (1979). Deficits in psychological and classroom performance of children with elevated dentine lead levels. *New England Journal of Medicine, 300,* 689–695.

———. (1991). The long-term effects of exposure to low doses of lead in childhood: An 11-year follow-up report. *New England Journal of Medicine, 322,* 83–88.

Neel, R.S., Meadows, N., Levine, P., & Edgar, E.B. (1988). What happens after special education: A statewide follow-up study of secondary students who have behavioral disorders. *Behavioral Disorders, 1,* 209–216.

Nelson, K.B., & Ellenberg, J.H. (1986). Antecedents of cerebral palsy: Multivariate analysis of risk. *New England Journal of Medicine, 315,* 81–86.

Neubert, D.A., & Moon, M.S. (2000). How a transition profile helps students prepare for life in the community. *Teaching Exceptional Children, 33*(2), 20–25.

Neubert, D.A., Tilson, G.P., & Ianacone, R.N. (1989). Postsecondary transition needs and employment patterns of individuals with mild disabilities. *Exceptional Children, 55,* 494–500.

Newcomer, P.L., & Barenbaum, E.M. (1991). The written composing ability of children with learning disabilities. A review of the literature from 1980–1990. *Journal of Learning Disabilities, 24,* 578–593.

Newell, W. (1991). ASL is not a four-letter word: Deaf education can dance with the boogieman. In S. Polowe-Aldersley, P. Schragle, V. Armour, & J. Polowe (Eds.), *Profession on parade: Proceedings of the Fifty-fifth Biennial Meeting, Convention of American Instructors of the Deaf and the Sixty-third Annual Meeting of the Conference of Educational Administrators Serving the Deaf, New Orleans, Louisiana, June 1991* (pp. 74–75). Silver Spring, MD: Convention.

Newland, T.E. (1976). *The gifted in socioeducational perspective.* Englewood Cliffs, NJ: Prentice-Hall.

Nietupski, J.A., & Hamre-Nietupski, S.M. (1987). An ecological approach to curriculum development. In L. Goetz, D. Guess & K. Stremel-Campbell (Eds.), *Innovative program design for individuals with dual sensory impairments.* Baltimore: Brookes.

Neitupski, J., Hamre-Nietupski, S., Donder, D.J., Houselog, M., & Anderson, R.J. (1988). Proactive administrative strategies for implementing community-based programs for students with moderate/severe handicaps. *Education and Training in Mental Retardation, 23,* 138–146.

Nihira, K., Foster, R., Shellhaas, M., & Leland, H. (1981). *AAMR adaptive behavior scale: School edition.* Monterey, CA: Publishers Test Service.

Nihira, K., Leland, H., & Lambert, N. (1993). AAMR Adaptive Behavior Scale - Residential and Community (2nd. ed.). Austin, TX: Pro-Ed.

Niparko, J.K. (2000). Introduction. In J.K., Niparko, K.I., Kirk, N.K., Mellon, A.M., Robbins, D.L., Tucci, & B.S. Wilson, (Eds.), *Cochlear implants: Principles and practices* (pp.1–6). Philadelphia: Lippincott Williams & Wilkins.

Noonan, M.J., & Kilgo, J.L. (1987). Transition services for early age individuals with severe mental retardation. In R.N. Ianacone & R.A. Stodden (Eds.), *Transition issues and directions* (pp. 25–37). Reston, VA: Council for Exceptional Children.

Northcott, W. (Ed.). (1984). *Oral interpreting: Principles and practices.* Washington, DC: Alexander Graham Bell Association for the Deaf.

Northern, J.L., & Downs, M.P. (1991). *Hearing in children* (4th ed.). Baltimore: Williams & Wilkins.

Oakes, J. (1985). *Keeping track.* New Haven: Yale University Press.

Oller, D.K., & Eilers, R.E. (1982). Similarity of babbling in Spanish- and English-learning babies. *Journal of Child Language, 9,* 565–577.

Oller, D.K., Weiman, L.A., Doyle, W.J., & Ross, C. (1976). Infant babbling and speech. *Journal of Child Language, 3,* 1–11.

Oller, J.W., & Damico, J. (1991). Theoretical considerations in the assessment of LEP students. In E.V. Hamayan & J.S. Damico (Eds.), *Limiting bias in the assessment of bilingual students* (pp. 77–110). Austin, TX: Pro-Ed.

Orel-Bixler, D.(1999). Clinical vision assessment for infants. In D. Chen (Ed.), *Essential elements in early intervention: Visual impairment and multiple disabilities.* New York: American Foundation for the Blind.

Orelove, F.P., & Sobsey, D. (1987). *Educating children with multiple disabilities: A transdisciplinary approach* (pp. 285–314). Baltimore: Brookes.

Orelove, F.P., & Sobsey, R. (1991). *Multiple disabilities: A transdisciplinary approach.* Baltimore: Brookes.

Ortiz, A.A., & Wilkinson, C.Y. (1991). Assessment and intervention model for the bilingual exceptional student (AIM for the BEST). *Teacher Education and Special Education, 14,* 35–42.

Osborn, A. (1963). *Applied imagination.* New York: Scribners.

O'Shea, D.J., O'Shea, L.J., Algozzine, R., & Hammitte, D.J.(2001). *Families and teachers of individuals with disabilities.* Boston: Allyn & Bacon.

Ostrosky, M.M., Drasgow, E., & Halle, J.W. (1999). How can I help you get what you want? *Teaching Exceptional Children, 31*(4), 5–61.

Owens, R.E., Jr. (1999). *Language disorders: A functional approach to assessment and intervention* (3rd ed.). Boston: Allyn & Bacon.

Padden, C. (1980). The deaf community and the culture of deaf people. In C. Baker & D. Cokely (Eds.), *Sign language and the deaf community: Essays in honor of William C. Stokoe* (pp. 89–103). Silver Spring, MD: National Association for the Deaf.

Padden, C., & Humphries, T. (1988). *Deaf in America: Voices from a culture.* Cambridge, MA: Harvard University Press.

Pahl, J., & Quine, L. (1987). Families with mentally handicapped children. In J. Oxford (Ed.), *Treating the disorder, treating the family.* Baltimore: Johns Hopkins University Press.

Paneth, N. (1995). The problem of low birth weight. *Future of Children, 5*(3), 19–34.

Parasnis, I. (1996). Interpreting the Deaf experience within the context of cultural and language diversity. In I. Parasnis (Ed.), *Cultural and language diversity and the Deaf experience* (pp. 3–19). New York: Cambridge University Press.

Parette, P. (1999). Transition and assistive technology planning with families across cultures. *Career Development for Exceptional Individuals, 22,* 213–231.

Park, C.C. (1998). Exiting nirvana. *The American Scholar, 67*(2), 28–43.

Patterson, D. (1987). The causes of Down syndrome. *Scientific American, 257*(2), 52–57.

Paul, P.(1998). *Literacy and deafness: The development of reading, writing, and literate thought*. Boston: Allyn & Bacon.

Paul, P.V. (1998). *Literacy and deafness.* Boston: Allyn & Bacon.

Paul, P.V., & Quigley, S.P. (1990). *Education and deafness.* New York: Longman.

Pauls, D.L. (1990). A review of the evidence for genetic factors in stuttering. In J.A. Cooper (Ed.), *Research needs in stuttering: Roadblocks and future directions.* (ASHA reports, #18). Rockville, MD: American Speech-Language-Hearing Association.

Pembrey, M. (1992). Genetics and language disorder. In P. Fletcher & D. Hall (Eds.), *Specific speech and language disorders in children* (pp. 51–62). San Diego: Singular Publishing.

Pendarvis, E.D., Howley, A.A., & Howley, C.B. (1990). *The abilities of gifted children.* Englewood Cliffs, NJ: Prentice-Hall.

Persson, B. (2000). Brief report: A longitudinal study of quality of life and independence among adult men with autism. *Journal of Autism and Developmental Disorders, 30,* 61–66.

Peterson, H.A., & Marquardt, T.P. (1990). *Appraisal and diagnosis of speech and language disorders* (2d ed.). Englewood Cliffs, NJ: Prentice-Hall.

Phelps, D. (1994). Retinopathy of prematurity: A neonatologist's perspective. In S.J. Isenberg (Ed.), *The eye of infancy* (2d ed., pp. 437–447). St. Louis: Mosby-Year Book.

Pierce, W.D., & Epling, W.F. (1995). *Behavior analysis and learning*. Englewood Cliffs, NJ: Prentice Hall.

Pintner, R., & Patterson, D. (1917). A comparison of deaf and hearing children in visual memory span for digits. *Journal of Experimental Psychology, 2*(2), 76–88.

Polloway, E.A., Patton, J.R., Payne, J.S., & Payne, R.A. (1989). *Strategies for teaching learners with special needs* (4th ed.). Columbus, OH: Merrill.

Polloway, E.A., Smith, J.D., Patton, J.R., & Smith, T.E.C. (1996). Historic changes in mental retardation and developmental disabilities. *Education and Training in Mental Retardation and Developmental Disabilities, 31,* 3–12.

Powell, T.H., & Gallagher, P.A. (1993). *Brothers and sisters: A special part of exceptional families* (2d ed.). Baltimore: Brookes.

Prelock, P. A.(2000). Epilogue: An intervention focus for inclusionary practice. *Language, Speech, and Hearing Services in Schools, 31* (3), 296–298.

Presley, J.A., & Hughes, C. (2000). Peers as teachers of anger management to high school students with behavioral disorders. *Behavioral Disorders, 25,* 114–130.

Pugach, M.C., & Warger, C.L. (1993). Curriculum considerations. In J.I. Goodlad & T.C. Lovitt (Eds.), *Integrating general and special education* (pp. 125–148). New York: Merrill/Macmillan.

Quay, H.C., & Peterson, D.R. (1983). *Behavior problem checklist: revised.* Coral Gables, FL: University of Miami.

Quigley, S.P., & Paul, P.V. (1984). *Language and deafness.* San Diego: College-Hill.

———. (1986). A perspective on academic achievement. In D.M. Luterman (Ed.), *Deafness in perspective* (pp. 55–86). San Diego: College-Hill.

Ramirez, M., & Casteñeda, A. (1974). *Cultural democracy, bicognitive development, and education.* New York: Academic Press.

Ramsey, E., & Walker, H.M. (1988). Family management correlates of antisocial behavior among middle school boys. *Behavioral Disorders, 13,* 187–201.

Raph, J.B., Goldberg, M.L., & Passow, A.H. (1966). *Bright underachievers.* New York: Teachers College Press.

Rapport, M.K. (1996). Legal guidelines for the delivery of special health care services in schools. *Exceptional Children, 62,* 537–549.

Raskind, M.H., Goldberg, R.J., Higgins, E.L., & Herman, K.L. (1999). Patterns of change and predictors of success in individuals with learning disaiblities: Results from a twenty-year longitudinal study. *Learning Disabilities Research and Practice, 14,* 35–49.

Raths, L.E., Wassermann, S., Jonas, A., & Rothstein, A. (1986). *Teaching for thinking.* New York: Teachers College Press.

Ratner, V., & Harris, L. (1994). *Understanding language disorders: The impact on learning.* Eau Claire, WI: Thinking Publications.

Reichard, A. (1995). The value of prenatal testing. *Exceptional Parent, 25*(8), 29–31.

Reichle, J., & Keogh, W.J. (1986). Communication instruction for learners with severe handicaps: Some unresolved issues. In R.H. Horner, L.H. Meyer & H.D.B. Fredricks (Eds.), *Education of learners with severe handicaps: Exemplary service strategies* (2d ed.) (pp. 189–219). Baltimore: Brookes.

Reid, D. Kim (2000). Ebonics and Hispanic, Asian, and Native American dialects of English. In K.R. Fahey & D.K. Reid (Eds.) *Language development, differences, and disorders,* pp. 219–244. Austin, TX: Pro-Ed.

Reid, D.H., Everson, J.M., & Green, C.W. (1999). A systematic evaluation of preferences identified through person-centered planning for people with profound multiple disabilities. *Journal of Applied Behavior Analysis, 32,* 467–477.

Reid, D.K. (2000). Discourse in classrooms. In K.R. Fahey & D.K. Reid (Eds.). *Language development, differences, and disorders.* Austin, TX: Pro-Ed.

Reid, R., Riccio, C.A., Kessler, R.H., DuPaul, G.J., Anastopoulos, A.D., Rogers-Adkinson, D., & Noll, M.B. (2000). Gender and ethnic differences in ADHD as assessed by behavior ratings. *Journal of Emotional and Behavioral Disorders, 8,* 38–48.

Reis, S.M., & McCoach, D.B.(2000). The underachievement of gifted students: What do we know and where do we go? *Gifted Child Quarterly, 44*(3), 152–170.

Reis, S.M., McGuire, J.M., & Neu, T.W.(2000). Compensation strategies used by high-ability students with learning disabilities who succeed in college. *Gifted Child Quarterly, 44*(2), 123–134.

Reis, S.M., Neu, T.W., & McGuire, J.M. (1997). Case studies of high-ability students with learning disabilities who have achieved. *Exceptional Children, 63*(4), 463–479.

Renner, P., Klinger, L.G., & Klinger, M.R. (2000). Implicit and explicit memory in Autism: Is Autism an Amnesic disorder? *Journal of Autism and Developmental Disorders, 30*, 3–14.

Renzulli, J.S. (1977). *The Enrichment Triad Model.* Mansfield Center, CT: Creative Learning Press.

———. (1978). What makes giftedness? *Phi Delta Kappan, 60*, 180–184.

———. (Ed.). (1986). *Systems and models for developing programs for the gifted and talented.* Mansfield Center, CT: Creative Learning Press.

———. (1996). Schools for talent development: A practical plan for total school improvement. *School Administrator, 53* (1), 20–22.

Renzulli, J.S., & Reis, S.M. (1985). *The schoolwide enrichment model: A comprehensive plan for educational excellence.* Mansfield Center, CT: Creative Learning Press.

———. (1991). The schoolwide enrichment model: A comprehensive plan for the development of creative productivity. In N. Colangelo & G.A. Davis (Eds.), *Handbook of gifted education.* Boston: Allyn & Bacon.

Reynolds, M.C., Wang, M.C., & Walberg, H.J. (1987). The necessary restructuring of special and regular education. *Exceptional Children, 53*, 391–398.

Richardson, G.A., & Day, N.J. (1994). Detrimental effects of prenatal cocaine exposure: Illusion or reality? *Journal of the American Academy of Child and Adolescent Psychiatry, 33*, 28–34.

Rimland, B. (1964). *Infantile autism: The syndrome and its implication for a neural theory of behavior.* Englewood Cliffs, NJ: Prentice-Hall.

Rimm, S.B. (1986). *Underachievement syndrome: Causes and cures.* Watertown, WI: Apple Publishing Company.

Roberts, J.E., Wallace, I.F., & Henderson, F.W. (1997). *Otitis media in young children.* Baltimore: Brookes.

Robertson, C.M., & Finer, N.N. (1993). Long-term follow-up of term neonates with perinatal asphyxia. *Clinics in Perinatology, 20*(2), 483–500.

Robinson, A. (1990). Cooperation or exploitation? The argument against cooperative learning for talented students. *Journal for the Education of the Gifted, 14*(1), 9–27.

Rodier, P. (2000). The early origins of autism. *Scientific American, 282*(2), 56–63.

Roessing, L.J. (1982). Functional vision: Criterion-referenced checklists. In S.S. Mangold (Ed.), *A teachers' guide to the special educational needs of blind and visually handicapped children* (pp. 35–44). New York: American Foundation for the Blind.

Rooney, K.J. (1988). *Independent strategies for efficient study.* Richmond, VA: J.R. Enterprises.

Rosen, L.A., Gabardi, L., Miller, C.D., & Miller, L. (1990). Home-based treatment of disruptive junior high school students: An analysis of the differential effects of positive and negative consequences. *Behavioral Disorders, 15*, 227–232.

Rosenberg, M.S., Wilson, R., Maheady, L., & Sindelar, P.T. (1992). *Educating students with behavioral disorders* (pp. 87–112). Boston: Allyn & Bacon.

Rosenshine, B., & Stevens, R. (1986). Teaching functions. In M.C. Wittrock (Ed.), *Handbook of research on teaching* (3d ed.) (pp. 376–391). New York: Macmillan.

Rosenthal, I. (1992). Counseling the learning disabled late adolescent and adult: A self-psychology perspective. *Learning Disabilities Research and Practice, 7*, 217–225.

Rosenthal-Malek, A., & Greenspan, J. (1999). A student with diabetes is in my class. *Teaching Exceptional Children, 31*(3), 38–43.

Ross, M. (Ed.). (1990). *Hearing-impaired children in the mainstream.* Washington, DC: Alexander Graham Bell Association for the Deaf.

Russ, S., Chiang, B., Rylance, B.J., & Bongers, J. (2001). Caseload in special education: An integration of research findings. *Exceptional Children, 67*, 161–172.

Rylance, B.J. (1998). Predictors of post–high school employment for youth identified as severely emotionally disturbed. *The Journal of Special Education, 32*, 184–192.

Sabornie, E.J., Kauffman, J.M., & Cullinan, D.A. (1990). Extended sociometric status of adolescents with mild handicaps: A cross-categorical perspective. *Exceptionality, 1*, 197–209.

Sacks, O. (1989). *Seeing voices: A journey into the world of the deaf.* New York: Harper Collins.

Sacks, S.Z. (1996). Psychological and social implications of low vision. In A.L. Corn & A.J. Koenig (Eds.), *Foundations of low vision: Clinical and functional perspectives.* New York: American Foundation for the Blind.

Sacks, S.Z., & Silberman, R.K. (2000). Social skills. In A.J. Koenig and M.C. Holbrook (Eds.), *Foundations of Education: Vol. II* (2d ed., pp. 616–652). New York: American Foundation for the Blind.

Safer, N. (1997). IDEA opens the door to a better future for students with disabilities and special educators. *Teaching Exceptional Children, 29*(60), 1.

Safran, S.P., & Safran, J.S. (1996). Intervention assistance programs and prereferral teams: Directions for the twenty-first century. *Remedial and Special Education, 17*(6), 363–369.

Saigal, S. (2000). Follow-up of very low birthweight babies to adolescence. *Seminars in Neonatology, 5*(2), 107–118.

Salisbury, C.L., Evans, I.M., & Palombaro, M.M. (1997). Collaborative problem-solving to promote the inclusion of young children with significant disabilities in primary grades. *Exceptional Children, 63*, 195–209.

Salvia, J., & Ysseldyke, J.E. (1991). *Assessment* (5th ed.). Boston: Houghton Mifflin.

Salvia, J., & Ysseldyke, J.E. (1998). *Assessment* (7th ed.) Boston: Houghton Mifflin.

Sameroff, A.J., & Chandler, M.J. (1975). Reproductive risk and the continuum of caretaking casualty. In F.D. Horowitz, M. Hetherington, S. Scarr-Salapatek & G. Siegel (Eds.), *Review of child development research* (Vol. 4) (pp. 187–244). Chicago: University of Chicago Press.

Sandall, S., McLean, M., & Smith, B.J. (2000). *DEC Recommended Practices in Early Intervention/Early Childhood Special Education*. Longmont, CO: Sopris West.

Sandall, S.R. (1997a). The family service team. In A.H. Widerstrom, B.A. Mowder & S.R. Sandall (Eds.), *Infant development and risk* (2d ed.). Baltimore: Brookes.

———. (1997b). The individualized family service plan. In A.H. Widerstrom, B.A. Mowder & S.R. Sandall (Eds.), *Infant development and risk* (2d ed.). Baltimore: Brookes.

Savelle, S., & Fox, J.J. (1988). Differential effects of training in two classes of social initiations on the positive responses and extended interactions of preschool-aged autistic children and their nonhandicapped peers. In R.B. Rutherford, Jr. & J.W. Maag (Eds.), *Monograph in Behavioral Disorders: Severe Behavior Disorders of Children and Youth, 11,* 75–86.

Scanlon, D., Deshler, D.D., & Schumaker, J.B. (1996). Can a strategy be taught and learned in secondary inclusive classrooms? *Learning Disabilities Research and Practice, 11,* 41–57.

Scarborough, H.S., & Dobrich, W. (1990). Development of children with early language delay. *Journal of Speech and Hearing Disorders, 33,* 70–83.

Scheuermann, B., & Webber, J. (1996). Level systems: Problems and solutions. *Beyond Behavior, 7*(2), 12–17.

Schildroth, A.N. (1986). Residential schools for deaf children: A decade in review. In A.N. Schildroth & M.A. Karchmer (Eds.), *Deaf children in America.* San Diego: College-Hill.

———. (1994). Congenital cytomegalovirus and deafness. *American Journal of Audiology* (July).

Schirmer, B.R. (1994). *Language and literacy development in children who are deaf.* New York: Merrill.

Schloss, P.J., & Smith, M.A. (1998). *Applied Behavior Analysis in the classroom* (2nd. ed). Boston: Allyn and Bacon.

Schoem, S.R.(1999). Update on otitis media in children. *Volta Review, 99* (5), 97–117.

Scholl, G.T. (1986). *Foundations of education for blind and visually handicapped children and youth: Theory and practice.* New York: American Foundation for the Blind.

Scholl, T.O., Hediger, M.L., & Belsky, D.H. (1994). Prenatal care and maternal health during adolescent pregnancy: A review and meta-analysis. *Journal of Adolescent Health, 15*(6), 444–456.

Schon, D.A. (1990). *Educating the reflective practitioner.* San Francisco: Jossey-Bass.

Schuler, P.A. (1997). Cluster grouping coast to coast. *Newsletter of the National Research Center on the Gifted and Talented* (Winter).

Schumaker, J.B., & Hazel, J.S. (1984). Social skills assessment and training for the learning disabled: What's on second? Part I. *Journal of Learning Disabilities, 17,* 422–431.

Schumaker, J.B., & Lyerla, K.D. (1991). The paragraph writing strategy instructor's manual. Lawrence, KS: University of Kansas.

Scorgie, K., Wilgosh, L., & McDonald, L. (1999). Transforming partnerships: Parents' life management issues when a child has mental retardation. *Education and Training in Mental Retardation and Developmental Disabilities, 34,* 395–405.

Scott, J., Clark, C., & Brady, M. (2000). *Student with autism: Characteristics and instructional programming.* San Diego, *CA:* Singular.

Scruggs, T.E., & Mastropieri, M.A. (1996). Teacher perceptions of mainstreaming/inclusion, 1958–1995: A research synthesis. *Exceptional Children, 63*(1), 59–74.

———. (2000). Mnemonic interventions for students with behavior disorders: Memory for learning and behavior. *Beyond Behavior, 10,* 13–17.

Seidel, J.F., & Vaugn. S. (1991). Social alienation and the learning disabled school dropout. *Learning Disabilities Research and Practice, 3,* 152–157.

Seidenberg, P.L., & Koenigsberg, E. (1990). A survey of regular and special education high school teachers and college faculty: Implications for program development for secondary learning disabled students. *Learning Disabilities Research, 5,* 100–117.

Seligman, M., & Darling, R.B.(1997). *Ordinary families, special children* (second ed.). New York: The Guilford Press.

Serna, L., Nielsen, E., Lambros, K., & Forness, S. (2000). Primary prevention with children at risk for emotional or behavioral disorders: Data on a universal intervention for Head Start Classrooms. *Behavioral Disorders, 26,* 70–84.

Shea, T.M., & Bauer, A.M. (1991). *Parents and teachers of children with exceptionalities: A handbook for collaboration* (2d ed.). Boston: Allyn & Bacon.

Sherburne, S., Utley, B., McConnel, S., & Gannon, J. (1988). Decreasing violent or aggressive theme play among preschool children with behavior disorders. *Exceptional Children, 55,* 166–172.

Shiono, P.H., & Behrman, R.E. (1995). Low birth weight: Analysis and recommendations. *Future of Children, 5*(3), 4–18.

Shutz, R.P., Williams, W., Iverson, G.S., & Duncan, D. (1984). Social integration of severely handicapped students. In N. Certo, N. Haring & R. York (Eds.), *Public school integration of severely handicapped students: Rational issues and progressive alternatives* (pp. 15–42). Baltimore: Brookes.

Shuy, R. (1988). The oral language basis for dialogue journals. In J. Staton, R.W. Shuy, J.K. Peyton & L. Reed (Eds.), *Dialogue journal communication* (pp. 73–87). Norwood, NJ: Ablex.

Siegel-Causey, E., McMorris, C., McGowen, S., & Sands-Buss, S. (1998). In Junior High you take Earth Science: Including a student with severe disabilities into an academic class. *Teaching Exceptional Children, 31*(1), 66–72.

Sienkiewicz-Mercer, R., & Kaplan, S.B. (1989). *I raise my eyes to say yes.* Boston: Houghton Mifflin.

Sigafoos, J. (2000). Communication development and aberrant behavior in children with developmental disabilities. *Education and Training in Mental Retardation and Developmental Disabilities, 35,* 168–176.

Silberman, R.K.(2000). Children and youths with visual impairments and other disabilities. In M.C. Holbrook and A.J. Koenig (Eds.), *Foundations of Education: Vol.1* (2d ed., pp.173–196). New York: American Foundation for the Blind.

Silliman, E.R., & Wilkinson, L.C. (1994). Discourse scaffolds for classroom intervention. In G.P. Wallach & K.P. Butler (Eds.), *Language learning disabilities in school-age children and adolescents* (pp. 27–52). New York: Merrill/Macmillan.

Silverstein, J. (2000). Parents of gifted culturally diverse youngsters. In G.B. Esquivel & J.C. Houtz (Eds.), *Creativity and giftedness in culturally diverse students*, pp. 193–214.

Cresskill, NJ: Hampton Press, Inc.

Simeonsson, R.J. (Ed.). (1994). *Risk, resilience, and prevention: Promoting the well-being of all children.* Baltimore: Brookes.

Simon, C.S. (1991). Functional flexibility: Developing communicative competence in speaker and listener roles. In C.S. Simon (Ed.), *Communication skills and classroom success: Assessment and therapy methodologies for language-learning disabled students.* Eau Claire, WI: Thinking Publications.

Simpson, R.L. (1988). Needs of parents and families whose children have learning and behavioral problems. *Behavioral Disorders, 14,* 40–47.

Simpson, R.L., & Souris, L.A. (1988). Reciprocity in the pupil-teacher interactions of autistic and mildly handicapped preschool children. *Behavioral Disorders, 13,* 159–168.

Singleton, D.K., Schuster, J.W., Morse, T.E., & Collins, B.C. (1999). A comparison of antecedent prompt and test and simultaneous prompting procedures in teaching grocery words to adolescents with mental retardation. *Education in Training in Mental Retardation and Developmental Disabilities, 34,* 182–199.

Siperstein, G.N., Leffert, J.S., & Widaman, K. (1996). Social behavior and the social acceptance and rejection of children with mental retardation. *Education and Training in Mental Retardation and Developmental Disabilities, 31,* 271–281.

Skinner, D., Bailey, D.B., Correa, V., & Rodriguez, P. (1999). Narrating self and disability: Latino mothers' construction of identities vis-à-vis their child with special needs. *Exceptional Children, 65,* 481–495.

Skinner, R. (1990). Genetic counseling. In A.E.H. Emery & D.L. Rimoin (Eds.), *Principles and practice of human genetics* (2d ed.) (Vol. 2). New York: Churchill Livingstone.

Slavin, R.E. (1988). Synthesis of research on grouping in elementary and secondary schools. *Educational Leadership* (Sept.), 67–77.

———. (1990). Ability grouping, cooperative learning and the gifted. *Journal for the Education of the Gifted, 14*(1), 3–8.

Smith, C.R. (1985). Identification of handicapped children and youth: A state agency perspective on behavioral disorders. *Remedial and Special Education, 6*(4), 34–41.

Smith, J.D. (1989). On the right of children with mental retardation to life sustaining medical care and treatment: A position statement. *Education and Training in Mental Retardation, 24,* 3–6.

Smith, S. B., Simmons, D. C. & Kameenui, E. J. (February 1995). Synthesis of research on phonological awareness: Principles and implications for reading acquisition. (*Technical Report No. 21*). Eugene: National Center to Improve the Tools of Educators, University of Oregon.

Smith, T. (1996). Are other treatments effective? In C.Maurice, G. Green, & S.C.Luce (Eds.), *Behavioral intervention for young children with autism: A manual for parents and professionals.* Austin, TX: Pro-Ed.

Smith, T., & Lovaas, O.L. (1997). The UCLA young autism project: A reply to Gresham and MacMillan. *Behavioral Disorders, 22,* 202–218.

Smith, T.E.C., & Dowdy, C.A. (1989). The role of study skills in the secondary curriculum. *Academic Therapy, 24,* 479–490.

Smith, T.E.C., Finn, D.M., & Dowdy, C.A. (1993). *Teaching students with mild disabilities.* Orlando, FL: Harcourt Brace Jovanovich.

Smith, T.E.C., Price, B.J., & Marsh, G.E. (1986). *Mildly handicapped children and adults.* St. Paul, MN: West.

Smith, T.M. (1994). Adolescent pregnancy. In R.J. Simeonsson (Ed.), *Risk, resilience, and prevention: Promoting the well-being of all children.* Baltimore: Brookes.

Snell, M.E. (1988). Curriculum and methodology for individuals with severe disabilities. *Education and Training in Mental Retardation, 23,* 302–314.

Snell, M.E., & Brown, F. (2000). Instruction of students with severe disabilities (5th ed.). Columbus, OH: Merrill.

Snell, M.E., & Drake, Jr., G.P. (1994). Replacing cascades with supported education. *Journal of Special Education, 27,* 393–409.

Snell, M.E., & Janney, R.E. (2000). Teachers' problem-solving about children with moderate and severe disabilities in elementary classrooms. *Exceptional Children, 66,* 472–490.

Snider, V.E. (1997). Transfer of decoding skills to a literature basal. *Learning Disabilities Research and Practice, 12,* 54–62.

Snow, C.E., Burns, M.S., & Griffin, P. (Eds.). (1998). *Preventing reading difficulties in young children.* Washington, DC: National Academy Press.

Snyder, L.S., & Downey, D.M. (1991). The language-reading relationship in normal and reading disabled children. *Journal of Speech and Hearing Research, 34,* 129–140.

Sobsey, D. (1994). *Violence and abuse in the lives of people with disabilities: The end of silent acceptance?* Baltimore: Brookes.

Solomons, G. (1983). Child abuse and neglect. In J.A. Blackman (Ed.), *Medical aspects of developmental disabilities in children birth to three* (pp. 31–37). Iowa City: University of Iowa.

Sparks, S.N. (1984). *Birth defects and speech-language disorders.* Boston: College-Hill Press.

———. (1993). *Children of prenatal substance abuse.* San Diego: Singular Publishing.

Sparrow, S.S., Balla, D.A., & Cicchetti, D.V. (1984). *Vineland adaptive behavior scales: Interview edition, survey form manual.* Circle Pines, MN: American Guidance Service.

Spencer, K.C., & Sands, D.J. (1999). Prediction of student participation in transition-related actions. *Education and Training in Mental Retardation and Developmental Disabilities, 34,* 473–484.

Sprague, J., & Walker, H. (2000). Early identification and intervention for youth with antisocial and violent behavior. *Exceptional Children, 66,* 367–379.

Stainback, G.H., Stainback, W.C., & Stainback, S.B. (1988). Superintendents' attitudes toward integration. *Education and Training in Mental Retardation, 23,* 92–96.

———. (1993). Schools as inclusive communities. In W. Stainback & S. Stainback (Eds.), *Controversial issues confronting special education* (pp. 29–43). Boston: Allyn & Bacon.

Stainback, S., Stainback, W., & Ayres, B. (1996). Schools as inclusive communities. In W. Stainback & S. Stainback (Eds.), *Controversial issues confronting special education: Divergent perspectives* (2d ed.) (pp. 31–43). Boston: Allyn and Bacon.

Stallman, A.C., & Pearson, P.D. (1990). Formal measures of early literacy. In L.M. Morrow & J.K.

Smith (Eds.), *Assessment for instruction in early literacy* (pp. 7–44). Englewood Cliffs, NJ: Prentice-Hall.

Stanovich, K. E. (1994). Romance and reality. *The Reading Teacher, 47,* 280–290.

Starko, A.J. (1986). Meeting the needs of the gifted throughout the school day: Techniques for curriculum compacting. *Roeper Review, 9*(1), 27–33.

Stecker, P.M., & Fuchs, L.S. (2000). Effecting superior achievement using curriculum-based measurement: The importance of individual progress monitoring. *Learning Disabilities Research and Practice, 15,* 128–134.

Stein, M., & Davis, C.A. (2000). Direct instruction as a positive behavioral support. *Beyond Behavior, 10,* 7–12.

Stella, J., Mundy, P., & Tuchman, R. (1999). Social and nonsocial factors in the Childhood Autism Rating Scale. *Journal of Autism and Developmental Disorders, 29,* 307–317.

Stephenson, J.R., & Dowrick, M. (2000). Parent priorities in communication intervention for young students with severe disabilities. *Education and Training in Mental Retardation and Developmental Disabilities, 35,* 25–35.

Sternberg, R.J. (1985). *Beyond IQ: A triarchic theory of human intelligence.* New York: Cambridge University Press.

———. (1991). Giftedness according to the triarchic theory of human intelligence. In N. Colangelo & G.A. Davis (Eds.), *Handbook of gifted education* (pp. 45–54). Boston: Allyn & Bacon.

———. (1997). What does it mean to be smart? *Educational Leadership, 54*(6), 16–20.

———. (2000). Wisdom as a form of giftedness. *Gifted Child Quarterly, 44* (4), 252–260.

Sternberg, R.J., & Clinkenbeard, P. (1995). A triarchic view of identifying, teaching, and assessing gifted children. *Roeper Review, 17,* 225–260.

Stetson, F. (1984). Critical factors that facilitate integration: A theory of administrative responsibility. In N. Certo, N. Haring & R. York (Eds.), *Public school integration of severely handicapped students: Rational issues and progressive alternatives* (pp. 65–82). Baltimore: Brookes.

Stewart, D.A., & Kluwin, T.N.(2001). *Teaching deaf and hard of hearing students: Content, strategies, and curriculum.* Boston: Allyn & Bacon.

Stinson, M., & Lang, H. (1995). Full inclusion: A path for integration or isolation? *American Annals of the Deaf, 139*(2), 156–159.

Stoel-Gammon, C. (1992). Prelinguistic vocal development: Measurement and predictions. In C.A. Ferguson, L. Menn & C. Stoel-Gammon (Eds.), *Phonological development: Models, research, implications* (pp. 439–456). Timonium, MD: York Press.

Stokoe, W. (1960). Sign language structure: An outline of the visual communication system of the American deaf. *Studies in Linguistics Occasional Papers No. 8.* Washington, DC: Gallaudet College Press.

Stoneman, Z., Brody, G.H., Davis, C.H., & Crapps, J.M. (1988). Childcare responsibilities, peer relations, and sibling conflict: Older siblings of mentally retarded children. *American Journal of Mental Retardation, 93,* 174–183.

Storey, K. (1997). Quality of life issues in social skills assessment of persons with disabilities. *Education and Training in Mental Retardation and Developmental Disabilities, 32,* 197–200.

Storey, K., & Provost, O. (1996). The effect of communication skills instruction on the integration of workers with severe disabilities in supported employment settings. *Education and Training in Mental Retardation and Developmental Disabilities, 31,* 123–141.

Stotland, J. (1984). Relationships of parents to professionals: A challenge to professionals. *Journal of visual impairment and blindness, 78*(2), pp. 69–74.

Strauss, M. (1999). Hearing loss and cytomegalovirus. *Volta Review, 99* (5), 71–74.

Strong, K., & Sandoval, J. (1999). Mainstreaming children with a neuromuscular disease: A map of concerns. *Exceptional Children, 65,* 353–366.

Stuckless, E.R., Avery, J.C., & Hurwitz, T.A. (Eds.). (1989). *Educational interpreting for deaf students: Report of the National Task Force on Educational Interpreting.* Rochester, NY: National Technical Institute for the Deaf, Rochester Institute of Technology.

Sugai, G., Sprague, J.R., Horner, R.H., & Walker, H.M. (2000). Preventing school violence: The use of office discipline referrals to assess and monitor school-wide discipline interventions. *Journal of Emotional and Behavioral Disorders, 8,* 94–101

Sullivan, C.A.C., Vitello, S.J., & Foster, W. (1988). Adaptive behavior of adults with mental retardation in a group home: An intensive case study. *Education and Training in Mental Retardation, 23,* 76–81.

Summers, J.A., Behr, S.K., & Turnbull, A.P. (1989). Positive adaptation and coping strengths of families who have children with disabilities. In G.H.S. Singer & L.K. Irvin (Eds.), *Support for caregiving families* (pp. 27–40). Baltimore: Brookes.

Swanson, H.L. (1993). Principles and procedures in strategy use. In L.J. Meltzer (Ed.), *Strategy assessment and instruction for students with learning disabilities* (pp. 61–92). Austin, TX: Pro-Ed.

———. (1999). Instructional components that predict treatment outcomes for students with learning disabilities: Support for a combined strategy and direct instruction model. *Learning Disabilities Research and Practice, 14,* 129–140.

Swanson, H.L., Cochran, K.F., & Ewers, C.A. (1990). Can learning disabilities be determined from working memory performance? *Journal of Learning Disabilities, 23,* 59–67.

Swarthout, D.W. (1988). Enhancing the moral development of behaviorally/emotionally handicapped students. *Behavioral Disorders, 14,* 57–68.

Swenson-Pierce, A., Kohl, F., & Egel, A. (1987). Siblings as home trainers: A strategy for teaching domestic skills to children. *Journal of the Association for Persons with Severe Handicaps, 12*(1), 53–60.

Szabo, J.L. (2000). Maddie's story: Inclusion through physical and occupational therapy. *Teaching Exceptional Children, 33*(2), 12–18.

Taylor, B.A., & McDonough, K.A. (1996). Selecting teaching programs. In C. Maurice, G. Green, & S.C. Luce (Eds.), *Behavioral intervention for young children with autism: A manual for parents and professionals* (pp. 63–177). Austin, TX: Pro-Ed.

Taylor, S.E. (1983). Adjustment to threatening events: A theory of cognitive adaptation. *American Psychologist, 38,* 1161–1173.

Taylor, S.J., Lakin, K.C., & Hill, B.K. (1989). Permanency planning for children and youth: Out-of-home placement decisions. *Exceptional Children, 55,* 541–549.

Terman, L.M. (1906). Genius and stupidity. *Pedagogical Seminary, 13,* 307–373.

Terman, L.M., et al. *Genetic studies of genius.* I. *The mental and physical traits of a thousand gifted children,* 1925; II: *The early mental traits of three hundred geniuses,* 1926; III: *The promise of youth,* 1930; IV: *The gifted child grows up,* 1947; V: *The gifted group at mid-life,* 1959. Stanford, CA: Stanford University Press.

Terman, L.M., & Merrill, M.A. (1973). *Stanford-Binet Intelligence Scale—Third Revision Form L-M.* Boston: Houghton Mifflin.

The new IDEA: A brief review of selected new statutes. (1997). *The Special Edge* (July-August), 6.

Thomas, S.B., & Hawke, C. (1999). Health-care services for children with disabilities: Emerging standards and implications. *Journal of Special Education, 32,* 226–237.

Thompson, L., Lobb, C., Elling, R., Herman, S., Jurkiewicz, T., & Hulleza, C. (1997). Pathways to family empowerment: Effects of family-centered delivery of early intervention services. *Exceptional Children, 64,* 7–18.

Thurstone, L.L. (1924). *The nature of intelligence.* London: Kegan Paul, Trench, Trubner.

Torgesen, J.K. (1977). Memorization process in reading disabled children. *Journal of Educational Psychology, 69,* 571–578.

———. (2000). Individual differences in response to early interventions in reading: The lingering problem of treatment resisters. *Learning Disabilities Research and Practice, 15,* 55–64.

Torrance, E.P. (1969). Creative positives of disadvantaged children and youth. *Gifted Child Quarterly, 13,* 71–81.

———. (1984). *Mentor relationships: How they aid creative achievement, endure, change and die.* Buffalo: Bearly Limited.

Townsend, B.L. (2000). The disproportionate discipline of African American learners: Reducing school suspensions and expulsions. *Exceptional Children, 66,* 381–391.

Treiman, R. (1993). *Beginning to spell.* New York: Oxford University Press.

———. (1993). Participatory research on cognitive coping: From concepts to research planning. In A.P. Turnbull, J.M. Patterson, S.K. Behr, D.L. Murphy, J.G. Marquis & M.J. Blue-Banning (Eds.), *Cognitive coping, families, and disability.* Baltimore: Brookes.

Turnbull, A., & Turnbull, R. (2001). *Families, professionals, and exceptionality: Collaborating for empowerment* (4th ed.). Upper Saddle River, NJ: Merrill/Prentice-Hall.

Turnbull, A.P., & Ruef, M. (1997). Family perspectives on inclusive lifestyle issues for people with problem behavior. *Exceptional Children, 63,* 211–227.

Turnbull, A.P., & Turnbull, H.R. (1997). *Families, professionals, and exceptionality: A special partnership* (3d ed.). Upper Saddle River, NJ: Merrill.

Turnbull, H.R. III, Buchele-Ash, A., & Mitchell, L. (1994). *Abuse and neglect of children with disabilities: A policy analysis.* Lawrence, KS: Beach Center on Families and Disability, University of Kansas.

Turnbull, H.R., Turnbull, A.P., Bronicki, G.J., Summers, J.A., & Roeder-Gordon, C. (1989). *Disability and the family: A guide to decisions for adulthood.* Baltimore: Brookes.

Tuttle, D.W., & Tuttle, N.R.(2000). Psychosocial needs of children and youths. In M.C. Holbrook and A.J. Koenig (Eds.), *Foundations of Education: Vol.1* (2d ed., pp. 161– 172). New York: American Foundation for the Blind.

U.S. Advisory Board on Child Abuse and Neglect. (1995). *A nation's shame: Fatal child abuse and neglect in the United States.* Washington, DC: U.S. Department of Health and Human Services.

U.S. Bureau of the Census (1995). Statistical Abstract of the U.S., 1995. Washington, DC: Government Printing Office.

U.S. courts affirm the need for a full continuum of services. (1996). *CEC Today, 3*(6), 4–5.

U.S. Department of Education (1991). Thirteenth Annual Report to Congress on the implementation of the Individuals with Disabilities Education Act. Washington DC: Author.

U.S. Department of Education. (1995). www.ed.gov. IDEA/amend95.backgrnd.html.

U.S. Department of Education (1999). Twenty-first Annual Report to Congress on the implementation of the Individuals with Disabilities Education Act. Washington, DC: Author

U.S. Department of Education. (2000). *Twenty-second Annual Report to Congress on the Implementation of the Individuals with Disabilities Education Act.* Washington, D.C.

U.S. Office of Education. (1977, December 29). Education of handicapped children. Assistance of the states: Procedures for evaluating specific learning disabilities. Federal Register, Part III. Washington, D.C: U.S. Department of Health, Education and Welfare

Utley, C.A., Delquadri, J.C., Obiakor, F.E., & Mims, V.A. (2000). General and special educators' perceptions of teaching strategies for multicultural students. *Teacher Education and Special Education, 23,* 34–50.

Vahidi, S. (1998). I learn, therefore I am: Descartes ideology in Cyberage. *The National Research Center on the Gifted and Talented Newsletter* (Winter), 5–8.

van Tassel-Baska, J. (Ed.). (1989). Introduction. *Patterns of influence on gifted learners: The home, the self, and the school* (pp. 1–10). New York: Teachers College Press.

Vaughn, S. (1991). Social skills enhancement in students with learning disabilities. In B. Wong (Ed.), *Learning about learning disabilities* (pp. 409–440). San Diego: Academic Press.

Vaughn, S., Bos, C.S., & Schumm, J.S. (1997). *Teaching mainstreamed, diverse, and at-risk students in the general education classroom.* Boston, Allyn & Bacon.

Vaughn, S., Schumm, J.S., & Arguelles, M.E. (1997). The ABCDEs of co-teaching. *Teaching Exceptional Children, 30*(2), 4–10.

Verharren, P., & Conner, F. (1981). Physical disabilities. In J.M. Kauffman & D.P. Hallahan (Eds.), *Handbook of special education.* Englewood Cliffs, NJ: Prentice-Hall.

Vernon, P.E. (1989). *Intelligence: Heredity and environment.* San Francisco: Freeman.

Villa, R.A., Thousand, J.A., Meyers, H., & Nevin, A. (1996). Teacher and administrator perceptions of heterogeneous education. *Exceptional Children, 63*(1), 29–45.

Voeltz, L.M. (1984). Program and curriculum innovations to prepare children for integration. In N. Certo, N. Haring & R. York (Eds.), *Public school integration of severely handicapped students: Rational issues and progressive alternatives.* Baltimore: Brookes.

Walker, B. (1989). Strategies for improving parent-professional collaboration. In G.H.S. Singer & L.K. Irvin (Eds.), *Support for caregiving families.* Baltimore: Brookes.

Walker, H., & Sylwester, R. (1991). Where is school along the path to prison? *Educational Leadership,* 14–16.

Walker, H.M., Colvin, G., & Ramsey, E. (1995). *Antisocial behavior in school: Strategies and best practices.* New York: Brooks/Cole.

Walker, H.M., Todis, B., Holmes, D., & Horton, G. (1988). *The Walker social skills curriculum: The ACCESS Program.* Austin, TX: Pro-Ed.

Walker, N. (1985). Impulsivity in learning disabled children: Past research findings and methodological inconsistencies. *Learning Disabilities Quarterly, 8,* 85–94.

Wallace, G., Larsen, S.C., & Elksnin, L.K. (1992). The nature of assessment. *Educational assessment of learning problems: Testing for teaching* (2d ed.) (pp. 1–29). Boston: Allyn & Bacon.

Walsh, K.K., Rice, D.M., & Rosen, M. (1996). Options and choices in residential service delivery. In W. Stainback & S. Stainback (Eds.), *Controversial issues confronting special education: Divergent perspectives* (2d ed.) (pp. 267–278). Boston: Allyn & Bacon.

Ward, M.E.(2000). The visual system. In M.C. Holbrook and A.J. Koenig (Eds.), *Foundations of Education: Vol.1*(2d ed., pp. 77–110). New York: American Foundation for the Blind.

Warren, D.H. (1984). *Blindness and early childhood development* (2d ed.). New York: American Foundation for the Blind.

Watlawick, J., Beavin, J., & Jackson, D. (1967). *The pragmatics of communication.* New York: Norton.

Weaver, C. (1991). Whole language and its potential for developing readers. *Topics in Language Disorders, 11*(3), 28–44.

Webb, B.J. (2000). Planning and organizing assistive technology resources in your school. *Teaching Exceptional Children, 32*(4), 50–55.

Wehman, P., West, M., & Krege, J. (1999). Supported employment program development and research needs: Looking ahead to year 2000. *Education and Training in Mental Retardation and Developmental Disabilities, 17,* 3–19.

Wehman, P., Wood, W., Everson, J., Marchant, J. & Walker, R. (1987). Transition services for adolescent age individuals with severe mental retardation. In R.N. Ianacone & R.A. Stodden (Eds.), *Transition issues and directions* (pp. 49–76). Reston, VA: Council for Exceptional Children.

Wehmeyer, M., & Schwartz, M. (1997). Self-determination and positive adult outcomes: A follow-up study of youth with mental retardation or learning disabilities. *Exceptional Children, 63,* 245–255.

Wehmeyer, M.L., & Kelchner, K. (1994). Interpersonal cognitive problem-solving skills of individuals with mental retardation. *Education and Training in Mental Retardation and Developmental Disabilities, 29,* 265–278.

Welsh, M.J., & Smith, A.E. (December, 1995). Cystic fibrosis. *Scientific American,* December, 52–59.

Werner, E.E. (1986). The concept of risk from a developmental perspective. In *Advances in special education* (Vol. 5) (pp. 1–23). Greenwich, CT: JAI Press.

———. (1999). Risk and protective factors in the lives of children with high-incidence disabilities. In R. Gallimore, L.P. Bernheimer, D.L. MacMillan, D.L. Speece, S. Vaughn (Eds.), *Developmental perspectives on children with high-incidence disabilities.* Mahwah, NJ: Lawrence Erlbaum.

Werner, E.E., $ Smith, R.S. (1982). *Vulnerable, but invincible: A longitudinal study of resilient children and youth.* New York: McGraw-Hill.

Whitmore, J.R. (1980). *Giftedness, conflict and underachievement.* Boston: Allyn & Bacon.

Whitmore, J.R., & Maker, C.J. (1985). *Intellectual giftedness in disabled persons.* Austin, TX: Pro-Ed.

Whitney-Thomas, J., & Hanley-Maxwell, C. (1996). Packing the parachute: Parents' experiences as their children prepare to leave high school. *Exceptional Children, 63*(1), 75–87.

Wieseler, N.A., Hanson, R.H., Chamberlain, T.P. & Thompson, T. (1985). Functional taxonomy of stereotypic and self-injurious behavior. *Mental Retardation, 23,* 230–234.

Will, M.C. (1984). *OSERS programming for the transition of youth with disabilities: Bridges from school to working life.* Washington, DC: Office of Special Education and Rehabilitative Services, U.S. Department of Education.

Willard-Holt, C. (1998). Academic and personality characteristics of gifted students with cerebral palsy: A multiple case study. *Exceptional Children, 65,* 37–50.

———. (1999). Dual exceptionalities. *ERIC Digest E574.* Available at http://www.ed.gov/databases/ERIC_Digests/ed430344.html/.

Williams, W., Vogelsberg, R.T., & Schutz, R. (1985). Programs for secondary-age severely handicapped youth. In D. Bricker & J. Filler (Eds.), *Severe mental retardation: From theory to practice* (pp. 97–118). Lancaster, PA: Lancaster Press, Inc.

Wissick, C.A., & Gardner, J.E. (2000). Multimedia or not to multimedia? That is the question for students with learning disabilities. *Teaching Exceptional Children, 32*(4), 34–43.

Withrow, F.B. (1976). Applications of technology to communication. *Volta Review, 78*(4), 107–112.

Witte, R. (1998). Meet Bob, a student with traumatic brain injury. *Teaching Exceptional Children, 30*(1), 56–60.

Witty, P.A. (1940). Some considerations in the education of gifted children. *Educational Administration and Supervision, 26,* 512–521.

Wolfensberger, W. (1972). *The principle of normalization in human services.* Toronto: National Institute on Mental Retardation.

———. (1977). The principle of normalization. In B. Blatt, D. Biklen & R. Bogden (Eds.), *An alternative textbook in special education* (pp. 305–327). Denver: Love.

———. (1983). Social role valorization: A proposed new term for the principle of normalization. *Mental Retardation, 21,* 234–239.

Wolffe, K.E.(2000). Growth and development in middle childhood and adolescence. In M.C. Holbrook and A.J. Koenig (Eds.), *Foundations of Education: Vol.1* (2d ed., pp. 135–160). New York: American Foundation for the Blind.

Wolk, S., & Schildroth, A.N. (1986). Deaf children and speech intelligibility: A national study. In A.N. Schildroth & M.A. Karchmer (Eds.), *Deaf children in America* (pp. 139–159). San Diego: College-Hill.

Wolozin, L. (1998). Teachers' Learning Center: A CD-ROM. Boston: Houghton Mifflin. In press.

Wolraich, M.L. (1983a). Myelomeningocele. In J.A. Blackman (Ed.), *Medical aspects of developmental disabilities in children birth to three* (pp. 159–166). Iowa City: University of Iowa.

———. (1983b). Seizure disorders. In J.A. Blackman (Ed.), *Medical aspects of developmental disabilities in children birth to three* (pp. 215–222). Iowa City: University of Iowa.

———. (1983c). Seizure disorders. In J.A. Blackman (Ed.), *Medical aspects of developmental disabilities in children birth to three* (pp. 31–37). Iowa City: University of Iowa.

Wong, B.Y.L. (1991). The relevance of metacognition to learning disabilities. In B.Y.L. Wong (Ed.), *Learning about learning disabilities* (pp. 232–261). San Diego: Academic Press.

Wood, D.K., & Frank, A.R. (2000). Using memory-enhancing strategies to learn multiplication facts. *Teaching Exceptional Children, 32*(5), 78–82.

Wood, D.K., Frank, A.R., & Wacker, D.P. (1998). Teaching multiplication facts to students with learning disabilities. *Journal of Applied Behavior Analysis, 31,* 323–338.

Wood, J.W. (1993). *Mainstreaming: A practical approach for teachers.* New York: Merrill/Macmillan.

Woodward, J., Baxter, J., & Robinson, R. (1999). Rules and Reasons: Decimal instruction for academically low achieving students. *Learning Disabilities Research and Practice, 14,* 15–24.

Woodward, J., & Gersten, R. (1992). Innovative technology for secondary students with learning disabilities. *Exceptional Children, 58,* 407–421.

Wright, D., Pillard, E.D., & Cleven, C.A. (1990). The influence of state definitions of behavior disorders on the number of children served under P.L. 94–142. *Remedial and Special Education, 11*(5), 17–22.

Yell, M. (1998). *The law and special education.* Columbus, OH: Merrill.

Yell, M.L., & Drasgow, E. (2000). Litigating a free appropriate public education: The Lovaas hearings and cases. *The Journal of Special Education, 33,* 205–214.

Yell, M.L., & Shriner, J.G. (1997). The IDEA amendments of 1997: Implications for special and general education teachers, administrators, and teacher trainers. *Focus on Exceptional Children, 30*(1), 1–19.

Yetman, N.R. (1985). *Majority and minority: The dynamics of race and ethnicity in American life* (4th ed.). Boston: Allyn & Bacon.

York, J., & Vandercook, T. (1991). Designing integrated programs for learners with severe disabilities. *Teaching Exceptional Children, 23*(2), 22–29.

Zanglis, I., Furlong, M.J., & Casas, J.M. (2000). Case study of a community mental health collaborative: Impact on identification of youths with emotional and behavioral disorders. *Behavioral Disorders, 25,* 359–371.

Zeaman, D., & House, B.J. (1979). A review of attention theory. In N.R. Ellis (Ed.), *Handbook of mental deficiency: Psychological theory and research.* Hillsdale, NJ: Erlbaum.

———. (1963). The role of attention in retardate discrimination of learning. In N.R. Ellis (Ed.), *Handbook of mental deficiency.* New York: McGraw-Hill.

Zigmond, N., & Baker, J.M. (1995). Concluding comments: Current and future practices in inclusive schooling. *The Journal of Special Education, 29,* 245–250.

Zimmerman, G.J. (1996). Optics and low vision devices. In A.L. Corn & A.J. Koenig (Eds.), *Foundations of low vision: Clinical and functional perspectives* (pp. 115–142). New York: AFB Press.

Zirpoli, T.J. (1986). Child abuse and children with handicaps. *Remedial and Special Education, 7*(2), 39–48.

Zuniga, M. (1998). Families with Latino roots. In E.W. Lynch & M.J. Hansen (Eds.), *Developing cross-cultural competence* (2d ed.) (pp. 209–245). Baltimore: Brookes.

Credits

p. 317 (box): From "Tests to Talking in the Classroom: Assessing Communicative Competency" by G. Zamora-duran and E.I. Reyes, Reducing Disproportional Representation of Culturally Diverse Students In Special And Gifted Education edited by A.J. Artiles and F. Zamora-duran. Copyright 1997 by The Council for Exceptional Children. Reprinted with permission.

Chapter 1
p. 13 Fig. 1.1: E. Deno, "Special Education as Developmental Capital," *Exceptional Children* 37 (1970), 229–237. Copyright 1970 by the Council for Exceptional Children. Reprinted with permission. **p. 14 Table 1.2:** Adapted from J. Lerner, D. Dawson, and L. Horvath, *Cases in Learning and Behavior Problems: A Guide to Individualized Education Programs* (Salem, WI: Sheffield Publishing Co., 1980), p. 3. Used by permission. **pp. 29–31 Fig. 1.3:** Adapted from Winifred Anderson, Stephen Chitwood, and Deirdre Hayden, *Negotiating the Special Education Maze: A Guide for Parents and Teachers,* 2d ed. (Rockville, MD: Woodbine House, 1990), pp. 122–123. Reprinted with permission. **pp. 27–28 Table 1.4:** Adapted from "Legal Foundations: The Individuals with Disabilities Education Act (IDEA)," *Teaching Exceptional Children,* Winter 1993, pp. 85-87. Copyright 1993 by The Council for Exceptional Children. Reprinted with permission. **p. 33 Table 1.5:** From "The ins and outs of special education terminology" by G. Vergason and J.L. Anderegg, *Teaching Exceptional Children*, 29, 1997, p. 36. Copyright 1997 by The Council for Exceptional Children. Reprinted with permission. **p. 6 (box):** "It's the 'Person First'—Then the Disability," *Pacesetter* (September 1989), p. 13. Reprinted by permission from *Pacesetter. Pacesetter* is published by PACER Center, Minneapolis, Minnesota. **p. 8 (box):** From "Lessons from a Boy Named David" by Sandy Banks, *Los Angeles Times,* February 21, 1999. Copyright 1999, Los Angeles Times. Reprinted by permission. **p. 15 (box):** From "Teacher perceptions of mainstraining/inclusion, 1958-1995: A research synthesis" by T.E. Scruggs and M.A. Mastropieri, *Exceptional Children,* 63, 1996, p. 72. Copyright 1996 by The Council for Exceptional Children. Reprinted with permission. **p. 20 (box):** Adapted from ERIC EC Digest E576, June 1999, "An Overview of the Individuals with Disabilities Education Act Amendments of 1997 (P.L. 105-17)." Reprinted by permission from The Eric Clearinghouse on Disabilities and Gifted Education. **p. 34 (box):** From M. Friend and L. Cook, *Interactions: Collaboration Skills For School Profesionals,* Third Edition. Copyright (c) 2000 by Allyn & Bacon. Reprinted by permission.

Chapter 2
p. 50 Table 2.1: From S.M. Pueschel and A. Goldstein in Johnny L. Matson and James A. Mulick, *Handbook of Mental Retardation.* Copyright (c) 1983 by Allyn & Bacon. Reprinted by permission. **p. 45 Fig. 2.2:** Adapted from *Before We Are Born,* Fifth Edition, by K.L. Moore. Copyright (c) 1998 by W.B. Saunders Company. Reprinted by permission. **p. 71 Table 2.2:** From "The Development of Competence in Favorable and Unfavorable Environments: Lessons from research on successful children" by A.S. Masten and J.D. Coatsworth. *American Psychologist,* 1998, 53, 205-220. Copyright (c) 1998 by the American Psychologist Association. Reprinted with permission. **p. 58 (box):** (c) Children's Defense Fund. www.childrensdefense.org. **pp. 54–57 (box):** From "Vietnam Ends Silence on Issues of Wartime Exposure to Agent Orange," by David Lamb, *Los Angeles Times,* September 26, 1998. Copyright, 1998, Los Angeles Times. Reprinted by permission.

Chapter 3
pp. 102–103 (box): Reprinted by permission of the author. Janice Fialka is the mother of two children, Micah (who has developmental disabilities) and Emma. This excerpt is published in a collection of her writings called "It Matters: Lessons from my son." To obtain a copy or to receive information about her speaking engagements, contact her at 10474 Lasalle Blvd., Huntington Woods, MI 48070 or by email: ruaw@aol.com **p. 86 (box):** From *Empowered Families, Successful Children* by S. Epps and B.J. Jackson, Copyright (c) 2000 by the American Psychological Association. Reprinted with permission. **p. 82 (box):** From *Building Cultural Reciprocity With Families: Case Studies In Special Education* by H. Harry et al. Copyright (c) 1999 by Paul H. Brookes Publishing. **p. 104 (box):** Box: "Questions About Cultural Competence" from *Serving Culturally Diverse Families Of Infants And Toddlers With Disabilities* by P. P. Anderson and E. S. Fenichel, p. 16. © 1989 by the National Center for Clinical Infant Programs. **p. 92 (box):** Adapted from "Addressing the challenges of families with multiple risks" by M.J. Hanson and J.J. Carta, *Exceptional Children,* 62, 1996, pp. 201-212. Copyright 1996 by The Council for Exceptional Children. Reprinted with permission. **p. 83 Fig. 3.1:** A. P. Turnbull, J. A. Summers, and M. J. Brotherson. *Working with Families with Disabled Members: A Family Systems Approach* (Lawrence: University of Kansas, Beach Center on Families and Disabilities, 1984), p. 60. Adapted by permission.

Chapter 4
p. 135 Fig. 4.2: Figure titled "Star Stragety" from "Effects of a problem-solving strategy on the introductory algebra performance of secondary students with learning disabilities" by P. Maccini and C. A. Hughes. From *Learning Disabilities: Research and Practice,* 15, pp. 10-21. © 2000 by Lawrence Erlbaum Associates. **p. 146 Fig. 4.4:** From S. Engelmann, L. Carnine, and G. Johnson, *Corrective Reading: Decoding Level A: Word-attack Basics,* pp. 225, 251. Copyright (c) 1978. Reprinted by permission of The Mcgraw-Hill Companies, Inc. **p. 155 Fig. 4.5:** Archive Vernon Huff, Jr., "The History of South Carolina," in *The Building Of The Nation* (Greenville, SC: Furman, 1991). Copyright (c) 1991. Reprinted by permission. **p. 135 (box):** From "Using memory-enhancing strategies to learn multiplication facts" by D.K. Wood and A.R. Frank, *Teaching Exeptional Children,* 32, 2000, pp. 78-82. Copyright 2000 by The Council for Exceptional Children. Reprinted with permission. **p. 166 (box):** "Peer-Assisted Learning Strategies (PALS)" from "Peer-assisted learning strategies: An evidence-based practice to promote reading achievement" by D. Fuchs, L. S. Fuchs, and P. Burish. From *Learning Disabilities: Research and Practice,* 15, 85-91. © 2000 by Lawrence Erlbaum Associates.

Chapter 5
p. 173 Fig. 5.1: S. A. Kirk and J. J. Gallagher, *Educating Exceptional Children,* 6th ed. (Boston: Houghton-Mifflin, 1988), p. 11. Copyright © 1988. Used with permission. **p. 175 Fig. 5.2:** AAMR Adaptive Behavior Scale. Reprinted by permission from PRO-ED. **p. 177 Fig. 5.3:** From "Promoting cultural competence through teacher assistance teams" by S. Craig et al, *Teaching Exceptional Children,* 32, 2000, pp. 6-12. Copyright 2000 by The Council for Exceptional Children. Reprinted with permission.

Chapter 6

p. 211 Table 6.1: From "How can I help you get what you want?" by M.M. Ostrosky et al., *Teaching Exceptional Children*, 31, 1999, pp. 56-61. Copyright 1999 by The Council for Exceptional Children. Reprinted with permission. **p. 223 Fig. 6.1:** M. E. Cronin & J.R. Patton, *Life Skills Instruction for All Students with Special Needs: A Practical Guide for Integrating Real Life Content into Curriculum* (Austin, TX: PRO-ED, 1993), p.13. Copyright © 1993. Used by permission of PRO-ED. **p. 218 Fig. 6.2:** From "In Junior High you take Earth Science: Including a student with severe disabilities into an academic class" by E. Siegel-causey et al, *Teaching Exceptional Children*, 31, 1998, pp. 66-72. Copyright 1998 by The Council for Exceptional Children. Reprinted with permission.
p. 208 (box): "Good Things Come in Small Packages" by Jessica Morgan. From *Exceptional Parent*, July 2000. Reprinted with the expressed consent and approval of *Exceptional Parent*, a monthly magazine for parents and families of children with disabilities and special health care needs. Subscription cost is $39.95 per year for 12 issues; Call (877) 372-7368. Offices at 555 Kinderkamack Rd. Oradell, NJ 07649.
p. 226 (box): From "Culturally sensitive transition plans for young children and their families" by D.A. Bruns and S.A. Fowler, *Teaching Exceptional Children*, 31, 1999, pp. 26-30. Copyright 1999 by The Council for Exceptional Children. Reprinted with permission. **p. 213 (box):** From *A Difference In The Family* By Helen Featherstone. Copyright (c) 1980 by Basic Books, Inc. Reprinted by permission of Basic Books, a member of Perseus Books, L.L.C. **p. 220 (box):** From *The Syracuse Community-Referenced Curriculum Guide For Students With Moderate And Severe Disabilities*, edited by Alison Ford et al. (c) 1989. Reprinted by permission from the Paul H. Brookes Publishing Company.
p. 221 (box): From *Special Education Technology Classroom Applications*, 1st edition, by R.B. Lewis (c) 1993. Reprinted with permission of Wadsworth, an imprint of the Wadsworth Group, a division of Thomson Learning. Fax 800-730-2215.

Chapter 7

pp. 256–257 (box): From "Anticipating Differences—celebrating Strengths" by Cartledge et al. *Teaching Exceptional Children*, February 2000 (v32 n2). Copyright 2000 by The Council for Exceptional Children. Reprinted with permission. **p. 243 Fig. 7.1:** From *Exceptional Children*, Summer 2000, (v66 n3), p. 391. Copyright 2000 by The Council for Exceptional Children. Reprinted with permission. **p. 261 Fig. 7.3:** From "Preventing School Violence: The Use of Office Discipline Referrals to Assess and Monitor School-wide Discipline Interventions" by G. Sugai, J.R. Sprague, R.H. Horner, and H.M. Walker (2000), *Journal of Emotional And Behavioral Disorders*, 8, pp. 94-101. Copyright 2000 by PRO-ED, Inc. Reprinted with permission.
p. 251 (box): Reprinted with permission from The Diagnostic and Statistical Manual of Mental Disorders, Fourth Edition, Text Revision. Copyright 2000 American Psychiatric Association.

Chapter 8

p. 287 (box): From *Let Me Hear Your Voice* by Catherine Maurice, copyright (c) 1993 by Catherine Maurice. Used by permission of Alfred A. Knopf, a division of Random House, Inc. **p. 273 (box):** Newsweek, Donna Foote and Heather Won Tesoriero. (c) 2000 Newsweek, Inc. All rights reserved. Reprinted by permission.
p. 271 (box): Reprinted from *The American Scholar*, Volume 67, No. 2, Spring 1998. Copyright (c) 1998 by the author. **pp. 290–291 (box):** Reprinted from *The American Scholar*, Volume 67, No. 2, Spring 1998. Copyright (c) 1998 by the author.
p. 281 Table 8.1: From *Students With Autism Characteristics And Instruction Programming*, 1st edition, by Jack Scott, Claudia Clark, and Michael Brady. **p. 275 Fig. 8.1:** (c) 2000 Terese Winslow. Reprinted with permission. **p. 284 Table 8.2:** Adapted from "Selecting Teaching Programs" by B.A. Taylor and K.A. Mcdonough, in *Behavioral Intervention For Young Children With Autism: A Manual For Parents And Professionals*, edited by C. Maurice, G. Green, and S.C. Luce. Copyright (c) 1996. Reprinted by permission from PRO-ED. **p. 280 Fig. 8.2:** From *Behavioral Intervention For Young Children With Autism* edited by Catherine Maurice, Gina Green, and Stephen Luce. Copyright (c) 1996 by PRO-ED. Reprinted with permission.

Chapter 9

p. 320 (box): From L. Mccormick et al., *Supporting Children With Communication Difficulties In Inclusive Settings.* Copyright (c) 1997 by Allyn & Bacon. Reprinted by permission. **p. 315 (box):** American Speech-Language-Hearing Association (1993). Implementation procedures for the standards for the certificates of clinical competence, *ASHA*, 35 (3), 76–83. Reprinted by permission of the American Speech-Language-Hearing Association.
p. 297 Fig. 9.1: M. Diane Klein, Division of Special Education, California State University, Los Angeles. Used with permission. **p. 300 Table 9.1:** From J.N. Bohannan and A.Warren-leubecker, "Theoretical Approaches to Language Acquisitions," as it appeared in Jean Berko Gleason *The Development Of Language*, Second Edition. Copyright (c) 1989. Reprinted by permission of Allyn & Bacon. **p. 302 Table 9.2:** From Robert E. Owens, Jr., *Language Development*, Third Edition. Copyright (c) 1992 by Allyn & Bacon. Reprinted by permission. **p. 299 Fig. 9.2:** From Lois Bloom and Margaret Lahey, *Language Development And Language Disorders.* Copyright (c) 1978 by Allyn & Bacon. Reprinted by permission.
p. 299 Fig. 9.3: From M.L. Edwards, *Introduction To Applied Phonetics.* Copyright (c) 1986 by Allyn & Bacon. Reprinted by permission. **p. 303 Table 9.3:** D. K. Oller and M. P. Lynch, "Infant Vocalizations and Innovations in Infraphonology," in C. A. Ferguson, L. Menn, and C. Stoel-Gammon, eds., *Phonological Development: Models, Research, Implications* (Timonium, MD: York Press, 1992), pp. 509–536. Used by permission. **p. 305 Table 9.4:** From *Language Instruction For Students With Disabilities*, Second Edition, by E.A. Polloway and Tom E.C. Smith, p. 38. Copyright (c) 2000. Reproduced by permission of Love Publishing Company. **p. 306 Table 9.5:** From L. Mccormick et al., *Supporting Children With Communication Difficulties In Inclusive Settings.* Copyright (c) 1997 by Allyn & Bacon. Reprinted by permission.
p. 312 (box): Adapted from "Teaching the silent student," by Amy Pyle, *Los Angeles Times*, June 11, 1996. Copyright, 1996, Los Angeles Times. Reprinted by permission.
p. 324 (box): Helen Exley, ed., *What It's Like to Be Me* (Watford, U.K.: Exley, 1981), p. 112. Reprinted with permission of Exley Publications, Ltd.

Chapter 10

p. 355 (box): Reprinted courtesy of Gallaudet University Laurent Clerc National Deaf Education Center. **pp. 362–363 (box):** Reprinted courtesy of Gallaudet University Laurent Clerc National Deaf Education Center. **pp. 346–348 (box):** Reprinted by permission from the Alexander Graham Bell Association for the Deaf and Hard of Hearing, Washington, Dc. www.agbell.org. **p. 418 (box):** From *Children and Epilepsy: The Teacher's Role*, pp. 3-4. Copyright (c) 1992. Reprinted by permission of the Epilepsy Foundation of America. **pp. 340–343 (box):** From *Odyssey*, Summer 2000 (Vol 1, Issue 3). (c) 2000 by Laurent Clerc National Deaf Education Center. Reprinted by permission from Gallaudet University. **p. 329 Fig. 10.1:** M. L. Batshaw and Y. M. Perret, *Children with Disabilities: A Medical Primer*, 3d ed. (Baltimore: Paul H. Brookes, 1992), p. 323. Used by permission of the authors.
pp. 336–337 Fig. 10.2: Reprinted with permission of the American Academy of Audiology. **p. 331 Table 10.2:** From *Hearing in Children*, 4/e by Jerry L. Northern and Marion P. Downs. Copyright (c)1991. Used by permission of Lippincott Williams & Wilkins, and the author.
p. 354 Fig. 10.3: T. Humphries, C. Padden, T. J. O'Rourke, *A Basic Bourse in American Sign Language* (Silver Spring,

MD: T. J. Publishers, 1980). Reprinted by permission. **p. 351 Table 10.4:** From David A. Stewart & Thomas N. Kluwin, *Teaching Deaf And Hard Of Hearing Students.* Copyright (c) 2001 by Allyn and Bacon. Reprinted by permission.

Chapter 11

p. 381 (box): Adapted from K.M. Finello, N.H. Hanson, & L.S. Kekelis, "Cognitive focus: Developing cognition, concepts, and language in young blind and visually impaired children," in R.L. Pogrund, D.L. Fazzi, & J.S. Lampert (eds.), *Early focus: Working with young blind and visually impaired children and their families.* (c) 1992 by American Foundation for the Blind. Reprinted by permission. **p. 377 Fig. 11.1:** Used by permission of National Society to Prevent Blindness. **p. 376 Table 11.2:** Used by permission of American Printing House for the Blind. **p. 390 Table 11.3:** From "The Core Curriculum for Blind and Visually Impaired Students, Including Those with Additional Disabilities" by P. Hatlen (2000). From *Foundations Of Education, Vol. 2, 2/e* edited by A.J. Koenig and M.C. Holbrook, pp. 779-784. (c) 2000 by American Foundation for the Blind. Reprinted by permission. **p. 395 Table 11.4:** From N.C. Barraga and J.N. Erin, *Visual Handicaps and Learning,* 1992, pp. 152-153. Copyright (c) 1992. Used by permission of PRO-ED Inc. **p. 396 Table 11.5:** From "Planning Instruction in Unique Skills" by A.J. Koenig and M.C. Holbrook (2000). From *Foundations Of Education, Vol. 2, 2/e* edited by A.J. Koenig and M.C. Holbrook, pp. 196-224. (c) 2000 by American Foundation for the Blind. Reprinted by permission. **p. 385 (box):** "Strategies for Promoting Social Inclusion at Home and at School" from "Social Skills" by S.Z. Sacks and S.K. Silbermann. From *Foundations Of Education,* Vol. 2, 2ed, edited by A.J. Koenig and M.C. Holbrook, pp. 633-634. (c) 2000 by American Foundation for the Blind. Reprinted by permission. **pp. 400–401 (box):** "Can Girls With Impaired Vision Be Mommies?," by Deborah Kendrick, *Envision,* August 1997, pp. 5-7. Copyright (c) 1997. Reprinted by permission of The Lighthouse Inc. **p. 402 (box):** Adapted from "Access to Information: Technology and Braille" by F.M. D'andrea and K. Barnicle. From *Instructional Strategies For Braille Literacy* edited by D.P. Wormsley and F.M. D'andrea, pp. 269-307. (c) 1997 by American Foundation for the Blind. Reprinted by permission.

Chapter 12

pp. 414–415 (box): "My Life," by Jessica Smallman, Ability Network Magazine, Vol. 5, Number 2, Winter 1996/97. Reprinted by permission of Ability Network Publishing Inc. **p. 444 Table 12.1:** From "I Learned How to Take Turns" by Cynthia Lau, *Teaching Exceptional Children,* v32 n4, March/april 2000, p. 9. Copyright 2000 by The Council for Exceptional Children. Reprinted with permission. **p. 413 Fig. 12.1:** M. L. Batshaw and Y. M. Perret, *Children with Handicaps: A Medical Primer,* 3d ed. (Baltimore: Paul H. Brookes, 1992), p. 444. Copyright © 1992. Used by permission of the author. Note: The darker the shading, the more severe the involvement. **p. 420 Fig. 12.2:** From "Mainstreaming Children with Neuromuscular Disease: A Map of Concerns" by Kristine Strong and Jonathan Sandoval, *Exceptional Children,* Spring 1999, pp. 353-366. Copyright 1999 by The Council for Exceptional Children. Reprinted with permission. **pp. 426–427 Fig. 12.3:** From "Children with Asthma" by Yvette Q. Getch and Stacey Neuharth-pritchett, *Teaching Exceptional Children,* v31 n3, Jan/feb 1999, pp. 34-35. Copyright 1999 by The Council for Exceptional Children. Reprinted with permission. **p. 423 (box):** From D.L Cates, M.A. Markell, and S. Bettenhausen, "At Risk for Abuse: A Teacher's Guide for Recognizing and Reporting Child Neglect and Abuse," *Preventing School Failure,* 39 (2), Winter 1995, pp. 6-9. Copyright (c) 1995. Reprinted by permission of the author. **p. 438 (box):** Used by permission of Disability Services. **p. 439 (box):** From "Maddie's Story: Inclusion Through Physical and Occupational Therapy" by Joanne Lockard Szabo, *Teaching Exceptional Children,* Nov/dec 2000 (v33 n2), pp. 49-53. Copyright 1999 by The Council for Exceptional Children. Reprinted with permission. **p. 443 (box):** From "Planning and Organizing Assistive Resources in Your Schools" by B.J. Webb, *Teaching Exceptional Children,* v43 n4, March/april 2000, pp. 50-55. Copyright 2000 by The Council for Exceptional Children. Reprinted with permission. **p. 448 (box):** "Tips for Eliminating Barriers," *Teaching Exceptional Children,* v32 n5, May/June 2000, p. 63. Copyright 2000 by The Council for Exceptional Children. Reprinted with permission.

Chapter 13

pp. 480–481 Table 13.1: Copyright material from *Gifted Child Quarterly,* a publication of the National Association for Gifted Children (NAGC), 1707 L Street, Nw, Suite 550, Washington, Dc 20036. (202) 785-4268. http://www.nagc.org. This mateiral may not be reproduced without permission from NAGC. **p. 469 (box):** Compiled from S.M. Reis, T.W. Neu, and J.M. Mcguire (1997), "Case Studies of High-ability Students with Learning Disabilities Who Have Achieved," *Exceptional Children* 63:4, 463-479 and S.M. Reis, J.M. Mcguire, and T.W. Neu (2000), "Compensation Strategies Used by High-ability Students with Learning Disabilities Who Succeed in College," *Gifted Child Quarterly* 44 (2), 123-134. **pp. 464–465 (box):** From "Where Budding Geniuses Can Blossom," by Elaine Woo, *Los Angeles Times,* November 22, 2000. Copyright, 2000, Los Angeles Times. Reprinted by permission. **p. 467 (box):** From *Smart Girls,* Revised Edition, by Barbara Kerr. Copyright (c) 1998 by Grifted Psychology Press, Inc. **p. 474–475 (box):** Excerpt from *Project Girl* by Janet Mcdonald. Copyright (c) 1999 by Janet Mcdonald. Reprinted by permission of Farrar, Straus and Giroux, Llc. **p. 487 (box):** Ennis, R.H., (October 1985). "A Logical Basis for Measuring Thinking Skills." *Educational Leadership,* 43, 2: 44-48. Reprinted with permission of the Association for Supervision and Curriculum Development. Copyright (c) 1985 by Ascd. All rights reserved. **pp. 490–491 (box):** Reprinted by permission from National Center for the Accelerated School Project. **p. 462 (box):** Copyright material from the National Association for Gifted Children (NAGC), 1707 L Street, Nw, Suite 550, Washington, Dc 20036 (202) 785-4268. http://www.nagc.org. This material may not be reproduced without permission from NAGC. **pp. 480–481 (box):** Copyright material from the National Association for Gifted Children (NAGC), 1707 L Street, NW, Suite 550, Washington, Dc 20036 (202) 785-4268. http://www.nagc.org. This material may not be reproduced without permission from NAGC.

Chapter 14

p. 507–511 Fig 14.1: From "A Tool to Encourage 'Best Practice' in Full Inclusion" by Vera Daniels and Sharon Vaughn, *Teaching Exceptional Children,* May/June 1999, pp. 49-53. Copyright 1999 by The Council for Exceptional Children. Reprinted with permission. **p. 512 Fig. 14.2:** From Marilyn Friend and William Bursuck, *Including Students With Special Needs.* Copyright (c) 1996 by Allyn & Bacon. Reprinted by permission.

Name Index

Subject Index

About the Authors

Dr. Nancy Hunt received her M.A. in Special Education from Teachers College, Columbia University, and her Ph.D. from the University of Southern California in 1982. She taught deaf children for nine years in New York and Los Angeles. Currently a professor at California State University, Los Angeles, Dr. Hunt teaches in the Early Childhood Special Education program and supervises teachers during practicum experiences. She frequently teaches the introductory special education course for which she wrote this text. Her interests include high-risk infants, hearing loss in children, and families of children with special needs. Dr. Hunt and her husband, Dewey Gram, have three daughters.

Dr. Kathleen Marshall received her Ph.D. in special education from the University of Virginia in 1983. She currently is Associate Professor and Coordinator of Programs in Special Education at the University of South Carolina. Dr. Marshall teaches courses for preservice, graduate, and doctoral level students in the areas of learning disabilities, special education curriculum, reading, and special education research. Her experience as a special educator includes teaching elementary and middle school children with learning disabilities and mild mental retardation. Her practical and research interests include teacher training and retention programs, curriculum development, and reading instruction.

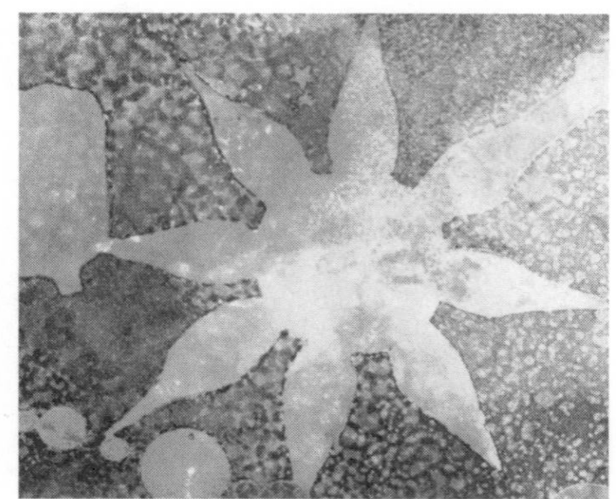